# Native Languages of the Americas

Volume 1

# Native Languages of the Americas

Volume 1

Edited by Thomas A. Sebeok
*Research Center for Language and Semiotic Studies*
*Indiana University*
*Bloomington, Indiana*

PLENUM PRESS · NEW YORK AND LONDON

Library of Congress Cataloging in Publication Data

Main entry under title:

Native languages of the Americas.

    Includes index.
    1. Indians–Languages. I. Sebeok, Thomas Albert, 1920-
PM108.N3                     497                    76-28216
ISBN 0-306-37157-X (Vol. 1)

© 1976 Plenum Press, New York
A Division of Plenum Publishing Corporation
227 West 17th Street, New York, N.Y. 10011

All the material in this volume was previously published by Mouton & Co., in the series *Current Trends in Linguistics*. With one exception, all the chapters first appeared in Volume 10: *Linguistics in North America* (© 1973 Mouton & Co., N. V., Publishers, The Hague). "Native North America," by Herbert Landar, first appeared in Volume 13: *Historiography of Linguistics* (©1975 Mouton & Co., N.V., Publishers, The Hague).

All rights reserved

No part of this book may be reproduced, stored in a retrieval system or transmitted, in any form or by any means, electronic, mechanical, photocopying, microfilming, recording, or otherwise, without written permission from the Publisher

Printed in the United States of America

# IN MEMORIAM
## Harry Hoijer
September 6, 1904 - March 4, 1976

# FOREWORD

Thirteen of the chapters that comprise the contents of this first volume of *Native Languages of the Americas* were originally commissioned by the undersigned in his capacity as Editor of the fourteen volume series (1963–1976), *Current Trends in Linguistics*. All appeared, in 1973, under Part Three of the quadripartite Vol. 10, subtitled *Linguistics in North America*. Two additional chapters are being held over for the volume to follow shortly, devoted to Central and South American languages and linguistics, where they more appropriately belong. A fourteenth chapter, on the "Historiography of native North American linguistics," was written similarly by invitation, for Vol. 13, subtitled *Historiography of Linguistics*, published in 1975. Both Volumes 10 and 13 were jointly financed by the United States National Science Foundation and National Endowment for the Humanities, with an enhancing contribution to the former by the Canada Council. The generosity of these funding agencies was, of course, previously acknowledged in my respective Editor's Introductions to the two books mentioned, but cannot be repeated too often: without their welcome and timely assistance, the global project could scarcely have been realized on so comprehensive a scale.

The *Current Trends in Linguistics* series was a long-term venture of Mouton Publishers, of The Hague, under the imaginative in-house direction of Peter de Ridder. Various spin-offs were foreseen, and some of them happily realized. The demand for pulling together all the contributions dealing with the native languages of the Americas was particularly insistent; accordingly, I am grateful to the present management of that publishing house I had been associated with until 1974 for having graciously yielded this important undertaking to Plenum Publishing Corporation.

Each of the authors was given an opportunity to correct, update, or otherwise alter his or her article, and a few even seized this opportunity to make major revisions. Thus at least some of the texts in this book are by no means identical with those published earlier under the same or a corresponding title, so the book, as a whole, may be viewed as a reasonably fresh and certainly comprehensive panoptic conspectus of the field in the last quarter of our century.

Both the first and the second volumes contain separate indices of personal names mentioned in that tome. These were compiled by May Lee. The second volume will feature two language checklists, one for the area north of the Rio Grande, the other covering the remainder of the Western Hemisphere. These are the fruit of years of labor by Herbert Landar; more about them in the Foreword to the next volume. I hope that provision of these two sets of guides to the entire contents of this work will increase its utility as a reference tool concerning the aboriginal tongues still spoken in the area, and of the past.

    The opening article in this volume was written by Harry Hoijer, who died some months after he gave his consent for its inclusion here, but a few weeks before his proofs became available. He was my once and only formal teacher in many of the subjects covered in this book. I was his student on two successive occasions, at two different institutions: first, in the Department of Anthropology at the University of Chicago, in the early 1940's, and, several Summers afterwards, in the frame of a Linguistic Institute held at the University of North Carolina. Although my chosen pursuit eventually forked off in quite another direction from his, and my few contributions to North and South American Indian linguistics (viz., Winnebago and Aymara) have remained altogether inconsequential, his craftsmanship and proficiency made an abiding impression on me as models of scholarship to be emulated. The interest that he sparked in me in the languages of this vast region—that could still be characterized by him in 1946 as being "of greater linguistic diversity than any other in the world"—has endured, indeed, flourished. In dedicating this collaborative volume to the memory of this master technician of American Indian linguistics in its full geographic extent as well as historical depth, I am sure that I am acting for the profession, not only as represented between these covers, but at large.

Bloomington, June 1, 1976

THOMAS A. SEBEOK

# CONTENTS

## VOLUME 1

FOREWORD .................................................... VII

LIST OF ABBREVIATIONS ...................................... XI

### PART ONE: NORTH AMERICA

#### General Chapters

History of American Indian Linguistics, by Harry Hoijer ................ 3
American Indian Linguistic Prehistory, by Mary R. Haas ................ 23
North American Indian Language Contact, by William Bright ............ 59
Philological Approaches to the Study of North American Indian Languages:
    Documents and Documentation, by Ives Goddard ..................... 73
Native North America, by Herbert Landar ............................ 93

#### Areal Groupings

Areal Linguistics in North America, by Joel Sherzer ................... 121
Eskimo-Aleut, by Michael E. Krauss ................................. 175
Na-Dene, by Michael E. Krauss ..................................... 283
The Northwest, by Laurence C. Thompson ........................... 359
California, by William Shipley ..................................... 427
Southwestern and Great Basin Languages, by C. F. and F. M. Voegelin .... 461
Algonquian, by Karl V. Teeter ...................................... 505
Siouan, Iroquoian, and Caddoan, by Wallace L. Chafe ................. 527
The Southeast, by Mary R. Haas .................................... 573

INDEX OF NAMES ............................................. 613

# CONTENTS

## VOLUME 2

FOREWORD .................................................... v

LIST OF ABBREVIATIONS ........................................ IX

### PART TWO: CENTRAL AND SOUTH AMERICA

Classical Languages, by Jorge A. Suarez ............................... 3
Writing Systems, by Thomas S. Barthel ............................... 27
Descriptive Linguistics, by Joseph E. Grimes ........................... 55
Areal Linguistics and Middle America, by Terrence Kaufman .............. 63
Indigenous Dialectology, by Marvin K. Mayers ......................... 89
Comparative Reconstruction of Indigenous Languages, by Robert E. Longacre  99
Mexico, by Marlys McClaran ........................................ 141
Otomanguean Isoglosses, by Calvin R. Rensch ......................... 163
Historiography of Native Ibero-American Linguistics, by Herbert Landar .... 185

### PART THREE: CHECKLISTS

North American Indian Languages, by Herbert Landar .................. 207
South and Central American Indian Languages, by Herbert Landar ........ 401

INDEX OF NAMES .............................................. 529

# LIST OF ABBREVIATIONS

## 1. JOURNALS AND BOOKS

| | |
|---|---|
| AAA-M | *American Anthropological Association*. Memoirs (Menasha, Wisc.). |
| AAAS-P | *Proceedings of the American Association for the Advancement of Science* (Washington, D.C.). |
| AAcadAS-M | *American Academy of Arts and Sciences*. Memoirs (Boston). |
| AAcadAS-P | *American Academy of Arts and Sciences*. Proceedings (Boston). |
| AAOJ | See AmAnt. |
| AAUP Bulletin | *American Association of University Professors*. Bulletin (Washington, D.C.). |
| Acta Salamanticensia | *Acta Salamanticensia iussu senatus universitatis edita*. Filosofia y Lettras (Salamanca). |
| AD | *American Documentation* (Washington, D.C.). |
| ADD | *American Dialect Dictionary*. |
| AES-M | *American Ethnological Society*. Memoirs (Seattle). |
| AES-T | *American Ethnological Society*. Transactions (Seattle). |
| AFS-M | *American Folklore Society*. Memoirs (Philadelphia). |
| AGI | *Archivio Glottologico Italiano* (Florence). |
| AGR | *American German Review* (Philadelphia). |
| AIAK | See PICAm. |
| AJPh | *American Journal of Philology* (Baltimore). |
| AJSoc | *American Journal of Sociology* (Chicago). |
| AL | *Acta Linguistica Hafniensia*. International Journal of Structural Linguistics (Copenhagen). |
| ALF | *L'Atlas linguistique de la France*. By Gillérion and Edmont. (1902-1912). |
| ALH | *Acta Linguistica Academiae Scientiarum Hungaricae* (Budapest). |
| AmA | *American Anthropologist* (Menasha, Wisc.). |
| AmAnt | *American Antiquarian* (Boston, Mass.). |
| AmAntiquity | *American Antiquity* (Salt Lake City). |
| AMCIA | See PICAm. |
| América Indígena | *América Indígena* (Mexico, D.F., Mexico). |
| AMNH-M | *American Museum of Natural History*. Memoirs (New York). |
| Anglia | *Anglia*. Zeitschrift für englische Philologie (Tübingen). |
| AnL | *Anthropological Linguistics* (Bloomington, Ind.). |
| Anthropologica | *Anthropologica*. Centre Canadien de Recherches en anthropologie (Université d'Ottawa). |

# LIST OF ABBREVIATIONS

| | |
|---|---|
| Anthropos | *Anthropos*. Revue internationale d'ethnologie et de linguistique/Internationale Zeitschrift für Völker- und Sprachenkunde (Freiburg, Switzerland). |
| AR | *Anthropological Record* (University of California Press, Berkeley and Los Angeles). |
| Archivum | *Archivum*. Revista de la Facultad de Filosofia y Letras (Universidad de Oviedo, Oviedo). |
| ArchL | *Archivum Linguisticum*. A review of comparative philology and general linguistics (Glasgow). |
| ArchSSL | *Archiv für das Studium der Neueren Sprachen (und Literatur)* (Braunschweig). |
| AS | *American Speech*.   Quarterly of Linguistic Usage (New York). |
| ASR | *American-Scandinavian Review* (New York). |
| ASNS | *Archiv für das Studium der Neueren Sprachen* (Brunswick). |
| AvglPhon | *Archiv für Vergleichende Phonetik* (Berlin). |
| BAAS-R | *British Association for the Advancement of Science*. Annual Report (London). |
| BAE-B | *Bureau of American Ethnology*. Bulletin (Washington, D.C.). |
| BAE-R | *Bureau of American Ethnology*. Annual Report (Washington, D.C.). |
| BCLC | *Bulletin du Cercle Linguistique de Copenhague* (Copenhagen). |
| BHS | *Bulletin of Hispanic Studies* (Liverpool). |
| BIA | *Bilingualism in the Americas*. A bibliography and research guide, by Einar Haugen. PADS 26. |
| BS | *Behavioral Science* (Ann Arbor, Mich.). |
| BSL | *Bulletin de la Société de Linguistique de Paris* (Paris). |
| CAnthr | *Current Anthropology*. A world journal of the science of man (Chicago). |
| CAIL | *Conference on American Indian Languages*. Conference held in conjunction with annual meetings of the American Anthropological Association. |
| CE | *College English* (Chicago). |
| CEACritic | *CEA Critic*. College English Association (Fullerton, Calif.). |
| ChiLing | *University of Chicago Publications in Anthropology*. Linguistic Series (Chicago). |
| CJL/RCL | *Canadian Journal of Linguistics/Revue Canadienne de Linguistique* (Toronto). (Formerly JCLA.) |
| CNAE | *Contributions to North American Ethnology*. Department of the Interior, U.S. Geographical and Geological Survey of the Rocky Mountain Region. Edited under the direction of J. W. Powell (Washington, D.C.). |
| CSlP | *Canadian Slavonic Papers* (Montreal). |
| CTA Journal | *California Teachers Association Journal* (San Francisco). |
| CTL 3 | *Current Trends in Linguistics*. Volume 3: Theoretical Foundations, ed. by Thomas A. Sebeok (The Hague, Mouton & Co., 1966). |
| CTL 4 | *Current Trends in Linguistics*. Volume 4: Ibero-American and Caribbean Linguistics, ed. by Thomas A. Sebeok (The Hague, Mouton & Co., 1968). |
| CTL 9 | *Current Trends in Linguistics*. Volume 9: Linguistics in Western Europe, ed. by Thomas A. Sebeok (The Hague, Mouton & Co., 1972). |
| CUCA | *Columbia University Contributions to Anthropology* (New York). |
| DA | *Dictionary of Americanisms on historical principles*. Ed. by M. M. Mathews (Chicago, 1951). |
| DAb | *Dissertation Abstracts*. A guide to dissertations and monographs available on microfilm (Ann Arbor, Mich.). |
| DAE | *Dictionary of American English on historical principles*. Ed. by Sir William Craigie and J. R. Hulbert (Chicago, 1938-1944). |
| Daedalus | *Daedalus*. Journal of the American Academy of Arts and Sciences (Boston). |
| DARE | *Dictionary of American Regional English*. Ed. by F. G. Cassidy. Forthcoming. |
| DC | *Dictionary of Canadianisms on historical principles*. Ed. by W. S. Avis (Toronto, 1967). |
| DN | *Dialect Notes*. Volume I (Boston), Volumes II-VI (New Haven). |
| EDD | *English Dialect Dictionary*. |
| EE | *Elementary English*. A magazine of the language arts. National Council of Teachers of English (Champaign, Ill.). |
| EETS | *Early English Text Society* (London). |

## LIST OF ABBREVIATIONS

| | |
|---|---|
| EJ | *English Journal* (Urbana, Ill.). |
| ES | *English Studies*. A Journal of English Letters and Philology (Amsterdam). |
| ETC. | *ETC. A review of general semantics* (Chicago). |
| Ethnohistory | *Ethnohistory*. Devoted to the original research in the documentary history of the culture and movements of primitive peoples and related problems of broader scope. American Society for Ethnohistory (Lexington, Ky.). |
| Ethnology | *Ethnology*. International Journal of Cultural and Social Anthropology (Pittsburgh). |
| ExSI | *Explorations and Field Work of the Smithsonian Institution* (Washington, D.C.). |
| FdaM | *Le Français dans le Monde* (Paris). |
| FL | *Foundations of Language*. International Journal of Language and Philosophy (Dordrecht, The Netherlands). |
| FLing | *Folia Linguistica*. Acta Societatis linguisticae Europaeae (The Hague). |
| Florida Anthropologist | *Florida Anthropologist* (Florida State University, Department of Anthropology, Tallahassee, Fla.). |
| Florida FLR | *Florida Foreign Language Reporter* (Tallahassee, Fla.). |
| FR | *The French Review* (Baltimore). |
| GK | *Gengo Kenkyū*. Journal of the Linguistic Society of Japan (Tokyo). |
| GL | *General Linguistics* (Lexington, Ky.). |
| Glossa | *Glossa* (Simon Fraser University, Burnaby, B.C.). |
| HAIL | *Handbook of American Indian Languages*. 4 Vols: 1 (1911) and 2 (1922) are BAE-B 40. Vols 3 and 4 (1940) published separately (J. J. Augustin, New York). |
| Hispania | *Hispania*. A journal devoted to the interest of the teaching of Spanish and Portuguese (Appleton, Wisc.). |
| HMAI | *Handbook of Middle American Indians*. Robert Wauchope, General Editor, Norman A. McQuown, editor of Vol. 5, Linguistics (Austin). |
| HO | *Human Organization*. Society for Applied Anthropology (Lexington, Ky.). |
| Homme | *L'Homme*. Revue française d'anthropologie (Paris and The Hague). |
| HUAIL | *Harvard University, Papers from the seminar in American Indian Linguistics* (Cambridge, Mass.). Mimeographed. |
| ICA | *See* PICAm. |
| ICSL | *International Conference on Salish Languages*. |
| IJAL | *International Journal of American Linguistics* (Baltimore). |
| IJSLP | *International Journal of Slavic Linguistics and Poetics* (The Hague). |
| IRAL | *International Review of Applied Linguistics in Language Teaching/Internationale Zeitschrift für angewandte Linguistik in der Spracherziehung* (Heidelberg). |
| IUPAL-M | *Indiana University Publications in Anthropology, [Folklore] and Linguistics*. Memoirs (Bloomington, Ind.). |
| IUP-LSM | *Indiana University Publications, Language Science Monographs* (Bloomington, Ind.). |
| JAbSocPsy | *Journal of Abnormal and Social Psychology* (Washington, D.C.). |
| JAcS | *See* JASA. |
| JAF | *Journal of American Folklore* (Philadelphia). |
| JanL | *Janua Linguarum*. Series maior, minor, practica, critica (The Hague, Mouton & Co.). |
| JAOS | *Journal of the American Oriental Society* (New Haven, Conn.). |
| JASA | *Journal of the Acoustical Society of America* (Lancaster, Pa. and New York). |
| JCLA | *The Journal of the Canadian Linguistic Association/Revue de l'Association canadienne de Linguistique* (Edmonton, Alberta). |
| JEGP | *The Journal of English and Germanic Philology* (Urbana, Ill.). |
| JEL | *Journal of English Linguistics* (Bellingham, Wash.). |
| JL | *Journal of Linguistics* (London). |
| JNH | *Journal of Negro History* (Washington, D.C.). |
| JSHD | *Journal of Speech and Hearing Disorders* (Ann Arbor, Mich.). |
| JSI | *Journal of Social Issues* (Ann Arbor, Mich.). |
| JSocAm | *Journal de la Société des Americanistes* (Paris). |
| JSocI | *See* JSI. |
| JVLVB | *Journal of Verbal Learning and Verbal Behavior* (New York). |

| | |
|---|---|
| JWAS | *Journal of the Washington Academy of Sciences* (Seattle). |
| KASP | *Kroeber Anthropology Society Papers* (Berkeley). |
| KDVS | *Det Konelige danske Videnskabernes Selskab. Hist.-Filo. Meddelelser* (Copenhagen). |
| Kybernetika | *Kybernetika* (Prague). |
| LANE | *Linguistic Atlas of New England.* |
| LenC | *Lenguaje y Ciencias* (Trujillo, Peru). |
| Lg | *Language*. Journal of the Linguistic Society of America (Baltimore). |
| Lingua | *Lingua*. International Review of General Linguistics/Revue internationale de linguistique générale (Amsterdam). |
| Linguistic Inquiry | *Linguistic Inquiry* (Toronto). |
| Linguistics | *Linguistics*. An International Review (The Hague). |
| Linguistique | *La Linguistique*. Revue internationale de linguistique générale (Paris). |
| LL | *Language Learning* (Ann Arbor, Mich.). |
| LPosn | *Lingua Posnaniensis*. Czasopiśmo poświęcone językoznawstwu porównawczemu i ogólnemu (Poznań). |
| L & S | *Language and Speech* (Teddington, Middlesex). |
| Man | *Man*. A Record of Anthropological Science (London). |
| META | *META*. Formerly *Journal des Traducteurs* (Université de Montréal). |
| MKAW | *Mitteilungen der kaiserlichen Akademie der Wissenschaften in Wien* (Vienna). |
| MLJ | *Modern Language Journal* (Ann Arbor, Mich.). |
| MLN | *Modern Language Notes* (Baltimore). |
| MLQ | *Modern Language Quarterly* (Seattle). |
| MLR | *The Modern Language Review* (Cambridge). |
| MPhil | *Modern Philology* (Chicago). |
| MPhon | *Le Maître Phonétique*. Organe de l'Association Phonétique Internationale (London). |
| MSLL | *Monograph Series on Language and Linguistics* (Georgetown University, Washington, D.C.). |
| MT | *Mechanical Translation* (Cambridge, Mass.). |
| Names | *Names*. Journal of the American Name Society (Berkeley). |
| NARN | *Northwest Anthropological Research Notes* (Moscow, University of Idaho). |
| NMC-B | *National Museum of Canada*. Bulletin (Ottawa, The Queen's Printer). |
| NoB | *Namn och Bygd*. Tidskrift för nordisk ortnamnsforskning (Uppsala). |
| Nph | *Neophilologus* (Groningen). |
| NPhM | *Neuphilologische Mitteilungen*. Bulletin de la Société neophilologique de Helsinki (Helsinki). |
| NRFH | *Nueva Revista de Filologiá Hispánica* (Mexico). |
| NTS | *Norsk Tidsskrift for Sprogvidenskap* (Oslo). |
| OED | *Oxford English Dictionary.* |
| OL | *Oceanic Linguistics*. Special Publication (Pacific and Asian Linguistic Institute, University of Hawaii, Honolulu). |
| Onomastica | *Onomastica*. Pismo poświecone nazewnictwu geograficznemu i osobowemu (Wrocław). |
| Orbis | *Orbis*. Bulletin international de documentation linguistique (Louvain). |
| OSlP | *Oxford Slavonic Papers* (London). |
| OSUWPL | *Ohio State University Working Papers in Linguistics* (Columbus). |
| PADS | *Publications of the American Dialect Society* (Gainesville, Fla. and University, Ala.). |
| PAES | *Publications of the American Ethnological Society* (Seattle and Leiden). |
| PAPS | *Proceedings of the American Philosophical Society* (Philadelphia). |
| Phonetica | *Phonetica*. Internationale Zeitschrift für Phonetik/International Journal of Phonetics (Basel and New York). |
| PhQ | *Philological Quarterly* (Iowa City). |
| PIAcadS | *Proceedings of the Indiana Academy of Sciences* (Indianapolis). |
| PICAm [3, 35, etc.] | *Proceedings of the [Third, Thirty-Fifth, etc.] International Congress of Americanists.* |
| PICL [7, 9, etc.] | *Proceedings of the [Seventh, Ninth, etc.] International Congress of Linguists.* |

# LIST OF ABBREVIATIONS

| | |
|---|---|
| PICPS 4 | *Proceedings of the Fourth International Congress of Phonetic Sciences*, held at the University of Helsinki, 4-9 September, 1961. Edited by Antti Sovijärvi and Pento Aalto (The Hague, Mouton, 1962). |
| PJE | *Philippine Journal of Education* (Quezon City). |
| PJL | *Philippine Journal of Language Teaching* (Quezon City). |
| Plateau | *Plateau* (Northern Arizona Society of Science and Art, Flagstaff, Ariz.). |
| PNQ | *Pacific Northwest Quarterly* (Seattle). |
| PMLA | *Publications of the Modern Language Association of America* (New York). |
| Poetics | *Poetics*. International Review for the Theory of Literature (The Hague). |
| POLA | *Project on Linguistic Analysis* (The Ohio State University Research Foundation, Columbus). |
| PRS[IHS] | *Prehistoric Research Series* (Indiana Historical Society, Indianapolis). |
| PSLM | *Publications de la Section de Linguistique, Faculté des Lettres, Université de Montréal.* |
| QJSp | *Quarterly Journal of Speech* (Columbia, Missouri). |
| RCAFL-P | *Publications of the Research Center in Antropology, Folklore and Linguistics* (Bloomington, Ind.). |
| RCB & B | *Royal Commission on Bilingualism and Biculturalism*. Preliminary Report + 4 vols. (Ottawa). 1965–. |
| RDialR | *Revue de dialectologie romane*. Société de dialectologie romane (Hamburg). |
| RFE | *Revista de Filología Española* (Madrid). |
| RHiM | *Revista Hispánica Moderna* (New York). |
| RJb | *Romanistisches Jahrbuch* (Hamburg). |
| RLing | *Revue Roumaine de Linguistique* (Bucharest). |
| Romania | *Romania* (Paris). |
| RomPh | *Romance Philology* (Berkeley and Los Angeles). |
| RTE | *Research in the Teaching of English* (National Council of Teachers of English, Champaign, Ill.). |
| SA | *Scientific American* (New York). |
| Saga och Sed | *Saga och Sed*. Gustav Adolfs Akademiens årsbok (Uppsala). |
| SAS-P | *Sacramento Anthropological Society*. Papers (Sacramento, Calif.). |
| SCA | *Smithsonian [Institution] Contributions to Anthropology* (Washington, D.C.). |
| Science | *Science*. American Association for the Advancement of Science (Washington, D.C.). |
| SCK | *Smithsonian [Institution] Contributions to Knowledge* (Washington, D.C.). |
| ScS | *Scandinavian Studies*. Publication of the Society for the Advancement of Scandinavian Studies (Menasha, Wisc.). |
| SEEJ | *Slavic and East European Journal* (Bloomington, Ind.). |
| Sefarad | *Sefarad*. Revista del Instituto Arias Montano de Estudios Hebraicos y Oriente Próximo (Madrid and Barcelona). |
| SG | *Studium Generale* (Berlin, Göttingen and Heidelberg). |
| SIL | *Studies in Linguistics* (Buffalo, N.Y.). |
| SJA | *Southwestern Journal of Anthropology* (Albuquerque, N.M.). |
| SL | *Studia Linguistica*. Revue de linguistique générale et comparée (Lund). |
| SMC | *Smithsonian [Institution] Miscellaneous Collections* (Washington, D.C.). |
| SocSciI | *Social Science Information/Information sur les sciences sociales*. International Social Science Council (Paris). |
| Southern FL Quarterly | *Southern Folklore Quarterly* (University of Florida, Gainsville, Fla.). |
| Sprache | *Die Sprache*. Zeitschrift für Sprachwissenschaft (Vienna). |
| SPh | *Studies in Philology* (Chapel Hill, N.C.). |
| Style | *Style* (University of Arkansas, Fayetteville). |
| SWES | *Selected Writings of Edward Sapir in Language, Culture and Personality*. Ed. by David G. Mandelbaum (University of California Press, Berkeley and Los Angeles, 1949). |
| TAPA | *Transactions and Proceedings of the American Philological Association* (Ithaca, N.Y.). |
| TAPS | *Transactions of the American Philosophical Society* (Philadelphia). |
| TCLC | *Travaux du Cercle Linguistique de Copenhague* (Copenhagen). |

| | |
|---|---|
| TCAAS | *Transactions and Collections of the American Antiquarian Society.* |
| TENES | *A Survey of the Teaching of English to Non-English Speakers in the United States.* By H. B. Allen (1966). |
| Thesaurus | *Thesaurus.* Boletin del Instituto Caro y Cueva (Bogotá). |
| TKAS | *Transactions of the Kansas Academy of Science* (Topeka). |
| TPhS | *Transactions of the Philological Society* (London). |
| TSLL | *Texas Studies in Language and Linguistics* (Austin). |
| UAS | *Uralic and Altaic Series.* Indiana University Publications (Bloomington, Ind., and The Hague). |
| UCPAAE | *University of California Publications in American Archaeology and Ethnology* (Berkeley and Los Angeles). |
| UCPL | *University of California Publications in Linguistics* (Berkeley and Los Angeles). |
| UHWPL | *University of Hawaii Working Papers in Linguistics* (Honolulu). |
| UNM-B | *University of New Mexico.* Bulletin (Albuquerque, N.M.). |
| UNM-PA | *University of New Mexico Publications in Anthropology* (Albuquerque, N.M.). |
| UPMAP | *University of Pennsylvania Museum Anthropological Publications* (Philadelphia). |
| UWPA | *University of Washington Publications in Anthropology* (Seattle). |
| VFPA | *Viking Fund Publications in Anthropology.* Wenner-Gren Foundation for Anthropological Research, Inc. (New York). |
| V & L | *Vie et Langage* (Paris). |
| VJa | *Voprosy Jazykoznanija* (Moscow). |
| WF | *Western Folklore* (California Folklore Society, University of California Press, Berkeley). |
| Word | *Word.* Journal of the Linguistic Circle of New York (New York). |
| WP-LBRL | *Working Papers, Language Behavior Research Laboratory* (University of California, Berkeley). |
| WSURS | *Washington State University Research Studies* (Pullman). |
| YFS | *Yale French Studies* (New Haven, Conn.). |
| YUPA | *Yale University Publications in Anthropology* (New Haven, Conn.). |
| ZDA | *Zeitschrift für Deutsches Altertum und deutsche Literatur* (Wiesbaden). |
| ZDPh | *Zeitschrift für deutsche Philologie* (Berlin). |
| ZEthn | *Zeitschrift für Ethnologie.* Organ der Deutschen Gesellschaft für Völkerkunde (Brunswick). |
| ZMaF | *Zeitschrift für Mundartforschung* (Wiesbaden). |
| ZPhon | *Zeitschrift für Phonetik, Sprachwissenschaft und Kommunikationsforschung* (Berlin). |
| ВЯ | See **VJa**. |

## 2. OTHER ABBREVIATIONS

| | |
|---|---|
| ADS | *American Dialect Society.* |
| ATESL | *Association of Teachers of English as a Second Language* (= English Language Section of NAFSA). |
| BIA | *Bureau of Indian Affairs.* |
| CAL | *Center for Applied Linguistics.* |
| CEA | *College English Association.* |
| CLA | *Canadian Linguistic Association.* |
| ERIC | *Educational Resources Information Centre* (London). |
| IEEE | *Institute of Electrical and Electronics Engineers.* |
| NACTEFL | *National Advisory Council on the Teaching of English as a Foreign Language.* |
| NAFSA | *National Association of Foreign Student Advisors.* |
| NCTE | *National Council of Teachers of English.* |
| TESL | *Teaching English as a Second Language.* |
| TESOL | *Teachers of English to Speakers of Other Languages.* |
| TOEFL | *National Council on the Teaching of English as a Foreign Language.* |

PART ONE

NORTH AMERICA

# GENERAL CHAPTERS

# HISTORY OF AMERICAN INDIAN LINGUISTICS

## HARRY HOIJER

The earliest studies of North American Indian languages were made in colonial times by missionaries. Two scholars of this period stand out: John Eliot, an Englishman who came to Boston in 1631 and Roger Williams, also English, who arrived at about the same time. Both men assumed pastorates in the Massachusetts colony, Eliot in Boston and Williams in Salem.

John Eliot soon left his Boston pastorate to assume a similar position in Roxbury, Massachusetts, where he remained until his death in 1690. In Roxbury Eliot soon became known as the Apostle to the Indians. He learned the language of the Indians with whom he worked, an Algonkian tongue (Natick) which is now extinct, so well that he was able in a few years to preach his sermons in Natick. Eliot then proceeded to translate the Bible and much other religious literature into Natick. Of more importance to linguistics, John Eliot published a grammatical study of Natick (Eliot 1666). This work probably represents the first scholarly study of a North American Indian language, the more valuable for the fact that the language described is now extinct. Eliot's grammar was for the period in which he wrote extremely well done. He avoided the error, so common in his day, of basing his study on some preconceived notion of universal grammar or, as was more often the case, on a Graeco-Latin model. Instead, he attempted to describe Natick in its own terms, based upon empirical observation (Wolfart 1967:154).

Roger Williams did not remain in Salem; he moved, a few months after his arrival, to assume a pastorate in Plymouth. Soon after, in 1631, Williams, because of his unorthodox views, was banished from the Massachusetts colony and with four other clergymen founded Providence, Rhode Island. Here Williams established friendly relations with the Narraganset Indians and learned their language. His contribution to the study of Indian languages was a phrase book of Narraganset (Williams 1643) so arranged as to be invaluable to travelers among the Indians of nearly all of New England. The work also contained pertinent ethnographic data which makes it probably the earliest example of what today is sometimes called anthropological linguistics.

The next considerable study of a native American language did not appear until the last half of the eighteenth century when we find two missionary studies of Greenlandic Eskimo. As Goddard puts it:

Eskimo were known in Europe long before the discovery of America. The natives of Greenland have been under the influence of the missionaries for about two centuries. During this time much of the Bible and a great deal of religious literature has been translated and composed in the dialects of Greenland. The grammars and dictionaries produced by two of these missionaries rank among the foremost contributions from missionary sources to the American languages (Goddard 1914:558).

The two missionaries to whom Goddard refers were Hans Egede and his son, Paul Egede, who laid the foundations of Eskimo linguistic studies and who also devised the first orthography with which to represent the complex sound system of Greenlandic. Paul Egede published a Greenlandic-Danish-Latin dictionary (Egede 1750) and, ten years later, one of the earliest grammars of Greenlandic Eskimo (Egede 1760).

Toward the end of the eighteenth century, in 1784, Catherine the Great of Russia began to collect wordlists of about 225 items each, largely from the many different languages spoken in the Russian empire. This collection, plus a great many more samples from languages elsewhere, formed the basis for the famous four volume work of Adelung and Vater published between 1806 and 1817. In volume 4 of this work (Adelung and Vater 1816) there appeared data from a considerable number of American Indian languages. According to Duponceau (1819a:xxxii) there were brief sketches of 'thirty-four American languages, and the Lord's Prayer in fifty-nine different idioms or dialects of native America'.

With the opening of the nineteenth century, the linguistic horizon began to broaden as reports of exotic languages came to the attention of scholars, European and American. Although much of the century was devoted to the historical study of the Indo-European languages and the development of the methods of historical linguistics, scholars could no longer ignore the exotic languages, reported from such regions as Africa south of the Sahara, Oceania, and the Americas. But practical difficulties stood in the way of adequate studies of exotic languages. Methods of fieldwork were crude; phonetics, an obvious prerequisite to the study of unwritten languages, was in its infancy, and many studies of exotic languages were still based very largely on Graeco-Latin models.

The Americas, it is evident, because of the enormous number and diversity of native idioms, provide an almost boundless laboratory for linguistic research. But, at the beginning of the nineteenth century, this laboratory was for the most part unexplored. Most of the studies of North American native languages were confined to languages spoken along the Atlantic coast; the languages of the rest of North America were still largely unknown. And when it became evident that the American languages were not only very different from each other but as well differed remarkably from the better known languages of Europe and the Middle East, a first problem that arose was that of somehow classifying these exotic tongues and so relating them to languages spoken elsewhere.

Two approaches to this problem were already evident: the genetic classification which, at the beginning of the nineteenth century, was only in an initial stage of development, and a typological classification, especially that proposed by Humboldt whereby languages might be divided into three groups: isolating, agglutinating, and inflectional.

When the [nineteenth] century opened [according to Haas] not even the constituency of the Indo-European stock was known, so it is not surprising that at first the problem of classifying the languages of the New World was not specifically or solely their genetic classification ... A new focus of attention was emerging in the problem of overall structural classification of these languages as differentiated from languages in other parts of the world, i.e. their typological classification, and, in consequence, their ranking in terms of higher and lower (Haas 1969a: 239).

One of the first to confront this problem was Peter Stephen Duponceau (1760–1844) who, born in France, came to the United States in 1777 as Steuben's secretary. Although Duponceau became famous as a lawyer, the study of language was one of his principal avocations. Among other languages he became interested in those of the Algonkian group, and translated from the German a grammar of Delaware originally written by David Zeisberger, a Moravian missionary (Zeisberger 1827). Duponceau also conducted an extensive correspondence with John Heckewelder, also a Moravian missionary, from whom he learned about and edited grammars of several other Algonkian tongues (Duponceau 1819b). Indeed, he became so well acquainted with languages of the Algonkian group that he 'was able to make the identification of many Algonkian cognates even though he had no real understanding of the nature of the sound correspondences' (Haas 1969a:241). Duponceau also provided a list of language families for most of the eastern part of North America. He set up four principal stocks: Karalit (= Greenlandic Eskimo), Iroquois, Lenni-Lenápe (=Delaware), and Floridian, or the Southern stock, a sort of wastebasket category often, but mistakenly, equated with Muskogean (see Haas 1969a:242).

In 1819, in a report to the historical and literary committee of the American Philosophical Society, Duponceau first characterized the American Indian languages as polysynthetic, a typological classification to which all American Indian languages belonged and which set them apart from languages spoken elsewhere in the world (Duponceau 1819a). Some ten years later, after Duponceau had examined many more grammars of American languages, all of which, however, were spoken in the eastern United States, he repeated his assertion that all American languages, from Greenland to Chile, were, without exception, polysynthetic (Duponceau 1838).

John Pickering (1777–1846) was, like his contemporary Duponceau, a lawyer by profession. He was also, however, both a general linguist and a first class classical scholar (Edgerton 1943:27, 28). Although Pickering won high distinction as a lawyer, and his classical studies won him an offer of a professorship in Greek from Harvard (which he declined), he also found time to make extensive studies of American Indian languages. One of his first publications in this field was an essay defining a uniform orthography for the Indian languages of North America (Pickering 1818). Edgerton describes this essay as 'nothing more nor less than a start towards an international phonetic alphabet' even though it is 'crude and rudimentary when judged by modern standards' (Edgerton 1943:27).

Pickering's principal contributions, however, consisted mainly of his editing and republishing many earlier studies of American languages, all of which he embellished with linguistic notes and comments of his own. Among these are Eliot's grammar (Pickering 1822), Jonathan Edwards' work on Mohegan (Pickering 1823), Josiah Cotton's vocabulary of Natick (Pickering 1830), and Sébastien Rasles' dictionary of Abnaki (Pickering 1833). Pickering also wrote an article on the Indian languages of North America for the *Encyclopedia Americana* (Pickering 1831).

Pickering, like Duponceau, classed all the languages of the Americas as polysynthetic, and maintained that this characterization set the American languages off from all others outside the Americas. He also suggested that there were no more than three or four principal language families east of the Mississippi, and that it was quite likely that future study of the languages of the West would not add greatly to this number. On this point he disagreed with Thomas Jefferson who had suggested, as early as 1787, that future study of the languages of the West would result in a large number of language families (Jefferson 1955).

Albert Gallatin (1761–1849), originally a language teacher, later became active in politics and finance and served for a time as Jefferson's Secretary of the Treasury. Later in his life he became interested in the native languages of North America and especially in the problem of classifying them. To this end, Gallatin, in 1826, prepared a list of some 600 words together with a few sentences and grammatical queries. This questionnaire was distributed widely by the Secretary of War to persons throughout the country who could provide data on American Indian languages. From the data so obtained, together with published and manuscript materials (the latter made available by Duponceau) Gallatin prepared the first systematic comparative study of the native languages of North America (Gallatin 1836). A revised and expanded version of this study appeared in 1848 as the introduction to Gallatin's study of the data on the Indian languages of the American Northwest collected by Horatio Hale (Gallatin 1848).

In the 1848 classification Gallatin set up thirty-two distinct linguistic families in and north of the United States but not including California. According to Haas, Gallatin's classification '... was a landmark in the history of the genealogical classification of North American languages and was not superseded until the work of Powell and his coworkers completed what Gallatin had begun' (Haas 1969a:244).

In the second half of the nineteenth century and continuing to the present day there appeared a considerable number of descriptive studies of North American native languages written by missionaries. Foremost among these is the work of Samuel Kleinschmidt, a Moravian missionary, on Greenlandic Eskimo.

Samuel Kleinschmidt was born in South Greenland in 1768, and died there in 1886. Since his father was a German, his mother a Dane, and his playmates were Eskimos, Kleinschmidt learned German, Danish and Eskimo as a child. According to Rosing,

'By playing with Greenlandic children [Kleinschmidt] learned, automatically, the thought processes of the Greenlanders and acquired the language as it was used and understood by the native population' (Rosing 1951:63).

Later Kleinschmidt went to school in Holland where, according to Rosing (1951:63), his linguistic training continued as he learned Latin, Greek, and Hebrew, along with Dutch, French, and English. Kleinschmidt returned to Greenland in 1840 as a missionary where he remained until his death in 1886. During his lifetime he wrote two major Greenlandic studies: a grammar, written in German (Kleinschmidt 1851) for which he was offered (but refused) an honorary degree from the University of Berlin, and a dictionary (Kleinschmidt 1871) written in Danish. According to Rosing, Kleinschmidt 'had not constructed his grammar according to the time-honored Latin systems, but instead, according to the language's own structure' (Rosing 1951:64).

Additional missionary studies include, among others, the following:

Cyrus Byington's grammar of Choctaw (Byington 1871).

Albert Lacombe's dictionary of Cree (Lacombe 1874).

Emile Petitot's comparative dictionary and grammar of the Athapaskan languages of northwestern Canada (Petitot 1876). This work, despite its cumbersome phonetic transcriptions, is still a valuable source of data on the northern Athapaskan languages.

Laurent Legoff's grammar of Chipewyan (or Montagnaise) (Legoff 1889).

Stephen R. Riggs' excellent studies of Dakota, a language he spoke fluently (Riggs 1890, 1893). These works were published after his death and edited by J. Owen Dorsey. Riggs began his publication of texts and translations as early as 1842, and a grammar and dictionary of Dakota was published by the Smithsonian Institution as early as 1851. Detailed bibliographic references to these earlier studies may be found in Pilling 1887.

Julius Jetté, a Jesuit missionary, spent most of his life among the Koyukon Indians of northern Alaska; he called them by the name Ten'a. Jetté wrote a long article on their language (Jetté 1907-09) and a detailed grammar and dictionary which runs to more than 2,000 manuscript pages. This work, still unpublished, is in the archives of the Crosby Library at Gonzaga University.

The Franciscan Fathers published two considerable dictionaries of the Navajo language (Franciscan Fathers 1910, 1912). Later, Father Berard Haile also published a dictionary (Haile 1950, 1951) as well as several volumes of texts which deal mainly with the elaborate ceremonies of the Navajo.

J.W. Chapman, a Protestant missionary stationed at Anvik, Alaska, published a volume of texts in the language (Chapman 1914) which he called Ten'a.

One of the most prolific of the missionaries, the Oblate Father A.G. Morice, wrote a great many articles and monographs on the language and culture of the Carrier Indians. His most important work, a two volume grammar and dictionary of Carrier, is still our principal source on this language (Morice 1932).

Today the most important missionary contributions to the study of American native languages are those of the Wycliffe Bible Translators (also referred to by the phrase

Summer Institute of Linguistics). Although their primary objective is to translate the Bible, many of this group have also produced excellent grammars and dictionaries. For a bibliography of their work, see Wares 1968.

We turn now to the scholars of the second half of the nineteenth century. Among these we find Henry Rowe Schoolcraft who acquired an excellent knowledge of Ojibwa, partly from having spent many years among them and in part from his wife, Jane Johnston, who was a native speaker of the language. Schoolcraft's most important work is a six volume study of the Indians of the United States (Schoolcraft 1851–57). Volume 5 of this work contains various grammatical and lexical materials. According to Edgerton, Leonard Bloomfield examined Schoolcraft's material on Ojibwa and found 'that Schoolcraft unquestionably had a sound and thorough knowledge of the language, and in general analyzed its forms quite intelligently. His weakest point is his orthography, which is fatally inconsistent' (Edgerton 1946:30). In this respect, however, he differed little from other scholars of his time.

J. Hammond Trumbull's principal work was an encyclopedia article on the Indian languages of America (Trumbull 1876). In this paper he queries the views of earlier scholars on the typological classification of the American languages, and emphasizes the need for historical studies based upon the comparative method.

In an earlier paper on the best method of studying the North American languages (Trumbull 1871) he presents an essentially modern view on synchronic studies. According to Haas, '... a new era in American linguistics has begun with Trumbull's programmatic statement. This is an early and clear formulation of the methodology which dominated American linguistic work until well into the second half of the twentieth century' (Haas 1969a:247).

Horatio Hale, who later in his life became a well known lawyer, went as a very young man as ethnologist and philologist of the Wilkes Exploring Expedition to the South Pacific. In 1841, when the expedition stopped at the Oregon Territory, Hale left it to conduct an extensive study of the many varied languages and customs of the Indians who lived there. It was these data, as we noted earlier, that formed the basis of Albert Gallatin's study of the Indian languages of the American northwest (Gallatin 1848).

Later, Hale did a comparative study of the Iroquoian languages, including in that stock the Cherokee (Hale 1883). Hale also was the first to discover that Tutelo, a language of the east coast formerly classed as Iroquoian, actually belonged to the Siouan family of languages (Hale 1884). More important than these contributions to American Indian studies is the fact that Hale supervised Boas' most important years of fieldwork and edited the reports which were their result (Wolfart 1967:166, quoting Gruber 1967). Wolfart later adds: 'Hale deserves to be remembered for his work on the languages of the American Northwest and for the influence which Gruber amply shows him to have had on Boas' (Wolfart 1967:168).[1]

---

[1] Gruber's argument depends on substantive parallels between Hale and Boas in their interest in ethnography and philology, as against the evolutionary ethnology that dominated the scene between

One of the dominant figures in the last half of the 19th century was William Dwight Whitney (1827-94) who, in addition to his outstanding reputation as a Sanskrit scholar, was also the first American to write on general linguistics (Whitney 1867, 1875). In the first of these books Whitney discussed the problem of classifying the native American languages and the further problem of relating them to languages outside the American continents. In this discussion, Whitney urged that

What we have to do at present ... is simply to learn all that we possibly can of the Indian languages themselves; to settle their internal relations, elicit their laws of growth, reconstruct their older forms, and ascend toward their original condition as far as the material within our reach, and the state in which it is presented, will allow (Whitney 1867:351).

One of the first to apply these principles to the American languages north of Mexico was John Wesley Powell (1834-1902). Powell followed many careers: he was an army officer during the Civil War, a geologist, and an explorer (the first to traverse the Colorado River in an open boat). He later became interested in ethnology and linguistics and became, in 1879, the founder and first director of the Bureau of American Ethnology. Powell also helped to organize both the Anthropological Society of Washington and its offshoot, the American Anthropological Association.

The publication for which Powell is best known is of course his classification of the Indian languages north of Mexico (Powell 1891). As Sapir has said: 'The cornerstone of the linguistic edifice in aboriginal North America ... is Powell's "Indian linguistic Families of America North of Mexico" ... This monumental work, with its appended map, has served ... as the basis of all classificatory work in North American linguistics' (Sapir 1917:79).

The Powell classification was based primarily on vocabulary; where he found obviously cognate forms between two or more languages, these were put into a single family; where any doubt existed, the languages were grouped separately. As a result, Powell listed 58 language stocks for American north of Mexico. Later studies reduced this number considerably. It is interesting to note, however, that in no case have any of the stocks established by Powell been discredited by later work. All modifications of the Powell classification have been to combine two or more of the Powell families into one.

In the preparation of his classification Powell was assisted by two men of considerable competence: Albert S. Gatschet and J. Owen Dorsey. Gatschet collected an enormous amount of data on languages all over the United States; his publications

---

Hale's main work at mid-century and Boas' emergence at the century's end, and on the fact of Hale's supervisory role for the British Association for the Advancement of Science in connection with work of Boas on the North Pacific Coast. Boas' letters, however, show him to have resented Hale's supervision, and to have been in conflict with Hale as to the work he should do (Rohner 1969:81-2, 106-9, xvii). Furthermore, Boas' interests and approach can be readily explained in terms of his own development, set against the background of his German training and prior field experience (cf. Stocking 1968: chs. 7, 9; 1972). Hale deserves attention, and Gruber's article says a good deal of interest about him, but the case for influence on Boas is at best circumstantial. [Note supplied by Dell Hymes at Professor Hoijer's request.]

extend over a period of more than twenty years from 1876 to 1900. A bibliography of his work may be found in Goddard 1914:596-7. Dorsey's studies were confined in large part to the Siouan languages, primarily the Ponca; see Goddard 1914:595. Gatschet and Dorsey, according to Goddard,

inaugurated the second period of linguistic work stimulated by scientific interest rather than missionary zeal in North America. Until their time the chief purpose has been to secure sufficient material to determine to which large group each language belonged. The new interest was two-fold: a psychological interest in the languages themselves ... and a historical interest in the changes that had taken place in a single language or in the various languages belonging to one family (Goddard 1914:560).

Of the many linguists associated with Powell, [Wolfart adds] Albert S. Gatschet and J. Owen Dorsey have to be singled out as more direct precursors of Boas and later anthropologists ... [The new lines of research inaugurated by Gatschet and Dorsey] required more thorough and much more detailed descriptions of individual languages than had been available so far; of this new type of description, Gatschet's monumental work on Klamath (1890) and Dorsey's on Ponca (1890) provide good examples (Wolfart 1967:163).

Daniel G. Brinton (1837-99) was a physician by profession who, early in his lifetime, developed a wide interest in the American Indians, their archeological past, their present condition, and their languages. In 1886, his accomplishments in these areas won him a professorship in American archeology and linguistics at the University of Pennsylvania.

Brinton's principal writings were on the languages and cultures of Middle America — in this area he wrote a grammar of Cakchiquel (a language of Guatemala, Brinton 1884) and published as well a collection of pre-conquest Nahuatl chants (Brinton 1890) and the *Annals of the Cakchiquels* (Brinton 1885).

Brinton's major work (Brinton 1891) is described by Wolfart as 'the first attempt at a systematic classification of all the tribes of America — North, Central, and South — on the basis of their languages' (Wolfart 1969:164-5).

Although Brinton's presentation for North America, because he could not gain access to the data collected by Powell and his associates, was almost at once superseded by the Powell classification, 'his classification of South American languages became the starting point for all subsequent classifications' (Rowe 1954:19). Brinton held essentially to Duponceau's view that all American languages were polysynthetic, but he also maintained that lexical comparisons must be a main standby in matters of classification. In this respect his position was not so very different from that held by Powell and his associates.

The major figure in what Goddard called the second period of linguistic research in North American languages was Franz Boas (1858-1942). Boas worked in all fields of anthropology: ethnology, archeology, physical anthropology, and linguistics, and in effect dominated both American anthropology and linguistics from about 1899 until his death in 1942.

Boas was born in Germany and received his Ph.D. in 1881; his thesis lay in the field of physics. Similarly, the six papers he published in 1881 and 1882 were also in physics and related subjects. It was not until 1883–84, when he joined an expedition to Baffinland, that he became interested in anthropology.

Boas visited the United States for the first time in the winter of 1884–85 and spent most of that period in the city of New York. On his return to Germany he studied with Bastian and Virchow and became Docent in Geography (1886) at the University of Berlin. In 1887 Boas returned to New York and decided to become a citizen of the United States. Boas became a docent at Clark University in 1888, where he spent four years. He resigned from Clark in 1892 to become an assistant to Putnam of the Department of Anthropology at the Chicago World Columbian Exposition, and later (1894) to become Curator of Ethnology and Somatology at the Field Museum, Chicago, a position he held for only one year. In 1895 Boas joined the staff of the American Museum of Natural History, a position wh ch was supplemented in 1896 when Boas became a lecturer in physical anthropology at Columbia University. In 1899 Columbia made him Professor of Anthropology, a position he held until his retirement. According to Kroeber,

In the teaching of linguistics, Boas' approach was wholly inductive and empirical. He set before students an interlinear text and proceeded to analyze it, developing the structure of the language as he proceeded ...
[This procedure] epitomized, of course, his own history of approach to linguistics; and served to ground firmly his cardinal principle of viewing each language in terms of its own pattern instead of a preconceived or theoretical one (Kroeber 1943:14, 15).

It was this approach to linguistics that was followed and further developed by his students and taught to their students until well into the present century. Boas' students included, among many others, Sapir, Kroeber, Jacobs, and Andrade. In the 1930s there were few linguistic students in the United States who had not been influenced by Boas, by one of Boas's students, or by Bloomfield, who, though not a Boas student, was nonetheless his devoted admirer and colleague.

The number and variety of American native languages recorded and investigated by Boas is truly remarkable. Most of these are languages of the American northwest, the area in which Boas did his first field studies; these include Chinook, Kathlamet, Tsimshian, Kwakiutl, Tlingit, Kutenai, and Bella Bella. In addition, Boas worked on Keresan, a Pueblo language, and Dakota, a language of the Plains. Boas also reworked earlier studies on Coos, Siuslaw, and Chukchi, the last named a language of northeastern Asia. Finally, we find a number of briefer studies on Eskimo, Chemakum, Salish, Ponca, Iroquois, and Tsetsaut. A full bibliography of Boas' work (in anthropology and in linguistics) is found in *Memoir* 61 (1943) of the American Anthropological Association, pp. 62–109.

Perhaps Boas' greatest achievement (in so far as American linguistics is concerned) is the *Handbook of American Indian Languages* (Boas 1911, 1922, 1933–38; Haas, 1940). These volumes contained twenty full length grammatical studies, each on a language representative of one of Powell's linguistic groupings. Boas himself wrote three studies, all to be found in Part 1 of the *Handbook*, and he probably aided in the writing of three more. The remaining grammars were written either by men who had studied under Boas (e.g. Sapir) or close associates of Boas (e.g. Thalbitzer).

Part I of the *Handbook* contained an Introduction written by Boas (Boas 1911:1–83). In this paper, Boas set forth his views on race and language; the characteristics, phonetic and grammatical, of languages in general; the problem of the classification of languages; the relationship of linguistics to ethnology; and a brief review of the unique characteristics of American native languages. Despite its age, the Introduction remains the best available general work on American native language, as is shown by the fact that it has twice been reprinted; once by the Georgetown University Press (an undated reprint) and again by the University of Nebraska Press in 1966.

In 1917 Boas founded the *International Journal of American Linguistics*, which he edited and maintained, often at heavy personal cost, until his death. Various individuals functioned as editorial assistants; among them were P.E. Goddard, William Thalbitzer, C.C. Uhlenbeck, Paul Rivet, Edward Sapir, and Leonard Bloomfield. The journal was genuinely international, both in the polyglot nature of its contributions and in the nationality of its writers and collaborators. It was, however, devoted alone to American native languages — the only American journal of its kind.

About 1925, the American Council of Learned Societies provided a considerable fund to be used to promote research in American Indian languages. The fund was administered by a Committee on Research in American Native Languages, a committee made up of Franz Boas, chairman, Edward Sapir, and Leonard Bloomfield. All of the money was to be used for field and living expenses of the researchers; no salaries were paid and no money was provided for publication. The fund thus provided for an immense amount of fieldwork but only a small proportion of the data collected was published; the major proportion of the data collected remains unpublished and is now stored in the library of the American Philosophical Society. An index to this collection is now available (Voegelin and Harris 1945). According to Kroeber: 'There has rarely been so vast a mass of wholly new data, many of them on the point of perishing, gathered at so low a cost in any field of scholarship; and Boas' was the greatest share of responsibility in the execution of the undertaking' (Kroeber 1943:39).

To summarize, we can do no better than to quote Emeneau:

Of [Boas'] success in dealing in a strictly linguistic way with the unfamiliar and difficult languages which he handled, we need say little. On perusal of the grammars which he wrote, we are struck by the combined ingenuity and soundness of his analysis in a field where the pedestrian had reigned for too long before him ... He brought to his descriptive work an almost complete freedom from preconceptions, at a time when linguistic scholarship had not yet quite freed itself from the last preconceptions of pre-scientific linguistic study ... He was able ... to analyze exotic material without forcing it into the straitjacket of the familiar. This was perhaps the most valuable single lesson in analysis that he taught his pupils and they theirs (Emeneau 1943:36–7).

Leonard Bloomfield adds to this praise in the following terms:

Perhaps [Boas'] greatest contribution to science ... was the development of descriptive language study. The native languages of our country had been studied by some very gifted men, but none had succeeded in putting this study on a scientific basis ... Boas amassed a tremendous body of observation, including much carefully recorded text, and forged, almost single-handed, the tools of phonetic and structural description (Bloomfield 1943:198).

Three men stand out in American linguistics from about 1920 until 1940 or 1950. Two of these were students under Boas: Alfred L. Kroeber (1876–1960) and Edward Sapir (1884–1939). The third was Leonard Bloomfield (1887–1949), a good friend and admirer of Boas. Kroeber took his Ph.D. at Columbia in 1901, and went immediately to the University of California (Berkeley) where he soon became Professor of Anthropology, a position he held until his retirement in 1946. Edward Sapir received his Ph.D. in 1909. In 1907–08 he served as research associate at the Berkeley campus and later spent a year or two as a research fellow and instructor at the University of Pennsylvania. In 1910, Sapir became chief of the newly created Division of Anthropology at the Victoria Museum at Ottawa (now the Canadian National Museum), a position he held until 1925. At that time he was appointed Professor of Anthropology at the University of Chicago, a post he held until 1931 when he went to Yale as Sterling Professor of Anthropology.

Leonard Bloomfield received his Ph.D. in 1909 at the University of Chicago. His principal area of research and teaching was in Germanic philology, and in 1913 and 1914 he studied at Leipzig and Göttingen. Until 1940, Bloomfield held teaching positions in Germanics at several universities, and in 1940, he was appointed Sterling Professor of Linguistics at Yale, a position he held until his death. While at the University of Illinois, Bloomfield became interested in Tagalog, a language of the Philippines, on which he published a volume of texts (Bloomfield 1917). Bloomfield's first contact with Boas probably took place shortly after the founding of the *International Journal of American Linguistics* when Bloomfield became one of the three co-editors of that journal. It was probably this contact that brought Bloomfield to the study of American Indian languages.

Kroeber, soon after he came to California, undertook an ethnological and archeological survey of the state. His purpose was in effect to define and describe the numerous cultures and languages found in California and to establish if possible the relationships of these to each other. In regard to the language problem, Kroeber asked and received aid from men whose linguistic training was far better than his own. Among those who, at one time or another, assisted Kroeber in his survey of linguistic problems were P.E. Goddard, who wrote primarily on the Athapaskan languages of the region; Edward Sapir, who spent a year in California working on the Yana languages; R.B. Dixon, T.T. Waterman, Samuel K. Barrett, and Paul Radin. Except for Sapir, all of these men, like Kroeber himself, were limited in linguistic research; their interests lay far more in anthropology than in linguistics.

Kroeber's linguistic studies fall into three principal categories:

1. Descriptive studies, confined essentially to languages that would soon become extinct.

2. Phonetic studies, an attempt to describe, as precisely as possible, the somewhat unusual phonetic characteristics of the Indian languages of California.

3. Classificatory studies, an attempt by Kroeber (aided by Dixon and Sapir) to reduce the large number of linguistic families set up by Powell for California to a smaller number.

In retrospect, the studies of category (3) stand out as the most important of Kroeber's linguistic contributions. Most of his descriptive studies have been replaced by later and more sophisticated work. Thus, for example, Kroeber's study of the Yokuts language of south central California (Kroeber 1907) is far superseded by Stanley Newman's more recent work (Newman 1944). It should be noted, however, that Kroeber, in a number of cases, did rescue from oblivion California languages that are now no longer spoken.

In the early 1900s, when Kroeber began his linguistic studies, California was remarkable for the number and diversity of its native American languages: of the 58 linguistic families set up by Powell for America north of Mexico, twenty-two families or parts of families were found in California. Kroeber and his co-workers set out to re-examine the Powell classification of California languages. To Kroeber, 'it seemed desirable to bring together all the readily available data [on the California languages] and determine the exact degree and nature of the [observed] similarities [between them]' (Dixon and Kroeber 1919:49).

The method employed is described as follows:

About two hundred and twenty-five English words were selected on which material was most likely to be accessible in reasonably accurate and comparable form, and the native equivalents in sixty-seven dialects of the twenty-one stocks were entered in columns. Comparisons were then instituted to determine all inter-stock similarities that seemed too close or too numerous to be ascribed to coincidence. The purpose of the study was three fold: first, to ascertain the nature and degree of borrowing between unrelated languages; second, to trace through these borrowings any former contacts or movements of language groups not now in contact; third, in the event of any relationship existing between languages then considered unrelated, to determine this fact (Dixon and Kroeber 1919:49).

The results provided by this methodology drastically reduced the number of Californian linguistic families set up by Powell. The major reduction was achieved by setting up two large families, Penutian, which combined Maidu, Yokuts, Wintun, Miwok, and Costanoan into one family; and Hokan, which similarly united Karok, Chimariko, Shastan, Pomo, Yana, Washo, Esselen, Salinan, Chumash, and Yuman. The Athapaskan languages of California had been recognized by Powell, as had the Shoshonean and Yukian groups. Kroeber, however, united two other Powell language isolates, Wiyot and Yurok.

As we mentioned earlier, Sapir participated in the attempts by Dixon and Kroeber to re-classify the California languages. It was he who extended the Hokan and Penutian groups to include a considerable number of languages outside of California. He also was the first to relate Dixon and Kroeber's Ritwan (i.e. Wiyot and Yurok) to Algonkian (Sapir 1913), a relationship severely criticized by Michelson, a long time student of the Algonkian languages (Michelson 1914). Sapir answered this criticism which provoked a second reply from Michelson (*AmA* 17.188-98, 1915). Although Dixon and Kroeber agreed with Sapir's Algonkian-Ritwan (Dixon and Kroeber 1919: 112) the controversy was not settled until 1958, when Haas presented irrefutable evidence of the Algonkian-Ritwan relationship (Haas 1958a).

In 1929 Sapir wrote his well-known classification, in which he grouped all of the languages of America north of Mexico and some in Mexico and Central America into six super-stocks: Eskimo-Aleut, Nadene, Algonkin-Wakashan, Penutian, Hokan-Siouan, and Aztec-Tanoan. This classification, too often assumed to be final, was instead highly tentative and, in Sapir's words, 'suggestive but not demonstrable in all its features at the present time' (Sapir 1929:137). Two of Sapir's super-stocks, Eskimo-Aleut and Aztec-Tanoan, have been confirmed (the latter by Whorf and Trager 1937). The Algonkin-Wakashan group (which combines Algonkin with Ritwan [i.e. Wiyot-Yurok], Kootenay, Mosan (i.e. Kwakiutl, Nootka, Chimakuan, and Salish) is not yet demonstrable in all respects. The Nadene super-stock, which unites Athapaskan, Haida, and Tlingit, is still unsupported. The remaining two super-stocks, Penutian and Hokan-Siouan, are still highly tentative, despite much recent work. This is especially so in regard to Hokan-Siouan which even Sapir regarded as exceptionally tentative. Indeed, Haas has recently suggested that the Muskogean languages, grouped with one branch of Hokan-Siouan by Sapir, may be distantly related to the Algonkian languages (Haas 1958b; see also Haas, this volume).

Sapir's field researches covered a considerable number of languages. At one time or another, he conducted extensive field studies of Wishram, Takelma, Yana, Southern Paiute, Nootka, Sarsi, Hupa, Kutchin, and Navajo. Less detailed studies were also made of Chasta Costa, Ingalik, Haida, Chinook, Tutelo, Wiyot, Yurok, and Kootenay. Much of this material remains unpublished except for brief articles. Sapir's published monographs are relatively few; these include *Wishram texts* (1909a), "Takelma texts" (1909b), "Yana texts" (1910), Takelma grammar (1922), an extensive study of Southern Paiute (1930) and *Nootka texts* (1930). Sapir's *Navaho texts* (1942) and *The phonology and morphology of the Navaho language* (Sapir and Hoijer 1967) were published posthumously.

Sapir's most extensive studies were of the Athapaskan languages; these began early in his life (ca. 1917) and continued until his death. On Navajo, an Athapaskan language of New Mexico and Arizona, Sapir brought together what is probably the most comprehensive data ever collected on an American Indian language. Most of these materials remain unpublished, as does the data Sapir collected on Hupa, Sarsi, and Kutchin, although some of the material is treated in brief articles. A complete bibliography of Sapir's publications (anthropological and linguistic) is found in his *Selected writings* (Mandelbaum, ed. 1949:601-17).

Although Leonard Bloomfield is best known for his book *Language* (1933), in which he laid the groundwork for the synchronic study of language, he was, as Haas puts it, 'one of the greatest historical linguists of this century' (Haas 1969b:21). Bloomfield, whose education and training lay in the field of Germanic philology, began, early in his career, to study the so-called 'exotic languages'. His first studies in this field related to Tagalog and the related languages of the Malayo-Polynesian family. Later, Bloomfield began his studies of the Algonkian languages of North America, and primarily on the central Algonkian languages: Fox, Cree, Menominee, and Ojibwa.

A great many historical linguists of the nineteenth century and even in the early twentieth century held that the historical and comparative study of unwritten languages was impossible, since these languages lacked written records attesting earlier stages in their history. Bloomfield proposed to refute this view and to demonstrate that the historical-comparative method, as developed by Indo-European scholars, could equally well be applied to languages that lacked a writing. Moreover, Bloomfield demonstrated that the phonemic system of the proto-language of a group of unwritten languages could be reconstructed with the same degree of rigor and reliability as had been achieved for the Indo-European languages (Haas 1969b:23). The first result of Bloomfield's demonstration appeared in his paper "On the sound-system of Central Algonquian" (Bloomfield 1925), a paper Haas describes as 'masterly' and one 'which paved the way for all future work in comparative Algonkian' (Haas 1969b:22, 23). A second and longer paper appeared in *Linguistic structures of Native America* (Hoijer and others, 1946:85-129) in which Bloomfield produced 'an outline descriptive grammar of the protolanguage' (Haas 1969b:24).

In addition to his historical studies Bloomfield published three collections of texts: *Menominee texts* (1928), *Sacred stories of the Sweet Grass Cree* (1930), and *Plains Cree texts* (1934). A grammar, *The Menominee language*, was published after his death (Bloomfield 1962). See Hockett (1948) for a full list of Bloomfield's publications on the Algonkian languages.

As we have seen, the scientific study of American native languages began with the work of Franz Boas, who was not only a highly competent linguist but was as well an anthropologist. It was his influence that accounts for the fact that linguistic studies in the United States were, until the 1940s, conducted by anthropologists who felt it their task to record and describe the native languages of America and who were, during this period, quite independent of the older Indo-European tradition. Indeed there were many linguistic scholars who looked with a disdain bordering on contempt upon linguists who concentrated upon languages that were not only 'primitive' but had as well no literary tradition.

During the years (approximately the first four decades of the twentieth century) there was considerable progress in the study of American native languages. This is manifest, not only in the greater number of languages that were described, but as well in the better quality of the descriptions. Much, if not all, of this advance is due to the efforts of Edward Sapir and Leonard Bloomfield, both of whom played a considerable role in training linguistic scholars.

Much of the research of this period remained unpublished, in large part due to the fact that funds provided for linguistic research did not, in general, provide for publication. Furthermore, the publication of Bloomfield's *Language* in 1933 led almost immediately to a prevailing and intensive concern with methodology. As a result descriptive data on American native languages were often presented only in journal articles as background material to illustrate one or other methodological problem. Complete structural studies, such as are illustrated by Stanley Newman's *Yokuts* (1944) or Mary Haas' "Tunica" (1940) were few in comparison to the flood of brief papers like those contained in *Linguistic structures of Native America* (Hoijer and others, 1946) and in the *International Journal of American Linguistics*. Also lacking were dictionaries and large collections of texts, a prime need in the study of American native languages.

The entry of the United States in World War II in 1941 and the establishment of the Intensive Language Program turned the attention of many linguists, including a number whose primary concern was with American Indian languages, to the problem of teaching languages essential to the war effort. According to Moulton, 'by the end of the year [1943] some 15,000 soldiers were being trained at 55 colleges and universities in 27 different languages' (Moulton 1961:85).

Linguists were considered essential to the Intensive Language Program, both in the problems of teaching and in the preparation of teaching materials.

One result of the war-time language program was enormously to increase the number of university departments of linguistics, and to begin the trend, today almost complete, to separate linguistic teaching from anthropology. Students, whether concerned with American Indian languages or with languages of other areas, are today encouraged to take their degrees in linguistics rather than, as previously, in departments of anthropology. However, this change did not necessarily discourage American Indian studies; at the University of California (Berkeley), for example, there was a considerable emphasis on American Indian studies, an emphasis which has led to the publication of a large number of grammars, collections of texts, and dictionaries on the native languages of California and the neighboring states. It may well be said that the California monograph series (*University of California Publications in Linguistics*) has published more on American native languages than on languages outside this area.

It should be noted, however, that the California situation is unique. Today many linguists have concentrated on languages of other regions, notably Africa, and especially on areas in which the languages are still very much alive. Studies of American native languages, a great many of which are on the verge of extinction, have in contrast been very few.

Some exceptions to this view should also be noted. Research on the Athapaskan languages for example, has in recent years shown a considerable advance. There are today a number of linguists working on these languages, and particularly on the Athapaskan languages of northwestern Canada and Alaska, the areas which are least known linguistically and which are exceedingly important in order that, first, an adequate description may be made of the Athapaskan stock as a whole and, second, that we may attack anew the problem first noted by Edward Sapir (1915) of the relationship of Athapaskan to Tlingit and Haida.

Similar advances are probably underway in other language families of America north of Mexico, notably in Algonkian and Uto-Aztecan (Haas 1969b: 76, fn. 8).

But there are still too few whose primary concern is with the North American languages, many of which will probably become extinct before any knowledge of them may be obtained.

## REFERENCES

ADELUNG, JOHANN CHRISTOPH, and JOHANN SEVERIN VATER. 1818. Mithridates oder allgemeines Sprachenkunde. Vol. 4. Berlin.
BLOOMFIELD, LEONARD. 1917. Tagalog texts. University of Illinois studies in language and literature 3.2–4. Urbana, Illinois.
———. 1925. On the sound system of Central Algonquian. Lg 17.130–56.
———. 1928. Menominee texts. PAES 12.1–607.
———. 1930. Sacred stories of the Sweet Grass Cree. NMC-B 60.
———. 1933. Language. New York, Holt.
———. 1934. Plains Cree texts. PAES 16.1–309.
———. 1943. Note [on Franz Boas]. Lg 19.198.
———. 1962. The Menominee language. New Haven and London.
BOAS, FRANZ, ed. 1911. Handbook of American Indian languages. Part 1. BAE-B 40.
———, ed. 1922. Handbook of American Indian languages. Part 2. BAE-B 40.
———, ed. 1933–38. Handbook of American Indian languages. Part 3. New York, Columbia University Press.
BRINTON, DANIEL G. 1884. A grammar of the Cakchiquel language of Guatemala. PAPS 21.345–412.
———. 1885. The annals of the Cakchiquels. Philadelphia.
———. 1890. Rig Veda Americanus. Philadelphia.
———. 1891. The American race: A linguistic classification and ethnographic description of the native tribes of North and South America. New York.
BYINGTON, CYRUS. 1871. Grammar of the Choctaw language. PAPS 2.317–67.
CHAPMAN, JOHN W. 1914. Ten'a texts and tales from Anvik, Alaska. With a vocabulary prepared by Pliny Earle Goddard. PAES 6.1–230.
DIXON, ROLAND B., and ALFRED L. KROEBER. 1919. Linguistic families of California. UCPAAE 16.47–118.
DORSEY, J. OWEN. 1890. The Ȼegiha language. CNAE 6.1–794.
DUPONCEAU, PETER STEPHEN. 1819a. Report of the corresponding secretary to the committee of his progress in the investigation committed to him of the general

character and forms of the languages of the American Indians. TAPS I.xvii–xlvi.

——. 1819b. A correspondence between John Heckewelder and Peter S. Duponceau. TAPA 1.351–448.

——. 1838. Mémoire sur le système grammatical des langues de quelques nations indiennes de l'Amérique du Nord. Paris.

EDGERTON, FRANKLIN. 1943. Notes on early American work in linguistics. PAPS 87.25–34.

EGEDE, PAUL. 1750. Dictionarium Grönlandico-Danico-Latinum. Hafniae.

——. 1760. Grammatica Grönlandica Danico-Latina. Havniae.

ELIOT, JOHN. 1666. The Indian grammar begun, or an essay to bring the Indian language into rules. Cambridge.

EMENEAU, MURRAY B. 1943. Franz Boas as a linguist. AAA-M 61.35–8.

FRANCISCAN FATHERS. 1910. An ethnologic dictionary of the Navaho language. St. Michaels, Arizona.

——. 1912. A vocabulary of the Navaho language: English-Navaho; Navaho-English. St. Michaels, Arizona.

GALLATIN, ALBERT. 1836. Synopsis of the Indians within the United States east of the Rocky mountains and in the British and Russian possessions in North America. Archaeologia Americana: TCAAS 2.1–422.

——. 1848. Hale's Indians of northwest America and vocabularies of North America. AES-T 2.

GATSCHET, ALBERT S. 1890. The Klamath Indians of southwestern Oregon. CNAE 2.1–711.

GODDARD, PLINY EARLE. 1914. The present condition of our knowledge of North American languages. AmA 16.555–601.

GRUBER, JACOB W. 1967. Horatio Hale and the development of American anthropology. PAPS 111.5–37.

HAAS, MARY R. 1940. Tunica. Extract from HAIL 4. New York, J.J. Augustin.

——. 1958a. Algonkian–Ritwan: The end of a controversy. IJAL 24.159–73.

——. 1958b. A new linguistic relationship in North America: Algonkian and the Gulf languages. SJA 14.231–64.

——. 1969a. Grammar or lexicon? the American Indian side of the question from Duponceau to Powell. IJAL 35.239–55.

——. 1969b. The prehistory of languages. The Hague, Mouton.

HAILE, BERARD. 1950. A stem vocabulary of the Navaho language: Navaho-English. St. Michaels, Arizona.

——. 1951. A stem vocabulary of the Navaho language: English-Navaho. St. Michaels, Arizona.

HALE, HORATIO. 1883. Indian migrations, as evidenced by language, part I. The Huron-Cherokee stock. AmAnt 5.18–28.

——. 1884. The Tutelo tribe and language. PAPS 21.1–47.
HOCKETT, CHARLES F. 1948. Implications of Bloomfield's Algonquian studies. Lg 24.117–31.
HOIJER, HARRY, and others. 1946. Linguistic structures of native America. VFPA 6.
JEFFERSON, THOMAS. 1955. Notes on the state of Virginia, ed. by William Peden. Chapel Hill, North Carolina.
JETTÉ, JULIUS. 1907–09. On the language of the Ten'a. Man 7.51–6 (1907); 8.72–3 (1908); 10.21–5 (1909).
KLEINSCHMIDT, SAMUEL PETRUS. 1851. Grammatik der grönländischen Sprache. Berlin.
——. 1871. Den grønlandske Ordbog, udg. ved H. F. Jorgensen. København.
KROEBER, ALFRED L. 1907. The Yokuts language of south central California. UCPAAE 2.165–377.
——. 1940. The work of John R. Swanton. Essays in historical anthropology of North America. SMC 100.1–10.
——. 1943. Franz Boas. AAA-M 61.14–15.
LACOMBE, ALBERT. 1874. Dictionnaire de la langue des Cris. Montreal.
LEGOFF, LAURENT. 1889. Grammaire de la langue Montagnaise. Montreal.
MANDELBAUM, DAVID, ed. 1949. Selected writings of Edward Sapir in language, culture, and personality. University of California Press.
MICHELSON, TRUMAN. 1914. Two alleged Algonquian languages in California. AmA 16.361–67.
MORICE, A.G. 1932. The Carrier language. St. Gabriel, Mödling bei Wien, Austria.
MOULTON, WILLIAM G. 1961. Linguistics and language teaching in the United States 1940–1960. Trends in European and American linguistics 1936–1960, edited by Christine Mohrmann, Alf Sommerfelt, and Joshua Whatmough, pp. pp. 82–109. Utrecht, Spectrum.
NEWMAN, STANLEY. 1944. Yokuts language of California. VFPA 2.
PETITOT, EMILE. 1876. Dictionnaire de la langue Dènè-Dindjié. Bibliothèque de linguistique et d'ethnographie Américaines, vol. II. Paris.
PICKERING, JOHN. 1818. On the adoption of a uniform orthography for the Indian languages of North America. AAcadAS-M 4.319–60.
——, ed. 1822. The Indian grammar begun, or an essay to bring the Indian language into rules, by John Eliot. Cambridge.
——, ed. 1823. Observations on the language of the Muhhekaneew Indians, by Jonathan Edwards. Cambridge.
——, ed. 1830. Vocabulary of the Massachusetts (or Natick) Indian language, by Josiah Cotton. Cambridge.
——. 1831. Indian languages of North America. Encyclopedia Americana 6.581–600. Philadelphia.
——, ed. 1833. Dictionary of the Abnaki language, by Sébastien Rasles. AAcadAS-M 1.375–565.

PILLING, JAMES CONSTANTINE. 1887. Bibliography of the Siouan languages. Washington, D.C.

POWELL, JOHN WESLEY. 1891. Indian linguistic families of America north of Mexico. BAE-R 7.

RIGGS, STEPHEN R. 1890. A Dakota-English dictionary. CNAE 7.1–665.

———. 1893. Dakota grammar, texts, and ethnography. CNAE 9.1–239.

ROHNER, RONALD P. 1969. The ethnography of Franz Boas. Letters and diaries of Franz Boas written on the Northwest Coast from 1886 to 1931. Chicago, University of Chicago Press.

ROSING, OTTO. 1951. Kleinschmidt Centennial II: Samuel Petrus Kleinschmidt. IJAL 17.63–5.

ROWE, JOHN HOWLAND. 1954. Linguistic classification problems in South America. UCPL 10.1–68.

SAPIR, EDWARD. 1909a. Wishram texts, together with Wasco tales and myths, collected by Jeremiah Curtin and edited by Edward Sapir. PAES 2.

———. 1909b. Takelma texts. UPMA-P 2.1–263.

———. 1910. Yana texts, together with Yana myths, collected by Roland B. Dixon. UCPAAE 9.1–235.

———. 1913. Wiyot and Yurok, Algonkin languages of California. AmA 15.617–46.

———. 1915. The Nadene languages: A preliminary report. AmA 17.534–58.

———. 1917. Linguistic publications of the Bureau of American Ethnology, a general review. IJAL 1.76–81.

———. 1922. The Takelma language of southwestern Oregon. HAIL 2, ed. by Franz Boas, pp. 1–296.

———. 1929. Central and North American languages. Encyclopedia Britannica, 14th edition. 5.138–41.

———. 1930. The Southern Paiute, language: Southern Paiute, a Shoshonean language; Texts of the Kaibab Paiutes and Uintah Utes; Southern Paiute dictionary. AAcadAS-P 65.1–296, 297–536, 537–730.

———. 1942. Navaho texts, with supplementary texts by Harry Hoijer. Edited by Harry Hoijer. LSA, Philadelphia.

SAPIR, EDWARD, and HARRY HOIJER. 1967. The phonology and morphology of the Navaho language. UCPL 50.

SAPIR, EDWARD, and MORRIS SWADESH. 1939. Nootka texts: Tales and ethnological narratives with grammatical notes and lexical materials. William Dwight Whitney Linguistic Series, LSA. Philadelphia.

SCHOOLCRAFT, HENRY ROWE. 1851–57. Historical and statistical information respecting the history, conditions, and prospects of the Indian tribes of the United States. 6 volumes. Philadelphia.

STOCKING, GEORGE W., JR. 1968. Race, culture, and evolution. Essays in the history of anthropology. New York, Free Press.

——. 1972. The Boas plan for American Indian languages: An historical re-examination. Traditions and paradigms: Studies in the history of linguistics, ed. by Dell Hymes. Bloomington, Indiana University Press.
TRUMBULL, J. HAMMOND. 1871. On the best method of studying the North American languages. TAPA 1869–70, 1.55–79. Hartford.
——. 1876. Indian languages of America. Johnson's New Universal Cyclopedia 2.1155–61. New York.
VOEGELIN, C.F., and Z.S. HARRIS. 1945. Index to the Franz Boas collection of materials for American linguistics. Language Monograph no. 22. Linguistic Society of America.
WARES, ALAN C. 1968. Bibliography of the Summer Institute of Linguistics, 1935–1968. Santa Ana, California.
WHITNEY, WILLIAM DWIGHT. 1867. Language and the study of language. New York, Charles Scribner and Co.
——. 1875. The life and growth of language, an outline of linguistic science. New York, D. Appleton and Co.
WHORF, B.L., and GEORGE TRAGER. 1937. The relationship of Uto-Aztecan and Tanoan. AmA 39.609–24.
WILLIAMS, ROGER. 1643. Key into the language of America. London.
WOLFART, H. CHRISTOPHER. 1967. Notes on the early history of American Indian linguistics. FLing 1.153–71.
ZEISBERGER, DAVID. 1827. Grammar of the Lenni Lenape or Delaware Indians. PAPS 86.65–250.

# AMERICAN INDIAN LINGUISTIC PREHISTORY

MARY R. HAAS

0. INTRODUCTION

Over the years a number of methods have been developed for the purpose of making some kind of determination about linguistic prehistory. The chief of these are (1) genetic classification, (2) the reconstruction of protolanguages, and (3) areal diffusion, or the delineation of linguistic areas. The discussion in the present paper will be confined to the first two of these, since linguistic areas and acculturation are the subject of papers to be found elsewhere in this volume.

1. PROBLEMS OF CLASSIFICATION

1.1 *Early Work*

The earliest question about the American Indians was, Where have they come from?, and many scholars hoped to find connections in their languages with the languages of the Old World. By the beginning of the nineteenth century it had become evident for the first time that ancient, unsuspected connections between peoples could be determined through their languages. Although there were few scholars indeed who turned their attention to North America, among these few there was no doubt that the determination of 'how many principal stocks, or families there are in North America' (Pickering 1831:581) was an important problem. The best summary of the situation in the first half of the century was achieved by Albert Gallatin (1836; with additions, 1848). However, new languages kept being discovered in the course of the relentless westward push, and it soon became clear that a still fuller and more complete delineation of the families of North America was needed. By ordering the collection of dozens of linguistic schedules and with the help of his talented staff at the Bureau of [American] Ethnology, John Wesley Powell achieved this goal in *Linguistic families of North America north of Mexico* (1891). At about the same time, Daniel G. Brinton was attempting a classification for both Americas in *The American race* (1891). Lacking access to the materials of the Bureau, his scheme for North America was not as complete as that of Powell and his coworkers, but Brinton did succeed in giving us the first comprehensive classification for South America (Rowe 1954).

In the early part of the twentieth century various attempts were made to reduce the fifty-five Powellian families by combining them into larger groupings. Several people began making attempts along these lines at about the same time, including John P. Harrington in the Southwest (1910), Roland B. Dixon and Alfred L. Kroeber in California (1913a, 1913b), and John R. Swanton in the Southeast (1919, 1924). The most drastic reduction of all was that of Paul Radin who proposed that all of the languages of North America except Eskimoan were related (1919). At the time this theory was considered little more than a tour de force and this fact, added to his very slight documentation, meant that his paper received very little attention. But within a decade Sapir's less drastic but still sweeping reduction of the various families into six superstocks (1921b, 1929) had received wide attention. However, Sapir's classification had been preceded by a number of earlier papers, some of which were extremely meticulous, which laid much of the groundwork (1913, 1915, 1917a, 1917c, 1921c, 1923b, 1925). He also built on the work of Harrington (1910), Dixon and Kroeber (1913a, 1913b, 1919), Kroeber (1915), Swanton (1919, 1924), and others. Nevertheless, some parts of the scheme were undocumented.

As might be expected, there were some who objected, often quite strenuously, to one or another of Sapir's proposals (e.g. Michelson 1914; P.E. Goddard 1917), even to the point of questioning the validity of making the attempt to find deeper connections (Boas 1920, 1929; Michelson 1921). And, as might also be expected, some of the controversies that arose have not yet been resolved. Nevertheless, Sapir's scheme gained ascendancy, in spite of some admitted weaknesses, particularly lack of evidence for some of the groupings (Hoijer 1941, 1946), and was made the basis of a widely-used map (C.F. Voegelin and E.W. Voegelin 1944) in which each of the superstocks was portrayed by a different color.

The year 1929 more or less marked the end of interest in classification problems for a number of years. Sapir himself seems to have lost interest, for, when his students at Yale wanted a seminar in the subject, he was not particularly eager to give it, though in the end he acquiesced for one session. It was among some of these students that the new interest in classificatory problems was beginning to arise, and later on, when they began to publish, their efforts were mostly directed toward testing out some of the least well-documented parts of Sapir's plan. One of the earliest and best of such articles was the test of the Aztec-Tanoan hypothesis presented by Benjamin L. Whorf and George L. Trager (1937).

Around this time Whorf was also actively engaged in making new amalgamations but none of this was ever published. Trager, in a review (1945) of the Voegelins' map, tells us that Whorf proposed to place 'Penutian, Sahaptian, Azteco-Tanoan [sic], Zuni, Kiowa, probably Mayan and Totonac, and possibly Tunica' into 'a phylum which he called "Macro-Penutian"' (188). Whorf was also said to believe that Hokan-Siouan was 'not a real phylum, but contained relics of several phyla' (188).

But all of this came at a time when interest in classificatory problems was at a low ebb and none of these surmises was followed up with published evidence.

The lull was only temporary, however, and the next two decades saw an ever-increasing interest in classificatory problems. This was instigated in large part by the fact that new descriptive materials based on new fieldwork were becoming available from all parts of this continent. It thus became possible to use new data to check old hypotheses that had previously rested on skimpy materials, sometimes no more than a poorly-recorded brief wordlist.

In the following paragraphs the new work is discussed in terms of interconnections between linguistic families, or between language isolates and linguistic families, but it is not arranged in terms of Sapir's superstocks. Moreover, new work carried on *within* a linguistic family (such as Muskogean, or Wakashan) is not included here but is reserved for discussion in the special section devoted to protolanguages.

## 1.2  *New Work on Interfamilial Connections*

The discussion of new work on interfamilial connections is divided into twelve subsections: (1) Siouan, Iroquoian, and Caddoan, (2) Muskogean and the other Gulf languages, (3) Salishan, Wakashan, and Chimakuan, (4) Algonkian, Wiyot, and Yurok, (5) Algonkian-Wiyot-Yurok and wider connections, (6) Athapaskan, Eyak, Tlingit, and Haida, (7) Hokan subfamilies and languages, (8) Hokan and wider connections, (9) Penutian subfamilies and languages, (10) Penutian and wider connections, (11) Uto-Aztecan, Kiowa, and Tanoan, (12) Other families and languages.

### 1.2.1  *Siouan, Iroquoian, and Caddoan*

It was certainly true that Hokan-Siouan was the most problematical of Sapir's superstocks. He himself had once referred to it as his 'waste-paper basket stock'. Some of the earliest suggestions for change consisted in rearrangements of the various subgroupings contained within this superstock. Thus Louis Allen (1931) brought forth evidence to suggest a special affiliation between Siouan and Iroquoian, whereas Sapir had placed Iroquoian closest to Caddoan without giving evidence. Today our knowledge of all three of these families is greater than in 1931. Wallace L. Chafe, who has done fieldwork in all of them, has followed up Allen's suggestion with new material supporting his thesis (Chafe 1964). This leaves Caddoan but insecurely placed, though Chafe thinks that 'Caddoan and Siouan are related' and since the relationship of Siouan and Iroquoian has been quite well established 'then Caddoan and Iroquoian must be related too' (1965:105; see also his paper in this volume). There is, however, as yet no published evidence to support this.

### 1.2.2  *Muskogean and the other Gulf languages*

The area of the lower Mississippi Valley and the adjacent coast of the Gulf of

Mexico contained a number of language isolates, including Natchez, Tunica, Chitimacha, and Atakapa. Swanton's scheme placed Tunica, Chitimacha, and Atakapa together in a group he named 'Tunican', and Natchez with Muskogean in 'Natchez-Muskogean'. Morris Swadesh, who had collected full materials on Chitimacha, tested and affirmed the relationship of Atakapa and Chitimacha in two articles (1946, 1947). Mary R. Haas, who had collected materials on Tunica, Natchez, and some of the Muskogean languages, particularly Creek, proposed combining Muskogean (Choctaw-Chickasaw, Alabama-Koasati, Hitchiti-Mikasuki, and Creek), Natchez, Tunica, Chitimacha, and Atakapa into a larger group called 'Gulf'. She tested this by tracing the words for 'water' (1951) and for 'land' (1952) in the several languages. In a separate paper she presented a series of cognates between Natchez and proto-Muskogean (1956).

In a recent lexical comparison of Atakapa, Chitimacha, and Tunica, Karl-Heinz Gursky (1969) concludes that the languages are related but only remotely. He adds that 'the relationship is approximately as remote as that of the Hokan grouping, i.e. it has to be placed at the upper limit of the stock level or, perhaps even at the phylum level' (106). Doubts of this sort are properly raised and are not surprisingly also being raised about some of the Hokan and Hokan-Coahuiltecan language isolates; see 1.2.8 below.

1.2.3 *Salishan, Wakashan, and Chimakuan*

Another of Sapir's superstocks, Algonkian-Wakashan (also called Algonkian-Mosan) included as its great western branch a grouping known as 'Mosan'. Even if taken by itself, Mosan would have to be rated as a superstock, since it was made up of three families, Salishan, Wakashan, and Chimakuan. Although strong phonological and structural resemblances had been noted from time to time, no evidence for genetic relationship had ever been published. Swadesh, who had done a great deal of work on Sapir's Nootka materials and who had also done fieldwork on Nitinat, was very knowledgeable about the Nootkan branch of Wakashan. He also familiarized himself with manuscript materials on Salishan and published several articles on this family (1949, 1950, 1952a). He then attacked the problem of Mosan and gave some of his results in a long article which appeared in two parts (1953a). It is significant that the subtitle of the first part was "A problem in remote origin". He presented probable or presumable cognates within and among the three families and sometimes added ad hoc reconstructions.[1] Later, however, Swadesh abandoned the idea of a special group known as Mosan and removed Wakashan and placed it in another large construct along with Eskimo-Aleut (1962b, 1964a). The matter is still far from being resolved. Further discussion is given under 1.2.5 below.

---

[1] These are ad hoc reconstructions since they are not based on rigorously assembled sound correspondences for each of which there is one reconstructed sound.

## 1.2.4 *Algonkian, Wiyot, and Yurok*

When Sapir (1913) presented his preliminary materials in support of a genetic connection between the Algonkian languages of the Northeast and the Plains and two small isolated languages of northern California, Wiyot and Yurok, he set in motion a rather sharp controversy. Truman Michelson, specialist in the Algonkian languages, found Sapir's thesis incredible (1914). There were supporters on both sides of the issue. When Gladys Reichard's extensive materials on Wiyot became available (1925), Boas still remained unconvinced of a connection (Uhlenbeck 1927b: 115). Finally in the 1950s extensive materials on Yurok and additional materials on Wiyot were collected. These materials, along with reliable reconstructions of proto-Algonkian forms (Bloomfield 1946), enabled Haas to make a reassessment of the situation (1958a). With new and better descriptive materials to utilize, she was able to present clearer evidence (though a few of her examples need revision) and her conclusion that Wiyot and Yurok are indeed related to Algonkian is now generally accepted. In a recent book, she has also presented some additional comparisons, particularly between Yurok and Algonkian (1969a:67–8).

Some unanswered problems remain, however. Before an Algonkian connection was suspected, Dixon and Kroeber had grouped Wiyot and Yurok together under the name 'Ritwan' (1913a, 1913b). Now that the Algonkian connection is clear, the need for a Ritwan subgroup is less clear. Karl V. Teeter (1964) published a preliminary comparison of Wiyot and Yurok stating that 'it is not at all obvious that they are more closely related to each other than either is to the Algonkian languages' (192). In a recent paper Eric Hamp (1970) suggested some refinements of Teeter's correspondences but did not adduce any new comparisons.

## 1.2.5 *Algonkian-Wiyot-Yurok and wider connections*

Sapir did not stop with his proposal of a relationship between the Algonkian family and the Wiyot and Yurok languages of northern California, but placed these together in a still larger construct known as Algonkian-Mosan (or Algonkian-Wakashan). Subincluded here were also Beothuk (on the Algonkian side) and Kutenai, as a separate branch. However, no evidence for these other connections was presented.

Our records for the extinct Beothuk language of Newfoundland are unusually poor and conflicting, but a careful reexamination of the material has made it appear very likely that it is somehow related to Algonkian (Hewson 1968). This had been assumed by Sapir (1929) but was later questioned by C.F. Voegelin and E.W. Voegelin (1946). Hewson has additional evidence forthcoming.

Kutenai shows strong structural resemblances to the Algonkian family but only a few possible cognates have been found. These are given in a paper entitled "Is Kutenai related to Algonkian?" (Haas 1965). In the same paper some resemblances to Salishan (probably borrowings) are also noted, and among these perhaps the most interesting are the first three numerals. At the same time both show resemblances to the first three numerals of Algonkian, while other resemblances are noted, particularly in the word for 'one', to Quileute (Chimakuan) and Nootka (Wakashan). The Kutenai problem remains unresolved. The Kutenai-in-relation-to-Algonkian problem is very similar to the Tlingit-in-relation-to-Athapaskan problem; see 1.2.6 below.

In 1958 an alignment quite different from the Algonkian plus Mosan one was proposed. This was that the Gulf languages may be related to Algonkian-Wiyot-Yurok (Haas 1958b) and a set of possible cognates was presented in support of this. This hypothesis split up two of Sapir's superstocks, Hokan-Siouan and Algonkian-Mosan, but of course could neither confirm or deny any of the other connections implied by Sapir. Some of these other possibilities have been examined in other papers. In a paper on "Some genetic affiliations of Algonkian" (Haas 1960) some possible comparisons between Algonkian and Chimakuan (Chemakum and Quileute) were given, but comparisons between Algonkian and Wakashan or Algonkian and Salishan (outside of the numerals mentioned above) were not adduced. Of these comparisons the best are between Algonkian and Chimakuan.

The Algonkian-Gulf hypothesis has also led to a search for other possible connections between Algonkian and some Hokan-Siouan groups, particularly Tonkawa (Haas 1959, 1967e) and some of the other languages of Texas (Gursky 1963). Gursky has also made lexical and morphological comparisons of Algonkian-Gulf and Hokan-Subtiaba (1965a, 1965b, 1966).

### 1.2.6 *Athapaskan, Eyak, Tlingit, and Haida*

The controversy started by Sapir's 1913 proposal of a relationship between Algonkian, Wiyot, and Yurok was still in full swing when he proposed still another relationship which provoked sharp controversy. Since Boas and others had noted important structural resemblances between Athapaskan, Tlingit, and Haida in the past, Sapir was surprised by the reaction to his attempts to find lexical comparisons among them (1915). Pliny Earle Goddard sought to disprove a relationship (1917). But Sapir's insight had been anticipated in Russia in the 19th century (Krauss 1964:128).

Sapir did not make use of the early Russian materials on Eyak, but interest in the latter language was later stimulated by the discovery of a few speakers in the 1930s. Fang-Kuei Li, Robert Austerlitz, and especially Michael Krauss have collected extensive data on the language. Li (1956) and Krauss (1964–65) have proven its relationship to Athapaskan while Krauss has further provided a protophonology and reconstructions of proto-Athapaskan-Eyak stems. But beyond this point, clear proof of relationship among the Nadéné languages (Athapaskan, Eyak, Tlingit, and Haida) is still lacking. No one doubts the strong and compelling structural resemblances, but there is still disagreement about whether this is to be interpreted as diffusion or genetic relationship. Krauss says, 'we begin to see Na-Dene as being a stratified set of relationships, in which degrees of correspondence between PAE [proto-Athapaskan-Eyak], Tlingit, and Haida, differ very widely, to the point of conflict, at the different strata' and in a footnote he adds, 'there is no agreement on a single historical interpretation [of these facts] and linguists are divided into conflicting camps' (1964–65:

27). Krauss himself found some favorable evidence in his paper on the classifiers in the Athapaskan, Eyak, and Tlingit verb (1969). And Heinz-Jürgen Pinnow regularly gives strong support to a genetic interpretation (1964a, 1966, 1968, 1970).

The ambiguous nature of the historical connections between the Nadéné languages, though deplored by some, has been amply compensated for by the stimulation it has provided. One of the most interesting papers to result has been Dell H. Hymes' "Na-Déné and positional analysis of categories" (1956). More recently Krauss has made an exhaustive study of "Noun-classification systems in Athapaskan, Eyak, Tlingit and Haida verbs" (1968); see also his paper "Na-Dene" in the present volume.

### 1.2.7 Hokan subfamilies and languages

Dixon, Kroeber, Harrington, Sapir, and others pieced together the Hokan stock by gradual stages (Dixon 1905; Dixon and Kroeber 1913a, 1913b; Kroeber 1915; Kroeber and Harrington 1914; Sapir 1917a, 1917b, 1921c). Although satisfactory proof of relationship of all the various families and language isolates subsumed under the term 'Hokan' has never been adduced, it will be easier to consider the more recent attacks on the problem by discussing them under one rubric.

An exceedingly large amount of fresh fieldwork has been done on the Hokan languages in the past two decades, particularly under the auspices of the Survey of California Indian Languages at Berkeley and, in Mexico, under the auspices of the Summer Institute of Linguistics. This has provided and is continuing to provide valuable materials for a fresh look at a variety of the problems. William Bright started the ball rolling again with a comparison of some of the northern Hokan languages (Karok, Shasta, Chimariko, Achumawi, Atsugewi) (1954) and this was followed not long afterwards by a series of studies of Palaihnihan (Achumawi-Atsugewi) and Shasta by David Olmsted (1956–59). In the meantime an important binary study of two quite distant languages, Karok and Washo, was published by William Jacobsen (1958). More on Shasta and its relation to other Hokan languages was given by Haas (1963a) followed by another paper by Olmsted (1965). The year 1964 saw the publication of several additional binary studies: Karok and Yana (Haas), Eastern Pomo and Yana (McLendon), and Shasta and Karok (Silver).

The chief difficulty in attacking the Hokan problem is that so many of the languages are actually language isolates and not closely related submembers of clearly identifiable families which lend themselves to phonological and lexical reconstruction. Thus the label of isolate has to be applied to Shasta, Karok, Chimariko, Washo, Esselen, Salinan, Tequistlatec, Seri, and others. In addition to such isolates, however, there are at least three families, namely Pomoan, Yuman, and Chumashan. It is in these families that the best clues to further advances in Hokan studies lie. Work is now under way on the reconstruction of proto-Pomoan and proto-Yuman, and as this work progresses it becomes increasingly clear that there are good cognates between the protoforms of these two families, as was already hinted by A.M. Halpern (1964: 92). Work on the reconstruction of proto-Chumashan has not yet really begun, but materials collected by M.S. Beeler, J.P. Harrington, and others will eventually make this possible.

### 1.2.8 *Hokan and wider connections*

Sapir presented materials connecting the Hokan stock with Subtiaba-Tlappanec (1925) and with the Coahuiltecan group (1917c) which had been suggested by Swanton (1915). Since the material on the languages of the Coahuiltecan group, except for Tonkawa, is not very extensive, the best part of Sapir's arguments have to do with the Subtiaba-Tlappanec connection. He called this larger group Hokan-Coahuiltecan and included it in the Hokan-Siouan superstock (1929). Little more was done on this problem for over thirty years. In 1953 Joseph H. Greenberg and Morris Swadesh proposed that Jicaque of Honduras, a language previously left unclassified, was connected with Hokan-Coahuiltecan. This was interesting in that the reaches of the combined stock was pushed southward. Haas made a study of the proto-Hokan-Coahuiltecan word for 'water' and proposed a reconstruction (1954). This paralleled her earlier study of the proto-Gulf word for 'water' (1951) which took in a large part of the remainder of Hokan-Siouan. William Bright presented the results of a study he had made of "Glottochronologic counts of Hokaltecan [Hokan-Coahuiltecan] material" (1956) and Greenberg and Swadesh also gave some material of this sort in their Jicaque paper.

Much remains to be done before all the problems raised by this proposed series of interconnections are resolved. A new kind of approach has been made by William Jacobsen in a very interesting paper on "Switch-reference in Hokan-Coahuiltecan" (1967). Here a syntactic device found in three of the languages, Washo, Kashaya (Pomo), and Tonkawa, is described. Although it had been hoped that this kind of study might yield a new kind of evidence for genetic relationship, the results were inconclusive (261). Nevertheless, the study remains a model of syntactic cross-language comparison in addition to being an interesting attempt to approach the age-old problem from a new direction.

Tonkawa has received considerable attention in recent years. Haas suggested that it might be related to Algonkian (1959, 1967e) though this is not to be taken to deny a possible Hokan connection. She also found several Uto-Aztecan loanwords (1967e: 318). Rudolph C. Troike, who has been making careful analyses of early Coahuilteco materials, presented a structural comparison of Tonkawa and Coahuilteco (1967) and concluded that on the basis of structure 'no evidence can be found to support a hypothesis of genetic relationship' (330). Indeed, he adds that 'it is not possible to demonstrate even the degree of relationship which Hymes (1956) has shown to obtain among Tlingit, Haida, and Athabascan' (331).

The doubts raised by Troike deserve careful consideration. Recently, also, doubts have been raised by Paul Turner (1967) about Kroeber's early proposal to connect Seri and Chontal (Tequistlatec). Bright (1970) expresses disagreement with Turner. However, it is important to keep reexamining the old hypotheses and to search for new ones, since many of the early suggestions are far from having been verified. We are used to them because they have been around for so long.

### 1.2.9 *Penutian subfamilies and languages*

The problems encountered in setting up the Penutian stock were the same as those faced in setting up Hokan. Indeed Dixon and Kroeber, in their early work on California languages, had met their greatest difficulties in separating the two (1913a, 1913b). Sapir (1929) added some languages of Oregon, Washington, and Idaho and even, in the case of Tsimshian, British Columbia. For the most part no real proof was adduced for this series of connections. And again very little was added to our knowledge of the problems posed for nearly thirty years. Swadesh, who had earlier reexamined the Mosan hypothesis, turned his attention also to "Problems of long-range comparison in Penutian" (1956). Dell H. Hymes, who was particularly knowledgeable about Chinook, also took up the problem (1957a). A year later particular attention was given to the so-called California Penutian languages (Miwokan, Costanoan, Wintun, Maidun, and Yokutsan) by Harvey Pitkin and William F. Shipley (1958) and they attempted to establish, in so far as possible, regular sound correspondences among these families. Since that time the greatest progress has been made in the reconstruction carried out within the subfamilies (as is discussed in the section on protolanguages) and in the comparison of pairs of subfamilies. Thus we have a systematic comparison of Miwokan and Wintun by Sylvia M. Broadbent and Harvey Pitkin (1964) and of Miwokan and Costanoan by Catherine A. Callaghan (1962, 1967). It is also important to mention here that M.S. Beeler (1955) showed that Saclan, which had long been thought to be the most northerly of the Costanoan languages, was actually a Miwok language; indeed it was 'the westernmost language of the eastern division' (109) of Miwok. Aoki has treated Sahaptin and Klamath (1963).

In 1966 Shipley added Klamath to his 'Penutian kernel' and later made some reconstructions of proto-Kalapuyan (1970) and of proto-Takelman (Takelma plus proto-Kalapuyan) (1969) based in part on suggestions made by Swadesh (1956, 1965). An interesting etymological study of some Penutian words for 'hail' and 'bead' was presented by Hymes (1964a) who in the same year also presented some lexical sets with initial *c- and *s- (1964b).

As was seen in the case of Hokan, doubts are also raised from time to time about some of the accepted subgroupings of Penutian. We have, for example, an article by Joe E. Pierce (1966) raising questions about Hanis, Miluk, Alsea, Siuslaw, and Takelma, and two articles by Bruce J. Rigsby on the problem of Cayuse and Molala (1966, 1969).

### 1.2.10 *Penutian and wider connections*

Sapir's six superstocks included many language isolates, some of which were only loosely connected or were queried. Zuni, long a problem to would-be classifiers, was placed with a query as a third branch of Aztec-Tanoan but no supporting material was ever presented. Recently Stanley S. Newman, who has been engaged in descriptive studies of Zuni, has presented materials showing a connection between Zuni and California Penutian (1964). In a more recent article Swadesh (1967b: 295–306) has discussed some of his own theories connecting it also with 'Mexican and South American languages' (296). Among these far-flung connections Swadesh includes 'Zuni, Penutian, Tarasco, Quechuan, Mayan, Zoquean, Totonacan and Nahua-Tanoan [Aztec-Tanoan]' (302). It will be noted that this is similar to one of Whorf's broad suggestions mentioned earlier in this paper. Suggestive as such theories may be, nothing is settled about them and a great deal more work needs to be done first on the closer connections.

1.2.11  *Uto-Aztecan, Kiowa, and Tanoan*

On the basis of plausible earlier suggestions by Harrington (1910) and others, Sapir recognized the connection between these families in his Aztec-Tanoan superstock (1929). Although the actual evidence for their relationship was not forthcoming until later, some of it much later, it is now well-documented. An excellent paper by Whorf and Trager (1937) established the connection between Uto-Aztecan and Tanoan by comparing reconstructed proto-Uto-Aztecan forms with reconstructed proto-Tanoan forms. This was made possible by Whorf's superb knowledge of Uto-Aztecan (1935, 1937) and Trager's of Tanoan (1942). But the evidence for the connection of Kiowa with Tanoan was slow in coming even though Harrington had suggested it as early as 1910. Wick R. Miller renewed the question in "A note on Kiowa linguistic affiliations" (1959b) and this prompted George L. Trager and Edith Crowell Trager, the latter of whom had done fieldwork on Kiowa, to present some of their comparisons of "Kiowa and Tanoan" (1959). More recently Kenneth L. Hale has presented some excellent material on Kiowa-Tanoan phonology (1962, 1967). As a result the time seems ripe for a full-scale treatment of Uto-Aztecan and Kiowa-Tanoan which presents all available material.

1.2.12  *Other families and languages*

In the time of the great push toward reduction which led to Sapir's widely accepted scheme of six superstocks, there seemed to be a great urgency to assign every language isolate and family to some larger grouping. Today there is a greater willingness to leave some things unassigned and to admit our inability to tie up all loose ends. A revised map of North American Indian languages by C. F. Voegelin and F. M. Voegelin (1966) reflects this, though it is marred by some errors in execution.

Some of the more troublesome cases have already been mentioned and some are closer to a resolution than they were forty years ago. Beothuk and Kutenai are discussed above under 1.2.5: Algonkian-Wiyot-Yurok and wider connections. Caddoan is discussed under 1.2.1: Siouan, Iroquoian, and Caddoan. Zuni, still somewhat troublesome, is discussed under 1.2.10: Penutian and wider connections. Kiowa, now firmly placed, is treated under 1.2.11: Uto-Aztecan, Kiowa, and Tanoan. In other cases new proposals have been made or new questions are being asked. Languages or families not already discussed are treated briefly below.

1.2.12.1 *Yukian*. Sapir placed Yukian (Yuki) in Hokan-Siouan but not in Hokan. In other words, he left it as an isolated branch. It is still a problem. There are four languages, Yuki, Coast Yuki, and Huchnom, which are quite close, and Wappo, which is geographically separate and the most divergent. What is needed is a reconstruction of proto-Yukian. In 1957 Shipley made a study of some Yukian-Penutian lexical resemblances but he did not consider these evidence of genetic relationship (p.c.). More recently Elmendorf has compared Yukian and Siouan in some detail in two papers (1963, 1964). The matter will not be definitely resolved, however, until proto-Yukian is compared with proto-Siouan.

1.2.12.2 *Keresan*. Some of the Keresan languages have been described in detail recently and a considerable amount of proto-Keresan has already been reconstructed (Miller and Davis 1963). Like Yukian, Keresan was also placed by Sapir in Hokan-Siouan but no evidence for this arrangement was ever given. Since the Keresan languages are very close, the time depth of proto-Keresan is not very great (perhaps 500–1000 years). Swadesh (1967b) explored the possibility of a relationship between Keresan and Iroquois-Caddoan (292–294). But since no evidence for the relationship of Caddoan to Iroquoian has yet been given (Chafe 1965), all this remains highly provisional, and Swadesh himself makes his suggestion in terms of his great 'Macro-Mayan chain phylum' (289). Moreover, just as with the Yukian and Siouan problem mentioned above, the matter needs to be explored in terms of a comparison between proto-Keresan and proto-Caddoan.

1.2.12.3 *Karankawa*. Karankawa is but poorly known and its affiliation is no longer considered quite as sure as formerly. Until very recently our only material came from three short vocabularies of widely separated dates. A few items are Nahuatl loans, as was first pointed out by Brinton in 1891. Herbert Landar (1968) has discovered another vocabulary of some 158 items, and with this added to the earlier vocabularies he compared the language to Cariban. This opens new possibilities and the whole question needs to be reexamined.

1.2.12.4 *Yuchi*. Yuchi is a language isolate which Sapir placed with Siouan, as Siouan-Yuchi, in Hokan-Siouan. No evidence for the connection was given, though the phonological structure is very similar to Siouan (Haas 1969a:90-1) and a few possible cognates between Siouan and Yuchi were also listed by Haas (1951:79). In general, suggestions about wider affiliations for Siouan include similar suggestions for Yuchi. Thus Elmendorf has drawn on Yuchi in his Yukian and Siouan work (especially 1964) and Haas has also drawn on Yuchi in "Athapaskan, Tlingit, Yuchi, and Siouan" (1964b). Clearly the Yuchi question is unresolved but a thorough comparison with Siouan, especially proto-Siouan, is still probably the best place to start.

1.2.12.5 *Timucua*. There is more material available on Timucua than on many of our problematical languages, but it has been long extinct and a reexamination of the synchronic materials and a restatement of the grammar would be very helpful

Located as it was in Florida, more than one would-be classifier has attempted to connect it with a South American family. Long ago A.S. Gatschet (1884) thought it showed some Carib and some Muskogean connections, and much more recently Swadesh (1964a) has argued for an Arawakan connection. Swanton thought he saw a Muskogean connection and this was accepted by Sapir (1929) though with a query. The problem remains unsolved. The material adduced by Swadesh (1964a:548) for an Arawakan connection is no more convincing than the possibility of a Siouan connection (Haas 1971).

## 2. PROTOLANGUAGES

Perhaps the most significant advances that have been made in our knowledge of American Indian linguistic prehistory in the past half century have been in the area of linguistic reconstruction. This involves the reconstruction of protophonologies, i.e. the phonologies of protolanguages, and eventually, roots and affixes, sometimes full words, of protolanguages. Fifty years ago almost nothing of this sort had been done with North American languages. Indeed, reputable scholars doubted that such work could be done with unwritten languages. Today such doubts have been completely refuted and many scholars are engaged in such work, not only in North America, but also in Mexico and South America, Africa, Asia, and the Pacific.

The momentum, however, was achieved only gradually at first. Sapir started out with Uto-Aztecan phonology (1913–14, 1915), Leonard Bloomfield laid firm foundations for Algonkian (1925, 1946), while Sapir (1931) and Fang-Kuei Li (1930, 1933) resolved many problems of Athapaskan. In 1931 Sapir even devoted an article to the description of the methodology used by Bloomfield and himself in their work on Algonkian and Athapaskan, respectively. This important early work on these families has put them in the forefront. Even today our knowledge of proto-Uto-Aztecan, proto-Algonkian, and proto-Athapaskan is more extensive and more advanced than our knowledge of most other North American (north of Mexico) protolanguages, at least those with a time depth in excess of 1500 years.

In the sections which follow mention is made of some of the materials that have been developed in several North American linguistic families. Particular attention is given to those families for which at least protophonologies have been developed and of course those for which stems (or stems and longer words) have been reconstructed are also treated. The discussion is arranged alphabetically by linguistic family.

### 2.1 *Algonkian*

Proto-Algonkian is probably the best-known protolanguage of North America north of Mexico. This can be attributed in part to the great geographic spread of the family, the availability of materials on many of the daughter languages, as well as the large number of people who have worked on the problem.

Limiting himself to four languages of the central area, Fox, Cree, Menomini, and Ojibwa, Leonard Bloomfield reconstructed the protophonology of Algonkian in 1925. Truman Michelson (1935) showed that Bloomfield's system would also work for languages of the western area, Cheyenne, Arapaho, and Blackfoot. Still working with his well-known four languages, Bloomfield (1946) presented an exemplary treatment of proto-Algonkian grammar together with the reconstruction of many protoforms. He had also assembled materials for a proto-Algonkian dictionary based on the four languages but the work was unfinished at the time of his death. Charles F. Hockett has reworked and expanded a part of these materials and published a large body of reconstructions based on proto-Algonkian stems in *k (1957). Reconstructions based on stems beginning in other consonants are promised for some future time. The reconstruction of the proto-Algonkian kinship system based on languages of the central area was published by Hockett in 1964. Languages of the eastern area have been treated particularly by Frank T. Siebert, who made a minor but important emendation of the reconstruction of one of Bloomfield's consonant clusters (Siebert 1941) and by Ives Goddard, who has added to the stock of reconstructions of words containing long *a· with special reference to its reflex in the eastern languages (1965). Haas has presented the sound correspondences for PA *θ, *l, and *n (and clusters containing these as their final members) for all the daughter languages for which information was available (1967a). She has also written on PA semivowels (1966b), the development of *awe (1967b) and a revised reconstruction of the word for 'sun' (1967c). Several studies of the historical phonology of individual daughter languages have appeared, viz. Blackfoot (Voegelin 1941a), Delaware (Voegelin 1941b), Potawatomi (Hockett 1942), Shawnee (Miller 1959a), Natick (Silver 1960), and Narragansett (Cowan 1969). Ives Goddard has an unpublished study of Arapaho. In addition, many unpublished studies have been carried out on Blackfoot, Arapaho, Abnaki, and Delaware by a number of students at Berkeley and at Harvard.

Other especially noteworthy contributions to our information about proto-Algonkian are Goddard's study of the independent indicative paradigm (1967b) and Siebert's reconstruction of words for flora and fauna by means of which he projects what he believes to be the original home of the proto-Algonkian people (1967a). In a map (35) he locates this as north of Lake Erie in the area between Lakes Huron and Ontario and he suggests 1200 B.C. as the probable date, i.e. about 2700 years ago. Nothing else like this has been worked out for any other linguistic family of North America, or, excepting Indo-European, elsewhere.

Other studies pertaining to Algonkian reconstruction or subgrouping include the following: Bloomfield 1927, 1947; J.A. Geary 1941, 1943, 1953, 1955; I. Goddard 1967a; Haas 1958c; Meeusen 1959; Michelson 1933, 1939; Heinz-Jürgen Pinnow 1958; Siebert 1967b; Karl V. Teeter 1965, 1967.

## 2.2 Algonkian-Wiyot-Yurok

In comparing Wiyot and Yurok with Algonkian, Haas (1958a) attempted to set up a protophonology for PAR (proto-Algonkian-Ritwan, i.e. Algonkian-Wiyot-Yurok) and made some reconstructions. Both the protophonology and the reconstructions are in need of some revision, and more morphological reconstruction will also be possible as our knowledge of these deeper relationships increases.

## 2.3 Athapaskan

The protophonology of the Athapaskan stem and prefix (they differ) was worked out by Sapir and Fang-Kuei Li, and a careful study was published by Li in 1933. Sapir also included his stem-initial reconstructions of two sibilant series (*$ts$, *$tš$) and a front palatal series (*$k^y$) and showed their differing reflexes in Hupa, Chipewyan, Navajo, and Sarcee in a paper on methodology (1931). The development of these same three series has been carried out for most of the other Athapaskan languages by Harry Hoijer (1963), who also used the type of reflex in the various languages as a means of arriving at subgroupings, especially in the north. Michael Krauss, working particularly with Athapaskan languages of Alaska, found that one of Sapir's sibilant series (the *$tš$-series) actually represented two different sets of protosounds which had fallen together in many languages, but not in Alaska (1964:118–23).

Special studies of the historical phonology of several daughter languages have also been undertaken, sometimes in considerable detail, as in Li's excellent study of Mattole (1930) and of Chipewyan (1933). More recently some information about the historical phonology of Tolowa (Smith River) is appended to a synchronic treatment by Jane Bright (1964). Hoijer has given special treatment to the Southern Athapaskan or Apachean (including Navajo) languages (1938), to Pacific Athapaskan (1960), and to Hare (1966). Victor K. Golla has made an etymological study of Hupa nouns, providing many cognates though no reconstructions (1964b).

The Athapaskan kinship system has been treated by Kroeber (1937) and by Hoijer (with reconstructions) (1956). Numerals, but without reconstructions, were the subject of a special study by Virginia D. Hymes (1955). The classificatory verb systems of several of the languages were compared by Davidson, Elford, and Hoijer (1963) and a comparison of the positional categories of the languages is to be found in D.H. Hymes (1956). Athapaskan comparative studies have been greatly advanced by Hoijer's recent study of Athapaskan protomorphology (1971).

## 2.4 Athapaskan-Eyak

Krauss has established beyond doubt that Eyak and Athapaskan are related (1964–

65) and he has accomplished this by working out the protophonology and reconstructing a few dozen stems (1964:125–127). Li has discussed a type of noun formation in Athapaskan and Eyak (1956) and Krauss has traced the development of the noun-classification systems in Athapaskan and Eyak verbs (1968) as well as the classifiers of Athapaskan and Eyak verbs (1969) in broader studies.

## 2.5 *Caddoan*

Until very recently Caddoan has been one of the most neglected families in North America. Although Alexander Lesser and Gene Weltfish did fieldwork on these languages in the 1920s, very little material was published and so comparative work could not be undertaken. Recently Paul Garvin, Wallace L. Chafe, and others have been doing extensive fieldwork on Wichita, Caddo, and Pawnee in particular, and Chafe expects in due course to work out proto-Caddoan. A suggestive preliminary study of the protophonology was made by Allan R. Taylor (1963b) and he has also provided the most recent intrafamilial classification (1963a).

## 2.6 *Gulf*

The Gulf stock includes Muskogean, which is treated separately below. Although Swadesh attempted to work out a protophonology for Atakapa and Chitimacha (1946, 1947) and Haas has presented proto-Gulf reconstructions for the words for 'water' (1951) and 'land' (1952), the languages are too remote from each other to expect more than the most limited kind of reconstruction. Gursky's studies (e.g. 1969), which are chiefly lexical and do not involve reconstruction, confirm their remoteness.

## 2.7 *Hokan and Hokan subfamilies*

Most of what is subsumed under Hokan consists of language isolates and, because of the difficulties inherent in such a situation, few attempts have been made to arrive at proto-Hokan reconstructions since some of Sapir's early work. Haas attempted the reconstruction of the word for 'water' (1954:59) and later of words for other basic terms, such as 'ear', 'liver', 'navel', 'nape', 'nose', 'nails', 'arm', 'tongue', and 'sleep' (1963b). Before much more progress can be made it will be necessary to reconstruct some of the subfamilies in some detail. A discussion of work undertaken to date follows.

### 2.7.1 *Palaihnihan*
Olmsted has worked out a protophonology for proto-Palaihnihan (1964) but there

are only two languages to compare (Achumawi, Atsugewi) and many problems remain (Bright 1965b; Silver 1966).

### 2.7.2 *Pomoan*

The Pomoan languages have been the object of fresh fieldwork in recent years and several of the investigators are currently working on problems of comparative Pomoan. The task was begun by A. M. Halpern in the 1930s but he published only a brief report (1964) which also contains a few reconstructions. Robert L. Oswalt (1964a) compares Kashaya (S.W. Pomo) and Central Pomo and shows that Kashaya is more archaic phonologically. Nancy M. Webb (1971) presents a statement of Pomo correspondences (some quite problematical); a brief earlier statement is by Webb, Carolyn W. Wall, and Louise Tanous (1965–66). More recently a monograph, "The reconstruction of proto-Pomo", has been prepared by Sally V. McLendon (in press). Internal classificatory problems have been treated by Halpern (1964) and by Oswalt (1964b).

### 2.7.3 *Yuman*

The Yuman family of languages has also been the object of fresh fieldwork in recent years and again several of the investigators are very much interested in comparative matters. A monograph on Yuman consonantism has been published by Alan Campbell Wares (1968) and the proto-Yuman demonstrative system has been worked out by Margaret Langdon (1968). An unusual piece of work has been undertaken by Howard W. Law, who attempted to reconstruct something of the protoculture by a comparative study of Yuman vocabularies (1961). Internal classificatory problems have been treated by Kroeber (1943) and by Judith Joel (1964).

As more and more reconstructions accumulate it will soon turn out to be profitable to compare proto-Pomoan and proto-Yuman. Halpern pointed out that 'in a limited number of instances there are unexpectedly close similarities between certain Pomo [Pomoan] and certain Yuma [Yuman] stems' (1964:92) and other investigators have been struck by the same thing.

### 2.7.4 *Chumashan*

The reconstruction of proto-Chumashan remains an important task for the future. The protophonology has not been reconstructed but enough is known about the languages to enable us to guess that it would be quite similar to the phonology of Barbareño (Beeler 1970). Perhaps the most striking thing about it is its similarity to Yokuts phonology. The Chumash languages are now all extinct, but J.P. Harrington collected a mass of material on Barbareño and a lesser but still respectable amount on Ventureño, Inezeño, and Obispeño. This material, when processed and added to Beeler's material on Barbareño, will make the reconstruction of proto-Chumashan a possibility for the future.

## 2.8 Iroquoian

One of the greatest needs in the field of North American comparative linguistics is published material on proto-Iroquoian. Although Floyd G. Lounsbury has worked out a great deal of it, he has published only a few reconstructions in his paper on "Iroquois-Cherokee linguistic relations" (1961). The paper also gives decisive information on the internal classification of the languages with projected time depths of separation.

## 2.9 Keresan

The Keresan family, as shown earlier, has not been positively connected with any other linguistic family. It consists of a group of closely related languages (almost dialects) which separated no more than 500–1000 years ago. Wick R. Miller and Irvine Davis (1963), each of whom has written a grammar on one of the languages (Miller on Acoma, Davis on Santa Ana), have worked out the protophonology as well as several hundred proto-Keresan reconstructions.

## 2.10 Muskogean

The protophonology of Muskogean has been worked out in a series of articles by Haas (1941, 1947a, 1949, 1950) and recapitulated in *The prehistory of languages* (1969a: 34–42). Reconstructions are to be found in all the papers except the 1941 one. Additional reconstructions are given in some papers comparing Muskogean with other languages and families, particularly Natchez (1956) but also some others (1951, 1952, 1958a,b,c). A comparative dictionary of the Muskogean languages will someday be possible, but more descriptive materials are needed first, particularly on Choctaw, Alabama, and Mikasuki. Some morphological comparison has also been undertaken for Muskogean, and the subject inflection of the active verb has been reconstructed (Haas 1946 and 1969a: 52–8).

## 2.11 Penutian and Penutian Subfamilies

Like Hokan, Penutian is made up of language isolates and small families. Pitkin and Shipley have postulated a protophonology (1958:176) for the 'Penutian kernel' (Miwokan, Costanoan, Maidun, and Wintun) but have not attempted any reconstructions at that level. Shipley added Klamath to this (1966) with more information on protophonology. In addition to these broader attempts, important progress has been made in the reconstruction of some of the smaller families.

### 2.11.1 *Miwokan*

The protophonology of Miwokan has been worked out by Sylvia M. Broadbent and Catherine A. Callaghan (1960) and they also include reconstructions. Other reconstructions are found in papers comparing Miwok with other families, e.g. Costanoan (Callaghan 1962, 1967) and Wintun (Broadbent and Pitkin 1964). Many additional reconstructions of proto-Miwok and proto-Western Miwok are given in Callaghan's recent dictionary of Bodega Miwok (1970).

### 2.11.2 *Costanoan*

All of the Costanoan languages are extinct, but J.P. Harrington collected valuable materials on many of them. There is a limited amount of material by other workers. In comparing Miwok with Mutsun, Callaghan (1962) proceeded without Costanoan reconstructions, but in a later paper on Miwok-Costanoan (1967) she was able to present some reconstructions. Other work on the reconstruction of this family, based largely on Harrington's materials, is being carried on under the direction of William F. Shipley. Some information on subgroups is presented by Beeler (1961b).

### 2.11.3 *Wintun*

No separate study of Wintun protophonology and no reconstructions have yet appeared, but Harvey Pitkin is engaged in this endeavor. When Wintun was compared with other Penutian families (Pitkin and Shipley 1958; Broadbent and Pitkin 1964) words from the separate languages were used in the comparisons.

### 2.11.4 *Maidun*

Work on the protophonology of Maidun is well-advanced. Shipley has compared Maidu and Nisenan (1961) and Russell Ultan has compared these two with Konkow (1964). Both papers also contain reconstructions.

### 2.11.5 *Yokutsan*

There were many languages and dialects of Yokuts, and Kroeber (1907) was early concerned with their internal classification. His results were corroborated by Stanley S. Newman (1944). Recently the protophonology of the family has been worked out by Victor K. Golla (1964a) on the basis of three of the languages. He also presents 333 reconstructions.

### 2.11.6 *Sahaptian*

Sahaptian consists of Nez Perce and Sahaptin (in three dialects). Haruo Aoki has made several studies of the protophonology (1962, 1966a), including the development of Nez Perce vowel harmony (1966a). The latter problem has also engaged the attention of several other people, including Bruce Rigsby (1965), William Jacobsen (1968), and Rigsby and Michael Silverstein (1969). Aoki has presented many reconstructions in his 1962 and 1966a papers and additionally in his careful reconstruction of proto-Sahaptian kinship terms (1966b).

## 2.12 *Salishan*

The sound shifts of Salishan received early attention from Boas and Herman Haeberlin (1927) and the problem of internal classification was also discussed. Hans Vogt (1940) treated the phonological development of four of the languages, including Kalispel which was his specialty. Swadesh (1952b) set up a protophonology and made a few reconstructions (239–40). Gladys Reichard (1958–60) presented a detailed comparison of five of the Salish languages, including Coeur d'Alene which she knew well. In particular she attempted to make progress in comparative grammar.

In recent years a number of linguists have undertaken a vast amount of new descriptive work on these languages and we can soon expect much more material on comparative Salish. Aert H. Kuipers presented a paper on the beginning of a Salish etymological dictionary at the Fourth International Conference on Salish Languages held in Victoria in 1969. Several other people are also actively at work on comparative Salish, including Laurence C. Thompson and M. Terry Thompson, M. Dale Kinkade (e.g. 1967), James E. Hoard, and others. Some of them have read important papers at meetings but these still remain unpublished.

## 2.13 *Siouan*

A considerable amount of work has been done on comparative Siouan. Protophonologies and reconstructions have been presented by Hans Wolff (1950–51) and by G. Hubert Matthews (1958 ms.). The proto-Siouan kinship system has also been reconstructed by Matthews (1959). Early treatment of some of the problems of Ofo and Biloxi was carried out by Voegelin (1939) and the discussion of an Ofo phonetic law was presented by Nils Holmer (1947). More recently some Southeastern Siouan (Biloxi, Ofo, and Tutelo) reconstructions have been published by Haas (1968a, 1969d) together with some emendations about the development of the sounds of these languages from proto-Siouan sounds. Internal classification of the family as a whole has been treated by Voegelin (1941d). Although much has been accomplished on Siouan, much more remains to be done. More descriptive work on the languages still spoken is urgently needed, and someone should undertake the task of preparing an etymological dictionary.

Catawba stands apart from the other Siouan languages and recognizable cognates are rare. There are, however, some very important morphological parallels which have been elegantly treated by Siebert (1945).

## 2.14 Tanoan and Kiowa-Tanoan

The protophonology of Tanoan has been worked out by Trager (Whorf and Trager 1937:614) as well as that of the Tiwa branch in particular (Trager 1942). Some reconstructed proto-Tanoan stems are included in the Whorf and Trager article (619–24) and some proto-Tiwa kin terms have also been published (Trager 1942). Much more reconstructed material is in Trager's hands and it is hoped he will eventually publish it.

Kiowa-Tanoan has received renewed attention lately. Brief comparative notes by Miller (1959b) and by G.L. Trager and E.C. Trager (1959) were followed by Kenneth L. Hale's more detailed comparisons between Jemez (a Tanoan language) and Kiowa (1962). But the most advanced material presented so far is Hale's protophonology of Kiowa-Tanoan including a number of reconstructions (1967).

## 2.15 Uto-Aztecan

Uto-Aztecan is one of the best-studied linguistic families of North America and, like Algonkian, it has attracted the attention of many scholars. The protophonology worked out by Whorf (1935) has been more recently slightly simplified by Voegelin, Voegelin, and Hale (1962). There are a great many sources for reconstructions, including Whorf (1935, 1937), Whorf and Trager (1937), Voegelin, Voegelin, and Hale (1962). Miller has prepared a monograph on Uto-Aztecan cognate sets (1967) and for each set he proposes a reconstruction (sometimes partial). Quite recently Ronald Langacker has made a new study of the protovocalic system (1970) and Richley H. Crapo has attempted to trace the origins of directional adverbs in the languages of this family (1970).

Several studies of the historical phonology of individual daughter languages or of subgroups have appeared in recent years. These include Numic (Davis 1966), Cupan (J.H. Hill and K.C. Hill 1968), Cahuilla (Bright 1965a; Seiler 1965), Cupeño (Bright and J.H. Hill 1967), and Papago (K.L. Hale 1970). Cognates from Classical Nahuatl have received the attention of Troike (1963) and, in a review of Miller 1967, of Bright (1968). The comparative reconstruction of Uto-Aztecan has also been discussed by Robert Longacre (1969). Problems of classification and internal diversity have been treated by several writers (Hale 1958–59; Lamb 1958, 1964; Mason 1936).

## 2.16 Wakashan

The Wakashan family consists of two branches, Kwakiutlan and Nootkan. Although the relationship of the two has been recognized for decades, progress in the actual reconstruction of proto-Wakashan has been very slow. In the course of his work on Nootka, Sapir at one time collected an extensive list of cognates between Nootka and

Kwakiutl but he did not publish his results. However, some of his very important insights, especially regarding morphophonemic problems, are reported in his elegant paper on "Glottalized continuants in Navaho, Nootka, and Kwakiutl" (1938). Swadesh presented a protophonology in his Mosan paper (1953a) but this is an ad hoc list arrived at by comparing phonemic systems, not by reconstructing the phonemes necessary to account for actually attested sound correspondences.

### 2.16.1 *Nootkan*

The greatest advance has been made in the Nootkan branch, which is comprised of Nootka, Nitinat, and Makah. In an important paper on Nootka pharyngeals, Jacobsen (1969) presented much valuable information about Makah, on which he has recently done extensive fieldwork, and made a thorough investigation of the historical problems involved in the development of pharyngeals in Nootka and, incidentally, in Nitinat also. The protophonology of Nootkan is given in Haas (1969b) together with Nootka and Nitinat cognates to back it up. Makah, which is critical in certain cases, is also quoted when available. A number of word reconstructions are included. The reconstruction of the Nootka-Nitinat pronominal suffixes is also attempted, and these in turn are compared with Kwakiutl to arrive at the proto-Wakashan system.

## 3. FOR THE FUTURE

Although the work of reconstructing the protolanguages of North America is at last beginning to receive the attention it deserves, what has been accomplished so far is just the beginning. We do not yet have a single etymological dictionary for any linguistic family, though materials are now accumulating which should make such a work eventually possible for several of the families, including Algonkian, Uto-Aztecan, Athapaskan-Eyak, Siouan, Muskogean, Salishan, Wakashan, Pomoan, and Yuman. But besides the etymological dictionary, of great importance also is the reconstruction of grammatical subsets, e.g. pronominals, demonstratives, instrumentals, and the like, and this work should lead to the preparation of protogrammars.

Alongside increased involvement with historical genetic problems we need more studies of linguistic diffusion areas so that outside influences can be assigned their proper place in the sequence of historical development. And out of this broader view of the proper nature of historical studies may come some new insights into old problems.

Perhaps it will seem that we have made very little progress toward the answer to our original puzzlement as to where the Indian came from. We still look to the Orient as the clue to the ultimate answer, but proof is as elusive as ever. In the meantime, though, we have truly begun to discover the New World, a world with a wealth of linguistic variety beyond our most extravagant expectations. Our major task now is to seek a better understanding of the ways in which this variety has come about.

## 4. BIBLIOGRAPHY AND REFERENCES

ALLEN, LOUIS. 1931. Siouan and Iroquoian. IJAL 6.185–93. [1.2.1]

AOKI, HARUO. 1962. Nez Perce and Northern Sahaptin: A binary comparison. IJAL 28.172–82. [2.11.6]

———. 1963. On Sahaptin-Klamath linguistic affiliations. IJAL 29.107–12. [1.2.9]

———. 1966a. Nez Perce vowel harmony and Proto-Sahaptian vowels. Lg 42.759–67. [2.11.6]

———. 1966b. Nez Perce and Proto-Sahaptian kinship terms. IJAL 32.357–68. [2.11.6]

BAUMHOFF, M. A., and D. L. OLMSTED. 1964. Notes on Palaihnihan culture history: Glottochronology and archaeology. Studies in Californian linguistics, ed. by William Bright, pp. 1–12. UCPL 34.

BEELER, MADISON S. 1955. Saclan. IJAL 21.201–9. [1.2.9]

———. 1959. Saclan once more. IJAL 25.67–8.

———. 1961a. Senary counting in California Penutian. AnL 3/6.1–8.

———. 1961b. Northern Costanoan. IJAL 27.191–7. [2.11.2]

———. 1970. Sibilant harmony in Chumash. IJAL 36.14–17. [2.7.4]

BLOOMFIELD, LEONARD. 1925. On the sound system of Central Algonquian. Lg 1.30–156. [2., 2.1]

———. 1927. The word-stems of Central Algonquian. Festschrift Meinhof, pp. 393–402. Hamburg. [2.1]

———. 1946. Algonquian. Linguistic structures of native America, by Harry Hoijer and others, pp. 85–129. VFPA 6. [1.2.4, 2., 2.1]

———. 1947. Proto-Algonquian *-iit-* 'fellow'. Lg 17.292–7. [2.1]

BOAS, FRANZ. 1920. The classification of American languages. AmA 2 2.367–76. [1.1]

———. 1929. Classification of American Indian languages. Lg 5.1–7. [1.1]

BOAS, FRANZ, and HERMAN HAEBERLIN. 1927. Sound shifts in Salishan dialects. IJAL 4.117–36. [2.12]

BRIGHT, JANE O. 1964. The phonology of Smith River Athapaskan (Tolowa). IJAL 30.101–7. [2.3]

BRIGHT, WILLIAM. 1954. Some Northern Hokan relationships: A preliminary report. Papers from the Symposium on American Indian Linguistics, pp. 63–7. UCPL 10. [1.2.7]

———. 1955. A bibliography of the Hokan-Coahuiltecan languages. IJAL 31.276–85.

———. 1956. Glottochronologic counts of Hokaltecan material. Lg 32.42–8. [1.2.8]

———. 1965a. The history of the Cahuilla sound system. IJAL 31.241–4. [2.15]

———. 1965b. Review of A history of Palaihnihan phonology, by D. L. Olmsted. Lg 41.175–8. [2.7.1]

——. 1968. Review of Uto-Aztecan cognate sets, by Wick R. Miller. IJAL 34.56–9. [Provides some corrections and additions, especially of Classical Aztec.] [2.15]
——. 1970. On linguistic unrelatedness. IJAL 36.288–90. [1.2.8]
BRIGHT, WILLIAM, and JANE HILL. 1967. The linguistic history of Cupeño. Studies in Southwestern ethnolinguistics, ed. by Dell H. Hymes and William E. Bittle, pp. 351–71. The Hague, Mouton. [2.15]
BRINTON, DANIEL G. 1891. The American race. Philadelphia, David McKay. [Reprinted in 1901.] [1.1, 1.2.1.2.3]
BROADBENT, SYLVIA M., and CATHERINE A. CALLAGHAN. 1960. Comparative Miwok: A preliminary survey. IJAL 26.301–16. [2.11.1]
BROADBENT, SYLVIA M., and HARVEY PITKIN. 1964. A comparison of Miwok and Wintun. Studies in Californian linguistics, ed. by William Bright, pp. 19–45. UCPL 34. [1.2.9, 2.11.1, 2.11.3]
CALLAGHAN, CATHERINE A. 1958. California Penutian: History and bibliography. IJAL 34.189–94.
——. 1962. Comparative Miwok-Mutsun with notes on Rumsen. IJAL 28.97–107. [1.2.9, 2.11.1, 2.11.2]
——. 1964. Phonemic borrowing in Lake Miwok. Studies in Californian linguistics, ed. by William Bright, pp. 46–53. UCPL 34.
——. 1967. Miwok-Costanoan as a subfamily of Penutian. IJAL 33.224–7. [1.2.9, 2.11.1, 2.11.2]
——. 1970. Bodega Miwok dictionary. UCPL 60. [2.11.1]
CALLAGHAN, CATHERINE A., and WICK R. MILLER. 1962. Swadesh's Macro Mixtecan hypothesis and English. SJA 18.278–85.
CHAFE, WALLACE L. 1959. Internal reconstruction in Seneca. Lg 35.477–95.
——. 1964. Another look at Siouan and Iroquoian. AmA 66.852–62. [1.2.1]
——. 1965. Discussion of Elmendorf's "Some problems in the regrouping of Powell units". CJL 10.105–6 passim. [1.2.1, 1.2.12.2]
COWAN, WILLIAM. 1969. PA *aˑ, *k, and *t in Narragansett. IJAL 35.28–33. [2.1]
CRAPO, RICHLEY H. 1970. The origins of directional adverbs in Uto-Aztecan languages. IJAL 36.181–9. [2.15]
DAVIDSON, WILLIAM, L.W. ELFORD, and HARRY HOIJER. 1963. Athapaskan classificatory verbs. Studies in the Athapaskan Languages, by Harry Hoijer and others, pp. 30–41. UCPL 29. [2.3]
DAVIS, IRVINE. 1963. Bibliography of Keresan linguistic sources. IJAL 29.289–93.
——. 1966. Numic consonantal correspondences. IJAL 32.124–240. [2.15]
DIXON, R.B. 1905. The Shasta-Achomawi: A new linguistic stock with four new dialects. AmA (n.s.) 7.213–17. [1.2.7]
DIXON, ROLAND B., and ALFRED L. KROEBER. 1913a. Relationship of the Indian languages of California. Science, n.s. 37.225. [1.1, 1.2.4, 1.2.7, 1.2.9]
——. 1913b. New linguistic families in California. AmA 15.647–55. [1.1, 1.2.4, 1.2.7, 1.2.9]

——. 1919. Linguistic families in California. UCPAAE 16/3. [1.1]
DORSEY, JAMES OWEN. 1893. The Biloxi Indians of Louisiana. AAAS-P 43.267–87.
DORSEY, JAMES OWEN, and JOHN R. SWANTON. 1912. A dictionary of the Biloxi and Ofo languages, accompanied with thirty-one Biloxi texts and numerous Biloxi phrases. BAE-B 47.
ELMENDORF, WILLIAM W. 1963. Yukian-Siouan lexical similarities. IJAL 29.300–9. [1.2.12.1]
——. 1964. Item and set comparison in Yuchi, Siouan, and Yukian. IJAL 30.328–40. [1.2.12.1, 1.2.12.4]
——. 1965. Some problems in the regrouping of Powell units. CJL 10.93–107.
——. 1969. Geographic ordering, subgrouping, and Olympic Salish. IJAL 35.220–5.
GALLATIN, ALBERT. 1836. A synopsis of the Indian tribes within the United States east of the Rocky Mountains and in the British and Russian possessions in North America. TCAAS 2.1–422. [1.1]
——. 1848. Hale's Indians of North-West America, and vocabularies of North America. AES-T 2.xxiii–clxxx, 1–130. New York. [1.1]
GATSCHET, ALBERT S. 1884. A migration legend of the Creek Indians. Vol. I. Brinton's Library of Aboriginal American Literature 4. Philadelphia. [1.2.12.5]
GATSCHET, ALBERT S., and JOHN R. SWANTON. 1932. A dictionary of the Atakapa language. BAE-B 108.
GEARY, J.A. 1941. Proto-Algonquian *çk: further examples. Lg 17.304–10. [2.1]
——. 1943. The Proto-Algonquian form for 'I — thee'. Lg 19.147–51. [2.1]
——. 1953. Strachey's vocabulary of Indian words used in Virginia, 1612. HSS 103.208–14. [2.1]
——. 1955. The language of the Carolina Algonkian tribes. HSS 105.873–900. [2.1]
GODDARD, IVES. 1965. The eastern Algonquian intrusive nasal. IJAL 31.206–20. [2.1]
——. 1967a. Notes on the genetic classification of the Algonquian languages. Contributions to Anthropology, Linguistics I, 7–12. NMC-B 214. [2.1]
——. 1967b. The Algonquian independent indicative. Contributions to Anthropology: Linguistics I. 66–106. NMC-B 214. [2.1]
GODDARD, PLINY EARLE. 1914. The present condition of our knowledge of North American languages. AmA 16.555–601.
——. 1917. Has Tlingit a genetic relation to Athapascan? IJAL 1.266–79. [1.1, 1.2.6]
GOLLA, VICTOR K. 1964a. Comparative Yokuts phonology. Studies in Californian linguistics, ed. by William Bright, pp. 54–66. UCPL 34. [2.11.5]
——. 1964b. An etymological study of Hupa noun stems. IJAL 30.108–17. [2.3]
GREENBERG, JOSEPH H., and MORRIS SWADESH. 1953. Jicaque as a Hokan language. IJAL 19.216–22. [1.2.8]
GREKOFF, GEORGE V. 1964. A note on comparative Pomo. Studies in Californian linguistics, ed. by William Bright, pp. 67–72. UCPL 34.

GURSKY, KARL-HEINZ. 1963. Algonkian and the languages of Southern Texas. AnL 5/9.17–21. [1.2.5]
——. 1965a. Lexical similarities between Caddoan and Algonkian-Gulf. AnL 7/4. 104–9. [1.2.5, 2.6]
——. 1965b. Ein lexikalischer Vergleich der Algonkin-Golf- und Hoka-Subtiaba-Sprachen. Orbis 14.160–215. [1.2.5, 2.6]
——. 1966. Ein Vergleich der grammatikalischen Morpheme der Golf-Sprachen und der Hoka-Subtiaba-Sprachen. Orbis 15.511–37. [1.2.5, 2.6]
——. 1967. Review of Die nordamerikanischen Indianer-sprachen, by Heinz-Jürgen Pinnow. IJAL 33.171–3.
——. 1968. Gulf and Hokan-Subtiaban: New lexical parallels. IJAL 34.21–41. [2.6]
——. 1969. A lexical comparison of the Atakapa, Chitimacha, and Tunica languages. IJAL 35.83–107. [1.2.2, 2.6]
HAAS, MARY R. 1941. The classification of the Muskogean languages. Language, culture, and personality, ed. by Leslie Spier, A. Irving Hallowell, and Stanley S. Newman, pp. 41–56. Menasha, Wisconsin. [2.10]
——. 1945. Dialects of the Muskogee language. IJAL 11.69–74.
——. 1946. A Proto-Muskogean paradigm. Lg 22.326–32. [2.10]
——. 1947a. The development of Proto-Muskogean *$k^w$. IJAL 13.135–7. [2.10]
——. 1947b. Some French loan-words in Tunica. RomPh 1.145–8.
——. 1948. Classificatory verbs in Muskogee. IJAL 14.244–6.
——. 1949. The position of Apalachee in the Muskogean family. IJAL 15.121–7. [2.10]
——. 1950. On the historical development of certain long vowels in Creek. IJAL 16.122–5. [2.10]
——. 1951. The Proto-Gulf word for *water* (with notes on Siouan-Yuchi). IJAL 17.71–9. [1.2.2, 1.2.8, 1.2.12.4, 2.6, 2.10]
——. 1952. The Proto-Gulf word for *land* (with a note on Proto-Siouan). IJAL 18.238–40. [1.2.2, 2.6, 2.10]
——. 1954. The Proto-Hokan-Coahuiltecan word for 'water'. Papers from the Symposium on American Indian Linguistics, pp. 57–62. UCPL 10. [1.2.8, 2.7]
——. 1956. Natchez and the Muskogean languages. Lg 32.61–72. [1.2.2, 2.10]
——. 1958a. Algonkian-Ritwan: The end of a controversy. IJAL 24.159–73. [1.2.4, 2.2]
——. 1958b. A new linguistic relationship in North America: Algonkian and the Gulf languages. SJA 14.231–64. [1.2.5]
——. 1958c. Notes on some PCA stems in /k-/. IJAL 24.241–5. [2.1]
——. 1959. Tonkawa and Algonkian. AnL 1/2.1–6. [1.2.5, 1.2.8]
——. 1960. Some genetic affiliations of Algonkian. Culture in history: Essays in honor of Paul Radin, ed. by Stanley Diamond, pp. 977–92. New York, Columbia University Press. [1.2.5]
——. 1961. Comment on Floyd G. Lounsbury's "Iroquois-Cherokee linguistic rela-

tions". Symposium on Cherokee-Iroquois culture, pp. 21-3. BAE-B 180.
——. 1963a. Shasta and Proto-Hokan. Lg 39.40-59. [1.2.7]
——. 1963b. The Muskogean and Algonkian words for *skunk*. IJAL 29. 65-6. [2.7]
——. 1964a. California Hokan. Studies in Californian linguistics, ed. by William Bright, pp. 73-87. UCPL 34. [1.2.7]
——. 1964b. Athaspaskan, Tlingit, Yuchi, and Siouan. PICAm 35/2.495-500. México. [1.2.12.4]
——. 1965. Is Kutenai related to Algonkian? CJL 10.77-92. [1.2.5]
——. 1966a. Wiyot-Yurok-Algonkian and problems of comparative Algonkian. IJAL 32.101-7.
——. 1966b. Vowels and semivowels in Algonkian. Lg 42.479-88. [2.1]
——. 1966c. Historical linguistics and the genetic relationship of languages. CTL 3. 113-54.
——. 1967a. Roger Williams's sound shift: A study in Algonkian. To Honor Roman Jakobson 1.816-32. The Hague-Paris, Mouton. [2.1]
——. 1967b. The development of Proto-Algonkian *-awe-. Studies in historical linguistics in honor of George Sherman Lane, pp. 137-45. Chapel Hill, University of North Carolina Press. [2.1]
——. 1967c. The Proto-Algonkian word for 'sun'. Contributions to Anthropology: Linguistics I, 60-5. NMC-B 214. [2.1]
——. 1967d. Language and taxonomy in Northwestern California. AmA 69.358-62.
——. 1967e. On the relations of Tonkawa. Studies in Southwestern ethnolinguistics, ed. by Dell H. Hymes and William E. Bittle, pp. 310-20. The Hague, Mouton. [1.2.5, 1.2.8]
——. 1968a. The last words of Biloxi. IJAL 34.77-84. [2.13]
——. 1968b. Notes on a Chipewyan dialect. IJAL 34.165-75.
——. 1969a. The prehistory of languages. JanL, series minor 57. [Revision and expansion of Haas 1966c.] [1.2.4, 1.2.12.4, 2.10]
——. 1969b. Internal reconstruction of the Nootka-Nitinat pronominal suffixes. IJAL 35.108-24. [2.16.1]
——. 1969c. Grammar or lexicon? The American Indian side of the question from Duponceau to Powell. IJAL 35.239-55. [2.13]
——. 1969d. Swanton and the Biloxi and Ofo dictionaries. IJAL 35.286-90.
——. 1970. Review of Benjamin Smith Barton, New views of the origin of the tribes and nations of North America. (Ann Arbor, Michigan, University Microfilms, 1968.) IJAL 36.68-70.
——. 1971. Southeastern Indian linguistics. Red, white, and black: Symposium on Indians in the Old South, ed. by Charles M. Hudson, pp. 44-54. Athens, University of Georgia. [1.2.12.5]
HALE, HORATIO. 1883a. Indian migrations, as evidenced by language. Part I: the Huron-Cherokee stock. AAOJ 5.18-28.
——. 1883b. The Tutelo tribe and language. PAPS 21.1-45.

HALE, KENNETH L. 1958–59. Internal diversity in Uto-Aztecan, I, II. IJAL 24. 101–7, 25.114–21. [2.15]

——. 1962. Jemez and Kiowa correspondences in reference to Kiowa-Tanoan. IJAL 28.1–5. [1.2.11, 2.14]

——. 1967. Toward a reconstruction of Kiowa-Tonoan phonology. IJAL 33. 112–20. [1.2.11, 2.14]

——. 1970. On Papago laryngeals. Languages and cultures of Western North America, ed. by Earl H. Swanson, Jr., pp. 54–60. Pocatello, Idaho State University Press. [2.15]

HALPERN, A. M. 1964. A report on a survey of Pomo languages. Studies in Californian linguistics, ed. by William Bright, pp. 88–93. UCPL 34. [1.2.7, 2.7.2, 2.7.3]

HAMP, ERIC P. 1960. Selected summary bibliography of language classification. SiL 15.29–45.

——. 1970. Wiyot and Yurok correspondences. Languages and cultures of Western North America, ed. by Earl H. Swanson, Jr., pp. 107–10. Pocatello, Idaho State University Press. [1.2.4]

HARRINGTON, JOHN P. 1910. On phonetic and lexical resemblances between Kiowan and Tanoan. AmA 12.119–23. [1.1, 1.2.11]

HEWSON, JOHN. 1968. Beothuk and Algonkian: Evidence old and new. IJAL 34. 85–93. [1.2.5]

HILL, JANE H., and KENNETH C. HILL. 1968. Stress in the Cupan (Uto-Aztecan) languages. IJAL 34.233–41. [2.15]

HOCKETT, CHARLES F. 1942. The position of Potawatomi in Central Algonquian. Papers of the Michigan Academy of Science, Arts and Letters 28.537–42. Ann Arbor, University of Michigan Press. [2.1]

——. 1957. Central Algonquian vocabulary: Stems in /k-/. IJAL 23.247–68. [2.1]

——. 1964. The Proto Central Algonquian kinship system. Explorations in cultural anthropology: Essays in honor of George Peter Murdock, ed. by Ward H. Goodenough, pp. 239–57. New York, Harper and Row. [2.1]

HOIJER, HARRY. 1938. The Southern Athapaskan languages. AmA 40.75–87. [2.3]

——. 1941. Methods in the classification of American Indian languages. Language, culture, and personality, ed. by Leslie Spier, A. Irving Hallowell, and Stanley S. Newman, pp. 3–14. Menasha, Wisconsin. [1.1]

——. 1946. Introduction. Linguistic structures of native America, by Harry Hoijer and others, pp. 9–29. VFPA 6. [1.1]

——. 1954. Some problems of American Indian linguistic research. Papers from the Symposium on American Indian Linguistics, pp. 3–12. UCPL 10.

——. 1956. Athapaskan kinship systems. AmA 58.309–33. [2.3]

——. 1960. Athapaskan languages of the Pacific Coast. Culture in history: Essays in honor of Paul Radin, ed. by Stanley Diamond, pp. 960–76. New York, Columbia University Press. [2.3]

——. 1963. The Athapaskan languages. Studies in the Athapaskan languages, pp. 1–29. UCPL 29. [2.3]

——. 1966. Hare phonology: An historical study. Lg 42.499–507.

——. 1971. Athapaskan morphology. Studies in American Indian languages, ed. by Jesse Sawyer, pp. 113–48. UCPL 65. [2.3]

HOIJER, HARRY and others. 1963. Studies in the Athapaskan languages. UCPL 29. [2.3]

HOIJER, HARRY, ERIC P. HAMP, and WILLIAM BRIGHT. 1965. Contributions to a bibliography of comparative Amerindian. IJAL 31.346–52.

HOLMER, NILS M. 1945. Sonant-surds in Ponca-Omaha. IJAL 11.75–85.

——. 1947. An Ofo phonetic law. IJAL 13.1–8. [2.13]

HYMES, DELL H. 1955. Positional analysis of categories: A frame for reconstruction. Word 11.10–23.

——. 1956. Na-Déné and positional analysis of categories. AmA 58.624–38. [1.2.6, 1.2.8, 2.3]

——. 1957a. Some Penutian elements and the Penutian hypothesis. SJA 13.69–87. [1.2.9]

——. 1957b. A note on Athapaskan chronology. IJAL 23.291–7.

——. 1959. Genetic relationship: Retrospect and prospect. AnL 1/2.50–66.

——. 1964a. 'Hail' and 'bead': Two Penutian etymologies. Studies in Californian linguistics, ed. by William Bright, pp. 94–8. UCPL 34. [1.2.9]

——. 1964b. Evidence for Penutian in lexical sets with initial *c- and –s-. IJAL 30.213–42. [1.2.9]

HYMES, VIRGINIA DOSCH. 1955. Athapaskan numeral systems. IJAL 21.26–45. [2.3]

JACOBS, MELVILLE. 1954. The areal spread of sound features in the languages north of California. Papers from the Symposium on American Indian linguistics, pp. 44–56. UCPL 10.

JACOBSEN, WILLIAM H., JR. 1958. Washo and Karok: An approach to comparative Hokan. IJAL 24.195–212. [1.2.7]

——. 1967. Switch-reference in Hokan-Coahuiltecan. Studies in Southwestern ethnolinguistics, ed. by Dell H. Hymes and William E. Bittle, pp. 238–63. The Hague, Mouton. [1.2.8]

——. 1968. On the prehistory of Nez Perce vowel harmony. Lg 44.819–29. [2.11.6]

——. 1969. Origin of the Nootka pharyngeals. IJAL 35.125–53. [2.16.1]

JOEL, JUDITH. 1964. Classification of the Yuman languages. Studies in Californian linguistics, ed. by William Bright, pp. 99–105. UCPL 34. [2.7.3]

KINKADE, M. DALE. 1967. Uvular-pharyngeal resonants in Interior Salish. IJAL 33.228–34. [2.12]

KLEIN, SHELDON. 1959. Comparative Mono-Kawaiisu. IJAL 25.233–8.

KRAUSS, MICHAEL E. 1964–65. Proto-Athapaskan-Eyak and the problem of Na-Dene I: Phonology; II: Morphology. IJAL 30.118–36; 31.18–28. [1.2.6, 2.3, 2.4]

——. 1968. Noun-classification systems in Athapaskan, Eyak, Tlingit, and Haida verbs. IJAL 34.194–203. [1.2.6, 2.4]
——. 1969. On the classifiers in the Athapaskan, Eyak, and Tlingit verb. IUPAL 24. [Title page misprinted as On the classification ...] [1.2.6]
KROEBER, ALFRED L. 1907. The Yokuts language of south central California. UCPAAE 2.165–377. [2.11.5]
——. 1915. Serian, Tequistlatecan, and Hokan. UCPAAE 11.279–90. [1.1, 1.2.7] [2.15]
——. 1937. Athabascan kin term systems. AmA 39.602–8. [2.3]
——. 1943. The classification of the Yuman languages. UCPL 1.21–40. [2.7.3]
——. 1955. Linguistic time-depth results so far and their meaning. IJAL 21.91–104.
KROEBER, ALFRED L., and JOHN P. HARRINGTON. 1914. Phonetic elements of the Diegueño language. UCPAAE 11.177–88. [1.2.7]
LAMB, SYDNEY M. 1958. Linguistic prehistory in the Great Basin. IJAL 24.95–100. [2.15]
——. 1959. Some proposals for linguistic taxonomy. AnL 1/2.33–48.
——. 1964. The classification of the Uto-Aztecan languages: A historical survey. Studies of Californian linguistics, ed. by William Bright, pp. 106–25. UCPL 34. [2.15]
LANDAR, HERBERT. 1968. The Karankawa invasion of Texas. IJAL 34.242–58. [1.2.12.3]
LANGACKER, RONALD W. 1970. The vowels of proto Uto-Aztecan. IJAL 36.169–80. [2.15]
LANGDON, MARGARET. 1968. The Proto-Yuman demonstrative system. FLing 2.61–81. [2.7.3]
LAW, HOWARD W. 1961. A reconstructed proto-culture derived from some Yuman vocabularies. AnL 3/4.45–57. [2.7.3]
LI, FANG-KUEI. 1930. Mattole, an Athapaskan language. Chicago, University of Chicago Press. [A largely historical treatment.] [2., 2.3]
——. 1933. Chipewyan consonants. The Ts'ai Yuan P'ei Anniversary Volume, pp. 429–67. (Supplementary Volume I of the BIHPAS). Peiping. [2., 2.3]
——. 1956. A type of noun formation in Athabaskan and Eyak. IJAL 22.45–8. [2.4]
——. 1965. Some problems in comparative Athapaskan. CJL 10.129–34.
LONGACRE, ROBERT E. 1961. Swadesh's Macro Mixtecan hypothesis. IJAL 27.9–29.
——. 1969. Comparative reconstruction of indigenous languages. CTL 4.320–60. [2.15]
LORIOT, JAMES. 1964. A selected bibliography of comparative American Indian linguistics. IJAL 30.62–80.
LOUNSBURY, FLOYD G. 1961. Iroquois-Cherokee linguistic relations. Symposium on Cherokee-Iroquois culture, pp. 1–20. BAE-B 180. [2.8]
MCLENDON, SALLY. 1964. Northern Hokan (b) and (c): A comparison of Eastern Pomo and Yana. Studies in Californian linguistics, ed. by William Bright, pp. 126–44. UCPL 34. [1.2.7]

———. In press. The reconstruction of proto-Pomo. [2.7.2]
MASON, J. ALDEN. 1936. The classification of the Sonoran languages (with an appendix by B. L. Whorf). Essays in anthropology presented to A. L. Kroeber ..., pp. 183–98. Berkeley, University of California Press. [2.15]
MATTHEWS, G. HUBERT. 1958. Handbook of Siouan languages. University of Pennsylvania dissertation. (MS). [2.13]
———. 1959. Proto-Siouan kinship terminology. AmA 61.252–78. [2.13]
———. 1970. Some notes on the Proto-Siouan continuants. IJAL 35.98–109.
MEEUSEN, A. E. 1959. Algonquian clusters with glottal stop. IJAL 25.189–90. [2.1]
MICHELSON, TRUMAN. 1914. Two alleged Algonquian languages of California. AmA 16.361–7. [1.1, 1.2.4]
———. 1921. The classification of American languages. IJAL 2.73. [1.1]
———. 1933. The linguistic classification of Powhatan. AmA 35.549. [2.1]
———. 1935. Phonetic shifts in Algonquian languages. IJAL 8.131–71. [2.1]
———. 1939–44. Contributions to Algonquian linguistics. IJAL 10.75–85. [2.1]
MILLER, WICK R. 1959a. An outline of Shawnee historical phonology. IJAL 25.16–21. [2.1]
———. 1959b. A note on Kiowa linguistic affiliations. AmA 61.102–5. [1.2.11]
———. 1966. Anthropological linguistics in the Great Basin. The current status of anthropological research in the Great Basin: 1964, ed. by Warren D'Azevedo, Wilbur A. Davis, Don D. Fowler, and Wayne Suttles, pp. 75–112. Reno, Desert Research Institute.
———. 1967. Uto-Aztecan cognate sets. UCPL 48. [2.15]
———. 1970. Western Shoshoni dialects. Languages and cultures of Western North America, ed. by Earl H. Swanson, Jr., pp. 17–36. Pocatello, Idaho State University Press.
MILLER, WICK R., and IRVINE DAVIS. 1963. Proto-Keresan phonology. IJAL 29.310–30. [1.2.12.2, 2.9]
NEWMAN, STANLEY. 1944. The Yokuts language of California. VFPA 2. [2.11.5]
———. 1964. Comparison of Zuni and California Penutian. IJAL 30.1–13. [1.2.10]
OLMSTED, DAVID L. 1956–59. Palaihnihan and Shasta I: Labial stops, II: Apical stops, III: Dorsal stops. Lg 32.73–7, 33.136–8, 35.637–43. [1.2.7]
———. 1964. History of Palaihnihan phonology. UCPL 35. [2.7.1]
———. 1965. Phonemic change and subgrouping: Some Hokan data. Lg 41.303–7. [1.2.7]
OSWALT, ROBERT L. 1964a. A comparative study of two Pomo languages. Studies in Californian linguistics, ed. by William Bright, pp. 148–62. UCPL 34. [2.7.2]
———. 1964b. The internal relationships of the Pomo family of languages. PICAm 35/2.413–27. [2.7.2]
PICKERING, JOHN. 1831. Indian languages of North America. Encyclopedia Americana 4.581–600. Philadelphia. [1.1]

PIERCE, JOE E. 1965. Hanis and Miluk: Dialects or unrelated languages. IJAL 31.323–5.
——. 1966. Genetic comparisons and Hanis, Miluk, Alsea, Siuslaw, and Takelma. IJAL 32.379–87. [1.2.9]
PINNOW, HEINZ-JÜRGEN. 1958. Bemerkungen zu den Konsonanten-verbindungen im Ur-Algonkin. ZPhon 11.350–5. [2.1]
——. 1964a. On the historical position of Tlingit. IJAL 30.155–64. [1.2.6]
——. 1964b. Die Nordamerikanischen Indianersprachen: ein Überblick über ihren Bau und ihre Besonderheiten. Weisbaden.
——. 1966. Grundzüge einer historischen Lautlehre des Tlingit: Ein Versuch. Wiesbaden. [1.2.6]
——. 1968. Genetic relationship vs. borrowing in Na-Dene. IJAL 34.204–11. [1.2.6]
——. 1970. Notes on the classifiers in the Na-Dene languages. IJAL 36.63–7. [1.2.6]
PITKIN, HARVEY. 1962. A bibliography of the Wintun family of languages. IJAL 28.43–54.
PITKIN, HARVEY, and WILLIAM SHIPLEY. 1958. Comparative survey of California Penutian. IJAL 24.174–88. [1.2.9, 2.11, 2.11.3]
POWELL, JOHN WESLEY. 1891. Indian linguistic families of America north of Mexico. B[A]E-R 7 (1885–1886) 7–142. [1.1]
RADIN, PAUL. 1919. The genetic relationship of the North American languages. UCPAAE 14/5.489–502. [1.1]
REICHARD, GLADYS A. 1925. Wiyot grammar and texts. UCPAAE 22.1–215. [1.2.4]
——. 1958–60. A comparison of five Salish languages: I–VI. IJAL 24.293–300; 25.8–15, 90–6, 154–67, 239–53; 26.50–61. [2.12]
RIGSBY, BRUCE J. 1965. Continuity and change in Sahaptian vowel systems. IJAL 31.312–22. [2.11.6]
——. 1966. On Cayuse-Molala relatability. IJAL 32.369–78. [1.2.9]
——. 1969. The Waiilatpuan problem: More on Cayuse-Molala relatability. NARN 3.69–146. [1.2.9]
RIGSBY, BRUCE, and MICHAEL SILVERSTEIN. 1969. Nez Perce vowels and Proto-Sahaptian vowel harmony. Lg 45.45–59. [2.11.6]
ROWE, JOHN HOWLAND. 1954. Linguistic classification problems in South America. Papers from the Symposium on American Indian Linguistics, pp. 13–26. UCPL 10. [1.1]
SAPIR, EDWARD. 1913. Wiyot and Yurok, Algonkin languages of California. AmA 15.617–46. [1.1, 1.2.4, 1.2.6]
——. 1913–14. Southern Paiute and Nahautl, a study in Uto-Aztecan. JSocAm 10.379–425, 11.443–88. [Part II also published in AmA 17.98–120, 306–28 (1915).] [2.]
——. 1915. The Na-Déné languages, a preliminary report. AmA 17.534–58. [1.1, 1.2.6, 2.]
——. 1916. Time perspective in aboriginal American culture: A study in method.

Canada Department of Mines, Geological Survey, Memoir 90, Anthropological Series no. 13. Ottawa. [Reprinted in SWES, pp. 389–462 (1949).]

——. 1917a. The position of Yana in the Hokan stock. UCPAAE 13.1–34. [1.1, 1.2.7]

——. 1917b. Linguistic publications of the Bureau of American Ethnology, a general review. IJAL 1.76–81.

——. 1917c. The Hokan and Coahuiltecan languages. IJAL 1.280–90. [1.1, 1.2,8]

——. 1921a. A characteristic Penutian form of stem. IJAL 2.58–67.

——. 1921b. A bird's-eye view of American languages north of Mexico. Science 54.408. [1.1]

——. 1921c. A supplementary note on Salinan and Washo. IJAL 2.68–72. [1.1, 1.2.7]

——. 1923a. A type of Athapaskan relative. IJAL 2.136–42.

——. 1923b. The Algonkin affinity of Yurok and Wiyot kinship terms. JSocAm 15. 36–74. [1.1]

——. 1925. The Hokan affinity of Subtiaba in Nicaragua. AmA 27.402–35, 491–527. [1.1, 1.2.8]

——. 1929. Central and North American Indian languages. Encyclopaedia Britannica, 14th edition, 5.138–41. [Reprinted in SWES, pp. 169–78 (1949).] [1.1, 1.2.5, 1.2.8, 1.2.9, 1.2.11, 1.2.12, 5.]

——. 1931. The concept of phonetic law as tested in primitive languages by Leonard Bloomfield. Methods in social science, ed. by Stuart A. Rice, pp. 297–306. Chicago, University of Chicago Press. [Reprinted in SWES, pp. 73–82 (1949).] [2., 2.3]

——. 1938. Glottalized continuants in Navaho, Nootka, and Kwakiutl (with a note on Indo-European). Lg 14.248–74. [Reprinted in SWES, pp. 225–50 (1949).] [2.16]

SAPIR, EDWARD, and MORRIS SWADESH. 1953. Coos-Takelma-Penutian comparisons. IJAL 19.132–7.

SEILER, HANSJAKOB. 1965. Accent and morphophonemics in Cahuilla and in Uto-Aztecan. IJAL 31.50–9. [2.15]

——. 1967. Structure and reconstruction in some Uto-Aztecan languages. IJAL 33.135–47. [2.15]

SHAFER, ROBERT. 1952. Athapaskan and Sino-Tibetan. IJAL 18.12–19.

——. 1957. Note on Athapaskan and Sino-Tibetan. IJAL 23.116–17.

——. 1967. A bibliography of Uto-Aztecan with a note on biogeography. IJAL 33.148–59.

SHIPLEY, WILLIAM. 1957. Some Yukian-Penutian lexical resemblances. IJAL 23. 269–74. [1.2.12.1]

——. 1961. Maidu and Nisenan: A binary survey. IJAL 27.46–51. [2.11.4]

——. 1966. The relation of Klamath to California Penutian. Lg 42.489–98. [1.2.9, 2.11]

——. 1969. Proto-Takelman. IJAL 35.226–30. [1.2.9]
——. 1970. Proto-Kalapuyan. Languages and cultures of Western North America, ed. by Earl H. Swanson, Jr., pp. 97–106. Pocatello, Idaho State University Press. [1.2.9]
SIEBERT, FRANK T., JR. 1941. Certain Proto-Algonquian consonant clusters. Lg 17.298–303. [2.1]
——. 1945. Linguistic classification of Catawba. IJAL 11.100–4, 211–18. [2.13]
——. 1967a. The original home of the Proto-Algonquian people. Contributions to Anthropology: Linguistics I, 60–5. NMC-B 214. [2.1]
——. 1967b. Discrepant consonant clusters ending in *-k in Proto-Algonquian, a proposed interpretation of saltatory sound changes. Contributions to Anthropology: Linguistics I, 48–59. NMC-B 214. [2.1]
SILVER, SHIRLEY. 1960. Natick consonants in reference to Proto-Central Algonquian: I, II. IJAL 26.112–19, 234–41. [2.1]
——. 1964. Shasta and Karok: A binary comparison. Studies in Californian linguistics, ed. by William Bright, pp. 170–81. UCPL 34. [1.2.7]
——. 1966. Review of A history of Palaihnihan phonology, by D.L. Olmsted. IJAL 32.210–12. [2.7.1]
SUTTLES, WAYNE, and WILLIAM ELMENDORF. 1963. Linguistic evidence for Salish prehistory. Symposium on language and culture, ed. by Viola E. Garfield and Wallace L. Chafe, pp. 41–52. Seattle, American Ethnological Society.
SWADESH, MORRIS. 1946. Phonologic formulas for Atakapa-Chitimacha. IJAL 12. 113–32. [1.2.2, 2.6]
——. 1947. Atakapa-Chitimacha *k$^w$. IJAL 13.120–1. [1.2.2, 2.6]
——. 1949. The linguistic approach to Salish prehistory. Indians of the urban Northwest, ed. by Marian W. Smith, pp. 161–73. New York, Columbia University Press. [1.2.3]
——. 1950. Salish internal relationships. IJAL 16.157–67. [1.2.3]
——. 1951a. Diffusional cumulation and archaic residue as historic explanations. SJA 7.1–21.
——. 1951b. Kleinschmidt centennial III: Unaaliq and Proto-Eskimo. IJAL 17. 66–70.
——. 1952a. Lexico-statistic dating of prehistoric ethnic contacts (with special reference to North American Indians and Eskimos). PAPS 96.452–63. [1.2.3]
——. 1952b. Salish phonologic geography. Lg 28.232–48. [2.12]
——. 1952c. Unaaliq and Proto-Eskimo II: Phonemes and morphophonemes; III: Synchronic notes; IV: Diachronic notes; V: Comparative vocabulary. IJAL 18.25–34, 69–76, 166–71, 241–56.
——. 1952d. Comment on Robert Shafer, Athapaskan and Sino-Tibetan. IJAL 18.178–81.
——. 1953a. Mosan I: A problem of remote common origin; II: Comparative vocabulary. IJAL 19.26–44, 223–36. [1.2.3, 2.16]

———. 1953b. Salish-Wakashan lexical comparisons noted by Boas. IJAL 19.290–1.
———. 1954a. Time depths of American linguistic groupings (with comments by George I. Quimby, Henry B. Collins, Emil W. Haury, Gordon F. Ekholm and Fred Eggan). AmA 56.361–77.
———. 1954b. Perspectives and problems of Amerindian comparative linguistics. Word 10.306–32.
———. 1955a. Towards a satisfactory genetic classification of Amerindian languages. PICAm (31st meeting), 1001–12. São Paulo.
———. 1955b. Towards greater accuracy in lexicostatistic dating. IJAL 21.121–37.
———. 1955c. The culture-historical meaning of Sapir's linguistic classification. Journal of the Colorado-Wyoming Academy of Science 4.23–4.
———. 1956. Problems of long-range comparison in Penutian. Lg 32.17–41. [1.2.9]
———. 1959a. Linguistics as an instrument of prehistory. SJA 15.20–33.
———. 1959b. The mesh principle in comparative linguistics. AnL 1/2.7–14.
———. 1960a. Tras la huella lingüística de la prehistoria. Suplementos del Seminario de Problemas Científicos y Filosóficas, 2a Serie, 26.97–145. México.
———. 1960b. On interhemispheric linguistic connections. Culture in history: Essays in honor of Paul Radin, ed. by Stanley Diamond, pp. 894–924. New York, Columbia University Press.
———. 1960c. The Oto-Manguean hypothesis and Macro-Mixtecan. IJAL 26.79–111.
———. 1961. The culture historic implication of Sapir's linguistic classification. A William Cameron Townsend, pp. 663–72. México, D.F.
———. 1962a. Afinidades de las lenguas Amerindias. AIAK 34.729–38.
———. 1962b. Linguistic relations across Bering Strait. AmA 64.1262–91. [1.2.3]
———. 1964a. Linguistic overview. Prehistoric man in the New World, ed. by Jesse D. Jennings and Edward Norbeck, pp. 527–56. Chicago, University of Chicago Press. [1.2.3, 1.2.12.5]
———. 1964b. Comparative Penutian glosses of Sapir. Studies in Californian linguistics, ed. by William Bright, pp. 182–91. UCPL 34.
———. 1965. Kalapuya and Takelma. IJAL 31.237–40. [1.2.9]
———. 1967a. Lexicostatistic classification. HMAI 5.79–115.
———. 1967b. Linguistic classification in the Southwest. Studies in Southwestern ethnolinguistics, ed. by Dell H. Hymes and William E. Bittle, pp. 281–309. The Hague, Mouton. [1.2.10, 1.2.12.2]
SWANTON, JOHN R. 1909. A new Siouan dialect. Putnam Anniversary Volume, pp. 477–86. New York.
———. 1915. Linguistic position of the tribes of southern Texas and northeastern Mexico. AmA 13.17–40. [1.2.8]
———. 1917. Unclassified languages of the Southeast. IJAL 1.47–9.
———. 1919. A structural and lexical comparison of the Tunica, Chitimacha, and Atakapa languages. BAE–B 68. [1.1]

——. 1924. The Muskhogean connection of the Natchez language. IJAL 3.46–75. [1.1]
——. 1929. The Tawasa language. AmA 31.435–53.
TAYLOR, ALLAN R. 1963a. The classification of the Caddoan languages. PAPS 107. 51–9. [2.5]
——. 1963b. Comparative Caddoan. IJAL 29.113–31. [2.5]
TEETER, KARL V. 1964. Wiyot and Yurok: A preliminary study. Studies in Californian linguistics, ed. by William Bright, pp. 192–8. UCPL 34. [1.2.4]
——. 1965. The Algonquian verb: Notes toward a reconsideration. IJAL 31.221–5. [2.1]
——. 1967. Genetic classification in Algonquian. Contributions to Anthropology: Linguistics I, 1–6. NMC-B 214. [2.1]
TRAGER, GEORGE L. 1942. The comparative phonology of the Tiwa languages. SiL 1/5.1–10. [1.2.11, 2.14]
——. 1943. The kinship and status terms of the Tiwa languages. AmA 45.557–71.
——. 1945. Review of Map of North American Indian Languages, compiled and drawn by C.F. Voegelin and E.W. Voegelin. IJAL 11.186–89. [1.1]
——. 1969. Taos and Picuris — how long separated? IJAL 35.180–2.
TRAGER, GEORGE L., and EDITH CROWELL TRAGER. 1959. Kiowa and Tanoan. AmA 61.1078–83. [1.2.11, 2.14]
TROIKE, RUDOLPH C. 1963. Uto-Aztecan cognates in Classical Nahuatl. IJAL 29. 72–4. [2.15]
——. 1964. The Caddo word for 'water'. IJAL 30.96–8.
——. 1967. A structural comparison of Tonkawa and Coahuilteco. Studies in Southwestern ethno-linguistics, ed. by Dell H. Hymes and William E. Bittle, pp. 321–32. The Hague, Mouton. [1.2.8]
TURNER, PAUL R. 1967. Seri and Chontal (Tequistlateco). IJAL 33.235–9. [1.2.8]
——. 1969. Proto-Chontal phonemes. IJAL 35.34–7.
UHLENBECK, C. C. 1927a. Algonkisch-klinkende woorden in het Wiyot. MKAW, Afdeeling Letterkunde 63.A.ix, 233–58. Amsterdam.
——. 1927b. Review of A. Meillet et M. Cohen, Les langues du monde ..., 1924. IJAL 4.114–15. [1.2.4]
——. 1939. Grammatische invloed van het Algonkisch op het Wiyot en het Yurok. MKAW, Afdeeling Letterkunde, n.s., II.iii, 41–9. Amsterdam.
ULTAN, RUSSELL. 1964. Proto-Maidun phonology. IJAL 30.355–70. [2.11.4]
VOEGELIN, CHARLES F. 1939. Ofo-Biloxi sound correspondences. Proceedings of the Indiana Academy of Science 48.23–6. [2.13]
——. 1941a. North American Indian languages still spoken and their genetic relationships. Language, culture, and personality, ed. by Leslie Spier, A. Irving Hallowell, and Stanley S. Newman, pp. 15–40. Menasha, Wisconsin.
——. 1941b. The position of Blackfoot among the Algonquian languages. Papers of the Michigan Academy of Science, Arts, and Letters 26.505–12. [2.1]

——. 1941c. Proto-Algonquian consonant clusters in Delaware. Lg 17.143–7. [2.1]
——. 1941d. Internal relationships of Siouan languages. AmA 43.246–9. [2.13]
VOEGELIN, CHARLES F., and ERMINIE WHEELER VOEGELIN. 1944. Map of North American Indian languages. PAES 20. [1.1]
——. 1946. Linguistic considerations of northeastern North America. Man in Northeastern North America. Papers of the Robert S. Peabody Foundation for Archaeology 3.178–94. Andover, Mass. [1.2.5]
VOEGELIN, CHARLES F., and FLORENCE M. VOEGELIN. 1965. Extinction of American Indian languages before and after contact periods. JCL 10.135–46.
——. 1966. Map of North American Indian Languages. PAES 20, Revised. [1.2.12]
VOEGELIN, CHARLES F., FLORENCE M. VOEGELIN, and KENNETH L. HALE. 1962. Typological and comparative grammar of Uto-Aztecan: I (Phonology). IUPAL 17. [2.15]
VOGT, HANS. 1940. Salishan studies: Comparative notes on Kalispel, Spokan, Colville, and Coeur d'Alene. Skrifter utgitt av Det Norske Videnskaps-Akademi, II, Hist.-Filos. Klasse no. 2. Oslo. [2.12]
WARES, ALAN CAMPBELL. 1968. A comparative study of Yuman consonantism. JanL, series practica 57. [2.7.3]
WATERHOUSE, VIOLA. 1969. Oaxaca Chontal in reference to Proto-Chontal. IJAL 35.231–3.
WEBB, NANCY M. 1971. A statement of some phonological correspondences among the Pomo languages. IUPAL 26. [2.7.2]
WEBB, NANCY M., CAROLYN F. WALL, and LOUISE TANOUS. 1965–66. Consonant and vowel correspondences among the Pomo languages. SiL 18.59–70. [2.7.2]
WHORF, BENJAMIN L. 1935. The comparative linguistics of Uto-Aztecan. AmA 37.600–8. [1.2.11, 2.15]
——. 1937. The origin of Aztec *tl*. AmA 39.265–74. [1.2.11, 2.15]
WHORF, BENJAMIN L., and GEORGE L. TRAGER. 1937. The relationship of Uto-Aztecan and Tanoan. AmA 39.609–24. [1.1, 1.2.11, 2.14, 2.15]
WINTER, WERNER. 1957. Yuman languages I: First impressions. IJAL 23.18–23.
WOLFF, HANS. 1950–51. Comparative Siouan I, II, III, IV. IJAL 26.61–6, 113–21, 168–78, 27.197–204. [2.13]
——. 1952. Osage I: Phonemes and historical phonology. IJAL 18.63–8.

# NORTH AMERICAN INDIAN LANGUAGE CONTACT

## WILLIAM BRIGHT

### 0. SCOPE

The proposed scope of this article includes the processes and effects of bilingualism and of linguistic acculturation involving the native languages of North American Indians in their contacts with each other and with European languages (specifically English, Spanish, French, and Russian). However, as will be seen below, there is relatively little work to report as regards ongoing processes of language contact; the bulk of published research deals with the post-facto results of such contact, especially as manifested in lexical borrowings. Geographically, the present survey covers mainly the area from the Arctic to the Rio Grande, with only a few incidental excursions into Mexico.

An important predecessor of this article is Haugen's monograph on *Bilingualism in the Americas* (1956), which provides bibliographical coverage and comment for both North and South America, and for colonial, immigrant, and creolized languages, as well as for the native languages. The successor to that work is Haugen's article, "Bilingualism, language contact, and immigrant languages in the United States", appearing in this volume, but only dealing briefly with American Indian languages. Both of these works by Haugen provide important orientation into research on the theory of language contact. I have attempted to avoid unnecessary duplication of Haugen's work; thus, major emphasis in what follows is placed on data-oriented research reported since 1956.

### 1. PROCESSES OF LANGUAGE CONTACT

The recent popularity of sociolinguistics has brought increasing attention to the dynamics and functions of language contact. Wherever speakers of two or more languages are interacting with each other, many questions can be asked: will speakers of A learn language B, or will B speakers learn A, or both? Will a pidginized language arise, instead of or in addition to other developments? In what situations will a bilingual choose to use one or the other of his languages? Given the existence of bilingualism, to what extent can linguistic borrowing be expected, as contrasted with new uses of native linguistic materials? Where borrowing occurs, what will be its effects on semantic, grammatical, and phonological structure? There are still more basic questions: in the language contact situation, how are the changes which occur related to speakers' attitudes toward their own languages and toward the languages with which they are in contact? What determines such attitudes toward languages? What role is played by political and social relationships between the groups in contact? What effect can deliberate language planning have? And, following a historical process which is typical of language contact in North America, we may ask: what factors bring about an end to bilingualism, when one language completely replaces another, as English tends to replace the native languages? What are the psychological and sociological circumstances of language obsolescence and extinction?

These are questions which have, for the most part, not yet been conclusively answered; the attempts to answer them constitute an exciting branch of current research. Regarding the processes of North American Indian language contact, however, our information is relatively scanty. The study of sociolinguistic process has become fashionable only in fairly recent years; but in the meantime, many aboriginal languages have become extinct, and most others have become obsolescent. Thus we have lost many opportunities to study, in vivo, the formative stages of bilingualism and of linguistic acculturation in native North America. Fortunately, however, a few languages are still in good health; Navajo, for instance, is spoken by a large and increasing number of Indians, including both monolinguals and bilinguals, and linguistic acculturation under the influence of English is an on-going process. Such present-day situations of language contact offer attractive research possibilities.

Two types of language contact may be distinguished in our area: (1) that between one Indian language and another, which has clearly been important since pre-Columbian times, and retains importance in some areas; and (2) that between Indian languages and European languages, this being of course the dominant type of language contact in the more recent past. The distinction of these two types is founded not on differences of linguistic structure, but on the sociological differences in contact situations: only the European contact was accompanied by massive forcible conquest, exploitation, and genocide.

## 1.1 *Contact between Native Languages*

Extensive bilingualism and borrowing between Indian languages in prehistoric times is attested by the continuing existence of well-defined linguistic areas, where languages of evidently distinct genetic origins have, through processes of diffusion, come to share features of semantic, grammatical and phonological structure; such areas are characterized in Joel Sherzer's paper in the present volume. However, we can at present only speculate as to the exact sociolinguistic processes which produced such areal phenomena. (Works focusing on the *results* of those processes are discussed in

§2.1, below.) A very few studies have discussed the dynamics of recent bilingualism between American Indian languages: Olmsted (1954) for Achumawi and Atsugewi in northeastern California, Mierau (1963) for Yavapai and Apache in Arizona, and Voegelin and Schutz (1967) for the Southwest generally.

## 1.2 Contact with European Languages

Where Indian and European languages have come together, it has been rare for any significant number of Whites to learn the Indian languages. In some regions, for limited periods, Whites and Indians have communicated through pidgin languages: the one best known, used in the Pacific Northwest, was Chinook Jargon, with a largely Indian lexical base (see 2.1, below); in some other areas, varieties of American Indian Pidgin English were used, with a largely English lexical base (Hall and Leechman 1955). The tendency which has prevailed, however, has been that Indians have learned a European language: Spanish in California and the Southwest, Russian in Alaska, French in Quebec and Louisiana, and English elsewhere. With the increasing dominance of Anglo society, Spanish, Russian, and (in some areas) French have been supplemented or supplanted by English as the Indians' language of contact with Whites. And from one generation to the next, Indians have tended to use the European languages more, to introduce more European elements into their native speech, and eventually to lose their native language entirely. A frequent result is that, although ethnically identifiable groups of Indians remain, there may — as in the case of the Chumash in Southern California — be no individual who remembers more than a few words of his ancestral language.

Glimpses of the processes of linguistic acculturation are provided by several of the contributors to the volume *Perspectives in American Indian culture change*, edited by E. H. Spicer (1961). For example, we may quote Dozier's article on the Rio Grande pueblos:

The addition of the Spanish language to the Pueblo dialects must be considered an important acquisition. Undoubtedly not all Pueblo adults spoke Spanish, but the records reveal that during the revolt [of 1680] and after the reconquest [of 1693] communication between the Indians and Spaniards presented no difficulties. It is very probable that the Spanish language, even at this early date, had become a lingua franca among the Pueblos. By adopting Spanish as the language for communicating with the outside world, the individual Pueblo linguistic communities retained their own indigenous languages as tools for retaining and perpetuating their cherished and closely guarded customs and beliefs (141) ... [In the contemporary period] English is now an important second language, but the native idioms continue to be dominant. Pueblo Indians are purists with regard to their language, a factor related to the phenomenon of compartmentalization. The native language is considered an area of culture that must not be polluted by foreign loans ... Pueblo speakers are keenly aware of borrowed terms and tend to delete or restrict their usage in the presence of outsiders ... The coinage of new words and the extension of old meanings to cover new cultural acquisitions are preferred to outright borrowing (Dozier 1961:141, 174–5).

Other aspects of English-Indian bilingualism are touched upon by Sasaki and Olmsted (1953), with reference to the Navajo; by Carroll and Casagrande (1958), who note the tendency of bilingual Navajo to operate more in terms of English semantic structures than monolingual Navajo; by Scott (1960), studying the Mescalero Apache; by Polgar (1960), in connection with Mesquakie (Fox) biculturation; by Ervin (1961), who comments further on Navajo bilingualism; by Fox (1968), for the Keresan of New Mexico; and by Bodine (1968), discussing trends in personal names at Taos. Voegelin (1959) reports on the 'expansion' of Hopi, through English loans, in the casual or non-formal usage of bilinguals.

Recently, there has been new interest in the theoretical and practical problems of teaching English to American Indians, in areas such as the Southwest where non-standard English or Indian monolingualism are still common; relevant publications include Shuy 1965, Cook and Sharp 1966, Ohanessian 1967, and Bauer 1968.

Finally, regarding the obsolescence and extinction of American Indian languages in the contact situation, one may refer to the pioneering article of Swadesh (1948). To end this section on a less gloomy note, however, it may be observed that several obsolescent languages are showing new signs of life; in southern California, for instance, during 1969, classes in the Luiseño, Cupeño, and Diegueño languages were being held by Indians, for Indians, and on Indian initiative, with some advice from White linguists. Such efforts may not guarantee the survival of the languages in question, but they are an encouraging sign of Indians' renewed interest and pride in their own cultural and linguistic heritage.

## 2. RESULTS OF LANGUAGE CONTACT

The majority of published studies of Amerindian language contact are in a sense philological, in that they take as their data the written records which reflect the results of the contact process; these may be published texts or dictionaries, or unpublished fieldnotes. Such data have been variously presented — either essentially unanalyzed, as of intrinsic interest; or interpreted in order to shed light on specific histories of culture contact; or used to illustrate supposed general principles of bilingualism and linguistic acculturation.

We may classify studies in the field by basically sociological criteria, as was done in §1.0 above. Thus we have the following types: (1) Contact occurs between two or more Indian groups; from the socio-cultural point of view, this is essentially a meeting of equals, and the linguistic results tend to show diffusion of semantic, grammatical, and phonological features. (2) Contact occurs between Indian and White, and the topic of interest involves features of the Indian's culture. As the White holds the dominant position, the areas of his interest in native culture are relatively limited: he wants to be able to identify geographical features in the territory originally occupied by the Indian; and he wants names for certain American flora and fauna known to the Indian, as well as for some of the more conspicuous features of the Indian's material culture. The linguistic results consist, then, of a large number of borrowed place names, from *Massachusetts* to *Alaska,* and of a much smaller number of common nouns such as *squash* (the vegetable, from New England Algonkian), *abalone* (a shellfish, from Costanoan of California), and *kayak* (from Eskimo). (3) Contact occurs between Indian and White, and the topic of interest involves features of the dominant white culture. In such cases the force of acculturation, whether forced or spontaneous, has of course generally tended to the replacement of the Indian culture and language; the linguistic results usually include extensive new usages of Indian lexical elements, plus varying amounts of lexical borrowing from European sources — commonly consisting mainly of nouns which designate features of White culture, but occasionally also including other parts of speech (see §2.3.2, below). It is of interest to note that, by contrast with the situation of contact between Indian languages, the Indian-White relationship in North America seems to result in little phonological borrowing, and almost no grammatical borrowing. Rather, it appears that obsolescence and extinction have overtaken most of the languages in our area before structural or deep-level borrowing could occur.

## 2.1 *Effects among Native Languages*

The results of past contact between Indian languages are reflected above all in the phenomenon of linguistic areas: see §1.1 above, and the article by Sherzer in this volume. Specific cases of apparent borrowing are discussed in Kroeber 1959 (from Athabaskan to Yuki, in central California), Bright 1959 (between Yurok and Karok, northwestern California), Callaghan 1964 (by Lake Miwok, from its neighbor languages in central California), Jacobsen 1966 (from Uto-Aztecan to Washo, in Nevada), Pinnow 1968 (in the Na-Dené phylum), and W. and M. Bright 1969 (between Hokan and Uto-Aztecan in southern California). Dozier (1955) reports the influence of Hopi on Arizona Tewa in the area of kinship, where borrowing has involved semantic structure rather than the forms of words (for other cases of semantic acculturation, see §2.3.1).

Cases are known of American pidgin languages used between different tribes in the contact situation. The Mobilian Jargon, used in the Southeast, is little known; much more documentation is available for the Chinook Jargon of the Pacific Northwest, e.g. in Shaw 1909, Boas 1933, and Jacobs 1932, 1936. In the Great Plains, a system of communication by hand gestures served a similar function (cf. Kroeber 1958; Voegelin 1958).

A few attempts have been made to generalize about results of prehistoric language contact in North America; thus Sapir (1916) discusses the detection of old loanwords as evidence for culture-historical reconstruction. Haudricourt (1961) hypothesizes that large phoneme inventories, such as are found in languages of the Pacific Northwest, are a reflection of extensive 'egalitarian' multilingualism (the Lake Miwok case reported by Callaghan, 1964, is another plausible example). Lamb (1964) argues that pre-Columbian language contact must have already resulted in the extinction of many languages and even whole language families, which are thus unrecoverable by reconstruction; this hypothesis is questioned by C.F. and F.M. Voegelin (1965).

## 2.2 *Indian Words in European Languages*

As noted above, the majority of these are place-names. The etymological literature on the subject is extensive but not of very good quality; the researchers involved have too often lacked sophistication either in general linguistics or in the structures of the relevant Indian languages. Typical examples are the place-name dictionaries for Arizona by Granger (1960), for California by Gudde (1960), and for New Mexico by Pearce (1965); these have been criticized in detail by Bright (1962a, 1962b, and 1967b, respectively). Specialists in American Indian linguistics have, however, produced some good place-name studies in recent years; excellent discussions of the general principles involved are provided by Beeler (1957) and by Lounsbury (1960); the latter work also gives exemplary etymological treatment for a number of Iroquois place-names. Other linguistically sophisticated treatments of particular place-names are those of Bright (1952b), Beeler (1954, 1955, and 1966), Oswalt (1960) (all the above relate to California), and Day (1961) (for New England). The name of *Taos* (New Mexico), for which a Spanish etymology was proposed by Jones (1960), has been shown by Trager (1960) to have an Indian source. And finally, Teeter (1958) has shown the name of *Loleta*, California, to be a classic put-on: it represents the Wiyot for 'Let's copulate!'

When place-names are set aside, the number of other loans from native North American languages is relatively small. Several important words for American plant foods are in fact borrowed, through Spanish, from Indian languages of the Caribbean, such as *potato* or *maize*, or from the Aztec (Nahuatl) of Mexico, such as *tomato*, *avocado*, *chocolate*, *cocoa* (cf. Watson 1938). The majority of words which have entered English from north of the Rio Grande are from the Algonkian languages encountered by the earliest English colonists; familiar examples are *persimmon*, *pecan*, *raccoon*, *opossum*, *chipmunk*, *skunk*, *papoose*, *wigwam*. A few such loans have undergone curious folk-etymologies — e.g., *whiskey-jack* 'Canada jay' from earlier *Whiskey-john*; cf. Cree *wiskitjân*. As settlement moved westward, the number of borrowings seems to have become less. The only cases known to me from Californian languages are the following: Spanish and English *islay* 'holly-leafed cherry' from Salinan; Sp. *aulón*, Eng. *abalone* from Costanoan; and Eng. *chuckwalla* 'lizard sp.' from Cahuilla *čáxwal*. The principal published reference for American Indian loans in European languages (other than place-names) is Friederici 1947.

## 2.3 *Effects of European on Native Languages*

As has been noted, the effects of contact between Europeans and Indians are more apparent in the Indian languages than in the European. We may distinguish three main types of development, which reflect the typology of linguistic innovation provided by Haugen (1956:101). (1) In certain types of culture contact, when bilingualism is minimal, there may nevertheless be motivation to name new cultural items. This can be done entirely with native lexical materials, by two processes: (a) semantic extension, as when the word for 'arrow' is extended to 'bullet', or 'dog' to 'horse' in many Indian languages; (b) new combination — by whatever morphosyntactic devices a language may have — as when a hotel is called an 'eating-place'. As reported by Voegelin and Hymes 1953, such processes are well attested in published dictionaries of American Indian languages. (2) Under more favorable conditions of culture contact, bilingualism increases, facilitating the admission of loanwords. (Note, however, that this development may chronologically precede a period of type 1, as described in Herzog 1941.) The degree to which such loans are found varies greatly from one Indian language to another: in areas of Spanish contact such as California, 'bullet' and 'horse' are frequently designated by native imitations of *bala* and *caballo*, but loans from English are in general less widely attested. Many languages have maintained European contacts for centuries and yet admitted very few loanwords. Thus Navajo has borrowed very little from Spanish, and this may be correlated with a low degree of Navajo-Spanish bilingualism. On the other hand, Pueblo languages such as Santa Clara Tewa have also been relatively conservative in their borrowing (Dozier 1956), though Indian-Spanish bilingualism was common for many years. (Possible explanations for such phenomena are discussed in §3, below.) Alongside loanwords, we also find occasional 'translation borrowings' ('loanshifts' or 'calques'): thus in Karok, a *pear* can be called *vírusur* 'bear', because the Indians, lacking voiceless stops, tended to equate the English *bear* and *pear*. Another possible type of loan — the borrowing of linguistic structure — is, as noted above, relatively rare in native North America. (3) In a third development, bilingualism prevails to the extent that the native language takes on secondary importance, becoming gradually obsolescent. In these circumstances, there is weakened motivation for new innovations in the native language, since communication about elements of European culture can simply be carried out in a European language. Some languages seem to have passed through the second type of development in contact with one European language, and then entered the third with another European language. Thus McLendon (1969) identifies about 150 Spanish loans in the Eastern Pomo languages of California, but notes (page 39, fn. 2): 'Curiously enough, despite more than 100 years of contact, hardly a dozen English-derived forms are used by EP speakers. Presumably this reflects (in part) the increasing preference, in the frame of an English-speaking environment, for bilingualism in lieu of expansion of the indigenous lexicon.'

Published accounts of lexical innovations in native languages, encompassing use of both native and borrowed materials, include the following works: Bright 1952a (on Karok of northwestern California) and Bright 1960a (on terms for introduced domestic animals in California as a whole); Casagrande 1954–55 (for Comanche — discussed by

Haugen 1956:16–19, 101, and by Troike 1956); Dozier 1956 and 1967 (for various languages of the Southwest); Garvin 1948 (for Kutenai of Idaho); Huot 1948 for Mohawk; Gross 1951 and Salzmann 1951 (for divergent reports on Arapaho); Herzog 1941 (for Pima in the Southwest); Johnson 1943 and Spicer 1943 (for Yaqui, originally spoken in northwestern Mexico, but now also in Arizona); Voegelin 1959 (for Hopi); and Lee 1943 (for Wintu of northern California).

### 2.3.1 *Use of native elements*

Some studies have focused particularly on innovation by use of native lexical resources, as being the dominant process reflected in the data for some languages. A particularly interesting approach to lexical innovation of this type is to view it as a partial restructuring of the native semantic system. Thus Basso (1967) shows that the Apache extension of body-part terms to automotive parts ('liver' to 'battery', etc.) is not a piecemeal process, but a well-motivated structural shift (cf. also the comment of Adams 1968). In Karok, a class of new coinages for colors not aboriginally distinguished ('smoke-like' for 'blue', 'grass-like' for 'green'), can be seen as exemplifying SEMAUTIC borrowing, a process seldom reported (Bright 1952a:56; cf. the Hopi-Tewa case reported in Dozier 1955, and mentioned in §2.1 above). The recent revival of semantics among linguists has also produced an interesting study by Lindenfeld (1971), in which semantic structure is seen as impeding borrowing in a language (Yaqui) which has otherwise been relatively hospitable to Spanish elements.

### 2.3.2 *Loanwords from European languages*

A relatively large amount of attention has been given to words borrowed from European sources. The richest materials are on borrowings from Spanish in the Southwest: literature includes Hoijer (1939) on Chiricahua Apache; Trager (1944) on Taos, with the note of Hall (1947); Spencer (1947) on Keresan, with Miller (1959–60) for Acoma Keresan in particular; and Dockstader (1955) for Hopi. Some complex developments of Spanish loanwords for 'cat' in the Southwest and in Latin America are discussed in Landar 1959, Bright 1960b, Landar 1961, and Crowley 1962, with the fullest and most final word to date being provided by Kiddle (1964). Spanish loans in Californian languages have also been well documented; see W. and E. Bright 1959 for Patwin, Shipley 1962 for Central California in general, Sawyer 1964a, b for Wappo, and McLendon 1969 for Eastern Pomo and neighboring languages. Borrowings from Spanish in the Southeast United States are discussed by Sturtevant (1962), and a surprising Spanish loan in Eskimo by Taylor (1962).

Studies of loans from other sources are harder to find. French has furnished some loans to Tunica in the Southeast (Haas 1947), and to Algonkian (Geary 1945; Haas 1968), though few data on French loans in the northeast are available. Russian has been a major source for loans in Alaskan Eskimo (Hammerich 1954; Worth 1963), and — because of the brief Russian attempt to colonize Central California — in one California language, Southwestern Pomo (Oswalt 1958; see also the note of

Worth 1960). English loans in a single Hopi text are reported by Kennard (1963). An instance of the English (actually Scottish) family name McKay being borrowed as an ethnonym, 'white man', in Northern California, is reported in Bright 1967a. Scattered data on other loanwords from all these European sources can be found among the references listed in §2.3.

## 3. EXPLANATIONS

As reported above, there have been few studies of Amerindian language contact in vivo; the bulk of publications, as reported in §2 above, simply present the lexical results of linguistic acculturation. An inspection of these results raises certain questions: why do some Indian languages borrow much more than others? Why have certain Indian languages, in contact with more than one European model, borrowed much more from one than another? Given that borrowings are most likely to be nouns, plus occasional adjectives and verbs, why do certain languages borrow significant numbers of 'function words' such as prepositions and conjunctions?

The general question of differential degrees of borrowing has been discussed most cogently by Dozier (1956), in a Southwestern context. His hypothesis is, essentially, that the amount of borrowing is mainly determined by socio-cultural rather than purely linguistic facts: it will be at a maximum where Europeans' policy toward the Indians is benevolent, and at a minimum where that policy is repressive. Support for this idea is provided from California languages in Bright 1960a and, for an Aztec dialect in Mexico, in Bright and Thiel 1965.

As to why certain types of words are borrowed, but not others, there has been very little discussion. Alongside nouns for artifacts, animals of acculturation, etc., we encounter items like Spanish *trabajo* 'work' as a loan into most languages of Central and Southern California (and, on phonological evidence, a very early loan). At this point we might ask: didn't the Indians, in aboriginal times, live by digging roots, carrying water, chopping wood, and other arduous activities classifiable as 'work'? And if so, why did they need to borrow a Spanish word for such activity? An answer is suggested by McLuhan (1964:129): '"Work" ... does not exist in a nonliterate world. The primitive hunter or fisherman did no work, any more than does the poet, painter, or thinker of today. Where the whole man is involved there is no work.' We may say, then, that the Indian borrowing of the Spanish word was prompted not so much by introduction of new modes of physical activity, but by a new semantic categorization of such activity.

Similar explanations may eventually be found for cases where even more abstract terms have apparently been borrowed, as when Cahuilla of Southern California uses Spanish *más* 'more'. A real challenge is presented by Indian languages of Mexico which show borrowing of many Spanish prepositions and conjunctions (e.g., cf. Hasler 1961; Bright and Thiel 1965). We must assume that the Indian languages involved had their own native systems of indicating abstract relationships; but we may speculate that those systems proved inadequate to the new world view which came in with Spanish civilization, and that a motive for the borrowing of Spanish function words was thereby provided. The testing of such speculations awaits new fieldwork, psycholinguistically and sociolinguistically oriented, on the dynamics of language contact in areas where — as among the Navajo — the process is still in full swing.

## REFERENCES

ADAMS, WILLIAM Y. 1968. Navaho automotive terminology. AmA 70.1181.
BASSO, KEITH H. 1967. Semantic aspects of linguistic acculturation. AmA 69.471–7.
BAUER, EVELYN. 1968. Teaching English to North American Indians in BIA schools. Linguistic Reporter 10:4.1–3. Washington, D.C., CAL.
BEELER, M.S. 1954. Sonoma, Carquinez, Umunhum, Colma: Some disputed California names. WF 13.268–77.
——. 1955. Yosemite and Tamalpais. Names 3.185–8.
——. 1957. On etymologizing Indian place-names. Names 5.236–40.
——. 1966. Hueneme. Names 14.36–40.
BOAS, FRANZ. 1933. Note on the Chinook Jargon. Lg 9.208–13.
BODINE, JOHN J. 1968. Taos names: A clue to linguistic acculturation. AnL 10/5.23–7.
BRIGHT, WILLIAM. 1952a. Linguistic innovations in Karok. IJAL 18.53–62.
——. 1952b. Some place names on the Klamath River. WF 11.121–2.
——. 1959. Review of The Yurok language, by R.H. Robins. Lg 35.100–4.
——. 1960a. Animals of acculturation in the California Indian languages. UCPL 4.215–46.
——. 1960b. A note on the Southwestern words for cat. IJAL 26.167–8.
——. 1962a. Review of Arizona place names, ed. by B.H. Granger. JAF 75.77–8.
——. 1962b. Review of California place names, by E.G. Gudde. JAF 75.78–82.
——. 1967a. Karok *mákkay* < Scottish *McKay*. Names 15.79–80.
——. 1967b. Review of New Mexico place names, by T.M. Pearce. WF 26.140–3.
BRIGHT, WILLIAM and ELIZABETH. 1959. Spanish words in Patwin. RomPh 13.161–4.
BRIGHT, WILLIAM and MARCIA. 1969. Archaeology and linguistics in prehistoric Southern California. UH WPL 10.1–26.
BRIGHT, WILLIAM, and R.A. THIEL. 1965. Hispanisms in a modern Aztec dialect. RomPh 18.444–52.
CALLAGHAN, CATHERINE. 1964. Phonemic borrowing in Lake Miwok. UCPL 34.46–53.
CARROLL, JOHN B., and JOSEPH B. CASAGRANDE. 1958. The function of language classifications in behavior. Readings in social psychology, ed. by Eleanor Maccoby et al., pp. 18–31. 3rd ed., New York, Holt.
CASAGRANDE, JOSEPH B. 1954–55. Comanche linguistic acculturation. IJAL 20.140–51, 217–37; 21.8–25.

Cook, Mary Jane, and Margaret Amy Sharp. 1966. Problems of Navajo speakers in learning English. LL 16.21–9.
Crowley, Cornelius J. 1962. Some remarks on the etymology of the Southwestern words for cat. IJAL 28.149–51.
Day, Gordon M. 1961. The name Contoocook. IJAL 27.168.
Dockstader, Frederick J. 1955. Spanish loanwords in Hopi: A preliminary checklist. IJAL 21.157–9.
Dozier, Edward P. 1955. Kinship and linguistic change among the Arizona Tewa. IJAL 21.242–57.
——. 1956. Two examples of linguistic acculturation: The Yaqui of Sonora and Arizona and the Tewa of New Mexico. Lg 32.146–57.
——. 1961. Rio Grande pueblos. *In* Spicer 1961, pp. 94–186.
——. 1967. Linguistic acculturation studies in the Southwest. Studies in Southwestern ethnolinguistics, ed. by Dell Hymes, pp. 389–402. Studies in general anthropology, 3. The Hague, Mouton.
Ervin, Susan M. 1961. Semantic shift in bilingualism. American Journal of Psychology 74.233–41. Urbana, Ill.
Fox, Robin. 1968. Multilingualism in two communities. Man (n.s.) 3.456–64.
Friederici, Georg. 1947. Amerikanistisches Wörterbuch. Hamburg, Cram.
Garvin, Paul L. 1947. Christian names in Kutenai. IJAL 13.69–77.
——. 1948. Kutenai lexical innovations. Word 4.120–6.
Geary, James A. 1945. Algonquian *nasaump* and *napōpi*: French loanwords? Lg 21.40–5.
Granger, Byrd H., ed. 1960. Will C. Barnes' Arizona place names. 2nd edition. Tucson, University of Arizona Press.
Gross, Feliks. 1951. Language and value changes among the Arapaho. IJAL 17.10–17.
Gudde, Erwin G. 1960. California place names. 2nd edition. Berkeley and Los Angeles, University of California Press.
Haas, Mary R. 1947. Some French loan-words in Tunica. RomPh 1.145–8.
——. 1968. The Menomini terms for playing cards. IJAL 34.217–19.
Hall, Robert A., Jr. 1947. A note on Taos kʼowena *horse*. IJAL 13.117–8.
Hall, Robert A., Jr., and Douglas Leechman. 1955. American Indian Pidgin English. AS 30.163–71.
Hammerich, Louis L. 1954. The Russian stratum in Alaskan Eskimo. Word 10.401–28.
Hasler, Juan. 1961. Juan del Oso en los Tuztlas. La Palabra y el Hombre 20.603–14. Xalapa, Universidad Veracruzana.
Haudricourt, André. 1961. Richesses en phonèmes et richesse en locuteurs. Homme 1.5–10.
Haugen, Einar. 1956. Bilingualism in the Americas: A bibliography and research guide. PADS 26. University, Ala., University of Alabama Press.
Herzog, George. 1941. Culture change and language: Shifts in the Pima vocabu-

lary. Language, culture, and personality, essays in memory of Edward Sapir, ed. by Leslie Spier et al., pp. 66–74. Menasha, Banta.

HOIJER, HARRY. 1939. Chiricahua loanwords from Spanish. Lg 15.110–15.

———. 1948. Linguistic and cultural change. Lg. 24.335–45.

HUOT, MARTHA C. 1948. Some Mohawk words of acculturation. IJAL 14.150–4.

JACOBS, MELVILLE. 1932. Notes on the structure of Chinook Jargon. Lg 8.27–50.

———. 1936. Texts in Chinook Jargon. UWPA 7.1–27.

JACOBSEN, WILLIAM H., JR. 1966. Washo linguistic studies. The current status of anthropological research in the Great Basin: 1964, ed. by W. L. d'Azevedo et al., pp. 113–36. Reno, University of Nevada.

JOHNSON, J. B. 1943. A clear case of linguistic acculturation. AmA 45.427–34.

JONES, WILLIAM M. 1960. Origin of the placename Taos. AnL 2/3.2–4.

KENNARD, EDWARD. 1963. Linguistic acculturation in Hopi. IJAL 29.36–41.

KIDDLE, LAWRENCE B. 1964. American Indian reflexes of two Spanish words for cat. IJAL 30.299–305.

KROEBER, A. L. 1958. Sign language inquiry. IJAL 24.1–19.

———. 1959. Possible Athabascan influence on Yuki. IJAL 25.59.

LAMB, SYDNEY M. 1964. Linguistic diversification and extinction in North America. PICAm 35/2.457–64.

LANDAR, HERBERT J. 1959. The diffusion of some Southwestern words for cat. IJAL 25.273–4.

———. 1961. The Southwestern words for cat. IJAL 27.370–1.

LEE, DOROTHY D. 1943. The linguistic aspect of Wintu acculturation. AmA 45.435–40.

LINDENFELD, JACQUELINE. 1971. Semantic categorization as a deterrent to grammatical borrowing: A Yaqui example. IJAL 37.6–14.

LOUNSBURY, FLOYD G. 1960. Iroquois place-names in the Champlain Valley. Champlain Basin, past-present-future: Report of the New York-Vermont Interstate Commission on the Lake Champlain Basin, pp. 23–66. (New York State legislative document, 1960, no. 9.) Albany.

MCLENDON, SALLY. 1969. Spanish words in Eastern Pomo. RomPh 23.39–53.

MCLUHAN, MARSHALL. 1964. Understanding media. New York, Signet.

MIERAU, ERIC. 1963. Concerning Yavapai-Apache bilingualism. IJAL 29.1–3.

MILLER, WICK R. 1959–60. Spanish loanwords in Acoma. IJAL 25.147–53, 26.41–9.

OHANNESSIAN, SIRARPI, ed. 1967. The study of the problems of teaching English to American Indians. Washington, D.C., CAL.

OLMSTED, D. L. 1954. Achumawi-Atsugewi non-reciprocal intelligibility. IJAL 20.181–4.

OSWALT, ROBERT L. 1958. Russian loanwords in Southwestern Pomo. IJAL 24.245–7.

———. 1960. Gualala. Names 8.57–8.

PEARCE, T. M. 1965. New Mexico place names. Albuquerque, University of New Mexico Press.

PINNOW, HEINZ-JÜRGEN. 1968. Genetic relationship vs. borrowing in Na-Dene. IJAL 34.204–11.

POLGAR, STEVEN. 1960. Biculturation of Mesquakie teenage boys. AmA 62.217–35.

SALZMANN, ZDENĚK. 1951. Contrastive field experience with language and values of the Arapaho. IJAL 17.98–101.

SAPIR, EDWARD. 1916. Time perspective in aboriginal American culture. Canada Dept. of Mines, Geological Survey, memoir 90, anthropological series 13. Ottawa. (Reprinted in SWES, pp. 389–462. 1949.)

SASAKI, TOM T., and D. L. OLMSTED. 1953. Navaho acculturation and English-language skills. AmA 55.89–99.

SAWYER, JESSE O., JR. 1964a. Wappo words from Spanish. UCPL 34.163–9.

———. 1964b. The implications of Spanish /r/ and /rr/ in Wappo history. RomPh 18.165–77.

SCOTT, RICHARD B. 1960. English language skills of the Mescalero Apache Indians. América Indígena 20.173–81. Mexico, D.F., Mexico.

SHAW, GEORGE C. 1909. The Chinook Jargon and how to use it. Seattle.

SHIPLEY, WILLIAM. 1962. Spanish elements in the indigenous languages of central California. RomPh 16.1–21.

SHUY, ROGER W. 1965. The problem of American Indian English. Social dialects and language learning, ed. by R. W. Shuy, pp. 52–4. Champaign, Ill., National Council of Teachers of English.

SPENCER, ROBERT F. 1947. Spanish loanwords in Keresan. SJA 3.130–46.

SPICER, EDWARD H. 1943. Linguistic aspects of Yaqui acculturation. AmA 45.410–26.

———, ed. 1961. Perspectives in American Indian culture change. Chicago, University of Chicago Press.

STURTEVANT, WILLIAM C. 1962. Spanish-Indian relations in southeastern North America. Ethnohistory 9.41–94.

SWADESH, MORRIS. 1948. Sociologic notes on obsolescent languages. IJAL 14.226–35.

TAYLOR, ALLAN R. 1962. Spanish *manteca* in Alaskan Eskimo. RomPh 16.30–2.

TEETER, KARL V. 1958. Notes on Humboldt County, California, place names of Indian origin. Names 6.55–56.

TRAGER, GEORGE L. 1944. Spanish and English loanwords in Taos. IJAL 10.144–60.

———. 1960. The name of Taos, New Mexico. AnL 2/3.5–6.

TROIKE, RUDOLPH C. 1956. Comanche linguistic acculturation: A critique. IJAL 22.213–15.

VOEGELIN, C. F. 1958. Sign language analysis, on one level or two? IJAL 24.71–6.

———. 1959. An expanding language, Hopi. Plateau 32.33–9.

VOEGELIN, C.F. and D.H. HYMES. 1953. A sample of North American Indian dictionaries with reference to acculturation. PAPS 97.634–44.
VOEGELIN, C.F. and F.M. 1965. Extinction of American Indian languages before and after contact periods. CJL 10.135–46.
VOEGELIN, C.F. and F.M., and NOEL W. SCHUTZ, JR. 1967. The language situation in Arizona as part of the Southwest Culture Area. Studies in Southwestern ethnolinguistics, ed. by Dell Hymes, pp. 403–51. Studies in general anthropology, 3. The Hague, Mouton.
WATSON, G. 1938. Nahuatl words in American English. AS 13.108–21.
WORTH, DEAN S. 1960. Russian *kniga*, Southwestern Pomo *kalikak*. IJAL 26.62–5.
——. 1963. Russian and Alaskan Eskimo. IJSLP 7.72–9.

# PHILOLOGICAL APPROACHES TO THE STUDY OF NORTH AMERICAN INDIAN LANGUAGES: DOCUMENTS AND DOCUMENTATION

IVES GODDARD*

0. INTRODUCTORY REMARKS

Philology may be thought of as that part of the discipline of linguistics that is concerned with getting from texts and other recorded attestations of languages systematic information that is not directly conveyed by such records as they stand. One branch of philology is concerned with obtaining information about cultures, especially about those aspects of culture which reveal themselves most directly in discourses of various sorts. Under this head may be put, on the one hand, the literary analysis of oral and written literature, both by traditional methods of textual interpretation and by more recently developed structuralist approaches, and, on the other hand, attempts to discover in the grammatical and semantic categories of languages more or less direct reflexes of the culture and psychology of their speakers. It is not possible to do more here than merely mention the existence of these facets of the broader field of philology, but it would be fair to say that, although the importance and applicability of these types of analysis to native North American languages has long been noted, they have not yet borne fruit in a way that is fully satisfying as to their linguistic aspects.[1]

A second branch of philology, that which is the topic of the present essay, subjects records to examination and interpretation in order to gain information about the languages in which these records are cast. It is written records that are the principal objects of study, but sound recordings are becoming increasingly important in philological investigations.

If the characterization of philology just given were taken broadly, then all descriptive linguistics might be considered philological. Whether the linguist works with his own fieldnotes or a three-hundred-year-old manuscript dictionary, he must base his analysis not on the actual, internalized, language — nor even on the actual 'performance' of speakers — but on a record, a second-hand attestation, of a finite number of verbal manifestations of the language. The task in each case is to use this record to reconstruct as closely as possible actual speech events of the language (or segments

---

* I am grateful to Dell Hymes for helpful suggestions regarding the present paper, although he is, of course, not responsible for the use made of them. The writing of this article was completed in April, 1970.
[1] For an early statement, see Boas *IJAL* 1.1–2 (1917). Examples of recent evaluations are Hymes 1965, 1966b, 1968.

of such events), and ultimately to gain an understanding of the grammatical system (in the widest sense) which is attested, however imperfectly, by these events. Nevertheless, there is a contrast in focus or emphasis. In the field of scientific descriptive linguistics as a whole, the completed analysis is foremost — it is the analyzed form that is of primary importance. In the branch of the field constituted by philology, however, attention is focused on the documentation of the stages through which linguistic raw material passes between the initial uttering and the eventual systematic description. Philological analysis explicitly recognizes the documentary filiation which characterizes all linguistic data as they are successively recorded, interpreted, and analyzed. It is concerned with establishing just what the facts of the primary record are, with specifying the degree to which the record is dependable, and with determining exactly what can or cannot be concluded from it.

There are, accordingly, two aspects to philology, depending on the direction from which it approaches the continuum of documentation. Given primary linguistic records, it considers what can be gotten from them; given secondary linguistic materials, it enquires after the more original data that support them. It might seem that philology ought simply to be part of the methodology of descriptive linguistics, and one may ask why it makes sense to discuss it as a separate topic in connection with the North American Indian languages. The answer to this is to be found not in an examination of the nature of philology, but in a consideration of the emphases and practices in the field of native American linguistics, as it has developed and as it looks to the future.

There is today in this field a de facto bias against the philological approaches to linguistic materials outlined above. Documents and documentation are rarely accorded the attention that they receive in the traditional study of Old World languages. There seems not to be a full appreciation of the value of earlier written records to the tasks and objects which concern contemporary linguists and anthropologists, not to mention the value of such records in themselves as linguistic monuments of the dead or doomed aboriginal societies of North America. This neglect of philological concerns results probably to a very great extent from the emphasis on fieldwork in the study of American Indian languages and from the nearly universal fact that the investigator has to rely so heavily on the data he himself collects. With the gradual perfection of systematic phonetics linguists have tended to look down on any record that does not measure up to the standards of accuracy of their own fieldnotes. As early as 1912 Truman Michelson wrote: 'It is simply a waste of time to attempt to unravel the vagaries of the orthography of the older writers in the case of dialects existing to-day.'[2] Furthermore, the fact that the collector and the analyst are the same person, and that as a result the primary data frequently have no existence independent of the analysis and the edited texts, has engendered a disregard for the necessity of full and explicit accountability in the publication of linguistic materials and a general negligent attitude

---

[2] *BAE-R* 28.280, fn. 1 (1912). There is discussion further below which may be taken to show that the distinction here between records of extinct languages and of those still spoken is specious.

towards the preservation of complete documentation of what eventually sees print. Fortunately, as the day of final extinction approaches for more and more American Indian languages — after which all study of them will have to be from whatever written records (or sound recordings) happen to survive — there is increasing attention being paid by Americanists to the preservation and use of documentary sources and to the problems of interpretation which they present.[3] The purpose of the present essay is to show the application of philological practices to the study of North American Indian languages, to exemplify what has been done in the past (including welcome exceptions to some of the generalizations made above), and to indicate what is required for the future. The philological interpretation of documents will be taken up first, followed by an examination of the question of linguistic documentation.

## 1. DOCUMENTS

The questions to be considered about the use of documents are principally: What kind of linguistic information is in them? How can it be gotten out of them? and What use can be made of it? In answering these, especially the last, it will not be possible to avoid trespassing to a slight extent on the field of investigation proper to that branch of philology which examines linguistic documents for the information they give about cultures (see the first paragraph of this essay). For the most part, however, this section will examine the use of documents from the point of view of linguistics.

It always seems to be of great concern to linguists to clarify the phonetic details of any documents they use, and it was suggested above that poor phonetics has been a significant factor leading to the general neglect of the use of earlier records. It is reasonable, accordingly, to begin by surveying the phonetic and phonological aspects of North American philology.

A very large topic is the problem of how to deal with materials on Indian languages that are recorded in phonetically inferior transcriptions. There are, of course, different degrees of inferiority and different approaches required, depending on the nature of the records and the purposes which they are expected to serve. But in every case the aim of the philologist in the first instance is to determine the phonetic key for the record under examination: what sound values are implied by the letters and symbols used? The recorder may have used letters with the values they have in his native language or in some other language or languages known to him, or he may have employed a standard or semi-standard phonetic alphabet. In general, however, it may be said that even when a standard alphabet is used, it will be used by different recorders in somewhat different ways, each one making his own idiosyncratic modifications, and the shifting caprice of fashion has probably had as much to do with the

---

[3] See for example the call for renewed philological interest by Hymes in *Lg* 32.600–1 (1965) and the apt remarks of William Bright in *Lg* 43.584 (1967). The present essay is intended to be illustrative and does not include mention of many recent studies which make use of older sources.

changing practices of transcription as has scientifically reasoned refinement. (In the present century, for example, after a shift in preference to unitary symbols — codified in a well known pronouncement (Herzog et al. 1934) — there is now a discernible trend back to compound symbols among some linguists.[4]) To a large extent, the standard alphabets used in recording North American languages have developed separately from the predominantly European phonetic tradition that culminated in the promulgation of the International Phonetic Alphabet (surveyed inadequately in Albright 1958). Important in the American tradition have been the systems put forth by John Pickering (1818), George Gibbs (1863), Wm. D. Whitney (1877),[5] John W. Powell (1880), and Franz Boas et al. (1916) (see Lounsbury 1953 for further bibliography). Yet even these well known attempts at standardization have never been brought together in a comparative or historical study, and each philologist is obliged to work out his own tables of equivalences. A prime desideratum in the field at present is a comprehensive survey of the phonetic alphabets and transcriptional practices which are encountered in the documents. As Hymes (1966a: 342) has stressed, such a handbook for North American philology should ideally include detailed information on such matters as the linguistic background and experience of the individual recorders. It may be symptomatic, however, that probably no Americanist has ever had the perspective and humility to furnish such information about himself.

In practice when Americanists have used older recordings they have generally preferred to summarize their interpretation of the notational system used by rewriting the original forms in some sort of normalized orthography. Where normalization is merely a matter of updating the symbolism it usually presents no difficulties. Thus it is almost automatic nowadays, for example, to replace older *t!* by *t'* and older *c* by *š*. But it is necessary, nevertheless, to continue to record the details of the original transcription, since different sets of symbols have different possibilities of miswriting and confusion and any future emendations must be made in terms of the system used in the primary record. Also, on a subtler level, different standard alphabets imply different sets of phonetic primes for the recorder to match against the stream of speech that he hears and thus may favor or disfavor the specification of different distinctions. That this is so is particularly obvious in the case of earlier investigators attempting to use inadequate phonetic alphabets to write sounds whose manner of articulation, or very existence, was unknown. Hymes has stressed the developmental nature of much early Americanist phonetics in comments on Boas[6] and Kroeber[7]. It also must be recognized, however, that more recent studies have not been immune to similar debilities, and it might even be fair to speak of an atrophy of phonetic

---

[4] Harry Hoijer exemplifies recent Athapaskanist usage in "Galice Athapaskan..." *IJAL* 32.320–7 (1966).
[5] Pp. 3–6 of Powell 1877.
[6] *AnL* 5/1.85 (1963).
[7] *Lg* 37.6, esp. fn. 16 (1961). Also in Dell Hymes, ed., *Language in culture and society*, p. 691 and fn. 12 (New York, Evanston and London, 1964).

knowledge among certain segments of the present-day anthropological and linguistic communities, not to mention the diminished phonetic explicitness in many contemporary linguistic descriptions.

In any event, normalization should be carried out only to the extent that it aids in the understanding of the forms and not for merely cosmetic purposes. Little would seem to be gained, for example, by following Granberry (1956:esp. 104) in transcribing the *qi* and *qui* of Pareja's Spanish-based Timucua orthography as *ki* and *k$^w$i*. Pareja explains his system quite fully, but where there are ambiguities (as there are in other places) no amount of normalization can overcome them; modernization can only obscure the real difficulties that exist. Mary Haas (1969) has discussed the instructive case of the over-normalization by modern Siouanists of Swanton's Ofo recordings.[8] Writing in the first decade of this century in a broad phonetic orthography, Swanton distinguished between a series of aspirated consonants and their plain counterparts: *ĭtho$^n$* 'big' but *to'pa* 'four'. Since the writing of the aspiration is not completely consistent, however, later scholars have omitted any indication of aspiration from their normalizations of Swanton's forms. In fact, though, comparative Siouan evidence shows that the aspiration is archaic, and even though Swanton did not always correctly note it, his recordings of this feature in Ofo are of considerable historical linguistic value; compare with the above forms Proto-Siouan *$*th\varrho$* 'big' and *$*tópa$* 'four'.

One type of normalization that has considerable potential value for the interpretation of older recordings is the method that Broadbent (1957) has called reconstitution. This can only be carried out 'if there are two or more vocabularies which partially duplicate each other, preferably collected by different individuals' (Broadbent 1957: 275). The various recordings of the same forms are compared, and by a sort of phonetic triangulation one can arrive at a better understanding of the phonetics of the language than could be gotten from any single source. Broadbent emphasizes, however, that the philologist cannot cut any finer than the distinctions made in the original records, and she makes it clear that she does not regard her reconstituted forms as taking the place of the originals. Rather, she envisions eventual publication of the reconstitutions together with all of the forms on which they are based, including a complete critical apparatus covering manuscript corrections and a full discussion of the transcriptional systems of the various recorders (Broadbent 1957:278–80).[9]

In many cases, when the multiple recordings necessary for Broadbent's method of reconstitution are not available, the philologist must attempt to learn what he can about a given language on the basis of documents written in a single, perhaps inconsistently used, orthography. Of great assistance under such circumstances may be the comparative evidence furnished by better known, related languages. As a concrete example, the case of the Massachusett language is instructive. The most important sources for this language are the seventeenth-century grammar and Bible

---

[8] The following discussion is based entirely on Haas 1969.
[9] The results of the investigation described in the article have not yet appeared.

translation of the missionary John Eliot, who used an English-based orthography that included certain special conventions intended to handle some of the phonetic features of Massachusett not found in English. This fairly well worked out system, however, was not employed any more consistently than was usual for the English orthography of the day. (Some later missionaries have left quite a bit of material in Massachusett, but they used Eliot's orthography, and though they sometimes applied it somewhat differently, they did not improve it.) A study of Massachusett phonology has been published by Shirley Silver (1960), which includes both a normalized rewriting of Eliot's forms and a comparison with other Algonquian languages (principally by reference to reconstructed Proto-Algonquian forms).[10] It is rather evident that in many cases the comparative evidence gives a better clue to the pronunciation of Eliot's forms than does the normalization (which is quite reasonable as such and close to what anyone would come up with solely on the basis of the vagaries of the orthography). Thus there is sufficient evidence for a series of preaspirated consonants ([hk], etc.) contrasting with a single series of plain ones — a common Algonquian feature — but the aspiration is somewhat erratically written. Silver normalizes, for example, *k*, *gk*, and *g* to /k/ and *hk* (including cases where *hk* alternates with *k* in the same form) to /ʰk/. Rather than reducing uncertainty, however, this actually increases it. Since Eliot's *k* can stand for either [k] or [hk], Silver's /k/ is still ambiguous to at least the same extent (when there are no attested alternants with *hk*); in addition, because of this, words with *gk* and *g*, which are unambiguously [k] in Eliot's forms, become ambiguous when rewritten as normalized /k/ by Silver. Thus Silver (1960: 236) normalizes the Massachusett word for 'shoe' as /makəs/, which does not reflect the fact that in this word the second consonant is always written with *k*, never with *g* or *gk*: *mokus*, *mokis* 'shoe', *mokussinash* 'shoes', and other forms. Other Algonquian languages attest for this word a cluster with second member *k* which reconstructs to \**xk*: Proto-Algonquian \**maxkeseni* giving Fox *mahkese·hi* (reshaped with diminutive ending), Cree *maskisin*, Munsee *máhksən*, etc. This (taken together with other evidence about the pattern of the reflexes of Proto-Algonquian clusters in Massachusett, which cannot be detailed here) makes it virtually certain that the Massachusett word for 'shoe' was phonetically [mahkəs].[11] In general it may be said about normalization that to be worthwhile it must be more than merely a transliteration; by itself it can never be a substitute for an interpretative analysis of an orthographic system based on all available internal and comparative evidence.

Just as the consideration of related languages can aid the philological interpretation of linguistic documents, so also philology can develop information from older recordings that may be of considerable significance in comparative and historical linguistics.

---

[10] In the discussion below Silver's normalization is in diagonals (though not to be considered phonemic — *ibid*.:113, fn. 7), and the square brackets enclose a broad phonetic interpretation. Natick, the name of Eliot's mission village, is sometimes used to designate the variety of Massachusett written by him.

[11] For further remarks on some details of Eliot's orthography, see Goddard 1965.

There might be objections to the use of comparative evidence, as suggested in outline above for Massachusett, on the grounds that there is a risk of circular reasoning. There has probably been among linguists some reluctance to use such evidence directly in reconstructing the phonetics of older recordings, no doubt in part for the same considerations of methodological purity that inhibit so thoroughly the introduction of any comparative evidence into descriptive treatments of American Indian languages. But the danger of circularity is really no greater than in other sorts of historical investigation, in which the investigator in general looks for mutual confirmation in his sources and seeks to reconstruct those possible real events which would be most likely to have resulted in the various records that are actually found. Thus in the Massachusett example, although there is no direct attestation of [hk] in the word for 'shoe', the fact that this word always is spelled with *k* and never with *g* or *gk* is fairly good indirect confirmation of the phonetic form postulated. This is not to deny the possibility of reading into an imperfect record more than was ever there; the philologist must, accordingly, adhere to strict standards of documentation, making his sources and his reasoning explicit enough so that others may reinterpret or correct his conclusions.

The comparative and historical information yielded by the philological examination of linguistic documents is of several sorts. It takes on a somewhat different character depending on whether the documents are early records of a language known largely from a later date, records of an extinct dialect fairly close to a better known language, or records of an extinct relatively isolated language, and depending, of course, on the nature and extent of the material recorded. Not all possibilities can be treated here, but particularly worthy of discussion — in direct rebuttal of the statement of Michelson quoted above[12] — are cases where earlier records of languages still spoken furnish information of historical and comparative value not recoverable from later attestations. For example, nineteenth- and twentieth-century recordings of the Algonquian language constituted by the various dialects of the Ojibwa type (Ojibwa, Ottawa, Algonquin, etc.) show a single phoneme *n* as the reflex of Proto-Algonquian *$n$, *$\theta$, and *$l$, but seventeenth- and eighteenth-century recordings by French missionaries have *r* or *l* as the reflex of *$\theta$ and *$l$ and *n* as the reflex only of *$n$: Proto-Algonquian *$a\theta emwa$ 'dog', seventeenth-century Algonquin *arim*, seventeenth-century Ottawa *alim*, contemporary Algonquin and Ojibwa *animošš* (diminutive); Proto-Algonquian *$wela\cdot kani$ 'dish', seventeenth-century Algonquin *8ragan*,[13] eighteenth-century Algonquin *8lagan*, contemporary *ona·kan* (Hanzeli 1961:128–31). Full use of these earlier recordings will clearly furnish significant comparative information on the many lexical items attested only from the languages in which *$n$, *$\theta$, and *$l$ fall together (e.g. Fox and Menomini in addition to Ojibwa). There is also the possibility that the

---

[12] That this attitude still prevails may be illustrated by the fact that Broadbent, whose suggestions for using older records of extinct languages have been discussed above, seems to agree with Michelson when it comes to records of languages still spoken; see Broadbent 1957:275, first paragraph.
[13] In these forms 8 represents a ligature that stands for *ou*.

documentary sources available for different areas and periods will provide the rare opportunity to observe the propagation of a sound change (l/r > n) across a dialect continuum.[14]

The number of instances in which an early record — even when made only a generation or two before the principal modern description — shows phonological features not present in the later material is probably greater than many Americanists realize. A Munsee text recorded by J.N.B. Hewitt in 1896 has *mxwəs* 'branch' (written by him [mhwoç]) for contemporary *xwəs* 'piece of wood', showing retention of the historically expected initial consonant found, for example, in Ojibwa *miššі* 'piece of firewood' (the noun stem is Proto-Algonquian *\*mehθ-*).[15] Notes on Tübatulabal made by A.L. Kroeber in the first years of this century have *nigi* 'I' (written 'nügi', 'nögi', etc.), while C.F. Voegelin recorded *nik* in 1931–33;[16] Kroeber's more archaic form shows the expected vowel in the first person element *ni-* (cognate with Nahuatl *ne-*, Luiseño *no-*, Hopi *ni*, etc., all from Uto-Aztecan *\*ni-*) and the full form of the enclitic element *-gi* appearing in other first-person pronominal forms. There are cases in which considerable phonological innovation exists in the speech of younger members of contemporary Indian communities, side by side with an archaic pronunciation among older members which agrees with recordings made earlier in this century; this situation has been reported by Elizabeth Brandt (1970) for Sandia and Paul Voorhis (1971) for Fox. In such cases philology clearly has contributions to make to sociolinguistics as well as to historical linguistics.

It should be stressed that even rather poor recordings can sometimes provide information on phonetics. In an eighteenth-century vocabulary of Atsina recorded in a very rough English-based orthography the word for 'four' is given as '*ne-an*'; the modern form *yéén*, on the other hand, lacks the initial *n*, as does Arapaho *yéín*. These words continue the Proto-Algonquian root *\*nye·w-* 'four' and attest a phonological change of *\*ny* to *y*; the value of the early Atsina form (which can now be seen to represent [*nyɛ·n*]) is that it shows that this innovation, though shared by Atsina and Arapaho, postdates the split-up of the two dialects and must have occurred independently in each. A significant piece of information about the relative chronology of the sound changes in Atsina and Arapaho can thus be recovered (on the above, see Taylor 1967:esp. 122).

Similarly, records of extinct dialects may be of considerable comparative value. Kroeber's 1899 recordings of the extinct Nawathinehena dialect of Arapaho (from one imperfect speaker) show many developments of Proto-Algonquian sounds which differ from those in the better known Arapaho (proper) and Atsina dialects. For example, Proto-Algonquian *\*l*, *\*n*, *\*w*, and *\*y* when not after consonants all fall

---

[14] Some statements in the seventeenth-century French sources indicate the existence of some dialects in which this change had already taken place (Hanzeli 1961:139, fn. 26). (See now the abridged discussion in Hanzeli 1969:70–1).
[15] Smithsonian Institution National Anthropological Archives, MS 16, p. 9.
[16] *UCPAAE* 2.355 (1907); 4.85, 96 (1907); 34.135 (1935).

together to Arapaho-Atsina $n$, $*s$ gives $n$ initially and $h$ elsewhere, and $*\theta$ gives Arapaho $\theta$ and Atsina $t$ and $c$;[17] in Nawathinehena, on the other hand, $*l$, $*s$, and $*\theta$ fall together to $t$ and $*w$ remains as a labial.[18] Thus, even though the recordings are scanty and rather unsatisfactory, they provide considerable information of the type furnished by the early Atsina vocabulary. Mary Haas (1963) has given information on a similar situation among the Shasta dialects. The comparison of apparently cognate forms in related Hokan languages suggests that there has been a contraction of $*ama$ to $a\cdot$ in the variety of Shasta still spoken. Haas shows that for some words assumed to attest this contraction the corresponding forms in the extinct Okwanuchu dialect recorded by R. B. Dixon (ca. 1905) and C. Hart Merriam (1925) show $VwV$, clearly an intermediate stage and evidence which confirms the postulated contraction. The recordings are poor and Merriam, who rejected modern phonetics, recorded Indian languages in a hopelessly inadequate English-based orthography — a fact which makes this an even more impressive example of the point here being made.

Early records of various types frequently furnish information on morphological features which had disappeared, or changed or declined in usage, at the time of the principal modern fieldwork on a language. An example of this is furnished by Luiseño. In this language the enclitic pronouns are fused with various tense and modal elements into an enclitic complex that follows the first word in the sentence: *-an* 'first singular present', *-ap* 'second singular present', *-nopo* 'first singular future', *-op* 'second singular future', etc. But while these frequently irregular combinations were a major feature of earlier Luiseño grammar, their use has declined and the full range of possible forms cannot be recovered from present-day speakers of the language. For an idea of the complete system, reference must be made to the grammatical sketches left by Pablo Tac (1822–1841), a native Luiseño, and Philip S. Sparkman (d. 1907), a linguistically gifted English storekeeper (see Kroeber and Grace 1960:60–67, 221–37; Tagliavini 1926:5ff.).[19] Valuable information on Delaware morphology is found in an early source of a type not yet discussed in this essay, an 1837 translation of a Harmony of the Gospels done by a Baptist missionary, Ira D. Blanchard, with the help of a Delaware named Jimmy.[20] Blanchard's translation regularly uses special future imperative forms, a grammatical category which has completely disappeared from later Delaware: Blanchard *lí* 'tell me (now)' and *lí·me* 'tell me (later)' but twentieth-century Delaware only *lí* 'tell me'. There are a number of formations for which Blanchard attests a more extensive use than that found in the

---

[17] The Atsina reflexes of $*\theta$ are conditioned by the vowel environment. The shift to $t$ from an intermediate affricate $\hat{\theta}$ postdates the eighteenth-century vocabulary mentioned above.

[18] A.L. Kroeber, *UCPAAE* 12.75–6 (1916); Truman Michelson, *IJAL* 8.131ff. (1935); Ives Goddard, "An outline of the historical phonology of Arapaho and Atsina," *IJAL* 40. 102–116 (1974).

[19] See also the discussion of a similar situation in Wiyot in Goddard 1966.

[20] For further particulars, see Pilling 1891:547. Pilling incorrectly gives David Zeisberger as the co-author; although Zeisberger also translated this work (*ibid.*:545), Blanchard's translation is entirely independent. Blanchard's forms are here transcribed phonemically from the special alphabet used by the Baptist missionaries in Kansas (*ibid.*:345). See further Goddard 1969.

modern language, as for example the preterite mode (see below). In some instances of this type Blanchard's text serves as a caveat against some possible hasty conclusions about linguistic change. Thus the special verb forms used with obviative (secondary third person) subjects are rarely used by contemporary speakers, but while Blanchard admittedly uses these forms much more frequently he nevertheless fails to employ them in a number of places (see Goddard 1969). Thus the decline in the use of the obviative verb forms may be seen as a gradual process extending back on the order of 150 years at least, and not, say, as simply grammatical atrophy among the last generations of largely bilingual speakers.

The existence of Blanchard's excellent translation, which is largely successful in its idiomatic Delaware renderings, suggests that a careful examination of the voluminous religious translational literature in American Indian languages would be rewarding. Such materials cannot be dismissed a priori simply because they are, to some extent, of non-native origin, even though many such productions are of quite poor quality. A number of religious translations, of course, have been done by native speakers.[21] Also, among some Indian groups translations of hymns have become an integral part of the modern culture and merit the attention of linguists and other specialists.[22]

In some cases writing systems introduced by missionaries or of other origins have been adopted by the Indians, resulting in the production of large numbers of mundane and usually ephemeral documents. Little collecting of personal letters, journals, public notices, and the like has been done for materials in the Cree, Eskimo, Fox and Kickapoo, Winnebago, or Cherokee syllabaries, or in the alphabetic scripts used for Dakota, Navajo, and other languages.[23] The Canadian Delawares learned to write their language in two ways, in the Unami dialect using a German orthography developed by Moravian missionaries, and in the Munsee dialect with the English orthography of the Methodists and Anglicans. People living today can recall members of their parents' generation sending and receiving letters written in Delaware. Yet, except for two letters sent to scholars who published them, not a single specimen of this extensive native literacy can be found today in any collection or in the Indian communities.[24] Only a few items of native composition in Eliot's Massachusett orthography survive in southeastern New England historical societies. Such documents, however, are clearly of great potential linguistic value, furnishing textual material undistorted by translation or the often unspontaneous fieldwork situation.[25]

---

[21] Alford 1929; the works of John Quinney and Hendrick Aupaumut given by Pilling 1891:415-17.

[22] This is true, for example, among some Ojibwa and Ottawa groups, and among the Cherokee.

[23] For example, such materials are reported to be very abundant among the Aleut; see Ransom 1945, esp. 339, 343. A recently published Cherokee document of this sort is Kilpatrick and Kilpatrick 1966. Linguists have made little use of this kind of material.

[24] See the Unami letter of Gottlieb Tobias in Brinton 1885:88, and the Munsee text of Nelles Montour in Prince 1902. Montour's text, which was printed not as written but with frequently incorrect emendations, was presumably lost in the fire which destroyed Prince's library in 1911; thus Tobias's letter, if it is in the Brinton papers at the University of Pennsylvania, would be the only surviving physical example of native Canadian Delaware written composition.

[25] More formal Indian-language productions of native origin, such as newspapers (e.g. the nine-

Bloomfield (MS.) reported that texts written out in the Cree syllabary were in some ways inferior to those dictated by his informants, but still felt them worthy of serious attention:[26]

> ... the [Sweet Grass] Cree ... who use the syllabary, [sic] do not use it enough to become skilful ... [C]onfusions ... are easily made ... [T]he ... diacritical marks are often misplaced or omitted.
> In writing, the Cree often lapses into meagre syntax or else is likely to lose track of his construction; he does not read readily enough to look back over what he has just written.
> Nevertheless, the syllabary texts avoid the errors of a foreigner's record, as well as some of the other difficulties of dictation.

Clearly documents written by Indians themselves in their own languages deserve more attention from linguists than they have been paid in the past.[27] It will be reasonable in most cases when publishing such texts to transcribe them into the standard phonemic orthography used for the given language. Difficulties of interpretation caused by ambiguities in the orthography can be indicated in explanatory notes.

The various types of documentary sources which have been mentioned also provide much lexical information which has so far been largely unused in the preparation of lexicons of Native American languages. Admirable from this point of view is Haas's *Tunica dictionary* (1953), which incorporates all interpretable items found in the largely unpublished notes of Gatschet and Swanton.[28] William Bright has recently compiled *A Luiseño dictionary* (1968) in which an attempt was made to gather together

---

teenth-century *Cherokee Phoenix* and *Cherokee Advocate*, and the twentieth-century Navajo *Adahooniligii* and *Diné Bizaad*, Eskimo *Messenger*, *Cherokee Newsletter*, and partly Cree *Native People*), are perhaps a category better known to linguists, but as with the more fugitive varieties little use has been made by them of this kind of material. Though the problem of native versus nonnative authorship is present, there is also much use to be made of Indian-language mission newspapers like the Dakota *Iape Oaye* and the Ojibwa *Anishinabe Enamiad*. Literacy and educational programs have produced large amounts of material in Cree, Eskimo, Navajo, Dakota, and Cherokee, such as the *Navajo Historical Series* and productions of the Carnegie Cherokee Project like Spade and Walker 1966 and Wahrhaftig and Nackedhead 1966.

[26] Franz Boas also stressed the value of native-written texts in spite of their occasional deficiencies; *IJAL* 1.1–2 (1917), *PAES* 3.68–9 (1912).

[27] In a different category, perhaps, from such everyday and relatively unpractised productions are the texts and letters written by Indians who have been taught to write their language in a scientific transcription. This sort of material has generally been treated as equivalent to that collected by field linguists, as, for example, the Nootka texts written by Alex Thomas (Sapir and Swadesh 1939:9 and passim, 1955:5 and passim), the Wishram Chinook texts of Pete McGuff (Sapir 1909:ix), and the voluminous amounts of Kwakiutl written out by the controversial George Hunt (White 1963:30–3; Rohner 1966:esp. 152 and 213ff., 1969:xi, xxix, etc.). All of Michelson's published Fox texts were written out in the Fox syllabary by his informants and then rewritten phonetically; many of Paul Radin's Winnebago texts were obtained in the same way. Michelson's statement on the value of such materials may be applied, mutatis mutandis, to the types mentioned above as well: 'The possible sources of error have been set forth ... because of their importance ... At the same time I am convinced that texts far more idiomatic in language and in better literary form may be obtained by having texts written by Indians and then dictated than those secured by dictation alone' (*BAE-R* 40.29 (1925)).

[28] Unclear words in these notes and the few Tunica words found in French historical sources are omitted.

materials obtained by Sparkman, Kroeber, G.W. Grace, J.P. Harrington, A. Malécot, and himself, all largely checked over by new fieldwork. Possible phonetic errors in the earlier sources are discussed in detail, but since the unchecked forms attested only in these sources are not indicated, this information is difficult to make appropriate use of. Proper names, place names, and tribal names are virtually entirely omitted (the first — and perhaps also the others — 'since the scanty data available on these were especially difficult to interpret' [Bright 1968:3]), though these are categories in which even poorly recorded data can be useful. Apparently, no use was made of the materials left by the Luiseño Pablo Tac. These shortcomings do not detract from the value of this dictionary as it stands, however, and more publications in the future with this kind of productive use of earlier sources would be welcome.[29] Linguists can also use with profit more of the lexical material collected by ethnographers, ethnobotanists, and the like than they have in the past; even when the phonetics in such sources are poor, the definitions are generally more accurate and complete than those obtained by investigators with no interest in the non-linguistic aspects of culture.[30] The present interest in ethnoscience and the 'new ethnography' among anthropologists will lead to the accumulation of much new lexical information of which linguists must take account. (For papers in this field which include further bibliographical material, see Tyler 1969.)

The philological examination of early vocabularies can sometimes lead to conclusions of ethnohistorical significance. In James Isham's "Small account of the Indian language in Hudsons Bay", written in 1743, there is, in addition to a considerable amount of Cree, Assiniboin, and Chippewyan vocabulary, a section on 'Different ways to count ten in the Indian language' (Rich 1949:34–37). One of these, called 'Earchithinu Language', is the earliest known sample of Blackfoot, spoken at the time on the South Saskatchewan River; another, labeled 'Earchethinue Language in an other part of the Country', is the earliest sample of Crow.[31] This shows that the Crow were distinct from the Hidatsa, and very likely north of the Missouri, at an earlier date than that assumed by some scholars (e.g. Bowers 1965:10–25).

So far this essay has reviewed various documentary sources on North American languages and discussed what more or less direct use may be made of them. It is worthwhile to consider also the kinds of creative interaction there can be between the use of documents and the more traditional activities of Americanist linguists. A concern for philology can broaden the range of questions which the linguist takes to

[29] Note also the discussion of several dictionaries from this point of view in Hymes 1969.
[30] See, for example, the remarks of Hymes, *Lg* 34.577 (1958), and the criticism of Eric Hamp, *IJAL* 32.183–4 (1966). Ideally, of course, linguists should make a habit of checking over ethnographers' wordlists with their informants; see below. Vigorous exception must be taken to Bright's (1968:3) implication that in lexicons expected to be used primarily for comparative purposes there is a justification for omitting ethnographic data. To do this is, in effect, to omit full semantic information, which is very often crucial to correct etymologies. See the instructive example in Calvert Watkins, "The etymology of Old Irish *ind-aim*" (1959), where the clue to the correct etymology of the word for 'to wash (hands or feet)' is furnished by ethnographic information on the method of washing the hands.
[31] Compare Hayden 1862:396; some innovations are evident in the numbers given in Lowie 1960.

the field, leading to the acquisition or confirmation of information that would otherwise remain unknown or uncertain. Conversely, fieldwork can contribute to the interpretation of the earlier documentary sources on a language. Checking over older lexical information with an informant is probably not uncommon among Americanists, and in many cases it may well become a necessary part of fieldwork, if pre-acculturation vocabulary is to be recovered to any great extent. More delicate is the pump-priming use of older grammatical materials to re-elicit parts of the morphology which may be used only rarely or in modified form at the time of fieldwork. Two examples from Oklahoma Delaware may illustrate the possibilities. In a text recorded by Truman Michelson in 1912 a woman rejects various animal suitors with insults, saying, for example, to the owl *sɔ́·mi kəmax·ahi·ná·kwsi* 'you are too ugly' and to the beaver *sɔ́·mi kəmax·ahi·na·kwší·š·i*, meaning ostensibly the same thing;[32] this last form and a few other of the woman's pejorative remarks attest an element -*š·i* (underlying /-ši/), before which *s* in certain cases shifts to *š*. When contemporary speakers were questioned about these forms in 1968, they readily accepted, repeated, and translated them, explaining that the ending had an ugly or unpleasant sound. Additional examples were elicited demonstrating that this pejorative /-ši/ is productively used in exactly parallel fashion to the well attested diminutive /-ti/, even though in four summers of fieldwork from 1966 to 1969 not a single spontaneous example turned up in texts or was observed in conversation (see Goddard 1969). The use of Michelson's text thus permitted the recovery of a morpheme that would otherwise not have been obtained from the informants, and the comments of the informants clarified the meaning of the imperfectly glossed forms in the text. More complex was the attempt to re-elicit paradigms of the moribund Delaware preterite, which, though abundantly attested in earlier records, is of rare and restricted use today, to the extent that speakers seem unsure of some of the forms. It was necessary to work back and forth between sometimes suspect elicited forms and sometimes phonetically ambiguous older recorded forms in order to fill out a paradigm that seemed to be reasonable. Although there is a certain risk of creating ghost forms with this method, it is minimal when there is proper rechecking with several informants; as in general, of course, all forms should be explicitly labeled as to their provenience.

A particularly fruitful area of collaboration between philology and field linguistics is in the restoration and interpretation of texts collected by earlier investigators. For example, J. N. B. Hewitt collected a Munsee origin-myth text in 1896, but added an interlinear English translation to only 13 of the 40 manuscript pages.[33] When reviewed with a Munsee speaker in 1968, the entire text proved to be recoverable and translatable, with the exception of a very few doubtful places. Without being worked over in the field, this manuscript would obviously have been of limited usefulness, but now it has the possibility of realizing its full potential (for some comments on the editing of texts, see below). In addition, though the Munsee no longer recall any

[32] Smithsonian Institution National Anthropological Archives, MS 2776.
[33] Smithsonian Institution National Anthropological Archives, MS 16.

traditional tales, there has now been recovered a mythological narrative of considerable interest. Along the same lines it should be borne in mind that many untranscribed sound recordings now in archives will clearly have their full value only if interpreted and explicated by fieldwork with living speakers.

It is cases such as the Munsee text just discussed that demonstrate — if proof be needed — that it simply will not do for Americanists to leave the study of written records till after the spoken languages have completely died out. For all the imperfections they may have, they are still — just as much as up-to-date fieldnotes — testimonial documents of the products of grammars. Poor phonetic transcription is, after all, no deterrent to those who wish to study Hittite, nor does calqued syntax cause the rejection of Wulfila's Gothic translation of the Bible.

## 2. DOCUMENTATION

The problems presented by earlier documents have been reviewed and methods for their philological interpretation discussed. But the linguist who has a philological approach looks not only to the past but also to the future; he must be concerned with minimizing the problems which the documents he produces will cause his successors. This means making explicit in the fullest practicable way all the information about a form or a corpus that a future investigator might seek. It is impractical, of course, to give full particulars for every form ever cited in print. But it is possible to do more along these lines than most Americanists have been accustomed to in the past.

There are two reasons in particular why the careful documentation of data on American Indian languages is so necessary: the fact that the analyst is usually also the principal source of information, and the fact that these languages are generally little known to anyone else. Most descriptive linguists probably feel that their finished grammars have a greater validity, in some sense, than their raw fieldnotes. But the field notes are the primary documents, the nearest thing to the actual speech events that there is, and they should always ultimately be deposited in a suitable library or public archive, together with explanatory information on dates of fieldwork, relevant characteristics of informants, changing transcriptional conventions, and indexes.[34] Only if this practice becomes more general can the present situation be improved, in which numerous cases of possible informant errors, artifacts of the elicitation methods, misprints, and miscopyings remain forever undetected or in doubt because of the impossibility of checking them against the primary documents. As an example of how significant information can be filtered out in the presentation of the analysis, a case may be cited in which the primary data are available in the form of a published text. In William Shipley's *Maidu grammar* (1964:30) the statement

---

[34] Two archives with large collections of primary American Indian linguistic materials are the American Philosophical Society, Philadelphia, and the Smithsonian Institution National Anthropological Archives Washington, D.C. For the former see Freeman 1966.

is made that for the citation form of a noun some speakers use the subject case and 'some younger speakers' the object case; presumably, since each idiolect is of equal validity, no further particulars were thought necessary. In a recorded conversation, however, in which two speakers use citation forms in the same context, it is a centenarian who uses the subject case *sòlím* 'song' and her daughter who uses the object case *sòlí* (Shipley 1968:68, text 18, paras. 41, 51).[35] This would seem to indicate, rather more clearly than the vague statement in the grammar, that the subject case citation form represents the older usage — a relevant fact about Maidu that many linguists would like to have included in full detail in any grammar.

Carelessness about documentation can lead to the creation of ghost forms, which are likely to be especially tenacious since not many control these languages sufficiently well to make corrections in them. For instance, few Algonquianists would be inclined to question the Fox forms *nesiči* 'my foot' and *nesitani* 'my feet' which Bloomfield gives in two papers of the 1940s;[36] many cognates in other Algonquian languages agree in form and meaning. These forms, however, are not attested in Fox;[37] they are Bloomfield's creations based on the regular patterns of Fox noun inflection as applied to a form he gives in an earlier paper[38] as *ositani* 'his feet'. This, in turn, is not found as such, but is an abstraction from an expression attested in a single Fox tale, as follows (Jones 1907:30, text 3): *mahkositani-me·tawa·čiki* (3X) 'Those-that-sulked-on-account-of-the-Bear('s)-Foot' (a legendary band of Fox who, having been left no boiled bear's foot after a hunt, separated from the rest of the tribe and are supposed to be living in some distant place); *mahkositani* 'the bear's foot'; *mahkosita·ni* 'the bear's foot' (cf. *mahkwa* 'bear'). It is not clear what the correct analysis of this form is, but it seems to be an archaism and cannot be made to yield up the word for 'his foot', which in Fox is *ohka·či*.[39] In this case there are sufficient records available to permit the correction of the error, but for much of the American Indian linguistic material published there is no guarantee that the forms are attested as printed, and no recourse to supporting documentation.

An important area in which questions of faithfulness to the record arise is in the editing of texts. Here the practices of Americanists must be said to fall far short of the standards adhered to by editors of textual materials in Old World languages. There seems to be little sympathy for the idea that published texts should follow as closely as possible the primary record, with emendations kept carefully apart. It is a common practice, often unavoidable, to take texts obtained from good, older narrators and review them with younger speakers who speak better English and have the stamina

---

[35] Calvert Watkins drew my attention to this problem.
[36] *Lg* 17.295 (1941); *VFPA* 6.119 (1946), no. 377. In this discussion, the spelling of the forms is modernized.
[37] They are not accepted by contemporary speakers, *fide* Paul H. Voorhis.
[38] *IJAL* 4.186 (1927).
[39] Truman Michelson, *IJAL* 8.141 (1935). Bloomfield interpreted this as 'his leg' on the analogy of the other languages; *IJAL* 4.182, *VFPA* 6.119, no. 380.

and interest necessary for fine linguistic work. When this is done, special care must be taken to insure that the archaisms and idiolectal peculiarities of the narrator are not filtered out. Bloomfield has given an example of the possible danger from his own Menomini texts. A formulaic expression in an old story contained a form of the verb *sɛ·ka·wekanɛ·hsemɛw* which appeared to mean 'he throws him (-*hsem*-) frightfully/ injuriously (*sɛ·k*-) with relation to X (-*a·wekanɛ·*-)'. The significance of the medial element was unknown to Bloomfield's best English-speaking informant, who insisted that the form was an error for *sɛ·ka·konɛ·hsemɛw* 'he throws him with injury on the snow' (with -*a·konɛ·*- 'snow'), and this emendation was incorporated into the published text. Subsequent fieldwork on Cree revealed the existence of a common element -*a·wikane·*- 'back (bone)' and convinced Bloomfield that the originally recorded Menomini form had been correct, with the meaning 'he throws him injuring his spine' (the sound correspondences are regular). Eventually a confirmatory Menomini example turned up in the word *moʔtawekanɛ·hsen* 'he lies with his back exposed' (with regular vowel-shortening).[40] Clearly, then, in editing texts the first aim must be to present as accurately as possible what the original narrator actually said; all emendation and explanation must be in addition to this. When it is desirable or necessary to publish a smoothly edited text, it would be advisable for the editor to make available as well — perhaps by deposit in a public collection — a close transcription of the primary record of the narration, whether written or tape-recorded. Where the text being edited was collected by an earlier fieldworker, there is an extra check against over-zealous editing, but care must still be taken in order to arrive at a restoration of the original and not merely a washed-out paraphrase. The Maidu texts originally published by R. B. Dixon which William Shipley has phonetically restored and retranslated (see Shipley 1968) show the fruitful possibilities of this approach, though one might wish for more explanatory notes at the points of disagreement.

Philology, one might say in conclusion, focuses on the fact that there are and will be only a finite number of documents recording the native languages of North America. It is necessary to make the fullest and most careful use of what there is, and to exercise the greatest diligence in preserving this corpus for the future in the most useful possible form.

### 3. SELECTED REFERENCES

ALBRIGHT, ROBERT W. 1958. The International Phonetic Alphabet: Its backgrounds and development. IUPAL 7 (= IJAL 24/1/3).
ALFORD, THOMAS WILDCAT. 1929. The four gospels of Our Lord Jesus Christ in Shawnee Indian language. Xenia, Ohio.
BLANCHARD, IRA D. 1837. The history of Our Lord and Saviour Jesus Christ... retranslated by I. D. Blanchard. Shawanoe Baptist Mission.

---

[40] Bloomfield 1928:188ff. and 189, fn. 1, which must postdate the work on Cree; *Festschrift Meinhof*, p. 401 (Hamburg, 1927); 1962; 390, section 18.54.

BLOOMFIELD, LEONARD. 1928. Menomini texts. PAES 12.
——. 1962. The Menomini language. New Haven.
——. Ms. Cree texts, series two, syllabary texts from Sweet Grass Reserve, pp. 522–733. Manuscript in the Library of the American Philosophical Society, Philadelphia (497.3/B63c/A1a.1).
BOAS, FRANZ, E. SAPIR, P.E. GODDARD, and A.L. KROEBER. 1916. Phonetic transcription of Indian languages. SMC 66/6.
BOWERS, ALFRED W. 1965. Hidatsa social and ceremonial organization. BAE-B 194.
BRANDT, ELIZABETH. 1970. On the origins of linguistic stratification: The Sandia case. AnL 12/2.46–50.
BRIGHT, WILLIAM, comp. 1968. A Luiseño dictionary. UCPL 51.
BRINTON, DANIEL G. 1885. The Lenâpé and their legends. Philadelphia.
BROADBENT, SYLVIA M. 1957. Rumsen I: Methods of reconstitution. IJAL 23.275–80.
FREEMAN, JOHN F. 1966. A guide to manuscripts relating to the American Indian in the library of the American Philosophical Society. Philadelphia.
GIBBS, GEORGE. 1863. Instructions for research relative to the ethnology and philology of America. SMC 7, article 11 (=Publication 160).
GODDARD, IVES. 1965. The Eastern Algonquian intrusive nasal. IJAL 31.206–20.
——. 1966. Review of Karl V. Teeter, The Wiyot language. IJAL 32.398–404.
——. 1969. Delaware verbal morphology: A descriptive and comparative study. Ph.D. dissertation, Harvard University.
GRANBERRY, JULIAN. 1956. Timucua I ... IJAL 22.97–105.
HAAS, MARY R. 1953. Tunica dictionary. UCPL 6/2.175–332.
——. 1963. Shasta and Proto-Hokan. Lg 39.40–59.
——. 1969. Swanton and the Biloxi and Ofo dictionaries. IJAL 35.286–90.
HANZELI, VICTOR. 1961. Early descriptions by French missionaries of Algonquian and Iroquoian languages ... Ph.D. dissertation, Indiana University.
——. 1969. Missionary linguistics in New France. The Hague, Mouton.
HAYDEN, F.V. 1862. Contributions to the ethnography and philology of the Indian tribes of the Missouri Valley. Philadelphia.
HERZOG, GEORGE, et al. 1934. Some orthographic recommendations. AmA 36.629–31.
HYMES, DELL H. 1965. The methods and tasks of anthropological philology (illustrated with Clackamas Chinook). RomPh 19.325–40.
——. 1966a. Some points of Siuslaw phonology. IJAL 32.328–42.
——. 1966b. Two types of linguistic relativity. Sociolinguistics, ed. by William Bright. The Hague, Mouton.
——. 1968. The 'wife' who 'goes out' like a man: Reinterpretation of a Clackamas Chinook myth. SocSciI 7.173–99.
——. 1969. Review of UCPL 31, 33, 39, 43, 45, and 46. AmA 71.131–38.

JONES, WILLIAM. 1907. Fox texts. PAES 1.

KILPATRICK, ANNA G., and JACK F. 1966. Chronicles of Wolftown: Social documents of the North Carolina Cherokees, 1850–1862. BAE-B 196, Anthropological Papers 75, pp. 1–111.

KROEBER, A. L., and GEORGE W. GRACE. 1960. The Sparkman grammar of Luiseño. UCPL 16.

LOUNSBURY, FLOYD G. 1953. Field methods and techniques in linguistics. Anthropology today, ed. by A. L. Kroeber et al., pp. 401–16. Chicago.

LOWIE, ROBERT H. 1960. Crow word lists. Berkeley.

PICKERING, JOHN. 1818. On the adaption of a uniform orthography for the Indian languages of North America. AAcadAS-M 4.319–57.

PILLING, JAMES C. 1891. Bibliography of the Algonquian languages. B[A]E-B 13.

POWELL, JOHN WESLEY. 1877. Introduction to the study of Indian languages. Washington, D.C. [On the alphabet, pp. 3–6, written by W. D. Whitney.]

——. 1880. Introduction to the study of Indian languages. 2nd ed. Washington, D.C. [Contains Powell's revision of Whitney's alphabet, pp. 1–16.]

PRINCE, J. DYNELEY. 1902. A modern Delaware tale. PAPS 41.20–34.

RANSOM, JAY E. 1945. Writing as a medium of acculturation among the Aleut. SJA 1.333–44.

RICH, E. E., ed. 1949. James Isham's observations on Hudsons Bay, 1743. Toronto.

ROHNER, RONALD P. 1966. Franz Boas: Ethnographer on the Northwest Coast. *And* Franz Boas among the Kwakiutl: Interview with Mrs. Tom Johnson. Pioneers of American anthropology, ed. by June Helm, pp. 149–222. AES-M 43. Seattle and London.

——. 1969. The ethnography of Franz Boas. Chicago and London.

SAPIR, EDWARD. 1909. Wishram texts. PAES 2.

SAPIR, EDWARD, and MORRIS SWADESH. 1939. Nootka texts. Philadelphia.

——. 1955. Native accounts of Nootka ethnography. IUPAL 1.

SHIPLEY, WILLIAM F. 1964. Maidu grammar. UCPL 33.

——. 1968. Maidu texts and dictionary. UCPL 41.

SILVER, SHIRLEY. 1960. Natick consonants in reference to Proto-Central Algonquian. IJAL 26.112–19, 234–41.

SPADE, WATT, and WILLARD WALKER. 1966. Cherokee stories. Tahlequah, Okla.

TAGLIAVINI, CARLO. 1926. La lingua degli Indi Luiseños... Biblioteca dell'Archiginnasio, ser. 2, no. 31. Bologna.

TAYLOR, ALLAN. 1967. Some observations on a comparative Arapaho–Atsina lexicon. Contributions to Anthropology: Linguistics I. NMC-B 214.113–27.

TYLER, STEPHEN. 1969. Cognitive anthropology. New York.

VOORHIS, PAUL H. 1971. New notes on the Mesquakie (Fox) language. IJAL 37.63–75.

WAHRHAFTIG, ALBERT L., and CALVIN NACKEDHEAD. 1966. The Cherokee people today. Tahlequah, Okla.
WATKINS, CALVERT. 1959. The etymology of Old Irish *ind-aim*. Lg 35.18–20.
WHITE, LESLIE A. 1963. The ethnography and ethnology of Franz Boas. Texas Memorial Museum Bulletin 6. Austin.

# NATIVE NORTH AMERICA

HERBERT LANDAR

MEN AND INSTITUTIONS

It is challenging to consider the Emersonian dictum that an institution is the lengthened shadow of one man. I can think of two men immediately, at the beginning of native North American historiography: Duponceau and Gallatin. Peter S. Duponceau was a justice of the Supreme Court of Louisiana; some of his linguistic materials were put into a docket book, now at the Library of the American Philosophical Society in Philadelphia. Albert Gallatin, whose picture appears on a $1\frac{1}{4}$ ¢ stamp and whose statue stands outside the Treasury Building in Washington, D.C., made his name as politician, diplomat and cabinet officer, retired from public life to become a bank president, and retired from income producing activities, at the end of his life, to be a scholar, president of learned societies, and as some have said the father of American linguistics. Some of the correspondence of the old men I have read in the Library just mentioned. They enjoyed trading information on the ravages of old age. Duponceau stayed with the American Philosophical Society; Gallatin helped to found the New York Historical Society, and the American Ethnological Society. I cannot see the shadow of the former living up to Emersonian expectations, though Duponceau as Secretary knew everybody in American colonial linguistic scholarship (or so I like to think he supposed); the shadow of the latter, however, gives one pause.

Gallatin left 90 portfolio boxes or so of papers to the New York Historical Society. Some years ago Margaret Blaker, Archivist of the Bureau of American Ethnology of the Smithsonian Institution, visited the Society's Library and sorted the linguistic papers into folders. She told me about her work and I spent some time there examining and indexing Gallatin's studies. The Library has a print-out of my notes which can be used as a rough guide for visitors, but my notes had to be revised slightly during later examinations and I am still working on a proper explication of the five boxes of linguistic manuscripts. I suspect that none of Gallatin's contemporaries had more comparative vocabularies and linguistic notes in hand than he. Most of his studies had to do with native languages of the United States and Canada, but he also had a passion for the study of native Ibero-American languages and he pleaded with correspondents for grammars of Mexican and more southerly languages. He did not get very many, but what materials he had helped him to support (or so he supposed) some of the Humboldtian typological presumptions which I have discussed in my earlier essay. Repeatedly he insists that American Indian languages are all of one type (except Otomi, perhaps), from the language of the Eskimo to the Araucanian language at Cape Horn. Here Gallatin set a theme for historiographers which it took a Boas to demolish.

Duponceau's institution, the American Philosophical Society, was established in 1743. Benjamin Franklin as Founder intended to 'Americanize a European idea,' to institute for the general welfare democratically what had been instituted in Europe about a century before under royal auspices. 'The academies in Europe were largely Royal Societies,' we are told by Goodenough (see Stevens 1949:154), 'the oldest of them not more than a hundred years old, and were essentially vehicles to get Royal patronage for the new encyclopedic learning.' The institution, rather than the man, has extended its shadow. It has archived American Indian linguistic manuscripts, the voluminous correspondence of Franz Boas, and studies of scholars who contemporaneously have collected linguistic data on the Phillips Fund; see Freeman (1962), Freeman and Smith (1966), and Bell and Smith (1966).

Thomas Jefferson was president of the APS from 1797 to 1814. He favored linguistic studies, collected data himself, and obliged Lewis and Clark to complete vocabulary schedules (which they brought back to him, but which later were lost). As secretary of the Committee of History, Moral Science, and General Literature, Peter Stephen Duponceau was encouraged by Jefferson's sympathy to collection of data. Jefferson collected vocabularies with the intention of doing what Gallatin later did; he and Barton were friendly rivals in this enterprise, which aimed to establish the patterns of migration of American tribes. For his part, Duponceau favored typological investigations while he did not slight the construction of comparative vocabularies. Duponceau became president of the APS in 1828 and remained in that position until 1844. His acquisitions for the Library and later linguistic acquisitions are detailed by Freeman (see Freeman and Smith 1966:1-14).

In Freeman's day there were almost 300 individual collections and over 50,000 items, taking up 150 feet of shelf space. Freeman observed that the Indian manuscripts equalled twenty per cent of the Library's total manuscript collections. More than 350 tribes and languages were represented, the greatest depth being in those of North America. While some items were written in the sixteenth century, most were produced in the periods 1780-1840 and 1890 to the present. Freeman, an authority on Schoolcraft, died before completion of his careful inventory, which uses a classification scheme devised by Swadesh, and Murphy Smith brought the inventory through the press.

The Boas Collection of American Indian Linguistics, 1875-date, with about 600 groups of items, was indexed in 1945 (see Voegelin and Harris 1945). The Boas Correspondence, 1878-1942, about 55,000 letters, has been microfilmed and was available in 1972 for a sum which can be managed by most university libraries.

A substantial call on the title of 'Center for the History of American Indian Linguistics', then, must be credited to Philadelphia. Between the APS and the University of Pennsylvania (the Museum Library there has the Brinton Collection, incorporating the Berendt Collection, and Dell Hymes has helped students in historiographical writing [see Sherzer 1968, Darnell 1967, 1969, Darnell and Sherzer 1971a, 1971b]) the claim is strong. The Smithsonian has a claim, too, as does the Newberry Library in Chicago. We shall deal with them later.

A sample entry from Freeman and Smith (1966:391; D. = document, A.D. = autograph document, L. = leaves) will show how thorough has been the groundwork intended to help the linguistic historian:

3976. SWADESH, MORRIS. Vocabularies in various Zapotec dialects [1941]. Mimeo. D. and A.D. 120L. In Spanish-Zapotec.
10 vocabulary lists of from 17 to 742 items, taken from informants at various villages; 4 Ixtlan, 5 Villa Alta lists, and 1 Tehuantepec list. [30(Z.5)]
Donor, Morris Swadesh, 1950.

The APS Latin American sources were described separately by Freeman in 1962. Bell and Smith (1966) deal with all the archives and manuscript collections of the APS and list (pp. 23-4) as No. 102 the American Indian Ethnology and Linguistics collection, containing miscellaneous studies. Also available at the APS Library are Middle American manuscripts from Chicago, on microfilm; see Tax (1948).

While regional institutions are strong in works reflecting their own history — the Bibliothèque Nationale is magnificent for French works, the British Museum for works on the former British colonies, but neither for recent American Indian linguistics on the scale of any major university in the United States — while we can expect strengths to reflect geography, it is remarkable that the APS Library has a strong collection of works on native Ibero-American languages. I list here languages, areas or tribes represented in Freeman and Smith, with their bibliographic serial numbers: Araucanian (406), Arawak and [Island] Carib (407-15, 501), Aztec or Nahuatl (434-45, 2337-54), Botocudo (467-8), Bribri (469), Cagaba (481), Cahita (482), Cakchiquel (483-97), Caingang (498), Central America (569-84), Chibcha (694), Chichimeca (695), Chinanteco (714-19), Chocho (737), Chontal [Tequistlatecan] (745-6), Chorti (747-50), Coroado (774), Cubeo (817), Cuicateco (818), Cuna (819-20), Guarani (1528-31), Huastec (1581-82), Huave (1583-97), Huichol (1598-1601), Jivaro (1863), Lenca (1962), Malali (2090), Mam (2103), Matlazinca (2136), Maya (2138-56), Mayo (2157-58), Mazatec (2159-60), Mexico (2169-216), Mixe (2248-53), Mixteco (2254-58), Mojo (2288), Oiampi (2496-97), Otomi (2614-15), Palicur (2644), Pima (2956-61), Pipil (2962), Quechua (3100-70), Quiché (3171-73), South America (3681-96), Taino (3708), Tarahumara (3726-29), Tarascan (3730-34), Tehuelche (3735), Tepehuan (3736-38), Totonac (3765), Tupi (3793-94), Tupinamba (3795), Tzeltal (3826), Uruba (3827), Uto-Aztecan (3832-34), Xinca (3909), Yao (3916-17), Yaqui (3918-19), Zapotec (3929-78).

The *Handbook of Middle American Indians*, edited by Robert Wauchope (with Vol.

5 edited by Norman McQuown, distinguished by William Bright's bibliography of descriptive linguistics [Bright 1967]); the present series, *Current trends in linguistics*, edited by Thomas A. Sebeok, with Vol. 10 on North America; and a projected revision of the *Handbook of North American Indians*, under the general editorship of William C. Sturtevant (with Vol. 15 on Languages edited by Ives Goddard), are all important historiographical monuments. While new information is presented in these series, there is also a fair amount of information about information, classifications and indexings of note. If we examine the centers at which editorial work is most indefatigable, we notice that New Orleans (and Austin), Chicago, Cambridge, Los Angeles, Bloomington, Philadelphia, and Washington, D.C., are prominent. Every reader, perhaps, has extended the list silently, but these will do for the moment.

New Orleans with Tulane University and the Middle American Research Institute is a center of American historiography. The Latin American collection at Tulane is filled with delightful surprises and rarities, many brought there by William Gates. Gates was an attorney whose connection with the Johns Hopkins University in Baltimore during the great depression was strained. He wanted to have his Middle American Research Institute at Johns Hopkins, but he moved to New Orleans because of a lack of salary and quarrels with the administration. At Tulane Gates quarreled with the administration over directing the Institute and he left eventually, taking with him part of his collection. Many of his books and manuscripts he sold; after his death Brigham Young University took some of his collection. Some of his manuscripts he sold to the Smithsonian; others have found their way to the magnificent Dulles Library at Princeton University (outstanding for the Mayan holdings which include the Chilam Balam of Chumayel and other such rareties). Howard Cline, of the Library of Congress, was doing a bibliography involving the Gates and other Middle American materials; his death in this connection as well as others is a great loss.

The University of Texas Press publishes the *Handbook of Middle American Indians*. The Library of the University of Texas is distinguished for its Latin American collection, which is world famous. I was told once that the University sends gunboats up South American rivers in search of books and manuscripts. The hyperbole in this story is scarcely to be discouraged by the recently issued set of about 30 volumes of card-catalogue entries for the Latin American Collection. Also at Austin Rudolph C. Troike has functioned as the American Indian bibliographer for the Modern Language Association International Bibliography. In 1967 the MLA began the separate bibliographical listing of native languages of North and South America. See Voegelin (1968).

The contrast between the American experience and the European is striking. Support for historiography in the United States derives very largely from private foundations, government agencies and foundations (such as the National Science Foundation), and educational institutions. In Europe private fortunes were devoted specifically to Americanist projects. The eccentric Lord Kingsborough brought together Mexican source materials and left a monument of nine huge volumes over his grave; he died of disease contracted in a jail where he had been thrown for debt (a paper bill).

The prime Maecenas in Europe at the turn of the century, however, was an American, Joseph Florimond. He was named Duc de Loubat for his benefactions to the Church. He was a moving force in Americanist affairs in Europe, he published Mexican manuscripts in facsimile, he set up a chair for Seler in Berlin, and he was an admiring patron of Hamy (whose bust is on display in the Musée de l'Homme) and other leaders of the Société des Américanistes de Paris. He was an institution of a kind.

Some of his contemporaries in America moved in parallel ways. The benefactions of Archer M. Huntington, son of the railroad and shipbuilding magnate Collis P. Huntington and Arabella Huntington, are well known. To Archer M. Huntington must go credit for huge contributions to the National Geographic Society and the Heye Foundation's Museum of the American Indian. Archer M. Huntington established the Hispanic Society of America, whose Library is a valuable resource on Latin American history. From this Library the Library of Congress acquired a surfeit of native Ibero-American linguistic materials.

Like the Duc de Loubat, Henry E. Huntington admired California — but Florimond was born there and left, and Huntington moved between New York and Pasadena (and contiguous San Marino) and finally developed his estate in California. His Library was richest in English and American literature and history, but it is strong in nineteenth-century materials relevant to American linguistics, it has more Eliot Bibles than any place else that I know of, and it has some very rare Mexican linguistic imprints. It also has a set of Lord Kingsborough's works, a set of Schoolcraft's *Indian tribes*, and other interesting materials, including one of Schoolcraft's questionnaires.

In Cambridge the anthropology library of the Peabody Museum, Harvard University, is outstanding. This Library has been more successful than most, I would suspect, in collecting offprints. The card catalogue volumes (by subject and by author, with supplements) are famous because they constitute probably the most extensive ethnographic bibliography available. Ives Goddard, editor of the volume on Languages mentioned above, is stationed at Harvard.

Bloomington, Indiana, is a small city but the work of linguists at Indiana University has made it well known in the world of linguistic historiography. C.F. Voegelin has edited the *International Journal of American Linguistics* there for many years. This journal is the most important single source of 'information about information', I think, in the midst of a wealth of such sources on American Indian languages. Another important source is *Anthropological Linguistics*, edited by F.M. Voegelin at the Archives of Languages of the World. Archived materials include tape recordings of native languages, and phonological analyses structured typologically (see Robinett 1954, Voegelin 1958). Thomas A. Sebeok, Secretary of the Linguistic Society of America and editor of *Current trends in linguistics*, is also stationed at Indiana.

Outstanding repositories of linguistic data include the Bancroft Library at Berkeley and the files of the Survey of California Indian languages of the Department of Linguistics. Guided by Mary Haas and others, a program to rescue native languages of California has been measured in part by a distinguished series of doctoral dissertations rich in grammars, texts and lexicons.

The books and manuscripts collected by Jesuit missionaries in the Province of Oregon were archived, when I examined them, in the Jesuit Archives, Crosby Library, Gonzaga University, Spokane, Washington. I believe they have been transferred to the Pacific Northwest Indian Center on the Gonzaga campus. They constitute a valuable resource for students of Eskimo and various languages of the Pacific Northwest.

Before I turn to Chicago and Washington I want to say a word about the library of the National Museum of Canada in Ottawa. Sapir enriched the anthropological section of this library and the ethnographic archives during his long residence in Canada. File drawers of his manuscripts remain in the archives.

The Geological Survey of Canada, established in 1842, included the museum functions which in 1920 were put under the Victoria Memorial Museum, whose name in 1927 was changed to the National Museum of Canada, a division of the Department of Mines and Resources till 1950, then a division of the Department of Resources and Development. Institutional bibliographies include Canada (1952). The Division of Anthropology was established around September 1, 1910. On the fathers of Canadian ethnology see Sapir (1911). On Sapir's career and his move to Chicago see Sapir, Lowie and Lowie (1965).

One of the major benefactors of the city of Chicago at the turn of the century was Edward Ayer. Like Henry E. Huntington, with whom he visited, Ayer was a passionate collector of books; he specialized, however, in Americana. Like Huntington, he came to wealth through business interests, rapidly. He manufactured railroad ties. After Pilling's death, Pilling's widow, with the aid of Pilling's friend, the bibliographer Wilberforce Eames, sold Pilling's collection of linguistic materials, purchased from other collectors like Brinton and Gatschet or from dealers like Nicolás Léon, or wheedled from correspondents during Pilling's bibliographic labors at the Smithsonian, and Edward Ayer, in buying the collection, established the Newberry Library in Chicago as preeminent in early American Indian linguistic imprints. Pilling had begged of his correspondents two or three copies of their works, one for Major Powell's collection, one for Pilling, and one for Eames. Much of the Eames Collection can be found at the New York Public Library. Major Powell sold his collection to a passionate collector of Americana named Horsford, who gave it to a college library which lost the major part of it in a fire.

The John Carter Brown Library in Providence, Rhode Island was established by another businessman with a passion for books. When Pilling died, Major Powell commissioned George Parker Winship, librarian to the Brown family, to complete the projected Mexican linguistic bibliography which had by turns attracted and terrified Pilling. Winship went on to better things at Harvard. Some years ago, Ives

Goddard found the letter books of Pilling in the John Carter Brown Library and in 1969 I studied them for several weeks. I wondered if Pilling meant to do just an Aztec bibliography or a set of bibliographies for various Mexican Indian language families; I think his letters to Icazbalceta and others are ambiguous on this point, but I suppose if he had lived long enough he would have exploited the Spanish which he and his wife tried to master in his last years. While Goddard was able to find the letter books, I have not been able to find the card file so frequently mentioned in Pilling's letters, on the basis of which we could have a firm answer.

## THE SMITHSONIAN INSTITUTION

Gallatin single-handedly ran an operation for the investigation of tribes and languages of the Americas (see Gallatin 1836, 1848) and he performed many of the functions later assumed by governmental agencies. In the United States the War Department took responsibility for Indian Affairs in 1789. George Washington looked to an Indian agent and to a general when he responded to Lafayette's communication of the request of Catherine the Great of Russia for Indian vocabularies. (The Manuscript Division of the Library of Congress has copies of these vocabularies.)

There were Indian agents during British colonial rule, of course, and I assume that they collected vocabularies, though I have found none earlier than those collected by the Revolutionary leaders. Early scholars issued printed lists (I call them "scout" lists) for the collection of vocabularies and grammatical data partly with the help of the War Department, and partly with the help of the Smithsonian Institution: Constantine S. Rafinesque, Jr., Albert Gallatin, Horatio Hale, Lewis Henry Morgan, George Gibbs, Henry Rowe Schoolcraft, and others. No one has made a complete survey of these scout lists yet, though I have plans and data for such a survey. (On the Bureau of Indian Affairs and allied organs see Schmeckebier 1927; a catalogue dictionary of library cards is now available through G. K. Hall.)

The preparation of scout lists and rules on how to collect data began with European explorations. The increased attention to basic vocabulary lists in connection with Swadesh's discoveries in the fields of lexicostatistics and glottochronology in the 1950's and 1960's stimulated the production of such lists, especially in English and Spanish, for use with all native American languages as well as others. Some of these European lists have been referred to in linguistic journals. For example, Kutscher (1958) has reported on the linguistic materials of W. Lehmann (who died in 1939) accepted by the Ibero-Amerikanischen Bibliothek zu Berlin. The Museum für Völkerkunde zu Berlin did a *Tabelle zur Aufnahme südamerikanischer Sprachen* which Lehmann used. The Commission d'Enquête Linguistique (of the Permanent International Committee of Linguists, now with UNESCO and sponsor of a monumental series of volumes of Linguistic Bibliography) has supervised research on questionnaires; see Commission d'Enquête Linguistique, C.I.P.L. (1931), and Cohen (1928,

1950, 1951a, 1951b). For more recent developments see the Summer Institute of Linguistics volumes of Robinson (1968, 1969a, 1969b).

The classification of tribes and languages which Gallatin prosecuted was continued by Major Powell in connection with explorations of the U.S. Geological Survey. Powell's chief clerk was James C. Pilling. In 1879 the Bureau of Ethnology was established and Pilling took on the chief clerkship there too. Helped by W. D. Whitney of Yale, Powell developed a phonetic alphabet and a series of questions; the first edition was published in 1877, the revised edition in 1880 (see Powell 1877, 1880; Sturtevant 1959). Pilling (1885:597–602) gives a detailed breakdown of categories that were investigated. The phonetic system of Powell found critics. In 1916 the American Anthropological Association proposed a new alphabet, which Edward Sapir favored; see American Anthropological Association (1916). The semantic analysis and assumptions of Powell also found critics. For a reflection of the sophistication of contemporary ethnosemantic investigations see Perchonock and Werner (1969).

Powell's main administrative concern, perhaps, in classification activities was bibliographic. He put Pilling to work in this field and supported him, as he observed in his funeral oration for Pilling, without stint. Powell also put many investigators to work collecting linguistic data in his scout lists, creating a rich store of manuscript data (see Sturtevant 1959). The classification was based largely on vocabulary comparisons supervised by Henry W. Henshaw; it was published in 1892 (see Powell 1891).

Among the important contributions of the Smithsonian Institution through the Bureau of Ethnology and its reincarnations under various names (Bureau of American Ethnology, Office of Anthropology, etc.) as far as linguistic historiographers are concerned one must list Pilling's bibliographies (Pilling 1885, 1887a, 1887b, 1888, 1889, 1891, 1892, 1893a, 1893b, 1894). For a view of the milieu in which Pilling worked, which needs to be supplemented, see Judd (1967).

Judd (1967:112–15) discusses the preparation of the Handbook of American Indians North of Mexico (Hodge 1907, 1910), supplementing Hodge's own remarks in his Preface. The work that went into the Handbook represented the entire experience of Powell's assistants and successors, and the two volumes are unrivaled to this day in certain respects, for example, in the list of tribal synonyms, perhaps 10,000 of them, tied to specific bibliographic sources. The Handbook is in process of revision, or rather of being superseded, with publication by the Smithsonian scheduled for June 25, 1976.

Current plans are for 18 to 20 volumes ranging in size from 500 to 750 pages, treating encyclopedically tribes north of Mesoamerica. The new Handbook is a program of the Center for the Study of Man of the Smithsonian, and its General Editor is William C. Sturtevant.

He and Margaret Blaker, among others, are members of the Archives Committee of the American Anthropological Association, whose function in ethnographic historiography has accelerated since its meeting in New Orleans in 1969, with George W.

Stocking as chairman. The purpose of the Committee is to build the National Anthropological Archives, to collect manuscripts on the history of anthropology, to poll departments of anthropology for historical matter, and to frame obituary notices.

## THE CENTER FOR APPLIED LINGUISTICS

The Center for Applied Linguistics, Washington, D.C., was established in 1959 and incorporated in 1964. It serves as a coordinating office for information on applications of linguistics to practical problems and services and data relevant to its function. It publishes the quarterly newsletter The Linguistic Reporter. It has published various useful works, including Zisa's checklist of American Indian languages (Zisa 1970). In 1970 it began publication for the International Committee on Computational Linguistics of the series Language and Automation: An International Reference Publication. Zisa's work was commissioned by the ERIC Clearinghouse for Linguistics and was published through EDRS, ERIC Document Reproduction Service (ERIC is an acronym for Educational Resources Information Center [U.S. Office of Education]). Facsimile copies of documents and microfiche records of them, available through EDRS or other outlets, were listed in the series of ERIC Bulletins. ERIC recently was moved to the Modern Language Association. In 1971 the Office of Education, through an award to the MLA, created the ERIC Clearinghouse on Languages and Linguistics. MLA/ERIC publishes a section in Foreign Language Annals (of the American Council on the Teaching of Foreign Languages). The U.S. Government Printing Office publishes a monthly record of ERIC accessions, RIE, which if available can be obtained through EDRS, Box O, Bethesda, Md. 20014.

While not every American doctoral dissertation in linguistics deals with an American Indian language, it is convenient to list here a series sponsored by the Center for Applied Linguistics, which helps the historiographer to save time in consulting Dissertation Abstracts: it opens with Rutherford (1968). Rutherford covers dissertations from 1900–1965. The LSA Bulletin adds titles every year. These will be cumulated every three to five years into a Supplement to Rutherford (1968).

## COMPUTERS IN HISTORIOGRAPHY

The computerized bibliography of the Summer Institute of Linguistics (see my essay on native Ibero-America) is the first American Indian list of its size to be made public. More, I am sure, will follow. As information retrieval problems are solved more and more libraries will be able, I think, to follow the lead of the Library of the University of Texas, whose Slavic collection I was able to have searched on request. I received a print-out showing which works of the collection involved the Eskimo-Aleut family. The larger the body of data in the computer's memory, however, the longer it takes to retrieve information, and the more expensive the search is. Of anthropologists who have specialized in computer applications, many are linguists who have studied

American Indian languages. Swadesh pioneered in programs, though with a punch-card system (Swadesh 1963). Pierce has specialized in typological indices; see Pierce (1962). Important sources on computers and their applications to the storage and use of information about American Indian linguistic data include Hymes (1965), Lamb (1965), Garvin and Spolsky (1966), Werner (1966), Murdock (1967, 1970), and Murdock and White (1969).

## INDEXING AND ABSTRACTING

One of the less noticed but very useful services in the monitoring of information is the journal index, a few examples of which are Sebeok (1945), Trager (1945), Canadian Research Center for Anthropology (1967). Abstracting services in anthropology often cover American Indian languages, their editors sometimes starting by scanning the lists of publications received which are printed in such journals as *Language* or *IJAL*. *Current Anthropology* reviews titles systematically. For the past few years *Abstracts in Anthropology* has abstracted Amerindian articles and books. Some of the entries of the *Arctic Bibliography* had to do with northern American Indian languages. Brief summaries of articles have been featured in the series, *Biennial Review of Anthropology* (for an example, see Siegel 1970). Materials abstracted by the Human Relations Area Files can be consulted through HRAF; see Murdock (1960).

The abstracts in *IJAL* stand out in their excellence. Hymes initiated the project in 1960 (see Voegelin 1960). In 1965 Werner published a comprehensive index to the abstracts (see Werner 1965). These include Latin American publications, translations of articles, and the like. One should include here reviews of journals such as *Lingua Posnaniensis* or other collections of articles. Representative samples: Hymes (1956), K. Hill (1963), Bright (1963a, 1963b, 1963c), Stark (1970). Announcements in *AnL*, *IJAL*, *Lg* and elsewhere of specialized conferences deserve notice as contributions to historians who will eventually try to trace movements and trends in Amerindian linguistics; samples are numerous in *IJAL*, as for example Voegelin (1971, 1972a).

Various genres of bibliography have appeared in Americanist historiography. Boggs (1949) and others specialized in native folklore texts. The Société des Américanistes de Paris has published more general bibliographies, and one of its members, Pottier, has begun a novel sort of fiche-oriented bibliography (Pottier 1967, 1969). The American Anthropological Association used to publish general bibliographies around the turn of the century. A similar endeavor is Swadesh's survey in *Lg* for 1936–37 (Swadesh 1938).

Another genre is the sort in which by means of bibliographic notes information is broadcast on material in a library collection or a journal, as in Schuller's notes on the Gates collection at Tulane and some small collections in Latin America, Landar's note on Quiché manuscript material at St. Louis University, Tax's note on the microfilm collection for Middle America at Chicago, the indexing of the Boas collection by Voegelin and Harris, and Swadesh's analysis of *Investigaciones Lingüísticas* (Schuller

1931a, 1931b, 1931c, Swadesh 1936–38, Voegelin and Harris 1945, Tax 1948, Landar 1967a).

Sometimes a review is designed to recover the history of the study of one or more American Indian languages, naming salient figures and giving fairly full bibliographies with annotational remarks; for particular figures data may be forthcoming which is intended to supplement data or correct them critically. A few examples here are Hymes (1969), Landar (1969), Goddard, Hockett and Teeter (1972), Hewson (1972).

## BIOGRAPHICAL MATTER

Pilling wrote to many of his correspondents to get biographical sketches from them, which he included in his publications; in this he conformed to tradition on the one hand, and he became the first major biographer of North American students of Indian languages on the other. Tovar (1961) has introduced an iconographic feature in his bibliography, portraits of linguists done by camera. Biographical notes on authors are almost as old as bibliographies; for an example of Eskimo bio-bibliography which may have influenced Pilling see Erslew (1843–53).

A basis for American Indian historiography has been developing in a genre which includes obituaries and reminiscences, appreciations, and presentations of correspondence and diaries. Dissertations and theses now can be added to this list (Darnell 1967, 1969). Representative obituaries and reminiscences include Sapir (1931) on Bloomfield, Boas (1931, 1939) on Goddard and Sapir, Jakobson (1939) and Harrington (1945) on Boas, Hockett (1948, 1970) on Bloomfield, Rosing (1951) on Kleinschmidt, Voegelin (1961b) on Lowie and Kroeber (1967) on Goddard. For diary and correspondence material see as samples MacCurdy (1921–23) on W. W. Turner and C. Byington, Yampolsky (1958) and Rohner (1969) on Boas, and Sapir, Lowie and Lowie (1965) for Lowie's views of Sapir's letters to him.

A word should be added about revivals and rescues of manuscripts. Mrs. Lowie's edition of the work just mentioned fits into a pattern not yet adequately traced, but which would include such works as Canestrelli and Boas (1927), Boas (1927), Kroeber 1967), and Hockett (1946, 1970), which bring fresh perspectives to happily preserved data.

The sensitive work of Victor E. Hanzeli deserves separate mention. He has established himself in American Indian historiography with his study of *Missionary linguistics in New France* (Hanzeli 1969).

## SPECIAL BIBLIOGRAPHIES

Sometimes an obituary article ends with a complete bibliography. Sometimes an individual's bibliography appears separately, either after his death or in celebration of some event in his life. For examples of the latter type see Bright (1964b), Connors (1966) and Thompson (1967), dealing with Hoijer, Jacobs and Li.

Bibliographical works of relatively recent date relating to American Indian languages of North America have been general, as in the case of Wolff (1947) and Croft (1948), who dealt with a bibliography of bibliographies of spoken languages and with one on extinct languages, respectively, or in the case of Loriot (1964), who dealt with comparative linguistics (cf. Stark 1965 and Hoijer, Hamp and Bright 1965 for supplements); or they have been aimed at specific languages, families or areas, as in the case of Croft on Nahuatl (1953), supplemented by Ulving (1953), Callaghan (1958) on California Penutian (1958), Salzmann (1961) on Arapaho, Day (1961) on Saint Francis Abnaki, Adler (1961) on Chimakuan, Kutenai, Ritwan, Salishan and Wakashan, Pitkin (1962) on Wintun, Davis (1963) on Keresan, Loewen (1963) on Chocó Hymes (1964) on Na-Déné, Landar (1967c) on Athapaskan, and Bright (1967) on Middle American languages.

If we establish a special category on checklists, census lists, handbooks and maps, important aids in historiographical research, an enumeration becomes difficult because of the diversity of materials. There are articles, for example, on Indian languages at Haskell Institute (Stuart 1962, Kinkade 1970), on speakers of North American Indian languages (Chafe 1962, 1965), and on linguists studying North American Indian languages (Kinkade 1971).

C. F. and F. M. Voegelin (1964, 1965, 1966) have produced at Indiana University a monumental summary of classifications of languages of the world. Native America Fascicle One, *AnL* 6, no. 6, June, 1964, deals with North American languages. Native America Fascicle Two, *AnL* 7, no. 7, Oct., 1965, revises the North American classification and covers South American languages. A complete index was published in 1966.

*Current Anthropology* prepares an international directory of anthropology; the fifth was scheduled for publication in 1972 (cf. *CA*, Vol. 12, No. 3, June, 1971 for an information form and other data).

W. C. Sturtevant's map for languages of the United States was published by the Atlas of the United States. I first saw it with pleasure in Sturtevant's office; it replaces what has been published previously; it is not as extensive, however, as the North American wall map of C. F. and F. M. Voegelin available from the American Ethnological Society.

The maps of Meillet and Cohen (1924) are being revised for a new edition of *Les langues du monde*. We lack a cartobibliography of native tribes — all I can give here, as a small fraction of what would go into such a listing, are a few motley references: Voegelin and Voegelin (1944), North America; the maps in Swanton (1952), North America; maps for North and South America of Murdock (1960), O'Leary (1963), and Murdock and White (1969); Heizer (1966), California; Johnson (1940), Mexico and Central America; Departamento de Asuntos Indígenas (1944), Mexico (cf. Wonderly 1947); Loukotka (1936) Brazil (cf. Trager 1948); cf. Voegelin 1954 on Rowe's map of South America. William Sorsby's maps of North America, based largely on the Swanton maps, have appeared in *Current trends in linguistics*, Vol. 10, with a checklist of classifications and tribes which I have prepared.

## TYPOLOGY

In my essay on native Ibero-America I took pains to distinguish between history and historiography. It would be a mistake to talk simply about methods used to monitor linguistic data if that would cause us to lose sight of motive and milieu. What needs to be investigated, I think, is the influence of Humboldt on scholars, and the counter-influence of Boas, as they have lengthened their intellectual shadows over great stretches of time and research.

A.A. Hill (1952) has contributed to this necessary investigation by evaluating nineteenth-century biases. His note on Cherokee verbs of washing is almost unique in its genre.

If we can distinguish two perspectives in typology, the Humboldtian and the Boasian, we would have to put Tovar (1961) with the former, in his typological comments on South American languages. In regard to ethnosemantic typologies perhaps the same division could be made; I will list here samples of contributions which indicate contemporary directions and trends: Landar (1967b), Berlin (1967), Friedrich (1969); see Scheppers (1970) for some other examples. Especially nice is Price (1967).

Chomsky in reviewing Hockett (1955) criticizes typological procedures which do not require objective tests. This sharpness works, of course, also against the Humboldtians, even those who talk about universals that can be diagrammed as deep structures.

The study of language dynamics, the interactions of languages, has involved a number of specialists in American Indian languages who would interest the scholar challenging the notion of two perspectives in typology. Some have engaged computers in their work or have thought about the matter; cf. Newman (1954), Wells (1954), Saporta (1957), Pierce (1957), Voegelin (1957, 1961a), Yegerlehner, Voegelin et al. (1957), Kroeber (1960), Moore (1961), Voegelin, Voegelin and Hale (1962) and Voegelin, Voegelin, Wurm, O'Grady and Matsuda (1963). A recent North American typological study is Nichols (1971). Greenberg has pioneered in typological analysis. He holds that synchronic and diachronic analyses are mutually supportive in reconstruction and he considers languages of various tribes of the Americas in his demonstrations; see Greenberg (1960, 1965, 1969, 1970). Mary Haas devotes a chapter of *The prehistory of languages* (1969) to native North American areal studies. Darnell and Sherzer overlooked her important work in their historical sketch of 1971 but corrected their oversight with a special note (Darnell and Sherzer 1971a, 1971b).

## BIBLIOGRAPHY

ADLER, F.W. 1961. A bibliographical checklist of Chimakuan, Kutenai, Ritwan, Salishan, and Wakashan linguistics. IJAL 27.198–210.

AMERICAN ANTHROPOLOGICAL ASSOCIATION. 1916. Phonetic transcription of Indian languages, Report of Committee of American Anthropological Association. Smithsonian Misc. Coll. 66.1–15. Washington, D.C.

BARTON, BENJAMIN SMITH. 1797. New views of the origin of the tribes and nations of America. Philadelphia. [Revised, Philadelphia, 1798.]

BEELER, M. S. 1972. An extension of San Francisco Bay Costanoan? IJAL 39.49–54.

BELL, WHITFIELD J., Jr., and MURPHY D. SMITH. 1966. Guide to the archives and manuscript collections of the American Philosophical Society. Memoirs, vol. 66. Philadelphia.

BERLIN, BRENT. 1967. Categories of eating in Tzeltal and Navaho. IJAL 33.1–6.

BLOOMFIELD, LEONARD. 1939. Menomini morphophonemics. Études phonologiques dédiées à la mémoire de N. S. Trubetzkoy, Travaux du Cercle Linguistique de Prague, 8, 105–15. Prague.

BOAS, FRANZ. 1895. The North-Western tribes of Canada (10th report). Report of the Sixty-fifth Meeting of the British Association for the Advancement of Science, pp. 587–92. London.

——. 1917. Introductory. IJAL 1.1–8. [Boas identifies research problems, including grammatical categories, areal linguistics, and genetic classification. See Voegelin (1939).]

——. 1920. The classification of American languages. AmA 22.367–76.

——. 1927. Additional notes on the Kutenai language. IJAL 4.85–104.

——. 1929. Classification of American Indian languages. Lg 5.1–7.

——. 1931. Pliny Earle Goddard. IJAL 6.1–2.

——. 1939. Edward Sapir. IJAL 14.58–63.

BOGGS, R. S. 1949. Bibliography of Indian folklore texts in Latin America: 1948. IJAL 15.251–2.

BRIGHT, WILLIAM. 1960. Animals of acculturation in the California Indian languages. UCPL 4.215–46.

——. 1963a. Publicações do Museu Nacional: Série lingüística especial, No. 1. Rio de Janeiro, 1959. Pp. 263. IJAL 29.79–81.

——. 1963b. On American Indian languages from Latin American publications. IJAL 29.264–9.

——. 1963c. Latin American publications. IJAL 29.372–7.

——. 1964a. Studies in Californian linguistics. UCPL 34.

——. 1964b. A bibliography of the publications of Harry Hoijer through 1963. IJAL 30.169–74.

——. 1967. Inventory of descriptive materials. In Handbook of Middle American Indians 5, ed. by R. Wauchope, pp. 9–62. Austin.

BUTLER, RUTH, LAPHAM. 1941. A bibliographical check list of North and Middle American Indian linguistics in the Edward E. Ayer collection. Chicago. [Vol. 1, A-M; Vol. 2, N-Z. Reviewed and indexed for languages by C. F. Voegelin, IJAL 12.246–7 (1946).]

CALLAGHAN, CATHERINE A. 1958. California Penutian: History and bibliography. IJAL 24.189–94.

CANADA, Dept. of Resources and Development, National Parks Branch. 1952.

Publications of the National Museum of Canada (1913–1951). Ottawa. [A mimeographed Supplementary list to publications catalogue was issued in August, 1959.]

CANADIAN RESEARCH CENTER FOR ANTHROPOLOGY. 1967. Index décennal (auteurs et titres), Anthropologica, 1955–1965. Decennial index (authors and titles). Ottawa.

CANESTRELLI, PHILIPPO, and F. BOAS. 1927. Grammar of the Kutenai language. IJAL 4.1–84. [In Latin. See Boas (1927).]

CHAFE, WALLACE L. 1962. Estimates regarding the present speakers of North American Indian languages. IJAL 28.162–71.

———. 1965. Corrected estimates regarding speakers of Indian languages. IJAL 31.345–6.

CHOMSKY, NOAM. 1957. Review of A manual of phonology, by Charles F. Hockett. IJAL 23.223–34.

COHEN, MARCEL. 1928. Instructions d'enquête linguistique. Paris.

———. 1950. Questionnaire linguistique. Instructions. Mâcon.

———. 1951a. Questionnaire linguistique. A. Mâcon.

———. 1951b. Questionnaire linguistique. B. Mâcon.

COMMISSION D'ENQUÊTE LINGUISTIQUE, C.I.P.L. 1931. Questionnaires linguistiques (A et B). Nimèque.

CONNORS, MAUREEN E. 1966. A selected bibliography of Melville Jacobs through early 1966. IJAL 32.388–9.

CROFT, KENNETH. 1948. A guide to source material on extinct North American Indian languages. IJAL 14.260–8. [Printed and manuscript materials, supplementing Wolff (1947).]

———. 1953. Six decades of Nahuatl: A bibliographical contribution. IJAL 19.57–73. [Supplemented by Ulving (1953).]

DARNELL, REGNA. 1967. Daniel Garrison Brinton: An intellectual biography. (Unpublished M.A. thesis, Univ. of Penn.) Philadelphia.

———. 1969. The development of American anthropology 1880–1920: From the Bureau of American Ethnology to Franz Boas. (Unpublished Ph.D. diss., Univ. of Penn.) Philadelphia.

———, and JOEL SHERZER. 1971a. Areal linguistic studies in North America: A historical perspective. IJAL 37.20–8.

———. 1971b. Addendum. IJAL 37.202.

DAVIS, IRVINE. 1963. Bibliography of Keresan linguistic sources. IJAL 29.289–93.

DAY, GORDON M. 1961. A bibliography of the Saint Francis dialect. IJAL 27.80–5.

D'AZEVEDO, WARREN L., W. A. DAVIS, D. D. FOWLER, and W. SUTTLES. 1966. The current status of anthropological research in the Great Basin. Reno. [Reviewed by Joel Sherzer, IJAL 34.304–6. Includes W.R. Miller, Anthropological linguistics in the Great Basin, etc.]

DEPARTAMENTO DE ASUNTOS INDÍGENAS. 1944. Mapas lingüísticos de la República Mexicana. México, D.F. [Reviewed by Wonderly (1947).]

DEPARTMENT OF ANTHROPOLOGY, Indiana University. 1957. Research scope of the Archives of Languages of the World. IJAL 23.304–5.

DIEBOLD, A. RICHARD. 1960. Determining the centers of dispersal of language groups. IJAL 26.1–10. [Descendants of homeland Maya and Salish are mapped.]

ERSLEW, THOMAS HANSEN. 1843–53. Almindeligt Forfatter-Lexicon for Kongeriget Danmark med Tilhorende Bilande, fra 1814 til 1840. Copenhagen. [Biographies of authors of Denmark and adjacent lands who have written in Eskimo, and lists of their works.]

FELDMAN, LAWRENCE H. 1972. A note on the past geography of southern Chiapas Languages. IJAL 38.57–8.

FREEMAN, JOHN FINLEY. 1962. Manuscript sources on Latin American Indians in the Library of the American Philosophical Society. APS-P 106.530–40.

——, and MURPHY D. SMITH. 1966. A guide to manuscripts relating to the American Indian in the Library of the American Philosophical Society. Memoirs of the APS, vol. 65. Philadelphia. [Covers in 3995 entries native Ibero-American as well as other native American languages. The Introduction, pp. 1–14, includes the history of Jefferson's efforts and those of Duponceau as well as more recent efforts to build the linguistic collections. Bibliography, 393–407.]

FRIEDRICH, PAUL. 1969. On the meaning of the Tarascan suffixes of space. IJAL Memoir 23.

——. 1971. Dialectal variation in Tarascan phonology. IJAL 37.164–87.

GALLATIN, ALBERT. 1836. A synopsis of the Indian tribes within the United States east of the Rocky Mountains, and in the British and Russian possessions in North America. Archaeologia Americana, Transactions and Collections of the American Antiquarian Society, Vol. II. [Gallatin's map appears here, the first of its kind: Map of the Indian tribes of North America.]

——. 1848. Hale's Indians of north-west America, and vocabularies of North America; with an introduction. Transactions of the American Ethnological Society, 2.xxiii-clxxxviii, 1–130. [Map faces title-page: Sites of the Indian tribes of North America.]

GARVIN, PAUL L., ed. 1970. Method and theory in linguistics. Janua linguarum, series maior, 40. The Hague. [Proceedings of a conference held in 1966.]

——, and BERNARD SPOLSKY. 1966. Computation in linguistics: A case book. [This volume is part of the series: Indiana University Studies in the History and Theory of Linguistics. The editorial committee in 1966 included E.P. Hamp, D.H. Hymes, J. Lotz, C.A. Ferguson and T.A. Sebeok.]

GAUDEFROY-DEMOMBYNES, J. 1931. L'oeuvre linguistique de Humboldt. Paris.

GODDARD, IVES. ms (1972). Publications on North American Indian languages issued by the Smithsonian Institution. [To be published in a volume on linguis-

———, C. F. HOCKETT, and K. V. TEETER. 1972. Some errata in Bloomfield's Menomini. IJAL 38.1–5.

GREENBERG, JOSEPH H. 1960. A quantitative approach to the morphological typology of language. IJAL 26.178–94. [Ranks Eskimo, etc., for ten averages.]

———. 1965. Some generalizations concerning initial and final consonant clusters. Linguistics 3.5–34.

———. 1969. Methods of dynamic comparison in linguistics. Substance and structure of language, ed. by Jaan Puhvel, pp. 147–204. Los Angeles.

———. 1970. Some generalizations concerning glottalic consonants, especially implosives. IJAL 36.123–45.

HAAS, MARY. 1969. The prehistory of languages. The Hague.

HAMP, ERIC P. 1972. Brief mention. IJAL 38.78–9. [Review of W.R. Miller's chapter on Language, with 15 pp. of bibliography, p. 78.]

HANZELI, V. E. 1969. Missionary linguistics in New France. A study of 17th and 18th century descriptions of American Indian languages. The Hague. [Review by H. Landar, 1971, Linguistics, 75.100–6.]

HARRINGTON, JOHN P. 1945. Boas on the science of language. IJAL 11.97–9. [See Jakobson (1939).]

HARVARD UNIVERSITY. 1963. Catalogue of the Library of the Peabody Museum of Archaeology and Ethnology, Harvard University. Authors, 26 vols. Subjects, 26 vols. and 1 vol. index. Boston.

———. 1963. Library of the Peabody Museum of Archaeology and Ethnology, Harvard University. Index to Subject headings. Boston.

———. 1970. Catalogue of the Library of the Peabody Museum of Archaeology and Ethnology, Harvard University. First Supplement. Authors. Boston. 6 vols. [About 64,800 entries made in 1963–69.]

HEIZER, ROBERT F. 1966. Languages, territories and names of California Indian tribes. Berkeley.

HEWSON, JOHN. 1972. Errata in Bloomfield's Algonquian sketch. IJAL 38.77.

HILL, ARCHIBALD A. 1952. A note on primitive languages. IJAL 18.172–7.

HILL, KENNETH. 1963. On American Indian languages from North American publications. IJAL 29.269–73.

HOCKETT, CHARLES F. 1946. Sapir on Arapaho. IJAL 12.243–5. [Edited from material given to Hockett by Swadesh in 1939.]

———. 1948. Implications of Bloomfield's Algonquian studies. Lg 24.117–31.

———. 1955. A manual of phonology. IJAL Memoir 11. [Discusses phonological typology. Reviewed by Chomsky (1957).]

———. 1970. A Leonard Bloomfield anthology. Bloomington. [Extracts of letters to B. Bloch and C.F. Hockett, 367–9, with perspectives on Algonquian data passim.

Corrected version of Algonquian study (1946) in Linguistic structures of native America. ed. by H. Hoijer et al., pp. 440-88. Viking Fund Publications in Anthropology 6. New York; Menomini morphophonemics (1939), 351-62; Menomini excerpt, 489-90; revision of Hockett (1948), 495-511.]
HODGE, FREDERICK WEBB, ed. 1907, 1910. Handbook of American Indians North of Mexico. BAE-B 30, Parts I and II. Republished by Rowman and Littlefield, New York, 1965.
HOIJER, HARRY. 1941. Methods in the classification of American Indian languages. Language, culture and personality, ed. by L. Spier, A. Hallowell and S. Newman, pp. 3-14. Menasha. [Powell's classification is taken as a first stage, historically, followed by one marked by descriptions, such as those of Gatschet, Dorsey and others. Sapir's methods and Boas's views are discussed.]
——. 1946. Introduction. Linguistic structures of native America, ed. by H. Hoijer, pp. 9-29. Viking Fund Publications in Anthropology, 6. New York. [Contains a conservative summary history of classifications.]
——. 1952a. Review of Linguistic bibliography for the years 1939-1947. Vol. I, 1949, Vol. II, 1950. IJAL 18.49.
——. 1952b. Review of Linguistic Bibliography for the year 1948 and Supplement for the years 1939-1947. IJAL 18.268-9.
——, E.P. Hamp, and W. BRIGHT. 1965. Contributions to a bibliography of comparative Amerindian. IJAL 31.346-53. [Supplements Loriot (1964) for all native American languages.]
HYMES, DELL, H. 1956. Review of Lingua Posnaniensis, Revue de Philologie Comparée et Linguistique Générale. Vol. I-V, 1949-55. IJAL 22.281-7.
——. 1958. Tradition trend in archaeology and linguistics. SJA 14.152-5. [Discusses shift of Wishram and Wasco tense-elaborate verbal system, from Chinookan aspect system, in the context of tradition trend.]
——. 1963. Notes toward a history of linguistic anthropology. AnL 5(2).59-103.
——. 1964. General bibliography. IJAL 30.165-8. [Covers Na-Déné references in IJAL 30, no. 2.]
——, ed. 1965. The use of computers in anthropology. The Hague.
——. 1969. Review of Language in relation to a unified theory of the structure of human behavior, by K.L. Pike. AmA 71.361-3. [Notes on Pike, Sapir, Trager, Hall.]
——. 1970. Linguistic method in ethnography: Its development in the United States, Method and theory in linguistics, ed. by P.L. Garvin, pp. 249-325. The Hague.
INSTITUTO NACIONAL INDIGENISTA. 1950. Densidad de la población de habla indígena en la República Mexicana. (Memorias del Instituto Nacional Indigenista, Vol. 1, No. 1.) Mexico. [Reviewed by H. Hoijer 1951. IJAL 17.134.]
JAKOBSON, ROMAN. 1939. Franz Boas' approach to language. IJAL 10.188-95. [Monitoring the milieu. This fine essay prompted Harrington's response of 1945.]
JAQUITH, JAMES R. 1970. The present status of the Uto-Aztekan languages of

Mexico. An index of data bearing on their survival, geographical location and internal relationships. Katunob. Occasional Publications in Mesoamerican Anthropology, No. 5, 1970. Greeley, Colorado, University of Northern Colorado, Museum of Anthropology.

JENNESS, DIAMOND. $1934^2$. The Indians of Canada. National Museum of Canada. Bull. 65, Anth. Ser., No. 15. Ottawa.

JOHNSON, FREDERICK. 1940. The linguistic map of Mexico and Central America. The Maya and their neighbors, ed. by C.L. Hay et al., pp. 88–114. New York.

JUDD, NEIL M. 1967. The Bureau of American Ethnology. Norman.

KINKADE, M. DALE. 1970. Indian languages at Haskell Institute. IJAL 36.46–52.

——. 1971. Roster of linguists studying North American Indian languages. IJAL 37.114–21.

KLOKEID, TERRY J. 1969. Index to AL 1 (1959)-10 (1968). AnL 11.24–47.

KROEBER, A.L. 1925. Handbook of the Indians of California. BAE-B 78. Republished by the California Book Co., Ltd., Berkeley, 1953.

——. 1960. On typological indices I: Ranking of languages. IJAL 26.171–7.

——. 1967. Goddard's California Athabascan texts. IJAL 33.269–75. [Edited by H. Landar.]

KUTSCHER, G. 1958. Ein von Walter Lehmann gesammeltes mexicanomärchen und vokabular (Mexicano de Chilapa, Staat Guerrero). Miscellanea Rivet 1.533–71. Mexico.

LAMB, SYDNEY M. 1965. Linguistic data processing. The use of computers in anthropology, ed. by D. Hymes, pp. 159–88. The Hague. [Discusses computer simulation of language change and language area dynamics, pp. 178–82. Refers to Siouans, Algonkians, Northern Athapaskans, p. 180.]

LANDAR, HERBERT. 1967a. Bibliographic note: Quiché. IJAL 33.76–8.

——. 1967b. Ten'a classificatory verbs. IJAL 33.263–8.

——. 1967c. Two Athapaskan verbs of being (with annotated bibliography). The verb 'Be' and its synonyms, ed. by J.W.M. Verhaar. FL, Supplementary Series, Vol. 1, Pt. 1. 40–74. Dordrecht.

——. 1969. Review of the Carib language, by B.J. Hoff. AmA 71.995–6.

——. 1972a. The language of Friendly Village. IJAL 38.55–7.

——. 1972b. Nutltleik. IJAL 38.208–9. [Response to R. Wilmeth on Friendly Village.]

——. 1973. The tribes and languages of North America: A checklist. CTL 10. 1251–1441. The Hague.

LOEWEN, JACOB A. 1963. Chocó I: Introduction and bibliography. IJAL 29.239–63. [Annotated bibliography, pp. 246–63, covering many historiographically relevant sources.]

LORIOT, JAMES. 1964. A selected bibliography of comparative American Indian linguistics. IJAL 30.62–80.

LOUKOTKA, ČESTMIR. 1936. Mapa de distribuicão dos idiomas indígenas no Brasil.

Revista do Arquivo Municipal de São Paulo. São Paulo. [Indexed by Trager 1948.]

——. 1942. Klassifikation der südamerikanischen Sprachen. Zethn 74.1–69. Berlin. [A rare item, most copies having been destroyed by bombing.]

——. 1950. Les langues de la famille Tupi-Guarani. Universidade de São Paulo, Faculdade de Filosofia, Ciências e Letras, Boletim 104, Etnografia e Lingua Tupi-Guarani, No. 16. São Paulo. [Reviewed by N.P. Smith, IJAL 17.193–5.]

MACCURDY, GEORGE GRANT. 1921–23. American linguistics in 1852. IJAL 2.74–5. [On C. Byington's Choctaw grammar, offered in 1852 to the BAE but published by the APS, ed. by D.G. Brinton, in 1870. Includes a letter of William W. Turner to Edward E. Salisbury, one of Byington's referees. Turner had classified American vocabularies for A.W. Whipple's Report: see p. 75. Turner also translated some of Humboldt for Gallatin.]

MANDELBAUM, D.G., ed. 1950. Selected writings of Edward Sapir in language, culture, and personality. Berkeley. [For a summary of the linguistic contents see IJAL 17.135 (1951).]

MANSUR GUÉRIOS. 1948–49. Dicionário das tribos e línguas indígenas da América meridional. Museu Paranaense, Publicações avulsas, No. 6. Tomo I, A, pp. 1–63; Tomo II, B-Cax, pp. 65–141. Curitiba. [Reviewed by Z. Salzmann, IJAL 17. 192–3 (1951). The final vol. will be a bibliography.]

MAYERS, MARVIN K., ed. 1966. Languages of Guatemala. The Hague.

MEILLET, ANTOINE, and MARCEL COHEN. 1924. Les langues du monde. (Collection linguistique publiée par la Société de Linguistique de Paris, XVI.) Paris. [Evaluated by C.C. Uhlenbeck, IJAL 4.114–6 (1927).]

MOHRMANN, CHRISTINE, F. NORMAN, and A. SOMMERFELT. 1963. Trends in modern linguistics. Utrecht. [Reviewed by A.A. Hill, IJAL 32.198–201 (1966). Contains H. Hoijer, Anthropological linguistics, 110–27; cf. also E.P. Hamp, General linguistics — the United States in the fifties, 165–95.]

——, ALF SOMMERFELT, and JOSHUA WHATMOUGH. 1961. Trends in European and American linguistics 1930–1960. Utrecht.

MOORE, BRUCE R. 1961. A statistical morpho-syntactic typology study of Colorado (Chibcha). IJAL 27.298–307.

MURDOCK, G.P. 1960. An ethnographic bibliography of North America. 3rd ed. New Haven.

——. 1967. Ethnographic Atlas: A summary. Ethnology 6.109–236. [North America, 218 societies; South and Central America, 89 societies. A bibliographical aid and guide to field-work opportunities with 862 societies. Coded on 170–233 are among others items 277–412, American societies. Column 64: Linguistic Affiliation, e.g. Mapuche is Ac or Araucanian.]

——. 1970. Kin term patterns and their distribution. Ethnology 9.165–207. [Some 220 American Indian tribes or groups (77 from South America) are tabulated, pp. 198–207.]

——, and Douglas R. White. 1969. Standard cross-cultural sample. Ethnology 8.329–69. [Maps for 65 sample American societies, pp. 346–7. On pp. 363–8 are items 122–86, for American societies. A sample item is (p. 368):
> 184. Mapuche (Sg2: 195) of Province 198 (Araucanians). Language: Aruacanian. Economy: A. Organization: I, P. Focus: The Mapuche in the vicinity of Temuco (38°30'S, 72°35'W) in 1950, just prior to Faron's field work. HRAF: SG4(c). Authorities: Faron, Hilger, Titiev.

This article reports on the first research results of the Cross-Cultural Cumulative Coding Center, established at the University of Pittsburgh, May, 1968, with NSF support.]

Newman, Stanley. 1954. Suggestions on the archiving of linguistic material. IJAL 20.111–5. [Data on Yokuts and Zuni.]

Nichols, Johanna. 1971. Diminutive consonant symbolism in western North America. Lg 47.826–48.

O'Leary, Timothy J. 1963. Ethnographic bibliography of South America. New Haven.

Perchonock, Norma, and Oswald Werner. 1969. Navaho systems of classification: Some implications for ethnoscience. Ethnology 8.229–42.

Pierce, Joe E. 1957. A statistical study of consonants in New World languages I: Introduction. IJAL 23.36–45.

——. 1962. Possible electronic computation of typological indices for linguistic structures. IJAL 28.215–26.

——, and James M. Ryherd. 1964. The status of Athapaskan research in Oregon. IJAL 30.137–43. [Census and survey of bibliographic items.]

Pilling, James Constantine. 1885. Proof-sheets of a bibliography of the languages of the North American Indians. Washington, D.C. Republished by Central Book Co., Inc., Brooklyn, N.Y., 1966.

——. 1887a. Bibliography of the Eskimo language. BAE-B 1.

——. 1887b. Bibliography of the Siouan languages. BAE-B 5.

——. 1888. Bibliography of the Iroquoian languages. BAE-B 6.

——. 1889. Bibliography of the Muskhogean languages. BAE-B 9.

——. 1891. Bibliography of the Algonquian languages. BAE-B 13. [Issued in February, 1892.]

——. 1892. Bibliography of the Athapascan languages. BAE-B 14.

——. 1893a. Bibliography of the Chinookan languages (including the Chinook Jargon). BAE-B 15.

——. 1893b. Bibliography of the Salishan languages. BAE-B 16.

——. 1894. Bibliography of the Wakashan languages. BAE-B 19.

Pinnow, Heinz-Jürgen. 1964. Die nordamerikanischen Indianersprachen: Ein Überblick über ihren Bau und ihre Besonderheiten. Wiesbaden.

Pitkin, Harvey. 1962. A bibliography of the Wintun family of languages. IJAL 28.43–54.

POTTIER, BERNARD. 1967. Bibliographie américaniste: Linguistique amérindienne, 1. Paris.
——. 1969. Bibliographie américaniste: Linguistique amérindienne, 2. Paris.
POWELL, JOHN WESLEY. 1877. Introduction to the study of Indian languages, with words, phrases, and sentences to be collected. Washington, D.C.
——. 1880. Introduction to the study of Indian languages with words, phrases and sentences to be collected. Second edition — with charts. Washington, D.C.
——. 1891. Indian linguistic families of America north of Mexico. BAE-R 7.1–142. [Issued in May or June, 1892.]
PRICE, P. DAVID. 1967. Two types of taxonomy: A Huichol ethnobotanical example. AnL 9(7).1–28.
RIOUX, LOUIS-PHILIPPE MARCEL, JACQUES ROUSSEAU, and JEAN-PAUL VINAY. 1954. Centre de recherches d'anthropologie amerindienne de l'Université d'Ottawa. Instructions pour une enquête ethno-linguistique. Ottawa. 5 vols.
RIVET, P., G. STRESSER-PÉAN, and Č. LOUKOTKA. 1952. Les langues de l'Amérique. Les langues du monde, ed. by A. Meillet and Marcel Cohen, 2.941–1097.
ROBINETT, FLORENCE M. 1954. First report on the Archives of Languages of the World. IJAL 20.241–7. [Inventory, native North America, 242–5, native South America, 245. A second report appeared in IJAL 21.83–8.]
ROBINSON, DOW F. 1968. Manual for bilingual dictionaries. Volume one. Textbook. Santa Ana. [Designed for Summer Institute of Linguistics students of Middle American languages and others, especially in Latin America.]
——. 1969a. Manual for bilingual dictionaries. Volume two. Word list: A-L. Santa Ana. [In Spanish.]
——. 1969b. Manual for bilingual dictionaries. Volume three. Word list: LL-Z. Santa Ana. [In Spanish.]
ROHNER, RONALD P. 1969. The ethnography of Franz Boas. Letters and diaries of Franz Boas written on the Northwest Coast from 1886 to 1931. Chicago.
ROSING, OTTO. 1951. Kleinschmidt Centennial II: Samuel Petrus Kleinschmidt. IJAL 17.63–5. [W. D. Preston's translation of the Danish text.]
RUTHERFORD, PHILLIP R. 1968. A bibliography of American doctoral dissertations in linguistics: 1900–1965. Washington, D.C. [A Center for Applied Linguistics publication. The linguistic Society of America adds titles every year, in the LSA Bulletin. These titles will be cumulated every three to five years into a Supplement to Rutherford's work.]
SALZMANN, ZDENĚK. 1951. Review of Klassifikation der südamerikanischen Sprachen, by Čestmír Loukotka, ZEthn. 74.1–69 (1942). IJAL 17.259–66. [Indexes Loukotka's work.]
——. 1961. Bibliography of works on the Arapaho division of Algonquian. IJAL 27.183–7.
SAPIR, EDWARD. 1911. An anthropological survey of Canada. Science 34.789–93. [Sapir credits Boas in his work for the British Association for the Advancement

of Science and G.M. Dawson in his work for Geological Surveys with fathering Canadian ethnology. Both collected linguistic as well as other materials.]

———. 1917. Linguistic publications of the Bureau of American Ethnology, a general review. IJAL 1.76–81. [Summary and evaluation. Hopes for success of the phonetic scheme of the American Anthropological Association; q.v. (1916). Note now Goddard (ms. 1972).]

———. 1931. The concept of phonetic law as tested in primitive languages by Leonard Bloomfield. Methods in social science, a case book, ed. by Stuart A. Rice, pp. 297–306, reprinted in Selected writings of Edward Sapir, ed. by D.G. Mandelbaum, Berkeley, 1950.

———, ROBERT H. LOWIE, and LUELLA COLE LOWIE, ed. 1965. Letters from Edward Sapir to Robert H. Lowie. With an introduction and notes by Robert H. Lowie. Berkeley. [R.H. Lowie's essay evaluating Sapir's life and work, pp. 2–14, was written in 1956.]

SAPORTA, SOL. 1957. Methodological considerations regarding a statistical approach to typologies. IJAL 23.109–13.

SCHEPPERS, EMILE. 1970. Some abstracts on lexical/semantic fields and ethnosemantics. IJAL 26.216–9.

SCHMECKEBIER, LAURENCE F. 1927. The Office of Indian Affairs: Its history, activities and organization. Baltimore.

SCHULLER, RUDOLF. 1931a. Materiales para el estudio de las lenguas aborígines del sur de Colombia, Suramerica. IJAL 6.34–6. [Describes materials in the library of Guillermo Valencia, in Popayán, Colombia.]

———. 1931b. Breve contribución a la bibliografía del idioma K'ak'čiq'el. Dialecto Maya-K'ičé de Guatemala. IJAL 6.37–40. [Manuscripts held by Daniel Sánchez García in El Salvador.]

———. 1931c. Beitrag zur bibliographie der sprache der Totonaca-Idianer. IJAL 6.41–2. [On manuscripts in the Gates collection, Tulane University.]

SEBEOK, THOMAS A. 1945. Index to volumes I to X. IJAL 11.1–12.

———. 1958. Review of Bibliographie des langues Aymara et Kičua. By Paul Rivet and Georges de Crequi-Montfort. IJAL 24.79–82. [A progressive philosophy of American linguistic bibliography is presented.]

SHAFER, ROBERT. 1967. A bibliography of Uto-Aztecan with a note on biogeography. IJAL 33.148–59.

SHERZER, JOEL. 1968. An areal-typological study of the American Indian languages north of Mexico. (Unpublished Ph.D. Diss., Univ. of Penna.) Philadelphia. [Devises "a framework for areal mapping."]

SIEBERT, F. 1967. The original home of the Proto-Algonquian people. In Contributions to Anthropology: Linguistics I (Algonquian). National Museum of Canada. Bulletin 214. Anthropological Series, 78.13–47.

SIEGEL, BERNARD J., ed. 1970. Biennial review of anthropology. Stanford.

STARK, LOUISA. 1965. Further bibliography on Quechumaran. IJAL 31.192-3. [Supplements Loriot (1964).]
——. 1970. Abstracts from Latin American publications. IJAL 36.53-6.
STEVENS, WALLACE. 1949. An ordinary evening in New Haven. (Transactions of the Connecticut Academy of Arts and Sciences 38.151-172, issued separately). New Haven. [The address of Edwin R. Goodenough (which touches on Benjamin Franklin's philosophy) is on pp. 154-5.]
STUART, C. I. J. M. 1962. American Indian languages at Haskell Institute. IJAL 28.151.
STURTEVANT, WILLIAM C. 1959. Authorship of the Powell linguistic classification. IJAL 25.196-8.
SUMMER, INSTITUTE OF LINGUISTICS. 1947. Linguistic and ethnographic bibliography of members of the Summer Institute of Linguistics. [Ann Arbor?]. [Reviewed by W. L. Wonderly, IJAL 14.61 (1948).]
SWADESH, MORRIS. 1936-38. Investigaciones Lingüísticas, Organo del Instituto Mexicano de Investigaciones Lingüísticas, 1933-. Mexico, D. F. Cuadernos Lingüísticos, Supplemento Escolar de "Investigaciones Lingüísticas". IJAL 9. 120-2. [Partial list of contents, 121-2.]
——. 1938. Bibliography of American Indian linguistics, 1936-1937. Lg 14.318-23.
——. 1963. A punchcard system of cognate hunting. IJAL 29.283-8.
SWANTON, JOHN R. 1915. Linguistic position of the tribes of southern Texas and northeastern Mexico. AmA 17.17-40.
——. 1952. The Indian tribes of North America. BAE-B 145. Republished by the Scholarly Press, Grosse Pointe, Mich., 1968.
TAX, SOL. 1948. Manuscripts on Middle American languages and cultures. IJAL 14.53-5. [Discusses the microfilm series on Middle American Linguistics and Cultural Anthropology, sponsored by the National Research Council, Committee on Latin American Anthropology, processed by the Library of the University of Chicago as Microfilm Collection of Manuscript Materials on Middle American Cultural Anthropology.]
THARP, GEORGE W. 1972. The position of the Tsetsaut among Northern Athapaskans. IJAL 38.14-25.
THOMAS, CYRUS, and J. R. SWANTON. 1911. Indian languages of Mexico and Central America and their geographical distribution. BAE-B 44.
THOMPSON, L. C. 1967. A bibliography of the publications of Fang-Kuei Li through 1967. IJAL 36.212-14.
TOVAR, ANTONIO. 1961. Catálogo de las lenguas de América del Sur. Buenos Aires. [Reviewed by Jorge A. Suárez, IJAL 28.286-93, with criticism of Tovar's typological notes, 288 ff.]
TRAGER, GEORGE L. 1945. Index to volume 11. IJAL 11.251-61. [Trager's system of classification, on which see SIL passim, is incorporated in this index.]
——. 1948. The Indian languages of Brazil. IJAL 14.43-8. [Discusses earlier maps

of Brazilian languages. Uses Loukotka's classification and indexes the map.]

ULVING, TOR. 1953. Additions to Croft's Six decades of Nahuatl. IJAL 19.245-6.

VAILLANCOURT, LOUIS-PHILIPPE. 1957. L'origine des caracters syllabiques. Anthropologica 5.125-9. Ottawa. [Cree syllabary history.]

VOEGELIN, C.F. 1939. Continuation of International Journal of American Linguistics. IJAL 10.109-112. [Summary of Boas (1917) with notes.]

———. 1941. North American Indian languages still spoken and their genetic relationships. Language, culture and personality: Essays in memory of Edward Sapir, ed. by Leslie Spier, A. Irving Hallowell and Stanley S. Newman, pp. 15-40. Menasha.

———. 1954. A map of the Indian tribes of South America. IJAL 20.241. [On John Howland Rowe's map. Rowe has helped in dissemination and collection of scout lists based on Swadesh's glottochronological basic vocabularies, done in Spanish and used in South America.]

———. 1957. Six statements for a phonemic inventory. IJAL 23.78-84.

———. 1958. Linguistic perimeters in Latin America. Miscellanea Rivet 1.197-208. Mexico. [Typological analysis of phonologies of languages of Mexico, Central and South America, including Totonac, Nahuatl, Cuna, Huichol, Chatino, Aguatec, Mixteco, Cuitlateco and Proto-Otomi. Describes archived phonological analyses at the Archives of Languages of the World.]

———. 1960. Abstracts and translations: An announcement. IJAL 26.357. [Inaugurated under editorship of Dell H. Hymes.]

———. 1961a. Typology of density ranges II: Contrastive and non-contrastive syntax. IJAL 27.287-97. [Towards a typology for sentences.]

———. 1961b. Review of Robert H. Lowie ethnologist: A personal record. IJAL 27.180-82.

———. 1968. MLA bibliography. IJAL 34.231. [Announces Rudolph C. Troike's position as MLA bibliographer for the MLA International Bibliography, with responsibility for native languages of North and South America. (In 1967 the Modern Language Association began its separate treatment of American Indian languages).]

———. 1971. Conference on Salish languages. IJAL 37.213. [Announces the Sixth Conference on Salish Languages.]

———. 1972a. SECOL VI (Sixth semi-annual meeting of the Southeastern Conference On Linguistics), April 20-22, 1972, University of Georgia, Athens, Georgia. IJAL 38.81.

———. 1972b. APS grants. IJAL 38.81.

———, and ZELLIG HARRIS. 1945. Index to the Franz Boas collection of materials for American linguistics. (Lg Monograph 21.) Baltimore.

———, and E.W. VOEGELIN. 1944. Map of North American Indian languages. (AES Pub. No. 20.) New York. [Reviewed by G.L. Trager, IJAL 11.186-9 (1945).]

——, and F. M. VOEGELIN. 1963. On the history of structuralizing in 20th century America. AnL 5(2).12–37.
——. 1964. Languages of the world: Native America fascicle one. AnL 6(6).1–149.
——. 1965. Languages of the world: Native America fascicle two. AnL 7(7).1–150.
——. 1966. Index of languages of the world. AnL 8.i-xiv, 1–202.
VOEGELIN, C. F. and F. M., and KENNETH L. HALE. 1962. Typological and comparative grammar of Uto-Aztecan: I (Phonology). (IJAL Memoir 17.) Baltimore. [Reviewed by Henry M. Hoenigswald, IJAL 28.210–13 (1962).]
VOEGELIN, C.F. and F.M., STEPHEN WURM, GEOFFREY O'GRADY, and TOKUICHIRO MATSUDA. 1963. Obtaining an index of phonological differentiation from the construction of non-existent minimax systems. IJAL 29.4–28. [Uto-Aztecan, Kiowa-Tanoan, Siouan and Athapaskan are treated, as well as other languages.]
VOEGELIN, C. F., A. K. RAMANUJAN, and F. M. VOEGELIN. 1960. Typology of density ranges I: Introduction. IJAL 26.198–205.
WELLS, RULON. 1954. Archiving and language typology. IJAL 20.101–7.
WERNER, OSWALD. 1965. Index for abstracts and translations, with number prefixed to each. IJAL 31.60–91.
——. 1966. Computers and anthropological linguistics. Computation in linguistics, ed. by P.L. Garvin and B. Spolsky, pp. 1–41. [Discusses specific computer programs and routines as applied to Navaho and other linguistic data.]
WOLF, HANS. 1947. Bibliography of bibliographies of North American Indian languages still spoken. IJAL 13.268–82.
WONDERLY, WILLIAM L. 1947. Review of Mapas lingüísticos de la República Mexicana. IJAL 13.122–5. [Census figures for speakers of "each of the Indian languages of Mexico", 123–5. Note 1, p. 123, contains a history of maps of or including Mexico, starting with that of Orozco y Berra (1864) and ending with that of Frederick Johnson (1940).]
——, and EUGENE A. NIDA. 1963. Linguistics and Christian missions. AnL 5(2). 104–44. [On the Americas see esp. pp. 125, 133, 135.]
YAMPOLSKY, HELENE BOAS. 1958. Excerpts from the letter diary of Franz Boas on his first field trip to the Northwest Coast. IJAL 24.312–20.
YEGERLEHNER, JOHN, FLORENCE M. VOEGELIN, et al. 1957. Frequencies and inventories of phonemes from nine languages. IJAL 23.85–93. [F. M. Voegelin: Hidatsa, G. Hubert Matthews: Winnebago, John Yegerlehner: Shawnee, Gordon Hirschy: Choctaw, Jerry Hopkins: Havasupai, Kenneth Hale: Navaho, Kathryn C. Keller: Mayan Chontal, Alan Wares: Tarascan.]
ZISA, CHARLES A. 1970. American Indian languages; classifications and list. Center for Applied Linguistics: ERIC Clearinghouse for Linguistics. Washington, D.C.

# AREAL GROUPINGS

# AREAL LINGUISTICS IN NORTH AMERICA

JOEL SHERZER

0. INTRODUCTION

At a conference on the *Universals of language* held in 1961, Roman Jakobson (1966: 274) stated that:

We most urgently need a systematic world-wide mapping of linguistic structural properties: distinctive features, inherent and prosodic — their types of concurrence and concatenation; grammatical concepts and the principles of their expression. The primary and less difficult task would be to prepare a phonemic atlas of the world.

With particular regard to North American Indian languages, Dell Hymes (1956) observed that such work was but in its initial stages and that what was greatly needed was a detailed study of the distribution of the phonological and morphological characteristics of North American Indian languages. The need was restated in Hymes' discussion (1961) of the pioneering work of Dixon and Kroeber. Emeneau (1953) also calls for the mapping of linguistic traits in North America.

This study attempts to respond to the needs made explicit by these scholars.[1] It will deal with the following topics:

1. The history of areal-typological studies in North America.

2. A framework for the presentation of areal linguistic phenomena and a discussion of the *culture area* and *linguistic area* approaches to culture and language.

3. A determination of the linguistic areas north of Mexico and a comparison of these with the culture areas north of Mexico, together with a discussion of the types of *sociolinguistic* or *communicative conditions* which gave rise to the various linguistic areas.

---

[1] This article is a revision and expansion of Chapters 1, 2, and 26 of my unpublished Ph.D. dissertation: *An areal-typological study of the American Indian languages north of Mexico*, University of Pennsylvania, 1968. In that study, the distributions of many phonological and morphological traits were investigated, using Driver's 'culture areas of North America' (1961) as a frame of reference. In the discussion of these distributions, an attempt was made to determine the relative roles of genetic relationship and language contact. Finally, linguistic areas were delineated on the basis of a number of diagnostic traits and these linguistic areas were compared with the culture areas. It is the results of this research which are reported here. The original research was supported by a Woodrow Wilson Dissertation Fellowship. More recent work has been supported by NSF-USDP Grant GU-1598. I would like to thank William Bright, Regna Darnell, Mary Haas, Dell Hymes, William H. Jacobsen, Jr., Michael Krauss, Brian Stross, and Rudolph Troike for their many helpful comments.

4. Implications of results for problems in North American Indian language history and for a theory of language change.

5. Suggestions for future research: ethnohistorical, linguistic, and sociolinguistic.

## 1. AREAL LINGUISTIC STUDIES IN NORTH AMERICA: AN HISTORICAL PERSPECTIVE

Similarities among languages are due to one of four causes:
a) retentions from a common ancestor
b) universals of linguistic structure
c) independent convergent development
d) diffusion

In the field of North American Indian linguistics, most discussion of language history has been concerned with a). People have argued about how many families or stocks there are in North America, if and how these families are related to one another (problems of relationship at great time depth), and how they are internally subdivided (problems of subclassification). Concern with b) has grown rapidly in recent years and implications for a study of language history have been drawn (see Greenberg 1966; Kiparsky 1968). Although c) and d) have received relatively little attention in the study of American Indian languages and, unfortunately, have often been viewed in opposition to a), we can nonetheless indicate the existence of an interest in areal-typological problems.

### 1.1 *The Areal and Typological Perspective of American Indian Linguistics in the Early Part of the 20th Century*

One of the reactions of Franz Boas against the evolutionary and psychological generalizations of the period which preceded him was to insist on the treatment of each language and culture in its own right, rather than forcing descriptions into supposed stages in the development of man. Grammars written by Boas or those influenced by him reflect the Boas point of view. These grammars describe the linguistic processes possessed by the language in question, contrasting them with languages in the area with which they disagree and showing similarities with other languages when they occur. In this sense, the Boas style might be termed 'areal-typological' as distinct from the 'diachronic' styles which were used previously.[2] The latter often merged synchrony and diachrony in the same study.

Contemporary readers of grammars written in the early 20th century might be surprised at the references made in the body of the text to other languages in the area.

---

[2] Boas' approach to linguistics seems to have been modelled on his approach to folklore (Dell Hymes, personal communication).

One might even be led to suspect that Boas' interest was in proving diffusion directly within grammatical descriptions. Actually, Boas' great concern with diffusion of grammatical traits came later, in his arguments with Sapir. The typological concern in the Boas-style grammar is in the tradition of von Humboldt and Steinthal, who greatly influenced Boas. Boas, with these predecessors, apparently believed that a grammar should represent the way(s) in which a particular group of people viewed and verbalized the world around them. Such a grammar is of course entirely synchronic; it is not at all concerned with how the linguistic structures described in it originated. The areal perspective in the Boas style is also essentially synchronic. It gives the reader a perspective by informing him of the ways in which this new language is similar to or differs from languages with which he may be familiar. The possibility of diffusion might be implicit; it is not explicit in the Boas style. It is, in fact, in Dixon, Kroeber, and Sapir that we find the transition from the Boasian areal-typological style of grammar writing to actual discussions of diffusion.

There are many examples of grammatical descriptions written with the areal-typological perspective. In the context of his "Notes on the Chemakum language" (1892), Boas discusses the occurrence of pronominal gender on the Northwest Coast. Boas' "Sketch of the Kwakiutl language" (1900) describes the grammatical processes of Kwakiutl in the context of the grammatical processes found in other languages of North America. Swanton's "Morphology of the Chinook verb" (1900) provides a general picture of Northwest Coast phonetics and shows the ways in which Chinook differs from other Northwest Coast languages. Kroeber's "The Washo language of east central California" (1907) is perhaps the best example of what is called here the areal-typological style of grammar writing. In this study, Kroeber refers constantly to other California languages and attempts to define Washo's areal and typological status within California. We are told that although the language exhibits the central California phonetic type, it is only partially included within the central California morphological type. Kroeber's "The languages of the coast of California south of San Francisco" (1904), and "The languages of the coast of California north of San Francisco" (1911b) are also both written in the areal-typological style. In Boas' "Tsimshian" (1911:296) there is an attempt to place Tsimshian within the framework of North American Indian languages:

In this respect Tsimshian resembles the Athapascan with its groups of verbal stems, the Salish and Takelma with their modes of reduplication, and the Iroquois with its classes of verbs.

Sapir is clearly in the tradition of his teacher Boas when he writes of Takelma (1922:8):

In its general phonetic character, at least as regards relative harshness or smoothness of acoustic effect, Takelma will probably be found to occupy a position about midway between the characteristically rough languages of the Columbia valley and the North California and Oregon coast (Chinookan, Salish, Alsea, Coos, Athapascan, Yurok) on the one hand, and the relatively euphonious languages of the Sacramento valley (Maidu, Yana, Wintun) on the other, inclining rather to the latter than to the former.

In concluding his discussion of Takelma, he writes (282):

> Some of the more important of these typical or at any rate widespread American traits, that are found in Takelma, are: the incorporation of the pronominal (and nominal) object in the verb; the incorporation of the possessive pronouns in the noun; the closer association with the verb-form of the object than the subject; the inclusion of a considerable number of instrumental and local modifications in the verb-complex; the weak development of differences of tense in the verb and of number in the verb and noun; and the impossibility of drawing a sharp line between mode and tense.

## 1.2 Attitudes Toward Language History in the First Part of the 20th Century among American Indian Scholars

At the beginning of the present century, the Powell classification of American Indian languages (1891) was generally accepted as a reference point, although efforts at revising it by combining the families Powell had identified into larger groupings were already beginning. Similarities among unrelated languages in the same area, whether lexical, phonetic, or grammatical, were often interpreted as due to diffusion. It must be stressed that this view was not limited to Boas, as is often supposed, but was shared by most scholars in the period. In fact, the real empirical work in areal linguistics in the period was done not by Boas, but by Dixon, Kroeber, and Sapir. The following quote from Sapir's "Preliminary report on the language and mythology of the Upper Chinook" (1907:542) is indicative of the attitude current at the time.

> It is of considerable theoretic importance, therefore, to note that the neighboring Sahaptian dialects, quite similarly to the Klamath, make an extended use of such case-suffixes. We would then have here a good example of the *grammatic*, not merely lexical, influence that dialects of one linguistic stock may exert on geographically contiguous dialects of a fundamentally distinct stock.

In "A Chinookan phonetic law" (1926), Sapir refers to the 'well known fact' that the change of 'k' sounds to 'tc' sounds is found in a (nearly) continuous area from a northern point on the west coast of Vancouver Island south to the mouth of the Columbia. In his famous "Time perspective" article (1916:458), Sapir states that

> It is well known to students of language that striking phonetic and morphologic similarities are not infrequently found between neighboring languages that, so far as can be ascertained, are in no way genetically related. Such resemblances, insofar as they are not merely fortuitous, must be due to the assimilatory influence exerted by one language over another.

In this article, Sapir uses evidence of grammatical diffusion to make historical inferences. He points out, for example, that resemblances between Tsimshian, Kwakiutl and Salish indicate a much earlier contact of Tsimshian with these languages than with its present neighbors, Haida and Tlingit. Similarly, the existence in Maidu of such Hokan features as instrumental prefixes and local suffixes in verbs leads him to infer long contact between the Penutian Maidu and Hokan speaking peoples.[3]

The only real areal studies in this period were carried out by Dixon and Kroeber in California. The quantity of work is impressive, especially when one considers the fact that practically no areal studies were to be undertaken in the following generations. We have: 1. Dixon and Kroeber, "The native languages of California" (1903), an attempt to describe the phonetic and grammatical types present in California and to place them areally; 2. Kroeber, "The Yokuts and Yuki languages" (1906), a study of the similarities and differences which are found in these two unrelated California languages; 3. Dixon, "The pronominal dual in the languages of California" (1906), a study of the distribution of one grammatical trait; 4. Dixon and Kroeber, "Numeral systems of the languages of California" (1907), a detailed discussion of the distribution of different types of numeral systems; 5. Kroeber, "Phonetic constituents of the native languages of California" (1911a), a preliminary areal study of California phonetics; and 6. Kroeber, "California kinship systems" (1917).

Kroeber also stresses the importance of recognizing areal influences in his "The determination of linguistic relationship" (1913) in which he points out that the types outlined by himself and Dixon in the 1903 article were as much a result of diffusion as of common origin. Kroeber's continuing or perhaps renewed interest in linguistic diffusion and typology is evidenced by two articles written near the end of his life: 1. "Possible Athapaskan influence on Yuki" (1959) and 2. "On typological indices I: Ranking of languages" (1960). Kroeber's contribution to the study of North American Indian language history (diffusional and genetic) is discussed in detail in Hymes 1961.

1.3 *Extension of Genetic Perspective: Relationship between Diffusion and Common Origin*

In the second decade of this century, students of American Indian languages began grouping the Powell units into larger genetic stocks. The former students of Boas lead the new trend. In 1913, Dixon and Kroeber announced new California groupings in "New linguistic families in California". In 1919, in "Linguistic families in California", the same authors admitted to an earlier conservatism and supplied sound correspondences for the linguistic stocks they now proposed. Swanton (1911, 1924) showed Natchez and Muskogean to be related and suggested a Haida-Tlingit-Athabascan relationship. Sapir (1917, 1921a, 1925) intensified work in both the Hokan and Penutian families as well as suggesting further relationships for each. He grouped Wiyot, Yurok, and Algonkian (1913b); Haida, Tlingit, and Athabascan (1915b); and the various Uto-Aztecan languages (1913a, 1915a).

[3] Sapir expresses similar views about the diffusion of linguistic traits (and uses the same examples) in a posthumously published paper (Sapir 1947). In order to better understand the development of Sapir's views with regard to language history, it would be useful to know exactly when this paper was written. Its style and general point of view suggest that it was written early in Sapir's career, although later additions (and perhaps editing by others) were no doubt made. I am grateful to Dell Hymes for calling this article to my attention.

In the light of the earlier focus on areal and typological relationships, the new trend in American Indian linguistics required a theoretical framework in order to explain the relationship between evidence of diffusion and evidence of common origin. This theoretical framework was provided by Sapir, who for many years to come was to represent the view that with careful scholarship, one can achieve great time depth in linguistic history. Sapir claimed that it is possible to separate those aspects of grammar which are superficial and likely to have resulted from diffusion from a 'deeper' and more 'profound' kernel of grammar which reveals genetic origins. As is pointed out by Hoijer (1941), perhaps the clearest account of Sapir's theoretical position as well as his methodological approach is to be found in his "The Hokan affinity of Subtiaba in Nicaragua" (1925). Here, Sapir states that (491):

> the most important grammatical features of a given language and perhaps the bulk of what is conventionally called its grammar are of little value for the remoter comparison, which may rest largely on submerged features that are of only minor interest to a descriptive analysis.

Sapir goes on to show that Subtiaba has undergone considerable structural influence from its unrelated neighbors. Nonetheless, he is still able to isolate traits which betray what he feels is an unmistakable relationship to Hokan.

It must be stressed that Sapir did not deny the possibility of considerable areal influence in grammatical structure, as the traditional 'Boas-Sapir controversy' view holds. Rather, he felt that one could reconstruct both internal and external developments in language. Thus, in "A characteristic Penutian form of stem" (1921a), Sapir shows that the 'fundamental type' of Penutian language is a predominantly inflective one. He then traces the various structural changes in the Penutian languages as having resulted from intimate contact with unrelated neighbors.

The 'Boas-Sapir controversy' cannot then be simplified to the view that one man saw all structural similarities as resulting from diffusion; the other, as resulting from common origin. Such a view is patently false; it is also an insult to the intellectual merit of both men. Boas was quite capable of accepting genetic relationships beyond the Powell framework. Sapir has provided us with some of the best analyses of the diffusion of structural traits. Boas felt, however, that at a certain time depth, one could no longer separate traits due to diffusion from those due to common origin. He even believed that under certain socio-cultural conditions, 'mixed-languages' might arise (see Boas 1929). Boas' articles on the subject are disappointing in that they repeat the same examples of diffusion from the Northwest coast which Sapir and others had already accepted.

In an important article, Emeneau (1956) has reviewed Sapir's position. He points out that although Sapir's view is very attractive, it is not always so easy to distinguish the 'superficial' from the 'profound' in grammatical structure. Emeneau feels that we should undertake areal studies in North America in order to better understand some of the historical problems which seem without solution.[4]

---

[4] See also Emeneau (1962). I am grateful to William H. Jacobsen, Jr. for calling my attention to this relevant article.

## 1.4 The 'Bloomfieldian' and 'Post-Bloomfieldian' Era: Little Emphasis on Areal-Typological Problems in American Indian Research

The 'Bloomfieldian' and 'post-Bloomfieldian' era of American linguistics can be characterized as one in which scholars applied newly codified descriptive techniques to grammar writing.[5] It was generally felt that actual grammars should be free from both historical and typological concerns (see Hockett 1954). Most historical studies were limited to listing phonemic correspondences between languages, whether the languages being compared were thought to be closely or distantly related. Arguments tended to focus on such questions as subgrouping within well established language families or how many cognates are necessary in order to prove relationship between two languages.

There are, however, a few exceptions to the above generalization. The earlier interest of Boas, Sapir, and Kroeber in areal and typological research was reflected in the work of a few scholars who had been influenced by these men. Jacobs continued to write linguistic descriptions in the areal-typological style characteristic of the early part of the century. Thus Jacobs (1931) writes of Northern Sahaptin (99):

> Acoustically northern Sahaptin is much less harsh than the neighboring Salish and Chinook stocks and somewhat less so than the related Molale-Cayuse language ... Occasional clusters of velar and exploded consonants remind one of the harsher phonetics of the north.

Of glottalized sounds in Northern Sahaptin, Jacobs writes (106):

> The glottalized sounds are on the whole uttered with almost as startling a crackle as the fortis glottalized sounds of the Salish language to the west and north. They are given far more explosive effect than is found in the coast Oregon languages such as Kalapuya and Athabaskan.

Jacobs (1937, 1954) also provides evidence of areal influences on the Northwest Coast as well as a socio-cultural explanation of the supposed direction of influences.

Velten's "The Nez Perce verb" (1943), although essentially a descriptive study, contrasts traits of the Nez Perce verb with those of Indo-European languages and shows similarities with other languages of the Nez-Perce area.

The late Morris Swadesh is thought of by most linguists as someone who tried to arrive at greater and greater linguistic time depth, including the possible reconstruction of the origin of language. This is true. However, Swadesh also continued Sapir's interest in tracing areal influences. In "A structural trend in Nootka" (1948), Swadesh points out that in the recent history of Nootka, many old postposed particles have become suffixes, under the influence of neighboring 'suffixing' languages of the North-

---

[5] The major basis of this codification was Bloomfield (1933). It is interesting to note that in this book, Bloomfield does briefly discuss the question of areal linguistic influences (468–75). He suggests that such influences are due to the imperfect learning of a second language by large populations. Bloomfield does not, however, undertake this type of research himself; nor did this section of his influential book receive subsequent attention by 'post-Bloomfieldian' scholars.

west coast. In "Salish phonologic geography" (1952), he traces sound changes which spread across genetic boundaries. In two recent books (1966, 1971), Swadesh stresses the importance of areal influences on linguistic structure, while at the same time attempting to demonstrate genetic relationships at great time depth.

Voegelin's "Culture area: Parallel with typological homogeneity and heterogeneity to North American language families" (1961) is the only attempt ever made to compare North American culture areas with linguistic areas (not genetic subgroupings!). (See also Voegelin 1941, 1945a, 1945b for some discussion of areal linguistic phenomena in North America.) Although this brief article suffers from a lack of an explicit framework and considers relatively little linguistic data, it is very important in that it indicates a fruitful area of research. A comparison of culture areas and linguistic areas is attempted in the present study.

One areal study in the Dixon-Kroeber tradition to come out of the period under discussion is V. Hymes' "Athapaskan numeral systems" (1955), inspired by the work of Harold Driver and his associates. Although Driver and Massey's very useful study (1957) maps many cultural traits in North America, the traits investigated are all non-linguistic.

With the exception of the studies listed above, then, most work concerning American Indian language history in the 'Bloomfieldian' and 'post-Bloomfieldian' era tended not to deal with areal-typological problems. Scholars worked on the details of relationship within such language families as Algonkian, Athabascan, Siouan, and Uto-Aztecan (or else tried to relate these units to other languages or language families). Language history, then, was viewed mainly in genetic terms. It seems to have been generally believed that neighboring languages did not seriously influence one another structurally.

It seems useful to indicate at this point that the present study is concerned with the distribution of phonological and morphological traits in the languages north of Mexico and not with lexical or vocabulary items. Information about lexical borrowing among American Indian languages would tell us much about the cultural relationships of the groups involved and throw further light on linguistic relationships as well. Unfortunately, there are very few studies dealing with this topic,[6] again apparently because of the predominant focus on genetic relationships. (Though, of course, one of the primary tasks of the student of genetic relationships ought to be to sift out lexical similarities among languages into those due to common origin, to borrowing, to chance convergence, etc.) Noteworthy in this regard, then, are Bright's discussion of lexical borrowing in the Karok-Wiyot-Yurok area of California (1959), Callaghan's collection of borrowed items in Lake Miwok (1964), Jacobsen's list of words borrowed into Washo from neighboring languages (1966), and Troike's study of Nahuatl loanwords in Coahuilteco (1961) and a Gulf loanword in Caddo (1964).

---

[6] Boas 1889 was an exciting suggestion of the value of lexical borrowing as a key to cultural contact among groups — this was never really followed up in subsequent Amerindian research.

## 1.5 Recent Trend in American Indian Research: A Return to Areal-Typological Interests

A survey of recent descriptive and historical studies shows renewed interest in areal and typological problems in North America. Aoki compares reduplication in Nez Perce with that of nearby languages (1963) and suggests that vowel harmony in Sahaptian might have resulted from an increase in the stock of vowels due to diffusion (Aoki 1966; for other views on this problem see Rigsby and Silverstein 1969 and Zwicky 1971). Haas studies consonant symbolism as an areal phenomenon in Northwestern California (1970). Jacobsen places Washo typologically and areally with respect to other languages of California and the Great Basin (1966, 1967) and discusses the role of areal pressures in the development of the proto-Sahaptian vowel system (1968). Langdon points to Athabascan languages as a source of lateral sounds in Yuman (1971). Diachronic studies by Callaghan (1964), Pitkin and Shipley (1958), Shipley (1966), Silver (1964), and Ultan (1964) discuss phonological diffusion in California. Finally, Kinkade (1969) argues that in spite of the striking structural similarities among the Chemakuan, Salishan, and Wakashan languages of the Northwest Coast, these language families are not genetically related (i.e. *Mosan* is not a valid genetic unit); and that the similarities must be due to diffusion. It is interesting that the typological similarities of the Mosan languages were once thought to be 'deep' in their linguistic structure. Armed with a richer or more abstract notion of what is 'deep' in language, it is now possible to argue that they are superficial or close to the 'surface' and perhaps due to diffusion rather than common origin.[7]

The aim of this section has been to show that there does exist an 'areal-typological' tradition in North American Indian linguistics. However, since this tradition has not been a dominant one, it has not developed rigorous frameworks or methods of analysis. Nor have areal-typological studies been carried out systematically. Therefore, it is not possible to speak of significant 'results' of such work. It is for this reason that the research which is reported here was undertaken.[8]

## 2. A FRAMEWORK FOR AREAL LINGUISTIC STUDIES

In Sherzer 1968, the distributions of many linguistic traits (phonological and morpho-

---

[7] Even if the Mosan languages are genetically related, the typological similarities discussed by Kinkade seem to reflect parallel developments due to intimate contacts; i.e. they are not retentions from a common ancestor.

[8] After this article was submitted I became aware of Mary Haas' recent book, *The prehistory of languages* (1969). An entire chapter of this book (Chapter 5: "Prehistory and diffusion") is devoted to areal linguistic studies, drawing on North American Indian languages for examples. This chapter is especially significant in that it provides a framework for the presentation of areal patterns in phonology. Haas' recent and important work in areal linguistics is also reflected in her "Language and taxonomy in Northwestern California" (1967) and "Consonant symbolism in Northwestern California: A problem in diffusion" (1970). Evidence of her earlier interest in North American Indian areal linguistic phenomena is her "Noun incorporation in the Muskogean languages" (1941) in which she shows that Muskogean, like several other American Indian language families, possesses noun incorporation.

logical) were presented, using Driver's 'culture areas of North America' (1961) as a frame of reference.[9] In such an investigation, some traits provide much more interesting results than others. Yet, no discussion of this question exists. For that reason, it was considered necessary to map as many traits as possible for all American Indian languages north of Mexico. It seems useful to indicate here the types of problems that are involved, as a way of offering suggestions for further research.

First, there is the problem of comparability. It is often difficult to relate one author's terminology with that of another, especially if the two descriptions are written in different periods or in different analytical frameworks or styles. It was thus decided to begin by studying those traits which have already been mentioned in the areal and typological literature, since, having attracted attention in this respect, they are thus fairly well reported. Some of these are: a glottalized stop series, a profusion of lateral sounds, a distinction between a k-series and a q-series of consonants, instrumental prefixes in the verb, the use of distinct verbal stems for singular and plural nouns (subjects or objects), prefixation and suffixation of personal pronouns in the noun and verb, a nominal case system, stem reduplication, incorporation of the noun into the verb, pronominal dual, nominal gender, the marking of the opposition between visibility and invisibility of objects in demonstratives, and the existence of nominal possession classes (inalienable/alienable). To these were added some others which seemed equally capable of being adequately handled in terms of available data. Some of these are: nasalized vowels, glottalized sonorants, locative-directional markers in the verb, source of information or evidential markers in the verb, an opposition between inclusive and exclusive in the first person dual or plural of pronouns, and numeral classifiers.

A second problem involves the adequacy of available descriptions which are used as sources. In phonology, for example, 'pre-phonemic' descriptions must be phonemicized, and errors (both in the original and secondary analysis) are of course possible. In both phonology and morphology, it is advisable to look at all available descriptions and to avoid using 'restatements' as much as possible, since these may manipulate the data in such a way as to conceal the trait being looked for.

A third problem concerns the relative universality of the trait in question. Traits which seem to be universal in language, e.g. the presence of consonants, the distinction between nouns and verbs, or the existence of a transformational component, are of course not interesting from the point of view of an areal linguistic study. On the other hand, areal-typological investigations may lead to the discovery of certain types of universals, especially of the implicational variety (see Greenberg 1966: Introduction). Even traits which are extremely common in language, although not universal, for example, the presence of a particular sound, like p or t, rarely lead to interesting results in an areal study (except in a negative sense, i.e. the absence of such common traits may characterize a small area — for example, nasal stops are lacking in a small

---

[9] See Chapters 3 and 15 for a list of the traits investigated and a discussion of them.

region of the Northwest Coast of North America). Most fruitful for areal-typological research seem to be traits which are relatively rare in language, such as glottalized sounds, voiceless laterals and nasals, nominal and verbal classifiers, nominal and pronominal dual, and a nominal case system overtly marked in the noun. It is precisely such relatively rare traits, often selected by scholars as identifying, characteristic, or diagnostic features of a language, a family, or an area, which proved useful here in the determination of linguistic areas.

Fourth, in an areal study, one wants to consider traits which are likely or susceptible to be borrowed from one language into another. Of course, we still know very little about how to identify such traits, although we suspect that they tend to be 'surface' rather than 'deep' aspects of linguistic structure (in terms of the dichotomy set up by generative-transformational grammar). By investigating many traits, we contribute to an understanding of this intriguing problem of language history.

Finally, one suspects that it will prove more rewarding to look for diffusion of linguistic traits in certain areas of the world than in others. It is by investigating all of North America north of Mexico that we have been able to draw inferences regarding the types of socio-cultural conditions under which such diffusion is likely to occur.

In the discussion of the relationship between *culture areas* and *linguistic areas*, the following terminology is used (adopted in part from Wolff 1959):

*whole areal trait*: a trait found in all languages of a given culture area.

*central areal trait*: a trait found in most languages of a given culture area and the locus of whose distribution is the center of this area.

*regional areal trait*: a trait with a continuous or almost continuous distribution within one region of a given culture area.

*family trait*: a trait in language x which x has retained from proto-language A. We can speak of a family trait of x or of A. (For example, obviation is a family trait of Cree or of Algonkian.)

In comparing culture areas with linguistic areas, it is important to recognize important differences between the two. A *culture area* has been traditionally defined as an area in which *many* cultural traits cluster (see, for example, Driver 1961; Kroeber 1939). In some cases, so many traits cluster in a particular culture area that it becomes difficult if not impossible to distinguish the cultures (or parts of them) in question *by this method*.[10] An example of this extreme case is the Hupa-Karok-Yurok region in northern California (see Sapir 1921b:214).

It has often been observed that language is the most self-contained or conservative part of culture. In spite of the great similarity of Hupa, Karok, and Yurok cultures, the languages, all unrelated (or, at best, extremely distantly related), are quite distinct from one another (for further discussion of this question, see Bright and Bright 1965; Haas 1967). Linguistic traits, especially grammatical traits, do not spread with the ease that many non-linguistic cultural traits seem to. This is apparently due to the

---

[10] Of course, there are approaches to the notion of culture other than the listing of traits.

fact that on the one hand, linguistic phenomena are usually less conscious than other cultural phenomena and on the other, that their diffusion requires very intimate contact between groups, including bilingualism.[11] We are arguing, then, that agreement in a few linguistic traits may often be more significant than agreement in many non-linguistic traits as an indication of the nature of relationships among groups in an area.[12] Any definition of linguistic area, then, cannot be strictly analogous to the above definition of culture area, since a cluster of *many* linguistic traits occurs only in areas where all the languages are related closely. As we shall see, there are instances in North America where the boundaries of a linguistic area (as defined below) and a genetic area (all languages in the area are members of one family) are considered to coincide. Nonetheless, there is also a sense in which it seems valuable to delimit linguistic areas which do not coincide with genetic areas.

A *linguistic area* is defined here as an area in which *several* linguistic traits are shared by the languages of the area and furthermore, there is evidence (linguistic and non-linguistic) that contact between the speakers of the languages contributed to the spread and/or retention of these traits and thereby to a certain degree of linguistic uniformity within the area.[13] It is important to remember that languages which are unrelated or distantly related may very well and probably do disagree with regard to many traits and yet still be in the same linguistic area according to the above definition, since they share *several* traits (which one might want to call diagnostic traits). What is significant, then, is that linguistic structure, usually impervious to influences coming from outside its own internal mechanism, has been affected by linguistic contact. A good example is the Northwest Coast-Plateau, here considered a linguistic area (see more complete discussion below). In this area are found languages belonging to eight families — Chemakuan, Hokan, Kutenaian, Na-Dene, Penutian, Ritwan, Salishan, and Wakashan; the cultures of the speakers of these languages are in some cases markedly similar. In spite of the fact that the languages are quite distinct from one another from a genetic point of view, they share a complex of traits which is not found in any other area of North America. Some of the traits in this complex are a glottalized stop series, nominal and verbal reduplication, and numeral classifiers.

There are problems involved in the delimitation of linguistic areas just as there are in the delimitation of culture areas. We have said that in a linguistic area several traits are shared by the languages. We have not said how many traits or what kind of traits. (For example, what exactly is a diagnostic trait?) Nor have we discussed the bound-

---

[11] It would no doubt be possible and useful to rank cultural phenomena according to such a dimension. At one end would be traits which diffuse rather easily (and often are related to ecological adaptation), such as various types of artifacts and clothing. At the other would be traits which require contacts between groups in order to spread in an area, such as certain aspects of social organization, folktales, and linguistic traits.

[12] Dell Hymes (1956) points to the presence of two sounds, f and $f^w$, in mutually unintelligible Kalapuya and Molala as evidence of intimate, face-to-face contacts between the two groups.

[13] We use the term *linguistic area* from Velten (1943) and Emeneau (1956) rather than 'convergence area', suggested by Weinreich (1958).

aries between areas — how does one decide in which area to place a borderline language? These are important questions that must be answered if areal-linguistic research is to proceed beyond the preliminary stage it is at now. In this study, areas which shared unique complexes of traits were considered linguistic areas. Some readers might not agree with the selection of complexes or feel that it was too arbitrary. Only future research will determine more rigorous methods of defining linguistic areas.

In the next section, each of the culture areas north of Mexico (see Driver 1961) will be examined and the following questions will be asked:

1. Is it possible to delineate linguistic areas in the sense discussed above?
2. Are there linguistic areas or subareas within a given culture area?
3. Are there linguistic areas or subareas which cut across the boundaries of culture areas?
4. Are there linguistic areas which are composed of two or more culture areas (or parts of them)?

Following the discussion of each linguistic area will be a discussion of the *communicative characteristics* of the area, with special emphasis on determining why a particular area actually became a linguistic area. We will try to focus on such questions as type of social organization, residence patterns, intermarriage, trade, bilingualism, density of population, and attitude towards one's own and others' languages. Often, it is impossible to obtain sufficient data in these domains. Nevertheless, an attempt will be made to give the general nature of the communicative characteristics of each linguistic area.

## 3. CULTURE AREAS AND LINGUISTIC AREAS: A COMPARISON

### 3.1 *Yukon and Mackenzie Subarctic*

There is one language family represented in the vast Yukon and Mackenzie Subarctic culture areas, Athabascan.[14] Thus, most individuals in these areas came into contact with either speakers of their own or a related language. With regard to the linguistic traits investigated here, there is a great deal of uniformity in the Yukon and Mackenzie Subarctic (see Sherzer 1968: Ch. 4, 5, 16).

*Whole areal traits* of the Yukon and Mackenzie Subarctic are:

1. three stop series system
2. voiced fricative series
3. sound: x
4. five lateral sounds: l, ł, λ, λ', λ
5. prefixation of the possessive pronouns of nouns

---

[14] I have not included Eskimo in this survey. Michael Krauss suggests (personal communication) that Eskimo has had an influence on various aspects of linguistic development in neighboring Athabascan dialects. I am grateful to him for extensive comments on this section. The remaining faults are, of course, my own responsibility.

6. alienable/inalienable opposition in nouns
7. pronominal plural
8. nominal locative suffixes
9. prefixation of the subject person markers in verbs
10. prefixation of tense-aspect markers in verbs
11. different verb stems for nouns (subject or object) of different form, shape, or number

The following are found in all Yukon and Mackenzie Subarctic languages, except some Koyukon, some Tanaina, and most Ahtena:

12. s/š opposition
13. c/č opposition[15]

It is on the basis of the distribution of the above traits that we group the Yukon Subarctic and the Mackenzie Subarctic into a single linguistic area. Notice that Kroeber (1939) groups them into a single culture area which he calls the Western Subarctic. Some of the above linguistic traits are rather common in the languages of North America. These are:

5. prefixation of the possessive pronouns of nouns
6. alienable/inalienable opposition in nouns
7. pronominal plural
8. nominal locative suffixes
9. prefixation of the subject person markers of verbs

The others are more restricted in occurrence outside the Yukon-Mackenzie Subarctic and serve to characterize this area as a linguistic area.

Traits characteristic of other linguistic areas, but lacking in the Yukon-Mackenzie Subarctic are:

1. one and two stop series systems
2. one fricative series systems
3. nominal case system
4. nominal reduplication to signify plurality, distribution, etc.
5. verbal reduplication to signify plurality, distribution, etc.
6. gender opposition
7. singular/plural opposition in nouns (there may be some languages in which this trait occurs, but it is certainly not well developed)
8. visibility/invisibility opposition in demonstratives
9. instrumental markers in the verb

The distribution of two traits suggests the existence of a western subarea within the Yukon-Mackenzie Subarctic linguistic area; this western subarea seems to have links with the Northwest Coast-Plateau linguistic area to be discussed below.

---

[15] It is interesting that the Athabascan dialects which lack traits 12. and 13. border on Eskimo, in which they are also lacking. These dialects also agree with Eskimo in having the k/q opposition. I am indebted to Michael Krauss for these observations.

1. two velar series are found in 'outer' Koyukon, 'outer' Ahtena, all Tanaina and all Ingalik (as well as in many languages of the Northwest Coast-Plateau area).[16]

2. glottalized continuants are found in Koyukon, Tanaina, and Tutchone (as well as in Bella Coola, Haida, Kwakiutl, Nootka, and Tsimshian on the Northwest Coast).

### 3.1.1 *Communicative characteristics of the Yukon-Mackenzie Subarctic*

Compared with the rest of North America, the Yukon-Mackenzie Subarctic was very sparsely populated in pre-Columbian times (see Kroeber 1939). Individuals were organized into loose bands which moved about a great deal. There is evidence of changes in habitat, invasions of one another's lands, and mixtures of various groups (see Spencer, Jennings, et al. 1965). Teit (1956) describes the nomadic nature of northern Athabascan groups and the absence of well-defined tribe or band boundaries. In some places, territories overlapped for long periods and families and bands migrated from territory to territory in search of better facilities for trading or hunting. The Athabascans apparently did not view themselves as being separated into distinct units. According to Teit (1965:42-3):

although tribes of other linguistic stocks are generally well differentiated in the minds of the Indians ... tribes of Athabascan lineage are not differentiated in the same way. The Indians seem to consider all within their ken as bands or scattered groups of the one family speaking the same kind of languages differing only in slight degree in certain localities.[17]

As stated above, since only one language family is represented in this vast area, most individuals came into contact only with speakers of their own or related languages. Krauss (1969) characterizes Northern Athabascan as a continuous linguistic community or dialect complex through which traits spread like waves. We can thus summarize the factors which underlie the linguistic uniformity of the Yukon-Mackenzie Subarctic:

1. one language family: speakers did not come into contact with very divergent linguistic traits.

2. mixtures of groups through moving about in hunting, incursions, etc. led to continual contact with individuals speaking languages with the same traits as one's own (other Athabascan languages) and perhaps checked idiosyncratic developments (multiple bilingual pressure for retention).

These two factors seem also to underlie the linguistic uniformity of the Uto-Aztecan Great Basin and the Algonkian Eastern Subarctic (see discussion below). A third factor, not known to be operative in these other areas, seems important in the Yukon-Mackenzie Subarctic. This is the well-known linguistic conservatism of Athabascan-speaking peoples. It is rare in North America that we have data concerning the attitude of a group of people toward linguistic change. The apparent reluctance of

---

[16] It is interesting that Eskimo also has two velar series. See footnote 15.

[17] According to Michael Krauss, however (personal communication), Athabascan dialect differentiation was sometimes sharp and when it was the groups in question felt themselves distinct.

Athabascan-speaking peoples to adopt alien traits in their languages, however, has been noted by many observers. For example, Dixon and Kroeber say the following of the Athabascan languages of California (1919:113–4):

These dialects seem not to have been influenced in the least, either lexically or structurally, by any of the neighboring non-Athabascan tongues. The California Athabascans are in geographical contact with Penutian, Hokan, Algonkin, and Yukian languages ... Yet they possess no loan words from any of these, and appear to have given none ... In short, the other languages and families of California have occasionally borrowed, or appeared to borrow, a stem from one another: Athabascan has reacted toward all of them like a jet of oil shot into water.

This uniqueness is intelligible on two grounds only. Either the Athabascans are too recent in the region to have taken over alien words, or there is something about their speech that prevents such purloining. The former alternative is disproved by the complete cultural assimilation of all the Athabascan groups in the state ... Such thorough acculturation requires at least a number of generations. The only interpretation that remains, accordingly, is that there is something in the character of Athabascan speech that causes it to cling with conservatism to its existing forms, and show a tenacious resistance to foreign elements and ideas. This inference is corroborated by the comparatively slight differentiation undergone by the Athabascan languages in regions so far separated as Alaska, Oregon and California, and New Mexico.[18]

It is interesting that this attitude toward language seems to continue to hold true for Athabascan languages no matter where they migrate to. Sapir (1921b:209) notes that 'The Athabaskan languages of America are spoken by peoples that have had astonishingly varied cultural contacts, yet nowhere do we find that an Athabaskan dialect has borrowed at all freely from a neighboring language'. And again (1921b:228): 'The cultural adaptability of the Athabaskan-speaking peoples is in the strangest contrast to the inaccessibility to foreign influences of the languages themselves.'[19]

The western linguistic subarea within the Yukon-Mackenzie Subarctic is interesting, especially the links with the Northwest Coast, considering our remarks above concerning the tendency of all Athabascan languages not to be influenced by their neighbors. There seems to have been a great deal of contact among the groups on the Northwest Coast and the Athabascan-speaking groups of the nearby interior. This contact was greatly increased by the white fur trade. There was much intermarriage and, no doubt, much bilingualism. Teit (1917) notes that folktales spread from the coast to the interior Athabascan groups. His discussion of the intimate contacts between the Tlingit and Tahltan is significant (1917:428–9):

The Tahltan assert that in the old trading-rendez-vous on the upper Stikine, members of the two tribes associated there for weeks together, and that one of the features of meeting was story-telling. Tahltan raconteurs told their stories one day, and Tlingit told theirs the fol-

[18] I am indebted to Dell Hymes for calling my attention to this passage.
[19] Athabascan languages seem to avoid influences not only from other languages, but from any source outside their own linguistic system, such as natural sounds or noises. Thus Sapir (1921b:8) notes that the Athabascan tribes of the Mackenzie River speak languages in which there is practically no onomatopoeia.

lowing day. Sometimes they thus told stories turn about for weeks. Occasionally the tribes competed in story-telling to see which had the most stories. As a result, it came to be acknowledged that the Tlingit had considerably more stories than the Tahltan. In this way, it is said, the Tahltan learned Tlingit stories, and vice versa.

It is hard to imagine how these story-telling sessions could have been successful without the participants being bilingual. It is also interesting that according to the Tahltan, it was the Tlingit who won the contests. Matrilineal descent is shared by most groups on the Northwest Coast and Athabascan-speaking groups of the nearby interior (see Driver and Massey 1957: map 156). There has been considerable debate concerning the direction of the diffusion of this trait of social organization. Driver and Massey (1957) present a good case for the argument that the influence was from the more affluent coast to the interior. The direction of the diffusion of the linguistic traits in question seems to be the same.[20] Some Athabascan groups located near the Northwest Coast apparently placed great value on learning the higher prestige languages along the coast. The Tahltan Indians, for example, sometimes placed a beaver's tongue in the mouth of a child during nursing to loosen the tongue and help it to later talk Tlingit and other languages without difficulty (Teit 1956:104).

## 3.2 *Eastern Subarctic*

There is only one language family represented in the Eastern Subarctic culture area, Algonkian. Furthermore, there are but two languages spread over this very large area, Cree and Ojibwa. Thus, as in the Yukon-Mackenzie Subarctic, most individuals in the Eastern Subarctic came into contact with speakers of either their own or a related language. As regards the linguistic traits investigated in this study, there is a great deal of uniformity in the Eastern Subarctic (see Sherzer 1968:Ch. 7, 18).

*Whole areal traits* of the Eastern Subarctic are:
1. one stop series (voiceless)
2. one fricative series (voiceless)
3. prefixation of possessive pronouns in nouns
4. alienable/inalienable opposition in nouns
5. suffixation of nominal diminutive marker
6. animate/inanimate gender
7. pronominal plural
8. nominal plural, marked by a suffix
9. inclusive/exclusive opposition in the first person plural of pronouns
10. nominal locative suffixes
11. prefixation (sometimes) of subject person markers in verbs
12. suffixation (sometimes) of subject person markers in verbs

---

[20] To the data presented here, Michael Krauss adds (personal communication) that Tahltan contains many words borrowed from Tlingit.

13. verbal reduplication signifies repetition, distribution, etc.
14. prefixation of tense-aspect markers in verbs
15. suffixation of tense-aspect markers in verbs
16. prefixation of locative-directional markers in verbs
17. obviation marked in verbs and nouns

Traits characteristic of other linguistic areas but entirely lacking in the Eastern Subarctic are:

1. vowels other than i, e, a, o, u
2. glottalized stop series
3. c/č opposition
4. sound: q
5. sound: k$^w$
6. sounds: f and v
7. sound: x
8. lateral sounds other than l
9. nasal consonants other than m and n
10. nominal case system
11. nominal reduplication
12. pronominal dual
13. active/static opposition in verbs
14. source of information markers in verbs
15. instrumental markers in verbs

It is on the basis of this linguistic uniformity (with regard to both traits shared and traits lacking) that we consider the Eastern Subarctic culture area to be a linguistic area.

### 3.2.1 *Communicative characteristics of the Eastern Subarctic*

Like the Yukon-Mackenzie Subarctic, the Eastern Subarctic was very sparsely populated in pre-Columbian times. Social organization in this area was also similar to that of the Yukon-Mackenzie Subarctic. It consisted of loose bands which moved about as they hunted. There are thus two principal factors which seem to underlie the linguistic uniformity of the Eastern Subarctic (see discussion above of same factors in the Yukon-Mackenzie Subarctic):

1. There is one language family in the area; speakers did not come into contact with alien linguistic traits.
2. Mixture of groups through moving about in hunting, etc. led to continual contact with individuals speaking languages possessing the same traits as one's own, thus providing additional pressure for retention.

### 3.3 *Northwest Coast*

The Northwest Coast culture area contrasts sharply with the Yukon-Mackenzie

Subarctic in that there are many language families represented in a relatively small area. The language families are Na-Dene (with three widely divergent branches: Haida, Tlingit, and Eyak-Athabascan), Wakashan, Salishan, Chemakuan, Penutian (with the widely divergent branches Tsimshian, Chinookan, Coos, and Yakonan), Hokan, and Ritwan. Thus, from the genetic point of view, there is much linguistic diversity on the Northwest Coast. Yet, the languages of the Northwest Coast were found to share many of the traits investigated in this study (see Sherzer 1968:Ch. 7, 18). Together with the Plateau, the Northwest Coast seems to form a single linguistic area (see discussion below).

*Central areal traits* of the Northwest Coast are:
1. glottalized stop series
2. s/š opposition
3. c/č opposition
4. sound: q
5. labiovelars phonemically distinct
6. one fricative series: voiceless
7. velar fricatives
8. sounds: l, ł, λ, and λ'
9. alienable/inalienable opposition in nouns
10. pronominal plural
11. nominal plural
12. numeral classifiers
13. verbal reduplication signifies distribution, repetition, etc.
14. suffixation of tense-aspect markers in verbs
15. evidential or source of information marker in the verb[21]
16. locative-directional markers in the verb

Of the above traits, 1., 5., 8., and 12. are especially characteristic of the Northwest Coast.

There are some traits which are found in the Northwest Coast which, although they are not *central areal traits*, are rarely found outside of this area and thereby contribute to the impression that the Northwest Coast (probably together with the Plateau) is a linguistic area. These traits (whose exact distribution will be discussed below) are:
17. pharyngeal phonemes[22]
18. glottalized continuants

---

[21] Traits 13., 14., and 15. are not found in Haida, Tlingit, or Eyak-Athabascan.
[22] The significance of this trait is given added weight when one considers the very interesting suggestion by Jacobsen (1969:152) that pharyngeal phonemes may only develop in languages which meet certain 'preconditions', namely 'the presence of glottalized consonants, and of contrasting k- and q-series of consonants'. This notion of precondition is related to Greenberg's concept of implicational universals (see Greenberg 1966:Introduction). Thus the development of pharyngeal phonemes in two Northwest Coast-Plateau regions (see below) is not surprising, in spite of the fact that the regions are not contiguous, because the precondition to these sounds is a Northwest Coast-Plateau central area trait.

19. sound: λ
20. masculine/feminine gender
21. visibility/invisibility opposition in demonstratives
22. nominal and verbal reduplication signifies the diminutive

The Northwest Coast can also be characterized for its

1. lack of one-stop-series languages (with the exception of Karok)
2. lack of languages with voiced fricative series (some languages have voiced fricative sounds, but none have complete series)
3. paucity of languages with 'r' sounds

Both Northwest Coast and Plateau languages have been noted for their 'complex' phonetics. The impression of 'complexity' is given by the fact that most languages have more than one stop series (usually including a glottalized stop series); the phonemic oppositions $k^w/k$, k/q, s/š, and c/č; and the sounds l, ł, λ, λ', and x.[23] As we shall see below, as one moves east in North America, the phonetics of languages becomes less complex, in the sense of complexity used here (for a discussion of this question, see Milewski 1953).

The distribution of a number of traits suggests the existence of a northern subarea within the Northwest Coast. This subarea includes Eyak, Tlingit, and Haida. Tsimshian and Kwakiutl may also be included in this subarea, although one might also want to consider them as a separate subarea, together with Nootka and perhaps Salishan and Chemakuan. As in delimiting the boundaries of culture areas, there are problems in delimiting the boundaries of linguistic areas. There are often intermediate areas which seem to belong as well with either of the adjacent areas. The traits which delimit a northern subarea are:

1. three stop series are found in Haida, Tlingit, Eyak, Tsimshian, Kwakiutl, Nitinat and Makah (Nootka dialects), Quileute and Comox (a coast Salish language).

2. three velar orders are found in Haida, Tsimshian, Kwakiutl, and Comox.

3. glottalized continuants are found in Haida, Tsimshian, Kwakiutl, Nootka and Bella Coola (a coast Salish language).

4. the sound λ is found in Eyak, Haida, Tlingit, and Kwakiutl.

5. prefixation of possessive pronouns in nouns is found in Eyak, Tlingit, and Haida.

6. the active/static opposition in verbs is found in Haida, Tlingit, and Tsimshian.

7. prefixation of the tense-aspect markers in verbs is found in Eyak, Tlingit, and Tsimshian.

8. different verbal stems for nouns of different form, shape, or number are found in Tlingit, Tsimshian, and Kwakiutl.

9. the visibility/invisibility opposition in demonstratives is found in Tsimshian and Kwakiutl.

The distribution of a number of traits suggests the existence of a central subarea

[23] William H. Jacobsen, Jr. points out (personal communication) that another reason for the phonetic 'complexity' of most Northwest Coast languages (especially Salish, Sahaptian, and Wakashan) is their syllable structure, which allows many consonant clusters.

within the Northwest Coast. This subarea seems to include Wakashan (Nootka and Kwakiutl), Chemakuan (Chemakum and Quileute), Coast Salish, and Lower Chinook. This central subarea together with the Plateau probably forms a linguistic subarea within a larger Northwest Coast-Plateau linguistic area. Kwakiutl and Tsimshian seem intermediate between this subarea and the northern one discussed above. Lower Chinook and Coast Salish perhaps form a subarea within the central subarea.

1. a three vowel system (high front, high back, low central) is found in Lower Chinook, Quileute, Chemakum, Kwakiutl, and Bella Coola.

2. pharyngeal phonemes are found in Nootkan: Nitinat and Nootka.

3. prefixation of possessive pronouns of nouns is found in Lower Chinook and Coast Salish. (Some pronouns are suffixed in Salishan.)

4. suffixation of possessive pronouns is found in Tsimshian, Kwakiutl, Nootka, Quileute, Chemakum, Coast Salish (some pronominal persons), Alsea, and Siuslaw.

5. prefixation of some tense-aspect markers in verbs is found in Coast Salish and Lower Chinook.

6. masculine/feminine gender is found in Chemakum, Quileute, Coast Salish, and Lower Chinook.

7. the visibility/invisibility opposition in demonstratives is found in Quileute, Coast Salish, and Lower Chinook.

8. verbal reduplication signifies the diminutive in Kwakiutl, Quileute, and Coast Salish.

Finally, the distribution of some traits enables us to postulate a southern subarea within the Northwest Coast; this southern subarea has links with the California culture area.

1. three stop series are found in all Pacific Coast Athabascan.

2. the sound $\gamma$ is found in Pacific Coast Athabascan as well as in neighboring Wiyot and Yurok.

3. prefixation of the possessive pronouns of nouns is found in Pacific Coast Athabascan, Karok, Yurok, and Wiyot.

4. prefixation of some tense-aspect markers of verbs is found in Pacific Coast Athabascan, Wiyot, and Yurok.

5. different verb stems for nouns of different form, shape, or number is found in Pacific Coast Athabascan.

6. consonantal alternation signifies the diminutive in Hupa, Karok, Yurok, and Wiyot.[24]

3.3.1 *Communicative characteristics of the Northwest Coast*

In pre-Columbian times, the Northwest Coast had the second greatest population density of all North American culture areas (only California was more densely popu-

---

[24] Trait 6. developed in Hupa as a result of contact with neighboring languages. This development was documented by Victor Golla in a paper presented at the Annual Meeting of the American Anthropological Association, 1970: "Symbolic processes in Pacific Coast Athabascan".

lated). This dense population consisted of many small groups speaking diverse languages (seven families, each family consisting of a number of quite distinct languages). Driver characterizes Northwest Coast social organization as follows (1961:331–2):

> Population in this area was much more dense than in the Sub-Arctic, and life depended mostly on fishing. Therefore the population was concentrated at the mouths of streams, where fishing was best, in villages numbering in the hundreds of persons. Before European contact there was probably no territorial unit that exceeded a thousand souls. These villages were often clans and demes, but some were aggregations of a number of clans and demes. Sometimes the villages were combined into larger territorial units which might be called tribelets, but the population of such tribelets was often no larger than that of one of the larger autonomous villages in another locality.

The great density of population in certain areas of the Northwest Coast, together with the genetic diversity of languages, enables us to imagine that most individuals came into intimate contact with languages other than their own (and perhaps quite distinct from their own). In addition, it has been reported by various authors (see Driver 1961; Driver and Massey 1957; Drucker 1955; Jacobs 1937, 1954; Suttles 1960) that there was a great deal of trade and intermarriage among the groups of the Northwest Coast. Driver (1961:230) notes that at certain trading rendez-vous near the coast, buyers and sellers spent days feasting, singing, and dancing. As stated earlier with regard to the nearby interior Athabascan groups, such events could only be successful if there was much multilingualism. Boas (1896) reports much diffusion of folktales among Northwest Coast groups. The areal spread of such a cultural trait also, of course, requires multilingualism. It is probable that for a long period of time (all groups represented in the Northwest Coast were located there for a very long time), bi- and multilingualism was the rule rather than the exception. It is the pressure from this multilingualism which no doubt led to the linguistic uniformity of the Northwest Coast. The uniformity results from both innovative developments in particular languages in the direction of others (development of areal traits) and retentions of traits found in neighboring languages (retention of areal traits).

Of the three linguistic subareas of the Northwest Coast delimited above, two have also been isolated by anthropologists as culture subareas. Drucker (1955), for example, states that (196): 'beginning in the north, it is fairly clear that the Tlingit, Haida and Tsimshian formed a sub-unit, or province, or areal culture, in which the northern divisions of the Kwakiutl, particularly the Haisla, participated in a marginal fashion.' Drucker lists a number of cultural traits shared by the groups in this subarea. One of these traits is 'matrilineal social organization with crests', a social organizational trait which one suspects is diffused under conditions of rather intimate contact (similar to the conditions under which linguistic traits are diffused).

Both Kroeber (1939) and Drucker (1955) delimit a Northwest California or Lower Klamath subarea within the Northwest Coast. In this are included Pacific Coast Athabascan, Wiyot, Yurok, and Karok, groups which, as was stated above, share a number of linguistic traits.

Between the northern and southern subareas of the Northwest Coast, Kroeber delimits five, and Drucker two subareas. Linguistically, as stated above, there seems to be a single central Northwest Coast subarea.

### 3.4 *Plateau*

There are three language families represented in the Plateau culture area, Penutian, Salishan, and Kutenaian. The genetic diversity within Penutian (especially if Upper Chinook is placed, following Driver, in the Plateau) leads to the impression of considerable genetic diversity (comparable to that described above for the Northwest Coast). As in the Northwest Coast, however, the languages of the Plateau were found to share many of the traits investigated in this study (see Sherzer 1968:Ch. 8, 19).

*Central areal traits* of the Plateau are:
1. glottalized stop series
2. sound: q
3. labiovelars phonemically distinct
4. one fricative series
5. velar fricatives
6. sounds: l, ɫ, λ, and λ'
7. pronominal plural
8. nominal plural
9. prefixation of the subject person markers of verbs
10. suffixation of tense-aspect markers in verbs
11. locative-directional markers in the verb

All of these traits, except 9., are also *central areal traits* of the Northwest Coast. Traits 1., 3., and 6. are especially characteristic of the Plateau culture area (as they are of the Northwest Coast culture area). There are some traits found in the Plateau which, although not *central areal traits*, are rarely found outside this area. These traits (whose exact distribution will be discussed below) are:

14. pharyngeal phonemes[25]
15. glottalized continuants
16. nominal and verbal reduplication signifies the diminutive
17. numeral classifiers

These four traits are also found in the Northwest Coast culture area. The complex of traits shared by most or all languages of the Northwest Coast and those of the Plateau (and which are relatively rare in the other culture areas) leads us to posit a single Northwest Coast — Plateau linguistic area.

The Northwest Coast — Plateau area can also be characterized for its
1. lack of one stop series languages (with the exception of Kutenai)

---

[25] See footnote 22.

2. lack of languages with voiced fricative series

The distribution of a number of traits suggests special links between some languages of the Plateau and the Northwest Coast (especially the central subarea of the Northwest Coast):

1. Pharyngeal phonemes are found in Cœur d'Alene, Columbia, and Okanagon, as well as in two languages of the Northwest Coast (see above).

2. Glottalized continuants are found in Cœur d'Alene, Columbia, and Kalispel, as well as in some languages of the Northwest Coast (see above).

3. Reduplication of the verbal stem signifies the diminutive in all Interior Salish, Sahaptin, and Nez Perce, as well as in some languages of the Northwest Coast (see above).

4. Reduplication of the nominal stem signifies the diminutive in all Interior Salish, Sahaptin, and Nez Perce, as well as in some languages of the Northwest Coast (see above).

5. Numeral classifiers are found in all Interior Salish and Sahaptin, as well as in most languages of the Northwest Coast (see above).

6. Consonantal alternation signifies the diminutive in all Interior Salish, Upper Chinook, and Sahaptin, as well as in some languages of the Northwest Coast (see above).

Kutenai, along the eastern border of the Plateau, seems to belong more in the Plains Algonkian linguistic area (see below) than in the Northwest Coast — Plateau linguistic area. It has a generally less complex phonetics than most Northwest Coast — Plateau languages. It has, for example, one stop series (voiceless) and no labiovelars.[26] In grammar, it marks obviation (as do neighboring Algonkian languages, to which it may be ultimately related).

### 3.4.1 *Communicative characteristics of the Plateau*

In pre-Columbian times, the Plateau had the fourth greatest population density of North American culture areas. As in the neighboring Northwest Coast, this population consisted of many small groups speaking diverse languages. Driver describes Plateau social organization as follows (1961:335):

A small minority of peoples in this area possessed only village organization, almost half were grouped in tribelets or aggregations of villages with slight tribal tendency, and the remaining acquired tribal organization from the Plains area in the historic period. The village unit was probably predominant before European contact and was rather small, those of the Sanpoil averaging only seventy-five persons. Fishing rights on rivers were jealously guarded, but the hunting territory between streams was normally shared by neighboring villages. *After the eastern peoples acquired tribal organization, they tended to exclude speakers of foreign languages from their entire territories.* (italics mine).

Spencer, Jennings, et al. (1965) describe a fair degree of movement of groups within the

---

[26] William H. Jacobsen, Jr. points out however (personal communication) that Kutenai is like most Northwest Coast languages in allowing many consonant clusters.

Mackenzie Subarctic and Yukon Subarctic (Spencer *et al.* 154) (see Section 3.1)

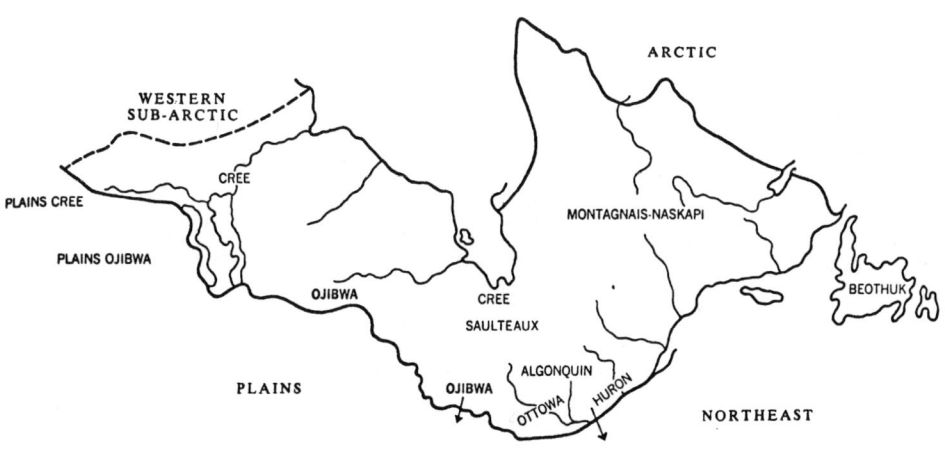

Eastern Subarctic (Spencer *et al.* 397) (see Section 3.2)

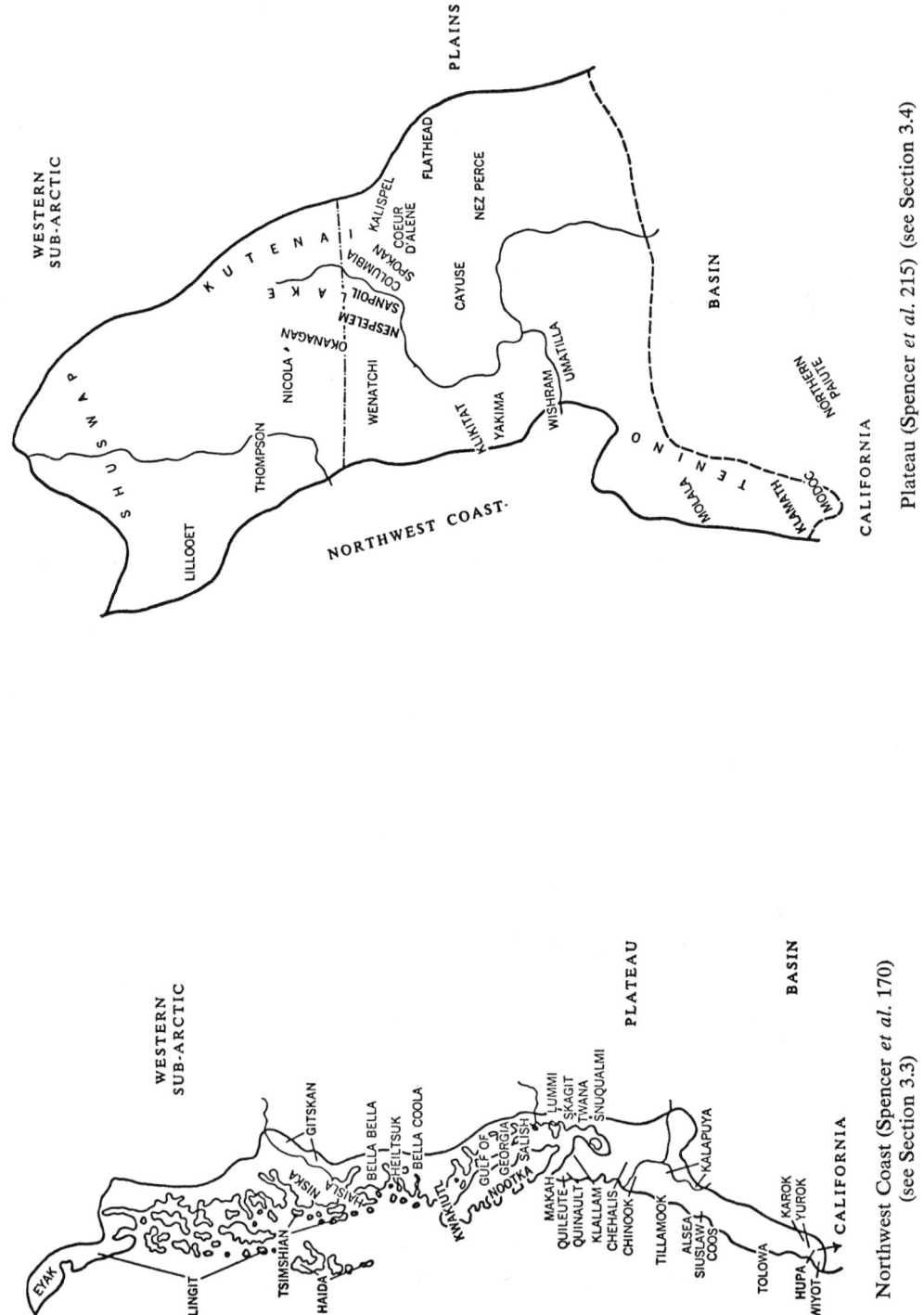

Plateau, good relationships between groups, and the buying of wives from other villages.

Thus, as in the Northwest Coast, individuals must have come into contact with several languages. Multilingualism must have been very common. Notice that in the quotation from Driver above, it is pointed out that it is only recently that speakers of foreign languages were excluded from territories. Earlier, there must have been a very long period of multilingual contact.

Evidence was presented above for considering the Northwest Coast — Plateau as a single linguistic area. Kroeber (1939) describes the Plateau as a 'hinterland' of the Northwest Coast, since the former has influenced the latter to a considerable degree. Driver and Massey (1957) discuss a lively trade carried on in pre-Columbian times among Northwest Coast and Plateau groups. Wealthier interior tradesmen bought wives from coastal villages, the coast being the area of higher prestige. Jacobs (1937) traces lines of prestige from the coast to the interior, and suggests that linguistic traits paralleled cultural traits and diffused eastward.

### 3.5 *Plains*

There are four language families represented in the Plains culture area, Athabascan, Algonkian, Siouan, and Aztec-Tanoan. The Plains is the most recently constituted of the culture areas of North America (late eighteenth and nineteenth century). The linguistic reflex of this fact is that languages share traits with related languages (whether or not they are neighbors) rather than with unrelated neighbors (see Sherzer 1968: Ch. 9, 20). It is thus not possible to speak of the Plains as a linguistic area in the same sense that we have spoken of the Northwest Coast — Plateau or the Yukon-Mackenzie Subarctic as linguistic areas. Since Plains languages are most often contiguous to *related* neighbors with which they share most of the linguistic traits investigated here, it seems valuable to view the Plains (and, as we shall see below, the Prairies and perhaps the East) as consisting of several linguistic areas, Plains Athabascan (Sarsi actually belongs in the Yukon-Mackenzie Subarctic, linguistically, although it has been placed in the Plains, culturally), Plains Algonkian, Plains Siouan, and Plains Aztec-Tanoan. It must be stressed that these units refer to linguistic areas and are not meant to be genetic subdivisions of the families in question.

*Whole areal traits* of the Plains are:
1. prefixation of possessive pronouns of nouns
2. prefixation of subject person markers in verbs
3. pronominal plural

These traits are *family traits* of all Plains languages. They are very common in the languages of North America. They provide some of the evidence for the impression that Plains languages have not developed new linguistic traits as a result of contact with unrelated languages, but rather have for the most part retained *family traits*.

*Central areal traits* of the Plains are:
1. one stop series system
2. the sound: x
3. alienable/inalienable opposition in nouns
4. nominal plural, marked by a suffix
5. inclusive/exclusive opposition in first person plural of pronouns
6. nominal diminutive suffix
7. animate/inanimate gender
8. evidential or source of information markers in the verb

All of these traits are found fairly frequently outside of the Plains; they cannot be used to isolate the Plains as a linguistic area. Each of these traits is a *family trait* of all Plains languages. Again, we see that Plains languages have not changed in the direction of unrelated neighbors; the distribution of these *central areal traits* can be explained as multiple retention of *family traits*.

The Plains can be characterized for its
1. lack of sound: q
2. paucity of sound: $k^w$ (found only in Comanche)
3. paucity of lateral sounds
4. lack of nasal consonants other than m and n
5. paucity of sound: r (found only in Crow and Comanche)

These five traits (or, more precisely, absence of traits) are probably *family traits* of all Plains languages; they contribute to the impression of 'phonetic simplicity' of the Plains. The eastern half of North America is found generally to be phonetically more 'simple' than the western half (in the sense of 'simplicity' used here).

### 3.5.1 *Communicative characteristics of the Plains*

As stated above, the Plains was constituted later than any other North American culture area. This constitution was partly the result of pressure from whites which caused Indians to move west; the acquisition of the gun and the horse led to the sudden and rapid development of 'classic' Plains culture. There was also the last stages of the southerly movement of the Athabascans and the late intrusion of Uto-Aztecan: Comanche. In sharp contrast to the Northwest Coast and the Plateau, then, we have here a case of diverse groups of people who were not at all in intimate contact, and a contact which lasted a relatively short period of time. The Plains, according to Secoy (1953:94):

> was newly formed out of a medley of tribes, some original inhabitants of the natural area and many others, immigrants from the diverse surrounding culture areas. Thus, in the Plains the largest social units tended to be coterminous with the largest cultural units ...

Secoy points out that the type of traits which are usually used to delineate the Plains as a culture area are not well integrated into the cultures in question. We might add that they are not the type of traits whose spread requires intimate, face-to-face contact among groups. In this light, then, it is interesting that Oliver (1962) shows that those cultural traits which are shared by all Plains groups are ecological adaptations, while those in which they differ are often well integrated patterns, retained from the period before the constitution of the Plains culture area.

Most Indians of the Plains achieved tribal organization during the period of their occupation of this area. According to Driver (1961:340), 'The Plains tribes occupied fairly well defined territories which, although sometimes shared with friendly neighbors, were at the same time defended against enemy tribes'. Communication occurred thus mainly among members of the same tribe, speaking the same language. Bilingualism must have been quite rare. It is on the Plains that the sign language developed, thus enabling individuals of diverse tongues to make themselves understood to one another. It is not at all surprising, then, that languages of the Plains have been so little influenced by unrelated neighbors.

### 3.6 *Prairies*

There are four language families represented in the Prairies culture area, Algonkian, Siouan, Caddoan, and Tonkawan. Like the Plains, the Prairies has been constituted fairly recently. Languages tend to share traits with related neighbors rather than with unrelated neighbors (see Sherzer 1968:Ch. 10, 21). The Prairies culture area seems thus best viewed as consisting of the linguistic areas: Prairies Algonkian, Prairies Siouan, Prairies Caddoan, and Prairies Tonkawan.

*Whole areal traits* of the Prairies are:
1. pronominal plural
2. suffixation of tense-aspect markers in verbs

These are *family traits* of all Prairies languages which are retained in all languages.

*Central areal traits* of the Prairies are:
1. voiced stop series
2. s/š opposition
3. sound: x
4. prefixation of possessive pronouns in nouns
5. alienable/inalienable opposition in nouns
6. nominal diminutive suffix
7. nominal plural
8. inclusive/exclusive opposition in the first person plural of the pronoun
9. nominal locative suffixes
10. prefixation of subject person markers in verbs
11. verbal reduplication signifies repetition or distribution
12. evidential or source of information markers in verbs
13. locative-directional markers in verbs

All of these traits are found fairly frequently outside the Prairies and cannot be used

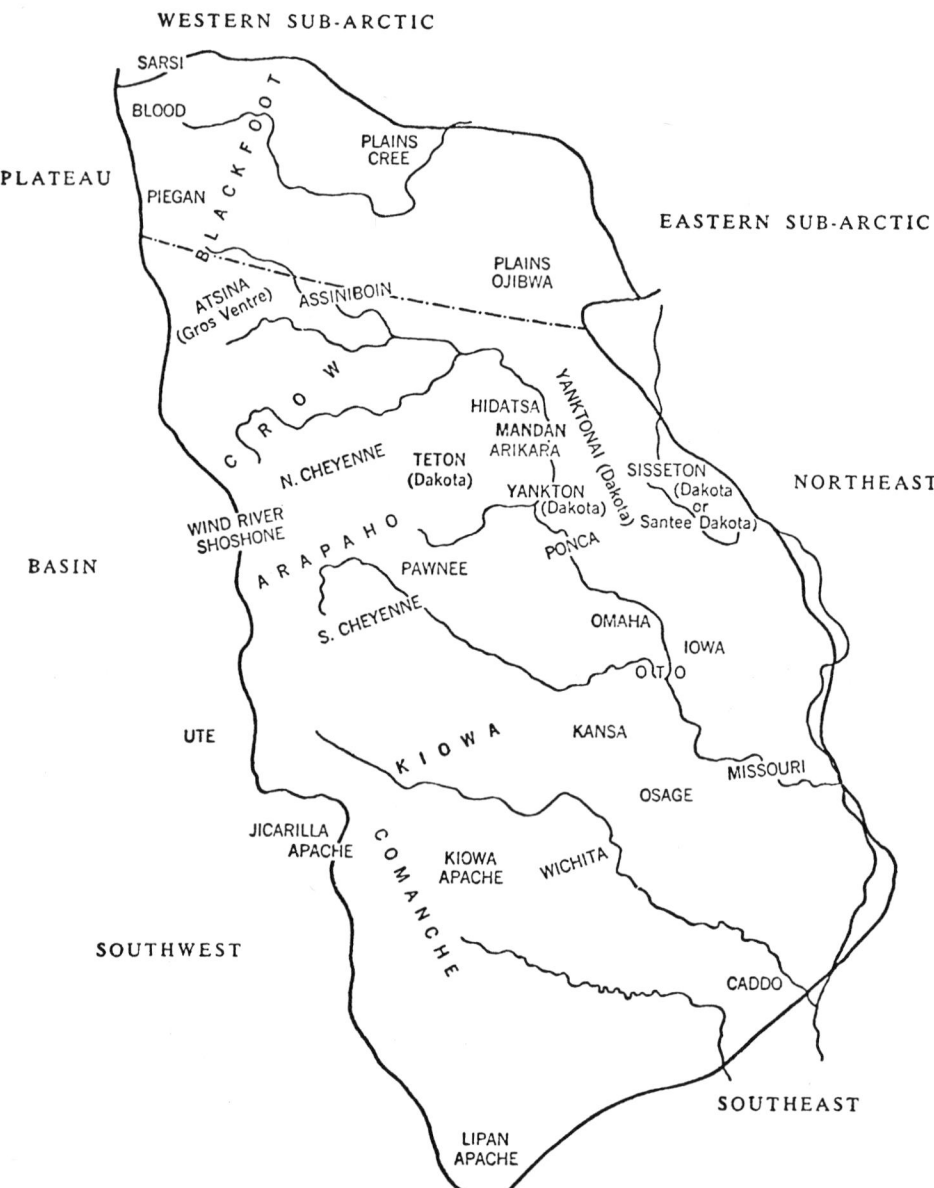

Plains and Prairies (Spencer *et al.* 339) (see Sections 3.5 and 3.6)

(Driver, 1961, map 43) (see Section 3.7)

to isolate the Prairies as a linguistic area. Each of these traits is a *family trait* of several or all Prairies language families. Like Plains languages, Prairies languages have not changed in the direction of unrelated neighbors; the distribution of *central areal traits* can be explained as multiple retention of *family traits*.

The Prairies can be characterized for its
1. lack of glottalized stop series (with the exception of Caddo)
2. lack of sound: q
3. lack of sound: $k^w$ (with the exception of Tonkawa and Wichita)
4. lack of sounds: f and v
5. lack of lateral sounds other than l
6. lack of nasal consonants other than m and n

These six traits (or absence of traits) are probably *family traits* of all Prairies languages; they contribute to the impression of phonetic simplicity of the Prairies.

### 3.6.1 *Communicative characteristics of the Prairies*

The Prairies, like the Plains, seems to have been constituted later than other North American culture areas. Contact between groups speaking unrelated languages occurred for only a short period of time and was not at all intimate. Social organization of the Prairies was probably similar to that of the Plains, although tribes were not quite as well developed. Both Kroeber (1939) and Lowie (1963) treat the Prairies as a subdivision of the Plains. As in the Plains, communication occurred mainly among members of the same tribe or village, speaking the same language. Bilingualism was rare. The communicative characteristics of the Prairies, like those of the Plains, were not at all conducive to the spread of linguistic traits across genetic boundaries. They rather encouraged linguistic uniformity within single languages or language families occupying a continuous area.

### 3.7 *East*

There are six language families represented in the Eastern culture area, Iroquoian, Algonkian, Siouan, Yuchian, Gulf, and Caddoan. These language families are spread over a rather large area; for the most part, each one forms a continuous area. Speakers of each language, then, tended to come into contact with speakers of their own or a related language rather than with speakers of unrelated languages, which are located at some distance. As in the Prairies and the Plains, language families in the East tend to be homogeneous with regard to the traits investigated here (see Sherzer 1968: Ch. 11, 22).

*Central areal traits* of the East are:
1. one fricative series system
2. sound: l
3. alienable/inalienable opposition in nouns

4. pronominal plural
5. prefixation of subject person markers in verbs
6. suffixation of tense-aspect markers in verbs
7. locative-directional prefixes in verbs

These traits are all found fairly frequently outside the East and cannot be used to isolate the East as a linguistic area. They are all *family traits* of the languages in which they are found. Multiple retention, then, rather than developments in the direction of neighbors, accounts for the distribution of these traits.

The East can be characterized for its

1. lack of glottalized stop series (with the exception of Chitimacha and Yuchi)
2. lack of sound: q
3. lack of sound: $k^w$ (with the exception of Natchez)

The distribution of a number of traits suggests the existence of a northeastern linguistic area and a southeastern linguistic area.

*Regional areal traits* of the Northeast are:

1. Nominal diminutives, marked by a suffix, found in all (?) Iroquoian and all Algonkian.

2. Nominal plural, marked by a suffix, found in all (?) Iroquoian and all Algonkian.

3. Inclusive/exclusive opposition in the first person plural of the pronoun, found in all Iroquoian and all Algonkian.

4. Nominal locative suffixes, found in all (?) Iroquoian and all Algonkian.

5. Nominal incorporation in verbs, found in all Iroquoian and all (?) Algonkian.

6. Prefixation of tense-aspect markers in the verb, found in all Iroquoian and all Algonkian.

*Regional areal traits* of the Southeast are:

1. Sound: f, found in all Muskogean, Yuchi, Ofo, and Tuscarora.

2. Possessive pronouns marked by independent morphemes, found in all Gulf languages, except Tunica.

3. Nominal diminutives, marked by a suffix, found in most Gulf languages.

4. Nominal plural, marked by a suffix, found in all Gulf languages except Atakapa.

5. Pronominal dual, found in most Gulf languages and Ofo.

6. Nominal locative suffixes, found in all Gulf, Yuchi, and Siouan.

7. Suffixation of subject person markers in verbs, found in all Gulf, except Natchez.

8. Active/static opposition in verbs, found in all Gulf languages, all Siouan, all Iroquoian, and Yuchi.

9. Reduplication of verbal stem signifies distribution or repetition, found in most Gulf and Yuchi.

### 3.7.1 *Communicative characteristics of the East*

According to Kroeber (1939), the East was one of the less dense areas of North America, with regard to population. Since five language families (for the most part forming continuous areas) are spread over a large area, there was little opportunity for intimate contact between genetically diverse languages. This situation contrasts sharply with the Northwest Coast — Plateau linguistic area, where there was much intimate contact among groups speaking genetically distinct languages.

Social organization in the East (again in sharp contrast with the Northwest Coast — Plateau) was unfavorable to the formation of linguistic areas across genetic boundaries. Tribal organization and, in the historic period, 'league' or 'confederacy' organization, was common, so that individuals had most or all contacts with persons speaking the same language or a closely related dialect. Most relations with alien peoples were not too friendly. Bilingualism was probably rather rare.[27] The distribution of folktales is a good indicator of lines of communication in an area. Unfortunately, we rarely have information concerning the density of diffusion of tales. A welcome exception is Thompson's report (1929) that the Iroquois tales are totally distinct from other groups. This state of affairs contrasts sharply with that reported earlier for the Northwest Coast, where there is a dense diffusion of tales across genetic linguistic boundaries.

It thus appears that the East, like the Prairies and the Plains, is best viewed not as a single linguistic area, but rather as several, corresponding to the genetic areas: Eastern Algonkian, Eastern Iroquoian, Eastern Siouan-Yuchian, Eastern Gulf, and Eastern Caddoan. Some modifications of this view, however, are relevant. First, the East, the Eastern Subarctic, the Prairies, and most of the Plains and the Great Basin can be contrasted with much of the western half of North America in that languages have simpler phonetic systems. Second, a clustering of linguistic traits in the Northeast and the Southeast suggests the possibility of a subdivision of the Eastern culture area into two basic linguistic areas, Northeast and Southeast. This would fit the traditional subclassification of the Eastern culture area into a northern and southern subarea (a subclassification based, of course, on the distribution of *nonlinguistic* cultural traits). Third, although the Gulf languages have recently been shown to form a genetic unit (see Haas 1958), this unit consists of a number of families (Muskogean, Natchez, Tunica, Chitimachan, and Atakapan). These families were neighbors in the Southeast for a very long period of time (well before the development of tribal organization). Thus, traits shared by the various Gulf languages may be the result of earlier conditions somewhat similar to those described above for the Northwest Coast culture area, i.e., small groups of people speaking distinct languages but in intimate contact with one another. Archeological and ethnohistorical research should throw some light on this question.

In summary, then, we have found that in the East (and the Plains and Prairies), lines of communication were for the most part within genetic linguistic boundaries; linguistic areas tend to coincide with genetic areas. This state of affairs contrasts with the Northwest Coast — Plateau, California, and the Oasis, in which lines of communication often cut across genetic linguistic boundaries, and linguistic areas and genetic areas tend not to coincide.

[27] Mary Haas, however, feels (personal communication) that in the Southeast, especially within the Creek Confederacy, there was considerable multilingualism.

### 3.8 *California*

California resembles the Northwest Coast — Plateau in that there is much linguistic diversity in a relatively small area. There are five language families represented in California: Athabascan, Yukian, Hokan (with widely divergent branches), Penutian (with widely divergent branches), and Uto-Aztecan. California also resembles the Northwest Coast — Plateau in that many traits were found to have distributions which cut across genetic boundaries. California contrasts with the Northwest Coast — Plateau, however, in that it seems to consist of several linguistic areas (not just one), although these several linguistic areas do not coincide with genetic areas (as they seem to in the East, the Prairies, and the Plains) (see Sherzer 1968: Ch. 12, 23).

*Central areal traits* of California are:
1. voiced stop series
2. sound: a central vowel (ə or i)
3. glottalized stop series
4. one fricative series
5. sound: l
6. nominal case system
7. possessive pronouns of nouns are independent morphemes
8. alienable/inalienable opposition in nouns
9. pronominal plural
10. nominal plural, marked by a suffix
11. pronominal dual
12. inclusive/exclusive opposition in the first person plural of pronouns
13. nominal locative suffixes
14. verbal reduplication signifies distribution, repetition, etc.
15. suffixation of tense-aspect markers in verbs
16. evidential or source of information markers in verbs

The distributions of these *central areal traits* do not coincide; they form, rather, a pattern with much overlapping at the center. This lack of coincidence in the distribution of *central areal traits* is one of the factors which leads us to treat California as consisting of several linguistic areas rather than forming a single area. Nonetheless, of the above traits, there are some which are especially characteristic of California, and may be sufficient to consider the California culture area as a whole as a linguistic area. These are:

2. central vowel
6. nominal case system
7. possessive pronouns of nouns are independent morphemes
11. pronominal dual
12. inclusive/exclusive opposition in the first person plural of pronouns

The distribution of a number of traits suggests the existence of a northern California linguistic area:

1. The sound θ is found in an almost continuous area in the north, consisting of Chimariko, Northern Wintu, Atsugewi (and Karok, along the boundary between the Northwest Coast and California culture areas).

2. The sound ł is found in Eastern Pomo, Lake Miwok, Northern Hill Patwin, and some Pacific Coast Athabascan.

3. The sound ƛ' is found in Lake Miwok, Northern Wintu, Northern Hill Patwin, and some Pacific Coast Athabascan.

4. The sound ŋ is found in some Athabascan, Hokan (Atsugewi), Penutian (Maidu [allophonically] and Sierra Miwok), and Uto-Aztecan (Northern Paiute).

5. Prefixation of the possessive pronouns of nouns is found in northern California.

6. The visibility/invisibility opposition in nouns is found in Pomo and Hupa.

7. Prefixation of the subject person markers of verbs is found in northern California.

8. Prefixation of tense-aspect markers in the verb is found in a small subarea of northern California, consisting of Pacific Coast Athabascan and Wappo.

9. Different verb stems for nouns of different form or shape are found in Pacific Coast Athabascan, Wappo, Pomo, and Yana.

The distribution of a number of traits suggests the existence of a north-central California linguistic area:

1. Four stop series are found in a small area consisting of Eastern, Southwestern, and Central Pomo, Lake Miwok, and all Wintun.

2. Retroflex apicals are found in an area in north-central California consisting of Yukian, Pomo, Miwok, Costanoan, Yokuts, and Salinan.

3. Instrumental prefixes in the verb are found in northern-central California in an area which links Penutian Maidu with northern California Hokan and Uto-Aztecan languages.

4. Locative-directional markers in the verb are found mainly in northern-central California in an area which links Penutian Maidu with northern California Hokan and Uto-Aztecan languages.

5. The inclusive/exclusive opposition in the first person dual of pronouns is found in Wintun, Sierra Miwok, Yokuts, Atsugewi, Shoshone, and Tubatulabal.

The distribution of a number of traits suggests the existence of a southern California linguistic area:

1. Retroflex dentals are found in the Yuman languages.

2. The sound $k^w$ is found in the Yuman languages.

3. The sound v is found in Cahuilla, Luiseño, Cupeño, Serrano, and Yuman.

4. The sound ł is found in Yuma and Diegueño.

5. The sound $l^y$ is found in Yuma, Mohave, Diegueño, Cahuilla, and Cupeño.

6. The sound ŋ is found in Penutian (Tule-Kaweah Yokuts) and Uto-Aztecan (Tubatulabal, Southern Paiute, Serrano, Luiseño, Cupeño, and Cahuilla).

7. The sound ñ is found in Yuman, Cahuilla, and Cupeño

8. The sound r is found in Uto-Aztecan (Southern Paiute, Serrano, Luiseño, and Cupeño) and Hokan (Yuman: Diegueño).

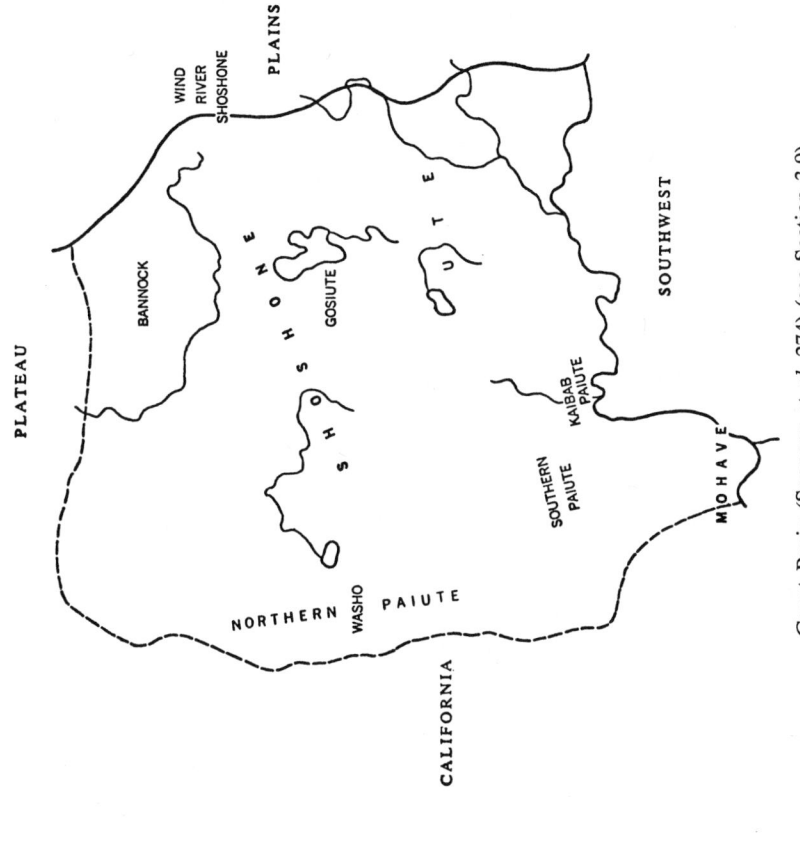

Great Basin (Spencer *et al.* 274) (see Section 3.9)

California (Spencer *et al.* 230) (see Section 3.8)

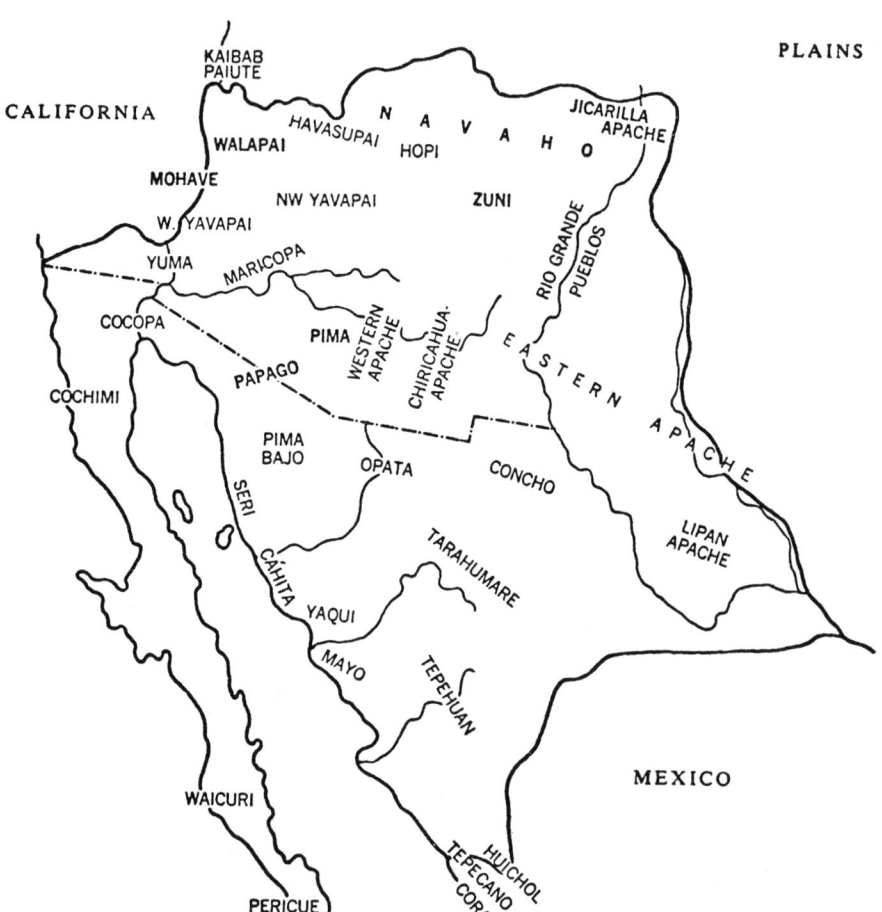

Greater Southwest (Spencer *et al.* 289) (see Section 3.10)

9. Prefixation of the possessive pronouns of nouns is found in southern California.

10. Prefixation of the subject person markers of verbs is found in southern California.

We have thus seen that the California culture area is probably best viewed as consisting of (at least) three linguistic areas, northern California, central or northern-central California, and southern California. Like the distributions of the *central areal traits*, the distributions of the *regional areal traits* (northern, central, or southern) overlap considerably. The differences in the distributions reflect differences in time depth and the nature of contacts between groups as well as differences in the susceptibility of particular linguistic traits to diffusion. Most traits investigated in this study exhibit rather small, continuous distributions in California.

3.8.1 *Communicative characteristics of California*

In pre-Columbian times, California had the greatest population density of all North American culture areas. The California population was concentrated along the coastal belt and at the mouths of streams. As in the Northwest Coast, this dense population consisted for the most part of many small groups speaking diverse languages. Tribes existed only among the marginal Mohave and Yuma. All other groups were organized into very small bands or villages, the only exception being the Yokuts, who approached 'tribelet' organization. Neighboring groups seemed to have good relationships with one another. These relationships must have lasted a relatively long period of time; the California culture area seems to have been constituted in its present form quite early. Thus, as in the Northwest Coast — Plateau, conditions were excellent for intimate contacts among groups speaking diverse languages. There was probably a considerable amount of trade, intermarriage, and bilingualism. The linguistic situation described above reflects these communicative characteristics of the California culture area. Although there is much genetic diversity linguistically (i.e. there are many unrelated or distantly related languages), many of the traits investigated here were found to have distributions which cut across genetic boundaries. The distributions of most traits were continuous but rather limited in extension. Relations with immediate neighbors, whether related or not, were quite intimate; while relations with distant groups (Kroeber 1939 says more than fifty miles away) were practically nonexistent.

Clear Lake is a good example of a California subarea in which groups speaking diverse languages had intimate contacts. There were speakers of Lake Miwok, Patwin, Pomo, and Wappo. There are a number of traits shared by several languages in the Clear Lake area:

1. four-stop-series system
2. retroflex dentals
3. sound: ł
4. glottalized semivowels

Catherine Callaghan (1964:47) says the following of the Clear Lake subarea: 'There was frequent contact, including some intermarriage, between groups of Indians around Clear Lake, and polylingualism was common.'

Students of California culture tend to divide the California culture area into three subareas: northern, central, and southern. The linguistic data suggest that California probably consists of three (main) linguistic areas, northern California, central California, and southern California (see above), thus paralleling the division made on non-linguistic, cultural grounds. Spencer, Jennings, et al. (1965) describe much trade and other contact between Yumans and Uto-Aztecans in southern California. Much more needs to be known about the details of interrelationships among other California Indian groups before we can definitively determine the geographic limits of and the nature of the communicative areas.

### 3.9 *Great Basin*

The Great Basin culture area resembles the Yukon-Mackenzie Subarctic and the Eastern Subarctic in that there is relatively little linguistic diversity from the genetic point of view. There are two language families represented in the Great Basin, Uto-Aztecan and Hokan. Hokan is only marginally represented. There is only one Hokan language, Washo, and it lies on the border between the California and Great Basin culture areas. Thus, most individuals in the Great Basin came into contact with speakers of either their own or a related language. With regard to the linguistic traits investigated in this study, there is a great deal of uniformity in the Great Basin (see Sherzer 1968:Ch. 13, 24).

*Whole areal traits* of the Great Basin are:
1. one fricative series (voiceless)
2. suffixation of nominal diminutive marker[28]
3. pronominal plural
4. suffixation of tense-aspect markers in verbs
5. different verb stems for nouns of different number

These traits are *family traits* of both Hokan and Uto-Aztecan.

*Central areal traits* of the Great Basin are
1. 3-2-1 vowel system
2. sound: ɨ
3. sound: ŋ
4. voiced stop series (often subphonemic)
5. sound: $k^w$
6. one fricative series
7. alienable/inalienable opposition in nouns
8. nominal locative suffixes
9. nominal reduplication signifies plurality, repetition, etc.
10. inclusive/exclusive opposition in the first person plural of pronouns

---

[28] William H. Jacobsen, Jr. notes (personal communication) that there is no productive diminutive in Washo. The diminutive suffix occurs with only two or three words.

11. suffixation of source of information markers in verbs
12. prefixation of instrumental markers in verbs

It is on the basis of these *whole areal traits* and *central areal traits* that we can consider the Great Basin to be a linguistic area as well as a culture area. Of the *whole areal traits*, 5. and of the *central areal traits*, 1., 2., 3., 5., 10., and 12. are especially characteristic of the Great Basin.

A number of traits are found mainly in the southern region of the Great Basin and suggest the existence of a southern subarea within the Great Basin linguistic area. These are:

1. sound: q
2. sound: v
3. sound: x
4. sound: ñ

These traits are also found in the southern California linguistic area (see above), thus providing evidence of links between southern California and the Great Basin.

### 3.9.1 *Communicative characteristics of the Great Basin*

The Great Basin was one of the more sparsely populated culture areas of North America in pre-Columbian times. A semi-nomadic life kept local groups in constant contact with one another. Social organization consisted of a continuous series of related villages which were at peace with, and intermarried into, one another. Wick Miller (1966:104) feels that 'the lack of divergence is more apt to be the result of recent occupation, but constant moving about must have played a part in the kind of dialect distribution that is found'. This semi-nomadic existence seems to have been characteristic not only of Great Basin groups (Hokan and Uto-Aztecan), but of some groups in nearby California as well. Downs (1966:42) says the following of the Great Basin:

We should further recall that these bands tended to move rather freely through their territory, despite general identification of certain groups with certain areas. Shortages or over-supply of wild crops or animals either forced bands to leave traditional gathering and hunting grounds or attracted people from less provident areas. For the most part decisions to make these translocations were made by the individual bands and not by larger entities. And we should recall that data from the Basin reflect a great deal of shifting of groups and of individuals, with intermarriage being quite common in some areas. In fact, were one to take all the groups in the Basin, it is possible to postulate a network of intermarriages between groups from the western foothills of the Sierra Nevada where the Washo intermarried with the Nisenan to the western slopes of the Rockies where Paiute, Ute, Shoshone, and Bannock intermingled.

Thus, the communicative characteristics of the Great Basin: small constantly interacting groups of people, intermarriage, and probable bilingualism, have led to a certain degree of linguistic uniformity. We can thus conclude that the Great Basin is a linguistic area as well as a culture area.

### 3.10 *Southwest*

In the Southwest, there is considerable linguistic diversity (from the genetic point of view) concentrated in a relatively small area. There are five language families, Aztec-Tanoan, Hokan, Athabascan, Zunian, and Keresan. All of the languages of the area (with the exception of Athabascan) have been there for a considerable length of time. In spite of this long period of languages in contact, there is relatively little agreement among languages as regards the traits investigated here (see Sherzer 1968: Ch. 14, 25).

*Whole areal traits* of the Southwest are:
1. pronominal plural
2. suffixation of tense-aspect markers in verbs

Both these traits occur frequently in the languages of North America (and in the languages of the world) and do not isolate the Southwest linguistically.

*Central areal traits* of the Southwest are:
1. voiced stop series
2. glottalized stop series
3. s/š opposition
4. sound: l
5. prefixation of possessive pronouns of nouns
6. alienable/inalienable opposition in nouns
7. nominal locative suffixes
8. prefixation of subject person markers of verbs

All these traits (except 2.) are also fairly common in the languages of North America. Traits found in other culture areas but entirely lacking in the Southwest are:
1. inclusive/exclusive opposition in pronouns
2. visibility/invisibility opposition in demonstratives
3. numeral classifiers
4. instrumental markers in verbs

Thus, the principal basis for considering the Southwest as a whole to be a linguistic area is the absence of four traits. For this reason, we conclude (see below) that although the Southwest is a culture area, it is not a linguistic area.

On the other hand, the distribution of a number of traits suggests the possibility of considering the Pueblo region of the Southwest to be a linguistic area.

1. A 2-2-1 vowel system is found in Zuni, Keresan, and some Tanoan.
2. Voiceless vowels, nasals, and semivowels are found in Hopi, Keresan, and Zuni.
3. Phonemic pitch is found in Keresan and Tanoan, as well as in Apachean.
4. The sound $k^w$ is found in Hopi, Zuni, and Tanoan, as well as in Navajo.
5. Pronominal dual is found in Zuni, Tanoan, and Keresan, as well as in Apachean.
6. Nominal plural is marked by a suffix in Hopi, Zuni, Keresan, and Tanoan, as well as in Walapai.
7. Nominal incorporation in verbs is found in Hopi, Zuni, Keresan, and Tanoan, as well as in Walapai.

8. Different verb stems for nouns of different number are found in Zuni, Keresan, and Tanoan, as well as in Papago and Apachean.

9. Locative-directional markers in verbs are found in no Pueblo language and in all non-Pueblo Southwest languages.

10. Switch reference is found in Hopi and Zuni.

Although the distributions of these traits sometimes include languages outside the Pueblo region and sometimes omit languages within this region, there is clearly a concentration of traits with a Pueblo locus.

The distribution of several traits suggests the existence of a westerly linguistic area within the Southwest, with links in southern California and the Great Basin. It is difficult to determine whether Hopi belongs in this linguistic area or in the Pueblo linguistic area described above. It clearly has links with both.

1. A one stop series system is found in all Yuman and in Hopi.

2. The sound q is found in Hopi and some Yuman, as well as in languages in southern California and the Great Basin (see above).

3. The sound v is found in Hopi and some Yuman, as well as in languages in southern California and the Great Basin (see above).

4. The sound ñ is found in Hopi, Papago, most Yuman, and Santa Clara Tewa, as well as in languages in southern California and the Great Basin (see above).

5. A nominal case system is found in Hopi and all Yuman, as well as languages in southern California and the Great Basin (see above).

3.10.1 *Communicative characteristics of the Southwest*

In pre-Columbian times the Southwest had the third greatest population density of all North American culture areas. The Pueblo subarea of the Southwest had by far the greatest population density in North America. Within the Southwest were found various kinds of social organization. The desert Yumans and Apacheans were organized into small, fluid bands. The river Yumans possessed large tribes. The Pueblo Indians lived in villages whose populations were in the hundreds.

It has long been noted that Southwest Indians share many non-linguistic, cultural traits while remaining quite distinct linguistically. The linguistic side of this picture is confirmed in this study. The Southwest culture area is not here considered to be a linguistic area. In the light of the degree of population density, the length of time groups have been neighbors, and the homogeneity of culture, it may seem difficult to determine why the Southwest did not become more uniform linguistically. In other areas with dense populations (Northwest Coast — Plateau, California), many linguistic traits were found to have continuous distributions cutting across genetic linguistic boundaries. In the Southwest, traits tend to be more randomly distributed, suggesting that little mutual linguistic influencing has occurred. The explanation of this situation may be found in a sociolinguistic factor about which we rarely have data— attitude toward language. The Southwest is one area for which many observers have reported attitudes towards one's own language and that of others, perhaps because these attitudes are often quite explicit. Southwest Indians are very conservative with respect to language, taking pride in their own language and often refusing to learn that of others. When they do learn other languages, they seem consciously to avoid allowing alien linguistic traits to penetrate their own linguistic system. We have here a good example of the interaction of several socio-cultural factors and linguistic change. Although the Southwest and the Northwest Coast are similar with regard to population density and availability of contact with alien languages, attitudes toward language have inhibited the spread of linguistic traits in one area and seemingly encouraged it in another.

Although the Pueblo subarea of the Southwest (like the Southwest as a whole) is known for its negative attitude toward alien linguistic traits (see Dozier 1951, 1956), some traits were found to be shared by all or most Pueblo languages, leading us to posit a Pueblo linguistic area (see above). It must be stressed, however, that the evidence for setting up the Pueblo area as a linguistic area is weak, when compared, for example, with that used in setting up the Northwest Coast — Plateau linguistic area. Pueblo groups have resided side by side in the Southwest for centuries, longer than non-Pueblo groups. (The Apacheans, for example, are relative newcomers to the Southwest.) Still, there is relatively little linguistic reflection of this long coresidence.

Traits shared by westerly Southwest languages and languages of southern California and the Great Basin are a reflection of relations which are known to have existed among groups in these areas (see Kroeber 1939).

## 4. LANGUAGE CHANGE IN NORTH AMERICA: IMPLICATIONS FOR A THEORY OF LANGUAGE CHANGE

In the last section, we summarized the results obtained in Sherzer (1968), comparing linguistic areas with culture areas. There have been relatively few attempts in American anthropology to apply the culture area concept to language. In the first decade of this century, Dixon and Kroeber (1903) tried to determine linguistic areas of California, considering the distribution of linguistic traits, irrespective of the genetic affiliation of languages. Although the culture area concept became dominant in anthropology, the analogous linguistic area concept (used by Dixon and Kroeber) found few adherents in linguistics (see 1. above: Areal Linguistic Studies in North America: A Historical Perspective). Wissler (1917) looked at language mainly from a genetic standpoint. He seemed to feel that families (or stocks) formed areas analogous to (or coincident with) the culture areas with which he operated.

The suggestion is, therefore, that the similarities of languages within a geographical, or culture area, are due to the expansion of the early parent stocks within their habitats, and to the long association made possible thereby. (333)

Sapir (1921b) pointed out that within the same culture area one often found languages with entirely different genetic affiliations. He seemed thus to conclude that language areas and culture areas do not coincide. In his earlier 1916 article, however, he distinguished two types of approach to language history — the genetic and the diffusional — and indicated the parallels between the latter approach and the culture area tradition in anthropology.

We have attempted here to integrate the culture area and the linguistic area concepts by determining to what degree North American culture areas and linguistic areas coincide and by trying to understand the communicative background to the various cases discussed. It was found that three sets of socio-cultural (or communicative) conditions correspond to three types of linguistic (or communicative) areas:

1. relatively sparsely populated area, individuals organized in small groups, little linguistic diversity from the genetic point of view, contact among groups, intermarriage, some bilingualism: Great Basin, Eastern Subarctic, Yukon-Mackenzie Subarctic.

2. densely populated area, individuals organized in relatively small groups, many language families, constant intimate contact among groups, much intermarriage and bilingualism: Northwest Coast — Plateau, Northern California, Central California, Southern California, Pueblo area.

3. village or tribal organization, few friendly contacts with groups speaking languages distinct from one's own, little or no bilingualism: Plains Athabascan, Plains Algonkian, Plains Siouan, Plains Aztec-Tanoan, Prairies Algonkian, Prairies Siouan, Prairies Caddoan, Prairies Tonkawan, Eastern Algonkian, Eastern Iroquoian, Eastern Siouan-Yuchian, Eastern Gulf, Eastern Caddoan.

In the development of culture areas, two types of socio-cultural phenomena are involved. On the one hand, there are ecological adaptations. In this category are such traits as subsistence techniques, clothing, and artifacts. Language enters here only in its lexical-semantic aspect (see Sapir 1912, Trager 1939). On the other hand, there are areal developments due to intimate, face-to-face contact among groups. Here we have in mind some types of social organization, folktales, expressive behavior, and most aspects of language. Anthropologists working in the culture area tradition have tended to think mainly in terms of ecological adaptations as the underlying factor in the formation of culture areas.[29] It seems to make more sense, however, to conceive of socio-cultural traits in terms of a continuum, ranging from traits which are highly sensitive to the environment to traits which are not so at all. Areal distributions of the latter, then, are more significant than those of the former as indicators of communicative contacts among groups. We stress that it is not mere contact in space which leads to diffusion and therefore to the development of linguistic areas. Rather, internal linguistic factors together with certain socio-cultural conditions (more precisely, *communicative conditions*: type of social organization; density of population; degree of trade, intermarriage, and multilingualism; attitudes toward language; etc.) can encourage or inhibit the diffusion of linguistic traits.

[29] For an excellent discussion of the positions taken on this question by various scholars, especially with reference to the problematic Plains culture area, see Oliver 1962, Chapter 2.

Students of American Indian language history have focused predominantly on genetic relationships. This is unfortunate for two reasons.

First, genetic relationships provide information about only one aspect of language history and an aspect which is often least important for students of culture history. According to Hymes (1968:41):

> the evidence for placing languages in genetic families consists of less adaptive features, i.e., those most resistant to reflecting the communicative adaptations of the users of the languages. The greater the time-depth of the relationship the smaller the portion of the present-day features of languages that are pertinent to the genetic connection, and the less likely it is that the genetically interesting features reflect communicative ties.

As we have seen here, areal-diffusional links among languages are important reflexes of communicative contacts among the speakers of the languages and of the nature of these contacts. In order to arrive at a true appreciation of culture history, one must study both genetic and areal-diffusional linguistic relationships (as was stated succinctly by Sapir 1916).

Second, even in the study of genetic relationships per se, it is important to distinguish resemblances in languages which are due to common origin from those which are due to diffusion. Areal-typological studies are an important aid to this task. They provide information about what traits are likely to be associated with particular areas, which traits are more susceptible to diffusion, and which groups have undergone the kind of contact in which diffusion takes place.

Areal-typological studies have certain implications for a theory of language change, especially the important question of the relationship between the synchronic and the diachronic pictures. A major contribution toward such a theory is provided by Weinreich, Labov, and Herzog (1968). These authors argue that we must assume that all speech communities are heterogeneous and study the ways in which this heterogeneity is projected in time and space. In the present study, of course, we are concerned with the nature of speech communities which lead to the formation of linguistic areas. We envisage speech communities in which speakers have repertoires of linguistic varieties; choices among varieties depend on sociolinguistic rules of usage (see Gumperz 1962, 1967; Hymes 1967). The linguistic varieties in a repertoire may be slight differences in pronunciation or grammatical patterns within one language (as in most of the examples given in Weinreich, Labov, and Herzog) or mutually unintelligible languages (as in Gumperz 1967). When the latter case is projected in space, the result is an overlapping of socio-cultural and linguistic boundaries. This is clearly the case in some of the linguistic areas which we have considered here, for example, the Northwest Coast — Plateau. In this area, for a long period of time, there must have been many communities in which two or more languages were spoken, each serving specific social functions. Apparently, when languages are in such intimate and constant contact, they begin to influence one another structurally. According to Gumperz (1967:49), 'code switching in everyday interaction sets up cross currents of diffusion which materially change the structure of local speech varieties.' It is many generations of such face-to-face language contact which led to the development of the linguistic areas described here.[30]

One might ask why it is that multilingual situations are maintained over long periods of time, i.e. why is it that some of the varieties in the repertoire are not eliminated, thereby simplifying the language learning process. The reason is social and not linguistic; i.e. multilanguage usage is maintained in a community because each of the varieties is needed to serve different social functions. Yet at the same time, the diffusion of linguistic traits and the resultant uniformization tends to minimize the differences between varieties, thus in a certain sense making the language learning task easier.

## 5. SUGGESTIONS FOR FURTHER RESEARCH

It is convenient to group the following remarks into three areas, linguistic, sociolinguistic, and ethnohistorical.

We reported here on a study which investigated many linguistic traits in the American Indian languages north of Mexico. A useful next step might be to look at certain of these in much greater detail. For example, with regard to reduplication, we might ask: What form does it take, i.e. initial, medial, or final? What types of meanings does it express: plurality, distribution or repetition in space, diminutive, adjective? Similarly, with regard to numeral or verbal classifiers: How do they categorize the world of objects? What are the underlying semantic dimensions? We suspect that such investigations will lead to the discovery of interesting areal patterns.

It will also be valuable to study traits which were not looked at here, for example, in the area of morphophonemics and syntax. Here we have in mind such questions as: What is the relationship between voiceless laterals and other sounds in the language — do they pattern with other laterals or with fricatives? What are the types of word order found in various areas?

In areal linguistic studies, we often want to know if a particular trait in a language is a retention from its ancestor or a recent development, perhaps due to contact with neighboring languages. For this purpose, we need much more information than we have now about the characteristics (especially morphological and syntactic) of the various proto-languages of North America, i.e. proto-Algonkian, proto-Athabascan, proto-Hokan, proto-Penutian, proto-Salishan, etc.

A number of traits which we might label sociolinguistic have been sporadically reported for the languages of North America, for example, baby talk, greeting patterns, men's and women's speech, onomatopoeia, and the role of silence. An areal investigation of these phenomena would be interesting. With regard to baby talk, one might ask: What form does it take: reduplication? consonantal alternation? special vocabu-

---

[30] One suspects that, other things being equal, the more intense and intimate this contact, the more linguistically uniform is the resulting linguistic area. As this study has attempted to show, however, other factors, such as attitudes towards languages, also play a role.

lary? When and by whom is it used? What is the society's attitude toward baby talk?

In the area of ethnohistory, there is a need for much greater documentation than now exists concerning the communicative conditions in various parts of North America. How much bilingualism was there? How long did it last? Was it restricted to certain individuals (e.g. traders) or was there societal bilingualism? How much intermarriage was there among groups speaking diverse languages? What was the direction of this intermarriage, i.e. was there an attempt to marry one's children with more prestigious neighbors? In general, what was the nature of communication among aboriginal groups in North America?

## BIBLIOGRAPHY

AOKI, HARUO. 1963. Reduplication in Nez Perce. IJAL 29.42–4.

———. 1966. Nez Perce vowel harmony and Proto-Sahaptian vowels. Lg 42.759–67.

BLOOMFIELD, LEONARD. 1933. Language. New York, Holt & Co.

BOAS, FRANZ. 1889. The Indians of British Columbia. Proceedings and Transactions of the Royal Society of Canada for the year 1888. 6 (section 2).47–57.

———. 1892. Notes on the Chemakum language. AmA 5.37–44.

———. 1896. The growth of Indian mythologies. JAF 9.1–11. Reprinted in Franz Boas, Race, language and culture, pp. 425–36. New York, Macmillan, 1966.

———. 1900. Sketch of the Kwakiutl language. AmA 2.708–21.

———. 1911. Tsimshian. HAIL 1.283–422 (= BAE-B 40).

———. 1929. Classification of American Indian languages. Lg 5.1–7. Reprinted in Franz Boas, Race, language, and culture, pp. 219–25. New York, Macmillan, 1966.

BRIGHT, JANE and WILLIAM. 1965. Semantic structures in Northwestern California and the Sapir-Whorf Hypothesis. AmA 67/5, Part 2.249–58.

BRIGHT, WILLIAM. 1959. Review of R. H. Robins, The Yurok language (UCPL 15, 1958). Lg 35.100–4.

CALLAGHAN, CATHERINE A. 1964. Phonemic borrowing in Lake Miwok. Studies in Californian linguistics, ed. by William Bright, pp. 46–53. (UCPL 34.)

DIXON, R. B. 1906. The pronominal dual in the languages of California. Boas Anniversary volume, pp. 80–4. New York.

DIXON, R. B., and ALFRED L. KROEBER. 1903. The native languages of California. AmA 5.21–6.

———. 1907. Numeral systems of the languages of California. AmA 9.663–90.

———. 1913. New linguistic families in California. AmA 15.647–55.

———. 1919. Linguistic families in California. UCPAAE 16.46–118.

DOWNS, JAMES F. 1966. The significance of environmental manipulation in Great Basin cultural development. The current status of anthropological research in the Great Basin: 1964, ed. by Warren L. D'Azevedo et al., pp. 39–56. Reno, University of Nevada Press.

DOZIER, EDWARD P. 1951. Resistance to acculturation and assimilation in an Indian Pueblo. AmA 53.56–66.
——. 1956. Two examples of linguistic acculturation. Lg 32.146–57. Reprinted in Hymes 1964 (q.v.), pp. 509–20.
DRIVER, HAROLD E. 1961. Indians of North America. Chicago, University of Chicago Press.
DRIVER, HAROLD E., and WILLIAM C. MASSEY. 1957. Comparative studies of North American Indians. TAPS 47.165–456.
DRUCKER, PHILIP. 1955. Indians of the Northwest Coast. New York, American Museum of Natural History.
EMENEAU, MURRAY. 1953. Dravidian kinship terms. Lg 29.339–53.
——. 1956. India as a linguistic area. Lg 32.3–16. Reprinted in Hymes 1964 (q.v.), pp. 642–53.
——. 1962. Bilingualism and structural borrowing. PAPS 106.430–42.
GREENBERG, JOSEPH H., ed. 1966. Universals of language. Cambridge, Mass., MIT Press.
GUMPERZ, JOHN J. 1962. Types of linguistic communities. AnL 4/1.28–40. Reprinted in Readings in the sociology of language, ed. by Joshua A. Fishman, pp. 460–72. The Hague, Mouton, 1968.
——. 1967. On the linguistic markers of bilingual communication. JSI 23.48–57.
HAAS, MARY R. 1941. Noun incorporation in the Muskogean languages. Lg 17.311–15.
——. 1958. A new linguistic relationship in North America: Algonkian and the Gulf languages. SJA 14.231–64.
——. 1967. Language and taxonomy in Northwestern California. AmA 69.359–62.
——. 1969. The prehistory of languages. The Hague, Mouton.
——. 1970. Consonant symbolism in Northwestern California: A problem in diffusion. Languages and cultures of Western North America, ed. by Earl H. Swanson, Jr., pp. 86–96. Pocatello, Idaho.
HOCKETT, CHARLES F. 1954. Two models of grammatical description. Word 10/2–3. 210–31.
HOIJER, HARRY. 1941. Methods in the classification of American Indian languages. Language, culture, and personality, ed. by Leslie Spier et al., pp. 3–14. Menasha, Wisconsin, Sapir Memorial Publication Fund.
——. 1948. Linguistic and cultural change. Lg 24.335–45. Reprinted in Hymes 1964(q.v.): pp. 445–66.
HYMES, DELL H. 1956. Review of Papers from the Symposium on American Indian Linguistics. Lg 32.585–602.
——. 1961. Alfred Louis Kroeber. Lg 37.1–28. Reprinted in Hymes 1964 (q.v.): pp. 689–710.

——, ed. 1964. Language in culture and society: A reader in linguistics and anthropology. New York, Harper & Row.
——. 1967. Models of the interaction of language and social setting. JSI 23.8–28.
——. 1968. Linguistic problems in defining the concept of 'tribe'. Essays on the problem of tribe, ed. by June Helm, pp. 23–48. PAES 1967.
HYMES, VIRGINIA DOSCH. 1955. Athapaskan numeral systems. IJAL 21.26–45.
JACOBS, MELVILLE. 1931. A sketch of Northern Sahaptin grammar. UWPA 4.
——. 1937. Historic perspectives in Indian languages of Oregon and Washington. PNQ 28.55–74.
——. 1954. The areal spread of sound features in the languages north of California. Papers from the Symposium on American Indian linguistics, pp. 46–56. UCPL 10.
JACOBSEN, WILLIAM H., JR. 1966. Washo linguistic studies. The current status of anthropological research in the Great Basin: 1964, ed. by Warren L. D' Azevedo et al., pp. 113–36. Reno, University of Nevada Press.
——. 1967. Switch-reference in Hokan-Coahuiltecan. Studies in Southwestern ethnolinguistics, ed. by Dell Hymes, pp. 238–63. (= Studies in General Anthropology 3). The Hague, Mouton.
——. 1968. On the prehistory of Nez Perce vowel harmony. Lg 44.819–29.
——. 1969. Origin of Nootka pharyngeals. IJAL 35.125–53.
JAKOBSON, ROMAN. 1966. Implications of language universals for linguistics. Universals of language, ed. by Joseph H. Greenberg, pp. 263–78. (q.v.)
KINKADE, M. DALE. 1969. Lexical suffixes in Mosan languages. Paper presented at the Annual Meeting of the American Anthropological Association, November, 1969.
KIPARSKY, PAUL. 1968. Linguistic universals and linguistic change. Universals in linguistic theory, ed. by Emmon Bach and Robert T. Harms, pp. 170–202. New York, Holt, Rinehart, and Winston.
KRAUSS, MICHAEL E. 1969. Classifying the Athapaskan languages. Paper presented at the Annual Meeting of the American Anthropological Association, November 1969.
KROEBER, A.L. 1904. The languages of the coast of California south of San Francisco. UCPAAE 2.28–80.
——. 1906. The Yokuts and Yuki languages. Boas Anniversary volume, pp. 64–79. New York.
——. 1907. The Washo language of east central California and Nevada. UCPAAE 4.241–317.
——. 1911a. Phonetic constituents of the native languages of California. UCPAAE 10.1–12.
——. 1911b. The languages of the coast of California north of San Francisco. UCPAAE 9.273–435.
——. 1913. The determination of linguistic relationship. Anthropos 8.389–401.

——. 1917. California kinship systems. UCPAAE 12/9.339-96.
——. 1939. Cultural and natural areas of native North America. Berkeley and Los Angeles, University of California Press.
——. 1959. Possible Athabaskan influence on Yuki. IJAL 25.59.
——. 1960. On typological indices I: Ranking of languages. IJAL 26.171-7.
LANGDON, MARGARET. 1971. Sound symbolism in Yuman languages. Studies in American Indian languages, ed. by Jesse Sawyer, pp. 149-74. (UCPL 65.)
LOWIE, ROBERT H. 1963. Indians of the Plains. New York, American Museum of Natural History.
MANDELBAUM, DAVID G., ed. 1949. Selected writings of Edward Sapir in language, culture, and personality. Berkeley and Los Angeles, University of California Press.
MILEWSKI, TADEUSZ. 1953. Phonological typology of American Indian languages. LPosn 4.229-76.
MILLER, WICK R. 1966. Anthropological linguistics in the Great Basin. The current status of anthropological research in the Great Basin: 1964, ed. by Warren D'Azevedo et al., pp. 75-112. Reno, University of Nevada Press.
OLIVER, SYMMES C. 1962. Ecology and cultural continuity as contributing factors in the social organization of the Plains Indians. Berkeley and Los Angeles, University of California Press.
PITKIN, HARVEY, and WILLIAM SHIPLEY. 1958. A comparative survey of California Penutian. IJAL 24.174-88.
POWELL, JOHN WESLEY. 1891. Indian linguistic families of America north of Mexico. BAE-R 7.
RIGSBY, BRUCE, and MICHAEL SILVERSTEIN. 1969. Nez Perce vowels and Proto-Sahaptian vowel harmony. Lg 45.45-59.
SAPIR, EDWARD. 1907. Preliminary report on the language and mythology of the Upper Chinook. AmA 9.533-44.
——. 1912. Language and environment. AmA 14.226-42. Reprinted in SWES (= Mandelbaum 1949, q.v.):89-103.
——. 1913a. Southern Paiute and Nahuatl, a study in Uto-Aztecan, Pt. I. JSocAm 10.379-425.
——. 1913b. Wiyot and Yurok, Algonkin languages of California. AmA 15.617-46.
——. 1915a. Southern Paiute and Nahuatl, a study in Uto-Aztecan, Pt. II. AmA 17.98-120, 306-28. Also JSocAm 11.443-88 (1914).
——. 1915b. The Na-Dene languages, a preliminary report. AmA 17.534-58.
——. 1916. Time perspective in aboriginal American culture: A study in method. Canada, Department of Mines, Geological Survey, Memoir 90. Anthropological Series No. 13. Ottawa. Reprinted in SWES (= Mandelbaum 1949, q.v.):389-462.
——. 1917. The position of Yana in the Hokan stock. UCPAAE 13.1-34.
——. 1921a. A characteristic Penutian form of stem. IJAL 2.58-67.

——. 1921b. Language. New York, Harcourt Brace & Co.
——. 1922. Takelma. HAIL 2.1–296 (= BAE-B 40).
——. 1925. The Hokan affinity of Subtiaba in Nicaragua. AmA 27.402–35, 491–527.
——. 1926. A Chinookan phonetic law. IJAL 4.105–10. Reprinted in SWES (= Mandelbaum 1949, q.v.): 197–205.
——. 1947. The relation of American Indian linguistics to general linguistics. SJA 3.1–4.
SECOY, FRANK RAYMOND. 1953. Changing military patterns on the Great Plains. Seattle, University of Washington Press.
SHERZER, JOEL. 1968. An areal-typological study of the American Indian languages north of Mexico. Ph.D. dissertation, University of Pennsylvania, Philadelphia.
SHIPLEY, WILLIAM F. 1966. The relation of Klamath to California Penutian. Lg 42.489–98.
SILVER, SHIRLEY. 1964. Shasta and Karok: A binary comparison. Studies in Californian linguistics, ed. by William Bright, pp. 170–81. (UCPL 34.)
SPENCER, ROBERT, JESSE D. JENNINGS, et al. 1965. The native Americans. New York, Harper & Row.
SUTTLES, WAYNE. 1960. Affinal ties, subsistence, and prestige among the Coast Salish. AmA 63.296–305.
SWADESH, MORRIS. 1948. A structural trend in Nootka. Word 4.106–19.
——. 1952. Salish phonologic geography. Lg 28.232–48.
——. 1966. El lenguaje y la vida humana. Mexico, Fondo de cultura económica.
——. 1971. The origin and diversification of language. Chicago, Aldine-Atherton.
SWANTON, JOHN R. 1900. Morphology of the Chinook verb. AmA 2.199–237.
——. 1911. Tlingit. HAIL 1.159–204 (= BAE-B 40).
——. 1924. The Muskhogean connection of the Natchez language. IJAL 3.46–75.
TEIT, JAMES A. 1917. Kaska tales. JAF 30.427–73.
——. 1956. Field notes on the Tahltan and Kaska Indians: 1912–15. Anthropologica 3.40–171.
THOMPSON, STITH. 1929. Tales of the North American Indians. Cambridge, Mass. (Reprinted, Indiana University Press.)
TRAGER, GEORGE L. 1939. 'Cottonwood' = 'Tree': A Southwestern linguistic trait. IJAL 9.117–18. Reprinted in Hymes 1964 (q.v.): pp. 467–8.
TROIKE, RUDOLPH C. 1961. A Nahuatl loan-word in Coahuilteco. IJAL 17.272–5.
——. 1964. The Caddo word for 'water'. IJAL 30.96-8.
ULTAN, RUSSELL. 1964. Proto-Maidun phonology. IJAL 30.355-70.
VELTEN, H. V. 1943. The Nez Perce verb. PNQ 34.271–92.
VOEGELIN, C. F. 1941. North American Indian languages still spoken and their genetic relationships. Language, culture, and personality, ed. by Leslie Spier et al., pp. 15–40. Menasha, Wisconsin, Sapir Memorial Publication Fund.
——. 1945a. Influence of area on American Indian linguistics. Word 7.54–8. Reprinted in Hymes 1964 (q.v.), pp. 638–41.

——. 1945b. Relative chronology of North American linguistic types. AmA 47. 47.232–4.
——. 1961. Culture area: Parallel with typological homogeneity and heterogeneity to North American language families. KASP 25.163–80.
WEINREICH, URIEL. 1958. On the compatibility of genetic relationship and convergent development. Word 14.374–9.
WEINREICH, URIEL, WILLIAM LABOV, and MARVIN L. HERZOG. 1968. Empirical foundations for a theory of language change. Directions for historical linguistics, ed. by W.P. Lehmann and Yakov Malkiel, pp. 95–188. Austin, University of Texas Press.
WISSLER, CLARK. 1917. The American Indian. New York. (3rd ed., Peter Smith).
WOLFF, HANS. 1959. Subsystem typologies and area linguistics. AnL 1/7.1–88.
ZWICKY, ARNOLD M. 1971. More on Nez Perce: On alternative analyses. IJAL 37.122–6.

# ESKIMO-ALEUT

## MICHAEL E. KRAUSS*

### 0. INTRODUCTION

The Eskimo-Aleut language family is a very well defined one, certainly distant from any other language family, and consisting of two clear-cut branches, Eskimo and Aleut.

The Aleut people was once perhaps 20,000 strong. It has been reduced to less than one-tenth that by the white man's civilizing influence. The Aleut language is by now largely abandoned, perhaps beyond the point of no return.

The case of Eskimo is very different from that of Aleut. The total world Eskimo population under four flags is probably higher now than ever before. A good estimate for 1972 would be 95,000 ($\pm 5\%$), with 43,000 ($\pm 5\%$) in Greenland, 17,000 ($\pm 5\%$) in Canada, 34,000 ($\pm 5\%$) in Alaska, and 1,000 ($\pm 5\%$) in Siberia. The Eskimo language itself, moreover, remains in full vigor over most of this vast territory, the most notable exceptions being certain larger population centers in Canada and northern Alaska (and now also Siberia), where the youngest generation no longer uses the language. The Eskimo language still seems to have a good chance of survival throughout most or even all of the American Arctic, and its dominant position in Greenland seems firmly established. Of those 95,000 Eskimos, figures for the number of *speakers* of Eskimo in 1972 (including infants learning it) might be estimated at 83,000 ($\pm 5,000$), with 43,000 ($\pm 5\%$) in Greenland; 16,000 ($\pm 10\%$) in Canada; 23,000 ($\pm 10\%$) (17,500 Yupik, 6,000 Inuit) in Alaska, and 800 ($\pm 10\%$) in Siberia.

In Greenland the Greenlandic Eskimo language is the first and usually only language of the entire indigenous population, virtually all of which is also literate in the language. Literature in written Greenlandic has been developing vigorously for well over 200 years in books and periodicals, in general use in education, in radio broadcasting, and as an official language of Greenland and its political life. Danish remains only an auxiliary

---

* The research on which this report is based was carried out at the University of Alaska (Department of Linguistics) as part of a program supported by the National Endowment for the Humanities (Grant H–69–0–65), and at the Massachusetts Institute of Technology (Research Laboratory of Electronics, Department of Linguistics) as part of a program supported by the National Institutes of Mental Health (Grant MH 13390–03). The author gratefully acknowledges this support; also the important bibliographical and critical assistance, ranging well beyond their own work, of K. Bergsland, A. Cearley, D.R.F. Collis, G.A. Menovščikov, O. Miyaoka, E.I. Reed, R.P.L. Schneider, O.M.I., R. Underhill; and the technical assistance of P. Regan. See also note on p. 281.

language of the elite, Greenlandic serving well for the daily domestic needs of the rapidly growing and advancing Greenlandic Eskimo population.

In Canada and Alaska the Eskimo language has not enjoyed the status it has in Greenland. It has managed to survive largely because the Eskimo minority population of the United States and Canada was geographically remote in the Arctic area, which until recently, at least, was very little exploited by any sizeable white population. With rapidly increasing pressure of white intrusion, both economic and cultural, the continued survival of Eskimo becomes increasingly uncertain. However, at the same time, other forces are at work in the form of greater pressure of political and cultural liberalism on the administrative and educational authorities (especially the Bureau of Indian Affairs in the United States, Department of Indian Affairs and Northern Development in Canada), making the traditional white cultural supremacist-assimilationist policy less easy to maintain in its usual uncompromising form. Bilingual education, native political and economic organization and activism, all serve to counteract the destructive pressures at work against the survival of the Eskimo people as such and of their language. There is very possibly another important factor at play in the remarkable survival of the Eskimo language, as in that of the Eskimo people themselves, a factor which is not easily evaluated objectively, but doubtless must be seen in terms of the extraordinary resourcefulness, strong sense of identity and also of unity of the Eskimo people. Many other languages and peoples of the world seem to have disappeared under less pressure than Eskimo has had to withstand.

The linguistic situation of the Eskimo people of Siberia has been also extremely remarkable, no doubt due also to the Soviet policy regarding the languages and cultures of the minority peoples of the Siberian North, vastly different from anything conceivable in the United States or Canada until very recently. Eskimo has been the first language of the school in Eskimo Siberia, with textbooks printed in Eskimo since 1932.

The United States and Canada are thirty to forty years behind the Soviets in their policy, despite the fact that the Eskimos constitute a vastly larger minority in the northern regions of America than of Siberia. In fact, one has cause to suspect that this very difference in proportion has something to do with the difference in policy. One senses that the Eskimos, especially united, could form a significant political force in the American (but not Siberian) Arctic, at odds with the actual and potential political and economic interests of the ruling class, which feels the need thus to undermine and eliminate the Eskimo people as such, through assimilationist 'education'. Where it is claimed that 'native traditions' are being encouraged, even this too, especially in Alaska, is all too often only a thinly disguised form of exploitation by cultural prostitution, by utilization of the population as a source of cheap labor for the white-run tourist and curio trade. Here, of course, the language would seem to have little value, and so is often the object of hostility on the part of the quasi-colonial local authority (teachers, administrators). Recently, with the penetration of concepts of bilingual education, there are still many who can accept the idea of learning first to read Eskimo only for the carryover value this may have in learning to read English: the Eskimo language is to serve as a 'bridge' to the acquisition of the more highly valued language, and then abandoned. The Eskimo language in Canada and Alaska clearly has a long way to go before it reaches the position it enjoys in Greenland, but it has perhaps already survived its period of gravest danger.

The present writer is not a qualified expert in Eskimo linguistics. He has, however, been in rather close contact with the field in Alaska, though mainly as peripheral to his other interests in Athapaskan and Eyak. This chapter will accordingly concentrate on the history of and applied aspects of work in Eskimo-Aleut linguistics, i.e. bibliography, and on the development of orthographies and literatures in the language, rather than on the actual content of the work, with which this writer is at best incompletely familiar. Also, though he does not read Russian easily, the writer has made a special effort to give detailed treatment to the recent history of Eskimo and Aleut in the Soviet Union, a subject very little-known outside the USSR, which deserves far wider attention for the remarkable developments which have taken place there. These are vastly different from and highly significant for the situation in the West, especially Alaska and Canada (which it is perhaps not unfair to label the most 'backward' states involved).

The text and bibliography of this chapter will be devoted mostly to work since World War II. The bibliography attempts to include, besides published materials, as much as possible of the titles of papers delivered at meetings, theses, mimeographed and typed and other organized though unpublished materials, and also items that are forthcoming or likely to appear in print before about 1972. The bibliography of linguistic studies on Eskimo and/or Aleut is thus reasonably exhaustive for the period 1945–1970, at least for published items. In the case of Siberia, Alaska, and Canada this includes any material published *in* the language as well as *on* the language, but nonlinguistic literature in the Greenlandic language is far too vast to be included. The other major omission is most of the late works of William Thalbitzer, whose contribution to all Eskimo studies has been enormous, but which was made mostly before 1945 and for which there exists an exhaustive bibliography (592). For work before 1945 or nonlinguistic items (neither in nor on the language itself, e.g. reports on missionary or educational activity or policy), the bibliography is not only incomplete but simply a selection of works cited according to the writer's convenience in the discussion. For work after 1970 coverage is less complete, especially for Canada and Greenland.

The world of Eskimo-Aleut scholarship (as well as Eskimo-Aleut society) has been badly divided by the political organization of the world, which cuts across the naturally unified Aleut-Eskimo Arctic with artificial and often impenetrable boundaries. Ironically, the situation might even be expressed in terms of the Stammbaum model: the 'Eastern branch' is the Soviet work, largely by G.A. Menovščikov, and the 'Western' is in turn subdivided into Greenland-Denmark, Canada, and Alaska-USA. The lack of communication between these three is exceeded in severity only by that between all of these and the Soviet Union. The leading figure in Eskimo-Aleut studies in the Soviet Union has obviously been G. A. Menovščikov. Probably the most outstanding contributor in the 'West' since the war has been Bergsland in Norway, who has made extremely important studies of Greenlandic and Northern Alaskan Eskimo, and in the field of Aleut and Comparative Eskimo-Aleut stands as alone as does Menovščikov in Siberia. Communication at the 'top', between Menovščikov and Bergsland, has not been entirely absent, but due to the situation just described, between workers at lower and more local levels, in Alaska, Canada, and Greenland, communication has been severely limited, and often with lamentable results, as in duplication of effort, and in uncoordinated developments of social significance, such as rival orthographies for Inuit Eskimo.

Publication in Eskimo-Aleut has been fitful and scattered, and often in obscure local outlets. There have been two major exceptions before 1970. Most important was the Kleinschmidt Centennial issue of the *International Journal of American Linguistics*, which on the occasion of the 100th anniversary of the publication of Samuel Kleinschmidt's fundamental classic, *Grammatik der Grönländischen Sprache*, published over a dozen papers on Eskimo and Eskimo-Aleut linguistics in 1951–53 (64, 176, 177, 179, 211, 237, 298, 476, 555, 556, 557, 558, 559, 593, 609, 613); though only a few before (193, 203, 458, 554, 588, 630) and a couple since (302, 648). The next occasion was the 32nd International Congress of Americanists in Copenhagen in 1956, in the *Proceedings* of which eight papers on Eskimo and Eskimo-Aleut were published (73, 74, 93, 131, 184, 185, 212, 563).

For fourteen years after that local activities in this language field continued in virtual isolation from each other, there being no major organized events to encourage or facilitate communication between them.

A visit of N. O. Christensen, Governor of Greenland, to Alaska in 1966, paved the way for a cultural exchange which resulted in an arrangement for Carl Chr. Olsen, a young Greenlander who had had training in Eskimo linguistics at the University of Copenhagen, to come to the University of Alaska to study Yupik Eskimo there from 1968 to 1969. The following year Olsen studied linguistics at the University of Chicago, at the invitation of Eric Hamp. Stimulated by the presence of Olsen, Hamp proposed to the National Science Foundation an international conference on Eskimo linguistics to fill the long-standing need. Supported by the National Science Foundation, this (first international) Conference on Eskimo Linguistics was held at the University of Chicago on June 5–7, 1970, hosted by Hamp, with organizational arrangements ably seen to by Eileen Petrohelos. In attendance and giving papers were Afcan (26), Bergsland (80), Cearley (110), Collis (118), Hammerich (189), Hamp (190), Heinrich (201), Jensen (239), Krauss (266), Landar (269), Mallon (292), Marsh (222), Mey (403), Miller (408), Miyaoka (417), Olsen (500), Reed (471), Sadock (500), Saladin d'Anglure (502), Silverstein (543), Teeluk (573), and Underhill (617). A paper by Webster and Zibell (645) was read by Reed, and Correll (121) was prevented at the last minute from attending. The majority of the delegates were from the United States (including six from Alaska), but Norway, Denmark, Greenland, France, Canada, and Japan were also represented. Most who were invited were able to come. The most serious and obvious exception was G.A. Menovščikov, who received his invitation too late to make arrangements to attend. Aside from the deeply regretted absence of Menovščikov., the conference was a very great success, not only because of the quality of the papers presented, but also because of the inestimable value of the personal contacts made between scholars with a deep mutual interest so long isolated from each other. The excitement and stimulation of the event will not soon be forgotten. It seems indeed safe to say that the Conference marks the beginning of a new period in Eskimo and Aleut linguistics.

In addition to the attention given the more conventional academic aspects of such a conference, considerable time was also devoted to plans for establishing the beginnings of an organization which would ensure continued coordination of efforts and future meetings. Most important of all, this organization has pledged itself additionally to certain ideals which have long been and still are all too often neglected by scholars in fields such as this, and all of which simply boil down to a concern for the welfare of the people whose languages have been the object of academic study. Recommendations and policy should deal with the following concerns:

(1) Cultural exchanges, of national and international scope, such as that by which the delegates were themselves benefitting, need even more to be established between the Eskimo people who are isolated even more unfortunately from each other and who would benefit at least as much from such exchange as has the academic world.

(2) Scholars have an obligation to make provision that the fruits of their labor benefit not only themselves but the people on whom it depends as well: scholars should make every effort to disseminate the scientific results of their work in such a way that it reaches these people also, through educational and other media.

(3) The obvious fact should be acknowledged that a native speaker of Eskimo is basically far better qualified to do Eskimo linguistics than anyone else. Linguists working in this area, very few of whom are Eskimos, have also a responsibility to stimulate Eskimo interest in Eskimo linguistics in the professional sense, both by the means mentioned above and by more direct recruitment and training and support, instead of maintaining a monopoloy in Eskimo studies whereby only Europeans can make a living or derive any benefit.

(4) The fate of the Eskimo language will be a central aspect of the fate of the Eskimo people. Students of the Eskimo language should also support and promote it within the establishment which they represent, with the goal of seeing the Eskimo language receive the full status it deserves, legislative recognition as an official language where it is the language of a significant proportion of the people. The Eskimo language should thus be recognized as an official language of the State of Alaska, the Yukon and Northwest Territories, Northern Quebec and Labrador (as it is already in Siberia and Greenland), for use in the legislature and courts, and in the appropriate schools and public media (radio, television, printed matter).

(5) Linguists should make efforts to promote similar ideals in the other academic

disciplines also closely associated with the Eskimos. Many of the same points apply with equal validity to or have obvious analogies in such fields as anthropology-ethnology-archaeology, all natural sciences pursued in the Arctic environment, and in applied fields such as game-management, social work, law, medicine, education, engineering, commerce, management, and government itself.

Two years after the Chicago Conference on Eskimo Linguistics, another event took place even more momentous for Eskimo-Aleut languages, at least those of Alaska. On June 9, 1972, the Alaska State Legislature in Juneau passed a series of bills concerning Alaska native languages. These bills recognize for the first time the importance of these languages for the peoples of the state, and its responsibility to give active support to their cultivation. Such support is absolutely necessary in order to balance the many other powerful forces, also supported by the State, which otherwise will surely lead to the destruction of these languages and peoples.

One pair of bills authorizes and appropriates funds for the establishment of an Alaska Native Language Center at the University of Alaska. The purposes of this Center are to '(1) Study languages native to Alaska; (2) develop literacy materials; (3) assist in the translation of important documents; (4) provide for the development and dissemination of Alaska Native literature; and (5) train Alaska native language speakers to work as teachers and aides in bilingual classrooms'.

The other pair of bills appropriates funds for bilingual education and stipulates that 'A state-operated school which is attended by at least 15 pupils whose primary language is other than English shall have at least one teacher who is fluent in the native language of the area where the school is located. Written and other educational materials, when language is a factor, shall be presented in the language native to the area.' The rationale is worth quoting: 'The legislature finds and declares the following:'

(1) Traditionally, basic language differences in Alaskan schools have been overlooked to the extent that the need for an educational program which incorporates both English and the Native language dialects has been vastly underestimated and often the program has tended to ignore and sometimes belittle classroom use of the Native dialect, a practice deplored by modern educators, concerned parents and students alike.

(2) The right to one's native language and culture is inherent in the concepts underlying our constitutional guarantees and continued disregard of this right has been protested by many who believe that Alaskan schools have an obligation to provide education which does not bypass this right and which is not designed to shift students unilaterally from one culture to another. Students in the villages of Alaska are representatives of a viable, valuable culture which is in a continual process of change, as are all cultures, but which has a right to continue its existence as a unique culture whether Indian, Eskimo, or Aleut.

(3) The absence of a bilingual program of education has worked a great learning handicap for those students who use English as a second language, placing a double burden of learning both the language and academic concepts simultaneously, while singular emphasis on English usage has contributed to a communications gap between parents and child, school and community, even though educational research has shown that the most successful educational method in primary programs is one that instructs in the Native dialect and then proceeds to promote literacy in English. It is a well-known fact that contrary traditional methods have

resulted in below-standard achievements by Alaskan Native students which, in turn, spawn difficulties in secondary and higher educational pursuits, exacerbate acculturation problems, present significant barriers in securing adequate employment and constitute a serious hindrance to the full enjoyment of life and its benefits.

(4) Establishment of a bilingual program of education for Native Alaskans will encourage the development of educational materials relevant to Native history, legends, folklore, artistic expression, and characteristic lifestyles by recognizing that the local culture is a legitimate source of study and interest. Adoption of a bilingual program of education will tend to bring about an end to the deprecation of local culture elements and values by the schools, stimulate better communication between the community and the school in solving educational problems, effect a positive student self-image, provide more effective use of both English and the Native dialect, foster higher achievement levels in academic performance, encourage more successful secondary and higher education careers, ease the obtaining of employment, allow genuine options for Native Alaskan students in choosing a way of life, and facilitate a more harmonious blending of Native Alaskan culture with the mainstream of society.

It should be noted that the bilingual education bill does not directly affect schools which are (a) operated by the Bureau of Indian Affairs (BIA) or by a local school district, and/or (b) where there are fewer than 15 students in the school who are fluent speakers of the native language. In terms of Eskimo and Aleut, then, this bill directly affects only about half of the Central Yupik schools (the other half are BIA-operated), about half of the Inuit schools (several are BIA-operated, and in several there are fewer than 15 speakers of Inuit), probably only one of the Aleut schools: Atka (probably none of the others have 15 fluent speakers of Aleut), neither of the St. Lawrence Island Yupik schools (BIA-operated), and none of the Pacific Yupik schools (mostly local districts, including English Bay, the only school with Eskimo-speaking children). The direct affect of the bilingual education bills is thus limited; but indirectly, of course, the entire state is at least influenced by the legislative policy. The Bureau of Indian Affairs, at best ambivalent in this regard, has permitted limited bilingual programs in Central Yupik, Barrow Inuit, and now St. Lawrence Island. None of the local school districts has yet implemented any such program either.

In all those Eskimo-Aleut (and Indian) areas which are thus not served by the bilingual education laws, the responsibility for research and development of linguistic and educational materials in the native languages devolves upon the University of Alaska Native Language Center alone.

Clearly, passage of these bills is an event of enormous importance in its effect, direct and indirect, on all Alaskan languages. It is probable, also, that this development in Alaska will have its influence on the policy for native languages, including Eskimo, in Canada and elsewhere.

As one result of this event, already a veritably explosive increase in the rate of production of materials in Alaska Native languages is now beginning. This report covers the development of postwar Eskimo and Aleut literature up to this historical point, through a period of what will no doubt prove to have been relatively slow production. The bibliography of books in Eskimo, 1945-1972, extensive as it may seem, may be expected to accumulate very much more rapidly after 1972.

## 1. ALEUT

The Aleut language in the eighteenth century was spoken on the extremity of the Alaska peninsula and on the Aleutian archipelago. Today it is still spoken, though by rapidly dwindling numbers, on parts of the peninsula, parts of the 'Chain', and also on the Pribilof Islands and, on the Siberian side, the Komandorskie Ostrova. Both pairs of islands were aboriginally uninhabited, but colonized during the Russian period. In a few places the Aleut language is still the everyday language of all generations, but generally, especially in the larger Aleut population centers, the language is little or not at all known to the youngest generations, having been replaced by English or Russian. The number of Aleuts has declined from perhaps 20,000 in 1741 to perhaps 2,000[1] at present, and the number of speakers of Aleut is now well below 1,000, perhaps already as low as 500.

### 1.1 *Alaska*

The Aleut language in Alaska has shown remarkable vitality considering the monstrous forces against which it has had to struggle. There was even widespread literacy in it until recently. The future of the language is now in very grave doubt, however; it has been the victim of the ignorance and inhumanity of the present educational and military establishments.

During the nineteenth century Aleut priests (Tikhon for Fox Island or Eastern Aleut, Netsvetov and Salamatov for Atkan) under Veniaminov translated the Gospels and other religious material, and established the foundation for written literature in Aleut, in a Slavonic alphabet which they adapted very well to the needs of Aleut, including e.g. special symbols for the uvulars and voiceless continuants. This written tradition was attacked with a vengeance by the American schools: it was in the wrong alphabet, it was the wrong language, and perhaps (above all) it represented the wrong religion. The American school system has struggled for three generations to eradicate this literacy, and has by now achieved almost complete success.

Also, a great many Aleut manuscripts perished in the destruction of Attu and Atka by the United States Navy during World War II. A number of such manuscripts have survived, however, in the Alaska Church Collection of the Library of Congress. Most important for linguistics, this writer discovered in that collection an uncatalogued Russian-Atkan dictionary by Netsvetov (669). This manuscript is truly a major lexical

---

[1] The native peoples of Alaska are generally, and rather stupidly, classed by popular tradition 'Eskimos, Aleuts, and Indians'. The category 'Aleut' includes about 6,000 Yupik Eskimos, of Bristol Bay, Alaska peninsula, Cook Inlet, Prince William Sound, and Kodiak Island. These Eskimos, who, like Aleuts, generally are Russian Orthodox in religion and have Russian surnames call themselves Aleuts, and are so classed also in the U.S. Census reports, which thus always return a much larger population of 'Aleuts' than actually exists of true Aleuts.

contribution, containing about 6,000 entries, no doubt one of the most extensive dictionaries of any American language for its time or even for now.

The Aleut language is now moribund everywhere in Alaska exept Atka (population 89, and possibly also Nikolski, population 45). Only there are the children still able to speak Aleut (along with English). In late 1972 two Atkans trained with Bergsland and Krauss to begin in Atka the first Aleut literary program since 1912.

There is significant dialectal variation within Aleut. Western Aleut (Attu only, nearly extinct) shows certain important innovations absent in the relatively conservative Central dialect (Rat-Andreanov-Atka, surviving only on Atka), which is in turn differentiated from Eastern Aleut (to Alaska Peninsula, the great bulk of Alaskan Aleut speakers) by significant isoglosses, but not sufficiently to impair very seriously mutual intelligibility. See Bergsland (70, 76) and Marsh and Swadesh (298) for more detailed discussion of Alaskan Aleut dialectology.

In 1944 under the devoted editorship of Frederica Martin there appeared Richard Geoghegan's *The Aleut language* (168), which is of no value whatever beyond that of being the best translation of Veniaminov's pioneering effort a century earlier (625), itself a very defective work, of the same vintage but not at all the same quality as Kleinschmidt's Eskimo grammar. Veniaminov's grammar had already been translated or restated twice during the nineteenth century, in French by Henry (201) and German by Pfizmaier (455). See also reviews of Geoghegan by J.P. Harrington (192), J.E. Ransom (464), and F. Lounsbury (287), and comments by Preston (458).

During the early 20th century Waldemar Jochelson had collected a considerable quantity of Aleut linguistic and folkloric materials and had published a number of articles (240, 241, 242, 243, 244, 245, 668). His work remains mostly unpublished, although partly in an advanced stage of preparation. Some of it is preserved at the New York Public Library. See Yarmolinsky (650) for a description of this and an important bibliography of all earlier Aleut material, and Vdovin (620, 624) for accounts of the work of Veniaminov, Jochelson, and others on Aleut. A number of scholars have since worked with Jochelson's collection: Ethel G. Aginsky before the war (33, 34), during the war Roman Jakobson, who published a very short but very valuable phonological statement (231), and after the war Gordon Marsh and Knut Bergsland; only part of this work has yet been published.

In 1936–37 and 1940 Jay Ellis Ransom did fieldwork with Umnak informants. This resulted in two articles of linguistic interest, on the remarkable tradition of native literacy and its importance amongst the Aleuts (463), and a good resumé of the state of development of Aleut studies as of the early 1950s (465). The grammar (a Master's Thesis presented at the University of Washington) that Ransom intended to publish in 1946 never reached the press, though Ransom later (1954, 1966) reports continued study of Aleut (466, 467).

In 1941 John Peabody Harrington of the Smithsonian Institution (as reported in 671) did extensive fieldwork with three Unalaska and Pribilof Aleut informants. Most of his notes consist of 'rehearings' and elaboration of earlier lexicon (Veniaminov and Jochelson), with good phonetics, and a few texts. None of this material has been published, though Harrington had prepared a significant partial typescript grammar (667). Harrington's six cartons of bulky fieldnotes are still uncatalogued, but now located and identified, at the National Anthropological Archives.

In 1948 Charles E. Shade also did fieldwork on Umnak, wrote an ethnological thesis (536), and left significant ms. lexical materials at the Peabody Museum (537), Harvard. Some of this material is in the hand of Afenogin Ermeloff, a native Aleut. Though Ransom speaks disparagingly of the linguistic results of the Harvard Expedition, he refers (467) to a published translation he made of a manuscript Aleut narrative by Afenogin Ermeloff (140).

In 1943 the Japanese linguist Takeshi Hattōri collected a short Aleut vocabulary from an Attuan interned for the period of the war in Japan (195, reported by Miyaoka in 412). Miyaoka has also called attention to an interesting manuscript (251) by Keoru Kasuga, a Japanese Army interpreter on Attu in 1942, which includes a few pages of observations about Aleut (in Japanese), and a list of about 250 words and phrases in Japanese, English and (Cyrillic) Aleut.

During the 1950s Gordon H. Marsh did fieldwork amongst the Aleut, and wrote a doctoral dissertation on part of the grammar (294). Marsh's fieldnotes (lexical and grammatical) and draft grammar remain unpublished. Marsh also reelicited and checked in the field a large number of the Jochelson texts, and prepared them in typescript with interlinear translation, but these also remain unpublished. Marsh's only publication on Aleut linguistics proper is a specialized lexical study on anatomical terms written in collaboration with William Laughlin (297), following an earlier paper on Aleut linguistics and prehistory with Laughlin (270). Marsh left academic life for the Russian Orthodox priesthood in 1958. His first association with the field since was at the Chicago conference in 1970 (222).

The greatest contribution to Aleut linguistics since the war has clearly been that of Knut Bergsland, who did fieldwork on Attuan and Atkan in 1950 and 1952. He has published several important articles on Aleut (see bibliography, especially 64, 70, 71, 81), but, above all, his *Aleut dialects of Atka and Attu* (76) is the most extensive and important contribution to Aleut linguistics to reach print in over a century. It contains an excellent section (p. 6–7) on the history of Aleut studies, including a valuable bibliography of the 19th century Russian religious text material, published and unpublished, much of which was composed by native speakers of Aleut and is of no small value as good Aleut text. Pages 11–55 are devoted to a study of Aleut proper names, mostly placenames, with maps and photographs. The final section of the book (56–128) contains Aleut texts with translations and notes: Iakov Netzvetov's folklore texts, first published in Veniaminov, reelicited modern Atka texts from dictation, and also about 60 minutes of taperecording (meticulously transcribed including indication of pauses, hesitation, unfinished forms, etc.), verified retranscription of 19th century religious material, and Jochelson's Attu texts. See also Swadesh (567) and Shimkin (538) for reviews of this excellent work.

Bergsland has continued his active interest in Aleut. Most recently he has published several articles (665, 80, 81, 666) on Aleut syntax, deeply penetrating an area into which no other linguist has seriously ventured. Some of his recent findings on the nature of Aleut syntax, fundamental aspects of which seem incompatible with phrase-structure and generative theory, promise to be major contributions to general linguistic theory. In fact, general linguistic theory may indeed have to be fundamentally revised in the light of Aleut syntax. Bergsland was able to revisit Atka during the summer of 1971, and to collect further materials for his syntactic work, as well as for the completion of his lexical and morphological materials on Atkan Aleut.

During his 1971 stay on Atka, Bergsland also made available in the island school versions of Atkan texts in a practical Roman orthography based on the Slavonic. The revival of literacy in Aleut in the Atka school is to be in both the Slavonic and Roman alphabet.

At the Chicago conference D. Gary Miller distributed an interesting mimeographed paper with a section on Aleut verb tense inflection (408), based on printed sources. A number of articles, especially by Bergsland (65, 66, 73, 77, 80) are devoted largely to Aleut, but also in comparison with Eskimo; these are mentioned in the comparative section.

### 1.2. *Commander and Kurile Islands*

On the Soviet side, as mentioned above, Aleuts were transplanted to the thitherto uninhabited Commander Islands, in 1826. Those on Bering Island (about 400, from Atka) were speakers of the Central (Rat-Andreanov-Atka) dialect; those on Copper Island (about 300) were speakers of Attuan or Western Aleut. Already in 1840 the population of these islands, especially Copper Island, began to include many Russians (and others: Eskimos, Chukchis, Zyrians, even Gypsies) in addition to and intermarrying with the Aleuts. Although in Soviet times they constitute their own administrative district ('rayon') and Aleut is recognized as a nationality and a national language, apparently the Commander Island Aleuts have dwindled in numbers from the original 700 and were too small a linguistic community to survive as such, especially with the heavy and steadily increasing non-Aleut admixture in the population of the islands. In 1932, when the Soviets began publishing schoolbooks in Siberian minority languages, according to Orlova (436) an Aleut primer-reader was in fact prepared for the press and sent to Leningrad for publication. It was apparently never published. The reason must have been not so such much that Aleuts constituted too small a linguistic community, but, far more importantly, that by then the language was being abandoned. In 1926–27 the Aleut population was reported at 345, of whom 332 spoke Aleut (49). A report from 1934 hints at a decline of the language (60). The 1959 census (227) reports the Aleut population at 421, of whom only 94 spoke Aleut. Menovščikov (375, p. 386) reports in 1968 that at most 50 persons, of the oldest generation, of the 300 Aleuts of the USSR had a command of the Aleut language.

Avrorin (57) obtained detailed figures for the status of the Aleut language in the Commander Islands in 1969, but none were published in his report. In any case, it is clear that children in the Commander Islands were no longer learning Aleut certainly by the early 1930s, at precisely the point when the primer was being prepared in Magadan.

Menovščikov included brief discussion of the Aleut language and the history of studies, especially Russian, in the Aleut language in two papers from 1959 (353, 354), and an encyclopedia article in 1957 (338). However, until 1963 there had apparently been no linguistic investigation of Commander Island Aleut, and until that year Menovščikov had had no first-hand experience of the language. In 1963 he made a field trip to the islands and published extremely interesting reports in 1964 (367) and 1965 (370), and a sketch in 1967 (375). The sketch is based largely on the Bering Island dialect (Central Aleut), though with notes also on the Copper Island (Attuan) dialect. Of very great interest is the remarkable development noted by Menovščikov in the sketch and especially in the 1964 report: the Copper Island dialect (more than the Bering) has become very deeply Russianized, to the point where the native inflectional suffixes to the verb (for person, number, tense, mood) have all been replaced with Russian affixes. Menovščikov is reportedly planning to publish a major study of Commander Island Aleut.

For further information on Aleut and the Commander Islands, note the additional references (673, 674, 676, 678) and especially the recent article by Gurvich (675), which confirms and details the decline of the Aleut language on the Commanders.

During the 18th and 19th centuries, the Russians deployed 'Aleuts' (i.e. Aleuts and Kodiak Eskimos) all along the North Pacific rim, from California to the Kuriles, as sea-otter hunters. Relatively permanent settlements of Aleuts were also established in the Kurile Islands, some Aleuts before 1800, and Kodiak Eskimos in 1826. There, also in contact with Ainus and Japanese, they led a meagre existence until the cession of the Kuriles to Japan. Miyaoka has called attention to and furnished an English summary of an article by Osamu Baba (672), which gives some of this history. In 1876 the Kurile Aleuts were moved to Kamchatka, and thence in 1888 to Bering Island in the Commanders. It is possible that two vocabularies of Kurile 'Aleut' (Aleut and probably Kodiak Eskimo) may yet be found: about 1880 the Polish naturalist Dybowski met the Kurile Aleuts at Cape Lopatka, Kamchatka. There he reportedly took down from them two Aleut vocabularies (677). In this series, Dybowski published several extensive vocabularies of Kamchadal, Koryak, and Ainu, but no Aleut vocabularies. Perhaps the manuscripts survive.

## 2. ESKIMO

The Eskimo section of this report is subdivided by political divisions: Siberia, Alaska, Canada, Greenland. The linguistic taxonomic subdivision of the Eskimo languages is very different from the political. It is seen by this writer as follows:

|  | Country | Est. Population | Est. Number of Speakers |
|---|---|---|---|
| A. Yupik languages | | | |
| 1. Siberian (two or three languages) | | | |
| a. Sirenik | Siberia | | 10 |
| b. (1) Chaplino | Siberia | 700 | 500? |
| St. Lawrence Island | Alaska | 1,000 | 1,000 |
| (2) Naukan | Siberia | 300 | 200? |
| 2. Alaskan (two languages) | | | |
| a. Central Yupik dialects | Alaska | 15,500 | 14,500 |
| b. Pacific Yupik dialects | Alaska | 5,500 | 2,000 |
| B. Inuit dialect continuum | Siberia (Imaklik) | 30 | 10 |
|  | Alaska | 11,000 | 6,000 |
|  | Canada | 17,000 | 16,000 |
|  | Greenland | 43,000 | 43,000 |

2.1 *Siberia*

The Eskimo population of Siberia is hardly over 1,000. Nevertheless, the variety of Eskimo dialects spoken in Siberia is equalled only in Alaska. There is also far more linguistic literature in print on Siberian Eskimo than on Alaskan or Canadian Eskimo. Moreover, there has been even a rather well-developed schoolbook and popular literature in Siberian Eskimo since the 1930s, far out of proportion to the minuscule population, if one compares the tiny minority that Eskimos constitute in the Siberian population with the relatively enormous groups of Eskimos in Greenland, Alaska, and even Canada.

2.11. *Imaklik*

Of the 1,000 Siberian Eskimos, only a very few are Inuit. These are the inhabitants of Big Diomede Island (in Russian Ostrov Ratmanova, in Eskimo Imaklik) in Bering Strait. They are certainly not numerous: 22 according to Bogoraz in 1929 (98). Their dialect is identical with that of Little Diomede on the American side, which in turn is practically identical with that of Wales, a Seward Peninsula Inuit dialect. Regular communication between the Diomedes continued on an informal basis until the Cold

War period. The Imaklik villagers were then cut off from their relatives on Little Diomede, and in 1948 were dispersed to the Siberian mainland, amongst Siberian Yupik speakers.

Menovščikov worked with Imaklik speakers in 1948, 1954–55, and 1960–61. His main publication on this dialect so far is a comparative study and sketch entitled "Yazyk Eskimosov Beringova Proliva", written in 1961, and published five years later (369, but see also data in 354, 364). The lack of any indication of consonant gemination in Menovščikov's transcriptions in this (very preliminary) sketch reflects either a serious inadequacy of the transcription or the alarmingly swift loss of what is a fundamental and highly functional consonantal contrast in all other attested Inuit (but not Yupik) dialects. Menovščikov lists a later manuscript study of Imaklik (388), and most recently has been completing a major study of the language.

### 2.12 *Siberian Yupik*

With this very minor and incidental exception of Imaklik, Siberian Eskimo languages are all Yupik. These are, however, all markedly divergent from Alaskan Yupik, and show the influence of Chukchi, with which they have been in intimate contact. Mutual intelligibility between Siberian Yupik and Central Alaskan Yupik is at best extremely marginal. Lexicostatistical tests show about 65 percent cognates between Chaplino and Central Alaska on the standard 100-word list.

Siberian Yupik (also known in the literature as Asiatic Eskimo, or Yuit) is divided according to Menovščikov into two or three languages, Chaplino-Naukan and the rather wildly aberrant Sirenik. Intelligibility between Chaplino and Naukan is partial, somewhat difficult, and between Chaplino and Sirenik it is extremely marginal or lacking. These judgments are confirmed by Krauss's experience with St. Lawrence Islanders' very partial comprehension of Sirenik and Naukan materials. Siberian Eskimo wordlists began to appear already in the late eighteenth century. A century later, V. F. Miller, working from fieldnotes by N. L. Gondatti taken in 1895, classified these three languages or dialects (Chaplino, Naukan, Sirenik) as such (169, 405, 406), and was confirmed by Bogoraz (94).

### 2.121 *Sirenik*.

Sirenik Eskimos formerly occupied a number of villages just to the west of the main Chaplino area, but the village of Sirenik is the only one in which the language survived until very recent times, and now, here too the Sirenik population has become mixed with and their language has become replaced by Chaplino Eskimo, Chukchi and Russian. The historical reasons for the aberrance of Sirenik Eskimo are not fully known. The lexicon shows especially extensive influence of and loans from Chukchi, and also lexicon of unknown origin, and perhaps also contact with Aleut. Certain phonological traits, e.g. spirant realization of final k and q as g and r, resemble developments in Nunivak (and probably elsewhere), and there are also phonological developments which are unique to Sirenik, e.g. reduction of short i a u in noninitial syllables all to [ə] (a rule that perhaps operates cyclically, and in absolute final position then [ə] > [a]). Inflection has simplified to a considerable extent: e.g. the dual category is lost. On the other hand, an important respect in which Sirenik is uniquely conservative is the degree to which it preserves intervocalic spirants which have elsewhere been lost, with resulting vowel clusters: e.g. Sirenik *atəyəsəx* 'one' (elsewhere *atauciq*, Chaplino *ataasiq*), *qayəx* 'forehead' (elsewhere *qauk*, but Chaplino *qayuk*), *acəx* 'blood' (elsewhere *auk*, Chaplino *aak$^w$*), *kucəx* 'river' (elsewhere *kuik*, Chaplino *kiik$^w$*).

G.A. Menovščikov had contact with Sirenik in the early 1930s, and again in 1948, and collected materials in 1954 and 1960 which he published first in 1962 (359) and has recently published in a major work, *Yazyk Sirenikskikh Eskimosov*, 1964 (364). This book consists of a grammar (to p. 106, essentially descriptive, with a few comparative comments but no attempt to develop systematic comparative-historical explanation), texts with translation (p. 107-175), a Sirenik-Russian lexicon (p. 176-203, containing about 2,700 items), and then a section of comparative vocabulary (p. 204-216, about 400 items compared in Sirenik, Chaplino, Naukan, Imaklik). Bergsland has written an important review of the work (79).

This important Eskimo language is on the verge of extinction. Besides the work of Menovščikov, and the earlier materials in Bogoraz (94) and Gondatti and Miller (179, 405, 406), E.S. Rubcova reportedly (364, p. 27 fn.) also transcribed some Sirenik texts, but these remain unpublished. Finally, Krauss in 1971 found one very old man in Savoonga, St. Lawrence Island, who had visited Sirenik and remembered fragments of the language. His older sister, the last competent speaker of Sirenik outside the USSR, died in Savoonga in 1969. It appears possible that there are aspects of the phonetics of this remarkable language not adequately covered in the published work, in which the phonological discussion is extremely sketchy. It will be regrettable if the language becomes extinct with no further supplement or verification of Menovščikov's work on it.

2.122 *Naukan.* The vast bulk of Siberian Eskimos speak the Chaplino-Naukan language. These two might be classified as dialects of the same language, but with poor mutual intelligibility. Naukan is spoken by the Eskimos of Naukan (Eskimo Nevuuqaq) and Uelen (Uulaq) on the East Cape (Cape Dezhnev), who were relocated in 1956 to Nunyagmo and Pinakul' in St. Lawrence Bay somewhat to the southwest. The number of speakers would probably not exceed 300, smaller than the number of speakers of Chaplino, which is also the base for the literary language. In 1953 (552, p. 138) it is reported that the problem of the value of publishing special textbooks for groups like the Naukan Eskimo would be considered. There has apparently been no literature published in the Naukan dialect, however, and no publications have yet been devoted to it, though it figures often in comparative remarks and lists in various of G.A. Menovščikov's works. Menovščikov has finished a major monograph to fill this gap, a manuscript grammar, texts, and dictionary (386, 387) forthcoming. Earlier Naukan wordlists have been published, e.g. by Gondatti and Miller (169, 406), Bogoraz (94), Jenness (235), Rasmussen (470). Naukan clearly shows some Inuit traits, especially in the lexicon. If indeed there is any area in which the Yupik-Inuit line is not clearly defined, it is probably Naukan. For a better understanding of the Yupik-Inuit relation, good documentation is badly needed of this very strategically situated Eskimo language.

2.123 *Chaplino*. The Chaplino (Eskimo Uŋaziq) dialect is spoken by the majority of Siberian Eskimos: 70%, according to Menovščikov, thus by about 700 souls in Siberia. It is the language of a number of villages of Cape Chaplin and Cape Chukotskiy, and of some families which moved in the early twentieth century to Uel'kal' in Kresta Bay some two hundred miles to the east, and of the (originally 45) Eskimos transplanted to Wrangell Island in 1925. Chaplino is furthermore identical with the language of the present population (over 800) of St. Lawrence Island on the American side.

The early history of the discovery and documentation and discussion of Siberian Eskimo (Merk, Robek, Lisyanskiĭ, Košelev, Kruzenštern) is detailed by Vdovin (620, p. 67, 74–9, 157–8; 100, p. 8–15). Non-Russian vocabularies of the middle and late 19th century period are not covered. The important Russian St. Lawrence Island vocabulary from before 1822 (681) is also omitted. The more modern period begins with the work of Gondatti and Miller (169, 405, 406), who identified the dialects or languages as mentioned above. Their work was continued by V. G. Bogoraz (1865–1936), who began his long association with easternmost Siberians, especially the Chukchi, in 1901 as a member of the Jesup Expedition. Bogoraz published a series of articles on Siberian Eskimo linguistics in 1909 (94), 1913 (95), 1919 (96), 1925 (97), and 1935 (99). An important general sketch from 1934 (98) included materials turned over to Bogoraz by A. S. Foršteĭn, who was a teacher amongst and who worked with the Siberian Eskimos to 1932 .The Gondatti-Miller-Bogoraz phase of Siberian Eskimo research is further detailed by Vdovin (620, p. 137–41, 162–63, and 624, p. 16–19, 58–59, 102–104 and in 100). Bogoraz's unpublished grammatical and textual materials were published posthumously in 1949 (100). The book begins with an extensive introduction (p. 3–24) by the editor, Vdovin, on Bogoraz's work and the history of work on Siberian Eskimo (including a description of manuscript material left by Bogoraz in Leningrad; for a description of the Bogoraz manuscripts in the New York Public Library, see Yarmolinsky, 651). Bogoraz's *Očerk Grammatiki Yazyka Aziatskikh Èskimosov* follows (p. 25–106), based on the 1901 material, devoted mainly to morphology. The following section (p. 107–178) contains 13 Chaplino texts with interlinear Chukchi version, the original Eskimo phonetics normalized (in Roman type) and edited by E. S. Rubcova, sentences numbered and provided with Russian translation also by Rubcova. Pages 179–220 contain Bogoraz's lexical material, edited by Menovščikov, mainly a list of Eskimo words with short Russian glosses, about 1800 items, and a list of about 60 postbases. Menovščikov appends a more systematized study of inflectional paradigms (p. 221–251), and the book closes with bibliographies of Bogoraz and of literature in Siberian Eskimo to 1948. It is to the credit of Bogoraz's successors that his important work is largely superseded.

The writing systems used by Soviet linguists for Eskimo have progressed only slowly towards phonemic adequacy from what they were in 1935, as taken over from Bogoraz. The Chaplino and St. Lawrence Island vowel system is a aa i ii u uu ə. Soviet publications in Eskimo continued to use o and e much of the time for uu and ii, and also for u and i next to uvulars. Vowel length and its interplay with stress, which is predictable (see Krauss, 698), were very little understood and not represented at all before Rubcova's efforts much later. According to Menovščikov (p.c.), when length was recognized it was considered impractical to write double vowels because of conflict with the rule for Russian that every vowel represent a distinct syllabic pulse, and the macron was reserved for scientific publication only. The consonant system of Chaplino-St. Lawrence Island is the following:

$$
\begin{array}{llllllllll}
p & t & k & k^w & q & q^w & & & & \\
v & z & \gamma & \gamma^w & \gamma & \gamma^w & r & l & y & \\
f & s & x & x^w & \underline{x} & \underline{x}^w & \underline{r} & \underline{l} & & h \\
m & n & \eta & \eta^w & & & & & & \\
\underline{m} & \underline{n} & \underline{\eta} & \underline{\eta}^w & & & & & & \\
\end{array}
$$

Bogoraz and Forštein and at first Sergeeva failed to recognize the voiceless nasals; the nature of the labialized velars and uvulars (now single segments, preceded by underlying au or iu, or followed by underlying ua or ui); h(rare); and worst of all, the distinction between x and x̱. Whether he heard the difference or not, Forštein also wrote r for both $\gamma$ and retroflex r. Later, after the switch to Cyrillic, Rubcova and Menovščikov did provide for x:x̱, r:$\gamma$, n:ṇ, and finally, began to eliminate e and o.

During the most recent period, a truly prodigious amount of scientific literature has been published on Siberian (Chaplino) Eskimo. Especially voluminious are the works of G.A. Menovščikov. These will be discussed last, following that of the contribution of others, also highly significant.

In 1941 E.S. Rubcova published a Russian-Eskimo dictionary, 141 pages long, containing 6,000 words (478), still by far the largest of its kind, designed for the schools; however, virtually the entire edition was destroyed in the war. A major part of Rubcova's contribution has been to the pedagogical literature, which will be treated below. A most recent publication by her is an article on adverbs (486). In 1949 she edited the texts in the posthumous Bogoraz volume (100). Her most important published scientific contribution to date, however, is an excellent large volume of Chaplino texts, with translation notes and illustrations, *Materialy po yazyku i fol'kloru Èskimosov*, part I (482, all that has so far appeared, though it is stated in the introduction that part II, containing 50 more texts, was forthcoming). Rubcova transcribed these texts in 1940, in Chaplino from a young man named Aivukhak (Ayvəx̱aq), reviewed them in 1948, and finished the work in 1950, with the help of a number of Eskimos, most of whose names also appear as contributors to other work:

Kalyanga, Kalya, Yata, Yu. M. Anko, V.A. Anal'kvasak, S.M. Gukhuge, A.M. Kavauge, and others.

E.S. Rubcova died in December 1971, in her 84th year. Before her death she finished two other major scientific works on Siberian Eskimo. In the fall of 1971 her definitive Eskimo-Russian dictionary (487) was published, a work that had absorbed much of the last decade of her life. Edited by Menovščikov, it contains about 19,000 entries, also with a supplement on postbases. This book is probably the most important single Soviet contribution to Eskimo linguistics.

Although Rubcova has not been the major linguist associated with Soviet Eskimo linguistics (and she herself has been involved even more prominently in the development of pedagogical material for Eskimos), her scientific contribution has been central and enduring. For instance, Rubcova was apparently the one who made the most serious effort to understand vowel length and its interplay with alternate-syllable stress, as can be seen in her 1954 *Materialy* (482), where both stress and length are marked, an attempt (only partially successful) being made to distinguish the two. In her 1966 article (486) and then in the new dictionary, the distinction is made with much more insight, attaining nearly complete observational adequacy. This critically important aspect of Siberian Yupik phonology is completely ignored at the same time by Menovščikov in his scientific works (e.g. his 1962-1967 grammar of the language, where generally no attempt is made to indicate stress or length, and treatment of it in the phonology discussion itself is completely inadequate).

In her eighties Rubcova finished yet one more work of great importance on Siberian Eskimo. Just before her death she finished preparing the long-awaited Part II of her *Materialy po yazyku i fol'kloru Èskimosov* (482). This is to appear posthumously under the editorship of Menovščikov.

I.M. Emel'yanova, a student with Menovščikov, has recently written a dissertation (132), and published some specialized articles on derivational processes in Eskimo, particularly stem-formation (133, 134, 135, 136). Scholars whose major activity has been elsewhere in linguistics have also sometimes written articles dealing with in one way or another Siberian Eskimo linguistics, e.g. Meščaninov (393, 394), and especially Vdovin. Vdovin has been the historian of Soviet Eskimo (and Paleoasiatic) studies. His contributions (620, 621, 623, 100, 696) have been very useful to this report. Another very interesting article (622) by Vdovin, however, deals extensively with lexical diffusion between Eskimo and the Chukotan groups, showing over 80 loans from Eskimo into Chukchi and /or the Alyutor dialect of Koryak, and over 100 loans in the other direction.

By far the most prolific of all writers on Eskimo of any nation since the war has been G.A. Menovščikov. His work on Imaklik, Sirenik, and Naukan has already been outlined above, and his central role in the development of popular and pedagogical literature in Eskimo will be outlined below. Here his extensive scientific writing on Chaplino will be discussed. Menovščikov spent some years during the thirties as a teacher in the Eskimo schools. His scientific publication begins after the war. After a return to the Eskimo district on an expedition in 1948 (312), and having done laboratory research on Eskimo phonetics and phonology under L.R. Zinder (333, 663), Menovščikov began publishing on inflections and agglutination in 1949–50 (100, 309, 313, 314, 316, 317, 318). Since then he has published nearly forty articles on various aspects of Eskimo (especially Chaplino) grammar and lexicology, also toponymy, and to some extent ethnology (322, 323, 324, 325, 332, 334, 335, 336, 337, 347, 348, 350, 353, 354, 356, 357, 358, 360, 361, 362, 364, 365, 367, 371, 372, 374, 375, 376, 377, 378, 379, 380, 381, 383, 384, 385, 389, 392, 682, 683, 684). Item 375 contains a good concise general sketch. Many of these articles are partly or even largely comparative and/or historical. In 1954 Menovščikov published a major, though not definitive, Eskimo-Russian school dictionary (330), containing 4,700 words, a list of postbases, and, on pages 189–320, his first Eskimo grammar. In 1960 he published an extensive pedagogical grammar (374 pages) for the use of teachers to the Eskimos (355). His magnum opus to date, however, is the two-volume *Grammatika yazyka aziatskikh Èskimosov* (360, 373). Totalling 588 pages, it is no doubt the most extensive Eskimo grammar yet published; it centers very heavily, however, on inflectional and derivational morphology. Volume I was published in 1962. Following the introduction is a brief section on phonology (pp. 16–50), i.e. phonetics and orthography, barely touching the morphophonemics, and including some comparative data, especially Sirenik. The rest of the volume (pp. 51–298) details the inflection and derivation of nominals (nouns, pronouns, numerals). Volume II, published in 1967, treats verb inflection and derivation (pp. 7–126), participles, adverbs, modals, conjunctions, particles, enclitics, interjections (p. 136–268). A chapter on Chukchi loans and their phonology in Eskimo follows (p. 258–276), and then an index of suffixes (postbases, p. 276–284). There is no section devoted to syntax (systematic description of sentence structure as such). The work is, again, basically descriptive, but with a number of comparative remarks and discussions, dealing especially with other Siberian Eskimo, but also to a lesser extent with Alaskan, Canadian, Greenlandic, and Aleut. The style of presentation is, by American scientific linguistic standards, very non-formal and non-concise, e.g. with detailed digressions on semantics.

Tor Ulving (695) has written a very important and helpful, if severe, critique of some of the weaknesses of this work, providing a great deal of sorely-needed insight in an area that has been dominated by an isolated scholar. In the morphophonemics, for example, the present writer might cite, in addition, Menovščikov's failure to explain that clusters of unlike vowels are entirely absent, and that this is because of the following transparent and simple assimilation rules: *ia, ai, iu, ui → ii; ua, au → aa*. There are also many alternations like *atəq ~ aatx-*, which Menovščikov not only fails to explain, but has no consistent need even to observe, since vowel length itself is generally ignored.

Soviet schools were established for the Siberian Eskimos in 1927, in Chaplino, Urelik (later Providenia), Kivak, and Sirenik. In 1932 the Northern Peoples' Institute at Leningrad began its program at the Khabarovsk Technical School of developing literatures in the languages of northern peoples, including (Chaplino) Eskimo (300, 436). The orthographies were to be in modified Roman phonetic symbols. Already by the end of that year the first Siberian Eskimo reader appeared, the bilingual and substantial *Xwankuta ihaput / Naša kniga*, by A. Byčkov and B. Leĭta or Legta, under the direction of Elizaveta Porfir'ievna Orlova (437, 685). Bilingual education began in 1933. Educators amongst the Eskimo at that time were Georgiĭ Alekseevič Menovščikov (1932–34, 1939–41), Aleksandr S. Foršteĭn (1929-32, died 1969), Katerina Semenovna Sergeeva (1934–41) and Ekatèrina Semenovna Rubcova (from the late thirties), all of whom were very productive in publishing school texts. Bibliographical sources are incomplete for this prewar period. The *Ežegodnik Knigi SSSR* was published for the year 1935 only, and for that year alone are listed no fewer than six Eskimo language books: readers, collections of traditional stories and stories for children, and a text on non-arctic animals, in the Roman phonetic orthography. Listed as authors, collaborators, translators, or editors are the teachers A.S. Foršteĭn (150, 151, 524, 525, 526, 527, 152, this last published in 1936), and K.S. Sergeeva, (524, 525, 526, 527, 690, 691), and the Eskimo V. Amkaun Nynlyuvak (150, 525, 526, 527). In 1936 another item translated by Amkaun (43), on the history of aviation, is listed in the bibliography of 100; this bibliography helps somewhat to fill in the 1936–1941 bibliographical gap. Not listed in either of these bibliographies, however, is the first arithmetic text, translated and countertranslated by Sergeeva in 1935 (690, 691).

After 1936 the Institut Narodov Severa changed its policy on orthographies, to convert them all to Cyrillic symbols. The Eskimo literature of the prewar Cyrillic period (1937–41) is probably very incompletely listed. The names credited with the work, with the exception of Sergeeva (529, 530, 531, 532, 533, 248, 253, 303) are new: these are the Eskimos Kasyga (252, 253, 390, 478), Ačirgin (1, 2, 3, 4, 253, 478), Tatak (253, 254, 478), Ashkamakyn (529), Tayu (529), Kaklya (478), and, perhaps to be identified with the preceding, Kalya (248, see also 482); except for the last, none of these names appear again after the war. Also associated with the work of this period, and appearing in print for the first time, though their scientific contributions after the war are far better known, are the names of G.A. Menovščikov (390, 303, 304), and E.S. Rubcova (1, 2, 3, 4, 253, 478). Some of these items were general readers and collections of stories of the type that had appeared before (253, 254, 303, 529, 530, 390, the last including a 27-page Russian-Eskimo dictionary as a supplement, the first of its kind and the first work of Menovščikov in print). In addition to these, however, the variety began to increase greatly, to include translations of poems for children (532), 'frontier stories' (248), works on arctic expeditions (1, 2), on health (4), 'meetings with' and a speech by Stalin (3, 252), an exposé of shamans (533); the arithmetic series was revised in Cyrillic and then expanded (531, first-year translated by Sergeeva in 1937; 304, expanded first-year, translated by Menovščikov in 1939; 457, second-year, translator not named). The final work of this period was the very important Russian-Eskimo dictionary (478), which of course falls also into the category of linguistics as such, and is mentioned above in the discussion of Rubcova's work. This work is the culmination of the great activity in Siberian Eskimo linguistic research in the prewar period. The war, not surprisingly, brought about a suspension of this work and publication in Eskimo.

Menovščikov and Rubcova continued their work after the war. The names of their Eskimo collaborators are all new. Publication resumed almost immediately, in 1946, with a Russian reader including a vocabulary by Menovščikov (305). There followed more specialized Russian manuals and readers: a manual for the preparatory year (editions in 1954 and 1959, 421, 422), a manual for the first year (1955, 264), and reader for the first year (editions in 1954 and 1959, 103, 104, 349, with vocabulary by Menovščikov and Kuyapa), a manual for the second year (editions in 1956 and 1961, 265, 629) and reader for the second year (editions in 1954 and 1959, 272, 268, with vocabulary by Kuyapa), and an advanced reader (editions in 1949 and 1955, 44, 273, with vocabulary by Anal'kvasak). These were all standard texts, adapted in Eskimo editions. There likewise continued a series on arithmetic: first year (editions in 1949 and 1954, 490, 495), and second year (1951, 492), translated by Rubcova, Anal'kvasak, Uïgakhpak, and Kalya.

Menovščikov between 1947 and 1957 published a whole series of *Učebniks* for the Eskimo language with accompanying translated teachers' manuals: for preparatory year (editions in 1951 and 1957, 320, 321, 339, 340), for first year (editions in 1947, 1953, and 1957, 307, 308, 325, 326, 341, 343), and for second year (editions in 1949, 1953, and 1957, 309, 310, 327, 328, 343, 344). Another series of texts for Eskimo was E. S. Rubcova's *Bukvar'* for preparatory year (488, 489, 493, 494, 497, 498; first edition, 1947, accompanied by translated teacher's manual, coauthored by Ayakhta and S. M. Gukhuge, second in 1953, coauthored by Gukhuge, with translated teacher's manual 1954, third and fourth editions in 1960 and 1965, coauthored by Gukhuge). For the first and second years she wrote the series *Naša Reč'*, with translated teacher's manual: two editions for first year (1950 and 1955, 491, 481 496, 483, the first coauthored by Vera A. Anal'kvasak and Tanuta, the second by Anal'kvasak), and two for second year (1948 and 1956, 479, 480, 484, 485, the second coauthored by L. Aïnana). The successive 'editions' of most of these books are almost completely rewritten works.

These series for Russian and arithmetic, and the series of *Učebniks* by Menovščikov and of *Bukvar'* and *Naša Reč'* by Rubcova and others constitute the great bulk of the postwar production in Eskimo books. Apparently the only other items are Menovščikov's second volume of traditional Eskimo stories in 1947 (306), a children's story in bilingual edition in 1948 (391, translation by Menovščikov and Uïgakhpak), in 1949–51 two volumes of stories for children by Čarušin (113, translated by Uïgakhpak 114, translator not cited) and one of skits for children by Maršak (299, translator not cited), and since then probably only one item, stories about Lenin in 1959 (262, translator not cited).

There appears to have been some development of belles-lettres in Siberian Eskimo. In an anthology of creative writing of peoples of the far Soviet north, published 1958 in Magadan (608), Menovščikov gives translations of unpublished prose stories by two Eskimo authors, Ktug'e and Numylen, both by then dead, and of works by two poets, the late Yuriĭ M. Anko (of Chaplino, 1932–1960; see also 482), and of Taĭsiya Gukhuv'e (a woman from Uel'kal'). Some of their works have been published in the periodicals *Sovetken Čukotka (Sovetskaya Čukotka), Pionerskaya Pravda, Na Severe Dal'nem*, and the manuscript periodical *Yunost'*, whether some in the Eskimo original or all in translation it is not clear. *Sovetskaya Čukotka*, published in Anadyr', is reported by Vdovin (696) to run a weekly Eskimo language page.

It is perhaps appropriate to include mention of volumes of Eskimo stories in translation (only) by Menovščikov (346, 383) and Sergeeva (534), and anthologies of traditional tales of northern peoples, including sections from the Eskimo by Menovščikov (318a, 693, 352, 319, 329, 345, the last three apparently successive editions of a very successful volume) and a similar anthology by Rubcova (687). Menovščikov also published a descriptive article (350) and a book on Eskimos (351) in Magadan 1959 for popular consumption. The latter contains much valuable information, e.g. about the recent cultural history of the Siberian Eskimos. Also significant for the social, educational, language and literature policy for Siberian Eskimos and other northern Soviet peoples are Vdovin (621, 623, 624, 696), the 1932 conference report (300), 1953 articles in *Voprosy Jazykoznaniya* (55 Avrorin, 228 editorial, 552 Sunik), a book by M. A. Sergeev (689), reports by Avrorin (56, 57), Onenko (434), Skorik (544), Sunik (694), Menovščikov (309, 385), and bibliographies of literature of northern peoples published in 1934, 1935, and 1951 (610, 611, 612).

Much of this primary and secondary material on Siberian Eskimo literature is not at all available in the United States. In spite of the incompleteness of the listing, and the still far more incomplete availability of the material for examination, one thing is abundantly clear: for a tiny and 'primitive' nation of 1,000 souls at the uttermost end of a vast continent, Siberian Eskimo literature, even incompletely described as it is here, amounts to a very remarkable achievement. It attests to an administrative policy enlightened in many ways and to which American and Canadian administrators could well pay heed, whatever the broader political considerations. On the other hand, in spite of the obvious recognition and support the Eskimo language has received in the Soviet Union, not all policy or developments there have remained in its favor. For instance, analysis of the bibliography of Siberian Eskimo school and popular literature reveals one very significant trend: whereas there are listed here 27 items for 1932–1941, and 52 more for the period 1946–1960, for the last decade 1961–1970 only two items appear, neither new: the second edition of the second-year Russian manual in 1961 and the fourth edition of the Rubcova-Gukhuge primer in 1965. Unless the bibliographical annual *Ežegodnik Knigi SSSR* and the *Knižnaya Letopis'* are less complete than before for materials of this type (the *Ežegodnik* is presently available to 1966 and the *Letopis'* to date), there clearly appears to be a very significant decrease in the rate of publication of Eskimo books. This significant decline, moreover, is accompanied by a decrease in the size of the *tiraž*: whereas through 1949 these materials were most commonly printed in 1000 copies, since then they have been coming out most commonly in only 500 or 300 copies.

A corresponding decline in the use of the Eskimo language by Eskimos can also clearly be seen. Onenko reports that in 1959 83.9% of Siberian Eskimos use the Eskimo language (434, p. 35, from the 1959 census (227) where it is reported that of the Eskimo population of 1118, those using the native language number 939); then, most recently in a report by Avrorin of the results of an extensive survey in 1969 (57, 1970) one may learn that only 19% of the Eskimo respondents speak exclusively Eskimo to their children, 22% speak both Eskimo and Russian, and 59% speak exclusively Russian to their children. And yet 63% of the Eskimos are in favor of using the Eskimo language as a medium of instruction in the schools, 97% are in favor of including it as a subject for study in primary schools, 89% also in secondary schools. It is not mentioned whether most adult Eskimos are still fluent in Chukchi, as reported in 1956, 336, p. 934. Also, with these figures may be compared those for the Chukchi, amongst whom the Eskimos live in very close contact and are largely interspersed; a group of about 12,000, more than ten times the size of the Eskimo: spoken to children 46% Chukchi only, 32% Chukchi and Russian, 22% Russian only. Chukchi too appears to be ceding to Russian, but much more slowly than Eskimo. But Chukchi interest in having their language in the schools in certainly no stronger than, if indeed as strong as, that of the Eskimos: 63% want Chukchi as a medium of instruction, 95% want it as a subject for study in primary school, 80% also in secondary.)

A clear explanation of the social policy behind these developments is to be found in Gurvich and Faineberg's (679) response to Hughes' observation (680) that in spite of economic and health conditions, which certainly must have vastly improved since 1900, the Soviet Eskimo population has failed to increase, has in fact decreased if anything, from 1,200 in Bogoraz's time to 1,100 or 1,000 today. Gurvich and Faineberg explain that this is true, and is due to a very high rate of intermarriage with Chukchi and Russian, the families then seldom identifying themselves as Eskimo. The Eskimo people no longer live in villages or collectives of their own unto themselves, but are everywhere mixed with Chukchis and Russians, amongst whom they are thus always a minority. In Gurvich and Faineberg's positive phraseology, 'the rapprochement of the few Asiatic Eskimos with the Chukchi and Russians has been strengthened on the basis of co-managing the general economy', in an 'interesting ethnic process of voluntary merging of two peoples who are already quite close in their cultures'. The social policy is thus quite clear. The reason for it, however, is not. Perhaps there is a reluctance to stimulate and strengthen Eskimo ethnic identity which might lead to feelings of allegiance with other Eskimos. The preface to Menovščikov's 1960 pedagogical Eskimo grammar (355) for teachers suggests this in the gingerly way it covers the subject of Eskimos in other countries: the population figures are underestimated, especially for Alaska (8,000, Canada 10,000, Greenland 22,000), and the Eskimo dialects of Alaska are listed as follows: Kuskokwim, Wales, Nunivak, 'Kan'yanegmit', Barrow, Unalakleet (in Norton Sound), and Sivukagmit (on St. Lawrence Island). There is no mention whatever of the fact that the dialect of St. Lawrence Island is at all special, though the fact that it is identical with standard Siberian Eskimo is certainly widely known to and of great interest to the Soviet Eskimos.

In fact, nowhere at all in the Soviet Eskimo schoolbooks are there any maps showing the location of Eskimos, even of Soviet Eskimos, any mention of Eskimo or even use of the word, or any content designed to increase consciousness of Eskimo identity as such, as distinct from any other Soviet identity. The illustrations and content are partly Eskimo, and the language is Eskimo, but apparently only for the purpose of being intelligible, for providing a bridge to assimilation into the larger Soviet society, and at the same time taking pains to include illustrations and content which the Eskimo child can readily understand and with which he can readily identify. The books thus do at least avoid being completely foreign and unintelligible, and at least they do not completely neglect or negate the child's Eskimo identity in a way that would be a destructive affront to his personality and culture. That much alone is more than has hitherto been provided the Eskimo schools in North America.

Another interesting characteristic of Soviet literary Eskimo, clearly in keeping with the political and social purposes of the schoolbooks, is the use of Russian words for most new or technical terms. These are very freely and copiously introduced, with unmodified spelling, throughout the Eskimo text, clearly in order to facilitate the shift to Russian, which is intended to be complete by the fourth year of elementary school. There is no systematic attempt made to coin new terms by using Eskimo morphemes, and no attempt to adapt the language for school use beyond the first few years of school.

## 2.2 *Alaska*

Alaska, like Siberia, or perhaps even more than Siberia, and certainly far more than Canada or Greenland, has a very full range of Eskimo dialects, Yupik and Inuit. Yet the Alaskan Eskimo dialects are the least well investigated by linguists. Alaska is clearly the Eskimo area most in need of linguistic investigation today.

There are three Yupik languages spoken in Alaska and one Inuit. The Yupik-Inuit borderline is at Unalakleet on Norton Sound, the older language of which is Yupik, the newer, Inuit.

The three Yupik languages are the Siberian of St. Lawrence Island, the Central Alaskan Yupik of the Yukon and Kuskokwim Deltas and Bristol Bay areas, and the Pacific Gulf Yupik, sometimes called Suk, Supik, '(Kad'iakskiĭ) Aleut', or, in that language itself, Sugcestun [suxt$^s$stun]. Mutual intelligibility between these three Yupik languages, according to experiments at the University of Alaska, is at a low level in each pairing of the three, but St. Lawrence Island seems still further removed from both Central and Pacific Yupik than those latter two are from each other. A count on the 100-word list showed about 65 cognates between Central and St. Lawrence Island Yupik, for instance. These findings agree fairly well with Hammerich's conclusions from his important Yupik dialectological fieldwork in 1950 and 1953 (184).

The total number of Eskimos in Alaska is difficult to estimate accurately, even from the 1971 census, which was done very inadequately for this purpose. A fairly safe guess for 1972 would be 34,000 $\pm 2,000$. About two-thirds of these, or 22,000, are Yupik: Siberian with 800 on St. Lawrence Island and 200 in Nome and elsewhere, Central by far the largest with 15,500 between Unalakleet and the Alaska Peninsula, and Pacific with about 5,500 on the Alaska Peninsula (South side), Kodiak and Afognak Islands, and Prince William Sound. Siberian is in full vigor in that all the people of St. Lawrence Island speak the language daily. Central Yupik is in full vigor in most areas, but eroded somewhat in the larger centers, especially Bethel and Dillingham, and in some of the fringe areas, where some of the children may have an inadequate knowledge of the language. It would nevertheless be safe to say that 14,500 of 15,000 Central Yupiks do speak the language. Pacific Yupik, on the other hand, is nearly everywhere moribund; only the older generations, perhaps 2,000 of 5,500, speak the language. The situation of each of the Yupik languages in Alaska will be detailed in order.

## 2.21 *St. Lawrence Island*

Not fifty miles from Siberia on the American side lies St. Lawrence Island, where about 800 Eskimos live, who speak virtually the same language as that of the Siberians, whose mountains are visible to them on a clear day. Since about 1947 there has been no contact between these two divisions of the only linguistic community in the world which is native to both hemispheres.

The Eskimos of St. Lawrence Island, as far as can be determined, have always spoken a variety of Siberian Eskimo. An 1822 vocabulary (681) shows clearly that the language of the island was then Siberian. In 1878 a severe famine and epidemic, no doubt connected with the depredation of the American whalers of the period, decimated the island population, leaving only about 200 at Gambell and 30 on the Southwest Cape. The present populations of Gambell and Savoonga are descendants of these, with some replenishment also from Siberia. There are minor dialectal differences between Southwest Cape and Gambell remembered, and some very old individuals can remember that the speech of one survivor of the famine from the Southeast Cape of the island spoke a markedly different dialect, though largely intelligible.

A Presbyterian school was established at Gambell in 1895. In 1910 the missionary Edgar O. Campbell published a pathetic little reader-pamphlet (108) of Bible quotations in a nearly unreadable orthography, for the Islanders and also the 'Siberian Kurds'. Half a century later, David and Marilene Shinen of the Wycliffe Bible Translators began a decade on the island. Mr. Shinen made available notes on the phonology

(539, 540). In 1966 the Shinens published a primer (541), in 1969 they published a hymnal (742) and in 1970 Mr. Shinen with Elinor Oozeva published a life of Christ (435), in an orthography which is very different from anything used for mainland Yupik and of course also from the Cyrillic Siberian.

During the period 1970–1972 Michael Krauss, Adelinda Womkon Badten, Dudley Hascall, and Sharon Pungowiyi Orr carried out research at the University of Alaska, supported in part by the National Science Foundation, on the phonology and morphology of St. Lawrence Island Eskimo. A chief problem was vowel length and its interplay with stress. This was worked out and described by Krauss in 1971 (702). An important applied result of this work was the development of a new orthography for St. Lawrence Island by Krauss, Badten, Hascall, and Shinen. Selections from Rubcova's *Materialy* (482), retranscribed in this orthography, were prepared by Krauss and Badten and presented to the Islanders with an introduction to reading in *Sivuqaghhmiit Atightullghit* (699). In 1972 they prepared a greatly expanded selection, *Ungazighmiit Ungipaghaatangit* (698). A characteristic of the orthography is the use of gh instead of r for $\gamma$, because the r is needed for retroflex r, a not infrequent sound in native Siberian Eskimo words. (This same problem also occurs in Alaskan Inupiat orthography.) Another characteristic is that the symbolization of intervocalic x x̣ r̥ ł m̥ n̥ ŋ̊ is by gg ghh rr ll mm nn ngng, as no consonant gemination of any kind occurs in St. Lawrence Island phonetics. Literacy in this orthography is now spreading on St. Lawrence Island. A teacher-training program was held in Savoonga in August, 1972, headed by Krauss, Shinen, and Orr. Bilingual education began in September, 1972. For the first time, this Eskimo language is being written and cultivated in St. Lawrence Island schools. This comes forty years after a similar beginning on the Soviet side, and at the same time as the language is apparently declining to obsolescence in the schools on the Soviet side. As part of the activity of the new Alaska Native Language Center at the University of Alaska, Badten and Krauss head a program of materials production under which it is anticipated that many books will be produced in St. Lawrence Island Eskimo at the University of Alaska and at St. Lawrence Island, already during 1972–1973. These will be, e.g., retranscriptions of the Soviet materials, translations and adaptations of materials produced at the University of Alaska in Central Yupik, and, above all the literature, history and culture of the St. Lawrence Islanders themselves.

2.22 *Central Alaskan Yupik*

The major Eskimo language of Alaska and the major Yupik language of the world is Central Alaskan Yupik. This will sometimes be called here Central Yupik or simply Yupik, in the language itself, Yup'ik [yúp·ik]. The total number of speakers is difficult to estimate closely (whole villages having been left out of the census): $14,500 \pm 1,500$. The total Central Alaskan Yupik population is perhaps 17,000, including those dispersed to Anchorage and elsewhere. Of these there are some of the younger generation in either the fringe situations or in the larger centers within the area

(Bethel, Dillingham), who do not speak the language. But in general Yupik is still the dominant language of its entire area. There are many adults who do not speak English well and most children upon entering school are monolingual in Yupik. The viability of Central Alaskan Yupik is far greater than that of any other native language in Alaska. Two factors contributing to the remarkable vitality of Yupik are clearly the sheer numbers relative to any other native language group, and also the relative density of the Eskimo population and the numerically relatively weak non-Eskimo population of the area.

The area extends from the north shore of the Alaska Peninsula across Bristol Bay and the Kuskokwim and Yukon Deltas to the south shore of Norton Sound, spreading far up the Kuskokwim to Sleetmute and the Yukon to Holy Cross, at the expense of the receding Athapaskan. The entire area is clearly a single language. There are significant dialect differences, sometimes troublesome, but all dialects are basically mutually intelligible. The three general regions appear to be Bristol Bay, Kuskokwim, and Yukon. The most aberrant dialects appear to be that of the Hooper Bay and Chevak area between the Yukon and Kuskokwim Deltas, and especially that of Nunivak Island, where initial y is often č and final q and k are r and g. Yet even Nunivak dialect is readily intelligible to the mainlanders. Central Alaskan Yupik thus constitutes a single linguistic community with considerable unity and strength. This fortunate circumstance and the recent developments to be reported here appear to portend a bright future for this Eskimo language. The situation of Central Alaskan Yupik is probably far more favorable than that of any Eskimo language except Greenlandic itself.

Before the war the major linguistic work done on Yupik was that of the missionaries: first Russian Orthodox throughout the area until the turn of the century, then the Jesuits at St. Michael in the Yukon Delta and in the Nelson Island area, and the Moravians at Bethel in the Kuskokwim Delta. The Jesuit priest Francis Barnum produced a grammar in 1901 (62), based on the dialect of Nelson Island which contains much valuable information, especially morphological, but the atrocious over- and under-differentiated and outdated system of transcription obscures the phonology to a point which makes this still unreplaced work rather difficult to use. The later liturgical material (284, 285, 286) published by the Jesuit fathers (Martin J. Lonneux and his associates, chiefly Margaret Hunt Andrews) fortunately employs a far superior, though still imperfect orthography. An enormous amount of manuscript Yupik material by Jesuits, mostly religious, is at the Archives of the Oregon Province Archives, Gonzaga University, Spokane. This material has been examined and catalogued by H. Landar (269).

The Moravian mission began to work at Bethel in 1885. Soon after, a useful and significant grammar of Yupik with vocabulary was published by A. Schultze (516, 517). The Moravian systems of transcription, like those of the Jesuits, evolved through several stages for the better, and the linguistic work of the Moravian Fathers (Frederick Drebert and John Hinz) culminated in a partial (5) and then complete New

Testament (250), a hymnal (653), largely the work of Fr. Drebert, and, most important for linguistics, in the Rev. John Hinz's *Grammar and vocabulary of the Eskimo language* (203, reviewed by Voegelin, 630). This is a sketchy work with many faults, but it profits not a little from the Kleinschmidt model on which it is based. Hinz, together with Barnum, certainly sums up what was available to linguists on Alaskan Yupik at the end of the war.

An extremely interesting development had taken place in Yupik toward the close of the nineteenth century in the form of a native writing system, originated largely by the Yupik Eskimo Helper Neck (Uyakoq, 1860–1924) with the Moravians at Bethel, and used by some of Neck's relatives and associates in religious and other composition. The writing evolved rapidly from pictographic to phonological. This remarkable phenomenon is dealt with at length by Alfred Schmitt (504, 505, but note also Schmitt's study of the Eskimo verb, 506). Though there are still a few Yupiks who know how to read it, this writing system never became very widespread or influential.

The first investigation of Yupik after the war that resulted in any publication was made by the Danes. E. Holtved and H. Larsen's expedition to Alaska in 1949–50 was mainly non-linguistic, but Birket-Smith and Holtved report (92, 209) that they recorded a large amount of text material in Bristol Bay (unpublished). In 1950 Helen Oswalt added 500-word lists (438, unpublished) from Mountain Village and Hooper Bay to those published by Birket-Smith (87). Most significantly, L. L. Hammerich visited Yupik Alaska in 1950, 1953 (reported in 183), and again in 1963. He surveyed large parts of the Central (as well as Pacific) Yupik area: Nelson Island, Nunivak Island, Marshall, Paimiut, Sleetmute, Dillingham, Iliamna, Egegik, Pilot Point. Hammerich's data remain mostly unpublished, but, besides deeply influencing all his subsequent publications on Eskimo, his Alaskan investigations resulted in a number of important articles, on the Nunivak dialect (180, see also 178, p. 39, and note the earlier Nunivak materials of Jenness, 236, and of Rasmussen, 470); on Yupik dialectology in general (184); and on Russian loans in Yupik (181, 182). Hammerich's articles on the loans apparently catalyzed a small flurry of publication on the subject by Menovščikov (322, 323, 334), Dean Stoddard Worth (648, 649), and (on a Spanish word) by Allan R. Taylor (572). In 1960 the late Svend Frederiksen collected a certain amount of lexical and textual material from Bethel and nearby villages (unpublished).

In 1961 Michael Krauss began a program of Yupik studies at the University of Alaska, first in the form of a fieldwork-type class with Martha Teeluk as informant. Amongst the students was Irene Reed, who took over the course the following year, and continued until 1963 when she left the University for four years. A very important development in the program began with the arrival in Alaska of Osahito Miyaoka in 1967. After a summer of fieldwork, especially on Nelson Island Yupik, Miyaoka undertook the teaching of the Eskimo courses at the University of Alaska, with Paschal Afcan as chief informant. Miss Reed joined the staff again in 1968. The program has developed into a flourishing curriculum under Miss Reed's direction, including the Eskimo Language Workshop, with all its creative and publishing activity.

During this period 1967–69, Miyaoka, Reed, Afcan, and Krauss, with the support of the National Endowment for the Humanities, worked on the development of a definitive Yupik orthography and grammar. This required a deep analysis of the phonology, probably much deeper than would have been required for a language for the phonology of which it does seem to make sense to discuss a 'taxonomic phonemic' level. To Krauss it seems that languages vary considerably in the extent to which their phonology presents anything resembling a consistent taxonomic phonemic level, and Central Yupik is one of those that least exhibits any such level in terms of consistent taxonomic phonological patterning. Judicious development of an orthography for Yupik therefore requires a relatively deeper understanding of the phonology through a continuum of morphophonemic levels, and then picking one's way through with a minimum of unavoidable inconsistencies and level-shifts, such that the orthography is an arbitrary but optimum compromise between surface phonetic and systematic phonological representation (one per morpheme). Another factor that must be kept in mind in the development of an orthography is the fact that a speaker's understanding of the phonology of his language deepens as he grows older. It probably takes at least ten years for the average speaker of English to progress in his tacit understanding from what Bloomfield's six-year-old was supposed to know of his phonology to what is claimed in Chomsky and Halle's *Sound pattern of English*. The Eskimo orthography is also a compromise, between what might be optimal for six-year-old learners and for adult learners.

Finally, a choice of symbols also requires consideration of several factors. At one extreme would have been a set with minimum resemblance to the dominant Roman, which would have the important advantage of e.g. the Eastern Canadian syllabary, in giving written Yupik a decidedly unique appearance, clearly a positive (conceivably even crucial) support to the prestige of the language. In this connection, Cyrillic, which was also the first used to represent Yupik, was considered, but rejected because of obvious political considerations ('are you trying to give Alaska back to the Russians?'). In fact, that chosen was the other extreme, a subset of the English type-font, which is designed to minimize printing costs and maximize carryover value (within limits) for English-language literacy. This required, for example, the artificial rule /ŋ/ → *ng* → [ŋ], i.e. (morpho)phonemic ŋ is orthographically written ng, and pronounced ŋ. Intervocalic voiceless fricatives are indicated by doubling the symbol for the voiced fricative, e.g. *alla* [ała], *agga* [axa], *arra* [axa], but [axta] is written *arta*. The letter *e* is used for /ə/, clearly the most problematical element in Yupik phonology. A consonant following the first vowel of a word is long if immediately followed by a sequence of two vowels, thus *anaa* → [anˑaˑ]. A sequence like [mikˑoq] 'it is small' requires the same type of interpretation, thus /mikeur/, and then e is deleted before another vowel. This is represented orthographically *mik'uq*, to avoid conflict with English writing patterns. Also, there is secondary vowel lengthening on the second of a sequence of three open syllables, so that the differences between [anˑaˑna] and [anaˑna] and [anˑana] are represented as *anaana* vs. *anana* vs. *an'ana*. The orthography is of course standardized in such respects. Real dialectal differences, however, are expected to be reflected in the writing.

The phonological analysis upon which the Yupik orthography is founded is also a part of the Yupik Eskimo classroom grammar (420), developed by Miyaoka and the University of Alaska group (Reed, Afcan, Krauss) during the period of his visit. This grammar is based primarily on Paschal Afcan's dialect (Southern Yukon Delta, Central Yupik) and is designed primarily to serve as the basis for college-level classroom instruction for those learning Yupik as a second language. It is organized accordingly, and contains a large amount of exemplification and exercise material. At the same time, since it does of course contain the necessary information for a scientific grammar of the language, it is also hoped that it may serve secondarily as such. This Yupik grammar, though still in preliminary version, is already of great interest to the field of Eskimo linguistics in general. During the period 1970–1972 work on Central Yupik grammar has been continued and further developed at the University of Alaska by Irene Reed, Dudley Hascall (719, 720, 721, 722), Jang Koo (724, 725, 726, 727), Martha Teeluk, Paschal Afcan, and Michael Krauss. This work also includes important further development of the classroom grammar. A continuing Central Yupik dictionary project has been established under the direction of Irene Reed (712) and Steven Jacobson. Miyaoka has already published two important papers on Central Yupik phonology (415, 418), and in Japan has also continued his Yupik work, with his forthcoming grammatical sketch of Central Yupik (728) for the new *Handbook of American Indian Languages*. This sketch will be the most important scientific publication on Central Yupik since Hinz's grammar.

Three items by other authors have recently appeared on Yupik phonology (302, 219, 724). They are perhaps interesting but must be recommended with very serious reservations. The first (Mattina) is grossly inaccurate, and the second (Hunns) leans heavily on the first and on Menovščikov, with predictably uncertain results. The Yupik Eskimo problem in Robert Langacker's recent *Fundamentals of linguistic analysis* (1972) is also unhappily based on 302.

After the development of the Central Yupik orthography, it became possible also for the Eskimo Language Workshop at the University of Alaska to launch the first Yupik periodical, *Naaqsugenarqelriit* ('things worth reading') (423).

A central objective of the University of Alaska program is the promotion of the Eskimo language in broadened sociopolitical use, in print, on radio and television, in education and in politics. A major issue has been the struggle for Eskimo cultural rights in the form of bilingual education, provided for by the Federal Bilingual Education Act. Proposals for including the Eskimo language in Eskimo public schools were initiated in 1968 by Donald Webster, Irene Reed, and Michael Krauss. This movement was given added strength by the results of the U.S. Senate Subcommittee hearings on Native Education, headed by Sen. Edward Kennedy, which held a session in Fairbanks in April of 1969. Agreement with Alaska and the Bureau of Indian Affairs was reached late in 1969. The Eskimo language was regularly used for the first time in

Alaskan public schools in the fall of 1970, both as a medium of some instruction and as an object of study in its own right, as a written language, in pilot programs at first grade level in these villages' schools and in experimental kindergarten at Bethel. For these purposes, programs were begun at the University of Alaska both for training native Eskimo teachers and for producing the pedagogical materials. At the Eskimo Language Workshop of the University of Alaska (for the Bilingual Education Program of the Alaska Rural Schools Project, the Bureau of Indian Affairs, and the Division of State Operated Schools), by September of 1972 already over fifty titles for early-grade schoolchildren had been produced, under the direction of Miss Reed. Miss Reed, Paschal Afcan and Kathy Morack have edited all the materials. Mr. Afcan is also the author of eleven of these titles (8, 9, 13, 15, 16, 18, 21, 23, 705, 28, 29), coauthor of ten others (31, 32, 707, 708, 709, 710, 711, 712, 246, 723), and translator or adaptor of seventeen more (6, 7, 10, 11, 12, 14, 17, 19, 20, 22, 24, 25, 27, 30, 704, 706, 249). Martha Teeluk is author of ten (574, 575, 578, 579, 581, 582, 584, 735, 736, 712), coauthor of seven (32, 585, 737, 738, 715, 716, 723), and also a translator-adaptor (577, 580, 583). Marie Nick Blanchett has translated or adapted six (426, 427–428, 429, 430, 713, 718), written two (425, 714), and coauthored six (585, 715, 716, 737, 738, 723). Moses Nick has written five (730, 731, 733, 734). Several other Eskimos have also written or composed in Eskimo: John Angaiak (32, 45), Anna Alexie and Elizabeth Worm (41), Joe Alexie (42), Joseph Coolidge (120, 718), Noah Jack (229), Anna Rose Afcan Joe (246), Mary Ann Lomack (8, 723), Elsie Mather (310), and Mary Toyukak (604). Many are traditional Eskimo literature, others new creative Eskimo literature, others translations or adaptations of European tales (e.g. Cinderella, Thumbelina, Peter Rabbit, Curious George, The Gingerbread Man in two different translations, Peter and the Wolf), many are instructional non-fiction (anatomy, anthropology, Eskimo life), some to be read by children, some to be read to children, all profusely and appropriately illustrated by Andrew Chikoyak, Geri Rudolph Keim, Diane S. Dart, Paschal Afcan, John Angaiak, Edward Hofseth, Dorothy Napoleon, Ida Jacomet, Cathy Hankinson, John Breiby, and Kathy Morack. Some of the production staff have also written original texts in English, which were then translated into Eskimo: Geri R. Keim (713, 20, 25), Diane S. Dart (11, 704), John Breiby (706), Kathy Morack (12). A five-volume elementary science series appeared in the summer of 1972 (Living Things 707, The Earth 710, The Universe 709, Matter and Energy 708, The Senses of the Human Body 711). This series, written in Yupik by Paschal Afcan, Irene Reed, and the staff, and finely illustrated by Geri R. Keim, is inspiring proof of the adaptability of the Eskimo language and of the potential of the Eskimo people to undertake successfully the challenge of adapting to modern Alaskan life literally on their own terms. The work of this remarkable group of Alaskans will certainly be of great importance in the survival and future development of the Yupik language.

The 1970-1971 bilingual education program in four schools was highly successful. During 1971-1972 it was expanded into ten more Yupik schools (both BIA and State-operated). The success of the program was also influential in the passage of the momentous Alaska Native Language Center and Bilingual Education bills in Juneau, June 9, 1972. These bills will in turn insure the further rapid spread of bilingual education throughout Central Yupik Alaska, at least where the schools are State-operated. It can be expected that by 1974 Central Yupik will be used in at least the majority of schools where the pupils speak that language.

In deciding the fate of the Eskimo language (and of course in a certain sense that of the Eskimo people with it), it is certain that the mass media of radio and eventually television will also be of very great importance. The first radio station in the Central Yupik area, KYUK, began broadcasting at Bethel in 1971. From the very beginning, the programming of this station has included three hours daily in Eskimo (news, information, specialties, announcements, and disc-jockeying). There seems little doubt that the prominent role given to Eskimo in local broadcasting will be another decisive factor for the survival of the language.

2.23 *Pacific Yupik*

This third Yupik language of Alaska has been variously called Pacific Yupik, Gulf Yupik, Suk, Supik, Sugcestun, and by the Russians (Kad'yakskiĭ) Aleut. Most popularly in Alaska it is called simply 'Aleut', and is not distinguished at all from the ('real') Aleut by the local white population or by the census. The census may return about 7,500 'Aleuts', who are thus considered a very important subdivision of the Alaska native population ('Eskimo, Indians, and Aleuts'). These Aleuts are united at least in the degree to which they have undergone Russian influence: in their Russian names, the use of Slavonic liturgy and Slavonic alphabet for their languages. Of these 7,500 'Aleuts', 1,500 are ('real') Aleuts, and perhaps 1,000 are Central Yupik of the Bristol Bay area. The great majority of Aleuts, over 5,000, are Pacific Yupik, who in their own language call that language Sugcestun [súxt$^s$stun].

This form of Yupik is, as mentioned above, very marginally or very partially intelligible to Central Alaskan Yupik, though it is apparently not as far distant from Central Alaskan Yupik as Siberian Yupik is from either Pacific or Central Alaskan Yupik. Pacific Yupik internally is reasonably uniform. There is easy intelligibility all along from the Chugach Eskimo of Prince William Sound to the Kenai and Alaska Peninsulas and to Kodiak and Afognak Islands.

Pacific Yupik once extended east of Prince William Sound to Controller Bay and Kayak Island. There are Eskimo place-names even as far east as Yakutat. Eskimo occupation of this area receded to the westward expansion of the Tlingit and even the Eyak. This eastern-most Eskimo group was known as Ugaliakhmiut or Ugalents (uŋalaɣmiut) and often confused with the Eyak. Miyaoka has recently pointed out (741) that, judging from the Voevodskiĭ wordlist (BAE ms. 334, 60 words, 1860) of the language of the 'Indians near Cape St. Elias' and contrary to all expectations, this dialect was not an extension of Chugach or Prince William Sound Yupik, but resembled a far more westerly Yupik, perhaps even Central rather than Pacific.

The first considerable postwar publication of any kind on Pacific Yupik was the appearance in 1953 of Kaj Birket-Smith's study of the Prince William Sound Eskimo (91), based on research carried out in 1933. This book contains a sketchy appendix on the language. But Chugach Eskimo remained very inadequately documented. This situation was alleviated somewhat by fieldwork in 1961 by Irene Reed of the University of Alaska. Miss Reed's materials remain unpublished, but are a very important source for this dying Yupik dialect.

In 1953 L.L. Hammerich, as part of his general survey of Alaskan Yupik, did fieldwork on Kodiak dialects and at Perryville on the Alaska Peninsula (183, 184). In 1962 his work was augmented by Miss Reed's linguistic survey of all the Kodiak settlements. Reed's and Hammerich's unpublished materials constitute considerable coverage of Kodiak dialectology. Aside from Hammerich's material from Perryville and Pilot Point, however, the Alaska Peninsula dialects are virtually undocumented, and thus constitute a still partly unknown border area between Central and Pacific Yupik.

During the mid-nineteenth century there was a promising beginning of Church literature in Kad'yakskii Aleut (an excellent Matthew 743, and a primer 744). With the Americanization of the area, this development was arrested and the use of the language was effectively discouraged. Also in this way then, this Pacific Yupik 'Aleut' is like ('real') Aleut and unlike the two other Yupik languages in Alaska. In the entire Pacific Yupik area, from Prince William Sound to the Alaska Peninsula, including Kodiak and the Afognak Islands, few or no one under twenty, in some locations no one under thirty, can speak the language well or at all. The only exceptions are Port Graham and English Bay at the southern tip of the Kenai Peninsula. At Port Graham, population 300, many under twenty can speak Yupik well, but none under ten. However, at English Bay, population 100, even the youngest children are still learning the language. English Bay village is thus the only place, like Atka for Aleut, where this language is still fully alive.

In 1971 Derenty Tabios, a student at Alaska Methodist University from Port Graham and a speaker of Pacific Yupik, began to transcribe and study the language under the direction of Richard Dauenhauer and Jeffrey Leer. In 1972, under the auspices of the University of Alaska Native Language Center, Leer, Tabios, Reed and Krauss collaborated to develop a new orthography for what they now call Sugcestun Aleut (739, 740). In September 1972 they printed the first book in over 100 years in the language (742), and this with the new orthography was presented by Leer and Tabios at a teacher-training workshop in English Bay and Port Graham. The chances for the survival of Sugcestun Aleut as a spoken language now appear somewhat less slim.

Among the phonological characteristics of the language are the placement of secondary accent (and vowel-lengthening in open syllables) on every *third* syllable (after primary accents, which fall on all long vowels, and on initial closed syllable or, failing that, the second syllable of the word), whereas both other Yupik languages have that accent on every *second* syllable. Another peculiarity of many Sugcestun dialects is the shortening of long vowels in closed syllables, so that they are then to be distinguished from short only by high-pitched stress. Another characteristic of Sugcestun is the late deletion of certain intervocalic voiced continuants, where the resulting vowel cluster fails to condition the expected gemination of the preceding consonant, as in [piŋáun] 'three', orthographically *pinga'un* (cf. Central Yupik *pingayun*).

2.24 *Alaskan Inuit*

The Inuit-speaking Eskimo population of Alaska (from Unalakleet north) is less dense and smaller than the Yupik. The area from Unalakleet in Norton Sound, Seward Peninsula, Northwest Alaska and the North Slope to Barter Island and the Canadian Border contains an Eskimo population of about 10,000, not counting perhaps another 1,000 natives of the area now dispersed, especially to Fairbanks. Of these ten or eleven thousand, however, there are perhaps five thousand who do not speak the language well or at all. In many of the settlements the younger generation is no longer learning the language, and is speaking English exclusively. This includes most of the youth of especially Kotzebue and Nome, two important population centers which alone constitute a third of the population. In many of the smaller settlements, especially Unalakleet and the Seward Peninsula villages, some of the Kobuk and Noatak villages, and Point Hope, the switch to English is far progressed, but in some places, especially the upper Kobuk and Wainwright, Eskimo is still the dominant speech of even the youngest generation.

The future of Alaskan Inuit as a spoken language seems precarious indeed. There are still very strong pressures working against its survival. In the large communities of Nome, Kotzebue, and Barrow, the white minority has entrenched political, social, economic, and cultural power far beyond its proportion, and until very recently, English has been the sole language of the schools. Finally in 1971 there began to be some changes. David Fauske began an Eskimo literacy project at the Barrow High School, and this is rapidly growing. Alaskan Inuit people are rapidly gaining in political power. The Alaska State Legislature now has two Eskimo Representatives and one Senator from this area. These men were influential in the passage of the 1972 Alaska Native Language bills, which will require and support more use of Eskimo in the schools of the area. But it is clear that the position of Inupiat is severely weakened. It remains to be seen whether the resurgence of Inuit pride and cultural self-respect has come soon enough to permit the people to retain their language.

The language and people are popularly called Eskimo or Iñupiat ('real people, Eskimos', <*iñuk* + *-piaq*, singular corresponding to Yup'ik), or here Inuit ('people') to continue the international academic tradition. Swadesh's term Inupik is an artificial bastardization, with the Inuit stem and the Yupik suffix.

Alaskan Inuit is of course the western end of the Inuit dialect complex or continuum. All Alaskan Inuit dialects are mutually intelligible to at least a very great extent, though a jump from Unalakleet to Barter Island, the two extremes, may entail some initial difficulty. With a little sophistication and good will, all Alaskan Iñupiat can certainly be considered to form a single linguistic community.

The subdialects seem to fall into three general areas: (1) Norton Sound and Seward Peninsula, (2) Kobuk and Noatak, Northwest, and (3) Wainwright, Barrow, Anaktuvuk Pass, Barter Island. A characteristic innovation of (1) is loss of some palatalization (e.g. *in > iñ > in = in < *ən), a characteristic innovation of (2) is flattening of diphthongs (see below), and a characteristic innovation of (3) is increasing consonant assimilation, as in Canadian Inuit. (3) is in fact nearly identical with Mackenzie Delta Inuit, so that the Alaska-Canada border is quite artificial linguistically.

As in the case of Yupik, after a period of exploration and wordlists, the first books in Inuit in Alaska were also by missionaries, but later, after the Russian period, and consisted mainly of liturgies and hymnals in impressionistic spelling. Perhaps the best of these was the work of the Jesuit Lafortune of Nome (746, perhaps also 137). The major linguistic works for the area were the vocabularies from several locations published by Jenness (235) and Rasmussen (470). Jenness (234, 236) had also written important grammatical notes on the language.

After the war, Roy Ahmaogak, native of Wainwright and a Presbyterian missionary, who had also had some linguistic training with the Summer Institute of Linguistics at Norman, Oklahoma, published parts of the New Testament (36, 37) and a primer-reader, *Iñupiat taiguanic* (35), which progresses to fully advanced levels. Note also the Wartes-Ahmaogak-Simmons-James-Chambers hymnals of 1959–66 (631, 111, 233; note also an earlier prephonemic hymnal, 143, of unidentified origin). Ahmaogak's orthography (developed with the collaboration of Eugene Nida and F. G. Klerekoper) is a truly remarkable achievement, entirely adequate to express efficiently the surface phonemics of the language. His transcriptions are very accurate, and his translations very good. The only defect of the orthography is strictly the practical disadvantage of retaining the linguist's symbols, e.g. ḳ and ġ for what in virtually all other Eskimo orthographies are q and r. A major trait of Alaskan Inuit phonology is the development of a surface contrast between palatalized and plain apicals after the vowels i and ə respectively, with subsequent merger of the vowels to i, thus e.g. in/ən > iñ/ən > iñ/in. Ahmaogak's orthography distinguishes at the phonetic level, between the plain and palatalized apicals, t and c, n and ñ, l and ḷ, ł and ł̣.

Ahmaogak was later joined by Donald H. Webster of the Summer Institute of Linguistics. Webster made a few changes in the orthography (ch for Ahmaogak's c, sr for ṣ, and r for Ahmaogak's z for retroflex [ẓ] or [r], which made impossible any later change of r for q̇). It is unfortunate that there was no coordination between this development and the efforts being made at exactly the same time in Ottawa to establish a standardized orthography for Canadian Eskimo. Both sides might have profited greatly thereby. After some preliminary materials by Webster (634, 636), in 1963 Ahmaogak, Kayutak, and Webster published a series of primer-readers in the finalized orthography (38, cf. the publication dates of R.C. Gagné's *Tentative standard orthography*, for Canada 1961, 1962).

In the early sixties, Eskimo collaborators in the SIL program, Ḳaġaḳpak, Tagarook, and Nashoalook, published some religious material (247, 571). In 1964 Ahmaogak and Webster published parts of the New Testament (39) and then in 1966 the complete New Testament (641, note also 640, 637). Webster clearly recognized, however, the need for establishment of the Eskimo language in broader use than for religious study alone. In 1966 and 1968 he published literacy aids (639, 642), and revised the primer-readers in 1969 (645). Webster also has published three papers on Alaskan Inuit linguistics (633, 635, 638). The last, especially, in spite of its title, is a brief descriptive sketch of the language including an appendix of tables of inflectional ending. The frequency of error in these tables is so extreme, however, as to render them nearly (or worse than) useless.

In the early sixties SIL in Northern Alaska was joined by Wilfried Zibell, working in the Kobuk River dialect. Coordination between Webster and Zibell's work has been maximal, it being agreed that Kobuk and Barrow (Webster's base) were similar enough to be handled by the same basic orthography. A peculiarity of Kobuk and other Northwestern subdialects, is that the sequences /ia/ and /ai/ are indistinguishable at the phonetic surface, both realized [e·], and likewise /ua/ and /au/ are both [o·]. This situation, with strict adherence to the biuniqueness principle, would require a system of three short vowels (i a u), five long (i· e· a· o· u·), and the diphthong iu only (iu > i·). Zibell decided to spell [e·], [o·] and sometimes [i·] (<iu) according to underlying form. This is easily determinable in most cases on internal grounds (morphophonemics, underlying representation), and in virtually all cases by simple dialect comparison. Zibell published some primary materials (655, 658, 752), religious materials (656, 172, with Arthur and Minnie Gray; 657, with Lilli Savok and Pauline Harvey; 661, 662, 663, New Testament portions, with Pauline Harvey; note also the earlier independent 194, in primitive orthography). In 1969 Zibell began publishing a series of three booklets of traditional stories from the Kobuk River (660), in Eskimo with English translations, of great interest to all Alaskan Inuit speakers.

In 1970 Webster left the field of Alaska, and in April 1972 Zibell died in a plane crash. In 1971, however, Zibell had begun experimenting with a revised orthography, which would eliminate all non-standard Roman symbols. He published an experimental second edition of *Unipchaat 1* (659) with partly revised orthography, whereby ḳ > q, ŋ > ng, ł > hl, ŋŋ > ngg, łł > hll, and then a new version of the alphabet book (658, 752), extending the revision with the further change ġ > gh, ġġ > ggh. (This last would presumably not be distinguished from the fairly rare cluster [γγ]. The projected final changes, l(l) > l(l)y, ł(ł) > hl(l)y, ñ(ñ) > n(n)y, were not yet introduced.) In order to avoid the danger of competing standards, in November 1972 Iñupiaq representatives met in Fairbanks and voted on a unified orthography which, in deference to widespread Literacy especially at Barrow, rejects the reform except that ḳ is now changed to q.

In 1971 James Nageak of Barrow and Michael Krauss began co-teaching a course in Iñupiaq at the University of Alaska. During the first year a set of corrected tables for the inflectional endings was produced, and a continuing program of research in the language has begun with that class. Involved are several Iñupiaq-speaking students, who along with Nageak are also transcribing traditional and taped materials in quantity. A related development is taking place in the Barrow literacy program under Fauske, mentioned above, and the instructors Martha Aiken and Alice Hopson, who with their students have produced two issues of the first Alaskan Inuit periodical *Tusaayugaat Miŋuaktuktuaniñ* (749). One of their 9th grade students, Janice Voss, has published *Aakagivigiñ?*, a translation of the Yupik and English *Aanakamken-qaa?/ Are You My Mother?* (750).

Webster and Zibell jointly published in 1970 an Inuit dictionary of considerable substance (644, 218 pp.; reviewed by Correll, 745), arranged by semantic category; this work is certainly a most important contribution to Alaskan Inuit lexicography and Eskimo linguistics in general. Earlier and also very substantial, although unpublished, are typescript dictionaries at the University of Alaska from the early 1950s, one by Albert Heinrich from Diomede and Wales (198), and one of uncertain authorship (137, Seward Peninsula, perhaps Lafortune, over 2,000 entries, English-Inuit). Heinrich (197) has also written important grammatical notes on Diomede and Wales Inuit.

Miscellaneous specialized contributions to Eskimo studies in Inuit Alaska are Irving's study of bird-names (225), Heinrich's extensive research on kinship terms throughout the area (199, 200) and D. J. Ray's study of Bering Strait place-names (751). Warren Tiffany's bilingual reader based on string-figure stories (601) is in an orthography unrelated to Ahmaogak-Webster's, but also too early (1959) to find wide use where it was intended. A primitive little 'conversation guide' was also published in 1965 by Strom in Nome (748).

During the fifties the Norwegian explorer Helge Ingestad visited the then still extremely isolated settlement of Nunamiut at Anaktuvuk Pass, and recorded a large amount of Nunamiut dialect on tape. The dialect is very similar to that spoken at Barrow. This material he turned over to Knut Bergsland, who has since spent much time transcribing and studying it. Bergsland's two mimeographed studies on the material (71, 80) are of great interest, and it is hoped that he will soon complete his analysis and publication of his Nunamiut work.

N. Gubser, then an honors student at Yale, spent some time with the Nunamiut during the early sixties. His excellent ethnographic report (174) includes some of his linguistic material.

Finally, it should be mentioned that the dialect of Imaklik, the village on Big Diomede Island in Bering Strait on the Russian side, is the same as that of Little Diomede on the American, a Seward Peninsula Inuit dialect. Imaklik is the only Inuit in Siberia. It has been studied by Menovščikov (369, 388; see further discussion under Siberia).

## 2.3 Canada

Canadian Eskimo dialects are of course all Inuit. They constitute a large continuous complex, the westernmost (Mackenzie Delta) intelligible or even nearly identical with Alaska, the easternmost (Ungava and Labrador) intelligible, to a large extent at least, with West Greenlandic. The extent to which Mackenzie and Labrador are mutually intelligible is much more doubtful, however. There is probably more linguistic distance, as there is geographical, between the extremes of Canada than between each of these extremes and its neighbor across the border or strait. The total Eskimo population of Canada has by now passed 17,000. Almost all of this is still Eskimo-speaking, but there are reports that in certain large settlements and centers of assimilation (e.g. Frobisher Bay, Inuvik) the younger generation is now abandoning the Eskimo language.

Canadian Eskimo will be discussed at times in terms of three large somewhat artificial districts: Eastern (Quebec, Labrador, Baffin Island), Central (Keewatin and north thereof), Western (Mackenzie District). From a point of view of writing systems in use, Canadian Eskimo is artificially divided in an increasingly unfortunate way. The Eastern and Central areas belong together in sharing the use of the syllabary adapted for Eskimo by E.J. Peck in the late 19th century from the system first invented by Evans for Cree (see Lewis 281, esp. 77–86; see also Peck's grammar, which went through several editions, the last of which, Flint's revision, 149, still does not make it a good grammar). This system consists of simple figures, the shapes of which symbolize the syllable-initial consonants, and the four orientations of which symbolize the following vowels (the language has only three vowels however; the fourth orientation is for the diphthong ai). It fails to distinguish consonantal and vocalic length, q from k, and ŋ (West of Hudson Bay also r) from g; perhaps even worse, it provides for syllable-closing consonants in the form only of miniature superscripts, and these in practice are seldom used. In adequacy the result is rather reminiscent of the Minoan Linear B syllabary. Nevertheless, Peck's syllabary had spread remarkably into very general use, such that the majority of Canadian Eskimos everywhere but in Mackenzie and Labrador were in fact literate in it by the beginning of the period in question, and this without any support from the schools. In spite of its grave shortcomings, Peck's syllabary unquestionably became firmly entrenched in general use and is a source of deep pride to its users, who regard it as graphic demonstration of the existence and uniqueness and worth of their own language. The system will not easily be replaced.

Oblate missionaries are responsible for an enormous amount of the work on Canadian Eskimo linguistics since before the war, published and unpublished (see Duthilly 128, and Carrière 759, 760, 761, 762). Since 1941 the Oblate missionary headquarters in Ottawa has been printing a periodical in syllabics (224), perhaps the first of its kind. Note another periodical from the Cambridge Bay mission since 1960 (432), and Fr. Schneider's from Ft. Chimo since 1962 (509), in syllabics, covering an amazingly broad and erudite range of topics. During the fifties the Oblates began to produce a large amount of linguistic literature, written in an alphabetic notation of varying quality, never entirely adequate, of very limited circulation, in manuscript, typescript or mimeo, but of very great lexicographic and dialectological value. Very notable contributions are by the Reverend Fathers Louis Lemer (280, 1951, Bathurst Inlet), Eugène Fafard (147, 1953, Chesterfield Inlet), and especially Maurice Métayer (395, 1953, Aklavik). All these materials are unpublished (to be found at the Oblate Archives in Ottawa), and were seen by Father Arthur Thibert, who consulted them but by no means exhausted them in compiling his English-Eskimo and Eskimo-English dictionary which he published first in 1954 (594, 598, also in French edition, 595; see also reviews by Swadesh, 562, and Menovščikov, 347), a very inadequate work in many respects, in spite of the pretentious claim (p. vii) that 'this dictionary covers practically all the words generally used by the Canadian Eskimo.' Listed by Carrière for Fr. Métayer are also unpublished studies on infixes (798), Pelly Bay dialectology (796), and a large collection of traditional texts (797). Fr. Métayer is reportedly still actively pursuing his work. Note also an earlier grammar by Fr. Kermal (787), and an anonymous collection of traditional texts (795, 280 pp.). The recently published *Atii, parlez esquimo* by Fr. Trinel (825), in spite of its title, is a typical Oblate reference grammar, concentrating heavily on inflections. It could hardly serve as a practical course in the language.

A very great contribution has been made by the Oblate priest Lucien Schneider in the Eastern district (Ungava). Father Scheider's great Eskimo-to-French *Dictionnaire alphabético-syllabique* (510, 1966, 1970, but with a preliminary edition in 1953; see also reviews by Mey, 396, and especially Rousselière, 477) and detailed study of postbases (512) contribute by far the richest source of organized lexical information yet available for any Eskimo other than Greenlandic or Asiatic. The orthography is good, phonologically adequate, a vast improvement over Thibert's, though it also overdifferentiates in minor ways (e.g. with *e* and *o*), mainly for the benefit of the European learner. Schneider has also published a grammar (511), based not on Peck but in the tradition of Kleinschmidt-Bourquin-Turquetil (see 102, and also 214, 605, 499). Schneider mimeographed in 1969 a tripartite pedagogical grammar (513) of Ungava Eskimo; the first part is a series of 41 basic lessons, the second a review including the above mentioned grammar, and the third a series of supplements. Schneider and B. Saladin d'Anglure are at present planning to combine the parts of this preliminary pedagogical grammar and further supplementary information which Schneider published as *Mélanges* in 1970 (514) into a revised new work.

Schneider reports as forthcoming a French-Eskimo dictionary (515). This will fill a major gap, as presently the only generally available French- (or English-) Eskimo dictionary is the second sections of Thibert (594, 595, 598), which themselves had not replaced the much older and still valuable Petitot (454). In this connection however, note another French-Eskimo dictionary reported as forthcoming (288), and a short practical French-Eskimo lexicon by Serge Pageau (805). A comparative Labrador-Ungava and West Greenlandic dictionary based on Schneider (510) and Schultz-

Lorentzen (519, 520), about 8,000 terms with English, French, and Danish translations, was written in 1967–68 by Dermot R. F. Collis, but remains unpublished (763).

Besides the Oblate fathers, also in the early fifties, certain agencies of the Canadian government in Ottawa began increasing activity on behalf of the Eskimo language and linguistics. In 1947 the Department of Mines and Resources published the *Book of Wisdom for Eskimo* in syllabics and English (773), adding a Roman version in 1949. Then, renamed the Department of Northern Affairs and Natural Resources, and finally in 1965 again renamed the Department of Indian Affairs and Northern Development (DIAND), it has published in Eskimo a sizable list of pamphlets and booklets on foods and health (293, 828, 786, 785, 820, 782, 800, 816, 771), on economics, government, and cooperatives (790, 817, 768), and on Eskimo art (218, 774, 823, 818, this last a very beautifully produced autobiography of the artist with prints of her work). Another recent and handsome production is the National Museum's collection of Pavungnituk stories by Zebedee Nungak and Eugene Arima (433), this time in standard Roman orthography.

In the middle fifties Gilles R. Lefebvre began his investigations of the dialect of the East coast of Hudson Bay, with a view towards establishing a standardized Roman alphabetic writing system (275). Lefebvre produced a number of reports and published articles (274, 276, 277, 278, 279) dealing, most importantly, with the "Draft Orthography for the Canadian Eskimo" for the Ottawa Department, a proposed orthography based on the dialect of the East Coast of Hudson Bay. Lefebvre's work benefits from the perspective of the structural linguistics ('phonemic principle') of the time, and certainly represents an important advance as a scientifically based orthography for a Canadian dialect. Lefebvre has been little active in the field since 1958.

Lefebvre's task has been taken up by Raymond C. Gagné, whose goal has been to establish and promote a standardized Roman orthography (eventually even a standard literary language) for all of Canadian Eskimo. Gagné in 1958 as a student with Lefebvre wrote his master's thesis on the (structural) phonemics of the dialect of Port Harrison on the East Coast of Hudson Bay (158), which includes also (Chapter X) the first version of his important article "In defense of a standard phonemic spelling..." (published the next year, 159, reprinted also as Appendix II in 161, 162). Gagné, who in 1957 had edited a small literary production in syllabics (157), here examines the syllabary system and observes that it is not based on such unscientific principles that its major defects as a phonemic writing system could not easily be remedied. (This has in fact been done by Fr. Schneider; see the end of the section on Canada.) Gagné makes certain gravely questionable judgements concerning the syllabary, however. One is in not believing 'that the Eskimos are sentimentally attached to their syllabics'. Gagné's orthography must indeed compete in Quebec, Baffin, and Keewatin (the vast majority of the Canadian Eskimo population) with the syllabary and 'overcome the tribal pride expressed by one Eskimo leader who stated that only the syllabary looked like Eskimo' (Webster-Zibell Report, 645, p. 7). Furthermore, Gagné is deeply interested in using Martinet's concept of 'functional yield' in developing an efficient writing system. The Port Harrison dialect he studied, being Eastern Canadian and more like Greenlandic than Western Canadian or Alaskan in this respect, assimilates clusters (progressively), so that syllable-closing consonants are manifested mainly as gemination of the consonant beginning the next syllable, and relatively little distinguished one from the other in the phonetic output. This is doubtless one of the reasons Gagné is not more dissatisfied with the syllabic system and also why writers of syllabics tend to omit syllable-closing superscripts. This applies even to word-final consonants, which Gagné also at one time considered dropping in his orthography. Though Gagné may have believed the functional yield of the distinctions between syllable-closing consonants, as he heard them in Port Harrison dialect, so low as to warrant suppression in orthography for Eastern Canadian, he was certainly wise to qualify the orthography he proposes as highly tentative and perhaps in need of change for dialects very far west of Hudson Bay. Doubtless, at least for the purpose of being as generally acceptable as possible, the orthography should have been revised to spell syllable-closing consonants more 'etymologically'. This policy would also have been more appropriate to Gagné's own to bring Canadian into closer contact with Greenlandic, the spelling of which is now notoriously 'etymological' in this respect.

Gagné's *Tentative standard orthography* has not been followed up by any modified versions taking into better consideration the Western and Central Dialects. Instead it has apparently come to be understood as a '[Definitive!] standard orthography' (see e.g. Spalding 549, p. iii: 'the orthography or spelling system used in this grammar is known as the *standard orthography* (SO) and is based on the system outlined in Mr. R.C. Gagné's booklet *Tentative standard orthography for Canadian Eskimos*. It is, without doubt, the best — because scientifically accurate — writing system now devised for the Eskimo language *bar none*'). Moreover, it has been followed up by very little literacy material, all in Eastern dialect: one primer (167), a few primers for children (1962–63, syllabic text by Rachel Erkloo, reprinted in 1965 including Roman version by Leah Idlout, 112, 220, 232, 664) and one very important book (462), with the Roman orthography in each case only as an adjunct to the text already in syllabics and English. Apparently only one story by Leah Illauq (Idlout, 233, Ungava) has been published exclusively in the orthography by the Ottawa Department. Ironically, in Eastern and Central Arctic Canada, where the orthography is linguistically more appropriate, it must compete with the syllabary in which there is already widespread literacy and strong pride. In the Western Canadian Arctic, where there is a real need for an improved writing system, the proposed orthographical standard is so inappropriate to the phonology as to be highly unacceptable to the people.

Among the items published in Standard Roman Orthography, syllabics, and English, the *Q-Book* (409), 1964, 302 pp., quarto, certainly deserves special mention as a major effort and probably the most important secular book in Canadian Eskimo. It is a very handsomely designed and illustrated guide for the Eskimo to government, education, health, welfare, safety, care of machines, etc., and is relatively free of the patronizing tone epitomized by its precursors, e.g. the Labrador *Eskimo Book of Knowledge* (814), and the *Book of Wisdom for Eskimo* (773). The names of some of those who worked on this book, Elijah Erkloo, Leah Idlout, Mary Panegoosho, Raymond Gagné, also appear in many other Canadian Eskimo publications.

It is a further misfortune that there was no coordination of effort between Lefebvre-Gagné and Ahmaogak-Webster in Alaska in the late fifties. The results of the general lack of coordination in developing writing systems for Alaska and Canada are surveyed in the Webster-Ahmaogak report (645), which contains a telling critique. One may hope, but without great confidence, that it is not too late for a renewed and broad cooperative effort at finding a better solution to the challenging but important problem of developing a unified writing system for Canadian and Alaskan Inuit.

More recently, Gagné has published an article (166) and, in limited mimeograph edition, an extensive practical pedagogical grammar of Eastern Canadian Eskimo, with copious exercises, and tapes (165). It is probably the most effective, practical learning grammar yet available for any Canadian Eskimo. Also useful, though much briefer, is Karl Kristiansen's 1964 grammar (267). S.T. Mallon, who has been engaged at Rankin Inlet in teaching Eskimo as a second language to English speakers, gave an interesting paper on that subject at the Chicago Meeting (292), and has produced local teaching materials (793, 794). Keith Crowe of the DIAND has played a very important role in the development and editing of many of its Eskimo language materials, and has himself contributed to the literature (767, 766). As anyone who has been faced with the problem will attest, it is a difficult matter to choose between presenting to the average learner the heavy but well organized Eskimo inflectional systems in large natural units as such and presenting them in small practical pedagogically sound doses.

A.E. Spalding, formerly also of the Ottawa Department, is a strong supporter of the Gagné orthography (546, 548, note also the evaluation from 549, quoted above). Spalding's recent second practical grammar (549) is almost entirely a different book from his first (547), and profits greatly from the adoption of Gagné's orthography.

The Ottawa Department has not endorsed the proposed standard orthography which it itself sponsors to the extent even of publishing reading material exclusively in it. On the contrary, it has, in fact, recently published e.g. the autobiography of John Ayaruaq exclusively in syllabics (58) and sponsored several periodicals and pamphlets exclusively in syllabics and English (e.g. 607, 632, 764, 765, 773).

The Government of New Quebec, on the other hand, though it has not sponsored the new orthography, is probably a stronger supporter of it than is the Ottawa Department. In 1966–69 it published for use in the schools two sets of primers and workbooks by Christiane Pageau and Paulusi Uqittuq, a set of two in syllabics (439, 804) and a more elaborate set of three in Roman (803, 802).

A very interesting and significant development has taken place in Northern Quebec with the growth of Eskimo authorship of native creative literature in syllabics, in a movement fostered by Bernard Saladin d'Anglure. He reports on the work of a large number of productive writers along the Ungava coast (558). Chief among these is Mitiarjuk of Wakeham, a woman born in 1931, mother of six. During the period 1954–58 and 1962–65 she composed in syllabics the long 'récit' *Sanaaq*, which Saladin d'Anglure transliterated into Gagné's orthography with interlinear translation, free translation, illustrations and notes, with the help of the Eskimos Marc-Uqittuq, Marie Nasaaluk, and Mitiarjuk herself, and Oblate priests Schneider, Dion, Trinel, Méeus, and Lecht, the last two of whom had also originally encouraged the author as she wrote (501). Mitiarjuk (and now also many others) has continued to write productively in the creation of a literature of great aesthetic and anthropological interest; so far only *Sanaaq* has been published. An English version of *Sanaaq* by Dermot Ronán F. Collis is reported forthcoming.

A similar development had begun to take place on Southampton Island a generation before. Thibert published in 1955 and 1960–61 (596, 598), in translation only, the syllabic journals from the late 1920s of two Eskimo hunters, Makik and Opartok. The original syllabic journal (801) of Opartok is reported in the Oblate Archives by Carrière. Carrière also reports another syllabic journal (784) by Bernard Irkrowaktok of Pelly Bay with Oblate romanization and translations at the Oblate archives, as well as a translation of the syllabic autobiography of John Ayaruaq (756), published by the DIAND in 1968 (58).

The Labrador dialect, though very close to and intelligible with that of Baffin Land and Ungava, has had imposed on it a separate writing tradition, due to its separate political and ecclesiastical history. Labrador was early missionized by the Herrnhut Moravians, already in the 18th century. Kleinschmidt's grammar (258) takes Labrador into consideration (mentions also a ms. Labrador grammar by Königseep ca. 1780). Erdmann's dictionary (138, translated into English by Peck, 442) and Bourquin's grammar (102) are in the Kleinschmidt tradition. Bourquin's influential grammar was translated into French in 1934 by the Oblate Balmès (757), and into English in 1966 by the Moravian Perrett (815). The Labrador hymnal was reissued in 1950 (255). The complete Bible had been translated into Labrador Eskimo by 1871, and parts were being reissued during the 1930s (latest edition of the New Testament 1952, 586). The orthography is expectably similar to the Greenlandic. Holtved's edition of Kleinschmidt's letters to Bourquin (214) reveals the relationship between the Moravian linguistic work in Labrador with that in Greenland. A most important Labrador publication of the 1930s was the bilingual *Eskimo Book of Knowledge* (814), Eskimo translation by the Moravian Walter W. Perrett, together with the original English, containing practical advice on e.g. hygeine and economics, eloquent but also a horrifyingly patronizing sermon on the benevolence and infallibility of King George and the Company (Hudson's Bay, the publisher): '[Strangers] cannot at heart possess the deep understanding of your lives through which our Traders have learned to bestow the care of a father upon you and your children. Remember then, in your dealings with strangers these three things: The things which the Company trades are good things. In times of sickness and scarcity the Company stands by you and helps you. There is no firmer or more faithful friend to the Innuit than the Company.' Until the appearance thirty-three years later of the *Q-Book* (462), the *Eskimo Book of Knowledge* was probably by far the most handsomely produced book in North American Eskimo, and the most important secular book printed for the people.

During the 1940s only a few locally produced minor ephemera appear to have been produced on or in Labrador Eskimo (191, 196, 440, 811). In 1950 the Hymnal was reissued (255), and in 1952 a revised version of the complete New Testament appeared (586), the work of Rev. Perrett and also Rev. Frederick W. Peacock. Rev. Peacock has since become the major figure in publishing in Labrador Eskimo. He has recently published at least six liturgical or Church items (792, 806, 807, 808, 809, 810, 812). In 1953 he mimeographed a small dictionary (440). Since his retirement in 1971 from active church work, Rev. Peacock has joined John Hewson and Lawrence Smith at Memorial University, St. John's, Newfoundland, where he is now working on a full-scale new Labrador dictionary (441). He has also very recently published, in connection with the Eskimo course at Memorial University, an *Eskimo Reader* (808) perhaps the most useful of its kind, a graded set of texts for non-speakers to read, with full vocabulary for each text.

The Eskimo population of Labrador is about 1,200, virtually all still Eskimo-speaking. The Eskimo language enjoyed some status in the Labrador Moravian Mission schools until the 1950s, after Labrador became an integral part of Newfoundland, Newfoundland became a Canadian province, and control of education in Labrador came under the jurisdiction of St. John's. Hope is again rising that the language may regain its position in the Labrador Eskimo schools. The Moravian writing system and literary language itself is by now rather far removed from the colloquial, presenting artificialities and difficulties at many levels. As the language becomes reintroduced into the schools, it is to be hoped that revisions can be made to bring written Labrador Eskimo closer into line with the Roman system used for Quebec (Ungava) Eskimo, with which colloquial Labrador is highly intelligible. Under such favorable circumstances, the Eskimo language would have good chances of survival in Labrador.

Several studies of interest on specialized areas of Canadian Eskimo lexicography are noted: Graburn, Heinrich, and Dorais on loans and recently coined terms in Labrador and Ungava (171, 775, 769), Graburn and Heinrich on kinship terminology (170, 200), Rousselière on string figures (821), Irving on bird names (226), MacPherson on bird and mammal names (290, 291), and Holmer, Wheeler, and Van de Velde on place names (207, 647, 619). This last, though unpublished, is remarkable for its very exact and detailed information on and analysis of 662 place names in the Pelly Bay region. Wheeler (647) has performed a similar feat for the Labrador coast (555 place-names). Yet far surpassing both in the forthcoming work of Saladin d'Anglure (822), reported to cover 4,000 place names of Ungava and the Belcher Islands.

Also during this period a Greenlander, the late Svend Frederiksen, collected large amounts of textual and lexical material, especially on the language of shamans in Chesterfield Inlet in 1946 and Rankin Inlet in 1960. This material, probably of considerable value, remains unpublished, typed in a Greenlandic-like orthography.

Reported in progress are a grammar and dictionary of the Upper Eskimo dialect (Cambridge Bay and Bathurst Inlet) by Duncan Pryde. Thomas Correll, who has worked also in Alaska (121), and who has spent a decade with the Caribou Eskimo, has headed courses in Eskimo at the University of Manitoba. He is reported to be nearing completion of a Caribou Eskimo grammar (122), and has completed two papers on Eskimo grammar (764, 765).

The following information may be of interest on recent publication of religious and periodical literature in Canadian Eskimo. For the Western (Mackenzie) region an expanded *Service Book* (535) appeared in 1949, and a new version of the Anglican Book of Common Prayer appeared in 1963 (46), portions of the Bible and a songbook have been printed (47, 51), and the Anglican Archdeacon John Sperry is reported to be finishing a complete New Testament for 1972 (550). A syllabic Book of Common Prayer was republished in 1950 (101) and a hymnal expanded (830). Bible portions in Baffin dialect have also appeared (123, 153, 154) and the whole syllabic Baffin New Testament was reprinted in 1962 (424). The Oblate Fathers (Thibert, Buliard L'Helgouac'h, Métayer, Fafard, Ducharme, Antoine, Didier, and especially Schneider) have been active in publishing religious materials during this period (597, 282, 148, 126, 48, 125, 507, 508, 824, 758, 772, 770, 829), some of which is in syllabics.

The development of periodical literature in Canadian Eskimo has been phenomenal in recent years. Three periodicals have already been mentioned, as published by the Oblate Fathers (224, 432, 509), which began in 1941, 1960, and 1962, respectively. In 1953 the Ottawa Department of Northern Affairs and Natural Resources began the syllabic and Roman *Eskimo Bulletin* (141). In 1959 this became *Inuttituut/Inuktitun* (223) in two separate editions, one syllabic and one Roman. The syllabic edition still continues, and has seen spring up during the late sixties and early seventies a veritable host of new periodicals and newsletters (40, 606, 607, 632, 789, 781, 783, 826) and community newspapers (754, 755, 788, 780, 819, 827). These are mostly in syllabics, often bilingual with English (e.g. the important *Inuit Nipingit/Keewatin Echo*, 781). However, the recent and promising *Inummarit* (783) of Igloolik, published by the Inuit Cultural Association to further the cause of Inuit cultural and linguistic survival, appears in syllabics and Roman.

At this point the Roman and syllabic orthographies are in direct conflict. In spite of their obvious shortcomings, the syllabics are much too powerful a force to be dismissed. They have recently been seriously studied at the University of Ottawa by T.R. Hofmann, who has developed a systematic pedagogy for teaching them (776, 779, 777, 778). The syllabics could easily be greatly improved, as Fr. Schneider proposes, by modifying the symbols for q + vowel and ŋ + vowel, to distinguish them from k + vowel and g + vowel, respectively. Another great improvement would be the use of the fourth orientation (obsolescent and unneeded, for consonant + ai) for consonant followed by no vowel, instead of being omitted entirely, as such consonants generally are in practice, as the superscripts which are supposed to be used to represent them are very unpopular. Besides improvements in the quality of the two writing systems, many other factors will influence the outcome of the conflict between them. These factors will include not only sociopolitical developments in Canada, but also developments and writing systems in Alaska and Greenland, as communications between the Inuit of these three nations improve.

The following remarks summarize and compare written Canadian Eskimo literature with Alaskan, and Siberian.

Written Canadian Eskimo literature, starting in Labrador in the late 18th century, for a long time was almost entirely church-sponsored and Christian-evangelical in nature. After the War, during the fifties, secular literature began to appear, sponsored mostly by the federal government (and also, more recently, the provincial government of Quebec). The secular literature is still largely instructional or primary material, but there are the beginnings of creative writing as well. Though Canadian Eskimo written literature is beginning to develop its own vitality, especially in the form of periodicals, the Eskimo language itself is still generally excluded from the schools in Arctic Canada.

The first books in Alaskan Eskimo were liturgies published by the Russian Orthodox Church for Kodiak in the mid-19th century, but these never proliferated into a continuing literature. Modern Alaskan (Yupik and Inuit) literature began to develop in any quantity again only since the 1920s, and then again was entirely church-sponsored and Christian-evangelical in nature. There were a very few desultory attempts (263, 601) to use written Eskimo in Juneau-sponsored educational booklets in the late 1950s, but the first major Alaskan Eskimo writings that were not church-sponsored developed from the University of Alaska programs in 1969, in fact as part of a program introducing the use of Eskimo to the schools.

Another notable difference between Alaskan and Canadian written Eskimo literature is that whereas the first Alaskan Eskimo periodical (423) began only in 1969, in Canada there have been periodicals, serials, or newsletters in Eskimo at least since 1941, and there are now about twenty, government-, church- and locally-sponsored.

In Siberia there were probably never any Christian missionaries to the Eskimo, and never any church-sponsored books in the language. There have apparently never been any periodicals in Eskimo there either (though a *stengazeta* or poster-type newspaper is mentioned in 528, and Vdovin mentions a weekly Eskimo page in the Chukotka newspaper). Sponsored of course entirely by the government, a written Siberian Eskimo literature began in 1932, and became very well developed not only in instructional materials but also along creative and traditional lines. In the 1960s, however, this literature seems to have declined completely, and the Eskimo language there may not long survive.

In Greenland, the situation is radically different from Siberia, Alaska, and Canada, as will be seen in the following section.

## 2.4 Greenland

Greenland has one of the most rapid natural population growth rates in the world. The population of Greenland has in fact recently passed the 47,000 mark. Danes compose only a small minority, about 5,000, in this group. All Greenlandic Eskimos speak Eskimo, and the status of Eskimo as the dominant language of Greenland now seems unshakeable. This situation was fostered by a relatively enlightened and benign Danish policy from the beginning of the modern colonial regime. The Danish administration and educational system has in the last few years, however, greatly increased its pressure in the schools to improve general competence in Danish, to the point of replacing many Greenlandic Eskimo teachers with unseasoned monolingual Danish ones. Yet only a minority of Greenlanders are very competent in Danish, which clearly remains only a secondary and administrative language for the Eskimo population of Greenland. At the same time, however (and also a strong reason for the resistance to Danish), there is near universal literacy in Greenlandic and a reasonably copious literature in it, going back some two hundred and thirty years, in a well-developed literary standard language which has long served local needs admirably and continues to grow and adapt itself to modern needs.

The position of the Eskimo language in Greenland (vs. Danish, especially in education) is not without its problems. For a sampling of the recent literature discussing the Greenlandic language situation, see Berthelsen (83, 84), Gad (155, 156), Jensen (239), Kleivan (260), R. Petersen (446, 447), N. Rosing (474), and especially, for a general summary and additional bibliography, Kleivan (261).

Greenlandic literature has grown to a point where it is far beyond the scope of this report to attempt to describe or list. Such a list would include thousands of entries. The bibliography and subsection of this report on Greenland, then, will omit all literature that is not linguistic in some sense other than being simply in Greenlandic, whereas all such literature in other Eskimo areas printed since 1945 is rather exhaustively listed even though it is linguistic only in the sense of being in Eskimo.

There are three major Greenlandic Eskimo dialects: East (Angmagssalik and Scoresbysund, total population about 3,000), Polar (Thule population perhaps nearly 700), and West (i.e. the whole West Coast from Kap Farvel north to beyond Upernavik, about 91% of the population nearly 40,000). The Eastern and Polar dialects are spoken by only a few hundred persons each, and enjoy no literary or official status as such. West Greenlandic, the literary and national standard, is taught everywhere; yet these two outlying groups still resist assimilation to the dominant standard.

East Greenlandic, at first contact, is only partly mutually intelligible with West. It is rather aberrant, especially because of extremely extensive lexical change due to tabu (see Bergsland 74, and Bergsland and Vogt 82). Apparently nothing has been published on East Greenlandic since the war. The major work on this dialect is still Thalbitzer's *The Ammassalik Eskimo* (589), especially Volume II, Part 3, a grammatical sketch and texts from a field trip to the area in 1905. The only more recent item of which this writer is aware is a 53-page vocabulary (59), of East Greenlandic, West Greenlandic, and Danish, by J. Balle, mimeographed in the thirties. Svend Frederiksen spent a month at Angmagssalik in 1961, and reports collecting about 135 pages of text, 100 pages of lexicon, and another 100 pages of shamanistic lexicon, all unpublished. Jens Rosing has recently investigated East Greenlandic language and folklore, collecting a large amount of material of linguistic interest, as yet unpublished.

The Polar dialect, phonologically somewhat more conservative than Greenlandic, and more similar to Baffin, has been the object of a major research effort by Erik Holtved, who has spent many years investigating Polar Eskimo archaeology and ethnology as well as linguistics. His major linguistic publication is a sizeable volume of texts (210), in very meticulous phonetic notation, with interlinear translation and a companion volume of free translations. The introduction to the volume and discussion of phonetics are also important, as is an article published the following year in *IJAL* (211). Apparently no other publication on Polar Eskimo linguistics has appeared during the recent period. Svend Frederiksen collected over 200 pages of lexical and textual material at Thule in 1961, and was also given two field notebooks of such material by Jens Olsen Pastor there, all unpublished.

The West Greenlandic language is itself not homogenous. There is significant difference between the southernmost and northernmost, but still not enough substantially to impair mutual intelligibility. The central dialects are slightly more innovative in some respects than the northern. The same central literary standard serves well for the whole range, which is in fact leveling and shrinking, due to increased communications and also centralization of population. This literary standard has evolved through the work of a series of missionary linguists starting soon after the arrival of the Egedes and Topp in Greenland two and a half centuries ago (72). Topp's ms. grammar of 1727 is now being published (603). Paul Egede published the first Greenlandic grammar in 1760 (130). Egede was followed by Königseer (ms. referred to in Kleinschmidt, never published) about 1780, then, more importantly, by Fabricius (145) in 1791. For details of the history of Greenlandic linguistics and literature to 1822, see Thalbitzer (850).

Samuel Petrus Kleinschmidt's brilliant *Grammatik der Grönländischen Sprache* (258) is an epoch-making achievement. The appearance of this book in 1851 marks a new era in Eskimo linguistics. It was in fact the first really good grammar not only of Eskimo but of any language of the new world. For a biography of Kleinschmidt see Bechler (63), Holtved (214, 215) and Otto Rosing (475, 476). All Eskimo linguistics is profoundly in debt to Kleinschmidt's great work, which reflects not only a solid knowledge of Greenlandic, but also amazing theoretical insight far in advance of its time; note Underhill (618) for an appreciation of this point. Kleinschmidt's letters to Bourquin are also very valuable for an understanding of his work (214). For further historical perspective and the development of Greenlandic linguistics see Collis (117, 119).

Later Greenlandic grammars included Chr. Rasmussen's (468, 1888, and still useful pedagogically, reprinted 1971) and then Schultz-Lorentzen, which is still in current use as the standard in Greenland. The first edition, in Greenlandic, appeared in 1904 (518), was translated in Danish in 1930 (521), revised in English in 1945 (522, reviewed by Preston, 459) and Danish in 1951 (521).

Swadesh published a restatement of Kleinschmidt in 1946 (553, reviewed very favorably by Hockett, 206). It was supplemented by an article by Swadesh (554), and also in turn itself abridged and restated by two other leading American linguists, first Harris in 1947 (193), and later Hill in 1958 (202).

In another way, however, perhaps an even greater contribution since Kleinschmidt in this relatively very advanced field of high-quality work, Greenlandic Eskimo grammar, is Knut Bergsland's *Grammatical Outline* of 1956 (67, 68), a mimeographed work of unfortunately limited distribution. Showing the influence of American structural linguistics and the author's stay at the University of Indiana, it is certainly the most original grammar of Greenlandic since Kleinschmidt, and an important source both of up-to-date information on and new insights for Greenlandic grammar.

A number of school grammars for Greenlanders have appeared since the war, by N. Rosing (473), Aa. Bugge (106), G. Thorning (600), H.C. Petersen (840), and also, for Danes to learn Greenlandic, a few new popular practical aids, by Aa. Bugge (105), Fr. Nielsen (431), K.P. Andersen (831), K.T. Petersen (841), and reprints of Schultz-Lorentzen (523), P. Vibæk (628), and Chr. Rasmussen (468).

Two very general articles were published by Holtved (212, 213) in 1958 and 1962, but with the exception of one study of Greenlandic inflection by M. Erichsen in 1944 (139) and an early article on phonology in Greenlandic by Robert Petersen in 1956 (445), apparently no published articles or conference papers on specialized topics in Greenlandic linguistics were produced until the late sixties, by scholars in Denmark (at the Institute for Eskimology founded in 1967 at the University of Copenhagen), Paris, and the United States. Some significant papers on Greenlandic phonology (including morphophonemics) have been presented by Robert Petersen, a native Greenlander (445, 448, 452, presenting a lot of valuable basic phonological information); and, also on phonology, in a generative framework, by Cearley and Mey (110), Underhill (615, 617, the latter also comparing Greenlandic with Yupik), Sadock and Olsen (500; Olsen is also a native Greenlander, who has studied Eskimology at the Copenhagen Institute, Yupik Eskimo at the University of Alaska, and linguistics at the University of Chicago), and Charles Pyle (461). Robert Petersen is currently doing research on statistical analysis (449), on the influence of Danish on Greenlandic (451) and on a thesis at the Copenhagen Institute concerning the relationship of the noun and verb in Greenlandic (453). Scholars in America have recently become rather active in exploring Greenlandic syntax from a point of view of transformational-generative theory, beginning a promising new phase of Eskimo linguistics: see Underhill (616) and Silverstein (543), both at Harvard, and above all, J. Mey of the University of Texas, who has presented several papers and published several articles of great interest on syntax (397, 398, 399, 400, 401, 402, 403, 839), and is currently preparing a major study on the syntax of the Greenlandic verbal constructions (404). J. Rischel at the University of Copenhagen has recently given a course on Eskimo phonology, making available valuable notes for that (847), articles on vowel patterns and noun phrases (848, 846), and, with Hideo Mase, a detailed laboratory phonetic study of consonant quantity(838).

Greenlandic lexicography has an even older history in print than Greenlandic grammar. The first Greenlandic dictionary published was by Paul Egede, in 1750 (129), but first in ms. in 1739; note also the 1750 ms. dictionary by Beyer, 833, listed in Pilling, 456). The next was Fabricius in 1804 (146), and then Kleinschmidt in 1871 (259, supplemented by Chr. Rasmussen in 1893 (469). Schultz-Lorentzen's Greenlandic-Danish dictionary of 1926 (519) and the Greenlandic-English version of it (520, 1927) are the latest and standard work, though not replacing Kleinschmidt-Rasmussen.

Two very important new Greenlandic dictionaries have appeared since the war however. One is a Danish-Greenlandic dictionary by Bugge et al. (107), a large (739 pp.) and excellent work, filling an obvious need. (The second edition of Barfod, 61, 35 pp., 1952, containing about 2,500 items, had been the only readily available one in print.) Bugge et al. is the first major non-Greenlandic to Greenlandic dictionary since Kjer and Rasmussen's of 1893 (256), which was apparently the first. Though Bugge et al. by no means completely replaces Kjer-Rasmussen, it contains a tremendous number of forms more recently attested in the vigorously developing Greenlandic language. The relationship between the two might be compared to that between Merriam-Webster's Unabridged Third and Second International.

The second new Greenlandic dictionary is Jonathan Petersen's *OrdbogêraK* (444). It first appeared in 1951, and was partly revised in 1968. *OrdbogêraK* is in a sense perhaps even more of a testimony than Bugge et al. to the enormous vitality of the Greenlandic language, in being a monolingual Greenlandic-Greenlandic work. The writer of this report is not aware of the existence of such a dictionary for any other North American language, perhaps for any American language at all. *OrdbogêraK*, being a work exclusively by a native Greenlander, is done with rare perspective and contains a wealth of lexical information not elsewhere available, e.g. on idiomatic usages. It also contains a very extensive list of postbases. *OrdbogêraK* moreover serves importantly as a standard popular reference for orthography, which is becoming increasingly problematical for Greenland. Discussion will return to this question below. To sum up, the Greenlandic dictionary situation is remarkably good: with *OrdbogêraK*, Schultz-Lorentzen, Bugge et al. (and Kjer-Rasmussen) the West Greenlandic lexicon is more accessible to linguistics than that of most other languages of the world. It would be especially unwise, however, to consider the coverage up-to-date for long, or even now, of a language so rapidly developing as Greenlandic.

Several minor Greenlandic wordlists also appeared during the period: two for the American military during the war (144, 257), a booklet for travellers and crew with the

Scandinavian Airlines System (142). There is a 1948 Danish-Greenlandic medical phrase-book (832). During the 1960s three little word-lists and phrase-books appeared for even Italian and Greenlandic (654, 837, 849).

A significant recent project in Eskimo lexicology, centering on Greenlandic, is development of methods for adapting computer programs for study of the lexicon (concordance, word-frequency) and on the general semiotics of Eskimo, by Dermot Rónan F. Collis in Paris. See articles in 1969 (116), and 1971 (836), and a paper at the Chicago conference (118). (Also in connection with Greenlandic and computers see J. Mey in 1969, 400.) Collis has studied Eskimo semantics in post-bases (835), and in 1971 published his dissertation on Greenlandic semiotics, a major contribution to the field of Eskimo semantics (119). The dissertation is also valuable for its historical survey of currents of thought in Eskimo linguistic studies, as are other articles by Collis (117, 834).

A word about the Greenlandic orthography and current issues. Greenlandic literature has a long enough history to have witnessed considerable phonological change in the language. Chief of these is the assimilation of the non-final diphthongs /ai/ and /au/ to /a·/ ([æ·] or, before uvulars, [a·]), and the assimilation of cluster-initial consonants, e.g. -ŋm- > -mm-. The base of the orthography is Danish (though Hans Egede was a Norwegian and Kleinschmidt a German). Thus a uvular spirant was easily recognized by the early missionaries, and spelled with an r, like the similar Danish (uvular or pharyngeal) sound. Doubtless, had the missionaries been Spaniards, or Englishmen, the results would have been different, and probably less felicitous. It was Kleinschmidt who established the standard orthography. Though the phonological changes mentioned above were no doubt already taking place, Kleinschmidt chose not only to ignore them, but in effect to reflect as much as possible of the underlying phonological structure. In this he clearly had remarkable insight, although of course many of his derivations are in fact incorrect; he also resorted even to comparative evidence (especially Labrador) for this purpose. Kleinschmidt may have gone too far in the conservatism and phonological depth of his orthography, especially considering the continued direction of phonological change since. For example, -aigdl-, -âvdl-, -autdl- (among others) are now all pronounced like -ãdl- ([æ·ł]), and it is often difficult or impossible for the ordinarily competent native speaker to figure out the underlying forms. Because of this and other matters standard literary Greenlandic is now considered very difficult by the general population and in need of spelling reform. Carl Chr. Olsen writes (p.c.) that 'not more than twenty persons in Greenland can use the spelling correctly'. Opinions by Robert Petersen, Frederik Nielsen, Jørgen Fleischer, Erik Holtved, Aage Bugge, Jens Poulsen, and others began to appear even before 1960 in the Greenlandic periodicals *Atuarfît Ilagîtdlo* (53), *Peкatigît Kalâtdlit* (443), *Grønland* (173), and especially the venerable and influential *Atuagagdliutit/Grønlandsposten* (52), e.g. Holtved and Bugge (216). A committee was appointed to investigate the possibilities for a spelling reform. In its 1967 report the committee did not yet see a radical reform advisable. During the sixties, however, Robert Petersen made serious experiments on the relative ease with which Greenlandic children learned to use an orthography radically reformed to represent phonetic consonant and vowel length directly by doubling (843, 449, 450). The reformed orthography of course resembles the Canadian Roman standard orthography of Gagné, including the adoption of q for κ (844). Late in 1971 the committee reconsidered the question, and has tentatively decided to undertake a radical reform (although certain aspects of it remain undecided, 842, 845). This decision is in any case of the utmost importance for Greenlandic. Its impact may also be felt in Canada and even Alaska.

The abandonment of the Kleinschmidt orthography also has significant bearing on the general theory of orthography design and the psychological nature of phonology itself. The Kleinschmidt orthography, lauded as optimal for the depth of insight with which it reflects underlying phonology (morphophonemics), as English orthography has been by Chomsky and Halle, proves in fact less practical and less direct a representation of phonological reality for the speaker than does a more 'shallow' representation of the phonetic 'surface'.

## 3. COMPARATIVE AND GENERAL STUDIES

Comparative-historical studies in Eskimo-Aleut logically fall into four groups: comparative Aleut, comparative Eskimo, comparative Eskimo-Aleut, and comparison of Eskimo-Aleut with other languages or families. These further seem to fall into three categories: historical-comparative studies (with systematic attempts to explain divergence from a common genetic prototype), typological-comparative (without such attempts), and lexicostatistic-glottochronological. For convenience, however, the present section will be divided into five subsections, concerning comparative Eskimo, comparative Eskimo-Aleut, broader comparisons, lexicostatistics-glottochronology, and general or miscellaneous. There have been no studies devoted primarily to systematic comparison within Aleut of Aleut dialects with a view to reconstructing proto-Aleut, and any attention this problem has received is in the literature cited in the section above on Aleut. Historical- or genetic-comparative studies will be mentioned here together with the typological-comparative in each section — and lexicostatistic-glottochronological studies, since these usually are primarily or exclusively such, but usually treat both internal Eskimo divergence and Eskimo-Aleut divergence (and Eskimo-Aleut divergence from other families), they most conveniently may be discussed in a separate subsection. Because this writer has not had the opportunity to study all the material mentioned with care, in some cases has not had the opportunity even to examine it at all, and is not qualified to make any authoritative critical evaluation of it, he must needs remain largely non-committal on the controversial issues involved.

## 3.1 Comparative Eskimo

The Eskimo languages or dialects are all so closely related that there has never been any question of the identity or genetic affiliation of any of them. Eskimo has always been recognized as such wherever it was encountered by scientific investigation. (Note, however, the popular confusion with 'Aleut' in Southwestern and Southern Alaska, mentioned in footnote under 'Alaska'.) Many 'comparative' vocabularies of Eskimo have been published since the eighteenth century. Chief amongst these and the most useful of those of the twentieth century are by Birket-Smith (87, vocabularies from West and North Greenland, and from three Central Canadian dialects), Jenness (235, vocabularies of Naukan in Siberia, from Alaskan Inuit dialects, Mackenzie and Coronation Gulf in Western Canada, Labrador, and Greenland), and K. Rasmussen (470, Naukan, Nunivak, Mainland Yupik, Unaaliq, three Alaskan Inuit dialects, Labrador, Greenland, not to mention his substantial contributions in other volumes of the *Report of the Fifth Thule Expedition on Canadian dialects*). In most cases the compilers, who were anthropologists and explorers who knew Eskimo but were not linguists, were satisfied simply to print the juxtaposed lists. Jenness, however, in his study of Wales phonology (234), attempts to make relatively systematic comparisons. Earlier work on Eskimo comparative phonology had also been done especially by Rink, Thalbitzer, and Uhlenbeck. By far the most important and systematic work on comparative Eskimo phonology before the war was L.L. Hammerich's classic 1936 monograph (175), mainly on inflectional morphology, but which also contains (pp. 17–35) a systematic study of comparative Eskimo phonology.

After the war Hammerich wrote articles on Eskimo cases (176) and on the dual (186), and made remarks on comparative Eskimo in several other of his articles of the period. Also concentrating in the area of comparative-historical Eskimo morphology are a significant paper and article by Osahito Miyaoka in 1967 (413, 424) identifying certain old derivational suffixes, remarks on the possessive by Underhill (855), and recent studies by D. Gary Miller (407, 408, 852) and by Alan H. Timberlake (853, not seen).

Morris Swadesh had worked in 1936 with an informant from St. Michael, the northernmost Yupik point, bordering on Inuit. He published the results in five installments much later, in *IJAL* 1951–52, a sizeable study of the dialect, synchronic and diachronic-comparative, which includes much important systematic work on comparative Eskimo phonology (555, 556, 557, 558, 559). Tor Ulving in two articles in the early fifties (613, 614) proposed a stress-theory of Eskimo historical phonology. This theory has been criticized by Miyaoka (412, pp. 102–3, 109, and personal communication), Bergsland (75, p. 8ff., and personal communication), and Underhill (personal communication). Very important and most recent contributors to systematic investigation of Eskimo historical phonology are by Miyaoka (410, 411, 412, 417, 419), Bergsland (78), and Underhill (617, 856). This last is in the generative framework, and in spite of its title includes a comparison of ordered rules and their chronology in Greenlandic and in Yupik (based on the Yupik grammar by Miyaoka et al., 420). The work of Hunns (194) on the other hand, attempts a phonological reconstruction restricted to Yupik, but is based only on Menovščikov and no adequate Alaskan source material (relying heavily e.g. on 302), so that accordingly the value of the results is severely limited.

Many, perhaps most, of the works of Menovščikov contain comparative data and remarks, though generally with no attempt at systematic historical explication. They are generally primarily from a Siberian point of view, comparing Chaplino, Naukan, Sirenik, Imaklik, but sometimes also Alaskan, Canadian, Greenlandic dialects as well. Amongst those seen may be cited especially (322, 323, 335, 360, 364, 369, 373, 375); especially important also in this connection is Bergsland's review of the Sirenik grammar (79). Menovščikov is reported to be planning extensive and systematic comparative work for the future.

Many of the articles cited in the subsections on comparative Eskimo-Aleut or on wider relationships of course also contain important studies of comparative Eskimo, above all those of Bergsland and Swadesh. Finally, since the Eskimo languages or dialects are in fact so closely related, a number of profound studies that are on specific dialects and non-comparative (e.g. the Greenlandic grammars of Bergsland and Swadesh, the Yupik grammar of Miyaoka et al., transformational studies by Mey on Greenlandic syntax) have important bearing on all Eskimo studies.

No one, surprisingly, seems to have been foolish enough to attempt seriously a Stammbaum-type classification of all Eskimo dialects. Eskimo generally presents so clearly the picture of a typical dialect complex (in spite of the enormous area over which it has spread) that linguists and usually even anthropologists have been content not to try to impose Stammbaum-type relationships on it. The main exception of course is the Yupik-Inuit split, which has long been recognized as fundamental, since the early days of Rink and Thalbitzer, though the borderline had been wrongly placed by Rink and Thalbitzer at the Alaska-Canada border, wrongly including Alaska Inuit with Western, in the 'Eastern' (Greenland-Canada) — 'Western' (Alaska-Siberia) dichotomy. It was not until the postwar publications of Hammerich, Swadesh, and Bergsland that it became clear that the border belongs in Alaska at Norton Sound between St. Michael (Swadesh's Unaaliq) and Unalakleet (note especially Correll, 121, on the Unalakleet boundary). Recent studies by Menovščikov on the Siberian dialects and by Bergsland on Alaskan Inuit (78) have shown, however, that even this split is not so simple and clean as hitherto believed. Especially needed for the resolution of these problems is a good description of the critically located East Cape Siberian Yupik.

## 3.2 *Comparative Eskimo-Aleut*

About 1820 Rasmus Rask, having had the opportunity to study both Greenlandic and Aleut, was the first to state the Eskimo-Aleut relationship. His notes were published by Thalbitzer nearly a century later (587), and then translated and elaborated in another study a few years later by Thalbitzer (588), which includes a good account of the history of comparative Eskimo-Aleut studies to 1921. The works of Sauvageot and especially Uhlenbeck contain some Eskimo-Aleut comparison, but their main concentration is on hypotheses of wider relationships. It was not until the publication of the Kleinschmidt Centennial volume of *IJAL* in 1951 that systematic proof of the genetic relationship was given, in the form of actual phonological correspondences. These are worked out independently in two excellent and fundamental articles in that volume, one by Marsh and Swadesh (298), and the other by Bergsland (64). Since 1951 Bergsland has been responsible for most of the progress made in comparative Eskimo-Aleut studies. He has made a very substantial contribution in about half a dozen articles and papers devoted principally to the problem (65, 66, 69, 73, 77, 80), dealing with phonology, morphology, lexicon, and, in the last two, also syntax; Bergsland points out that in the area of sentence structure there are deep differences between Eskimo and Aleut. In two articles (69, 75) which focus on the possible relationship of Eskimo-Aleut to Uralic, Bergsland has further significant observations to make on comparative Eskimo-Aleut. Also important for Eskimo-Aleut are comparisons made by Miyaoka in articles and papers dealing primarily with comparative Eskimo (411, 412, 413, 414). Menovščikov has written three rather general sketches comparing Eskimo and Aleut (353, 354, 375), and has dealt with both Eskimo and Aleut in at least two articles on syntax (the ergative construction, 365, 374).

## 3.3 *Lexicostatistics and Glottochronology*

Morris Swadesh was the originator and chief proponent of the method of dating linguistic divergence by cognate count on a test list. Since Swadesh was also deeply involved in Eskimo studies, it is natural that there should have been a fair amount of activity in attempting to date Eskimo and Eskimo-Aleut divergence. Already in 1951 (555) Swadesh proposed some tentative dates, 1500–2000 years for the age of the Yupik-Inuit split, and 4000 years for Eskimo-Aleut. In 1952 (560) these dates are revised to 1000 and $2900 \pm 400$ years respectively, which would appear too low. David I. Hirsch made a serious and detailed lexicostatistical study of Eskimoan divergence at that point in a masters thesis (204) and article (205). A symposium was devoted to the subject in 1954 (561), with discussion especially by Quimby, Collins, and Eggan on Swadesh's presentation. In 1956 at the 32nd International Congress of Americanists in Copenhagen, Swadesh presented new figures (563), increasing the depth to 1400 and 4600 years minimum, which seem more realistic and harmonious with the non-linguistic data. Also at that Congress Eskimo-Aleut glottochronology was discussed by Fred Eggan (131) and also by Knut Bergsland (74). Bergsland there and in a later paper (82) attacked Swadesh's figures on important theoretical grounds, by pointing out that lexical change does not take place at a uniform rate, so that time-depths cannot be reliably calculated on the basis of cognate percentages; some languages would show absurdly short divergence-time, e.g. Icelandic, and others absurdly long, e.g. East Greenlandic, where lexical change has been unusually rapid and extensive because of tabu on words connected with names of the dead. Swadesh continued to include Eskimo-Aleut data and figures in his later papers (1959–66) on wider relationships (564, 565, 566, 568, 569, 570), but since 1962 discussion of Eskimo-Aleut divergence dates has subsided completely. A resumé and review of studies on Eskimo-Aleut and Eskimo glottochronology and dialect classification in the light of archaeological evidence is included in an article published by Don Dumond in 1965 (127).

### 3.4 Broader Comparative Hypotheses

There has long been speculation about relationships of Eskimo and/or Aleut with a variety of other language groupings of the world. The oldest such hypothesis is the Eskimo(-Aleut)-Ural(-Alta-)ic, which was suggested in fact in 1576 by Martin Frobischer at the very first contact with Eskimo. It was taken up again in various forms during the eighteenth and nineteenth centuries by half a dozen scholars, and more importantly and elaborately during the twentieth century by C.C. Uhlenbeck, who was a student of Eskimo, in a series of articles between 1905 and 1941, and by A. Sauvageot, who was not a student of Eskimo, in a number of publications from 1924 to 1953. Knut Bergsland, himself an expert also in Uralic as well as Eskimo and Aleut, took up the question in an important article in 1956 (69), and then in 1959 reviewed very competently the whole subject and its history and bibliography in a paper (75) which itself remains by far the most important discussion of the hypothesis in print.

C.C. Uhlenbeck increasingly later (1935–41) took up the question of a relationship between Eskimo and Indo-European, but in terms of convergence, i.e. some ancient Asiatic contact, revealed in the lexicon, rather than genetic relationship (genetic relationship, on typological grounds, being more plausible with Uralic). Thalbitzer, who had in 1926 severely attacked Sauvageot's Eskimo-Uralic hypothesis, gives very serious and largely sympathetic evaluation to Uhlenbeck's Eskimo-Indo-European hypothesis in a 1944 paper (590), which (like Bergsland on Eskimo-Uralic in 1959) contains further comparisons and remains the most important discussion in print on that subject. Later discussion by Thalbitzer and by Hammerich appeared in their necrologies of Uhlenbeck in *IJAL* in 1953 (609). Thalbitzer in one of his last papers on the subject (591) considered the Eskimo-Indo-European hypothesis much more plausible than any other distant relationship posited for Eskimo-Aleut. Hammerich has also discussed the Eskimo-Indo-European hypothesis sympathetically, especially in an article in *IJAL* in 1951 (177), and in a number of subsequent general treatments of the Eskimo language and prehistory, most recently in 1970 (188).

In 1953 D. Jenness suggested the possibility that even Yahgan of Tierra del Fuego might be related to Eskimo (237), but this idea has not received any further attention in print.

In 1942, and more plausibly, Roman Jakobson in a footnote to an article on Paleoasiatic studies (230) cited nine very striking similarities between Aleut and Gilyak grammatical suffixes. Thalbitzer had noted, in 1923 (589, pp. 577–80), similarities between Eskimo and Kerek (Chukotan). Also in this direction, in his review (538) of Bergsland's 1958 Aleut monograph D.B. Shimkin made 18 suggestive comparisons between Aleut and Chukotan (Chukchi, Kamchadal, Koryak).

Certainly the most important development during the postwar period in exploring distant relationships for Eskimo-Aleut has been in this direction of Chukotan. The major work is that of Morris Swadesh, who toward the end of his career was deeply involved in a theory relating all the languages of the world, a theory which many have, probably not always with justification, considered too radical or visionary. In this scheme, Eskimo-Aleut is part of the Vascodéné (Basque to Na-Dene) network (in his Mexican publications: 564, 565, 566) or the somewhat more restricted Finno-Déné (569, in Russian). This grouping includes Uralic, but not Indo-European. The closest neighbors to Eskimo-Aleut in these networks are not Uralic (or, of course, Indo-European, which belongs much farther away), but Kutenai, Wakashan, and Chukotan. Eskimo-Aleut, itself with 3700 years internal divergence, is separated from each of these by about 4500 years. In the Russian article on Finno-Déné (569) Swadesh illustrated these relationships with 24 lexical similarities ('cognate pairs') between Aleut and Kutenai, 26 between Aleut and Kwakiutl (Wakashan), and 22 between Inuit and Chukchi. Apparently no further elucidation of the relationship with Kutenai has been published; for that with Wakashan, in one of his last papers Swadesh elaborated briefly on an Eskaleut-Chukotan-Wakashan triangle (570). However, for Eskaleut-Chukotan, Swadesh published in 1962 a detailed study (568) of the relationships between Eskimo-Aleut and Chukchi-Koryak-Kamchadal, which is clearly one of Swadesh's finest late works. The article begins with an excellent general discussion of the problem and its history, moves on to an evaluation of the grammatical similarities, and then presents a systematic and detailed comparative phonology, based on a large number of comparisons given, many of which appear reasonably convincing. It seems to this writer (and also to Eric Hamp, 190), that Swadesh has assembled and presented an impressive argument for a genetic relationship between Eskimo-Aleut and Chukotan in Asia. Swadesh has perhaps here succeeded in demonstrating convincingly a genetic relationship between an old-world family and a new-world family (if one discounts Eskimo, itself in both Siberia and America, as already an instance). It should come as no surprise, however, that the the first such genetic relationship to be demonstrated between the hemispheres should be between those language families closest on both sides to the Bering Strait.

### 3.5 General and Bibliographical

In connection with current trends in Eskimo-Aleut linguistics a number of papers also deserve mention which are of too general a scope to have been included in any of the above subsections. A series of papers by Birket-Smith on problems and progress in Eskimo research, especially reports on Danish activity in the field, is a useful contribution to the history of the subject (88, 89, 90, 92, 93). A number of papers and lectures by L. L. Hammerich (178, 185, 187, 188, 189) give excellent general introductions to the nature of the Eskimo language and the role of Eskimo-Aleut linguistics in the perspective of what is known and of the intriguing problems that remain in the prehistory of these peoples. Very important as general discussions of the same scope are papers by the Americans Dumond (127) and Hirsch (204, 205). Miyaoka has written an article on the history of Eskimo linguistic studies as an introduction for the Japanese audience (409). Collis's recent paper (117) and dissertation (119) might again be mentioned here as being especially useful as general introductions to the basic scientific literature of Eskimo. Note further a general paper by Holmer (208). L. L. Hammerich has reportedly undertaken to write the major study of Eskimo work for the forthcoming new *Janua Linguarum*, Series critica (851).

Already cited as including studies of the history of Eskimo and/or Aleut linguistic research are papers and monographs especially by Vdovin (100, 620, 621, 623, 624), and of course a number of major studies by Menovščikov, Bergsland, Hammerich, Thalbitzer, and others have been cited above as including important discussions of previous literature. More purely bibliographical, however, are, for the early periods, Lauridsen (271), and especially Pilling's monumental work (456). More recent are the contributions of Yarmolinsky (650, 651), and, not yet published, but probably most extensive of all, the computerized list compiled and described by Landar (269). The bibliography of the work of William Thalbitzer is also of major importance here (592). The standard more general bibliographies which are the most useful are the *Arctic bibliography* (Arctic Institute of North America, 50), *Linguistic bibliography/Bibliographie linguistique* (85), and the Modern Language Association *Bibliography* (86), but these are all far from complete for Eskimo-Aleut linguistics. Useful also are the Stefansson Collection and Arctic Institute Library catalogues (109, 124).

Finally, a cooperative effort to establish a standardized system of phonetic notation for Eskimo and Aleut studies by Thalbitzer, Hammerich, Holtved and Bergsland published in 1952 (395) certainly ought to be recommended.

## 4. BIBLIOGRAPHY

The following bibliography consists of a main and a supplementary section. The main section is a single alphabetical sequence. The supplementary section, which lists items which were not included in the earlier drafts of this report, is subdivided by area.

1. Ачиргин (translator). Байдуков, Г. Полюскун Американум/Через полюс в Америку [для дошкол. возраста] пер. Ачиргина при участии Е. С. Рубцовой, рис. А. Дейнека, Л., Главсевморпуть 1939, 52 стр., ill., bilingual.
2. —— (translator). Ляпидевский, А. В. Челюшкинцат/Челюшкинцы [для мл. возраста] пер. Ачигрина при участии Е. С. Рубцовой, рис. Б. Кожина, Л., Главсевморпуть 1939, 60 стр., ill., bilingual.
3. —— (translator). Речын'а тутунак'ым сивун'ани, собраниен'итни тугуты-стихк'ат Сталинмын' атик'ами тугутфигым округани городми Москвами/ Сталин, И. В. Речь на предвыборном собрании избирателей сталинского избирательного округа с Москвы 11 декабря 1939 года в Большом театре, на эскимос. яз., пер. Ачигрина при участии Е. С. Рубцовой, Л., Главсе-вморпут 1939, 28 стр.
4. —— (translator). Свердлов, В. С. Ак'ниг'нын'унани киях'тыл'ыхк'амун/За здоровою жизнь, пер. Ачиргин под ред. Е. С. Рубцовой, рис. Н. Г. Басмано-вой, Л., Учпедгиз 1940, 64 стр., ill., bilingual.

Ачиргин, see also 253, 478.

5. Acts, Galatians, Philippians, 1 Peter, Jas., Colossians (Kuskokwim Yupik, Moravian Fathers). American Bible Society, New York, 1950.
6. AFCAN, PASCHAL (translator). Aanakamken-qaa? (P. D. Eastman, Are You My Mother?). Eskimo Language Workshop, University of Alaska, 1971, 57 pp. Ill. Andrew Chikoyak.
7. —— (translator) Alrakum Qupai (O. Avey, E. Hammermeister, C. Allen, Stories of the Seasons). Eskimo Language Workshop, University of Alaska, forthcoming.
8. ——. Amirelucuar (Little Cloud). Eskimo Language Workshop, University of Alaska, 1972, 24 pp. Ill. Diane S. Dart.
9. ——. Angalegaam Qimugtai (Pat's Dogs). Eskimo Language Workshop, University of Alaska, 1971, 16 pp. Ill. P. Alcan and Andrew Chikoyak.
10. —— and MARIE N. BLANCHETT (translators). Angelan Kegeluneq-llu (S. Prokofiev, Peter and the Wolf). Eskimo Language Workshop, University of Alaska, 1972, 21 pp. Ill. Andrew Chikoyak.
11. —— (translator). Angnilria Asriq Issuriyagaq (Diane S. Dart, Little Mischief, also with Kuskokwim version by Marie N. Blanchett). Eskimo Language Workshop, University of Alaska, 1973, Ill. Diane S. Dart.
12. —— (translator). Anuga (K. Morack, The Wind)
13. ——. Canek Amllerenek Nalluneritua (I Know Many Things). Eskimo Language Workshop, University of Alaska. 1972, 14 pp. Ill. Diane S. Dart.
14. —— (translator). Cat Assikellrenka (Françoise, The Things I Like). Eskimo Language Workshop, University of Alaska, 1971, 30 pp. Ill. Diane S. Dart.
15. ——. Cikemeyaq (Blinky, a rabbit). Eskimo Language Workshop, University of Alaska, 1972, 26 pp. Ill. Andrew Chikoyak.
16. Erenerput (Our Day). Eskimo Language Workshop, University of Alaska, forthcoming, 28 pp.

17. —— (translator). Goldilocksaaq Pingayun-llu Taqukaat (Goldilocks and the Three Bears). Eskimo Language Workshop, University of Alaska, 1972, 46 pp. Ill. Cathi Hankinson, see also 574.
18. ——. Iqmik, Iingaq, Pameyuq-llu (Snuffy, Eyeball, and Tail). Eskimo Language Workshop, University of Alaska, 1973, Ill. Pascal Afcan.
19. —— (translator). Nacacuar (Elizabeth Orton Jones, Little Red Riding Hood). Eskimo Language Workshop, University of Alaska, 1971, 20 pp. Ill. Andrew Chikoyak.
20. ——. Kaviaq Angniilnguq (Geri Keim, The Sad Little Fox). Eskimo Language Workshop, University of Alaska, 1973, 21 pp. Ill. Geri Keim.
21. ——. Napam Cuyaa (The Tree Leaf). Eskimo Language Workshop, University of Alaska, 1972, 13 pp. Ill. Edward Hofseth.
22. —— (translator). Nayirculeriik (Seal Hunt, Department of Indian Affairs and Northern Development, Ottawa). Eskimo Language Workshop, University of Alaska, forthcoming, 17 pp., Ill. Edward Hofseth.
23. ——. Nunamtni (In Our Village). Eskimo Language Workshop, University of Alaska, forthcoming, 52 pp.
24. —— (translator). Paqnatareli Cuucicuar (H.A. Rey, Curious George). Eskimo Language Workshop, University of Alaska, forthcoming.
25. —— (translator). Qanganacuar (Geri Keim, The Little Squirrel). Eskimo Language Workshop, University of Alaska, 1973, 19 pp. Ill. Geri Keim.
26. ——. Qaillun Piciqat Yupiit Yugtun Alengareyaureskuneng Ataucitun (How a Unified Writing System Will Affect the Yupiks). Text and translation, paper read at the Conference on Eskimo Linguistics, Chicago, 5–7 June, 1970.
27. —— (translator). Qimalleq (Beatrix Potter, Peter Rabbit). Eskimo Language Workshop, University of Alaska, 1972, 20 pp. Ill. Andrew Chikoyak.
28. ——. Upsankut (Upsaq's Family). Eskimo Language Workshop, University of Alaska, 1971, 1972, 17 pp. Ill. P. Afcan. See also 575.
29. ——. Uqumyak (The Obnoxious Mouse). Eskimo Language Workshop, University of Alaska, 1971, 15 pp. Ill. Andrew Chikoyak.
30. —— (translator). Yuguaq Kelipaq (Nancy Nolte, The Gingerbread Man). Eskimo Language Workshop, University of Alaska, forthcoming.
31. ——, and IRENE REED. Qanereyarat Ayagenerita Nepait (The Sounds That Begin Words). Eskimo Language Workshop, University of Alaska, 1971, 28 pp. Ill. Diane S. Dart.
32. ——, MARTHA TEELUK, JOHN ANGAIAK, and IRENE REED. Qunguturaq Naruyayaguq (The Little Pet Seagull). Eskimo Language Workshop, University of Alaska, 1971, 29 pp. Ill. John Angaiak.

AFCAN, PASCHAL, see also 45, 246, 249, 420, 423.

33. AGINSKY, ETHEL G. A critical review of Waldemar Jochelson's unpublished Aleutian Grammar and an analysis of some text materials. Master's Thesis, Columbia University, 1933.

34. ——. Aleut Dictionary (based on Jochelson materials). New York, 1933 ms.
35. AHMAOGAK, ROY. Iñupiat taiguanic/Eskimo Primer. Board of National Missions of the Presbyterian Church in the U.S.A. New York, 1947, 24 pp.
36. —— (translator). Tusaayugaaġiksuat Uḵaluŋigun Maagum (Mark). American Bible Society. New York, 1948, 92 pp.
37. —— (translator). Tuyuutiŋi Paulum Tilizam Zuummiunun (Romans). American Bible Society. New York, 1948, 62 pp.
38. ——, MICHAEL J. KAYUTAK, and DONALD H. WEBSTER. Iñupiam Uḵaluŋi (Primer). Summer Institute of Linguistics. Fairbanks, 1963, three volumes, 16+20+24 pp. See 643.
39. ——, and DONALD H. WEBSTER (translators). God-im Uḵaluŋi (John, Ephesians, James, 1 John). American Bible Society. New York, 1964, diglot.
AHMAOGAK, ROY, see also 571, 631, 641, 642, 643.
40. Ajagait (periodical). Direction générale du Nouveau-Québec. Québec, 1967–.
41. ALEXIE, ANNA and ELIZABETH WORM (translators). Uutacuggluar Angun (Nancy Nolte, The Gingerbread Man). Eskimo Language Workshop, University of Alaska, forthcoming. See also 30.
42. ALEXIE, JOE. Iralunkuk Akerta-llu (The Moon and Sun). Eskimo Language Workshop, University of Alaska, forthcoming. Ill. Joe Alexie.
43. АМКАУН, В. (translator). Тамби, В. Natьn juk paxqeima tьŋanьgtьŋ/Как человек научился лететь, Перевел на эскимоский Амкаун Нынлювак, Л., Детгиз, 1936.
АМКАУН, В. (Амкагун нын'лювак), see also 150, 524, 526, 527.
44. АНАЛЬКВАСАК, ВЕРА А. (translator). Русско-эскимосский словарь (к книгам для чтения в III и IV классах школ народов Крайнего Севера) составленный С. М. Лазуко и М. Я. Басиной. Перевод В. А. Анальквасак, Л., Учпедгиз, 1949, 74 стр. (containing about 3,500 words) (see 273).
АНАЛЬКВАСАК, В. А., see also 273, 490, 491, 492, 495, 496.
ANDREWS, MARGARET HUNT. See 284, 285, 286.
45. ANGAIAK, JOHN. Maketaacuaraanka (My Little Book). Eskimo Language Workshop, University of Alaska, forthcoming, 68 pp. Ill. J. Angaiak, ed. P. Afcan.
ANGAIAK, JOHN, see also 32, 423.
46. Anglicanmiut Kengnotait Atuaitlo (Coppermine Dialect revision of earlier Mackenzie River dialect translation of: Book of Common Prayer). Edmonton, 1963.
АНКО, Ю. М., see 608, 482.
47. Annaodji Nunamiun (Bible portions, Genesis to Revelation, Coppermine Dialect [translated by Archdeacon John Sperry]). Scripture Gift Mission. Toronto, 1961, 64 pp.
48. ANTOINE, R. P. JOSEPH, O.M.I. Nungusuittuq Inuusiq (Four Gospels, commentary, Ungava Dialect). Wakeham, 1964, 272 pp., mimeograph.

49. Антропова, В. В. Алеуты. Народы Сибири. АН СССР, М.-Л. 1956, стр. 986-90.
50. Arctic Bibliography. Arctic Institute of North America.
51. Arctic Song Book (Cambridge Bay Hymnal).
    ARIMA, EUGENE, see 433.
    АШКАМАКЫН, see 529.
52. Atuagagdliutit/Grønlandsposten. Godthåb, periodical 1852-.
53. Atuarfît Ilagîtdlo/Skole og Kirke. Grønland. Godthåb, periodical 1954-.
54. Avangnâmiok. Godhavn, periodical, 1966-.
55. Аврорин, В. А. Литературные языки народов севера и местные диалекты. ВЯ 1953, № 2.3-27.
56. ——. Итоги и задачи изучения языков малых народностей Сибирского Севера. Языки и фольклор народов Сибирского Севера. АН СССР М.-Л., 1966, стр. 3-26.
57. ——. Опыт изучения функционального взаимодействия языков и народов Сибири. ВЯ 1970, № 1.33-43.
    АЯХТА, see 488, 489.
58. AYARUAQ, JOHN. Autobiography (in syllabics). Welfare Division, Northern Administration Branch, Department of Indian Affairs and Northern Development. Ottawa, 1968, 123 pp.
    Айнана, Л., see 484.
59. BALLE, J. Ordliste. Mimeographed, n.p., n.d. (Greenland, 193?), 53 pp.
60. Барабаш, И. И. Командорские острова. Советский Севера 1934, № 4.41-51.
61. BARFOD, H. P. Dansk-Grønlandsk Ordliste til Skolebrug. First Edition 1943, Second Edition, Godthaab, 1952, 35 pp.
62. BARNUM, FRANCIS P., S.J. Grammatical Fundamentals of the Innuit Language as Spoken by the Eskimo of the Western Coast of Alaska. Boston, 1901, xxv, 384 pp.
63. BECHLER, THEODOR. Samuel Kleinschmidt, der Sprachmeister Grönlands. Herrnhuter Missionsstudien Nr. 26, 1930.
64. BERGSLAND, KNUT. Aleut Demonstratives and the Aleut-Eskimo Relationship. IJAL 17.167-79, 1951.
65. ——. Litt om Nomen og Verbum i Eskimoisk og Aleutisk. Festskrift til L. L. Hammerich på tresårsdagen. Copenhagen, 1952, 44-52.
66. ——. Aleutisk-Eskimoisk 1953 (trykt som manuskript). Oslo, 173 pp.; also Nordisk Sprog og Kulturforlag, Copenhagen.
67. ——. The Eskimo Language. Doctoral Dissertation. University of Oslo, 1955. Microfiche copy available from Inter Documentation Co. AG, Poststrasse 9, Zug, Switzerland (= 68, see NTS 16.480-6, 1952, 18.489-94, 1958).
68. ——. A Grammatical Outline of the Eskimo Language of West Greenland. Oslo, 1956, mimeographed.

69. ——. The Uralic 'Half-Eye' in the Light of Eskimo-Aleut. Ural-Altaische Jahrbücher 28.165–72, 1956, Wiesbaden.
70. ——. Some Problems of Aleut Phonology. For Roman Jakobson, 38–43. The Hague, 1956.
71. ——. Näytteitä aleutti- ja Eskimokielistä/Specimens of the Aleut and Eskimo Languages. Oslo, 1957, mimeographed.
72. ——. Hans Egedes betydning for utforskningen av det grønlandske språk. Minneskrift om Hans Egede. Oslo, 1958.
73. ——. Aleut and Proto-Eskimo. PICAm 32.624–31, 1958.
74. ——. Is Lexicostatistic Dating Valid? PICAm 32.654–7, 1958.
75. ——. The Eskimo-Uralic Hypothesis. Journal de la Société Finno-Ougrienne 61.1–29, 1959.
76. ——. Aleut Dialects of Atka and Attu. TAPS 49.3, 1959. Reviewed by Swadesh (567), Shimkin (538).
77. ——. Morphological Analysis and Syntactic Reconstruction in Eskimo-Aleut. PICL 9.1009–15, 1964.
78. ——. The Eskimo Shibboleth inuk/yuk. To Honor Roman Jakobson. The Hague, 1966, 1.203–21.
79. ——. Review of Меновщцков (364). ВЯ, 1966, No. 4.140–8.
80. ——. Questions of Subordination in Aleut and Eskimo. Conference on Eskimo Linguistics. Chicago, June 5–7, 1970, with handout. 15 pp.
81. ——. An Aspect of Subordination in Aleut. Studies in General and Oriental Linguistics presented to Shirō Hattori on the Occasion of his 60th Birthday. Tokyo, 1970, 10–20.
82. BERGSLAND, KNUT and HANS VOGT. On the Validity of Glottochronology. CAnthr. 3.115–53, 1960, esp. 126–9, 149–51.
83. BERTHELSEN, CHRISTIAN. Hvor meget Dansk og hvor meget Grønlandsk? Grønland, 1965, No. 10.346–53.
84. ——. Sprogproblemet og Skolelovsforslaget. Grønland, 1966, No. 2.61–9.
85. Bibliographie Linguistique. Utrecht.
86. Bibliography. Modern Language Association. New York.

BIRD, CHARLES, see 280.

87. BIRKET-SMITH, KAJ. Five Hundred Eskimo Words: A Comparative Vocabulary from Greenland and Central Eskimo Dialects. Report of the Fifth Thule Expedition 1921–24. Vol. III, No. 3. Copenhagen, 1928, 64 pp.
88. ——. Danish Activities in Eskimo Research since 1940. PICA 28.231–6, 1948.
89. ——. Recent Achievements in Eskimo Research. Journal of the Royal Anthropological Institute 77.145–56, 1951, London.
90. ——. The Present Status of the Eskimo Problem. Tax, Sol, ed. Indian Tribes of Aboriginal America, Selected Papers of the 29th ICA. Chicago, 1952 (= PICAm 29.).
91. ——. The Chugach Eskimo. Copenhagen, 1953, 235–248.

92. ——. Danish Activities in Eskimo Research 1949–1954. PICAm 31/2.1119–28, 1955.
93. ——. The Significance of Eskimology. PICAm 32.46–50, 1958.
94. Богораз, В. Г. Материалы для изучения языка азиатских эскимосов. Живая старина, вып. II–III, кн. 70/71, СПб. 1909, 178–90, reprinted 1910, 13 pgs.
95. ——. The Eskimo of Siberia. Jesup North Pacific Expedition, VIII. New York, 1913.
96. ——. О так называемом языке духов (шаманском) у различных ветвей эскимосского племени. Изв. АН, Серия VI, т. XIII, № 8–11, Пг. 1919, стр. 489–95.
97. ——. Early Migrations of the Eskimo between Asia and America. ICA 9/2.216–34. Göteborg, 1925.
98. ——. Юитский (азиатско-эскимосский) язык. Сб. Языки и письменность народов Севера, ч. III, 1934, Л., стр. 105–28.
99. ——. Древнейшие элементы в языке азиатских эскимосов. Сб. Академия наук СССР академику Н. Я. Марру. Л., 1935, стр. 353–66.
100. ——. Материалы по языку азиатских эскимосов. (Подготовили к печати Г. А. Меновщиков и Е. С. Рубцова. С приложением таблиц склонения имен и спряжения глаголов в современном языке азиатских эскимосов, составленных Г. А. Меновщиковым. Под редакцией И. С. Вдовина). Л., Учпедгиз, 1949, 256 стр.
101. Book of Common Prayer (tr. Edmund Peck, W. G. Walton, J. M. Turner, et al.). Diocese of the Arctic, Church of England, Toronto 1950 (reprint), 589 pp., syllabics.
102. BOURQUIN, THEODOR. Grammatik der Eskimo-Sprache ... an der Labrador-Küste. London, 1891. (See also translations, 757, 815).
103. Бойцова, А. Ф., Л. А. Варковицкая, и Л. А. Воблова. Книга для чтения в первом классе начальной школы народов Севера. Л., Учпедгиз, 1954, с рус.-эскимосс. постатейным словарем, 204 стр.
104. ——. Книга для чтения в первом классе нач. школы народов Севера. С прил. русско-нац. постатейных словарей, изд. 2, переработ. Л., Учпедгиз, 1959, 208 стр. (АПН РСФСР нац. школ). Русско-эскимосский словарь, 33 стр.
105. BUGGE, AAGE. Grønlandsk Rejseparlør. Nyt Nordisk Forlag. Kjøbenhavn, 1952, 132 pp.
106. ——. Dansk-Grønlandske Stiløvelser. Ministeriet for Grønland. Kjøbenhavn, 1957, 1966.
107. ——, KRISTOFFER LYNGE, AD. FUGLSANG-DAMGAARD, and FREDERIK NIELSEN. Dansk-Grønlandsk Ordbog. Ministeriet for Grønland. Kjøbenhavn, 1960, 739 pp.

BUGGE, AAGE, see also 161.

BRUCE, TOMMY, see 596.
108. CAMPBELL, Rev. EDGAR O., M.D. Pē nēl lŭ r ghā- O͡ong wē ē pŭk. Ō ko͞ot- ŏ ko͞oz ē tĭt- Kē yŏ ghŭ nŭ ghum- ē yŏ'ŏ nŭng. Gambell, St. Lawrence Is., Alaska, 1910, 27 pp.; also Women's Board of Home Missions of the Presbyterian Church of the U.S.A. Philadelphia, 1910.
109. Catalogue of the Library. Arctic Institute of North America, 4 vols. Boston, 1968.
110. CEARLEY, ALVIN, and JACOB MEY. Metathesis in Eskimo Plurals. Abstract and handout, paper read at the Conference on Eskimo Linguistics. Chicago, 5–7 June, 1970.
111. CHAMBERS, Rev. JOHN R., and Rev. SAMUEL SIMMONS. The Iñupiat Eskimo Hymnbook. Fellowship Book Store. Barrow, Alaska, 1965 (Cuernavaca, 1966) [232] pp. See 631.
112. CHARPUT, THÉRÈSE, and RACHEL ERKLOO. The Story of Papik, an Eskimo Boy (reader). Department of Indian Affairs and Northern Development. Ottawa, 1963 (in English and syllabics), 1965 (in English, syllabics and standard Roman orthography), 50 pp. Translated into Yupik (426).
113. ЧАРУШИН, Е. Рассказы, рис. автора. Л., Учпедгиз, 1949, 187 стр., in Eskimo.
114. ——. Большие и маленькие [Рассказы]. Л.-М., Учпедгиз, 1951, 24 стр., ill., in Eskimo.
115. COLLINS, HENRY B. Comments (on Swadesh: Time Depths of American Indian Linguistic Groupings). AmA 56.364–72, 1954.
116. COLLIS, DERMOT RÓNAN F. On the Establishment of Visual Parameters for the Description of Eskimo Semantics. Folk 11.309–28, 1969.
117. ——. Etudes philologiques et linguistiques des langages esquimaux. Internord. 11.263–82, Paris, 1970.
118. ——. The Intermediary Application of Mechanographic Concordances in Eskimo Descriptive Semiotics, abstract and handout. Conference on Eskimo Linguistics. Chicago, June 5–7, 1970.
119. ——. Contributions à la sémiologie esquimaude: la reconnaissance et les ensembles sémantiques. Dissertation. Centre de Linguistique Quantitative de la Faculté des Sciences de l'Université de Paris, 1971, 166 pp.
120. COOLIDGE, JOSEPH. Kguterpalek (Big-Teeth). Eskimo Language Workshop, University of Alaska, forthcoming.
121. CORRELL, THOMAS C. Unalakleet: Modern and Traditional Aspects of the Yupik-Inupik Boundary. Paper read by title only. Conference on Eskimo Linguistics. Chicago, 5–7 June, 1970.
122. ——. Grammar of Central Canadian (Caribou) Eskimo. Forthcoming.
123. DAULBY, Rev. Canon T. (translator). Daily Strength (Bible verses in Baffin Land dialect, syllabics). Scripture Gift Mission. Toronto, 1959, 31 pp.
124. Dictionary Catalogue of the Stefansson Collection on the Polar Regions. Dartmouth College Library. 8 vols. Boston, 1967.

125. DIDIER, R. P., O.M.I. New Testament (Repulse Bay dialect). In progress.
DREBERT, FREDERICK, see 5, 250, 653.
126. DUCHARME, R. P. LIONEL, O.M.I. Jesusib, piniarningillu, ajokrertusingillu (Four Gospels, Chesterfield Inlet Dialect). Montréal, 1950, 378 pp., edition in Roman orthography, also edition in syllabics.
DUCHARME, see also 224.
127. DUMOND, DON. On Eskaleutian Linguistics, Archaeology, and Prehistory. AmA 67.1231–57, 1965.
128. DUTHILLY, ARTHÈME. An Inexhaustible Source of Linguistic Knowledge. PAPS 87.403–6, 1944.
129. EGEDE, PAUL. Dictionarium Grönlandico-Danico-Latinum. Havniae, 1750, 312 pp.
130. ——. Grammatica Grönlandica-Danico-Latina. Havniae, 1760, 256 pp.
131. EGGAN, FRED. Glottochronology: A Preliminary Appraisal of the North American Data. PICAm 32.645–53, 1958.
132. ЕМЕЛЬЯНОВА, N. M. Образование глагольных основ в языке азиатских эскимосов. Диссертация рукопись в ленинградских отделении, Инст. яз., АН СССР.
133. ——. Способы образования производных глагольных основ в эскимосском языке. Сб. В помощь учителю школ Севера, вып. 12. М.–Л., 1964.
134. ——. К вопросу о конверсии в эскимосском языке. Изв. АН СССР, ОЛЯ, том XXIII, 1964, вып. 1.36–43.
135. ——. Об агглютинации в эскимосском языке. Сб. Морфологическая типология и проблема классификации языков. М.–Л., 1965, стр. 205–16.
136. ——. О соотношении эргативной и номинативной конструкций в эскимосском языке. Эргативная конструкция в языках различных типов, стр. 269–76, 1967.
137. English-Inuit Dictionary [Seward Peninsula dialect, authorship uncertain, perhaps Lafortune]. n.d., n.p., typescript, 161 pp.
138. ERDMANN, FRIEDRICH. Eskimoisches Wörterbuch gesammelt von den Missionären in Labrador. Budissin, 1864, 360 pp.
139. ERICHSEN, MICHELLE. Désinences casuelles et personnelles en Eskimo. AL 4.67–88, 1944.
ERKLOO, ELIJAH, see 607.
ERKLOO, RACHEL, see 112.
140. ERMELOFF, AFENOGIN K. The wreck of the Umnak Native. Alaska Sportsman 7/2.14–15, 25–28, 1941 (tr. by J.E. Ransom).
ERMELOFF, AFENOGIN K., see also 537.
141. Eskimo Bulletin 1953–1958 (later Inuktitut = 223). Department of Northern Affairs and Natural Resources. Ottawa (syllabic and Roman versions). Ed. by Mary Panegoosho and Robert Williamson.

142. Eskimo Dictionary. Scandinavian Airlines System, Company Training Library, 1956, 69 pp. Reprint of USAF dictionary, 144 or 257.
143. Eskimo Hymnal. The Fountain Press. Freeport, Pennsylvania, ca. 1955, 62 pp.
144. Eskimo Word List. Anonymous, compiled by U.S. Army. Before 1950, 20 pp. typescript, mimeographed (Stefansson Collection).
145. FABRICIUS, OTHO. Forsøg til en forbedret grønlandsk Grammatika. Kjøbenhavn, 1791, 1801, 388 pp.
146. ——. Den grønlandske Ordbog forbedret og forøget. Kjøbenhavn, 1804, 795 pp. (incl. Danish-Greenlandic index, p. 545–795).
147. FAFARD, R.P. EUGÈNE, O.M.I. Dictionnaire Esquimau-Français. Chesterfield Inlet, 1953, ms. # R40 at Archives Deschatelets, 146 pp., containing ca. 6000 items.
148. ——. Prières et Cantiques en Esquimau. Ottawa, 1957, 375 pp., Roman and syllabics.

FLEISCHER, JØRGEN, see 52.

149. FLINT, MAURICE S., ed. Revised Eskimo Grammar (revision of Peck, Rev. E. J., Eskimo Grammar, 1883, 1919, 1931, 1943). Toronto, 1954, ix + 79 pp.
150. Форштейн, Александр С. Jupigьm akuziłha/Эскимосское слово (Букварь). Проверен на занятиях по эскимос. яз. в Ин-те народов Севера с эскимосом Амкаун. М.–Л., Учпедгиз, 1935, 90 стр., ill.
151. ——. Jupigьm uŋьparataŋi/Сказки азиатских эскимосов. Записаны в поселке Унгазик А. С. Форштейном. Л., Детгиз 1935, 22 (2) стр., рис. Ю. Петрова.
152. ——. Jupigьm uŋьparataŋi/Сказки азиатских эскимосов. Записаны в поселке Унгазик А. С. Форштейном. М.–Л., 1936, 21 (3) стр.

Форштейн, А. С., see also 98, 524, 525, 526, 527.

153. FOSTER (translator, editor). Proverbs (Baffin Island dialect). British and Foreign Bible Society. Toronto, 1950, 77 pp., syllabics.
154. —— (translator, editor). Psalms, Genesis, Isaiah (Baffin Island dialect). Canadian Bible Society. Toronto, 1966, syllabics.

FUGLSANG-DAMGAARD, AD., see 107.

155. GAD, FINN. Grønlands Sprogsituation. Grønland, 1954, 10.382–92.
156. ——. The Language Situation in Greenland. ASR 45.377–83, 1957.
157. GAGNÉ, RAYMOND C., ed. Shadows. Hamilton, 1957, 10 pp., mimeographed, in syllabics.
158. ——. A Phonemic Analysis of an Eastern Hudson Bay Eskimo Dialect (with special reference to orthographic unification). M.A. Thesis, University of Montreal, 1958, 153 pp.
159. ——. In Defense of a Standard Phonemic Spelling in Roman Letters for the Canadian Eskimo Language. Arctic 12.203–13, 1959; reprinted as Appendix II of 161; early version is Ch. X of 158.

160. ——. On the Importance of the Phonemic Principle in the Design of an Orthography. Arctic 13.20–31, 1960, reprinted as Appendix III of 161.
161. ——. Tentative Standard Orthography for Canadian Eskimos. Welfare Division, Department of Northern Affairs and Natural Resources. Ottawa, first edition 1961, revised edition 1962, 1965, 75 pp. (see also 159, 160, 162, 163).
162. ——. Projet d'orthographe Uniforme à l'Intention des Esquimaux du Canada. Welfare Division, Department of Northern Affairs and Natural Resources. Ottawa, 1962, 89 pp. (French version of 1962 edition of 161).
163. ——. Towards a Canadian Eskimo Orthography and Literature. CJL 7.95–107, 8.33–9, 1962 (see also Appendix IV of 161).
164. ——. Language Culture in Canada. Northern Welfare, 44–6. Department of Northern Affairs and Natural Resources. Ottawa, 1962.
165. ——. Eskimo Language Course. Department of Indian Affairs and Northern Development. Ottawa, [1966], mimeographed, with 35 7" tapes, ca. 364 pp.
166. ——. Spatial Concepts in the Eskimo Language, in Victor F. Valentine and Frank G. Vallee, Eskimo of the Canadian Arctic. Princeton, 1968, 30–8.
167. ——, and PAUL KOOLERK. Uqalimartaa (primer, Pond Inlet dialect). Education Branch, Department of Indian Affairs and Northern Development. Ottawa, 1968, 79 pp.

GAGNÉ, RAYMOND C., see also 462.

168. GEOGHEGAN, RICHARD HENRY. The Aleut Language (The Elements of Aleut Grammar, with a Dictionary in Two Parts Containing Basic Vocabularies of Aleut and English), edited by Frederica I. Martin. Washington, U.S. Department of the Interior, 1944, 169 pp., reviewed by Lounsbury (287), Harrington (192), Ransom (464).
169. Гондатти, Н. Л. Материалы по наречиям инородцев Анадырского округа. Живая старина, вып. II, год 7-й. СПб., 1897, стр. 218–29.
170. GRABURN, NELSON H. Taqagmiut Eskimo Kinship Terminology. Ph.D. Thesis, University of Chicago, 1963.
171. ——. Some Aspects of Linguistic Acculturation in Northern Ungava Eskimo. KASP 32.11–46, 1965.
172. GRAY, ARTHUR, MINNIE GRAY, and WILFRIED ZIBELL (translators). Jesus-ŋum iñuułhanik (Gospel Stories in Kobuk River Eskimo). Wycliffe Bible Translators Berghausen [Germany], 1966, 37 pp.
173. Grønland. Det Grønlandske Selskab. Kjøbenhavn.
174. GUBSER, N. J. The Nunamiut Eskimos, Hunters of Caribou. New Haven and London, 1965.

Гухуге, С. М., see 488, 489, 493, 494, 497, 498.

175. HAMMERICH, L. L. Personalendungen und Verbalsystem im Eskimoischen. Det Kgl. Videnskabernes Selskab, Hist.-filol. Meddelelser 23.2. Copenhagen, 1936, 226 pp.
176. ——. The Cases of Eskimo. IJAL 17.18–22, 1951.

177. ——. Can Eskimo Be Related to Indo-European? IJAL 17.217–23, 1951.
178. ——. Humanisme en taalkunde (Scripta Academica Groningana), 1952, 46 pp. (Eskimo, taal en volk, 32–40, 46).
179. ——. C. C. Uhlenbeck: I. IJAL 19.75, 1953.
180. ——. The Dialect of Nunivak. PICAm 30.110–3, 1953.
181. ——. Russian Loanwords in Alaska. PICAm 30.114–26, 1953.
182. ——. The Russian Stratum in Alaskan Eskimo. Word 10.401–28, 1954, reviewed by Меновщиков, 334.
183. ——. Report on my Journeys of 1950 and 1953 to Investigate the Language of Some Eskimos of North Alaska. Copenhagen, 1954, 22 pp. (Arctic Institute of North America Project No. O[ffice of] N[aval] R[esearch] 49, 102).
184. ——. The Western Eskimo Dialects. PICAm 32.632–39, 1958.
185. ——. The Origin of the Eskimo. PICAm 32.640–44, 1958.
186. ——. Wenn der Dualis Lebendig ist. Sprache 5.16–26, 1959.
187. ——. Some Linguistic Problems of the Arctic. Acta Arctica 12.83–9, 1960.
188. ——. The Eskimo Language. Fridtjof Nansen Minneforelesninger VI, October 10, 1969. Det Norske Videnskaps Akademi i Oslo, Universitetsforlaget. Oslo, 1970, 5–42.
189. ——. Eastern and Western Eskimo. Some basic remarks. Abstract, paper read at the Conference on Eskimo Linguistics. Chicago, June 5–7, 1970.
190. HAMP, ERIC. On Eskimo and Luoravetlan. Paper read at the Conference on Eskimo Linguistics. Chicago, 5–7 June, 1970.
191. HARP, Rev. GEORGE. An English-Eskimo Conversation Book. Hopedale, 1941, 24 pp., mimeographed.
192. HARRINGTON, JOHN P. Review of Geoghegan (168). IJAL 13.197–9, 1947.
193. HARRIS, ZELLIG. Structural Restatements: I. IJAL 13.47–54, 1947 (see 553).
194. HARVEY, PAULINE, BERT HARVEY, PAUL MILLER, PATSY MILLER (translators). Moo me ting itch Tay yote (Gospel quotations, Iñupiat dialect). Granada Heights Friends Church of California, ca. 1963, 12 pp. mimeographed.
195. HATTORI, TAKESHI. Attuan Aleut Vocabulary. Otaru, 1943, unpublished ms., containing ca. 300 items.
196. HAYS, GEORGE. Conversation-Book (Labrador Eskimo). Hopedale, 1941, 20 pp., mimeographed.
197. HEINRICH, ALBERT. A partial analysis of Bering Straits Innupiaq. University of Alaska, 1955, 151 pp., typescript.
198. ——. A Bering Straits Innupiaq, i.e. Inupiat, Word List. University of Alaska, 1955, 110 pp., typescript.
199. ——. Structural Features of Northwestern Alaskan Eskimo Kinship. SJA 16.110–26, 1960.
200. ——. Linguistic Errors and the Formulation of the Concept 'Eskimo Type Kinship', handout. Conference on Eskimo Linguistics. Chicago, 5–7 June, 1970.
201. HENRY, VICTOR. Esquisse d'une Grammaire raisonnée de la Langue Aléoute

d'après la Grammaire et le Vocabulaire d'Ivan Veniaminov. Paris, 1879, 79 pp.
202. HILL, ARCHIBALD. Eskimo: A grammatical sketch. Appendix to Introduction to Linguistic Structures. New York, 1958, pp. 419–40.
203. HINZ, Rev. JOHN. Grammar and Vocabulary of the Eskimo Language, as spoken by the Kuskokwim and Southwest Coast Eskimos of Alaska. Bethlehem, Pa., 1944, 199 pp., reprinted 1955; reviewed by Voegelin (630).
HINZ, Rev. J., see also 5, 250, 653.
204. HIRSCH, DAVID L. Some Aspects of Eskimo and Eskimo-Aleut Prehistory in the Light of a New Technique for Linguistic Dating. M.A. Thesis, University of Chicago, 1953.
205. ——. Glottochronology and Eskimo and Eskimo-Aleut Prehistory. AmA 56.825–38, 1954.
206. HOCKETT, CHARLES F. Review of Swadesh (553). Lg 24.186–8, 1948.
207. HOLMER, NILS M. The Native Place-Names of Arctic America. I: Names 15.182–96, 1967, II: Names 17.138–48, 1969.
208. ——. On the Amerindian Character of Aleut and Eskimo. In: Bolognesi, Giancarlo, et al., eds., Studî linguistici in onore di Vittore Pisani. Brescia, 1969.
209. HOLTVED, ERIK. Blandt sagafortællere i Grønland og Alaska. Det Grønlandske Selskabs Årsskrift. Kjøbenhavn, 1950, 69–80.
210. ——. The Polar Eskimos: Language and Folklore. I: Texts. Meddelelser om Grønland 152/1.1–366, 1951, 152/2.1–153, 1951.
211. ——. Remarks on the Polar Eskimo Dialect. IJAL 18.20–4, 1952.
212. ——. Remarks on Eskimo Semantics. PICA 32.617–23. Copenhagen, 1958.
213. ——. Er Eskimoisk et primitivt Sprog? Grønland, 1962, No. 8.281–97.
214. ——, ed. Kleinschmidts Briefe an Theodor Bourquin. Meddelelser om Grønland, 140.3, 1964, 124 pp. Copenhagen.
215. ——. Samuel Kleinschmidt, i anledning af 150-året for hans fødsel. Grønland, 6.217–30, 1964.
216. ——, and A. BUGGE. Retskrivningsmuligheder undersøges i øjeblikket. Atuagagdliutit 20.5, 1962.
217. ——, and ——. Omkring det grønlandske Retskrivning. Ministeriet for Grønland. Kjøbenhavn, 1967, mimeographed.
218. HOUSTON, JAMES. Eskimo Handicrafts. Canadian Handicraft Guild and Department of Indian Affairs and Northern Development. Ottawa, 1951, 32 pp., bilingual.
219. HUNNS, DEREK. A Reconstruction of Proto-Yupik Phonology. Ph.D. Dissertation. Cornell University, 1970, 229 pp.
220. Igloolik (reader). Curriculum Section, Education Division, Northern Affairs Branch, Department of Indian Affairs and Northern Development. Ottawa, 1962 (in English and syllabics), 1965 (in English, syllabics, and standard Roman orthography), 52 pp.
221. ILLAUQ (IDLOUT), LEAH. Imirqutailakuluk nanuaalullu (La petite hirondelle de

mer et le gros ours blanc). Welfare Division, Department of Northern Affairs and Natural Resources. Ottawa, 1962, 14 pp.

222. INNOCENT, R.P. (formerly Gordon H. Marsh). The Grammatical Category of Definite and Indefinite in the Aleutian Aleut Language (Unalaska-Umnak Dialect). Abstract and handout, paper read at the Conference on Eskimo Linguistics. Chicago, 5–7 June, 1970.
223. Inuktitut/Inuktitun 1959– (Earlier Eskimo Bulletin 141; Inuktitut, Western Arctic Edition, in Roman alphabet; Inuktitut, Eastern Arctic Edition, in syllabics). Department of Indian Affairs and Northern Development. Ottawa.
224. Inungnut Tamainut. Institut de Missiologie. Ottawa, 1941–64. Since 1965 renamed Inungnit Inungnut. Periodical in syllabics, ed. by R.P.L. Ducharme, O.M.I.

Йохельсон, В. И., see JOCHEL'SON.

225. IRVING, LAURENCE. On the Naming of Birds by Eskimos. University of Alaska Anthropological Papers 6.61–77, 1958.
226. ——. Stability in Eskimo Naming of Birds in Cumberland Sound, Baffin Island. University of Alaska Anthropological Papers 10.1–12, 1961.
227. Итоги всесоюзной переписи населения 1959 года. СССР сводны том Гостатиздат ЦСУ СССР. М., 1962, стр. 186–7, 192–3, 198–9.
228. Из постановления совещания по языкам народов Севера. ВЯ 1953, № 2. 139–42.
229. JACK, NOAH. Elluarrlua Auluklerkaqa Wangnek (The Ways I Take Care of Myself). Eskimo Language Workshop, University of Alaska, 1971, 15 pp. Ill. Diane S. Dart. Dittoed.
230. JAKOBSON, ROMAN. The Paleo-Siberian Languages. AmA 44.602–20, 1942.
231. ——. Note on Aleut Phonology. Bulletin of the New York Public Library, 48.677, 1944.
232. JAMASSEE, NICOTYE. Nicotye and her Family (reader). Curriculum Section, Education Division, Northern Affairs Branch, Department of Indian Affairs and Northern Development. Ottawa, 1963 (in English and syllabics), 1965 (in English, syllabics, and standard Roman orthography), 27 pp.
233. JAMES, ROBERT (translator). Atuutit Mumiksat. Wycliffe Bible Translators, ca. 1961 (not to be identified with 657, of same title).
234. JENNESS, DIAMOND. Notes on the Phonology of the Eskimo Dialect of Cape Prince of Wales, Alaska. IJAL 4.168–80, 1927.
235. ——. Comparative Vocabulary of the Western Eskimo Dialects. Report of the Canadian Arctic Expedition 1913–1918, 15A. Ottawa, 1928, 134 pp.
236. ——. Grammatical Notes on Some Western Eskimo Dialects. Report of the Canadian Arctic Expedition 1913–1918, 15B. Ottawa, 1944, 34 pp.
237. ——. Did the Yahgan Indians of Tierra del Fuego Speak an Eskimo Tongue? IJAL 19.128–31, 1953.

238. JENSEN, BENT. Grønlandsk (Arbejdshæfte til Læsebog for 9. skoleår). Red. K. Helveg Petersen, G. Nyborg Jensen, 1965.
239. ——. Remarks on Social Aspects of the Greenlandic Language Question. Paper presented at the Conference on Eskimo Linguistics. Chicago, 5–7 June, 1970.
240. JOCHELSON, V. I. The Aleut language and its relation to the Eskimo dialects. PICAm 18/1.96–104, 1912.
241. Йохельсон, В. И. Заметки о фонетических и структурных основах алеутского языка. Изв. АН, серия VI, 1912, № 17, стр. 1031–46.
242. ——. Опись фольклорных и лингвистических материалов В. И. Иохельсона, хранящихся в Азиатском музее Российской Академии наук. I. Алеуты. Изв. АН, серия VI, 1918, т. XII, вторая часть, № 17, стр. 1979–2003, Пг., 1919.
243. ——. Алеутский язык в освещении грамматики Вениаминова. Изв. АН, 1919, сер. VI, № 2, Пг., 1920, стр. 133–54; № 4–7, Пг., 1920, стр. 287–315 (tr. by E. Aginsky, 70 pp., typescript).
244. ——. Материалы по изучению алеутского языка и фольклора, собранные и обработанные В. И. Иохельсоном, т. I. Образцы народной словесности, вып. 1. Тексты на уналашкинском наречии. Пг., 1923 (2), IV, 28 стр. (tr. by E. Aginsky, 73 pp., typescript).
245. ——. Унанганский (алеутский) язык. Сб. Языки и письменность народов Севера, ч. III, 1934, стр. 129–48.
246. JOE, ANNA ROSE AFCAN, and PASCHAL AFCAN. Tukutukuaraller (The Old Snipe). Eskimo Language Workshop, University of Alaska, 1971, 22 pp. Ill. Andrew Chikoyak.
247. K̇AG̈AK̇PAK (KAGAK, D. O.) K̇uliak̇tuat Taimani. Summer Institute of Linguistics. Santa Ana, ca. 1962, 15 pp.
    КАКЛЯ, see 478.
    KALLUAK, see 606.
248. КАЛЯ (translator). Ун'ипамсюгыт пограничнигнын'/Рассказы о пограничниках. Пер. на эскимос. яз. Каля под ред. К. Сергеевой, рис. В. Морозова. Л., Главсевморпут, 1938, 68 стр., ill., bilingual.
    Каля, see also 482, 490, 492, 495.
249. KAMERLING, LEONARD. Kassigeluremiut (The people of Kasigluk in pictures and poems). Rural School Project and Eskimo Language Workshop. University of Alaska, 1970, 46 pp. tr. into Eskimo by P. Afcan and M. Nick.
250. Kanearakgtar (New Testament, Kuskokwim Eskimo). American Bible Society. New York, 1956, 1967, 627 pp.
251. KASUGA, KAORU. Aryuutogo Ippan; Aryuuto-zoku ni taisuru Nihon-go Kyooju-an (A Glimpse of the Aleut Language; a First Step in Japanese for the Aleuts). Attu, 1942, 21 pp., ms. (in Japanese, original at Hokkaido University).
252. КАСЫГА (translator). Байдуков, Г. Схасюхвал'хыт илямнын' Сталинмын'/ Встречи с товарищем Сталиным. [Для дошкол. возраста] на эскимос. и

рус. яз., пер. Касыга и К. Сергеевой, рис. Б. Дехтерева. Л., Главсевморпут, 1939, 36 стр.
253. ———. и Татак. Атехтуг'ьяхк'ак' книга/Книга для чтения. Для нач. эскимос. школы. В работе над книгой принимали участе Ачиргин и Рубцова, утв. НКП РСФСР. Л., Учпедгиз 1940, ч. I, для I класса, 140 стр., ill.
254. ——— и ——— (translators). Книга для чтения, ч. 1, для 1 класса, перевод с эскимосского языка, под ред. Е. С. Рубцовой, 1940, 54 стр.
255. Kattangutiget tuksiarutingit (Moravian Hymn Book), Imgerutit attoraksat illagektunut Labradoremetunut. United Society for Christian Literature for the Moravian Missions. Muswell Hill (England), (A. Martin 1900, W. W. Parrett 1918), reprint. 1950, xv + 383 pp.
Касыга, see also 390.
Kayutak, Michael J., see 38.
Храковский, В. С., see 392.
256. Kjer, O., and Chr. Rasmussen. Dansk-Grønlandsk Ordbog. Kjøbenhavn, 1893 (published together with 469).
257. Klausen, A. Greenlandic Dictionary of Useful Phrases and Military Terms. 1942, Washington, D.C., 58 pp., mimeographed (Stefansson Collection).
258. Kleinschmidt, Samuel Petrus. Grammatik der grönländischen Sprache (mit teilweisem Einschluss des Labradordialekts). Berlin, 1851, 182 pp., reprinted by Georg Olms Verlag Buchhandlung, Hildesheim, 1968.
259. ———. Den Grønlandske Ordbog Omarbejdet (H. F. Jørgensen, ed.). Copenhagen, 1871, 460 pp.
Kleinschmidt, S. P., see also 214, 215, 475, 476.
260. Kleivan, Inge. Sprogproblemet i folkeskolen i Grønland, en kommentar til lovudkastet til en ny lov om skolevæsenet i Grønland. Grønland, 1965, No. 6.211–24.
261. ———. Language and Ethnic Identity-Language Policy and Debate in Greenland. Folk 11/12.235–85, 1969/1970.
262. Колонов, А. Рассказ о Ленине (Школьная б-ка для нерусских школ. Для семилет. школы, Изд. на эскимос.). Л., Учпедгиз, 1959, 95 стр.
Koolerk, Paul, see 167.
263. Kowalczyk, Emil, and students. Kasigluk Eskimo-English Reader (Adult Education Series) I–II. Department of the Interior, Bureau of Indian Affairs, Branch of Education. Juneau, 1957, 8 + ca. 8 pp.
264. Красинская-Воблова, Л. А. Учебник русского языка, 1 класс. Л., Учпедгиз, для эскимос. школы, 1955, 143 стр.
265. ———. Учебник русского языка, 2 класс. Л., Учпедгиз, 1956, для эскимосской школы, 188 стр.
266. Krauss, Michael E. Eskimo-Athapaskan Areal Contacts in Alaska. Paper presented at the Conference on Eskimo Linguistics. Chicago, June 5–7, 1970.
Krauss, Michael E., see also 420, 698, 699, 702–703.
267. Kristensen, Karl. A Brief Introduction to the Eskimo Language of the

Eastern Arctic. Adult Education Section, Education Division, Northern Administration Branch, Department of Northern Affairs and Natural Resources. Ottawa, 1964, 1966, 1967, 73 pp., mimeographed for restricted distribution.

268. Куяпа, Ф. Русско-эскимосский постатейный словарь. Приложение к Книге для чтения во втором классе начальной школы народов Севера, С. М. Лазуко. На эскимосский язык перевел Ф. Куяпа. Л., Учпедгиз, 1959, 31 стр. (С. М. Лазуко. Книга для чтения во втором классе нац. школы народов Севера. С прил. русско-нац. постатейных словарей. Изд. 2, испр., 215 стр., Русско-эскимосский словарь, 32 стр. Л., Учпедгиз, 1959; see also 272.)

Куяпа, Ф., see also 103, 104, 272, 349.

269. LANDAR, HERBERT. Eskimo Bibliography, abstract. Paper read at the Conference on Eskimo Linguistics. Chicago, June 5–7, 1970.

270. LAUGHLIN, WILLIAM S., and GORDON H. MARSH. A New View of the History of the Aleutians. Arctic 4.74–88, 1951.

LAUGHLIN, WILLIAM S., see also 297.

271. LAURIDSEN, P. Bibliographica Groenlandica. Meddelelser om Grønland 13.199–217, 1890, Copenhagen.

272. Лазуко, С. М. Книга для чтения во втором классе начальной школы народов Севера. Л., Учпедгиз, 1954, с рус.-эскимос. постатейным словарем, 220 стр., see also 268.

273. ——. Книга для чтения в третьем классе начальной школы народов Крайнего Севера [для эскимос. школы], 1955, 303 стр., see also 44.

274. LEFEBVRE, GILLES R. A Comparative and Annotated Glossary of the East Hudson Bay Eskimo Dialect. Montreal, 1956, 74 pp., unpublished, mimeographed (report prepared for the National Museum, Ottawa, 1955, 100 pp., 1 map).

275. ——. Remarques phonologiques pour une orthographie du dialecte esquimau de l'Est de la Baie d'Hudson. Anthropologica 2.39–59, 1956.

276. ——. L'Expression du temps dans le verbe. Stylistique et Linguistique. Montreal, 1956.

277. ——. An Eskimo Ethnolinguistic Questionnaire for Phonological Investigation. Montreal, 1956, mimeographed.

278. ——. A Draft Orthography for the Canadian Eskimo: Towards a Future Unification with Greenlandic. Northern Co-ordination and Research Centre, Department of Northern Affairs and Natural Resources. Ottawa, 1957, 13 pp., mimeographed (NCRC-57-1).

279. ——. Le Nouveau-Quebec dans la perspective de l'Unité linguistique esquimaude. In: Malaurie, Jean, and Jacques Rousseau, eds., Le Nouveau-Quebec. Paris, La Haye, 1964, 277–313.

Легта, Лейта, see 437.

280. LEMER, R.P. LOUIS, O.M.I. Dictionnaire Esquimau-Français-Anglais. Partie

Anglaise par Charles Bird (Northern Insect Survey, National Museum, Ottawa), Bathurst Inlet, 1951, #R31 at Archives Deschatelets. Ottawa, typescript, 113 pp., containing ca. 3000 items.
281. LEWIS, Rev. ARTHUR. The Life and Work of the Rev. E. J. Peck among the Eskimos. London, 1904, 349 pp.
282. L'HELGOUAC'H, R.P. JEAN, O.M.I., and R.P. MAURICE MÉTAYER, O.M.I. Angadjutitka (Roman Catholic Missal and Hymn Book). Toronto, 1953.
283. LOMACK, MARY ANN. Acsialriit (Berrypickers). Eskimo Language Workshop, University of Alaska, 19 pp., 1971. Ill. Ida Jacomet.
284. LONNEUX, MARTIN J., S.J., et al. Mass Book and Hymnal in Innuit/Missarchutit Kalikat. Chaneliak, Hamilton P.O., Alaska, 1950, 129 pp.
285. ——. The Graded Catechism in Innuit. Chaneliak, Hamilton P.O., Alaska, 1951, 292 pp.
286. ——. Catholic Manual of Prayers in Innuit. Chaneliak, n.p. (Chaneliak?), n.d. (ca. 1950), 107 pp.
287. LOUNSBURY, FLOYD. Review of Geoghegan (168). Word 2.165–167, 1946.

LYNGE, KRISTOFFER, see 107.

288. MACGREGOR, RODERICK. Lexique Français-Esquimau. Direction Generale du Nouveau-Quebec, Ministère de Richesses naturelles. Forthcoming.
289. MACMILLAN, DONALD BAXTER. Eskimo Place Names and Aid to Conversation. Washington, Hydrographic Office, U.S. Navy, 1943, 154 pp.
290. MACPHERSON, ANDREW. Arviligjuarmiut Names for Birds and Mammals. Arctic Circular 12.2, 1958, 4 pp.
291. ——. Names for Birds and Mammals from the Interior Barrens. Arctic Circular 12.4, 1959, 6 pp.

MAKIK, see 599.

292. MALLON, S. T. Some Problems in the Teaching of Eskimo as a Second Language. Paper read at the Conference on Eskimo Linguistics. Chicago, 5–7 June, 1970.
293. MANSFIELD, A. W. Aivit/Walrus. Fisheries Research Board of Canada. Montreal, 1960, 51 pp. (syllabics and English).
294. MARSH, GORDON H. A Grammatical Analysis of the Noun Structure of Eastern Aleut. Ph.D. Dissertation. Columbia University, 1956, 206 pp.
295. ——. Aleut grammatical and lexical materials. Unpublished.
296. ——. Aleut texts of Jochelson. Typescript.
297. ——, and WILLIAM S. LAUGHLIN. Human Anatomical Knowledge among the Aleutian Islanders. SJA 12.38–78, 1956.
298. ——, and MORRIS SWADESH. Kleinschmidt Centennial V: Eskimo-Aleut Correspondences. IJAL 17.209–16, 1951.

MARSH, GORDON H., see also INNOCENT.

299. МАРШАК, С. Двенадцать месяцев. Пьеса-сказка. М., Исскуство, 1950, 115 стр., bilingual.

300. Материалы I. Всероссийской конференции по развитию языков и письменности народов Севера. М.-Л., 1932.
301. MATHER, ELSIE. Qessanquq Avelengaq (The Lazy Mouse). Eskimo Language Workshop, University of Alaska, 1971, 18 pp. Ill. Andrew Chikoyak.
302. MATTINA, ANTHONY. Phonology of Alaskan Eskimo, Kuskokwim Dialect. IJAL 36.38–45, 1970.
303. Меновщиков, Георгий Алексеевич. Ун'ипаг'атыт/Эскимосские сказки. Записаны и переведены Г. А. Меновщиковым. Л., изд-во Главсевморпути, 1939, 80 (4) стр., ill., под ред. К. С. Сергеевой.
304. —— (translator). Попова, Н. С. К'ырн'ухл'ыга арифметикам задачан'ита ама упражнениен'ыта/Сборник арифметических задач и упражнений, для нач. школы, утв. НКП РФСФР, для I класса, пер. с 7-го изд. на эскимос. языке пер. Г. А. Меновщикова. Л., Учпедгиз, 1939, 136 стр., see 457, 531.
305. ——. Русско-эскимосский словарь. Приложение к Первой книге по русскому языку для школ народов Крайнего Севера, Д. Б. Эльконина. На эскимосский язык перевел Г. А. Меновщиков. Л., Учпедгиз, 1946, 44 стр.
306. ——. Ун'ипаг'атыпут (эскимосыг'мит ун'ипаг'атылг'утан'ит)/Наши сказки (сборник эскимосских сказок). Составил и перевел на русский язык Г. А. Меновшиков. Л., Учпедгиз, 1947, рис. И. В. Вальтер, trl., для эск. школы, 228 стр., bilingual.
307. ——. Учебник эскимосыстун улюн'истун/Учебник эскимосского языка, для 1 класса. Л., Учпедгиз, 1947, 176 стр., ill.
308. ——. Учебник эскимосыстун улюн'истун/Учебник эскимосского языка, пер. с эскимос. Л., Учпедгиз, 1947 (В помощь учителю эскимос. школы) [ч. 1], Грамматика, правописание, развитие речи, для 1 класса, 63 стр.
309. ——. Программа по эскимосскому языку для эскимосской начальной школы (приложением грамматических таблиц). Составил Г. А. Меновщиков, Утв. министерством просверщения РСФСР. Л., Учпедгиз, 1948, see 324.
310. ——. Учебник эскимосыстун улюн'истун/Учебник эскимосского языка, для 2 класса. Л., Учпедгиз, 1949, 204 стр.
311. ——. Перевод учебника эскимосского языка, для 2 класса. Л., Учпедгиз, 1949, 111 стр. (В помощь учителю эскимос. нач. школы.)
312. ——. Новые материалы по эскимосскому и чукотскому языку. (Сообщение об экспедиции на Чукотку в 1948 г.). Изв. АН СССР, ОЛЯ, 1949, т. VIII, вып. 6, стр. 570–2.
313. ——. О роли агглютинации в оформлении слов языка азиатских эскимосов. (В кн. Научная сессия молодых ученых, посвященная памяти Н. Я. Марра. Тезисы докладов). М.-Л., 1949, стр. 12–3.
314. ——. Агглютинация и основные конструкции простого предложения в эскимосском языке. Изв. АН СССР, ОЛЯ, 1949, т. VIII, вып. 4, стр. 355–68.
315. ——. Эскимосско-русский словарь к текстам и список словообразователь-

ных суффиксов. Приложение к кн. В. Г. Богораз, Материалы по языку азиатских эскимосов, стр. 179–220, see also 100.

316. ——. Таблицы склонения имен и спряжения глаголов в современном языке азиатских эскимосов (чаплинский диалект). Приложение к кн. В. Г. Богораз, Материалы по языку азиатских эскимосов, стр. 221–51, see also 100.

317. ——. Склонение в эскимосском языке. Рукопись кандидатской диссертации, ЛО ИЯ АН СССР, 1950.

318. ——. Склонение в эскимосском языке. Автореферат канд. дис. Л., 1950, 15 стр.

318a. ——. Чукотские, эскимосские, корякские сказки. Хабаровск, 1950, 155 стр.

319. ——. Сказки Севера. В обработке Г. А. Меновщикова. Л.-М., Учпедгиз, 1951, 92 стр., ill., see 329, 345.

320. ——. Учебник эскимосского языка, для подготовит. класса. Л., Учпедгиз, 1951, 116 стр.

321. ——. Перевод учебника эскимосского языка, для подготов. класса эскимосской начальной школы. Л., Учпедгиз, 1951, 40 стр. (В помощь учителю эск. нач. школы.)

322. ——. Об устойчивости грамматического строя и основного словарного фонда эскимосского языка. (По материалам эскимосских диалектов). Сб. Вопросы теории и истории языка в свете трудов И. В. Сталина по языкознанию. М., 1952, стр. 430–60.

323. ——. (в соавторстве с Н. М. Терещенко и В. Д. Колесников). О русских заимствованиях в языках народов Севера. Тезисы докладов на Совещании по языкам народов Севера. М.-Л., 1952.

324. ——. Сведения по некоторым разделам грамматики эскимосского языка. (См. Приложение к Программе по эскимосскому языку для эскимосской начальной школы. М.-Л., Учпедгиз, 1953, стр. 57–120), see 309.

325. ——. Учебник эскимосского языка, для 1 класса. М.-Л., Учпедгиз, 1952, 152 стр.

326. ——. Перевод учебника эскимосского языка, для первого класса эскимос. нач. школы. Л.-М., Учпедгиз, 1952, 72 стр.

327. ——. Учебник эскимосского языка, для 2 класса. Л.-М., Учпедгиз, 1952, 119 стр.

328. ——. Перевод учебника эскимосского языка, для 2 класса эскимос. начал. школы. Л.-М., Учпедгиз, 1952, 64 стр.

329. ——. Сказки Севера. В обработке Г. А. Меновщикова. М.-Л., Детгиз, 1953, 79 стр., ill., see 319, 345.

330. ——. Эскимосско-русский словарь. С кратким указателем суффиксов и очерком грамматики эскимосского языка. Л., Учпедгиз, 1954, 320 стр., 4,700 words.

331. ——. О некоторых структурных особенностях эскимосского языка.

Ученые Записки ЛГПИ им. А. И. Герцена, т. 101, ф-т народов Севера. Л., 1954, стр. 255–80.

332. ——. Указательные местоимения в эскимосском языке. ВЯ, 1955, № 1, стр. 26–41.

333. ——. Звуковой состав эскимосского языка. (Рукопись Инст. языкозн. АН СССР, в работе установленнию фонем эскимосского языка непосредственное участие принимал Л. Р. Зиндер), 1956.

334. ——. Русские заимствования в языке эскимосов Аляски (рецензия на работу Л. Хаммериха). ВЯ, 1956, № 2, стр. 124–6.

335. ——. Из истории образования числительных в эскимосском языке. ВЯ, 1956, № 4, стр. 60–71.

336. ——. Эскимосы. Народы Севера. АН СССР. М.–Л., 1956 (translated by Charles C. Hughes, The Eskimo. Anthropological Papers of the University of Alaska, 12.1–13, 1964).

337. ——. Эскимосский язык. БСЭ, 2 изд., т. 49, 1957, стр. 180.

338. ——. Алеутский язык (статья). Бюллетень БСЭ, 1957.

339. ——. Учебник эскимосыг'мит улюн'истун/Учебник эскимосского языка, для подготовительного класса, [изд. 2, переработ.]. Л., Учпедгиз, 1957, 100 стр.

340. ——. Перевод учебника эскимосского языка для подготовительного класса эскимосской начальной школы: грамматика, правописание развитие речи, издание второе, переработ. Л., Учпедгиз, 1957, 32 стр. (В помощь учителю эскимос. нач. школы.)

341. ——. Учебник эскимосского языка, для 1 класса, [изд. 2, переработ.]. Л., Учпедгиз, 1957, 111 стр.

342. ——. Перевод учебника эскимосского языка, для первого класса начальной школы, 2-е изд., испр., и переработ. Л., Учпедгиз, 1957, 50 стр. (В помощь учителю эскимос. нач. школы.)

343. ——. Учебник эскимосского языка, для 2 класса, [изд. 2, переработ.]. Л., Учпедгиз, 1957, 109 стр.

344. ——. Перевод Учебника эскимосского языка, для второго класса эскимосской начальной школы, изд. 2, переработ. Л., Учпедгиз, 1957, 54 стр. (В помощь учителю эскимос. нач. школы.)

345. ——. Сказки Севера. Сборник сост. Г. А. Меновщиков. Л., Учпедгиз, 1958, 122 стр., see 319, 329.

346. ——. Эскимосские сказки. (Запись, перевод, предисловие и примечание Г. А. Меновщикова). Магадан, 1958, 180 стр.

347. ——. Review of Thibert (594). ВЯ, 1958, № 1, стр. 164–5.

348. ——. Имена обладания в эскимосском языке. Доклады и сообщения Ин-та языкознания АН СССР, вып. XI, 1958, стр. 86–94.

349. ——. Русско-эскимосский постатейный словарь. Приложение к Книге для чтения в первом классе начальной школы народов Севера, А. Ф. Бойцовой,

Л. А. Варковицкой, Л. А. Вобловой. На эскимосский язык перевел Г. А. Меновщиков, при участии Куяпы. Л., Учпедгиз, 1959, 36 pp., see 104.

350. ———. Зарубежные эскимосы. Альманах На севере дальнем, 1.162–76. Магадан, 1959.

351. ———. Эскимосы. (Научно-популярный историко-этнографический очерк об азиатских Эскимосов). Магадан, 1959.

352. ———. Сказки народов Севера. Составление, редакция, предисловие и примечания М. Г. Воскобойникова и Г. А. Меновщикова. Л., Гозлитиздат. 1959. (Переводы сказок 28 народностей Севера с примечаниями и словарем терминов), 627 стр.

353. ———. Эскимосско-алеутские параллели. Ученые записи ЛГПИ им. Герцена, том 167, кафедра языков народов Крайнего Севера. Л., 1959, стр. 170–91.

354. ———. Эскимосско-алеутские языки. Сб. Младописьменные языки народов СССР. М.–Л., 1959, стр. 300–17.

355. ———. Эскимосский язык. Фонетика, лексика, морфология. Учеб. пособие для пед. училищ. Л., Учпедгиз, 1960, 374 стр.

356. ———. О категории переходности и залога в эскимосском языке. Сб. Вопросы грамматики, изд-во АН СССР, 1960, стр. 81–102.

357. ———. Моносемия суффиксов в эскимосском языке. Понятие агглютинации и агглютинативного типа языков. Л., 1961, стр. 44–6, see 368.

358. ———. О пережиточных явлениях родовой организации у азиатских эскимосов. Советская этнография, № 6, 1962.

359. ———. Язык сиреникских эскимосов. ВЯ, 1962, № 3, стр. 107–14.

360. ———. Грамматика языка азпатских эскимосов. Фонетика и морфология именных частей речи, ч. I. М.–Л., 1962, 300 стр. (ч. II. М.–Л., 1967, 321).

361. ———. Wissen, religiose Vorstellungen und Riten der asiatischen Eskimos. In: Glaubenswelt und Folklore der sibirischen Völker. Budapest, 1963.

362. ———. Палеоазиатские топонимы северо-восточно Сибири. ВЯ, 1963, № 6, 117–25.

363. ———. Устное народное творчество азиатскии эскимосов как историко-этнографический источник, УП МКАЭН. М., 1964.

364. ———. Язык сиреникских эскимосов. М.–Л., 1964, 220 pp.

365. ———. Эргативная конструкция предложения в эскимосско-алеутских языках. Тезисы докладов на конференции: Эргативная конструкция предложения в языках различных типов. Л., 1964.

366. ———. О влиянии русского языка на развитие эскимосской лексики. Сб. Вопросы развития литературных языков народов СССР. Алма-Ата, 1964, 333–8.

367. ———. К вопросу о проницаемости грамматического строя языка. ВЯ, 1964, № 5, 100–6.

368. ———. Моносемия суффиксов в эскимосском языке. Сб. Морфологическая

типология и проблема классификации языков. М.–Л., 1965, 198–204, see 357.
369. ——. Язык эскимосов Берингова пролива. Сб. Языки и фольклор народов Сибирского Севера. М.–Л., 1965, 69–83.
370. ——. Новые данные о языке алеутов Командорских островов. Изв. Сиб. отд. АН СССР. Серия общественных наук, вып. I, № 1, 1965.
371. ——. Грамматика языка азиатских эскимосов, ч. I и II. Автореферат докторской диссертации. Изд. ИЯ АН СССР. М., 1965.
372. ——. О топонимической работе в районах Северо-Восточной Сибири. Тезисы докладов Всесоюзной конференции по топонимике ВГО. Л., 1965.
373. ——. Грамматика языка азиатских эскимосов, ч. II. М.–Л., 1967, 288 стр.
374. ——. Об основых конструкциях в эскимосско-алеутских языках. Эргативная конструкция предложения в языках различных типов, 1967, 261–8. Translated as: Les constructions fondamentales de la proposition dans les langages esquimau-aléoutes (en liaison avec la construction ergative. Langages 15.127–33, 1969.
375. ——. Эскимосско-алеутская группа. Язык народов СССР V, под ред. П. Я. Скорик, изд. Наука. Л., 1968, 352–406. (Введение, 352–65; Эскимосский язык, 366–85; Алеутский язык, 386–406).
376. ——. Popular Conceptions, Religious Beliefs and Rites of the Asiatic Eskimos. Popular Beliefs and Folklore Tradition in Siberia. Budapest, 1968.
377. ——. Этимологии названий месяцев у азиатских эскимосов. Доклады отделений и комиссий, ВГО СССР, вып. 5. Л., 1968.
378. ——. Об изучении топонимики в районах Северо-восточной Сибири. Записки Чукотского Краеведческого музея. Магадан, 1968.
379. ——. Оронимы Чукотского полуострова. Сб. Ономастика. М., 1969.
380. ——. О некоторых социальных аспектах эволюции языка. Сб. Вопросы социальной лингвистики. Л., 1969.
381. ——. О лингвистических контактах на Крайнем Северо-Востоке Сибири. Сб. Происхождение аборигенов Сибири и их языков. Томск, 1969.
382. ——. К вопросу топонимических исследований на Северо-Востоке Сибири. Материалы конференции: Этногенез народов Сибири. Новосибирск, 1969.
383. ——. Эскимосские сказки и легенды. Магадан, 1969.
384. ——. Способы выражения единичности и множественности в языках различного типа. ВЯ, 1970, 1.82–8.
385. ——. Некоторые типы языковых контактов у аборигенов крайнего северо-востока сибири. Советская социологическая ассоцияция советский оргкомитет по подготовке VII международного социологического конгресса (Варна, Болгария). М., 1970, 11 pp.
386. ——. Язык науканских эскимосов (монографическое исследование грамматического строя, тексты, словарь), рукопись. ИЯ АН СССР, 1970.
387. ——. Словарь Науканских Эскимосов, рукопись.

388. ——. Материалы по Имакликскому диалекту, тетр. АНГ № 3, дополнение 4, лист 3, рукопись ЛО ИЯ АН СССР.
389. ——. Падежи и типы склонения в эскимосско-алеутских языках. Тезисы докладов на конференции: Склонение в палеоазиатских и самодийских языках. ЛО ИЯ АН СССР. Л., 1970.

Меновщиков, Г. А., see also 487, 608.

390. —— и Касыга. Русско-юитский словарь. К учебнику русского языка для II класса юитской (эскимосской) школы Г. П. Васильева. Перевод Меновщикова, Г. А. и Касыги, Л. Учпедгиз, 1938, 27 стр.
391. —— и Г. Уйгах'пак (translators). Тихон Захарович Семушкин. Талько ынкам льн'ам якун'илн'ук' к'икмик' Лилит/Талько и его храбый Лилит. Учпедгиз, 1948, 67 стр., ill., bilingual.
392. —— и В. С. Храковский. Каузативные конструкции в эскимосском языке. ВЯ, № 4, 1970.
393. Мещанинов, И. И. Притяжательное склонение в унанганском (алеутском) и абхазском языках. Язык и мышление, т. IX, 1940, стр. 15–28.
394. ——. Эргативной строй предложения. Проб. сравит. филол. 273.19–25, 1964.
395. Métayer, R.P. Maurice, O.M.I. Dictionnaire Esquimau-Français. Aklavik, 1953, #R3 at Archives Deschatelets. Ottawa, typescript, 158 pp., containing ca. 7000 items. On last page: NB. il reste encore 118 pages consacrées aux 'infixes' de la langue Esquimaude.

Métayer, see also 282.

396. Mey, Jacob. Review of Schneider (510). AmA 70.833, 1968.
397. ——. On the Notion 'To Be' in Eskimo. FL, Supplementary Series 6.1–34, 1968. (John M. Verhaar, ed., The Verb 'Be' and its Synonyms 2.)
398. ——. The Eskimo Transitive Verb: A Reappraisal. Read at the 1968 Winter Meeting of the Linguistic Society of America, 30 December, 1968 (earlier version of Possessive and Transitive in Eskimo).
399. ——. Possessive and Transitive in Eskimo. JL 6.47–56, 1969.
400. ——. The Analysis of Reference in Eskimo and the Computer. Festskrift Carl Hj. Borgstrøm. Oslo, 1969, 97–110.
401. ——. Reflexives in Eskimo. Abstract and handout, 68th Annual Meeting of the American Anthropological Association, November 1969, New Orleans. IJAL 37.1–5, 1971.
402. ——. The Cyclic Character of Eskimo Reflexivization. AL 13.1–31, 1970.
403. ——. Comparatives in Eskimo. Abstract and handout, Conference on Eskimo Linguistics, Chicago, June 5–7, 1970, to be published.
404. ——. The Syntax of the Eskimo Verbal Constructions (in preparation).

Mey, Jacob, see also 110.

405. Миллер, Б. Ф. Об эскимосских наречиях Анадырского округа. (На осно-

вании материалов, собранных Н. Л. Гондатти). Живая старина, вып II, год 7-й. СПб., 1897, стр. 133–59.

406. ———. Материалы по наречиям инородцев Анадырского округа, собранны Н. Л. Гондатти. Живая Старина, вып. II, год 7-й. СПб., 1897, стр. 218–29.

407. MILLER, D. GARY. Present Tense Formations in Eskimo. Papers from the Seminar in American Indian Linguistics, Vol. IV. Department of Linguistics, Harvard University, 1970, mimeographed (earlier version of 408).

408. ———. Reconstruction in the Eskimo-Aleut Verbal System (Part I: Origin of the Verbal Suffix -wu-/-wa- in Eastern Eskimo; Part II: History of the Present, Perfect, and Imperfect Tenses in Eastern Aleut). University of Illinois, 1970, unpublished mimeograph, 35 pp., read in part at the Conference on Eskimo Linguistics, Chicago, 5–7 June, 1970, Tokyo.

MITIARJUK, see 501.

409. MIYAOKA, OSAHITO. A Perspective of Eskimo Linguistics (in Japanese). Minzokugakū-Kenkyū 26.96–9, 1961.

410. ———. A Comparative Study of Eskimo Dialects: Consonant System. M.A. Thesis. Kyoto University, 1963.

411. ———. On Eskimo and Aleut Metathesis. Paper read at the First Conference of Students of Northern Languages (Hoppo-gengo Kenkyusha Kyogikai). Hokkaido University, 4–6 September, 1965 (preliminary version of 412).

412. ———. Metathesis in Eskimo. Jinmon-Kenkyu 31.97–125. Otaru University, 1966.

413. ———. Two Obsolete Suffixes in Eskimo. Jinmon-Kenkyu 33.99–117. Otaru University, 1967 (see 414).

414. ———. Suffixes in Bodily Terms of Eskimo. Paper read at the 56th Conference of the Linguistic Society of Japan. Tokyo University, 1967, resumé in GK 52 (see 413).

415. ———. Vowel Lengthening in Western Eskimo. Hoppo Bunka Kenkyu (Bulletin of the Institute for the Study of North Eurasian Cultures) 4.157–68. Hokkaido University, 1970.

416. ———. A Linguistic Survey of the Alaskan Eskimos: An Interim Report. Paper read at the 9th Annual Meeting of the Ethnological Society of Japan, May 1970, published in Minzokugakū-Kenkyū 35.307–08, 1971, Tokyo.

417. ———. A Few Problems in Yuk Phonology. Handout, paper read at the Conference on Eskimo Linguistics, Chicago, 5–7 June, 1970 (see 419).

418. ———. On Syllable Modification and Quantity in Yuk Phonology. IJAL 37,219–26, 1971.

419. ———. Word-Initial Differentiation in Western Eskimo. Otaru University, 1970, 23 pp. typescript (revised version of 418).

420. ———, et al. Yupik Eskimo Classroom Grammar (preliminary edition). University of Alaska, 1969–1970.

421. Молл, Т. А. Букварь. Первая книга по рус. яз. для подготовит. класса эскимос. школы. Л., Учпедгиз, 1954, 120 стр.
422. ———. Букварь. Первая книга по русскому яз. для подготовит. класса эскимос. школы, изд. 2, испр. и доп. Л., Учпедгиз, 1959, 125 стр.
423. Naaqsugnarqellriit. Eskimo Language Workshop, University of Alaska, College, 1969–: 1.1 November 1969, 18 pp., 1.2 February 1970, 32 pp., 1.3 September 1970, 1.4 June 1971, 20 pp., Paschal Afcan, editor.

NASHOALOOK, A., see 571.

424. New Testament (Baffin Land Eskimo). British and Foreign Bible Society, 1962 (reprint of 1927 edition, in syllabics), 922 pp.
425. NICK, MARIE. Cetugpak (Long-Nails). Eskimo Language Workshop, University of Alaska, 1971, 22 pp. Ill. Andrew Chikoyak.
426. ——— (translator). Ciukam Yupiim Qalangssaa (The Story of Papik, an Eskimo Boy, see 112). Eskimo Language Workshop, University of Alaska, forthcoming.
427–428. ——— (translator). Kavirelit Kalikanka (Jean Forshaug, My Red Book, ill. Arne Randall). Eskimo Language Workshop, University of Alaska, 1972, 26 pp.
429. ———(translator). Neqa Piitam Pitaqesciigatellra (The Fish That Pete Could Not Catch, by students at Mekoryuk). Eskimo Language Workshop, University of Alaska, 1972, 61 pp.
430. ——— (translator). Waniwa Cing'aq (Sylvia Fulton and Kathleen Breckman, Here's Jack, DIAND, Ottawa, 1962). Eskimo Language Workshop, University of Alaska, 1972, 25 pp. Ill. Geri Keim.

NICK, MARIE. See also 249, 110, 11.

431. NIELSEN, FREDERIK. Kalâdtlisut ilíniutit/Undervisning i Grønlandsk. Det Grønlandske Forlag, Godthåb, Hefte I, 1957, 1961, 1965, 30 pp.; Hefte II, 1959, 1965.

NIELSEN, FREDERIK, see also 107.

432. Nuna, Inuinain Makperaksan (Magazine for Eskimos). Cambridge Bay, NWT, Our Lady of the Arctic Mission, 1960–, quarterly, ed. M. Lemer.
433. NUNGAK, ZEBEDEE, and EUGENE ARIMA. Unikkaatuat sanaurngaik atyingualiit Puvirngiturngmit/Eskimo Stories from Pavungnituk Quebec. Bulletin No. 235. National Museum of Canada, Anthropological series No. 90, 196?, vii + 139 pp.

НЫНЛЮВАК, see АМКАУН.

OLSEN, CARL CHRISTIAN, see 500.

434. Оненко, С. Н. Роль родного языка в условиях двуязычиния. Языки и фольклор народов Сибирского Севера. АН СССР. М.–Л., 1966, стр. 27–40.
435. OOZEVA, ELINOR, and DAVID SHINEN (translators). Kiyaḫtałha Jesus Christ-m (The Life of Jesus Christ in Yupik Eskimo, St. Lawrence Island, Alaska). Bibelmission Dr. Kurt Koch, 7501 Berghausen, Germany, 1970, 91 pp.

ÒPARTOK, see 596.

436. Орлова, Елизавета Порфирьевна. К вопросу создания письменности у народов Севера. Советский Севера, 1932, № 4.103–6.

437. ——, А. Бучков, и Б. Легта. Xwankuta ihaput/Наша книга. Первая эскимосск. книга сост. учащимися эскимосам Бучковым и Легта, под. руководством Е. Орловой. Л., Учпедгиз, 1932, 72 стр., ill. (Науч.-иссл. асс-ция народов Севера ЦИК'а СССР.)
438. Oswalt, Helen. Eskimo Vocabulary Study (Mountain Village and Hooper Bay Wordlists), typescript. University of Alaska, ca. 1951, 55 pp.
439. Pageau, Christiane, and Paulusi Uqittuq. Allagit Allaniarit/Ecris lis I–II (primer, two volumes). Direction générale du Nouveau Québec, Ministère des Richesses Naturelles, (I) 1966, 96 pp., 1967, 95 pp.; (II) 1966, 99 pp., 1969, 115 pp.
440. Peacock, Rev. Frederick W. English-Eskimo Dictionary. Nain, Labrador, 1953, 53 pp., and 1954, 50 pp., mimeographed.
441. ——. Labrador Eskimo Dictionary, in progress.
Peacock, F., see also 586.
442. Peck, Rev. Edmund J. A Dictionary of the Eskimo Language. Hamilton, 1925, 310 pp. (based on 138).
Peck, Rev. E.J., see also 101, 149, 281.
443. Peҟatigît Kalâtdlit (periodical of the Greenlandic Association in Denmark). Kjøbenhavn.
444. Petersen, Jonathan. Ordbogêraҟ. Nûngme, 1951, Ministeriet for Grønland, København, 1968.
445. Petersen, Robert. Oqausileríssutigssatut misiliut (On Phonetic Change). Atuarfît Ilagîtdlo 5, 1956.
446. ——. Det Grønlandske Sprog. Bogen om Grønland. Politikkens Forlag, ed. P. Barfod. Copenhagen, 1962, 1968, 1970.
447. ——. The Greenlandic Language. Greenland, Past and Present. Copenhagen, 1970.
448. ——. On Phonological Length in the Eastern Eskimo Dialects. Folk 11/12, 329–44, 1969/1970 (revised as 452).
449. ——. Stikprøver i fordeling af bogstaver og Stavelseslængder in Grønlandsk/ Agdlangnerit taineritdlo sivitsornerisa atorneκarnerinik migiliutit. Atuarfît Ilagîtdlo/Skole og kirke 17/8.1–9, 1970.
450. ——. Rapport: Retskrivningsprøver (report to the Committee on Orthography) 1970, 30 pp; mimeographed.
451. ——. Greenlandic in Contact with Danish. Grønland (forthcoming), in Danish.
452. ——. The Phonological Length as an Element of Expression in the Eastern Eskimo Dialects, abstract. Paper read at the Conference on Eskimo Linguistics, Chicago, 5–7 June, 1970.
453. ——. Noun and Verb in Greenlandic. Dissertation, University of Copenhagen, in preparation.
454. Petitot, R.P. Emile, O.M.I. Vocabulaire Français-Eskimo, dialecte des Tchiglit des Bouches du Mackenzie ... Paris, 1876.

455. PFIZMAIER, A. Die Sprache der Aleuten und Fuchsinseln. Sitzungsberichte, Phil.-Hist. Kl., Kais. Ak. der Wissenschaft, 105–6. Vienna, 1884.
456. PILLING, JAMES C. Bibliography of the Eskimo Language. Washington, 1887 (Bureau of American Ethnology), 112 pp.
457. Попова, Н. С. Сборник арифметических задач и упражнений, для нач. школы, утв. НКП РСФСР. Л., Учпедгиз, 1939, ч. 2, для 2 класса, 92 стр., Eskimo edition, see 304, 531.
458. PRESTON, W. D. Some Methodological Suggestions based on Aleut Linguistic Material. IJAL 13.171–4, 1947.
459. ——. Review of Schultz-Lorentzen (522). IJAL 14.271–4, 1948.
460. PRYDE, DUNCAN. Dictionary and Grammar of Copper Eskimo. Cambridge Bay, Bathurst Inlet, in preparation.
461. PYLE, CHARLES. West Greenlandic Eskimo and the representation of vowel length. Papers in Linguistics 3.112–44, 1971.
462. Q-Book/Qaujivaallirutissat (in English, standard Roman orthography and syllabics). Department of Northern Affairs and Natural Resources. Ottawa, 1964, 302 pp. (includes preface, 14–9, by Raymond C. Gagné).
463. RANSOM, JAY ELLIS. Writing as a Medium of Acculturation among the Aleut. SJA 1.333–44, 1945.
464. ——. Review of Geoghegan (168). IJAL 13.196–7, 1947.
465. ——. Aleut Linguistic Perspective. SJA 2.48–55, 1946.
466. ——. Aleut Linguistics and Anthropology, abstract. Paper presented at the 5th Alaskan Science Conference, September 7–10, 1954. Science in Alaska 1954. American Association for the Advancement of Science, Alaska Division, 1957, p. 118.
467. ——. The Aleut Language and Anthropology. Explorers Journal 44.163–8, 1966 (adapted from 466).
468. RASMUSSEN, CHRISTIAN. Grønlandsk Sproglære. Kjøbenhavn, 1888, reprint 1971, 201 pp.
469. ——. Supplement til Den Grønlandske Ordbog. Kjøbenhavn, 1893 (published together with 256).
RASMUSSEN, CHR., see also 256.
470. RASMUSSEN, KNUD. Alaskan Eskimo Words. Report of the Fifth Thule Expedition 1921–1924, Vol. III, No. 4. Copenhagen, 1941, 83 pp.
471. REED, E. IRENE. The Beginnings of Bilingual Education for Alaskan Eskimos. Paper read at the Conference on Eskimo Linguistics, Chicago, 5–7 June, 1970.
472. ——. Preliminary Yupik vocabulary: University of Alaska ditto, 1969, 60 pp.
REED, E. IRENE, see also 31, 420, 423.
473. ROSING, NIKOLAJ. Kalâdtlisut agdlangnek I. Godthåb, 1945, 1952, 66 pp.
474. ——. Sprogproblemet i Grønland og det grønlandske Sprog. Grønland, 1966, 2.55–60.
475. ROSING, OTTO. Samuel Kleinschmidt. Nûngme, 1949, 94 pp.

476. ——. Kleinschmidt Centennial II: Samuel Petrus Kleinschmidt. IJAL 17.63–5, 1951.
477. ROUSSELIÈRE, R.P. MARY, O.M.I. Review of Schneider (510). Arctic 20.273–4, 1967.
478. Рубцова, Е. С. Русско-эскимосский словарь для эскимосской начальной школы. В переводе слов на эскимосский язык принимали участие Ачиргин, Какля, Касыга, Татак. Л., Учпедгиз, 1941, 131 стр. (6000 сл.).
479. ——. Хуан'кута акузилъых'пут/Наша речь. Книга для чтения, для 2 класса. Л., Учпедгиз, 1948, 200 стр., ill.
480. ——. Наша речь. Пер. книга для чтения для 2 класса эскимос. школы. Л., Учпедгиз, 1948, 120 стр. (В помощь учителю эскимос. школы.)
481. ——. Перевод книги для чтения, в первом классе эскимосской начальной школы. Л.-М., Учпедгиз, 1950, 88 стр. (В помощь учителю эскимос. нач. школы.)
482. ——. Материалы по языку и фольклору эскимосов (чаплинский диалект), ч. I. М.-Л., изд-во АН СССР, 1954, 556 стр. (ч. II forthcoming).
483. ——. Перевод книги для чтения, в первом классе эскимосской начальной школы. Л., Учпедгиз, 1955, 66 стр. (В помощь учителю эскимос. нач. школы.)
484. ——. Хуан'кута алых'к'улъых'пут/Наша речь. Книга для чтения для 2 класса. В работе над книгой принимала участие Л. Айнана. Л., Учпедгиз, 1956, 130 стр.
485. ——. Наша речь. Перевод книги чтения для 2 класса эскимос. школы. Л., Учпедгиз, 1956, 72 стр. (В помощь учителю эскимос. нач. школы.)
486. ——. К вопросу о наречиях в эскимосском языке. Языка и фольклор народов Сибирского Севера, 116–27, изд. Наука. М.-Л., 1966.
487. ——. Эскимосско-русский словарь. Рукопись ЛО ИЯ АН СССР, in preparation, ed. Г. А. Меновщиков.
488. ——, Аяхта, и С. М. Гухуге. Букварь, для подготовит. класса эскимос. школы. Л., Учпедгиз, 1947, 116 стр., ill.
489. ——, ——, и ——. Букварь, для подготовит. класса эскимос. школы, пер. с эскимос. Л., Учпедгиз, 1947, 39 стр. (В помощь учителю эскимос. школы.) [Translation, teacher's manual for 488.]
490. ——, Анальквасак, Уйгахпак, и Каля (translators). Н. Н. Никитин, Г. Б. Поляк и Л. Н. Володина. Сборник арифметических задач и упражнений, изд. 5. М., Учпедгиз, 1949, 157 стр., Eskimo edition.
491. ——, В. Анальквасак, и Танута. Хуан'кута акузилъых'пут/Наша речь. Книга для чтения в 1 классе. Л.-М., Учпедгиз, 1950, 203 стр.
492. ——, Анальвасак, Уйгахпак, и Каля (translators). Н. Н. Никитин, et al. Сборник арифметических задач и упражнений, изд. 7. М., Учпедгиз, 1951, для 2 класса, Eskimo edition.
493. ——, и С. М. Гухуге. Букварь юпигыт улюн'истун аюк'ылг'и подготови-

тельнимун классимун пиюхаг'ми игаг'вигим/Букварь для подготовительного класса эскимосской начальной школы. Второе переработанное издание. М.-Л., Учпедгиз, 1953, 133 стр.

494. ——, и ——. Букварь для подготовительного класса эскимосской начальной школы, пер. с эскимос. яз. 2-е переработ. изд. М.–Л., Учпедгиз, 1954, 44 стр. [Translation, teacher's manual for 493.]

495. ——, АНАЛЬКВАСАК, УЙГАХПАК, и КАЛЯ (translators). Н. Н. НИКИТИН, et al. Сборник арифметических задач и упражнений, для 1 класса. Сухуми, Абгиз, 1954, 139 стр., Eskimo edition.

496. ——, и В. А. АНАЛЬКВАСАК. Хуан'кута акузилъых'пут/Наша речь. Книга для чтения в 1 классе. Л., Учпедгиз, 1955, 142 стр.

497. ——, и С. М. ГУХУГЕ. Букварь, для подготовит. класса, 3-е изд. Л., Учпедгиз, 1960, 129 стр.

498. ——, и ——. Букварь, для подготовит. класса [изд. 4]. М.–Л., Просвещение, 1965, 127 стр., Разрезная азбука.

РУБЦОВА, see also 1, 2, 3, 4, 253.

499. SABEAN, B. Outline of Eskimo Grammar, n.p. (Montreal?), n.d. (ca. 1950?), mimeographed.

SABEAN, B., see also 551.

500. SADOCK, JERROLD, and CARL CHRISTIAN OLSEN. Phonological Processes across Word Boundaries in West Greenlandic, handout. Paper read at the Conference on Eskimo Linguistics, Chicago, 5–7 June, 1970.

501. SALADIN D'ANGLURE, BERNARD. Sanaaq: Récit esquimau composé par Mitiarjuk (document ethnographique translittéré du syllabique et traduit littéralement). Thèse de Doctorat de Troisième Cycle, Cinquième Section, sous la direction de Madame E. Lot-Falck. Volume I (free translation, notes), forthcoming. Volume II (orthographical transliteration and interlinear translation). Paris, 1969, vii + 227 pp.

502. ——. Eskimo Writers in Syllabics (results of five years of ethnographic experience based on the encouragement of the Eskimos of New-Quebec to write about their own culture), handout. Paper read at the Conference on Eskimo Linguistics, Chicago, 5–7 June, 1970.

503. SAUVAGEOT, AURELIEN. Charactère ouraloïde du verbe eskimo. BSL 49.107–21, 1953.

504. SCHMITT, ALFRED. Untersuchungen zur Geschichte der Schrift: Eine Schriftentwicklung um 1900 in Alaska. Leipzig, 1940, 534 pp.

505. ——. Die Alaska-Schrift und ihre Schriftgeschichtliche Bedeutung. Marburg, 1951, 200 pp. and Abbildungsheft [16] pp. (Münstersche Forschungen, Heft 4).

506. ——. Der nominale Charakter des sogenannten Verbums der Eskimo-Sprache. Zeitschrift für vergleichende Sprachforschung 73, 1/2.27–45, 1955, Göttingen.

507. SCHNEIDER, R.P. LUCIEN, O.M.I. Bambo (exposé de la Doctrine Catholique avec Bambo). Issy-les-Moulineaux, Seine, 1958, 304 pp. (in syllabics).

508. ——. Catholic Prayer Book. Issy-les-Moulineaux, Seine, 1958, 304 pp. (in syllabics).
509. ——. Eskimo. Ft. Chimo, mimeographed periodical, from 1962, 35 issues, 354 pp. as of 1970 (in syllabics).
510. ——. Dictionnaire alphabético-syllabique du langage esquimau de l'Ungava et contrées limitrophes. Travaux et Documents du Centre d'Etudes nordiques, 3. Québec, Les Presses de l'Université Laval, 1966, 380 pp.; reviewed by Mey (396), Rousselière (477), (preliminary mimeographed edition 1953, 184 pp.) augmented second edition, forthcoming.
511. ——. Grammaire Eskimaude du sous-dialecte de l'Ungava. Direction générale du Nouveau-Québec, Ministère de Richesses naturelles, 1967, 149 pp. (first edition mimeographed, 1953, 42 pp.).
512. ——. Dictionnaire des infixes de l'Esquimau de l'Ungava. Direction générale du Nouveau-Québec, Ministère de Richesses naturelles, 1968, 150 pp. (first edition mimeographed, 1957, 71 pp.).
513. ——. Cours de Langue esquimaude. Dialecte de l'Ungava. Mimeographed, 1969, 146 pp.
514. ——. Mélanges de Linguistique esquimaude I. Mimeographed, 1970, 16 pp.
515. ——. Dictionnaire Français-Esquimau du Langage esquimau de l'Ungava et Contrées limitrophes. Travaux et documents du Centre d'Etudes nordiques 5, Université Laval, Québec, 1970, 421 pp.
516. SCHULTZE, AUGUSTUS. A Brief Grammar and Vocabulary of the Eskimo Language of Northwestern Alaska. Bethlehem, Pa., 1889, 21 pp.
517. ——. Grammar and Vocabulary of the Eskimo Language. Bethlehem, Pa., 1894, 70 pp.
518. SCHULTZ-LORENTZEN, C. W. Kalâtdlit oĸausînik oĸausileríssutit. Nûngme, 1904, 1929 (see 521, 522).
519. ——. Den Grønlandske Ordbog. Kjøbenhavn, 1926, 1964, 360 pp.
520. ——. Dictionary of the West Greenland Eskimo Language (Meddelelser om Grønland, 59). Copenhagen, 1927, 1964, 303 pp.
521. ——. Det Grønlandske Sprog i grammatisk Fremstilling. København, 1930, 1951, 100 pp. (see 518, 522).
522. ——. A Grammar of the West Greenland Eskimo Language (Meddelelser om Grønland, 129.3). Copenhagen, 1945, 103 pp. Reviewed by Preston (459). (First version in Greenlandic 1904, reprinted 1929, Danish version 1930; see 518, 521.)
523. ——. Undervisning i Grønlandsk. 1. Hefte. København, 1939, 1952 (reprint), 44 pp.
524. СЕРГЕЕВА, КАТЕРИНА СЕМЕНОВНА. Igaq Atehturjahqaq/Книга для чтения, ч. I для класса начальной школы. При сост. этой книги использованы: Книга для чтения, ч. I, П. Н. Жулева. В работе над настоящей книгой помогал Амкаун Нынлювак, сост. под ред. А. С. Форштейна, 1935, 95 стр., ill.

525. ——. Книга для чтения, пер. с эскимос. яз. А. С. Форштейна. М.–Л., Учпедгиз, 1935, 24 стр. (Метод. пособие. В помощь учителю эскимос. школы), ч. I.
526. —— (translator). Чарушин, Е. И. Puqłaŋłagьm nunaŋan treikusi/Животные жарких стран [для детей] пер. К. С. Сергеева и Амкаун Нынлювака под ред. А. С. Форштейна. Л., Детгиз, 1935, 12 стр., color illustr., in Eskimo.
527. —— (translator). Якобсон, А. Ajvan Jugwi/Люди Севера. (Рассказ для детей) пер. К. С. Сергеева при участии Амкаун Нынлювака, под ред. А. С. Форштейна. Л., Детгиз, 1935, 24 стр.
528. ——. В уреликском нацсовете. Советский Севера, 1935, № 1.95–101.
529. ——. Книга Атехтур'ьяхк'ак'/Книга для чтения, ч. 1, для первого класса юитской (эскимосской) начальной школы, в работе над этой книгой помогали Ашкамакын и Таю. Л., Учпедгиз, 1937, 112 стр., (revision of 524 in Cyrillic).
530. ——. Букварь на юитском (эскимосском) языке. Л., Учпедгиз, 1937 (listed only in 100, p. 253; perhaps to be identified with 529).
531. —— (translator). Попова, Н. С. Учебник арифметики для начальной школы. Перевод К. С. Сергеевой. Л., Учпедгиз, 1937, see also 304, 457.
532. —— (translator). Маршак, С. Я. Школым илякул'хит/Школьные товарищи (стихи для младш. возраста). Нарисувк'ат А. Пахомовым, Мумихтыка К. Сергеевам. М.–Л., Детиздат, 1938, 24 стр., in Eskimo only.
533. ——. Ухпык'игатанка алигналг'ит/Не верю шаманам. Рассказы и сказки, разоблачающие обманы шаманов. Сборник сост. и пер. К. Сергеевой, рис. Королева. Л., Главсевморпут, 1939, 60 стр., ill., bilingual.
534. ——. Сказочник Кивагме. Магадан, 1962.
Сергеева, Катерина Семеновна, see also 248, 252, 303.
535. Service Book of the Western Eskimo (New and Enlarged Edition). Society for Promoting Christian Knowledge. London, 1949, 365 pp.
536. Shade, Charles E. Ethnological Notes on the Aleuts. B.A. Thesis, Harvard University, 1949, at Peabody Museum Library, Harvard.
537. ——. Aleut Vocabulary. Nikolski, 1948, ms. at Peabody Museum Library (ref. N. A. Ling. Sh 12e, case book 2), partly in hand of Afenogin Ermeloff, cyrillic.
538. Shimkin, Dmitri B. Review of Bergsland (76). AmA 62.729–30, 1960.
539. Shinen, David. Notes on St. Lawrence Island Yupik Phonology. Alaskan Science Conference 12, College, August 28–September 1, 1961, Science in Alaska, American Association for the Advancement of Science, Alaska Division, 1962, 13–14.
540. ——. Some Notes on the Sound System of St. Lawrence Island Yupik. Ca. 1965, 10 pp. ditto.
541. ——, and Marilene Shinen. Yopigum Atiḫtoosi (A Beginning Reading Book in Yupik Eskimo). Summer Institute of Linguistics. Gambell, Alaska, 1966, 28 pp.

542. SHINEN, MARILENE R., and DAVID C. SHINEN. Yopiguston Momiḥḳoḳat Ilagaatut (hymnal). Fairbanks, 1969, 56 pp.

SHINEN, DAVID C., see also 435.

543. SILVERSTEIN, MICHAEL. On the Typology of Eskimo Ergativity. Abstract and handout, paper read at the Conference on Eskimo Linguistics, Chicago, 5–7 June, 1970.

SIḲUPSIĠAḲ, see HARVEY, PAULINE.

SIMMONS, S., see 111, 631.

544. Скорик, П. Я. О роли родного и русского языков в культурном развитии малых народностей Севера. Вопросы развития литературных языков народов СССР. Алма-Ата, 1964, стр. 313–23.

545. Совещание по языкам народов Севера. Тезисы докладов. (Brochure). М.–Л., 1952.

546. SPALDING, ALEC E. An Orthography for the Canadian Eskimo Language. Northern Affairs Bulletin 6.22–6, 1959.

547. ———. A Grammar of the East and West Coasts of Hudson Bay. Northern Administration Branch, Department of Northern Affairs and Natural Resources. Ottawa, 1960, 178 pp.

548. ———. No Frigate Like a Book. North 9.17–20, 1962.

549. ———. Salliq: An Eskimo Grammar. Education Branch, Department of Indian Affairs and Northern Development. Ottawa, 1969, 128 pp.

550. SPERRY, Archdeacon JOHN (translator). New Testament (Coppermine District dialect). Forthcoming, 1972.

551. STEINMANN, Rev., and B. SABEAN. Possessive Declension and Verb Conjugation in Eskimo, n.p. (Montreal?), n.d. (ca. 1950?), typescript.

552. Суник, О. П. Совещание по языкам народностей Севера. ВЯ 1953, № 2.132–9.

553. SWADESH, MORRIS. South Greenlandic (Eskimo). In: H. Hoijer et al., eds. Linguistic Structures of Native America. VFPA 6.30–54, 1946; reviewed by Hockett (206), restated by Harris (193), Hill (202).

554. ———. South Greenlandic Paradigms. IJAL 14.29–36, 1948.

555. ———. Kleinschmidt Centennial III: Unaaliq and Proto-Eskimo. IJAL 17.66–70, 1951.

556. ———. Unaaliq and Proto-Eskimo II: Phonemes and Morphophonemes. IJAL 18.25–34, 1952.

557. ———. Unaaliq and Proto-Eskimo III: Synchronic Notes. IJAL 18.69–76, 1952.

558. ———. Unaaliq and Proto-Eskimo IV: Diachronic Notes. IJAL 18.166–71, 1952.

559. ———. Unaaliq and Proto-Eskimo V: Comparative Vocabulary. IJAL 18.241–56, 1952.

560. ———. Lexicostatistical Dating of Prehistoric Ethnic Contacts. PAPS 96.453–63, 1952.

561. ———, G. I. QUIMBY, H. B. COLLINS, E. W. HAURY, G. F. EKHOLM, and F. EGGAN.

Symposium on: Time Depths of American Linguistic Groupings. AmA 56.361–377, 1954.
562. ——. Review of Thibert (94). Word 11.350–2, 1955.
563. ——. Some New Glottochronological Dates for Amerindian Linguistic Groups. PICAm 32.671–4. Copenhagen, 1958.
564. ——. Mapas de clasificación lingüística de México y de las Américas. Cuadernos del Instituto de Historia, Serie Antropológica, No. 8. University of Mexico, 1959.
565. ——. Tras la huella lingüística de la historia. Suplementos del Seminario de problemas scientíficos y filosóficos, Núm. 26, segunda serie, 1960, 97–145.
566. ——. Afinidades de las lenguas amerindias. PICAm 34.729–38, 1962.
567. ——. Review of Bergsland (76). Lg 38.101–3, 1962.
568. ——. Linguistic Relations across Bering Strait. AmA 64.1262–91, 1962.
569. ——. Лингвистические связи Америки и Евразии. Этимология, 1965, p. 271–322.
570. ——. The Relation of Wakashan to Eskimo-Aleutian and Chukchian. Eleventh Pacific Science Congress. Tokyo, 1966.
SWADESH, MORRIS, see also 298.
571. TAGAROOK, PETER, and ALVA NASHOALOOK (translators). Kamanaktuat Savaaŋi Jesus. Ed. R. Ahmaogak. Wycliffe Bible Translators, ca. 1962, 26 pp.
ТАНУТА, see 491.
ТАТАК, see 253, 254, 478.
572. TAYLOR, ALLAN R. Spanish 'manteca' in Alaska. RomPh 16.30–2, 1962.
ТАЮ, see 529.
573. TEELUK, MARTHA. A Personal Reaction to Eskimo Linguistics Research. Handout, paper read at the Conference on Eskimo Linguistics, Chicago, 5–7 June, 1970.
574. ——. Caarkat Goldilocksaamek (Workbook for Goldilocks, 13). Eskimo Language Workshop, University of Alaska, forthcoming, 35 pp.
575. ——. Caarkat Upsankunek (Workbook for Upsankut, 20). Eskimo Language Workshop, University of Alaska, 1971, 21 pp.
576. ——. Igareyarat (Writing). Eskimo Language Workshop, University of Alaska, 1971, 70 pp.
577. —— (translator). Inupiat Ayuquciat (Eskimos' Way of Living, by children at Chesterfield Inlet, NWT, 1959). Eskimo Language Workshop, University of Alaska, 1971, 46 pp.
578. ——. Kaviarem Kavirillra (How the Fox Became Red). Eskimo Language Workshop, University of Alaska, 1971, 12 pp. Ill. Edward Hofseth.
579. ——. Kuk'uq. Eskimo Language Workshop, University of Alaska, forthcoming, Ill. Ida Jacomet.
580. —— (translator). Kumlucekaq (Andersen-Tenggren, Thumbelina). Eskimo Language Workshop, University of Alaska, 1971, 32 pp. Ill. Diane S. Dart.

581. ——. Nuk'ankut (Nukaq and his Family, preprimer). Eskimo Language Workshop, University of Alaska, 1971, 1972, 23 pp. Ill. Andrew Chikoyak.
582. ——. Qangqiyaaq, Tulukaruq, Angeyayagaq-llu (The Ptarmigan, the Crow, and the Shrew). Eskimo Language Workshop, University of Alaska, 1971, 14 pp. Ill. Diane S. Dart.
583. —— (translator). Wiinguuq (It's Me!, Dorothy Napoleon, Sincerely Yours, Wheenuk, ill. D. Napoleon). Eskimo Language Workshop, University of Alaska, forthcoming, 16 pp.
584. ——. Wii Makut Pikanka (These Belong to Me, human anatomy). Eskimo Language Workshop, University of Alaska, 1971, 95 pp. Ill. John Angaiak and Paschal Afcan. dittoed.
585. ——, and MARIE NICK BLANCHETT. Nuk'aq Pre-primer I., Eskimo Language Workshop, University of Alaska, 1971, 1972, 13 pp. Ill. Paschal Afcan and Andrew Chikoyak.

TEELUK, MARTHA, see also 32, 420, 423, 652.

586. Testamentitak tamadja nalegapta piulijipta Jêsusib Kristusib Apostelingitalo piuiarningit ajokertusingallo (Labrador New Testament, revision by Peacock and Perrett). British and Foreign Bible Society. London 1952, 490 pp.
587. THALBITZER, WILLIAM. Et Manuskript av Rasmus Rask. Oversigt over det kgl. Danske Vidensk. Selskabs Forhandl. 3.211–49, 1916.
588. ——. The Aleutian Language Compared with Greenlandic. IJAL 2.40–57, 1921.
589. ——. The Ammassalik Eskimo (Meddelelser om Grønland, 39, 40), Copenhagen, 1914, 1923.
590. ——. Uhlenbeck's Eskimo-Indoeuropean Hypothesis. TCLC 1.66–96, 1944.
591. ——. Possible Early Contacts between Eskimo and Old World Languages. PICAm 29/3.50–4, 1952.
592. ——. Bibliografi 1900–1953 (Meddelelser om Grønland 140.1). Copenhagen, 1954, 28 pp.
593. ——, L. L. HAMMERICH, E. HOLTVED, and K. BERGSLAND. Eskimo-Aleut Phonetic Notation. IJAL 18.112–3, 1952.
594. THIBERT, R.P., ARTHUR, O.M.I. English-Eskimo–Eskimo-English Dictionary. Ottawa, 1954, 184 pp.; reviewed by Swadesh (562), Menovščikov (347).
595. ——. Dictionnaire Français-Esquimau et Esquimau-Français. Centre de Recherches d'Anthropologie Amérindienne. University of Ottawa, 1955, 200 pp.
596. —— (translator). Le Journal quotidien d'un Esquimau de l'Ile de Southampton 1926-1927. Anthropologica 1.49–98, 1955 (syllabic original ms. by Tommy Bruce or Òpartok, in Oblate Archives, Ottawa).
597. ——. Ayokertuserk (Catéchisme en Images). Ottawa, 1956, 128 pp. (in syllabics).
598. ——. English-Eskimo, Eskimo-English Dictionary (revised edition). Research Centre for Amerindian Anthropology, University of Ottawa. Ottawa, 1958, 173 pp., reprinted.
599. —— (translator). Journal de l'Esquimau Makik, Southampton Island, 1925–

1931. Anthropologica, n.s. 2.190–211, 3.95–110, 1960, 1961 (syllabic original ms., by Makik, in Oblate Archives, Ottawa).
600. THORNING, GÁBA. Kalâdtlisut oκausilerinermik ilitsersûtit. Ministeriet før Grønland, 1966, 24 pp.
601. TIFFANY, WARREN. Stories in String. Bureau of Indian Affairs, Branch of Education. Juneau, 1959, 50 pp.
602. Toosahyuuauk Eneupanune/Message to the Eskimos. Alaska Teaching Committee, National Spiritual Assembly of the Baha'is of the United States. Anchorage, Alaska, 1954, 24 pp.
603. TOPP, ALBERT. Relation om Grønlændernes Brugelige Sprog. Ms., 1727, in preparation for publication. Oslo.
604. TOYUKAK, MARY. Qanqiirenkuk Iggiayuli-llu (The Ptarmigan and the Owl). Eskimo Language Workshop, University of Alaska, 1972, 10 pp. Ill. Diane S. Dart.
605. TURQUETIL, Mgr. S. E., O.M.I. Grammaire Esquimaude. Composée en 1928, 2nd edition, mimeographed, 245 Rue Bloomfield, Outremont, P.Q., 1938, 89 pp. (50 copies), #R21 at Archives Deschatelets, Ottawa.
606. Tusautit (Community Newspaper). Eskimo Point, NWT, –1970 Mark Kalluak, ed. (in syllabics).
607. Tusarqvik/The Listening Post. Produced monthly by the Baffin Region Adult Education Office, Department of Indian Affairs and Northern Development. Frobisher Bay, 1969–, ed. Elijah Erkloo, 1971 Joanassie Salomonie (syllabics and English).
608. Творчество народов дальнего Севера. Магадан, 1958, 203 стр.
609. UHLENBECK, C. C. Necrology by K. Bouda, L. L. Hammerich, and W. Thalbiter. IJAL 19.74–7, 1953.

Уйг'ах'пак, Г. И., see 391, 490, 492, 495.
610. Указатель литературы, изданной на языках народов Севера в 1931–1933 гг. Л., Изд. ИНС'а, 1934, 25 стр.
611. Указатель литературы, изданной на языках народов Севера в 1931–1934 гг. Л., Изд. ИНС'а, 1935, 31 стр.
612. Указатель учебно-методической литературы для школ народов Крайнего Севера за 1945–1950 гг. Л.–М., 1951, 48 стр.
613. ULVING, TOR. Consonant Gradation in Eskimo. IJAL 19.45–52, 1953.
614. ——. Two Eskimo Etymologies. Studia Linguistica 8.16–33, 1954, Lund.
615. UNDERHILL, ROBERT. Morphophonemics of the Noun in Greenlandic. Abstract and handout, paper read at the Winter Meeting of the American Anthropological Association. Washington, November 30, 1967.
616. ——. The Absolutive and Relative in Eskimo. Abstract and handout, paper read at the Summer Meeting of the Linguistic Society of America. Urbana, 1968.
617. ——. Greenlandic Morphophonemics. Handout, paper read at the Conference on Eskimo Linguistics, Chicago, 5–7 June, 1970.

618. ——. Kleinschmidt's Grammar and Modern Linguistic Theory. 69th Annual Meeting of the American Anthropological Association. San Diego, 1970.

UQITTUQ, PAULUSI, see 439.

UYAKOQ, see 504, 505.

619. VAN DE VELDE, R.P., F., O.M.I. Lexique géographique de noms esquimaux de la carte de Pelly-Bay et environs, 1959, #R23 at Archives Deschatelets, Ottawa, typescript, 97 pp., exact information on and analysis of 662 place-names.

620. Вдовин, И. С. История изучения палеоазиатских языков. АН СССР, Инст. яз., изд. АН ССР. М.–Л., 1954, 166 стр.

621. ——. Общие сведения о создании письменности на языках народов Севера. АН СССР, инст. языкозн. Младописьменные языки, 1959, 284–99.

622. ——. Эскимосские элементы в культуре Чукчей и Коряков. АН СССР, инст. этн. Труды 64/3.27–63, 1961.

623. ——. Малые народности Севера на социалистическом пути развития за 50 лет советской власти. Сов. этнография, 1967, № 5.78–91.

624. ——, и Н. М. ТЕРЕЩЕНКО. Очерки истории изучения палеоазиатских и самодийских языков. АН СССР, инст. яз., серия: История отечественного языкознания, вып. 3-й. Л., Учпедгиз, 1959, 117 стр.

Вдовин, И. С., see also 100.

625. ВЕНИАМИНОВ, И. Е. Опыт грамматики алеутско-лисьевского языка. СПб., 1846, XV, 120 стр.

626. ——. Замечания о колошенском и кадьякском языках. Отчасти о прочих российско-американских, с присовокуплением российско-колошенского словаря, содержащего более 1000 слов, из коих на некоторые сделаны пояснения. СПб., 1846, 81, 11 стр.

627. ВЕСЕЛЕЦКИЙ, В. В., ed. Словари, изданные в СССР, библиографический указатель 1918–1962, изд. Наука. М., 1966 (Eskimo-Russian/Russian-Eskimo dictionaries listed on p. 189).

628. VIBÆK, PAUL. 100 Timer i Grønlandsk. Kjøbenhavn, 1900, 1917, 1952.

629. ВОБЛОВА, Л. А. Учебник русского языка. Для эскимос. школы, 2 класса. Л., Учпедгиз, 1961, 226 стр.

630. VOEGELIN, CARL F. Review of Hinz (203). IJAL 11.248–249, 1945.

631. WARTES, Rev. WILLIAM C., Rev. ROY AHMAOGAK, and SAMUEL SIMMONS. The Utkiaġvik Inupiat Hymn Book. Cuernavaca, 1959, [70] pp. (See also 111).

632. We Co-operate. Cooperative Union of Canada and Northern Administration Branch, Department of Indian Affairs and Northern Development. Ottawa, quarterly, 1967– (syllabics and English).

633. WEBSTER, D. H. A Tagmemic Analysis of the Barrow Eskimo Verb Complex. Alaskan Science Conference 12, College, August 28–September 1, 1961; Science in Alaska. American Association for the Advancement of Science, Alaska Division, 1962, 10–3.

634. ——. Iñupiat Taiguangich I–II (Adult Reader). Summer Institute of Linguistics, Fairbanks, ca. 1961, 10 + 17 pp., mimeographed.
635. ——. A Brief Introduction to Eskimo (Arctic Slope Dialect). Wainwright, Alaska, ca. 1962, 14 pp.
636. ——. Iḷisaaġviṇich Iñupiam (Adult Primer). Summer Institute of Linguistics. Santa Ana, ca. 1962, 24 pp.
637. ——. Ḳuliaḳtuaḳ Iñuusiagun Jesus (Life of Jesus). Summer Institute of Linguistics, ca. 1967, 16 pp.
638. ——. Let's Learn Eskimo. Summer Institute of Linguistics. Fairbanks, first edition 1967, 53 pp., revised edition 1968, vi + 66 pp.
639. ——. Can You Read English? Then You Can Read [Eskimo]. Summer Institute of Linguistics. Fairbanks, 1968, 60 pp.
640. ——. Ikaayutit (New Testament Helps). Wycliffe Bible Translators. Fairbanks, ca. 1968, [8] pp.
641. ——, and ROY AHMAOGAK (translators). Iñupiat New Testament (North Alaskan Eskimo and Today's English Version). American Bible Society. New York, 1966, 1503 pp.
642. ——, compiler and ed. Iñupiat Suuvat?/What About the Eskimo? Summer Institute of Linguistics. Fairbanks, 1968, 29 pp.
643. ——. Iñupiam Uḳaluṇi/Eskimo Reading Course I–II (revised edition of 38, with tapes). Summer Institute of Linguistics. Fairbanks, 1969, 8 + 68 pp.
644. ——, and WILFRIED ZIBELL. Iñupiat Dictionary. University of Alaska and Summer Institute of Linguistics. Fairbanks, 1970, 218 pp.
645. ——, and WILFRIED ZIBELL. Report of the Canadian Eskimo Language Survey, 1968. Summer Institute of Linguistics. Fairbanks, unpublished, 37 ill., read in part at the Conference on Eskimo Linguistics, Chicago, 5–7 June, 1970.

WEBSTER, DONALD H., see also 38, 39.

646. WELLS, ROGER, and JOHN W. KELLY. English-Eskimo and Eskimo-English Vocabularies. U.S. Bureau of Education. Washington D.C., 1890, 72 pp.
647. WHEELER, EVERETT PEPPERELL. List of Labrador Eskimo Place Names. NMC-B 131. Ottawa, 1953, 109 pp.

WORM, ELISABETH, see 41.

648. WORTH, DEAN STODDARD. Russian 'kniga', Southwestern Pomo 'kalikak'. IJAL 26.62–6, 1960.
649. ——. Russian and Alaskan Eskimo. IJSLP 7.72–9, 1963.
650. YARMOLINSKY, AVRAHM. Aleutian Manuscript Collection; a list of works relating to the Aleut language. Bulletin of the New York Public Library 48.678–80, 1944.
651. ——. Kamchadal and Asiatic Eskimo Manuscript Collections, a Recent Accession. Bulletin of the New York Public Library 51.659–69, 1947.
652. Yuarutet (Songs in Yupik Eskimo; composed or translated by Mary Ann

Lomack, Molly Lomack, Elsie Mather, Marie Nick, Sophie Parks, Martha Teeluk). Eskimo Language Workshop, University of Alaska, 1971, 5 pp., ill.
653. Yuarutit (Liturgy and Hymns in the Eskimo Language of the Kuskokwim District, Alaska). Society for Propagating the Gospel. Bethlehem, Pa., 1945, 190 pp.
654. ZAVATTI, SILVIO. Dizionarietto Italiano-Groenlandese. Istituto Geografico Polare. Bologna, 1964 (contains ca. 300 items), 22 pp.
655. ZIBELL, WILFRIED. Iñupiam Ukałhi (Eskimo Reader for the Kobuk River – Kotzebue Sound area). Summer Institute of Linguistics. Fairbanks, 1966 (trial edition), 1968, 41 pp.
656. ——. Jesus-ŋum Iñuułha (Life of Jesus). Summer Institute of Linguistics. Fairbanks, 1966, 16 pp.
657. ——. Atuutit Mumiksat (Hymnal). Fairbanks, 1967, (22) pp. [not to be identified with 233, of same title].
658. ——. Suŋŋuat (Eskimo Alphabet Coloring Book). Summer Institute of Linguistics. Fairbanks, 1969, [24] pp.
659. ——. Unipchaat: Animal Stories of the Kobuk River Eskimos 1, 2, 3. Summer Institute of Linguistics. Fairbanks, 1969, $1969^2$, 1970; 22, 26, 25 pp.
660. ——, and PAULINE HARVEY (translators). Thessalonians I–II. Summer Institute of Linguistics. Fairbanks, 1968, 28 pp.
661. ——, and —— (translators). Timothy I. Summer Institute of Linguistics. Fairbanks, 1968, 22 pp.
662. ——, and —— (translators). Timothy I–II, Thessalonians I–II, Titus. Evangelizationsverlag. Berghausen, Germany, 1971.
ZIBELL, W., see also 172, 644, 645.
663. Зиндер, Л. Р. Экспериментальное изучение фонетики северных языков. Изв. АН СССР, ОЛЯ т. VIII, 1948, вып. 6.
Зиндер, Л. Р., see also 333.
664. ZUK, WILLIAM M. Inuit pinnguarusingit (Eskimo Games, syllabic and Roman version). Department of Indian Affairs and Northern Development. Ottawa, 1967, 26 pp.

SUPPLEMENTARY BIBLIOGRAPHY

1.1 *Alaskan Aleut*

665. BERGSLAND, KNUT. A Problem of Transformation in Aleut. Word 25/3.24–38, 1969.
666. ——. Object and Reference in Aleut Syntax. Forthcoming.
667. HARRINGTON, JOHN P. Unalaska Aleutian Grammar. BAE ms. #4783, typescript, ca. 1949, 217 + 85 pp.

668. Иохельсон, В. И. Образцы материалов по Алеутской живой старине, собранных на Алеутских островах в експедиции Ф. П. Рябушинского. Петроград, 1916, 16 pp. (separate from: Живая старина XXIV, 1915, 293–308).
669. NETSVETOV, JAKOV. Russian-Aleut Dictionary. ms., Library of Congress.
670. RANSOM, JAY ELLIS. A Brief Grammar of Fox Island Aleut. University of Washington, M.A. Thesis, 1941.
671. Smithsonian Annual Report 1941–1942 (1943) p. 50.

### 1.2 *Commander Island and Kurile Aleut*

672. BABA, OSAMU. Chishima ni okeru Aryuuto-zoku (The Aleuts in the Kurile Islands) Minzokugaku Kenkyū (Journal of Ethnology) 8.773–794, 9.877–890 (1943). [English resumé by Miyaoka 1971.]
673. Барабаш-Никифоров (И. И.?). В стране ветров и туманов. М., 1934.
674. Вдовин, И. С. К вопросу о происхождении названия "алеут" страны и народы востока, вып. 8, 101–104. АН СССР географическое общество. СССР Восточная комиссия. Изд. "Наука". М., 1968.
675. Гурвич, Т. С. Алеуты командорских островов. Советская Этнография 5, 112–123, 1970.
676. Орлова, Е. П. У алеутов на командорских островах. Изв. Сибирского Отделения АН СССР. Сер. общесть наук, № 8, 3–10, 1962.
677. RADLIŃSKI, IGNACY. Słowniki narzeczy ludów Kamczackikh. Ze zbiorów Prof. B. Dybowskiego. Polska Akademja Umiejętności. Wydział Filologiczny. Rozprawy, Series II 1.53–119, 130–217, 2.103–124, 3.81–164, 1892; 7.149–229, 1895. Krakow.
678. Суворов, Е. К. Командорские острова и пучиной промысел на них. СПб., 1912, 98 стр.

### 2.12 *Siberian Yupik*

679. GURVICH, I.S., and L.A. FAINBERG. Reply to Hughes (680). CAnthr 6.59–60, 1964.
680. HUGHES, CHARLES C. Under Four Flags: Recent Culture Change Among the Eskimo. CAnthr 6.3–69, 1964.
681. Хромченко, Г. Открывки из журнала плавания Г. Хромченки, в 1822 году. Северный Архив 11. 254–276, 12. 303–314, 13/14. 38–64, 15. 119–131, 16. 177–186, 17. 235–248, 18. 297–312, 1824.
682. Меновщиков, Г. А. 30 лет Чукотского национального округа. Магадан, 1960.
683. ——. Топонимический Чукотского побережья. 1968. (В Меновщикове, 1971, стр. 116.)

684. ——. Эскимосский субстрат в топонимике Чукотского побережья. (Советская этнография? 1971, № ?, 116–120.
685. Орлова, Е. П. Азиатские Эскимосы. Известия всесоюзного географического общества 2., 1941.
686. Рубцова, Е. С. Сказки народов Северо-Востока. Магадан, 1956.
687. ——. Эскимосско-русский словарь. 17.000 слов, составила Е. С. Рубцова, под редакцией Г. А. Меновщикова, Ленинградское отделение института Языкознания АН СССР, издательство советская энциклопедия. М., 1971, 644 стр.
688. ——. Материалы по языку и фольклору Эскиимков, ч. 2, forthcoming.
689. Сергеев, М. А. Некапиталистический путь развития малых народов севера. М.-Л., 1955.
690. Sergeeva, K. S., Wbje Serejnegmi, and Amkagun Nbŋluvak (translators). N. S. Popova. Arifmetika Nutan Hatarjuhwałhanun Apьhturevigmun. Sivuleq Noŋehqełeq, Učpedgiz, L., 1935, 68 pp.
691. Сергеева, К. С. Учебник Арифметики. Часть первая. Контрперевод с Юитского (эскимоского) языка К. С. Сергеевой. Л., Учпедгиз, 1935, 20 стр.
692. ——. Школа в бухте провидения. Советский Север. 2, 54–59. М., 1935.
693. Советская Чукотка/Советкен Чукотка. Газета. Анадырь.
694. Суник, О. П. Некоторые проблемы языкого стройтельства в СССР. ВЯ 1971, № 6, 16–30.
695. Ulving, Tor. Observations on the Language of the Asiatic Eskimo as Presented in Soviet Linguistic Works. Linguistics 69/87–119, 1971.
696. Vdovin, I. S. Politique législative, économique, sociale, et culturelle de l'U.R.S.S. en faveur du développement des Esquimaux et des Tchouktches. Internord 11.113–122, 1970.
697. Zobarskas, Nola M., ed. Tundra Tales: Chukchi, Koryak, other Eskimos. Manyland Books, Woodlawn New York 1967, 17 pp., translation, unacknowledged as such, of 318a.

### 2.21 St. Lawrence Island Yupik

698. Badten, Adelinda (Aghnaghaghpik), and Michael E. Krauss. Ungazighmiit Ungipaghaatangit. Eskimo Language Workshop, University of Alaska. 1971, 85 pp.
699. ——, ——, and Dudley Hascall. Sivuqaghhmiit Atightullghit/Reading St. Lawrence Island Eskimo. Eskimo Language Workshop, University of Alaska, 1971, 47 pp.
700. Hascall, Dudley, Jang H. Koo and Adelinda Badten. Some Morphophonemics in St. Lawrence Island Eskimo. University of Alaska ms. 1971. 4 pp.

701. Koo, Jang H. The E-element and Its Related Morphophonemics in St. Lawrence Island Eskimo. University of Alaska ms. 1971, 2 pp.
702–703. Krauss, Michael E. St. Lawrence Island Eskimo Phonology. Paper presented at the 70th Annual Meeting of the American Anthropological Association, New York, 1971, with handout.

### 2.22 *Central Alaskan Yupik*

704. Afcan, Paschal (translator). Angnilria Asriq Issuriyagaq (Diane Dart, The Playful Little Seal. Kuskokwim version by Marie N. Blanchett). Eskimo Language Workshop, University of Alaska, 1973. Ill. by Geri Keim.
705. ——. Qanemcicuaraak Angalgaam: Avelngayagaq Kameksiigka-llu (Two Little Stories by Angalgaq: The Little Mouse and My Boots). Eskimo Language Workshop, University of Alaska, 1972. 21 pp. Ill. by Geri Keim.
706. ——, and Marie Nick (translators). Taqukaq Qanganaq-llu. (John Breiby, The Bear and the Squirrel), Eskimo Language Workshop, University of Alaska, 1971, 50 pp. Ill. by John Breiby.
707. ——, Irene Reed, and the Eskimo Language Workshop Staff. Cat Anerteqellriit: Unguvalriit Naunraat-llu (Living Things: Animals and Plants). Eskimo Language Workshop, University of Alaska, 1972. 39 pp. Ill. by Geri Rudolph.
708. ——, ——, ——. Cauciun Piniun-llu (Matter and Energy). Eskimo Language Workshop, University of Alaska, 1972. 40 pp. Ill. by Geri Rudolph.
709. ——, ——, ——. Ella Iquilnguq (The Universe). Eskimo Language Workshop, University of Alaska, 1972. 36 pp. Ill. by Geri Keim.
710. ——, ——, ——. Nunarpak (The Earth) Eskimo Language Workshop, University of Alaska, 1972. 48 pp. Ill. by Geri Rudolph.
711. ——, ——, ——. Yuum Temiin Elpeksuutai (The Senses Of the Human Body). Eskimo Language Workshop, University of Alaska, 1972. Ill. by Geri Keim.
712. ——, Steven Jacobson, Irene Reed, Martha Teeluk, and the Eskimo Language Workshop Staff. Yupik Dictionary, in preparation.
713. Blanchett, Marie Nick (translator). Caurluq (Geri Keim, 'Caurluq, a version of Cinderella'). Eskimo Language Workshop, University of Alaska, 1973. 60 pp. Ill. by Geri Keim.
714. ——. Kaukak Naucetaarpak-llu (Jack and the Beanstalk). Eskimo Language Workshop, University of Alaska, (forthcoming).
715. ——, and Martha Teeluk. Caliluta Aquiluta-llu Pre-primer II. Eskimo Language Workshop, University of Alaska 1972. 20 pp. Ill. by Paschal Afcan.
716. ——, and ——. Nuk'aq Ilai-llu Pre-primer III. Eskimo Language Workshop, University of Alaska, 1972, 21 pp. Ill. by Paschal Afcan.
717. Cacirkat. Eskimo Language Workshop, University of Alaska, 1971, 1972. 22 pp. Ill. by Geri Rudolph.

718. COOLIDGE, JOSEPH, Sr., and MARIE NICK (translators). Wangnek Tamalkurma (Virginia W. Jones and Joel Bartholet, All About Me) Alaska Rural School Project, University of Alaska [1971], 59 pp. Ill. by John Breiby.
719. HASCALL, DUDLEY. Yupik Eskimo Person Endings. University of Alaska typescript, 1971. 26 pp.
720. ——. Yupik /-lr-/, Past Marker. University of Alaska typescript, 1971, 3 pp.
721. ——. The Verbalizer 'to be' and the Third Person Intransitive verb Marker in Yupik Eskimo. University of Alaska typescript, 1971, 8 pp.
722. ——, LINDA BADTEN, JANG KOO, and IRENE REED. Classes of Eskimo Noun Bases. University of Alaska typescript, 1971, 16 pp.
723. Igaryaraq 1–2–3. Eskimo Language Workshop, University of Alaska (Mary Ann Lomack, Molly Lomack, Paschal Afcan, Marie Nick Blanchett, Andrew Chikoyak, Diane Dart, Martha Teeluk, Irene Reed) 1971, 20, 24, 26 pp.
724. KOO, JANG H. The Copulative 'u' in Yupik Eskimo and Crossover convention. IJAL 37.215–218, 1971.
725. ——. The intransitive marker t in Eskimo. Proceedings of the IXth International Congress of Anthropological and Ethnological Sciences, Chicago, 1973.
726. ——. Vowel Polarization and Third Person Possessed Endings in Eskimo. University of Alaska, typescript, 1971, 13 pp. Presented at the annual meeting of the International Linguistic Association, New York, 1972.
727. ——. Reinterpretation of r in Eskimo. ms. University of Alaska, 1971.
728. MIYAOKA, OSAHITO. A Grammatical Sketch of Yupik Eskimo. Otaru University, 1972, typescript, 78 pp. forthcoming, new Handbook of American Indian Languages.
729. Naaquteliuryarat Caliarkait I (Mary Ann Lomack, Molly Lomack, and Bernadine Featherly, Mathematics Worksheets) Eskimo Language Workshop, University of Alaska, 1971. 100 pp., Eskimo text by Marie N. Blanchett, Martha Teeluk, ed. Irene Reed, Ill. by Geri Rudolph.
730. NICK, MOSES. Iqalluaq Uksiloria (A Smelt in Winter), Eskimo Language Workshop, University of Alaska, (forthcoming).
731. ——. Qanganaq Meqsartulria. Eskimo Language Workshop, University of Alaska, 1972, 20 pp. Ill. Diane Dart.
732. ——, Taqukaq Ayalria (The Bear That Went on a Journey). Eskimo Language Workshop, University of Alaska, forthcoming.
733. ——, Tusairnar Ayalria. Eskimo Language Workshop, University of Alaska, forthcoming.
734. ——, Tuutangayak Ayalria (The Goose That Went on a Journey). Eskimo Language Workshop, University of Alaska, forthcoming.
735. TEELUK, MARTHA. Ilanka (My Family, primer) Eskimo Language Workshop, University of Alaska, 1972 23 pp. Ill. by Dorothy Napoleon.
736. ——. Tanegurraq Nervallalleq (The Boy Who Ate Too Much). Eskimo Language Workshop, University of Alaska, forthcoming. Ill. by Dorothy Napoleon.

737. ——, and MARIE N. BLANCHETT. Naaqiyugngaunga (I Can Read) Elementary Reader. Forthcoming.
738. ——, ——. Wangkuta Kalikaput (Our Book) Elementary Reader. Forthcoming.

## 2.23 *Pacific Yupik*

739. LEER, JEFFREY A. Notes on Sugcestun Phonology, Alaska Methodist University 1972, 4 pp., mimeographed.
740. ——. Stem-file for Sugcestun Aleut, Alaska Methodist University, 1972, 60 pp.
741. MIYAOKA, OSAHITO. An Eskimo Tribe Near Mount St. Elias, Alaska. Otaru University, typescript 1971, 19 pp.
742. TABIOS, DERENTY, and JEFF LEER, eds. Sugcestun Unigkuat: Paluwigmiut Nanwalegmiut-hlu Quli'anguahlrit. (Stories in the Sugcestun Language from the Villages of English Bay and Port Graham, coll. by Derenty Tabios and Seraphim Meganack). Division of Alaska Native Languages, Center for Northern Educational Research, University of Alaska, Fairbanks. Sept. 1972. 36 pp.
743. Тыжнов, Илья (translator). Отъ Матѳея святое благовѣствованіе. На Алеутско-Кадьякскій языкъ перевелъ И. Тыжнов. СПб. 1949, 217 pp.
744. ——. Алеутско-Кадьякскій Букварь. СПб., 1848, 52 pp.

## 2.24 *Alaskan Inuit*

745. CORRELL, THOMAS C. Review of Webster and Zibell, Iñupiat Eskimo Dictionary. IJAL 38.76–77, 1972.
746. [LAFORTUNE, BERNARD]. A Collection of Prayers, Hymns, and Instructions for the use of the Catholic Eskimos on the Seward Peninsula, Alaska. [n.p., Nome?], [n.d., ca. 1915]. 38 pp.
747. RAY, DOROTHY JEAN. Eskimo Placenames in Bering Strait and Vicinity. Names 19.1–33, 1971.
748. STROM, R.P. "Speedy". Say It in Eskimo: An Informal Phonetic Guide to Northern Alaska Eskimo Speech. Nome, 1965. 76 pp.
749. Tusaayugaat Miŋuaktuktuaniñ (Inupiat School Newspaper, Barrow Day School, edited by Marsha Aiken, Alice Hopson and Marilyn Gamboa, teachers), Dec. 22, 1971, May 15, 1972.
750. VOSS, JANICE (translator). Aakagivigiñ? (P.D. Eastman, Are You My Mother?). Barrow Day School, 1972. 57 pp.
751. WEBSTER, THELMA. Unipkaat (Coloring Book in Iñupiat). Summer Institute of Linguistics, Fairbanks, 196, 1971. 28 pp. Ill. by Thelma Webster.
752. ZIBELL, WILFRED. Aglaich (Alphabet Book). Summer Institute of Linguistics, Fairbanks, 1971. 32 pp.

753. ——. Iñupiat Noun Classes. Typescript, Noorvik, ca. 1970. 4 pp.

### 2.3 *Canada*

754. Arctic Star. Frobisher Bay, N.W.T. Community newspaper.
755. Ariviat Nipi. Eskimo Point, N.W.T. Community newspaper.
756. AYARUA, JEAN. L'Esquimau Jean Ayarua de Rankin Inlet écrit ses aventures (1915–1960). Trad. par Arthur Thibert, 1961, typescript. 35 pp.
757. BALMÈS, JOSEPH, O.M.I. (1874–1935) (translator) Grammaire de la langue Esquimaude... 373 [+1136] pp. 1934.
758. BULIARD, ROGER, O.M.I. Inukpian katolgit krinraotikasangitlu atutikeangitlu ... Montréal, Beauchemin, 1949. 366 pp.
759. CARRIÈRE, GASTON, O.M.I. Contributions des Oblats de Marie immaculée de langue française aux études de linguistique et d'ethnologie du nord canadien. Culture 12.213-226, 1951, Québec.
760. ——. Catalogue des manuscrits en langues indiennes conservés aux archives oblates, Ottawa. Anthropologica n.s. 12.151-179, 1970.
761. Manuscrits microfilmés conservés au Centre de Recherche en Anthropologie, Ottawa, typescript, 1970. 16 pp.
762. ——. Manuscrits en langues indiennes conservés sur microfilms aux archives historiques oblates, Ottawa, typescript. 10 pp.
763. COLLIS, DERMOT R. F. A Comparative vocabulary of Two Eastern Eskimo Dialects, Labrador-Ungava and West Greenlandic, Paris. ms. 1967–68.
764. CORRELL, THOMAS C. The Eskimo Verb: A Transformational Sketch of Obligatory Components. Paper prepared for the Annual Meeting of the Linguistic Circle of Manitoba and North Dakota, October 24, 1970. 22 pp., typescript.
765. ——. Dramatis Personae in the Eskimo Language: A Precis (paper read before the Annual Meeting of the Linguistic Circle of Manitoba and North Dakota, Nov. 15, 1968), published in Proceedings of the Linguistic Circle of Manitoba and North Dakota. 6 pp., mimeographed.
766. CROWE, KEITH J. Beginning Eskimo, First Steps Toward Learning the Language of the Canadian Eastern Arctic. DIAND, Ottawa, 1970. 15 pp.
767. ——. The Eskimo Language in Adult Education, Northern, 1969.
768. ——, and ELIJAH ERKLOO. Kunapamut Ilisarutitsaat/Introduction to Artic Cooperatives, Adult Education, Arctic District, DIAND, Ottawa 1968. 60 pp. (syllabics and English).
769. DORAIS, LOUIS-JACQUES. L'Acculturation lexicale chez les Esquimaux du Labrador. Languages 18.65-77, 1970.
770. DUCHARME, LIONEL, O.M.I. Tamaja piulijita yisusi-kritusi. Les quatre evangiles, Vicariat apostolique de la Baie d'Hudson, 1945. 442 pp. (syllabics).
771. ERKLOO, ELIJAH, JOANASSIE SALOMINIE, MARK KALLUAK (translators). Niqitsat

Inuusigingiqsamut/Foods for Health, DIAND. Ottawa, 1966. 24 pp. (syllabics and English).
772. FLINT, Rev. MAURICE. Pilgrim's Progress. (syllabics).
773. FORD, SAMUEL G., and CYRIL WINGNEK (translators). Book of Wisdom for Eskimo/Khaoyimayum Titiganigit Inuinnangmun. Department of Mines and Resources, Ottawa, 1947. 1949, 28+28+39 pp. (syllabics and English).
774. ——, and FREDERICK WOODROW (translators). Sanayaqsak/Eskimo (by James A. Houston). Canadian Handicraft Guild, Ottawa 1951. 30 pp. (syllabics).
775. HEINRICH, ALBERT. Some Borrowings from German into Eskimo. AnL 13. 96–99, 1971.
776. HOFMANN, T.R. Basic Guide for the Use of Syllabic Finals. Inuit Nipingit/Keewatin Echo (87), vi 1971, p. 5–6.
777. ——. Notes. Eskimo Language Course. University of Ottawa, 1971. 13 pp. mimeographed.
778. ——. Teaching the Eskimo Syllabics. University of Ottawa, 1970. 9 pp. mimeographed.
779. ——. Writing in the Eskimo Classroom. University of Ottawa, 1971. 7 pp. mimeographed, to appear in Cahiers linguistiques d'Ottawa.
780. Imianik. Cambridge Bay, N.W.T. Community newspaper.
781. Inuit Nipingit/Keewatin Echo, monthly, Adult Education Staff, Government of the N.W.T., Churchill, ed. Mark Kalluak, 1967–, syllabics and English.
782. Inuk Agnak Igagutik Aglait (Eskimo Woman's Cookbook) by Nurse Big Joe and Daisy Watt. Ft. Chimo, [1961]. 18 pp. (syllabics).
783. Inummarit. Igloolik, N.W.T., 1972– (roman and syllabics).
784. IRKROWAKTOK, BERNARD. Journal (Pelly Bay, syllabics, ms. 125 pp.), with Roman version and French translation by Franz Van de Velde O.M.I., 1958–1962, ms., and partial English and French translations by Arthur Thibert, O.M.I., 1967, ms., 53 pp.
785. Kano Inuktitauyuunangmangata Urraqsimayut Tuktu (How to Conserve Caribou). Northern Affairs and Natural Resources, Ottawa, [ca. 1960]. 16 pp. (syllabics).
786. Kanuinginilmik Uqaquk (Talking About Health). Northern Affairs and Natural Resources, Ottawa, 1957. 18 pp. (syllabics).
787. KERMAL, ALAIN, O.M.I. Grammaire esquimaude 1929–1930, ms. 238 pp.
788. Koglotomiut. Coppermine N.W.T., Community newspaper.
789. Kungo/Kanguk. La Federation des Cooperatives des Nouveau-Québec 1971–, 51, rue Bel Air, Lévis, Quebec (syllabics and English).
790. Kuup/Co-op. Northern Affairs and Natural Resources, Ottawa, 1959. 26 pp. (syllabics and English).
791. LEFEBVRE, G.R. Canadian Eskimo Orthography. Department of Northern Affairs and Natural Recources, Ottawa, 1958, 130 pp.

792. Litaraiit Liturgiillo Attoraksat illagêktunut. Labradoremêtunut Herrnhutime, 1913, Revised, Green Bay, Wisconsin, 1971. 277 pp.
793. MALLON, S.T. Eskimo Language Course. DIAND, Rankin Inlet, N.W.T., [n.d., ca. 1971].
794. ——. Notes on the Eskimo Phonological System. DIAND, Rankin Inlet N.W.T., 1971. 14 pp. mimeographed, syllabified by T.R. Hofmann.
795. Manuscrits Esquimaux, compositions d'enfants et contes. 280 pp.
796. MÉTAYER, MAURICE, O.M.I. Notes sur le dialecte de Pelly-Bay. ms.
797. ——. Collection de légends, contes, et fables en langue esquimaude. ms., n.d. [ca. 1953].
798. ——. Etude des infixes en esquimau. ms. [118 pp. cf. 395].
799. Nipisuilak/The Midnight Sun. Igloolik, N.W.T. Community Association 1968– (in English and syllabics).
800. Niqirsiat Inusirinatuq/Good Food for Good Health. Northern Affairs and Natural Resources, Ottawa, 1983. 13 pp. (syllabics and English).
801. ÒPARTOK (TOMMY BRUCE). Journal (Southampton Island, 1925–1927). ms., syllabics, 138 pp., (translated by A. Thibert, 596).
802. PAGEAU, CHRISTIANE, and PAULUSI UQITTUQ. Alaniakunga inutitu/Je lis comme les Esquimaux. Ministère de Richesses Naturelles, DGNQ, Wakeham, 1966. 119 pp. (syllabics).
803. ——, and ——. Alasiakunga Inutitu/J'écris comme les Esquimaux (Cahier d'exercises). Ministère de Richesses Naturelles, DGNQ, Wakeham. 99 pp. (syllabics).
804. ——, and ——. Allasiarlugit./Cahier d'exercises, complément des 1er et 2ième livres de lecture, Governement du Québec, Ministère de Richesses Naturelles, DGNQ Wakeham, 1967. 107 pp.
805. PAGEAU, SERGE. Lexique Français-Esquimau. Gouvernement du Québec, Ministère des Richesses Naturelles, DGNQ, 1970. 54 pp. (ca. 1200 items).
806. PEACOCK, Rev. FEDERICK W. Doctrine and Church Order. Happy Valley, 1969, mimeographed (revision of 1926 version).
807. ——. Erkaumajaksat 1972-imut. Kattangutigêt Labradorimêtut Aglaktangit Englisetortunit. Happy Valley, 1972. 36 pp.
808. ——. Eskimo Reader. Memorial University of Newfoundland, [1971 or 1972]. 32 pp.
809. ——. Illaget Moraviamiut Labradorimetut. Angijorornek Kristuseme. Aglait Kommunionetaksanut. Happy Valley, [ca. 1965]. 28 pp. mimeographed.
810. ——. The Labrador Church Book/Kattangutiget Illa Labradoremiut Malligaksangit. Happy Valley, 1969. 85 pp. (bilingual).
811. ——. Story of the Moravian Church in Labrador 1771–1971, St. John's, 1971 (in Eskimo).
812. SeκκInek, Uvleriallu TaκκerIo, 1942, mimeographed.
813. PEARCE, TERRY. Learning to Speak Eskimo. North 18.28–31, 1971.

814. PERRETT, Rev. WALTER WHATLEY (translator). Aglait Ilisimatiksat Inungnut Ilingnajut (George Binney, The Eskimo Book of Knowledge), Hudson's Bay Co., London, 1931, 237 pp. (bilingual).
815. ——. English translation of Bourquin (102). Happy Valley, 1966. 225 pp.
816. Pilagitsanatut/What You Should Know About Rabies. Department of National Health and Welfare, Ottawa, 1965. 31 pp. (syllabics and English).
817. Pillautauningit Uqartansimajut Taakkunaungat Qaujinasuttinit Gavamakkunik Inuit Naranganniittunut (Information proposals for Government of the Northwest Territories) Welfare Division, DIAND, Ottawa, 1966. 57 pp. (syllabics and Roman).
818. PITSEOLAK. Pictures of My Life. Ed. by Dorothy Harley Eber from tape-recorded interviews with Pitseolak. Design Collaborative Books, Montréal, Oxford University Press, Toronto. Eskimo text published by DIAND [1971], [95] pp. (syllabics and English).
819. Pond Inlet Newsweek. Pond Inlet, N.W.T. Community newspaper.
820. Puvadlungnaq Piyunaititauyunaktuk (T.B. Can be Prevented). Northern Affairs and Natural Resources, Ottawa, ca. 1960. 30 pp. (syllabics).
821. ROUSSELIÈRE, GUY MARY. Les jeux de ficelle des Arviligjuarmiut. Musées nationaux du Canada, Bulletin 233, Ottawa, 1969, 18 pp.
822. SALADIN D'ANGLURE, BERNARD. La toponomie littorale du Nouveau-Québec. Ministère des Richesses Naturelles, Québec, forthcoming.
823. Sananguaksimayut/Sculpture. A competitive exhibition of Eskimo sculpture organized by the Canadian Eskimo Arts Council as a contribution to the Centenial of the Northwest Territories, 1970. Canadian Eskimo Arts Council, Ottawa. 40 pp. (syllabics, English, and French).
824. THIBERT, ARTHUR, O.M.I., ed. Sennektailigiutit (Missel Dominical). Institut de Missiologie de l'Université d'Ottawa, 1955 (2nd editions, roman and syllabic), 296 pp.
825. TRINEL, ERNEST, O.M.I. Atii, parlez esquimau. Essai de grammaire esquimaude d'après le dialecte d'Ivujuvik, Nouveau-Quebec. Centre Canadien de Recherches en Anthropologie, Université Saint-Paul, Ottawa, 1970, xxi+206 pp.
826. Tukisinatut/Message. Newsletter produced for Arctic Québec, Adult Education Staff, Regional Headquarters, DIAND Québec, ed. Zebedee Nungak 1970– (in syllabics, English, and French).
827. Tukisiviksaat. DIAND, Yellowknife. ed. Peter Irniq 1971–.
828. Tuktut/Caribou. Northern Affairs and Natural Resources, Ottawa, 1957. (syllabics, Roman, and English).
829. Tuqsiutit. Ingerutillu, Qatoliq oqpisiakatigeqtut Atoraqsangit (Hymnal and Missal) Wakeham, 1950. Mimeograph, 204 pp. (syllabics and roman).
830. WHITBREAD, Rev. D. H. Additional Hymns and Choruses in Use at the Anglican Mission of the Good Shepherd, Spence Bay, N.W.T., 48 pp. syllabics.

## 2.4 Greenland

831. ANDERSEN, KARL PETER. Grønlandsk for Begyndere. København. 1970.
832. BERTELSON, ALFRED. Dansk-Grønlandsk Sproghjælp for Læger og Sygeplejersker. J. H. Schultz Universitets Bogtrykkeri, Kjøbenhavn, 1948.
833. BEYER, JOHN FREDERIC. Greenlandic-German Dictionary. ms., 1750, 163 pp. (at Moravian Archives, Bethlehem, Pennsylvania, listed in Pilling, 456).
834. COLLIS, D. R. F. Attività dell'istituto Eschimologico dell'Università di Copenhagen. Atti del 1 Congresso Internazionale Polare, Istituto Geografico Polare. Cittanova, Marche, 1971.
835. —. De grønlandske tilhæng (affikser og suffikser), Copenhagen 1968, ms.
836. ——. Semiotica Eschimese. Il Polo (Rivista del Istituto Geografico Polare) Macerata, 1971.
837. FANTIN, MARIO. Idioma Groenlandese (in Montagne di Groenlandia 353–367, Documenti d'esplorazione e d'Alpinismo) Bologna, 1969.
838. MASE, HIDEO, and JORGEN RISCHEL. A Study of Consonant Quantity in West Greenlandic. Annual Report of the Institute of Phonetics, University of Copenhagen 5.175–247, 1971.
839. MEY, JACOB. Is Reflexivization Always a Cyclical Process? Papers in Linguistics 2.90–109, 1970.
840. PETERSEN, H. C. Kalâtdlisut oĸausînik oĸausileríssutit imarĸarniliornerat (Grammar of Greenlandic Words and Word-formation). Knud Rasmussens Højskole. Holsteinsborg, 1967. 18 pp.
841. PETERSEN, KJELD THOR. [Grønlandsk Grammatik] in progress. Copenhagen.
842. PETERSEN, ROBERT. Nogle forudsætninger for sprog- og retskrivningsudvalgets forslag til en ny retskrivning på grønlandsk. 1972, 7 pp. mimeographed.
843. ——. Rapport: Læseprover i Grønlandsk, 1964. mimeographed.
844. ——. K' eller Q, k eller q. Atuagagdliutit/Grønlandsposten 1968, No. 19.
845. ——. Kommentarer til udtalelserne vedrørende retskrivningsforslaget. Tåstrup, 1972, 4 pp. mimeographed.
846. RISCHEL, JØRGEN. Some Characteristics of Noun Phrases in West Greenlandic. ALH 13.213–245.
847. ——. Grønlandsk Fonologi (notes for course). University of Copenhagen, 1971. typescript. 40 pp.
848. ——. Vowel Patterns of Greenlandic Eskimo. BCLC–ALH, forthcoming.
849. SOZZO, CIRO, and MARIO FANTIN. Manuale di Conversazione Italiano-Groenlandese. Bologna 1962.
850. THALBITZER, WILLIAM. Fra Grønlandsforskningens første dage. København 1932.

## 3. Comparative and General Studies

851. HAMMERICH, L.L. Eskimoisch. JanL, Series Critica, forthcoming
852. MILLER, D. GARY. A Justification of Historical Grammars: Evidence from Eskimo (Prince of Wales Dialect). University of Illinois, 1969. 80 pp. dittoed.
853. TIMBERLAKE, ALAN H. Eskimo Nominal Morphology. Papers from the Seminar in American Indian Linguistics. Harvard University, 1971.
854. UNDERHILL, ROBERT. Noun Bases in two Eskimo Dialects: A Study in Comparative Morphophonemics. Harvard University, 1971. 30 pp. typescript (revised version of 617).
855. ——. Remarks on Possessives (in Eskimo) Paper presented at the 46th Annual Meeting of the Linguistic Society of America, 1971.

This report reflects the state of Eskimo-Aleut studies in 1970 in what has remained a rapidly developing field. In a special sense, 1970 might well be considered an appropriate date for a report since it marked the end of an era of scholarship, one in which the speakers of the language were primarily objects of observation, and the dawn of a new era in which the active participation of native speakers has dramatically increased, not only in the field of language-study, but in all areas of academic, cultural, and educational activity.

# NA-DENE

### MICHAEL E. KRAUSS*

#### 0. INTRODUCTION

This report covers academic research activity on the Athapaskan, Eyak, Tlingit, and Haida languages since approximately 1945, though some of the more important work before 1945 may for various reasons also be mentioned. Coverage since 1945 is fairly complete, including most if not all of the significant unpublished as well as published work in this area, up to 1970, with some last minute addenda and corrigenda up through December 1971. Depth of coverage nevertheless varies considerably, e.g. significant psycholinguistic papers dealing with certain areas of Navajo lexicon, or editions of texts of Navajo ceremonials, or the entire New Testament in Apache, are not mentioned at all, whereas the possibility that J.P. Harrington may have gotten a few words of Nicola in 1940 is fully reported. The line has somehow been drawn to exclude that which is not systematically linguistic (includes ethnobotanical wordlists but excludes articles with many Indian technical terms occurring throughout running text; excludes translations of the Bible, even though these can be used, especially with the English Bible concordance, as convenient sources of primary data). Works on vigorous languages with many speakers and a relatively large literature, e.g. Navajo, are covered in less depth than those at the other extreme, e.g. Kwalhioqua-Tlatskanai or Eyak.

The author has himself been deeply involved since 1960 in work in this language group. He makes no claim to lack of bias, especially where his own conclusions are at odds with those of other researchers.

In 1969 the author sent form letters to a large number of personnel known to be active in linguistic work in this language group. He wishes to acknowledge the generally very cooperative response of all those who supplied information on their own and others' recent activities. This information has contributed very greatly to making possible a report as current and complete as it is hoped this may be.

---

* The research on which this report is based was carried out at the University of Alaska (Department of Linguistics) as part of a program supported by the National Science Foundation (Grants G-23994 and GS-733), and at the Massachusetts Institute of Technology (Research Laboratory of Electronics, Department of Linguistics) as part of a program supported by the National Institutes of Mental Health (Grant MH 13390-03). The author gratefully acknowledges this support. See also note on p. 358.

At the outset, the author wishes to lament the fact that there are practically no American Indians working in this American Indian linguistic field, just as there are very few American Indians working in any professional academic capacity connected with American Indians. This is bad for Indians and bad for linguistics. American Indian linguistics, as it still is, remains simply one facet of the nearly universal pattern of the exploitation of the American Indian. Many non-Indians have increased their earning power, social security and prestige, by writing a dissertation or publishing an article on an American Indian language or culture, but which in no way or to a far lesser extent has benefitted the Indians upon whose cooperation it fully depends, and whose culture and language are in fact the victims of unabated cultural genocide.

In some ways it is absurd, although it is written here, to write something to the effect that e.g. 'The X language is virtually unknown'. X is in fact very well known to the X Indians, but it is as if Western society cannot rest content until this wealth too has been taken from the Indians, until well-paid non-Indian professionals have acquired the language for 'science' (libraries and archives of academic and government institutions), while it becomes lost, through 'education' and 'assimilation', to the Indians themselves. The academic community takes few real pains to prevent this tragic injustice, rather only profits itself from the opportunity presented.

## 1. ATHAPASKAN[1]

The organization of this section into subdivisions is simply one of convenience, like the organization of this report as a whole, and is in no way meant to imply that the language areas treated in each subdivision are coordinate branches in any scheme of genetic relationship.

### 1.1 *Alaska*

Though the political state of Alaska of course has no meaning as a subdivision of Athapaskan, it does include the original American home of the Athapaskans and is the sector longest inhabited by Athapaskans. This history is clearly reflected in the fact that far greater variety and divergence in Athapaskan is found within Alaska than anywhere else. For instance, the divergence between Koyukon and Kutchin, neighbors in northern Alaska, is greater than that between e.g. Navajo and Sarsi, or Hupa and Chipewyan. In addition, many of the Alaskan Athapaskan languages are conservative in various unique ways, and thus preserve still more information on Proto-Athapaskan (PA) which is not available (though sometimes in existence in the form of difficult irregularities) outside Alaska. Therefore, from the compara-

---

[1] It is perhaps time to standardize the spelling of the term Athapaskan. This writer personally prefers and proposes adoption of the present spelling with p and k to 'Athabaskan, Athabascan, Athapascan', but also happens to pronounce it [æθibǽskin], with a b.

tive Athapaskan point of view (not to mention Eyak and Tlingit, also Alaskan), Alaska is by far the most interesting area. Far more about PA can be learned from a comparison of what is in Alaska than from what is elsewhere. Yet there is not in print a single grammar or even grammatical sketch of any consequence for any Alaskan Athapaskan language. It can, incredibly but accurately, be said that no linguist has ever done any fieldwork on any Alaskan Athapaskan language under the auspices of any university outside Alaska. A number of ethnologists have worked in Athapaskan Alaska, e.g. Cornelius Osgood from Yale, Robert McKennan from Dartmouth, Frederica de Laguna from Bryn Mawr, but their training and work has not been primarily linguistic. The only exception is E. Benveniste from Paris, who, as a result of a short stay for fieldwork in Kutchin, published a flora-fauna list entitled "Le vocabulaire de la vie animale chez les Indiens du Haut Yukon (Alaska)" (1953a).

The only other near-exception is the earlier work of Sapir, still unpublished, but of course important, especially in the development of Sapir's thinking about Athapaskan: Sapir worked with an Anvik Ingalik informant for a few hours in 1923 in Ottawa, and, under the same circumstances, got a rather good amount of material from John Fredson, a Ft. Yukon Kutchin, also in 1923. Sapir's Kutchin material was later worked on at Yale under Sapir by Mary Haas and still later at Berkeley by Victor Golla, who have prepared a manuscript stem list from this material. Sapir understood the phonology of Kutchin at least as well as any linguist has, but this is still not well. Kutchin has undergone very severe, almost complete, loss of stem-final obstruents, with resulting development of tone (early, from glottalization and gradation), diphthongization of stem-vowel which simplified with the development of a system of palatalization, in at least two waves, of stem-initial consonants (still the situation in Han, which might be regarded as a kind of 'medieval Kutchin'), and then mergers of certain of the resultingly multiplied series, but with certain differences in the mergers in the various dialects, and then, increasingly, dialect mixture. It should therefore not be surprising that even Sapir found Kutchin phonology extraordinarily difficult, and the Haas-Golla interpretation of Sapir's work, though very important, is not meant, of course, to be considered definitive. Additional Kutchin data from Ft. McPherson on the Canadian side have recently been collected by Michael Krauss, Marshall Durbin, Harry Hoijer, Geoffrey O'Grady, and John Ritter.

Sapir's Anvik material is much less extensive than his Kutchin, and the place of his Anvik work in Sapir's thought is discussed in the section on Comparative Athapaskan below.

Another effort on Ingalik from outside Alaska should be mentioned here, that based on his own earlier fieldwork by Cornelius Osgood, published in his *Ingalik material culture* (1940) and reprinted in *Ingalik mental culture* (1959), consisting mainly of a fairly extensive vocabulary as an appendix. Along with this should be mentioned Osgood's comparative vocabularies from six Tanaina subgroups appended to his *The ethnography of the Tanaina* (1937), especially because this too has served as an often misleading source for studies in comparative Athapaskan, and also for two derivative articles on Tanaina dialectology, Herbert Landar's "Tanaina subgroups" (1960a), and H.A. Gleason Jr.'s "A note on Tanaina subgroups" (1960). Osgood makes no claim to being a linguist, but his use of symbols such as $k'$ or $q$ has misled some linguists, like Pinnow, discussed below in the section on comparative Na-Dene, into taking Osgood's transcriptions too seriously as being consistent and observationally adequate transcriptions of the Athapaskan forms, which they most certainly are not. F. de Laguna, although not a linguist, has transcribed extensive Ahtena linguistic data in the course of her ethnographic work in the Upper River region.

All fieldwork by linguists on Alaskan Athapaskan since well before World War II (with the one minor exception of Benveniste from Paris) has been done exclusively either from the University of Alaska or the Summer Institute of Linguistics, which has a branch base in Fairbanks. If a large group of Indo-European languages were found, like Anatolian with 'laryngeals' still overt in some form and/or many other archaic and/or unexpected features, a large crowd of linguists would be expected to come flocking, even if these languages were in central Amazonia or Antarctica. It is to be hoped that more Athapaskanist linguists will do work in Alaska.

At the University of Alaska since 1960, Michael E. Krauss has conducted a field survey of Alaskan Athapaskan. He has collected data from over sixty Athapaskan checkpoints in the state, adequate for a reasonably complete mapping of the development of at least the surface stem-phonology of the whole area. He has more extensive information from certain points, especially Minto, but his Alaskan fieldwork has been essentially a phonological survey, and his publication on it entirely from a comparative-historical point of view. It has accordingly been discussed in greater detail in the historical-comparative sections below.

In 1956 Gordon Marsh, then of the University of Alaska, did fieldwork with the Han. Krauss and Nancy McRoy have since also collected significant Han material, and Mrs. McRoy further data on nearly extinct transitional Tanana dialects. Also, Krauss and Ruby Tansy have worked together on Miss Tansy's native Ahtena. And, under the University of Alaska program in 1961, Clark A. Davis collected some Tanaina data and Robert O.H. Peterson some Ahtena. None of these materials have been published.

The rest of the Alaska Athapaskan work has all been done by linguists of the Wycliffe Bible Translators/Summer Institute of Linguistics. Raymond and Sally Jo Collins have been in Nikolai since 1963, and have published, besides a primer, a noun dictionary entitled *Dinak'i* (1966, 74 pp.), of the Upper Kuskokwim language, which, though intended for popular use, is of very great benefit to the linguist. The Upper Kuskokwim language, spoken in an area Osgood (1940) erroneously assumed to be Ingalik, is not Ingalik (of the Anvik, Shageluk, Holy Cross, Middle Kuskokwim type) at all, but is mutually unintelligible with Ingalik, and much more closely related to Central Tanana (Minto-Nenana). This language, still spoken, incidentally, by the children at Nikolai, is perhaps, all told, phonologically the most conservative Athapaskan language extant. It preserves stem final glottalization and the $*q : *\underline{k}$ series contrast stem finally, lost there in Minto-Nenana, and preserves the $\underline{k}^w$-series distinct as $tr$, like Minto-Nenana. However, for all Nikolai speakers except optionally for the oldest, the PA $*c$ ($> t\theta$ or $t\underline{s}$) and $*\check{c}$ ($> ts$) series have fallen together as $ts$. The Collins dictionary does not record the archaic distinction.

David C. and Kay Henry of SIL have been with the Koyukon since 1959. In addition to primers, a reader and portions of Gospel in Koyukon, the Henrys have published a noun dictionary, like the Collins one mentioned above, entitled *Dinaak'a* (1969a, 81 pp.), and two significant articles: "Koyukon classificatory verbs" (1965), and "Koyukon locationals" (1969b), probably the only one of its kind in print of a very highly developed system within Koyukon; all other Alaskan Athapaskan languages also have a very elaborate system of locationals, and most of the rest probably do too, but the Henry article seems to be the only published specific study of the problem. There are two major dialects of Koyukon, called by Krauss the 'Inner Koyukon' (Tanana Village, Stevens Village, Crossjacket, Kantishna, Roosevelt, Manley, Bearpaw: essentially upriver extensions into the interior) characterized by the interior trait of velar fronting, PA $*q > k$, $*\underline{k} > \check{c}$, and the 'Outer Koyukon' characterized by the peripheral ('Eskimoid') trait $*q > q$, $*\underline{k} > k$. The language of the Henry materials is Outer Koyukon. Two striking unique characteristics of Koyukon are 1) the innovation PA $*c (> t\theta) > tl$ ($= t\ł < *\lambda$), and the conservation of certain final clusters, especially $*$-C-$l > $ -C-$\lambda$ (in future-progressive of verbs, and also $-l$ 'instrumental' suffix, e.g. Koyukon $s\partial x\lambda$ 'hook') and $*$-C-$g$ in repetitive of verbs (e.g. PA $*$-$\Omega a\check{s}$-$g$ 'sneeze', Outer Koyukon -$\Omega \partial sg$, Inner -$\Omega \partial s\check{z}$). These clusters, though certainly predictable from comparative Athapaskan, are overtly attested only in Koyukon.

Richard J. Mueller of SIL has been with the Alaskan Kutchin since 1959. He has published a *Kutchin dictionary* (1964, 52 pp.), of the type that Henry produced for Koyukon and Collins for Upper Kuskokwim, which is a valuable addition to Kutchin (noun) lexicography. In addition to religious materials, Mueller has recently published elementary popular materials for learning Kutchin (1970, 1971).

Paul and Trude Milanowski have been with the Upper Tanana since 1959. Milanowski has so far published, in addition to gospel and primer material, a short dittoed wordlist in 1961, and a paper on the phonology, entitled "Sound system of Upper Tanana Athapaskan: A preliminary view" (1962).

The following is a brief summary of the Alaskan Athapaskan 'languages' as defined (in part arbitrarily) by Krauss as a result of his 1961-62 survey. Very rough estimates of the number of speakers and indications of the age of the youngest speakers are also given.

AHTENA A. Chitina, Tonsina, Copper Center, Glenallen, Tazlina, Louise-Tyone, Gulkana-Gakona, Denali-Cantwell.
    B. Chistochina, Batzulnetas.

C. Mentasta.

ca. 250; very few, if any, under 20.

TANAINA A. 'Inner': Knik, Eklutna, Susitna-Talkeetna, some Tyonek.
B. 'Outer': Kenai, Ninilchik, Seldovia, some Tyonek, Iliamna, Nondalton, Lime-Hungry-Stoney.

ca. 400; very few, if any, under 20.

INGALIK A. Kuskokwim: nearly extinct, except for a few individuals at Sleetmute, Stoney River, Aniak, all bilingual in Eskimo.
B. Yukon: Anvik, Shageluk, Holy Cross.

ca. 150; very few, if any, under 30.

HOLIKACHUK (now moved to Grayling on Tukon; intermediate language between Ingalik and Koyukon).

ca. 50; very few, if any, under 30.

KOYUKON A. 'Outer': Kaltag, Nulato, Koyukuk, Ruby, Galena, Kokrines, Allakaket, Huslia, Hughes, some at Rampart.
B. 'Inner': 1. Tanana Village, Stevens Village, some at Rampart, some at Beaver, few at Allakaket ('South Fork'); 2a. Crossjacket, Manley Hot Springs; 2b. Roosevelt-Mindumina (extinct), Bearpaw.

ca. 600; very few under 30, except at Hughes, very few under 20.

UPPER KUSKOKWIM: Nikolai, Telida, McGrath (closely related to Tanana A, but separated by Koyukon B2b).

ca. 100, including all children at Nikolai.

TANANA A. 'Central': Minto-Tolovana, Toklat, Nenana, Wood River.
B. 'Transitional' 1. Chena, Salcha, Goodpaster; 2. Healy Lake, Tanacross.

ca. 250; ca. 150 of A, very few under 35, probably none under 25; fewer than 10 of B1, none young; ca. 100 of B2, including some children at Tanacross.

UPPER TANANA: Tetlin, Northway, Nabesna, Scottie Creek.

ca. 300; including all children at Tetlin, many at Northway.

HAN: Eagle (also Moosehide, near Dawson, Yukon Territory).

ca. 30 at Eagle, few, if any, under 20.

KUTCHIN (dialects not defined, largest difference perhaps between American and Canadian): Circle, Fort Yukon, Venetie, Arctic Village, Chalkyitsik, Birch Creek, Canyon Village, some at Beaver (also in Canada: Old Crow, Fort MacPherson, Inuvik).

ca. 900 in Alaska (1,000–1,200 in Canada); including all or most children in some locations, e.g. Arctic Village, Venetie, some children at others, e.g. Fort Yukon.

Total for Alaska ca. 3,000.

Very recently there have been stirrings of pride spreading through Athapaskan Alaska, including a resurgence of interest in the language. In most cases, unfortunately, this is probably too late to maintain the language (Ahtena, Tanaina, Ingalik, Holikachuk, Koyukon, most Tanana, Han). Very recently, State-Operated Schools at Northway (Upper Tanana, Paul Milanowski), Nikolai (Upper Kuskokwim, Ray Collins), and Fort Yukon (Kutchin, Richard Mueller), have begun to consider programs to include the Athapaskan language in the classroom. It remains uncertain, however, that any Alaskan children will know Athapaskan in the year 2000.

## 1.2 Canada

It is still largely unknown what Athapaskan languages are spoken in Canada; the structure and interrelationships within the enormous Athapaskan complex of linguistic communities in Canada are at best only very partially explored. Also, very little has been published in the way of descriptive information on Canadian Athapaskan languages. Nevertheless, this forbidding apparent vacuum conceals a fair amount of linguistic research by a fair number and variety of personnel in the field. There are a few unpublished or forthcoming items to be added to the generally known bibliography, but the bulk of the unreported information is still in the form of fieldnotes by academic linguists and anthropologists, and especially linguistically trained missionaries of the Summer Institute of Linguistics (SIL) or Northern Canada Evangelical Missions (NCEM), some of whom have spent several years in the Athapaskan communities and gained an active command of the language.

Before discussing recent academic linguistic work on Canadian Athapaskan, it is perhaps appropriate to mention briefly here the enormous amount of Canadian Athapaskan that has been written down by the Oblate Fathers, who have established their missions throughout most of the area for a century. The Oblate Fathers made a practise of learning the indigenous languages, to preach and write religious materials in them. In the process they often compiled for themselves extensive dictionaries and paradigms, mostly as an aide-mémoire and also for practise, usually for personal use only. Most of what was published was religious text (for a bibliography of this see Carrière 1951). The best-known linguistic works in this literature are Petitot's *Dictionnaire de la langue Déné-Dindjié* (1876), Legoff's Chipewyan grammar of 1898 and dictionary of 1916, and Morice's monstrous study of Carrier (1932) (for a bibliography of Morice see Carrière n.d.). But the great bulk of the Oblate Athapaskan material has never been printed. Some has been typed or mimeographed for limited circulation, but by far the greatest part of it is only in manuscript and microfilm at the Oblate Archives at Edmonton and Ottawa. For catalogues of these holdings see Carrière 1957, 1969a, 1969b, 1970. A cursory analysis of these lists discloses huge amounts of material in Chipewyan, Slave, and Hare, and lesser collections in Beaver, Loucheux (Kutchin), and Dogrib. Over twenty dictionaries apiece are listed for each of the first three, and about half a dozen apiece for each of the latter three. 'Grammars' (mostly compilations of verb paradigms) are about half as numerous as the dictionaries, and religious texts about twice as numerous. It must be added, however, that probably none of these materials are written with anything approaching adequacy for phonological purposes, so that their usefulness is seriously limited in this way to begin with.

Wallace P. Chafe, in "Estimates regarding the present speakers of North American Indian languages" (1962, see also Chafe 1965), reports for all Canadian Athapaskan languages listed that they are spoken by speakers of 'all ages', with the exceptions of Tagish (approx. 5, all over 50 years of age) and Sarsi (approx. 50, all over 20 years of age; but according to E.-D. Cook, the number of Sarsi speakers is now less than 10, see below). How true it was in 1962 or remains in 1970 that all these languages are maintained by the youngest generation is questionable in certain cases, but in general it can certainly be said that the Athapaskan languages in Canada are likely to be spoken for longer into the future that those in Alaska. It would be indeed an interesting subject for study to determine precisely what differences in history and educational and social policies between the Canadian and the Alaskan have brought about such a contrasting picture, profound cultural loss in Alaska, relative vitality in Canada. The following shows the Canadian Athapaskan languages as listed by Chafe (1962) with estimated number of speakers, and indication of the age of the younger speakers. These figures are followed in brackets by those listed in the Department of Indian Affairs and Northern Development's report *Linguistic and cultural affiliations of Canadian Indian bands* (1970) for the total population of each group.

BEAVER 300, all ages [789]
CARRIER 1,000–3,000, all ages [5,155, including 606 at Anaham]
CHILCOTIN 500–1,000, all ages [795, excluding 606 at Anaham, 1,000 estimated by Q. King]
CHIPEWYAN 3,400–5,600 (including 400–600 Yellowknife), all ages [5,612, including 504 Yellowknife (Dogrib?)]
DOGRIB 800, all ages [1,202] (+504 "Yellowknife"?)
HARE 600, all ages [715, probably including Bearlake at Fort Franklin]
KASKA 200–500, all ages [533 Liard River 'Nahani']
KUTCHIN 1,200 (total Alaska and Canada) all ages [1,205 'Loucheux'; 1,000–1,200 Canadian Kutchin estimated by Mueller]
SARCEE 50, all over 20 [467; fewer than 10 speakers according to Cook]
SEKANI 100–500, all ages [450; 350 estimated by Wilkinson, with no children speakers]
SLAVE 1,000–2,000, all ages [3,334, probably including some Bearlake and Mountain at Fort Norman]
TAGISH ca. 5, all over 50 [not listed as Athapaskan]
TAHLTAN 100–1,000, all ages [702]
TUTCHONE 1,000, all ages [1445 'Kutchin' and 'Nahani' excluding Liard River]
Total for Canada 10,000 to 17,000 according to Chafe (1962), ca. 22,000 according to 1970 report.

CHIPEWYAN, with over 5,000 speakers, is no doubt the largest Athapaskan linguistic community in Canada, or, for that matter, anywhere north of Apachean. It is also the best known language. Fang-Kuei Li, who had done fieldwork on

Chipewyan in 1928 and already published his well-known "A list of Chipewyan stems" in 1932, published "Chipewyan" in 1946, a brief classic sketch which probably remains the best single introduction to the general structure of an Athapaskan language available in print. This is a most highly recommended reading for those embarking on the study of Athapaskan, in spite of the fact that Chipewyan is by no means the least innovative (in fact rather typically so) of Athapaskan languages (e.g. shows fairly extensive loss of stem-final obstruent system, though less extensive than in Han, Kutchin, Hare-Bearlake-Dogrib, Tutchone, Slave, or, apparent replacement of the general Athapaskan 'future' by the optative). Li later published "A Chipewyan ethnological text" (1964), which would be a very useful supplement as a reading exercise in an introduction to Athapaskan studies. Murray W. Richardson, formerly of NCEM, who spent more than a decade amongst the Chipewyan, published "Paradigmatic prefixes in Chipewyan" (1963). Less widely known in academic quarters, but far more important, is Richardson's *Chipewyan grammar* (1968, 65 pp.). This sketch is intended for a more popular audience than Li's, and supplements it in a number of ways, particularly in sentence syntax. In fact, Richardson's *Chipewyan grammar* is virtually unique in treating at any length at all the sentence structure of any Athapaskan language north of Apachean or Hupa. L.W. Elford and Hélène Labadie, both of NCEM, have spent a considerable period of time with Chipewyan, and are at present working on a noun dictionary of the language. Note also a treatment of Chipewyan classificatory verbs by Elford in *Studies in the Athapaskan languages* (Davidson, Elford and Hoijer 1963:33–5). Unpublished Chipewyan data have also been obtained by Beryl Gillespie in 1970 and Virginia Lawson in 1971 for the Iowa University Survey under Robert Howren.

Very closely related to, in fact a dialect of Chipewyan, is Yellowknife, reported on by Mary Haas in "Notes on a Chipewyan dialect" (1968), on the basis of a few hours' work with an informant in 1967. The article consists mainly of a wordlist (about 300 items) demonstrating the closeness to Li's Chipewyan, and introductory sections on the classificatory verb system, French loans and card-playing terms, and most interestingly, on Haas's discovery that in Yellowknife PA $*t (>[t^x]) > k$ [kh], precisely as in Kiowa-Apache, Jicarilla, and Lipan in the South. Haas wisely attributes this similarity to parallel development.

HARE, BEARLAKE, MOUNTAIN, and DOGRIB are four fairly well defined dialects of one fairly well defined language. This group runs a poor second to Chipewyan for published literature since World War II, but is perhaps ahead of Chipewyan in terms of research activity and unpublished materials. Fang-Kuei Li in 1929 had gathered a considerable amount of Hare from which Hoijer has prepared a typescript "Hare stem list" (104 pp.) and "English-Hare index" (40 pp.). This list is more useful even than Li's Chipewyan stem-list in listing actual forms showing the derivational prefixes, and in having an English index; but Hare is, unfortunately for comparative purposes, one of the furthest evolved of all the Athapaskan languages in terms of loss of stem-final consonantism and stem-variation. Also based on Li's material is Hoijer's "Hare phonology: An historical study" (1966c), discussed at further length in the section on comparative Athapaskan. More recent fieldwork in this language group has tended to concentrate on Dogrib. William Davidson, formerly of SIL, worked for several years in Dogrib, and published "A preliminary analysis of active verbs in Dogrib" (1963a), and an account of Dogrib classificatory verbs (Davidson, Elford and Hoijer 1963:35-7). Since 1965, Herbert Zimmerman of SIL and Dean Annis of NCEM have done fieldwork with Dogrib, but have not published any results. Unpublished Hare fieldnotes and vocabulary collected by Hiroko Sue in 1961 are available at the American Philosophical Society (items 1546-8 in the Freeman Catalogue; see also Hiroko Sue 1964 and 1962, 59 pp. (unpublished)); the R.P. Bernard Brown, OMI, at Colville Lake is working on a Hare grammar and dictionary. George Tharp collected some Hare data for the Iowa Survey in 1970.

Very important work in this area has been done, with fieldwork on Dogrib (and to a lesser extent on Hare and Bearlake) since 1965, by Robert Howren. Howren has produced two papers on Dogrib phonology, in a generative framework. The first, "Stem phonology and affix phonology in Dogrib (Northern Athapaskan)" (1968), is a brief description of certain aspects of Dogrib phonology, of some theoretical interest as well in highlighting the difference between stem-rules and affix-rules. These and other points are expanded in Howren's 'The phonology of Rae Dogrib' (forthcoming) perhaps the best phonology of a Northern Athapaskan language yet available. Dogrib phonology of course figures in Howren's "A formalization of the Athapaskan d-effect" (1971), discussed in the section on comparative Athapaskan. Howren provides an excellent resumé of his findings on the Hare-Bearlake-Dogrib dialect group in a mimeographed report to the National Science Foundation, 1969, showing e.g. that Bearlake is intermediate between Hare and Dogrib. He notes $u > i$ in Dogrib ($ti$ 'water', Hare-Bearlake $tu$; this shift occurs also in Ingalik and Tanaina in Alaska), voicing of initial spirants ($l > l$, $W$ ($< *\theta < *s$) $> w$), and spirantization of aspirate affricates in Hare ($\lambda$, $c$, $č$, $k^w > l$, $s$, $š$, $f^w$; cf. PCA), loss of possessive suffix in Dogrib ($\lambda'i \sim -\lambda'i$ 'rope', Hare-Bearlake $*\lambda'u \sim -\lambda'ul-e\text{?}$). Howren's most recent paper, "A century of phonological change in a Northern Athapaskan dialect group" (1970), details in a very interesting way this PCA-like spirantization of the aspirate affricates which has taken place progressively over the last century, from 1876 in E. Petitot's *Dictionnaire de la langue Dènè-Dindjié*, through 1929 (Li's fieldnotes), to the present. The anthropologist June Helm and other associates of Howren at Iowa, Charles Pyle (see comparative Athapaskan), Phyllis Coleman, and Beryl Gillespie, have also recently done fieldwork among the Dogrib, some of it linguistic.

In certain ways intermediate between Chipewyan-Yellowknife and Hare-Bearlake-Mountain-Dogrib is an extremely ill-defined group of dialects and/or languages grouped together vaguely under the name SLAVE or Slavey. This term should probably also apply to the group designated 'Mountain', by Osgood in 1936, according to findings by Michael Krauss and Geoffrey O'Grady in a session at Camsell Hospital in Edmonton 1964 with informants from Ft. Norman, Wrigley, and Fort Simpson, whose dialects appear each to be different gradations between what is known as Hare and what is known as Slave. In 1966–67 Terry Klokeid collected additional Slave material from informants from Ft. Simpson and Ft. Providence. Published linguistic information on 'Slave' during the recent period has been very little. Philip Howard, an independent Protestant missionary presently at Hay River, published a very short study on Netla — Ft. Liard — South Nahanni in "A preliminary presentation of Slave phonemes" (1963), and is currently working on a grammar. Victor and Anita Monus of SIL, working at Jean-Marie River in the Ft. Simpson district since 1958, have produced some primers and gospel translations, but have not yet published any linguistic studies. Virginia Lawson and Stanley Witkowski also collected some Slave data for Howren in 1970.

Howren's most recent paper (1971b) confirms this grouping of Hare-Bearlake-Mountain-Dogrib and Chipewyan-Yellowknife, with Slave intermediate between the two groups, and proposes to classify this whole grouping as a Northeastern substock within Northern Athapaskan. Aside from the danger of relying too heavily on a Stammbaum model within a dialect complex, it is perhaps also too early to make this claim knowing as little as we still do of neighboring languages like Tutchone, Kaska, Beaver. Howren's paper adds some interesting detail on the Hare-Bearlake-Mountain-Dogrib, including the hitherto nearly unknown Mountain (with new data obtained in 1970 by George Tharp, who also collected supplementary data that year on Hare and Bearlake), showing Hare, Bearlake, and Mountain to be close dialects, and Dogrib somewhat divergent and more innovative still, and showing Dogrib in turn intermediate between this grouping and Slave, to oversimplify somewhat a picture complicated with crossing isoglosses. Howren also shows in this paper that the ə-syncope and spirant-voicing rules proposed by Krauss (1969b) for the prefixes (tense-mode, subject, classifier) of the Proto-Athapaskan-Eyak verb can still be seen to function synchronically even in these very highly evolved modern Athapaskan languages.

In the dialect area known as (Northern and Southern) TUTCHONE, also linguistically still rather ill-defined, there has been nothing published, but nonetheless significant recent research. In 1964 Michael Krauss transcribed some Tutchone at Snag and other points. During the last decade the ethnologist Catharine McClellan has spent much time in the area, and her notes include a large amount of linguistic material. Her students, Glenda and Carter Denniston, gathered in 1965 some Tutchone linguistic data for classifying some of the bands of the area, and include this work as part of their mimeographed report "The place of the Upper Pelly River Indians in the network of Northern Athapaskan Groups" (1966). In 1971 Howren and Tharp obtained Tutchone data from a number of points, so that this area can now be included in the perspective of the Iowa Survey.

The TAGISH language is now nearly extinct, with fewer than five speakers. It is the former Athapaskan speech now replaced by that of the Inland Tlingit. In 1953, Gordon Marsh collected some Tagish data, and at the 1958 Annual Meeting of the Canadian Linguistic Association presented a paper entitled "Tentative placing of the

Tahgish language within the Athapaskan Stock". Marsh sent some Han data and a copy of this paper to Hoijer, who included Tagish in his "The Athapaskan languages" (1963). Hoijer there has Tagish in a class by itself, as apparently all three (four) consonant series in question, PA *ts, *tš (and *$k^w$), and *$k$, had in Tagish merged as ts, at least in the speech of Marsh's informant, who had not used the language for forty years. However, Catharine McClellan subsequently gathered Tagish data from another informant, and this material reveals that at least the *ts series is still distinct in Tagish (ts as opposed to tš for *tš, *$k^w$, *$k$), and that Tagish on this and other grounds is to be classed, as Marsh had also conjectured, as most closely related to Kaska, on the other side of the Inland Tlingit intrusion into the Yukon. It is therefore highly likely that the former Taku-Athapaskan area between Tagish and Kaska was also of the Tagish-Kaska rather than Tutchone type.

For KASKA there was virtually no recent linguistic investigation to report, except, in a sense, that of the anthropologist John Honigmann, who published a small amount of linguistic material *passim* in 1954, until 1971, when some Kaska data were obtained by E.-D. Cook and G. Tharp.

Tagish, Kaska, Sekani, Tahltan form perhaps a grouping which might be called Western Canadian, having in common at least the property of being in recent times very little investigated and being virtually unrepresented in the published linguistic literature. J. Honigmann has a little SEKANI linguistic material, but for Sekani the major linguistic effort has been by David B. Wilkinson of SIL, since 1963 at MacLeod Lake and Ware. In addition to forthcoming primers and gospel material, Wilkinson has been working on phonological and grammatical analysis of Sekani. Wilkinson by 1970 found that the Sekani language was moribund, no longer vital enough to warrant a continued SIL program there, and has since joined Richard Walker at Ft. St. James (Carrier). V. Lawson obtained some Sekani material in 1971 for Howren's survey.

There has been very little linguistic investigation of TAHLTAN during the recent period, and that so far without published results. Marshall Holdstock and Henry Hildebrandt of SIL spent a week in the area in 1965, and Michael Krauss did some fieldwork with a Tahltan informant in Fairbanks during the early 1960s. But most significantly, Kenneth Hale and Geoffrey O'Grady collaborated on fieldwork with a Tahltan informant in summer 1965, resulting in fieldnotes of very high quality, including elicitation of sentences of special interest for the study of sentence structure. In 1971 G. Tharp obtained some Tahltan data for Howren's survey, and E.-D. Cook also did some fieldwork in the language. Cook reports that Tahltan, somewhat surprisingly, is not a tone-language.

BEAVER is yet another ill-defined area in Northern Athapaskan, certainly with significant internal differentiation, and certainly also shading into intelligibility with neighboring dialects of Slave and Sekani. William Davidson transcribed some Beaver wordlists during the 1950s, apparently from more than one location (i.e. more than one 'Beaver' dialect), and this material was used by Hoijer in his "The Athapaskan languages" (1963). Kenneth Hale and G. N. O'Grady obtained a small amount of Beaver data in 1965. Far more extensive has been the work of Marshall E. Holdstock of SIL, who has been with the Beaver since 1964. He has published a Beaver primer and some gospel texts, and has also been working on phonological and grammatical analyses of the language. V. Lawson obtained Beaver data in 1970 and 1971 for Howren's survey.

SARSI has been the object of two major research efforts, fortunately, because the language is now on the verge of extinction. E.-D. Cook reports that there are now only 'half a dozen Sarcee speakers, all over seventy years old'. In 1922 Edward Sapir did fieldwork with Sarsi, and published his important "Pitch accent in Sarcee, an Athapaskan language" (1925). His discovery of tone in Sarsi deeply influenced Sapir's thought about Athapaskan, to the point where he felt that an Athapaskan language without tone would be well-nigh inconceivable. F.-K. Li published from Sapir's material "A study of Sarcee verb stems" (1930a), a well-known landmark in Athapaskan studies. But it remained for Harry Hoijer and Janet Joël 33 years later to publish "Sarsi nouns" (1963) from Sapir's material. Since then, Eung-Do Cook has continued Sarsi studies, working with Sapir's fieldnotes and, since 1966, doing fieldwork with the surviving informants. Cook reports three unpublished papers: "A sketch of Sarcee phonemics" (1966), "An introductory sketch of Sarcee grammar" (1967), and most important, "Vowels and tones in Sarcee" (1971a). This last is an important contribution to Athapaskan studies, showing very interestingly, within the framework of generative phonology, e.g. that all three Sarsi tone-levels can be predicted in the verbal prefix-complex in terms of underlying segments and the tone of the stem (there are still three lexically fixed tones on stems and on certain prefixes). Cook has thus not gone so far as R. Stanley for Navajo in reducing the verb-complex to a string of segments in underlying representation from which the phonetic surface can be predicted by a set of rules, but it may not be possible to go so far in the synchronic analysis of Sarsi as in that of Navajo (if indeed, it is possible to justify as a description of the Navajo speaker's competence the analysis of Navajo taken to the depth that Stanley has taken it). Most recently Cook has written "Morphophonemics of Sarcee classifiers" (1971b), elegantly reconstructing the Sarcee classifiers including *l* (never actualized as such). Cook has continued his productivity in Sarcee linguistics with three more recent papers. Cook 1971c discusses the deletion of four prefixes (*mi-* 3rd person obj., *ni-* 2sg. subj., *ni-* terminative, *si-* perfective) and the theoretical implications of the constraint which forbids their deletion when the result would be a verb with no syllabic prefixes, though it does not explain the apparently very complex rules conditioning the deletions. Cook 1971d gives a very nice account of the complete Sarcee numeral system, phonologically and morphologically: cardinals, multiplicatives, counting humans and animals. Cook 1971e discusses sets of Sarcee verb stems which include inherent number (of subject of intransitives, of object of transitives) in their meaning ('go, sit, stand, awake/be angry, dance, rush, dream [lie], swim'), in which the number categories can be sg, du, pl, sg/du, du/pl, and shows the interaction of these stems with the prefixes *gi-* 'du/pl' and *da-gi-* 'pl'. Such phenomena occur, it is well known, in all Athapaskan languages, and it is helpful to have this account of them in Sarcee.

On CARRIER, a relatively well-defined language, but certainly with rather significant internal subdivision, there has been virtually nothing published since A.G. Morice's massive but chaotic two-volume *The Carrier language* (1932). Carrier is a close second to Chipewyan in terms of numbers of speakers, with about 5,000, for whom the language is reportedly quite vital. However, there are apparently three major dialects of Carrier, the Northern (or Babine), Central (or Stuart Lake Upper, Higher), and Southern (or Lower, Ulgatcho, Ulkatcho). Research is now being done on each of the three dialects. Henry Hildebrandt of SIL has been working on Northern Carrier at Burns Lake since 1967. He says (p.c.) that there is 'little comprehension' between Northern and Central Carrier. Richard Walker of SIL has been working at Fort St. James (Central Carrier) since 1961. He verifies (p.c.) that the Northern and Central dialects are 'almost mutually unintelligible'. Walker has a paper on the phonemics of Central Carrier forthcoming in the *Bulletin of the National Museum*, Ottawa; has published primers, readers, and religious materials in the language; is preparing a Central Carrier ethnobotany, toponymy, and dictionary; and is working towards a bilingual literacy program through the local schools. Since 1970 Walker has had the assistance of Wilkinson, who formerly worked with Sekani. The divergence between Southern Carrier and Central is perhaps somewhat less great than that between Central and Northern. Since 1967 Clark A. Davis of the National Museum, Ottawa, has spent long periods of time in the Ulgatcho (or Lower, Southern) Carrier field. Davis published (1970) a note on the identity of this group, who now live at Anahim (or Anaham) Lake, which used to be Chilcotin territory. In his most recent paper (1971) Davis shows that Harrington's 'Chilcotin' data are in fact Northern Carrier.

Southernmost of the Northern Athapaskan languages is CHILCOTIN, a very different language from Carrier. Since 1964 Quindel King of NCEM has been doing fieldwork with Chilcotin, and has a description of Chilcotin phonology forthcoming in the *Bulletin of the National Museum*, Ottawa. King reports (p.c.) that there are about 1000 speakers of Chilcotin, and that they are tenaciously maintaining their language. King's new research on Chilcotin, apparently the first of any linguistic significance in the twentieth century, is particularly welcome because of the position of Chilcotin as southernmost of the Northern Athapaskan languages, which may well throw important light on the origin and relationship to the North of Nicola, Kwalhioqua-Tlatskanai, Pacific Coast Athapaskan, and Apachean.

Finally, mention may be made of TSETSAUT, an Athapaskan language of Portland Canal, British Columbia and Alaska, of which Boas got a rather skimpy corpus in 1894 (Boas and Goddard 1924b), when he could locate only three surviving speakers. The material that Boas got is extremely difficult to interpret with any high degree of phonological precision, but it is nevertheless very clear that Tsetsaut shows phonological developments of great importance for the study of comparative Athapaskan. Tsetsaut very probably represents the end of a migration from the interior of the

North, in that it resembles especially the languages of that area in having undergone severe loss of stem-final obstruents. It further resembles especially the Hare-Bearlake-Dogrib group in that it has developed a stem-initial labial affricate series. But whereas this type of series developed in Hare-Bearlake-Dogrib from the PA *$c$ series (probably through $t\theta$), the Tsetsaut $pf$ series developed from the PA *$\underset{\sim}{k}^w$ series, and from the *$\underset{\sim}{k}^w$ series alone, which Tsetsaut thus uniquely preserves distinct from all other series (PA *$\check{c}$ > Tsetsaut $c$). The only other Athapaskan languages which preserve PA *$\underset{\sim}{k}^w$ series distinct from the *$\check{c}$ are the Alaskan languages, far removed from Tsetsaut, where *$\underset{\sim}{k}^w$ > $tr$ (Ingalik, Upper Kuskokwim, Tanana, Kutchin, Han). Unfortunately, the conditions under which Boas worked with Tsetsaut were very difficult, and the resulting materials are accordingly of limited scope and quality. It has apparently been assumed that this extremely interesting language has been extinct since about the turn of the century. It is probable, however, that Tsetsaut speakers survived until long past then: Marius Barbeau reported at least one, not mentioned by Boas, alive in 1927. The chances that any survive today are exceedingly slim, but have not been, yet should still be, investigated. The Boas material, however, will probably forever be the only documentation of Tsetsaut. M.E. Krauss in his studies on comparative Athapaskan has already made important use of this problematical Boas Tsetsaut material. It clearly deserves much attention, for Tsetsaut was indeed the most strikingly aberrant, at least phonologically, of all Athapaskan languages. Tharp (1972) and Tsetsaut will be further discussed in sections 5.1 and 5.2.

## 1.3 *Kwalhioqua-Tlatskanai and Nicola*

Since these isolated islets of Athapaskan speech were all extinct before the period in question, and very little represented in the printed literature, it is not surprising that there is little new work to be reported in this dead area. Nonetheless, at least from a historical-comparative point of view, these languages merit some attention, and some space will be devoted here to the more recent unpublished literature that is behind the few remarks on these languages that have appeared in print since 1940.

The inimitable J.P. Harrington writes in a letter to the Smithsonian Bureau of American Ethnology (Harrington carton No. 415) dated Oakville, Washington, April 7, 1942, as follows:

This letter is worthy of a telegram. They say blessings never come singly, and I have by doing long detective work located descendants of BOTH the Kwalhioqua and Tlatskanay, Lizzie Johnson here, whose Kwalhioqua-speaking mother died in 1910, and Willie Andrew at Tahola, whose father was a pure Tlatskanay, and who spoke it until his father died when was eight years old; now he is eighty years old and has recently had a stroke, but can work with me. This Kwalhioqua-Tlatskanay language is vital to connecting the Chilco[tin]s with the Hupas, is the only half-way link. Slowly after decades of disuse I am building up the vocabulary just as the words were pronounced, with glottal stops and all ...

Harrington further reports in print (1943b:51): 'he was able to discover individuals who had in their remote youth actually spoken the extinct Kwalhioqua and Tlatskanai dialects of Washington and Oregon, and to recover vocabularies of these with all their original phonetics'. Examination of the rather voluminous materials that Harrington got in this area (in BAE cartons) reveals that Harrington's informants knew or remembered virtually nothing of the Athapaskan; that beyond two or three forms which appear to be genuinely remembered, Harrington for the most part, at least, forced spurious responses in attempts to reelicit from an earlier manuscript Tlatskanai wordlist (Alexander Caulfield Anderson, "Vocabulary of the Klatskanai dialect of the Tahculli [Carrier]", 185 items, 1856, in BAE collection). In addition, Harrington got about five authentic Athapaskan items from Clara Pearson, a Nehalem Tillamook woman, the same items that she had remembered for Melville Jacobs in 1935. Harrington's material is thus a serious disappointment, though not an unexpected one at such a late date.

Nevertheless, the documentation of Kwalhioqua-Tlatskanai is significantly better than indicated by what is generally taken to be the definitive source for this language, Franz Boas and Pliny Earle Goddard's "Vocabulary of an Athapascan dialect of the state of Washington" (1924a). The material in that article is not only full of errors in the printing of its sources, all of which are still available in print or manuscript (Hale, Teit, Gibbs), but though it gives the impression of being complete, it published only a fraction of the Gibbs list (which Boas had earlier published in 1896), and unaccountably omits two other lists in the BAE collection, the Frachtenberg from 1910 which both Boas and Teit certainly knew about, which Boas had in fact corresponded with Frachtenberg about, and the Anderson list mentioned above. Still another source not included in the Boas-Goddard article was already in print, collected about 1912 by E.S. Curtis who published it under "Willapa" in Volume 9 (1913) of his monumental *The North American Indian*. A more understandable omission was another Kwalhioqua list collected by James Wickersham at Boisfort, Washington, ca. 1888, now at the Alaska State Historical Museum. The Boas-Goddard (1924a) article is thus an error-filled copy of something less than half the Kwalhioqua-Tlatskanai material available; but it is also true that the materials not included are of the same type and primitive quality as those included. The only running text is a tiny one in Frachtenberg, about a dozen words long, and for which there is unfortunately no translation. Hoijer remarks in "Athapaskan Languages of the Pacific Coast" (1960:960–61) the following:

Two languages formerly spoken near the mouth of the Columbia River (i.e. Kwalhioqua and Clatskanie) are sometimes included in this group [PCA], but the fragmentary data [Hoijer is here referring probably to the Boas-Goddard article and also copies by Melville Jacobs of the Wickersham and Frachtenberg materials] remaining on these two languages indicate that they do not belong linguistically with the Pacific Coast sub-stock.

Study of all the available materials by Krauss indicates that Hoijer's remark is entirely justified, at least phonologically. Kwalhioqua and Tlatskanai, clearly very closely related dialects of one language, are definitely unlike PCA in showing none of the typical PCA breakdowns within series, and clearly showing, on the other hand, a typical (evolved) Northern pattern of merger of the PA $*c$, $*č$ and $*\underline{k}^w$ series all to $c$. Their position by morphological and lexical criteria appears less clear, perhaps intermediate between the North and PCA. J.P. Harrington (1943a) considered them to be branches of Chilcotin, the southernmost Northern Athapaskan language, as he considered also all of PCA to be. From the limited material so far readily available on Chilcotin, it is already clear that this hypothesis of Harrington's is untenable for PCA at least, and no special affinity between Chilcotin and Kwalhioqua-Tlatskanai is yet easy to spot.

Harrington is far more likely to be correct in considering the other Athapaskan islet, Nicola in British Columbia, a branch of Chilcotin. This hypothesis was already examined by Franz Boas in "Vocabulary of an Athapascan tribe of Nicola Valley, British Columbia" (1924), on the basis of the materials available. The language was virtually extinct by about 1900, though Teit was able to get a few words as late as 1920, and there is a little Teit Nicola material in the American Philosophical Society Library that is not included in Boas's article. There were perhaps fifty different Nicola forms recorded (and of these about a dozen were Salishan).

Then in 1942 J.P. Harrington reports that he 'recovered traditions that the Chilcotin languages had formerly occupied the Nicola Valley, and was able to obtain a large number of Chilcotin words in that region, handed down in individual families' (1943b:50–51), and (1943a:204), 'working separately with eight different informants, I swept their memory clean of the former [Nicola Athapaskan] language and obtained a sizable and important list of vocables, the best results coming from the aged chief Ernest Billy and from his sister Matilda'. Harrington's Nicola material has not yet been located at the BAE, but there is some hope that with this new material and/or better documentation available for Chilcotin, the position of Nicola will become still better defined. According to Davis (1970), however, it is doubtful that Harrington ever worked in the Chilcotin or Nicola areas, and according to archivist Margaret Blaker of the Smithsonian BAE, there is serious doubt that the Harrington 'box marked Merritt, B.C.' ever existed.

## 1.4 Pacific Coast Athapaskan

The Pacific Coast Athapaskan (PCA) languages constitute a geographical branch of Athapaskan which, though now nearly extinct and of practically no sociopolitical importance, is more divergent from the North than is Apachean, shows more internal divergence than does Apachean, and was probably never an undifferentiated linguistic community even if, as is historically somewhat improbable, it split off from the North as one group. Nevertheless, it is clear that Pacific Coast Athapaskan split off from a relatively restricted or linguistically homogeneous sector of the North, and that a number of important phonological and morphological innovations are unique to and universal in PCA.

There are perhaps no speakers of any PCA language under 70 years of age, and most language groups are now extinct (surely Nongatl, Mattole, Bear River, Lassik, Sinkyone, Chasta Costa, Umpqua, Galice, Applegate, though there were surviving speakers of a number of these until much later in certain cases that was generally supposed: e.g. Harrington's Chasta Costa in the 1940s; Mary Haas was able to elicit a few Mattole forms in the 1950s). One elderly man with a limited competence in Coquille was reported by Bruce Rigsby (personal communication) in 1963. There are still alive today perhaps five people with some memory of various dialects of the Tolowa-Tututni complex. The only Pacific Coast Athapaskan language not quite yet at the brink of extinction is Hupa, for which about ten fluent speakers remain, all elderly.[2] Fortunately for comparative purposes, Hupa also happens to be the most conservative generally, at least from a phonological point of view, of all the Pacific Coast Athapaskan (PCA) languages. In 1971 Victor Golla, investigating reports that speakers of Kato and/or Wailaki might yet survive, succeeded in locating and eliciting some material from one informant who had a fragmentary memory of a dialect apparently intermediate between Wailaki and Lassik. She also informed him that her mother, who spoke it fluently, had died only a year or so before. The possibility that Kato or Wailaki might still survive should not yet be completely discounted.

Though many PCA languages are extinct, virtually all of them are documented, however inadequately, in a rather extensive literature, much of it still unpublished. Many of the major contributors were the California linguists and ethnologists of 1900–40: above all P.E. Goddard, but also E.W. Gifford, C.H. Merriam, A.L. Kroeber, G.A. Nomland, F. Essene, E.S. Curtis, P. Drucker, all of whom gathered data, sometimes extensive, rather widely in the area. In this class are also the earlier materials mostly in the Smithsonian (especially G. Gibbs and J.O. Dorsey). Of far better quality is the work of Sapir on Chasta Costa (published in 1914) and Hupa (1927, unpublished), of Melville and Elizabeth Jacobs (Galice, Euchre Creek, Chetco, Coquille, Umpqua, virtually all still unpublished — Melville Jacobs "Historic perspective on Indian languages of Oregon and Washington", 1937, and "Survey of Pacific Northwest anthropological research", 1941 — through Mrs. Jacobs published one short Chetco text 1968), and of Fang-Kuei Li on Hupa and especially Wailaki, unpublished, and Mattole, published in the classic *Mattole: An Athapaskan language* (1930b).

Much of the earlier material is catalogued at the Smithsonian and the American Philosophical Society. Note further the Pilling Catalogue, C.H. Merriam *Studies of California Indians* (1955), A.L. Kroeber and Dale Valory "Ethnological manuscripts in the Robert H. Lowie Museum of Anthropology" (1967), A.L. Kroeber "Goddard's California Athapaskan texts" (1967), Joe E. Pierce and James M. Ryherd's "The

---

[2] It has recently been reported that there may be one young Hupa speaker in his twenties.

status of Athapaskan research in Oregon" (1964), and Joe E. Pierce "The field situation in Oregon: 1964" (1965). The bibliography of Pacific Coast Athapaskan material is being actively pursued by Michael Krauss and Dale Valory. The publication of such a detailed bibliography would demonstrate that PCA is rather richly documented for Amerindian 'philology'. In spite of the extinction of nearly all the languages, with these materials and in-depth work still possible on some languages, PCA studies hold promise of being a richly productive field.

Discussion of the activity in PCA linguistics since 1940 will include much of that which has not yet led to publication. In 1942 J.P. Harrington of the Smithsonian Institution gathered some Coquille and a little Umpqua data, and also found Wolverton Orton, Sapir's old informant from 1906, still alive. His notes marked 'Wolv.' in the Smithsonian archives, with Harrington's meticulous phonetic notations, clear up certain phonetic problems in Sapir's 1914 publication on Chasta Costa: what Sapir writes as $ts$ and $t\theta$ Harrington transcribes $t\theta$, $ts$, $t\underset{\cdot}{s}$, $t\dot{s}$, or $t\check{s}$, varying freely, for the PA $*c$ series, contrasting optionally with what Harrington transcribes $ts$ or $t\underset{\cdot}{s}$, Sapir $ts$, for the PA $*\check{c}$ (and $*k^w$) series. This is a situation which may eventually explain some of the phonetic problems in the documentation of the rest of the Tolowa-Tututni complex, to which Chasta Costa intimately belongs.

During the summer of 1953 Morris Swadesh gathered some Tututni material, about 420 items, on tape for the Penutian language survey (see Swadesh 1954). Tolowa-Tututni data from the field have been gathered by Mary Woodward (1952, Tolowa), Harry Hoijer (1956, Tolowa, Coquille), Jane Bright (1962–63, Tolowa), Victor Golla (1963–64, Tututni), Dale Valory (1965–68, Tolowa), Gary Hawthorne (1968, Tolowa). So far, only that of Jane Bright has led to publication: "The phonology of Smith River Athapaskan (Tolowa)" (1964); Mrs. Bright's untimely death was a major loss to PCA studies.

Somewhat outside the Tolowa-Tututni complex in Oregon is Galice, which has received a relatively great amount of attention. In 1956, Harry Hoijer visited the late Hoxie Simmons, the last speaker of Galice. Hoijer was thus able to supplement the already fair amount of material Melville Jacobs had obtained on Galice from Mr. Simmons during the thirties. Of his Galice material, Jacobs has published one text in "An historical event text from Galice Athapaskan in Southwestern Oregon" (1960). Hoijer published a brief "Galice Athapaskan: A grammatical sketch" (1966a) and there exists a typescript Galice stem-list by Hoijer based on his and Jacobs's materials. Swadesh recorded some 450 items from Mr. Simmons on tape in 1953 (Swadesh 1954).

Hupa, as mentioned above, is remembered by a larger number of speakers, by far, than any other PCA language. Phonologically conservative in many respects, more than other PCA languages, Hupa is especially important for comparative Athapaskan. Mary Woodward began fieldwork on Hupa in 1953 and later published "Hupa phonemics" (1964). Victor Golla began intensive and extensive study of Hupa with fieldwork since 1962–63, integrated with study of Sapir's extensive and high quality materials from the field in 1927. Golla recently finished a doctoral dissertation entitled *Hupa grammar*, University of California, Berkeley, 1970. It centers, as do several Athapaskan grammars, on verb morphology, which is indeed the most complex and central aspect of Athapaskan grammar. Golla's *Hupa grammar* accounts not only for the morphophonemics of the stem and prefixes, and for the paradigmatic prefixes, but also accounts for the derivational prefixes and derivational processes in a far more satisfactory way than any other Athapaskan grammar available. This grammar is not only a milestone in PCA studies, it is indeed a very important event for Athapaskan linguistics in general.

Golla has published "An etymological study of Hupa noun stems" (1964), a very welcome and well-presented contribution to comparative Athapaskan, and, perhaps even more useful, though distributed still only in typescript, a list of 'Hupa verb themes', a model study of its type both for succinctness and comprehensiveness. It is a truly 'sophisticated' stem-list, including all the derivational prefixes, in such a way that no unjustified meaning is assigned to the stem which belongs partly or largely in fact to the prefixes.

(The omission of these derivational prefixes is a source of major frustration in using e.g. Fang-Kuei Li's classic "A list of Chipewyan stems" (1932), which lists only the stem-variants and classifiers, thus e.g. Chipewyan *-ní, -ní, -ní* 'to hum' (*1*), *-ní, -ní, -ní* 'to keep' (*1*), *-ní, -ní, -ní* 'to remark' (*1*), or *-ní, -ní, -ní* 'to respect, to act respectfully toward' (zero), *-ní, -ní, -ní* 'to wave (one's hand)' (zero), or *-ní, -ní, -ní* 'to say' (zero), *-ní, -ní, -ní* 'to be easy, capable, to have luck, to be brave' (zero), *-ní, -ní, -ní, -dí* 'to guess' (zero). These sets of verbs are distinguished semantically surely more by prefixes (besides the classifier) than by the stem with its variations, which is obviously the standard Athapaskan simply for 'do, act'. It is certainly of little use to list *-ní, -ní, -ní* 'to hum' (*1*), 'to keep' (*1*), 'to remark' (*1*) as separate entries so long as the prefixes which in fact distinguish and carry the meanings are not shown. There has been a strong tendency to neglect for too long the challenging study of derivational prefixes in the Athapaskan verb. Golla's Hupa verb-theme list and grammar are major contributions in this area.)

The most general and a very important publication on PCA during the period is Harry Hoijer's "Athapaskan language of the Pacific Coast" (1960). It begins with a brief survey of the PCA state of affairs, which is of course to be supplemented by the Pierce-Ryherd article of 1964, and the present discussion. In his introduction, Hoijer makes the misleading statements that 'no data are available' or 'there is too little information on these languages to include them in the present discussion' in the case of Chetco, Tututni, Nongatl, Lassik, Sinkyone. In the case of Nongatl, for instance, P.E. Goddard from 1907–08 left an enormous amount of material: twenty-three fieldnote-books and thirty-seven texts therefrom in typescript (354 leaves), C.H. Merriam left some vocabulary from 1922, G.A. Nomland some vocabulary from 1928, and H.E. Driver got a few forms in 1935; all of this material is probably at Berkeley. For Chetco there are e.g. J.O. Dorsey's 1,345-item vocabulary from 1884 in the Smithsonian (BAE ms. 73), and Elizabeth Jacobs's fieldnotes from 1935. By far the most poorly documented PCA language is probably Applegate, for which there are only three short 19th century vocabularies in the Smithsonian (G. Gibbs "Nabiltse" ca. 1852, 100 items; W.G. Hazen 1857, 180 items; J.O. Dorsey "Dakubetede" 1884, ca. 250 items), and Sapir obtained nine Applegate bird-names in 1906, which he published in 1914, with the note that 'these two Athapascan dialects [Galice and Applegate] are probably practically identical' (1914:339–40). Of Applegate Hoijer states that he has 'seen no data in this language (except for a very small amount included in Sapir, 1914) but it is said to be essentially like Galice'. Even in this worst case, the available (if unpublished) data are in all likelihood at least adequate to provide a rough idea of how close Applegate was to Galice. In the case of the other languages, it will eventually be possible, with the development of a science of 'Amerindian philology', to determine much more from these older and phonologically (and otherwise also) very inadequate materials, especially by comparison with data from closely related languages which will be relatively well documented, such as Hupa.

Hoijer's 1960 article under discussion is a fine comparative study of the development of certain stem-initial obstruents in the PCA languages other than the omitted ones mentioned above. Like other Athapaskan, the PCA languages differ most strongly in the way the PA $*c$, $*č$, $*\underline{k}^w$, and $*\underline{k}$ series develop and tend to merge, and in this respect, phonologically at least, the PCA languages are not clearly set off from the rest of Athapaskan, but in fact share developments typical in the North. However, PCA is on the other hand rather clearly distinguished from most other Athapaskan (but cf. especially Hare and some Tutchone in the North) phonologically by the strong tendency for certain of the manner contrasts within the series also to break down, thus in the apicals e.g. $ʒ$, $c$, $s(\sim z)$ all $>s$ or $s \sim c$, i.e. the lenition of affricates to (voiceless) fricatives, and in the velars, broadly, $*k$, $*x>k$ and $*g$, $*\gamma$ ($*\gamma<$ intervocalic $x$) $>g$ in Galice and in all Californian except Hupa, and $*k$, $*x>x$, $*g>g$, $*\gamma>\gamma$ in Hupa and all Oregonian except Galice. The glottalized member of every series remains distinct as such. Hoijer summarizes (1960:969): 'The evidence presented in the preceding sections (1) clearly differentiates a PCA sub-stock of the greater Athapaskan family, and (2) strongly supports the hypothesis that this sub-stock has two main divisions, the Californian (Hupa, Wailaki, Mattole, and Kato) and the Oregonian (Tolowa, Chasta Costa, Galice, Coquille, Euchre Creek, and Umpqua).' This seems to be essentially correct, and seems also supported, as far as it goes, by morphology and lexicon. Hoijer carries his classification a step further, however, though with a strong note of caution (p. 970): 'As a provisional hypothesis, subject to change after a more detailed comparison has been made, the following grouping of PCA languages is proposed.

  A. California Division

    1. Hupa
    2. Wailaki-Kato-Mattole
      a) Wailaki

       b) Kato
       c) Mattole

  B. Oregon Division
    1. Southern group
       a) Euchre Creek-Coquille
         i. Euchre Creek
         ii. Coquille
       b) Tolowa
       c) Chasta Costa
    2. Galice (and Applegate?)
    3. Umpqua.'

Hoijer expects revisions in this scheme to become advisable, but he apparently does not expect the Stammbaum system itself to become untenable with further investigation. Hoijer's own data themselves clearly show however conflicting cross-classification, necessitating arbitrary weighting of one type of change over another in evaluating degrees of divergence; and further evidence from other sources, mostly unpublished, makes any Stammbaum most inappropriate as a model for the description of PCA relationships (beyond a fairly clear California-Oregon branching, but that too includes some cross-cutting isoglosses). This PCA dialect-complex situation was graphically presented in terms of isogloss patterns by Krauss in "Classifying the Athapaskan languages" (Handout, 68th Annual Meeting of the American Anthropological Association, New Orleans, November 1969). Generally, this much can be said: Hupa is rather aberrant (and relatively conservative) from the rest of the California group, which then shades through perhaps two or three stages of mutual unintelligibility or low intelligibility from Mattole (and Bear River) through Lassik, Nongatl, Sinkyone, to Wailaki, and then Kato. In Oregon Umpqua is the most aberrant, and most of the rest are perhaps mutually intelligible to a rather high degree, shading from Tolowa through Chetco into the Tututni (sub-)dialects (of which Euchre Creek is one), and eastward through Chasta Costa to Coquille, with Galice-Applegate as an isolated (but still not distant) extreme. The only major point that is somewhat unexpected from the geography is that Umpqua shares a number of traits in common with the Californian group.

Subsequent treatments by Hoijer of comparative PCA within the larger context of comparative Athapaskan are to be found especially in his "The Athapaskan languages" (1963, especially pp. 9–13), "Athapaskan classificatory verbs" (Davidson, Elford and Hoijer 1963, especially pp. 37–9 (Mattole and Galice)), and in his writings on Athapaskan glottochronology.

Krauss feels that it is correct to consider PCA a separate and earlier offshoot than Apachean from the North, and that there are indications (e.g. tonelessness, certain consonant developments) that its closest relatives in the north are in Western British

Columbia, especially perhaps Tahltan, as much or more than Chilcotin. Far too little is still known about that northern area, however. Certainly Californian areal influences have also been very important in shaping PCA (in this connection see Golla 1970 on consonant symbolism and diminutives).

## 1.5 *Apachean*

### 1.5.1 *Navajo*

Of the Southern Athapaskan or Apachean languages — and also of all the Athapaskan languages — indeed of all American Indian languages — Navajo[3] is by far the most important sociopolitically in terms of number of speakers. In spite of the decline in number of speakers of most Athapaskan languages, more persons now speak Athapaskan than probably ever before, the number of Navajos now having surpassed 120,000, perhaps even 140,000 and still growing, and most of these speak Navajo. (Recently published estimates of 80,000 — Chafe 1962, Sapir and Hoijer 1967 — are certainly far too low.) Accordingly, the quantity of linguistic (as well as anthropological) literature on Navajo dwarfs that on most other American Indian linguistic communities. The present account of work in Navajo will perforce be somewhat selective.

Harry Hoijer, who had studied Navajo as a student of Sapir's in the pre-war period, continued his and Sapir's joint work in Navajo, publishing their *Navaho texts* in 1942, and only much later, *The phonology and morphology of the Navaho language* in 1967 (for reviews of the latter, see Richard Stanley 1969, and Michael E. Krauss 1970a). Hoijer's fundamental *Navaho phonology* appeared in 1945c. Zellig Harris published a highly interesting restatement of part of Hoijer's phonology in "Navaho phonology and Hoijer's analysis" (1945). Additional publications by Hoijer on Navajo during the period, aside from those concerned more broadly with general Apachean or Athapaskan, include two articles on Navajo semantics: "Cultural implications of some Navaho linguistic categories" (1951a), and "Semantic patterns of the Navaho language" (1959). For a bibliography of the work of Harry Hoijer see *IJAL* 30:169-74, 1963, complete to that date. To this may be added, for Navajo, "Navaho" on word-classes and parts of speech (1966b), "Navaho reference verbs and verb expressions made up of two verb forms" (1968), and "Internal reconstruction in Navaho" (1969).

Closely related to the Sapir-Hoijer tradition in Navajo studies is the work of the late Berard Haile, also continuing his long association with Navajo from before the war. Most important here are his *Learning Navaho* in four volumes (1941-48), and his *A stem vocabulary of the Navaho language: Navaho-English* (1950), and *English-Navaho* (1951). The former, intended as a pedagogical work, is rather chaotically organized and difficult to use as a reference work, though fairly well indexed, but it

---

[3] The spelling with -*j*- is that officially adopted, in preference to the also current one with -*h*-, by the Navajo Nation.

contains a great deal of interesting grammatical and semantic information. The *Stem vocabulary* volumes, for all their serious defects, still constitute the most detailed lexicon of an Athapaskan language in print. Father Berard also leaves a vast collection of unpublished materials on and in Navajo at the Library of the University of Arizona, Tucson, and at the Department of Anthropology, University of Chicago. See further H. Hoijer 1951b, for a bibliography and appraisal of Father Berard's work to 1950.

Somewhat less closely related to the Sapir-Hoijer-Haile work is that of Robert W. Young and William Morgan. In addition to volumes of texts in and translations into Navajo, Young and Morgan published jointly in 1943 *The Navaho language* (reprinted 1967). This work consists of a grammar and Navajo-English and English-Navajo dictionary. It is probably the most useful reference work for many purposes (both comparative and descriptive) in existence for Navajo, indeed for any Athapaskan language, especially because of the Navajo-English dictionary, which is arranged essentially by stem, but includes excellent detailed and extensive derivational and paradigmatic information on verbs. Important supplements to this work are Young and Morgan's *The function and signification of certain Navaho particles* (1948), and especially, *A vocabulary of colloquial Navaho* (1951). More recently Young published a grammatical resumé as a section entitled "The Navajo language", in *The Navajo Yearbook* (1959), which he edited. In addition, William Morgan has collaborated with Leon Wall in Wall and Morgan's mimeographed *Talking Navajo before you know it* (1954), and a *Navajo-English dictionary* (1958) arranged alphabetically by word rather than by stem.

In 1940 Gladys A. Reichard published in collaboration with Adolph E. Bittany a significant booklet entitled *Agentive and causative elements in Navajo*, raising certain points that have yet to be integrated into other accounts of the language. Miss Reichard subsequently published a number of Navajo texts and articles on the language, notably and still significant "Linguistic diversity among the Navaho Indians" (1945), "Significance of aspiration in Navaho" (1948), and "The character of the Navaho verb stem" (1949). Her Navajo work culminated in her *Navaho grammar* (1952). This grammar is motivated in considerable part by Miss Reichard's general dissatisfaction with the approach of the Sapir-Hoijer-Haile 'school' of Navajo grammar, dissatisfaction largely misplaced on theoretical grounds, for which Reichard's grammar was severly criticized by Hoijer in his review in 1953 (see also G. Trager 1953; D.L. Olmsted 1953; A.G. Haudricourt 1954). In spite of glaring faults, the book remains of very great importance in Navajo studies, if for no other reason than the head-on attack on the derivational prefixes of the verb to which nearly half of the book is devoted. In this area the Sapir-Hoijer grammar is indeed very weak, and Reichard's account, chaotic though it is, remains the only serious systematic attempt in print at describing the derivational prefix system of the verb for Navajo (or, for that matter, of any other Athapaskan language). Not published, but significant as the only other major study dealing squarely with the derivational prefixes of the verb in more than a phonological way, and thoroughly systematic, though rather limited in scope, is Kenneth Hale's "The distribution of the class II prefixes in Navaho" (1956).

A final major 'pretransformational' contribution to Navajo linguistics is that of Herbert Landar, whose first article on the subject was "The Navaho intonational system" (1959), which was followed by a series of articles on e.g. word order (1960b, 1961), the optative (1962), and lexical notes, mostly in *IJAL* (see Landar 1967d:69). Most important, however, is Landar's *Navaho syntax* (1963), a phrase-structure (nontransformational) study of Navajo sentences, which is noteworthy also for its radical departure from conventional Navajo transcription. Landar's "Syntactic pattern in Navaho and Huichol" (1967a) deals especially with 'operators' (like Young and Morgan's 'particles'), and explores the application of transformations to Navajo sentence structure.

Transformational work on Navajo has begun to develop. Most of it is still in the form of theses and papers with limited distribution, but much of this is also of enough interest to warrant mention here. There have already appeared two doctoral dissertations on Navajo morphophonemics in terms of underlying representations and distinctive feature analysis. Muriel Saville's "Navajo morphophonemics" (1968), contains a review of the Sapir-Hoijer-Haile literature, on which it is based (e.g. Young and Morgan's *The Navaho language* is not even listed in the bibliography). Mrs. Saville has since been concentrating her research on Navajo dialectology.

A study of major importance is Richard Stanley's "The phonology of the Navaho verb" (1969b). Stanley boldly attempts to analyze the entire Navajo verb into single underlying representations for each morpheme, from which the phonetic representation can be generated by ordered rules, for both the entire prefix-complex, and also stem. The work has the advantage of being based on data from Young and Morgan's *The Navaho language*, and on work with Navajo informants. Though Stanley has lost an important source of insightful hypotheses in choosing not to investigate comparative Athapaskan evidence, and his analysis seems unrealistic at a number of important points to those who have studied other Athapaskan languages, it is still quite clear that Stanley has made an enormous and bold contribution at least to the study of Navajo. For instance, with regard to the verb stem, the intricate variations of which Hoijer documents but leaves unexplained as 'suppletive', Stanley not only segments into stem + a series of suffixes (a rather obvious step from a comparative point of view, and already attempted as internal reconstruction in Kenneth Pike and Alton L. Becker's "Progressive neutralization in dimensions of Navaho stem matrices" (1964), which was somewhat naive from an Athapaskan point of view but otherwise highly sophisticated and suggestive; see also Krauss, review of Sapir-Hoijer (1970a)); but Stanley attempts also to predict tone by positing an underlying glottal segmental suffix. That Stanley associates high tone with glottalization is counter to very clear historical evidence that Navajo high tone developed in the absence of glottalization, and low in its presence, but Stanley is certainly correct e.g. in attempting to account for Navajo tone in terms of glottalization.

Finally, Kenneth Hale and some students at the Massachusetts Institute of Technology produced a series of transformational studies on Navajo, concerned mostly with sentence structure. Of these papers, mimeographed at MIT in 1968, only one is published (Adrian Akmajian and Stephen Anderson's "On the use of the fourth person in Navajo, or Navajo made harder" (1970)); it is greatly to be hoped that further such studies will soon be printed. These papers are of great importance for Athapaskan studies in their originality and in constituting a beginning of research in the syntax (sentence structure) of an Athapaskan language, where they have already brought to light facts about Navajo of fundamental importance. For instance, in "Remarks on pronominalization and the passive in Navaho", by James E. Parrish, Stephen R. Anderson, Adrian Akamjian, and Kenneth Hale, Navajo nouns are discovered to be ranked in the order 1) human, 2) animal, and 3) inanimate, such that the passive transformation (*bi-* as pronominal object) applies only when the object is animate or human, and is equal in rank or outranks the subject; it is obligatory when the object outranks the subject, but optional when object and subject are of equal rank.

Hale (1971c), Frishberg (1971), and Taptto (1971, a native speaker of Navajo who has studied with Hale) have further investigated the complexities of this highly developed Navajo noun-ranking in a series of recent papers.

There are a number of important specialized contributions to certain areas of Navajo lexicology and semantics. Leland C. Wyman has contributed extensively in ethnobotany and ethnoentomology: with S. K. Harris in "Navajo Indian medical ethnobotany" (1941), and *The ethnobotany of the Kayenta Navaho* (1951), and most recently with Flora L. Bailey in *Navaho Indian ethnoentomology* (1964). In 1941 Adolph Bitanny made available a mimeographed Navajo medical dictionary. In anatomy there is Oswald Werner and Kenneth Begishe's mimeographed *Anatomical Atlas of the Navajo* (1966), now being revised and expanded. These works document the existence of a far more elaborate, extensive, and systematic development of areas of the scientific vocabulary of a North American Indian language than might otherwise be believed, even though the Franciscan Fathers' *Ethnologic dictionary of the Navaho language* (1910) was already remarkable for its ethnoscientific vocabularies. That work listed 200 insect names, but that already impressive number was increased to a stupendous total of 700 insect names by Wyman and Bailey's 1964 study. Also to be noted in this class is Norma Perchonock and Oswald Werner's "Ethnoscience methodology and categories of Navajo foods" (1969), Werner's "Semantics of Navajo medical terms" (1965), and (with Kenneth Begishe), "A lexemic typology of Navajo anatomical terms I: The foot" (1970), and "The classification of the Navajo universe" (1970). A number of articles by Herbert Landar also fall into this class: see Landar's bibliography in 1967d:69, items 69, 71, 74, 76, 80, 81.

To this list should be added Landar's "Class co-occurrence and Navaho gender" (1965b) and "The language of pain in Navaho culture" (1967b). (Oswald Werner's "Problems of Navajo lexicography" (1967) discusses especially the adaptation of the Navajo writing system to use in computers; see also H.-J. Pinnow's review of the volume, 1968a). Recent studies on noun-classification in Navajo verbs are by Simmons (1969) and Witherspoon (1971).

In the category of pedagogical grammars since those of Haile (1941-48) and Wall-Morgan (1954) mentioned above, at least three extensive and systematic Navajo learning grammars have recently been published: Irvy Goosen's *Navajo made easier* (1967); Robert W. Blair, Leo Simmons, and Gary Witherspoon's programmed *Navajo basic course* (1969); and Alan Wilson's *Breakthrough Navajo* (1969) and reader with full apparatus (Wilson and Dennison 1970). Pinnow has recently begun publishing one for German speakers, "Wir lernen Navaho" (1970b). Also to be noted is Oswald Werner, Kenneth Begishe, and Jeannette Frank's *A programmed guide to Navajo transcription* (1967). Irvy Goosen is preparing an expansion of the Wall-Morgan Navajo-English word dictionary, to include also an English-Navajo section. This veritable abundance of high quality practical materials for non-speakers to study Navajo is no doubt a reflection of the vitality of Navajo and its unquestionable and increasing sociopolitical importance. This category of linguistic literature exists in fact practically only for Navajo of all the Athapaskan languages.

Navajo is also unique among the Na-Dene languages in possessing its own reasonably extensive and varied literature published in the language itself, e.g. ethnography, religion (Navajo mythology and ceremonies), a newspaper, and translations into Navajo of western materials, secular and religious. (For a brief recent history of Navajo literacy see Penny Murphy in Spolsky et al. 1970). This literature cannot be detailed here; however, a bibliography of it (Spolsky et al. 1970) is in its second edition at the University of New Mexico under the direction of Bernard Spolsky. Spolsky's Navajo Reading Study Project at the University of New Mexico has published a series of reports on the status of the Navajo language in its so far successful struggle to maintain itself against the relentless pressures of Anglicization ("Navajo Language Maintenance", Spolsky 1970, 1971a, 1971b). This series also includes a report by Spolsky and Wayne Holm (1971) on literacy in Navajo, studies on Navajo orthography by Holm (1971a, 1971b, see also *Conference on Navajo Orthography*, 1969), reports on a conference on the teaching of reading in Navajo (Murphy 1970), on the development of reading materials (Atcitty et al., 1971), and on the Navajo vocabulary of six-year-olds (Spolsky et al. 1971a, 1971b; Holm et al. 1971).

At least four studies have been published concerning the teaching of English as a second language to Navajos, contrasting Navajo and English structures; see Pedtke and Werner (1969), Saville and Troike (1970), and Young (1959:473-510, 1968).

Another unique contribution in connection with Navajo is Oswald Werner's "A typological comparison of four Trader Navaho speakers" (1963) (see also *Linguistics* 13.121-3, 1965), a study of the (non-standardized) or rudimentary Navajo spoken by white traders with the Navajo. The existence of this phenomenon is also evidence of the vigor of Navajo.

There even exists an outstanding sketch of certain aspects of Navajo grammar of very general and popular interest, by Clyde Kluckhohn and Dorothea Leighton,

Chapter 8 entitled "The tongue of the people", pp. 182-214, of *The Navaho* (1946).

Finally, Kenneth Hale has written an inspired series of papers on Navajo linguistics for Navajos themselves in the study of their own language as a scientific and educational discipline. In this connection Hale also reports a paper by Higgins (1971) on the Navajo classifiers.

### 1.5.2 *Apache and Comparative Apachean*

All the other Apachean languages and comparative Apachean together have received far less attention than Navajo. There have been several significant studies in this area, however, where linguistic divergence is rather slight compared to that found in the rest of Athapaskan, such that Apachean in general is far better attended to linguistically than any other Athapaskan division.

Basic descriptive works in print on Apache (non-Navajo) are not numerous. Fundamental is Hoijer's early work on Chiricahua and Mescalero, which resulted in his *Chiricahua and Mescalero Apache texts* (1938a), which include important grammatical sketches of both languages or dialects, as well as fairly extensive texts. Hoijer also has stem lists for both in typescript, never published. Hoijer's "Chiricahua Apache" (1946a), is a typical sketch by Hoijer of part of the grammar of an Apachean language; like his *Phonology and molphology of the Navaho language* (1945c), this Chiricahua sketch is two-thirds devoted to the phonetics and morphophonemics, and the rest to the morphology, especially the verb inflexional prefixes. There is nothing on sentence structure. More recent work on Mescalero is in papers by Elaine Clark and Grace Sutton, both of SIL, who have gathered a considerable amount of field data which they are analyzing along the lines of the tagmemic model. As for Jicarilla and Lipan, no recent work whatever has come to this writer's attention. Lipan is probably on the verge of extinction.

The Apachean linguistic community next largest to Navajo is the group of very closely related and mutually intelligible dialects including San Carlos, White Mountain, Cibecue, Northern and Southern Tonto, with nearly 10,000 speakers total. This group, especially San Carlos, has been the object of a few major papers. Faye E. Edgerton's "The tagmemic analysis of sentence structure in Western Apache" (1963) is, as the title indicates, strictly drawn up in Pike's framework, and rather confirms what one would expect from Navajo if such a study for Navajo were available (see also Landar 1965a for a criticism of this paper). Not seen at date of writing is Marshall E. Durbin's "A componential analysis of the San Carlos dialect of Western Apache: A study based on analysis of the phonology, morphophonics, and morphemics" (1964), where, according to the abstract, 'the author proposes to demonstrate that the phoneme as a cultural unit produces a generative phonology, while distinctive features alone do not'.

Faith Hill's article "Some comparisons between the San Carlos and White Mountain dialects of Western Apache" (1963) gives a fair notion of the degree and kind of dialectal or subdialectal divergence, especially phonological, within the group. A significant unpublished work on this language is Faith Hill's "Tone in Western Apache". Recent papers on specialized semantic areas of the Western Apache lexicon are by Basso (1967, 1968), and Philip J. Greenfield (1971). Finally, Greenfield is working on a dissertation entitled "The phonological hierarchy of the White Mountain dialect of Western Apache", a work in the tagmemic framework.

Kiowa-Apache is by far the most divergent of all the Apachean languages. It is also near extinction, with fewer than ten speakers, all elderly. Two students with William Bittle have recently done specialized lexicographical work with the language: Julia A. Jordan on ethnobotany, and Michael G. Bross on body-parts and disease terms. William Bittle's "Kiowa-Apache" (1963 is the only published work on this language, and is largely a condensation of Bittle's doctoral dissertation "The position of Kiowa-Apache in the Apachean Group" (1956). Its title notwithstanding, this dissertation is essentially a descriptive work. It is based closely on the model Hoijer had developed for Apachean and published during the forties, and which has been very influential in Athapaskan studies. Bittle's work in Kiowa-Apache has the same strengths and limitations.

The fundamental work alluded to above, and probably the most influential in the history of Athapaskan studies, is Harry Hoijer's "The Apachean verb", which appeared serially as follows: "Part I: Verb structure and pronominal prefixes" (1945a); "Part II: The prefixes for mode and tense" (1946b); "Part III: The classifiers" (1946c;) "Part IV: Major form classes" (1948a); "Part V: The theme and prefix complex" (1949), supplementary to which should be added "Classificatory verb stems in the Apachean languages" (1945b) and "The structure of the noun in the Apachean languages" (1948b). These studies are profoundly the product of Hoijer's discipleship to Sapir in Athapaskan studies, but also clearly in keeping with the development of American linguistics during the first decade after the untimely death of Sapir, because of which certain ideas germinal in Sapir's thought failed to develop in Athapaskan, e.g. further 'internal reconstructive' treatment of the phonology, now resumed by the transformationalist work, instead of the rather 'hard-line' biuniqueness-taxonomic phonemics in ascendance during this period. Hoijer's "Apachean verb" remains nevertheless a classic landmark in Athapaskan studies. It is truly remarkable as a detailed descriptive analysis of at least the paradigmatic workings of the Apachean verb, in fact a tour-de-force in handling all the Apachean languages together, with copious exemplification, from Hoijer's own first-hand field data on them all.

Based also on this fieldwork is another earlier classic study by Hoijer on the comparative phonology of Apachean, "The Southern Athapaskan languages" (1938b), which is a very clear and reasonably detailed exposition of phonological differentiation within Apachean. Less felicitous is the Stammbaum-type classification of the Apachean languages Hoijer develops as a conclusion, arbitrary and not justified by the data as so well presented in the article itself (see Krauss 1969a), where in fact Apachean can clearly be seen as a typical dialect complex with many crossing isoglosses and cross-classifications. It is particularly important to stress the problem of 'Stammbaum vs. wave' in connection with Athapaskan, because of the apparent perennial hunger of anthropologists for neat family-tree genetic classifications from linguists for American languages, a hunger which Sapir and also Hoijer have often been tempted to satisfy, their footnoted reservations and qualifications unfortunately going unheeded. Hoijer amends his 1938 subclassification of Apachean in a paper presented at the 68th Annual Meeting of the American Anthropological Association, New Orleans, November, 1969, entitled "The position of the Apachean languages in the Athapaskan stock". On the basis of lexicostatistics, Hoijer shows that Kiowa-Apache is a separate Apachean language equidistant from the rest, and that the rest are dialects of one language. It is not clear whether the earlier Stammbaum for the rest still holds for Hoijer or is to be repudiated, and in any case the role of wave or convergence, certainly crucial in the development of the relationships within dialect complexes such as these, is not explicitly considered.

## 2. EYAK[4]

Eyak is not an Athapaskan language, but is in fact the only language clearly related to Athapaskan in the untroubled classical genetic sense. Clear cognates in Athapaskan can be found not only for Eyak affixes, but for stems also, with regular phonological correspondences. Eyak is coordinate with all of Athapaskan as one branch of the two-branch Athapaskan-Eyak family, and seems equidistant lexically to all Athapaskan (see section 5.3 below). On the other hand, areally, Eyak shares with Ahtena and Tanaina the peripheral ('Eskimoid') trait of PAE $*q > q$, $*\underline{k} > k$. Eyak, of very great value, in fact unique value by virtue of its comparative position, is of all the more crucial value for historical linguistics because of its extreme archaism in very many respects, both phonological and morphological, at least. For example, the Eyak verbal prefix-complex and stem-suffix system, compared with the Athapaskan, is relatively transparent and regular, and the source of many fundamental insights on the origin and development of the Athapaskan verbal prefix-complex. The study of Athapaskan can be immensely enriched by comparison with Eyak.

Eyak was neglected by American science, in fact forgotten by it, until discovery by Frederica de Laguna in 1930, and the publication of the very limited linguistic results of the 1933 Danish-American expedition, in Kai Birket-Smith and Frederica de Laguna's *The Eyak Indians of the Copper River Delta, Alaska* (1938). This monograph was based on about seventeen days' work with a few Eyak informants, and the linguistic material is limited mainly to a wordlist of about 500 forms and a few partial paradigms in a not very adequate phonetic transcription. Almost all the linguistic

---

[4] Pronounced [íyæk] in local English by Indians and whites, < Eyak /ʔi·ya·ɢ/, the name of one Eyak village-site, in later times the most important, < Chugach Eskimo /iiɣiaraq/, placename, 'neck (narrowing, at outlet of lake into river)'. The occasional English pronunciation /áyæk/, though included in Merriam-Webster's *Third International*, must be a spelling-pronunciation.

material in the fieldnotes is published in the monograph, the most notable exception being a short text, transcribed in the hand of Norman Reynolds. Reynolds was a graduate student at the University of Washington, along on the expedition. He has since disappeared, perhaps with unpublished Eyak data.

Although it was too late in his life for Sapir to do anything about it, it was easy for him to see from this material that Eyak was a most important discovery for comparative Athapaskan and for Na-Dene studies.

The Eyak tribe is a victim of genocide and White greed. Already in the thirties the Birket-Smith and de Laguna monograph shows the Eyaks nearing extinction, suffering cruel injustice that apparently is to continue to plague them until the last Eyak is gone in Cordova. The monograph actually lists by name the surviving Eyaks of the thirties, who did not number many more than thirty-eight. At present there are about three persons still capable of serving at all competently as informants for Eyak. The tragic decline of the Eyaks was not as well known to linguists as it should have been. For instance, Hoijer much later still gravely overestimates the Eyak population at 200 in his preface to *Language in culture* (1954).

The first American linguist to work with Eyak was John Peabody Harrington of the Smithsonian, who spent a few weeks with the Tlingit-Eyak bilingual George Johnson in Yakutat during the spring of 1940. Mr. Johnson's Eyak was already rusty but fairly adequate for Harrington's purposes. Harrington's voluminous notes, mostly ethnographic and anecdotal, contain about 500 Yakutat Tlingit forms, usually with their Eyak equivalents, mainly nouns, especially flora-fauna, and place-names, in a meticulous phonetic transcription often adequately observing all the necessary details, and more. Harrington's ear was superb, and his experience with languages of this part of the world was vast. But his perspective from a point of view of most linguistic theory was rather naive. Harrington never published any of this material, but it is preserved (at least most of it) at the Smithsonian. Harrington also left an unpublished typescript paper on the Yakutat flora-fauna terms, in which, simplifying his transcription for the typewriter, he comes amazingly close to a reasonable and adequate transcription of Eyak, a feat not approached before, and not surpassed for more than twenty years thereafter. Harrington never published any of this material, and his Eyak work remained largely unknown.

Then in 1952 Fang-Kuei Li spent some summer weeks on Eyak fieldwork, in Yakutat with Harrington's informant George Johnson and Anna Nelson Harry, widow of Galushia Nelson, Birket-Smith and de Laguna's chief informant from 1933, and also in Cordova with the late Scar and Minnie Stevens. Li got extensive vocabulary, and for the first time, extensive paradigms, and also for the first time, connected text in any quantity. His only publication concerning Eyak is "A type of noun formation in Athapaskan and Eyak" (1956), a short but very tantalizing article largely concerned with the *-l* 'instrumental' suffix.

In the summer of 1961 Robert Austerlitz spent several weeks with the three main surviving speakers of Eyak: Anna Nelson Harry of Yakutat, Lena Nacktan of

Cordova, and Marie Smith, daughter of Scar and Minnie Stevens, also of Cordova. Austerlitz collected some more paradigmatic and textual and general lexical material, but his main concentration was on flora and fauna terms, where his material, though unpublished, constitutes an especially significant contribution to Eyak studies.

In 1963 Michael E. Krauss began fieldwork on Eyak with all the surviving informants, especially Lena Nacktan and Anna Nelson Harry. Working in the field for several summers, and intensively on analysis of the available materials, Krauss has devoted a major effort to preserving a record of the Eyak language before it perishes. To this effort, Li and Austerlitz, and also Frederica de Laguna, have generously donated copies of their unpublished fieldnotes. Krauss has taken all these materials into account, as well as all the other earlier work (Harrington, and the nineteenth century Russian wordlists), in connection with his major objective; to elicit as much information as possible from the memory of the surviving speakers for as complete as possible a description of the Eyak language. By pooling the strengths of each of the informants, one can piece together a reasonably comprehensive account of the Eyak language.

In all of Krauss's publications on Comparative Athapaskan, Eyak, and Na-Dene, the Eyak material figures centrally. With the exception of his sketch "Eyak: A preliminary report" (1965a), which is mainly descriptive with only a few comparative notes, Krauss's publications concerning Eyak are more appropriately discussed in the comparative sections above. His Eyak material itself has at present reached the following stage: *Eyak Texts* in typescript, 912 p., Eyak text, edited, with translation and extensive annotation, and introduction, is ready for publication or reproduction for limited distribution; at approximately the same stage of preparation as the *Eyak Texts* is his massive *Eyak Dictionary*, ca. 4,000 pages, a virtually complete lexical account of the entire corpus of texts and elicitations, arranged by stem, and with English-Eyak index containing perhaps 10,000 English glosses. In 1970 the *Eyak texts* and *Eyak dictionary* were published in a limited edition of 50 copies, greatly reduced in bulk by microfilming and xerography, four pages of the original to a page. In 1971 Krauss paid a short visit to the Eyaks and collected some supplementary data and texts. Krauss has transcribed and edited about six hours of narrative Eyak text from Mrs. Harry. This is only a fraction, however, of the Eyak folklore the aged Mrs. Harry is now the only person to know. The author hopes that the publication or distribution of the Eyak materials will greatly enrich and provide new impetus to the field of comparative Athapaskan(-Eyak) and Na-Dene. Krauss is presently (1970) at the Massachusetts Institute of Technology, where several students are investigating with him various aspects of Eyak grammar.

One other publication concerning Eyak might be mentioned here: Uwe Johannsen's "Versuch einer Analyse dokumentarischen Materials über die Identitätsfrage und die kulturelle Position der Eyak-Indianer Alaska" (1963), which serves as a supplement — though it by no means completes the story — to Birket-Smith and de Laguna's already long account of the lengthy and involved series of errors in the literature concerning the identity of the Eyak and their language. Suffice it to say here that the true identity and significance of Eyak was discovered at the eleventh hour, and that Krauss's work notwithstanding, Eyak urgently deserves more scientific attention than it has received.

## 3. TLINGIT[5]

Tlingit is a relatively bright spot in the documentation of Na-Dene languages. Ever since F. Boas's *Grammatical notes on the language of the Tlingit Indians* (1917) (a remarkable production for about six weeks' fieldwork) and H. V. Velten's "Two Southern Tlingit tales" (1939) and "Three Tlingit tales" (1944), with their notes and vocabulary, it has been possible e.g. to do comparative work with Tlingit.

Some Tlingit materials of interest were gathered by J. P. Harrington in the 1940s, and are now in the BAE collection and the collection of Melville Jacobs. These include some notes from Yakutat, which include Eyak forms, and are described in the Eyak section of this report. Far less valuable is Harrington's "Phonematic daylight in Lhiinkit, Navajo of the north," (1945), discussed here under the subheading of Na-Dene.

A great amount of incidental Tlingit linguistic information has been gathered by the non-linguist ethnologists Frederica de Laguna, especially at Yakutat, and Catharine McClellan, especially inland Tlingit, during the 1950s and 1960s. None of their linguistic materials have been published systematically, but abound in their fieldnotes and ethnographic publications.

The work of H.-J. Pinnow on Tlingit is essentially historical-comparative, and will be dealt with under the subheading of Na-Dene.

Tlingit linguistics has been enormously advanced by the work of Constance Naish and Gillian Story, of the Summer Institute of Linguistics. Miss Naish's *A syntactic study of Tlingit* and Miss Story's *A morphological study of Tlingit* have appeared in mimeograph as M.A. theses at the University of London (1966). The style of both is 'tagmemic' but also 'London' or 'Prosodic', especially in the terminology. The organization and terminology, somewhat unfamiliar to many American linguists, make these theses relatively difficult (at any rate for the usual American linguist) to read quickly and use quickly as reference material, but the information available in these two works affords more complete coverage of the grammar of Tlingit from phonetics to the structure of complex sentences than is yet available in print for any other Na-Dene language. In addition to these theses, Naish and Story have made available an *English-Tlingit Dictionary: Nouns* (1963), a list of Tlingit nouns arranged by subject heading, and are currently preparing a similar list for verbs. These are on a more popular level, in the Tlingit orthography designed by the authors, primarily for the use of the Tlingit people, but also of very great usefulness to linguists. They will

---

[5] Pronounced variously in Alaska by Tlingits and local non-Indians as [kliŋkit, tliŋkit], or, perhaps best [tlíŋgít], < Tlingit /łengíd/ or /łɪngíd/ or /łɪngíd/ 'person, Indian, Tlingit', etymology uncertain.

soon publish a much more extensive and more systematic, but still popularly useful, dictionary of verb stems and themes, a work certainly eagerly awaited by students of Na-Dene. Naish and Story have also published primers, a hymnal and gospel materials in the Tlingit orthography. Naish, furthermore, has made available a mimeographed set of practical lessons for learning Tlingit (1968), which is encountering great and ever-increasing demand as classes for learning Tlingit continue to spring up in the Tlingit area schools. Andrew P. Johnson of Sheldon Jackson College, Sitka, is a native-speaking teacher of one such class, who also began a set of elementary conversational Tlingit lessons (1969).

The future of the language, however, seems very doubtful. Though there are over 1,000 persons still speaking Tlingit, almost none of these are children. The proportion of those under twenty years of age competent in Tlingit is low everywhere, and extremely low in most Tlingit communities. At the same time as the Tlingit language continues to be thus abandoned, probably beyond the point of no return as a normally living language, a native cultural renaissance, as part of the general movement of social upheaval concerning minority groups or cultures in the United States and Canada, has definitely invaded and already affected the Tlingit. These two powerful opposing forces for assimilation and against assimilation have converged now on the Tlingit people, who are caught in powerful cross-currents. Classes in Tlingit are becoming common in the Tlingit schools, but there is a lack of trained teachers and of materials, and the movement lacks organization. With these problems remedied, however, it would be difficult to predict to what extent and in what sense or function the Tlingit language may yet survive.

To answer the need for organization and training of teachers, the first Tlingit Language Teachers' Conference was held at Sitka, June 2–8, 1971. arranged by Elaine Ramos of Sheldon Jackson and directed by Michael Krauss. Tlingit teachers from several communities there agreed to adopt the Naish-Story orthography as a standard, and began to learn its use. Several resolutions were passed for the perpetuation, documentation, teaching and study of the Tlingit language and literature. A repository of Tlingit linguistic materials and center for Tlingit language publication is planned.

A course in Tlingit has been taught at the University of Alaska, College, by Michael Krauss and Walter Soboleff.

Richard Dauenhauer of Alaska Methodist University, and Mrs. Nora Florendo, a native Tlingit speaker, have collaborated in teaching and investigating Tlingit language and literature in Anchorage. They are preparing scholarly interpretative editions of Tlingit potlatch oratory, an art developed to exquisite poetic heights by traditional Tlingit people. Dauenhauer and Florendo have recently been joined by Jeffrey A. Leer, who is making important advances in Tlingit linguistics. Leer is currently preparing a badly needed extensive set of practical Tlingit lessons. He is also further continuing the study of Tlingit classificatory verb stems, begun by Dauenhauer and Florendo. It turns out that the noun-classificatory system in the Tlingit verb is much more complex than was hitherto supposed, that function being filled by a large set of stems as well as by certain positions in the prefix-complex (see further discussion in connection with Krauss 1968 under 5.1 and 5.5).

## 4. HAIDA

Though our information on the subject of Haida dialectology is still extremely meagre, Haida is apparently a single language with two major dialect groups, which we will call here the Northern and the Southern. They are mutually intelligible, to at least a great extent, but reportedly with considerable difficulty and difference between the Northern and Southern groups.

All that is left of Southern Haida is Skidegate. Another Southern dialect was Ninstints, at the southern extremity of Queen Charlotte Islands. Swanton (1911:209, 213) states that Ninstints 'differed so far from Skidegate that it may also have been entitled to dialectic rank, but so few of those who used to speak it now survive that we have no absolute knowledge on this point', and 'all that is known of the peculiarities of the Ninstints dialect is that it tended to substitute $k$ for $g$, and that the manner of its enunciation was esteemed by the Haida to resemble Athapaskan'. The dialect survived in fact until 1970, when the centenarian last speaker died at Skidegate. No one had done any linguistic work with her. Nancy Turner reports that the Ninstints dialect was considered to be quite close to the Skidegate, and that the Ninstints few plant names recorded ca. 1901 by C.F. Newcombe bear this out.

The Northern group is called Masset, from the name of the only settlement on the Queen Charlotte Islands where it survives. An offshoot of this group moved to the nearby islands of southern Alaska, in the eighteenth century, where they were known in the literature as the Kaigani, settling at Kaigani, Howkan, Sukwan, Klinkwan, Koiandlas, and Kasaan, later all at New Kasaan, and since about 1913 all at Hydaburg. The Hydaburg dialect is fairly close to Masset.

The number of speakers of Haida, who were once 8,000, has declined tragically, to a point much lower than is generally supposed. For example, Chafe (1962) estimates 700, fewer than 100 of these being Skidegate, most over 50 years of age. The total number of speakers in the Queen Charlotte Islands is probably under 50, of the very oldest generation only, perhaps a dozen at Skidegate and two or three dozen at Masset. Perhaps a dozen old speakers are living scattered in Canadian west coast cities. Of the Hydaburg dialect there are about a dozen speakers, of the older generation, at Hydaburg, with a few more scattered throughout southeastern Alaska and in Seattle. The total number of Haida speakers is in any case well below 100, and very rapidly diminishing. It seems extremely unlikely that living memory of any Haida will survive the twentieth century.

In the field of Haida linguistics, there are practically no results of any new work available since Sapir published "The phonetics of Haida" (1923, from a few hours' work with a Haida informant in 1920, half a century ago!) For fifty years the dying

Haida language has been virtually ignored. Perhaps the relative bulk of the work Swanton published on Haida (during the period 1902–12, including grammatical sketches, many texts from Masset, and a few from Skidegate) has misled potential investigators into believing that Haida has been reasonably well documented. This also is by no means the case: Swanton's transcriptions themselves are not even observationally adequate, do not even approach phonemic reliability. They are, however, an extremely valuable source of literary text, the like of which could not be obtained in the field today, but which probably could be retranscribed, with the help of an informant, in a verbatim rehearing of the originals, thus updating Swanton's material and using ('rehearing') materials no longer otherwise available. At this point the only Haida linguistics based on new work in print since Sapir are the few very general remarks (no data) of another illustrious linguist, E. Benveniste, "Les traits caractéristiques de la langue des indiens Haïda" (1953b), also the result of a very short period of fieldwork. In the early 1960s G. Bursill-Hall of Simon Fraser University tape-recorded a considerable number of Haida songs and texts, but has not been able to pursue the work. In 1968 Joseph F. Kess of the University of Victoria published a short article including a bibliography of published Haida materials and in the summer of that year did some fieldwork with three Skidegate informants, recording on 34 five-inch reels and transcribing about 1,200 forms in his fieldnotes, mostly lexical, though including some paradigmatic and syntactic elicitations.

Work on Haida for the last fifty years unfortunately can be reported on in detail on one page. Published results are so far virtually nil. All comparative work dealing with Haida in any way remains purely speculative. Good new primary information on Haida is urgently needed.

Very recently there seems at last to be a beginning of increased activity in Haida linguistics. Mrs. Nancy Turner, a University of British Columbia botanist, collected extensive Masset and Skidegate ethnobotanical lexicon in fieldwork during 1970 and 1971. In 1971 Randy Bouchard of the British Columbia Provincial Museum collaborated with Mrs. Turner in developing a new transcription-system, and on the basis of fieldwork with a very able Skidegate informant (Mrs. Peter Kelly, widow of Sapir's informant in 1920), and with taperecordings, developed a preliminary phonological analysis of the dialect (Bouchard 1971). Michael Krauss, working with Skidegate tapes and materials sent by Bouchard, did some further analysis of the phonology, and has observed, among other things, that Haida is a tone-language, like e.g. Navajo, with each syllable marked with either high tone or low tone. That Sapir did not fully understand this in 1920 is perhaps due to the fact that he became acutely aware of tone in the Na-Dene language group only somewhat later, in his 1922 work with Sarcee (see discussion of Sarcee in 1.2 above).

Carol M. Eastman and Paul K. Aoki of the University of Washington have recently begun work with Hydaburg informants in Seattle and have developed a preliminary analysis of the vowels (Eastman and Aoki 1971). In 1971 Margaret B. Blackman of

Ohio State University recorded some Masset and Hydaburg material on tape. Finally, Robert D. Levine, a graduate student at Columbia University, is to begin a full-scale field investigation of Skidegate Haida in early 1972.

## 5. COMPARATIVE ATHAPASKAN, ATHAPASKAN-EYAK, GLOTTOCHRONOLOGY, NA-DENE, AND BEYOND

This section is devoted to discussion of recent comparative or historical studies of broader scope than the local (local defined as confined to some subgroup of Athapaskan), such as Apachean (all of Hoijer's work before 1956), or Pacific Coast Athapaskan (Hoijer 1960), or some narrower subsection of the North (Howren's report on Hare-Bearlake-Dogrib, 1968, or Marsh, McClellan, Hoijer, Krauss on the position of Tagish), though Krauss's survey of Alaska is included because of its implications for the whole of Athapaskan. All such narrower studies are discussed in the non-comparative sections.

The line thus once drawn, it is not always practical here to separate further comparative studies of various scope, from general comperative Athapaskan (Proto-Athapaskan, PA) through Athapaskan-Eyak (PAE) and Athapaskan-Eyak-Tlingit (AET) and Athapaskan-Eyak-Tlingit-Haida (Na-Dene), to Sapir's Sino-Tibetan-Na-Dene or Swadesh's Vasco-Dene. Discussion will center first on studies of narrower scope, however, and proceed to the broader.

### 5.1 Comparative Athapaskan

The Athapaskan languages are so clearly and closely related that in spite of the late European contact with most of the Athapaskan realm and its relative inaccessibility, the Athapaskan family had been established and reasonably well defined in the scientific literature already over a century ago.

The founder of modern comparative Athapaskan was Edward Sapir, in that he was the first to organize any concrete hypothesis about the nature of proto-Athapaskan. Sapir's first publication on Athapaskan (1914) is already comparative. Sometime between his first Athapaskan fieldwork, in 1906, and the publication of his report on Na-Dene, in 1915, Sapir had already established the fundamentals of his reconstruction of Proto-Athapaskan (PA), although he did not explicitly explain how he arrived at this reconstruction in print until much later (1931). The symbols Sapir uses for PA in 1915 are the following: $d\ t^c\ t!\ tl!\ l\ l\ ts\ ts!\ s\ z\ dj\ tc^c\ tc!\ c\ g\ \underline{k}\ \underline{x}\ g\ k^c\ k^{\prime}\ \underline{x}\ \gamma\ \gamma w\ h^{\prime}$ $m\ n\ \eta\ y\ i\ e\ a\ o\ \check{e}$, which imply that Sapir was thinking in terms of the following system:

| | | | | | | | | | |
|---|---|---|---|---|---|---|---|---|---|
| d | λ | z | ž | g̱ | g | (gʷ?) | | | |
| t | ƛ | c | č | ḵ | k | (kʷ?) | | i | u |
| tʼ | ƛʼ | cʼ | čʼ | ḵʼ | kʼ | (kʼʷ?) | ʔ | ə | |
| | l | s | š | x̱ | x | (xʷ?) | h | e | a |
| | l | z | (ž?) | y | γ | γʷ | | | |
| m | | n | | | ŋ | | | | |

At this point Sapir did not consider tone at all in Na-Dene languages. Some of this reconstruction seems to have been influenced by extra-Athapaskan (Tlingit and Haida comparative) considerations, and Sapir is vague about alternations between voiced and voiceless fricatives. He also has (1915:539) Ath *ts!ai, *ts!a· 'dish', where especially the a· is puzzling. In any case, Sapir never explains the system as such and never explains distributions beyond the principle that the canonic form of stems is CV(C). Sapir's system becomes clearer in its functioning and detail and distributions in the 1930s with the work of Li and Hoijer, who were Sapir's students starting in the late 1920s. In the 1930s Li published a series of fundamental studies of Mattole (1930b), Sarsi (1930a), and Chipewyan (1932, 1933), which though still not explicit formulations of Proto-Athapaskan structure, were largely historical-comparative and (especially 1933) contained the most highly developed and detailed elaboration of Sapir's system that ever reached publication. Hoijer made excellent use of Sapir's reconstruction of PA in his 1938b account of the development of Apachean phonology, but it was not until the 1950s that Hoijer began publishing on Athapaskan more widely than Apachean. Hoijer's first publications that go beyond Apachean were in 1956 in the field of lexicostatistics, and will be discussed with the other lexicostatistic studies. In 1956 Hoijer also published a comparative study of Athapaskan kinship terms (1956c), collating from a very large number and wide variety of sources. This is the only published study by Hoijer containing explicit PA reconstructions, and follows Sapir's general framework, but Hoijer himself does not claim that his reconstructions are based on any rigorous formulations. Hoijer continued making good use of Sapir's reconstruction, though not further developing it, in his 1958 and 1960 papers. By far his most ambitious paper of this sort is "The Athapaskan languages" (1963a). The purpose of these papers, especially the latter, is to use the differentiation in development of Sapir's PA occlusive series, especially the affricate *c, *č and *ḵ series, to classify the Athapaskan languages, presumably into a genetic family tree, a problem of primary interest to Hoijer.

Sapir's reconstruction of Proto-Athapaskan had remained fundamentally unchanged for about 50 years, when in (a paper entitled "Recent linguistic research in Alaska and a new look at Proto-Athapaskan") 1961 Michael Krauss showed from his work in Alaskan languages, and from material already in the ms. of Hoijer 1963a, that Sapir's *č series had been in fact two PA series, which Krauss reconstructed *č and *ḵʷ, in order to explain the oppositions ts : tr in certain Alaskan languages (Minto, Ingalik, Kutchin, Han) which correspond with each other and also with ts : pf in Boas's data from the extinct Tsetsaut. This first reconstruction of the new PA series as *$ḵʷ$ was made on a purely internal Athapaskan basis, but is obviously reinforced by the correspondence with Eyak č : k(ʷ). Krauss published a formulation of the new reconstruction of PA in "Proto-Athapaskan-Eyak and the problem of Na-Dene I: The phonology" (1964a); this paper, though seriously marred by many glaring printer's errors, constituted a major and fundamental revision of Sapir's long-standing PA reconstruction. It included e.g. the new PA *$ḵʷ$- series, prediction of voiced fricatives as intervocalic variants of the voiceless, reconstruction of the vowels as a system of four full vowels and three reduced (both *i* and *e* reducing to ə), and also, for the first time, formulated explicit tone correspondences. Krauss also proposed a relatively explicit definition of the PA stem, in terms of a formula CVT, where T is a string of stem-final consonant and/or glottalization and/or suffixes, which ultimately may explain both tone and gradation in the stem-vowel.

Hoijer's "Hare phonology: An historical study" (1966c) is based on materials collected by Li in 1929 (see section on Canada); the historical discussion in this paper is the first by Hoijer taking as point of departure the PA phonological system as revised by Krauss.

Fang-Kuei Li, who was the major contributor to comparative Athapaskan studies during the 1930s, maintained his interest but not his former activity in this area. Li's only recent publication in comparative Athapaskan is "Some problems in comparative Athapaskan" (1965), which touches briefly on various points. Li's "A type of noun formation in Athapaskan and Eyak" (1956), mentioned here also under the heading of Eyak, is especially interesting in demonstrating for the first time the extraordinary usefulness of Eyak in comparative Athapaskan(-Eyak) studies.

Two articles on PCA languages, V. K. Golla on Hupa nouns (1964) and Jane Bright on Tolowa phonology (1964), are partly historical-comparative. Charles Pyle, a student with R. Howren at Iowa University, completed there a Master's thesis, "Proto-Athapaskan stem consonants" (1968), on certain problems of PA phonology not well accounted for by Krauss's 1964 formulation. G. Tharp in his paper (1972) on the position of Tsetsaut, in spite of some errors, makes the important point that in Proto-Athapaskan Krauss's *$ḵʷ$ series was probably coronal, not velar (i.e. no longer velar as Krauss had reconstructed it for Proto-Athapaskan-Eyak).

Robert Howren's "A formalization of the Athabaskan 'd-effect'" (forthcoming) is particularly important as being the first and still so far the only historical-comparative study of Athapaskan in the transformational-generative framework. It deals with the restricted problem of formulating phonological rules for the 'd-effect' (reflex of the PA *də-classifier) in Dogrib especially, then also in Chipewyan, Sarsi, Carrier, and Navajo. Howren then formulates a general d-effect rule (e.g. (-də-s- >) -d-z- > -ʒ-) for a wide area of Athapaskan. It turns out, incidentally, that this area for some reason is roughly coterminous with that in which syllabic tone has developed (Canadian [including Han, Kutchin] and Apachean, but not PCA or Alaska, or Eyak).

Comparative Athapaskan studies as such are virtually limited to phonology at this point still, though Hoijer has completed a manuscript on comparative Athapaskan morphology (Hoijer 1971), and there is a fair amount of discussion of comparative Athapaskan morphology in the broader Na-Dene literature, to be discussed below. The comparative study of Athapaskan sentence structure (syntax) is completely undeveloped. In addition to lexicostatistic-glottochronological study of the Athapaskan lexicon, also to be discussed below, there are a number of studies published in specialized areas of the Athapaskan lexicon: Virginia D. Hymes's "Athapaskan numeral systems" (1955), Hoijer's article, mentioned above, on Athapaskan kinship terms, and a paper by Marshall Durbin, "Proto-Athapascan pronouns", read at the Annual Meeting of the American Anthropological Association, November 1968 (see *Abstracts* for the Meeting). Classificatory verbs have received a great deal of attention, starting with Hoijer's "Classificatory verb stems in the Apachean languages" (1945b). Very important here is William Davidson, L. W. Elford, and H. Hoijer's "Athapaskan classificatory verbs" (1963), which compares the Navajo, Chipewyan, Dogrib, Mattole, and Galice. After the publication of this article there ensued a veritable flurry of (uncoordinated) publication on this subject: see Mary Haas "Language and taxonomy in Northwestern California" (1967), and *The prehistory of languages* (1969:93–96), David and Kay Henry "Koyukon classificatory verbs" (1965), Herbert Landar "Seven Navaho verbs of eating" (1964), "Class co-occurrence and Navaho gender (1965a) and "Tena'a classificatory verbs" (1967c), Keith Basso "The Western Apache classificatory verb system: A formal analysis" (1968), Leon Simmons "A transformational generative analysis of Navaho classificatory verbs" (1969), Gary Witherspoon "Navajo categories of objects at rest" (1971), and most broadly M. E. Krauss "Noun-classification systems in Athapaskan, Eyak, Tlingit, and Haida verbs" (1968). This last item is of course not restricted to Athapaskan and will be discussed under Na-Dene. See also section 3, for study of this problem in Tlingit.

Also to be mentioned here is a paper by Landar on verbs of 'being' (1967d); one by Pinnow (1966) on some of the well-known special characteristics of Athapaskan morphological and lexical structure generally; and a discussion by Voegelin (1951) on Sapir's much overemphasized theory that Athapaskan verb stems are nominal in origin, the converse being equally often the case: various types of nominalization are very productive in Athapaskan, and a large number of stems serve equally in nouns and in verbs. Finally, Voegelin et al. (1963) typologizes the phoneme inventories of languages of several families, including Athapaskan (p. 19–23), and comes up with figures evaluating the degree of differentiation of phoneme inventories within the Athapaskan groups, Apachean showing an internal differentiation index of 5, Pacific Coast Athapaskan 8, Northern Athapaskan 15, within a maximum of 22 for all Athapaskan. These figures compare and coincide very nicely with Hoijer's (1956) glottochronological figures (see section 5.4).

## 5.2 Classifying the Athapaskan Languages

Another major goal in comparative Athapaskan studies, especially in Hoijer's work, as a continuation of Sapir's, has been the reconstruction of the external as well as internal history of the Athapaskan languages, i.e. their genetic subclassification. Attempts to accomplish this have been largely disastrous, based largely on two false premises. The first false premise is that the Stammbaum model (implying pure divergence, 'campfire'-theory) is adequate to explain the relationships. The second false premise is that even if Athapaskan were in fact a group of languages thus related (by pure divergence), the Athapaskan 'languages' as now known (i.e. more or less the units set up by Cornelius Osgood in his 1936 pioneering classic *The distribution of the Northern Athapaskan Indians*, which has apparently been taken as a definitive working map of Athapaskan) are very largely mythical and arbitrary groupings. Osgood often separates communities with virtually complete mutual intelligibility (e.g. Chipewyan and Yellowknife, Bear Lake and Hare); or groups together what are two very different linguistic communities: there are certainly dialects of 'Slave' which are hardly or not at all mutually intelligible; or includes in 'Ingalik' the language of the Upper Kuskokwim, profoundly different from Ingalik and not at all mutually intelligible with it, and also includes therein part of the Tanaina area. Yet of the Athapaskan world, Osgood knew Tanaina relatively well, and best of all Ingalik, both of which he had studied at first hand (publishing one ethnographic monograph on Tanaina, and three on Ingalik; 'Ingalik', incidentally, is an opprobrious term, still resented by many of the group). Areas such as those designated by 'Tanana' or 'Beaver' or, especially, 'Slave' are extremely vague perhaps from any point of view, certainly so from a point of view of what languages they designate.

Krauss has repeatedly emphasized (1964b, 1969a) that it is not possible to subclassify the Athapaskan languages meaningfully solely or even largely on the basis of the Stammbaum model, but that Athapaskan must be viewed as a dialect complex with many convergence ('wave') as well as divergence (Stammbaum) relationships, and further, that PCA and Apachean are each themselves dialect complexes which are in turn parts of the greater Athapaskan dialect complex.

In Sapir's time reliable Northern Athapaskan data came from checkpoints generally so few and far between that most points were isolated enough from each other (artificially, by simple ignorance of what lay in between) to make Athapaskan look like a group of discrete languages. This image dies hard. Sapir was able to notice certain close relationships, e.g. Hare and Dogrib, but was understandably hesitant to make strong claims.

Hoijer has been especially persistent (1938b, 1960, 1962a, 1963a, 1969a) in his attempts to make a genetic subclassification of the Athapaskan languages according to a Stammbaum model. His very important paper "The Athapaskan languages" (1963a) is by far the most ambitious — and therefore the most disastrous — along this line. It includes, for the first time for Hoijer, the Northern Athapaskan languages, 'classifying' the whole of Athapaskan into (presumably) genetic 'substocks', according to the differential development of Sapir's PA *$ts$-, *$t\check{s}$- (Krauss's *$t\check{s}$- and *$\underset{\sim}{k}{}^w$-), and *$\underset{\sim}{k}$-series, in stem-initial position. This is an admittedly tiny set of criteria on which to base 'substocks'. The result is interesting from a purely typological point of view, perhaps. But due to the obvious inadequacy of the criteria, and what should be an equally obvious inadequacy of the theory based exclusively on divergence (and ignoring all diffusion, convergences, and simple parallel innovations or retentions), and extremely frequent inadequacy of the data and often of the interpretation of the data, the results are predictably absurd from a genetic point of view. Hoijer's Northern 'substocks' 3(a, b, c), 5, and 7 are especially meaningless. For 7 (Tagish) see section 1.2. 'Substock' 3 has in common only a $t\theta$-like reflex of *$ts$, and as such should include all of 'substock' 4, and also much of Pacific Coast Athapaskan (e.g. Chasta Costa and Tututni). PA *$ts$ may well have been fronted [ts] or even [tθ], and [tθ] was also no doubt an intermediate stage in the development to $tl$ characterizing 'substock' 2 (Koyukon) and the labials characterizing 'substock' 6 (Hare, Dogrib [but also Mountain, Bear Lake, and, from 'substock' 3a, some Slave]). 'Substock' 5 is characterized by a further merger, of *$ts$ with (Sapir's) *$t\check{s}$, i.e. of three series, a trait so widespread throughout Athapaskan that it includes languages otherwise as disparate as Ahtena and Sarcee (and according to Hoijer also Tahltan, Sekani, Beaver, [and should also include some Tanaina, Kwalhioqua-Tlatskanai, some Oregon Athapaskan]). In this scheme no consideration is given to the development of vowels, of tone, or of consonants in any other position (in stem-final position many or most consonants have been lost altogether in Kutchin and Han of 'substock' 4, Hare-Dogrib of 'substock' 6, Tutchone of 'substock' 3c, Slave of 'substock' 3a); to say nothing of morphology, syntax, lexicon, which are left entirely out of account.

It is possible to apply this restricted set of criteria much more completely, and to include therein the fourth series, reconstructed by Krauss as *$\underset{\sim}{k}{}^w$. Krauss reconstructs the four series as follows: | $ts$ | $\underset{\sim}{k}$ | or more abstractly | $c$ | $\underset{\sim}{k}$ |, or still more | $t^y$ | $\underset{\sim}{k}{}^y$ | | $t\check{s}$ | $\underset{\sim}{k}{}^w$ | | $c^w$ | $\underset{\sim}{k}{}^w$ | abstractly | $t^{yw}$ | $\underset{\sim}{k}{}^{yw}$ |. With the loss of the oppositions (whatever their exact nature), the following patterns are attested in Athapaskan-Eyak, without regard, for the moment, to the actual phonetic nature of the reflexes:

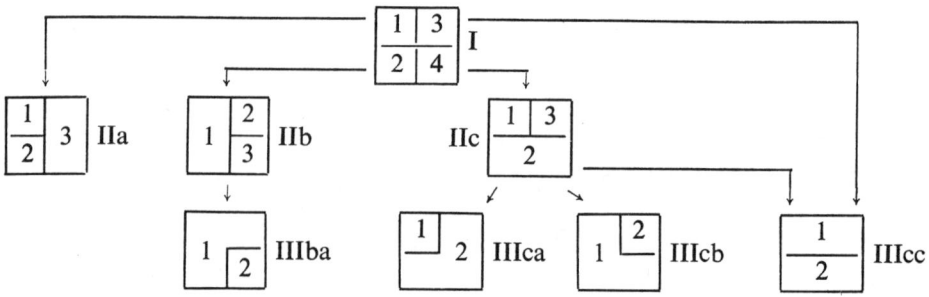

Since lost oppositions are not restorable, patterns are uniquely derivable (except that IIIcc may also be derived directly from I; and that theoretically IIIca might be derived from IIa and IIIcb from IIb, but IIa is Eyak, IIb is mainly Tsetsaut, whereas IIc is very widespread). As Krauss (1964a:120) points out, there is never a merger of diametrically opposed series without involving also a third series, a necessary and very telling condition for the validity of the pattern of oppositions as shown. The numerals within the boxes refer to the reflexes themselves, which are now given below in the order indicated by the numerals:

| | | | | | |
|---|---|---|---|---|---|
| I | tθ | ts | tš | tr | Central Tanana, Kutchin, Han, Yukon Ingalik (but Han and Kutchin have also palatalized versions of all series, and all Ingalik has a split, tš and k, for *ḳ) |
| | tṣ | ts | tš | tr | a few older speakers of Upper Kuskokwim |
| IIa | ts | tš | k | | Eyak |
| IIb | ts | tš | pf | | Tsetsaut (the informants Levi and Jonathan) |
| | ts | tš | tr | | Upper Kuskokwim (most speakers) |
| IIc | ts | tš | k | | Outer Tanaina, Hupa, Wailaki |
| | tθ | ts | k | | Holikachuk |
| | tł | ts | k | | Outer Koyukon |
| | tł | ts | tš | | Inner Koyukon |
| | tθ | ts | tš | | Kuskokwim Ingalik, Transitional Tanana, Upper Tanana, Tutchone, Chipewyan, most Slave |
| | tṣ | ts | tš | | at least some Carrier, some Beaver, some Tututni, Chasta Costa |
| | W* | ts | tš | | Hare, Bearlake, Mountain, Dogrib, at least Wrigley Slave (*W = various labials) |
| | ts | tš | tšʸ | | Mattole, Bear River |
| IIIba | ts | pf | | | Tsetsaut (the informant Timothy)[6] |

[6] Tharp (1972.19) fails to clarify this point, that Timothy has simply merged Levi's ts- and tš-series, actualizing them both as something Boas usually heard as ts-, as the following examples will demonstrate:

| | | Timothy | Levi |
|---|---|---|---|
| 1. | mosquito | dzəsdzɔ·' | ts'esdja, ts'əsdjɔ·' |
| 2. | sing thou! | ɪndzɛ' | ɪ'ndjɪ |
| 3. | rain | -tsa | -tca' |
| 4a. | strong (big) man | adətsxa | adəntcxa' |
| 4b. | sea (big water) | txu tsxo' | txu tcxo, tsxə |
| 4c. | big house | ŭntsxa' kxə' | khu tcu'la |
| 5. | small | utsa'ə | utcɛye·' |
| 6. | younger brother | tse·'e | -tce·'e, -tcce·'ɛ |
| 7. | old man | sa·'na | ca·n |
| 8. | thumb | -'łatsxa | (cf. Chipewyan -làtcɛ́ð) |
| 9. | tomorrow | tsatsa·" | tcatca·'lɛ |
| 10. | moccasins | tse·qa·'' | -cika- |

It may well be that Timothy's further merger is due to his defective command of a moribund

| | | | |
|---|---|---|---|
| IIIca | *ts* | *tš* | at least some Tahltan, Tagish(?), Kato, Lassik, Sinkyone, Nongatl, Umpqua |
| IIIcb | *tṣ* | *k* | Ahtena (except Mentasta), Inner Tanaina |
| | *ts* | *tš* | Mentasta Ahtena, the youngest Waska brother speaking Kuskokwim Ingalik, Kaska, Sekani, Sarcee, Chilcotin(?), Nicola(?), Kwalhioqua, Tlatskanai, some Tututni, Coquille, Galice. |
| IIIcc | *ts* | *tš* | all Apachean |

Though this classification is not without some interest, there are many obvious absurdities. The youngest Waska brother would no doubt be surprised not to belong to the same 'substock' of Hoijer's (5) as his brothers (3a)! Many nearly identical idiolects or dialects of single languages end up in different 'substocks' (e.g. Ingalik, Tsetsaut, Tututni, Tanaina, Upper Kuskokwim), while vastly different languages end up in the same (e.g. Upper Kuskokwim and Tsetsaut, Tanaina and Hupa, Tahltan and Kato, Mentasta Ahtena and Sarcee and Kwalhioqua and Galice).

Krauss in his review (1964b) of Hoijer (1963a) and subsequently (e.g. 1969a, 1970b) has repeatedly stressed the limitations of this type of approach, and also the danger that some anthropologists, ignoring any footnoted qualifications or reservations, will inevitably take such schemes quite seriously as the genetic substocks they have so long and eagerly awaited. Robert Howren has continued somewhat in this vein, for parts of Canada, talking of 'substocks' (see section 1.2), but treading with due caution on what he knows to be shaky ground. George Tharp, on the other hand, in his attempt to 'classify' Tsetsaut (1972) falls headlong into the pit: he puts Tsetsaut into Hoijer's 'substock' 5, along with Tahltan, Beaver, Kaska, Sekani, Sarcee, Ahtena, and closest of all to Tahltan and Beaver because these latter two show both *tš*- and *ts*-type reflexes of Sapir's **tš*-series. In reality, however, the apparent dual reflexes in Tahltan and Beaver do not correspond in any way with the two Tsetsaut series (*ts* from **tš* and *pf* from **k̭*$^{w}$), but are reflexes of **ts* and **k̭*$^{w}$ completely undifferentiated, the variation arising from free phonetic variation and/or inconsistent transcription and/or dialect mixtures. Tsetsaut may indeed be closest to Tahltan (as well as geographically) in terms of morphology, syntax, and/or lexicon, but surely not in phonology. It is greatly to be hoped that there will soon be enough good documentation of Tahltan so that we may investigate this possibility. From a phonological point of view, the really striking thing about Tsetsaut (aside from the *pf* from **k*$^{w}$) is the very severe loss of stem-final consonants, in which it strongly resembles not any of Hoijer's

language, very much as in the case of the youngest Waska brother, the youngest speaker of the moribund Kuskokwim Ingalik, nearly replaced by Eskimo, which does not encourage the maintenance of more than one sibilant affricate series. The same may be said of Nass River Tsimshian, Timothy's favored language, which, according to Boas (BAE-B 40.289, 291), has only one sibilant affricate series, the affricates of which 'have a clear continued *s*-sound, the tip of the tongue touching the teeth; while *s* has a decided tinge of English *sh*'.

'substock' 5 languages, but Kutchin, Han, Hare, Mountain, Bearlake, Dogrib, Slave, and is the only language not contiguous to that group to undergo such loss so severely. There is a further typological resemblance also, to Kutchin and Han in preserving *$ḵ^w$* distinct (*tr* in Kutchin and Han, *pf* in Tsetsaut), and to Hare, Mountain, Dogrib, Bearlake, Wrigley Slave in developing a labial series (from *$ts$ in the Canadian group, from *$ḵ^w$ in Tsetsaut), suggesting, along with the ethnographic evidence, some such interior geographic origin perhaps. And this does by no means eliminate probable similarities of Tsetsaut with Tahltan at other levels, which could easily be accounted for by a theory allowing for diffusions and convergences. These are fundamental concepts which have been recognized for at least a century in comparative-historical linguistics, and which can hardly be ignored in the study of a single family of languages spoken over a contiguous area, in fact a classic instance of a dialect complex.

Krauss's blanket survey of the whole of Alaska for (at least) the (surface) phonology of stems proved beyond any doubt that even in this area of deepest Athapaskan divergences, Athapaskan relationships must still be viewed as those of a dialect complex. A few schematic examples will suffice to illustrate this point. PA *$q$ (and *$q^w$) and *$ḵ$ remain $q$ and $k$ in some (Outer) Koyukon, all Ingalik (but there *$ḵ > č$ before front vowels), all Tanaina, and most Ahtena (except interiormost Mentasta), whatever the differences in the rest of the phonology of these languages. It can be no coincidence that this non-fronting of velars occurs uniquely (though also in Hupa, Wailaki) in contiguous languages (which themselves, incidentally, are also largely contiguous with Eskimo). In Ingalik *$c$, *$č$, *$ḵ^w > tθ, ts, tr$ respectively, but in Outer Tanaina *$c > ts$, *$č$ and *$ḵ^w > tš$, and in Inner Tanaina and in Ahtena *$c$, *$č$, *$ḵ^w$ all $> tš$, i.e. Ahtena and Inner Tanaina share the further merger of $ts$ ($< *c$) and $tš$ ($< *č, *ḵ^w$). The only major phonological difference between Ahtena and Inner Tanaina is the vowel shift which all Tanaina shares with Ingalik, *$u > i$ ($= i < *i$), though Tanaina and Ingalik are otherwise very different (though sharing also the velar non-fronting). Krauss (1971) has made a preliminary presentation of some of these patterns in terms of isogloss maps, and is at present planning a major publication of them for 1972.

Another interesting point brought out by Krauss's survey of Alaska is the areal similarity to Eskimo of 'Peripheral' Alaskan Athapaskan: (Outer) Koyukon, Ingalik, Tanaina, (Outer, i.e. all but Mentasta) Ahtena, all of which keep *$ḵ : q$ as such, surely an Eskimo trait, whereas in the interior *$ḵ : *q > č : k$. Furthermore, in (all) Koyukon and Tanaina and Ahtena the number of obstruent series is reduced by mergers (instead of fronted, but generally without mergers, as in the interior). In Koyukon *$c$ ($> *tθ$) $> λ$ ($= λ < *λ$), and in all these languages *$ḵ^w$ and *$č$ merge, to $ts$ in Koyukon, $tš$ in Outer Tanaina, and then in Inner Tanaina and Ahtena the resulting $ts$ and $tš$ merge to $tš$, with the general Eskimo-like result of only one or two (non-laterally) affricated series, thus:

| | | | | | | |
|---|---|---|---|---|---|---|
| Inner Koyukon | t | tl | ts | tš | k | |
| Outer Koyukon | t | tł | ts | | k | q |
| Ingalik | t | tł tθ | ts | tr | k | q |
| Proto-Athapaskan | t | tł | ts | tš | ḵʷ k | q |
| Outer Tanaina | t | tł | ts | tš | k | q |
| Inner Tanaina and Ahtena | t | tł | tś | | k | q |
| Mentasta | t | tł | ts | | tš | k |
| Minto, Upper Kuskokwim | t | tł tθ | ts | tr | tš | k |
| Eyak | t | tł | ts tš | | k | q |

Compare especially Outer Koyukon and Inner Tanaina-Ahtena with Eskimo (*p t*) *č k q*. Inner Koyukon and Mentasta are clearly cases of 'interiorized peripherals', i.e. affricates merged (peripheral trait, Eskimoid), but velars fronted (interior trait, non-Eskimoid).

In the vowel system, the reduction of the four full vowels to three in Tanaina (*\*i, \*u > i, \*e > a, \*a > u*) and Ingalik (*\*i, \*u > e, \*e > a, \*a > o*), and reduction of the three reduced vowels probably to one (*\*ə, \*a, \*v > ə*) is also no coincidence in the context of (Yupik) Eskimo, which has the vowel system *i a u ə*. All these phonological convergences with Eskimo seem to have taken place in the virtually complete absence of any other type of convergence. Lexical borrowing is very recent and superficial, and grammatical borrowing seems virtually out of the question. Exactly how this areal situation has come about remains a very interesting mystery and an important theoretical question. See also Melville Jacobs "The areal spread of sound features in the languages north of California" (1954) and Mary Haas *The prehistory of languages* (1969, Ch. 5 "Prehistory and diffusion", especially pp. 84–89, 93–96).

Another major set of phonological wave-traits in Athapaskan is the deterioration of the PA stem-final consonant system as such. This system was at one time complex, as still in Eyak, consisting of a string of zero to perhaps, with suffixes, as many as four consonants clustered. With Koyukon as almost the sole exception, no modern Athapaskan language preserves overt clusters, though of course there is plenty of indirect evidence for them in variations in the shape of the stem in all the languages, and of course comparatively. The glottalized/nonglottalized distinction in stem-finals is lost as such in a very large sector of the North, and within that sector there are further mergers and reductions in stem-final consonants, to the point in the Kutchin-Hare-Slave core of the area where very few or virtually no obstruents any longer occur stem-finally, and there are compensating developments such as tone, more vowels, diphthongization and palatalization of stem-initials. This progressive change of the shape of the stem from a string of several successive linear segments to a compressed sequence of two or three within which an enormous amount of information is piled up, clearly has taken place as a series of waves, concentrically spreading outward from the north-central sector of Northern Athapaskan in Canada.

Everywhere in Athapaskan such examples of the spread of characteristics in 'waves' can be shown very easily. One memorable and very simple case is the change *$\lambda' > t'$, which takes place in PCA only, and there only in the contiguous Nongatl, Sinkyone, Lassik, Wailaki, and also shows up again in Tolowa. This type of situation is entirely typical of Athapaskan, which can eventually, once adequately surveyed, be very adequately and realistically and simply and interestingly described in terms of isogloss maps, with many overlapping areas, crossings of single isoglosses and bundles of isoglosses. The basic unit for the linguistic community must be the tribelet, with boundaries of the fairly well defined area within which the tribelet lived as the lines of the base map, along which to draw isoglosses.

Canada is badly in need of a survey. With present day roads and transportation and communications this should be a relatively easy matter to negotiate physically. In fact, the very conditions (communications and transportation, centralization of population, assimilation and education, bilingualism in English) which would make such a survey so easy are also conditions which contribute to the rapid decay of the aboriginal situation and the eventual extinction of many of the languages and dialects. There is thus this short interim period during which one can have one's cake and eat it too, but which will soon end with the disappearance of many of the languages and dialects in dialect-levelling or replacement by English. It is worse than useless in the meanwhile to speculate further on the internal relationships of the Athapaskan languages, before such a survey is completed, and it is fully to be expected that virtually the only meaningful internal relationships will be those which can be shown far better in terms of isogloss maps than by any other means.

For a Canadian survey, it might be possible to gather sufficient information in a careful study of the entire literature, published and unpublished, for Canadian Athapaskan. This literature, after two centuries, is now rather vast, but mostly unpublished, scattered, and mostly not of the quality of work than can be done today. Such an assemblage and analysis of materials would doubtless be at far greater cost and be far less satisfactory than a rather simple modern survey. In this connection, a few limited surveys can already be reported for this recent period. Emil Otto Höhn's "The names of economically important or conspicuous mammals and birds in the Indian languages of the District of Mackenzie, N.W.T., and in Sarcee" (1962), gives 33 mammal and 62 bird names in Kutchin from Ft. McPherson, Hare from Ft. Good Hope, 'Slave' from Ft. Norman, Dogrib from Ft. Rae, Chipewyan from Ft. Resolution, and Sarsi, collected in 1949. Höhn's transcriptions are primitive, but tapes and better phonetic transcriptions are reported to be available from the Secretary of the Department of Modern Languages, University of Alberta. In the early 1960s, Irvine Davis of SIL organized and mimeographed some wordlists, mostly the Swadesh-

Hoijer 100-word list, some incomplete and some with supplements, from various Canadian points, transcribed by various SIL workers: Doig River, Upper Hay River, Ft. Vermillion (all 'Beaver'?), Sekani, Ft. Graham, Ware (all Sekani?), Lower Post (Kaska?), Cold Lake, Churchill, Ft. Resolution (all Chipewyan), Dogrib, Hare, Hay River and Jean-Marie River (both 'Slave'), Tahltan, Alexis Creek Chilcotin, Anahim Reservation (Carrier, or Chilcotin?). Finally, Robert Howren and student assistants from the University of Iowa have conducted a survey over most of the Canadian area in 1970 and 1971 (see section 1.2), the results of which remain to be determined.

## 5.3 *Athapaskan-Eyak*

The only truly clear-cut branching to be observed in the Athapaskan-Eyak family is that between Athapaskan and Eyak. Sapir, when late in his life he saw Eyak material, easily observed that Eyak was genetically related to Athapaskan but outside Athapaskan. Li and Krauss have confirmed this point, that Eyak is one branch, coordinate with Athapaskan as a whole, of the two-branched Athapaskan-Eyak language family.

It is this position of Eyak, and its archaism, and the fact that it is on the brink of extinction, that has placed such high priority on Eyak research, to the point where Krauss has devoted nearly all his research activity since 1963 to Eyak.

Krauss has shown (1969a, 1970b) that Eyak is in fact lexicostatistically equidistant to all Athapaskan, e.g. both Navajo and Ahtena (closest Athapaskan neighbor to Eyak) show virtually the same percentage of cognates, 33%, with Eyak on the Swadesh-Hoijer 100-word list, and that Eyak shows quite regularly $33 \pm 4\%$ (with insignificant variation) with all Athapaskan, well below the lowest percentages (ca. 58%) within Athapaskan, indicating that the Athapaskan-Eyak split antedated by about a thousand years the earliest attested divergences within Athapaskan.

Discussion will return to lexicostatistics and glottochronology after taking up briefly the subject of Proto-Athapaskan-Eyak (PAE). The reconstruction of PAE as such is not well developed yet, but Eyak has contributed enormously to the study of PA, and serves ideally in some respects as a link between PA and Tlingit. Krauss, virtually the only author who has worked in PAE, has not always carefully distinguished PA phonology from PAE, and has not yet attempted to solve certain problems of PAE phonology which are certainly of considerable interest. The same can be said for PAE morphology and syntax and semantics, for which, however, see also the discussion of Na-Dene below.

## 5.4 *Glottochronology*

At the end of his "Pacific Coast Athapascan discovered to be Chilcotin" (1943a) John P. Harrington makes the following negative statement, very remarkable for its date: 'CONVERSION OF LINGUISTIC CHANGE INTO CHRONOLOGY: One may ask ... the practical question: How long have the Chilcotin languages been developing asunder? To this question no answer can probably ever be given. Linguistic change has had for various features various and varying rates, and no amount of study will convert as a whole the duration of the linguistic change sundering these languages to time reckoning, even to the extent of a good guess.' As if to challenge this statement, there developed since 1951 the following literature on Athapaskan and Na-Dene lexicostatistics and glottochronology, listed together here in order of appearance:

1. Swadesh, Morris, "Diffusional cumulation and archaic residue", *SJA* 7.14–21, 1951.
2. ——, "Lexicostatistic dating of prehistoric ethnic contacts", *PAPS* 96.452–63, 1952.
3. ——, "Time depths of American linguistic groupings", *AmA* 56.361–4, 1954.
4. Kroeber, A. L., "Linguistic time depth results so far and their meaning", *IJAL* 21.91–104, 1955.
5. Hoijer, Harry, "Lexicostatistics: A critique", *Lg* 32.49–60, 1956.
6. ——, "The chronology of the Athapaskan languages", *IJAL* 22.219–32, 1956.
7. Hymes, Dell, "A note on Athapaskan glottochronology", *IJAL* 23.291–6, 1957.
8. Swadesh, Morris, "Some new glottochronological dates for Amerindian linguistic groups", *Proceedings of the 32nd International Congress of Americanists*, Copenhagen, 1958, p. 670–4.
9. ——, *Mapas de clasificación lingüística de México y de las Américas* (Cuadernos del Instituto de Historia, Serie antropológica, No. 8), University of Mexico, 1959.
10. ——, "Afinidades de las lenguas amerindias", Akten des 34. Internationalen Amerikanistenkongresses, 1960, Wien, 1964, p. 729–38.
11. ——, *Tras la huella lingüística de la prehistoria* (Suplementos del Seminario de Problemas cientéficos y filosóficos 26, Segunda Serie), 1960, p. 97–145.
12. Milke, Wilhelm, "Athapaskische Chronologie: Versuch einer Revision", *IJAL* 25.182–8, 1959.
13. Kroeber, A. L., "Reflections on Athapaskan glottochronology", *UCPAAE* 47.241–58, 1959.
14. Hoijer, Harry, personal communication to Hymes.
15. Hymes, Dell, "Lexicostatistics so far", *CAnthr* 1.3–44, 1960a.
16. ——, "More on lexicostatistics", *CAnthr* 1.338–45, 1960b.
17. Hoijer, Harry, "Linguistic subgrouping by glottochronology and by the comparative method", *Lingua* 11.192–8, 1962a.
18. ——, "Comments on the validity of glottochronology", *CAnthr* 3.135, 1962b.
19. ——, personal communication to Krauss.

Before discussing these items it must be stated generally that the Athapaskan cognate counts are based on a reasonably clear notion of correspondences and cognation, whereas the Athapaskan-Tlingit(-Haida) counts are invariably based only on notions of surface similarity. A survey of the conclusions follows. Swadesh 1951 (1.) guesses 2000 to 5000 years separation between Athapaskan (Hupa) and Tlingit, then in 1952 (2.) specifies 2000 years for Athapaskan-Tlingit, 2900 for Na-Dene including Haida, and states 2000 years for Athapaskan-Tlingit in 1954 (3.). Kroeber in 1955 (4.) considers Swadesh's figures too low. He is certainly right in so doing. Hoijer in 1956a revises Swadesh's 100-word list for Athapaskan (explained in 5.), and publishes an excellent and explicit presentation of the basic data (6.), coming up with the maximum (again surprisingly low) divergence within Athapaskan of 1300 years.[7] Hymes in 1957 (7.) noted that Hoijer had used an inappropriate rate for his wordlist; his recalculations increased Hoijer's figure to 1800 years, with Hoijer's approval. Milke (1959) (12.) attempted to apply another mathematical approach and Kroeber (1959) (13.) also reassessed the figures, both proposing increased time depths (see also Hymes (19.) criticizing Milke). Swadesh in 1958 (8.) now sees 1500 years as a *minimum* for maximum divergence within Athapaskan. Then in 1959 Swadesh (9.) greatly increases his Athapaskan-Eyak-Tlingit minimum divergence to 5000 years, and for Na-Dene including Haida to 9000 years. However, in 1960 (10.) and 1962 (11.) Swadesh, for what are apparently his last published dates for Na-Dene, indicates a maximum time-depth for divergence within the group as 4700 years, but it is not clear how he includes Haida within this. Hoijer (14.) by 1960 tells Hymes (p.c) that 'the addition of some twelve northern languages gives considerably greater time-depth — 2000 years as compared with the 1500 of the original article. The greater distances come in relation to the Alaskan languages and particularly Tanaina', and Hymes (15.) gives a good general discussion and bibliography of the whole problem. Hymes in the same article also agrees with Swadesh's higher dates (6.) for Athapaskan-Eyak-Tlingit and Na-Dene. By 1962 Hoijer (17., 18.) is clearly disenchanted with glottochronology if not with lexicostatistics, and, in spite of the title of his article (17.) does not mention dates. By 1963 (19.) Hoijer told Krauss (p.c.) that he was thoroughly discouraged with glottochronology and further repudiated earlier dates, as new data from the North and Alaska were yielding absurdly deep divergence. Part of this disenchantment is unjustified, in that the Alaskan materials were collected by investigators who were not trained in linguistics or in Athapaskan, with the result that there was far less uniformity in style of elicitation and, especially, far less communication between informant and investigator as to what was wanted. Krauss has remarked that glottochronology is simply a means for the linguist to quantify precisely

---

[7] One of Hoijer's most interesting and probably most valid conclusions is that there is greater lexical divergence within Pacific Coast Athapaskan than within Apachean, and greater within Northern than within Pacific Coast. These figures compare interestingly with the conclusions of Voegelin et al. (1963). Hoijer here significantly also shows greater distance between Pacific Coast and Northern Athapaskan than between Apachean and Northern.

the degree to which he subjectively believes or wishes the languages to be related; that by knowing the list and the potential responses to it in the languages of the family quite well, he can, consciously or unconsciously, have considerable control over the outcome, from the way he elicits from the informant and from the way he judges cognation, and, of course, from the formula he chooses to convert to time-depth. Krauss, having experimented several times, consistently comes up with a maximum divergence within Athapaskan of $2400\pm500$ years, and between Athapaskan and Eyak of $3400\pm500$ years.

Na-Dene figures have been published only by Swadesh (1951, 1952, 1954) who started out at 2000 years for Athapaskan-Tlingit and 2900 for Na-Dene with Haida (1., 2., 3.). Kroeber (4., on extralinguistic grounds, and certainly correctly) thought these dates too low. Swadesh then increases the figures to 5000 and 9000 years (9.), a change welcomed by Hymes, and no doubt also by Hoijer. Krauss believes that these latter figures are not extremely far from correct, though 5000 years between Athapaskan-Eyak and Tlingit would seem rather low for a case where it has still not been possible, so Krauss believes, to demonstrate regular phonological correspondences to prove genetic relationship in the lexica (stem-inventories), though the languages are decently enough documented for the purpose, and PAE goes back a large part of the way, presumably. In other words, because he remains unconvinced that any regular correspondences have yet been demonstrated between Athapaskan-Eyak and Tlingit stems, it is impossible to calculate with confidence any cognate percentages. The minimum date of 5000 years is perhaps realistic as that short of which correspondences ought, given the circumstances, to be reasonably easy to detect. 5000 years is also, ironically enough, not far off from what might be calculated from the percentages of surface similarities between Athapaskan-Eyak and Tlingit. Krauss, in several attempts, consistently has come out with a figure of about $8\pm1\%$ cognates on the list for both Tlingit-Athapaskan and Tlingit-Eyak, based on excellent data (the Tlingit contributed by Naish and Story), elicited with considerable sophistication concerning the potential responses, alternatives, semantic shifts, etc.

One conclusion is certain from these figures. The relationship between the Athapaskan-Eyak and the Tlingit stem-inventories, if genetic at all, is far more distant than the relationship between certain prefixes central to the Athapaskan-Eyak and the Tlingit verb. Whatever the relationship between Haida and Tlingit-Eyak-Athapaskan, all writers agree that it is clearly much more distant in every respect than that between Tlingit and Athapaskan-Eyak. Furthermore, since Haida is so poorly documented, since nothing in fact has been published on the Haida language for almost fifty years, Haida must needs figure relatively little in the present discussion.

## 5.5 Na-Dene

The Na-Dene hypothesis most certainly did not originate with Sapir. Krauss (1964a) gives some account of the history of the hypothesis. Tlingit-Haida was first examined in 1798, Athapaskan-Eyak-Tlingit in 1805. Mithridates (1816) contains a good discussion of the problem. By the mid nineteenth century, the Russian literature had reached essentially the same understanding of the relationship (including Eyak, unknown to Sapir) and its problems as is presented in this report.

In "The Na-Dene languages, A preliminary report" (1915), Sapir states that 'a full presentation of the comparative lexical, phonological and morphological evidence that serves to show, beyond all reasonable doubt, that Athabaskan, Haida, and Tlingit are indeed but divergent representatives of a common prototype is given in an extensive paper on "The Na-Dene Languages" now in the course of preparation as a memoir of the Anthropological Series of the Geological Survey of Canada. The present sketch, prepared at the request of Dr. P.E. Goddard, is merely a rapid abstract of some of the leading points involved. I wish expressly to emphasize the fact that it does not present all the evidence at my disposal.' In 1925:186 Sapir still claims that he 'hopes to publish fuller studies on the Nadene languages (Athabaskan, Tlingit, Haida) in the future. Since the preliminary report was published more new evidence has come to light.' Sapir never published either the fuller study he promised or for that matter any new evidence for the Na-Dene hypothesis after 1915. New data tore down as much as built up his hypothesis. Sapir discovered tone in Sarsi in 1922 (with which he was so impressed that he figured tone must be fundamental to all Athapaskan); and Kutchin, which he studied in 1923 also had tone, similar to that of Sarsi. Since he knew from Boas that Tlingit had tone of sorts, the discovery of tone in Athapaskan (Sarsi 1922, Kutchin 1923) was probably primarily what Sapir had in mind as the 'new evidence' for Na-Dene as he wrote about Sarsi in 1925 (the same year, incidentally, that his only published reference to Sino-Tibetan-Na-Dene appeared). On the other hand, Ingalik, which Sapir had also done a few hours' fieldwork on in 1923, and Hupa, with which Sapir worked extensively in 1927, turned out to have no tone. Furthermore, the Haida work which Sapir did in 1920, though it improved his knowledge of Haida phonology, invalidated some of his claims about correspondences with Haida stem-initial clusters made from Swanton's data, which turned out to be faulty. Sapir's fuller paper for the Geological Survey of Canada certainly never materialized. This writer has never seen proof that it ever existed on paper. The large ledger that Sapir kept his Na-Dene comparisons in, now in Hoijer's possession, contains virtually nothing of significance not published in Sapir's 1915 'preliminary' report.

An important task that should no longer be neglected is that of collecting and copying and cataloguing Sapir's notes and manuscripts and correspondence, now scattered in various institutions and private hands, and making accessible in some form these materials, which doubtless contain much of importance and interest. It is this writer's guess that no major unpublished monograph by Sapir on Na-Dene will turn up, though comments in his letters to various correspondents in support of Na-Dene may contain a limited amount of evidence that he never published. Most probably, however, it will be revealed that Sapir's earlier comments and promises were due to an excess of enthusiasm and overconfidence, and that though he never retreated from this position, in fact advanced to still broader hypotheses (Sino-Tibetan-Na-Dene), Sapir experienced a growing frustration for lack of productive regular phonological correspondences in the lexicon, which prevented him from publishing further on Na-Dene.

Boas remained skeptical. The late Melville Jacobs reported that Boas was finally convinced by work done on the problem by Elizabeth Jacobs during the 1930s. Krauss has examined Mrs. Jacobs manuscript material and found in it no more convincing evidence than in Sapir's published work.

Hoijer and Li, who since Sapir have known the most about it, have remained silent or noncommittal on the question of a regular genetic relationship between Athapaskan(-Eyak) and Tlingit. However, in 1940 John P. Harrington visited the Tlingit (see under section 3., Tlingit), and reported exuberantly on this in "A field comparison of Northwestern and Southwestern Indians" (1941:91–4) and in "Phonematic daylight in Lhiinkit, Navajo of the north" (1945): 'I pried into the Lhiinkit language for genetic relationship with Navajo and found it, amounting to practical identity in sounds and structure and lexical co-inheritance extending to some 400 vocables.' Harrington gives only a few examples of this 'practical identity': Tlingit *thé* 'stone', Navajo *tshé* 'stone', and Tlingit *khèł* 'dog', Navajo *łįiʔ* 'pet'. This latter pair 'reflects some ancient metathesis. In order to correctly understand correspondences, one would have to know the ancient development of forms, which lack of record forever deprives us of knowing'. This gives a fair idea of the quality of Harrington's judgement and the nature of his comparative method. In this article Harrington also gives a short Tlingit wordlist, but makes no mention of Eyak.

The only writers on the subject of Na-Dene since Harrington have been Dell Hymes, Heinz-Jürgen Pinnow, and Michael Krauss. Hymes published "Positional analysis of categories: A frame for reconstruction" in 1955, essentially a comparison of Apachean, Chipewyan, Hupa and Mattole verbal prefix-class positions and reconstruction of the PA system assumed to be a daughter system of Sapir's Na-Dene. Hymes further elaborated in "Na-Dene and positional analysis of categories" (1956), including a comparison of Athapaskan, Tlingit, and Haida, with a serious attempt at reconstructing the Na-Dene system of prefix categories in the verb. Adequate Eyak information was at that point still not available. Hymes also gives some account of the history and state in 1956 of the Na-Dene hypothesis, and also adds a few Athapaskan-Tlingit rapprochements. But the article is devoted mainly to discussion of similarity in morphological structure (the abstract prefix positions with their linear order and semantic or grammatical function, more than the phonological shape and meaning of the specific morphemes which fill these positions) as opposed to common inheritance of lexicon as demonstrated by regular phonological correspondence (as though granting that this is indeed the problematical part of the Na-Dene hypothesis) in the determination of genetic relationship.

Since Hymes's paper in 1956, the problem of Na-Dene has become the subject of a rather lively dialogue exclusively between Heinz-Jürgen Pinnow and Michael Krauss, both of whom have devoted considerable research effort to it. The pertinent published bibliography is:

P1. Pinnow, Heinz-Jürgen, "Zwei Probleme der historischen Lautlehre der Na-Dene-Sprachen", *ZPhon* 11.128–159, 1959, abstracted at length in *IJAL* 28.61–6, 1962, by Dell Hymes.
P2. ——, "On the historical position of Tlingit", *IJAL* 30.155–64, 1964.
P3. ——, *Grundzüge einer historischen Lautlehre des Tlingit: Ein Versuch*. Wiesbaden, 1966.
P4. ——, "Genetic relationship vs. borrowing in Na-Dene", *IJAL* 34.204–11, 1968.
P5. ——, "Entlehnungen von Tiernamen im Tsimshian und Na-Dene sowie Grundsätzliches zur Entlehnungsfrage bei Indianersprachen", *ZEthn* 94.82–102, 1969.
P6. ——, "Sprachhistorische Studie zur Verbstammvariation im Tlingit", *Orbis* 17.509–31, 1968.
P7. ——, "Notes on the classifiers in the Na-Dene languages", *IJAL* 36.63–7, 1970.
K1. Krauss, Michael E., "Proto-Athapaskan-Eyak and the problem of Na-Dene I: The phonology", *IJAL* 30.118–31, 1964.
K2. ——, "Proto-Athapaskan-Eyak and the problem of Na-Dene II: The morphology", *IJAL* 31.18–28, 1965.
K3. ——, "Eyak: A preliminary report", *CJL* 10.167–87, 1965.
K4. ——, "Noun-classification systems in Athapaskan, Eyak, Tlingit, and Haida verbs", *IJAL* 34.194–203, 1968.
K5. ——, *On the classifiers in the Athapaskan, Eyak, and Tlingit verb*, *UPAL-M* 24 (= *IJAL* 35:4, Part II), 1969. [Title on jacket and title-page erroneously given as "On the classification in the Athapascan, Eyak, and the Tlingit verb."]

P1. is early and isolated in this series, germinal but frankly speculative and far from definitive in the development of Pinnow's thought on Na-Dene. Even though it antedates the reconstruction (in K1.) of the PA(E) *$k^w$-series, which renders completely congruent the PAE and Tlingit obstruent series, Pinnow already senses that there are few direct phonological resemblances or correspondences and that, in order to show any significant number of phonological correspondences between the Tlingit and Athapaskan (or Haida) lexica, it will be necessary to show the Na-Dene consonant systems as having gone through each a separate complex evolution and reshaping, in spite of their surface similarity. In this he is entirely correct, of course, in much the way that the same is true of e.g. the modern French and German (surface) vowel systems. Though both are more or less *i e a o u ü ö*, the correspondences between the French and German are practically nowhere direct (except of course in the loans). In order to find the correspondences, one must go very deep in history to show both systems as having undergone a long and complex evolution, starting with a system that was very different from the modern type, and through long independent development finally to have converged typologically again (or, perhaps, to have remained typologically similar for a long time through superficially parallel development). P1. examines the possibilities for Na-Dene largely in terms of the components of the consonants and the role of labialization and labials, for Na-Dene is certainly peculiar in its lack of labial obstruents. This article is, however, highly abstract, dealing mainly with the consonant systems themselves as data rather than with the actual morphemes to be compared, and so is far more speculative than substantive.

P2. is Pinnow's first serious attempt to prove genetic relationship of the Na-Dene lexica (though it is conceded that the position of Haida remains uncertain). Pinnow concedes a very wide divergence (i.e. much real lexical as well as simply phonological change). He expressly rejects the notion that there has been language-mixture or creolization, however, and prefers to attribute this divergence (in lexicon, as opposed to the sensibly closer relationship in the morphology) to an (extraordinarily?) strong tendency for new descriptive terms or circumlocutions to be coined and replace old forms. Many of the replacing forms, morphologically complex, then undergo various types of regular and irregular change and contraction, it is claimed. P2. suffers severely from some major weaknesses. First, the sources are not reliable, and often not judiciously interpreted. For Haida the best source is still Swanton, for Eyak Pinnow's best source was still Birket-Smith and de Laguna, and these and even the Athapaskan and Tlingit (which do have some reliable, observationally adequate, documentation in print) need to be supplemented by still more primitively transcribed nineteenth- and twentieth-century sources. In Na-Dene such sources are far less adequate for these purposes than in e.g. Algonkian, where e.g. the symbols *g* or *k* both are simply to be read /k/. Here, however, the symbol *k* may typically stand for any one of at least six contrasting units: *g k k' G q q'*, perhaps also sometimes even e.g. *x'* or *G*ʷ, not to mention e.g. *hG ʔk'*. It can well be imagined then how inconclusive a resemblance between two instances of, say, *kak* in such transcriptions must be considered, admitting of literally dozens, even hundreds, of contrasting readings. A particularly deceptive source in this respect is Osgood's Tanaina (see under section 1.1., Alaska), because this is relatively recent, and respectable-looking because it employs such symbols as *g k k' G q q'*. Osgood uses these symbols because, though not a linguist himself, he has been instructed to do so by linguists who know what kind of distinctions are likely to exist in such languages. Osgood, however, did not learn to hear or transcribe such distinctions consistently, in fact uses these symbols arbitrarily and interchangeably for all *k*-like sounds. Thus, as P2. quotes (1964:160), in the varieties of Tanaina (in reality closely related and mutually intelligible dialects), Osgood has for 'brown bear' variously *q'áq'á, q'aq'a, qágá, gaagaa*. These transcriptions all stand in fact for /GaGa/ (checked in the field by this writer). Pinnow's conclusion, however, is (p. 160) that 'the exact nature of these laws cannot be established and that many special developments have occurred. Even within the A[thapaskan] languages and the individual A[thapaskan, e.g. Tanaina] subgroups, there are numerous divergences which are hard to explain and which seem to contradict the phonetic laws which have been postulated. Thus within Tanaina there is an interchange of *k* and *q*, *k* and *g*, and of glottalized and unglottalized consonants. There is also frequent interchange of vowel quantity, tones, etc. ... And, if this is the situation within one A [Athapaskan] group, even greater difficulties can be expected [and greater liberties taken!] in comparisons of the far more distantly related subdivisions of Na-Dene.' Pinnow is of course right in expecting great difficulties, but wrong to conclude from these sources that phonological development in these languages is so unsystematic or capricious or complex. Pinnow's claim permits him to posit a large variety of ad hoc explanations, e.g. contractions with affixes, metatheses, shifts in position of glottalization, and also folk-etymology. Pinnow concedes in P2. that some of his comparisons may later need to be rejected, and that the 'problem' of the relationship of Tlingit, Eyak, Athapaskan, and Haida is still unsolved, though a genetic relationship, at least for the first three, is claimed to be proven.

The explicit and systematic reconstruction of Proto-Na-Dene (PND) phonology is not yet developed in P2., though Pinnow's thought on it is clearly beginning to take shape, e.g. for Haida *gʸuu* 'ear', Tlingit *-gúkʷ* (actually *-gúg*), and various transcriptions of Athapaskan (PA clearly /-ǯəx-əʔ/) and Eyak (actually /-ǯehx ~ -ǯəx-/), 'the PND word may have been something like *\*giakʷ*'.

Two years later Pinnow published P3. (*Grundzüge einer historischen Lautlehre des Tlingit* (1966)) still highly tentative (subtitled 'Ein Versuch'), but a serious elaborate systematic explicit formulation of a theory of Na-Dene phonology based on comparisons of concrete data. It is surely a very important contribution to Na-Dene. It is a model of clear organization and exposition, also with truly excellent indices and bibliography. But the book suffers from all the weaknesses of P2. mentioned above. The theory of PND, however (if not the actual comparison of forms), is very explicit and systematic, and has the virtue of being on what appears perforce to be the right track, in taking the recent similar (Tlingit, and PA(E), now including the *\*ḵʷ*-series) systems completely apart. Whether the *Grundzüge* does this in the right way is another question; see also the discussion of Kl. below. According to P3., early PND had *d g G t k q s x x̣ l n ʔ i e a u*, consonant clusters like *dl, tl, ds, dʔ, tʔ*, etc., and all 16 possible two-vowel clusters. This system later developed *š* from *x* or *s*, *h* from *ʔ, G, q*, or *x*, and then reduced vowels, and also rising and falling diphthongs, e.g. *i̯e, i̯e, i̯e*, thus allowing for 64 syllable nuclei. With various ensuing palatalizations, labializations, resegmentations, metatheses, lenitions, and contractions with prefixes or suffixes posited ad hoc for the purpose, Pinnow constructs a theory that is easily powerful enough to show systematic correspondences in his data. The theory is in fact so powerful that the inadequacies of the data matter very little. This is not the place to attempt a tedious and futile negative proof of Na-Dene (see P.E. Goddard in *IJAL* 1.266–279, 1920 for a notorious earlier attempt), but to this writer it seems clear that with the kind of machinery constructed by Pinnow in P3., virtually any language could as easily be included in Na-Dene.

Pinnow's *Grundzüge* is easy to criticize. It would be easy to fill many pages demonstrating with better and more accurate data than Pinnow had at his disposal, especially Eyak and Athapaskan, how at least most of his comparisons do not stand up under such closer scrutiny. But although he is largely wrong, as Pinnow himself might concede, there is the possibility that the PND theory contains some grains of truth, and/or that the direction taken, the complete taking apart of converged modern systems, is justified. Then too, a few of the more direct comparisons are certainly arresting, e.g. (made also by Sapir) Haida *t'aa-, t'ao*, Tlingit *t'aw* 'feather', PAE *-t'a-* 'leaf, feather'.

In P2. Pinnow had begun to deal with the question of certain items, especially fauna terms, like PAE *naGac'e*, Tlingit *naGas'é*, Haida *na·Gaže·* 'fox', Tlingit and PAE [Gəx] 'rabbit' (both of which also occur, incidentally, in e.g. Tsimshian). In P2. it is cautiously stated 'it is difficult to tell when borrowing occurred and when not. In many cases it may be necessary to decide in favor of a genetic relationship'. In P3., however, this reservation is explicitly abandoned (p. 35) for most items. The question then remains as to why the fauna terms so clearly tend to show direct correspondences and other sections of the lexicon tend not to. Pinnow's next two articles are attempts to close the gap. P4. contains an attempt to show that there are numerous non-fauna terms with simple correspondences, but in fact none of these are quite so direct or contain so many simply corresponding segments as e.g. the 'fox' item. P4. also examines affixal morphemes, which do indeed sometimes show striking direct correspondence, but these are not stems, and here is part of the enigma of Na-Dene. In P4. Pinnow also attempts to demonstrate some cases of indirect correspondences in fauna terms. A prime example is 'wolverene', where Pinnow claims that Tlingit and Haida *nusg*, Eyak *kənaʔs* (also, for this purpose Birket-Smith and de Laguna's '*kýnd'əs*: or *kýná·'ə̀s*' with strong final aspiration' is cited by Pinnow as *kʋnaaʔsh*, though in fact it is absolutely incorrect insofar as it differs from *kənaʔs*), and Minto *nəltriθ* < PA *\*nəlkʷis* (Krauss), are cognates from PND *\*nausk-u* or *-a*. Pinnow lines these up essentially as follows:

|              |        |       |   |          |
|--------------|--------|-------|---|----------|
| Tlingit-Haida |       | n     | u | s    g   |
| Eyak (BSdL)  | kʋ –   | na·ʔ  | s | h        |
| Eyak (Krauss)| kə –   | naʔ   | s |          |
| Minto        |        | nə    | l | t – riθ  |
| PA           |        | nə    | l | k̲ – ʷis. |

The reality here is very probably that the Tlingit-Haida is a diffusion, which, incidentally, also turns up in Tsimshian. The form *nusg* is certainly not related to the Athapaskan or Eyak. Ironically, however, the Athapaskan and Eyak forms may well be cognate, but in a way entirely unlike that proposed by Pinnow: the Athapaskan appears clearly to be analyzed *nə-l-k̲ʷis*, a nominalized verb with one of several very well attested prefixes of the form *nə-*, *l*-classifier, and stem *-k̲ʷis*, of perfectly regular shape but unknown meaning. This stem could, however, well be cognate with Eyak *kənaʔs*. There are many stems ('broken' stems) in Eyak of the form CVRV(C) where R is /wmlny/, some of which alternate with unbroken stems, and though *-naʔs* could conceivably be a stem in Eyak, stems beginning with -*n*- are exceedingly rare, and, above all, there is most definitely no prefix in Eyak of the form *kə*- or *ku*-, not even in any single odd Eyak item that is not clearly a loan. Pinnow nevertheless states that 'according to Krauss no prefix is involved in E *kə*- in *kənaʔs*; the historical relations [i.e. this comparison, and this alone], however, point to one'.

Sapir is guilty of the same thing in comparing $C_1VC_2$ in one language with $C_1V(C_3)$ in the other simply by claiming but not proving $C_2$ (and $C_3$) to be suffixal. Solid proof cannot be based on such procedures as these used by Pinnow and Sapir.

In P4. Pinnow does, however, allow for the possibility of some diffusion in addition to these 'cognates'. In P5. he takes up many more examples, and also the problem of diffusion outside Na-Dene, especially Na-Dene to Tsimshian, where, as noted above, many of these same terms are encountered. Pinnow has undertaken to treat here a very interesting and difficult problem, one badly neglected but extremely important for Amerindian and general linguistics. As studies of diffusion and as collocations of relevant published data, P4. and P5. are very useful and stimulating, but as studies in genetic comparison, they are of less value, so far as this writer is concerned.

P6. undertakes a very different sort of task, the explanation of verb-stem variation in Tlingit, now approachable, thanks to the work of Naish and Story in their M.A. theses. As a systematic effort at internal reconstruction, not attempted by Naish and Story, P6. is a very interesting study, from a point of view of generative phonology also, even though the actual reconstruction may seem unnatural in certain respects (e.g. two contrasting tones on stems [a strong position], and three on suffixes [a weak position, where vowels drop]). The section at the end, comparing the Tlingit variations and suffixes with the Athapaskan and Eyak, treads of course on far less solid ground. Pinnow is very probably essentially correct here, however, in his claim that the structure of the Tlingit verb stem (if not the individual stems themselves) is so similar typologically to the Athapaskan-Eyak that there must be between them more than chance resemblance. There still remains the question to what extent and in what way this resemblance is connected with the inescapable fact that there has been and is now geographical proximity between Tlingit and Athapaskan-Eyak; the answer to this question might partly or even largely disallow Pinnow's conclusion of simple genetic relationship.

Krauss in Alaska has had the advantage of access to a large variety of conservative dialects of Athapaskan, and also, especially, Eyak, and has a considerable amount of still unpublished data on these, not yet available to Pinnow. Krauss's work is perhaps less amenable to criticism than Pinnow's also because his claims are less ambitious, at least in attempting to prove systematic relationship only between PAE and Tlingit, and there only between certain affixes and of course basic morphological structure. These claims were certainly adequately proven already by Sapir and Hymes, and the work of Krauss simply investigates the actual detail. In addition, however, Krauss makes the negative claim that Sapir and Hymes and Pinnow are wrong about the relationship of the lexica (stem-inventories) of PAE and Tlingit (and Haida), that these are not (or at least are not yet proven to be) genetically related. I.e. Krauss claims that the Na-Dene lexica are either not genetically related at all, or that if they are genetically related (either pair or all three), the divergence is much greater than could possibly be congruent with the obvious and intimate relationship exhibited in the general morphological structure and in certain specific affixes, especially the 'classifiers'. Krauss is thus himself making a strong claim, that there is this incongruence and that such is not entirely 'normal' or 'ordinary' in relationships between (e.g. Indo-European) languages, and that some sort of historical explanation involving some kind of intimate borrowing, language-mixture, or creolization is required. Pinnow rejects the creolization theory, and minimizes the incongruence.

As Krauss 1964, 1965a, 1965b, and 1968 (K1.–K4) are discussed elsewhere in this report, only a few remarks concerning these will be added here. In K1 Krauss calls attention to the fact that in PA stems of the form CVC ('closed' stems, as opposed to 'open', CV), there are the following severe and interesting restrictions on the choice of C: the $c$- and $č$-series, and also the $č$- and $ḵ^w$-series, are mutually exclusive, i.e. a stem having as initial C any member of the $č$-series cannot have as final C any member of the $c$- or $ḵ^w$-series, and the converse. Also, a stem having as initial C any member of the $c$-series cannot have as final C any member of the $ḵ^w$-series, but the converse here is not true, as some stems of the form $ḵ^wVc$ (e.g. Minto -$triθ$ in 'wolverine') do occur. It is probably also true that the $q^w$- and $q$-series are mutually exclusive, and it is, curiously, definitely true that the $t$-series ($d, t, t'$) is self-exclusive, i.e. there are no PA(E) stems of the form e.g. $dVt'$. All these same selection-restrictions hold also for Eyak (except that here the $q$- and $q^w$-series are early and completely merged, also the $ḵ$- and $ḵ^w$-series, but later and less completely so), so that we are faced here with a set of very interesting and potentially useful facts about PAE as well as PA. These restrictions selecting consonant series which cooccur in closed stems, i.e. the partial predictability of stem-finals from stem-initials, and/or vice-versa, this non-randomness, clearly implies that some processes of assimilation (and dissimilation) have taken place in the prehistory of PAE. Tlingit closed stems, on the other hand, do not show such selection-restrictions. Krauss feels that the exact nature of these processes that have led to this property of PAE might well prove the key to the discovery of productive regular phonological correspondences between PAE and Tlingit stems. So far, however, neither Pinnow nor Krauss has attempted to follow this promising lead. It must also be considered a point in disfavor of Pinnow's theory of Na-Dene phonological correspondences that it fails to account for these PAE constraints.

K4. shows that both PAE and Tlingit had a double system of classifying nouns in the verb-complex, that there were two positions in both verb-complexes which together cross-classified the subject of intransitive or the object of transitive verbs. In Tlingit it is the function of a (diminutive) prefix leftward in the prefix-complex combined with part of the function of the 'classifiers' (which immediately precede the stem). In PAE however, though there were two positions also with partly noun-classificatory function, these were not the same two positions as in Tlingit.[8] Some of the prefixes occurring in the position immediately preceding those for mode-aspect were partly noun-classificatory, and there were some noun-classificatory stems (at least two, -*ta* 'longish' and -*ʔa* 'roundish'). In Eyak the prefixal position is now very elaborately developed as noun-classificatory, and this function is only very vestigial in the stem. In modern Athapaskan exactly the opposite is now true. And in both Athapaskan and Eyak, and therefore in PAE, there is no evidence whatever that the 'classifiers' ever had any noun-classificatory function, such as they do in Tlingit. It is ironic that these prefixes in Tlingit, where they do have some classificatory function, are now called 'extensors' by Naish and Story, whereas the term 'classifier' remains in use in the Athapaskan and Eyak literature for those prefixes for which they are a complete misnomer.

K2. attempted to deal especially with the inflectional function and variation in the Tlingit and PAE classifiers, but without benefit of the Naish-Story grammars for Tlingit. K5. greatly profited from the advances made by Naish and Story, and succeeds in demonstrating the relationship between the forms of the PAE and Tlingit classifiers and their variation in inflection. This relationship is so exquisitely intimate that, for the first time in Na-Dene studies, it becomes possible not only to show resemblances or only prove a relationship, but also for Tlingit and PAE to be mutually explanatory in a very rewarding way in the comparison. The PAE-Tlingit classifier thus proves to have been a sequence of three components, $\pm d \pm l \pm y$ (in Tlingit also $s$ or $š$ as a middle component), each with a different and definable function. The $y$-component is no longer functional in Eyak in the same way as in Tlingit, and in Athapaskan the $y$-component has left only traces, e.g. in Navajo in the high tone of the optative prefix when the classifier is zero or $l$, or, especially in the stem 'sg. sj. goes', which has a zero initial in some forms, but irregularities implying alternation of zero with $y$-initial in perfectives and optative.

Here, certainly, is a very close relationship, where comparison of PAE and Tlingit sheds powerful light on the history of both, but only in this very restricted segment of the verb-complex. K5. thus serves to accentuate the incongruence, which Pinnow seeks to minimize, in closeness of relationship in different aspects or at different levels of the structure of Athapaskan-Eyak and Tlingit.

In P7. Pinnow would revise the third component of the PAE-Tlingit classifier in K5., such that $+y$ is ι, and $-y$ is ∅ and $a$. The ∅ : $a$ contrast, however, can be justified only by comparison with Haida, the transcriptions and analysis of which and comparability of which to PAE-Tlingit is still doubtful. Though Pinnow's ι may well be better that Krauss's $y$, this is not proven by Pinnow's claim that $y > ι$ is 'very improbable', or less probable than '*ι to yι and finally to yα', but depends on the advisability of attempting to include Haida here.

As regards the classifiers, and certainly the general structure of the verb-complex,

---

[8] Danenhauer, Florendo, and Leer have recently shown that Tlingit also has classificatory stems (see 3.).

Pinnow and Krauss are in complete agreement that in these respects, at any rate, PAE and Tlingit are descendants of a common prototype. The real disagreement is that Pinnow believes regular phonological correspondences have been discovered which demonstrate how at least a considerable proportion of the stem-inventories of PAE and Tlingit can be traced back to a common prototype. Krauss, however, does not believe that such correspondences have yet been discovered, notwithstanding the insightful work of Pinnow and Sapir.

## 5.6 Beyond Na-Dene

Finally, there is the question of broader genetic relationships of Na-Dene or parts of Na-Dene with other language groups. So far three serious hypotheses have been proposed: 1) Sino-Tibetan-Na-Dene, 2) Vasco-Dene, and 3) Athapaskan-Tlingit-Yuchi-Souian.

Of these three hypotheses, Sino-Tibetan-Na-Dene is the oldest and best known. Though the idea is attributed largely to Edward Sapir, A. G. Morice and others had earlier speculated on such ideas in print: aside from Petitot's works see e.g. Rev. John Campbell "The Dénés of America identified with the Tungus of Asia" (1898, criticized by Morice 1899); and Morice's "Northwestern Dénés and Northeastern Asiatics" (1914). Sapir's only publication on his hypothesis is "The similarity of Chinese and Indian languages" (1925), a short note designed for popular consumption. One of the highlights of this note is that both Sino-Tibetan and Na-Dene are tonal. Ironically, it is becoming increasingly clear that tone as shown today in both Sino-Tibetan and Na-Dene (at least PAE) is in fact largely or entirely a relatively recent development compensating for deterioration of stem-final consonantism and suffixation in earlier stages of both language groups. There is a file of correspondence between Sapir and Berthold Laufer at the Field Museum in Chicago. From a sample of that correspondence seen by this writer, it does not appear that Sapir had ever gotten beyond his 'intuitive speculative' stage on Sino-Tibetan-Na-Dene. Sapir was in fact clearly carried far beyond any objectively justifiable conclusions by his enthusiasm for the idea, and clearly was in no position to publish any organized or detailed hypothesis. His frustrations here must also have increased along with those he must have had in Na-Dene itself.

However, Robert Shafer attempts to demonstrate a genetic relationship between Sino-Tibetan and Athapaskan (without regard to the rest of Na-Dene) in "Athapaskan and Sino-Tibetan" (1952) (see also Swadesh, *IJAL* 18.178–81) and "A note on Athapaskan and Sino-Tibetan" (1957). Shafer is a recognized authority on Sino-Tibetan, but his handling of the Athapaskan is less than sophisticated. For this and the usual other reasons (lack of clear productive rigorous phonological correspondences based on a large enough number of well-established forms, and the inevitable semantic indeterminacy), the Sino-Tibetan-Na-Dene hypothesis remains not so much better substantiated than e.g. the Rev. Campbell's "Déné-Tungus" that it does not belong essentially in the same category of speculation.

Another hypothetical genetic relationship for Na-Dene was proposed and examined by Mary Haas in "Athapaskan, Tlingit, Yuchi, and Siouan" (1964). Haida (and Eyak) are left out because of lack of available data. Haas makes only 34 lexical comparisons between Tlingit-and/or-Athapaskan and Yuchi-and/or-Souian. These attempt to show some regularities, but of course are not extensive or precise enough to be very convincing. Nevertheless, Haas's hypothesis appears to be as plausible at least as the Sino-Tibetan.

Finally, the broadest and most dramatic claim of all is that made by Morris Swadesh as part of his scheme of world-wide linguistic relationships, where the grouping Vasco-Déné figures centrally, as a network of genetic relationships involving Basque at one end and Na-Dene at the other, all going back to a very ancient hypothetical common parent language. See especially Swadesh 1959, 1960a, 1960b, 1962a, 1962b, esp. pp. 1264, 1266, and 1965 (written in 1960; important, but published in Russian and little known). Within the supergroup of Vasco-Dene, Na-Dene would be closest to Wakashan, Kutenai, and Japanese, and somewhat less close to Macro-Hokan, Hamitic, and Indo-European.

It is this writer's opinion that though these relationships for Na-Dene are still purely speculative, Swadesh and Haas cannot fail ultimately to be on the right track in looking to other American families as well as to Asia for genetic affiliations for Na-Dene. In fact, since Krauss does not consider a genetic relationship for at least the large bulk of the Athapaskan-Eyak and Tlingit (and Haida) lexica (of stems) by any means yet proven, there are also strong reasons yet to examine the possibilities of relating one or two of these alone to non-Na-Dene groupings, thus to increase chances for explaining the enigma of Na-Dene itself, which still needs explanation, as well as establishing broader relationships.

However, clearly not much progress in these directions can be made before there is great improvement in the quality and amount of primary data from all the pertinent languages available for study.

That science will outstrip genocide in North America by enough of a margin in enough cases to preserve adequate record of extirpated languages is perhaps a vain hope. However, if the scientific community could see its responsibility to do everything within its power to deter further oppression of American Indians, and at the same time to welcome the ultimate authorities on the subject, the Indians themselves, into the scientific community for what they potentially can contribute, there is real hope that American Indian linguistics can be a scene of bright progress instead of continued tragedy both for American Indians and for linguistics.

The following list of references cited includes only a few of the unpublished materials discussed or mentioned in the body of the report. Likewise, none of the materials published *in* any Na-Dene languages are listed here, and only a selected few of the scientific works on Na-Dene linguistics published before 1945 are listed. Then, with the exception of some of the works of Harry Hoijer and of Herbert Landar (for which see *IJAL* 30.169–74, 1970, and Landar 1967d below), the following list might be considered a fairly exhaustive bibliography of published work on Na-Dene linguistics from 1945 to 1971. The term mimeographed is used loosely here for a variety of duplicating processes.

REFERENCES CITED

AKMAJIAN, ADRIAN, and STEPHEN ANDERSON. 1970. On the use of the fourth person in Navajo, or Navajo made harder. IJAL 36.1–8. [1.5.1]

ATCITTY, MARLENE, et al. 1971. Preparing reading materials in Navajo. Navajo Reading Study Progress Report No. 15, University of New Mexico. [1.5.1]

BASSO, KEITH. 1967. Semantic aspects of linguistic acculturation. AmA 69.471–77. [1.5.1]

———. 1968. The Western Apache classificatory verb system: A formal analysis. SJA 24.252–66. [1.5.1]

BENVENISTE, E. 1953a. Le vocabulaire de la vie animale chez les Indiens du Haut Yukon (Alaska). BSL 49.79–106. [1.1]

———. 1953b. Les traits caractéristiques de la langue des indiens Haida. BSL 49.iii–iv. [4.]

BIRKET-SMITH, KAI and FREDERICA DE LAGUNA. 1938. The Eyak Indians of the Copper River Delta, Alaska. KDVS [2.]

BITANNY, ADOLPH E. 1941. Medical Dictionary, English to Navajo. Window Rock, Arizona. Mimeographed. [1.5.1]

BITTLE, WILLIAM E. 1956. The position of Kiowa-Apache in the Apachean Group. Doctoral Dissertation, University of California, Los Angeles. [1.5.2]

———. 1963. Kiowa-Apache. Studies in the Athapaskan languages, pp. 149–54. UCPL 29. [1.5.2]

BLAIR, ROBERT W., LEON SIMMONS and GARY WITHERSPOON. 1969. Navajo basic course. Salt Lake City, Utah, Brigham Young University Press. [1.5.1]

BOAS, FRANZ. 1917. Grammatical notes on the language of the Tlingit Indians. UPMAP 8/1. [3.]

———. 1924. Vocabulary of an Athapascan tribe of Nicola Valley, British Columbia. IJAL 3.36–38. [1.3]

BOAS, FRANZ, and P. E. GODDARD. 1924a. Vocabulary of an Athapascan dialect of the state of Washington. IJAL 3.39–45. [1.3]

———. 1924b. Ts'ets'aut, an Athapascan language from Portland Canal, British Columbia. IJAL 3.1–35. [1.2]

BOUCHARD, RANDY. 1971. Haida [tentative Skidegate phonology]. Victoria, ms. [4]

BRIGHT, JANE. 1964. The phonology of Smith River Athapaskan (Tolowa). IJAL 30.101–07. [1.4, 5.1]

CAMPBELL, Rev. JOHN. 1898. The Dénés of America identified with the Tungus of Asia. Transactions of the Canadian Institute 5.167–223. [5.6]

CARRIÈRE, GASTON, O.M.I. 1951. Contribution des Oblats de Marie Immaculée de langue française aus études de linguistique et d'ethnologie du nord canadien. Culture 12.213–226. [1.2]

——. 1957. Une riche collection de manuscrits en langues indiennes. Culture 18.105–112. [1.2]

——. 1969a. Manuscrits microfilmés conservés au Centre de Recherche en Anthropologie. Ottawa, typescript. [1.2]

——. 1969b. Manuscrits en langues indiennes conservés sur microfilms aux archives historiques oblates. Ottawa, typescript. [1.2]

——. 1970. Catalogue des manuscrits en langues indiennes conservés aux archives oblates, Ottawa. Anthropologica n.s. 12.151–179. [1.2]

——. n.d. Tentative bibliography of Adrien-Gabriel Morice, O.M.I. (1859-1938). Ottawa, typescript. [1.2]

CHAFE, WALLACE L. 1962. Estimates regarding the present speakers of North American Indian languages. IJAL 28.162–71. [1.2]

——. 1965. Corrected estimates regarding speakers of Indian languages IJAL 31. 345–46. [1.2]

COLLINS, RAYMOND, and SALLY JO. 1966. Dinak'i. Fairbanks. [1.1]

*Conference on Navajo orthography*. 1969. Center for Applied Linguistics, English for Speakers of other Languages Program. Prepared under contract with The Bureau of Indian Affairs, Department of the Interior. Washington, D.C.

COOK, E.-D. Ms. 1966. A sketch of Sarcee phonemics. The University of Alberta. [1.2]

——. 1967. An introductory sketch of Sarcee grammar. The University of Alberta. [1.2]

——. 1971a. Vowels and tones in Sarcee. 1947.164–79. [1.2]

——. 1971b. Morphophonemics of Sarcee classifiers. IJAL 37.152–55. [1.2]

——. 1971c. Phonological constraint and syntactic rule. Linguistic Inquiry 2.465–78. [1.2]

——. 1971d. Sarcee numerals. University of Calgary, mimeographed, forthcoming in AnL. [1.2]

——. 1971e. Number categories in Sarcee verbs. University of Calgary, mimeographed, 19 pp., with appendix, 3 pp., also paper read at the 70th Annual Meeting of the American Anthropological Association, New York, 1971. [1.2]

CURTIS, E.S. 1913. Willapa. The North American Indian, vol. 9. [1.3]

DAVIDSON, WILLIAM. 1963a. A preliminary analysis of active verbs in Dogrib. Studies in the Athapaskan languages, pp. 48–56. UCPL 29. [1.2]

DAVIDSON, WILLIAM, L. W. ELFORD, and H. HOIJER. 1963. Athapaskan classificatory verbs. Studies in the Athapaskan languages, pp. 30–41. UCPL 29. [1.2, 1.4, 5.1]

DAVIS, CLARK A. 1970. The identity of the Netca'ut'in. IJAL 36.59–60. [1.2]

———. 1971. Some notes on Plateau Athapaskan. Ottawa, mimeographed. [1.2]
DENNISTON, GLENDA and CARTER. 1966. The place of the Upper Pelly River Indians in the network of Northern Athapaskan Groups. Department of Anthropology, University of Wisconsin. [Mimeographed.] [1.2]
DEPARTMENT OF INDIAN AFFAIRS AND NORTHERN DEVELOPMENT. 1980. Linguistic and cultural affiliations of Canadian Indian bands. Ottawa. [1.2]
DURBIN, MARSHALL. E. 1964. A componential analysis of the San Carlos dialect of Western Apache: A study based on analysis of the phonology, morphophonics, and morphemics. Dissertation, State University of New York at Buffalo. Available from University Microfilms, Ann Arbor Michigan, order no. 65–3743. DAb. 27.1357–B. [1.5.2]
———. 1968. Proto-Athapascan pronouns. Paper read at the 67th Annual Meeting of the American Anthropological Association, New Orleans, November 1968. [See the Abstracts of the Meeting.] [5.1]
EASTMAN, CAROL M., and PAUL K. AOKI. 1971. The vowels of Haida. University of Washington, typescript. [4.]
EDGERTON, FAYE E. 1963. The tagmemic analysis of sentence structure in Western Apache. Studies in the Athapaskan languages, pp. 102–48. UCPL 29. [1.5.2]
FRANCISCAN FATHERS. 1910. Ethnologic dictionary of the Navaho language. St. Michaels, Arizona. [1.5.1]
FREEMAN, JOHN F. 1966. A guide to manuscripts relating to the American Indians in the Library of the American Philosophical Society. APS-M 65. [1.2]
FRISHBERG, NANCY. 1971. Navaho subject markers and the great chain of being. University of California at San Diego, mimeographed. [1.5.1]
GLEASON, H. A., JR. 1960. A note on Tanaina subgroups. IJAL 26.348–51. [1.1]
GODDARD, P. E. 1920. Has Tlingit a genetic relation to Athapascan? IJAL 1.266–79.
GOLLA, VICTOR K. 1964. An etymological study of Hupa noun stems. IJAL 30.108–17. [1.4, 5.1]
———. 1970a. Hupa grammar. Dissertation, University of California, Berkeley. [1.4]
———. 1970b. Symbolic processes in Pacific Coast Athabascan. 69th Annual Meeting of the American Anthropological Association, San Diego. [1.4]
GOOSEN, IRVY. 1967. Navajo made easier. Flagstaff, Northern Arizona University. [1.5.1]
GREENFIELD, PHILIP J. 1971. Playing cards in Western Apache. IJAL 37.195–6. [1.5.2.]
HAAS, MARY. 1964. Athapaskan, Tlingit, Yuchi, and Siouan. XXX Congreso internacional de Americanistas, Mexico, 1962, 2.495–500. = PICAm 30. [5.6]
———. 1967. Language and taxonomy in Northwestern California. AmA 96.358–62. [5.1]
———. 1968. Notes on a Chipewyan dialect. IJAL 34.165–75. [1.2]
———. 1969. The prehistory of languages. JanL, series minor 57. [5.1, 5.2]

HAILE, FR. BERARD. 1941–1948. Learning Navaho. 4 vols. St. Michaels, Arizona. [1.5.1]
——. 1950. A stem vocabulary of the Navaho language: Navaho–English. St. Michaels, Arizona. [1.5.1]
——. 1951. English–Navaho. [1.5.1]
HALE, KENNETH. 1956. The distribution of the Class II prefixes in Navaho. Master's Thesis, Department of Linguistics, Indiana University, Bloomington. [1.5.1]
——. 1957. [Navajo phoneme inventory]. IJAL 23.86. [1.5.1]
——. 1970. Navajo linguistics I (prepared for the Hunter's Point Workshop). M.I.T., mimeographed. [1.5.1]
——. 1971a. Navajo Linguistics II. M.I.T., mimeographed. [1.5.1]
——. 1971b. Some comments on the role of American Indian linguistics in bilingual education. M.I.T., mimeographed. [1.5.1]
——. 1971c. A note on subject-object inversion in Navajo. M.I.T., mimeographed, forthcoming in Papers in linguistics in honor of Henry and Renee Kahane, ed. by Braj Kachru et al. [1.5.1]
HARRINGTON, JOHN P. 1941. A field comparison of Northwestern and Southwestern Indians. Smithsonian Institution, Explorations and Field-Work ... in 1940, pp. 91–94. Washington, D.C. [5.5]
——. 1943a. Pacific Coast Athapaskan discovered to be Chilcotin. Journal of the Washington Academy of Sciences 33.203–13. [1.3, 5.4]
——. 1943b. Smithsonian Institution, Annual Report for 1941–42, pp. 50–51. [1.3]
——. 1945. Phonematic daylight in Lhiinkit, Navajo of the north. Journal of the Washington Academy of Sciences 35.1–6. [3., 5.5]
HARRIS, ZELLIG. 1945. Navaho phonology and Hoijer's analysis. IJAL 11.239–46. [1.5.1]
HAUDRICOURT, A. G. 1954. Review of Reichard 1952. Word 10.114–15. [1.5.1]
HENRY, DAVID C. and KAY. 1965. Koyukon classificatory verbs. AnL 7/4.110–16. [1.1, 5.1]
——. 1969a. Dinaak'a. Fairbanks. [1.1]
——. 1969b. Koyukon locationals AnL 11.136–42 [1.1]
HIGGINS, ROGER. 1971. A Dialogue on the Navajo classifier. M.I.T., mimeographed. [1.5.1]
HILL, FAITH. 1963. Some comparisons between the San Carlos and White Mountain dialects of Western Apache. Studies in the Athapaskan languages, pp. 149–54. UCPL 29. [1.5.2]
HÖHN, EMIL OTTO. 1962. The names of economically important or conspicuous mammals and birds in the Indian languages of the District of Mackenzie, N.W.T., and in Sarcee. Arctic 15.299–308. [5.2]
HOIJER, HARRY. 1938a. Chiricahua and Mescalero Apache texts. Chicago, University of Chicago Publications in Anthropology. [1.5.2]
——. 1938b. The Southern Athapaskan languages. AmA 40.75–87. [1.5.2]

——. 1945a. The Apachean verb I: Verb structure and pronominal prefixes. IJAL 11.193–203. [1.5.2]
——. 1945b. Classificatory verb stems in the Apachean languages. IJAL 11.13–23. [1.5.2, 5.1]
——. 1945c. Navaho phonology. UNMPA 1. [1.5.1]
——. 1946a. Chiricahua Apache. Linguistic structures of native America, pp. 55–84. VFPA 6. [1.5.2]
——. 1946b. The Apachean verb II: The prefixes for mode and tense. IJAL 12.1–13. [1.5.2]
——. 1946c. The Apachean verb III: The classifiers. IJAL 12.51–59. [1.5.2]
——. 1948a. The Apachean verb IV: Major form classes. IJAL 14.247–59. [1.5.2]
——. 1948b. The structure of the noun in the Apachean languages. Actes du XXVIIIe congrès international des Américanistes, pp. 173–84. PICAm 28. [1.5.2]
——. 1949. The Apachean verb V: The theme and prefix complex. IJAL 15.12–22. [1.5.2]
——. 1951a. Cultural implications of some Navaho linguistic categories. Lg 27.111–20. [1.5.1]
——. 1951b. Review of Father Berard Haile, papers and monographs on Navaho language and culture. IJAL 17.124–26. [1.5.1]
——. 1953. Review of Reichard 1952. IJAL 19.78–83. [1.5.1]
——. 1954. Preface to Language in culture. AAA-M 79. [2.]
——. 1956a. Lexicostatistics: A critique. Lg 32.49–60. [5.4]
——. 1956b. The chronology of the Athapaskan languages. IJAL 22.219–32. [5.4]
——. 1959. Semantic patterns of the Navaho language. Sprache — Schlüssel zur Welt, Festschrift für Leo Weisgerber, ed. by Helmut Gipper, pp. 361–73. Düsseldorf. [1.5.1]
——. 1960. Athapaskan languages of the Pacific Coast. Culture in history, ed. by Stanley Diamond, pp. 960–76. New York, Columbia University Press. [1.3, 1.4, 5.1]
——. 1962a. Linguistic subgrouping by glottochronology and by the comparative method. Lingua 11.192–98. [5.4]
——. 1962b. Comments on the validity of glottochronology. CAnthr 3.135. [5.4]
——. 1963. The Athapaskan languages. Studies in the Athapaskan languages, pp. 1–29, UCPL 29. [1.2, 1.4., 5.1]
——. 1966a. Galice Athapaskan: A grammatical sketch. IJAL 32.320–27. [1.4]
——. 1966b. Navaho. Lingua 17.88–102. [1.5.1]
——. 1966c. Hare phonology: An historical study. Lg 42.499–507. [1.2, 5.1]
——. 1968. Navaho reference verbs and verb expressions made up of two verb forms. IJAL 34.176–82. [1.5.1]
——. 1969a. The position of the Apachean languages in the Athapaskan stock. Paper read at the 68th Meeting of the American Anthropological Association, New Orleans, November 1969. [1.5.2]

——. 1969b. Internal reconstruction in Navaho. Word 25/3.155–59. [1.5.1]
——. 1971. Athapaskan morphology UCPL 65.113–47. [5.1]
HOIJER, HARRY, and JANET JOËL. 1963. Sarsi nouns. Studies in the Athapaskan languages, pp. 62–75. UCPL 29. [1.2]
HOLM, AGNES, WAYNE HOLM, and BERNARD SPOLSKY. 1971. English loan words in the speech of six-year-old Navajo children. Navajo Reading Study Progress Report No. 16, University of New Mexico. [1.5.1]
HOLM, WAYNE. 1971a. Navajo spelling lists. Navajo Reading Study Progress Report No. 11, University of New Mexico. [1.5.1]
——. 1971b. Grapheme and unit frequencies in Navajo. Navajo Reading Study Progress Report No. 12, University of New Mexico. [1.5.1]
HONIGMANN, JOHN. 1954. The Kaska Indians: An ethnographic reconstruction. YUPA 51. [1.2]
HOWARD, PHILIP. 1963. A preliminary presentation of Slave phonemes. Studies in the Athapaskan languages, pp. 42–47. UCPL 29. [1.2]
HOWREN, ROBERT. 1968. Stem phonology and affix phonology in Dogrib (Northern Athapaskan). Papers from the Fourth Regional Meeting of the Chicago Linguistic Society, ed. by B. J. Darden et al., pp. 120–29. Department of Linguistics, University of Chicago. [1.2, 5.]
——. 1969. Report to the National Science Foundation. Mimeographed. [1.2]
——. 1970. A century of phonological change in a Northern Athapaskan group. University of Iowa, mimeographed, and handout, 69th Annual Meeting of the American Anthropological Association, San Diego. [1.2]
——. 1971a. A formalization of the Athapaskan d-effect. IJAL 37.96–113. [1.2, 5.1]
——. 1971b. Some isoglosses in Mackenzie drainage Athapaskan: First steps toward a subgrouping. Working paper for the Athapaskan Conference, Ethnology Division, National Museum of Man, Ottawa, mimeographed.
——. Forthcoming. The phonology of Rae Dogrib. Bulletin of the National Museum of Canada. [1.2]
HYMES, DELL. 1955. Positional analysis of categories: A frame for reconstruction. Word 11.10–23. [5.5]
——. 1956. Na-Dene and positional analysis of categories. AmA 58.624–38. [5.5]
——. 1957. A note on Athapaskan glottochronology. IJAL 23.291–96. [5.4]
——. 1960a. Lexicostatistics so far. CAnthr 1.3–44 [5.4]
——. 1960b. More on lexicostatistics. CAnthr 1.338–45. [5.4]
HYMES, VIRGINIA D. 1955. Athapaskan numeral systems. IJAL 21.26–45. [5.1]
JACOBS, ELIZABETH D. 1968. A Chetco Athabaskan myth text from Southwestern Oregon. IJAL 34.192–93. [1.4]
JACOBS, MELVILLE. 1937. Historic perspective on Indian languages of Oregon and Washington. PNQ 28.55–74. [1.4]
——. 1941. Survey of Pacific northwest anthropological research. PNQ 32.79–106. [1.4].

———. 1954. The areal spread of sound features in the languages north of California. UCPL 10.46–56. [5.2]

———. 1960. An historical event text from Galice Athapaskan in Southwestern Oregon. IJAL 34.183–90. [1.4]

JOHANNSEN, UWE. 1963. Versuch einer Analyse dokumentarischen Materials über die Identitätsfrage und die kulturelle Position der Eyak-Indianer Alaska. Anthropos 58.868–96. [2.]

JOHNSON, ANDREW P. 1969. Thlingit language [lessons]. Sheldon Jackson College, Sitka, mimeographed. [3.]

KESS, JOSEPH F. 1968. A bibliography of the Haida language. CJL 14.63–5. [4.]

KING, QUINDEL. Forthcoming. Chilcotin phonology. NMC-B [1.2]

KLUCKHOHN, CLYDE and DOROTHEA LEIGHTON. 1946. Chapter 8, The tongue of the people. The Navaho, pp. 182–214. Cambridge, Harvard University Press. [1.5.1]

KRAUSS, MICHAEL E. 1961. Recent linguistic research in Alaska and a new look at Proto-Athapaskan. Paper read at the Annual Meeting of the Linguistic Society of America, Chicago. [5.1]

———. 1964a. Proto-Athapaskan-Eyak and the problem of Na-Dene I: The phonology. IJAL 30.118–31. [5.1, 5.5]

———. 1964b. Review of Hoijer et al., Studies in the Athapaskan languages. IJAL 30.409–15. [5.2]

———. 1965a. Eyak: A preliminary report. CJL 10.167–87. [2., 5.5]

———. 1965b. Proto-Athapaskan-Eyak and the problem of Na-Dene II: The morphology. IJAL 31.18–28. [5.5]

———. 1965c. Eyak lexicon and prehistory. 64th Annual Meeting of the American Anthropological Association, Denver, Abstracts p. 40. [2.]

———. 1968. Noun-classification systems in Athapaskan, Eyak, Tlingit, and Haida verbs. IJAL 34.194–203. [5.1, 5.5]

———. 1969a. Classifying the Athapaskan languages. Paper read at the 68th Annual Meeting of the American Anthropological Society, New Orleans, November, 1969. Also handout. [1.4, 1.5.2, 5.2, 5.3]

———. 1969b. On the classifiers in the Athapaskan, Eyak, and Tlingit verb. IUPAL-M 24 (=IJAL 35/4/2). [5.5]

———. 1970a. Review of Sapir and Hoijer 1967. IJAL 36.220–28 [1.5.1]

———. 1970b. Proto-Athapaskan-Eyak. Informal report, 10th Annual Meeting of the Northeastern Anthropological Association, Ottawa, May 7–9, 1970. [5.3]

———. 1970c. Eyak texts. Boston. [2.]

———. 1970d. Eyak dictionary. Boston. [2.]

———. 1971. Alaskan Athapaskan isoglosses. Handout, Athapaskan Conference, Ethnology Division, National Museum of Man, Ottawa. [5.1, 5.2]

KROEBER, ALFRED L. 1955. Linguistic time depth results so far and their meaning. IJAL 21.91–104. [5.4]
——. 1959. Reflections on Athapaskan glottochronology. UCPAAE 47.241–58. [5.4]
——. 1967. Goddard's California Athapaskan texts. IJAL 33.269–75. [1.4]
KROEBER, ALFRED L. and DALE VALORY. 1967. Ethnological manuscripts in the Robert H. Lowie Museum of Anthropology. KASP 37.1–22. [1.4]
LANDAR, HERBERT. 1959. The Navaho intonational system. AnL 1/9.17–19. [1.5.1]
——. 1960a. Tanaina subgroups. IJAL 26.120–22. [1.1]
——. 1960b. A note on accepted and rejected arrangements of Navaho words. IJAL 26.351–54.
——. 1961. A note on preferred arrangements of Navaho words. IJAL 27.175–7.
——. 1962. Navaho optatives. IJAL 28.9–13.
——. 1963. Navaho syntax. Language Dissertations, no. 57. Supplement to Lg. 39. [1.5.1]
——. 1964. Seven Navaho verbs of eating. IJAL 30.94–6.
——. 1965. Class co-occurrences and Navaho gender. IJAL 31.326–51. [1.5.1, 5.1]
——. 1967a. Syntactic pattern in Navaho and Huichol. IJAL 33.121–27. [1.5.1]
——. 1967b. The language of pain in Navaho culture. Studies in Southwestern ethnolinguistics, ed. by Dell H. Hymes and William E. Bittle, pp. 119–44. (=Studies in General Anthropology 3.) The Hague, Mouton. [1.5.1]
——. 1967c. Ten'a classificatory verbs. IJAL 33.263–68. [5.1]
——. 1967d. Two Athapaskan verbs of 'being'. The verb 'be' and its synonyms: philosophical and grammatical studies, ed. by John W. M. Verhaar. FLss 1.40–74. [1.5.1]
LEER, JEFFREY A. 1971. Tlingit language lessons. Alaska Methodist University, Anchorage, ms. in progress. [3.]
LI, FANG-KUEI. 1930a. A study of Sarcee verb stems. IJAL 6.3–27. [1.2, 5.1]
——. 1930b. Mattole: An Athapaskan language. Chicago, University of Chicago Press. [1.4, 5.1]
——. 1932. A list of Chipewyan stems. IJAL 7.122–51. [1.2, 1.4, 5.1]
——. 1933. Chipewyan consonants. BIHP Ts'ai Yüan P'ei anniversary volume (supplementary volume I, pp. 429–67). [5.1]
——. 1946. Chipewyan. Linguistic structures of Native North America, ed. by H. Hoijer, pp. 398–423. VFPA 6. [1.2]
——. 1956. A type of noun formation in Athapaskan and Eyak. IJAL 22.45–48. [2., 5.1]
——. 1964. A Chipewyan ethnological text. IJAL 30.132–36. [1.2]
——. 1965. Some problems in comparative Athapaskan. CJL 10.129–34. [5.1]
MARSH, GORDON. 1958. Tentative placing of the Tahgish language within the

Athapaskan stock. Paper presented at the Annual Meeting of the Canadian Linguistic Association, 1958. [1.2]

MERRIAM, C. H. 1955. Studies of California Indians. Berkeley, University of California Press. [1.4]

MILANOWSKI, PAUL. 1962. Sound system of Upper Tanana Athapaskan: A preliminary view. Alaskan Science Conference 12.7–10. College, Alaska, August 28–September 1, 1961. AAAS, Alaska Division. [1.1]

MILKE, WILHELM. 1959. Athapaskische Chronologie: Versuch einer Revision. IJAL 25.182–88. [5.4]

MORICE, A. G. 1899. Review of Campbell 1898. Transactions of the Canadian Institute 6.84–100. [5.6]

——. 1914. Northwestern Dénés and Northeastern Asiatics. Transactions of the Canadian Institute 10.131–93. [5.6]

——. 1932. The Carrier language. 2 vols. Vienna. [1.2]

MUELLER, RICHARD J. 1964. Kutchin dictionary. Fairbanks. [1.1]

——. 1970. Let's speak Kutchin. Summer Institute of Linguistics, Fairbanks, mimeographed.

——. 1971. Kutchin grammar. Summer Institute of Linguistics, Fairbanks, mimeographed.

MURPHY, PENNY. 1970. Teaching initial reading in Navajo: Report of a conference of educators held at Kayenta, January 30–31, 1970. Navajo Reading Study Progress Report No. 6, University of New Mexico. [1.5.1]

NAISH, CONSTANCE. 1966. A syntactic study of Tlingit. Master's Thesis, University of London. [Mimeographed; to appear, The Hague, Mouton.] [3.]

NAISH, CONSTANCE and GILLIAN STORY. 1963. English-Tlingit dictionary: Nouns. Fairbanks. [3., 5.4]

[Naish]. 1968. [Lessons in Tlingit]. Angoon, mimeographed. [3.]

——. n.d. A brief outline of Tlingit word classes and word and phrase structures, N.p., n.d. (ca. 1965), mimeographed. [3.]

OLMSTED, D. L. 1953. Review of Reichard 1952. SIL 11.49–50. [1.5.1]

OSGOOD, CORNELIUS. 1936. The distribution of the Northern Athapaskan Indians. YUPA 7. [1.1, 5.2]

——. 1937. The ethnography of the Tanaina. YUPA 16. [1.1]

——. 1940. Ingalik material culture. YUPA 22. [1.1]

——. 1959. Ingalik mental culture YUPA 56. [1.1]

PARRISH, JAMES E., STEPHEN R. ANDERSON, ADRIAN AKMAJIAN, and KENNETH HALE. Ms. 1968. Remarks on pronominalization and the passive in Navaho. Cambridge, M.I.T. [1.5.1]

PEDTKE, DOROTHY, and OSWALD WERNER. 1969. English for speakers of Navajo. Part II of Teaching English to speakers of Choctaw, Navajo, and Papago, a contrastive approach. Indian Education Curriculum Bulletin No. 6. Washington, D.C., Center for Applied Linguistics. [1.5.1]

PERCHONOCK, NORMA and OSWALD WERNER. 1967. Ethnoscience methodology and categories of Navajo foods. Ethnology 229–42. [1.5.1]
PIERCE, JOE E. 1965. The field situation in Oregon: 1964. CJL 10.120–28. [1.4]
PIERCE, JOE E. and JAMES M. RYHERD. 1964. The status of Athapaskan research in Oregon. IJAL 30.137–43. [1.4]
PIKE, KENNETH L. and ALTON L. BECKER. 1964. Progressive neutralization in dimensions of Navaho stem matrices. IJAL 30.144–54. [1.5.1]
PINNOW, HEINZ-JÜRGEN. 1959. Zwei Probleme der historischen Lautlehre der Na-Dene-Sprachen. ZPhon 11.128–59. Abstracted IJAL 28.61–66, 1962. [5.5]
——. 1964. On the historical position of Tlingit. IJAL 30.155–64. [5.5]
——. 1966a. Grundzüge einer historischen Lautlehre des Tlingit: Ein Versuch. Wiesbaden. [5.5]
——. 1966b. Einige Züge indianischen Denkens, dargelegt an der Sprachen der Athapaskan. Anthropos 61.9–32.
——. 1968a. Review of Hymes and Bittle 1967. Anthropos 63–64.1019–23. [1.5.1]
——. 1968b. Genetic relationship vs. borrowing in Na-Dene. IJAL 34.204–11. [5.5]
——. 1968c. Sprachhistorische Studie zur Verbstammvariation im Tlingit. Orbis 17.509–31. [5.5]
——. 1969. Entlehnungen von Tiernamen im Tsimshian und Na-Dene sowie Grundsätzliches zur Entlehnungsfrage bei Indianersprachen. ZEthn 94.82–102. [5.5]
——. 1970a. Notes on the classifiers in the Na-Dene languages. IJAL 36.63–67. [5.5]
——. 1970b. Wir Lernen Navaho. Kalumet 19/1.23–26. 19/2.23–26, 19/3.23–26, 19/4.23–26, 19/5.23–26, 19/6.23–26, to be continued. [1.5.1]
PYLE, CHARLES. 1969. Proto-Athapaskan consonants. Master's Thesis, Iowa University. [5.1]
REICHARD, GLADYS A. 1945. Linguistic diversity among the Navaho Indians. IJAL 11.156–68. [1.5.1]
——. 1948. Significance of aspiration in Navaho. IJAL 14.15–19. [1.5.1]
——. 1949. The character of the Navaho verb stem. Word 5.55–76. [1.5.1]
——. 1952. Navaho grammar. PAES 21. New York, J.J. Augustin. [1.5.1]
REICHARD, GLADYS and ADOLPH E. BITTANY. 1940. Agentive and causative elements in Navajo. New York, J.J. Augustin. [1.5.1]
RICHARDSON, MURRAY W. 1963. Paradigmatic prefixes in Chipewyan. Studies in the Athapaskan languages, pp. 56–61. UCPL 29. [1.2]
——. 1968. Chipewyan grammar. Cold Lake, Alberta, Northern Canada Evangelical Mission. [1.2]
SAPIR, EDWARD. 1914. Notes on Chasta Costa phonology and morphology. UPMAP 11/2. [5.1]
——. 1915. The Na-Dene languages: A preliminary report. AmA 17.534–58. [5.1, 5.5]

——. 1923. The phonetics of Haida. IJAL 2.143–58. [4.]
——. 1925. Pitch accent in Sarcee, an Athapaskan language. JSAm 17.185–205. [1.2, 5.5]
——. 1925c. The simularity of Chinese and Indian languages. Science 62/1607 (October 16). xii. [5.5, 5.6]
——. 1942. Navaho texts, with supplementary texts by Harry Hoijer. Edited by Harry Hoijer. Linguistic Society of America, Philadelphia. [1.5.1]
SAPIR, EDWARD, and HARRY HOIJER. 1967. The phonology and morphology of the Navaho language. UCPL 50. [1.5.1]
SAVILLE, MURIEL. 1968. Navajo morphophonemics. Doctoral Dissertation, University of Texas at Austin. Available from University Microfilms, Ann Arbor, Michigan, order number 69–6208. DissAb 29.3600-A. [1.5.1]
SAVILLE, MURIEL, and RUDOLPH C. TROIKE. 1970. A handbook for bilingual education. Washington, D.C., Center for Applied Linguistics. [1.5.1]
SHAFER, ROBERT. 1952. Athapaskan and Sino-Tibetan. IJAL 18.12–19. [5.6]
——. 1957. A note on Athapaskan and Sino-Tibetan. IJAL 23.116–17. [5.6]
SIMMONS, LEON V. 1969. A transformational generative analysis of Navaho classificatory verbs. M.A. thesis, Brigham Young University. [1.5.1, 5.1]
SPOLSKY, BERNARD. 1970. Navajo language maintenance I: Six-year-olds in 1969. Navajo Reading Study Progress Report no. 5, University of New Mexico, reprinted in Language Sciences 13.19–24. [1.5.1]
——. 1971a. Navajo language maintenance II. Six-year-olds in 1970. Navajo Reading Study Progress Report No. 13, University of New Mexico. [1.5.1]
——. 1971b. Navajo language maintenance III: Accessibility of school and town as a factor in language shift. Navajo Reading Study Progress Report No. 14, University of New Mexico. [1.5.1]
SPOLSKY, BERNARD, AGNES HOLM, and PENNY MURPHY. 1970. Analytical bibliography of Navajo reading materials (revised and enlarged edition of NRS Progress Report No. 3, 1969). Navajo Reading Study Progress Report No. 7, University of New Mexico, reprinted as Curriculum Bulletin No. 10, United States Bureau of Indian Affairs, 1970. [1.5.1]
SPOLSKY, BERNARD, and WAYNE HOLM. 1971a. Literacy in the vernacular: The case of Navajo. Navajo Reading Study Progress Report No. 8, University of New Mexico, reprinted in Studies in language and linguistics, 1970–71, edited by Jacob Ornstein, University of Texas at El Paso Press. [1.5.1]
——. 1971b. Bilingualism in the six-year-old Navajo child. Conference on Child Language, Chicago.
SPOLSKY, BERNARD, WAYNE HOLM, and JONATHAN EMBRY. 1971. A computer assisted study of the vocabulary of six-year-old Navajo children. Navajo Reading Study Progress Reports No. 9, University of New Mexico. [1.5.1]
SPOLSKY, BERNARD, WAYNE HOLM, BABETTE HOLLIDAY, JUDY HARVEY, MARLENE ATCITTY, IRENE SILENTMAN, and JONATHAN EMBRY. 1971. A spoken word count

of six-year-old Navajo children. Navajo Reading Study Progress Report No. 10, University of New Mexico. [1.5.1]

STANLEY, RICHARD. 1969a. Review of Sapir and Hoijer 1967. Lg. 45.927–39. [1.5.1]

——. 1969b. The phonology of the Navaho verb. Doctoral Dissertation, M.I.T. [1.5.1]

STORY, GILLIAN. 1966. A morphological study of Tlingit. Master's Thesis, University of London. [Mimeographed; to appear, The Hague, Mouton.] [3.]

SUE, HIROKO. Ms. 1962. Report on ethnographic field research at Ft. Good Hope, N.W.T., Summer 1961. Bryn Mawr, Pa. [1.2]

——. 1964. *Hare* zoku no shakai kōzō. Minzokugakū kenkyū 27.181–96. [1.2]

SWADESH, MORRIS. 1951. Diffusional cumulation and archaic residue. SJA 7.14–21. [5.4]

——. 1952. Lexicostatistical dating of prehistoric ethnic contacts. PAPS 96.452–63. [5.4]

——. 1954a. Time depths of American linguistic groupings. AmA 56.361–64. [5.4]

——. 1954b. On the Penutian vocabulary survey. IJAL 20.123–133. [1.4]

——. 1958. Some new glottochronological dates for Amerindian linguistic groups. Proceedings of the 32nd International Congress of Americanists, pp. 670–74. = PICAm 32. [5.4]

——. 1959. Mapas de clasificación lingüistica de México y de las Americas. Cuadernos del Instituto de Historia, Serie antropológica, no. 8. University of Mexico. [5.4]

——. 1960a. On interhemispheric linguistic connections. Culture and history, Essays in honor of Paul Radin, ed. by Stanley Diamond, pp. 894–924. New York. [5.6]

——. 1960b. Tras la huella lingüistica de la prehistoria. Suplementos del Seminario de Problemas Científicos y Filosóficos 26.97–145. [5.4]

——. 1962a. Afinidades de las lenguas Amerindias. Akten des 34. Internationalen Amerikanistenkongresses, 1960 Wien, pp. 729–38. = PICAm 34. [5.4, 5.6]

——. 1962b. Linguistic relations across Bering Strait. AmA 64.1262–91. [5.6]

——. 1965. Lingvisticheskie svyazi Ameriki i Evrazii. Etimologiya 5.271–322. [5.6]

SWANTON, JOHN R. 1911. Haida. BAE-B 40.205–282. [4.]

TAPTTO, MARY HELEN. 1971. Ranking in Navajo nouns. 70th Annual Meeting of the American Anthropological Associtation, New York. [1.5.1]

THARP, GEORGE W. 1972. The position of Tsetsaut among the Northern Athapaskans. IJAL 38.14–25. [1.2, 5.1, 5.2]

TRAGER, GEORGE. 1953. Review of Reichard 1952. AmA 55.428.29. [1.5.1]

VELTEN, H.V. 1939. Two southern Tlingit tales. IJAL 10.65–74. [3.]

——. 1944. Three Tlingit tales. IJAL 10.168–80. [3.]

VOEGELIN, CARL F. 1951. A query on the nominal origin of verb stems in Athapaskan. IJAL 17.80–83. [5.1]

——, et al. 1963. Obtaining an index of phonological differentiation from construction of non-existent minimal systems. IJAL 29.4–28. [5.1, 5.4]

WALKER, RICHARD. forthcoming. Central Carrier phonemics. NMC-B [1.2]

WALL, LEON and WILLIAM MORGAN. 1954. Talking Navajo before you know it. Window Rock, Arizona. Mimeographed. [1.5.1]

——. 1958. Navajo-English dictionary. Phoenix, Arizona. [1.5.1]

WERNER, OSWALD. 1963. A typological comparison of four trader Navaho speakers. Doctoral Dissertation, Indiana University. Available from University Microfilm, Ann Arbor, Michigan, order number 64–5507. DissAb. 25.752 1964.; see also Linguistics 13.121–23, 1965. [1.5.1]

——. 1965. Semantics of Navaho medical terms: I. IJAL 31.1–17. [1.5.1]

——. 1967. Problems of Navajo lexicography. Studies in Southwestern ethnolinguistics, ed. by Dell Hymes and William E. Bittle, pp. 145–64. (= Studies in general Anthropology 3.) The Hague, Mouton. [1.5.1]

——. 1970a. A typology of the principles of naming anatomical terms. IJAL 36.247–265. [1.5.1]

——. 1970b. The classification of the Navajo universe. Proceedings of the 10th Congress of Americanists, Lima, Peru, August 1970. [1.5.1]

WERNER, OSWALD and KENNETH BEGISHE. 1966. Anatomical atlas of the Navajo. [Mimeographed.] [1.5.1]

——. 1970. A lexemic typology of Navajo anatomical terms I: The foot. IJAL 36.247–265. [1.5.1]

WERNER, OSWALD, KENNETH BEGISHE, and JEANNETTE FRANK. 1967. A programmed guide to Navajo transcription. Mimeographed. [1.5.1]

WILSON, ALAN. 1969. Breakthrough Navajo. Gallup, New Mexico, University of New Mexico. [1.5.1]

WILSON, ALAN, and GENE DENNISON. 1970. Laughter: The Navajo way. Gallup, University of New Mexico. [1.5.1]

WITHERSPOON, GARY. 1971. Navajo categories of objects at rest. AmA 73.110–27. [1.5.1, 5.1]

WOODWARD, MARY. 1964. Hupa phonemics. Studies in Californian linguistics, ed. William Bright, pp. 199–216. UCPL 34. [1.4]

WYMAN, LELAND C. and FLORA L. BAILEY. 1964. Navaho Indian ethnoentomology. UNMPA 12. [1.5.1]

WYMAN, LELAND C. and S. K. HARRIS. 1941. Navajo Indian medical ethnobotany. University of New Mexico Bulletin 5. Albuquerque. [1.5.1]

——. 1957. The ethnobotany of the Kayenta Navaho. University of New Mexico Publications in Biology 5. Albuquerque. [1.5.1]

YOUNG, ROBERT W. 1959. The Navajo language. The Navajo yearbook, pp. 197–228. Window Rock, Arizona. [1.5.1]

YOUNG, ROBERT W. and WILLIAM MORGAN. 1943. The Navaho language. Education

Division, Office of Indian Affairs, Phoenix, Arizona. Reprinted 1967, Deseret Book Company, Salt Lake City, Utah. [1.5.1]

——. 1948. The function and signification of certain Navaho particles. Phoenix, Arizona. Reprinted, Farmington, New Mexico, Navajo Mission's Press. [1.5.1]

——. 1951. A vocabulary of colloquial Navaho. United States Indian Service, Phoenix, Arizona. [1.5.1]

——. 1968. English as a second language for Navajos: An overview of certain cultural and linguistic factors. Albuquerque (1967, revised 1968). [1.5.1]

This report reflects the state of Eskimo-Aleut studies in 1970 in what has remained a rapidly developing field. In a special sense, 1970 might well be considered an appropriate date for a report since it marked the end of an era of scholarship, one in which the speakers of the language were primarily objects of observation, and the dawn of a new era in which the active participation of native speakers has dramatically increased, not only in the field of language study, but in all areas of academic, cultural, and educational activity.

# THE NORTHWEST

LAURENCE C. THOMPSON

0. INTRODUCTION

The story of linguistic research in the Northwest is a complex and varied one.[1] Inextricably intertwined with the rich and varied cultures of the indigenous peoples who speak those languages, it has drawn fascinated field researchers from all over the world, and it promises to yield yet untold riches in the variety of human expression and the ways human beings systematize the natural and supernatural phenomena of their universe and their reactions and attitudes in response to them. Not surprisingly, the linguists who have attempted to record and study these tongues have usually been to greater or lesser extent also anthropologists — interested as well in the cultural relationships, and concerned about the fate of those earlier Americans.

It is a fascinating story, involving as it does some of the world's richest diversity of linguistic structures, and some of the most extraordinary cases of diverging semantic organization. And it is offering a valuable challenge to researchers concerned with testing assumptions — both explicit and, insofar as it becomes possible, hidden — about universal features of language design.

In terms of areal linguistic studies, too, the Northwest offers a multifaceted fabric of interwoven trait patterns which, with a better understanding, may give us fresh insights into the ways languages in contact affect one another. Work on genetic relationships in the area furnishes not only the necessary basis for consideration of further linguistic alignments, but much significant information which should increase our understanding of patterns of linguistic change.

---

[1] I am grateful to a number of scholars for supplying information on their own and others' activities in order to afford improved current coverage; several of them have also been good enough to make detailed suggestions on a draft of this chapter: Haruo Aoki, Barbara Efrat, William Elmendorf, R. J. Gregg, Mary Haas, Eric Hamp, Thomas Hess, Dell Hymes, Melville Jacobs, William Jacobsen, M. Dale Kinkade, Bruce Rigsby, Michael Silverstein, Wayne Suttles. I must retain, however, the responsibility for the form and substance of the chapter; none of them should be blamed for any of its inadequacies. I am likewise grateful to J. V. Powell for checking the bibliography and references. I should also like to acknowledge here the generous support over many years of the National Science Foundation for research related to this area. Thanks are due as well to the Pacific and Asian Linguistics Institute of the University of Hawaii for support of this research and assistance in its administration. Finally, I am most indebted to my wife, M. Terry Thompson, for assistance at all levels of the preparation of this survey. The information offered is as up-to-date as possible through the summer of 1970.

Additional data from the area have stimulated further thought also about linguistic typologies — and challenged researchers to attempt to capture and define those elusive features that characterize linguistic systems.

The area, then, challenges universal considerations with its very diversity — or dares researchers to find the recurrent, general and underlying in the wealth of superficial disparity. But the strong suspicion remains, for at least some of us, that the organization of human thought has some fundamental diversity. In any case, if we can manage to devise approaches which avoid the superficial projection of structure on one new language after another, we are about to stumble on the reality of just what universal features underlie the world's languages, and to what extent we must recognize fundamental differences in the human experiencing and structuring of the universe.

We may think of the Northwest[2] as an interlocking set of linguistic areas extending roughly from the Oregon-California border north along the Pacific coast to the panhandle of Alaska, and inland across the coastal mountain ranges, up the great river valleys, and often far across the interior highlands to still other mountains beyond. It is the country par excellence of the great Salishan linguistic family and its smaller neighbors Chemakuan and Wakashan; it also embraces the isolated Kutenai, all the northern portion of Sapir's Penutian stock, and various enclaves of Athapaskan speech.

In the north it abuts on Na-Dene, with Haida and Tlingit on the coast and the great spread of Canadian Athapaskan in the interior — which because of their linguistic affiliation are best treated with Alaskan Athapaskan and Eyak. In the east and south it meets Uto-Aztecan over a long frontier-fringe of the Great Basin speech groups, belonging linguistically with the Southwest. In the south it faces Hokan and melts into California Penutian. In the center the area bulges far inland across the interior plateaus to Idaho and Western Montana. The eastern frontier approaches the Algonkian Blackfoot and the Siouan Crow.

The central focus of the area, then, is that group of families which were early proposed as a Mosan stock — Salishan, Wakashan and Chemakuan. Although Swadesh (1953a, 1953b) offered evidence to support the hypothesis originally suggested by Frachtenberg (1920a:295) and adopted by Sapir (1929a), further work of Swadesh (e.g. 1962:1266, 1964b:547) suggested that the relationship is a far more remote one, and the question still awaits more detailed study when more extensive materials become available and, especially, when reliable reconstructions of early stages of

---

[2] The following description presents a reconstruction of language distributions in the pre-reservation period — around the early nineteenth century — with some notes about apparent recent movements. The discussion uses linguistic names with the -*an* suffix for language families and stocks to assist the uninitiated in distinguishing them from single languages (which are sometimes confusingly identified by the same unsuffixed terms). For some helpful linguistic maps, in addition to the better known ones, see Barnett (1955:opposite 24); Elmendorf and Suttles (1960:2); Jacobs (1945:154); Kotschar (1951); Oregon Historical Society (1958); Ray (1936); Suttles (1954:30); and Suttles and Elmendorf (1963).

Salishan and Wakashan are made. Supplying these needs, then, is one of the principal aims of current research activities.

The Chemakuan family consists of just two languages — the extinct Chemakum, originally spoken at the northeast corner of Washington's Olympic Peninsula, present Port Townsend and vicinity; and Quileute, still spoken by a few elders on the opposite side of the Olympic Peninsula, facing the Pacific Ocean. The Wakashan family is more ramified: it has two main divisions, Nootkan and Kwakiutlan. Nootkan (three languages) extends from Makah, just north of the Quileute and occupying the northwestern tip of the Olympic Peninsula, up along the west coast of Vancouver Island, with closely related Nitinat at the southern end, and several dialects of Nootka proper further north. Beyond that lies the domain of the three Kwakiutlan languages — Kwakiutl proper in several dialects occupying all the north of Vancouver Island and extending onto the mainland of British Columbia opposite, Bella Bella (or Heiltsuk) further north, and finally Haisla.

Salishan is a large, complex family. The main body lies in Washington and southern British Columbia, extending in its center back from the Pacific coast straight across the Cascade Mountains and the plateau beyond, to the Rockies in Montana and originally perhaps on into the plains. The languages fall into two great divisions, Interior Salishan east of the Cascades, and Coast Salishan to the west, and the peoples belong accordingly also to two different cultural areas, the Plateau and the Northwest Coast, respectively. Although the Coast division is indeed oriented to salt water, the peoples occupied primarily land that did not face the open ocean and, with a few exceptions, were not oriented toward exploitation of it in the way the Nootkan groups were. In a detached enclave to the south, Tillamook commanded the north Oregon coast from the mouth of the Nehalem River south to that of the Siletz; the language is clearly closer to those of the Coast division than to those of the Interior. In another detached area far to the north lies Bella Coola, separating the northern Kwakiutlan territories, on the shores of the Bella Coola River and the inland waterways into which it empties (North and South Bentinck Arm), as well as the connected Dean Channel and the lower reaches of the Dean and Kimsquit Rivers which feed it. This language is still more divergent than Tillamook, but again seems to align with the Coast rather than the Interior division of the main body.

Interior Salishan separates into a northern branch (three languages: Lillooet, Shuswap and Thompson spread along the river valleys and lake shores of south central British Columbia), and a southern branch (four languages — Okanagan-Colville sweeping southward into Washington; Columbian, centering around Wenatchee, Washington; and Kalispel and Coeur d'Alene, occupying the easternmost territory of the stock).

Coast Salishan is still more ramified. Besides the two separated enclaves of Tillamook and Bella Coola, we can recognize a separate Olympic Branch in southwestern Washington (in two sets of closely related languages — inland Upper Chehalis and [Lower] Cowlitz, and downriver/coastal Lower Chehalis and Quinault), and a long spread of even more closely related branches which together can be called Central Coast Salishan. At the southern end of this continuum are two branches — close-knit Twana (around the Hood Canal) and Puget Sound Salish (two sets of mildly differentiated dialects surrounding Seattle). Further north we encounter Straits Salish (Clallam on the northern shores of the Olympic Peninsula, and an intergrading set of dialects extending along the southern end of Vancouver Island and the San Juan Islands to the mainland around Bellingham, Washington); and the isolated Nooksack and Squamish on each side of a long dialect continuum, Halkomelem, which stretches from around the head of navigation of the Fraser River at Yale, British Columbia, down to its mouth and across to the southeastern littoral of Vancouver Island, including the islands of the Gulf of Georgia between. Finally, the northernmost group includes Seshelt, just north of Squamish on the British Columbia mainland; Pentlatch on the east shore of Vancouver Island north of Halkomelem; and a considerable dialect spread of Comox from Powell River to Bute Inlet on the mainland and from Courtenay to Campbell River on the island.

On the eastern fringe of our region is the language isolate Kutenai, in northern Idaho, northwestern Montana and adjacent British Columbia.

The northern complex of the putative Penutian stock is less cohesive. The northernmost family, Tsimshian, occupies a far removed enclave on the north coast and river drainage of British Columbia, around the valleys of the Skeena and Nass Rivers; it is divided into two dialect sets, Coast Tsimshian and Nass-Gitksan. Other constituent families claim much of southern Washington and the largest part of Oregon.

Plateau Penutian is for the moment primarily a geographical grouping. It includes the Sahaptian family (two languages: Nez Perce around the point where Oregon, Washington and Idaho come together; and Sahaptin proper, a long series of dialects stretching from northeastern Oregon down the Columbia Valley and up along the Yakima River), Klamath on the eastern flank of the Cascades at the Oregon-California border, and the troublesome Waiilatpuan (two languages, Cayuse and Molale, which have been thought to form a group but which had only limited coverage before their extinction, so that comparison is difficult).

From the eastern slope of the Cascades to the sea the Columbia Valley was occupied by speakers of Chinookan languages — Coastal Chinook (or Chinook proper) around the river's mouth and a few miles upstream, then a long set of dialects that Boas called Upper Chinook extending up the river to The Dalles. To the south, in the drainage of the Willamette River, is the Kalapuyan family (three languages — Tualatin, Santiam, and Yonkalla). This, in turn, seems not too distantly related to Takelma along the upper Rogue River in southern Oregon. Finally, along the Oregon coast, south of the Salishan Tillamook, were three groups: Yaquina and Alsea; Siuslaw; and the Coosan languages (Hanis and Miluk).

Besides the Na-Dene neighbors in the northeast and northwest (Athapaskan, Haida and Tlingit), there were enclaves of Athapaskan speech within the area of the families just discussed. In the north, in the Upper Nicola Valley of southern British

Columbia, was Nicola — a small island in Salishan territory, now apparently extinct. Two Athapaskan groups in the region of the lower Columbia also disappeared early: Kwalhioqua and Clatskanie. On the southern Oregon Coast, however, there was a considerable area of Athapaskan languages, some still surviving. Together with languages of northwestern California they form the Pacific Coast subgroup of the Athapaskan family, extending from the Umpqua River in Oregon to the head of the Eel in California.

It is possible to recognize three periods in the modern pursuit of linguistic research in the Northwest. The early period runs roughly from the end of the last century to the late 1920s, and is dominated by the vigorous and wide ranging fieldwork and rich documentation of Franz Boas (cf. the bibliography of Boas' work: Andrews and others 1943) and the keen insights and brilliant syntheses of Edward Sapir (cf. the bibliography by Leslie Spier 1958).

The middle period brought a decline in interest in the area: while a number of scholars began research there they were mostly drawn away to other concerns until World War II, when the preoccupation with foreign areas reduced Amerindian studies to almost total neglect. During this interim, however, Melville Jacobs of the University of Washington's Department of Anthropology pursued the recording and study of language after language on the verge of extinction, and campaigned to rekindle interest. His survey of Northwest anthropological research in the 1930s (M. Jacobs 1941) affords a good sense of the needs and problems of the times. After the war Jacobs' efforts began to pay dividends, and his influence was strengthened by others' endeavors during the current period — the 1950s and '60s.

Anthropological work with more marginal linguistic interest[3] continued through the middle period — carried on in particular by a number of anthropologists at the Universities of Washington, Oregon and British Columbia. One individual contribution should be mentioned here as important background for the understanding of the Plateau languages: Verne F. Ray as a student and faculty member at the University of Washington provided detailed information on the location of village sites in the Plateau area (1936; see also Ray and others 1938), and on cultural relations (1939). Convenient summaries of tribal distributions are Berreman (1937) for Oregon and Spier (1936) for Washington. Allan H. Smith (1953) has provided a more recent ethnographic summary for Washington. Fred Adler (1961) has supplied a bibliography of linguistic studies covering much of the Northwest, including listings of unpublished data; however, it does not include references to Penutian.[4]

Over the full extent of his life John P. Harrington of the Bureau of American Eth-

---

[3] Coverage here of general anthropological interests is suggestive rather than in any sense comprehensive: works mentioned are primarily those relating directly to linguistics or valuable for references. Consult recent items for further bibliography.

[4] Many comparative studies relating to the area are included in the more general bibliographies of Amerindian comparison — see Loriot (1964) and Hoijer, Hamp and Bright (1966).

nology continued collecting linguistic materials on the native languages of western North America. The full coverage of languages in his literary estate, now deposited in the Bureau, has yet to be determined. Beyond the material now identified some important (perhaps extensive) samples of now extinct Northwest languages may appear from this source.

While the intention here is to emphasize the work currently under way, it is desirable to relate this to earlier research. Thus many older publications are cited. For further references to the early work and to ethnographic publications, see pertinent sections of Murdock (1960), Newberry Library (1961), and the Pilling (1885) proofsheets of a general North American Indian language bibliography, as well as his later bibliographies of individual families (Pilling 1893a, 1893b, 1894). For a recent summary of the linguistic situation in Native America, which integrates this area into the rest and, in fact, into the world linguistic community, see C. F. and F. M. Voegelin (1964, 1965), now revised and to appear in a separate series on the languages of the world.

Work on the various languages and their inter-relationships, as well as more general discussions and byproduct work, are best discussed topically. However, to give a sense of the continuity of the current work it may be useful to outline some of the programmed research that has developed in the recent period.

When I joined the faculty of the University of Washington in 1957 my primary objective was to help advance the linguistic coverage of the Northwest, and I began work on Salishan languages in my spare time as soon as it was possible. I recognized, however, that anything approaching adequate coverage of Northwest languages before their extinction would have to be accomplished by teamwork of a number of trained researchers, and resolved to develop a research program patterned on the successful survey of native languages conducted by Mary R. Haas at the University of California, Berkeley (hereafter called the California Survey). In such a program graduate students in linguistics are supported in field research on inadequately studied languages and prepare descriptions of those languages as their doctoral dissertations. From 1959 to 1966 it was possible to interest linguistics graduate students at the University of Washington in Northwest indigenous languages. In 1962 the National Science Foundation granted generous funds to back this work, and the project has continued training new researchers for the area, moving to the University of Hawaii with me in 1966. Two other faculty members participated in the project at the University of Washington: William H. Jacobsen, Jr., and George V. Grekoff.

M. Dale Kinkade developed an interest in the area as an undergraduate at the University of Washington and began field researches in Olympic Salishan in 1960 as a graduate student at Indiana University. Now at the University of Kansas, he has joined in the effort to train further researchers, and the National Science Foundation has supported his work since 1966. It is convenient to refer to these two cooperative projects under a collective title, the Northwest Survey.

The National Science Foundation has also given funds for work on Oregon indigenous languages close to extinction, under a grant to Joe E. Pierce at Portland

State University (henceforth the Oregon Survey). Considerable coverage in the Northwest, especially in Oregon and Idaho, has been afforded by the California Survey mentioned above. Recently Washington State University has supported some field research in the Plateau under the direction of James Goss.

The Phillips Fund of the American Philosophical Society has continued to sponsor a variety of individual field trips in the Northwest, and the Society's library has worked to assure use of its important Boas Collection of materials on Amerindian languages, which is rich in documentation of Northwest languages (cf. the recent catalogue, Freeman and Smith 1966).

There are many pertinent manuscripts besides Harrington's in the archives of the Bureau of American Ethnology at the Smithsonian Institution, and the Bureau has continued to assure their availability to scholars.

A special collection in Spokane, Washington, holds many early records of Indian languages of the Northwest: in the Archives of the Oregon Province of the Society of Jesus are both manuscripts and publications on these and related topics, centering around the core of materials prepared by Jesuit missionaries. The archivist, Rev. Wilfred P. Schoenberg, S.J., has acquired also many museum pieces relating to the Indians and has directed the development of the new Spokane Indian Center. The collection will move from its present location in Crosby Library at Gonzaga University to the Indian Center as soon as the specially designed archive accommodations there are completed.

On the Canadian side, the Canada Council has taken an important interest in the research on indigenous languages. In addition to awarding a number of individual grants, it has supported an institutional project for the study of neglected British Columbia languages, under the direction of Geoffrey N. O'Grady and Henry J. Warkentyne, in the University of Victoria Linguistics Department (henceforth the Victoria Survey). The Canada Council is supporting the same university in establishing archives of tape recordings and fieldnotes on Northwest languages; it is planned to duplicate the materials so that one copy will be held by the Curator of Ethnology, British Columbia Provincial Museum, Victoria, while the other remains at the Department of Linguistics at the University. In this connection the department is conducting a survey aimed at dialectal classification.

The British Columbia Provincial Museum has also instituted a newsletter (see Bouchard, Kew and McNair 1970) describing ongoing research on Indians of the region. Geoffrey L. Bursill-Hall encouraged staff members of his Department of Modern Languages at Simon Fraser University to undertake researches on local languages. And interest is now developing at the University of British Columbia, with its growing linguistics program, for the study of languages of the province.

The Canadian National Museum in Ottawa and the British Columbia Provincial Museum in Victoria have also supported research on the indigenous languages and have helped toward the preservation of information for the future through the microfilming of manuscript material and the copying of recorded tapes.

The Summer Institute of Linguistics opened a training program at the University of Washington in the summer of 1959 under the direction of Benjamin Elson. The intention was to utilize informants of local indigenous languages in the Northwest for the two-week practical exercise with which the introductory courses end. In this way it would be possible for staff to make a contribution by working with students each summer on these languages, and there would be an accumulation of understanding of the structures. Informants were brought in from several local groups, including Northern Puget Sound (Skagit), Southern Puget Sound (Nisqually), Clallam, Upper Chehalis, and Quileute. The languages proved to be so difficult to deal with for these purposes that the organization abandoned the plan in favor of languages into which students in the summer program could be expected to develop some insight during the intensive two-week exercise. This was one in a series of practical experiences with Northwest languages which helped make clear that they present considerably more than average difficulty for recording and analysis.

Leon V. Metcalf of Seattle, working on his own time, providing his own equipment, materials and transportation, has made a contribution to the collecting of samples of disappearing languages. In the 1950s he traveled about the Northwest contacting the oldest and best informed speakers of many languages and making magnetic tape recordings of vocabulary, short sentences and connected conversations or narratives wherever possible. In some instances he reached informants who were able to record connected texts; as these informants have since died and the languages are now represented at best by speakers who can interpret the texts but could not produce them, these tapes provide the only sound-recorded samples of connected speech for the languages.

This matter calls attention to what is a considerable difference between current and earlier fieldwork in the area. Until recently very few sound recordings were made of any of these languages. However, with the advent of the portable tape recorder with good fidelity it is possible to make many recordings — in fact, the practice has been to tape record the greatest part of notes taken in the field as well as making the more obvious permanent records of whatever textual material can be had. This means that for future generations of linguists there may be records of these languages which will make them come more alive, and may lead to new discoveries about the languages long after they are already extinct.

The Language Master machine has provided a valuable special adaptation of tape recordings: it plays material which has been recorded on short segments of tape laminated on cards. This device makes possible comparative listening with a maximum of flexibility and selectivity, and it has contributed to analytical work on the languages as well as affording a means to create sample 'speaking dictionaries' of them for archiving purposes. Recordings made on regular tape recorders in the field are dubbed off onto Language Master cards for these purposes.

In 1966, acting on the suggestion of M. Dale Kinkade, I arranged a conference of researchers then actively working on Salishan languages, held at the University of

Washington for two days at the end of the summer. Ongoing research was discussed, problems reviewed, priorities for further work explored, and cooperative efforts enlisted. It was decided that it would be useful to plan a continuing annual conference with papers on topics of mutual interest circulated in advance. The annual meeting later drew scholars interested in languages of the Northwest outside the Salishan family, and so it has developed into a wider Northwest conference. It met again at the University of Washington in 1967; then the University of Victoria sponsored it in 1968 and 1969; and sponsorship passed to the Spokane Indian Center and Gonzaga University for 1970. There has been an increasing number of native speakers of the languages and their descendants in attendance, showing a growing interest in work on the languages. This continuing conference has proven valuable in stimulating further work, in encouraging cooperation among researchers, and in assuring discussion of needs and interests, as well as by furnishing a forum for presentation of ideas for consideration. Many of the papers presented have found their way into print in various journals. Selected papers from the 1970 conference have now been published as a volume (Hoard and Hess 1971).

The current trend is a reintegration of all theoretical and practical interests, coupled with an intensifying industry in collecting material on the languages before it is too late — in short, a revitalization of general linguistic studies with a firm base in the data of the area.

## 1. PENUTIAN

The groupings of the languages of the putative northern extension of California Penutian are still in question — indeed the relationship of many of the languages remains not yet established, for some not even proven, in Hymes' (1959a:52) sense of those terms. Let us proceed in terms of geographic location and cultural areas.

The province of northern Penutian is essentially the present state of Oregon, with spillover into Washington and Idaho (and the separate enclave, Tsimshian, in British Columbia). A recent survey of the field situation in Oregon by Joe E. Pierce (1965b) affords an introduction, especially read in conjunction with M. Jacobs' (1941) earlier depiction of the overall anthropological scene.

To the Northwest in the summer of 1926 came a student of Franz Boas, Melville Jacobs, to whom we owe more than to any other single person in the rescue from oblivion of so many cultural expressions (language, folklore, music) of the area. Although a general anthropologist, he was strongly influenced by Boas' example of responsibility for the languages involved, and a great deal of his work has remained strongly centered around language. That first summer and the next he collected material on dialects of a language which has come to be known as Sahaptin,[5] present-

---

[5] There has been variation of usage on the name of the Sahaptin language and of the family to which it belongs. Adopted here is a current usage, in keeping with the general naming pattern: Sahaptin for the language, Sahaptian for the family, which includes just Nez Perce and Sahaptin. Sahaptin seems to have had a dozen or more dialects, which group into two divisions, northern and southern; the northern division includes northwest and northeast clusters, the Columbia River cluster constitutes

ing a grammar as his doctoral dissertation at Columbia University. He soon made available a collection of texts (M. Jacobs 1929, 1934–37), his grammar (1931), and an article on kinship terms (1932a). (Note Swadesh's [1936] review of the first volume of texts.) He also at this time outlined (1929:241, 1931:93) a broader stock, including this language and Nez Perce to the east (Powell's Shahaptian) together with Klamath in southern Oregon and northern California (Powell's Lutuamian) and the extinct Cayuse and nearly extinct Molale languages in north-central Oregon and nearby Washington (which had earlier been combined as Waiilatpuan). This is the same grouping which Sapir (1929a) designated Plateau Penutian. In addition to these publications he has extensive unpublished myth and worldview texts in Klickitat, the northwestern dialect on which he concentrated.

Verne Ray collected ethnological texts in a southern (Columbia River) dialect of Sahaptin (Umatilla) during the course of his survey of the Plateau in the 1930s. But the main thread of work on the language has now been taken up by Bruce Rigsby, who began his interest in the area by a critical summary of linguistic relations in the southern part of the Plateau for his doctoral dissertation at the University of Oregon (1965b). Beginning in 1963, he undertook fieldwork under the auspices of the Oregon Survey at Portland State University. He concentrated on the Umatilla dialect of the Columbia River cluster and Yakima of the northwestern group, but collected materials in all the extant dialects, including tape recordings in all but one. He presented a discussion of Sahaptin internal relations (1965c) and went into the complexities of vocalic developments in the language, contributing to an understanding of the Proto-Sahaptian picture (1965a; cf. also Rigsby and Silverstein 1969 and discussion under Nez Perce below).

The eastern Sahaptian language, Nez Perce (spoken in an unknown number of dialects which separate basically into Upper and Lower clusters), was studied during the middle period by Archie Phinney, who published a collection of texts (1934). Later Harry V. Velten (1943) discussed the verbal system. More recently the California Survey has joined with the Idaho State Historical Society in sponsoring extensive field research on the language by Haruo Aoki, who presented a grammar as his doctoral dissertation in 1965 at the University of California, Berkeley; he has now published a revised version (Aoki 1970b). He has also written on reduplicative elements (1963b), vowel harmony (1966b, 1968), glottalized consonants (1970a), and referential kin term usage (1970d), and has offered specific proof of the Sahaptian relationship — a binary comparison of Nez Perce and Sahaptin with reconstructions (1962). Later he continued his reconstruction of Proto-Sahaptian in the area of kinship terms (1966a) and vowel harmony (1966b). He also presented evidence for the earlier proposed further relationship of Sahaptian with Klamath (1963a) and summarized broadly the status of the Penutian hypothesis with regard to languages of

---

the southern division (cf. Rigsby and Silverstein 1969:45 fn. 1, and Swadesh 1956:21). The larger grouping of Plateau Penutian remains unproven (cf. Rigsby 1969b).

Oregon (1965). Recently he has begun the exploration of diffusion of features in the North Plateau area (1970c).

Aoki's discussion of problems of vocalic harmony led to more general considerations of this typological matter (Aoki 1968). It is a useful example of the way careful data-oriented work in a particular area often leads outside and affords advances in general understanding of important topics. Karl Zimmer (1967:168–9) mentions the Nez Perce case in connection with a general discussion of vowel harmony, and Paul Kiparsky (1968) brings it up in a still wider context; Chomsky and Halle (1968: 377–8) also summarize Aoki's (1966b) view. William Jacobsen (1968a) returns to the matter in detail, considering different hypotheses about the Proto-Sahaptian system and the transition to the two daughter languages, and bringing up some areal similarities. Rigsby and Silverstein (1969) review the matter, showing evidence for earlier vocalic harmony in Sahaptin dialects and concluding that historically vowel harmony can be viewed as a phonetic process arising in the dialects by parallel restructuring from a Proto-Sahaptian system of morphological ablaut. Indications are that the topic is far from exhausted, as evidenced by Arnold Zwicky's (1970) discussion of the alternative analyses from the point of view of synchronic handling of the 'deep structure'.

Back from the coast at the southern border of our area, where the Northwest meets California, lies the territory of Klamath and Modoc. These are probably best considered slightly divergent dialects of the same language (cf. Voegelin 1946). Following the account of deAngulo and Freeland (1931) we now have M. A. R. Barker's extensive grammar (1964), dictionary (1963a) and texts (1963b), based on field research conducted under the California Survey in the summers of 1955–57. The grammar and dictionary are interesting in a more general way: they are prepared in response to an early version of Sydney Lamb's model for language description. At the same time they reflect the time-honored responsibilities of careful detailed documentation of the language and extensive exemplification of generalizations. William Shipley (1966) presented evidence for the relationship of Klamath to the California Penutian kernel.

Leslie Spier studied the culture of the Klamath and Modoc; he presented his ethnography of the Klamath (1930), and shortly thereafter conducted an ethnographic field school which focused attention on the other group. He later turned over the class notes to one of the participants, Verne Ray, who checked the data in the field and utilized it in combination with his own material in the composition of a Modoc ethnography (Ray 1963). We should also note here research extending over several years on the same group of Indians by Theodore Stern of the University of Oregon; cf. his treatments of their folklore (Stern 1953, 1956) and of culture change on the reservation (1965). There is an annotated bibliography of anthropological works on the Klamath Basin by B.K. Swartz, Jr. (1967).

The remaining portion of the putative Plateau Penutian stock, Waiilatpuan, is seriously problematic. Cáyuse, originally spoken in northeastern Oregon and adjacent Washington, was going out of use well before the middle of the nineteenth century, replaced in the mouths of the younger generation of Cayuse Indians largely by a lower Nez Perce dialect, and became extinct in the 1930s. Molale (also spelled Molele, Molala, Molalla) survived until about 1965, but its background is shrouded in mystery. The pre-contact distribution seems to have been in two discontinuous areas: one was in the uplands extending north from the upper Rogue River in southern Oregon along the western slopes of the Cascades to a point roughly east of Eugene; the second was in the Mt. Hood area. In Aoki's (1965) review of the evidence for the Penutian hypothesis with respect to languages of Oregon, he noted that Cayuse and Molale show enough inspectional resemblances so that their relationship to other Penutian languages seems likely. Further there are some positive indications that Waiilatpuan may yet prove a meaningful grouping — at least areal, if not genetic. And there are also indications that Plateau Penutian may yet turn out to be more than a geographical assemblage. Rigsby (1966) reviewed the putative Waiilatpuan relationship, citing salient examples from his collection of all the available Cayuse material compared with Molale, and concluded that the relationship could not be demonstrated on this basis. More recently (1969b) he published a monograph describing in detail the materials available on the two languages and appending a lexicon of all the Cayuse forms with comparative data from Molale wherever pertinent. The Cayuse material is skimpy and frustratingly contradictory, including only fragmentary incidental notes by recent workers (Jacobs, Ray, Stern). Molale is extensively represented, but the materials are unpublished and are very likely difficult to structure and describe; the principal sources are Frachtenberg's fieldnotes from 1910–11 and Jacobs' from 1928 and following years. Michael Silverstein (p.c.) and William Elmendorf (p.c.) have independently expressed similar conclusions: they suspect that Molale may well prove to be Penutian, but caution that loan material must be carefully culled from the inspectional resemblances. If this is difficult at present for Molale, it is virtually impossible for Cayuse because of the nature of the material, so that this part of the question may remain unanswerable. Dell Hymes (p.c.), on the basis of some etymologies he has studied, thinks it likely that Molale will find its place in the Penutian spectrum.

The languages which Sapir (1929a) grouped as 'Oregon Penutian' include several of Powell's families (listed here in forms that are familiar today, rather than Powell's original spellings) — Takelma, Kalapuyan, Coosan, and Yakonan (from which Siuslaw was later extracted as separate).

Takelma, originally spoken in southwestern Oregon, along the middle to upper portion of the Rogue River and some of its tributaries, is now apparently extinct, but fortunately we have Edward Sapir's texts (with vocabulary) (1909a) and grammar (1922), based on fieldwork in the summer of 1906. We also owe to him practically all we have of Takelma ethnography (for this and other references, see 1922:7–8).

The Kalapuyan languages are now also apparently extinct. Material was collected by Gatschet in 1877 and by Frachtenberg around 1914. Frachtenberg (1918) identified several dialects, which he organized in three groups — northern, central and southern; the paper is mainly, however, notes on his comparison of Kalapuyan with Takelma and Chinookan, and it is there also that he indicated he was assembling proof of relationship between Klamath, Sahaptian and Waiilatpuan, and had already collected material establishing a probable common origin for the Coosan, Siuslaw, Yakonan and perhaps Kalapuyan languages. He went on to suggest that these latter languages, and perhaps Chinookan, might eventually be proven to relate to California Penutian.

But it is to Melville Jacobs that we owe the preservation of rich material on the Kalapuyan languages, accomplished in a number of brief sessions between 1928 and 1936. Besides recording texts on his own, he also rechecked as far as it was possible those collected by Gatschet and Frachtenberg, publishing the entire collection (M. Jacobs 1945). He makes clear that some eight tribal groups originally inhabited the Willamette drainage from the southern part of the present Portland metropolitan area southward, the dialects falling into three mutually unintelligible groups: Yamhill and Tualatin (Atfalati, Tfalati) in the north; a large central cluster typified by Santiam and Mary's River or Kalapuya proper; and Yonkalla, spoken in a few bands extending south from Eugene. J.P. Rumberger, Jr. (1949) utilized the text collection to make some interesting ethnolinguistic observations — an example of the constructive use of positive qualities as opposed to the all too common destructive approach of some reviewers; cf. the programmatic but unproductive criticisms of the same collection by Preston (1946) and Lisker's (1946) phonemic comments. Jacobs also has extensive lexical and grammatical files on the languages which will provide the essential basis for future descriptive and comparative work.

Morris Swadesh collected some material in the summer of 1953 in the course of a survey of Penutian languages. He also extracted forms from Jacobs' files and other unpublished earlier materials preserved in the library of the University of Washington and presented results of a glottochronological comparison of the various Kalapuyan forms of speech with Takelma (Swadesh 1965). He also offered as confirmation of the Takelma-Kalapuya relationship some of the more obvious of the lexical evidence in preliminary form, advancing the name Takelman for the stock. William Shipley has carried on, utilizing Swadesh's Kalapuyan materials, and has presented some reconstructions of Proto-Kalapuyan (1970) and Proto-Takelman (1969). M. Jacobs (1970) calls attention again to the more extensive resources on Kalapuyan languages and questions Shipley's conclusion that the glottalized stops, apparently unpatterned in correspondences in the comparison, were the result of diffusion.

On the central Oregon coast were several groups of Indians with distinct forms of speech. It is again to Frachtenberg and Jacobs that we owe most of our records of them. The southernmost of these were the Coos Indians, who lived in aboriginal times around Coos Bay, and along the Coos and Coquille Rivers near the ocean. It now seems clear that the dialects, which have been called collectively Coos (Coosan, Kusan), belonged to two separate languages — Miluk, spoken in the south along the lower Coquille and South Slough of Coos Bay; and Hanis, further north along Coos

Bay and on the Coos River. In 1903 H. H. St. Clair collected texts in Hanis and made limited notes on Miluk. Frachtenberg recorded further material in 1909 and published his and St. Clair's texts (Frachtenberg 1913), some notes on Coosan dialects (1914: 141-9), and a grammatical sketch (1922a). The language represented is primarily Hanis; Frachtenberg elicited only limited material on Miluk. Jacobs turned to these disappearing languages in the period 1932-34, collecting further texts in Hanis but, on the discovery of an excellent informant for Miluk, devoted more effort to recording that language, since Hanis boasted still a number of speakers and had already been represented in Frachtenberg's studies. Jacobs also made some phonograph recordings of narratives and songs by one informant. His texts appeared in two collections — one of narrative and ethnologic pieces (1939) and one of myths (1940).

Joe E. Pierce (1965c) studied the published Coosan materials with a kind of inspectional and sampling technique and raised the question whether the two speech forms are related at all — he suggested rather that they may be two unrelated languages which have come to have resemblances as the result of convergence because of an intimate social relationship in comparatively recent times. Otherwise we are forced to conclude either that there was a great period of separation or an exceedingly rapid rate of morphological replacement. The following year he pursued the question further, and extended it to include other languages in the putative Oregon Penutian grouping — Alsea, Siuslaw and Takelma (1966). Here he applied a technique of analysis of grammatical morphemes in order to determine the basic forms for each and compared these among the several languages. He compared pronominal elements and numerals up to ten, and found that they suggest different sorts of alignments. Again the conclusions are rather negative, but the paper is intended to raise certain fundamental questions about the way comparative work is conducted with Amerindian languages — Pierce suggests that Americanists need to develop special techniques to handle the kind of data available to them.

The phrasing of Pierce's question — whether Hanis and Miluk are dialects of the same language or unrelated languages — raises a point which has wider significance in the area as a whole. In recent times there has been some attempt to find a meaningful dividing point between a dialect boundary (marking differences in speech without impairing mutual intelligibility) and a language boundary (where intelligibility becomes difficult or nonexistent). Earlier writers, however — e.g. Boas, Frachtenberg, Haeberlin — spoke of dialects more loosely, with a different sort of emphasis: they were identifying diverse forms of speech which were obviously related, belonging to the same family. Understanding of this difference in usage should clear up a number of puzzling passages.

Aoki (1965) has pointed out that there may, in fact, have been a period of separation between Hanis and Miluk, mentioning that only Miluk among the Oregon Penutian languages has a numeral system identical in type to that of Oregon Athapaskan (cf. V. Hymes 1955). Hanis, on the other hand, has an entirely different modified quinary system, indicating an association with Alsea and Siuslaw, which have quinary systems.

Aoki suggests, then, that the unquestionable contiguity of Miluk to and its possible displacement by an adjacent Oregon Athapaskan language just south of it may account for the lexical and grammatical discrepancy between Miluk and Hanis. Silverstein (p.c.) has observed that 'there are syntactic determinants for the apparent divergence which makes the two languages look less similar than they are. In Miluk, a number of tense, pronominal, and aspectual particles are sentence enclitics so that they occupy, in a string, the second position in a clause, while in Hanis these rules have been eliminated — these elements are rather bound as prefixes to verbs and nouns. Thus one's notion of what are the constituents of a morphological word can potentially eliminate from the comparison the appropriate series of elements. At the same time it is clear that the verbal inflectional endings are the same, and these are bound forms.'

Recently Mrs. Jane Sokolow, a graduate student at the University of California, Berkeley, has undertaken field research with a speaker of Hanis Coos, which may afford still further helpful materials on this family.

Immediately to the north of the Coos, living along the lower courses of the Umpqua and Siuslaw Rivers, were people speaking two closely related dialects. J. Owen Dorsey collected brief samples of both Lower Umpqua and Siuslaw dialects in 1884, and shortly concluded that this language (which we shall call Siuslaw) was related to Alsea and Yaquina to the north in a stock called Yakonan; this classification was adopted by Powell. In the spring of 1911 Frachtenberg took up the study, working primarily with the Lower Umpqua dialect. The informants were far from ideal and were working under various difficulties, so that Frachtenberg felt dissatisfied with the results. He presented his texts shortly (1914) and his grammatical sketch (1922b) appeared in the second volume of the *Handbook of American Indian Languages*. In the introduction to the latter he allows that Siuslaw may be ultimately related to Alsea and Yaquina, and, in fact, perhaps also to Coosan and Kalapuyan, but he finds indefensible the Yakonan stock as envisaged.

It was not until 1953 that any further material was collected on Siuslaw — this by Swadesh in the course of his Penutian vocabulary survey (cf. Swadesh 1954); at that time he obtained songs and a test vocabulary in Lower Umpqua and a test vocabulary in Siuslaw dialect proper. Material was recorded on tape and is in the Archives of the Languages of the World (Indiana University). The following year Dell Hymes was able to follow up this work briefly, checking in particular a number of troublesome (and important) points of phonology. His study (1966a) is essential for further interpretation of the earlier materials and also affords a good view of the kinds of problems Frachtenberg had as a pioneer field phonetician and analyst. Hymes (p.c.) reports that the Harrington material at the Smithsonian includes a rechecking of Frachtenberg's Siuslaw lexicon, which may provide a still better control of the phonology.

North of Siuslaw were two languages which apparently were quite closely related, perhaps only mildly different dialects of the same language — Alsea and Yaquina (Yakwina, Yakona). Unfortunately the latter, investigated briefly along with Alsea in 1884 by Dorsey, disappeared before modern records could be made. Livingston Farrand took down some Alsea texts in 1900, and Frachtenberg investigated the language in 1910 and 1913, integrating Farrand's texts with his own and publishing the whole collection (Frachtenberg 1917a, 1920b). To the book of texts (1920b) are appended vocabularies and a list of formative elements which cover all the stems in the materials available to him. Pierce (1965a) is currently engaged in a computerized analysis of this text collection.

Jacobs again followed Frachtenberg, recording extensive lexical and grammatical material on Alsea in 1935, so that we have a more modern file upon which to draw for information on the language. Harrington is also reported (Rigsby, p.c.) to have rechecked much of Frachtenberg's Alsea material. Jacobs corroborated the Frachtenberg claim about a genetic relationship of Alsea, Siuslaw and Coos. It now seems clear that this relationship was not close, and Powell's Yakonan family, including the two northern sets of dialects, is probably to be dissolved, as Frachtenberg insisted. Aoki (1965) examined lexical sets which showed that there is a slightly better case for grouping Alsea and Siuslaw against Coos than for grouping Siuslaw and Coos against Alsea, little evidence for an Alsea-Coos grouping; the best course would seem to be setting up three coordinate groups, leaving open the question of what proto-language (within Penutian) they go back to. In any case, there seems at present little justification for Sapir's Oregon Penutian grouping (Takelma-Kalapuya plus Alsea, Siuslaw and Coosan).

From Willapa Bay and the tidewater area at the mouth of the Columbia River back along its valley to the Cascades, and a dozen miles up the Willamette Valley, was the territory of the Chinookan family of languages. Essentially two languages are involved. Dialects of Coastal Chinook were spoken by the Clatsop on the south bank of the Columbia at its mouth and by the Chinook proper on the north bank and on nearby Shoalwater and Willapa Bay. The rest of the Chinookan territory was riverine, occupied by speakers of Upper or River Chinook dialects — Kathlamet on the lower course of the Columbia, Clackamas around the present Portland area, and other intergrading dialects up to Wasco and Wishram about four miles east of The Dalles.

Coastal Chinook speech died out by the 1930s; our best source of information on it is Boas' materials. His major publications are *Chinook texts* (1894) and a grammar (1911a) in the first volume of the *Handbook of American Indian Languages*. The grammar contains also some notes on differences in certain dialects of Upper Chinook. John R. Swanton utilized Boas' fieldnotes for his analysis of the Chinook verbal system, which he presented as his doctoral dissertation at Harvard and made available in print (Swanton 1900). Dell Hymes (p.c.) is preparing for publication Boas' sizable collection of Clatsop (Coastal Chinook) vocabulary.

Boas also collected texts in Kathlamet (1901) — his Coastal Chinook informant also knew that dialect — and a few samples in other dialects. But it is primarily to Edward Sapir that we owe our first modern treatment of Upper Chinook: in fact, Wishram was the language on which Sapir did his first fieldwork, in the summer of

1905. Following Boas's example, he trained Pete McGuff to write texts in phonetic transcription, thus enriching what he could himself collect in the field. He presented these texts, editing also the few others in Upper Chinook collected by Boas and those in English by Jeremiah Curtin for the same volume (Sapir 1909b). His grammatical notes on special features of Upper Chinook appear inserted at pertinent places in Boas' (1911a) grammar. He returned to the language, of course, in connection with his comparative work; note also the famous piece of internal reconstruction (Sapir 1926). The constant association of language and culture that characterizes so much of Sapir's work is apparent in the Spier and Sapir (1930) Wishram ethnography.

In the course of his work in Oregon, Melville Jacobs also added much material to the attestation of Upper Chinook. He collected extensive texts in Clackamas during the summer of 1929 and the following winter, concentrating on getting down all the possible myths (almost fifty) which the informant could give. He published these native versions with translations in two volumes (1958, 1959b). At the same time he obtained miscellaneous ethnographic notes and a collection of songs. He also studied the content and style of this material in depth, presenting his method and theory of analysis of an oral art form together with translations and detailed analyses of eight myths (1959c). The balance of the summaries and analyses appeared as a separate book (1960a). He also had drawn on the material in his discussion of titles (1957) and his thoughts on methodology for comprehension of an oral literature (1960b).

Upper Chinook (Wishram speech) also furnished the basis for a doctoral dissertation at Yale University by Walter Dyk (1933). And it was Upper Chinook to which Dell Hymes first turned, conducting field research on Wasco-Wishram in 1951 and presenting a grammar of Kathlamet based on the Boas (1901) texts as his doctoral dissertation at Indiana University (D. Hymes 1955). This served as a springboard for broader work in Penutian comparison (e.g. 1957, 1964a, 1964b). He also studied linguistic features peculiar to Chinookan myths (1958), myth and tale titles of the Coastal Chinook (1959b), and drew on the Chinookan experience in discussing the typology of cognitive styles in languages (1961). There is also a joint paper (Dyk and Hymes 1956) on stress accent in Wishram. In his discussion of linguistic relativity Hymes (1966b) presented a lengthy ethnographic reconstruction of patterns of the use of language among the Wishram, important as an attempt to portray in detail a sociolinguistic aspect of an Amerindian community. Hymes (1969) studied 'fourth person' and phonesthematic aspects of personal pronoun systems in three languages, including Wishram Chinook; he presents a componential analysis of the Wishram pronouns and a discussion of correlations between these semantic features and phonological shapes.

Over a number of years David French of Reed College, and his wife Kay of the University of Oregon Medical School, have collected linguistic material on Wishram-Wasco, as well as on Sahaptin, in connection with their continuing ethnographic work. David French (1958) has presented a system of cultural matrices of Chinookan non-casual language. Linguistic field research has lately been undertaken by Michael

Silverstein, who is engaged in reworking Chinookan grammar. He has studied 'thematization' and underlying ergativity in the Chinook verb (1969a).

Coastal Chinook furnished the base for the lingua franca, Chinook jargon, which spread rapidly over the greater Northwest. Beside the many popular and semipopular writings on this jargon, we are indebted again to Melville Jacobs for a more serious treatment. He has made available a structural summary (1932b) and a short set of texts (1936b). Rena V. Grant (1945) discussed it more from the point of view of history and interest, with some details on usage; she also provides references to other works.

It has now grown much more difficult to obtain extensive materials on Chinook jargon, but a number of fieldworkers in the present period record what is possible as they pursue work on other languages. There is a need to document as well as possible the varying forms which the jargon took in the different Northwest districts. Terrence Kaufman of the University of California, Berkeley, is currently assembling a dictionary of the jargon, based on all the materials available to him, in which he is attempting to identify the sources of the forms. He presented a preliminary report at the Salish Conference in 1968 and has circulated a draft of materials for the dictionary, soliciting help from the many people working in the area. Silverstein (1970) has studied the jargon from the point of view of language contact and multi-level generative systems.

The northernmost family of the putative Penutian stock occupies the northern portion of the British Columbia coast in the drainage of the Nass and Skeena Rivers. It was again Boas who collected early material, including texts from the Coast Tsimshian (1895b, 1912) and from Indians at the mouth of the Nass (1902). Boas had trained a native speaker, Henry W. Tate, to write his language (which Boas termed Tsimshian proper), and on the basis of extensive texts thus afforded, Boas prepared a study of the mythology, which contains the texts in translation but also considerable linguistic material (1916). He also prepared a grammar treating Nass and Coast Tsimshian together (1911d). Sapir (1920) published on Nass terms of relationship. Considerably later Viola Garfield (1939) presented a description of Tsimshian kinship and clanship.

More recently (beginning in the summer of 1966) Bruce Rigsby has taken on the responsibility for serious linguistic and ethnographic field research on the Tsimshian peoples of the Nass and Skeena River valleys. He has also done some surveying on the Coast Tsimshian, and directed the research of a doctoral candidate on that language: John Dunn (1970) presented a systematic phonology as his dissertation at the University of New Mexico. Rigsby (1967) presented a preliminary report on his studies, including a comparative vocabulary of Coast Tsimshian, Nass and Gitksan of nearly three-hundred forms, together with notes toward a Nass-Gitksan systematic phonology. He has also written a note on Gitksan speech-play (1970) and has begun the study of Tsimshian linguistic history (forthcoming).

Researchers in Oregon have progressively opted for the affinity of various languages to the Penutian stock. Much of this has been mentioned in connection with individual languages or smaller groupings and need not be repeated here. The more general aspects of Northwest Penutian are largely associated with the names of Sapir and Swadesh in the past, more recently with Hymes, Shipley, Aoki, Rigsby and Silverstein.

It was Sapir (1921) who discussed first in intuitive terms, but with reference to material he planned to present later, the grand extension of the Penutian kernel in California to include those languages of western Oregon which Frachtenberg had suggested as possibly affiliated, and beyond to include the northerly Tsimshian. By 1929 he had included as well the Plateau languages.

Swadesh pursued this direction in particular after he had begun his glottochronological work, undertaking himself a field vocabulary survey (described in Swadesh 1954). He had also seen into print the Coos-Takelma-Penutian comparisons of Sapir (Sapir and Swadesh 1953). He subsequently summarized the problems of long-range comparison (1956), published some comparative Penutian glosses which Sapir had entered in the margins of various books and reprints (1964a), and offered his comparisons between Takelma and Kalapuyan (1965).

Dell Hymes (1957) discussed the comparison of some Penutian grammatical elements, focusing on reconstruction of one, and reviewed the Penutian hypothesis in general. Later (1964a) he showed that some northern languages often were revealing in cases where comparisons within the California kernel were vague or ambiguous; this article introduces a methodological device and provides comparisons with all the Northwest Penutian languages, as well as those of Mexico. He has studied two etymologies in considerable detail (1964b), and has assembled grammatical and lexical evidence for the relationship of Tsimshian and Chinookan (1965b).

In addition to his comparative work with individual languages in the Northwest, Shipley (1965) has surveyed the scope and limits of Penutian in general. Aoki (1965) explored the Penutian hypothesis in particular with regard to the languages of Oregon. Rigsby (1965b) reassessed linguistic relations in the southern part of the Plateau, out of which grew his concern with the Waiilatpuan problem (described above).

Probably the most extensive review of Penutian is being accomplished by Silverstein, who is preparing his doctoral dissertation at Harvard on this subject. He has been particularly concerned with the problems of subgrouping — the place of Coosan and Siuslaw (1965a), and California Penutian as a model for subgrouping arguments (1967) — and with bringing in grammatical considerations, rather than depending so much on lexical comparisons (1965b); in this vein he has also studied Tsimshian and Penutian possessives (1969b). He has outlined a general statement of approach to the Penutian problem (1966).

## 2. WAKASHAN

In contradistinction to Penutian, Wakashan is a clearly defined family of long standing, consisting of two sub-families, Kwakiutlan and Nootkan.

Of the three Kwakiutlan languages, it is the southernmost, Kwakiutl proper, which is overwhelmingly represented in the literature. It is this language on which Boas concentrated so much energy, although he also recorded quite extensive Bella Bella texts (1928, 1932a) and surveyed the family broadly. He was again able to train a native speaker, George Hunt, so that he could write texts and furnish various kinds of ethnographic information; thus the ethnology (1921) 'based on data collected by George Hunt', and the joint publication of texts (Boas and Hunt 1902–05, 1906). Beside these and other collections of texts (1910, 1935–43), there are a number of descriptive pieces on the language — the early grammar (1911c), the revised list of suffixes (Boas and Goddard 1924a), and the posthumous revised grammar (Boas 1947), notes on vocabulary (1931), and some observations of differences in the speech of younger speakers (1932b). Note the reviews of the later grammar by Hall (1950), Newman (1950) and Swadesh (1948b).

It is perhaps at least partly because of Boas' lifelong preoccupation with the Kwakiutlan family that so little work has been undertaken by others. However, in more recent times Geoffrey O'Grady has identified the group as one which the Victoria Survey should take responsibility for, and has himself collected survey material in several dialects. David Grubb (1969) presented as his M.A. thesis at the University of Victoria a phonological analysis of Kwakiutl as now spoken at Alert Bay. While working with Tsimshian Bruce Rigsby took advantage of an opportunity to take a vocabulary list in Heiltsuk in the summer of 1967. Emmon Bach of the University of Texas has recently undertaken study of Kwakiutlan languages. During the summer of 1969 he worked with some Alert Bay informants who were available in Victoria. In the summer of 1970, he and his wife, Reed Bates, spent several weeks in Kitimat and began intensive study of the northern language, Haisla, developing a practical orthography. They discussed several aspects of the work in a paper for the fifth Salish Conference (Bach and Bates 1971).

Of the Nootkan family, it is Nootka proper, the northern language stretching along the west coast of Vancouver Island, and the immediate neighbor of Kwakiutl, that is best represented in the literature. It is the language on which Sapir focused attention, and he had the good fortune to be able to train a very able native speaker, Alex Thomas, to write his language, thus greatly expanding the extensive texts which he himself had collected. This resulted in our best account of Nootka — doubtless one of the best accounts of any language in the area — the texts with grammatical summary and lexicon prepared jointly by Sapir and Swadesh (1939). Sapir's ethnologic interests are again apparent in his work on the language — cf. his early presentation of texts (1919, 1924–25), his discussion of the wolf ritual (1911) and of abnormal types of speech (1915a) and baby words (1929b). And much of the writing is diachronically oriented (see below). There remains in Ottawa a large quantity of Sapir's unpublished material on Nootka.

Sapir also trained two students in Nootkan who were to go on to important work. Morris Swadesh and Mary Haas, then just married, spent the summer of 1931 collecting Nootka and Nitinat material; they presented a Nitinat text the next year (Haas and Swadesh 1932). Swadesh continued working with Sapir's and Thomas' Nootka texts, treating the morphology, which afforded the basis of his doctoral dissertation at Yale University (Swadesh 1933). He later published a reduced version as an article on word structure (1939) and incorporated his analytical knowledge into the grammatical appendix (for which he is primarily responsible) to the text collection (Sapir and Swadesh 1939). He presented a further view of the language with interesting areal typological overtones (1948a), and utilized difficulties of translating many Nootkan entities, especially bound forms, in his theoretical treatment of translation problems (1960). He also prepared for publication a volume comprising native accounts of Nootka ethnography (Sapir and Swadesh 1955), and discussed linguistic and ethnological aspects of Nootka songs (Roberts and Swadesh 1955:310–27).

In recent years Alex Thomas has offered further contributions to the Nootka material. Eugene Arima of the National Museum of Canada transferred to tape the songs and other material which Sapir had recorded on wax cylinders, and in 1967 he arranged for Thomas to transcribe the songs and translate the words. George Grekoff, at the University of Victoria in 1967–68, also contacted Thomas and made tape recordings of spontaneous reminiscences about the work with Sapir.

Haas has maintained an interest in Nootkan studies, returning recently to untangle the fused pronominal suffixes in Nootka and Nitinat (1969a) and to suggest the existence of stem extending suffixes with elusive meanings as important formatives in the two languages (1969b).

Beginning fieldwork in 1966 as an undergraduate on the Victoria Survey, O'Grady's student Terry J. Klokeid has collected considerable material on Nitinat, as well as adjunct recordings of some Nootka and Kwakiutl dialects. He presented a study of lexical innovations in Nitinat (1968) at the Third Salish Conference. A University of Washington student, Ernest Clifton, is also working on Nitinat and has collected some material on Nootka.

The third language of the family, Makah, spoken at the tip of Washington's Olympic Peninsula, has until recently had little attention. Aside from some early vocabularies and a brief note by Frances Densmore (1927), it was until recently unrepresented in published sources, although we should note the assimilation study of Elizabeth Colson (1953). The speech of the Makah was originally thought of as simply another dialect of Southern Nootka or Nitinat (Sapir 1911:15, 1924–25:76), but later Sapir (e.g. 1938:254) listed three separate languages in the family. Only fuller evidence on both Nitinat and Makah will make it possible to determine the subgrouping; for recent discussions see Haas (1969a:115, 120) and Jacobsen (1969b:141).

Since Makah was so poorly known, Jacobsen assumed responsibility for this language as part of his labors under the Northwest Survey, beginning field research in the summer of 1962. During the academic year 1963–64 he directed students working with a Makah informant in the year-long field methods course at the University of Washington. Now at the University of Nevada, he has continued with the collection of an extensive body of data on the language, meanwhile making important contributions to comparative Wakashan. He presented a paper on Makah neologisms (1967), studied the effects of glottalized resonants which have been lost in Makah (1968b), and offered convincing proof that the development of pharyngeal elements in Nootkan is recent (1969b). He has also discussed the special distribution of labialized velars in Nootkan (1969a).

The genetic relationship of Kwakiutlan and Nootkan languages was signalled by Boas (1890), and he also recognized the morphophonemic processes of 'hardening' and 'softening' which have such important historical meaning. But it was Sapir who developed Wakashan comparison into a fine art. He early (1911) cited the principal correspondences between the two languages and discussed their structural similarities and differences. He also drew on Wakashan examples among the many others in his important general methodological paper on "Time perspective in aboriginal American culture" (1916). Later (1938) he recapitulated a great deal of Wakashan linguistic history in his discussion of glottalized continuants in these and some other languages.

There have also been attempts to deal with further relationships: Swadesh (1949, 1953a, 1953b) supporting the Mosan hypothesis, and, in the same connection, calling attention to lexical comparisons which Boas had noted (Swadesh 1953c) and editing for publication Andrade's (1953b) notes on relations between Nootka and Quileute; Haas (1960, 1965) more cautiously exploring possible connections of Wakashan and other Northwest languages with Algonkian. More recently Swadesh (1962, 1964b) would align Wakashan rather with Eskimo-Aleut and some Asiatic connections. Elmendorf (p.c.) reports Swadesh told him in 1964 that he had (unpublished) evidence for connecting Wakashan with Eskimo-Aleut 'at least as good' as that which he had published (Swadesh 1962) relating Eskimo-Aleut with Chukchi-Koryak-Kamchadal.

Klokeid (1969) suggested that the notion of rule sharing to demonstrate genetic relationship (eliminating universal rules characteristic of all languages and typological rules shared without concomitant sharing of phonological realization) can be applied to the Mosan problem. His sample application yielded negative results for Wakashan-Salishan comparison. M. Dale Kinkade (1969a) approached the Mosan question from the point of view of a typological feature the languages share — the lexical suffixes. With an interim reconstruction of Salishan suffixes he compared corresponding semantic entities in individual Wakashan and Chemakuan languages. Results were again negative.

### 3. CHEMAKUAN

Chemakuan, consisting of just the two languages Chemakum and Quileute, is a close-knit family of limited time depth.

Unfortunately Chemakum (Chimakum) was scarcely spoken any longer by the time there were scholars curious about it. Aside from some brief early collections (cf. Adler 1961:199) our knowledge of the language is limited to the forms which Boas was able to elicit in 1890 and which Andrade subsequently checked with the same informant in the summer of 1928 (M. Jacobs 1954:48, fn. 9). Boas (1892) published some brief notes on the basis of his experience. June Collins' (1949) suggestion of a somewhat wider area for the language is misleading; Wayne Suttles (1957:166-7, note esp. fn. 29) controverts her argument and the information on which it was based.

Quileute (Quillayute), however, is still spoken by a small number of people, primarily at LaPush on Washington's west coast. Frachtenberg collected materials on the language, including texts, in 1915–16; he discussed abnormal types of speech which he had observed (1920a) and also presented an article on the eschatology of the Quileute (1920c). About 1926 Boas encouraged Manuel J. Andrade to make a serious study of Frachtenberg's unpublished notes; this he did, deriving from them such a careful analysis that Boas was convinced he should be sent to check his hypotheses about the workings of the grammar in the field and to collect further texts. This resulted eventually in publication of all the texts, edited by Andrade (1931) (note M. Jacobs' [1936a] review), and in a grammar (Andrade 1933) (reviewed by Swadesh 1934). There is also Frances Densmore's (1939) study of Quileute music, along with that of Nootka.

Andrade had made notes on similarities between Quileute and Chemakum, and confirmed that the two languages are related. Swadesh edited the manuscript for posthumous publication (Andrade 1953a), as well as Andrade's (1953b) similar notes on possible comparisons with Nootka. Swadesh (1955) himself restudied the Chemakum-Quileute comparison and utilized all these materials in his Mosan studies (cf. Swadesh 1953a, 1953b).

More recently Eric P. Hamp of the University of Chicago has shown interest in Quileute, taking advantage of residence in Seattle during the 1962 summer Linguistic Institute of the Linguistic Society of America to elicit material from a speaker then hospitalized there, and making subsequent short field trips to elicit further material. He hopes to tape record the published texts under the best possible recording circumstances. He has read papers on Quileute at various meetings: reanalyzing Andrade's prosodics (Hamp 1963b), commenting on the implications of Quileute place name study (1963a), and comparing Quileute lexical suffixes with those of Salishan (1968).

James E. Hoard, who became interested in Northwest languages while a graduate student at the University of Washington, has also undertaken study of Quileute, making field trips to LaPush under the auspices of the Northwest Survey while he was on the staff at the University of Kansas. Hoard continues his Northwest interests in his new position at the University of Victoria. He has read a paper on Quileute prosody (1968).

The importance of the language, isolated as it is, looms greater when we consider the difficulties of long-range comparisons. From this point of view I have encouraged James V. Powell, a graduate student at the University of Hawaii, to assume a major responsibility for Quileute. He began field research under the Northwest Survey in the summer of 1969 with the goal of adding as much as possible to the lexicon and preparing the way for internal reconstruction and further comparative work. He has presented a study of deictic elements in the language (1971), and has collaborated with Quileute speakers in studies on place names (Powell, Penn and others, in press) and on ethnobotany (Powell and Woodruff 1971).

### 4. SALISHAN

In the very early period much attention was paid to this family, so that Pilling (1893b:v) was able to say: 'Of the numerous stocks of Indians fringing the coast of northwest America few have been as thoroughly studied or their languages so well recorded as the Salishan.' Ironic it is, then, that this family moved into the second half of the twentieth century as one of the most neglected of all American families. This is partly because so much of the material collected remained in a raw state, largely lacking the careful processing and reworking that makes for progress in understanding. On the other hand, it is important to recognize that so many of the best trained and capable linguists either skirted this family entirely or at best did only limited work with a few languages or attempted overall syntheses. For example, Sapir (1915b) presented some limited material on noun reduplication in Comox, collected from his Nootka informant, whose mother was Comox, and collected vocabulary in Thompson and Lillooet, numeral forms in Okanagan (see Freeman and Smith 1966 for references to these and other manuscript materials in the Boas Collection), but never became seriously involved with any of the languages. Even Boas, despite his great interest in Salishan and a good deal of field experience with several languages (most of it early), published relatively little to advance our knowledge of their structure, although he secured a mass of grammatical material on Chehalis in 1927. A good deal of linguistic material from various Salishan groups appeared in connection with ethnographic reports in the early period, including some in which characterization of the languages themselves was the primary focus. Space does not permit their citation here, but they can be located quickly by referring to Murdock (1960) listings under the Northwest Coast and Plateau headings; note especially numerous items by Boas, C. Hill-Tout, and James A. Teit. We are only now beginning to have depth studies of Salishan languages, and much remains to be done.

The two branches of Interior Salishan are perhaps less close to one another than Swadesh's (1950) glottochronological figures suggest. The South Interior (also referred to as eastern or southeastern) includes four separate languages. Coeur d'Alene occupied a considerable area in what is now northern Idaho and adjacent Washington. Extending in pre-contact times from east of the Rockies in present-day Montana westward, around to the north of Coeur d'Alene and to its west flank, was a crescent of intergrading dialects: Sematuse, Flathead, Kalispel, Spokane; Spokane is a divergent set of dialects at the western end. The language is perhaps best called Kalispel, although the Indians themselves have a term suggesting the linguistic unity from which the English word Salish (Selish; Latinized as Lingua Selica) is derived. Further west and extending northward into a large area of British Columbia is Okanagan-Colville, spoken in mildly differentiated dialects by such groups as the Okanagan (Okanogan), Sanpoil, Nespelem, Lakes and Colville Indians. Finally, to the southwest of Okanagan-Colville lies Columbian, spoken by a number of groups such as the Moses, Wenatchee and Chelan.

Of the Interior Salishan languages Coeur d'Alene was the first to receive detailed attention in recent times. Beginning under Boas' guidance, Gladys Reichard collected material on the language over a period of several years, in fact bringing a young informant, Lawrence Nicodemus, to New York for his education while she continued work with him. She taught him to write his language in broad phonetic transcription and apparently learned a good deal about its phonetic and phonological complexities from his reactions to this experience. She produced a grammar of the language (Reichard 1938), provided a stem list, at least the beginning of a dictionary (1939), and attempted to see through some of the difficult vocalic alternations in the language (1945). She also commented on imagery in the vocabulary (1943) and presented an analysis of mythological texts (1947).

In 1963 Clarence Sloat expressed an interest in undertaking some work with the language and, sponsored by the Northwest Survey, spent one summer and part of another in the field. Relocating Mr. Nicodemus, he checked through a great many of Reichard's forms and worked out phonological redundancy rules for the language based on her material and his own, which he presented for his doctoral dissertation at the University of Washington (Sloat 1966) — one of the first full applications of this approach to phonology. Since then he has made available a systematized report of his reevaluation of her phonological writing (1968), in order to help a reader to rephonologize her writing of Coeur d'Alene forms, and has considered the phonetic and phonological similarity of /r/ and pharyngeal elements in the language (1971). He has also studied the vexing problem of vocalic alternations in the language, arriving at a system of vowel harmony (1972).

James E. Hoard utilized materials from Coeur d'Alene to exemplify the theoretical points concerning the foundations of phonological theory which comprised his doctoral dissertation at the University of Washington (1967). More recently James Goss of the Department of Anthropology at Washington State University has sent students Robert Johnson, Paul Nesbitt, and John Schultz to work on the language.

Hans Vogt of the University of Oslo, who was for a time a student of Sapir at Yale, also pioneered with Interior Salishan, coming to the field in the summer of 1937 and collecting an impressive amount of material on Kalispel, with adjunct vocabulary on Spokane and Colville, in a short span of eleven weeks. He presented his findings as a grammar with an accompanying short collection of texts and dictionary (Vogt 1940a) and a brief monograph listing the adjunct vocabulary with comparative notes (1940b) (note the review by Ethel Aginsky 1947). Although modest in scope and pretensions,

Vogt's is still the most penetrating account of this language, and one of the few overall grammatical treatments of any of the family. This is the same language that is represented in the nineteenth-century dictionary of Giorda (1877-79) and the Latin-based grammatical statement of Mengarini (1861). Besides early vocabulary lists, there are several more recent collections of forms — e.g. in connection with ethnography (Turney-High 1937), ethnozoology (Weisel 1952), and music (Merriam 1967). We may note also the recent publication of a collection of hymns and prayers (Quáy-Lem u En-chów-men 1958).

Allan H. Smith of Washington State University has studied the Kalispel for several years and has in addition to anthropological notes a considerable collection of unpublished folktales and other texts. He has also been influential more broadly in encouraging Salishan studies by others.

Merriam (1967:148 ff.) raises the problem of the obviously Plains connected music of the Flathead in the face of the clear linguistic affiliation with the Salishan group, and calls for more investigation of the musicology of other Salishan groups of the Plateau area. This appeal is surely correct, but his suggestion that the Flathead may have been originally a Plains people that took on Salishan speech seems less likely than the possibility he also envisions that at least the more easterly of the Plateau groups will turn out to have a music of Plains origin like that of the Flathead. From the linguistic point of view it still appears that the ancestors of the present Flathead, Kalispel, and Spokane must have been in a more compact area in the not too distant past. Both the divergence of Spokane and the homogeneity of the Kalispel dialects to the north and east suggest that in comparatively recent times speakers of the ancestor of Spokane and Kalispel spread out around and to the east of Coeur d'Alene, which — itself quite divergent from the rest of the family — was probably the easternmost of the languages. The important general Salishan pattern should be reaffirmed here: the diversity and complexity of the Coast Salishan languages over short distances suggests that the original spread began from near the coast, while the relative homogeneity of the Interior languages over great distances (even with the difference of topography) suggests more recent split and spread. (On positions of the northern Plateau languages and their implications, see Elmendorf 1965a; on Salishan distribution more broadly and the question of original homeland, see Suttles and Elmendorf 1963.) In order to gather important material to study this whole question, as well as to supplement and extend the earlier work, Barry Carlson, a graduate student at the University of Hawaii working under the Northwest Survey, began research on Spokane in the summer of 1969.

The other area which Vogt began to explore — the Okanagan-Colville language — is likewise an important subject for investigation. Verne F. Ray has provided us with some items of vocabulary in connection with his ethnographic study of the Sanpoil and Nespelem (1933a); he has also made available folkloristic material in English translation (1933b). Other ethnographic coverage is afforded by Cline and others (1938). A student at the University of Washington, Gary Arrowsmith, collected material for the Survey in the summer of 1965. The project was taken over in the summer of 1968 by Anthony Mattina, who is now preparing a grammar of the language (eastern Colville dialect) for his doctoral dissertation at the University of Hawaii. Independently, Donald Watkins of Red Deer Junior College is making a study of the Lakes dialect in British Columbia, and preparing a doctoral dissertation at the University of Alberta. The language as spoken at the north end of Okanagan Lake has been the subject for summer study of Professor Alex Wainman of the University of British Columbia since 1964. Material on Canadian Okanagan is also being collected by Randy Bouchard, supported in part by the Victoria Survey and the provincial government. His work is primarily oriented toward Indian literacy and educative and research programs; he has developed a practical orthography and trained native speakers in its use.

Columbian has been scantily covered until recently. William Elmendorf, in addition to his major work on the coast (see below), collected some material, and some forms are cited in earlier ethnographic discussions. But our main source for the language is M. Dale Kinkade, who began field research in 1963. He has discussed deictic elements in the language (1967a) and is assembling lexical, grammatical and textual coverage. He trained a speaker, Mrs. Mary Wippel, to write the language, and she is now assisting with the ongoing analysis and with the collection of texts. Recognizing a wealth of pharyngeal continuants in Columbian, Kinkade (1967d) went on to consider the distribution of uvular-pharyngeal continuants in the rest of Interior Salishan, drawing also on recent reports of other researchers on Lillooet, Thompson and Shuswap, as well as his own survey notes on the languages further east. He has also straightened out for us the question of the placement of Methow speech (1967b), which previously had been assigned to Columbian, but which emerges as a divergent dialect of the Okanagan-Colville complex, and he has sponsored work on that dialect by two University of Kansas students under the Northwest Survey: Michael O'Brien (1967) presented a basic sketch of the phonology; Philip Young has undertaken work related to native cognitive systems.

Ranging across the east Interior ground is some auxiliary work carried on by a devotee of Salishan studies who has had only limited time for field research. While a graduate student at the University of Washington, John Krueger (now of Indiana University) took opportunities to make short field trips beginning in the summer of 1957 and collected lexical material on Flathead to supplement earlier contributions, making them available as topical lists (Krueger 1960, 1961a, 1961b). Another brief trip in 1963 made possible the collection of a basic vocabulary in Columbian (1967a). He has also supplied an English index of the words in his own lists as well as Vogt's (1940a) dictionary and vocabulary list (1940b) (Krueger 1967b).

After a considerable lapse of time since the early work on the northern Interior Salishan area (e.g. by Boas, Teit and Hill-Tout), studies are now under way on all of the languages.

Shuswap covers the largest area, with villages along the upper drainage of the

Thompson and Fraser Rivers and by the lakes of the region, to the north of Canadian Okanagan. James A. Gibson of the University of Nebraska undertook research under the Northwest Survey on easterly dialects (primarily at Chase, but also at Salmon Arm and Kamloops) while a graduate student at the University of Washington and the University of Hawaii, 1966-69, and is preparing a grammar as his doctoral dissertation at the latter institution. Aert H. Kuipers collected some material in an earlier period and is now expanding it on northern dialects. He has presented a preliminary study of the transitive verb system (1970a).

My wife and I are collecting material on Thompson for the Northwest Survey, working primarily with the southernmost dialect around Spuzzum, with adjunct material on Lytton and Merritt speech. The language seems to be quite homogeneous, but rather more different from Shuswap than one would suppose from Swadesh's (1950) glottochronological computations.

The Northwest Survey has also supported collection of material on Lillooet, primarily as spoken on the Fountain Reserve, by Lillian Nakai Campbell, when she was a student at the University of Washington, 1964-66. More recently a graduate student at the University of British Columbia, Leo Swoboda, has undertaken research on the language, working in the Mount Currie area, under the direction of R.J. Gregg.

Randy Bouchard, while focusing attention on Okanagan, has also collected considerable material on Lillooet and adjunct vocabulary in Thompson and Shuswap.

The northernmost Salishan language, the isolated Bella Coola, was one with which Boas spent considerable time during his early work. He published several pieces on the language and culture; here we may mention his treatment of the mythology (1898) (cf. Adler 1961:203 for other references). He encouraged Stanley Newman to undertake the study of the language — another well known linguist who had baptism in field research in the Northwest. Newman (1947) presented his analysis of Bella Coola phonology, startling readers with this account of long stretches of speech without significant vocalisms, even whole utterances without voiced sounds. It thus appears to have carried to a logical extreme the tendency observable in most Salishan speech to eliminate vowels and foster long strings of consonants. More recently, Newman has returned to further analysis of his field materials, making available information on the overall aspect of the grammar (1969a) and presenting the basic paradigms with pronominal and demonstrative elements (1969b). The two-volume ethnography of McIlwraith (1948) should be noted; it contains a lexicon of vocabulary collected incidental to the ethnographic work. Ross Saunders of Simon Fraser University, and Philip Davis (formerly at Simon Fraser, now at Rice University) have been studying the language during the last few years.

Tillamook, also isolated from the rest of the family, represents its southern extreme. Boas recorded vocabulary and some myth texts early in his own career, and later directed work by May (Mandelbaum) Edel, who spent the summer of 1931 collecting data on the language. Even then there were very few persons left who remembered it.

Boas subsequently requested Melville Jacobs to take additional material from any available informants in order to supplement Mrs. Edel's notes. Her grammar (Edel 1939) represents an insightful analysis of these quite different and often conflicting materials, but leaves many unsolved problems. She recognized two major dialects — Siletz in the south, on which Frachtenberg (1917b) had also collected a brief vocabulary, but which was apparently extinct by the time she reached the field; and Tillamook proper in the north.

Leon Metcalf made a tape recording of vocabulary and a brief text in 1951 from an informant in Portland. Although the language had been presumed extinct for several years, 1965 brought discovery of an informant, and my wife and I immediately undertook work with her. We described the circumstances and reviewed the background of Tillamook studies in a paper giving new details on the phonology (L.C. and M.T. Thompson 1966). Since the informant's memory of the language is rusty, the only workable procedure turned out to be stimulation by reading earlier phonetic notations of phrases and sentences, and for this purpose Jacobs' notes proved extremely productive. Much has been straightened out about the phonology which was earlier obscure; there remains an arduous philological task to advance understanding of the grammatical structure. Eric Hamp (1967) reconsidered our phonological analysis in terms of distinctive features and suggested that the complete lack of labials is compensated for by the rounded velar elements.

While Jacobs was collecting linguistic material on Tillamook in 1933, Mrs. Jacobs took advantage of the opportunity to take down in English a sizable body of Tillamook tales, which her husband subsequently edited for publication (E. Jacobs 1959). In addition to their folkloristic value, these texts in English may be important in another way. They seemed to Mrs. Jacobs to be sentence-by-sentence translations from the informant's memory of the Tillamook originals. It is expected they will provide the essential key to the unanalyzed native texts which Mrs. Edel has left in manuscript, taken from the same informant. (After Mrs. Edel's death, these manuscripts were donated to the University of Washington Archives by her husband, Professor Abraham Edel of City University of New York.)

The Olympic branch of Coast Salishan is distinguished from the rest of the coastal continuum by lexical and grammatical peculiarities. It divides into two subgroups — one centered away from the ocean, the other in the lower drainage of the rivers and coastal plains of southwestern Washington. Inland languages are Upper Chehalis, with a mildly divergent Satsop dialect, now apparently extinct; and closely related (Lower) Cowlitz. The coastal subgroup includes Quinault in the north, and Lower Chehalis in several dialects to the south.

From the earlier period we have for published linguistic material only an analyzed text in Upper Chehalis by Boas (1934a) and scattered vocabulary in Olson's (1936) ethnography of the Quinault. It was thus logically on Upper Chehalis that Kinkade began his work in the area in 1960, and he presented as his doctoral dissertation an analysis of the phonology and morphology, shortly made available in print (Kinkade

1963-64). It combines conciseness of formulation with readability and generous exemplification, and suggests a deep penetration of the structure. He has also presented studies of vowel alternation in the language (1966) and of prefix-suffix constructions (1967c).

Kinkade surveyed the area of southwestern Washington carefully, covering both the Salishan and non-Salishan languages. This survey had one unexpected outcome: he located a few speakers of Lower Cowlitz (usually called simply Cowlitz[6]), a form of speech very closely related to Upper Chehalis, but not quite mutually intelligible with it. Thelma Adamson had worked intensively on Cowlitz in 1927, but her notes have vanished. However, we have her folktales in English (1934), drawn primarily from the inland Olympic peoples. Kinkade elicited extensive lexical and grammatical material in Cowlitz and supervised a graduate student, Erik J. Beukenkamp, in further collecting. Kinkade plans an integrated dictionary of Cowlitz and Upper Chehalis.

The same survey turned up some dozen speakers of Lower Chehalis, of which only four or five were willing to serve as informants; unfortunately this did not include any of those who remember the language best. However, considerable vocabulary could be collected, and Kinkade undertook the task, directing also a graduate assistant, Charles Snow, in work on the language. Snow (1969) presented a generative phonology as his M.A. thesis at the University of Kansas.

While a graduate student at the University of Washington, James Gibson undertook fieldwork on the Quinault (Quinaietl) language under Northwest Survey sponsorship. It proved difficult to secure informant time and cooperation, but he managed to collect enough material for a phonological analysis, which he presented as his M.A. thesis (Gibson 1964). Kinkade's efforts to establish further work on the language have been even more discouraging. Quinaults in key political positions have apparently felt embittered by earlier associations with the academic community so that team work between Indians remembering the old culture and academics specially trained in the investigation of such matters has become impossible. Nevertheless, the Quinault Tribal Council recently decided it wished to have the language taught to youngsters in the local school, and arrangements were made in 1965 for Mrs. Ruth Modrow, who had had brief training with the Summer Institute of Linguistics at the University of Oklahoma, to undertake the work. She has developed a writing system for the language and produced an introductory booklet of topically organized words and sentences for limited circulation among those involved locally in the project (Modrow 1967).

Eric Hamp (1966) has provided a footnote to Kinkade's study of Upper Chehalis, re-analyzing some modal particles which seem to have wider Salishan relatives and Quileute parallels — this, then, adds some more detail to speculations about Chemakuan-Salishan relationships (perhaps genetic, perhaps diffusional).

---

[6] We should recall at this point that Lower Cowlitz is a Salishan language, while further up the Cowlitz River Valley were speakers of a northern Sahaptin dialect (Taitnapam), and they are often referred to as Upper Cowlitz.

The southernmost of the long central Coast Salishan continuum is Twana (also known by the name Skokomish), originally spoken in the area around Hood Canal. William W. Elmendorf made a detailed ethnological study during the course of which he collected a good deal of linguistic material (cf. especially Elmendorf 1946, 1951, 1960) and some samples of the oral literature in translation (1961a). He kindly made available unpublished material from his linguistic files in order to help advance the work of the Northwest Survey.

Gaberell Drachman, now of Ohio State University, as a University of Chicago graduate student undertook fieldwork on Twana under the sponsorship of the Northwest Survey, spending three summers, 1963–65, collecting extensive material from the few speakers remaining; the language is all but extinct. He presented a generative phonology for his doctoral dissertation at Chicago (now published, Drachman 1969), in which he studies in great detail the motivations for underlying forms. He has presented papers at several national meetings using Twana materials. We may hope for further grammatical studies of rich detail from him.

The group of dialects which surrounded Puget Sound in aboriginal times divides naturally into two sets, approaching distinct languages. The southern set, extending roughly from present-day Seattle to the head of Puget Sound and on up into the Nisqually River drainage, was spoken by such groups as the Duwamish, Suquamish,[7] Snoqualmie, Puyallup and Nisqually. It was this language which was investigated summarily by Ransom (1945: Duwamish speech), and subsequently by two students of the Department of Anthropology at the University of Washington. The first of these researches resulted in an M.A. and the manuscript was later edited for publication by Melville Jacobs — this is Colin E. Tweddell's (1950) preliminary phonological and morphological study of Snoqualmie-Duwamish, based on material collected in 1946–47. The second resulted in a doctoral degree; it affords a deeper analysis of material collected during three summers, 1953–55, from Suquamish, Snoqualmie and Duwamish informants; it has now been revised and published (Warren A. Snyder 1968a). Snyder has also made available his collection of texts and native place names, together with a dictionary (1968b).

During the summers of 1964 and 1965 the Northwest Survey sponsored adjunct work on the language by Mrs. Angeliki Malikouti Drachman. While her husband was studying Twana, she collected lexical and grammatical materials in the southernmost dialects for which informants could be located. More recently the Northwest Survey has supported additional collections in several localities by Thomas Hess and James Hoard. In an earlier period Arthur C. Ballard (1927, 1929, 1935, 1950) presented material on this language in connection with his ethnologically oriented studies. Marian W. Smith's (1940) ethnography of the Puyallup-Nisqually represents this group, as does Haeberlin and Gunther's (1930) description. There is also an early dictionary of Nisqually (Gibbs 1877). The northern dialects, extending north from

[7] Chief Seattle's own group; note that this is not to be confused with Squamish, an independent language further north.

around Everett, Washington to the Skagit Valley, were spoken by such groups as the Snohomish and Skagit. They are not well represented in the earlier research, so that it seemed important to focus attention on them early in the Northwest Survey. It was possible to bring a Skagit speaker to the University of Washington to serve as informant for the course in linguistic field methods twice a week over the period of several years (1960–66). In this year-long course successive classes of graduate students in linguistics worked with the informant eliciting material and analyzing it under the guidance of George Grekoff and myself. In this way a number of students became interested in languages of the area, and one, Thomas M. Hess, took on a serious commitment for work on this language itself, focusing mainly on Snohomish speech: it furnished the basis of his subsequently published M.A. thesis, a study of reduplicative patterns in the language (1966), and his doctoral dissertation, a full outline of the grammar (1967a). The grammar presents a rigorous and thorough analysis of the language with clarity and precision. Hess also has a draft of a dictionary at an advanced stage. He has contributed separate papers on analytical problems (1967b, 1968, 1969, 1971). He has a considerable collection of texts in Snohomish and Skagit, and is making efforts to obtain native versions of texts collected in English by an anthropologist, Sally Snyder, who presented an analysis of the mythology of the Skagit as her Ph.D. dissertation in anthropology at the University of Washington (1964). This analysis and the collection of texts on which it was based are now to be printed by the American Folklore Society. Another anthropology student at the University of Washington is pursuing studies on semantic domains in the area: Mrs. Pamela Amoss (1969), who began her Northwest interests with work on Nooksack (see below), has recently offered an exploration of the domain of food in Skagit.

Hess has also assisted a Skagit speaker, Mrs. Violet Hilbert of Seattle, in studying the analysis and writing of her language; Mrs. Hilbert has taken considerable interest in recording on tape as many texts in the language as older people in the community are able and willing to give, and her entree may prove especially important for the preserving of much valuable material for posterity.

A close-knit dialect complex belongs to the area of the coast along the international boundary between the United States and Canada. Since it centers around the narrow arms of the sea separating land masses in that area, it is logically termed Straits Salish (Suttles 1954:29–31). One language, Clallam (Klallam), is somewhat removed from the rest of the dialect continuum; it occupied most of the north shore of the Olympic Peninsula. The rest of the dialects extend from Lummi and some nearly identical dialects around the area of Bellingham and Blaine, Washington, and aboriginally on the islands of the San Juan group, across to Songish (Lkungen) around modern Victoria, on Vancouver Island, and on northward to include Saanich on the peninsula that bears its name and westward on the island to Sooke.

Coverage of the Straits peoples in the literature has been uneven. Erna Gunther of the University of Washington studied the Clallam, providing an ethnography (1927) and a collection of folktales in English (1925). A convenient ethnographic summary and references to studies of the other groups are provided in Wayne Suttles' (1954) monograph on culture change among the Lummi. Suttles collected extensive linguistic material on several Straits dialects in the course of his ethnologic research; he has generously made unpublished materials available to the Northwest Survey. Melville Jacobs has also turned over to the Survey his notes on Lummi and Saanich.

I began a study of Lummi in 1958, working in spare time and as informants were available. In 1964 I located a speaker of Clallam, which seemed in even more urgent need of recording. My wife and I prepared a preliminary grammatical sketch of the latter language in 1968 (L.C. and M.T. Thompson 1971), and drew on experience with both languages in calling attention to the use of metathesis as a grammatical device (1969b). More recently I have begun the study of Lummi umlaut (Thompson 1972). Both these languages are so close to extinction that they present special difficulties for collection of useful data.

In 1969 Elizabeth Bowman of Western Washington State College at Bellingham became interested in Lummi and has taken over responsibility for the language, training also a student, William Seaburg, to assist with the work. My wife and I were pleased to offer what help was possible from our experience, and to arrange for Northwest Survey support. Seaburg has now undertaken graduate studies at the University of Hawaii, where he continues his interest in Lummi. Two graduate students at the University of Washington also collected some material on Lummi for the Northwest Survey: Mrs. Elaine Phelps in 1964 and Duane Mylerberg in 1965.

The Vancouver Island dialects of Straits Salish are also close to extinction, but some skillful informants have been available. Barbara S. Efrat of the University of Victoria undertook the recording of Sooke beginning in 1962, extending the work to Saanich in 1967, and collecting also some material on Songish. She has treated Sooke structure with some notes on differences in Saanich in her University of Pennsylvania doctoral dissertation (Efrat 1969), and has in preparation a paper on the problems of unstressed vowels which is likely to have important overtones for other languages of the area, having as they do very similar problems. She has also trained assistants in the work, interesting in particular Michael Pidgeon, who took up fieldwork with Saanich under the Victoria Survey, preparing his M.A. thesis on lexical suffixes (1970). Thomas Hess has also used a Saanich informant in classroom training in field methods at the University of Victoria.

A separate enterprise was undertaken by another graduate student at the University of Victoria, resulting in an M.A. thesis which is a dictionary of Songish, reflecting strong ethnographic interests (Marjorie Mitchell 1968). Since 1969 a graduate student from the University of Kansas, Miss Yolanda Raffo, has been sponsored by the Northwest Survey for further work in Songish. She has presented a study of the Songish aspectual system (1971).

In his ethnographic work, Wayne Suttles has also collected extensive material over the last two decades on neighboring Halkomelem (Swadesh's Nanaimo-Fraser), focusing attention particularly on Musqueam, spoken at Vancouver, British Columbia, at the mouth of the Fraser River, but also covering other dialects. He collaborated with Elmendorf in a discussion of some basic patterns and changes in the Musqueam, Cowichan and Chilliwack dialects (Elmendorf and Suttles 1960), which also makes available basic vocabulary in all three. Suttles has assembled material for a grammar of the language and in 1968–69 offered a seminar at Portland State University in which students studied the language structure and analyzed texts in a wider context of the culture, thus learning a great deal about the significance of linguistic studies in ethnological research. One of these students, Dawn Stuart, has continued her study of the language; another, Bonnie McCay, went to the field in the summer of 1969 to collect further texts in Musqueam with some assistance from the Northwest Survey in addition to support from Portland State University.

Ethnographic data on the Salish peoples around the Georgia Strait (speakers of Central Coast Salishan languages on the Canadian side) are provided by Homer Barnett (1955); the book is also useful for its bibliography of earlier work on the Central Coast Salish more broadly, including the groups in Washington. For the upriver Halkomelem peoples there is Wilson Duff's (1952) ethnography.

While a student at the University of Washington, Jimmy G. Harris studied the upriver Halkomelem dialect Chilliwack, collecting a good body of texts on tape. He presented a phonological analysis for his M.A. thesis (Harris 1966). In the summer of 1970, Brent Galloway took up the study of this dialect under sponsorship of the California Survey.

Vancouver Island Halkomelem is more a going concern than the Fraser Valley dialects; Cowichan, in particular, has a fairly large number of speakers. In connection with his direction of the Victoria Survey, Geoffrey N. O'Grady has worked with Cowichan and has used informants of that dialect in the classroom to train students in linguistic fieldwork. One student, Miss Tiiu Kava, went on to collect further data and presented a phonological analysis for her M.A. thesis (1969); she is now continuing grammatical research on the language along with doctoral studies at the University of Hawaii, under a grant from the Canada Council. Further north on the Island, the Nanaimo dialect has had little investigation in recent times; Suttles (p.c.) indicates that it shows some interesting special features. In summer 1970 the Victoria Survey sponsored a student, Adrian Leslie, to begin work on this dialect.

Lying between the upriver Skagit of Puget Sound Salish and the Fraser Valley portion of the Halkomelem complex, facing the Lummi to the west, was a small enclave of independent speech — Nooksack (Nuksack, Nootsack). The custom of importing wives from other communities contributed to early obsolescence of the distinctive language originally spoken there; by the time of White contact this process seems to have been at an advanced stage, so that now only a few persons recall the time when a number of old men in the villages spoke among themselves 'the old language', while for general purposes other languages were in use — primarily Chilliwack Halkomelem and Skagit. It is now difficult to determine very surely what the original Nooksack language was like, because the materials that have been collected all bear the marks of borrowing from the neighboring languages, especially from Halkomelem.

Although several persons have collected data on the language, it is not represented as well as we should like. Thelma Adamson's mass of notes from 1932 is lost. Paul Fetzer, an anthropology student of Jacobs at the University of Washington who around 1950 undertook ethnologic and linguistic research on the community, sadly succumbed to early cancer, leaving lexical and grammatical notes and some texts. In 1954–55 another Jacobs student, Pamela (Thorsen) Amoss, picked up the thread of the work, producing a phonological study as an M.A. thesis in anthropology (1961). Recently she has returned to anthropological inquiry involving the Nooksack people, and the Northwest Survey has supported her in tape recording texts from the one of her earlier informants who is still living. She has also made available her earlier fieldnotes to the Survey.

In the course of the work of the Survey it was discovered that a speaker of Skagit could recall a surprising amount of the Nooksack speech of her grandfather, and I was able to check a good deal of lexical and grammatical material with her during the winter of 1967. Barbara Efrat has now assumed this responsiblity, collecting further material from the same informant and proceeding on an analysis of taped texts collected by Mrs. Amoss. The two plan further field research and collaboration.

To the north of Halkomelem on the shore of the mainland was Squamish territory, centering around Howe Sound and the valley of the Squamish River. Modern work on this language was undertaken by Aert H. Kuipers while he was on the staff of the University of British Columbia in 1951–54; it was supplemented by further collection during the autumn of 1956 and the summer of 1967. He has presented a handbook in classic style, grammar with accompanying texts and dictionary, appearing in two parts (Kuipers 1967b, 1969). (The first part has been reviewed by Kinkade 1969b and Thompson 1969.) Rich in examples, it accounts for all the material collected, affording the most extensive and informative description of any Salishan language so far. At the University of Leiden for several years now, he has continued his deep interest in Salishan, making annual trips for summer field research, recently concentrating on Shuswap (see above). He has also embarked on comparative studies (see below).

North of Squamish on the British Columbia coast the next language is Seshelt (Sechelt, Sisiatl), on which George Grekoff undertook research beginning in 1965 under the Northwest Survey. More recently Ronald Beaumont of the University of British Columbia has begun work on the language. There are few speakers left with extensive knowledge, and indications are (Grekoff p.c. and my own field survey notes) that it should prove to be of considerable comparative interest.

In 1964 I conducted a search along the east shore of Vancouver Island between Nanaimo and Comox in hopes that someone remembering at least some words of Pentlatch (Puntlatch, Puntledge) might be found, but it proved fruitless. This language seems to have been spoken by a small community and to have become extinct quite early, replaced either by English or by neighboring Comox or Nanaimo. We must then rely on materials collected in the earlier period for our knowledge of this language: Boas has left us considerable material in manuscript.

The northernmost of the central coast complex, however, has a large number of speakers, even some monolinguals in the more remote communities. Comox territory lies on both sides of the passage between Vancouver Island and the mainland to the east, extending northward from around the town of Comox on the Island and Powell River on the mainland opposite. A considerable northwestern area of original Comox territory seems to have been taken over by southward-moving Kwakiutl speakers in the post-contact period (Taylor and Duff 1956). There are a number of subgroups — Comox proper, which probably centered originally around Campbell River; Sliammon in the area around Powell River; Klahuse along the shores of Toba Inlet; and Homalco at the head of Bute Inlet. Dialect cleavages remain to be worked out.

Boas studied Comox, in the very early period, and left a large amount of manuscript material. Sapir (1915b) took advantage of the fact that one of his Nootka informants had learned Comox from his mother, a native of that group, and recorded a sizable collection of noun-like forms with plurals or collectives, which he published together with phonological indications. The dialect of this speaker was clearly Island Comox, which has lost certain distinctions still preserved in Sliammon (reaffirmed by my field survey notes in 1964). The Northwest Survey sponsored Thomas Hess in beginning work on Sliammon in 1965, and he has continued as time has permitted, considering his prior obligations to Puget Sound work where the dialects are faced with nearly immediate extinction. He also interested a student, John Davis, who worked at Sliammon under the Victoria Survey in the summer of 1969, and presented as his M.A. thesis a generative phonology with some comparative-oriented wordlists (1970). He has summarized some results of his work in a paper for the Salish Conference (1971). In summer 1970 the Northwest Survey sponsored University of Kansas student Herbert Harris for further study of Island Comox.

Comparative work in Salishan was an early interest. Most of the basic sound correspondences and indirect suggestions about sensible reconstructions were presented by Boas and Haeberlin (1927), including a fair number of etymologies. Swadesh (1950) utilized this monograph, together with the comparative list of basic vocabulary items covering some 35 dialects which Boas had assembled and prepared for the printer (ms. S2 in the Boas Collection), but which never appeared, for the first application of his glottochronological subgrouping and dating, presenting his technique along with percentages and implied time depths for 30 Salishan languages and dialects. He also drew on other manuscripts in the same collection and on some other (primarily more recent) published material to round out comparison — on Kalispel by Vogt (1940a), on Coeur d'Alene by Reichard (1938), on Upper Chehalis by Boas (1934a), on Southern Puget Sound Salish by Tweddell (1950), and on Comox by Sapir (1915b) — and presented a summary of the apparent phonological developments in the family in a kind of wave theory approach (Swadesh 1952). In these articles we may be impressed with the order he was able to create from a diversity of difficult and inconsistent source material. At the same time we must recognize that the brilliant outline tends to obscure the tentative nature of the results. For actual evidence we find only nine etymologies (1952:239–40) and a few scattered forms, with reference to the Boas-Haeberlin (1927) sketch of sound shifts and to Swadesh's own unpublished comparisons ('Salish cognates', slip file in the Boas Collection, ca. 1950). The latter shows extensive work, but reveals that correspondences were apparently not systematically worked out and reconstructions were primarily impressionistic. Certain preconceptions prevented Swadesh's deeper understanding of the comparative picture: for example, he assumed that no Salishan language had significant vowels of the schwa type, and he generally edited them out (although, interestingly enough, not systematically in the unpublished notes). This made it impossible for him to observe the far-reaching effects of accentual shifts in the development of the languages.

If Swadesh's treatment conveys the notion that basic work on comparative Salishan has been done and that it remains to work out some problems of detail, a different impression emerges from a reading of Gladys Reichard's (1958–60) detailed comparison of the five languages on which there was available fairly extensive grammatical material (Coeur d'Alene, Kalispel, Tillamook, Upper Chehalis, and Southern Puget Sound — cf. references cited above). She explores as much as possible of the grammatical correspondences among the languages, departing, as one might expect, from her own experience with Coeur d'Alene, and utilizing Boas' unpublished fieldnotes on Upper Chehalis. While she does advance our notions of comparative Salishan grammar, what we are most struck by in reading her monograph is the great need for better and more extensive descriptive materials on the languages she discusses, to say nothing of those languages for which no adequate materials were available at the time of her study.

Swadesh's work, of course, set off a good deal of discussion over the validity of his approach to subgrouping through percentages of cognates in 'basic vocabulary', and to corresponding computation of time elapsed since divergence of languages. (For more general treatment of these matters, see Hymes 1960a, 1960b, and the comments and further references in Hymes 1964c: 567–73, 622.)

Swadesh (1953a, 1953b, 1953c) himself went on to study further connections of Salishan within the framework of the Mosan stock (as described above). He also explored the implications of the percentages that could be worked out for putative cognates between Salishan, Wakashan and Chemakuan languages, in connection with his amassing of evidence for the grouping; it is interesting to note that implicit in this discussion (cf. esp. Swadesh 1953a:41–4) is an early suggestion of the limitations and uncertainties of this method when applied to great time depths. In his later far-flung comparisons, in which Mosan is completely dissolved (e.g. 1962, 1964b) these reservations seem to have evaporated.

Gordon Fairbanks (1955) raised important questions about the identification of cognates on the basis of which lexicostatistic percentages are computed, and particularly about the possibility that in long-range comparisons like the Mosan one, where little detail work has been done, the chance of mistaking accidentally resemblant forms for genetic cognates is far greater than Swadesh presumed. A.L. Kroeber (1955:97–101) called attention to the great time depth computed within Salishan, although the languages had been recognized right away as related, in contrast to stocks like Hokan and Penutian, where the time depths computed were similar or less but where the genetic relationships were far less obvious — relationships which Boas, in fact, had regarded as unprovable. He concluded that the continued contiguity of the Salishan languages must account for their retention of similarities that render the relationship transparent, pointing out that peripheral languages regularly seemed to change more rapidly than those in more central positions in a family area. It now appears, as more material becomes available on the various Salishan languages and more details of their comparison are worked out, that the time depth as computed was in any case too great. (See also Suttles and Elmendorf 1963:42–5.)

Elmendorf (1951) raised the possibility that the kind of tabooing pattern which he had observed in Twana was more widespread and that it could have caused a greater than usual pace of replacement of items in the basic vocabulary of Coast Salishan languages. He went on to explore lexicostatistic problems in Central Coast Salishan (Elmendorf 1962a) and developed the notion of lexical relation models as a possible check on lexicostatistic inferences (1962b). At the same time he was considering the implications for subgrouping of Salishan languages on the basis of the numerical systems, with special concern for the placement ot Tillamook (1962c). Recently James Hoard (1971) studied comparatively another limited system — the pronominal elements — in all the languages for which he could obtain pertinent material.

Suttles and Elmendorf (1963) reviewed the comparative picture for the family in broader perspective, offering some reinterpretations and pointing out needs for further research. Elmendorf (1970) has also returned to consider further the matter of word taboo and change rates.

Some suggestions have been made about Salishan solely on the basis of Swadesh's (1950) original figures, without familiarity with the languages themselves. Thus Diebold (1960) used the Salishan case to apply Isidore Dyen's (1956) language distribution and migration theory, concluding (unsurprisingly) that the original Salishan homeland lay within the area now occupied by the Central Coast and Interior languages. Dyen (1962) himself also turned to the Salishan family (again using the same figures) to exemplify his principles for recognizing inflated percentages between adjacent languages and arriving at subgroups of a language family on the basis of significant breaks (discussed more fully in Dyen 1963). He then reworked the Salishan figures and arrived at a different subgrouping.

Elmendorf (1965a) employed a concept of chain relation of languages which is different from the approaches of Swadesh and Dyen and explored the distribution and subgrouping of Interior Salishan languages. Later Elmendorf (1969) challenged Dyen's manipulation of Swadesh's figures especially with respect to abolishing the

Olympic subgroup as an entity, and, on the other hand, setting up two sub-members of Swadesh's Olympic branch (Quinault-Lower Chehalis vs. Satsop-Upper Chehalis-Cowlitz) as separate branches coordinate with the other coast branches. The telling point is that those percentages of Olympic languages which prompted Dyen to see no significant break between the branch and other coast languages are precisely those for languages geographically adjacent and with which there has been well-known extensive contact. In other words, if Dyen's method is valid it should point out the inflation of percentages between adjacent languages of Olympic and neighboring groups so as to prevent the conclusion to which he came. The matter is interesting and instructive for those wishing to pursue this kind of lexicostatistic classificatory work in Dyen's footsteps: Dyen's reanalysis of the figures is not accompanied by any familiarity with the Salishan material, whereas one can recognize that Swadesh had developed a great deal of sensitivity about Salishan languages, and Elmendorf has done considerable first-hand work with them. Elmendorf's conclusion, using precisely the same figures again, squares with the convictions of several others who have worked intimately with the languages. Joseph G. Jorgensen (1969) took Swadesh's basic glottochronological study and its updating for the linguistic foundation of a statistical comparison of Salishan language and cultural relations. Problems with these various statistical approaches raise questions and doubts about lexicostatistical methods more generally.

Further comparison and reconstruction in Salishan has necessarily awaited the availability of fuller and more accurate materials on the various languages. Kuipers (1967a) suggested some proto-language consonantal alternations as bases for divergence in cases where apparent cognates in various languages fail to present the expected correspondences. More recently (1970b) he has offered the beginnings of a Salishan etymological dictionary, presenting cognates in Squamish and Shuswap from his own materials, together with related forms in several other languages as they were available. The paper also makes proposals about vowel alternations. His Squamish handbook (1967b, 1969) offers etymological notes with forms in the dictionary. And at the end of the first part (1967b:401–5) he has appended detailed comments on similarities between Squamish (as representative of Salishan) and Indo-European, making the significant point that in some other cases of the sort such similarities have been used to bolster claims of long-range relationship.

Wayne Suttles and I independently observed a set of correspondences in Salishan which had been overlooked earlier. Boas and Haeberlin (1927:134–5) observed that Straits Salish languages frequently show a velar nasal corresponding to $m$ in other languages, and treat it as a change $m$ to $\eta$; Swadesh (1952:241) considers this apparent shift a Straits innovation which had not yet spread to any surrounding languages. However, there are parallel correspondences in the stops: Straits palatals $č$ $č̓$ corresponding to $p$ $\dot{p}$ in other languages. At the same time, Straits languages have a large number of forms with labials. Suttles (1965b) hypothesized that all forms with labials must be borrowings in Straits, and outlined an impressive categorization covering a large number of these forms. I (Thompson 1965) suggested that where velars and palatals correspond to labials we may well be dealing with original labiovelars, which remained without change only where they were protected in original consonantal clusters or contiguous to rounded vowels; at the same time many of the labiovelars attested in the modern languages today may have arisen as rounding of original plain velars in assimilation to former adjacent rounded vowels, many of which have since been lost — a pattern common in the area. This leaves open the question of origin of the forms with labials in Straits languages — obviously many of them are borrowings from nearby languages, and as material on all the languages becomes more available it will be possible to trace the routes of borrowing; but it appears that there are a good many forms with labials which are not to be explained in this way.

M. Dale Kinkade and I have also worked on the general Salishan comparative picture. It seems clear that further progress will result best from careful detailed comparative studies of the various subgroups of the family before the reconstruction of Proto-Salishan grammar and lexicon is attempted. To this end Kinkade and Sloat (1972) have begun with some southern Interior languages (primarily Coeur d'Alene, Kalispel and Columbian) and have focused attention on the difficult problems of the vowel correspondences. Beginning in December 1969, under the Northwest Survey, Barbara Efrat has entered into collaboration with my wife and myself on Central Coast Salishan comparative studies.

## 5. KUTENAI

Kutenai (Kootenay) is an isolated language spoken in two mildly differentiated dialects, Lower (around the international border where Idaho and Montana meet British Columbia) and Upper (further north and upstream along the Kutenai River). Alexander F. Chamberlain recorded a series of texts, some in each dialect, in 1891. In the summer of 1914 Boas worked with Upper Kutenai informants, collecting fuller texts and revising those of Chamberlain; he published these together, with an appended vocabulary (Boas 1918). Drawing on his experience with the language he edited a grammar of the language by Father Philippo Canestrelli (Canestrelli 1926), adding essential phonetic detail wherever possible and otherwise increasing the lucidity of the sketch, and appending extensive notes of his own (Boas 1926). Sapir (1918) discussed Kutenai kinship terms.

Paul Garvin took up the study of the language, collecting material in two summer field trips, 1946 and 1950, and presenting a grammar in several installments (1948a, 1951a) and a few texts (1953, 1954). He also described the handling of Christian names in the language (1947) and the nature of lexical innovations (1948b), and provided a summary grammatical sketch in connection with detailed discussion (in French) of the obviative — a system of considerable typological interest (1951b). This latter also exemplifies a descriptive technique for handling semantic analysis, and he later (1958) presented a revised version in English. While his earlier texts (1953) were narratives recorded from dictation, the later presentation (1954) is of special interest: it is a spontaneous conversation recorded on tape and analyzed with the help of an informant. He has also commented on the analytical difficulties of a language like Kutenai (1957).

Einar Haugen (1956) utilized Garvin's phonological description to study phoneme distribution in the language, offering this as evidence that the syllable furnishes a valuable descriptive unit for distributional studies in a language with a large number of consonant clusters. Eric Hamp (1958) also utilized Garvin's description to reanalyze Kutenai vowel length. Recently two students havs begun further work with the language: Marvin Kramer of the University of California, Berkeley, sponsored by the California Survey; and Lawrence Morgan of the University of Wisconsin. We should also note ethnographic coverage of Kutenai by Harry Turney-High (1941).

From the genetic point of view Kutenai stands alone, surrounded by languages of sure — and differing — affiliations. Sapir (1929a) placed it in his putative Algonkin-Wakashan superstock as a separate branch, without suggesting a closer relationship to any of the other members. No evidence for such relationships had been advanced until Mary Haas (1965) offered comparisons which she had managed to cull for Kutenai with Algonkian on the one hand, with Salishan, Chemakuan and Wakashan on the other; she also provides an excellent summary of speculations on the matter up to that time. The results are suggestive that Kutenai may indeed find its place in the general context that Sapir suggested, but nothing conclusive can be said at this time. Meaningful comparison must await the availability of more extensive Algonkian reconstructions and — particularly — general reconstructive work and further comparisons in the Salishan, Chemakuan and Wakashan area.

## 6. ATHAPASKAN

Northern Na-Dene — Haida, Tlingit, Eyak and northern Athapaskan — forms the heart of another area to the north, treated elsewhere in this volume by Michael Krauss. However, there were enclaves of Athapaskan speech within the region we have delineated as Northwest, and in the long run they may turn out to have exerted important influences in the development of areal typologies. Their investigation also played an interesting part in the development of work on the Northwest more generally, so that some words should be added about them here.

Between the territories of the Thompson and Okanagan Salishan peoples in southern British Columbia's Upper Nicola Valley and the region to the south was an Athapaskan group speaking a language which is best called Nicola. Now apparently long extinct, it was only very meagerly recorded; Boas (1895a, 1924) summarized what was known and published the vocabularies available. In general the material suggests a close relationship to nearby Chilcotin to the north.

The patch of Athapaskan speech near the mouth of the Columbia River has now disappeared. The Clatskanie (Klatskanai, Tlatskanai) of northwestern Oregon may have lived, in a remoter era, on the prairies along the Chehalis River in southwestern Washington, near the mouth of the Skookumchuck, but it has been urged that because of a failure of game in relatively recent times they moved across the Columbia River, where they were located on White contact. They were extinct by 1930 or 1932, according to Jacobs (p.c.). The Kwalhioqua, on the other hand, lived in a nearby area in Washington along the Willapa River; their form of speech appears to have died out by 1920. Again the recordings were very limited. Boas and Goddard (1924b) summarized the information and presented a short vocabulary; there is additional data in Curtis (1913:153–4). While these two speech forms were apparently very similar to one another, they seem to form a separate subgroup of the Athapaskan family.

On the southern Oregon coast and for some distance up the Umpqua and Rogue Rivers there was a considerable area occupied by Athapaskan speaking peoples, some still surviving. Together with languages of the northern California coastal area they form a subgroup of the family, extending continuously from the Umpqua River in Oregon to the head of the Eel River in California. Naming generally from north to south, the languages in Oregon are (Upper) Umpqua, (Upper) Coquille, Galice, Chasta Costa, Euchre Creek, and Chetco. They seem to fit into a coastal group — Euchre Creek, Coquille, Chasta Costa and Chetco (grouping with Tolowa in California) — and a coast range group — Umpqua and Galice.

For the largest amount of information on Oregon Athapaskan (aside from the yet undetermined material which may be found in the literary estate of J.P. Harrington) we are again indebted to Melville Jacobs and to his wife Elizabeth D. (Langdon) Jacobs. During the early 1930s he recorded a short (Upper) Umpqua wordlist and a large array of myth and other texts in Galice from the last living speaker. Mrs. Jacobs recorded Euchre Creek, (Upper) Coquille and Chetco speech from the last survivors. She has worked out sound correspondences and filed cognate sets for a number of Athapaskan languages. (She also examined Boas' Tlingit publication and made available to him — independently of Harrington — comparisons proving its kinship with Athapaskan.) The Jacobs have published short sample texts in Galice (M. Jacobs 1968) and Chetco (E. Jacobs 1968). In 1956 Jacobs made available his unpublished Galice texts to Harry Hoijer, who collected additional material from the same informant that same year. On the basis of these sources Hoijer (1966) presented a grammatical sketch of Galice in Jacobs' honor.

The special characteristics of Pacific Coast Athapaskan are outlined by Hoijer (1960) and are of course reflected in others of his publications treating the family more broadly (see elsewhere in this volume). Virginia Dosch Hymes (1955) made a detailed study of Athapaskan numeral systems (originally presented as her M.A. thesis at Indiana University), including important observations about the Pacific Coast languages. For further discussion of the Oregon Athapaskan situation, see the survey by Pierce and Ryherd (1964) and the references cited there, as well as the chapter covering Na-Dene in this volume.

## 7. AREAL AND OTHER STUDIES

The Northwest as a linguistic area has interested many scholars over the years. Boas (1911b) in his general introduction to the *Handbook of American Indian Languages* keeps coming back to Northwest areal features, and Sapir has drawn on problems of this nature in many of his writings. We should pause here to note that the continuity of phonological systems in the Northwest was probably an important factor influencing Boas to conclude that it was futile to pursue long-range genetic relationships in North America.

More specifically, Melville Jacobs (1937) discussed the shifting boundaries of languages and language families and offered convincing evidence that these resulted from the advance of less privileged groups into areas more richly endowed with natural resources through marriage into bands and hamlets whose people originally occupied these areas. Moving downstream along the less populous water courses, newcomers gradually increased the non-native population of marginal villages, which became bilingual until the newcomers predominated, their language then replacing the original one. In this way it can be seen how it happens that upriver communities of the coastal areas so often relate to interior groups across the mountains, rather than to their downstream neighbors. Later (Jacobs 1954) he discussed in a more general and encompassing way the areal spread of sound features in the Northwest. In a review Norman McQuown (1955:77) called for utilizing the techniques of historical linguistics to separate diffused elements from genetically inherited ones. However, the matter is not so simple: it seems obvious now that languages in a diffusion area develop inherited systems in the direction of types characteristic for the area. Hymes (1956:588–91) signalled the importance of such efforts and added revealing detail and some revisions to Jacobs' picture. With so many new descriptions of languages in the area now it will be possible to advance such studies further.

Mary Haas (1968) studied the areal distributions and interrelationships of consonantal systems more broadly in western North America, drawing on languages from Alaska to California. She identified a Pacific Coast phonological diffusion area which she used as an example in her treatment of diffusional phenomena as they relate to linguistic prehistory (1969c: chapter 5; cf. esp. 84–9). In the same work (1969c:92–5) she discussed diffusion of classificatory schemes apparently from Pacific Coast Athapaskan languages into neighboring Penutian Takelma and Klamath. Johanna Nichols (1971) utilized available descriptions in a survey of diminutive consonant symbolism in western North American languages, and studied the areal distribution and apparent dynamics of the systems.

In the general survey of areal-typological features of Amerindian languages north of Mexico which Joel Sherzer (1968) presented as his doctoral dissertation at the University of Pennsylvania, we find again special emphasis on the Northwest; he has provided a summary and some expansion of his study for the present volume.

Earlier Morris Swadesh (1948a) discussed the apparent development of all-suffixing synthetic structure for Wakashan and Chemakuan, suggesting diffusion from Eskimo-Aleut in an earlier period, and studying in detail the evidence presented in Nootka. Swadesh's later conviction (1962, 1964b; see also above under Wakashan) of a genetic connection between Wakashan and Eskimo-Aleut may now place this in a different light.

Areal and general typological questions also arose in connection with the study of vowel harmony in Sahaptian (see discussion above). Another putative long-range relationship was also proposed: Kiparsky (1968) points out the striking similarity of Sahaptian vocalic harmony to the system in Chukchi, and suggests on this basis a genetic connection between the two families. The two systems could, however, have arisen quite independently (Jacobsen, p.c., reporting also similar views of Rigsby and Silverstein). We should also note here Hymes' (1969) discussion of 'fourth' person and phonesthematic aspects of personal pronouns (see discussion under Chinookan above).

Reduplication is widespread in the Northwest, and reduplicative morphemes denoting collectives or distributives on the one hand and attenuative or diminutive on the other are common. Aoki (1963b) describes the patterns in Nez Perce and calls attention to the likelihood we are dealing with an areal feature. Others have singled out reduplication for special treatment: Sapir (1915b) for Comox, Hess (1966) for Puget Sound Salish, and Haeberlin (1918) for Salishan more broadly.

Lexical borrowings between Tsimshian and neighboring Na-Dene languages have been studied by Pinnow (1969). As Haas (1969c:78) points out, such studies are interesting and valuable in themselves and constitute an important part of linguistic history — not merely as explanations of divergent forms in a genetic comparison. It is of course also true that poor control of borrowed elements causes serious problems in genetic studies. It is clear that for the area as a whole much work must be done on diffusion. Perhaps the most serious problems lie with intimate borrowing among closely related languages and dialects.

There have been several studies of more limited typological features in the Northwest. M. Dale Kinkade (1967d) noted the distribution and special characteristics of uvular-pharyngeal resonants in the Interior Salishan languages. The appearance of similar sounds in Wakashan, and more generally the conditions apparently favorable for their development, have been investigated by William Jacobsen (1969b) in connection with his quest for the origin of the Nootka pharyngeals.

At the third Salish Conference, Stanley Newman (1968) offered a preliminary comparison of Salishan lexical suffixes, including a discussion of both their morphological and semantic aspects. This prompted a discussion on the same occasion of the semantic categories such entities cover in Quileute in comparison with the Salishan (Hamp

1968). Later Dale Kinkade (1969a) took up the matter in connection with the Mosan hypothesis, with negative results (see above). He links the similarities of these systems to the broader picture of similarities among the three families and calls for more investigation of areal features of this sort. Such studies also underline the need for careful and full investigation of such systems in all the languages involved.

Still other features of the area are interesting in general typological terms. Thus Kinkade (1967c) reports that for Upper Chehalis words are formed with prefixes and suffixes alone, lacking the usual root or base. Further studies may reveal more of this sort of morphological construction in the area. In the course of work on Straits Salish my wife and I observed metathesis operating in the grammatical system signalling aspectual distinctions (L. C. and M. T. Thompson 1969b). We also noted (1966) that due to a method of internal rounding replacing the usual lip-rounding, Tillamook Salish is totally devoid of labial sounds (aside from a few borrowings). On the other hand, the opposition between plain and rounded velars seems to be neutralized in more environments in Wakashan than in Salishan. Jacobsen (1969a) discussed the distribution of such elements in Nootkan.

Some areal features have been seen to relate importantly to general questions about linguistic universals. Charles Ferguson (1963) hypothesized that every language has at least one nasal, and if only one, then it is fundamentally *n*. He mentioned 'three Salishan languages' as marginal exceptions in which original nasals had been converted to voiced stops. Since the literature has treated this question unclearly and rather misleadingly, my wife and I (L. C. and M. T. Thompson 1969a) detailed the facts, pointing out that in addition to Puget Sound dialects and Twana of the Salishan family, there are also Quileute of the Chemakuan family, and Makah and Nitinat of the Wakashan family which lack nasals completely except for borrowings and other marginal forms, adding that upriver dialects of Halkomelem have *m*, not *n*, as their only nasal. We went on to explore ways of explaining why languages which apparently formerly had more usual inventories should have developed such unusual ones, and in the course of discussion brought out some other areal features as well. This contradiction of a putative universal and the misleading statements about the languages and families involved were also remarked by Haas (1969a:112, fn. 16). Kuipers (1968b:74) mentions the problem of nasal-less languages as well as Bella Coola's vowel-less utterances in his appeal for more responsible handling of data in the construction of general hypotheses; he cites also the urgent need for more concentrated work on American indigenous languages (1968b:84–6) in his general attack on the theoretical preoccupations of current American linguistics.

Another widely accepted universal is the opposition of noun and verb in grammar. Some Northwest linguistic structures are thought-provoking in this connection as well. R. H. Robins (1952) discusses the matter in general terms, cautioning against projection of categories onto structures where they do not belong. He concludes, however, that the opposition will likely be shown to be universal. He mentions the Nootka case discussed below, but seems not to recognize the depth of the difference between it and familiar Indo-European structures — he refers in the same breath to verbless adjectival predications in Russian, without noting that in past or future the verb *be* reappears. (Nominal predications in Russian, of course, have the same characteristics.) In his analysis of Nootka, Swadesh (1939:78) recognized the contradiction: he makes clear that non-particles are either predicative or non-predicative, depending on their paradigmatic ending. Salishan structure is if anything more contradictory of a noun/verb type opposition, except in the most superficial sense. Edel (1939:5) already recognized that Tillamook has no rigorous distinction between noun and verb stems. Kinkade (1963:345–6) adopts the opposition for Upper Chehalis, but his description makes clear the tenuous quality of the distinction; he has privately (p.c.) indicated great dissatisfaction with the dichotomy. Barbara Efrat (1969: see especially section 4.4.3) utilizes a nominal-verbal distinction as an expedient in her description, but calls attention to the disparity between the Sooke entities designated nominals and the traditional use of that term, and indicates the need for deeper study. Newman (1969a:176–7) finds in Bella Coola no inflectional criteria for distinguishing nouns and verbs; even inflected transitive words can have either a predicative or substantival function and these functions can be defined only in syntactic terms. My wife and I (L.C. and M.T. Thompson 1971:287–88) discuss the problem in Clallam, concluding that all non-particles have a fundamental predicative function; their appearance in positions complementary to the predicate of a clause reflects a secondary syntactic use, and the opposition of the two uses is quite dissimilar from that of nouns and verbs in languages like English. Independently Kuipers (1968a) studied this problem in detail with reference to Squamish in contrast with English, relating it to the transitive-intransitive opposition. He concludes that Squamish, too, is better described without a noun/verb opposition. The matter is of considerable importance in relation to both typology and work on linguistic universals; we may expect further interesting investigations as more languages are probed in depth.

Languages of the area have furnished a stimulation for adapting methods of using the computer for analysis, especially in connection with material collected at an earlier period. In addition to the Jorgensen (1969) statistical study of Salishan linguistic and cultural elements, we find that Pierce (1963) has attacked study of a Sahaptin dialect (as well as Turkish) in a statistical manner and has embarked on a computerized analysis of Frachtenberg's Alsea texts (Pierce 1965a). Earlier (1962) he used some Sahaptin and Chinookan examples in developing his methodology for the electronic computation of typological indices for linguistic structures. This reflects a continuation of earlier interest in statistical investigations going back to his doctoral dissertation (Pierce 1957b), which includes some Northwest languages in its statistical study of New World languages (cf. also Pierce 1957a, a published version of the study of consonants).

In a broader framework we should note some investigations of ethno- and psycholinguistic interest. Edwin M. Lemert (1952) observed the existence of stutterers in a number of Indian groups on the British Columbia coast and Vancouver Island, and offered evidence that stuttering existed also in pre-contact times. He relates the problem to psychological pressures in the cultures involved. Joseph L. Stewart's (1960) monograph discusses the matter in fuller terms from the background of the speech pathologist, comparing data from a smaller area on Vancouver Island where stuttering was reported with data from the 'non-stuttering' Ute group in the Great Basin and relating them to differences in attitudes and tensions in the two societies. Herbert Landar (1961) mentions some Northwest cases in his attempt to uncover connections between stuttering and reduplication.

More familiar ethnolinguistic concerns are reflected in the numerous studies of kinship systems. Most of these have already been mentioned above in connection with the various languages. Here we should add Elmendorf's (1961b) overall study of the Salishan usages, combining reconstruction of a proto-system on a linguistic basis with discussion of both linguistic and sociocultural factors producing the historically attested systems. There are also some ethnobotany studies. Erna Gunther (1945) has provided information on the uses of specific plants by various peoples in a broad area of western Washington. More detail for a single group (the Thompson Indians) is afforded by James Teit's notes, edited by Elsie Steedman (Teit 1928). Suttles (1951) discussed the early diffusion of the potato among the Coast Salish, utilizing linguistic forms along with other kinds of evidence. Later (1957) he wove linguistic factors skillfully in with cultural and archaeological evidence in his demolition of Marian Smith's (1956) constructs, the Middle Fraser and Foothill cultures. He has also drawn various examples from his experience to demonstrate anthropological ends which linguistic investigations can serve (Suttles 1965a).

There have been some studies of linguistic acculturation — e.g., in Kutenai by Garvin (1948b), in Makah by Jacobsen (1967), and in Nitinat by Klokeid (1968). Special linguistic subsystems have received some attention — e.g. Sapir's (1929b) treatment of Nootka baby words, the discussion of abnormal forms of speech in Nootka (Sapir 1915a) and Quileute (Frachtenberg 1920a), and Hymes' (1958) treatment of linguistic features peculiar to Chinookan myths, as well as sporadic mention of sound symbolism in other connections (e.g. in Jacobsen 1969b). But the mention here may hopefully serve primarily as a stimulant for further investigation of expressive systems, in which the region is rich.

This is not the place to detail studies of oral literature and indigenous music, but some mention should be made of the concern for such studies and of the need for further collections while it is still possible. M. Jacobs (1959a), in the course of surveying Boas' contribution to folklore studies as a researcher, editor and teacher, affords a valuable summary of work in the Northwest because so much of Boas' activity centered here. He also (Jacobs 1962) discusses directly the great difficulties for work along these lines in Oregon — similar comments apply to the rest of the area as well. However, there have been some beginnings made with the music and literatures of various peoples — these have been cited above in connection with work on the individual languages. Here we should mention George Herzog's (1949) analysis of the music of several Salishan peoples; he also provides a survey of studies and materials.

Jacobs' (1959c, 1960a) analysis of Clackamas Chinook texts should be mentioned outside the narrow context of Chinookan studies for its general approach to content and style, and, together with the Indian texts themselves (1958, 1959b), as an important sample of anthropological philology. Hymes (1965a) discusses this set of contributions from the several points of view — that of the Chinookan specialist, that of the ethnographer and folklorist, that of the linguist, and that of the anthropological philologist. He calls attention to the important further work needed to establish a meaningful philology for preliterate peoples, particularly for those cultures which are obsolescent or in process of extreme transformation. (Note also William Lessa's [1960] review of Jacobs' *Content and style* ...)

Hymes has himself drawn on Chinookan materials in discussing the typology of cognitive styles in language (1961) and in reconstructing patterns of language use among the Wishram (1966b). He has also made a beginning in analysis of poetics from several Northwest cultures (1965c). More recently (1968) he has re-analyzed a Clackamas myth, following the import of his earlier (1959b) discussion of titles in Chinookan myths and utilizing certain methods of Lévi-Strauss. The methods, however, lead to interesting different conclusions, and expressive as well as referential structure emerges. The study also provides the opportunity to refute the Lévi-Strauss position that myth structure can be analyzed without attention to linguistic form.

Another general trend should be noted. As elsewhere in North America, there has been a revival of interest in things Indian on the part of Indians themselves. This healthy resurgence of pride in their background has often carried with it a wish to re-establish the old language, to teach it to the children who now typically grow up speaking only English. Despite the severe difficulties that such efforts at relinguistification always face, there has been some impact. In addition to the Quinault instance mentioned above, the neighboring Quileute have resolved to teach their language to the children of the tribe. The Office of Economic Opportunity supported a worker for the purpose, and James Hoard and J.V. Powell gave their time during the summer of 1970 to prepare lesson materials. There have also been school organized programs for the Lower Elwha Clallam and the Lummi; in both these cases my wife and I were able to offer assistance. On Vancouver Island similar work is under way — in particular, materials are being developed for Cowichan, Kwakiutl and Sliammon, with the assistance of O'Grady, Hess and Davis. Bouchard is working toward a similar goal for Okanagan, Lillooet, Shuswap and Thompson. He has helped Larry Pierre of the northern Okanagan and Priscilla Ritchie of the Lillooet in learning to write their languages; they are transcribing texts and preparing materials to teach others on their reserves how to write. Lawrence Nicodemus is teaching Coeur d'Alene to young Indians and offers an extension course in the language at Eastern Washington State College (Cheney). Interest among the northern Shuswap along these lines has been furthered by Aert Kuipers' assistance. A parallel movement has gotten under way on the Yakima Reservation, where Rigsby has assisted. Rigsby (p.c.) reports that at

Warm Springs in 1969 Linton Winishut conducted a class in Sahaptin for adults. Rigsby also reports that Mrs. Mary Halfmoon and others on the Umatilla Reservation have been offering classes for young adults mainly in Nez Perce, and he has assisted by correspondence. He has identified a fluent young Yakima-Umatilla woman, Pauline Sam, who lived for a number of years with her bilingual grandmother (who spoke Nez Perce and Sahaptin only); he has arranged for her to study the writing of Sahaptin and develop some linguistic background at the University of New Mexico.

An important byproduct of these efforts, taken together with the work of trained linguists, can be the psychologically and culturally important contribution of some native scholarship. It is surely essential to increase the sense of cooperation between a developmental indigenous scholarship and the wider scholarly community — something which has been exceedingly difficult in the past. In these terms efforts are in order to encourage younger tribal members with background in their own language and culture to train their capacities in this direction.

## 8. FOR THE FUTURE

So today we stand on the threshold of a period of great progress in the documenting and understanding of Northwest indigenous languages and their background. The recent period has seen an increasing interest and a rising number of qualified participants. Nevertheless the research team is still short-handed for the accomplishment of the basic job — that of documenting fully all of the languages and oral genres, including mythology, in the short time before their extinction. Directions for work are clear. Obviously fundamental is the continued effort to obtain and analyze as full material as possible on all the surviving languages. For comparative purposes special care needs to be taken to collect the most extensive possible lexical files on those isolated languages or families whose genetic affiliations are clouded (e.g. Kutenai, Quileute) or simply remote from their congeners (e.g. Tsimshian, Chinookan). On the other hand, certain languages (e.g. Comox) have interesting grammatical complexities which appear old — again special care should be taken to insure full coverage of their non-productive morphological forms which may well furnish important evidence for comparison.

For typological and areal studies the same kind of basic collections will be important; in addition, there need to be thorough explorations of various special and marginal systems — phonological, grammatical, and expressive. This leads on to concern for a host of things related to the cultural expression of the peoples. Again, obviously, we must obtain wherever possible full collections of folkloristic and historical texts, and whatever samples are possible from those situations where only fragmentary collections are available. In order to obtain the most valuable collections the linguist must be experienced with the language and must have established an advanced working relationship with the informant. Only then is it possible to minimize those damaging suppressions and transformations of content which the imposition of White values has made so likely; only then can the special linguistic and interpretive difficulties of the texts themselves be successfully dealt with. Similar qualities are needed to get at songs, and at verbal play and humor. The wealth of abnormal speech and special semantic systems should likewise be fully documented. Successful pursuit of these goals requires the cooperation of well trained anthropologists and linguists — where the skills are available in the same person, so much the better, but failing that we should hope for close integration of research of two or more collaborators.

In some circumstances it is still possible to work with living speech communities rather than with last survivors of fragmentary cultures (e.g. in Comox and Shuswap areas, or on the Yakima Reservation). In these cases it is important to bring to bear the developmental techniques of dialectal variation patterns. Even in some less favorable circumstances (e.g. Cowichan Halkomelem, several Interior Salishan groups, Nootkan and Kwakiutlan groups) much can still be worked out on the dialectal patterns. Sociolinguistic studies can and should be done in circumstances where the patterns of assimilation and acculturation are under observation.

Analysis of the materials being collected must continue apace. Work toward the simple goals of grammatical description and lexical compilation will serve also to clarify urgent collecting needs and will provide bases for genetic and typological comparisons. The concern of researchers for all levels of textual and grammatical work will help keep their perspective about the need for overall descriptions as well as detailed exhaustive analyses of portions of a language structure.

Work on genetic relationships must proceed on several levels at once. Full intimate comparisons must be completed using all available material and yielding the maximum possible reconstructions for the putative proto-languages. At the same time, comparisons must be continued at deeper levels, so that, for example in Penutian, lower level work can draw on the results emerging from consideration of broader patterns. All this is necessarily intimately connected with increasing control of overall areal development, so that gradually more and more of the diffused elements can be sorted out from among the tokens of genetic relationships, and more can be worked out about earlier patterns of diffusion.

Beyond this there is the need for development of a high level of philological approach to the area as a whole and to the constituent languages and cultures. In order are new editions of texts (critical and interpretive), definitive dictionaries utilizing all available materials, old and new. This area of human culture is as deserving as any other, and as valuable to the understanding of mankind — in fact, there are some respects in which it is unusually endowed, and fortunately we do already have a fair amount of material for comprehensive study. There are at least some indications that concentration on this and a few other areas of the world may afford a far greater than proportionate insight into the developmental diversity of human cognitive systems — a diversity which under the present world pressures is disappearing rapidly. It is imperative to collect and analyze details and patterns which may be crucial in puzzling out the ways human beings think and develop systems of thought.

All this calls for the highest qualities of scholarship, and for scholarship that is mutually reinforcing, more than the sum of its parts. Only with the intensive cooperative effort of well trained scholars — linguists, ethnohistorians, folklorists, anthropologists and others — can this essential work be done. It is thus a serious responsibility for those involved in the area not only to accomplish what they can themselves and make their work available to others, but also to train students who can extend and revise and integrate beyond what is now feasible. A review of encouraging current developments should also emphasize the vast dimensions of the job still at hand.

BIBLIOGRAPHY

ADAMSON, THELMA. 1934. Folk-tales of the Coast Salish. AFS-M 27.
ADLER, FRED W. 1961. A bibliographical checklist of Chimakuan, Kutenai, Ritwan, Salishan and Wakashan linguistics. IJAL 27.198–210.
AGINSKY, ETHEL. 1947. Review of Hans Vogt, 1940b. IJAL 13.274–75.
AMOSS, PAMELA THORSEN. 1961. Nuksack phonemics. Univ. of Washington M.A. thesis.
——. 1969. The domain of food in Skagit. Paper presented at 4th ICSL, Victoria.
ANDRADE, MANUEL J. 1931. Quileute texts. CUCA 12.
——. 1933. Quileute. HAIL 3.149–292.
——. 1953a. Notes on the relations between Chemakum and Quileute, ed. by Morris Swadesh. IJAL 19.212–15.
——. 1953b. Relations between Nootka and Quileute, ed. by Morris Swadesh. IJAL 19.138–40.
ANDREWS, H. A., and others. 1943. Bibliography of Franz Boas. AAA–M 61.67–109.
AOKI, HARUO. 1962. Nez Perce and Northern Sahaptin: A binary comparison. IJAL 28.172–82.
——. 1963a. On Sahaptian-Klamath linguistic affiliations. IJAL 29.107–12.
——. 1963b. Reduplication in Nez Perce. IJAL 29.42–4.
——. 1965. An exploration of the Penutian hypothesis with regard to the languages of Oregon. Paper presented at 4th CAIL, Denver.
——. 1966a. Nez Perce and Proto-Sahaptian kinship terms. IJAL 32.357–68.
——. 1966b. Nez Perce vowel harmony and Proto-Sahaptian vowels. Lg 42.759–67.
——. 1968. Toward a typology of vowel harmony. IJAL 34.142–5.
——. 1970a. A note on glottalized consonants. Phonetica 21.65–74.
——. 1970b. Nez Perce grammar. UCPL 62.
——. 1970c. North Plateau linguistic diffusion area. Paper presented at 5th ICSL, Spokane.
——. 1970d. Usage of referential kin terms in Nez Perce. Languages and cultures

of western North America: Essays in honor of Sven S. Liljeblad, ed. by Earl H. Swanson, Jr., pp. 61–73. Pocatello, Idaho State University Press.

BACH, EMMON, and REED BATES. 1971. Some notes on Xa'isla. SAS-P 11.1–11.

BALLARD, ARTHUR C. 1927. Some tales of the Southern Puget Sound Salish. UWPA 2.57–81.

———. 1929. Mythology of Southern Puget Sound. UWPA 3.31–150.

———. 1935. Southern Puget Sound Salish kinship terms. AmA 37.111–16.

———. 1950. Calendric terms of the Southern Puget Sound Salish. SJA 6.79–99.

BARKER, M.A.R. 1963a. Klamath dictionary. UCPL 31.

———. 1963b. Klamath texts. UCPL 30.

———. 1964. Klamath grammar. UCPL 32.

BARNETT, HOMER G. 1955. The Coast Salish of British Columbia. University of Oregon Monographs, Studies in Anthropology 4. Eugene.

BERREMAN, J.V. 1937. Tribal distribution in Oregon. AAA-M 47.

BOAS, FRANZ. 1890. The Kwakiutl. BAAS-R 60.604–32, 655–8.

———. 1892. Notes on the Chemakum language. AmA 5.37–44.

———. 1894. Chinook texts. BAE-B 20.

———. 1895a. The Tinneh tribe of Nicola Valley. BAAS-R 1895.551–5.

———. 1895b. [Tsimshian texts] Indianische Sagen von der Nord-pacifischen Küste Amerikas, pp. 272–305. Berlin, A. Asher.

———. 1898. The mythology of the Bella Coola Indians. AMNH-M 1.25–127.

———. 1901. Kathlamet texts. BAE-B 26.

———. 1902. Tsimshian texts. BAE-B 27.

———. 1910. Kwakiutl tales. CUCA 2.

———. 1911a. Chinook. HAIL (BAE-B 40) 1.559–677.

———. 1911b. Introduction. HAIL (BAE-B 40) 1.1–83.

———. 1911c. Kwakiutl. HAIL (BAE-B 40) 1.423–557.

———. 1911d. Tsimshian. HAIL (BAE-B 40) 1.283–422.

———. 1912. Tsimshian texts (new series). PAES 3.65–285.

———. 1916. Tsimshian mythology. BAE-R 31.27–1037.

———. 1918. Kutenai tales. BAE-B 59.

———. 1921. Ethnology of the Kwakiutl based on data collected by George Hunt. BAE-R 35.1388–1466.

———. 1924. Vocabulary of the Athapaskan tribe of Nicola Valley, British Columbia. IJAL 3.36–8.

———. 1926. Additional notes on the Kutenai language. IJAL 4.85–104. (See also Canestrelli 1926)

———. 1928. Bella Bella texts. CUCA 5.

———. 1931. Notes on the Kwakiutl vocabulary. IJAL 6.163–78.

———. 1932a. Bella Bella tales. AFS-M 25.

———. 1932b. Note on some recent changes in the Kwakiutl language. IJAL 7.90–3.

——. 1934a. A Chehalis text. IJAL 8.103–10.
——. 1934b. Geographical names of the Kwakiutl Indians. CUCA 20.
——. 1935–43. Kwakiutl tales (new series). CUCA 26.
——. 1947. Kwakiutl grammar, with a glossary of the suffixes, ed. by Helene Boas Yampolsky and Zellig S. Harris. TAPS 37.201–377.
BOAS, FRANZ and PLINY E. GODDARD. 1924a. A revised list of Kwakiutl suffixes. IJAL 3.117–31.
——. 1924b. Vocabulary of an Athapaskan dialect of the State of Washington. IJAL 3.39–45.
BOAS, FRANZ and HERMAN HAEBERLIN. 1927. Sound shifts in Salishan dialects. IJAL 4.117–36.
BOAS, FRANZ and GEORGE HUNT. 1902–05. Kwakiutl texts. AMNH-M 5.
——. 1906. Kwakiutl texts (2nd series). AMNH-M 14.1–269.
BOUCHARD, RANDY, MIKE KEW and PETER L. MCNAIR. 1970. Newsletter for research relating to British Columbia Indians. British Columbia Provincial Museum, Victoria.
CANESTRELLI, P. PHILIPPO, S.J. 1926. Grammar of the Kutenai language (annotated by Franz Boas). IJAL 4.1–84. (see also Boas 1926)
CHOMSKY, NOAM, and MORRIS HALLE. 1968. The sound pattern of English. New York, Harper and Row.
CLINE, WALTER, RACHEL S. COMMONS, MAY MANDELBAUM, RICHARD H. POST, and L. V. W. WALTERS. 1938. The Sinkaietk or Southern Okanagan of Washington, ed. by Leslie Spier. General Series in Anthropology, No. 6. Menasha, Wisc.
COLLINS, JUNE M. 1949. Distribution of the Chemakum language. Indians of the urban northwest, ed. by Marian W. Smith. CUCA 36.147–60.
COLSON, ELIZABETH. 1953. The Makah Indians. Manchester, Manchester University Press.
CURTIS, EDWARD S. 1913. The North American Indian. Vol. 9, Norwood, Massachusetts, Plimpton.
DAVIS, JOHN H. 1970. Some phonological rules in mainland Comox. University of Victoria M.A. thesis.
——. 1971. Notes on mainland Comox phonology. SAS-P 11.12–31.
DEANGULO, JAIME, and LUCY S. FREELAND. 1931. The Lutuami language. JSAm 23.1–45.
DENSMORE, FRANCES. 1927. The language of the Makah Indians. AS 2.237.
——. 1939. Nootka and Quileute music. BAE-B 124.
DIEBOLD, A. RICHARD, JR. 1960. Determining the centers of dispersal of language groups. IJAL 26.1–10.
DRACHMAN, GABERELL. 1969. Twana phonology. OSU WPL 5.
DUFF, WILSON. 1952. The Upper Stalo Indians. Anthropology in British Columbia, Memoir 1. Victoria, B.C., Provincial Museum,

DUNN, JOHN. 1970. Coast Tsimshian systematic phonology. University of New Mexico Ph.D. dissertation.

DYEN, ISIDORE. 1956. Language distribution and migration theory. Lg 32.611–26.

——. 1962. The lexicostatistically determined relationship of a language group. IJAL 28.153–61.

——. 1963. Lexicostatistically determined borrowing and taboo. Lg 39.60–6.

DYK, WALTER. 1933. A grammar of Wishram. Yale University Ph.D. dissertation.

DYK, WALTER, and DELL H. HYMES. 1956. Stress accent in Wishram Chinook. IJAL 22.238–41.

EDEL, MAY MANDELBAUM. 1939. The Tillamook language. IJAL 10.1–57.

EFRAT, BARBARA S. 1969. A grammar of non-particles in Sooke, a dialect of Straits Coast Salish. University of Pennsylvania Ph.D. dissertation.

ELMENDORF, WILLIAM W. 1946. Twana kinship terminology. SJA 2.420–32.

——. 1951. Word taboo and lexical change in Coast Salish. IJAL 17.205–8.

——. 1960. The structure of Twana culture. [With comparative notes on the structure of the Yurok culture, by A. L. Kroeber.] WSU RS, Monographic Supplement 2.

——. 1961a. Skokomish and other Coast Salish tales. WSU RS 29.1–37, 84–150.

——. 1961b. System change in Salish kinship terminologies. SJA 17.365–82.

——. 1962a. Lexical innovation and persistence in four Salish dialects. IJAL 28.85–96.

——. 1962b. Lexical relation models as a possible check on lexicostatistic inferences. AmA 64.760–70.

——. 1962c. Relations of Oregon Salish as evidenced in numerical stems. AnL 4/2.1–16.

——. 1965a. Linguistic and geographic relations in the northern plateau area. SJA 21.63–78.

——. 1965b. Some problems in the regrouping of Powell units. CJL 10.93–107.

——. 1969. Geographic ordering, subgrouping, and Olympic Salish. IJAL 35.220–5.

——. 1970. Word taboo and change rates: Tests of a hypothesis. Languages and cultures of western North America: Essays in honor of Sven S. Liljeblad, ed. by Earl H. Swanson, Jr., pp. 74–85. Pocatello, Idaho State University Press.

ELMENDORF, WILLIAM W., and WAYNE SUTTLES. 1960. Pattern and change in Halkomelem Salish dialects. AnL 2/7.1–32.

FAIRBANKS, GORDON H. 1955. A note on glottochronology. IJAL 21.116–20.

FERGUSON, CHARLES A. 1963. Assumptions about nasals: A sample study in phonological universals. Universals of language, ed. by Joseph H. Greenberg, pp. 53–60. Cambridge, Mass., MIT Press.

FRACHTENBERG, LEO J. 1913. Coos texts. CUCA 1.

——. 1914. Lower Umpqua texts and notes on the Kusan dialects. CUCA 4.

——. 1917a. Myths of the Alsea Indians of Northwestern Oregon. IJAL 1.64–75.

——. 1917b. A Siletz vocabulary. IJAL 1.45–6.

——. 1918. Comparative studies in Takelman, Kalapuyan, and Chinookan lexicography. IJAL 1.175–82.
——. 1920a. Abnormal types of speech in Quileute. IJAL 1.295–9.
——. 1920b. Alsea texts and myths. BAE-B 67.
——. 1920c. Eschatology of the Quileute Indians. AmA 22.330–40.
——. 1922a. Coos. HAIL (BAE-B 40) 2.297–430.
——. 1922b. Siuslawan (Lower Umpqua). HAIL (BAE-B 40) 2.431–629.
FREEMAN, JOHN F., and MURPHY D. SMITH. 1966. A guide to the manuscripts relating to the American Indian in the Library of the American Philosophical Society. MAPS 65.
FRENCH, DAVID. 1958. Cultural matrices of Chinookan non-casual language. IJAL 24.258–63.
GARFIELD, VIOLA E. 1939. Tsimshian clan and society. UWPA 7.167–349.
GARVIN, PAUL L. 1947. Christian names in Kutenai. IJAL 13.69–77.
——. 1948a. Kutenai. IJAL 14.37–42, 87–90, 171–87.
——. 1948b. Kutenai lexical innovations. Word 4.120–6.
——. 1951a. Kutenai IV: Word classes. IJAL 17.84–97.
——. 1951b. L'obviation en Kutenai: Échantillon d'une catégorie grammaticale amérindienne. BSL 47.166–212.
——. 1953. Short Kutenai texts. IJAL 19.305–11.
——. 1954. Colloquial Kutenai text: Conversation II. IJAL 20.316–34.
——. 1957. On the relative tractability of morphological data. Word 13.12–23.
——. 1958. A descriptive technique for the treatment of meaning. Lg 34.1–32.
GIBBS, GEORGE. 1877. Dictionary of the Niskwalli. CNAE 1.285–361.
GIBSON, JAMES A. 1964. Quinault phonemics. University of Washington M.A. thesis.
GIORDA, JOSEPH. 1877–79. A dictionary of the Kalispel or Flathead Indian language. St. Ignatius Mission, Montana.
GRANT, RENA V. 1945. Chinook jargon. IJAL 11.225–33.
GRUBB, DAVID McC. 1969. A Kwakiutl phonology. University of Victoria M.A. thesis.
GUNTHER, ERNA. 1925. Klallam folktales. UWPA 1/4.113–69.
——. 1927. Klallam ethnography. UWPA 1/5.171–314.
——. 1945. Ethnobotany of western Washington. UWPA 10/1.
HAAS, MARY R. 1960. Some genetic affiliations of Algonkian. Culture in history, ed. by Stanley Diamond, pp. 977–92. New York, Columbia University Press.
——. 1965. Is Kutenai related to Algonkian? CJL 10.77–92.
——. 1968. Phonological convergences of western North America. Paper presented at 7th CAIL, Seattle.
——. 1969a. Internal reconstruction of the Nootka-Nitinat pronominal suffixes. IJAL 35.108–24.

———. 1969b. Stem extenders in Nootka-Nitinat. Paper presented at 4th ICSL, Victoria.

———. 1969c. The prehistory of languages. JanL, series minor 57.

HAAS (SWADESH), MARY, and MORRIS SWADESH. 1932. A visit to the other world, a Nitinat text. IJAL 7.195–208.

HAEBERLIN, HERMAN K. 1918. Types of reduplication in the Salish dialects. IJAL 1.154–74.

HAEBERLIN, HERMAN(N), and ERNA GUNTHER. 1930. The Indians of Puget Sound. UWPA 4/1.

HALL, ROBERT A., JR. 1950. Review of Franz Boas 1947. IJAL 16.101–2.

HAMP, ERIC P. 1958. Prosodic notes. IJAL 24.321–2.

———. 1963a. The danger of place names for history. Paper presented at the annual meeting of the Linguistic Society of America, Chicago.

———. 1963b. An interim report on Quileute prosodics. Paper presented at the summer meeting of the Linguistic Society of America, Seattle.

———. 1966. Upper Chehalis $qa\ł \sim q̓es$-. IJAL 32.84–6.

———. 1967. Another look at Tillamook phonology. Paper presented at 2nd ICSL, Seattle.

———. 1968. Quileute and Salish lexical suffixes. Paper presented at 3rd ICSL, Victoria.

HARRIS, JIMMY G. 1966. The phonology of Chilliwack Halkomelem. University of Washington M.A. thesis.

HAUGEN, EINAR. 1956. Syllabification in Kutenai. IJAL 22.196–201.

HERZOG, GEORGE. 1949. Salish music. Indians of the urban northwest, ed. by Marian W. Smith. CUCA 36.93–109.

HESS, THOMAS M. 1966. Snohomish chameleon morphology. IJAL 32.350–6.

———. 1967a. Snohomish grammatical structure. University of Washington Ph.D. dissertation.

———. 1967b. The morph -əb in Snohomish. Paper presented at the 2nd ICSL, Seattle.

———. 1968. Directive phrases: A consideration of one facet of Puget Salish syntax. Paper presented at the 3rd ICSL, Victoria.

———. 1969. Secondary suffixation in Puget Salish. Paper presented at 4th ICSL, Victoria.

———. 1971. Prefix constituents with /x^w/. SAS-P 11.43–69.

HOARD, JAMES E. 1967. On the foundations of phonological theory. University of Washington Ph.D. dissertation.

———. 1968. Quileute prosody. Paper presented at the annual meeting of the Linguistic Society of America, New York.

———. 1971. Problems in Proto-Salish pronoun reconstruction. SAS-P 11.70–90.

HOARD, JAMES E., and THOMAS M. HESS, eds. 1971. Studies in Northwest Indian languages. SAS-P 11.

HOIJER, HARRY. 1960. Athapaskan languages of the Pacific Coast. Culture in history, ed. by Stanley Diamond, pp. 960–76. New York, Columbia University Press.

———. 1963. The Athapaskan languages. Studies in the Athapaskan languages, ed. by Harry Hoijer and others. UCPL 29.1–29.

———. 1966. Galice Athapaskan: A grammatical sketch. IJAL 32.320–7.

HOIJER, HARRY, ERIC P. HAMP, and WILLIAM BRIGHT. 1966. Contributions to a bibliography of comparative Amerindian. IJAL 31.346–53.

HUNT, GEORGE. 1916. Myths of the Nootka. BAE-R 31.888–935.

HYMES, DELL H. 1955. The language of the Kathlamet Chinook. Indiana University Ph.D. dissertation.

———. 1956. Review of Papers from the Symposium on American Indian Linguistics (UCPL 10.1–67). Lg 32.585–602.

———. 1957. Some Penutian elements and the Penutian hypothesis. SJA 13.69–87.

———. 1958. Linguistic features peculiar to Chinookan myths. IJAL 24.253–7.

———. 1959a. Genetic classification: Retrospect and prospect. AnL 1/2.50–66.

———. 1959b. Myth and tale titles of the Lower Chinook. JAF 72.139–45.

———. 1960a. Lexicostatistics so far. CAnthr 1.3–44.

———. 1960b. More on lexicostatistics. CAnthr 1.338–45.

———. 1961. On typology of cognitive styles in languages (with examples from Chinookan). AnL 3/1.22–54.

———. 1964a. Evidence for Penutian in lexical sets with initial *c- and *s-. IJAL 30.213–42.

———. 1964b. 'Hail' and 'bead': Two Penutian etymologies. Studies in Californian linguistics, ed. by William Bright. UCPL 34.94–8.

———, ed. 1964c. Language in culture and society. New York, Harper and Row.

———. 1965a. The methods and tasks of anthropological philology (illustrated with Clackamas Chinook). RomPh 19.325–40.

———. 1965b. On the relationship of Tsimshian and Chinookan. Paper presented at the 4th CAIL, Denver.

———. 1965c. Some Northwest Coast poems: A problem in anthropological philology. AmA 67.316–41.

———. 1966a. Some points of Siuslaw phonology. IJAL 32.328–42.

———. 1966b. Two types of linguistic relativity. Socio-linguistics, ed. by William Bright, pp. 114–67. The Hague, Mouton.

———. 1968. The 'wife' who 'goes out' like a man: Re-analysis of a Clackamas Chinook myth. SocSciI 7/3.173–99.

———. 1969. On personal pronouns: 'Fourth' person and phonesthematic aspects. (mimeo.)

HYMES, VIRGINIA DOSCH. 1955. Athapaskan numeral systems. IJAL 21.26–45.

JACOBS, ELIZABETH D. 1959. Nehalem Tillamook tales, ed. by Melville Jacobs. University of Oregon Monographs, Studies in Anthropology 5. Eugene.
——. 1968. A Chetco Athabaskan myth text from southwestern Oregon. IJAL 34.192–3.
JACOBS, MELVILLE. 1929. Northwest Sahaptin texts. UWPA 2/6.174–244.
——. 1931. A sketch of Northern Sahaptin grammar. UWPA 4/2.85–292.
——. 1932a. Northern Sahaptin kinship terms. AmA 34.688–93.
——. 1932b. Notes on the structure of Chinook jargon. Lg 8.27–50.
——. 1934–37. Northwest Sahaptin texts. 2 vols. CUCA 19.
——. 1936a. Review of M.J. Andrade 1931. AmA 38.314–15.
——. 1936b. Texts in Chinook jargon. UWPA 7/1.1–32.
——. 1937. Historic perspectives in Indian languages of Oregon and Washington. PNQ 28.55–74.
——. 1939. Coos narrative and ethnologic texts. UWPA 8/1.1–126.
——. 1940. Coos myth texts. UWPA 8/2.127–260.
——. 1941. Survey of Pacific Northwest anthropological research, 1930–1940. PNQ 32.79–106.
——. 1945. Kalapuya texts. UWPA 11.
——. 1952. Psychological inferences from a Chinook myth. JAF 65.121–37.
——. 1954. The areal spread of sound features in the languages north of California. Papers from the Symposium on American Indian Linguistics. UCPL 10.46–56.
——. 1955. A few observations on the world view of the Clackamas Chinook Indians. JAF 68.283–9.
——. 1957. Titles in an oral literature. JAF 70.157–72.
——. 1958. Clackamas Chinook texts, Part 1. RCAFL-P 8.
——. 1959a. The anthropology of Franz Boas: Folklore. AAA-M 89.119–38.
——. 1959b. Clackamas Chinook texts, part 2. RCAFL-P 11.
——. 1959c. The content and style of an oral literature: Clackamas Chinook myths and tales. Chicago, University of Chicago Press. [Also VFPA 26.]
——. 1960a. The people are coming soon; analyses of Clackamas Chinook myths and tales. Seattle, University of Washington Press.
——. 1960b. Thoughts on methodology for comprehension of an oral literature. Selected papers of the Fifth International Congress of Anthropological and Ethnological Sciences, ed. under chairmanship of Anthony F.C. Wallace, pp. 123–29. Philadelphia, University of Pennsylvania Press.
——. 1962. The fate of Indian oral literatures in Oregon. Northwest Review 5.90–9.
——. 1968. An historical event text from a Galice Athabaskan in southwestern Oregon. IJAL 34.183–91.
——. 1970. Resources in Kalapuyan languages. IJAL 36.67.
JACOBSEN, WILLIAM H., JR. 1967. Notes on Makah neologisms. Paper presented at the 20th Northwest Anthropological Conference, Seattle.
——. 1968a. On the prehistory of Nez Perce vowel harmony. Lg 44.819–29.

——. 1968b. Traces of glottalized resonants in Makah. Paper presented at the annual meeting of the Linguistic Society of America, New York.
—— 1969a. Labialization in Nootkan. Paper presented at the 4th ICSL, Victoria.
——. 1969b. Origin of the Nootka pharyngeals. IJAL 35.125–53.
JORGENSEN, JOSEPH G. 1969. Salish language and culture. A statistical analysis of internal relationships, history, and evolution. IUP-LSM 3.
KAVA, TIIU. 1969. A phonology of Cowichan. University of Victoria M.A. thesis.
KINKADE, M. DALE. 1963–64. Phonology and morphology of Upper Chehalis. IJAL 29.181–95, 345–56; 30.32–61, 251–60.
——. 1966. Vowel alternation in Upper Chehalis. IJAL 32.343–9.
——. 1967a. Deictics in Columbian: A work paper. Paper presented at the 2nd ICSL, Seattle.
——. 1967b. On the identification of the Methows (Salish). IJAL 33.193–7.
——. 1967c. Prefix-suffix constructions in Upper Chehalis. AnL 9/2.1–4.
——. 1967d. Uvular-pharyngeal resonants in Interior Salish. IJAL 33.228–34.
——. 1969a. Lexical suffixes in Mosan languages. Paper presented at the 8th CAIL, New Orleans.
——. 1969b. Review of Aert H. Kuipers 1967b. Lingua 22.293–300.
KINKADE, M. DALE, and CLARENCE SLOAT. 1972. Proto-Interior Salish vowels. IJAL 38.26–48.
KIPARSKY, PAUL. 1968. How abstract is phonology? Publications of the Indiana University Linguistic Club. Bloomington.
KLOKEID, TERRY J. 1968. Linguistic acculturation in Nitinat. Paper presented at 3rd ICSL, Victoria.
——. 1969. Notes on the comparison of Wakashan and Salish. UH WPL 1/7.1–19.
KOTSCHAR, VINCENT F. 1951. Tribal and linguistic map of Vancouver Island and adjacent territory. Fighting with property, by Helen Codere (end map). AES-M 18.
KROEBER, A.L. 1955. Linguistic time depth results so far and their meaning. IJAL 21.91–104.
KRUEGER, JOHN R. 1960. Miscellanea Selica I: A Flathead supplement to Vogt's Salishan studies. AnL 2/7.33–8.
——. 1961a. Miscellanea Selica II: Some kinship terms of the Flathead Salish. AnL 3/2.11–18.
——. 1961b. Miscellanea Selica III: Flathead animal names and anatomical terms. AnL 3/9.43–52.
——. 1967a. Miscellanea Selica IV: An interim Moses' Columbia (Wenatchee) Salishan vocabulary. AnL 9/2.5–11.
——. 1967b. Miscellanea Selica V: English–Salishan index and finder list. AnL 9/2.12–25.

KUIPERS, AERT H. 1967a. On divergence, interaction and merging of Salish language communities. Paper presented at 2nd ICSL, Seattle.
——. 1967b. The Squamish language: Grammar, texts, dictionary. JanL, series practica 73.
——. 1968a. The categories verb-noun and transitive-intransitive in English and Squamish. Lingua 21.610–26.
——. 1968b. Unique types and typological universals. Pratidanam (F.B.J. Kuiper Festschrift), pp. 68–88. The Hague, Mouton.
——. 1969. The Squamish language: Grammar, texts, dictionary, part 2. JanL, series practica 73/2.
——. 1970a. Shuswap transitive verbs. Paper presented at 5th ICSL, Spokane.
——. 1970b. Towards a Salish etymological dictionary. Lingua 26.46–72.
LANDAR, HERBERT J. 1961. Reduplication and morphology. Lg 37.239–46.
LEMERT, EDWIN M. 1952. Stuttering among the North Pacific coastal Indians. SJA 8.429–41.
LESSA, WILLIAM A. 1960. Review of Melville Jacobs 1959c. IJAL 26.161–2.
LISKER, LEIGH. 1946. Review of Melville Jacobs 1945. IJAL 12.178.
LORIOT, JAMES. 1964. A selected bibliography of comparative American Indian Linguistics. IJAL 30.62–80.
MCILWRAITH, THOMAS F. 1948. The Bella Coola Indians. Toronto, University of Toronto Press.
MCQUOWN, NORMAN. 1955. Review of Papers from the Symposium on American Indian Linguistics (UCPL 10.1–68). IJAL 21.73–7.
MENGARINI, P. GREGORIO, S.J. 1861. Grammatica linguae selicae. Library of American Linguistics 2. New York, Cramoisey Press.
MERRIAM, ALAN P. 1967. Ethnomusicology of the Flathead Indians. Chicago, Aldine. [Also VFPA 44.]
MITCHELL, MARJORIE R. 1968. A dictionary of Songish, a dialect of Straits Salish. University of Victoria M.A. thesis.
MODROW, RUTH. 1967. Introduction to the Quinault language. Taholah, The Quinault Tribe (ditto).
MURDOCK, GEORGE P. 1960. Ethnographic bibliography of North America. 3rd ed. New Haven, Human Relations Area Files.
NEWBERRY LIBRARY, Chicago. 1961. Catalog of the Edward E. Ayer collection of Americana and American Indians. 8 vols. Boston, G.K. Hall.
NEWMAN, STANLEY. 1947. Bella Coola I: phonology. IJAL 13.129–34.
——. 1950. Review of Franz Boas 1947. IJAL 16.99–101.
——. 1951. Review of Marian W. Smith, ed., 1949. IJAL 17.56–7.
——. 1968. A comparative study of Salish lexical suffixes. Paper presented at 3rd ICSL, Victoria.
——. 1969a. Bella Coola grammatical processes and form classes. IJAL 35.175–9.
——. 1969b. Bella Coola paradigms. IJAL 35.299–306.

NICHOLS, JOHANNA. 1971. Diminutive consonant symbolism in western North America. Lg 47.826–48.

O'BRIEN, MICHAEL. 1967. A phonology of Methow. Paper presented at 2nd ICSL, Seattle.

OLSON, RONALD L. 1936. The Quinault Indians. UWPA 6/1.1–194.

OREGON HISTORICAL SOCIETY. 1958. Indian tribes and languages of the old Oregon country (map). Data compiled by Claude Schaeffer, Curator. Portland, Oregon Historical Society.

PHINNEY, ARCHIE. 1934. Nez Percé texts. CUCA 25.

PIDGEON, MICHAEL. 1970. Lexical suffixes in Saanich, a dialect of Straits Coast Salish. University of Victoria M.A. thesis.

PIERCE, JOE E. 1957a. A statistical study of consonants in New World languages. IJAL 23.36–45, 94–108.

——. 1957b. A statistical study of New World languages. Indiana University Ph.D. dissertation.

——. 1962. Possible electronic computation of typological indices for linguistic structures. IJAL 28.215–26.

——. 1963. A statistical study of grammar and lexicon in Turkish and Sahaptin (Klikitat). IJAL 29.96–106.

——. 1965a. Computer analysis of Alsea. IJAL 31.128–31.

——. 1965b. The field situation in Oregon: 1964. CJL 10.120–8.

——. 1965c. Hanis and Miluk: Dialects or unrelated languages. IJAL 31.323–5.

——. 1966. Genetic comparisons and Hanis, Miluk, Alsea, Siuslaw, and Takelma. IJAL 32.379–87.

PIERCE, JOE E., and JAMES M. RYHERD. 1964. The status of Athapaskan research in Oregon. IJAL 30.137–43.

PILLING, JAMES C. 1885. Proof sheets of a bibliography of the languages of the North American Indians. BAE Miscellaneous Publication No. 2. [Photographic facsimile by Central Book Co., Inc., Brooklyn, N.Y., 1967.]

——. 1893a. Bibliography of the Chinookan languages. BAE-B 15.

——. 1893b. Bibliography of the Salishan languages. BAE-B 16.

——. 1894. Bibliography of the Wakashan languages. BAE-B 19.

PINNOW, HEINZ-JÜRGEN. 1969. Entlehnungen von Tiernamen im Tsimshian und Na-Dene sowie Grundsätzliches zur Entlehnungsfrage bei Indianersprachen. ZEthn 94.82–102.

POWELL, J.V. 1971. Quileute deixis — a study of grammatical markedness. SAS-P 11.91–109.

POWELL, J.V., WILLIAM PENN, and others. (in press). Place names of the Quileute Indians. PNQ.

POWELL, J.V., and FRED WOODRUFF. 1971. A note on the Quileute entries of *Ethnobotany of Western Washington* (by Erna Gunther). SAS-P 11.110–16.

PRESTON, W.D. 1946. Problems of text attestation in ethnography and linguistics. IJAL 12.173–7.

QUÁY-LEM U EN-CHÓW-MEN. 1958. A collection of hymns and prayers in the Flathead-Kalispel-Spokan Indian language. Worley, Idaho.

RAFFO, YOLANDA ADELA. 1971. Songish aspectual system. SAS-P 11.117–22.

RANSOM, JAY ELLIS. 1945. Notes on Duwamish phonology and morphology. IJAL 11.204–10.

RAY, VERNE F. 1933a. The Sanpoil and Nespelem: Salishan peoples of northeastern Washington. UWPA 5.

——. 1933b. Sanpoil folk tales. JAF 46.129–87.

——. 1936. Native villages and groupings in the Columbia Basin. PNQ 27.99–152.

——. 1938. Lower Chinook ethnographic notes. UWPA 7.29–165.

——. 1939. Cultural relations in the plateau of northwestern America. Publications of the Frederick Webb Hodge Anniversary Publication Fund, Southwest Museum, 8.

——. 1963. Primitive pragmatists: The Modoc Indians of northern California. PAES 38.

RAY, VERNE F., and others. 1938. Tribal distribution in eastern Oregon and adjacent regions. AmA 40.384–415.

REAGAN, ALBERT B. 1935. Some myths of the Hoh and Quillayute Indians. TKAS 38.43–85.

REAGAN, ALBERT B., and L.V.W. WALTERS. 1933. Tales from the Hoh and Quileute. JAF 46.297–346.

REICHARD, GLADYS A. 1938. Coeur d'Alene. HAIL 3.517–707.

——. 1939. Stem-list of the Coeur-d'Alene language. IJAL 10.92–108.

——. 1943. Imagery in an Indian vocabulary. AS 19.96–102.

——. 1945. Composition and symbolism of Coeur d'Alene verb-stems. IJAL 11.47–63.

——. 1947. An analysis of Coeur d'Alene Indian myths. AFS-M 41.1–218.

——. 1958–60. A comparison of five Salish languages, ed. by Florence M. Voegelin. IJAL 24.293–300; 25.8–15, 90–6, 154–67, 239–53; 26.50–61.

RIGSBY, BRUCE J. 1965a. Continuity and change in Sahaptian vowel systems. IJAL 31.306–11.

——. 1965b. Linguistic relations in the Southern Plateau. University of Oregon Ph.D. dissertation.

——. 1965c. Sahaptin internal relations. Paper presented at 4th CAIL, Denver.

——. 1966. On Cayuse-Molala relatability. IJAL 32.369–78.

——. 1967. Tsimshian comparative vocabularies with notes on Nass-Gitksan systematic phonology. Paper presented at the 2nd ICSL, Seattle.

——. 1969a. Incorporation and the ergative in Nass-Gitksan. Paper presented at the annual meeting of the American Anthropological Association, New Orleans.

——. 1969b. The Waiilatpuan problem: More on Cayuse-Molala relatability. NARN 3.68–146.
——. 1970. A note on Gitksan speech-play. IJAL 36.212–15.
——. (Forthcoming). Some linguistic insights into recent Tsimshian prehistory.
RIGSBY, BRUCE, and MICHAEL SILVERSTEIN. 1969. Nez Perce vowels and Proto-Sahaptian vowel harmony. Lg 45.45–59.
ROBERTS, HELEN H., and MORRIS SWADESH. 1955. Songs of the Nootka Indians of western Vancouver Island. TAPS 45.199–327.
ROBINS, R. H. 1952. Noun and verb in universal grammar. Lg 28.289–98.
RUMBERGER, J. P., JR. 1949. Ethnolinguistic observations based on Kalapuya texts. IJAL 15.158–62.
SAPIR, EDWARD. 1909a. Takelma texts. UPMA-P 2.1–267.
——. 1909b. Wishram texts. PAES 2.
——. 1911. Some aspects of Nootka language and culture. AmA 13.15–28.
——. 1915a. Abnormal types of speech in Nootka. Canada Dept. of Mines, Geological Survey, Memoir 62 [No. 5, Anthropological Series]. Ottawa, Government Printing Bureau. [Reprinted in SWES, 179–96.]
——. 1915b. Noun reduplication in Comox. Canada Department of Mines, Geological Survey, Memoir 63 [No. 6, Anthropological Series]. Ottawa, Government Printing Bureau.
——. 1916. Time perspective in aboriginal American culture: A study in method. Canada Dept. of Mines, Geological Survey, Memoir 70 [No. 13, Anthropological Series]. Ottawa, Government Printing Bureau. [Reprinted in SWES, 389–467.]
——. 1918. Kinship terms of the Kootenay Indians. AmA 20.414–18. Corrigenda 1919: AmA 21.98.
——. 1919. A flood legend of the Nootka Indians. JAF 32.351–5.
——. 1920. Nass River terms of relationship. AmA 22.261–71.
——. 1921. A characteristic Penutian form of stem. IJAL 2.58–67.
——. 1922. The Takelma language of southwestern Oregon. HAIL (BAE-B 40) 2.1–296.
——. 1924–25. The rival whalers, a Nitinat story [Nootka text with translation and grammatical analysis]. IJAL 3.76–102.
——. 1926. A Chinookan phonetic law. IJAL 4.105–10. [Reprinted in SWES, 197–205.]
——. 1929a. Central and North American languages. Encyclopaedia Britannica, 14th ed., 5.138–41. [Reprinted in SWES, 169–78.]
——. 1929b. Nootka baby words. IJAL 5.118–19.
——. 1938. Glottalized continuants in Navaho, Nootka, and Kwakiutl (with a note on Indo-European). Lg 14.248–74. [Reprinted in SWES, 225–50.]
SAPIR, EDWARD, and MORRIS SWADESH. 1939. Nootka texts: Tales and ethnological narratives, with grammatical notes and lexical materials. Philadelphia, Linguistic Society of America.

——. 1953. Coos-Takelma-Penutian comparisons. IJAL 19.132-7.
——. 1955. Native accounts of Nootka ethnography. RCAFL-P 1.
SHERZER, JOEL F. 1968. An areal-typological study of the American Indian languages north of Mexico. University of Pennsylvania Ph.D. dissertation.
SHIPLEY, WILLIAM F. 1965. The present scope and limits of Penutian. Paper presented at 4th CAIL, Denver.
——. 1966. The relation of Klamath to California Penutian. Lg 42.489-98.
——. 1969. Proto-Takelman. IJAL 35.226-30.
——. 1970. Proto-Kalapuyan. Languages and cultures of western North America: Essays in honor of Sven S. Liljeblad, ed. by Earl H. Swanson, Jr., pp. 97-106. Pocatello, Idaho State University Press.
SILVERSTEIN, MICHAEL. 1965a. Coos and Siuslaw: The relevance of subgrouping in Sapir's Penutian. HU AIL 2.
——. 1965b. Penutian: The grammatical dimensions of Sapir's hypothesis. (Harvard University Bachelor's Honors Thesis.) HU AIL 2.
——. 1966. An approach to comparative Penutian. Paper presented at 5th CAIL, Pittsburgh.
——. 1967. On the validity of subgrouping in Penutian. Paper presented at 6th CAIL, Washington.
——. 1969a. Chinook verb 'thematization' and underlying ergativity. Paper presented at the 8th CAIL, New Orleans.
——. 1969b. Tsimshian and Penutian possessives. Paper presented at the annual meeting of the American Anthropological Association, New Orleans.
——. 1970. Chinook jargon: Language contact and the problem of multi-level generative systems. Paper presented at the 5th ICSL, Spokane.
SLOAT, CLARENCE. 1966. Phonological redundancy rules in Coeur d'Alene, University of Washington Ph.D. dissertation.
——. 1968. A skeleton key to Reichard's Coeur d'Alene transcriptions. AnL 10/5.8-11.
——. 1971. The phonetics and phonology of Coeur d'Alene /r/. SAS-P 11.123-37.
——. 1972. Vowel harmony in Coeur d'Alene. IJAL 38.234-39.
SMITH, ALLAN H. 1953. The Indians of Washington. WSU RS 21.85-113.
SMITH, MARIAN W. 1940. The Puyallup-Nisqually. CUCA 32.
——, ed. 1949. Indians of the urban Northwest. CUCA 36.
——. 1956. The cultural development of the Northwest Coast. SJA 12.272-94.
SNOW, CHARLES T. 1969. A Lower Chehalis phonology. University of Kansas M.A. thesis.
SNYDER, SALLY. 1964. Skagit society and its existential basis: An ethnofolkloristic reconstruction. University of Washington Ph.D. dissertation.
SNYDER, WARREN A. 1968a. Southern Puget Sound Salish: Phonology and morphology. SAS-P 8.

——. 1968b. Southern Puget Sound Salish: Texts, place names and dictionary. SAS-P 9.
SPIER, LESLIE. 1930. Klamath ethnography. UCPAAE 30.
——. 1936. Tribal distribution in Washington. General Series in Anthropology 3. Menasha, Banta.
——. 1958. Bibliography of Edward Sapir. SWES 601–14.
SPIER, LESLIE, and EDWARD SAPIR. 1930. Wishram ethnography. UWPA 3/3.
STERN, THEODORE. 1953. The trickster in Klamath mythology. WF 12.158–74.
——. 1956. Some sources of variability in Klamath mythology. JAF 69.1–12, 135–46, 377–86.
——. 1965. The Klamath tribe. AES-M 41.
STEWART, JOSEPH L. 1960. The problem of stuttering in certain North American Indian societies. JSHD Monograph Supp. 6.
SUTTLES, WAYNE. 1951. Early diffusion of the potato among the Coast Salish. SJA 7.272–88.
——. 1954. Post-contact culture change among the Lummi Indians. British Columbia Historical Quarterly 18.29–102.
——. 1957. The 'Middle Fraser' and 'Foothill' cultures: A criticism. SJA 13.156–83.
——. 1965a. Linguistic means for anthropological ends on the Northwest coast. CJL 10.156–66.
——. 1965b. Multiple phonologic correspondences in two adjacent Salish languages and their implications. Paper presented at the 18th Northwest Anthropological Conference, Bellingham.
SUTTLES, WAYNE, and WILLIAM W. ELMENDORF. 1963. Linguistic evidence for Salish prehistory. Symposium on language and culture: Proceedings of the 1962 Annual Spring Meeting of the American Ethnological Society, pp. 41–52.
SWADESH, MORRIS. 1933. The internal economy of the Nootka word. Yale University Ph.D. dissertation.
——. 1934. Review of M. J. Andrade 1933. IJAL 8.219–20.
——. 1936. Review of Melville Jacobs 1934–37, part 1. PNQ 27.179–80.
——. 1939. Nootka internal syntax. IJAL 9.77–102.
——. 1948a. A structural trend in Nootka. Word 4.106–19.
——. 1948b. Review of Franz Boas 1947. Word 4.58–63.
——. 1949. The linguistic approach to Salish prehistory. Indians of the urban Northwest, ed. by Marian W. Smith, pp. 161–73. CUCA 36.
——. 1950. Salish internal relationships. IJAL 16.157–67.
——. 1952. Salish phonologic geography. Lg 28.232–48.
——. 1953a. Mosan I: A problem of remote common origin. IJAL 19.26–44.
——. 1953b. Mosan II: Comparative vocabulary. IJAL 19.223–36.
——. 1953c. Salish-Wakashan lexical comparisons noted by Boas. IJAL 19.290–1.

———. 1954. On the Penutian vocabulary survey. IJAL 20.123–33.
———. 1955. Chemakum lexicon compared with Quileute. IJAL 21.60–72.
———. 1956. Problems of long-range comparison in Penutian. Lg 32.17–41.
———. 1960. On the unit of translation. AnL 2/2.39–42.
———. 1962. Linguistic relations across Bering Strait. AmA 64.1262–91.
———. 1964a. Comparative Penutian glosses of Sapir. Studies in Californian Linguistics, ed. by William Bright. UCPL 34.182–91.
———. 1964b. Linguistic overview. Prehistoric man in the New World, ed. by Jesse D. Jennings and Edward Norbeck, pp. 527–56. Chicago, University of Chicago Press.
———. 1965. Kalapuya and Takelma. IJAL 31.237–40.
SWANTON, JOHN R. 1900. Morphology of the Chinook verb. AmA (n.s.) 2.199–237.
SWARTZ, B.K., JR. 1967. A bibliography of Klamath Basin anthropology, with excerpts and annotations (revised edition). NARN 1/2.
TAYLOR, HERBERT C., and WILSON DUFF. 1956. A post-contact southward movement of the Kwakiutl. WSU RS 24.56–66.
TEIT, JAMES A. 1928. The ethnobotany of the Thompson Indians, ed. by Elsie Viault Steedman. BAE-R 45.441-522.
THOMPSON, LAURENCE C. 1965. More on comparative Salish. Paper presented at 4th CAIL, Denver.
———. 1969. Review of Aert H. Kuipers 1967b. AmA 71.138–9.
———. 1972. Un cas de métaphonie en lummi. Langues et technique, nature et société, ed. by Jacqueline M.C. Thomas and Lucien Bernot; vol. 1, Approche linguistique, pp. 257–60. Paris, Klincksieck.
THOMPSON, LAURENCE C., and M. TERRY THOMPSON. 1966. A fresh look at Tillamook phonology. IJAL 32.313–9.
———. 1969a. Language universals, nasals, and the Northwest Coast. UH WPL 1/11. 1–36.
———. 1969b. Metathesis as a grammatical device. IJAL 35.213–9.
———. 1971. Clallam: A preview. Studies in American Indian languages, ed. by Jesse Sawyer. UCPL 65.251–94.
TURNEY-HIGH, HARRY H. 1937. The Flathead Indians of Montana. AAA-M 48.
———. 1941. Ethnography of the Kutenai. AAA-M 56.
TWEDDELL, COLIN ELLIDGE. 1950. The Snoqualmie-Duwamish dialects of Puget Sound Coast Salish. UWPA 12.
VELTEN, HARRY V. 1943. The Nez Perce verb. PNQ 34.271–92.
VOEGELIN, C.F. 1946. Notes on Klamath-Modoc and Achumawi dialects. IJAL 12.96–101.
VOEGELIN, C.F., and F.M. VOEGELIN. 1964. Languages of the world: Native America, fascicle one. AnL 6/6.
———. 1965. Languages of the world: Native America, fascicle two. AnL 7/7(1).

VOGT, HANS. 1940a. The Kalispel language. Oslo, Det Norske Videnskaps-Akademi.

——. 1940b. Salishan studies: Comparative notes on Kalispel, Spokan, Colville, and Coeur d'Alene. (Skrifter utgitt av Det Norske Videnskaps-Akademi, II, Hist.-Filos. Klasse No. 2.) Oslo.

WEISEL, GEORGE F. 1952. Animal names, anatomical terms and some ethnozoology of the Flathead Indians. Journal of the Washington Academy of Sciences 42.345-55.

ZIMMER, KARL E. 1967. A note on vowel harmony. IJAL 33.166-71.

ZWICKY, ARNOLD M. 1970. More on Nez Perce: An alternative analysis. OSU WPL 4.115-26.

# CALIFORNIA

## WILLIAM SHIPLEY

### INTRODUCTION

The place now called 'California' was, in aboriginal times, one of the most diverse speech areas in the world. For many thousands of years its peaceful inhabitants, living mostly in villages near water courses or in high mountain meadows, maintained an ancient linguistic particularism. Often, two groups living in adjacent valleys spoke languages which were, so far as we know, totally unrelated. It is impossible for us ever to know precisely what the situation was in pre-Spanish times; the number of Chumash languages, for example, may have been five or seven or nine — some dwellers in the old Chumash hinterland vanished with no trace of their speech left behind.

A rough-and-ready tabulation based on what we do know of the old days results in a count of about seventy-five languages for the area, including such languages as Modoc and Washo, which spill over into Oregon and Nevada respectively. Perhaps there were a dozen more.

Since the nineteenth century linguists and anthropologists have been attracted to this feast. The earliest researcher on Californian languages was the Spanish priest, Father Felipe Arroyo de la Cuesta (1780–1840), who spent twenty-five years at Mission San Juan Bautista. In addition to doing extensive work on Mutsun, the Costanoan language of the region, he collected materials on various other languages in the central coastal region of California, notably Esselen and the Northern Costanoan languages around San Francisco Bay.

Later work may be divided into three great periods of linguistic research. In the latter part of last century, there was a period of preliminary exploration and data collecting, dominated by such scholars as J. Buschmann, Jeremiah Curtin, Albert Gatschet and Pliny Goddard. Much information of variable value was also collected by amateurs in those years. With the turn of the century, A. L. Kroeber arrived at the University of California to initiate a second phase of the research, concentrating on the difficult and virtually untouched problems of identifying deeper historical relationships. Over a period of some twenty years the work of Kroeber, R. B. Dixon, Edward Sapir and others brought vast insights into the tangle of genetic relations among the California languages.

The third period only got under way after a thirty year hiatus. This phase, from about 1950 on, was essentially set into motion by the Survey of California Indian Languagues, based at Berkeley under the direction of Mary R. Haas. Haas' incredible capacity to attract and stimulate students has resulted in a spate of new, precise and sophisticated data on virtually every extant Californian language. This, of course, has brought about a new interest in genetic questions, not only among Haas' students but also among other scholars like Madison Beeler, Dell Hymes and Stanley Newman. This third phase continues today with undiminished vigor and shows every sign of leading eventually to really subtle insights and to a clearer understanding of the genetic relationships among the languages of old California.

## EARLY CLASSIFICATIONS

The very large amount of invaluable research carried on in the nineteenth century by such workers as Gallatin, Latham, Powers and Gatschet was summarized most elegantly by J.W. Powell in his now famous classification of the North American Indian languages north of Mexico (Powell 1891:12–25). We may thus conveniently take his monograph as a starting point for examining the successively more inclusive proposals made up until Edward Sapir's publication of his six superstocks (Sapir 1929).

Of the 58 families in Powell's classification 22 were wholly or partly in California. These are:

1. Athabaskan.
    (A northern group in Alaska and Canada).
    (A southern group in the Southwest)
    Pacific group (A few Oregon languages)
    Hupa
    Kenesti = Wailakki [Wailaki][1]
    Saia
2. Chimarikan.[2]
    Chimálakwe
    Chimariko
3. Chumashan.
    San Buenaventura [Ventureño]
    Santa Barbara [Barbareño]
    Santa Inez [Inezeño]

---

[1] Where relevant, names in current usage will be supplied in square brackets. Many of Powell's language and family names have fallen partly or entirely into disuse.

[2] 'Although a study of these [Chimariko] vocabularies reveals a number of words having correspondences with the Kulanapan [Pomo] equivalents, yet the greater number show no affinities with the dialects of the latter family, or indeed with any other' (Powell 1891:63). Thus Powell adumbrated a fragment of Hokan.

Purísima
San Luis Obispo [Obispeño]
Santa Rosa Island
Santa Cruz Island
4. Copehan [+ Nomlaki = Wintun].
Patwin
Wintu
5. Costanoan.[3]
Five groups are mentioned, apparently village names, all in the vicinity of Mission Dolores, i.e. in or near modern San Francisco. They probably all spoke the the same language. The names are: Ahwaste, Ohlon, Romonan, Tulomo, and Altatmo. Curiously enough, no mention is made of any of the other Costanoan languages to the south or east.
6. Esselenian.
Esselen
7. Kulanapan [Pomo].
A list of 30 'tribes' is given with no identification as to language.
8. Lutuamian [Klamath–Modoc].
9. Mariposan [Yokutsan].
24 'tribes' are listed, some of which (e.g. Chukchansi, Tachi, Wikchumni) correspond to presently known dialect names.
10. Moquelumnan [Miwokan].
No languages are identified; 35 'tribal' names are listed.
11. Palaihnihan [Achomawi (+Atsugewi?)].[4]
Of the 8 'tribes' listed, one — Achomawi — corresponds to a presently-used language name.
12. Pujunan [Maiduan].
Most of the 26 names listed are identifiable as village names. No languages are identified.
13. Quoratean [Karok].
The three names mentioned are probably all village names. Bright found no dialect differentiation (Bright 1957:1).
14. Salinan.
San Antonio [Antoniano]
San Miguel [Migueleño]
15. Sastean [Shasta].[5]

---

[3] '... in 1877, Mr. Gatschet, under the family name Mutsun, united Costano dialects with the ones classified by Latham under Moquelumnan [Miwokan] ... More recent comparison ... revealed very decided and apparently radical differences between the two groups of dialects ... The result seems fully to justify the separation of the two groups as distinct families' (Powell 1891:70). Another adumbration.

[4] The term 'Palaihnihan' has been revived by Olmsted in recent years (Olmsted 1964).

[5] Powell quotes Gatschet: '... ultimately it [Palaihnihan] will be found to be linguistically related to the Sastean [Shasta] languages' (Powell 1891:98).

16. Shoshonean.
> (Many non-Californian groups.)
> Chemehuevi
> Pai Ute [Southern Paiute]
> Paviotso
> A group, designated Tobikhar, at Mission Agency, California, probably subsuming all the other Uto-Aztecan groups of Southern California.

17. Washoan.
> Designated as a single language, i.e. Washo.

18. Weitspekan [Yurok].
19. Wishoskan [Wiyot].
20. Yanan.
21. Yukian.
> The family is respresented as consisting of a single language. The five groups or 'tribes' named do not correspond to any language names in current use.

22. Yuman.
> (Several groups in Arizona and lower California)
> Diegueño
> Mohave (partly in Arizona)
> Yuma (partly in Arizona)

Twelve years later Dixon collaborated with Kroeber on what was essentially a typological examination of the California languages (Dixon and Kroeber 1903). Insofar as it was possible, the presence or absence of the following grammatical features was noted: pronominal incorporation; syntactic cases; locative and instrumentals; noun plurals; noun duals; noun gender; sex differences in usage; number of deictics. In spite of poor data and of the relative grossness of the categories, there was a clear tendency for (what later would be called) Penutian, Uto-Aztecan, Yukian and sometimes Pomo to cluster as over against Hokan, with the Northwestern languages forming a third group.

The first combinatory revision of Powell's classification was made by Dixon. Two new dialects of Shasta had been discovered — Okwanuchu and New River — as well as a separate Shastan language, Konomihu. Dixon proposed that these Shastan groups be combined with Palaihnihan to form a new stock which he called Shasta-Achomawi (Dixon 1905). A few years later, Chimariko was tentatively proposed as an addition to the group which, thus redefined, was called Shastan (Dixon 1910).

In that same year Kroeber cautiously reintroduced the proposal of a genetic link between Miwok and Costanoan (Kroeber 1910). This proposal had been made much earlier by Latham (1856). Although Kroeber considered the possibility of accounting for lexical similarities as entirely diffused, he really believed Miwok and Costanoan to be related.

This earlier mood of over-cautiousness gave way to an exhaustive examination of the data during the next few years leading to a much bolder and more comprehensive grouping of the California languages (Dixon and Kroeber 1913). Lexical and formal comparisons were made; the following new families were proposed:

1. Penutian.

   The name is based on the words for *two* in Maidu and Costanoan.[6] The diagnostic structural attributes for the family (never found all together in any single language) were: (a) vowel gradation; (b) no prefixes; (c) noun cases — object, possessive, instrumental, locative, ablative, terminative [allative] and comitative. Curiously enough, no subject case was postulated, though all the languages have one; (d) 'Indo-Germanic' type verbs, expressing voice, mode, tense, person, etc. The Penutian family included Wintun, Maiduan, Yokutsan, Miwokan and Costanoan.

2. Hokan.

   This name was also derived from the word for *two* in some of the relevant languages.[7] The diagnostic features for the family were: (a) no noun plurals for most nouns; (b) some suppletive verb stems for singular and plural; (c) pluralizing verb suffixes; (d) locative verb suffixes; (e) instrumental prefixes; and (f) pronominal prefixes. The Hokan family subsumed Karok, Shasta, Chimariko, Achumawi-Atsugewi, Pomo, Yana, Esselen and Yuman.

3. Iskoman.

   The name comes from the Chumash word for *two*.[8] Although the connection to Hokan was postulated, this separate group was nevertheless set up. Twelve lexical comparisons were given in evidence. The Iskoman family contained Chumash and Salinan.

4. Ritwan.

   This name is from the Wiyot word for *two*.[9] The family was postulated on the basis of 48 lexical comparisons, though Kroeber had taken note of structural similarities between Yurok and Wiyot (the only two languages in the group) a couple of years earlier (Kroeber 1911).

In addition to these new families, Athapaskan, Lutuamian, Shoshonean, Yukian and Washo were retained intact from the Powell classification.

During this same period Sapir made the dramatic and fascinating discovery that the Ritwan languages were related to Algonkian (Sapir 1913). His evidence was copious and varied, including lexical, phonological and grammatical comparisons. Though he deferred decision on subgrouping, he suggested the inclusion of Wiyot-Yurok in Algonkian proper.

---

[6] The modern reconstructions for these forms are: Proto-Maiduan *pé·n* 'two' (Ultan 1964) and Proto-Costanoan *utxi* 'two' (based on unpublished research carried out by Richard Levy at the University of California, Santa Cruz).

[7] The actual forms from which the term was derived are unidentified; cf. Karok *ʔaxak* (Bright 1957: 445), Yana *ux(si)-* (Sapir and Swadesh 1960:256), Achumawi *haʔaq* (Olmsted 1966:132), Atsugewi *hoqi* (Olmsted 1959:639). Shasta *xukʔwa* (Shirley Silver, unpublished notes). The Atsugewi and Shasta forms appear to be the likeliest candidates for Dixon and Kroeber's original sources.

[8] A Chumash prototype is quoted from a J.P. Harrington manuscript, published by M.S. Beeler. The form is Ventureño: *piskoʔm* 'two' (Beeler 1964).

[9] Wiyot *dit-* 'be two' (Teeter 1964a:91). The /d/ is an apico-dental voiced flap (Teeter 1964a:14).

Sapir's postulation was vigorously challenged by Truman Michelson (1914), to whom Sapir replied in the following year (Sapir 1915).[10] The issue stood unresolved for 43 years, though Sapir did lend further credence to his theory with the publication of an article comparing Ritwan and Algonkian kinship terms (Sapir 1923).

By 1919, Dixon and Kroeber had taken further combinatory steps by bringing Iskoman and Washo[11] into Hokan, thus bringing the postulated genetic situation for

TABLE 1

| Powell 1891 | Dixon 1903 | Dixon and Kroeber 1910 | 1913 | 1919 | Sapir Superstock 1929 |
|---|---|---|---|---|---|
| 1. Sastean | Shasta- Achomawi | Chimariko- Shastan (Dixon) | | | |
| 2. Palaihnihan | | | | | |
| 3. Chimarikan | | | | | |
| 4. Kulanapan | | | Hokan | | |
| 5. Quoratean | | | | | |
| 6. Yanan | | | | Hokan | Hokan-Siouan |
| 7. Esselenian | | | | | |
| 8. Yuman | | | | | |
| 9. Salinan | | | Iskoman | | |
| 10. Chumashan | | | | | |
| 11. Washoan | | | | | |
| 12. Yukian | | | | | |
| 13. Moquelumnan | | Miwok-Costanoan (Kroeber) | | | |
| 14. Costanoan | | | | | |
| 15. Mariposan | | | | Penutian | Penutian |
| 16. Pujunan | | | | | |
| 17. Copehan | | | | | |
| 18. Lutuamian | | | | | |
| 19. Weitspekan | | | Ritwan | | Algonkian-Wakashan |
| 20. Wishoskan | | | | | |
| 21. Shoshonean | | | | | Uto-Aztekan |
| 22. Athabaskan | | | | | Na-Déné |

*Summary of Early Classifications*

[10] In the same issue of the *American Anthropologist* there was a further rejoinder by Michelson (1915) and an epilogue by Sapir.
[11] This was done as the result of Sapir's evidence (Sapir 1917b).

California proper more or less to the state in which it has remained since (Dixon and Kroeber 1919).[12]

Mention must be made of Radin's paper postulating a genetic relationship among all the North American languages (Radin 1919).

The penultimate combinatory step was taken by Sapir in 1921 when he published an early version of his six super-stock classification (Sapir 1921b). The more famous version, published eight years later, actually differs in only one detail from the earlier one — but, for California, that detail is most important. It involves the inclusion of Lutuamian, Waiilatpuan and Sahaptian in the Penutian superstock. Thus, Klamath-Modoc (along with other Oregon languages) was brought into the Penutian fold (Sapir 1929). We may consider this general grouping as the culmination of the early period in Californian genetic research. Sapir's proposed classification, established by 1930, became, for many years, a kind of basic doctrine for anthropologists and linguists engaged in research on aboriginal North America. A summary of the period from 1891 to 1929 is provided in Table 1.

## PENUTIAN

Even before he had made the decision to group the Plateau languages with Penutian, Sapir published a diagnostic for Penutian, i.e. a canonical statement of a characteristic Penutian stem-form (Sapir 1921a). This is, essentially,

$$C \; V_1 \; C \; V_1$$

that is, a disyllabic stem exhibiting total vowel harmony. Examples were given from Takelma, Coos and Siuslaw in Oregon as well as for Wintu, Patwin, Maidu, Yawdanchi Yokuts, Coast Miwok and various Costanoan languages. This seems to have been the last article published by Sapir on the details of the Penutian relationship during his lifetime. We do have, however, some marginal notes of his, published in an article by L. S. Freeland on the possible relationship of Mixe to Penutian (Freeland 1930). These proposals assumed, at least for the argument, that Mixe is a Penutian language. We learn from one of Freeland's footnotes that a connection between Zoque and Penutian had been proposed by Dixon in a letter to Sapir. This seems to have been the origin of Sapir's inclusion of Mixe-Zoque and Huave in his final version of the Penutian superstock.

A decade later, a still wider proposal was made — a Macro-Penutian phylum including Aztec-Tanoan, Mayan, Totonacan, Xincan and Lencan (Mason 1940; Johnson 1940). This vast collocation was primarily due to Benjamin Lee Whorf — at least, according to Mason and to Trager, who made the following (now somewhat incredible) statement (1945):

[12] Mary Haas has written an excellent short history and evaluation of the Dixon-Kroeber contributions to language classification in California (Haas 1964:73-4).

Whorf established, to the satisfaction of those who saw his material, that the grouping of Penutian, Sahaptian, Azteco-Tanoan, Zuni, Kiowa, probably Mayan and Totonac, and possibly Tunican, as stocks constituting a phylum which he called Macro-Penutian, was at least as good as the Algonkian-Mosan, or Na-Déné groupings of Sapir.

It would be most interesting to see Whorf's evidence for this vast collocation. His only published statement on Macro-Penutian is a simple adumbration (Whorf 1935).

Except for Swadesh's work (about which more later), the Macro-Penutian hypothesis marks the broadest proposal ever made for Penutian affiliations. Since that time most of the work in Penutian has concentrated on consolidating and refining our understanding of the details, of augmenting the evidence and of confirming or refuting the various groupings made before 1940.

This trend was resoundingly initiated by Robert Shafer in two closely related articles (1947, 1952). He says:

Setting up such far flung linguistic empires with little or nothing to hold them together except the authority of their builders has gone so far that one of the founders of the original Penutian group, A.L. Kroeber, has protested.[13] It seems preferable to examine in some detail the data in support of the Penutian family proposed by Dixon and Kroeber and establish such phonetic equations as one can for the five languages [sic][14] and many dialects ... Linguists will then have a more substantial basis for deciding *first whether there is such a family*, then *whether they can expand it or not* [italics mine].

Shafer's work was much more disciplined and organized than any earlier efforts. He set up eight velar consonants for which reasonable recurrent correspondences could be found. He also brought together the possible cognates for the famous Penutian case suffixes, thus bringing some consideration of the grammar into the discussion for the first time.

Shafer's main difficulties had to do with paucity of data, clumsy and inaccurate recordings and the lack of a certain 'feel' for the languages. His work was valuable in setting a new direction and in the establishing of a sense of restraint and responsibility toward the genetic problem, at least within the specific context of Penutian studies.

A notable exception to this tendency for consolidation and restraint was the work of Morris Swadesh, the originator of the concepts of glottochronology and lexicostatistics. In the earlier relevant paper Swadesh (1954a) was generally concerned with the hypotheses of a common origin for all of the languages of the New World, submitting as evidence his basic glottochronological wordlist. A couple of years later he focused his attention specifically on Penutian, arguing for the expansion of Whorf's Macro-

---

[13] Kroeber said, in part (1941): 'Rather different has been the effect of another type of classification in which Sapir was the leader in America. These may be called provisional classifications by speculative intuition .... The process is essentially one of ... guessing .... But the dangers of the procedure are obvious; especially as soon as the tenuous working hypotheses begin to be construed as established findings.'

[14] The current view is that there were about thirty languages in the California Penutian group — Maiduan, 3; Wintun, 3; Miwokan, 7; Costanoan 8 or 9; Yokutsan uncertain — perhaps 10 or so.

Penutian group into a huge phylum of languages which he designated as 'Penutioid' (Swadesh 1956). He excluded Aztec-Tanoan, Kiowa and Tunican; thus Penutioid was not simply an expansion of Macro-Penutian, but actually a different theory — the boldest and most far flung collocation with which the 'Penutian' has been associated. There were twenty subgroups, as follows:

1. Coosan
2. Siuslaw
3. Alsea
4. Tsimshian
5. Chinookan
6. Sahaptian, including Klamath-Modoc (Lepitan)
7. Takelman
8. Wintu-Maiduan (Palpenan)
9. Yokutsan
10. Miwok-Costanoan (Utian)
11. Totonacan
12. Mixe-Zoque (Mechan)
13. Huave
14. Mayan
15. Coconucan
16. Paez
17. Cholonan
18. Quechua-Aymará
19. Tarasco
20. Zuni

Only illustrative examples of Swadesh's evidence for Penutioid were published. Phonologically, the criteria used were: symbolic vowel and consonant interchange, consistent traces of vowel harmony, in line with Sapir's earlier formulations (Sapir 1921b), and, of course, resemblant forms based on inspection. Grammatically, the criteria were: reduplication, affixation, similarity of pronominal systems, and the inflectional categories of dual and plural number and case in the substantives, voice and aspect in the verb.

One of the unfortunate things about this whole formulation would seem to be (in the face of no published evidence) that Swadesh's phonological, as well as some of his grammatical, criteria might well be the result of diffusion, typological similarities or mere chance. On his own admission, much of his material was scanty; often, what little structural information he had was gleaned from fortuitous bits of evidence attached to lists of forms quoted in isolation.[15]

---

[15] These objections need not be further elaborated here; the pitfalls and inadequacies of working with scanty, inaccurate or unanalyzed data have been discussed again and again in the literature, e.g. Pitkin and Shipley 1958, Silverstein 1965, Shipley 1966.

Hymes took a skeptical, though essentially positive, view of Penutioid in the course of a discussion of plural and other affixes in Penutian (Hymes 1957). Accepting Sapir's Penutian grouping as very probably correct, he went on to say of Swadesh's Penutioid features: 'Individually none of them is very significant. Collectively, they are not conclusive, but they are significant ... At present the best test possible is to see if the general features to which Swadesh calls attention illuminate particulars in the individual languages.' Hymes then discussed some features in Chinookan which do, indeed, strengthen the hypothesis.

Until the early fifties, only a few detailed grammatical descriptions were published on the California Penutian languages. Such existed for Maidu (Dixon 1911), Central Sierra Miwok (Freeland 1951), Yokuts (Kroeber 1907; Newman 1944) and Mutsun Costanoan (Mason 1916). In addition, for Penutian languages outside California, there were published works on Takelman (Sapir 1922), Coos (Frachtenberg 1922a), Siuslaw (Frachtenberg 1922b), Northern Sahaptin (Jacobs 1931), Chinook (Boas 1911a) and Tsimshian (Boas 1911b).

During the middle fifties and later, a new upsurge of fieldwork in Penutian was getting under way, largely supported by the Survey of California Indian Languages, under the direction of Mary R. Haas. Extensive studies were done on Klamath (M.A.R. Barker), Wintu (Harvey Pitkin), Patwin (Elizabeth Bright, Donald Ultan), Maidu (William Shipley), Konkow (Russell Ultan), Lake Miwok (Catherine Callaghan) and Southern Sierra Miwok (Sylvia Broadbent).

These activities resulted in a spate of new source material. In a single year, three grammars were published: Klamath (Barker 1964), Maidu (Shipley 1964) and Southern Sierra Miwok (Broadbent 1964). There were also new collections of texts: Klamath (Barker 1963a), Maidu (Shipley 1963), and Nisenan (Uldall and Shipley 1966). New dictionaries appeared: Lake Miwok (Callaghan 1965), Central Sierra Miwok (Freeland and Broadbent 1960), Southern Sierra Miwok (Broadbent 1964a), Bodega Miwok (Callaghan 1967), Klamath (Barker 1963b), Maidu (Shipley 1963) and Nisenan (Uldall and Shipley 1966). All this material was the direct result of fieldwork carried on under the auspices of the Survey of California Indian languages except the Nisenan, which was based on data collected by H.J. Uldall in 1930-32. Previously, the only published material on Uldall's extensive work with Nisenan was a description of the phonetics (Uldall 1954).

Various other interesting and valuable contributions were made. Using materials recorded by de la Cuesta in 1821, Beeler (1955, 1959) demonstrated that Saclan, an extinct language once spoken in the area to the west of Mt. Diablo, was not, as Kroeber had earlier surmised, Costanoan but Miwokan, specifically a member of what is now known as the eastern division. Beeler also (1961b) made a study of the senary elements in Penutian number systems. Broadbent (1957) evolved methods of reconstituting the inconsistent and inaccurate recordings of Rumsen made in the nineteenth century by H.W. Henshaw and Alphonse Pinart (Heizer 1952, 1955). The phenomenon of borrowing from (principally) Spanish into the native tongues of

California was investigated by several persons (Bright, W. and E. 1959; Bright 1960; Shipley 1962; Sawyer 1964). Restatements were made of Newman's Yokuts grammar (or parts of it) by Harris (1944), Hockett (1967) and Kuroda (1967). In this same vein, Hamp (1966) made a restatement of certain aspects of Broadbent's Southern Sierra Miwok.

In an important sense, the main line of Penutian research during the last twenty years has been concerned with establishing the internal relationships of the various subfamilies and with validating and defining the scope and limits of the Penutian stock.

The problem of internal relationship has been attacked on several fronts.

For Yokuts, two late publications of Kroeber's have been of great value: first, some northern Yokuts vocabularies, previously unpublished, collected by various persons in the late nineteenth and early twentieth centuries (Kroeber 1959a), and second, the results of his Yokuts dialect survey (published posthumously) giving forms for 304 English glosses in 21 Yokuts dialects, with, of course, some lacunae (Kroeber 1963). Golla (1964a) reconstructed 333 Proto-Yokuts forms by comparing reliable lexical material from Yawelmani (Valley Division, Southern group), Yawdanchi (Foothill Division, Tule-Kaweah group) and Chukchansi (Foothill Division, Northern Foothill group). These three forms of Yokuts are widely separated within the general Yokuts speech area, so that Golla's reconstructions for Yokuts consonants are probably accurate in the main. He did not even attempt to handle the complex vocalization for which Yokuts is so notorious, though nominal vowel reconstructions are made for the (usually) identical vowels found in citation forms for the three languages. A few forms from Tachi, Koyeti and Gashowu are included.

In Utian,[16] much progress has been made. Broadbent and Callaghan (1960) did a segmental reconstruction based on five of the seven known Miwok languages.[17] The subgrouping into Eastern and Western Miwok was firmly established on the basis of interim reconstructions. Two hundred ninety-five (295) lexical sets were examined; 134 tentative Proto-Miwokan lexical reconstructions were made. Later, Callaghan (1962) extended the scope of the study with a comparison of Miwokan with Mutsun; still later (1967) she rounded off this phase of her research with a summary paper on the nature of the Miwok-Costanoan relationship.[18] Beeler (1961a) brought about

---

[16] I now prefer this term to 'Miwok-Costanoan' since recent researches by Richard Levy, a former student of mine, makes it look as if Eastern Miwok — Western Miwok — Costanoan may form a chain, with Western Miwok as close to Costanoan as to Eastern Miwok.

[17] Saclan has long been extinct (Beeler 1955). A speaker of Coast (Bodega) Miwok was discovered by Callaghan, but too late for the 1960 comparative study (Callaghan 1970).

[18] As Callaghan pointed out, J.P. Harrington amassed a great amount of excellent material on Costanoan. Much of this has already been incorporated into current research. Specifically, there are large manuscripts on Chochenyo (East Bay Costanoan), Mutsun and Rumsen. Richard Levy, now a graduate student at the University of British Columbia, did his senior honors thesis in Anthropology at the University of California, Santa Cruz, on Proto-Costanoan, incorporating materials from all available sources including Harrington. I am currently involved (in collaboration with Marc Okrand, now a graduate student in Linguistics at Berkeley) in writing a description and dictionary of Rumsen, based on the Harrington materials.

considerable order by setting up East Bay Costanoan as a subgroup of Northern Costanoan and by establishing Karkin as a third major dialect group, coterminous with Northern and Southern Costanoan.

For Maiduan, a binary survey of the segmental-lexical relationship between Maidu and Nisenan was made by Shipley (1961), followed by a fuller treatment of Proto-Maiduan phonology by Ultan (1964), based on reliable material from all three Maiduan languages. Three hundred seventy-three (373) lexical sets were given, all involving a tentative Proto-Maiduan reconstruction. The special difficulty with Proto-Maiduan phonology is a particularly interesting one: although identity correspondences abound in the lexical correspondences (indeed, there is little else except a few h/ʔ sets and some differences in vowel length), the grammatical structures of Maidu, Konkow and Nisenan are very disparate, particularly in the verb. The current tentative explanation for this is that lexical diffusion and reinforcement have been extensive within the total speech area.

The problem of broad relationships in Penutian generally was reopened, as has been mentioned earlier, by Shafer. Swadesh published a list of resemblant forms noted by Sapir (Sapir and Swadesh 1953) comparing Coos and Takelma on the one hand with various California Penutian forms on the other. Pitkin and Shipley (1958) carried out an exhaustive lexical survey of the California Penutian material then available. Their evidence was assembled in 320 lexical sets, the most numerous and reliable aggregation of such material up to that time (cf. Hymes 1959). A segmental system was tentatively established, though no morphemic sequences were reconstructed. The system was:

```
p   ph   b                    m   w
t   th   d    s   ƛ           n              l   r
c                                 j=[y]
k             x
q
ʔ             h
```

Clearly, the $x$ and $ƛ$ are superfluous, representing reflexes which are positional variants of $k$ ($kh?$) and $r$ respectively.

As a reaction against the very broad proposals for Penutian affinity made by Sapir, Whorf and Swadesh, Pitkin and Shipley returned to the original Dixon-Kroeber hypothesis as the basis for their investigations. The publication of new data on the Oregon languages, notably Klamath (Barker 1963, 1964), along with a growing familiarity with the research resources brought about a retreat from this reactive view. This was focused by Hymes (1964b) in a beautiful discussion of the Penutian hypothesis and problem. There would seem to be little general dissent from his proposed characterization of Penutian research (p. 213):

a) the possibility, and necessity, of working in Penutian at the level of the hypothesis proposed by Sapir;

b) evidence that the hypothesis must be given the status of a fact;

c) projection of the implications of the evidence for the further study of Penutian;

d) introduction of a technical device for handling work at a level approaching, but short of, reconstruction and the starred form.

With regard to (d), there may be some methodological argument (we need not explore this issue here), but the main thrust of Hymes' view — that Sapir's hypothesis is essentially correct — now seems beyond cavil.

A particularly interesting bit of evidence for Sapir's Penutian was proffered by Hymes (1964a) in his discussion of the semantically linked etymologies for Proto-Penutian 'hail' and 'bead'.

Newman (1964), working from his dual control of Yawelmani Yokuts (1944) and Zuni (1958, 1965), brought forth provocative lexical evidence (along with some discussion of structural similarities) in support of a possible distant relationship between Zuni and California Penutian, thus reintroducing, on much firmer ground, a fragment of Swadesh's Penutioid hypothesis. He brought forth 187 lexical sets, including 57 tentative reconstructions.

An entirely different track was taken by Silverstein in his (unpublished) Harvard senior honors thesis (Silverstein 1965). He took as his reference point the structural relations and morphophonemic shapes of pronouns and verbal morphemes in Tsimshian, Coos, Chinook, Takelma and Yokuts. The Tsimshian and Chinook data were taken from Boas (1911a, b) the Coos from Frachtenberg (1922a), the Takelma from Sapir (1922) and the Yokuts from Newman (1944). After summarizing the relevant grammatical material from these five languages, he arrived at a basic sentence pattern:

$$S \rightarrow VP + NP$$

$$VP \rightarrow (PREV+) \begin{cases} Verb_{TR} + NP \\ \\ Verb_{INTR} \end{cases}$$

This describes all the languages he examined (except Takelma) at some level, thus giving a possible fundamental diagnostic for Proto-Penutian structure.[19] A further degree of explicitness is attained: in the terminal string, the grammatical tagging of NPs from left to right (i.e. away from the verb) are subject, object, indirect object, Silverstein's work makes an elegant initiatory contribution to the formal study of Penutian historical grammar. As he correctly pointed out, lexical and grammatical comparisons are complementary, with a certain minimal grammatical sophistication

---

[19] If I understand correctly, the optional PREV should be deleted from Silverstein's basic pattern. It was included because there is, in Chinook, an *obligatory* PREV (Mode?) which Silverstein has tagged as a recent phenomenon. Even if it were not, its *obligatory* presence in Chinook does not imply its *optional* presence in Proto-Penutian.

as prerequisite to any sensible and valid analysis of the phonological-lexical relationships.

Shipley (1966) carried the problem of lexical analysis along by attempting to establish, on the basis of recurrent sound correspondences, the genetic relationship of Klamath to California Penutian.[20] It was taken as demonstrated that the four California subgroups do, indeed, form a genetic kernel; the assumption was made that any language which could be systematically linked to this kernel was Penutian. A tentative heuristic for the consonant system was proposed (elements in parentheses are those for which the evidence is scanty, ambiguous or non-recurrent; inferred segments are in square brackets):[21]

|  |  |  |  |  |  |  |
|---|---|---|---|---|---|---|
| p | [t] | [c]? | k | (kʷ) | q | [ʔ] |
| ph | [th] | [ch]? | [kh] | [kʷh]? | qh | |
| m | n | | | | | |
| | (s) | (ł)? | | | | (h) |
| (w)? | | [y]? | | | | |
| | r | | | | | |
| | (l)? | | | | | |

Current research in California Penutian is proceeding along several important lines. Callaghan is consolidating and reworking the descriptive and genetic materials for Miwok and Miwok-Costanoan.[22] Richard Levy is preparing a monograph on Proto-Costanoan, based on the lately available data from Harrington, and including analyses of both grammar and phonology. Harvey Pitkin is assembling the materials for a comparative Wintun dictionary. William Shipley is writing (with Marc Okrand) a description and dictionary of Rumsen and is also continuing to adduce evidence for the expansion of the Penutian kernel. The time is at hand when a much more detailed linkage with Penutianists working outside the California area — Haruo Aoki, Dell Hymes, Stanley Newman, Bruce Rigsby — will be made, defining the scope and limits of the language family so brilliantly adumbrated by Dixon, Kroeber and Sapir.

## HOKAN

A picture much different from Penutian appears when the history of research on the Hokan family of languages is examined. At least superficially, the nut is a much

---

[20] And thereby, presumably, all of Sahaptian (cf. Aoki 1963).

[21] Working along these same lines, it would now be possible to remove the brackets or parentheses from *kh, h, w* and *l*. The most interesting thing about the chart is the dearth of evidence for the dentals and palatals. Perhaps this is due, at least to some extent, to the depredations of old sound-symbolism systems.

[22] Several new Proto-Miwok reconstructions are to be found in Callaghan's *Bodega Miwok dictionary* (1970).

harder one to crack: the Hokan relationship would seem to lie very deep in time; its erstwhile linkage (by Sapir) with Coahuiltecan and Siouan may have added to the obscurity of the situation.

The identification of Hokan was made, as has been discussed earlier, by Dixon and Kroeber (1913, 1919). However, it is to Sapir that we owe the basic characterization of Hokan which is used, even today, as a springboard for research. In two articles (1917a, 1925), Sapir described the phonological and grammatical attributes of Proto-Hokan as they are reflected in the daughter languages, leading not only to a convincing argument for the reality of the classification but also to the subgrouping which has now become classic.[23] The phonological evidence, presented earlier (1917a) had to do with patterns of initial, medial, and final vowel loss in the various languages. The later morphological evidence (1925) was based on the inferential detection of nominal and verbal prefixes in Proto-Hokan.

Sapir's resultant subgrouping for Hokan was:
1. Northern Hokan
    a) Karok; Chimariko; Shasta-Achomawi
    b) Yana
    c) Pomo
2. Washo
3. Esselen; Yuman
4. Salinan; Chumash; Seri
5. Chontal

At the same time, the Hokan-Siouan superstock was presented. Sapir said of this:

The evidence for this 'Hokan-Siouan' construction is naturally morphological rather than lexical, though the lexical bonds that unite Natchez-Muskogean and Hokan, for instance, are by no means negligible. This evidence will be given in due time. It is of a general rather than specific nature, though specific elements constantly enter into the argument, and can hardly receive its due weight unless one contrasts the underlying 'Hokan-Siouan' features with the markedly different structures that we encounter in Eskimo-Aleut, in Nadene, in Algonkian-Wakashan, and in Penutian.

It can only be regretted that here, as so often elsewhere, Sapir's evidence for the classification was never made public.

Twenty years passed before anything further was published on general comparative Hokan.

Haas (1954) carefully analyzed the evidence for the genetic link between Hokan, Subtiaba-Tlappanec, Coahuiltecan, Gulf and Yuki in terms of a single etymology — the word for 'water'. The reconstructions involved are of great interest for Hokan studies. They are:

---

[23] Though this subgrouping has been strongly challenged in recent years (cf. Bright 1954:67; Olmsted 1956, 1957, 1959; Haas 1963:56-8). Sapir's criteria are never really explicit; they must be inferred from his phonological and morphological discussions.

Proto-Coahuiltecan: *ax
Proto-Subtiaba-Tlappanec: *ixya (< *axyi?)
Proto-Hokan: *axa (Sapir) or *axi
Proto-Gulf: *ak^win
Yuki: uk'

By further reconstruction:

Proto-Hokan-Coahuiltecan: *axi

Then, PHC can be postulated as related to Proto-Gulf with the equation PHC x : PG $k^w$, with the possibility of a more distant connection to Yuki by an equation of the Yuki *u* with the *w* in Proto-Gulf.[24]

Bright (1954) focused on the problem of Northern Hokan relationships — those between Karok, Chimariko, Shasta, Achumawi and Atsugewi. In spite of inadequate data, particularly for Achumawi and Atsugewi, he managed to establish a reasonably symmetrical system of proto-segments. His reservations about the 'Shastan' subgroup of Northern Hokan were further explored in three articles by Olmsted (1956, 1957, 1959) who, after analyzing the stop correspondences for Palaihnihan, Shasta and (for the velars) Karok, concluded that Palaihnihan proper was the only subgroup which could be set up in Northern Hokan on the basis of available evidence.

The latter part of Olmsted's work, i.e. the dorsal series, was much helped, as Hokan research in general has been, by the publication (1957) of Bright's grammar of the Karok language. This work, Halpern's grammar of Yuma (1946–7), and Langdon's grammar of Diegueño (1970b) are the only modern full-scale treatments of Hokan languages available in print. The situation with dictionaries is somewhat better; in addition to the lexicon included in Bright's work on Karok there are published dictionaries of Yana (Sapir and Swadesh 1960) and Achumawi (Olmsted 1966).[25]

A most interesting trend in comparative Hokan research was initiated by Jacobsen (1958). This was the technique of binary comparison, applied by Jacobsen to Washo and Karok, by Silver (1964) to Shasta and Karok, and by McLendon (1964) to Eastern Pomo and Yana.

---

[24] But the Yuki situation is very complex and problematical; cf. the discussion in the section on Yukian which follows.

[25] However, what has been a trickle of published source materials shows every sign of turning into a flood. In the northern group, the extensive field studies of Shasta (Shirley Silver), Washo (William Jacobsen) and Atsugewi (Leonard Talmy) will, hopefully, soon be in print. Some of David Olmsted's Atsugewi materials have appeared (Olmsted 1961); we may hope for more in future, as well as more of his work on Palaihnihan generally (cf. Olmsted 1964). George Grekoff is working on Chimariko, provided with new data and insights by materials collected by the late J.P. Harrington. Basic sources in the Pomoan languages are in preparation by Robert Oswalt (Kashaya), Sally McLendon (Eastern Pomo), Julius Moshinsky (Southeastern Pomo) and Eero Vihman (Northern Pomo). Further south, Madison Beeler's synchronic studies in Barbareño Chumash will soon be published. For the Yuman languages, too, the prospect is brilliant: extensive resources will soon be made available by James Crawford for Cocopa, Alan Shaterian for Yavapai, Mauricio Mixco for Kiliwa, and Edwin Kozlowski for Havasupai. James Redden has briefly sketched the phonology and morphology of Walapai in two recent papers (Redden 1966a, b); an even briefer treatment is Winter's (1966).

The Washo-Karok comparison was arbitrarily dictated by the then available data; clearly, no proto-language could be assumed. The work was nevertheless of great heuristic value with its utilization of sophisticated recordings and its slicing through a hitherto unexplored dimension of the Hokan relationship.

McLendon's comparison of Yana with Eastern Pomo, though also dictated in part by available data, was nevertheless based on an important rationale: much of the earlier investigation had centered on the Kahi group (cf. Bright 1955:277), coterminous with Sapir's subgroup (a) of Northern Hokan. McLendon, for the first time, looked into the specific evidence for the relationship between Sapir's group (b) — Yana — and his group (c) — Pomoan. The quality of her data was likewise excellent. She cited 163 English glosses for which suggestive forms could be found.

The Kahi group was reexamined by Silver (1964), resulting in the proposal that the languages in the Kahi group (except for Palaihnihan) showed no more closeness of relationship internally than did any one member of the group with, say, Yana or Pomo. Though her focus was on the binary comparison of Karok and Shasta (again because of the quality of the data), relevant forms from the other Kahi languages were occasionally brought into the 117 sets examined.

The problem of internal relationships and subgroupings among the Pomoan languages was reopened by Oswalt in a paper read in 1962 at the International Congress of Americanists in Mexico City (Oswalt 1964a). Using Swadesh's 100-word glottochronological list, Oswalt made a careful count of shared cognates among the seven Pomoan languages on the basis of which he proposed a subgrouping as in Table 2.

TABLE 2

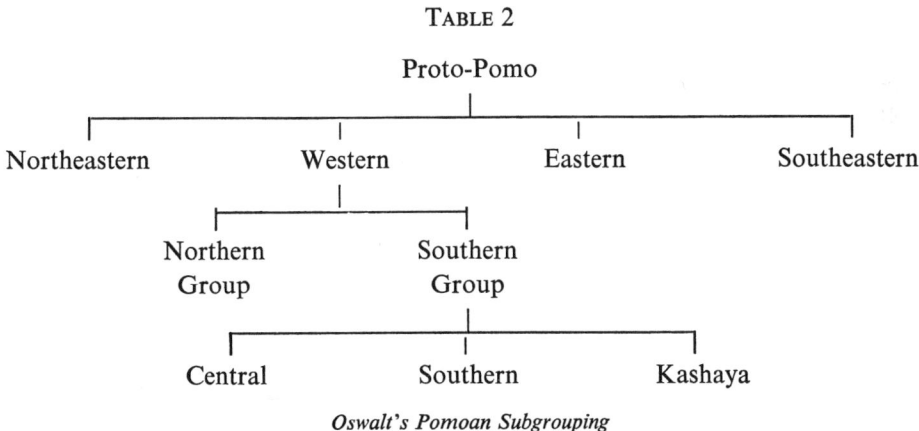

*Oswalt's Pomoan Subgrouping*

This was shortly followed by a phonological study of the close relation between Kashaya and Central Pomo (Oswalt 1964b). Grekoff also examined briefly the initial syllable correspondences between Southeastern Pomo, Southern Pomo and Kashaya, basing his work on S. M. Barrett's manuscript vocabularies (Grekoff 1964).

At about the same time, Halpern (1964) published his classification of Pomoan, based on his own extensive fieldnotes for the seven languages. His criteria were primarily phonological. The chart, which has been rearranged to facilitate comparison with Oswalt's findings shown above, is shown in Table 3.[26]

TABLE 3

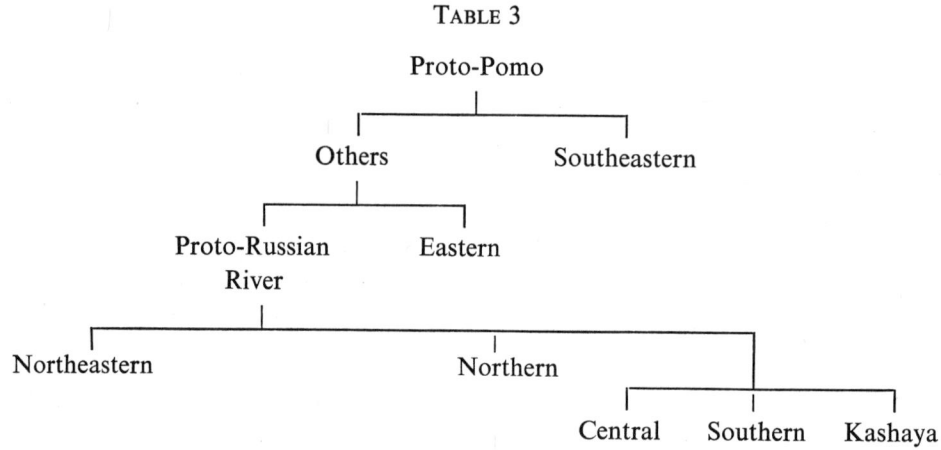

*Halpern's Pomoan Subgrouping*

It may be seen that, except for more elaborate branching in Halpern, the two classifications are essentially similar.

The problem of subgrouping for Hokan in general was raised by Haas (1963). Using as a springboard her own discovery that Proto-Hokan *ama* > Shasta /aˑ/ and Proto-Hokan *ima/*ami* > Shasta /eˑ/, she carried out a detailed analysis of the etymologies for Proto-Hokan *ear, liver, navel, neck (nape), nose, nails (claws), arm, tongue,* and *sleep*. These etymologies were then examined for evidence pointing to any solution of the subgrouping problem in Hokan. Her conclusion was that, short of good interim reconstructions (Proto-Yuman, Proto-Pomoan, Proto-Palaihnihan), no changes in, or refinements of Sapir's original conservative listing (Sapir 1929) was feasible.

In the course of her discussion, she questioned the negative conclusions of Bright (1954) and Olmsted (1956, 1957, 1959) concerning the closeness of Shasta to Palaihnihan. A short time later Olmsted (1965) contested this point, basing his argument on the proposal that though Shasta /aˑ/ and /eˑ/ may have come from Proto-Hokan *ama* and *ima/*ami* respectively, this did not warrant the postulation of the sequences *ama, ima* or *ami* in Proto-Shastan itself.

Haas expanded the horizons of her Proto-Hokan investigations in a later paper (1964), pointing out possible Hokan affinities with Penutian, Yukian and Ritwan in the set for *ear* and with Penutian in the set for *navel*.

---

[26] Halpern actually presented two alternative chartings; I have taken the liberty of quoting the one more similar to Oswalt.

The value of a specific *grammatical* criterion, i.e. switch reference, was weighed by Jacobsen (1967) in the determination of genetic relationship. Among the Hokan-Coahuiltecan languages, switch reference is found in Tonkawa, Washo and Kashaya. Though his conclusions were that switch reference was inadequate as a diagnostic for genetic relationship in Hokan, his delineation of the phenomenon was of great value and interest.

In line with Haas' exhortations with regard to the reconstruction of intermediate families in Hokan (cf. Haas 1963), the problem of Proto-Yuman classification was reopened by Joel (1964). Twenty years earlier, Kroeber (1943) classified the Yuman languages into four groups, basing his work on his own (and Gifford's) field data. These were: Delta, River, Arizona, and California. Three of these groups were agreed to by Winter (1957), though he found Kroeber's California group invalid. Joel separated Kroeber's California group into three, at the same time pointing out the extreme divergence of Kiliwa from all the other Yuman languages. Her grouping was:

Group A: 1. Arizona
         2. River
         3. Delta
         4. Diegueño
         5. Paipai
Group B: 6. Kiliwa

In a much longer work, Wares (1968) returned to a four way subgrouping:
1. Northern: Havasupai, Walapai, Yavapai, Paipai
2. Central: Mohave, Maricopa, Yuma
3. Delta-California: Cocopa, Diegueño, Tipai
4. Kiliwa

In commenting on this classification, Langdon (1970a) made some trenchant and extremely valuable remarks on the whole pastime of 'pigeonholing', derived as it is from the family tree model of genetic language relationships. As she so beautifully pointed out, the technique fails to capture the meaningful relationships among languages which are so close genetically and geographically. Indeed, at much greater time depths, the family tree model, particularly in North America, may prove to be simplistic to the point of uselessness.

A subtle combination of phonological, morphological and syntactic criteria were brought into play by Langdon in her work on the Proto-Yuman demonstrative system (Langdon 1968). By means of internal reconstruction and the making of cross-language deductions she produced a virtuoso exercise in the practice of comparative-historical linguistic research. This published work was preceded by two other papers on Proto-Yuman — "Proto-Yuman verb morphology" (read at the annual meeting of the American Anthropological Association in 1966) and "Sound symbolism in Yuman languages" (1971).

In the spring of 1970 an event took place of inestimable value to Hokan studies and, in a sense, to American Indian linguistics in general. Margaret Langdon organized a conference on Hokan languages at the University of California at San Diego from April 23 to 25, 1970. Supported by funds from the National Science Foundation, the conference brought together some 26 or so official delegates from all over the United States and (in one case) from Europe. In addition, there were numerous unofficial visitors and auditors. Five sessions were held — on Pomoan, on Yuman, on syntactic topics in certain Hokan languages, on subjects concerned with various Hokan matters and on Proto-Hokan.[27] The meetings were permeated by a general mood of intellectual excitement; vast insights into the nature of the Hokan relationship were broadly sketched in, particularly with regard to Proto-Pomoan and Proto-Yuman. Methodological questions were aired, particularly those having to do with the nature of grammatical, lexical and phonological relationships in an old, worn down, un-Indo-European-like milieu such as the Hokan hypothesis must necessarily presuppose.

Though the conference as a whole was intensely interesting, there were certain peaks of excitement generated by the specific aspect of Hokan being brought into focus or by the uniqueness of the idea or approach being discussed. Some of these were (in the writer's opinion): Julius Moshinsky's brilliant statement of Proto-Pomoan phonology, Margaret Langdon's analysis of the Proto-Yuman vowel system, Leonard Talmy's beautiful synchronic discussion of Atsugewi instrumental prefixes, Madison Beeler's rich and satisfying characterization of Barbareño Chumash structure and lexicon (particularly since nothing at all for many, many decades has been made available on the Chumash languages), William Jacobsen's jewel-like vignette on the Yana stop series, Shirley Silver's fine discussion of methodology (particularly her concept of morphemicization) and, finally, Mary Haas' insightful and sophisticated characterization of the sound systems, numerals and pronouns of the Northern California area.

More than anything else, this conference demonstrated the viability of North American Indian linguistic research — its excitement, its promise for meaningful and profitable future work.

[27] The program of the conference was as follows: Eero Vihman, 'Accent in Northern Pomo'; Julius Moshinsky, 'Historical Pomo phonology'; Sally McLendon, 'Internal reconstruction of some Eastern Pomo morphemes'; Robert Oswalt, 'Comparative verb morphology in Pomo'; Alan Shaterian, 'Northern Yuman vocalism'; Martha B. Kendall and William L. Coleman, 'Directions in the study of Upland Yuman'; Leanne Hinton, 'Object-subject pronominal prefixes in La Huerta Diegueño'; Margaret Langdon, 'The Proto-Yuman vowel system'; Mauricio Mixco, 'Kiliwa and Proto-Yuman'; Rudolph Troike, 'Cochimi and Yuman'; James Redden, 'Walapai syntax'; George Grekoff, 'The structure and function of the nominalized clause in Chimariko'; Bruce Nevin, 'Discourse analysis and string-transformational structure in Yana'; Edwin Kozlowski, 'Havasupai syntax'; Werner Winter, 'Switch reference and absolute case: A functional parallelism between Hokan-Coahuiltecan and Indo-European'; Leonard Talmy, 'The Atsugewi instrumental prefix-system'; David Olmsted, 'The linguistic career of Jeremiah Curtin, early-day Atsugewist'; Madison Beeler, 'Topics in Barbareño Chumash grammar'; Paul Turner, 'Pluralization of nouns in Seri and Chontal'; Viola Waterhouse, 'Another look at Chontal and Hokan'; Eric Hamp, 'On methods and goals in comparative Hokan studies'; James Crawford, 'Some cognate sets from Chimariko and Yuman'; William Jacobsen, 'The Yana stop series'; Shirley Silver, 'Comparative Hokan and the Northern Hokan languages'; Mary Haas, 'The Northern California linguistic area'; William Bright, 'Summary and conclusions'.

## YUKIAN

In many ways, the Yukian family of languages is the most intriguing and problematical in California. There are four languages: Coast Yuki, Yuki, Huchnom, and Wappo.[28] Although the first three languages are clearly and closely related, there is some question with regard to the genetic status of Wappo.[29]

Internal genetic work on Yukian is but little advanced, principally because of the paucity of reliable descriptive materials. The only published phonologically reliable source is on Wappo (Sawyer 1965). There are but two published grammars, one of Wappo (Radin 1929) and one of Yuki (Kroeber 1911). Early wordlists were published for all four families (Barrett 1908). Materials collected by Kroeber, H.J. Uldall, Sydney M. Lamb and Roy Siniard are extant but have not yet found their way into print.

The *external* relationships of this small family have stimulated the speculations of researchers since the early part of the century when Kroeber compared Yuki to Yokuts (1906). He pointed out a striking similarity between the structures of Yuki and Yokuts, but rejected the classification of Yukian as genetically related to Penutian. A little later, Radin (1919) characterized Yukian and Penutian as closer to each other than either was to anything else.

Included by Sapir in Hokan-Siouan (Sapir 1921b, 1929), Yukian has, nevertheless, not been systematically or convincingly linked with any other language group. The whole question was reviewed in the late fifties in a brief examination by Shipley (1957) of lexical resemblances between Yukian and Penutian, thus complementing Kroeber's structural evidence. The 32 sets of forms adduced by a thorough perusal of the (then) available data were suggestive though far from convincing.[30]

The Yukian problem was touched on earlier by Swadesh (1954a), who included Yukian in his Hokogian category. On the basis of the cultural and linguistic anomalies of the Yukians vis-à-vis California, he proposed that they might have migrated from some area in the South, perhaps in the vicinity of New Orleans. If any credence could be given this theory it would certainly strengthen the case, not for Hokan affiliation as we now perceive things, but for affinities with Macro-Algonkian, the stock to which Muskogean and the Gulf languages are now tentatively assigned.[31]

A more direct examination of the Yukian-Hokan theory was made by Gursky (1965), who assembled 94 suggestive sets, including some 50-odd comparisons of

---

[28] The situation with regard to Yukian speakers is terminal: Coast Yuki and Huchnom are extinct; at this writing there is one known speaker of Yuki (Mrs. Minnie Fulwiler) and one of Wappo (Mrs. Laura Fish Somersal).

[29] J.O. Sawyer, who has worked with Wappo for many years, has expressed his doubts to me as to whether Wappo is, in fact, a Yukian language. These doubts are implied, though not discussed, in the introduction to his "English-Wappo vocabulary" (Sawyer 1965:vii).

[30] In fact, in view of our present insights into Penutian comparative phonology, many of the Yukian-Penutian sets now seem far less convincing than they did when they were assembled.

[31] But Swadesh was later very partial to the idea of a Yukian-Hokan link (personal communication) though in the face of his monogenetic theory for (at least) the languages of the New World he never felt that one genetic connection precluded another (cf. Swadesh 1969).

Wappo and Yana. Since most of the glosses were of the 'basic vocabulary' type, Gursky minimized the possibility of diffusion: 'Dagegen reicht dieser Artikel meines Erachtens aus, um zu zeigen, dass eine ernst zu nehmende Möglichkeit einer der artigen Sprachverwandschaft besteht, die einer genaueren Untersuchung wert ist.' Nevertheless, no systematic or really convincing case was made.

The most sedulous and informed researcher on Yukian internal and external relationships is clearly William Elmendorf. His careful and balanced evaluations of others' work are admirable; his own efforts are painstaking and imbued with modesty and common sense. Following up a lead from Radin (1919), Elmendorf (1963) explored the possibility of a Yukian-Siouan link, adducing from his carefully organized evidence the possibility of a real, though distant, genetic connection. The 95 sets which he brought together provide an impressive number of tabulated recurrent segmental correspondences. These were not taken as pointing to a Proto-Siouan-Yukian but to the presence of both Siouan and Yukian in some larger genetic configuration. Taking Wiyot-Yurok as a precedent, Elmendorf made the interesting speculation that the Yukians, too, might have been wanderers who had strayed far from their linguistic kinsmen. This suggests, of course, Swadesh's notion in connection with Hokogian.

Yuchi was also brought into consideration, proceeding from Sapir's linkage of Siouan-Yuchi in Hokan-Siouan (Sapir 1921b, 1929). In a later paper (1964), Elmendorf expanded his consideration of Yuchi, proposing a cognate triad: Yuchi-Siouan-Yukian. This was examined in the context of sets — i.e. groups of stems within one language closely related in meaning and segmentable into smaller meaningful elements.[32] He found a parallelism among Yuchi, Siouan and Yukian (particularly Wappo) with regard to the forms and meanings of such stem sets, thus providing a considerably more convincing argument for the relationship than one based on simple lexical resemblance.

Elmendorf recently explored, in as much detail as presently available data will allow, the internal relations of Yukian (Elmendorf 1968). His findings were: (1) that Coast Yuki, Huchnom and Yuki were very close — perhaps little more than dialects, with Huchnom in an intermediate position; (2) that Wappo is very divergent — that, indeed, it must be characterized as a distinct 'branch' of Yukian with a separation of, perhaps, 3,000 years from its northern congeners; (3) that Wappo is about equally distant from all of the three northern languages and; (4) that the percentage of cognates between Wappo and the others varies markedly from one semantic domain to another,

---

[32] An example from Wappo will make this clear. To quote Elmendorf (1964:332): 'There is a Wappo stem set *tooth* ~ *bite* ~ *scrape* in which the base stem CV shows modifications C (s, c, ć, š, č, č̣) and V (e, a, o, u) for some members ... Among augments appearing with modifications of this base stem is an element *-te/-ti* seen in the following: *cute* "peel skin", *ćute* "scrape pan", *šote* "scrape with knife, whittle, pare off", *šoti* "scrape", *čate* "scrape with fingers." These seem to be the only members of the set involving a common semantic component *remove by scraping or cutting along surface* ... We assign this meaning to the element *-te/-ti*.'

with highest percentages for plant names and natural phenomena, and lowest percentages for verbs, adjectives and especially animal terms.

The position of Yukian thus remains ambiguous, both internally and externally. Is Wappo 'really' a Yukian language? Is Yukian related to Penutian or Hokan or Siouan-Yuchi, or to some or all of them or none of them? We may only hope that the unpublished materials on Yuki may soon be brought into play and that perhaps a little more Yuki may be collected in the field so that we may be provided with more conclusive answers to these most intriguing questions.

PERIPHERAL GROUPS

Aside from Penutian, Hokan and Yukian there were numerous languages spoken in California genetically related to families essentially outside the California area.

Perhaps the most fascinating of these groups is that one, earlier known as Ritwan and now established as part of a larger Algon-Ritwan family.[33] We have taken brief note of the Sapir-Michelson controversy in the section above on early classifications. This question, though referred to by various writers from time to time, lay unresolved for more than forty years, mainly because the requisite data for proof were not available. In the fifties, Mary Haas was in a position to assemble these data and to distill from them 93 lexical sets demonstrating recurrent sound correspondences.[34] The result was an exceedingly convincing display of the nature of the Algonkian-Ritwan relationship.

Teeter (1964b) briefly surveyed the Wiyot-Yurok connection, refraining from reconstructing without bringing in Algonkian. Later (1965), he pointed out that Wiyot and Yurok were not, indeed, Algonkian languages in the strict sense, but congeners external to Algonkian proper; a fact which he interpreted as supporting Michelson's old argument (Michelson 1914). Soon thereafter, Haas (1966) made clear that this misrepresented Michelson's view — that Michelson was clearly opposed to the idea of any genetic connection between Ritwan and Algonkian.

Three branches of the great Uto-Aztecan family are, or have members in, California. These are:

Takic: Luiseño-Juaneño, Cupeño, Cahuilla, Gabrielino-Fernandeño, Serrano.
Tubatulabal.

---

[33] This term, a shortened form of Algonkian-Ritwan, was proposed by Haas (1967) as less cumbersome than the more precise Algonkian-Wiyot-Yurok, specifying that it implies no closer relation between Wiyot and Yurok than either has with Algonkian. An equivalent term, revived by Karl Teeter, is Algic — a term, he pointed out, used by Schoolcraft in the early nineteenth century (Teeter 1965).

[34] The Wiyot and Yurok data were from new manuscript sources; Wiyot from Karl Teeter (1964a) and Yurok from R. H. Robins (1958). Some forms from Reichard (1925) were also used. Algonkian reconstructions were from Bloomfield (1946), Hockett (1957), Michelson (1935), Voegelin (1941) and Siebert (1941).

Numic: Monachi-Paviotso, Panamint-Shoshoni, Kawaiisu-Ute.[35]

Published descriptive and lexical sources on these languages are not copious. For Luiseño, there are a grammar (Kroeber and Grace 1960) and a dictionary (Bright 1968) as well as a somewhat briefer structural analysis (Malécot 1963a, b, 1964a, b). For Tubatulabal there are a grammar, a dictionary and a collection of texts (Voegelin 1935a, b, 1958). For Ute (Southern Paiute) there is the classic study of Sapir (1930). Paviotso, Shoshoni and Ute are outside of California.

There are unpublished materials for several more of the languages: for Cahuilla (Hansjakob Seiler), for Serrano (Kenneth Hill), for Monachi (Sydney M. Lamb) and for Kawaiisu (Sheldon Klein). Currently, fieldwork is under way on Paviotso (Michael Nichols).

Two general works on Proto-Uto-Aztecan naturally involve consideration of the Californian languages: Miller's monograph on Uto-Aztecan cognate sets (Miller 1967) and Langacker's article on Proto-Uto-Aztecan vocalism (Langacker 1970). In the specific area of Numic there are Lamb's basic discussion of the Numic group (1958), and a binary Monachi-Kawaiisu lexical comparison by Klein (1959).

Only a few California languages belonged to the vast and far-flung Na-Déné stock. Published grammars are extant for three of them — Mattole (Li 1930), Kato (Goddard 1912), and Hupa (Goddard 1905). There are published texts for Wailaki (Goddard 1922). There is a recent description of Tolowa phonology (J. Bright 1964). Hoijer (1960) has discussed in general terms the Pacific Coast Athabaskan languages, of which the California group forms only a part.

Hupa has been carefully and elaborately studied in the field by Victor Golla, whose forthcoming grammar, texts and dictionary will be a major contribution to North American Indian linguistics. He has published an etymological study of Hupa noun stems (Golla 1964a), the discussion of which properly belongs with the examination of genetic relationships in Athabaskan and Na-Déné generally.

## EPILOGUE

The conceptualization of the genetic relationships among the California Indian languages has remained essentially stable for fifty years (Dixon and Kroeber 1919). The Sapir classification (1929) made little change in Dixon and Kroeber's formulations within the California area — Klamath was added to Penutian, a postulation confirmed by later research (Shipley 1966), and Yukian was classified as distantly related to Hokan, a linkage which is still being investigated (Elmendorf 1963, 1964). Even the results of the conference on the classification of North American Indian

---

[35] This classification and listing is a composite. The term 'Takic' is from Kroeber (1934), though the list of Takic languages is from a later source (Kroeber and Grace 1960). The term 'Numic' was coined by Lamb (1958), based on the word for *person* in the Numic languages. The list of Numic languages is also from Lamb.

languages, convoked by C.F. Voegelin at Bloomington in the summer of 1964, left the earlier California configuration undisturbed internally, though a fundamental reorganization of the broader scheme for North America was effected. It is likely that the groupings as we now see them will prove out with the insights and advances of future research. Two questions of great interest are: (1) what are the grammatical and lexical factors which will make a subtler subgrouping possible within genetic groups; (2) what are the *external* connections of the groups which essentially center in California — Penutian, Hokan and Yukian? Though the finding of Old World congeners for these families seems very unlikely indeed as contrasted with the possibilities, say, for Na-Déné or Algonkian, still there is hope, particularly as our techniques of comparison and reconstruction become more refined. The language situation in California is very, very old and does not yield easily to historical research. Nevertheless, great strides have been taken, and still greater and more interesting possibilities undoubtedly lie ahead.

## REFERENCES

AOKI, HARUO. 1963. On Sahaptian–Klamath linguistic affiliations. IJAL 29.107–12.
——. 1966. Nez Perce vowel harmony and Proto-Sahaptian vowels. Lg 52.759–67.
BARKER, M.A.R. 1963a. Klamath texts. UCPL 30.
——. 1963b. Klamath dictionary. UCPL 31.
——. 1964. Klamath grammar. UCPL 32.
BARRETT, S.A. 1908. The ethno-geography of the Pomo and neighboring Indians. UCPAAE 6.
BEELER, MADISON S. 1955. Saclan. IJAL 21.201–10.
——. 1959. Saclan once more. IJAL 25.67–68.
——. 1961a. Northern Costanoan. IJAL 27.191–7.
——. 1961b. Senary counting in California Penutian. AnL 3/6.1–8.
——. 1964. Ventureño numerals. UCPL 34.13–18.
——. 1970a. Sibilant harmony in Chumash. IJAL 36.14–17.
——. 1970b. Topics in Barbareño Chumash grammar. Paper read at the Conference on Hokan Languages, University of California at San Diego, April 1970.
BLOOMFIELD, LEONARD. 1946. Algonquian. Linguistic structures of native America, ed. by Harry Hoijer, pp. 85–129. VFPA 6.
BOAS, FRANZ. 1911a. Chinook. BAE-B 40/1.559–677.
——. 1911b. Tsimshian. BAE-B 40/1.283–422.
BRIGHT, JANE O. 1964. The phonology of Smith River Athapaskan (Tolowa). IJAL 30.101–7.
BRIGHT, WILLIAM. 1954. Some northern Hokan relationships: A preliminary report. UCPL 10.63–7.
——. 1955. A bibliography of the Hokan-Coahuiltecan languages. IJAL 21.276–85.

——. 1956. Glottochronologic counts of Hokaltecan material. Lg 32.42–48.
——. 1957. The Karok language. UCPL 13.
——. 1960. Animals of acculturation in the California Indian languages. UCPL 4.215–46.
——, ed. 1964. Studies in Californian linguistics. UCPL 34.
——. 1965. The history of the Cahuilla sound system. IJAL 31.241–44.
——. 1968. A Luiseño dictionary. UCPL 51.
BRIGHT, WILLIAM and ELIZABETH. 1959. Spanish words in Patwin. RomPh 13.161–4.
BROADBENT, SYLVIA M. 1957. Rumsen I: Methods of reconstitution. IJAL 23.275–80.
——. 1964. The Southern Sierra Miwok language. UCPL 38.
BROADBENT, SYLVIA M., and CATHERINE CALLAGHAN. 1960. Comparative Miwok: A preliminary survey. IJAL 26.301–16.
BROADBENT, SYLVIA M., and HARVEY PITKIN. 1964. A comparison of Miwok and Wintun. Studies in Californian linguistics, ed. by William Bright, pp. 19–45. UCPL 34.
CALLAGHAN, CATHERINE A. 1958. California Penutian: History and bibliography. IJAL 24.189–195.
——. 1962. Comparative Miwok-Mutsun with notes on Rumsen. IJAL 28.97–107.
——. 1964. Phonemic borrowing in Lake Miwok. Studies in Californian linguistics, ed. by William Bright, pp. 46–53. UCPL 34.
——. 1965. Lake Miwok dictionary. UCPL 39.
——. 1967. Miwok-Costanoan as a subfamily of Penutian. IJAL 33.224–7.
——. 1970. Bodega Miwok dictionary. UCPL 60.
CRAWFORD, JAMES M. 1970a. Cocopa baby talk. IJAL 36.1–13.
——. 1970b. Some cognate sets from Chimariko and several Yuman languages. Paper read at the Conference on Hokan Languages, University of California at San Diego, April 1970.
DIXON, R.B. 1905. The Shasta-Achomawi: A new linguistic stock with four new dialects. AmA (NS) 7.213–17.
——. 1910. The Chimariko Indians and language. UCPAAE 5.335–38.
——. 1911. Maidu. BAE-B 40.679–734.
——. 1913. New linguistic families in California. AmA 15.647–55.
——. 1919. Linguistic families of California. UCPAAE 16.3.
DIXON, R.B., and A.L. KROEBER. 1903. The native languages of California. AmA (NS) 5.1–26.
ELMENDORF, WILLIAM W. 1963. Yukian-Siouan lexical similarities. IJAL 29.300–9.
——. 1964. Item and set comparison in Yuchi, Siouan and Yukian. IJAL 30.328–40.
——. 1968. Lexical and cultural change in Yukian. AnL 10/7.1–41.
FRACHTENBERG, LEO J. 1922a. Coos. BAE-B 40/2.297–430.
——. 1922b. Siuslawan. BAE-B 40/2.431–630.
FREELAND, L.S. 1930. The relationship of Mixe to the Penutian family. IJAL 6.28–36.

———. 1951. Language of the Sierra Miwok. IUPAL Memoir 6.
FREELAND, L. S., and SYLVIA M. BROADBENT. 1960. Central Sierra Miwok dictionary. UCPL 23.
GALLATIN, ALBERT. 1848. Hale's Indians of Northwest America, and vocabularies of North America; with an introduction. AES-T 2.xxiii–clxxxviii, 1–130.
GODDARD, P. E. 1905. Morphology of the Hupa language. UCPAAE 3.1–344.
———. 1912. Elements of the Kato language. UCPAAE 11.1–176.
———. 1922. Wailaki texts. IJAL 2.77–135.
GOLLA, VICTOR K. 1964a. Comparative Yokuts phonology. Studies in Californian linguistics, ed. by William Bright, pp. 54–66. UCPL 84.
———. 1964b. An etymological study of Hupa noun stems. IJAL 30.108–17.
GREKOFF, GEORGE V. 1964. A note on comparative Pomo. Studies in Californian linguistics, ed. by William Bright, pp. 67–72. UCPL 34.
———. 1970. The structure and function of the nominalized clause in Chimariko. Paper read at the Conference on Hokan Languages, University of California at San Diego, April 1970.
GURSKY, KARL-HEINZ. 1965. Zur Frage der historischen Stellung der Yuki-Sprachfamilie. Abhandlung der Völkerkundlichen Arbeitsgemeinschaft, Heft 8.
HAAS, MARY R. 1954. The Proto-Hokan-Coahuiltecan word for 'water'. UCPL 10.57–62.
———. 1958. Algonkian-Ritwan: The end of a controversy. IJAL 24.159–73.
———. 1963. Shasta and Proto-Hokan. Lg 39.40–59.
———. 1964. California Hokan. Studies in Californian linguistics, ed. by William Bright, pp. 73–87. UCPL 34.
———. 1966. Wiyot-Yurok-Algonkian and problems of comparative Algonkian. IJAL 32.101–7.
———. 1967. Language and taxonomy in Northwestern California. AmA 69.358–62.
———. 1970. The northern California linguistic area. Paper read at the Conference on Hokan Languages, University of California at SanDiego, April 1970.
HALPERN, A. M. 1946–1947. Yuma. IJAL 12.25–33, 147–51, 204–12; 13.18–30, 92–107, 147–56.
———. 1964. A report on a survey of Pomo languages. Studies in Californian linguistics, ed. by William Bright, pp. 88–93. UCPL 34.
HAMP, ERIC P. 1966. Studies in Sierra Miwok. IJAL 32.236–41.
———. 1970. On methods and goals in comparative Hokan studies. Paper read at the Conference on Hokan Languages, University of California at San Diego, April 1970.
HARRIS, ZELLIG. 1944. Yokuts structure and Newman's grammar. IJAL 10.196–211.
HEIZER, ROBERT F., ed. 1952. California Indian linguistic records: The mission Indian vocabularies of Alphonse Pinart. AR 15:1, University of California Press.
———. 1955. California Indian linguistic records: The mission Indian vocabularies of H. W. Henshaw. AR 15:2, University of California Press.

HILL, JANE H. 1966. A grammar of the Cupeño language. Unpublished Ph.D. dissertation, University of California, Los Angeles.

HILL, KENNETH C. 1967. A grammar of the Serrano language, Unpublished Ph.D. dissertation, University of California, Los Angeles.

HINTON, LEANNE. 1970. Object-subject pronominal prefixes in La Huerta Diegueño. Paper read at the Conference on Hokan Languages, University of California at San Diego, April

HOCKETT, CHARLES F. 1957. Central Algonquian vocabulary: Stems in /k-/. IJAL 23.247–68.

——. 1967. The Yawelmani basic verb. Lg 43.208–22.

HOIJER, HARRY. 1960. Athapaskan languages of the Pacific Coast. Culture in history, essays in honor of Paul Radin, ed. by Stanley Diamond, pp. 960–76. New York, Columbia University Press.

HYDE, VILLIANA. 1971. An introduction to the Luiseño language. Banning, Calif., Malki Museum Press.

HYMES, DELL H. 1957. Some Penutian elements and the Penutian hypothesis. SJA 13.69–87.

——. 1959. Genetic classifications: Retrospect and prospect. AnL 1/2.50–66.

——. 1964a. 'Hail' and 'bead': Two Penutian etymologies. Studies in Californian linguistics, ed. by William Bright, pp. 94–8. UCPL 34.

——. 1964b. Evidence for Penutian in lexical sets with initial *c- and *s-. IJAL 30.213–42.

JACOBS, MELVILLE. 1931. A sketch of Northern Sahaptin grammar. UWPA 4.85–292.

JACOBSEN, WILLIAM H., JR. 1958. Washo and Karok: An approach to comparative Hokan. IJAL 24.195–213.

——. 1967. Switch-reference in Hokan-Coahuiltecan. Studies in Southwestern ethnolinguistics, ed. by Dell Hymes and William E. Bittle, The Hague, Paris: Mouton.

——. 1970. The Yana stop series. Paper read at the Conference on Hokan Languages, University of California at San Diego, April 1970.

JOEL, JUDITH. 1964. Classification of the Yuman languages. Studies in Californian linguistics, ed. by William Bright, pp. 99–105. UCPL 34.

JOHNSON, FREDERICK. 1940. The linguistic map of Mexico and Central America. Chapter 6, The Maya and their neighbors, ed. by C. L. Hay, et al. New York, Appleton-Century.

KENDALL, MARTHA B., and WILLIAM L. COLEMAN. 1970. Directions in the study of Upland Yuman. Paper read at the Conference on Hokan Languages, University of California at San Diego, April 1970.

KLEIN, SHELDON. 1959. Comparative Mono-Kawaiisu. IJAL 25.233–6.

KOZLOWSKI, EDWIN. 1970. Havasupai syntax. Paper read at the Conference on Hokan Languages, University of California at San Diego, April 1970.

KROEBER, A.L. 1906. The Yokuts and Yuki languages. Boas Anniversary Volume, 64–79.
——. 1907. The Yokuts language of south central California. UCPAAE 2.165–377.
——. 1910. The Chumash and Costanoan languages. UCPAAE 9.259–63.
——. 1911. The languages of the coast of California north of San Francisco. UCPAAE 9.
——. 1934. Uto-Aztecan languages of Mexico. Ibero-Americana 8.1–28.
——. 1941. Some relations of linguistics and ethnology. Lg 17.287–91.
——. 1943. Classification of the Yuman languages. UCPL 1.21–40.
——. 1958. An Atsugewi word list. IJAL 24.213–15.
——. 1959a. Northern Yokuts. AnL 1/8.1–19.
——. 1959b. Possible Athabascan influence on Yuki. IJAL 25.59.
——. 1963. Yokuts dialect survey. AR 11:3, University of California Press.
KROEBER, A.L., and GEORGE WILLIAM GRACE. 1960. The Sparkman grammar of Luiseño. UCPL 16.
KURODA, S.Y. 1967. Yawelmani phonology. Research monograph no. 43, M.I.T. Press, Cambridge, Massachusetts.
LAMB, SYDNEY M. 1958. Linguistic prehistory in the Great Basin. IJAL 24.95–100.
——. 1959. Some proposals for linguistic taxonomy. AnL 1/2.33–49.
LANGACKER, RONALD. 1970. The vowels of Proto-Uto-Aztecan. IJAL 36.169–80.
LANGDON, MARGARET. 1968. The Proto-Yuman demonstrative system. FLing 2. 61–81.
——. 1970a. Review of A comparative study of Yuman consonantism, by Alan C. Wares. Lg 46.533–44.
——. 1970b. A grammar of Diegueño: The Mesa Grande dialect. UCPL 66.
——. 1970c. The Proto-Yuman vowel system. Paper read at the Conference on Hokan Languages, University of California at San Diego, April 1970.
——. 1971. Sound system in Yuman languages. Studies in American languages, ed. by Jesse Sawyer, pp. 149–74. UCPL 65.
LATHAM, R.G. 1856. On the languages of northern, western and central America. London: Transactions of the Philological Society, 57–115.
LI, F.-K. 1930. Mattole, an Athabaskan language. University of Chicago, Publications in Anthropology, Linguistic Series. Chicago.
MALÉCOT, ANDRÉ. 1963a. Luiseño, a structural analysis I: Phonology. IJAL 29.89–95.
——. 1963b. Luiseño, a structural analysis II: Morphology, morphophonemics, syntax. IJAL 29.196–210.
——. 1964a. Luiseño, a structural analysis III: Texts and lexicon. IJAL 30.14–32.
——. 1964b. Luiseño, a structural analysis IV: appendices. IJAL 30.243–50.
MASON, J. ALDEN. 1916. The Mutsun dialect of Costanoan based on the vocabulary of de la Cuesta. UCPAAE 11.399–72.
——. 1940. The native languages of Middle America. Chapter 5, The Maya and their neighbors, ed. by C.L. Hay. New York, Appleton-Century.

McLendon, Sally. 1964. Northern Hokan (b) and (c): a comparison of Eastern Pomo and Yana. Studies in Californian linguistics, ed. by William Bright, pp. 126–44. UCPL 34.

——. 1970. Internal reconstruction of some eastern Pomo morphemes. Paper read at the Conference on Hokan Languages, University of California at San Diego, April 1970.

Michelson, Truman. 1914. Two alleged Algonkian languages of California. AmA(NS) 16.361–7.

——. 1915. Rejoinder to Sapir. AmA(NS) 17.194–8.

——. 1935. Phonetic shifts in Algonquian languages. IJAL 8.131–71.

Miller, Wick R. 1967. Uto-Aztecan cognate sets. UCPL 48.

Mixco, Mauricio. 1970. Kiliwa and Proto-Yuman. Paper read at the Conference on Hokan Languages, University of California at San Diego, April 1970.

Moshinsky, Julius. 1970. Historical Pomo phonology. Paper read at the Conference on Hokan Languages, University of California at San Diego, April 1970.

Nevin, Bruce E. 1970. Internal reconstruction of Yana transformations. Paper read at the Conference on Hokan Languages, University of California at San Diego, April 1970.

Newman, Stanley S. 1944. Yokuts language of California. VFPA 2.

——. 1958. Zuni dictionary. RCAFL-P 6.

——. 1964. Comparison of Zuni and California Penutian. IJAL 30.1–13.

——. 1965. Zuni grammar. UNMPA 14.

——. 1967. Yokuts. Lingua 17.182–99.

Olmsted, David L. 1954. Achumawi-Atsugewi non-reciprocal intelligibility. IJAL 20.181–4.

——. 1956. Palaihnihan and Shasta I: Labial stops. Lg 32.73–75.

——. 1957. Palihnihan and Shasta II: Apical stops. Lg 33.136–8.

——. 1958. Atsugewi phonology. IJAL 24.215–20.

——. 1959. Palaihnihan and Shasta III: Dorsal stops. Lg 35.637–44.

——. 1961. Atsugewi morphology I: Verb inflection. IJAL 27.91–113.

——. 1964. A history of Palaihnihan phonology. UCPL 35.

——. 1965. Phonemic change and subgrouping: Some Hokan data. Lg 41.303–7.

——. 1966. Achumawi dictionary. UCPL 45.

——. 1970. The linguistic career of Jeremiah Curtin, early-day Atsugewist. Paper read at the Conference on Hokan Languages, University of California at San Diego, April 1970.

Oswalt, Robert. 1964a. The internal relationships of the Pomo family of languages. PICAm 35, 413–27.

——. 1964b. A comparative study of two Pomo languages. Studies in Californian linguistics, ed. by William Bright, pp. 149-62. UCPL 34.

——. 1964c. Kashaya texts. UCPL 36.

———. 1970. Comparative verb morphology in Pomo. Paper read at the Conference on Hokan Languages, University of California at San Diego, April 1970.
PITKIN, HARVEY. 1962. A bibliography of the Wintun family of languages. IJAL 28.43–54.
PITKIN, HARVEY, and WILLIAM SHIPLEY. 1958. Comparative survey of California Penutian. IJAL 24.174–88.
POWELL, J.W. 1891. Indian linguistic families of America north of Mexico. BAE-R 7.7–139.
RADIN, PAUL. 1919. The genetic relationship of the North American Indian languages. UCPAAE 14.489–502.
———. 1929. A grammar of the Wappo language. UCPAAE 27.
REDDEN, J.E. 1966a. Walapai I: Phonology. IJAL 32.1–16.
———. 1966b. Walapai II: Morphology. IJAL 32.41–63.
———. 1970. Walapai syntax. Paper read at the Conference on Hokan Languages, University of California at San Diego, April 1970.
REICHARD, GLADYS A. 1925. Wiyot grammar and texts. UCPAAE 22.1–215.
ROBINS, R.H. 1958. The Yurok language. UCPL 15.
SAPIR, EDWARD. 1913. Wiyot and Yurok, Algonkin languages of California. AmA (NS) 15.617–46.
———. 1915. Algonkin languages of California: A reply. AmA(NS) 17.188–94. (Also Epilogue, p. 198).
———. 1917a. The position of Yana in the Hokan stock. UCPAAE 13.1–34.
———. 1917b. The status of Washo. AmA(NS) 19.449–50.
———. 1921a. A characteristic Penutian form of stem. IJAL 2.58–67.
———. 1921b. A bird's-eye view of American languages north of Mexico. Science 54.408.
———. 1922. The Takelma language of south-western Oregon. BAE-B 40(2).1–296.
———. 1923. The Algonkian affinity of Yurok and Wiyot kinship terms. JAS 15.37–74.
———. 1925. The Hokan affinity of Subtiaba in Nicaragua. AmA 27.402–35, 491–527.
———. 1929. Central and North American languages. Encyclopaedia Britannica (14th ed.) 5.138–41. Reprinted in SWES.
———. 1930. The Southern Paiute language. AmAAS-P 65.
SAPIR, EDWARD, and MORRIS SWADESH. 1953. Coos-Takelma-Penutian comparisons. IJAL 19.132–37.
———. 1960. Yana dictionary. UCPL 22.
SAWYER, JESSE O., JR. 1964. Wappo words from Spanish. Studies in Californian linguistics, ed. by William Bright, pp. 163–69. UCPL 34.
———. 1965. English-Wappo vocabulary. UCPL 43.
———, ed. 1971. Studies in American languages. UCPL65.
SEILER, HANSJAKOB. 1957. Die phonetischen Grundlagen der Vokalphoneme des Cahuilla. ZPhon 10.204–23.
———. 1970. Cahuilla texts with an introduction. LSM 6.

SHAFER, ROBERT. 1947. Penutian. IJAL 13.205-19.
——. 1952. Notes on Penutian. IJAL 18.211-16.
——. 1961. Tones in Wintun. AnL 3/6.17-30.
SHATERIAN, ALAN. 1970. Aspects of Yavapai vocalism. Paper read at the Conference on Hokan Languages, University of California at San Diego, April 1970.
SHIPLEY, WILLIAM. 1956. The phonemes of Northeastern Maidu. IJAL 22.233-37.
——. 1957. Some Yukian-Penutian lexical resemblances. IJAL 23.269-74.
——. 1961. Maidu and Nisenan: A binary survey. IJAL 27.46-51.
——. 1962. Spanish elements in the indigenous languages of California. RomPh 16.1-21.
——. 1963. Maidu texts and dictionary. UCPL 33.
——. 1964. Maidu grammar. UCPL 41.
——. 1966. The relation of Klamath to California Penutian. Lg 42.489-98.
SIEBERT, FRANK T., JR. 1941. Certain proto-Algonquian consonant clusters. Lg 17.298-303.
SILVER, SHIRLEY. 1964. Shasta and Karok: A binary comparison. Studies in Californian linguistics, ed. by William Bright, pp. 170-81. UCPL 34.
——. 1970. Comparative Hokan and the northern Hokan languages. Paper read at the Conference on Hokan languages, University of California at San Diego, April 1970.
SILVERSTEIN, MICHAEL. 1965. Penutian: The grammatical dimensions of Sapir's hypothesis. Unpublished honors thesis in linguistics, Harvard University.
SWADESH, MORRIS. 1954a. Perspectives and problems of Amerindian comparative linguistics. Word 10.306-32.
——. 1954b. On the Penutian vocabulary survey. IJAL 20.123-33.
——. 1956. Problems of long-range comparison in Penutian. Lg 32.17-41.
——. 1959. The mesh principle in comparative linguistics. AnL 1/2.7-14.
——. 1964. Comparative Penutian glosses of Sapir. Studies in Californian linguistics, ed. by William Bright, pp. 182-91. UCPL 34.
TALMY, LEONARD. 1970. The Atsugewi instrumental-prefix system. Paper read at the Conference on Hokan Languages, University of California at San Diego, April 1970.
TEETER, KARL V. 1959. Consonant harmony in Wiyot (with a note on Cree). IJAL 25.41-3.
——. 1964a. The Wiyot language. UCPL 37.
——. 1964b. Wiyot and Yurok: A preliminary study. Studies in Californian linguistics, ed. by William Bright, pp. 192-98. UCPL 34.
——. 1965. The Algonquian verb: Notes toward a reconsideration. IJAL 31.221-5.
TRAGER, GEORGE L. 1945. Review of Map of North American Indian languages by C.F. and E.W. Voegelin. IJAL 11.188.
TROIKE, RUDOLPH. 1970. Cochimi and Yuman. Paper read at the Conference on Hokan Linguistics, University of California at San Diego, April 1970.

TURNER, PAUL. 1970. Pluralization of nouns in Seri and Chontal. Paper read at the Conference on Hokan Languages, University of California at San Diego, April 1970.
ULDALL, H.J. 1954. Maidu phonetics. IJAL 20.8–16.
ULDALL, H.J., and WILLIAM SHIPLEY. 1966. Nisenan texts and dictionary. UCPL 46.
ULTAN, RUSSELL. 1964. Proto-Maidun phonology. IJAL 30.355–70.
ULVING, TOV. 1959. Additions to Catherine A. Callaghan's California Penutian. IJAL 25.136.
VIHMAN, EERO. 1970. Accent in northern Pomo. Paper read at the Conference on Hokan Languages, University of California at San Diego, April 1970.
VOEGELIN, C.F. 1935a. Tübatulabal grammar. UCPAAE 34.55–190.
——. 1935b. Tübatulabal texts. UCPAAE 34.191–246.
——. 1941. Proto-Algonquian consonant clusters in Delaware. Lg 17.143–7.
——. 1958. Working dictionary of Tübatulabal. IJAL 24.221–28.
WARES, ALAN C. 1968. A comparative study of Yuman consonantism. JanL, series practica, 57.
WATERHOUSE, VIOLA. 1970. Another look at Chontal and Hokan. Paper read at the Conference on Hokan Languages, University of California at San Diego, April 1970.
WHORF, BENJAMIN LEE. 1935. The comparative linguistics of Uto-Aztecan. AmA 37.60-08.
WINTER, WERNER. 1957. Yuman languages I: First impressions. IJAL 23.18–23.
——. 1966. Yuman languages II: Wolf's Son — a Walapai text. IJAL 32.17–40.
——. 1967. The identity of the Paipai (Akwʔala). Studies in southwestern ethnolinguistics, ed. by Dell Hymes and William E. Bittle, pp. 372–8. The Hague, Mouton.
——. 1970. Switch reference and absolute case: A functional parallelism between Hokan-Coahuiltecan and Indo-European. Paper read at the Conference on Hokan Languages, University of California at San Diego, April 1970.

# SOUTHWESTERN AND GREAT BASIN LANGUAGES

### C. F. AND F. M. VOEGELIN

#### INTRODUCTION

Those who have not been faced with the task of giving a reasonable account of languages whose varieties do not include a standard may fail to appreciate the difficulty of the task. The linguistic varieties within different native languages in the Great Basin and in the Southwest of America are easier to account for than those of aboriginal Australia, for example, because the Australian languages are virtually all related, and because any language may consist — or have consisted — of a chain of dialects such that the dialect of a given small area is intelligible to the dialects in the flanking small areas, while the dialects at the geographical ends of the linguistically interlocking or intermeshing small areas are separated by as much of a language barrier as could be expectable between any two separate languages that are in fact related, but most distantly so. Any non-contiguous dialect is apt to be not quite intelligible to its once removed neighbor; yet since adjacent dialect links in the chain are mutually intelligible, the dialect chain as a whole can be claimed to constitute a single language — though one which is not amenable to the usual criterion of intelligibility based on sharing a high percentage of cognates. The correlation alleged to exist between percentage of same or recognizable lexical items and some degree of intelligibility in dialect distance testing would yield an increase in 'separate' language count — but, paradoxically, would isolate 'separate' languages which are never separated by a language barrier at any particular point along the unbroken dialect chain. Furthermore, where the dialect chain is broken by relocation of societies in the historical or the protohistorical period, the distinction between separate languages and dialects of the same language would be impossible to attest even with the dubious definiteness of dialect distance testing of unbroken chains of dialects.

#### 1. LANGUAGE BARRIERS

The closest approximation to this typical Australian situation is found among the native American languages still spoken in the Great Basin, since all of these — with the exception of Washo — are genetically related. On the other hand, since several different language families are represented in the Southwest, it is possible to say with complete certainty that a barrier separates one language from its near and distant neighbors when they belong to a different language family. For example, even though the Southern Paiute now living at Willow Springs and Navajo Mountain have adopted the dress and some of the house types of the neighboring Navajo, one can assume without further investigation that Southern Paiute and Navajo are separate languages; or in addition one can test this assumption by observing that it is always the case — except for those who are bilingual in the two languages — that speakers cannot communicate with each other when one speaks Southern Paiute and the other Navajo. (Today, of course, the two would use what for them is a lingua franca, English, in verbal communication.) Less obvious is the possibility that the same can be said for languages which belong to different subfamilies in the same family, as Southern Paiute in the Numic subfamily of the Uto-Aztecan family, and Hopi, also in the Uto-Aztecan family, but in a different subfamily.

Hence, the continuing work on establishing the internal relationships of language families in the Great Basin and the Southwest, though strictly a matter of autonomous linguistics, is also relevant to the ethnography of communication.

## 2. SCOPE

It seems appropriate to preface our review of the continuing work on internal relationships (Sections 10–15, following) with an extended note on the sociolinguistic implications of modern relationships. This prefatory note is based on the solid foundation of comparative method linguistics, as far as it has been carried, but it is oriented in respect to the modern and post-modern expectations which are now animating American Indians, and in respect to work in ethnographic semantics (ethnoscience) and oral literature which goes beyond the language-linked semantics of autonomous linguistics.

Work in any of these new directions which neglects the historical background of which the present situation is an outgrowth cannot hope to find a perspective to anticipate the near future — say the remainder of the twentieth century. The bland assumption sometimes implied (if not explicitly expressed) that American Indians are about to give up both their languages and their cultures — rather than to keep them intact — lacks an appreciation of what has taken place in the past (change in both), and what can be reasonably expected for the rest of this century (change in both).

In the preparation of this paper we followed the following order of writing (and autonomous linguists may wish to read in the same order): (a) first the sections on historical background and internal relationships of language families, as determined so far (e.g. Yuman Family, Hokan relatives of Yuman, Uto-Aztecan Family, Tanoan relatives of Uto-Aztecan, and so on); (b) then the less formal reports on the present status of societies in respect to their languages which we had identified genetically under successive center heads (10–15) as mentioned. But in presentation, we give (b) first — the less systematic reports on aspects of the ethnography of speaking, and on various sociolinguistic and on occasional psycholinguistic implications, and on beginning work in ethnoscience — and on the changes these less formal kinds of work appear to be bringing to a host of important questions, from the native speaker's intuition of the semantics of his mother tongue to factors effecting the maintenance and/or replacement of languages native to America which are now spoken, for the most part, by bilinguals.

3. IDENTIFICATION OF LANGUAGE AND SMALLER NATIONALITY

The Indian Reorganization Act of 1934 'widened alternatives', as Shimkin and Reid (1970) express it — self-government reinforced by economic aid, opportunity to learn new skills associated with construction and the handling of motor cars and heavy machinery and so on — and the bridge to entering any of the new cultural spaces was to speak English as a second language. This opening of a new phase of history among American Indians generally is now undergoing a second acceleration, or rather a third acceleration, since the first acceleration is said to have begun as early as 1920 for the Algonquian Powhattan — by Speck (1928) who sensed that the 'desire to exist as smaller nationalities is behind the move'. It appears to be possible for a 'smaller nationality' to have self-identification without having a 'smaller language' peculiar to it; but having one no doubt facilitates the present-day striving toward the ideal of a 'small nationality' — certainly so in the case of the Hopi, and possibly so for the Navajo in the Southwest.

But in the case of the Great Basin languages, it is difficult to see how a particular language can have a 'small nationality' identification. The distribution given by Wick Miller (1970) for the 'Shoshoni language', for example, extends beyond the Great Basin: it includes the Panamint Shoshoni in California, and although Shoshoni dialects are centered in Nevada they extend continuously into Utah, Idaho and Wyoming, and discontinuously into the southern Plains.

Though it may be argued that relationships within the dialect continuum or chain of linked dialects extending from California to Wyoming are not expressible in family tree terms, something approximating a family tree appears possible when one distinct area is designated as having greater dialect diversity than others — e.g. the Panamint Shoshoni area where California and Nevada adjoin versus the vast area covered by the Shoshoni proper versus the geographically discontinuous Comanche (Shoshoni who migrated into the southern Plains from Wyoming only a few centuries ago). Something like two or three different Shoshoni languages might be postulated, but — from the evidence of lexical items alone — it appears that a single language is involved. And phonological differences along the dialect chain contribute little interpretive help. A velar nasal appears only in Panamint dialects but this may be a very recent innovation; other items of phonological variation occur, but are less localized areally. Some dialect variation which Miller (1970) calls 'subphonemic' is reminiscent of the slight differences in different village varieties of Hopi which are, nevertheless, completely intelligible to speakers of other varieties.

In the case of the Shoshoni, it is said that dialects can no longer be studied in their local homelands; hence isoglosses cannot be interpretively plotted because available informants these days move about too much, while those who stay at home have been influenced by the majority who move about.

But the moving about of Western Shoshoni speakers in a sense represents a continuity from the period before the availability of horses and automobiles facilitated communication. As hunters and food gatherers associated in bands of from a single family to a half dozen families (varying from season to season and year to year), the Shoshoni did not stay in one locality; and a dozen of these small bands would join forces for a week or so every year to participate in a communal rabbit hunt, to enjoy dancing, gambling, and exchange of women in marriage — and no doubt to exchange lexical items by borrowing — borrowings which would later diffuse as the bands dispersed over the 'wide areas' representing the total territory in which the seasonal migrations took place.

With the coming of Anglo ranchers and guns in the last century, domesticated animals consumed much of the wild seeds, and hunting with guns depleted the wild game upon which the Shoshoni had depended. The modern consequence is an exchange of the old widespread hunting and gathering for modern residence in one place — in 'Indian colonies' found at the outskirts of many towns in Nevada and Utah, or in one of the numerous but small Indian Reservations established in this century, which accommodate a hundred or fewer Indians, except for Owyhee (500 Shoshoni and 400 Northern Paiute) which was established in the last century. There remains much visiting between reservations and Indian colonies in towns, but verbal communication can take place in English today. It is only on the small and isolated Gosiute Reservation that children still acquire Shoshoni as their native language. The prevalence of the old propensity for occasional change of residence is not less now than formerly, but it is translated from seasonal migration to social visits over a wide territory by automobile travel. Since Shoshoni is still spoken by most adults, the language is viable for the rest of this century, but probably not longer, unless the smaller nationality interest serves to revive an interest in Shoshoni as a 'national' symbol — such an interest (even if borne by a minority) might continue the language into the next century, just as Irish and Welsh might continue into the distant future, if sufficiently subsidized through the offices of Irish and Welsh nationalists.

But the last sure opportunity to study Shoshoni dialects as a problem in sociolinguistics and the ethnography of communication remains in this century.

Intermarriage with Northern Paiute has probably increased the propensity for travel beyond the 'wide areas' that visiting Shoshoni bands formerly covered. Since Northern Paiute and Shoshoni belong to the same subfamily (Numic), the question of whether any intelligibility is possible between the two is better subjected to research than to conjecture.

We know that the Southern Paiute do not find Northern Paiute speech intelligible; at least speakers of these two apparently separate Numic languages use English as a lingua franca when they meet. Many Shoshoni, however, use not only English but also Northern Paiute, and Southern Paiute, as second languages.

## 4. ACQUISITION OF LANGUAGE WITHOUT A PEER GROUP

It is not always the case that Numic speakers acquire their first or native language in large part from hearing other children talk, rather than from a purely adult model, as is usually the case in societies like the Hopi, in which children are surrounded by age-mates, and in which a 'baby language' version of Hopi is spoken by young children. In the scattered and locally sparse population of the Great Basin, 'aboriginally (and still in some cases today) there were no peer groups', as Miller (1966) reports. Questions that this unusual situation suggests, and their implication for language change — as in the psycholinguistic theory that reformulation and reordering of grammatical rules is affected by children while adults merely add rules — can still be investigated.

Research by Lamb (1958), Hopkins (1965), Miller (1966, 1970) and Goss (1970) has nevertheless been largely concerned with the evolution of Numic diversity — has been past-oriented rather than present- or future-oriented.

## 5. INDETERMINATENESS OF NUMIC LANGUAGE BOUNDARIES

The first differentiation after proto-Numic times led ultimately to the present situation. Today the largest Numic group of dialects is, as already mentioned, centrally distributed (from Panamint in California, to the Shoshoni in Wyoming with their Comanche offshoot); this central group is flanked by another group of Numic dialects (Mono and Paviotso, Northern Paiute, Bannock) to the north. The northern Numic dialects occupied more territory than the flanking Numic dialects to the south (Kawaiisu and Southern Paiute, Ute, Chemehuevi). The interlocking and intermeshing within each of these three groups of Numic dialects occasionally encounters a low barrier to intelligibility — but still some kind of barrier (greater than that encountered among dialects which unquestionably belong to the same language); in such cases it is tempting to postulate more than one separate language in each of the three groups of Numic dialects, thereby yielding a total of six or seven rather than three or four separate languages.

As already mentioned, it is not possible to use dialect distance testing to determine language boundaries in a dialect chain because the extremes of such a chain would always turn out to indicate a language barrier while closer links in the chain would not; and lexicostatistic counts of shared cognates are difficult to interpret.

Some attempts have been made to determine language boundaries within the Numic dialect complex by the application of Swadesh's glottochronological techniques — i.e. by the percentage of shared cognates. These reflect phenomena more relevant to areal linguistics, typology, and sociolinguistics than to genetic proximity, which can be gauged only by shared innovations, and not even then when the innovations are sporadically distributed.

Until some new evaluation is proposed, the question of whether there are six separate Numic languages — or only three — appears at the moment to be either not interesting or not amenable to expression in terms of the family tree model. Beside the alternative classification of three versus six Numic languages, mentioned above, there is a five language classification which differs from the six language classification chiefly in merging Panamint with other dialects in the central group of Numic (Goss 1970, following Lamb 1958): '(1) Mono, (2) Paviotso (Northern Paiute), (3) Shoshone (including Comanche dialect), (4) Kawaiisu, and (5) Ute (including the dialects of the Ute, Southern Paiute, and Chemehuevi) ...'

## 6. YUMAN AND UTO-AZTECAN LANGUAGES IN CONTACT

Languages from four subfamilies of Uto-Aztecan — Numic, Takic, Hopi, and Piman — make contact with languages belonging to a wholly unrelated family (Yuman) in Arizona and California. See now section 10, Yuman Family, for details supplementing the rather over-simplified estimate made earlier in a paper by us and Schutz (1967) ('... we know, at least, where the language barriers [in the Yuman family] lie — namely between the groups of dialects labeled (A) the Upland or Pai language and (B) the Up River or Mohave-Maricopa-Yuma language, and (C) the Delta River or Cocopa (plus) language'); this is followed by oral history and ethnohistorical information on the relationships between speakers of these Yuman languages and their Uto-Aztecan neighbors. It would be interesting, now, to find out, from a modern ethnography of communication, the persistence as well as the shifts in intertribal alliances and trading relationships and hostilities that exist today.

The Havasupai gave succor to hundreds of Hopi refugees suffering from a late 18th century drought, thereby initiating — or continuing — a period of friendly intertribal relations that extended throughout the 19th century, despite (a) the existence of a language barrier and (b) the non-existence of agreed-upon boundaries between the two. English became available as a lingua franca only in the 20th century; this now permits communication between most members of both societies. Apparently the relationship between the Yuman Mohave and the Uto-Aztecan Chemehuevi was also non-hostile after the latter settled near the Mohave between 1776 and 1840. Here again verbal communication was formerly restricted to occasions when a bilingual was available. The non-Yuman, non-Uto-Aztecan Zuni also served as hosts for Hopi families who sought refuge among the Zuni in the 19th century. Until the 20th century friendly relations existed between societies speaking Uto-Aztecan languages north of Mexico and those non-Apachean Indians with whom they had contact, so far as is known in ethnohistory — despite the need of occasional bilinguals to effect any verbal communication at all. It might be argued that the very lack of easy communication among the majority in contact tended to preserve the peace. On the other hand, much friendly communication existed among the Shoshoni of the Great Basin; some degree of communication could be established between visitor and host, but visitors to another's territory and their hosts — during the occasional season when piñons were bearing in the host's territory but not at home — were uniformly friendly and hospitable. This friendliness may well have been motivated: a reciprocal visit from the host would operate something like a gift exchange at another season, when food was plentiful in the other territory.

However in the case of societies speaking Yuman languages, there are instances of discord between ethnic groups in contact, even though the majority could communicate with each other in varieties of the same language. Though the Havasupai and Walapai were not hostile to the Southern Paiute, separated from them by the Grand Canyon and a language barrier, they were indeed hostile to the Yavapai, who spoke the same Yuman language on the other side of the Aquarius mountains. Despite the 1857 success of the Yuman Maricopa in defeating the Yuman Mohave and Yuma, the Maricopa withdrew from the Colorado River and moved eastward along the Gila River. It might be argued that easy verbal contact between different ethnic groups in contact does not tend to keep peace among the majority in frequent contact; though the Shoshoni, as mentioned, enjoyed relatively easy contact with one another, it cannot be said that they had frequent contact — rather, no more than seasonal contact on ceremonial occasions, as when rabbit hunts or peyote meetings occurred.

## 7. DIFFERENT SOCIOLINGUISTIC SITUATIONS IN THE SAME LANGUAGE

Ethnic differences among the speakers of the fairly homogeneous Pai language in the Yuman family make for great sociolinguistic differences — while the Pai language as such does not. Thus, the Havasupai are bilingual in English. Many of the Walapai are more truly Walapai-Mohave bilinguals than speakers of Walapai with English as a second language; still others speak Hopi or Navajo as a second language, and English as a third. Whatever kind of bilingual a Walapai may be, he speaks Walapai at wakes, in courtship, in joking or with joking relatives, and alternates with English at community fiestas, when answering charges of arrest, and when hospitalized — even Walapai nurses switch to English after first talking in Walapai. The Yavapai have had so much intermarriage with the Apache that many speak three wholly unrelated languages — Yavapai and Apache, as well as English. Some say that more Apache is spoken by the Yavapai at San Carlos than Yavapai. The first of these three languages to be lost in replacive bilingualism is Yavapai; the first to be learned is English. Spanish, which was also conspicuous a century ago, has become so old-fashioned as to be hardly ever used by those who retain a smattering of it. Those who now have only a passive knowledge of Yavapai find that they cannot understand the slightly divergent Havasupai-Walapai dialect at all. However much communication results, it is considered good form for a Yavapai to speak Yavapai when he meets a speaker of another Yuman dialect; perhaps Yavapai will remain viable as long as it functions as a symbol of being a Yuman Indian.

There are two languages of the Yuman family that are celebrated for their dialectal differentiation: (a) the Pai language which includes a divergent non-contiguous dialect in Baja California as well as contiguous dialects in Arizona, reviewed above; (b) Diegueño, which seems to have developed greater dialectal differentiation than Pai, even though Diegueño does not include widely separated dialects as Pai does.

## 8. THE EFFECT OF SOCIAL INTERACTION ON LANGUAGE BOUNDARIES

In Uto-Aztecan, the Numic subfamily is celebrated for the problems it offers for determining clear-cut language barriers. The vagueness or indeterminateness in establishing language barriers in the Great Basin may be accounted for in part by seasonal migrations and, more generally, a fondness for moving about in 'wider areas', whether economically motivated or to relieve the isolation of living (otherwise) in contact with none other than members of a few families. One suspects that the difficulty of saying exactly how many Numic languages are spoken in the Great Basin could be matched by the difficulty speakers of these languages have in estimating how many dialects or different Numic languages they have learned or picked up quite casually while visiting among neighboring languages and dialects ever since early childhood.

In contrast, the pueblo societies in the Southwest (whose economy is based on a continuity of New World neolithic horticulture) do not go in for seasonal migrations, nor do they suffer any sense of social isolation which stimulates visiting for non-economic and non-ceremonial purposes. One might expect less vagueness in determining where the language barriers lie in pueblo societies — i.e. in distinguishing between separate languages and dialects of the same language. This expectation is wholly realized for Zuni and Hopi pueblos and partly realized for Keresan. But since only one language is spoken in each of these three cases, it is not surprising that the linguistic variety problem can be treated as a matter of simple dialectology.

Tanoan is in a sense a test case for the thesis that clear-cut language boundaries are a functional consequence of pueblo culture. As appears below (under 13, Tanoan relatives of Uto-Aztecan), our latest Tanoan authority concurs with our first Tanoan authority on the number of different Tanoan language groups — namely three — but our latest Tanoan authority casts doubt on whether this was the case before some Tanoan dialects became extinct. It is when pueblos are abandoned, and their former inhabitants move into a still flourishing pueblo that dialect leveling takes place, or that speakers of a formerly different language become so assimilated to the dominant group that they adopt its language. A possible Tanoan example of this is found in the so-called Towa 'language-group', which was formerly represented in two pueblos, Jemez and Pecos. The latter was abandoned after an epidemic in 1838; a score of survivors moved to the Jemez pueblo, which includes today well over a thousand individuals, a third of whom maintain a cultural self-identification as descendants of the fugitives from Pecos in contrast to their co-residents at Jemez today — but they have not maintained their linguistic differentiation. Today only one leveled dialect is spoken in the Jemez pueblo — under the assumption that Pecos was once dialectally differentiated from Jemez — or else replacive bilingualism has resulted in the replacement of Pecos by Jemez, if Pecos was a separate language, whether or not it was a Tanoan language.

It is also possible to cite a Tanoan example of language maintenance despite the fact that speakers of one language (Tewa as spoken at Hano) live on a single mesa with and are intermarried with speakers of another language (Hopi). The result is non-reciprocal bilingualism: the Hopi do not learn Tewa, while all Tewa living on First Mesa speak both Hopi and Tewa.

## 9. PARTICIPANTS IN FIELDWORK: AMERICAN INDIANS AND EXTERNAL INVESTIGATORS

Cultural and social anthropology characteristically comes to focus on the 'other society' and on another language than that of the external investigator, as does ongoing work in ethnolinguistics (in which language is used to explicate culture), and in sociolinguistics (in which language is used to explicate social relationships), and in autonomous linguistics (in which language is represented as a self-sufficient system). But neither in ethnoscience nor in autonomous linguistics that seeks to investigate language-linked semantics will the psychology of the 'other' long remain the appropriate psychology, since persons-in-the-society are increasingly working as collaborators or as independent investigators of their own society. All kinds of fieldwork problems are still open to investigation in the societies of the Southwest and the Great Basin, since the Indians in these areas, for the most part, still live, with adaptations to modern conditions, where their forebears traditionally lived; they have neither been removed nor have they removed themselves into these areas (except for the Yaqui) as have most Indians in modern Oklahoma. Of all the possible varieties of fieldwork mentioned, the following sample of on-going work is confined to ethnolinguistics, ethnoscience, sociolinguistics and to various kinds of autonomous linguistics.

Our sample of current ethnolinguistic work on Uto-Aztecan languages in the

Southwest and Great Basin is limited to Hopi, Papago and Ute. Much more ethnolinguistic work than this also appears in the non-current literature, for ethnolinguistics is the oldest of the several special interest subfields that now seek to relate language to societies, to particular social spaces within a given society, to cognitive psychology, and to various applied problems in teaching and in political anthropology; indeed, in the older anthropological literature, 'ethnolinguistics' was used as a cover term for any research that attempted to relate language to any aspect of culture, including the Sapir-Whorf kind of linguistic relativity.

For Hopi we cite in our bibliography Kennard's paper on linguistic acculturation (1963); this paper was a by-product of a larger study of post-war acculturation. Another paper by Kennard on Hopi, now in press, is concerned with magic and metaphor. Black's (1967) paper on Hopi chanting treats different aspects of chanting. Lévi-Strauss' student, Arlette Frigout, has written several articles on Hopi space orientation (e.g. 1966); Ortiz's student Louis Hiel is doing fieldwork on Hopi clowning. Titiev has published a monograph on a diary of his 1933 fieldwork and on changes in Hopi culture since then.

Nagata's recently published book (1970) on the most acculturated Hopi village (Moencopi) includes interpretations derived from ethnolinguistic work, and is also relevant to our own current interest in sociolinguistic aspects of the adaptation of Hopi who live off-mesa. The former use of Moencopi as a dormitory while working in their fields (but returning to Oraibi for ceremonies) anticipates the practice of many modern Hopi — using nearby Anglo towns as dormitories while working for wages (but returning to their Mesa villages regularly for ceremonies, and eventually for retirement).

Fred Eggan's (1967) paper giving a Hopi example of the distinction between history and myth is concerned with theory which is ethnolinguistically oriented. Dorothy Eggan's work on Hopi dreams (1955) was also so oriented, though concerned primarily with psychological theory.

A. F. Whiting remains our chief contributor to Hopi ethnolinguistics, pure and simple. He is not only working on a revision of his published monograph on ethnobotany (1939) but has 'in progress' much additional work on the scope of naming in Hopi of ethnozoology (mammals and birds), astronomy (names of stars) and costumes and costuming. In one sense or another our own monograph on *Hopi domains* (1957) is also ethnolinguistic in scope, though our intent was not, like Whiting's, to present an encyclopedic compendium in any one domain.

We can cite only three current contributors of ethnolinguistic papers on Papago, and one for Ute. Alvarez, a native speaker of Papago, explicates Papago puns (1965); Donald Bahr has worked with Alvarez on aspects of Papago culture as expressed in the language; and Madeleine Mathiot has written several papers and monographs which are at once ethnolinguistic and psychological in interest and throw new light on the whole question of linguistic relativity. She has done extensive work on cognitive categories in the Papago lexicon and morphology; see for example her 1967 paper and others cited therein. James Goss's (1968) ethnolinguistic studies of the Ute language include a study of the relationship of kin behavior, kin terms and the names and behavior of characters in Ute myths.

Our sample of ethnolinguistic work on the Tanoan and Keresan languages includes the ethnographies of two native speakers of Tewa — Ortiz's *Tewa world* (1969) and Dozier's *The Hopi-Tewa of Arizona* (1954). Dozier has also done linguistic acculturational work on Tewa (and Yaqui) and has recently (1967) summarized this and earlier work on linguistic acculturation in other Southwestern languages. Richard Ford has recently worked on the cultural ecology and ethnobotany of Tewa, Picuris and Cochiti. G. Trager and his recent students have also done ethnolinguistic work on Tanoan languages, e.g. the Tragers' paper (1970) on cardinal directions and Leap's (1970) on noun class semology.

Our sample of ethnolinguistic work on Navajo and Apache is more extensive than that on any other language group in the Southwest. In his paper which questions whether a singer's 'fee' is payment or prestation, Aberle (1967) makes use of Navajo lexicon to clarify a number of fine points in his ethnography; and in his on-going work in economic anthropology, he is making use of Navajo words for households and families, kin, ecological niches and some religious concepts relevant to economics. Rather than lexicon, David McAllester is presently concerned with the translation of Navajo poetry (versions of the Horse Songs in the Blessingway ceremony), and finds that his translations result in better English poetry the closer they get to the Navajo source language; in addition to current work on all the songs in Blessingway ceremony, he has recorded a nine-day chant with several hundred songs (Shootingway). Between 1957 and 1970 Leland C. Wyman has edited Father Berard Haile's translation of four Navajo ceremonies (Beautyway, Windways, Red Antway, Blessingway), and written monographs with long lists of Navajo terms for plants and insects. He is now engaged in preparing for eventual publication Navajo texts and their translations from the Mountainway and a monograph on the Nightway, the latter a study of ceremonial procedure and sandpaintings, and has recently published a paper on sandpaintings of the Shootingway (1970). Keith Basso's work with Apache, as that of his former student Everett, is in part ethnolinguistically oriented. The latter based his doctoral dissertation (1970) on a ten month's study of medical decision making among the White Mountain Apache, e.g. ailments defined in one way in Apache are taken to a medicine man while those defined in another way are not (rather, the patient is taken to the Public Health Service for treatment by white physicians). Much of Everett's other work is in ethnoscience, as is much of Basso's, but the latter's article on linguistic acculturation (1967) is clearly ethnolinguistic in scope and the question which Basso is now formulating for future discussion might be treated ethnolinguistically: 'Why do some domains ... appear to get readily (and more or less completely) extended, while others do not?'

Our sample of recent ethnolinguistic work on Zuni includes Walker's paper in press on the domain of household items in the Zuni lexicon, and Tedlock's chapter on pueblo literature in the monograph edited by Ortiz, as well as other papers in press dealing with oral literature and 'Zuni narrative paralinguistics' (also discussed under ethnoscience, following).

The remaining ethnolinguistic work in our sample indicates a widely scattered interest in large dictionary projects. Thus, Maring (1967) notes that the Keresan speakers at Acoma are anxious to have a dictionary of their language prepared; various plans are underway to implement this, and space is being provided in the offices of the Acoma Community Action Program. For the summer of 1970, Turner directed the work of a half dozen beginning students from the University of Arizona on an on-going dictionary project which is intended to be cumulative as future students work on the same languages (Yaqui, Papago, Pima, Mohave, Apache, Pima Bajo) until a doctoral candidate can make use of the lexical accumulation on a given language to prepare a bilingual dictionary. Fontana at the Arizona State Museum has tape-recorded lexical lists of various Southwest languages, including a tape spoken by possibly the last speaker of Lipan Apache.

Our sample of beginning work in ethnoscience in the Southwest is limited to work on a few languages — Papago, Hopi, and Zuni (e.g. Tedlock's work), and Apache (e.g. Basso's work), as well as on Navajo. This sparseness in the sample is surely not unconnected with the fact that ethnoscience appeared last among the special interests that have (in the second half of this century) given new directions to fieldwork, and a new sense of collaborative cooperation between outside investigators of the 'other' society and persons in the 'other' society; the latter appear to become more readily intrigued with ethnoscience problems than with problems in ethnolinguistics (above) or with sociolinguistics or autonomous linguistics (following).

For ethnoscience problems concerned with monolingual verbal definitions, note the brilliant diversity of such definitions made by Luke Preston in Papago, translated by Kenneth Hale, and arranged in terms of logical relations in Casagrande and Hale 1967. This paper shows that it is possible for a native speaker of a language, as Papago, to formulate 'definitions for common words which seldom if ever require explanation' in the cultural spaces which a Papago would enter in traditional Papago society. But the Papago, like the Hopi, the Navajo and Apache, are increasingly sharing our cultural spaces and academic interests; they can be intrigued into testing whether it is possible to define all words in a native language by means of other words in that language. The exercise that Luke Preston performed in his own language — and successfully so — shows at least that the test is worth trying in other languages, as an empirical basis for discussing ethnoscience universals.

For ethnoscience problems concerned with folk-taxonomies, we refer especially to the collaborative work between a native speaker of Navajo, Kenneth Y. Begishe, and Oswald Werner (e.g., Werner and Begishe 1966). Together they prepared a half dozen preliminary versions of a monumental anatomical atlas which, so far, lists 400 body-part terms in Navajo, thereby offsetting the false conclusion previously held by the health personnel on the Navajo Reservation — namely, that their Navajo patients spoke a language which included no more than 50 terms for body-parts. Their anatomical atlas is by no means a terminological compilation based on verbal information supplied by Begishe (qua informant) and typologized by Werner (qua external investigator); in short, it is not an example of traditional ethnolinguistic work. Rather, it is a clear example of a folk-taxonomy of the encyclopedic sort — the sort that represents the total lexical resources of a particular domain in a particular language; like all encyclopedic knowledge, this exceeds the knowledge interiorized individually by any one speaker of the language. Instead of reflecting our typological notions of the natural order for listing body parts (from head to neck to shoulder to arms to hands to trunk to hip to leg to foot), the Navajo anatomical atlas lists body parts in a folk-taxonomic order which is the inverse of ours (from foot to leg to hip to trunk to shoulder to arms to hands to neck and head). This folk-taxonomic order is the order in which many Navajo speakers discussed body parts with Begishe (an aspect of sentence-oriented ethnoscience, as noted below); it is also the order of creation of various parts of the body as attested in oral literature that has been collected by anthropologists engaged in ethnolinguistic work (see above); it is the order which the Navajo literature motivates mythologically and expresses explicitly, as in the following translation of a sentence in that literature: *from the bottom of the sole to the top of the head.* In addition to anatomy, many other folk-taxonomies have been assembled by Begishe and Werner and their students, as in the Perchonock and Werner paper on the classification of Navajo food (1969).

For ethnoscience problems concerned with applied anthropology, we refer especially to the many studies undertaken in the last decade by Levy and Kunitz and their medical students on anomie and social pathologies and social deviance, on alcoholic cirrhosis and drinking patterns, on medical interpreting and decision-making, on peyotism, on schizophrenics, homicide, and suicide — among the Navajo and their ethnic neighbors, the Hopi, the Yavapai and the Apache.

It will someday be possible to compare the extensive work on various Navajo folk-taxonomies with parallel taxonomies beginning to be prepared by several workers for Yuman and Pueblo societies, including Zuni, that enjoy occasional contact with the Navajo. A theoretical difficulty that has always been found in treating ethnolinguistic domains and that reappears in ethnoscience work might well be illuminated by comparative study of a problem which, as Basso puts it, concerns 'the extension of whole (i.e. multi-lexemic) taxonomies from one domain to another, and possible reasons why' (personal communication) (1970a).

For the use of folk-taxonomies as a basis for attesting dummy nodes (the no-name problem) by means of asking questions and obtaining answers in Hopi on the relation of unnamed nodes to adjacent nodes that have Hopi names available for a tree diagram, we refer to our own papers on sentence-oriented ethnoscience.

Everyone who works on any kind of ethnoscience problem is aware that ethnoscience (no less than new directions in autonomous linguistics) is bringing about a transition in fieldwork that is changing the relationship between American Indians in the Southwest and external investigators who formerly probed them as 'informants' but now work together with them as collaborators on problems of mutual interest, with the consequence that our American Indian co-investigators (and co-authors of publications which result from the joint investigations) become our personal friends and colleagues in a way that was scarcely possible when American Indians were 'used' as informants. What remains, for the remainder of this century, is to effect academic social change so that a fieldworker who is a native speaker in a society under investigation, working in close cooperation with a fieldworker who is not, may be rewarded by attaining professional security. Some other way is needed for effecting such social change than that of having the doctoral degree a prerequisite to professional security, as it is in colleges and universities.

Our sample of beginning work in sociolinguistics for the native American languages of the Southwest turns out to include fewer activities than can be readily found for ethnoscience work in the same area. This is surprising, since sociolinguistics, or the sociology of language (as Joshua Fishman prefers to call it), might be said for some other parts of the world to have attracted more specialized personnel, to have produced more papers, monographs, and readers, and to be more diversified in its different aspects than is ethnoscience, so far. For the Southwest, only a few types of sociolinguistic interest have been expressed, as in language maintenance.

Concerning this first and most conspicuous type, Levy and Kunitz have noted that Navajo who leave their reservation to live in Flagstaff recognize each other as Navajo but do not talk to each other at all unless they are closely related; they send their children to Anglo schools where English is the language of instruction and of the playground. Replacive bilingualism in the children's generation seems more likely than language maintenance by them, though there is no doubt that Navajo will continue to be spoken, beside English, by those who remain on their reservation.

The environment of the Hopi who move to Flagstaff from their villages on the mesas differs in some ways from that of the Navajo, so far as language maintenance is concerned, chiefly by the fact that the Hopi children often return for weekends to watch ceremonial dances in the villages from which they came. In fact, the off-mesa Hopi of Flagstaff have been — for the last two years — practicing dances for weeks each spring and early summer using the Museum of Northern Arizona's hospitable accommodations, in order to be able to contribute their share by performing at the mesa villages. A study of language maintenance (and the kind of changes that are occurring in 'expanded Hopi') was recently initiated by LaVerne Masayesva, a native speaker of Hopi. She and Harry King interviewed most Hopi families in their Flagstaff homes, and intend to continue the interviewing and sampling of Hopi language in other towns that are close enough for off-mesa Hopi to return to the mesas on weekends to renew their self-identification.

Elizabeth Brandt (1970) has investigated the correlation between age of speakers and their relative competence in Sandia, Spanish and English, and amount of phonological change in their Sandia. Mary Miller (1970) investigated the language preferences of (mostly Pima) children on the Salt River reservation in terms of which languages were used to speak to playmates and certain relatives, and questions such as which languages were believed to be 'best', correlating the information with information on the native languages of the parents and the children's ages.

Basso's work in sociolinguistics is on types of situational factors which accompany the absence of verbal communication among the Western Apache — i.e. under what circumstances the Apache do not speak (1971). And Cox (1970) has studied how Hopi groups use gossip to make a political point. Our own survey of the modern language situation in Arizona includes a few points of minor sociolinguistic interest.

The Boasian model dominated autonomous linguistic work on languages of native America since the turn of this century; with minor shifts of emphasis, it continues today and results in the production of grammars which are designed to be morphologically comprehensive, to account for the classification of words, and all their constituents, and to be accompanied by a separate body of texts which have ethnolinguistic uses besides serving as a corpus to attest the correctness of the grammatical analysis for each language treated. The survey of California Indian languages — extending to languages spoken in the Great Basin and the Southwest — called in addition for the production of a separate lexical corpus — a bilingual dictionary — for each language. Rules for the production of sentences in grammars following the Boasian model are conspicuously, if not entirely, absent; syntax is treated last, if at all.

Much of the current work in autonomous linguistics in the Southwest and Great Basin is still done within this Boasian framework, or in other essentially taxonomic frameworks, as the tagmemic model (most frequently used by members of the Summer Institute of Linguistics), and as the 'phonological syntax' of Trager and Smith.

Beside continued work in taxonomic linguistics, work has begun in the transformational-generative frame of reference, in which syntax comes first; and with the centrality of syntax, semantic problems are given attention that they never receive in grammars that follow the Boasian model, and the lexicon is treated as a component of the grammar. Some of the new generative work is based on earlier published sources rather than on fresh fieldwork (e.g. Harm's 1966 generative statement of Southern Paiute phonology on the basis of Sapir's published Southern Paiute materials), but generative fieldwork is also being done, especially with the assistance of native speakers of Southwestern languages as collaborators rather than as informants.

Examples of work done within both kinds of framework are given under the headings of the various language families, following, except for current work on Apachean languages, since such work is discussed fully by Krauss in this volume.

Transformational-generative work is conducive to presenting the grammar of a language as a basis for learning to generate sentences in it. Ronald Langacker, Roderick Jacobs, and their students at La Jolla, in collaboration with a Luiseño speaker, have produced an *Introduction to Luiseño* which would facilitate learning Luiseño (Hyde 1971). The concomitant interest in language acquisition and the new attitudes toward the education of Indians — including the possibility of using Indian languages as the initial languages of instruction — have inspired work throughout the Southwest on the speech of Indian children and the preparation of materials not only to teach Indian languages to non-native speakers (as Langacker's for Luiseño and the several Navajo teaching grammars cited by Krauss) but also for the elementary education of speakers of Indian languages. Work of this sort includes projects that are being directed by linguists at two universities for the Navajo language — at the University of New Mexico (by Bernard Spolsky and his colleagues) and at the University of Texas (by Muriel Saville); and for the Keresan languages at the University of Southern Illinois (by Joel Maring, working in collaboration with Acoma students).

## 10. YUMAN FAMILY

More Yuman languages are spoken in the Southwest than in the continuous Yuman area extending into California and Baja California. Two of the three branches of the family are found mostly in the Southwest; the third in California and Baja California.

(1) The Pai branch had been previously identified either as Upland Yuman, or as Arizona Yuman or as Northern Yuman; all these previous identifications became misleading as soon as it was realized that Paipai (Akwaʔala) in Baja California belongs in the same Yuman branch as Havasupai, Walapai and Yavapai in Arizona. It is not probable that another language, Kiliwa, may turn out to belong to this branch rather than to any other Yuman branch; Kiliwa is spoken south of Paipai in Baja California.

In recent years doctoral dissertations have been finished or nearly finished on Havasupai (William Seiden (1963) and Edwin Kozlowski (1972), Indiana University), on Yavapai (Robert Madigan and Bonnie Kendall (1972), Indiana University; Alan Shaterian, University of California, Berkeley), on Walapai (James Redden (1965), Indiana University), Paipai (Judith Joel (1967), U.C.L.A.). The similarity between Paipai in the south and the other Pai languages in the north justifies placing all Pai languages in one branch — a branch that flanks the two other branches of the Yuman languages.

(2) Mohave, Maricopa and Yuma — the languages of the central branch of the Yuman family — are still spoken in the Colorado River drainage. Halpern's doctoral dissertation on Yuma was written a generation ago, but Yuma remains the only language in this branch for which something approaching a comprehensive taxonomy of grammatical formatives is available; however, work is currently being done on Maricopa (Bary Alpher, Arizona State University, Henry Harwell, Indiana University), and has begun on Mohave (Susan Penfield, University of Arizona).

(3) Cocopa and Diegueño are spoken in the delta region of the Colorado and on both sides of the California-Mexican border. Cocopa has been comprehensively studied (Crawford 1966), as have the various Diegueño dialects — the latter by Margaret Langdon (1970a) and her students, who also have worked on the reconstruction of Proto-Yuman (Langdon 1970b), as has A.C. Wares (1968).

To return to (1), the Pai branch, two salient problems need to be discussed. The first is the geographical separation of the Paipai in Mexico from the Pai dialects in Arizona, and the second is to account for the dialect differentiation in Arizona.

Three different ways of explaining the geographical separation were reviewed by D. Walker in 1970. One was that innovations occurred in the two geographical branches of Yuman which are flanked by the Pai branch, while the latter remained conservative during the innovating period. This is the strongest claim of the three and the most vulnerable: it can be proved or disproved, after comparative evidence is brought forward to show what is innovative in the Yuman languages and what is not. The second claim, made by Werner Winter (1967), is that Paipai represents a recent migration to the south; this is the least vulnerable claim, for aside from the acknowledged linguistic similarities that constitute the basis for the classification of Pai languages in one branch, there is apparently no ethnohistorical or ethnographic evidence available either to support or to cast doubt on any particular migration. Walker argues that the third claim — that the Pai-like features of Paipai represent some continuum of dialect features between Paipai and the neighboring Yuman dialects in the Delta branch (Diegueño and Cocopa) — fails to support the migration claim and, further, that the dialect continuum cannot be adequately explained by the family tree model. The adjacent dialects of the Diegueño language, as Tipai and Ipai, are more numerous than those of any other Yuman language except possibly the Pai language in Arizona.

Ethnographers have treated the Havasupai and the Walapai as culturally distinct, though their speech is virtually identical; the two were apparently ethnically one until relatively recently — the distinction having been externally imposed upon them, first by the Army, and then by the Bureau of Indian Affairs for administrative purposes.

The Yavapai are possibly overly distinguished from the Havasupai-Walapai in the minds of anthropologists, because of the self-designation of the Yavapai-Apache tribe. Whatever the effect of their close association with Apache has had on the culture of the Yavapai, and it has been considerable, the association has had no apparent effect on their language, though widespread intermarriage has resulted in frequent bilingualism.

The differences between Yavapai and Havasupai-Walapai are trivial differences in phonology; some slight differences in descriptive terms and idioms, the bases of which are cognates; and some differences in syntax, especially in inflections. The differences in inflections are apparently the chief source of the less than complete mutual intelligibility between the Pai dialects spoken in Arizona.

## 11. HOKAN RELATIVES OF YUMAN

Until recently, Hokan-Siouan was taken to be a phylum which included language families scattered from the Pacific to the Atlantic, and from Mexico into Canada. In 1964, Americanists at the First Conference on American Indian Languages agreed that evidence for the Hokan-Siouan hypothesis, first proposed by Edward Sapir, had failed to materialize. On the other hand, evidence for a Hokan phylum, including the Yuman family, had been increasingly found since Sapir's day.[1]

In the context of the weaker hypothesis — a Hokan phylum, bereft of Siouan and other eastern language families — it can be said that languages of the Yuman family are the only Hokan languages in the Southwest; and that the non-Yuman Washo is the only Hokan language in the Great Basin. Though the Hokan phylum includes several families or branches beyond the Southwest, it is not necessarily the case that such Hokan branches (to the west, northwest and southwest of the Yuman languages) will turn out to be more closely related to each other than to the Yuman branch. Problems such as these, and anticipation of really attesting rather than guessing at internal Hokan relationships, were discussed from three points of view in the 1970 Hokan Conference held at San Diego, and are now reviewed below.

First, it was noted by Troike (1970) that a case can be made for a 'special relationship' between the Yuman family and the non-Yuman Cochimi, a Hokan language formerly spoken in Baja California. This was noted in the light of Kroeber's 1931 estimate that Cochimi and Yuman are closer to each other than either is to Seri, still spoken on Tiborón Island in the Gulf of California.

Note that this, in turn, is reminiscent of the intermediate status of Eyak, between the Athapascan family and its distant relatives in the Na-Dene phylum. Krauss (in this volume of *Current Trends*) clearly states that Eyak, nevertheless, does not belong in the Athapascan family. So also, Troike's interpretation is that an occasional Hokan language or two which is closer to Yuman than are other Hokan languages may nevertheless be counted as non-Yuman.

Any such bold claim as that Seri and Cochimi are somewhat divergent members of the Yuman family would be jumping from the frying pan into the fire. Though comparative linguistic work in general subscribes to the tenet that two putative daughter languages can never be demonstrated not to have descended from some same ancestral proto-language — i.e. though negative interpretations are impossible to demonstrate — Turner (1970) nonetheless attempts just this (to show that Seri and Chontal are not genetically related). On the other hand, if Seri and Yuman are notably similar, and if Chontal and Seri are too, as Kroeber thought, is Chontal to be taken as a member of the Yuman family?

In short, one consideration of the San Diego conference was to discuss the possibility of extending a particular language family, as Yuman, to include other languages within the Hokan phylum.

---

[1] This is reflected on the two wall maps, both called 'Map of North American Indian Languages' (*PAES* 20 and *PAES* 20 revised). The Hokan-Siouan phylum, as well as other phyla proposed by Sapir, appeared on the first edition of *PAES* 20 (1946). Though the Hokan-Siouan phylum does not, the western extension of the discarded phylum does appear, as Hokan, on the second edition of *PAES* 20 (1966). For a critique of the compromise classification between the early Powell and early Sapir classifications, see our review of Pinnow in a recent issue of *Language* (1967).

Secondly, we face the consideration that the Hokan phylum consists of little language families and 'language isolates' (in Mary Haas' sense — language isolates having no close family relatives) which are necessarily interconnected and interlocking without anything comparable to the clear break between the Athapascan family and Haida and Tlingit in the Na-Dene phylum. Mary Haas, in reference to the Northern California linguistic area, shows (1970) that non-Yuman Hokan, as well as Yuma (a single, but sufficient, example of the Yuman languages) all include the same prefix (*m-*) for second person (Karok, Shasta, Chimariko, Pomo), while the non-Hokan Wiyot and Yurok have a different second person prefix, a prefix which is cognate with the prefix reconstructed for proto-Algonquian (*$ke$-). Crawford (1970) cites rather extensive cognate sets to attest the relationship of a non-Yuman Hokan language in California (Chimariko) to Cocopa and Mohave and other languages of the Yuman family. The motivation in this second consideration is to attest the genetic relationship of Hokan languages, irrespective of subbranch or small family relationships (such as of Yuman).

Thirdly, we face the consideration that groups of Hokan languages might be distinguished more efficiently in terms of areal linguistics, rather than in terms of a family tree model depending on a single assertion of brachiation; the latter would lead to controversy — if more than one brachiation were to be postulated — as in occasional former attempts to include Seri in the Yuman family in the south within Hokan (our second consideration, above); similar alternative branching can be controverted for the Pomo family in northern California. At any rate, when groups of Hokan languages were discussed at the Hokan conference under the apparent influence of areal linguistic considerations, the Yuman family was often left unmentioned. Pomo was more often included, either as a branch of Hokan which permitted self-sufficient reconstruction, or as a type of Hokan structure which might, with other northern Hokan languages, permit a theory of proto-Hokan phonology.

Jacobsen had the following criticism to make of such paired comparisons as Atsugewi-Achumawi and Shasta, Shasta and Karok, Karok and Washo, Karok and Yana, Yana and Eastern Pomo, without assuming that each pair descended from a single proto-language; in fact, cognates from other Hokan languages were often cited as 'additional forms' beside the focus on a paired comparison. Different patterns of correspondence did emerge, but the patterning of a proto-language would not emerge. Anomalous correspondences also resulted from Bright's comparisons of five northern Hokan languages, and sparse evidence for recurrent correspondence could, of course, only be expected from Haas' comparisons restricted to nine items of basic vocabulary in a wide range of Hokan languages.

Jacobsen eschewed the paired comparisons and areal linguistic borrowings which give emphasis to recent innovations, and relied instead on internal reconstruction — on the best single study of Hokan, that of Sapir and his students on Yana (Yahi) (see Bibliography). There are three stop series in Yana (neutral, aspirated, and glottalized), and three also in Washo, Salinan, and Chimariko; these are exceeded by the four series in Pomo languages; other Hokan languages appear to have two series (Chumash and Shasta) or one (Karok and Yuman). The working hypothesis obtained from this diversity in stops is a proto-Hokan two stop system (plain and glottalized); additional series are supposed to have originated from consonant clusters. (The merging of two series into one must have been different in the north (Karok), in a linguistic area in which glottalized consonants are characteristic, than in the Southwest (Yuman), where the surrounding languages do not all include glottalized stops.)

Recent descriptive works on the non-Yuman Hokan languages which are most relevant to the Great Basin or Southwest languages include William Jacobsen's Ph.D. thesis on Washo (1964) and the work of Edward Moser (e.g. 1970) of the Summer Institute of Linguistics on Seri.

## 12. UTO-AZTECAN FAMILY

The northern Uto-Aztecan languages are spoken in the Great Basin and in the Southwest, as well as in the flanking adjacent areas. Most of these languages were traditionally thought to belong to that major branch called Shoshonean in which four subfamilies could be distinguished; recent comparative work has tended to focus on these four subfamilies as units in reconstruction rather than on the major branch.

Languages in the northernmost subfamily which extend south from the Plateau culture area and which are distributed throughout the Great Basin and into California and the Southwest (and more recently into the Plains) were labelled 'Numic' by Sydney Lamb (1958). 'Numic' is appropriately derived from the term for *person* in the languages to which it applies. The new name, Numic, is an improvement over the old name, Plateau Shoshonean, because the languages in this subfamily are by no means restricted to the Plateau culture area; in distribution, they center in the Great Basin. In fact, however, the motivation for the renaming to Numic was to avoid the implication of any special relationship among the subfamilies of the traditional major branch (Shoshonean), i.e. to avoid terminological confusion in arguing for a new perspective — that the sound system of the Numic subfamily developed directly from the proto-Uto-Aztecan system. The combined sample of Numic sound systems presented by Hale and us in 1962 (hereinafter VVH) and by Miller in 1967 includes Southern Paiute, Mono, and Comanche. Sven Liljeblad has for the last few decades been investigating the northernmost Numic dialects or languages (Northern Paiute and Bannock), and James Goss has recently completed a Ph.D. dissertation on Ute. Additional Numic languages are mentioned in the preface to this paper; the problem of determining language barriers and distinguishing separate languages from dialects of the same language is also discussed there.

The Takic subfamily was so named by Wick Miller. 'Takic' is derived from the term for *man*, but inappropriately so, since cognates for *man* appear not only in the languages which fall in the Takic subfamily but also in languages which do not, as in Hopi (ta·qa) and in languages of the Aztec subfamily (ta·ka-t, λa·ka-λ, teke-t). The motivation for changing the name of this subfamily from Southern California Shoshonean to Takic is parallel to that for innovating Numic, i.e. to avoid implication of development of a sound system through an intermediate major branch (Shoshonean). In addition to Miller's 'Takic', Bright and Hill (1967) have innovated 'Cupan' as a cover-term for Luiseño, Cahuilla and Cupeño, and postulated a closer genetic relationship between Cahuilla and Cupeño than that of either to Luiseño; all three languages in the Cupan subfamily then stand apart from Serrano which is regarded as more distantly related within the Takic subfamily. The relationship among the languages still spoken in the Southern California subfamily of Uto-Aztecan can be shown in a tree diagram as follows:

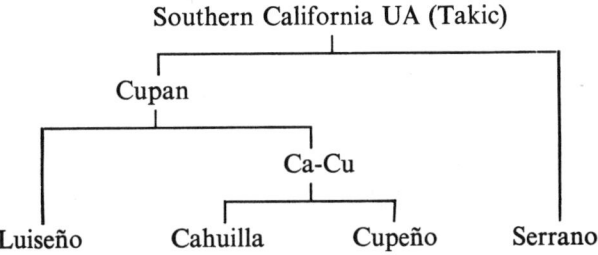

Doctoral dissertations by Kenneth Hill (1967) and Jane Hill (1966) on Serrano and Cupeño, respectively, have been completed. Most recently Langacker and his colleagues have produced a grammar of Luiseño (Hyde 1971), and Seiler is continuing his fieldwork and publications on Cahuilla (e.g. 1970).

In addition to Numic and Takic, the two remaining subfamilies in the northern major branch of U-A are each represented by a single language — Hopi and Tübatulabal.

These four subfamilies were correctly recognized in 1907 by Kroeber who did not contrive Shoshoneless terms for them, since he worked under the assumption that the four subfamilies were descended from an intermediate Shoshonean parent rather than directly descended from proto-Uto-Aztecan.

The correctness of Kroeber's assumption was challenged by Whorf in 1935, largely on the grounds that Whorf could find no evidence of shared phonology or shared innovations to justify the major traditional branch (Shoshonean); smaller groups of languages, stated in terms of four subfamilies, could naturally be expected to show shared features in each subfamily. If no comparative light can be obtained through considering a major Shoshonean brachiation, then Shoshoneless labels for the four subfamilies are of course needed.

Since Whorf, the possibility of an alternative historical interpretation to the subfamily classification has been flatly rejected, except in VVH where the question is raised as to whether subfamilies descended directly from reconstructed proto-Uto-

Aztecan or else descended from reconstructable intermediate parent languages — proto-Shoshonean for the subfamilies discussed above, as well as proto-Sonoran and proto-Aztec — to be discussed below — for the other two major branches of the Uto-Aztecan family. The question can of course be raised, but it is not certain that the question can be resolved within the framework of common descent utilizing the family tree model, without areal and typological considerations.

It is obvious that consensus can be reached on the reconstruction of the sound system of proto-Uto-Aztecan from which the daughters ultimately descended, whether directly or with intermediate brachiation. In fact, the independent reconstructions of proto-U-A consonants postulated in VVH and in Miller 1967 are identical for the obvious reason stated by Langacker: '... the essential validity of this reconstruction is easily confirmed by an examination of cognate sets'. It is less obvious why less than complete consensus would be expected in reconstructions of the traditional major branches of the Uto-Aztecan family (Shoshonean, Sonoran and Aztec).

It would be anachronistic — after Bloomfield's work in Algonquian and Sapir's work in Athapascan — to suggest that written records of earlier stages in a language family are necessary for the reconstruction of a proto-language for a given family, as Indo-European. Where such written records are available, as for Classical Greek, Latin, Persian and Sanskrit, it is tempting to first reconstruct the sound systems of proto-Romance or proto-Italic, and proto-Indic or proto-Indo-Iranian, and then, thereafter, to reconstruct proto-Indo-European largely on the basis of the older Indo-European languages. Where such written records of older stages in a family are unavailable, as in the case of Uto-Aztecan, it is tempting to first reconstruct the apex sound system of the family as a whole, and subsequently to look for evidence of intermediate brachiation between the apex node in the family tree, as proto-Uto-Aztecan; and the terminal nodes — the still spoken languages in the family — with either a single level or more than one level for intermediate stages represented by nodes for major branches, as Shoshonean, and/or (without a major branch) nodes for subfamilies, as Takic. (Note that Classical Nahuatl is at best comparable to Middle English rather than to one of the older Indo-European languages in time depth).

It is not anachronistic to suggest that the difficulty in reaching as much consensus on intermediate brachiation in Algonquian and Athapascan and Uto-Aztecan as has been reached on the intermediate brachiation of Indo-European is due to the fact that the older Indo-European languages served as points of departure in research on the major branches of that family, while other points of departure have to be found for all language families in native America — as well as for the vast majority of languages in other parts of the world — bereft of written records of earlier stages within a given family. The typical point of departure for families lacking older written languages is to group together geographically contiguous languages and then to distinguish among areally overlapping languages those which are typologically distinct. Thus the northern Uto-Aztecan daughters, when first placed in a Shoshonean branch, were not confused with the daughters in the Sonoran branch that were found as far north as the Southwest, as Papago.

For any postulated brachiation, whether of a major branch or of a small subfamily, it is not always possible to distinguish between (a) features in the daughters which reflect common descent, and (b) features which reflect borrowings between related languages that have remained in contact or resumed contact in some prehistoric or historic areal linguistic situation, and (c) typological features which may arise among related languages at different times and places, even though they are not in contact, after the fashion of Sapir's 'drift' process. There is no doubt that it is easier to distinguish (a) and (b), above, in several small subfamilies than in a few major branches; but it is equally difficult to distinguish (b) from (c), not to mention (d) — language universals. A possible example of (c) is implicit in the recent Hale-Voegelin papers on modal particles in Papago and in Hopi — particles which are not cognate but are still semantically and syntactically parallel to a high degree. This does not contribute to the intermediate brachiation problem in Uto-Aztecan, since one could argue equally well that the parallel particles appear or reappear in two different major branches of the family (Sonoran and Shoshonean), or in two different subfamilies (Pimic and Hopi) without reference to major brachiation.

Of the three major branches of Uto-Aztecan, the southernmost (Aztec) and the geographically middle branch (Sonoran) go beyond the scope of languages spoken in the Great Basin and Southwest culture areas, though Sonoran languages are spoken in Arizona today as well as in western Mexican states. They overlap the languages treated by Robert Longacre in volume 4 (1968) of *Current Trends in Linguistics* (Ibero-American and Caribbean Linguistics). Longacre's views on the three major branches of Uto-Aztecan are stated in reference to the view stated in VVH: '... we have reconstructed where we had evidence to reconstruct, typologized whether or not reconstruction was possible, and quantified rather casually whenever the quantification promised to be interpretable'; VVH include reference to the kind of recent innovations which must constitute the chief objects of research in areal linguistics within culture areas that is followed by Joel Sherzer in this volume of *Current Trends*.

In Longacre's opinion the evidence for the VVH reconstruction of proto-Aztec 'is clear', and certainly stronger than the evidence for reconstructing the other two major branches of the family. In his 1935 challenge of the major brachiation, however, Whorf did not spare skepticism, even of the traditional Aztec or 'Nahuatlan' branch which, he thought, might well be enlarged into an 'Aztecoid' branch by the inclusion of some Sonoran languages.

Longacre discusses the VVH reconstruction of the Sonoran branch from the point of view of consonantal mergers, and from this point of view there is obviously no basis for grouping the Sonoran languages into one commonly descended group. Innovations cited for languages of the Sonoran branch occur not only in languages of the Aztec branch to the south but also in those of the Shoshonean subfamilies in the north. For common descent classification, Longacre prefers a set of subfamilies in place of the traditional Sonoran branch. The Sonoran subfamilies might nevertheless exhibit evidence for typological retentions and for drift-like typological emergence of features found also, but sporadically, in the daughters of the flanking subfamilies to the north and south. Languages of the central Sonoran region might well retain linguistic area and culture area relics, since they are now spoken in regions over which early migrants from the north travelled to become, protohistorically, the conquering Aztecs in the Valley of Mexico (and in Middle America generally) from which, even before the Aztec period, cultural diffusion spread north from Middle America — as far as the Pueblo societies that once flourished in the Great Basin.

How many subfamilies are to be included in the set of Sonoran subfamilies? Longacre (1968), following Lamb (1964), favors three: Taracahitan (Tarahumara, Yaqui-Mayo and Cahita), Cora-Huichol and Piman. Miller (1967) favors four: Pimic (including the upper and lower Pima-Papago and northern and southern Tepehuan), Corachol (including Cora and Huichol), Tarahumara (including Tarahumara and Varohio), and Cahita (including Yaqui and Mayo). These three or four subfamilies are then taken to be coordinate with the four subfamilies to the north and with one to the south, thereby making a total of eight or nine subfamilies in a Shoshoneless, Sonoranless Uto-Aztecan family.

The traditional Sonoran classification given in VVH finds no support for the three or four subfamilies in terms of shared cognates which are 'no more numerous between Tarahumara and Yaqui-Mayo than those between Papago and Yaqui-Mayo' — or in other words, the languages within the Taracahitan subfamily are no closer to each other lexically than one of them is to one of the languages in the Piman subfamily. At least one of these subfamilies (Piman or Pimic, recently renamed Tepiman by Burton Bascom) includes languages with shared innovations in phonology, and in this respect the attestation of Piman follows the criterion for genetic proximity which requires a set of shared structural innovations. Though Piman is now attested as a subfamily this means only that two or at most three separate languages are closely related; the other subfamilies also include only two or three separate languages — two in the general case.

One is reminded of Jacobsen's criticism (mentioned under 11, Hokan relatives of Yuman) of the practice of comparing pairs of Hokan languages. This tended to give undue emphasis to recent innovations, especially when internal reconstructions were not utilized to narrow the range of phenomena to be accounted for.

Returning now to the northern Uto-Aztecan languages in the traditional Shoshonean branch, note how the subfamily situation differs from the paired language constituency of subfamilies in the Sonoran group: (1) the northern subfamilies consist either of one language each — Hopi and Tübatulabal, respectively — or of geographically contiguous clusters of more than two languages, as in the case of the Numic and Takic subfamilies; and (2) instead of showing sporadic sets of phonological innovations, all four Shoshonean subfamilies reveal phonological retentions from the proto-Uto-Aztecan period. Hence, the reconstruction of the apex proto-language (U-A) and the intermediate proto-Shoshonean in VVH is virtually identical for consonants and completely identical for vowels.

All questions converge on an apparently binary alternative, but an alternative which cannot be evaluated. Does the recognition of numerous small subfamilies (each including a few languages, or a pair of languages, or a single language, as Hopi and Tübatulabal) yield more interpretive insights than the reconstruction of a low number of large branches (including many languages for most branches)? The question is not whether the family tree model to account for brachiation within language families is an adequate model or an inadequate model in some vague general case, but rather whether serious attempts to operate with the family tree model in a particular family yield results upon which serious investigators can agree or, failing agreement, envisage a way of resolving differences — in short, whether evaluation procedures can, or cannot, be applied to resolve differences of interpretation. Typically, there are no evaluation procedures for resolving the kind of brachiation problems encountered in Uto-Aztecan.

An example of the possibility of resolving reconstructive differences — but without direct dependence upon the family tree brachiation within the Uto-Aztecan family — appears in evaluation procedures which apply to the reconstruction of the Uto-Aztecan vowel system. There is complete agreement among recent workers upon the reconstruction of four of the five vowels — *i *u *a *o — while Whorf's former reconstruction was deviant, because it was overly influenced by language-particular considerations of Hopi. For the fifth vowel, Wick Miller reconstructs *e, Kenneth Hill *ə, and VVH *ɨ.

The alternatives for reconstructing the fifth vowel are evaluated positively and negatively by Ronald Langacker (1970) who demonstrates that it is possible to determine which alternative reconstruction is the correct one. In the following summary of some of the positive evaluations, we relate the languages cited by Langacker to the family tree brachiation proposals reviewed above in order to show that the family tree model, with its apparently unresolvable alternatives, is not necessarily relevant to the following sample of evaluation arguments.

(1) Most languages which show /ɨ/ as the fifth vowel are vocalically conservative because they also retain the other four vowels of proto-U-A — e.g. in the Numic subfamily (Comanche), in the Piman subfamily (Papago), and in Tübatulabal — while most languages which show /e/ as the fifth vowel are vocalically innovative because they alter at least one of the other four vowels of proto-U-A — e.g. in the Corachol subfamily (Cora), in the Takic subfamily (Cahuilla), and in Aztec.

(2) A backing rule can be stated as $*k > q / \_\_ [\overset{V}{_{-\text{HIGH}}}]$ if *i is reconstructed, as reflected in daughters in the Takic subfamily (Cahuilla, Cupeño, Luiseño), in Tübatulabal and in Hopi, but the backing rule must be stated as $*k > q / \_\_ [\overset{V}{_{-\text{HIGH} \atop -\text{FRONT}}}]$ if *e is reconstructed. In Takic languages, the consonantal backing can be said to occur before reflexes of vowels that were simply non-high, if *i is reconstructed; but if *e were reconstructed, the rule would have to be stated with an additional feature

specification — that backing occurred before vowels that were non-front as well as non-high.

(3) The strongest argument that favors *i as the correct reconstruction depends in part on showing the relative strengths of the alternative reconstructions to emphasize the conclusion that with *i reconstructed, the development of the vowel systems in the daughters can be more naturally explained than if *ə or *e were reconstructed for the fifth vowel of proto-U-A. A mere example or two of the relative unnaturalness of postulating either *ə or *e is given below before a sample of the positive argument that shows *i to be the correct choice among the three alternative reconstructions proposed. The third proposal (for *i) listed below can be shown to have stronger support than the preceding two proposals. (But in alternative proposals for brachiation, as Michael Krauss shows for Athapascan in this volume of *Current Trends*, alternatives are equally valid — or invalid — and their difference depends on the data selected to set up different arrangements of subfamilies or branches; hence the alternative proposals in brachiation cannot be formally evaluated, as can the alternative proposals for reconstructing the fifth vowel in proto-U-A.)

The weakest proposal favors the reconstruction of *ə; it seems impossible to find a valid argument in favor of *ə, but possible to find some arguments against setting up *ə — e.g. many sound changes would have had to occur to account for the reflexes of *ə in most of the daughters; only Cupeño would have retained *ə as /ə/. With *i the backing rule can be stated naturally and simply, as above; with *ə, the backing rule has to be reformulated, since it operates neither before non-high *ə nor high *u and high *i, but does operate before non-high *a and *o. Hence the reformulation would have to specify the environment for backing disjunctively.

In essence, the argument against reconstructing *e for the fifth vowel of proto-U-A is that this choice fails to reveal phonological developments that can be captured when *i is reconstructed. For example, with *e one is bereft of the strong argument that is possible with *i — namely, to show a development from proto-U-A *o to Cahuilla /i/, via intermediate stages — not a plethora of 'increments of articulatory slippage' but instead a low number of discrete changes from *o to /i/.

This claim for intermediate stages of development requires *i to be reconstructed as the fifth vowel of U-A. The argument is confined for the most part to three of the four Takic languages.

The first step postulates a development from *o to /ö/ in three daughters (Cahuilla, Cupeño, Luiseño), even though these daughters do not now include a front rounded non-high vowel in their vocalic systems; but both Serrano (in the same subfamily) and Hopi (in another subfamily) do, and thereby show that *o > ö is a natural and possible development in the Uto-Aztecan family, and incidentally — as in the case of most phonological developments in this family — not confined to any one subfamily.

The second step postulates a change from /ö/ to /e/ in the same three daughters. These shared innovations are ordered so that they can be said to precede the following unshared innovations; but note first that this second intermediate development from *o — namely from /ö/ to /e/ — is a final development for Luiseño, but not a final development for the other two daughters in the set (Cahuilla and Cupeño).

The next step goes from intermediate stage /e/ to final stage /i/ in the two daughters noted above — a development which they do not share with Luiseño. Though one of these daughters (Cahuilla) does in fact develop /e/, this final development is from *i rather than *o, while the other does not include /e/ among its final vocalic developments.

Modern research in comparative Uto-Aztecan generally proceeds by (a) proposing phonological reconstructions, and then (b) attesting a particular reconstruction among tentative reconstructions; both (a) and (b) are derived on the basis of daughter phonologies that have been described in autonomous phonemic terms, for the most part, rather than in morphophonemic terms or in a generative framework.

This raises the question of what we may expect from post-modern research in comparative Uto-Aztecan. Kenneth Hale's (1969) paper on Papago morphophonemics is cited by Langacker as a harbinger of future work on the basis of which it will be possible to test his prediction: 'The strongest evidence in favor of one vowel or the other [among tentative proposals for reconstructing the vowel system of proto-Uto-Aztecan] would be likely to emerge from the comparison of comprehensive generative phonological analyses of the daughter languages.' This prediction is curiously modest; Langacker has already found sufficiently strong evidence for making his points (as our sample of his arguments, above, suggests), on the basis of a comparison of daughters described in modern rather than in post-modern frames of reference. Phonemicizing in modern research is bi-unique only in principle; whenever the bi-unique principle leads to indecision in the analysis of any language, silent recognition of partial morphophonemic information has been used in practice to resolve the indecision, as in our own so-called 'phonemic' treatment of Tübatulabal. Subsequently, under the guidance of Sapir and Swadesh, we avoided 'blinding in' morphophonemic evidence silently, by presenting an explicit statement of Tübatulabal morphophonemics — the first such treatment of a Uto-Aztecan language. This earlier analysis has now been restated by McCawly (1969) in the framework of genesative phonology, and is being stated again in an Indiana dissertation (1973) on Tübatulabal phonology by James Jensen, who also discusses Lightner's restatement.

Our answer to the question raised by Langacker — what would emerge from 'the comparison of comprehensive generative phonological analyses of the daughter languages'? — parallels his. Our prediction is that such comprehensive analyses of the daughter language phonologies would also permit the treatment (hitherto impossible) of length and stress in the proto-language through the formulation of rules of alternation of stress that involve some alternation of length.

### 13. TANOAN-KIOWA RELATIVES OF UTO-AZTECAN

In his 1929 classification of North American Indian languages Sapir listed the Uto-Aztecan family, the Tanoan-Kiowa family, and the Zuni isolate as remotely related;

in the next decade Whorf and Trager (1937) brought together evidence to show that the postulated relation between the Uto-Aztecan and Tanoan families could be supported.

Note that in distribution these phylum relatives of the Uto-Aztecan family — languages in the Tanoan-Kiowa family — extend in the eastern range of the Southwest, and beyond into the Plains, somewhat as the phylum relatives of the Yuman languages extend in the western ranges of the Southwest and beyond.

Trager (1969) has recently confirmed the correctness of Harrington's 1910 classification — but only for languages that are still spoken — of the three existing Tanoan 'language groups': (1) Tiwa, including Taos-Picuris and Sandia-Isleta-Isleta del Sur and Piro dialects; (2) Towa, including Jemez and Pecos dialects, and (3) Tewa. Like the languages and/or dialects in the two preceding 'language groups', Tewa is spoken in pueblos along the Rio Grande in New Mexico (San Juan, Santa Clara, San Ildefonso, Nambe, Pijoaque, and Tesuque); but since 1700 a Tewa dialect has also been spoken at Hano, on the Hopi First Mesa in Arizona. Trager concedes that at least three Tanoan languages — Tiwa, Towa, and Tewa — can be differentiated in the Tanoan-Kiowa family, but suggests there may be more than these three. For example, Taos and Picuris may be two languages separated by a language barrier in the Tiwa 'language subgroup'; the inclusion of Piro among Tiwa dialects is questionable, since Piro may have constituted a fourth Tanoan language; so also, the inclusion of Pecos in Towa is not certain, since it may have constituted a fifth language, possibly not even a Tanoan language. Trager also suggests that a language barrier may separate Santa Clara from 'Central Tewa' (San Juan-San Ildefonso-Nambe-Tesuque). Trager repeats his earlier conclusion — 'that Kiowa and Tanoan are related to each other so as to form a family related as a whole to Uto-Aztecan' — but rejects his former conclusion concerning genetic relationship between Zuni and the phylum comprising the Uto-Aztecan and Tanoan-Kiowa families.

When the proto-language of Tanoan-Kiowa is reconstructed, an earlier stage of contrasts between oral and nasal vowels will be postulated, since all the daughters show some such distinction; but the reconstruction of the proto-Uto-Aztecan vowel system, as already shown, includes only oral vowels. In general the vowel systems of Tanoan-Kiowa languages are fairly homogeneous and symmetrical, while those of Uto-Aztecan languages are not — in fact the vowel systems of some of the daughters in the latter are quite asymmetrical — e.g. Hopi contrasts *i ɨ* [HIGH] without rounding for front-back, but with the rounding feature for each front and back vowel that is not high: *e ö a o* [-HIGH]. Tones distinguish vowels in Tanoan languages, but not in Uto-Aztecan languages. And so on. There are sufficient similarities among the daughters in each family — especially in the Tanoan-Kiowa family — and such striking differences in surface structure between the languages of the two families, that no one has been tempted to reconstruct the phylum parent of both in any great detail before reconstructing proto-Uto-Aztecan and proto-Tanoan-Kiowa.

Much active work is on-going among languages of the Tanoan-Kiowa family, mostly under the direction of George Trager. We distinguish, following, between studies concerned with Tiwa languages or dialects from those concerned with Tewa, and with Towa, and include items which are not primarily devoted to autonomous linguistics but which nevertheless use linguistic data.

Tiwa: M. Estellie Smith's (1967) dissertation was on Taos governing structures, of which part is published, and part in press — an article on Tiwa government. Felicia Trager (1968) wrote a dissertation on the Picuris language, in an ethnographic frame of reference, and is now preparing papers on the basis of this as well as of other than linguistic data which she has gathered; her Picuris data were used by George Trager in the paper discussed below: "Taos and Picuris — how long separated?" (1969). John Collins, whose dissertation was directed by the late David Stout, worked on a peyote problem at Toas under Trager's direction. William L. Leap has written a grammar of Isleta with Trager-Smith phonological syntax, and supplied the linguistic data for M. Estellie Smith's work on Isleta. Elizabeth A. Brandt lived at the Sandia pueblo and participated in various activities not usually opened to outsiders, working with the language in its ethnographic context. James Bodine, who is related to some Taos families, worked at Toas for a summer to check linguistic data with Trager; his Tulane dissertation (1967), directed by Edmondson, is on the 'three cultures' of Taos.

Tewa: Randall H. Speirs wrote a dissertation (1966) on San Juan Tewa, and is now engaged with his wife in compiling an ethnographically oriented dictionary and in native-language teaching at San Juan pueblo. John Yegerlehner and Edward Dozier have also made important contributions to Tewa linguistics.

Towa: The Summer Institute of Linguistics has a linguist working on Jemez — Hazel Shorey; Hale and Miller have also worked on Jemez.

George Trager is of course our chief authority on Tanoan in general and on Taos in particular, as is apparent in the bibliography.

Trager concludes that the relationship between the two families in the 'Azteco-Tanoan phylum' has been 'put on reasonably firm ground', but that the distance of the relationship cannot be gauged until proto-Tanoan-Kiowa and proto-Uto-Aztecan are reconstructed. As noted above (under Uto-Aztecan Family), reconstructions made recently now agree on the consonant system for proto-Uto-Aztecan; the differences in the reconstructions of the proto-Uto-Aztecan vowel system have been shown to be subject to a kind of evaluation that makes it probable that a single reconstructed vowel system, among the alternatives postulated, can be relied upon in further comparative work. As much as this will surely be forthcoming before long for proto-Tanoan-Kiowa, thanks largely to the work of George Trager, and the work of others that he has stimulated. At the moment, the internal relations of daughters in this family can be reasonably outlined in terms of 'subfamilies' and 'language-family subgroups' and 'language-groups'. Trager's Tanoan 'subfamily' dominates at least two 'language-family subgroups' (Towa and Tiwa-Tewa); the second 'subgroup' listed dominates two 'language-groups' (Tiwa and Tewa). Even Kiowa may be close enough to be included as another 'subgroup' of the 'subfamily', i.e. of Tanoan, which leaves the extinct Piro — the only extinct Tanoan language for which evidence was recorded before extinction — to be still classified. Piro might turn out to have belonged 'to one of the three divisions in New Mexico' — i.e. to have belonged to one of those 'language groups' which have living representatives today (Tewa, Tiwa or Towa — Harrington had placed Piro in what Trager calls the Tiwa 'language group'); or, if not, to provide evidence for a Piro 'language-family subgroup' coordinate with those in New Mexico (Towa and Tiwa-Tewa) and in the southern Plains (Kiowa). (Rudolph Troike reports that there may still be speakers of Piro among the survivors in the El Paso area; if so, it might be possible to obtain the necessary data for its more certain classification.)

An explanation should be given of the terminology above: 'language-groups' instead of 'languages' which are dialectally differentiated for Tewa, Tiwa and Towa. This reflects Trager's implicit skepticism of the usefulness of the language-dialect distinction in general, and of glottochronology or lexicostatistics in particular. An explicit critique of both appears in his recent paper "Taos and Picuris — how long separated?" which ends on a satirical note: 'To return to the question in the title: Taos and Picuris became separate languages 700 years ago, or possibly only 350 years ago, or maybe they are still one language! This kind of technical "precision" is only a little more useless than most of the "precise numerical" data that some social scientists are fond of.'

In two other recent papers Shafer (1967) gives a bibliography of Uto-Aztecan, and Hale (1967) a partial reconstruction of Kiowa-Tanoan phonology. Shafer's bibliography runs to more than two hundred items even though its 'common focus' is that the references should contribute 'lexical data for research in ethnobotany, ethnozoology, migration theory ... where the geographical distributions of lexemes are of interest'; scores of workers have contributed to Uto-Aztecan, while recent contributors to Tanoan-Kiowa have been those trained by Trager for the most part. There are not many other scholars like Kenneth Hale and Wick Miller who make contributions to and evaluations of work in both Uto-Aztecan and Tanoan-Kiowa, in reference to the claim that there is a 'close relationship' between the two families (Hale) or between Kiowa and the rest of the Tanoan-Kiowa family (Hale; Miller). Hale is not alone in believing that the proto-languages of each family should be independently reconstructed before the two are compared.

The Whorf-Trager reconstruction of proto-Tanoan is based on Tiwa. Hence it is not a reconstruction of proto-Tanoan-Kiowa, nor even a reconstruction of the 'language-family subgroup' to which Tiwa belongs (namely Tiwa-Tewa); it is, in effect, an internal reconstruction of a 'language group' (Tiwa) two of the constituents of which, as Trager now says — but satirically so (see above) — may still be one language or may now represent separate languages.

Several consonantal features which are found generally in Tanoan-Kiowa languages are conspicuously absent in Uto-Aztecan languages. This observation is not to be taken as a negative argument — against the postulated phylum connection of the two families; rather, it makes possible a positive argument — that the genetic connection which is granted is quite remote, since the daughters in the two families differ importantly in their vowel systems (see above) and in their consonant systems. The latter is most succinctly realized by noting how Hale's reconstruction of proto-Tanoan-Kiowa (based on representatives of Tiwa — i.e. Taos; Tewa — i.e. Santa Clara; Towa — i.e. Jemez; and Kiowa) reveals a consonantal system which includes not only plain stops, much as in the recent reconstructions of proto-Uto-Aztecan, but includes also glottalized stops ($*p'$ $*t'$ $*c'$ $*k'$ $*k^{w'}$) and aspirated stops ($*p^h$ $*t^h$ $*c^h$ $*k^h$ $*k^{wh}$) and voiced stops ($*b$ $*d$ $*z$ ($*g$) $*g^w$), which are not reconstructed for proto-Uto-Aztecan. The reconstructions tabulated above are based on correspondences in stem-initial position among four Tanoan-Kiowa daughters.

The close resemblance of the Whorf-Trager reconstruction based on one 'language group' and the Hale reconstruction of Tanoan-Kiowa, based on representatives of all four 'language groups' of the family, suggests what Hale says it suggests — that this 'testifies further to the extreme closeness of the relationship between the languages comprising the Kiowa-Tanoan family'. The same could not be said for any four languages selected from the Uto-Aztecan family — not even if four languages were selected from one subfamily.

## 14. APACHEANS IN MODERN HISTORY

Michael E. Krauss disclaims (in his treatment of the Athapascan family in this volume) the possible implication that the language areas treated in each subdivision of his paper might be intended to represent 'coordinate branches in any scheme of genetic relationship'. The organization in terms of five Athapascan subdivisions (Alaska, Canada, Kwalhioqua-Tlatskanai and Nicola in the 'North', and Pacific Coast, and Apachean) 'is simply one of convenience'.

The Southwestern Navajo and Apache (whence 'Apachean' for both) are most distantly separated from the other 'subdivisions' listed above — in terms of geographic rather than genetic distance. All subdivisions in the 'North' are more or less contiguous; the two subdivisions which are non-contiguous to those in the 'North' are the Pacific Coast and the Apachean Athapascans.

Of these two, the languages of the Pacific Coast are not only 'more divergent from the North than is Apachean' but also show 'internal divergence' — i.e. they differ from one another conspicuously. Hence, the Pacific Coast subdivision was 'probably never an undifferentiated linguistic community even if' — a possibility that invites disbelief — 'it split off from the North as one group'. On the other hand, it is easy to believe that the Apacheans entered the Southwest as a single undifferentiated linguistic community.

The light that the linguistic prehistory of the Athapascan family casts on the entry of the Apacheans into the Southwest in protohistoric times also illuminates interpretations made by the Spaniards who arrived subsequently in the Southwest but left written records, thereby initiating 'history' in this part of the world. These first Spaniards did not distinguish Navajo from Apache dialects or languages.

Later Spaniards — those of the 18th century — did begin to make a Navajo-Apache distinction, but more on the basis of geographic distribution (much like the subdistinction of Eastern Apache versus Western Apache) than of systematic 'internal divergence' in a linguistic rather than cultural sense. Cultural differentiation among the different Apachean societies began to be studied soon after these societies became located on different reservations, but the problem of linguistic varieties among these societies has only recently been appreciated as a neglected but still researchable problem.

Of the 18th century Spanish identifications of Western Apache tribal or band societies and their habitats, three can be clearly translated into modern reservation locations, as follows.

(1) The Coyoteros formerly located between the headwaters of the Salt River and the Mogollon Rim are now centered on the Fort Apache Reservation in and about Cibicue, Carrizo, and North Fork.

(2) The Pinaleños, formerly living along the middle Gila and San Carlos Rivers, are now known as the San Carlos Apache; on this reservation there are also found today some Chiricahua and Tonto Apache and two or three score of Yuman-speaking Yavapai.

(3) The Tonto Apache, formerly located in an area extending from the Mogollon Rim and Tonto Basin to the San Francisco Peaks or modern Flagstaff, are now represented as a minority at Camp Verde which today includes twice as many descendants of other Apache societies as Tonto — not to mention the Yavapai who are found at Camp Verde as well as at San Carlos.

In addition, the Chiricahua and Mescalero Apache still reside in the southern parts of Arizona and New Mexico and in northern Mexico (in the Sierra Madre Mountains from which they are rumored to have continued raiding neighboring villages until 1958). The Eastern Apache — Jicarilla and Lipan — are found east of Arizona; the Lipan, who formerly extended into the Plains, are now apparently extinct. The Kiowa-Apache are Apache who went off into the Plains to live with the Kiowa (of the Tanoan-Kiowa family). The question is: Can any language barrier be demonstrated to exist now between any of these 'in addition' Apache and the Apache numbered (1), (2), (3), above, between whom easy communication can be demonstrated by dialect distance testing?

But even between the Navajo dialects, which seem relatively homogeneous, and the more differentiated Apache dialects there may not be a language barrier. Though Navajo speakers regard Apache speech to be separate in some vague way from their own, they are still able to recognize the resemblance between the two, whether or not they are able to understand natural utterances in Apache; no one seems certain they can — or that they cannot.

The question does not seem a very important one to modern Apachean peoples since they have — except for a diminishing number of monolingual Navajo — the availability of English to use on occasions when they wish to communicate verbally. Little is known of what those occasions may be, how the differences among the Apachean linguistic varieties relate to the ethnography of communication, political anthropology, teaching in the native language, and other theoretical and applied interests.

The most studied and best known of all the Apachean varieties and the variety with by far the most speakers is Navajo, as Krauss (1970) makes clear in his review of the recent Sapir and Hoijer monograph (*The phonology and morphology of the Navajo language*), and in the section on Navajo in his Na-Dene paper (this volume). Krauss also reviews the published work on 'Apache and comparative Apachean' (following his review of Navajo) and emphasizes the divergence of Kiowa-Apache — now spoken by only ten individuals — from all other varieties of Apachean — i.e. 'On the basis of lexicostatistics, Hoijer shows that Kiowa-Apache is a separate Apachean language equidistant from the rest, and that the rest are dialects of one language'.

When a language is spoken by a remnant of ten bilinguals, its sociolinguistic function in the larger society of monolinguals shrinks also. We can forsee the extinction of Kiowa-Apache upon the death of its few remaining speakers with as much certainty as we can assume that the forbears of the Kiowa-Apache spoke a variety of Apache intelligible to other Apacheans in the Southwest. These twin assumptions, leading to the expectation that the near future will resume the language situation existing in the historic past (a single Apachean language) seems reasonable enough until one considers that the present resurgence of 'smaller nationalities' tends to reinforce the tendency to relexification to accommodate the on-going acculturation of the 'smaller nationalities'.

But, in fact, more evidence can be brought to support the twin assumption, even though it is weak, than the assumption that lexicostatistics reflecting a sufficiently high percentage of shared cognates is enough to guarantee that dialects in question constitute a single language. No one knows exactly how language barriers can be clearly recognized, but it is probably safe to say that enough is known to cast doubt on the establishment of the existence — or in the case of the Apachean dialects, the non-existence — of a language barrier on the basis of lexicostatistics alone.

## 15. ZUNI AND KERESAN

Zuni is spoken in a single dialect in a single pueblo in western New Mexico; until this century its monolingual speakers were separated by a language barrier from monolingual speakers of every other language in the Southwest. What external verbal communication did occur was of the kind that has to pass through channels — the channels of Zuni-Navajo and Zuni-Spanish bilinguals, for example. However, in this century English gradually became a second language for virtually all Zuni and thereby has come to serve as a lingua franca for communicating with all other Indians, including those west of the Rio Grande who had not used Spanish as a second language and who therefore remained monolingual until they became bilingual in English.

The same single pueblo, single language, single dialect isolation cannot be claimed for Keresan which is spoken both along the Rio Grande, and also in one of the culturally — but not linguistically — homogeneous Western Pueblos whose social organization differs from that of the Eastern Pueblos.[2] Indeed, individuals in Hopi and Zuni and the Keres pueblo of Acoma spoke three distinctive languages but shared a common culture.

Acoma is today a ceremonial rather than a dormitory pueblo, since most Keres people known as 'Acoma' are now living at nearby Acomita and Santa Maria de Acoma (McCartys). All other Keres people live in Eastern pueblos. Hence the dialects of Keresan, no less than the cultures of the Keres pueblos, extend or stretch over a 'Keresan bridge' — as Fred Eggan (1950) has called it — between the Western Pueblos (Hopi, Zuni, Acoma) and the Eastern or Rio Grande Pueblos which include all of the Tanoan pueblos and some of the Keres pueblos: Cochiti, San Felipe, Santa Ana, Zia and Santa Domingo — all established in prehistoric times — as well as Laguna, which was established in 1699 and is today the largest of the Keres pueblos, with a total population exceeding 3000, if Keres people in the outlying settlements (Paguate, Mesita, Encinal, Paroje, Seams, Casa Blanca) are counted together with the Keres in Laguna proper.

The Eastern Keres pueblos, somewhat like the Tanoan pueblos which are entirely Eastern, had adopted Spanish as a widespread second language long before this century and therefore could communicate in Spanish when dialects in their own languages were not mutually intelligible. Navajo raids on the Eastern pueblos were much more frequent than on the Western pueblos; and Navajo, after Spanish, may also have served as a lingua franca for Keres speakers as well as for Zuni speakers. Thus, there is at least some ethnohistoric indication that when the Hopi fled as refugees to the Zuni (see 6. above), Navajo came to be used as the lingua franca for the Hopi (rather than Zuni or Spanish).

The degree of genetic proximity between either Zuni or Keresan and any other language of native America can be stated either in vague classificatory terms available

---

[2] Information on the present degree of differentiation among the Keresan dialects is not available. In a modern ethnography of communication it would be noted that English is used as a lingua franca when people speaking uncomfortably divergent dialects encounter one another. Without some lingua franca, attempts at communication between speakers of different Keresan dialects might well have been made. But now that such attempts are unnecessary, relexification and lexical expansion — if Keresan is expanding as 'expanded Hopi' is — might well go on differently in the different pueblos speaking Keresan, with the consequence that Keresan dialects may have become more differentiated now than they were formerly, before the stabilizing or leveling influence of interpueblo communication in Keresan was interrupted by the widespread use of Spanish and English as second languages.

for stating remote genetic relationships, or in less imprecise terms of glottochronological quantification, even though the latter are subject (a) to counter-examples and (b) to being wholly rejected. Quantification in glottochronology is falsely precise, since it interprets for the whole on the basis of selected data which are representative of a tiny fraction of the whole. How is one to choose between this devil (of quantification) and this deep blue sea (of vague classification)? But the two are not really contradictory; they can be combined to obtain the following perspective in prehistory.[3]

Pre-Zuni must have long ago split from its Penutian phylum relatives in California, as is suggested by the number of lexical retentions which Stanley Newman (1964) discovered to connect Zuni with the Yokuts language which surely belongs in the far-flung Penutian phylum which extends continentally in Western America from the Tsimshian in Canada southward. If the Uru-Chipaya languages of South America in the Bolivian altiplano are remotely related to the Mayan family in Middle America, and if it is assumed that Mayan, Mixe-Zoquean, Totonacan, are also related, and if Whorf's unpublished evidence for including the Azteco-Tanoan phylum in the larger Macro-Penutian phylum is substantial, then there may still be a genetic connection — but a most indirect one — between Zuni and a family of languages still spoken in the Southwest (Tanoan via Azteco-Tanoan via Penutian via the connection shown by Newman to exist between Zuni and Penutian Yokuts of California). The claims are very 'iffy'; the relevant bibliography (cited in Trager 1967, and Longacre 1968) does not always give the evidence to support claims of such very remote relationships.

That Zuni is a language isolate related to California Penutian has been shown, with solid evidence; by glottochronological reckoning, pre-Zuni separated from pre-Yokuts seven or eight millenia ago — i.e. twice as long ago as proto-Indo-European was spoken on the shores of the Baltic (or else on the northern shores of the Black Sea).

Keresan was once classified in the now abandoned Macro-Hokan-Siouan phylum. Can it be reclassified in the currently acceptable Hokan phylum?

A reasonable conclusion can be drawn from the preceding critique: the degree of proximity (a) between Zuni and Keresan and (b) between either and any other language in the Southwest-Great Basin approximates zero. Nonetheless, this negative conclusion can generate a faint but possible light on the order of puebloization in the Southwest-Great Basin.

[3] The following perspective in prehistory reflects much more than current work in linguistics which, in one sense, is extrinsic to this perspective, but in another sense provides the foundation for any perspective of the past or future. Current work in Keresan linguistics includes Wick Miller's (1965) and Joel Maring's (1967) Acoma grammars, as well as Irvine Davis' work on Santa Ana (see also his bibliography of Keresan), and his and Miller's joint work on reconstructing a phonology of proto-Keresan. Zuni has recently engaged the attention of more linguists than has Keresan. The point of departure for all current work on Zuni clearly lies in the publications of Stanley Newman — a dictionary (1958) followed by a 1965 grammar which made possible the comparison of Zuni and California Penutian, already noted. Under the auspices of the Summer Institute of Linguistics, Curtis Cook is continuing to work on Zuni. Julian Granberry (1967) wrote a dissertation on Zuni grammar, as did Willard Walker (1964), whose "Inflectional class and taxonomic structure in Zuni (with a note by Stanley Newman)" (1966) is worthy of special note.

In general, the neolithic culture which evolved in Middle America diffused as far north as the Great Basin in western America, where it was creatively reconfigurated as distinct pueblo cultures in societies that have had languages, for as long as modern history can attest, which belong to four different language families: Uto-Aztecan (Hopi), Tanoan (Tiwa, Tewa, Towa), Zunian (Zuni), and Keresan dialects. The less general or more specifically oriented problem is how to infer the relative order of puebloization of pueblos known in modern history.

The last shall be considered first — Hopi and Tanoan pueblos; then those puebloized earlier can even be related to some prehistoric sites known archaeologically, as Trager has shown.

That pre-Hopi speakers were the last to have transformed themselves from a pre-pueblo to a pueblo culture might be inferred from the fact that they have fewer language family relatives in the Southwest, in modern history, than in areas flanking the Southwest. Hence the inference that the pre-Hopi entered the Southwest from an adjacent non-pueblo culture area.

That the Tanoans were the next to last to have become puebloized can be inferred from the fact that their languages are close relatives of Kiowa, now spoken in the southern Plains; and the modern Kiowa have a tradition of former residence in the northern Plains.

But where were the Zuni and Keresan speakers before they became puebloized? Aside from possible but often dubious phylum relationships, they have no language family relatives known to be in the Southwest or in any area adjacent to the Southwest in any past that can be reconstructed with reasonable certainty. Ergo, they were in the Southwest at the time the neolithic cultural diffusion reached the Southwest; and since there is no good evidence one way or the other, it is possible that Zuni and Keresan were simultaneously affected by the earliest neolithic influence, one to develop in the direction of Western Pueblo social organization (which the pre-Hopi adopted upon their emergence as pueblos), and the other to have settled in the east (except for Acoma), where the incoming Kiowa-Tanoans from the Plains served to alter the social organization but not the base of subsistence economy that characterizes all pueblo societies known in modern history.

BIBLIOGRAPHY

ABERLE, DAVID F. 1967. The Navaho singer's 'fee': Payment or prestation? Studies in southwestern ethnolinguistics, ed. by Dell H. Hymes and William E. Bittle, pp. 15–32. The Hague, Mouton.

ALVAREZ, ALBERT. 1965. Some Papago puns. IJAL 31.106–7.

BASCOM, BURTON WILLIAM, JR. 1965. Proto-Tepiman. Unpublished manuscript, University of Washington.

BASSO, KEITH H. 1967. Semantic aspects of linguistic acculturation. AmA 69.471–7.

——. 1971. 'To give up on words': Silence in Western Apache culture. Studies in Apachean culture history and ethnology, ed. by Morris Opler and Keith H. Basso. Tucson, University of Arizona Press.

——. In press. Western Apache witchcraft. Anthropological Papers of the University of Arizona 1971.

BLACK, ROBERT A. 1967. Hopi grievance chants: A mechanism of social control. Studies in southwestern ethnolinguistics, ed. by Dell H. Hymes and William E. Bittle, pp. 54–67. The Hague, Mouton.

BODINE, JOHN JAMES. 1967. Attitudes and institutions of Taos, New Mexico: Variables for value system expression. Ph.D. Dissertation, Tulane University.

BRANDT, ELIZABETH. 1970. On the origins of linguistic stratification: The Sandia case. AnL 12.46–50.

BRIGHT, WILLIAM, and JANE HILL. 1967. The linguistic history of the Cupeño. Studies in southwestern ethnolinguistics, ed. by Dell H. Hymes and William E. Bittle, pp. 351–71. The Hague, Mouton.

CASAGRANDE, JOSEPH B., and KENNETH HALE. 1967. Semantic relationships in Papago folk-definitions. Studies in southwestern ethnolinguistics, ed. by Dell H. Hymes and William E. Bittle, pp. 165–93. The Hague, Mouton.

COX, BRUCE. 1970. What is Hopi gossip about? Information management and Hopi factions. Man 5.88–98.

CRAWFORD, JAMES M. 1966. The Cocopa language. Ph.D. Dissertation, University of California, Berkeley.

——. 1970. Some cognate sets from Chimariko and several Yuman languages. Paper presented at the Hokan Conference, University of California, San Diego.

DOZIER, EDWARD P. 1954. The Hopi-Tewa of Arizona. UCPAAE 44/3.

——. 1967. Linguistic acculturation studies in the southwest. Studies in southwestern ethnolinguistics, ed. by Dell H. Hymes and William E. Bittle, pp. 389–402. The Hague, Mouton.

EGGAN, DOROTHY. 1955. The personal use of myth in dreams (Hopi). JAF 68.445-53.

EGGAN, FRED. 1950. The social organization of the Western Pueblos. Chicago.

——. 1967. From history to myth: A Hopi example. Studies in southwestern ethnolinguistics, ed. by Dell H. Hymes and William E. Bittle, pp. 33–53. The Hague, Mouton.

EVERETT, MICHAEL W. 1970. White Mountain Apache medical decision making. Ph.D. Dissertation, University of Arizona.

FRIGOUT, ARLETTE. 1966. L'espace cérémoniel des indiens Hopi (Arizona—Etats Unis.) ICA.

GOSS, JAMES A. 1968. Cultural-historical inference from Utaztekan linguistic evidence. Occasional Papers of the Idaho State University Museum 22.1–42.

——. 1970 Voiceless vowels (?) in Numic languages. Languages and cultures of Western North America, ed. by Earl H. Swanson, Jr., pp. 37–46. Pocatello, University of Idaho Press.

GRANBERRY, JULIAN. 1967. Zuni syntax. Ph.D. Dissertation, State University of New York at Buffalo.
HAAS, MARY. 1970. The northern California linguistic area. Paper presented at the Hokan Conference, University of California, San Diego.
HALE, KENNETH. 1962. Jemez and Kiowa correspondences in reference to Kiowa-Tanoan. IJAL 28.1-5.
——. 1967. Toward a reconstruction of Kiowa-Tanoan phonology. IJAL 33.112-20.
——. 1969. Papago /čim/. IJAL 35.203-21.
HALPERN, A. M. 1946-47. Yuma I, II, III, IV, V. IJAL 12.25-33, 147-51, 204-12, 13.18-30, 147-66.
HARMS, ROBERT. 1966. Stress, voice, and length in Southern Paiute. IJAL 32.228-35.
HARRINGTON, JOHN P. 1910. An introductory paper on the Tiwa language, dialect of Taos, New Mexico. AmA 12.11-48. (Reprinted as no. 14 of the Papers of the School of American Archaeology.)
HILL, JANE H. 1966. A grammar of the Cupeño language. Ph.D. Dissertation, University of California, Los Angeles.
HILL, KENNETH. 1967. A grammar of the Serrano language. Ph.D. Dissertation, University of California, Los Angeles.
——. 1969. Some implications of Serrano phonology. Papers from the Fifth Regional Meeting of the Chicago Linguistic Society, ed. by Robert I. Binnick et al., pp. 357-65. Chicago.
HOPKINS, NICHOLAS A. 1965. Great Basin prehistory and Uto-Aztecan. AmAntiq 31.46-60.
HYDE, VILLIANA. 1971. Introduction to Luiseño, ed. by Ronald Langacker. Banning, Calif., Malki Museum.
JACOBSEN, WILLIAM H., JR. 1964. A grammar of the Washo language. Ph.D. Dissertation, University of California, Berkeley.
——. 1970. Observations on the Yana stop series in relationship to problems of comparative Hokan phonology. Paper presented at the Hokan Conference, University of California, San Diego.
JOEL, JUDITH DINA. 1967. Paipai phonology and morphology. Ph.D. Dissertation, University of California, Los Angeles.
KENNARD, EDWARD A. 1963. Linguistic acculturation in Hopi. IJAL 29.36-41.
——. In press. Metaphor and magic: Key concepts in Hopi culture and their linguistic forms. Studies in linguistics, ed. by M. Estellie Smith.
KRAUSS, MICHAEL E. 1970. Review of: Sapir and Hoijer, The phonology and morphology of the Navaho language. IJAL 36.220-8.
——. 1973. Na-Dene. CTL 10.903-78.
KROEBER, A. L. 1907. Shoshonean dialects of California. UCPAAE 4.65-165.
——. 1931. The Seri. Southwest Museum Papers 6.
KUNITZ, S. J., J. E. LEVY, P. BELLET and T. COLLINS. 1969. Census of Flagstaff Navajos. Plateau 41.156-63.

KUNITZ, S.J., J.E. LEVY and M. EVERETT. 1969. Alcoholic cirrhosis among the Navajo. Quarterly Journal of Studies on Alcohol 30.672–85.

KUNITZ, S.J., J.E. LEVY and C.L. ODOROFF. 1970. A one year follow-up of Navajo migrants to Flagstaff, Arizona. Plateau 42.92–106.

LAMB, SYDNEY M. 1958. Linguistic prehistory in the Great Basin. IJAL 24.95–100.

——. 1964. The classification of the Uto–Aztekan languages: A historical survey. Studies in California linguistics, ed. by William Bright, pp. 106–25. UCPL 34.

LANGACKER, RONALD W. 1970. The vowels of proto Uto–Aztecan. IJAL 36.169–80.

LANGDON, MARGARET. 1970a. A grammar of Diegueño: The Mesa Grande dialect. UCPL 66.

——. 1970b. The Proto-Yuman vowel system. Paper presented at the Hokan Conference, University of California, San Diego.

LEAP, WILLIAM L. 1970. Tiwa noun class semology: A historical view. AnL 12.38–45.

LEVY, JERROLD E. 1961. Navajo health concepts and behavior: The role of the Anglo medical man in the Navajo healing process. Tuba City Hospital Bulletin 2/2. Tuba City, Calif.

——. 1962. Medical decision making in a Navajo outfit. United States Public Health Service, Window Rock Field Office. Window Rock, Arizona.

——. 1965. Navajo suicide. HO 24.308–18.

LEVY, J.E., and S.J. KUNITZ. 1969. Notes on some White Mountain Apache social pathologies. Plateau 42.11–19.

——. In press. Indian reservations, anomie, and social pathologies. Studies of contemporary Indian reservations, ed. by R. Hackenberg and D. Walker.

LEVY, J.E., S.J. KUNITZ and M. EVERETT. 1969. Navajo criminal homicide. SJA 25.124–52.

LEVY, J.E., S.J. KUNITZ, C.L. ODOROFF and J. BOLLINGER. In press. Hopi deviance: An historical and epidemiological survey. Essays in honor of Fred Eggan, ed. by A. Spoehr.

LINDENFELD, JACQUELINE. 1969. A transformational grammar of Yaqui. Ph.D. Dissertation, University of California, Los Angeles.

LONGACRE, ROBERT E. 1968. Comparative reconstruction of indigenous languages. CTL 4.320–60.

MCCAWLEY, JAMES D. 1969. Length and voicing in Tübatulabal. Papers from the Fifth Regional Meeting of the Chicago Linguistic Society, ed. by Robert I. Binnick et al., pp. 407–15. Chicago.

MARING, JOEL M. 1967. Grammar of Acoma Keresan. Ph.D. Dissertation, Indiana University.

MATHIOT, MADELEINE. 1967. The cognitive significance of the category of the nominal number in Papago. Studies in southwestern ethnolinguistics, ed. by Dell H. Hymes and William E. Bittle, pp. 197–237. The Hague, Mouton.

MILLER, MARY R. 1970. The language and language beliefs of Indian children. AnL 12.51–61.

MILLER, WICK R. 1959. A note on Kiowa linguistic affiliations. AmA 61.102–5.

———. 1965. Acoma grammar and texts. UCPL 40.

———. 1966. Anthropological linguistics in the Great Basin. The current status of anthropological research in the Great Basin: 1964, ed. by Warren L. d'Azevedo, et al., pp. 75–112. Reno, University of Nevada Press.

———. 1967. Uto-Aztecan cognate sets. UCPL 48.

———. 1970. Western Shoshoni dialects. Languages and cultures of western North America, ed. by Earl H. Swanson, Jr., pp. 17–36. Pocatello, University of Idaho Press.

MOSER, EDWARD. 1970. Some Seri morphophonemic data *and* Inflectional verb affixes: Seri data sheet. Papers presented at the Hokan Conference, University of California, San Diego.

NAGATA, SHUICHI. 1970. Modern transformations of Moenkopi Pueblo. Illinois Studies in Anthropology 6. Urbana, Ill.

NEWMAN, STANLEY S. 1958. Zuni dictionary. IUPAL 6.

———. 1964. Comparison of Zuni and California Penutian. IJAL 30.1–13.

———. 1965. Zuni grammar. UNMPA 14.

ORTIZ, ALFONSO. 1969. The Tewa world. Chicago.

———, ed. In press. New perspectives on the Pueblos. Monographs of the School of American Research.

PERCHONOCK, NORMA, and OSWALD WERNER. 1969. Navaho systems of classification: Some implications for ethnoscience. Ethnology 8.229–42.

REDDEN, JAMES E. 1966. Walapai I, II. IJAL 32.1–16, 141–63.

SAPIR, EDWARD. 1910. Yana texts. UCPAAE 9.

———. 1922. The fundamental elements of Northern Yana. UCPAAE 13.215–34.

———. 1923. Text analyses of three Yana dialects. UCPAAE 20.263–94.

———. 1929. Central and North American languages. Encyclopaedia Britannica, 14th ed., pp. 5.138–41. [Reprinted in SWES ..., pp. 169–75.]

SAPIR, EDWARD, and MORRIS SWADESH. 1960. Yana dictionary, ed. by Mary Haas. UCPL 22.

SAPIR, EDWARD, and HARRY HOIJER. 1967. The phonology and morphology of the Navajo language. UCPL 50.

SEIDEN, WILLIAM. 1963. Havasupai phonology and morphology. Ph.D. Dissertation, Indiana University.

SEILER, HANSJAKOB. 1970. Cahuilla texts with an introduction. LSM 6.

SHAFER, ROBERT. 1967. A bibliography of Uto-Aztecan with a note on biogeography. IJAL 33.148–59.

SHIMKIN, DEMITRI B., and RUSSELL M. REID. 1970. Socio-cultural persistence among

Shoshoneans of the Carson River basin (Nevada). Languages and cultures of western North America, ed. by Earl H. Swanson, Jr., pp. 172–200. Pocatello, Idaho University Press.

SMITH, M. ESTELLIE. 1967. Aspects of social control among the Taos Indians. Ph.D. Dissertation, State University of New York, Buffalo.

SPECK, FRANK G. 1928. Chapters on the ethnology of the Powhatan tribes of Virginia. Indian Notes and Monographs 1.227–455.

SPEIRS, RANDALL H. 1966. Some aspects of the structure of Rio Grande Tewa. Ph.D. Dissertation, State University of New York at Buffalo.

SWADESH, MORRIS, and C.F. VOEGELIN. 1939. A problem in phonological alternation. Lg 15.1–10.

TEDLOCK, DENNIS. In press. Pueblo literature: Style and verisimilitude. New perspectives on the Pueblos, ed. by Alfonso Ortiz. Monographs of the School of American Research.

———. 1971a. On the translation of style in oral narrative. JAF.

———. 1971b. Finding the Center: Narrative poetry of the Zuni Indians. New York, Dial Press.

TITIEV, MISCHA. 1972. The Hopi Indians of Old Oraibi. Ann Arbor, University of Michigan Press.

TRAGER, FELICIA HARBEN. 1968. Picuris Pueblo, New Mexico: An ethnolinguistic 'salvage' study. Ph.D. Dissertation, State University of New York, Buffalo.

TRAGER, GEORGE L. 1948, 1954, 1960, 1961. Taos I, II, IV. IJAL 14.155–60, 20.173–80, 27.211–22; Taos III. AnL 2:2.24–30.

———. 1967. The Tanoan settlement of the Rio Grande area: A possible chronology. Studies in southwestern ethnolinguistics, ed. by Dell H. Hymes and William E. Bittle, pp. 335–50. The Hague, Mouton.

———. 1969. Taos and Picuris — How long separated? IJAL 35.180–2.

TRAGER, GEORGE L., and FELICIA HARBEN TRAGER. 1970. The cardinal directions at Taos and Picuris. AnL 12.31–7.

TROIKE, RUDOLPH C. 1970. The linguistic classification of Cochimi. Paper presented at the Hokan Conference, University of California, San Diego.

TURNER, PAUL R. 1970. Pluralization of nouns in Seri and Chontal. Paper presented at the Hokan Conference, University of California, San Diego.

VOEGELIN, C.F. 1935. Tübatulabal grammar. UCPAAE 34.55–190.

———. 1959. An expanding language, Hopi. Plateau 32.33–9.

VOEGELIN, C.F. and E.W. 1946. Map of North American Indian languages. PAES 20.

VOEGELIN, CHARLES F., and FLORENCE M. VOEGELIN. 1957. Hopi domains: A lexical approach to the problem of selection. IUPAL 14.

———. 1966. Map of North American Indian languages. PAES revised 20.

———. 1967. Review of: Heinz-Jürgen Pinnow, Die nordamerikanischen Indianersprachen. Lg 43.573–83.

——. 1969. Hopi /ʔas/. IJAL 35.192–202.

——. 1970a. Hopi names and no names. Languages and cultures of western North America, ed. by Earl H. Swanson, Jr., pp. 47–53. Pocatello, Idaho University Press,

——. 1970b. Cross-cultural typologies and folk taxonomies. Echanges et communications: Mélanges offerts à Claude Lévi-Strauss, II, pp. 1132–47. The Hague, Mouton.

——. 1971. The autonomy of linguistics and the dependence of cognitive culture. Studies in American Indian languages, Papers in honor of Mary Haas, ed. by Jesse O. Sawyer (UCPL 65, pp. 303–17).

VOEGELIN, C.F., F.M. VOEGELIN and KENNETH L. HALE. 1962. Typological and comparative grammar of Uto-Aztecan: I (phonology). IUPAL 17.

VOEGELIN, C.F., F.M. VOEGELIN and NOEL W. SCHUTZ, JR. 1967. The language situation in Arizona as part of the Southwest culture area. Studies in Southwestern ethnolinguistics, ed. by Dell H. Hymes and William E. Bittle, pp. 403–51. The Hague, Mouton.

WALKER, DOUGLAS. 1970. Diegueño plural formation. Linguistic Notes from La Jolla 4.1–16. La Jolla, Calif., University of California at San Diego.

WALKER, WILLARD. 1964. Reference, taxonomy, and inflection in Zuni. Ph.D. dissertation, Cornell University.

——. 1966. Inflection class and taxonomic structure in Zuni. IJAL 32.217–27.

——. In press. A lexicon of Zuni household items with contextual definitions. New Haven, Human Relations Area Files.

WARES, A.C. 1968. A comparative study of Yuman consonantism. The Hague, Mouton.

WERNER, OSWALD, and KENNETH BEGISHE. 1966. Anatomical atlas of the Navajo. Mimiographed, Evanston, Illinois.

WHITING, ALFRED F. 1939. Ethnobotany of the Hopi. Museum of Northern Arizona Bulletin 14.

WHORF, BENJAMIN L. 1935. The comparative linguistics of Uto-Aztecan. AmA 37.600–08.

WHORF, BENJAMIN LEE, and GEORGE L. TRAGER. 1937. The relationship of Uto-Aztecan and Tanoan. AmA 39.609–24.

WINTER, WERNER. 1967. The identity of the Paipai. Studies in southwestern ethnolinguistics, ed. by Dell H. Hymes and William E. Bittle, pp. 372–8. The Hague, Mouton.

WYMAN, LELAND C. 1951. The ethnobotany of the Kayenta Navaho. University of New Mexico Publications in Biology 5.

——. 1957. Beautyway: A Navaho ceremonial. Bollingen Series 53. New York, Bollingen Foundation.

——. 1962. The Windways of the Navaho. Colorado Springs, Colo.

——. 1965. The Red Antway of the Navaho. Santa Fe, New Mexico.

——. 1970a. Blessingway. Tucson, Arizona.

——. 1970b. Sandpaintings of the Navaho Shootingway and the Walcott Collection. SCA 13.
WYMAN, LELAND C., and FLORA L. BAILEY. 1964. Navaho Indian ethnoentomology. UNMPA 12.
WYMAN, LELAND C., and S. K. HARRIS. 1941. Navajo Indian medical ethnobotany. UNM-B 366.
YEGERLEHNER, JOHN. 1957. Phonology and morphology of Hopi-Tewa. Ph.D. Dissertation, Indiana University.

# ALGONQUIAN

KARL V. TEETER

## 1. INTRODUCTORY: EARLY RESEARCH

From as early as the fifteenth century, the explorers of the Atlantic coast of North America mostly received their first impressions of New World natives from speakers of different languages of the same family, Algonquian. At the time of the first foreign settlements, Algonquian languages were spoken from Labrador to as far south as the Carolinas along the Atlantic coast, and extended inland in present Canada and the northern United States as far west as the Great Plains. This gives the family one of the widest distributions of any group of indigenous languages, a geographical spread emphasized by the confirmation of Edward Sapir's bold hypothesis, published in 1913, that Wiyot and Yurok, languages found on the Pacific coast in northern California, bear a genetic relationship to Algonquian.[1]

There are more than two dozen distinct languages belonging to the family. Despite this their interrelationship has been evident ever since scholars began to realize that the diversity of American Indian languages was more than random, a recognition first found widely in the work of American amateur anthropologists of the early nineteenth century (an example is Schoolcraft 1839; some relationships were seen much earlier, as shown in Haas 1967). This recognition was aided by the availability of descriptions of many Algonquian languages by Christian missionaries and divines from the seventeenth century on, which all together amount to an extensive literature and give Algonquian studies a chronological depth rare for indigenous languages of America. The value of many of these works extends to the present, especially in those cases where missionaries believed in the utility of aiming for a native speaker's competence in the language. Most noteworthy are the studies of the more northerly languages by French Jesuits and Sulpicians, but seventeenth century work on Massachusett and Narragansett, along with eighteenth and early nineteenth century studies of Delaware by Moravian missionaries, are also of primary importance. Twentieth century Mennonite work on Cheyenne is basic in published material on this western language, and current research on several languages, including Anglican study of Cree, continues the tradi-

---

[1] Evidence of the relationship and references to pertinent papers may be found in Haas 1958; the details are not yet clear. The wider group has been referred to as Algic (National Museum of Canada 1967:3-4).

tion. Many missionary sources are referred to directly or indirectly in the bibliography which constitutes section 6 of this article.

Early sources such as these, together with accounts by travellers, gave impetus to the recognition of the unity of the Algonquian family, as stated, and yet tend to be forgotten amid emphasis on more recent work, which too often comes down to meaning exclusively one's own fieldwork. Such a narrow view is particularly unfortunate not only because a number of the languages are no longer spoken and hence cannot be approached directly, but also since older sources, as well as providing valuable control, contain data on former periods, before the disruptive changes which followed displacement of the natives during white settlement. Many such sources are yet unpublished, and their discovery and utilization still underway; a hint of what exists is contained in a recently published study of work in New France (Hanzeli 1969), and a model of how older material may be used is found in Goddard 1967.

## 2. THE ALGONQUIAN LANGUAGES: LOCATION AND PRESENT STATUS

Algonquian languages and dialects are numerous, and major efforts at a comprehensive list do not exactly match.[2] Any language list is subject to the general difficulty of drawing the line between language and dialect; the list I present here for Algonquian is further influenced by the accident of which have attracted workers and by the state of subclassification in the field, which is still in its infancy. In some cases a language is no longer spoken and available data on it limited. There may even be languages which have disappeared without record; in at least one instance (Beothuk, once spoken in Newfoundland) the data are so limited that even the question of affiliation with the family, though likely, is not decided to the general satisfaction of scholars.

In the tabular list the order of the roman alphabet is followed, and indications are also given as to relative locations of the languages and their current status. There have been many changes in location since the time of white occupation, systematic for the more westerly languages, which moved westward and southward into the Great Plains area, and sporadic for others. Changes in location as well as status were most striking for those languages directly in the path of intensive settlement. Thus the coastal languages lead the list of those no longer spoken, the remnants of Delaware are now found in two groups in Ontario and Oklahoma, and Kickapoo, once contiguous with Fox and Sauk around present Illinois, is now spoken in Oklahoma and Mexico. Languages on the border of main areas of European incursion absorbed speakers of

---

[2] The name 'Algonquian' is pronounced with -*qui*- as 'key' in the French style. The language names listed here in large part follow Michelson 1912 and Bloomfield 1946, but the grouping of dialects is somewhat more conservative. This and other usages are adjusted to reflect the current state of knowledge in the field, including instances where less is known than may have once been thought. Two innovations should be noted here. The splitting of Abnaki into Eastern and Western branches follows the current practice of the principal workers in the field, Day and Siebert. Connecticut is a convenient cover term for Quiripi, Shinnecock and other dialects on which we have very little data.

other dialects once distinct, and hence have a specially complex history; such is strikingly the case for Abnaki.

The notations as to present status mostly follow Chafe (1962). Half of the indigenous languages of North America presently spoken are due to pass out of currency in this generation, and Algonquian languages are no exception except insofar as their obsolescence somewhat precedes the general trend.[3] In the list I have used the symbol + for those languages presently spoken by all ages, and × for those no longer spoken. More impressionistic is the use of ? as against no indication, the distinction being between those which (being exclusively spoken by members of the oldest generation) are due to die within this generation and those which may survive it. Abbreviations of location are E(ast), C(entral), W(est), N(orth), and S(outh), and refer to directions within the general Algonquian area.

| LANGUAGE | LOCATION | | STATUS |
|---|---|---|---|
| Abnaki (Eastern) | E | N | ? |
| Abnaki (Western) | E | N | ? |
| Arapaho-Atsina-Nawathinehena | W | | + |
| Blackfoot | W | N | + |
| Carolina Algonquian | E | S | × |
| Cheyenne | W | S | + |
| Connecticut-Unquachog-Shinnecock | E | | × |
| Cree | C, W | N | + |
| Delaware | E | | ? |
| Fox-Sauk | C | | + |
| Illinois-Peoria-Miami | C | | × |
| Kickapoo | C | | + |
| Loup | E | | × |
| Mahican | E | | × |
| Malecite-Passamaquoddy | E | N | |
| Massachusett | E | | × |
| Menomini | C | | ? |
| Micmac | E | N | + |
| Mohegan-Pequot-Montauk | E | | × |
| Montagnais-Naskapi | E | N | + |
| Nanticoke-Conoy | E | | × |
| Narragansett | E | | × |
| Ojibwa-Algonquin-Ottawa | C | N | + |
| Potawatomi | C | | |
| Powhatan | E | S | × |
| Shawnee | C | S | |

[3] In round numbers, of perhaps 300 languages spoken at the coming of the white man, Chafe lists 210. Of these some 80 were spoken around 1960 only by the generation over fifty years of age, with 85 languages, many of them the same ones, used by groups of people numbering less than a hundred.

## 3. COMPARATIVE ALGONQUIAN: TWENTIETH CENTURY STUDIES

From the time the unity of the languages was recognized in the nineteenth century, various scholars studied aspects of Algonquian comparative grammar. The name of J. Hammond Trumbull may be singled out; author of a dictionary of Massachusett (1903) and other papers on the languages, he was perhaps the first to attempt a sketch of grammar for several languages in a paper on the verb (1876). Other works of interest, in respect to comparative grammar and other matters, appear in the references gathered in Pilling 1891, a bibliographical source of outstanding value. The reports of meetings of the American Philological Association from about the 1870s include, in *TAPA* (among which the above mentioned paper by Trumbull was published), summaries of reports and discussions involving Algonquian, some of them reporting comments on the subject by the pioneer American linguistic scholar William Dwight Whitney.

Comparative studies on a scale both broad and detailed began with the papers of Truman Michelson early in the twentieth century, and were brought to a new height of systematization by Leonard Bloomfield, who made the description and history of Algonquian a principal life work. Michelson, son of a distinguished physicist, passed his career with the Bureau of American Ethnology (now absorbed in the Department of Anthropology) of the Smithsonian Institution in Washington, D.C. He published papers and reports over several decades, and was the first to formulate sound laws illuminating the development of the family as a whole. He was also the first, in an uncharacteristically long paper (1935), to bring extensive data from the more westerly languages, Arapaho, Cheyenne, and Blackfoot, into Algonquian reconstructions. We owe to Michelson much ethnographic information as well, and linguistic description of the languages along with his comparative studies. His papers are numerous in each of these areas but, unfortunately, are typically very short — a paragraph or a page is not uncommon — and scattered in periodical sources often difficult to come by. A thorough bibliographical study and evaluation of his work is much to be desired.

Bloomfield worked extensively on Algonquian from around 1920, gathering original data through fieldwork and analyzing material already available. His papers are fundamental both for description and comparison of the languages, and he left much important material still unpublished at his death in 1949. One such manuscript was a grammar of Menomini based on direct fieldwork, which appeared posthumously (1962) under the editorial care of C. F. Hockett and constitutes easily the most thorough description to date of an Algonquian language.[4] Another, among his earliest papers in the field, is an exemplary statement of Fox grammar (1925, 1927) derived from published textual material. His own work and that of others from the perspective of comparative study is brilliantly summarized and pursued in a paper referred to by Algonquianists as 'The sketch' (1946). This work, simultaneously descriptive and

---

[4] This book is reviewed by the present author, from different points of view, in *Lg* and in *IJAL* (Teeter 1970a, 1970b).

comparative, is based primarily on four languages, but Bloomfield claims, citing Michelson (1935) as support, that his reconstructions 'will, in the main, fit all the languages and can accordingly be viewed as Proto-Algonquian' (1946:85). The claim has been borne out by subsequent studies, although much detail needs to be added and refinements made in the analysis, as I indicate presently. The four languages Bloomfield's Sketch describes and compares are Fox, Cree, Menomini, and Ojibwa, all located in the central Algonquian area. He himself did fieldwork on the last three and, as mentioned, published a detailed secondary study of Fox early on.

The Sketch is articulated first according to the divisions of grammar in a relatively traditional scheme, with major subheadings such as Sounds, Internal Combination, Inflection, and so forth, and subordinate numbered but untitled sections organized according to topics of Algonquian grammar, such as semivowels, vowel syncope, orders and modes (of the verb). In the sections, Bloomfield names and describes categories, processes, and paradigms, including with each such statement a reconstructed form with its reflexes in the modern languages treated, occasionally bringing in forms from other Algonquian languages. These reconstructions are chosen so as to illustrate the grammatical statements and numbered serially throughout the paper, which contains 404 in all.

The relatively similar patterning of rather complex forms in the languages on which he focuses allows Bloomfield to reconstruct such complex forms as wholes in a large majority of cases. This achievement obviates a major fault of the Sketch, at least in part, since he refrains in general from stating abstract rules of grammar to connect his categorized lists, an abstention based, it would seem, on principled grounds.[5] Despite the difficulty this entails, Bloomfield's success in reconstructing complex forms means that the forms in themselves contain much of grammar, so that the Sketch is not just a list, however detailed, of classified partial similarities, but a first approximation to a true comparative grammar. Complexity of the forms is related to the typology of Algonquian languages, which is in itself, as I shall argue when presenting typology (section 4), a factor mitigating the terseness of Bloomfield's manner of presentation. It would be improper not to stress, however, that if his organization of Algonquian grammar and choice of categories is not elaborated and justified as we might wish, it reflects a superb intuition and an intimate first-hand knowledge of the languages dealt with, both too rarely encountered. The Sketch is and will remain the indispensable starting point for Algonquian studies and is a strong foundation on which to build.

The problems which must be faced in this task of building are principally two. The first has just been alluded to, and is that the description needs to be made more comprehensive in a particular sense: under Bloomfield's system, when partially similar forms with analogous functions occur in different categories, there is no principled way to connect them, and similarly, accumulation of different functions on the same form

---

[5] The influence of behaviorist psychology and positivist philosophy is the major factor in Bloomfield's atheoreticalism, as I have contended (1964); his method may nevertheless be seen as based on an implicit and interesting theory of language use (Teeter 1970a).

cannot be clearly motivated. The second problem is also one of refinement rather than any correction of the facts given, but it is very important: despite the achievement of the Sketch as a comparative grammar, its comparisons finally fall short of true history. This result is not unrelated to the philosophical abstemiousness of which I have complained (footnote 5).

The technique followed in the Sketch is in general to reconstruct only when reflexes in two or more of the languages studied show a regular phonological development from a prototype. When analogical or other interference with such development would have to be postulated to explain a modern form, most commonly Bloomfield stops with characterizing it as 'discrepant', often even omitting the offending word from citation. He thus shuns the very inferences necessary to link language system with language system historically, and the result is that only forms in a direct line from the protolanguage, historically the least interesting, are comprehensively considered. This is one of the directions in which the comparisons in the Sketch stop short of history. True historical study must not only account for the picture, but show how it was painted, and thus discrepant forms must be closely examined. It is precisely the explanation of such forms which often turns out to be most important in understanding earlier stages, in linking the systems, and ultimately in subclassifying the languages and studying their relative chronology, a major tool being the discovery of shared discrepancies. A case in point is the creative paper, already cited, of Ives Goddard (1967), who starts with forms left by Bloomfield as 'discrepant' (or, in one case, accounted for tentatively and, it turns out, incorrectly), and is led finally to a revealing and original scheme for the history of the principal verbal paradigms of Algonquian.

The other direction in which comparison short of history may lead us is to the postulation of too many distinctions in the protolanguage. Indeed, this is inevitably the case in early stages of comparison, given only that we insist on accounting for the data rigorously, and that their origins are complex. Here I may cite as an example a celebrated problem of reconstruction in Algonquian, one still not adequately solved, the matter of consonant clusters. In scrupulously tabulating the regular correspondences found among modern forms, Bloomfield is led to postulate three consonants for the protolanguage which occur exclusively as prior members of consonant clusters. He is aware of the difficulty, of course, referring to these as 'obscure elements which we render by arbitrary symbols' (1946:88), but this is where he leaves affairs. Various modern languages also show other consonant clusters whose place in his system is not clear. So although it seems highly unlikely that the protolanguage will have to bear the weight of all of these directly, only closer study both of individual forms and of the language systems themselves can transcend this consequence. Some such study has been done, on consonant clusters specifically, and has thrown light both on subclassification and on borrowing relationships among the languages, interfering factors scarcely touched in the Sketch. Here see especially the two important papers of Siebert on the subject (1941, 1967a).

The basic importance of the Sketch is that of great scholarly landmarks in general:

it gives a system solid enough to add to and incisive enough to point to places where such addition may improve the system itself. It does what it does so definitively that new areas are opened in previously unpenetrated territory.

## 4. TYPOLOGY AND SUMMARY DESCRIPTION

The morphological typology of the Algonquian languages is neatly summed up in the capsule characterization of Edward Sapir (1929; the quotation is found on p. 134 of Sapir's *Selected works*, 1963): The languages

are 'polysynthetic' and ... inflective; make use of suffixes; to a much less extent ... of prefixes; have important inner stem modifications, including reduplication; have a weak development of case; and illustrate to a marked degree the process of building up noun and verb themes by suffixing to stems local, instrumental, adverbial, and concretely verbalizing elements.

It may be added that there are different techniques of synthesis according to the stage of word formation; the derivation of themes involves a fair degree of fusion, but their inflection, which can also be rather complex, is generally agglutinative.

Syntax in Algonquian is parallel to morphology in a way not universal to the world's languages, and hence of typological interest. It is usual for constructions and relations to be associated with concrete morphemes; and syntactic and morphological features, while the correspondence is far from perfect, are commonly in one-to-one relationship. Though I can only mention such a typological property here in a tentative way, it bears particular importance in evaluating previous work on Algonquian as well as utility in overall characterization of the grammar. I think it may be argued that the same technique which provides an effective and revealing description for one language may fail for another not because of the technique itself but because of the different nature of the languages involved, and that Algonquian and the past work on it is a case in point as contrasted, for example, with English or with Chinese, for which analysis along the lines of Bloomfield's Algonquian would be quite inadequate.

The typological feature of which I speak may be termed GRAMMATICAL CONCRETE-NESS,[6] and ranges Algonquian most particularly, among languages with which I have some familiarity, with the classical Indo-European languages, with modern English and Chinese at the opposite pole. But grammatical concreteness is something quite distinct from degree of synthesis — I mean by it the characteristic I have just described, that most grammatical categories and functions have unique morphemes associated with them, and that conversely, there is rather limited cumulation of functions on single forms.

[6] I use this term with some hesitation because of possible confusion with the view, discredited but not dead, that logical abstraction cannot be accomplished with the languages spoken by peoples who lack a tradition of writing. Perhaps the ascription of grammatical concreteness to Greek and Latin as well as Algonquian will help avoid this confusion.

It is not always easy to separate a theory of language from the typology of the specific languages one wishes to approach. Modern transformational grammar grew historically, in the first instance, from attempts at the adequate description of English, a grammatically abstract language where specifying only morphemes and their constructions is strikingly insufficient. English passivization, many types of nominalization, and so on, are quite unintelligible described only as morphemes in construction, for homonymous constructions are plentiful. Once this is seen, there is a strong temptation to try to absorb morphology into syntax, and indeed this has become a core issue in current theoretical discussion, as it has been under the surface in American linguistics ever since students of Sapir tried to do something similar for certain American Indian languages (an example is Swadesh 1946, for Eskimo). The temptations of Algonquian are rather the opposite, and like those of Greek and Latin; seeing the concreteness of the grammar, one is tempted to concentrate on morphology, explaining syntactic features by simply pointing to the morphemes uniquely associated with them. Indeed, insofar as this is the situation, one can do this and at least not seriously distort the language in describing it. Even features such as word order need little mention at a basic level; in contrast with English, word order in Algonquian, or in Latin, is secondary, and the arrangement of words is more a matter of rhetorical style than of primary grammatical relations. In one case the language type seduces one to try absorbing morphology into syntax, in the other to slight syntax and treat it as a reflection of morphology, and this is quite apart from higher theoretical predilections.[7] Many cases of grammatical concreteness, of syntactic features as expressed in morphemes, might be cited, but perhaps the point is most quickly exemplified by the category/process of PREDICATION. Morphemes expressing predication are widespread in Algonquian, and the expression of this feature seems to be most fully developed in Menomini, the single Algonquian language which Bloomfield knew most intimately. In Menomini every sentence regardless of complexity has one and only one predicative phrase, marked by a unique inflected form of either verb, particle, or pronoun. Distinct inflectional patterns are employed to show that other phrases are non-predicative, so that in fact predication is doubly marked. The practical consequence of grammatical concreteness as a typological feature is that one can go further in accounting for the facts of such a language, by careful description, than otherwise possible without invoking a level of abstract syntax. Given, on the part of Bloomfield, this very reluctance to make theoretical abstractions, the typology itself of Algonquian is a saving grace.

The languages are all sufficiently similar that they may be summarily described as a

---

[7] For form's sake I must here disclaim advocacy of either extreme. Clearly word and sentence are not mutually assimilable without going beyond the realm of natural languages altogether (as some current discussion does); whether their difference is predictable on the basis of human cognitive structure is not a linguistic question. My purpose in stressing the contrast here is only that it seems to inform modern work on Algonquian, particularly that of Bloomfield and Hockett. It may not be too much to say that Algonquian was (typologically!) a language on which one could do honest work with minimal interference with prevailing philosophical prejudice.

whole without undue violence. The three westerly languages, Arapaho, Blackfoot, and Cheyenne, are most different at first glance, but this disparity comes about through historical changes which are generally superficial, though sometimes striking, as the development in Arapaho of an accent based on pitch. I shall give here a very brief sketch of Algonquian grammar.[8]

Phonologically, Algonquian languages are rather simple, though features of tone, accent, and voicing, mostly nondistinctive, have interfered with fieldworkers' ability to make accurate reports. For vowels Proto-Algonquian has four qualities *i e o a*, long and short. Semivowels *y w* are nonsyllabics virtually in complementary distribution with *i o*, and the historical development of vowel and semivowel combinations is difficult and diverse. Simple consonants are *p t c k* and perhaps *kw*, with *c* a palatal affricate often morphophonemically related to *t*, and *s θ š*, sonorants *l m n*, and laryngeal *h*. The consonant *$\theta$ undergoes a complex development, typically yielding *θ, t, l,* or *n* in various modern languages, as does *$l$, of which the common reflexes are *l, n, r,* or *y*. Historical development of other consonants is mostly straightforward, with various contractions and abbreviations, in respect to particular sequences or positions in the word. Consonant clusters especially are subject to change of various sorts in the modern languages. In Proto-Algonquian they are limited to two consonants, commonly with an obstruent as second member. One exceptionally widespread variety has *h* as initial member with obstruent or sonorant consonant, and the distinction between these and the simple consonants of the protolanguage is often realized in later languages as tense vs. lax consonant, a distinction which tends to be obscured in fieldwork records. Internal combination of phonemes is sometimes complicated, but does not offer unusual phenomena; many are adjustments which preserve the sequential alternation of consonants and vowels.

Syntactically, the Algonquian word is generally complex, represented at minimum by a theme, inflected or uninflected. A theme consists of a root plus a suffix called a final, and it is the final which in principle determines the part of speech; roots may function in more than one word class. Themes may be compounded or further derived. Such processes, particularly of derivation, are multifarious but not treated here. Algonquian themes are verbs, nouns, pronouns, or particles, with the last term, as usual, covering a multitude of syntactically disparate forms. Verb and noun themes are inflected by the use of endings of various kinds, and specifiable types have also one of a class of personal prefixes.

Inflection of themes, particularly verbal themes, is very hard to sort out neatly piece by piece, on the most concrete level of analysis. Algonquian verbal inflection used to provide favorite examples of so-called discontinuous morphemes in textbooks of

[8] For more detail the reader should begin with Bloomfield's Sketch. My summary here is informed by my own fieldwork on Malecite, carried out at various times since 1963, and largely based on a recent paper of mine (1971), but also influenced by Goddard's perspicuous study of the Delaware verb in his Ph.D. dissertation (1969 ms.). Perhaps needless to add, both of us are also fundamentally indebted to Bloomfield. My terminology does not always follow his, however; one difference of importance is in the conception of the theme.

structural morphological analysis, and indeed, the determination of inflectional reference to subject or object for verbs or to possessor for nouns often requires consideration both of a prefix and certain suffixes. There are still interesting problems here which must be passed over in a summary treatment such as this, but the categories themselves are clear enough, as for example in Goddard's description (1969 ms.). According to his scheme, there are nominal, pronominal, and verbal categories. All of these are expressed in respect to the verb, the first two with a possessed noun, the first alone with the noun otherwise.

Nominal categories are GENDER, NUMBER, OBVIATION, and PRESENCE. The first is inherent in the noun; every noun is classified as either animate or inanimate. There is a semantic correspondence in the main for these genders (thus in Malecite 'tree' is animate, 'rock' inanimate), and where this is not clear rules to predict gender on semantic grounds can usually be formulated. As is usually the case for such categories, however, there is a residuum where application of the distinction seems essentially arbitrary. For example, in Malecite 'blueberry' is inanimate but 'strawberry' animate. The other three inflectional categories offer assymetrical binary oppositions; for number, plural is marked as against singular, and for obviation and presence the marked feature is referred to as obviative and absentative, respectively. Briefly, obviative is applied to all but the first noun in a particular focus, so that for example in a 'raw' sentence such as 'John ... Bill ... hit' one of the persons named (independent of subject and object distinctions) must be marked as obviative — Bloomfield uses 'the other' as a convenient translation tag for an obviated noun. Absentative, of rather limited use in the modern languages, applies to a noun stigmatized as removed from the focus of discourse. A noun is typically so inflected to refer to a deceased friend or relative, but may equally be marked as absentative, in at least some of the languages, to characterize a person or object out of the room, not in sight, and so forth. Thus a canoe the speaker once owned but no longer does when referred to by him with this inflection (and a possessive) expresses in compact compass a range of meaning such as 'the canoe I used to have, my former canoe'.

Pronominal categories express PERSON, and are defined by the set of personal pronouns used independently. These are seven, expressing first, second, and third person singular and plural, with first person plural divided into inclusive and exclusive. The exclusive 'is a first plural which excludes the addressee' (Goddard 1969 ms.:30). The expression of pronominal categories so conceived is quite straightforward, in contrast to the tangled forms found in traditional analyses. First, there are the simple singular categories. Second, there is a marked feature of pluralization. Third, each of the four plural categories indicates two persons involved, according to the following scheme:

| *Category* | *Persons* |
| --- | --- |
| First plural exclusive | First and third |
| First plural inclusive | First and second |
| Second plural | Second and third |
| Third plural | Third and third |

In opposition to the seven definite person categories there is a category for indefinite person.

The nominal and pronominal categories together specify one or more PARTICIPANTS (Goddard's term; the participants are also characterized by concrete grammatical features as subject or object) in relation to verbal forms. The verbal categories of ORDER and MODE point out how the participant(s) are related to the verbal notion. The modern languages differ widely among themselves as to how these categories subdivide. There are cases in some languages where functions of a given type can be shown to have been taken over by forms which in their origin belong to another, but there are also many differences which for the present can only be described and not yet explained. The situation is generally as follows: there are five verbal orders, the independent, the conjunct, the imperative, the prohibitive, and the interrogative. Each order has forms for one or more modes; but after the indicative mode of the independent order, certain conjunct modes, and the imperative mode of the imperative order, the list varies according to the language, including such modes as relative (independent order) and potential (prohibitive order). Some languages have a negative order or mode. The functions are more or less those which would be expected from the conventional use of the terms: the details cannot be gone into here. In respect to the two most commonly encountered orders, the independent is used by and large for predications, the conjunct for subordinations.

Phrase and sentence types are numerous, and there are nominal as well as verbal sentences; but in the nature of the language, the verb with its internal elaborations is central, the verb alone typically amounting to a sentence in microcosm. In the average verbal sentence, nouns, when used at all, often do no more than give a more specific name to an entity already signalled within the verb as to its presence and function. Yet in turn a noun itself may be derived from a verb, rich in grammatical content as it already is. Semantic content of single words may also be rich, for, as the quotation from Sapir given at the beginning of this section indicates, elements subordinate to roots may also be quite concrete in their signification, and there are compound stems and themes within the compass of single words as well; we have been unable to exemplify these properties properly in this summary sketch, but they are nonetheless important. In fact, as might be expected in a language called polysynthetic, single Algonquian words not infrequently constitute sentences in themselves. Recent linguistic theory has underplayed the importance of the word as a fundamental unit in grammar. Progress in the description and the understanding of Algonquian languages can provide a valuable corrective.

## 5. CONTINUING RESEARCH AND DESIDERATA

In the Foreword to a volume of papers resulting from a 1964 conference on Algonquian linguistics (National Museum of Canada 1967:iii), A. D. DeBlois writes that the conference 'was attended by twelve linguists, very nearly the total for all of North America who are actively engaged in research on Algonquian linguistics'. Although a few younger scholars have since joined this small group, the statement points up a basic problem not only for Algonquian but for American Indian linguistics in general. Twelve people cannot adequately handle twenty-six languages. Given that more languages will pass to extinction over the next decade or so than has been the case since the coming of the white man to the New World, and that many of these languages lack even adequate description, much mitigation of the situation cannot be expected. At least Algonquian linguistics has a solid beginning, and recent research continues to add results, if slowly. I shall cite briefly in this section some results obtained and hoped for, treating first historical and second descriptive research, indissolubly related as these two may be in practice. Some work in progress is also referred to in the bibliography along with published and unpublished papers; mention here is more selective.

In the subclassification of the languages, at least one important concrete result has been achieved since Bloomfield. This is to show that Eastern Algonquian constitutes a subgroup marked by shared innovations, at the same time confirming Bloomfield's claim that the scheme for Proto-Algonquian given in the Sketch will by and large cover all the languages. Common Eastern Algonquian includes more than half of the languages as listed; specifically, all of those with an 'E' for location in the previous list except Montagnais-Naskapi. The result comes from the work of Goddard, principally his paper already cited (1967). A first step in a valuable project assembling Algonquian comparative vocabulary is Hockett 1957; further installments are yet to appear. An interesting and pioneering attempt to locate the Algonquian homeland is found in Siebert 1967b, which arrives at a center of diffusion in the eastern upper Great Lakes region. In the same paper Siebert also gives us an educated guess as to the dates for latest Algonquian unity, which he finds from 1200–900 B.C. In addition to these, a number of papers on specific points of history or comparative study have appeared, references to many of which are found in the bibliography or in works listed therein, especially National Museum of Canada 1967. The teaching of Mary R. Haas has directly and indirectly stimulated much work on Algonquian, including that of Taylor on Blackfoot and other western languages and that of the present writer, and Haas herself is engaged in important research on several aspects of the subject, as well as on the history of American Indian linguistics as a whole. In historical Algonquian studies the data exist for further rapid progress in many specific areas.

In descriptive studies a major difficulty is that much work remains to be published, as seen for example in the listing of recent doctoral dissertations on Blackfoot, Delaware, Kickapoo, Micmac, and Plains Cree in the bibliography. Another outstanding case is the thorough and extensive work on modern Penobscot carried out since the 1930s by Frank T. Siebert, Jr., which is finally now being prepared for publication and which will prove of incalculable value to Algonquianists. A monument among published works is Bloomfield's Menomini grammar which came out posthumously under Hockett's editorship (Bloomfield 1962); a Menomini-English lexicon of comparable importance in Hockett's possession has yet to appear. C.F. Voegelin has provided us with several basic papers, particularly on Shawnee and Delaware. A model restatement of part of an earlier description of Cheyenne is found in a paper by the European scholar Meeussen (1962).

Current needs in Algonquian studies begin of course with more fieldwork. Perhaps the most serious deficiency at present is the lack of materials on the dialects of the northern languages, Montagnais-Naskapi, Cree, and Ojibwa-Algonquin-Ottawa. There are numerous dialects, the subgrouping has yet to be thoroughly understood, and it may well be that there are more than three separate languages involved. This is only one salient example; basic fieldwork is either needed or remains unpublished for the majority of the languages remaining.

Field research is of course no longer possible on the ten Algonquian languages no longer spoken of the twenty-six listed, but this does not foreclose our knowledge of these thanks to earlier works, particularly those of missionaries. Scholars such as Goddard and Meeussen have shown how much can be accomplished by intelligent reinterpretation of these works. Besides Goddard's paper (1967) cited already several times, his Ph.D. dissertation on Delaware (1969 ms.) combines in an exemplary manner fieldwork on a language going out of currency and painstaking study of earlier literature with restatement of relevant portions.

Despite the need for more data, finally, enough exists so that a great deal of real history can be recovered and the grammar well understood working with available sources. Again, Goddard's results are the proof of this fact. Languages without a written tradition develop historically as all others, as Leonard Bloomfield demonstrated. Further study is a desideratum, not only to deepen his demonstration, but as well to enrich our knowledge of the history of languages by examining the history of widely diverse linguistic types. Algonquian linguistics offers one valuable laboratory for such research.

## 6. SELECTED ANNOTATED BIBLIOGRAPHY

This bibliography[9] is intended to include the principal published sources (with a few unpublished doctoral dissertations) on Algonquian and the Algonquian languages, that is, those works to which one may profitably refer for basic information. Where the most recent treatment is in an article of somewhat restricted scope, it has been listed as well; also included are some sources of poor quality that contain the only information available on a given language. Some information on work in progress is given, but this was not systematically gathered.

[9] The bibliography is based on one compiled by Ives Goddard, to whom I am grateful.

## General and Comparative

BLOOMFIELD, LEONARD. 1946. Algonquian. Linguistic structures of native America, ed. by Harry Hoijer et al., pp. 85–129 (= VFPA 6). The fundamental work in the field of Algonquian, with an extensive bibliography.

HOCKETT, CHARLES F. 1957. Central Algonquian vocabulary: Stems in /k-/. IJAL 23.247–68.

———. 1966. What Algonquian is really like. IJAL 32.59–73.

MICHELSON, TRUMAN. 1912. Preliminary report on the linguistic classification of Algonquian tribes. BAE-R 28.221–90b. Contains much information not found elsewhere, though the analysis has generally been superseded.

———. 1935. Phonetic shifts in Algonquian languages. IJAL 8.131–71.

MURDOCK, GEORGE P. 1960. Ethnographic bibliography of North America. 3rd ed. New Haven, Conn.

NATIONAL MUSEUM OF CANADA. 1967. Contributions to anthropology: Linguistics I (Algonquian) (= Bulletin 214). Ottawa, 1967. Useful papers reflecting the state of the art as of 1964.

PILLING, JAMES C. 1891. Bibliography of the Algonquian languages. B[A]E-B 13.

Except for the most significant items, material in the above collections is not repeated below.

### Abnaki (Eastern)

RASLES, SEBASTIAN (Sébastien Râle). 1833. A dictionary of the Abnaki language in North America, ed. by John Pickering. AAcadAS-M, new series, 1.375–565. Cambridge, Mass.

SPECK, FRANK G. 1920. Penobscot transformer tales. IJAL 1.187–244.

———. 1928. Wawenock myth texts from Maine. BAE-R 43.165–97. A better collection linguistically than the preceding.

A great deal of material on modern Penobscot has been collected by FRANK T. SIEBERT, JR.

### Abnaki (Western)

DAY, GORDON. 1964. A St. Francis Abnaki vocabulary. IJAL 30.371–93.

LAURENT, JOSEPH. 1884. New familiar Abenakis and English dialogues. Quebec.

MASTA, HENRY LORNE. 1932. Abenaki Indian legends, grammar and place names. Victoriaville, P.Q.

Laurent and Masta were native speakers of Abnaki.

### Arapaho-Atsina-Nawathinehena

KROEBER, A. L. 1916. Arapaho dialects. UCPAAE 12.71–138.

SALZMANN, ZDENĚK. 1956a. Arapaho I: Phonology. IJAL 22.49–56.

——. 1956b. Arapaho II: Texts. IJAL 22.151–58.
——. 1956c. Arapaho III: Additional texts. IJAL 27.266–72.
——. 1961. Arapaho IV: Interphonemic specification. IJAL 27.151–55.
——. 1965a. Arapaho V: Noun. IJAL 31.39–49.
——. 1965b. Arapaho VI: Noun. IJAL 31.136–51.
——. 1967. Arapaho VII: Verb. IJAL 33.209–23.

### Blackfoot

FRANTZ, DONALD G. 1966. Person indexing in Blackfoot. IJAL 32.50–8.
UHLENBECK, C.C. 1938. A concise Blackfoot grammar. Verhandelingen der Koninklijke Akademie van Wetenschappen, Afdeeling Letterkunde, n.s., 41. 1–120. Amsterdam.
UHLENBECK, C.C., and R.H. VAN GULICK. 1930. An English-Blackfoot dictionary (= Verhandelingen der Koninklijke Akademie ..., n.s., 29, no. 4, pp. 1–261). Amsterdam.
——. 1934. A Blackfoot-English dictionary. Verhandelingen der Koninklijke Akademie ..., n.s., 33, no. 2, pp. 1–380. Amsterdam.

There have been recent dissertations by DONALD G. FRANTZ (University of Alberta, 1970) and ALLAN R. TAYLOR (University of California at Berkeley, 1969).

### Carolina Algonquian

GEARY, JAMES A. 1900. The language of the Carolina Algonquian tribes. Appendix II in The Roanoke Voyages 1584–1590, ed. by David B. Quinn, pp. 873–900. 2 vols. Works issued by the Hakluyt Society, second series, 104, 105.
LAWSON, JOHN. 1709. A New Voyage to Carolina. London, 1709, and subsequent editions. Pampticough vocabulary on pp. 225–30.

### Cheyenne

DAVIS, IRVINE. 1962. Phonogical function in Cheyenne. IJAL 28.36–42. Reflects the large amount of unpublished work on Cheyenne by members of the Summer Institute of Linguistics.
MEEUSSEN, A.E. 1962. The independent order in Cheyenne. Orbis 11.260–88. Useful organization of some of Petter's data.
PETTER, RODOLPHE. 1907. Sketch of the Cheyenne grammar. AAA-M I/6.443–78.
——. 1915. English-Cheyenne dictionary. Kettle Falls, Washington.
——. 1952. Cheyenne grammar. Newton, Kansas.

## Connecticut-Unquachog

HARRINGTON, MARK R. 1924. An ancient village site of the Shinnecock Indians. Anthropological Papers of the American Museum of Natural History 22.5.227–83. The few known words of this dialect are on p. 282; compare JAF 16.39 (1903).

JEFFERSON, THOMAS. 1836. [Vocabulary of Unquachog recorded in 1791], in Albert Gallatin, "A synopsis of the Indian tribes", Transactions and Collections of the American Antiquarian Society (= Archaeologia Americana) 2.305–367 (1836). Not an accurate and complete publication of the manuscript, which is in the library of the American Philosophical Society.

PEIRSON, ABRAHAM (Abraham Pierson). 1658. Some helps for the Indians. Cambridge, 1658, and later editions. A poor composition using jargonized grammar.

## Cree

BLOOMFIELD, LEONARD. 1930. Sacred stories of the Sweet Grass Cree. NMC-B 60.
———. 1934. Plains Cree texts. PAES 16.
    These two volumes of superb texts are both from the Plains Cree of the Sweet Grass Reserve.

EDWARDS, MARY. 1954. Cree: An intensive language course. 2nd ed. 1961. Meadow Lake, Saskatchewan. Plains Cree.

ELLIS, C. DOUGLAS. 1961. The so-called interrogative order in Cree. IJAL 27. 119–24. Moose Cree.
———. [1962?] Spoken Cree, West Coast of James Bay: Part I. Toronto.

HORDEN, JOHN. 1881. A grammar of the Cree language. London. Moose Cree.
———. 1934. A grammar of the Cree language, revised edition in Plain[s] Cree. London.

LACOMBE, ALBERT. 1874. Dictionnaire et grammaire de la langue des Cris. Montreal. Plains Cree.

WATKINS, E. A. 1938. A dictionary of the Cree language. Revised edition edited by R. Faries. Toronto.

There is a recent doctoral dissertation on Plains Cree by H. CRISTOPH WOLFART (Yale, 1970).

## Delaware

VOEGELIN, C. F. 1945. Delaware texts. IJAL 11.105–19.
———. 1946. Delaware, an Eastern Algonquian language. Linguistic structures of native America, ed. by Harry Hoijer et al., pp. 130–57. (= VFPA 6.)

A recent doctoral dissertation by IVES GODDARD (Harvard, 1969) lists and evaluates some additional sources.

## Fox-Sauk

BLOOMFIELD, LEONARD. 1925, 1927. Notes on the Fox language. IJAL 3.219–32; 4.181–219. Based on materials published by Jones and Michelson.

JONES, WILLIAM. 1907. Fox texts. PAES 1. Leyden.

MICHELSON, TRUMAN. 1925. Accompanying papers. BAE-R 40.21–658. With stem list and grammatical notes; may be taken as representative of the volumes of texts Michelson published as *Bulletins* of the Bureau of American Ethnology.

VOORHIS, PAUL H. 1971. New notes on the Mesquakie (Fox) language. IJAL 37.63–75. Intended to supplement Bloomfield's "Notes", listed above.

## Illinois-Peoria-Miami

DUNN, JACOB P. [English-Miami Dictionary], incorporated into C.F. Voegelin, "Shawnee stems" (1938–40) (see under Shawnee, below). See further CAROLINE DUNN, "Jacob Piatt Dunn: His Miami language studies and Indian manuscript collection", Prehistory Research Series 1.25–59 (Indiana Historical Society, Indianapolis, 1937).

## Kickapoo

JONES, WILLIAM. 1915. Kickapoo tales. PAES 9. Leyden.

A grammar of this language is now available in the doctoral dissertation of PAUL VOORHIS (Yale, 1967).

## Loup

JEAN-CLAUDE MATHEVET's manuscript "Mots Loups" is now being edited by Gordon Day.

## Mahican

PRINCE, J. DYNELEY. 1905. A tale in the Hudson River Indian language. AmA, n.s. 7.74–84.

The moderately extensive materials on this language remain largely unpublished and unanalyzed.

## Malecite-Passamaquoddy

BARRATT, JOSEPH. 1851. The Indian of New England. Middletown, Conn.

CHAMBERLAIN, MONTAGUE. 1899. Maliseet vocabulary. Cambridge, Mass.

PRINCE, J. DYNELEY. 1921. Passamaquoddy texts. PAES 10. New York.
TEETER, KARL V. 1971. The main features of Malecite-Passamaquoddy grammar. Studies in American Indian languages dedicated to Mary R. Haas, ed. by Jesse Sawyer, pp. 191–249. UCPL 65.

## Massachusett

COTTON, JOSIAH. 1830. Vocabulary of the Massachusetts (or Natick) Indian language. Collections of the Massachusetts Historical Society, series 3, 2.147–257. Cambridge.
ELIOT, JOHN. 1666. The Indian grammar begun. Cambridge, 1666, and later editions.
TRUMBULL, JAMES HAMMOND. 1903. Natick dictionary. BAE-B 25.

## Menomini

BLOOMFIELD, LEONARD. 1928. Menomini texts. PAES 12. New York. Bloomfield also left at his death a manuscript Menomini-English lexicon of 439 typed pages, including over 10,000 entries.
——. 1962. The Menomini language. New Haven and London. The best grammar of an Algonquian language.

## Micmac

PACIFIQUE, RÉVÉREND PÈRE ——. 1939. Leçons grammaticales théoriques et pratiques de la langue Micmaque. Sainte-Anne de Ristigouche, P.Q.
RAND, SILAS T. 1888. Dictionary of the language of the Micmac Indians. Halifax. English-Micmac.
——. 1902. Rand's Micmac dictionary. Charlottetown, P.E.I. Micmac-English.

A generative phonology of Micmac has been submitted as a doctoral dissertation by JAMES FIDELHOLTZ (MIT, 1968).

## Mohegan-Pequot-Montauk

GARDINER, JOHN LYON. 1824. A vocabulary of the Indian language spoken by the Montauk Tribe. In Silas Wood, Sketch of Long Island (Brooklyn, 1924), p. 28, footnote. Not satisfactorily published.
SPECK, FRANK G. 1928. Native tribes and dialects of Connecticut: A Mohegan-Pequot diary. BAE-R 43.199–287.

## Montagnais-Naskapi

LEMOINE, GEO. 1901. Dictionnaire Français-Montagnais. Boston.

MICHELSON, TRUMAN. 1939. Linguistic classification of Cree and Montagnais-Naskapi dialects. BAE-B 123.67–95 (= Anthropological Papers 8).

ROGERS, JEAN H. 1960. Notes on Mistassini phonemics and morphology. NMC-B 167.90–113 (= Contributions to Anthropology, 1958).

SIROIS, LUC. [1937?]. Montagnais sans maître. Bersimis, P.Q. Bersimis dialect.

## Nanticoke-Conoy

SPECK, FRANK G. 1927. The Nanticoke and Conoy Indians, with a review of linguistic material from manuscript and living sources. Papers of the Historical Society of Delaware, new series 1. Wilmington.

## Narragansett

WILLIAMS, ROGER. 1643. A key into the language of America. London, 1643; fifth edition, Providence, 1936. Contains a few errors of grammar, but far ahead of its time in its implicit perception that a language is profitably studied within the framework of the culture of those that speak it.

## Ojibwa-Algonquin-Ottawa

BARAGA, FREDERIC. 1850. A theoretical and practical grammar of the Otchipwe language. Detroit.

———. 1853. A dictionary of the Otchipwe language. Cincinnati. A second edition of these two important works was issued at Montreal, 1878–1880; the revisions consist mostly of omissions in the grammar.

BLOOMFIELD, LEONARD. 1957. Eastern Ojibwa. Ann Arbor. Complements but does not replace Baraga.

CUOQ, JEAN ANDRÉ. 1886. Lexique de la langue Algonquine. Montréal. Algonquin-French.

———. 1891, 1892. Grammaire de la langue Algonquine. Proceedings and Transactions of the Royal Society of Canada 9 (Section I), 85–114; 10 (Section I), 41–119. The culmination of nearly three centuries of work on Algonquian languages by French and French-Canadian missionaries, this grammar, though rarely cited, laid the foundations for the subsequent development of the field.

JONES, WILLIAM. 1917, 1919. Ojibwa Texts. PAES 7 (Part 1, Leyden; Part II, New York).
LEMOINE, GEO. 1911. Dictionnarie Français-Algonquin. Québec.
ROGERS, JEAN H. 1963. Survey of Round Lake Ojibwa phonology and morphology. NMC-B 194.91–154 (= Contributions to Anthropology, 1961–62, Part II).

*Potawatomi*

HOCKETT, CHARLES F. 1939. Potawatomi syntax. Lg 15.235–248.
———. 1948. Potawatomi, I-IV. IJAL 14.1–10, 63–73, 139–49, 213–25.

*Powhatan*

SMITH, JOHN. 1612. A map of Virginia. Oxford. Contains a short vocabulary reprinted in Smith's Generall Historie of Virginia (London, 1624, and later editions).
STRACHEY, WILLIAM. 1612. The historie of travell into Virginia Britannia. (= Works issued by the Hakluyt Society, second series, 103, London, 1954). Vocabularies on pp. 174–207; see also BAE-B 157.189–202 (= Anthropological Papers 26) (1955).

*Shawnee*

VOEGELIN, C. F. 1935. Shawnee phonemes. Lg 11.23–37.
———. 1936. Productive paradigms in Shawnee. Essays in anthropology in honor of Alfred Louis Kroeber, pp. 391–403. Berkeley.
———. 1938–40. Shawnee stems and the Jacob P. Dunn Miami Dictionary. Prehistory Research Series 1.61–108, 131–67, 287–341, 343–89, 407–78. Indiana Historical Society, Indianapolis.

7.

Listed here are the items referred to in the first five sections of this paper. Many of these are fully cited in the selected annotated bibliography which constitutes section six; the letters SAB plus a word or phrase in the entries below are used to refer to the appropriate subdivision in the bibliography under which they are found.

BLOOMFIELD, LEONARD. 1925, 1927. SAB Fox-Sauk.
———. 1946. SAB General and Comparative.
———. 1962. SAB Menomini.

CHAFE, WALLACE L. 1962. Estimates regarding present speakers of North American Indian languages. IJAL 28.162–71.
GODDARD, IVES. 1967. The Algonquian independent indicative. NMC-B 214 (SAB General and Comparative), 66–106.
——. 1969 ms. SAB Delaware.
HAAS, MARY R. 1958. Algonkian-Ritwan: The end of a controversy. IJAL 24.159–73.
——. 1967. Roger Williams's sound shift: A study in Algonquian. To honor Roman Jakobson 1.816–32. The Hague, Mouton.
HANZELI, VICTOR E. 1969. Missionary linguistics in New France. JanL, series maior 29.
MEEUSSEN, A. E. 1962. SAB Cheyenne.
MICHELSON, TRUMAN. 1912. SAB General and Comparative.
——. 1935. SAB General and Comparative.
NATIONAL MUSEUM OF CANADA. 1967. NMC-B 214. SAB General and Comparative.
PILLING, JAMES C. 1891. SAB General and Comparative.
SAPIR, EDWARD. 1929. Central and North American languages. Encyclopedia Britannica 5.138–41. Reprinted in SWES, pp. 169–78. 1963.
SCHOOLCRAFT, HENRY ROWE. 1839. Algic researches. New York, Harper and Brothers.
SIEBERT, FRANK T., JR. 1941. Certain Proto-Algonquian consonant clusters. Lg 17.298–303.
——. 1967a. Discrepant consonant clusters ending in $*$-$k$ in Proto-Algonquian. NMC-B 214 (SAB General and Comparative), 48–59.
——. 1967b. The original home of the Proto-Algonquian people. NMC-B 214. 13–47.
SWADESH, MORRIS. 1946. South Greenlandic (Eskimo). Linguistic structures of native America, by Harry Hoijer and others, pp. 30–54. VFPA 6.
TEETER, KARL V. 1964. Descriptive linguistics in America: Triviality vs. irrelevance. Word 20.197–206.
——. 1970a. Review of The Menomini language, by Leonard Bloomfield. Lg 46.524–33.
——. 1970b. Review of The Menomini language, by Leonard Bloomfield. IJAL 36.235–9.
——. 1971. SAB Malecite-Passamaquoddy.
TRUMBULL, J. HAMMOND. 1876. The Algonkin verb. TAPA 146–71.
——. 1903. SAB Massachusett.

# SIOUAN, IROQUOIAN, AND CADDOAN

WALLACE L. CHAFE

0. INTRODUCTION

Apart from the Algonquian, Muskogean, and Gulf languages, the three language families that will be discussed in this chapter account for most of the aboriginal languages spoken in North America east of the Rocky Mountains. They are treated under a single heading because of the likelihood that they are remotely related, forming a linguistic unit which might be referred to as 'Macro-Siouan'. The first part of the chapter will be taken up with discussions of the work that has been done so far on the languages of these families. The Caddoan languages will be discussed first, then the Iroquoian, and finally the Siouan. The author is more directly familiar with the Caddoan and Iroquoian languages and with past and present linguistic work conducted in those areas. For that reason it is possible that his treatment of the Siouan languages is less complete, and he would be happy to be informed of relevant information that he has not included. The latter part of the chapter is concerned with remote relationships, particularly the Macro-Siouan hypothesis, and presents for the first time certain evidence tending to link Caddoan with both Siouan and Iroquoian.

1. CADDOAN

There are essentially three extant Caddoan languages: Caddo, Wichita, and Pawnee. A geographically separated and quite aberrant dialect of Pawnee known as Arikara (or Ree) is usually listed as a separate language. Another language, Kitsai, lost its last speaker a few decades ago. Caddo, Wichita, and Pawnee are now spoken in Oklahoma, Arikara in North Dakota. There are no more than a few hundred speakers of any of these languages remaining; in the case of Wichita and Arikara the number is smaller than that. None of the languages is being learned by children. An excellent discussion of all but the most recent history of Caddoan linguistics is Taylor (1963a), on which much of the following is based.

1.1 *Caddo*

The ancestors of the present Caddo, when first encountered by Europeans, formed a far-flung group of individual bands of varying size on the western edge of the Southeast culture area. Aside from a few isolated groups, these bands were clustered into several larger entities, chief among which were the Hasinai, in what is presently eastern Texas, and the Kadohadacho, farther to the north in approximately the area where the Red River now forms the boundary between Texas and Arkansas. Other bands lived farther south on the Red River in Louisiana and farther east and north in Arkansas. Linguistically, these bands differed at least to the extent that they spoke a number of distinct dialects. The present Caddo represent a melting pot of these different bands, created by an amalgamation of all of them in Texas in the nineteenth century. In 1859 they fled from Texas into what is now Oklahoma, where they were settled in the neighborhood of the present towns of Anadarko, Binger, and Ft. Cobb. Remnants of the earlier dialect differences are still found distributed among them in a manner that would repay further study.

A group of Caddo may have been visited by the DeSoto expedition as early as 1541, but these people seem not to have been seen by Europeans again until the 17th century, when a variety of contacts took place between them and both Spanish and French explorers and traders. It seems that LaSalle may have been the first to record some words of their language, in 1687. It was not until the beginning of the 19th century, however, that we have anything more than a few sporadic words preserved. During the first decade of that century, just after the Louisiana Purchase, John Sibley collected for Thomas Jefferson vocabulary lists of Caddo, of a divergent dialect called Natchitoches, and of a distinct language called Adai whose affiliation remains problematic. The Natchitoches vocabulary has been lost, but the Caddo list was later published (Claiborne and Mason 1879), as was the Adai (Gallatin 1836:307–67). Sibley was the first Indian agent in this area. One of his successors, George Gray, also collected a Caddo vocabulary and some sentences, and it was this material (with nineteen additional words from Sibley) which was published by Gallatin (1836:307–67, 383–97, 409–13). Schoolcraft (1853:790–12) published a Caddo vocabulary which had been collected by Captain Randolph B. Marcy. Twenty words of Caddo collected by Lieutenant Amiel Weeks Whipple were also published at about the same time (Whipple 1856:70). Still later in the 19th century, James Mooney included a short Caddo glossary in his ghost-dance study (Mooney 1896:1102–3).

In the present century, a set of Caddo kinship terms was discussed by Leslie Spier (1924), and a number of Caddo words were included among some ethnographic notes published by Elsie Clews Parsons (1941). In 1956 and early 1957 Daniel da Cruz, at that time an undergraduate student at Georgetown University, worked with a Caddo informant and subsequently wrote a provisional phonemic analysis of the language as a senior essay (da Cruz 1957). In the first half of the 1960s Wallace L. Chafe spent four summers working with the language. The results of that work should eventually be published, but at present reference can be made only to some Caddo examples in work dealing with phonological theory (Chafe 1968).

## 1.2 Wichita

The Wichita are generally thought to have been the inhabitants of the 'Province of Quivira', which represented the farthest penetration into the North American continent by the Coronado expedition in 1541. At that time the Wichita were probably located in central Kansas. After moving into what is now Oklahoma, where they were found by Frenchmen in the early 18th century, they were gradually forced further south into Texas before the end of that century. Later they returned to Oklahoma, fled to Kansas during the Civil War, and were finally placed together with the Caddo in the vicinity of Anadarko, Oklahoma, particularly in and about the town of Gracemont.

As with the Caddo language, there is a small amount of poorly transcribed Wichita vocabulary material from the 19th century. In particular, there are two different vocabulary lists collected by Marcy (Marcy 1853:307–8 and Schoolcraft 1853:709–11), plus Whipple's vocabulary of the now extinct dialect called Waco (Whipple 1856: 65–8). Spier's article on kinship (1924) dealt with Wichita as well as Caddo terms. Edward S. Curtis (1907–30:vol. 19, 230–7) also gives a Wichita vocabulary. In 1949 the Wichita were visited by Paul L. Garvin, who subsequently published an article on Wichita phonemes (Garvin 1950), and who also recorded the kinship terms that were discussed in Schmitt (1952). More recent and more extensive work has been done by David S. Rood, who began fieldwork on the language in 1965, and who has completed a grammar of the language as a doctoral dissertation (Rood 1969).

## 1.3 Kitsai

The Kitsai may have been located prehistorically in Oklahoma, but Europeans first found them living in what is now Texas between the Red River and the upper Trinity. In 1858 they fled to Oklahoma, where they have been living among the Wichita ever since. In recent times, at least, the Wichita have considered the Kitsai to be part of their own tribe, and all the last speakers of Kitsai also spoke Wichita. The last fluent speaker of Kitsai evidently died during the 1930s. A vocabulary of Kitsai appears in Whipple (1856:65–8). Kitsai data were recorded by Alexander Lesser in the summers of 1929 and 1930. His extensive notes, to be deposited in the Library of the American Philosophical Society, provide the only important source of information on this language. Bucca and Lesser (1969) is based on this material.

## 1.4 Pawnee

Coronado's guide through the plains area in the 16th century is thought to have been a Pawnee. Significant European contact, however, awaited the coming of French explorers in the early 18th century. At that time the Pawnee were located principally in the area of what is now Nebraska, in the neighborhood of the Platte River. They seem to have been divided into four distinct bands (or five, including the Arikara, to be discussed separately below). Three of these bands spoke approximately the same dialect. The fourth, known as the Skidi (Skiri), spoke a distinguishable but not radically different dialect. In the 19th century the Pawnee moved to what is now Oklahoma, where they presently live in and about the town of Pawnee.

The first systematic recording of the Pawnee language seems to have been a list of vocabulary items collected for Thomas Jefferson by the Lewis and Clark expedition in 1804–05. The earliest published vocabulary was collected by Thomas Say, a member of the Long expedition in 1819–20, and was published in the report on that expedition by Edwin James (Thwaites 1904–07: vol. 17, 290–8, 305). Say's vocabulary also appeared in Gallatin (1836:307–67). The German nobleman, Alexander Philip Maximilian, Prince of Wied, during his travels in the West in the 1830s, collected a brief Pawnee vocabulary from a non-Indian who spoke Pawnee (Maximilian 1839–41: vol. 2, 630–2; also in Thwaites 1904–07: vol. 24, 293–4). A lengthier vocabulary of Pawnee was published by Ferdinand Vandeveer Hayden (1863:347–51), who received his material from William Hamilton, a missionary among the Pawnee. Hayden himself collected additional Pawnee material, both lexical and grammatical, which he published a few years later (Hayden 1869:390–406). Lewis Henry Morgan (1871: 293–382) included kinship terms from two different bands of Pawnee collected by himself and B. F. Lushbaugh. A short grammar of Pawnee by John Brown Dunbar appeared in 1890 as an appendix to a collection of Pawnee stories (Grinnell 1893: 409–37). Texts of some Pawnee songs are found in Fletcher (1902) and Densmore (1929). Gilmore (1919:139–45, 149–50) gives the Pawnee names of some plants. Gene Weltfish has devoted much of her career to ethnographic (including linguistic) study of the Pawnee. She published a Pawnee text with a detailed grammatical analysis (1936), and some further texts with word for word translations (1937). Douglas R. Parks began working with the language in the summer of 1965, and is, at the time of this writing, preparing a description of it as a doctoral dissertation.

## 1.5 *Arikara*

Beginning as a northern offshoot of the Pawnee, the Arikara have in historic times gradually moved northward along the Missouri River from South Dakota into North Dakota. They moved to Fort Berthold in North Dakota in 1862, and eventually became one of the three tribes (with the Mandan and Hidatsa) on the Fort Berthold Reservation.

Gallatin (1836:129) mentioned the Arikara, saying, 'All the accounts of the Indians and of the interpreters agree in the fact of their speaking Pawnee, but we have no vocabulary of their language'. A significant vocabulary had, however, been collected by Maximilian shortly before Gallatin's work was published. Unusually accurate for the time, it was first published in Maximilian (1839–41:465–74), and can be found also in Thwaites (1904–07:vol. 24, 210–4). Another list of Arikara words, less satisfactorily recorded than those of the Maximilian list, was published by the well-known painter of Indian subjects, George Catlin (1841:vol. 2, 262–5). There is evidence that this list was made, not by Catlin, but by an official of the American Fur Company named Kenneth Mackenzie (Latham 1846:32). A third Arikara vocabulary appeared in Hayden (1863:356–63). Morgan (1871:293–382) includes Arikara kinship terms. Curtis (1907–30:vol. 5, 169–77) also contains an Arikara vocabulary. In more recent years occasional brief fieldwork on Arikara has been done by Gene Weltfish, Melvin Gilmore, Allan R. Taylor, Wallace L. Chafe, and Douglas R. Parks. Parks contemplates further work with Arikara as an extension of his Pawnee studies.

1.6 *Relationships within Caddoan*

The relationship of Wichita and Kitsai to Pawnee is not so distant that it would escape any scholar possessed of sufficient data from these three languages. The first published mention of this relationship seems to have been that included in a footnote in Josiah Gregg's *Commerce of the prairies* (1844:vol. 2, 251): 'The Pawnees and Rickaras of the north, and the Wacoes, Wichitas, Towockanoes, Towyash and Keechyes, of Red River, are of the same origin.' Documentation was provided in Whipple, Ewbank, and Turner (1855:68–9), based on the vocabulary collected by Whipple. In that same work, Turner also mentioned the possible inclusion of Caddo in this family, and he gave a list of half a dozen possible cognate sets (70). Subsequent classifications of Indian languages accepted the inclusion of Caddo, at first tentatively, but as time went on with increasing conviction (Latham 1860–400; Buschmann 1859: 448; Keane 1878:478; Gatschet 1884:42; Brinton 1891:95–7). During this period reference was usually made to the 'Pawnee' family or stock, but the Powell classification established the name 'Caddoan', which has been used ever since (Powell 1891: 58–62).

The inclusion of Adai in the Caddoan family has been at various times suggested. Our knowledge of the language is so limited, however, that no definitive statement on this point may ever be possible (see discussion in Taylor 1963a:57–8).

As far as subgrouping within the Caddoan family is concerned, the statement of Lesser and Weltfish (1932:1) is probably as accurate as any that can be given at the present time: 'Pawnee, Wichita, and Kitsai are, in relation to each other, about equally divergent, save that Kitsai in phonetic structure and some forms is probably closer to Pawnee than Wichita is to Pawnee. All three, however, are mutually unintelligible. Caddo is the most divergent of the four languages.'

The only systematic comparative work on the Caddoan languages is Taylor (1963b), which does not take into account the more recent descriptive work of Chafe, Parks, and Rood.

## 2. IROQUOIAN

The Iroquoian languages divide themselves into two major branches, Northern Iroquoian and Southern Iroquoian. The degree of difference between these two branches is only a little less than that between the most divergent languages of the Indo-European family. The Northern Iroquoian languages which are still spoken are six in number. They include the very closely related languages of the original Five Nations of the Iroquois — Mohawk, Oneida, Onondaga, Cayuga, and Seneca — plus Tuscarora, now the Sixth Nation, a language somewhat more divergent. These languages are spoken largely in New York State and neighboring Canada, although there are a number of Oneida speakers in Wisconsin and a few speakers of Cayuga in Oklahoma. None of the languages has more than a few thousand speakers, most of them middle-aged or older, and Onondaga, Cayuga, and Tuscarora have well under a thousand, with Tuscarora probably the closest to extinction. A seventh Northern Iroquoian language, Huron (Wyandot), was spoken by a few individuals in Oklahoma until recently. In earlier times the number of Northern Iroquoian languages was larger. Various other languages of this family were spoken in Ontario and Quebec, in western New York, in Pennsylvania, and northern Ohio, as well as in parts of Maryland, eastern Virginia, and eastern North Carolina. All these other languages were obliterated in the early days of European colonization, and we know next to nothing about them. A short vocabulary of one group living along the Susquehanna River, variously called Susquehannock, Conestoga, Andaste, or Minqua, is preserved in Campanius (1696: 155-60). Gallatin (1836:305-67) gives some words from Nottoway, a language spoken in southeastern Virginia and apparently closely related to Tuscarora. The record of another language on the St. Lawrence River is discussed immediately below under 'Laurentian'.

There is only one Southern Iroquoian language, Cherokee, although it is spoken in at least half a dozen dialects. There are roughly ten thousand speakers of Cherokee of all ages, most of them in eastern Oklahoma, but some still occupying a small part of their original territory in western North Carolina.

### 2.1 *Laurentian*

The first North American language to be recorded by a European was a Northern Iroquoian language. Jacques Cartier, after his voyage to the Gulf of St. Lawrence in 1534, took back to France two young men who were part of a fishing party which was temporarily in that area, but whose home was farther to the west. After his second voyage in 1535-36 he returned to France with other captives from the neighborhood of Quebec City. The accounts of these two voyages have appended to them vocabularies which may have been elicited in France from some of these people by the first North American Indian linguist, whoever he may have been. They are published in Biggar (1924:80-1, 241-6). The language of these 'Cartier vocabularies' is often assumed to have been Huron, or partly Huron and partly Mohawk (Barbeau 1959), but it seems more likely that it was some third language, not unlike Huron, that was spoken along the St. Lawrence River in the early 16th century (Chafe 1962; Tooker 1964:3-4). Champlain, at the beginning of the 17th century, did not find Iroquoian speakers in this area. The name 'Laurentian' has been used to refer to this earliest recorded Iroquoian language.

During the 17th, 18th, and 19th centuries a great deal of missionary work was performed among the speakers of Northern Iroquoian languages. The missionaries focused much attention on linguistic matters, for they were generally desirous of preaching to the Indians in their own language, in translating sections of the Bible, prayers, and hymns, and in providing language materials for the training of new missionaries. A number of grammars, vocabularies, and religious texts of various sorts remain in manuscript. The interested reader should consult Pilling (1888) for a list of these and other sources, both published and unpublished. The summaries below will focus on those published sources which are most directly relevant to linguistic studies. Adelung and Vater (1806–17) will not be cited for each language, but a listing of its various Iroquoian vocabularies, reprinted from other sources, is given in Pilling (1888:2). As always, it must be remembered that the transcription systems devised by pre-20th century missionaries suffered from serious inadequacies, and that their grammatical descriptions were generally hampered by a commitment to Latinate models.

## 2.2 *Huron*

The Huron, on first European contact, occupied an area in present Ontario southeast of Georgian Bay. They were visited by Champlain in 1615, but more important linguistically was the visit of the Recollet missionary Gabriel Sagard-Théodat in 1623–24. Sagard prepared a dictionary of the Huron language that was first published a few years later (Sagard 1632). In 1634 Jesuit missionaries from France began intensive work among the Huron, which lasted until the devastating defeat of these people by the Iroquois in 1649–50. Many Huron words are scattered through the Jesuit Relations for this period (Thwaites 1896–1901). Of particular interest are the comments on the language by Jean de Brébeuf (Thwaites 1896–1901:vol. 10, 117–23; also in Gallatin 1836:236-8), and the grammar prepared by Pierre Joseph Marie Chaumonot, which was evidently the source of a work published in translation at a much later date (Wilkie 1831).

The Huron who survived the defeat at the hands of the Iroquois scattered in all directions, and groups of them eventually settled in a variety of locations. In the mid-18th century another Jesuit, Pierre Potier, working at the Huron mission at Sandwich, Ontario, put together an extensive grammar and dictionary, based to a large extent on earlier manuscripts, especially Chaumonot's. A facsimile edition of Potier's manuscripts is now available (Fraser 1920). Potier's work can be viewed as the culmination of all the Jesuits' linguistic work among the Huron.

Another Huron group, after many vicissitudes, finally settled in northeastern Oklahoma, where they have been known as the Wyandot. The language spoken there was recorded in 1911–12 by Marius Barbeau of the National Museum of Canada. This material was used in Barbeau 1915, a work comparing Wyandot 'pronominal prefixes' with those in some other Northern Iroquoian languages. Texts collected at that time were published in Barbeau 1960. Barbeau's lexical material remains in manuscript form in the National Museum of Canada.

## 2.3 *Mohawk*

In earliest recorded times the Mohawk, the easternmost of the Five Nations, occupied a half dozen or more villages in the Mohawk River valley in present New York State, approximately from Schenectady to Utica. They were first encountered by Champlain in 1609, and shortly after by the Dutch. Provided with guns by the Dutch and later the English, they occupied an important military position until the time of the American Revolution. Having sided with the English at that time (as did most of the other Iroquois, except for the Oneida and Tuscarora), many of them then moved to Canada, where they lived with other Iroquois on the Grand River Reserve in Ontario. Still in the 17th century a group of converted Mohawk were settled by the Jesuits at Caughnawaga near Montreal. In the mid-18th century an offshoot from this group formed a settlement further up the St. Lawrence, and their descendants now inhabit the St. Regis Reservation in northernmost New York and adjacent Canada. Smaller groups of Mohawk settled at Tyendinaga and Gibson in Ontario and at Oka in Quebec. Still others now live in Brooklyn, attracted by high steel work.

The first significant linguistic work on Mohawk was carried on by Jacques Bruyas, a Jesuit, whose dictionary (1863), with a few accompanying grammatical notes, was compiled during the 1670s. In the next century a Moravian missionary, Johann Christoph Pyrlaeus, came up from Pennsylvania to work with the Mohawk, but none of his extensive notes on the language have been published. In the 19th century Jean André Cuoq, a Sulpician missionary, worked at Oka on both the Mohawk and Algonkin languages. Several scholarly works by Cuoq on the nature of Indian languages drew heavily on both these languages for examples. From the point of view of Mohawk descriptive material, Cuoq's most important publications are his chapters on Mohawk grammar (1866) and his Mohawk dictionary (1882). Cuoq's work was based in part on manuscripts left by Joseph Marcoux, a missionary at St. Regis and Caughnawaga earlier in the century. Other 19th century sources on Mohawk include the vocabularies published by Gallatin (1836:305–67, 383–97) and by Schoolcraft (1846:264–70; 1851–57:vol. 2, 482–93), the kinship terms in Morgan (1871:291–382), and Horatio Hale's grammatical discussion and glossary (1883b:9–113, 191–215). Numerous minor sources are listed in Pilling (1888:121–3).

In the present century we have, first of all, the long and carefully transcribed cosmological texts published by J. N. B. Hewitt, one of which is in Mohawk (1903:255–339), plus a short ritual text (Hewitt 1928b). Huot (1948) discusses the manner in which Mohawk words have been adapted or invented to apply to items of white culture. More recently, an intensive investigation of Mohawk was undertaken by Paul M. Postal. His dissertation (1962) remains unpublished. There have appeared in print an article on the generation of Mohawk prefixes (Postal 1964b) and on vowel doubling (Postal 1969), as well as discussions of various points of Mohawk phonology in an article on Boas's phonological practice (Postal 1964a) and in a book on phonological theory (Postal 1968).

## 2.4 *Oneida*

Earliest records show the Oneida settled south of Oneida Lake in New York. A remnant of them remains in their original location in Oneida County, New York. Others, however, joined the Iroquois on the Grand River Reserve in Ontario, and still another group entered Canada in 1849 to settle on the Thames River, where they are known as the Oneidas of the Thames. The largest number of Oneida, however, left New York in 1846 and traveled to land on Green Bay, Wisconsin, where they remain today.

The early missionary grammars and dictionaries that we have for Mohawk are lacking for Oneida, which is, however, so closely related that it verges on being an aberrant Mohawk dialect. Nineteenth century vocabularies include those published in Gallatin (1836:305–67), Schoolcraft (1846:279–81), and Schoolcraft (1851–57:vol. 2, 482–93), as well as the kinship terms in Morgan (1871:291–382). Further sources are listed in Pilling (1888:132). In the present century we have, first of all, a grammatical sketch by Franz Boas (1909), and the authoritative description of the Oneida verb by Floyd G. Lounsbury (1953). This last work established much of the framework and terminology followed by subsequent Iroquoian scholars, particularly Postal and Chafe.

## 2.5 *Onondaga*

The earliest known home of the Onondaga was in the same area in New York of which they occupy a small part today. Its center was more or less the present Onondaga County, and it extended northward to Lake Ontario. After the American Revolution some of the Onondaga moved to the Grand River Reserve in Ontario, while some remained in New York, where they now live on a small reservation just south of Syracuse.

What may be the earliest record of the Onondaga language is a dictionary believed to have been compiled by one of the Jesuits at the end of the 17th century. It was published by Shea (1860), who says concerning the identity of the language that it was asserted to be Onondaga by a missionary at Caughnawaga who was a competent

Mohawk scholar, and who noted 'as the most striking differences the substitution of *h* for the Mohawk *r*, and in the preterites of *i* for the Mohawk *on*'. (The *h* referred to is that at the beginning of the masculine pronominal prefix, and the *i* is that of an aspect suffix; both are indeed features by which Onondaga differs from Mohawk.) In the mid-18th century the Onondaga were visited by a Moravian missionary, David Zeisberger, whose grammar and dictionary were also published during the 19th century (Horsford 1887; Zeisberger 1888). It is a curious fact that both the Shea dictionary and the Zeisberger material show a language which differs from Onondaga as it is spoken today. Most notably, the language of the earlier records contains *r*, whereas in modern Onondaga, as in Seneca, *r* has been lost in all environments. Whether Onondaga has undergone a highly significant sound change since the mid-17th century, or whether the language described by Zeisberger (and the Shea dictionary) is not directly ancestral to modern Onondaga remains problematic.

Gallatin (1836:305-67) contains an Onondaga vocabulary taken from Zeisberger's materials, but Schoolcraft (1851-57:vol. 2, 482-93) gives material obtained independently. Again Morgan (1871:291-382) provides a list of kinship terms. Pilling (1888: 133) can be consulted for further, less important sources. Toward the end of the 19th century a great deal of ethnographic work was done by a clergyman named William M. Beauchamp, and he published various works that contain many items of Onondaga vocabulary. An 'ethnobotanical' example is Beauchamp (1902). Hewitt published two cosmological texts in Onondaga (1903:141-220; 1928a:612-791). A recent treatment of Onondaga is Chafe (1970).

### 2.6 *Cayuga*

Earliest records locate the Cayuga on the shores of what is now Cayuga Lake. The majority of them moved to the Grand River Reserve in Ontario after the American Revolution. Those who remained behind were scattered among the other Iroquois tribes, but some, together with other Iroquois, moved westward into Ohio and eventually settled in northeastern Oklahoma, where a small number of them still speak the language. In Oklahoma this slightly deviant dialect of Cayuga is usually called 'Seneca'.

Published sources on Cayuga are remarkably few. Gallatin (1836:376) lists a few words, said to have been taken from Barton. Schoolcraft (1846:271-7; 1851-57:vol. 2, 482-93) gives longer lists. Morgan (1871:291-382) includes Cayuga kinship terms. Speck (1949) contains some Cayuga vocabulary, particularly ceremonial terms. Floyd G. Lounsbury has worked extensively with Cayuga, but has not published on the language, and further work is currently being performed by Michael K. Foster.

### 2.7 *Seneca*

When first encountered the Seneca were situated between the Seneca Lake area and the Genesee River. After the neighboring Erie and Neutrals were defeated during the 17th century, the Seneca spread westward to Lake Erie. After the American Revolution some of them settled on the Grand River Reserve in Ontario, but many remained in western New York, where they now inhabit the Tonawanda, Cattaraugus, and Allegany Reservations. The small Cornplanter Grant in Pennsylvania, formerly inhabited by Seneca, was recently obliterated by the Kinzua Dam.

There is little record of Seneca before the 19th century. The most important early material is found in the works of Asher Wright, a Protestant missionary who worked among the Seneca, first at Buffalo Creek and then at Cattaraugus, from 1831 to 1875. Wright published a great deal of material in Seneca, some of it on his own Mission Press. Most of the material was religious in nature, for example hymnals and a translation of the Gospels, but he also published a Spelling Book (1842) and even a periodical, called in English the 'Mental Elevator', which ran to at least nineteen numbers. Wright at one time devised a unique set of letters to be used in printing Seneca, but they were never adopted. Other 19th century sources on Seneca include a vocabulary published by the Quaker, Halliday Jackson (1830:114–20), two vocabularies and some sentences in Gallatin (1836:305–67, 383–97, 415), a vocabulary in Schoolcraft (1846:393–400) obtained from Ely S. Parker, and Morgan's kinship terms (1871:291–382). Morgan's classic ethnography (1851) also contains a number of Seneca terms, as well as a chapter dealing with the language (394–411). Other sources are listed in Pilling (1888:153).

One of the three texts in the first part of Hewitt's Iroquoian cosmology is in Seneca (Hewitt 1903:221–54). Curtin and Hewitt (1911:715–43, 756–90) also has texts in Seneca. Curtin (1923:513–6) contains a glossary. A number of ethnographic works subsequent to Morgan contain scattered Seneca terms. A few representative examples of such works are Mark R. Harrington (1908), Frederick W. Waugh (1916), Arthur C. Parker (1910, 1913), William N. Fenton (1953), and Harold C. Conklin and William C. Sturtevant (1953). Several articles on Seneca appeared in *IJAL* at mid-century; one by W. D. Preston and C. F. Voegelin (1949), and two based on fieldwork by Nils M. Holmer (1952–53). Holmer subsequently collected all his Seneca material in a single monograph (1954). Wallace L. Chafe's dissertation on Seneca morphology was first published in installments in *IJAL* (Chafe 1960–61), and later republished together with a dictionary (Chafe 1967). Some ritual texts with morphological analysis were published in Chafe 1961. Chafe 1963 was intended as a practical guide to the language, containing orthographic instructions, a sketch of Seneca word structure, and a glossary of ethnographically relevant terms. Chafe (1959a) illustrated a theoretical point with Seneca examples, and Chafe (1959b, 1964b) involved principles and examples of certain kinds of historical reconstruction.

## 2.8 *Tuscarora*

The early colonists found the Tuscarora located in eastern North Carolina. Difficulties with the whites led to their migration to New York State early in the 18th century, where they were subsequently accepted as the sixth nation of the Iroquois League. At the end of the 18th century most of them settled on the small reservation near Niagara Falls which they occupy today. A few, however, moved to the Grand River Reserve in Ontario.

The earliest Tuscarora linguistic material of any consequence seems to be John Lawson's vocabulary from the North Carolina period (Lawson 1709:225–30). Vocabularies published in the 19th century include those in Gallatin (1836:305–67), Catlin (1841:vol. 2, 262–5), and Schoolcraft (1846:251–8). Morgan (1871:291–382) includes Tuscarora kinship terms. Other sources are listed in Pilling (1888:162–3). J. N. B. Hewitt, himself a Tuscarora, prepared a large dictionary of the language, but it remains in manuscript (see Pilling 1888:81–2). More recently there is an article by Frans M. Olbrechts in Dutch dealing with Tuscarora pronominal prefixes (Olbrechts 1929). Anthony F. C. Wallace wrote an account of linguistic materials, mainly wire recordings, collected by him in 1948 (Wallace 1949), and Wallace and Reyburn (1951) contains a text in Tuscarora. Joan Fickett, a student at the State University of New York at Buffalo, wrote an M.A. thesis on Tuscarora phonology which was subsequently published (Fickett 1967). It includes a useful background discussion of the Tuscarora and their language, as well as a brief English-Tuscarora wordlist. Floyd G. Lounsbury has unpublished notes from his own fieldwork on the language.

With respect to the Northern Iroquoian languages in general, there are a few brief articles from the late 19th century dealing with various points of detail. Several by Erminnie A. Smith (1883a, 1883b, 1884) are worth mentioning. There is an interesting controversy between Horatio Hale and J. N. B. Hewitt regarding the etymology of the word *Iroquois*, and various other etymological points (Hewitt 1888, 1891; Hale 1888). Another article on Iroquoian etymology is Hewitt 1892. All these writings show a concern for detail that was characteristic of the period in American Indian linguistic studies.

### 2.9 *Cherokee*

Except for the rather distant linguistic relationship, the Cherokee have little in common — culturally, historically, or geographically — with the Northern Iroquoian groups discussed above. De Soto may have encountered the Cherokee in 1540, but extensive European contact awaited the settlement of Virginia and the Carolinas. In the 17th century these people occupied the southern Appalachian region in Tennessee and North Carolina, as well as neighboring parts of Virginia, South Carolina, Georgia, and Alabama. More than most tribes, the Cherokee made a concerted effort to adapt to white ways. In spite of this effort, most of them were forced to move into what is now northeastern Oklahoma in 1838–39. A few of them hid in the mountains, and were subsequently permitted to remain on the land which forms the Qualla Reservation in North Carolina.

Aside from their relatively large numbers for an American Indian linguistic group, the speakers of Cherokee are of special interest because of their adoption, in 1821, of a unique writing system devised by one of their own number, George Guess (Sequoya). The system was widely used into the first part of the 20th century. In recent time familiarity with it has declined, although most recently there has been a conscious attempt to revive it.

Little systematic attention was paid to the Cherokee language before the 19th century. In 1825 Samuel A. Worcester began missionary work among the Cherokee which lasted until his death in 1859. Worcester was to the Cherokee what Asher Wright was to the Seneca. He arranged for the publication of a large amount of material in the Cherokee syllabary, including portions of the Bible, hymns, and almanacs. Worcester provided most of the material on Cherokee that is scattered throughout Gallatin (1836:241–50, 276, 305–67, 398–404, 415–21), and the notes on Cherokee included in Schoolcraft (1851–57:vol. 2, 443–56). During this same period several periodicals were published in the syllabary: the *Cherokee Phoenix* (1928–34), the *Cherokee Advocate* (1844–54, 1870–1906), and the *Cherokee Messenger* (1844–46).

Two grammars of the language were written by scholars at about this time. The first, by John Pickering (1830), was never completed, but was published in unfinished form. It was based on direct work with an informant. The second, by Hans Georg Conon von der Gabelentz (1852b), was based on Pickering, on Worcester's material in Gallatin, and on copies of the *Cherokee Messenger*. Both these grammars (the second in translation) were republished in Krueger (1963). Thomas Say, of the Long expedition in 1819–20, collected a vocabulary of Cherokee which was published in the report of that expedition (Thwaites 1904–07:vol. 17, 290–8). Lewis Henry Morgan included Cherokee kinship terms from two different dialects, obtained from missionary sources (Morgan 1871:291–382). Other early sources are listed in Pilling (1888:42–4). The ethnologist James Mooney worked with the Cherokee toward the end of the 19th century, and produced several important works in which a variety of linguistic material is embedded. Mention might be made of his collection of Cherokee sacred formulas, an important literary genre in the language (Mooney 1891), and the long glossary at the end of his comprehensive volume on Cherokee history and myths (Mooney 1900: 506–48).

In the present century there have been, first of all, a few brief texts in Cherokee published in *IJAL* (Speck 1926; Olbrechts 1931). Frans M. Olbrechts also edited further sacred formulas collected by Mooney (Mooney and Olbrechts 1932). Mary R. Haas (1948), writing on classificatory verbs in Muskogee (Creek), compared them with the same phenomenon, more highly developed, in Cherokee. A series of articles on Cherokee grammar, originating at the University of Pennsylvania, appeared in *IJAL* during the 40s and 50s. The first (Bender and Harris 1946) dealt with the phonemes of the North Carolina dialect. The second (Bender 1949) contained a morphemic analysis of several short texts. There followed a three-part series on Cherokee verb morphology (Reyburn 1953–54). These relatively brief and tentative articles by

Reyburn constitute the only modern description of the language of any consequence. Again, Floyd G. Lounsbury possesses extensive notes from his own fieldwork on the language. Mention should also be made of the amusing article by Archibald A. Hill (1952) on the alleged primitivism of Cherokee. A number of recent publications by Jack Frederick Kilpatrick and Anna Gritts Kilpatrick contain miscellaneous linguistic items (for example Kilpatrick and Kilpatrick 1965; see also Willard Walker 1967). Gulick (1958) presents a sociolinguistic study of the use of the language in North Carolina. The many works that have dealt with the Sequoya syllabary and its use will not be listed here, but mention can be made of the recent articles by Chafe and Kilpatrick (1963), and by John K. White (1962). The latter work mentions a manuscript bibliography and history of Cherokee printing by Raymond Yamachika (1961).

## 2.10 *Relationships within Iroquoian*

The Northern Iroquoian languages are so closely related that the fact of their relationship has always been obvious. It has long been clear, also, that the languages of the original Five Nations belong together in a subgroup as opposed, for example, to Tuscarora. The precise relations within that subgroup, however, are not entirely clear. The close affinity of Mohawk and Oneida is apparent, but whether Onondaga is to be more closely identified with them or with Seneca and Cayuga remains problematic, and perhaps it is best to regard these languages as forming a dialect continuum. One investigation of this question is reported in Hickerson, Turner, and Hickerson (1952). Use was made of a technique whereby intelligibility across seven languages (including Tuscarora and Cherokee) was tested by means of tape recordings. Bernard G. Hoffman (1959) attempted to subgroup a larger collection of Iroquoian languages (including Huron, Laurentian, Andaste, and Nottoway) on the basis of the number of shared cognates in a limited vocabulary sample.

The relation of Cherokee to the northern languages is not immediately obvious, although anyone reasonably familiar with Cherokee and one of the other languages could hardly help being aware of it. The first writer to have pointed it out seems to have been Benjamin Smith Barton (1797:xlv, lxvii). He mentions a few similarities between Cherokee words and words of the Six Nations languages. Gallatin (1836: 91-2) referred to Barton's statement and expressed hesitant agreement. A more substantive demonstration of the relationship was given by Horatio Hale (1883a:26-8), who set forth a small but convincing collection of lexical and grammatical correspondences. Further correspondences were given by Albert S. Gatschet a few years later (Gatschet 1886). Additional evidence substantiating the relationship was compiled by J. N. B. Hewitt at about the same time, but was never published (see Pilling 1888:81).

Aside from the small amount of comparative material in Barbeau (1915) and some unpublished work done by Lounsbury, no systematic comparative work on the Iroquoian languages is available. Lounsbury (1961), however, provides some glottochronological time depths for the historical branchings within this family, and points to some evidence which suggests an ancient split between Cherokee, Laurentian, Huron, and Tuscarora on the one hand and the Five Nations languages on the other — a split which was later superseded by the major branching into Northern and Southern Iroquoian.

### 3. SIOUAN

With respect, at least, to those languages which are still spoken or have been spoken in recent times, the languages of the Siouan family are somewhat more numerous and more widely distributed than those of the other two families discussed above. The most conspicuous Siouan language is Dakota (Sioux proper), which is still spoken in its various dialects by perhaps twenty thousand people of all ages on reservations in North and South Dakota, Nebraska, Montana, Minnesota, Manitoba, Saskatchewan, and Alberta. Iowa and Oto, two closely related dialects of a language which has sometimes been referred to as Chiwere, are still spoken by perhaps a few hundred older people in Oklahoma, Kansas, and Nebraska. A third Chiwere dialect, Missouri, is now extinct. A language closely related to Chiwere, and sometimes included under the same label, is Winnebago, of which there may still be a thousand or more speakers in Wisconsin and Nebraska. Those in Wisconsin may still include some children. Another language consisting of several dialects with distinct names is Dhegiha. Dialects still spoken in Oklahoma include Ponca, Osage, Kansa (Kaw), and Quapaw (Arkansas). There are no more than a few hundred speakers altogether. Kansa and Quapaw are the closest to extinction, if they are still spoken at all. Ponca, as well as a fifth Dhegiha language, Omaha, is also spoken in Nebraska, where Omaha remains the most viable language of this group with a thousand or more speakers, some of whom may still be children. Turning back to the north, we find the Crow language spoken by a few thousand people, including children, in Montana. The Hidatsa language in North Dakota has fewer than a thousand speakers, and perhaps no children are learning it. On the same reservation in North Dakota there remain about a dozen speakers of Mandan.

Two Siouan languages, Ofo and Biloxi, were once spoken in Mississippi. Both languages became extinct in the early years of the present century. A number of Siouan languages were once spoken east of the Appalachians in Virginia and the Carolinas. The early historical situation is confused, and we have data from only three of these languages, all now extinct: Tutelo, Catawba, and Woccon. Tutelo and Catawba will be discussed below. Woccon is known to us only from a vocabulary of about 140 items first published in John Lawson (1709:225–30).

#### 3.1 *Dakota*

Europeans first encountered the Dakota in the general area of the upper Mississippi

River, in what is now Minnesota and western Wisconsin. Under pressure from other Indians, caused indirectly by white pressure further to the east, the Dakota gradually moved westward, displacing other tribes in turn. They spread across the Missouri River in the 18th century, and by the 19th century occupied a large territory in the states and provinces mentioned above, where their present-day reservations remain. There are usually said to be four major Dakota dialects: Santee (Dakota proper), Teton (Lakota), and Yankton and Assiniboine (collectively Nakota). Each has various minor subdialectal divisions. The Canadian variety of Assiniboine is called Stoney.

The Dakota were first mentioned in recorded history by the Jesuits, in 1640, but the first mention which has any linguistic interest appears in the account by Louis Hennepin, a Recollet missionary who spent a few months among the Dakota in 1680. Hennepin wrote that he compiled a dictionary of the language, but it has not survived (see Marion E. Cross 1938:109). A century later Jonathan Carver, a Captain of provincial troops in the area during the 1760s, published an account of his observations, and included a vocabulary of Santee (Carver 1778:433-40). Carver's material appears also in Barton (1797). Edward Umfreville, an 18th century fur trader, provided a short wordlist of Assiniboine (Umfreville 1790:facing 202), republished in Gallatin (1836:374), as well as in Adelung and Vater (1806-17:vol. 3, pt. 3, 263-5). The latter work also contains grammatical remarks on Dakota (256-64), under the early name Naudowessi (Nadowessier). Thomas Say of the Long expedition in 1819-20 collected a Yankton vocabulary (Thwaites 1904-07:vol. 17, 290-8), also republished in Gallatin (1836:307-67) along with a vocabulary of Dakota proper compiled from several other sources. Gallatin (1836:251-2) also included a few brief remarks on Dakota grammar from a General Cass. In the early 1830s Alexander Philip Maximilian collected vocabularies of Assiniboine, Yankton, and Teton, which are most easily found in Thwaites (1904-07:vol. 24, 215-7, 223-6). Horatio Hale collected a Dakota vocabulary and a shorter Yankton vocabulary which were published in Gallatin (1848:83-9, 116). Catlin (1841:vol. 2, 262-5) also contains a Dakota vocabulary.

The 19th century saw considerable Protestant missionary activity centered in the Minnesota area. One of the earliest of these missionaries was Jedediah Dwight Stevens, the author of a Sioux spelling book (Stevens 1836). Another, Samuel W. Pond, compiled a Hebrew-Dakota dictionary in 1842, with a view toward translating the Bible directly from Hebrew into Dakota. It was never published, but the manuscript is discussed by W. Gunther Plaut (1953). Certainly the most important of these missionaries from a linguistic point of view was Stephen Return Riggs, who worked among the Dakota for about 40 years beginning in 1837. He provided an abundance of material for the Indians in their own language, including a catechism, hymns, lesson books, the Minnesota Constitution, and *The Pilgrim's progress*. In collaboration with Thomas S. Williamson he eventually translated the entire Bible into Dakota (Williamson and Riggs 1880). He also published a number of more specifically linguistic works. The first version of his Dakota grammar and dictionary appeared at mid-century (S. R. Riggs 1852), and an abridgment of the dictionary was prepared by his wife (M. A. C. Riggs 1852). The materials he collected were posthumously edited by J. Owen Dorsey in the form of an expanded Dakota-English dictionary (Riggs 1890) and a volume containing a grammar, texts, and ethnographic description (Riggs 1893). Several briefer works include a general discussion of the language (Riggs 1881a), as well as a short text (Riggs 1881b). The Riggs dictionaries, especially, remain of great value to linguists today despite certain shortcomings (above all his failure to distinguish between aspirated and unaspirated consonants). Other works from the 19th century include a grammar by Hans Georg Conon von der Gabelentz (1852a), vocabularies of both Teton and Assiniboine collected by Ferdinand Vandeveer Hayden (1863:375–8, 389–91), a vocabulary prepared by two army lieutenants (Hyer and Starring 1866), and a general discussion of the language by F. L. O. Roehrig (1873), who suggested very tentatively that Dakota might be related to the Turanian (Ural-Altaic) languages. This speculation was improved upon by A. W. Williamson (1881, 1882), the son of Thomas S. Williamson, who presented evidence that Dakota was instead related to Indo-European. Lewis Henry Morgan (1871:291–382) included kinship terms from nine Dakota dialects, the Santee obtained from Riggs and the rest collected by himself. Hale (1883c:36–45) made use of Rigg's material. J. Owen Dorsey (1885) compared Dakota with several other Siouan languages. Other early sources on Dakota can be found in Pilling (1887).

The Protestant missionary tradition begun in the 1830s produced its last important linguistic work with the publication of an English-Dakota dictionary by another son of Thomas S. Williamson (John P. Williamson 1902). Most of that work had been focused on the Santee dialect. Subsequently, however, the Teton dialect was given a great deal of attention by a Jesuit missionary, Eugene Buechel. Father Buechel published a grammar of Teton (1939), and left a vast amount of unpublished lexical material.

It was, however, Franz Boas who was responsible for the most important linguistic work on Dakota in the present century. The first volume of the *Handbook of American Indian Languages* contained a combined description of the Teton and Santee dialects. The Teton material was extracted by John R. Swanton from some manuscript texts, but the Santee was taken by Boas from Riggs's publications (Boas and Swanton 1911). Most of Boas's later work was done in collaboration with Ella Deloria, a native speaker of Teton. The two authors produced a sketch of the language which appeared in *IJAL* in the early 1930s (Boas and Deloria 1933), and Deloria herself had published a major volume of texts in the preceding year (Deloria 1932). Boas subsequently wrote an article describing several features of the language which he found to be of general linguistic interest (Boas 1937). The culmination of this work, however, was the joint publication of a full-fledged Dakota grammar (Boas and Deloria 1941). This work undoubtedly stands as one of the high points in American Indian linguistics. Many years later Deloria saw to the publication of some brief textual material (Deloria 1954).

Robert H. Lowie worked with the Assiniboine in the early years of this century.

Lowie (1909:263-70) has short texts with interlinear translation, and other texts, collected between 1907 and 1913, were published by his wife after his death (Lowie 1960c). There is a long Dakota wordlist in Fred M. Hans (1907:309-58). James R. Walker (1914) contains Teton kinship terms, as well as a text in Teton dealing with the kinship system. Melvin R. Gilmore (1919:139-47) has a list of Dakota plant names. G. Hubert Matthews (1955) gives a phonemic analysis of the speech of a single individual with an atypical linguistic background. An attempt to delimit Dakota sentences and clauses by means of phonological and grammatical (non-semantic) criteria is described by Donald S. Stark (1962). Still more recently, a grammar of Assiniboine has been published by Norman Balfour Levin (1964). Further work on Assiniboine (Stoney) is being done in Alberta by Warren Harbeck of the Summer Institute of Linguistics.

### 3.2 *Chiwere (Iowa, Oto, and Missouri)*

The Iowa were a small group which, in earlier times, occupied various spots within the present state of Iowa and neighboring states. In 1836 they were given a reservation in Nebraska and Kansas. Some of them later settled in Oklahoma. The Oto were at first located south and west of the Iowa, near the confluence of the Platte River with the Missouri. For a time in the 19th century they occupied land in Nebraska and Kansas, but in the 1880s they moved to Oklahoma. The Missouri were once located on the Missouri River, near the point where it is joined by the Grand River in the state of Missouri. At the end of the 18th century they were badly defeated by the Sauk and Fox, and they suffered further in a war with the Osage in the early 19th century. From that time on, most of them lived with the Oto and moved with the latter to Oklahoma.

It would appear that the earliest linguistic record of Chiwere is the brief Oto vocabulary collected by Thomas Say during the Long expedition of 1819-20 (Thwaites 1904-07:vol. 17, 290-8, 300). Say's material was also printed in Gallatin (1836: 307-67). Gallatin (1836:377) also gives a very brief vocabulary of Iowa. A somewhat longer vocabulary of Oto was collected by Maximillian in the 1830s (Thwaites 1904-07:vol. 24, 285-93). Another brief vocabulary of Oto collected by Horatio Hale was printed in Gallatin (1848:117). William Hamilton and Samuel M. Irvin were two Protestant missionaries who worked among the Chiwere tribes for many years during the 19th century. They published an Iowa spelling book and a 'primmer' (Hamilton and Irvin 1843, 1849), but their most important linguistic work was an Iowa grammar (Hamilton and Irvin 1848). Hamilton also provided the remarks on the Iowa language contained in Schoolcraft (1851-57:vol. 4, 397-406). Hayden (1863:452-6) gives a vocabulary of 'Iowa, or Oto'. Morgan (1871:291-382) lists two sets of kinship terms — for Iowa and for Oto-Missouri. J. Owen Dorsey did considerable work with Chiwere in the latter part of the 19th century, but most of it remains unpublished in the Smithsonian archives. Reference can be made to a brief published text in Oto with interlinear translation (Dorsey 1880–81), and to the Chiwere forms in Dorsey (1885). Other 19th century sources are listed in Pilling (1887). The only more recent source is the very brief grammar of Iowa-Oto by William Whitman (1947). Whitman's material is used for examples in Voegelin (1947).

### 3.3 *Winnebago*

Closely related linguistically to Chiwere, the Winnebago (often called the Hochangara in the early literature) once lived south of Green Bay in what is now Wisconsin. Some have remained in that state while others, after many changes of location, eventually settled on a reservation in northeastern Nebraska.

There is not much early material on Winnebago. A brief vocabulary taken down by Major Stephen H. Long in 1817 can be found in Thwaites (1904–07:vol. 17, 306–8). Nicholas Boilvin, an Indian agent, collected a Winnebago vocabulary sometime before his death in 1924. It, together with material from other sources, is given in Gallatin (1836:307–67). Another brief vocabulary obtained by Horatio Hale appears in Gallatin (1848:116). Ferdinand Vandeveer Hayden (1869:411–21) collected and published some 'grammatical forms and phrases' as well as a vocabulary. Morgan (1871:291–382) gives Winnebago kinship terms. Most of J. Owen Dorsey's material remains in manuscript, but some of it can be found in Dorsey (1885). A few other early sources are mentioned in Pilling (1887).

Melvin R. Gilmore (1919:139–45, 148–9) lists a number of Winnebago names for plants. The ethnologist Paul Radin worked among the Winnebago from 1908 to 1913. His linguistic material was used by Boas in presenting comparative remarks on Winnebago in the Boas and Swanton (1911) work on Dakota. Radin (1923) contains some ritual speeches in Winnebago with free translations, and there are many Winnebago words scattered throughout the work. Much later, two monographs were published containing texts in Winnebago accompanied by extensive commentaries (Radin 1949, 1950). Radin's notes also formed the basis for the Winnebago dictionary recently prepared as a dissertation by Mary Marino (1968). Several other works appeared during the 1940s. One was a brief article on word play in Winnebago by Amelia Susman (1941), incidental to a larger but unpublished dissertation (Susman 1943). Some of Susman's data were utilized in Hockett (1942). Three years later there appeared a small but useful grammar written by William Lipkind (1945). Two short Winnebago texts were published by Thomas A. Sebeok shortly after, in 1947. Besides the Susman and Marino dissertations mentioned above, a recent dissertation on Winnebago phonology was completed by Anita Marten (1964).

### 3.4 *Dhegiha (Omaha, Ponca, Kansa, Osage, Quapaw)*

In prehistoric times the ancestors of the Dhegiha speakers may have lived farther to the east (according to tradition, near the junction of the Wabash and Ohio Rivers), but earliest European contact found them in the central plains. The Omaha and Ponca were on the southwest bank of the Missouri River in northeastern Nebraska, the Kansa on the Kansas River in the present state of Kansas, the Osage on the river of that name in Missouri, and the Quapaw near the junction of the Arkansas River with the Mississippi. The Omaha still live in Nebraska, as do some of the Ponca, but the majority of the latter have been in Oklahoma since 1877. The Kansa have been in Oklahoma since 1873. During much of the 19th century the Osage were located chiefly in Kansas, but in the early 1870s they were established on a reservation in Oklahoma where they now live. The Quapaw occupied various spots in Arkansas, Kansas, and Oklahoma, until they were finally restricted to a small area in northeastern Oklahoma in 1867.

Perhaps the earliest published record of a Dhegiha dialect is the vocabulary of Quapaw (Arkansas) in the second edition of Benjamin Smith Barton (1798), collected by someone named Bossu. From the beginning of the 19th century there are several vocabularies of Osage: one in Adelung and Vater (1806–17: vol. 3, pt. 3, 273–4) collected by Albert Pike, another in John Bradbury (1817:213–9), and still another, collected by one Dr. Murray, in Vater (1821:53–62). Both the Bradbury and the Murray materials were used in Gallatin (1836:307–67). In the 1830s Maximilian collected vocabularies of Kansa, Omaha, Ponca, and Osage (Thwaites 1904–07: vol. 24, 229, 280–5, 294, 296–300). At about the same time two missionaries, William B. Montgomery and W.C. Requa, published an *Osage first book* (1834). Gallatin (1848: 83–9) contains some Osage words collected by Horatio Hale.

In 1819–20 Thomas Say of the Long expedition took down vocabularies of Kansa and Omaha (Thwaites 1904–07: vol. 17, 290–8, 301–3), which also appear in Gallatin (1836:307–67). Hale's very brief vocabularies of Omaha and Quapaw appear in Gallatin (1848:117). Edward McKenney (1850), another missionary, prepared an Omaha primer. Hayden (1863:448–52) also has an Omaha vocabulary. Morgan (1871:291–382) includes kinship terms for Ponca, Omaha, Kaw (Kansa), and Osage-Quapaw. Other early sources are mentioned in Pilling (1887).

A great deal of work was done on the Dhegiha dialects in the latter part of the 19th century by J. Owen Dorsey, who was in fact responsible for grouping them together under that name. His most voluminous published work (Dorsey 1890) consists of texts in Omaha and Ponca, with interlinear and free translations, and notes. Much earlier, while still a missionary, he prepared a Ponca primer (Dorsey 1873). Omaha texts with interlinear and free translations can be found in Dorsey (1879–80) and Dorsey (1881), and Osage texts are given similar treatment in Dorsey (1888). Dorsey (1884) contains a number of Omaha words and sentences. Dorsey (1885) includes comparative phonological information and vocabulary from Ponca, Kansa, and Osage. References to other publications and manuscripts of Dorsey can be found in Pilling (1887:24–6) and Dorsey (1890:xvii–xviii). Working from Dorsey's materials, particularly Dorsey (1890), Franz Boas wrote an article on Ponca grammar (1907), and interspersed remarks on Ponca (as well as Winnebago) in Boas and Swanton

(1911). The large ethnographic description of the Omaha by Alice C. Fletcher and Francis La Flesche (1911) contains a number of Omaha words scattered throughout. There is an ethnobotanical study of Omaha by Melvin R. Gilmore (1913), plus a list of Omaha plant names in Gilmore (1919:139-45, 147-8). More recently there has been an article by Nils M. Holmer (1945) on certain aspects of the Ponca-Omaha and related sound systems. Osage has been documented in this century, first through the dictionary by La Flesche (1932), and later by two articles on Osage phonology and morphology by Hans Wolff (1952). Wolff also discussed (1958) attempts by his informant to write Osage words.

## 3.5 Crow

The Crow (earlier often called Upsaroka) have, in historic times, always been located near the Yellowstone River in Montana, their present reservation being on the Big Horn River, a southern tributary of the Yellowstone.

Perhaps the earliest recording of the Crow language that can be found in a published source is the very brief vocabulary collected by Thomas Say of the Long expedition in 1819–20 (Thwaites 1904–07:vol. 17, 299). It was reprinted in Gallatin (1836:377). Another brief vocabulary was collected by Maximilian (Thwaites 1904–07:vol. 24, 222). Gallatin (1848:83–9) gives a somewhat longer list obtained by Horatio Hale. Ferdinand Vandeveer Hayden (1863:395–420) presents not only a vocabulary, but also some remarks on the grammar. Morgan (1871:291–382) includes Crow kinship terms. For other early sources see Pilling (1887:22).

Recent work on Crow is somewhat more extensive than that on most of the other Siouan languages. Much of it was done by the ethnologist Robert H. Lowie, who paid a great deal of attention to the language. His most important linguistic works include a text accompanied by grammatical notes (Lowie 1930), a grammatical sketch followed by a text and analysis thereof (Lowie 1941), and a large volume of posthumously published texts accompanied by Crow-English and English-Crow vocabularies in a separate volume (Lowie 1960a, 1960b). Lowie had a special interest in literary style in Crow, in which connection reference can be made to Lowie (1932, 1950, and 1959).

Still more recent work on Crow has been done by Dorothea V. Kaschube. Her principal work is a grammar (Kaschube 1967). An earlier article on tones in Crow (Kaschube 1954) was followed by a restatement by Eric P. Hamp (1958), and still another interpretation, in terms of ordered rules, by G. Hubert Matthews (1959a.)

## 3.6 Hidatsa

The Hidatsa, formerly often called the Minitari and locally still referred to as the Gros Ventres, have always, within historic times, been located within what is now the state of North Dakota, at various points along the Missouri River. Having been earlier slightly farther south, in 1845 they moved to the Fort Berthold area, where they still are.

The earliest published vocabulary of Hidatsa again appears to be that collected in 1819–20 by Thomas Say, now available in Thwaites (1904–07: vol. 17, 290–8, 304). Maximilian contains a Hidatsa vocabulary collected in the 1930s (Thwaites 1904–07: vol. 24, 261–76). Gallatin (1836:307–67) repeats the material from Say, and a short wordlist obtained by Horatio Hale is published in Gallatin (1848:117). Schoolcraft (1851–57: vol. 3, 256) also repeats some of Say's material. Another vocabulary of Hidatsa appears in Hayden (1863:424–6). Morgan (1871:291–382) includes Hidatsa kinship terms. Other early sources are listed in Pilling (1887:35, 51).

Of considerably more importance is the work of Washington Matthews, an army surgeon who was stationed in the Hidatsa area between 1865 and 1872. Matthews gave a great deal of time and attention to the Hidatsa language, and wrote up what he found. His principal publication is the grammar and dictionary contained in Matthews (1877), compiled and revised from his earlier grammar and Hidatsa-English dictionary (Matthews 1873) and English-Hidatsa dictionary (Matthews 1874). His material was used by Horatio Hale (1883c:36–45).

Robert H. Lowie collected a number of Hidatsa texts in 1911. Almost thirty years later this material was linguistically annotated and published by Zellig Harris and C.F. Voegelin (Lowie 1939). R.H. Stetson (1946) subsequently wrote about certain aspects of Hidatsa phonetics. Work done at the 1953 Linguistic Institute led to a discussion by C.F. Voegelin and Florence M. Robinett (1954) of what they called Hidatsa 'mother language' — the manner in which a speaker may modify his pronunciation 'for the benefit of children or of strangers struggling to acquire the language'. From a present-day point of view it is interesting that they found such speech to 'coincide with or resemble' their tentative morphophonemic representations. Shortly thereafter Robinett (1955) published a three installment description of the language. More recently there has appeared an extensive transformational treatment of Hidatsa written by G. Hubert Matthews (1965). The first chapter of that work includes a useful critical discussion of the earlier works by Washington Matthews, Harris and Voegelin, and Robinett.

### 3.7 *Mandan*

In historic times the Mandan have lived in approximately the same area of North Dakota as the Hidatsa, and are presently located with the latter (as well as the Arikara) on the Fort Berthold Reservation. They were first encountered by Verendrye in 1783, and were described in some detail by Maximilian and Catlin in the 19th century. They attracted special attention because they were said to have a lighter skin color and to differ in other ways from other Indians, and they were thus supposed by some to have had a European origin.

The first published Mandan vocabulary may be that in C.S. Rafinesque (1832–33), obtained principally from George Shannon, said to have been a member of the Lewis and Clark expedition. In the 1930s Maximilian gave more attention to Mandan than to any of the other languages he recorded, and he subsequently published not only a vocabulary but also a small grammar (Thwaites 1904–07: vol. 24, 234–61). Catlin (1841:261–5) includes a Mandan vocabulary, and compares a few Mandan and Welsh words (with the idea that the Mandan were descended from misplaced Welshmen). A Mandan vocabulary provided by James Kipp was published in Schoolcraft (1851–57: vol. 3, 255–6, 446–59). Hayden (1863:435–44) also includes grammatical remarks as well as a vocabulary. Mandan kinship terms appear in Morgan (1871:291–382). Other early sources are given in Pilling (1887:48). Early in the present century two Harvard students put together a description of Mandan, including a grammatical sketch and a vocabulary, based on the various published sources then available (G. F. Will and H.J. Spinden 1906:188–219). Edward Kennard later published a grammar of Mandan (Kennard 1936) which has been the principal modern source of information on the language, but a Mandan dictionary accompanied by considerable phonological and grammatical information has just been completed (Robert C. Hollow 1970).

### 3.8 Ofo and Biloxi

The Ofo were located historically on the Yazoo River in the present state of Mississippi. After various sojourns on or near the Mississippi River, they seem to have been entirely lost from history between the years 1784 and 1908, when a single Ofo survivor was found by John R. Swanton living among the remnants of the Tunica in Louisiana (Swanton 1909). The Biloxi were once located on the lower Pascagoula River in Mississippi. They subsequently lived in several locations in Louisiana, and some of them in Texas and Oklahoma. They too seem to have dropped out of sight for a time, until in 1886 a group of them was discovered by Albert S. Gatschet in Louisiana. Gatschet collected some linguistic material, evidently the first to have been recorded for either of these languages.

Gatschet's material itself has never been published, but it was enough to enable the linguists at the Bureau of American Ethnology to determine the Siouan affiliation of Biloxi, and it stimulated J. Owen Dorsey to visit these people for extensive linguistic work in 1892 and 1893. His report on the Biloxi included a grammatical sketch of the language (Dorsey 1894). The material which he left at his death two years later was subsequently edited by Swanton, and published in a single volume together with Swanton's own material on Ofo (Dorsey and Swanton 1912). In addition to Biloxi and Ofo dictionaries, this work contains a number of annotated texts in Biloxi, and a collection of Biloxi sentences. It formed the basis for several later publications. C.F. Voegelin (1939) discusses sound correspondences between Ofo and Biloxi. Nils M. Holmer (1947) talks about the development of a prothetic vowel in Ofo (as well as

Biloxi and Tutelo). Mary R. Haas (1969) provides several kinds of advice for users of the Dorsey and Swanton volume. Swanton's Ofo material was all that was ever recorded for that language. For Biloxi, however, Mary Haas and Morris Swadesh collected some 54 words in 1934 from a woman living in Texas who had evidently been an able speaker of the language many years earlier. This material has been published very recently (Haas 1968).

### 3.9 *Tutelo*

In the 17th century the Tutelo were living in western Virginia. They subsequently moved northward, and in 1753 were adopted by the Cayuga in New York State, with whom they moved to Canada after the Revolution. The principal source of information on the language is the article by Horatio Hale (1883c), based on work which he did with the last fluent speaker in 1870, supplemented by material subsequently obtained from others who remembered the language to some degree. In the early years of the present century a few scattered words were resurrected from the memory of people who had once heard the language (Edward Sapir 1913 and Leo J. Frachtenberg 1913). A few kinship terms recorded in the early 1930s by Frank G. Speck are given in Speck and Schaeffer (1942:573-4).

### 3.10 *Catawba*

Since European contact, at least, the Catawba have always been located in an area centered in northern South Carolina. They were already known to Europeans in the 16th century, and during the early colonization period they and the Cherokee were the two most important Indian groups of the Carolinas. During the 18th century, however, wars and smallpox reduced them to a state of comparative insignificance. They have for many years occupied a tiny reservation near Rock Hill, South Carolina, but the language is no longer spoken.

Some Catawba words appear in the second edition of Benjamin Smith Barton (1798). This material as well as a larger vocabulary collected by one J.L. Miller was included in Gallatin (1836:307-67). Another and still longer wordlist is to be found in Oscar M. Lieber (1858), along with a few grammatical notes. Albert S. Gatschet worked with the language in 1881, and published a grammatical sketch some years later (Gatschet 1900). Gatschet (1902) also contains a few Catawba words. John R. Swanton did linguistic work on Catawba in 1918, and Swanton (1918) contains some ethnobotanical information. Frank G. Speck worked with Catawba informants intermittently between 1913 and 1944. Texts collected in 1913 from a Catawba woman living among the Cherokee were published with interlinear and free translations in Speck (1913). Speck (1924) gives a few Catawba words tending to confirm the notion that there were Siouan peoples on the coast of South Carolina in the 16th century. More texts were published in Speck (1934), and a last brief one, obtained from the man who was probably the last fluent informant, appeared in Speck (1946). Speck and Schaeffer (1942) is based on kinship terms from several sources, including Speck's own material. Frank T. Siebert, Jr. worked with the last few Catawba speakers in 1914. His two-part comparative article (Siebert 1945) cites some of the material which he collected, more of which remains in manuscript. More recently, G. Hubert Matthews has worked with a man who once spoke some Catawba with his grandfather and a cousin. Matthews and Red Thunder Cloud (1967) discusses the phonology and morphology of material obtained from this informant, and gives some texts and a wordlist.

## 3.11 *Relationships within Siouan*

The relatedness of the western Siouan languages was the first to be recognized. With the exception of Winnebago they occupied a geographically contiguous area, and their similarities were readily apparent. In Gallatin's classification (1836:120–8, 306) they were grouped together under the name Sioux. (He also hesitantly included Cheyenne, whose Algonquian affiliation was not then recognized.) Nothing was known of the Biloxi and Ofo languages at that time. When Biloxi was first recorded by Gatschet in 1886 its Siouan nature was immediately seen, and the same can be said of Ofo when it was recorded by Swanton in 1908. As for the eastern languages, Hale's description of Tutelo emphasized the Siouan affiliation of that language, and he included a comparative vocabulary of Tutelo, Dakota, and Hidatsa (Hale 1883c: 36–45).

The Siouan nature of Catawba was not so obvious. A good discussion of the history of this problem is available in Siebert (1945:100–1). Gallatin (1836:87, 306) listed Catawba as an independent language family, including also Woccon as originally suggested by Adelung and Vater (1806–17:vol. 3, pt. 3, 308). Although the staff of the Bureau of American Ethnology credited Gatschet with being the first to discover that Catawba was related to Siouan (e.g. Powell 1891:112), Siebert points out that the credit should really go to Lewis Henry Morgan (1870:54), although Morgan did not support his suggestion with concrete evidence. Perhaps, however, Latham (1860:327) should be given some credit also. A brief work by A.F. Chamberlain (1888) made use of the same Gallatin material on which Morgan had based his conclusion. But no extensive verification of this hypothesis appeared until Siebert (1945) settled the matter. A useful survey of the work that has been done to establish the existence of Siouan languages in the East is Sturtevant (1958).

The early subgroupings of the Siouan languages were based as much on geographic as on linguistic criteria. Gallatin (1836:120) mentioned four subdivisions: Winnebago, Sioux proper, the 'Minetare group' (Crow, Hidatsa, and Mandan), and Osage 'and other southern kindred tribes'. With more languages recognized, and with considerably more data available, Swanton (1923) suggested a classification of Siouan into four subgroups: (1) a northeastern group including Hidatsa, Dakota, Biloxi, Ofo, and

Tutelo; (2) a southeastern group including Catawba and Woccon; (3) a southwestern group including the Dhegiha dialects; and (4) a northwestern group including the Chiwere dialects and Winnebago. He purposely left Mandan outside this subgrouping, being uncertain of its proper assignment. Swanton (1936) emphasized the fact that Tutelo and Catawba belonged to different subgroups. Voegelin (1939) strengthened the idea that Biloxi and Ofo belong within the same subgroup, and Voegelin (1941a) did the same for Crow and Hidatsa. Joe E. Pierce (1954) also discussed the degree of relatedness of Crow and Hidatsa. The overall subgrouping proposed in Voegelin (1941b) has become the standard generally referred to. Voegelin also established four subgroups, but they differed in certain respects from Swanton's. They included: (1) an eastern group consisting only of Catawba; (2) a so-called Ohio valley group consisting of Ofo, Biloxi, and Tutelo (with the idea that the prehistoric location of these peoples was in the Ohio valley area); (3) a Missouri River group consisting of Hidatsa and Crow; and (4) a Mississippi River group consisting of Chiwere, Winnebago, Dhegiha, Dakota, and Mandan. The presence of Mandan in the last group is questionable, however; at the present time it would seem preferable to place Mandan in a subgroup by itself, although one that is more closely tied to the other Siouan languages than is Catawba.

In contrast to the Caddoan and Iroquoian families, where the amount of comparative work to date has been minimal, several scholars have paid a great deal of attention to comparative Siouan. The earliest was J. Owen Dorsey, who published a comparative phonology of Dakota, Dhegiha, Chiwere, and Winnebago (Dorsey 1885). A more recent and more thorough study is that of Hans Wolff (1950–51). G. Hubert Matthews has also worked in this area, and has written a dissertation on the subject (Matthews 1958) as well as an article dealing with the reconstruction of the Proto-Siouan kinship terminology (Matthews 1959b). Terrence S. Kaufman has also done unpublished work on comparative Siouan. It can hardly be said, however, that all the problems in this area have been laid to rest. The work accomplished so far has clearly been only a prelude to what might eventually be done within this diverse and interesting language family.

## 4. MACRO-SIOUAN

From time to time there have been suggestions that the three language families discussed in this chapter are remotely related to each other. At the beginning of this chapter the name 'Macro-Siouan' was suggested for this hypothetical linguistic stock. In what follows, the possible relationships of Siouan and Iroquoian, of Siouan and Caddoan, and of Iroquoian and Caddoan will be discussed in that order.

### 4.1 *Siouan and Iroquoian*

It is this relationship which is the best documented of the three, as might be expected from the fact that the Siouan and Iroquoian languages themselves have been better documented than the Caddoan. The possibility of such a relationship was perhaps implied by Robert G. Latham (1846:44), but it was explicitly stated in Latham (1860: 327). Lewis Henry Morgan (1971:150-1) asserted his belief that the Iroquois were 'an early offshoot' of the Sioux. Edward Sapir, in his famous 1929 proposal concerning the classification of North American languages, placed both Iroquoian and Siouan in his large Hokan-Siouan grouping, but did not posit any special closeness of relationship between them (Sapir 1951:173). Shortly thereafter, however, Louis Allen (1931) published the first real evidence supporting the Siouan-Iroquoian relationship. More recently the hypothesis has been strengthened by Chafe (1964a), who listed 67 possible cognates with tentative Proto-Siouan-Iroquoian reconstructions and a tabulation of phonological correspondences.

## 4.2 Siouan and Caddoan

Latham (1860:327) tentatively suggested a Siouan-Caddoan connection, and again Sapir (1951:173) placed both families within Hokan-Siouan without positing any special closeness of relationship. The following evidence in support of a Siouan-Caddoan relationship is presented in written form for the first time, having been given orally at the annual meeting of the American Anthropological Association in Denver in 1965.

It is not possible at present to set down a list of hypothetical cognates which would be subject to explanation on the basis of a plausible Proto-Siouan-Caddoan phonological system. Some lexical resemblances have indeed been noted, but they are not of the quantity or nature that would permit one to forcefully reject the explanation that they are fortuitous (cf. English *cut* and Caddo *kat* 'knife'). Then too, there are some resemblances between Caddo and Siouan which are in all likelihood the result of diffusion, probably from Osage (La Flesche 1932) into Caddo:

|  | Caddo | Osage |
|---|---|---|
| 'mother' | ʔinaʔ | ina |
| 'deer' | daʔ | ta |

Resemblances such as the following are tantalizing, if inconclusive:

|  | Caddo | Winnebago | Dakota |
|---|---|---|---|
| 'bird' | banit | waník |  |
| 'blood' | bahʔuh | waʔíh | wé |
| 'arrow' | baʔ | mą́ | wą-(híkpe) |
| 'earth' | wádat | mą́ | mą-(khá) |
| 'man' | wit 'self' |  | wičhá |
|  | (Pawnee *pita* 'man') |  |  |

More convincing are facts like the following.

A well known feature of Siouan languages is their use of 'instrumental' prefixes in the derivation of verb bases. An instrumental prefix is typically represented by a consonant-vowel syllable; for example, Winnebago *ną-, mą-, wa-, gi-, ra-, ru-, ta-, bo-*. It usually carries a meaning which is in some sense instrumental. The meaning may be generalized and impersonal, such as 'by heat' or 'by cutting', or it may be specific and personal, such as 'with the mouth' or 'with the foot'; there are in fact two distributionally distinct classes which roughly reflect this semantic distinction. As would be expected, many of the meanings associated with particular combinations of these prefixes with verb roots are idiomatic: not predictable from any consistent meaning assignable to either the root or the prefix. The following examples from Winnebago (Lipkind 1945) show some of the occurrences of the prefix *gi-*, said to have the meaning 'by striking':

| | |
|---|---|
| *gi-sák* | 'to kill, knock unconscious' |
| *gi-kúnuk* | 'to chop, hammer off' |
| *gi-pére* | 'to hammer thin' |
| *gi-híri* | 'to mash' |
| *gi-žé* | 'to break up' |
| *gi-xúx* | 'to break something brittle' |
| *gi-xóro* | 'to strip off' |
| *gi-gás* | 'to tear' |
| *gi-šára* | 'to cut bare' |

In Caddo most verb bases contain two formally distinguishable parts, which may be called the preverb and the verb root. Examples are *ka-dís* 'to wash', *ya-ʔah* 'to be', *yi-bahw* 'to see'. Usually these two parts are contiguous, but there is a 'plural' element (usually *-wa-*; see below) which intrudes between them: compare *hákkadíssaʔ* 'he is washing' with *hákkawadíssaʔ* 'they are washing'. With a few exceptions, one particular verb root will occur always and only with one particular preverb. A preverb is typically represented by a consonant-vowel syllable; for example, *bi-, ka-, ki-, na-, ni-, pa-, ya-, yi-, ʔa-*. There are about as many of them as there are instrumental prefixes in Siouan languages. For the most part these Caddo preverbs must be accepted as simply arbitrary appendages to the verb roots. It is usually problematic whether they can be associated with any consistent semantic feature. The preverb *yi-*, for example, is found in such bases as the following:

| | |
|---|---|
| *yi-bahw* | 'to see' |
| *yi-šuki* | 'to write' |
| *yi-yah* | 'to proceed' |
| *yi-ʔaʔn* | 'to plant' |

There is at least once case, however, in which there does seem to be an identifiable common element of meaning among many of the bases which contain a specific preverb:

| | |
|---|---|
| ki-cʾákiʔni | 'to chew' |
| ki-čʾud | 'to peel' |
| ki-duk | 'to bite, break' |
| ki-kʾas | 'to shell' (e.g. corn) |
| ki-kʾúd | 'to suck' |
| ki-náhʔy | 'to cut' |
| ki-paáhnuʔ | 'to scratch oneself' |
| ki-saki | 'to pound, mash, crack' |
| ki-sáwʔ | 'to scrape' |
| ki-súd | 'to sew' |
| ki-wawík | 'to tear' |

All these bases have to do with inflicting some sort of violence with an instrument, either part of one's body or a separate tool. The coincidence with the Winnebago examples cited earlier is threefold: there is a clear semantic resemblance (it would be hard to say how the common semantic element in these Caddo examples differs from that in the Winnebago examples); there is a correspondence in position (direct prefixation to the verb root); and there is a similarity in shape. Winnebago *gi-* is, in fact, apparently a reflex of Proto-Siouan *\*ki-*. (The Winnebago vowel is anomalous; other Siouan prefixes said to have the meaning 'by striking' go back to a Proto-Siouan *\*ka-*.)

At least one more parallel of the same kind can be mentioned. There is a Siouan instrumental prefix reconstructable as *\*ra-* which has the general meaning 'with fire or heat'. It appears in Winnebago as *ta-*; for example (Lipkind 1945:20):

| | |
|---|---|
| ta-xú | 'to burn' |
| ta-xére | 'to fry' |
| ta-jók | 'to cook till tender' |
| ta-wús | 'to dry' |

Caddo has several bases containing the preverb *na-* (alternating with *ta-* in initial position) in which the meaning of fire or heat is also involved:

| | |
|---|---|
| na-bahn | 'to catch fire' |
| na-hak | 'to dry' |
| na-hasi | 'to be cooked' |
| na-hásiʔni | 'to dry' (causative of the preceding) |

Although there are fewer Caddo examples available, the coincidence here seems to parallel that which exists in the case of *ki-*. There is, however, a complication in the Caddo forms. Internal evidence shows that the preverb in these bases developed out of an incorporated noun root *nak-* 'fire'. There are other bases in which this noun root is the first element; for example, *nak-háh* 'to burn'. In the above examples one can identify a preverb *na-* only on the basis of the plural forms, since it is only in the plural that the difference between *na-* and *nak-* is clear. The first element in these examples has evidently been reshaped from *nak-* to *na-* in the plural, probably on the model of numerous other bases that begin with one of two other elements having the shape *na-*. This derivation of Caddo *na-* fron *nak-* does not necessarily vitiate the parallel to Siouan, however. It may, on the contrary, be a useful clue to the way these instrumental prefixes came into being. It is certainly possible, although probably demonstrable only through such indirect shreds of evidence as this, that the instrumental prefixes were once incorporated noun roots which took on specialized function and perhaps underwent reshaping in the process.

Another parallel between Caddoan and Siouan languages is the common occurrence within verbs of an element that specifies whether a lying, sitting, or standing posture is involved in the verb's total meaning. This element is prefixed to the verb root in Caddoan, but suffixed in Siouan. The following are possible reconstructions of the Siouan forms. There is probably a morpheme boundary between the syllables (some languages show reflexes of the first syllable only):

     *-wáki*  'lying'
     *-ráki*  'sitting'
     *-háki*  'standing'

The Caddo element which has the most suggestively similar shape is *Paniki-* 'standing'. In Caddo, too, it would appear that the *-ki-* was at one time a separate element; cf. the other two forms, *Pini-* 'lying' and *Pawi-* 'sitting'. Thus there is agreement of the two language families in specifying these three postures within verbs, in the shape of the Siouan forms when compared with Caddo 'standing', and in the ancient segmentability of these comparable forms.

### 4.3 *Iroquoian and Caddoan*

Latham (1846:44) suggested more specifically that Caddo is related to the Iroquoian languages, and Sapir (1951:173) placed Iroquoian and Caddoan together in a special subgroup within Hokan-Siouan. He never made clear his reasons for doing so, however, and this relationship, like that between Siouan and Caddoan, has remained undocumented up to the present time. The following evidence, also presented orally in Denver in 1965, is, like that above, given in written form for the first time. It is taken largely from the Caddo and Seneca languages, but the implication is that the features described for these two are retentions from Proto-Caddoan and Proto-Iroquoian respectively.

There are just a few lexical resemblances which can be cited:

|  | Caddo | Seneca |
|---|---|---|
| 'to pound corn' (verb root) | *(na)-dáʔ* | *-theʔt-* |

| | | |
|---|---|---|
| 'to make' (verb root) | (ʔa)-ʔnih | -ǫni- |
| 'to dye' (verb root) | (nača)-súʔ | -(ah)-so- |
| 'feces' (noun or noun root) | ʔidah | -iʔta- |

Perhaps more will appear as work on the Caddoan languages progresses, but for the moment the following kinds of evidence are more substantial.

A somewhat oversimplified but useful generalization about both Caddo and Seneca verbs is that they consist of four major parts. The first part, counting positionally from left to right, is a motley collection of prefixes and prefix combinations involving meanings of tense, aspect, subordination, location, relation, negation, and so on. The second part is a group of 'pronominal' prefixes which relate to the subject or object of the verb, or to a combination of subject and object. The third part is a verb base, which may include anything from a simple verb root to an elaborate combination of compounded roots and modifiers. The fourth part is a relatively small set of suffixes expressing aspect or tense or, in Caddo, location. Let us concentrate here on the pronominal prefixes and on certain items immediately adjacent to them in the verb base.

We can begin by comparing those prefixes which are associated with singular subjects and objects in the various persons. For Caddo we will consider only the 'real' prefixes; there is a parallel 'unreal' set which is used in negations, questions, conditions, and elsewhere. Caddo does not overtly express third person (when 'real'), but its 'indefinite' person relates suggestively to one of the Seneca third persons:

| | CADDO | | SENECA | |
|---|---|---|---|---|
| | Subject | Object | Subject | Object |
| 'first person' | ci- | ku- | k(e)- | wak(e)- |
| 'second person' | yahʔ- | si- | s(e)- | sa- |
| 'indefinite' (Caddo)/ 'feminine-indefinite' (Seneca) | yi- | yu- | ye- | (ya)ko- |
| 'neuter' | | | ka- | yo- |
| 'masculine' | | | ha- | ho- |

(Seneca (e) is subject to different morphophonemic treatment than e, and (ya) is lost in word-initial position. These facts are not relevant to the hypothesis presented here, and must be explained on some other grounds.)

We might imagine a regular model such as the following as a basis for stating the Caddo-Seneca similarities:

| | Subject | Object |
|---|---|---|
| 'first person' | ke- | ko- |
| 'second person' | se- | so- |
| 'indefinite' | ye- | yo- |

Not that an arrangement of precisely this form need be assumed to have existed in the remote past. For the purpose mentioned it is a convenient arrangement to work from, but it may overlook complications which are here extraneous.

For Caddo we need state only the following developments (equating *e* of the model with Caddo *i*, and *o* with *u*; Caddo has only the vowels *i*, *u*, and *a*):

1. $k > c$ before the front vowel.
2. By a 'push-chain' development an innovational 'second person subject' form *yah?-* displaced *si-*, which in turn displaced *su-*, which in turn was lost.

For Seneca the following statements are necessary:
1. Two new ways of representing the 'objective case' arose; specifically, the prefixing of *wa-* in the 'first person' and the use of *a* rather than *o* in the 'second person'. In the 'first person object' form, however, other Iroquoian languages (including at least Cayuga, Oneida, Tuscarora, and Cherokee) show an anomalous *w* after the *k* in some environments, suggesting that an earlier shape of the Iroquoian 'first person object' was *\*kw-* (Lounsbury 1953:69).
2. The meaning 'indefinite' was extended to include 'feminine', while 'neuter' and 'masculine' prefixes were added to form the following intermediate arrangement:

|  | Subject | Object |
|---|---|---|
| 'feminine-indefinite' | *ye-* | *yo-* |
| 'neuter' | *ka-* | *ko-* |
| 'masculine' | *ha-* | *ho-* |

It might alternatively be posited that these three third person genders were originally present and were lost in Caddo(an). The reasons they were treated here as innovations in Seneca (or Northern Iroquoian) are:
 a) The retention of the 'indefinite' meaning alongside the 'feminine' in Iroquoian, suggesting that the three genders were not always on a par.
 b) The different vowel in the innovational subject forms.
 c) The absence of the 'neuter' category outside the singular, where it fuses with 'feminine-indefinite'.
 d) The absence of all third person gender distinctions in Cherokee.
3. An interchange of 'feminine-indefinite' and 'neuter' object forms, but with retention of (*ya*) < *yo* as part of the 'feminine-indefinite' object.

The plausibility and simplicity of this model intriguingly suggest a common origin for these Caddo and Seneca prefixes.

In both Caddo and Seneca it is possible to specify 'dual' or 'plural' number for the subject or object of the verb. (The same device is used for the number of both subject and object, and sometimes there can be ambiguity as to which pronominal referent a number morpheme affects.) 'Plurality' is expressed in Caddo by a syllable *-wa-* that usually occurs between the preverb and the verb root. Thus, *yi-bahw* means 'to see' and *yi-wa-bahw* is the same base with specification of a plural subject or object. In Seneca 'plurality' is also expressed by a syllable *-wa-*. Seneca verb bases do not have the two parts described above for Caddo verbs, but consist of either a single root or a root with various prefixes and/or suffixed extensions. The syllable *-wa-* occurs between the pronominal prefix and the total verb base, whatever the latter may consist of; thus, *se-kęh* 'you see' and *s-wa-kęh* 'you (plural) see' or 'it sees you (plural)'. Here again, with this plural morpheme, there is a clear similarity between meaning, form, and function in Caddo and Seneca.

The Caddo 'dual' indicator does not occur in the same position as the 'plural', but in a position analogous to both the 'dual' and 'plural' in Seneca; that is, directly following the pronominal prefix. The Caddo 'dual', however, is *-wiht-*, while the Seneca 'dual' is *-ni-*. Just possibly Caddo *-wiht-*, which alternates with *piht-* initially, is relatable to the Siouan 'plural' suffix *-pi*. It may be noted that Caddoan postural prefixes ('lying', 'sitting', 'standing') also correspond to Siouan suffixes.

In addition to its regular pronominal prefixes, Caddo shows in some verbs a prefix from the following set:

*hani-*   'nonsingular subject'
*haka-*   'nonsingular object'
*kani-*   'indefinite transitive' (involvement of the indefinite category in a subject-object combination)

Such a prefix occurs between the regular pronominal prefix and the verb base. Each has a number of peculiarities associated with its occurrence, but all that needs to be said here is that these three forms are evidently relics of an earlier pronominal prefix system — perhaps one that occurred only with verbs of a certain kind — on which the modern pronominal system has been superimposed. A relationship of these relic prefixes in Caddo to the following Seneca pronominal prefixes is suggested:

*hęn-* (alternating with *hati-*)   'masculine plural subject'
*hakǫ-*   'nonsingular object acted upon by masculine singular subject'
*khni-* < **kani-*   'nonmasculine dual subject'

It might be further speculated that the *ha-* in the Caddo forms bears an ultimate relationship to Seneca *ha-* 'masculine subject', Caddo *ka-* to Seneca *ka-* 'neuter or nonmasculine subject', Caddo *-ni-* to Seneca *-ni-* 'dual', and Caddo *-ka-* to an Iroquoian indicator of nonsingularity — an element *ka-* which is prefixed to pronominal forms in Cayuga, Tuscarora, and Cherokee (Lounsbury 1961:12–13). It most often affects the number of the object of a transitive prefix; note that Caddo *haka-* indicates 'nonsingular object'.

There is a syllable *ʔi-* which occurs before some Caddo noun and verb roots, and whose only function seems to be to protect the left flank of the root from occurring initially or from coming into direct phonemic contact with a pronominal prefix. For example, the verb root *wayuh* 'to climb' (with a variant shape -'*wyuh*) will tolerate an immediately preceding plural, as in *páwyuhah* 'they climb', but adds *ʔi-* to protect itself initially (*ʔíwyuhah* 'he climbs') and from a pronominal prefix (*ci·wayuhah* < *ciʔiwayuhah* 'I climb'). There is also in Seneca a syllable *ʔi-* which occurs at the beginning of some verbs, and whose only function is to prevent the occurrence of a verb that would contain only one vowel. Thus, one would otherwise expect the imperative 'hit it!' to be *\*jet*, but it is in fact *ʔijet* (Chafe 1967:14). This use of *ʔi-* as a protective device to prevent the occurrence of something the language seems unable to tolerate is thus another feature that unites Caddo and Seneca, even though the intolerable conditions are not identical in the two languages.

One last resemblance that seems worth mentioning here is that which exists between Caddo *-t-* 'dative' and Seneca *-at-* 'reflexive' (or 'middle voice'). There is an obvious similarity in shape. Both elements, moreover, occur as the leftmost constituents of verb bases. In addition, both affect transitivity in some of their occurrences, although in opposite ways. The Caddo 'dative' sometimes transitivizes bases otherwise intransitive, while the Seneca element sometimes has the opposite effect.

### 4.4 *Macro-Siouan phonology*

The phonological inventories of Caddoan languages appear superficially to be quite different from those of either Siouan or Iroquoian languages. In traditional phonemic terms, for example, Caddo has three vowels and nineteen consonants while Seneca has seven vowels and eight consonants. It is interesting and suggestive that the greatest differences between these various languages show up at the 'systematic phonetic' level, while at the morphophonemic or 'systematic phonemic' level, which undoubtedly reflects an earlier stage of the languages' history, they look much more alike. Finally, when one reconstructs phonological inventories for the three proto-languages, the similarities are even more striking. It is useful to line up these reconstructed inventories side by side in a way that will emphasize their common characteristics:

| Proto-Siouan | | | Proto-Northern-Iroquoian | | | Proto-Caddoan | | |
|---|---|---|---|---|---|---|---|---|
| i | | u | i | | | i | | u |
| e | | o | e | | o | | | |
| | a | | | a | | | a | |
| į | | ų | ę | | ǫ | | | |
| | ą | | | | | | | |
| p | t | k | (p) | t | k | p | t | k |
| w | y | r | w | y | n | r | w | y | n | r |
| s | š | x | s | | | s | | |
| h | ʔ | | h | ʔ | | h | ʔ | |

There are controversial points in each of these reconstructions. The nasal consonants *m* and *n* have been omitted from the Proto-Siouan inventory on the advice of Terrence S. Kaufman, who argues that these consonants in the modern Siouan languages can be explained as reflexes of other consonants or consonant clusters which were followed by nasalized vowels. The labial stop *p* is included in the Proto-Northern-Iroquoian inventory on the basis of suggestions which have been made by Paul M. Postal. The Proto-Caddoan list differs slightly from that published in Allan R. Taylor (1963b). His *c*, $k^w$, and *ks* have been omitted on the grounds that they may ultimately be explainable as clusters, and *y* has been added because it seems to be needed to explain developments in Caddo. Affricates, labiovelars, and resonants may be considered to be the most problematic aspects of Caddoan linguistic history at the moment.

However these questions are resolved, the similarity between the three families will not be greatly affected. The point is that the phonological inventories of Siouan, Iroquoian, and Caddoan appear to converge as one traces them back in time. This kind of evidence for relationship may not be inconsequential when it is coupled with evidence of other kinds.

## 5. OTHER REMOTE RELATIONSHIPS

The relationships which link the members of the Macro-Siouan stock to each other are not the only remote relationships involving these language families that have been suggested. Most important are the several relationships outside this stock that have been suggested for the Siouan family. There is, of course, the fact that Sapir included Siouan, along with Iroquoian and Caddoan, in his extensive and diverse Hokan-Siouan stock. More interesting, however, is Sapir's suggestion of a special closeness of relationship between Siouan and Yuchi. Yuchi is a linguistically isolated language originally spoken in Tennessee and the western part of the Carolinas, and presently still spoken by a few people in Oklahoma. The principal description of the language is by Günter Wagner (1934); there is a more recent but brief article by Hans Wolff (1948), as well as an analyzed text (Wolff 1951). Mary R. Haas (1951) has published a few lexical resemblances which support Sapir's hypothesis of a Siouan-Yuchi relationship. Haas (1964) presents some evidence that Siouan is related not only to Yuchi, but also to the Nadene languages (specifically Athapaskan and Tlingit). Haas (1951), as well as Haas (1952), also suggests a relationship between Siouan and the 'Gulf' languages (the Muskogean family plus Natchez, Tunica, Chitimacha, and Atakapa), based on reconstructions of the words for 'water' and 'land'. It may be noted that if Siouan is related to the Gulf languages and the latter in turn are related to Algonquian (Haas 1958), there is essentially but one superstock of languages east of the Rocky Mountains. A relationship as geographically far-flung as that suggested by Haas between Siouan and Nadene has been given some documentation by William W. Elmendorf (1963), who has found some resemblances between Siouan (as well as Yuchi) and the Yukian languages of California (Yuki, Huchnom, Wappo). Elmendorf was led to look for such resemblances by an earlier suggestion of Paul Radin. Elmendorf (1964) presents further evidence for the Siouan-Yuchi-Yukian relationship. If all these suggestions are valid, they mean that Macro-Siouan is only part of a great linguistic stock which covered North America east of the Rockies, which extended with Nadene into the Northwest, Southwest, and all the way to the West Coast, and which had a further West Coast representative in Yukian, the latter perhaps providing a further link to Penutian, Hokan, or both. At the moment it would be well to remain aware of the speculativeness of these ideas.

## 6. REFERENCES

ADELUNG, JOHANN CHRISTOPH, and JOHANN SEVERIN VATER. 1806–17. Mithridates oder allgemeine Sprachenkunde mit dem Vater Unser als Sprachprobe in bey nahe fünf hundert Sprachen und Mundarten. Berlin.

ALLEN, LOUIS. 1931. Siouan and Iroquoian. IJAL 6.185–93.

BARBEAU, C. MARIUS. 1915. Classification of Iroquoian radicals with subjective pronominal prefixes. Canada Department of Mines, Geological Survey, Memoir 46, Anthropological Series No. 7. Ottawa.

———. 1959. The language of Canada in the voyages of Jacques Cartier (1534–1538). NMC-B 173.108–229.

———. 1960. Huron-Wyandot traditional narratives in translations and native texts. NMC-B 165.

BARTON, BENJAMIN SMITH. 1797. New views of the origin of the tribes and nations of America. Philadelphia. 2nd ed. 1798.

BEAUCHAMP, WILLIAM M. 1902. Onondaga plant names. JAF 15.91–103.

BENDER, ERNEST. 1949. Cherokee II. IJAL 15.223–8.

BENDER, ERNEST, and ZELLIG S. HARRIS. 1946. The phonemes of North Carolina Cherokee. IJAL 12.41–21.

BIGGAR, H.P. 1924. The voyages of Jacques Cartier. Publications of the Public Archives of Canada 11.

BOAS, FRANZ. 1907. Notes on the Ponka grammar. PICAm 15/2.317–37.

———. 1909. Notes on the Iroquois language. Putnam anniversary volume, pp. 427–60. New York, G.E. Stechert.

———. 1937. Some traits of the Dakota language. Lg 13.137–41.

BOAS, FRANZ, and ELLA DELORIA. 1933. Notes on the Dakota, Teton dialect. IJAL 7.97–121.

———. 1941. Dakota grammar. Memoirs of the National Academy of Sciences 23, Part 2.

BOAS, FRANZ, and JOHN R. SWANTON. 1911. Siouan (Dakota). HAIL I (= BAE-B 40.875–965).

BRADBURY, JOHN. 1817. Travels in the interior of America, in the years 1809, 1810, and 1811. London, Sherwood, Neely, and Jones.
BRINTON, DANIEL G. 1891. The American race. New York, N.D.C Hodges.
BRUYAS, JACQUES. 1863. Radices verborum Iroquæorum. Radical words of the Mohawk language, with their derivatives. New York, Cramoisy Press. Also published in the same year as Appendix E, 16th Annual Report of the Regents of the University of the State of New York, Albany.
BUCCA, SALVADOR, and ALEXANDER LESSER. 1969. Kitsai phonology and morphophonemics. IJAL 35.7–19.
BUECHEL, EUGENE, S.J. 1939. A grammar of Lakota, the language of the Teton Sioux Indians. Saint Francis, S.D., Saint Francis Mission.
BUSCHMANN, JOHANN CARL EDUARD. 1859. Die Spuren der aztekischen Sprache im nördlichen Mexico und höheren amerikanischen Norden. Berlin, Königl. Akademie der Wissenschaften.
CAMPANIUS, JOHAN. 1696. Lutheri catechismus ofwersatt på american-virginiske språket. Stockholm. Republished 1937, Stockholm, I. Hæggstrom.
CARVER, JONATHAN. 1778. Travels through the interior parts of North America, in the years 1766, 1767, and 1768. London. [Numerous republications and translations.]
CATLIN, GEORGE. 1841. Letters and notes on the manners, customs and conditions of the North American Indians. 2 vols. New York, Wiley and Putnam.
CHAFE, WALLACE L. 1959a. The classification of morphs in Seneca. AnL 1/5.1–6.
——. 1959b. Internal reconstruction in Seneca. Lg 35.477–94.
——. 1960–61. Seneca morphology. IJAL 26.11–22, 123–9, 224–33, 283–9; 27.42–5, 114–8, 223–5, 320–8.
——. 1961. Seneca thanksgiving rituals. BAE-B 183.
——. 1962. Review of Marius Barbeau 1959. AmA 64.679–81.
——. 1963. Handbook of the Seneca language. New York State Museum Bulletin 388. Albany.
——. 1964a. Another look at Siouan and Iroquioan. AmA 66.852–62.
——. 1964b. Linguistic evidence for the relative age of Iroquois religious practices. SJA 20.278–85.
——. 1967. Seneca morphology and dictionary. SCA 4.
——. 1968. The ordering of phonological rules. IJAL 34.115–46.
CHAFE, WALLACE L., and JACK FREDERICK KILPATRICK. 1963. Inconsistencies in Cherokee spelling. Proceedings of the 1962 Annual Spring Meeting of the American Ethnological Society 60–3.
CHAMBERLAIN, A.F. 1888. The Catawba language. Toronto, Imrie and Graham.
CLAIBORNE, JUDGE J.F.H., and OTIS T. MASON. 1879. Anthropological news. American Naturalist 13.788–90.
CONKLIN, HAROLD C., and WILLIAM C. STURTEVANT. 1953. Seneca Indian singing tools at Coldspring Longhouse. PAPS 97.262–90.

CROSS, MARION E., translator. 1938. Father Louis Hennepin's Description of Louisiana. University of Minnesota Press.

CUOQ, JEAN-ANDRÉ. 1866. Études philologiques sur quelques langages sauvages de l'Amerique. Reprinted 1966 by S.R. Publishers Ltd., Johnson Reprint Corp., and Mouton and Co.

——. 1882. Lexique de la langue iroquoise. Montréal, J. Chapleau.

CURTIN, JEREMIAH. 1923. Seneca Indian myths. New York, E.P. Dutton.

CURTIN, JEREMIAH, and J.N.B. HEWITT. 1911. Seneca fiction, legends and myths. BAE-R 32.

CURTIS, EDWARD S. 1907–30. The North American Indian. Cambridge, University Press.

DA CRUZ, DANIEL. 1957. A provisional analysis of segmental phonemes in Caddo. [Mimeographed.]

DELORIA, ELLA. 1932. Dakota texts. PAES 14.

——. 1954. Short Dakota texts, including conversations. IJAL 20.17–22.

DENSMORE, FRANCES. 1929. Pawnee music. BAE-B 93.

DORSEY, JAMES OWEN. 1873. Ponka ABC wa-bá-ru. New York.

——. 1879–80. How the rabbit killed the (male) winter. An Omaha fable. AmAnt 2.128–32.

——. 1880–81. The rabbit and the grasshopper: An Otoe myth. AmA 3.24–7.

——. 1881. How the rabbit caught the sun in a trap. An Omaha myth, obtained from F. La Flèche by J. Owen Dorsey. BAE-R 1.581–3.

——. 1884. Omaha sociology. BAE-R 3.205–370.

——. 1885. On the comparative phonology of four Siouan languages. Smithsonian Institution, Annual Report for 1883, pp. 919–29. Washington, D.C.

——. 1888. Osage traditions. BAE-R 6.373–97.

——. 1890. The Ȼegiha language. CNAE 6.

——. 1894. The Biloxi Indians of Louisiana. AAAS-P 42.267–87.

DORSEY, J.O., and JOHN R. SWANTON. 1912. A dictionary of the Biloxi and Ofo languages. BAE-B 47.

ELMENDORF, WILLIAM W. 1963. Yukian-Siouan lexical similarities. IJAL 29.300–9.

——. 1964. Item and set comparison in Yuchi, Siouan, and Yukian. IJAL 30.328–40.

FENTON, WILLIAM N. 1953. The Iroquois Eagle Dance: An offshoot of the Calumet Dance. BAE-B 156.

FICKETT, JOAN GLEASON. 1967. The phonology of Tuscarora. SIL 19.33–57.

FLETCHER, ALICE C. 1902. The Hako, a Pawnee ceremony. BAE-R 22.

FLETCHER, ALICE C., and FRANCIS LA FLESCHE. 1911. The Omaha tribe. BAE-R 27.

FRACHTENBERG, LEO J. 1913. Contributions to a Tutelo vocabulary. AmA 15.477–9.

FRASER, ALEXANDER. 1920. Huron manuscripts from Rev. Pierre Potier's collection. Fifteenth Report of the Bureau of Archives for the Province of Ontario. Toronto.

GABELENTZ, HANS GEORG CONON VON DER. 1952a. Grammatik der Dakota-Sprache. Leipzig, F.A. Brockhaus.

———. 1852b. Kurze Grammatik der Tscherokesischen Sprache. Zeitschrift für die Wissenschaft der Sprache 3.257–300. [Also published separately.]

GALLATIN, ALBERT. 1836. A synopsis of the Indian tribes within the United States east of the Rocky Mountains, and in the British and Russian possessions in North America. Transactions and Collections of the American Antiquarian Society 2. Cambridge.

———. 1848. Hale's Indians of North-West America, and vocabularies of North America; with an introduction. AES-T 2.xxiii-clxxxviii, 1–130.

GARVIN, PAUL L. 1950. Wichita I: Phonemics. IJAL 16.179–84.

GATSCHET, ALBERT S. 1884. Migration legend of the Creek Indians. (Library of Aboriginal American Literature 4.) Philadelphia, D.G. Brinton.

———. 1886. On the affinity of the Cherokee to the Iroquois dialects. TAPA 16.xl-xlv.

———. 1900. Grammatic sketch of the Catawba language. AmA 2.527–49.

———. 1902. Onomatology of the Catawba River basin. AmA 4.53–6.

GILMORE, MELVIN R. 1913. A study in the ethnobotany of the Omaha Indians. Collections of the Nebraska State Historical Society 17.314–57.

———. 1919. Uses of plants by the Indians of the Missouri River region. BAE-R 33.43–154.

GREGG, JOSIAH. 1844. Commerce of the prairies. 2 vols. New York, H.G. Langley. [Numerous republications.]

GRINNELL, GEORGE BIRD. 1893. Pawnee hero stories and folk tales. New York, C. Scribners Sons.

GULICK, JOHN. 1958. Language and passive resistance among the Eastern Cherokees. Ethnohistory 5.60–81.

HAAS, MARY R. 1948. Classificatory verbs in Muskogee. IJAL 14.244–6.

———. 1951. The Proto-Gulf word for *water* (with notes on Siouan-Yuchi). IJAL 17.71–9.

———. 1952. The Proto-Gulf word for *land* (with a note on Proto-Siouan). IJAL 18.238–40.

———. 1958. A new linguistic relationship in North America: Algonkian and the Gulf languages. SJA 14.231–64.

———. 1964. Athapaskan, Tlingit, Yuchi, and Siouan. PICAm 25.495–500.

———. 1968. The last words of Biloxi. IJAL 34.77–84.

———. 1969. Swanton and the Biloxi and Ofo dictionaries. IJAL 35.286–90.

HALE, HORATIO. 1883a. Indian migrations as evidenced by language. AmAnt 5.18–28.

———, ed. 1883b. The Iroquois book of rites. Philadelphia: D.G. Brinton. Reprinted 1963 with an introduction by William N. Fenton, University of Toronto Press.

———. 1883c. The Tutelo tribe and language. PAPS 21.1–47.

———. 1888. Indian etymologies. AmA 1.290–1.

HAMILTON, WILLIAM, and SAMUEL M. IRVIN. 1843. An elementary spelling book of the Ioway language. Indian Territory, Ioway and Sac Mission Press.

——. 1848. An Ioway grammar. Ioway and Sac Mission Press.
——. 1849. The Ioway primmer. Ioway and Sac Mission Press.
HAMP, ERIC P. 1958. Prosodic notes. IJAL 24.321–2.
HANS, FRED M. 1907. The great Sioux nation. Chicago, M.A. Donohue. [Republished 1964. Minneapolis, Ross and Haines.]
HARRINGTON, MARK R. 1908. Some Seneca corn-foods and their preparation. AmA 10.575–90.
HAYDEN, FERDINAND VANDEVEER. 1863. Contributions to the ethnography and philology of the Indian tribes of the Missouri Valley. TAPS 12.231–461.
——. 1869. Brief notes on the Pawnee, Winnebago, and Omaha languages. PAPS 10.389–421.
HEWITT, J.N.B. 1888. Etymology of the word Iroquois. AmA 1.188–9.
——. 1891. Iroquoian etymologies. Science 17.217–20.
——. 1892. The etymology of the two Iroquoian compound stems, $-ske^m\text{-}ra\text{-}keq'\text{-}te'$ and $-ndu\text{-}ta\text{-}keq'\text{-}te'$. Science 19.190–2.
——. 1903. Iroquoian cosmology, first part. BAE-R 21.127–339.
——. 1928a. Iroquoian cosmology, second part. BAE-R 43.449–819.
——. 1928b. A Mohawk form of ritual of condolence, 1782, by John Deserontyon. Indian Notes and Monographs 10.87–110.
HICKERSON, HAROLD, GLEN D. TURNER, and NANCY P. HICKERSON. 1952. Testing procedures for estimating transfer of information among Iroquois dialects and languages. IJAL 18.1–8.
HILL, ARCHIBALD A. 1952. A note on primitive languages. IJAL 18.172–7.
HOCKETT, CHARLES F. 1942. A system of descriptive phonology. Lg 18.3–21.
HOFFMAN, BERNARD G. 1959. Iroquois linguistic classification from historical materials. Ethnohistory 6.160–85.
HOLLOW, ROBERT C., Jr. 1970. A Mandan dictionary. Ph.D. dissertation, University of California, Berkeley.
HOLMER, NILS M. 1945. Sonant-surds in Ponca-Omaha. IJAL 11.75–85.
——. 1947. An Ofo phonetic law. IJAL 13.1–8.
——. 1952–53. Seneca II, III. IJAL 18.217–22; 19.281–9.
——. 1954. The Seneca language, a study in Iroquoian. Upsala Canadian Studies 3.
HORSFORD, E.N., ed. 1887. Zeisberger's Indian dictionary. Cambridge, Mass., John Wilson and Son.
HUOT, MARTHA CHAMPION. 1948. Some Mohawk words of acculturation. IJAL 14.150–4.
HYER, JOSEPH K., and WILLIAM STARRING. 1866. Dictionary of the Sioux language. Facsimile edition published by Yale University Press, 1968.
JACKSON, HALLIDAY. 1830. Civilization of the Indian natives. Philadelphia, Marcus T.C. Gould.
KASCHUBE, DOROTHEA V. 1954. Examples of tone in Crow. IJAL 20.34–6.

———. 1967. Structural elements of the language of the Crow Indians of Montana. University of Colorado Studies, Series in Anthropology 14. Boulder.
KEANE, AUGUSTUS H. 1878. Ethnography and philology of America. Stanford's compendium of geography and travel, ed. by Henry W. Bates, pp. 443–545. London, E. Standford.
KENNARD, EDWARD A. 1936. Mandan grammar. IJAL 9.1–43.
KILPATRICK, JACK FREDERICK, and ANNA GRITTS KILPATRICK. 1965. The shadow of Sequoyah: Social documents of the Cherokees, 1862–1964. Norman, University of Oklahoma.
KRUEGER, JOHN R. 1963. Two early grammars of Cherokee. AnL 5/3.1–57.
LA FLESCHE, FRANCIS. 1932. A dictionary of the Osage language. BAE-B 109.
LATHAM, ROBERT G. 1846. Miscellaneous contributions to the ethnography of North America. Proceedings of the Philological Society 2.31–50. London.
———. 1860. Opuscula: Essays chiefly philological and ethnographical. London, Williams and Norgate.
LAWSON, JOHN. 1709. A new voyage to Carolina. London.
LESSER, ALEXANDER, and GENE WELTFISH. 1932. Composition of the Caddoan linguistic stock. SMC 87/6.
LEVIN, NORMAN BALFOUR. 1964. The Assiniboine language. IUPAL 32.
LIEBER, OSCAR M. 1858. Vocabulary of the Catawba language. Collections of the South Carolina Historical Society 2.327–42.
LIPKIND, WILLIAM. 1945. Winnebago grammar. New York, King's Crown Press.
LOUNSBURY, FLOYD G. 1953. Oneida verb morphology. YUPA 48.
———. 1961. Iroquois-Cherokee linguistic relations. BAE-B 180.11–17.
LOWIE, ROBERT H. 1909. The Assiniboine. AMNH 4/1.
———. 1930. A Crow text with grammatical notes. UCPAAE 29/2.155–75.
———. 1932. Proverbial expressions among the Crow Indians. AmA 34.739–40.
———. 1939. Hidatsa texts. With grammatical notes and phonograph transcriptions by Zellig Harris and C. F. Voegelin. PRS 1.173–239.
———. 1941. The Crow language: Grammatical sketch and analyzed text. UCPAAE 39.
———. 1950. Observations on the literary style of the Crow Indians. Beiträge zur Gesellungs- und Völkerwissenschaft, 271–83. Berlin, Gebrüder Mann.
———. 1959. The oral literature of the Crow Indians. JAF 72.97–104.
———. 1960a. Crow texts. Berkeley and Los Angeles, University of California Press.
———. 1960b. Crow word lists. Berkeley and Los Angeles, University of California Press.
———. 1960c. A few Assiniboine texts. AnL 2/8.1–30.
MCKENNEY, EDWARD. 1850. Omahaw primer.
MARCY, RANDOLPH B. 1853. Exploration of the Red River of Louisiana in the year 1852. Washington.
MARINO, MARY CAROLYN. 1968. A dictionary of Winnebago: An analysis and refer-

ence grammar of the Radin lexical file. Ph.D. dissertation, University of California, Berkeley.

MARTEN, ANITA ELMA. 1964. The morphophonemics of the Winnebago verbal. Ph.D. dissertation, University of Wiconsin.

MATTHEWS, G. HUBERT. 1955. Phonemic analysis of a Dakota dialect. IJAL 21. 56–9.

——. 1958. Handbook of Siouan languages. Ph.D. dissertation, University of Pennsylvania.

——. 1959a. On tone in Crow. IJAL 25.135–6.

——. 1959b. Proto-Siouan kinship terminology. AmA 61.252–78.

——. 1965. Hidatsa syntax. The Hague, Mouton.

MATTHEWS, G. HUBERT, and RED THUNDER CLOUD. 1967. Catawba texts. IJAL 33.7–24.

MATTHEWS, WASHINGTON. 1873. Grammar and dictionary of the language of the Hidatsa (Minnetarees, Grosventres of the Missouri). New York, Cramoisy Press.

——. 1874. English-Hidatsa (Minnetaree) dictionary. New York: Cramoisy Press.

——. 1877. Ethnography and philology of the Hidatsa Indians. U.S. Geological and Geographical Survey, Miscellaneous Publications 7.

MAXIMILIAN, ALEXANDER PHILIP, PRINCE OF WIED. 1839–41. Reise in das Innere Nord-America in den Jahren 1832 bis 1834. 2 vols. Coblenz, J. Hoelscher.

MONTGOMERY, WILLIAM B., and W. C. REQUA. 1834. The Osage first book. Boston, American Board of Commissioners for Foreign Missions.

MOONEY, JAMES. 1891. The sacred formulas of the Cherokee. BAE-R 7.301–97.

——. 1896. The ghost-dance religion, and the Sioux outbreak of 1890. BAE-R 14, pt. 2.

——. 1900. Myths of the Cherokee. BAE-R 19, p. 1.

MOONEY, JAMES, and FRANS M. OLBRECHTS. 1932. The Swimmer manuscript. BAE-B 99.

MORGAN, LEWIS H. 1851. League of the Ho-de'-no-sau-nee, or Iroquois. Rochester, Sage and Brother. [Numerous republications.]

——. 1870. Indian migrations. The North American Review 110.33–82.

——. 1871. Systems of consanguinity and affinity of the human family. SCK 17.

OLBRECHTS, FRANS M. 1929. De pronominale prefixen in het Tuscarora. Donum natalicium Schrijnen, pp. 154–61. Nijmegen-Utrecht, N.V. Dekker and Van de Vegt.

——. 1931. Two Cherokee texts. IJAL 6.179–84.

PARKER, ARTHUR C. 1910. Iroquois uses of maize and other food plants. New York State Museum Bulletin 144. Albany.

——. 1913. The code of Handsome Lake, the Seneca prophet. New York State Museum Bulletin 163. Albany.

PARSONS, ELSIE CLEWS. 1941. Notes on the Caddo. AAA-M 57.

PICKERING, JOHN. 1830. A grammar of the Cherokee language. Boston, Mission Press.
PIERCE, JOE E. 1954. Crow vs. Hidatsa in dialect distance and in glottochronology. IJAL 20.134–6.
PILLING, JAMES C, 1887. Bibliography of the Siouan languages. B[A]E-B 5.
——. 1888. Bibliography of the Iroquoian languages. B[A]E-B 6.
PLAUT, W. GUNTHER. 1953. A Hebrew-Dakota dictionary. Publication of the American Jewish Historical Society 42.361–70.
POSTAL, PAUL M. 1962. Some syntactic rules in Mohawk. Ph.D. dissertation, Yale.
——. 1964a. Boas and the development of phonology: Comments based on Iroquoian. IJAL 30.269–80.
——. 1964b. Mohawk prefix generation. PICL 9.346–55.
——. 1968. Aspects of phonological theory. New York, Harper and Row.
——. 1969. Mohawk vowel doubling. IJAL 35.291–8.
POWELL, JOHN W. 1891. Indian linguistic families of America north of Mexico. BAE-R 7.1–142.
PRESTON, W. D., and C. F. VOEGELIN. 1949. Seneca I. IJAL 15.23–44.
RADIN, PAUL. 1923. The Winnebago tribe. BAE-R 37.35–560.
——. 1949. The culture of the Winnebago: As described by themselves. IJAL Memoir 2.
——. 1950. The origin myth of the medicine rite: Three versions. The historical origins of the medicine rite. IJAL Memoir 3.
RAFINESQUE, CONSTANTINE S. 1832–33. American languages. Wahtani or Mandan. Atlantic Journal, and Friend of Knowledge 132–3. Philadelphia.
REYBURN, WILLIAM D. 1953–54. Cherokee verb morphology. IJAL 19.172–80, 259–73; 20.44–64.
RIGGS, MARY ANN CLARK. 1852. An English and Dakota vocabulary. New York, American Board of Commissioners for Foreign Missions.
RIGGS, STEPHEN R. 1852. Grammar and dictionary of the Dakota language. SCK 4.
——. 1872. The Dakota language. Minnesota Historical Society Collections 1.89–107.
——. 1881a. Of the Dakota language. AmAnt 3.243–4.
——. 1881b. A dog's revenge. A Dakota fable, by Michel Renville. BAE-R 1.587–9.
——. 1890. A Dakota-English dictionary. Ed. by James Owen Dorsey. CNAE 7.
——. 1893. Dakota grammar, texts, and ethnography. CNAE 9.
ROBINETT, FLORENCE M. 1955. Hidatsa I, II, III. IJAL 21.1–7, 160–77, 210–6.
ROEHRIG, F. L. O. 1873. On the language of the Dakota or Sioux Indians. Annual Report of the Board of Regents of the Smithsonian Institution for the year 1871, pp. 434–50. Washington, D.C.
ROOD, DAVID S. 1969. Wichita grammar: A generative semantic sketch. Ph.D. dissertation, University of California, Berkeley.
SAGARD, GABRIEL. 1632. Dictionnaire de la langage huronne. Paris, Denys Moreau.

Republished in Gabriel Sagard-Théodat, 1866, Histoire du Canada, vol. 4. Paris, Librairie Tross.

SAPIR, EDWARD. 1913. A Tutelo vocabulary. AmA 15.295–7.

———. 1951. Central and North American languages. SWES, pp. 169–78.

SCHMITT, KARL, and IVA OSANAI SCHMITT. 1952. Wichita kinship past and present. Norman, Oklahoma.

SCHOOLCRAFT, HENRY R. 1846. Notes on the Iroquois. New York, Bartlett and Welford.

———. 1851–57. Information respecting the history, condition, and prospects of the Indian tribes of the United States. 6 vols. Philadelphia, Lippincott, Grambo.

SEBEOK, THOMAS A. 1947. Two Winnebago texts. IJAL 13.167–70.

SHEA, JOHN GILMARY. 1860. A French-Onondaga dictionary, from a manuscript of the seventeenth century. New York, Cramoisy Press.

SIEBERT, FRANK T., JR. 1945. Linguistic classification of Catawba. IJAL 11.100–4, 211–8.

SMITH, ERMINNIE A. 1883a. Accidents or mode signs of verbs in the Iroquois dialects. AAAS-P 32.402–3.

———. 1883b. Studies in the Iroquois concerning the verb to be and its substitutes. AAAS-P 32.399–402.

———. 1884. Disputed points concerning Iroquois pronouns. AAAS-P 33.606–9.

SPECK, FRANK G. 1913. Some Catawba texts and folk-lore. JAF 26.319–30.

———. 1924. The possible Siouan identity of the words recorded from Francisco of Chicora on the South Carolina coast. Journal of the Washington Academy of Sciences 14.303–6.

———. 1926. Some Eastern Cherokee texts. IJAL 4.111–3.

———. 1928. Recording the Catawba language. El Palacio 24.307–8.

———. 1934. Catawba texts. CUCA 24.

———. 1946. Catawba text. IJAL 12.64–5.

———. 1949. Midwinter rites of the Cayuga Longhouse. Philadelphia, University of Pennsylvania.

SPECK, FRANK G., and C. E. SCHAEFFER. 1942. Catawba kinship and social organization with a resume of Tutelo kinship terms. AmA 44.555–75.

SPIER, LESLIE. 1924. Wichita and Caddo relationship terms. AmA 26.258–63.

STARK, DONALD S. 1962. Boundary markers in Dakota. IJAL 28.19–35.

STETSON, R. H. 1946. An experimentalist's view of Hidatsa phonology. IJAL 12.136–8.

STEVENS, JEDEDIAH DWIGHT. 1836. Sioux spelling book. Boston, American Board of Commissioners for Foreign Missions.

STURTEVANT, WILLIAM C. 1958. Siouan languages in the East. AmA 60.738–43.

SUSMAN, AMELIA. 1941. Word play in Winnebago. Lg 17.342–4.

———. 1943. The accentual system of Winnebago. Ph.D. dissertation, Columbia.

SWANTON, JOHN R. 1909. A new Siouan dialect. Putnam anniversary volume, 477–86. New York, G.E. Stechert.

———. 1918. Catawba notes. Journal of the Washington Academy of Sciences 8.623–9.

———. 1923. New light on the early history of the Siouan peoples. Journal of the Washington Academy of Sciences 13.33–43.

———. 1936. Early history of the eastern Siouan tribes. Essays in anthropology presented to A.L. Kroeber, pp. 371–81. Berkeley, University of California.

TAYLOR, ALLAN R. 1963a. The classification of the Caddoan languages. PAPS 107.51–9.

———. 1963b. Comparative Caddoan. IJAL 29.113–31.

THWAITES, REUBEN G. 1896–1901. Jesuit Relations and allied documents. 73 vols. Cleveland, Burrows Brothers.

———, ed. 1904–07. Early western travels: 1784–1846. 32 vols. Cleveland, A.H. Clark.

TOOKER, ELISABETH J. 1964. An ethnography of the Huron Indians, 1615–1649. BAE-B 190.

UMFREVILLE, EDWARD. 1790. The present state of Hudson's Bay. London.

VATER, JOHANN S. 1821. Analekten der Sprachenkunde. Leipzig.

VOEGELIN, C.F. 1939. Ofo-Biloxi sound correspondences. Proceedings of the Indiana Academy of Science 48.23–6.

———. 1941a. Historical results of Crow-Hidatsa comparisons, according to three methods. Proceedings of the Indiana Academy of Science 50.39–42.

———. 1941b. Internal relationships of Siouan languages. AmA 43.246–9.

———. 1947. A problem in morpheme alternants and their distribution. Lg 23.245–54.

VOEGELIN, C.F., and F.M. ROBINETT. 1954. 'Mother language' in Hidatsa. IJAL 20.65–70.

WAGNER, GÜNTER. 1934. Yuchi. HAIL 3.295–384.

WALKER, JAMES R. 1914. Oglala kinship terms. AmA 16.96–109.

WALKER, WILLARD. 1967. Review of Kilpatrick and Kilpatrick 1965. IJAL 33.82–4.

WALLACE, ANTHONY F.C. 1949. The Tuscaroras: Sixth nation of the Iroquois Confederacy. PAPS 93.159–65.

WALLACE, ANTHONY F.C., and WILLIAM D. REYBURN. 1951. Crossing the ice: A migration legend of the Tuscarora Indians. IJAL 17.42–7.

WAUGH, FREDERICK W. 1916. Iroquois foods and food preparation. Canada Department of Mines, Geological Survey, Memoir 86. Ottawa.

WELTFISH, GENE. 1936. The vision story of Fox Boy. IJAL 9.44–75.

———. 1937. Caddoan texts. PAES 17.

WHIPPLE, AMIEL WEEKS. 1856. Reports of explorations and surveys to ascertain the most practicable and economical route for a railroad from the Mississippi River to the Pacific Ocean. Washington, D.C.

WHIPPLE, AMIEL WEEKS, THOMAS EWBANK and WILLIAM W. TURNER. 1855. Report upon the Indian tribes. Whipple 1856: vol. 3, pt. 3.

WHITE, JOHN K. 1962. On the revival of printing in the Cherokee language. CAnthr 3.511–4.

WHITMAN, WILLIAM. 1947. Descriptive grammar of Ioway-Oto. IJAL 13.233–48.

WILKIE, JOHN, translator. 1831. Grammar of the Huron language. Transactions of the Literary and Historical Society of Quebec 2.94–198. Quebec.

WILL, G. F., and H. J. SPINDEN. 1906. The Mandans: A study of their culture, archaeology and language. Peabody Museum of American Archaeology and Ethnology, Papers 3.81–219. Cambridge, Mass.

WILLIAMSON, A. W. 1881. Is the Dakota related to the Indo-European languages? Minnesota Academy of Natural Sciences, Bulletin 2.110–42.

——. 1882. The Dakotan languages. AmAnt 4.110–28.

WILLIAMSON, JOHN P. 1902. An English-Dakota dictionary. New York, American Tract Society.

WILLIAMSON, THOMAS S., and STEPHEN R. RIGGS. 1880. The Holy Bible, in the language of the Dakotas. New York, American Bible Society.

WOLFF, HANS. 1948. Yuchi phonemes and morphemes, with special reference to person markers. IJAL 14.240–3.

——. 1950–51. Comparative Siouan. IJAL 16.61–6, 113–21, 168–78; 17.197–204.

——. 1951. Yuchi text with analysis. IJAL 17.48–53.

——. 1952. Osage I: phonemes and historical phonology. IJAL 18.63–8. Osage II: morphology. IJAL 18.231–7.

——. 1958. An Osage graphemic experiment. IJAL 24.30–5.

WRIGHT, ASHER. 1842. A spelling-book in the Seneca language. Buffalo-Creek Reservation, Mission Press.

YAMACHIKA, RAYMOND. 1961. Cherokee literature: Printing in the Sequoyan syllabary since 1828 with a bibliography. Ms., University of Oklahoma.

ZEISBERGER, DAVID. 1888. Essay of an Onondaga grammar, or a short introduction to learn the Onondaga al. Maqua tongue. Reprinted from The Pennsylvania Magazine of History and Biography. Philadelphia.

# THE SOUTHEAST

MARY R. HAAS

0. INTRODUCTION

It is a commonplace of anthropological literature that the greatest diversity of aboriginal North America was that found in the California-Oregon area.[1] But we know this largely because of the relative recency of contact, since the northern part of the area was little affected by the inroads of European civilization until around the middle of the nineteenth century while the southern part was similarly unaffected until the latter part of the eighteenth century.

Another area of great linguistic diversity in North America was certainly the Southeast and the adjacent coast of the Gulf of Mexico. However, it is seldom spoken of in these terms and is certainly not likely to be compared to California. The principal reason for this is the far longer period of contact — nearly five centuries — and the sparseness of information about the most critical period, namely that before the tribes had been seriously dislocated by the pressures of the competing European nations.

Many smaller tribes in the Southeast have almost certainly vanished without a trace. Many others are known to us by name only, and in this event (in spite of frequent claims to the contrary) linguistic affiliation is unknown. Our linguistic knowledge of the Southeast, then, is based chiefly on some of the larger and more powerful tribes of the area, such as the Cherokee, the Creek, and the Choctaw, and only rarely on the much smaller ones, such as the Biloxi, the Ofo, or the Tunica.

Although our knowledge of the Southeast is much poorer than we could wish, the literature on the known languages is nevertheless quite extensive. In the section which immediately follows, the various linguistic families and language isolates are taken up in order: the Muskogean family, Natchez, Tunica, Chitimacha, Atakapa, Timucua, southeastern representatives of the Siouan family, Yuchi, southeastern representatives of the Iroquoian family, and southeastern representatives of the Algonkian family.

Besides specific references to be mentioned later, general coverage of the area is to be found in a number of sources. Extensive information on both printed and manu-

[1] There is some overlap between this paper and an earlier paper on "Southeastern linguistics" (1971) which was presented at the 1970 meeting of the Southern Anthropological Society in Athens, Georgia.

script sources for materials known at the time of publication is to be found in Pilling's famous bibliographies of the Siouan languages (1887), of the Iroquoian languages (1888), of the Muskogean languages (1889), and of the Algonkian languages (1891). More recent coverage of printed materials, including ethnographic as well as linguistic items, can be gleaned from Murdock's *Ethnographic bibliography of North America* (1960). Manuscript materials in the collections of the American Philosophical Society are listed in Freeman and Smith (1966). Special bibliographies which should also be consulted are "A guide to source material on extinct North American Indian languages" by Croft (1948), "A selected bibliography of comparative American Indian linguistics" by Loriot (1964), and "Contributions to a bibliography of comparative Amerindian" by Hoijer, Hamp, and Bright (1966).

Various of Swanton's monographs cover the history and general ethnography of the several tribes of the Southeast, particularly, *Indian tribes of the lower Mississippi Valley and adjacent coast of the Gulf of Mexico* (1911), and *The Indians of the Southeastern United States* (1946). A recently translated book, Berlandier's *The Indians of Texas in 1830*, edited by John C. Ewers (1969), gives a good description showing that many Southeastern Indians had moved to Texas by the early nineteenth century. Grant Foreman's books on the more recent history of some of these peoples are also noteworthy, especially *Indian removal* (1932) and *The five civilized tribes* (1934).

1. DESCRIPTIVE MATERIALS

1.1 *The Muskogean Family*

The extant Muskogean languages are Choctaw and Chickasaw (originally in Mississippi, Alabama, and eastern Louisiana), Alabama and Koasati (Alabama), Hitchiti and Mikasuki (southern Alabama and Florida), and Creek or Muskogee (Alabama Georgia, and Tennessee). The extinct Apalachee (Florida) was also of this family. Since many of these tribes were forced to relocate during the great Indian removal in 1836–40 (Foreman 1932), their present location needs separate mention. Choctaw, Chickasaw, Creek, and Seminole are now spoken in eastern Oklahoma (formerly Indian Territory) in the areas of the old Indian Nations bearing their respective names. Choctaw is also spoken by a large group living in eastern Mississippi and smaller groups in Louisiana, while Seminole is spoken by a large part of the Seminole Indians of Florida. Mikasuki is spoken by a few individuals living in the Seminole Nation (Oklahoma), but the majority of the speakers comprise a part of the Florida Seminoles. Alabama and Koasati are spoken in eastern Texas and western Louisiana, respectively, and Hitchiti, virtually, if not actually, extinct, was still remembered thirty years ago by a few individuals living in the Seminole Nation.

Of the several languages mentioned above, not all merit the rank of a separate 'language'. Choctaw and Chickasaw are actually subvarieties of the same language —

in other words, Chickasaw is one of several Choctaw dialects — but the political separation of the two tribes is very ancient. Hitchiti and Mikasuki are also similarly related and the same is true of Creek and Seminole.

There are not many sources in which all or most of these languages are treated together on a descriptive basis. The presence of differences between men's and women's speech in Koasati, Hitchiti, and Creek is described by Mary R. Haas (1944). Noun incorporation in Muskogee (Creek), Koasati, Hitchiti, and Choctaw is discussed in Haas (1941d). John R. Swanton presents, in translation, a number of animal stories told by the various tribes of the Muskogean family (1913) and a larger collection of myths and tales of the Creek, Hitchiti, Alabama, and Koasati, as well as Natchez, who are not, strictly speaking, Muskogean (1929). Other items which treat the family as a whole tend to be of a comparative or classificatory nature. These will be discussed in a later section.

### 1.1.1 *Choctaw and Chickasaw*

Cyrus A. Byington, a missionary to the Choctaw in the early part of the nineteenth century, has left us the most extensive materials available on their language, including translations of parts of the Bible as well as grammatical and lexical materials. His *Grammar*, edited by Daniel G. Brinton, appeared in 1870. His *Dictionary*, edited by John R. Swanton and Henry S. Halbert, did not become available until 1915. Swanton, in his editing of dictionaries (Haas 1969b), was prone to modify the orthography to conform to current usage even though this introduced considerable probability of error. In the case of the Choctaw his modifications were minimal but, unfortunately, the one change he made in the consonants (the substitution of ł for hl everywhere) removed an ambiguity that should have remained. Choctaw does have the voiceless lateral spirant [ł] but it also has medial clusters of h + l. Many words have thus been mistranscribed, e.g. *mali* instead of the correct *mahli* 'wind'.

Some material on another dialect is provided in a monograph on *The Choctaw of Bayou Lacomb* (Bushnell 1909), and a description of an anonymous manuscript on a dialect in Southwest Louisiana is given by William A. Read (1940). Choctaw kinship terms appear in Lewis Henry Morgan (1871) and in Swanton (1931), and Fred Eggan (1940) discusses "Historical changes in the Choctaw kinship system" induced by changing cultural patterns under white influence. Choctaw music has been treated by Frances Densmore (1943a). Other facets of Choctaw culture are taken up by Swanton in "Source material for the social and ceremonial life of the Choctaw Indians" (1931).

In the late 1930s Haas collected brief vocabularies of a Louisiana dialect (Glenmora, La.) and of an Oklahoma dialect (Quinton, Okla.). Important recent work is that of T. Dale Nicklas, who, on the basis of several months' fieldwork in southeastern Oklahoma in 1967-68, is writing a modern grammar of Choctaw.

Albert S. Gatschet collected some Chickasaw words and phrases in 1889-90 (BAE Mss. 588-a and 588-b). A few words from an earlier collection are to be found in his

*A migration legend of the Creek Indians* (1884:56, 96). Frank G. Speck provided "Notes on Chickasaw ethnology and folk-lore" in 1907(b), but the most extensive treatment of Chickasaw ethnography is Swanton's "Social and religious beliefs of the Chickasaw Indians" (1928b).

In the spring of 1970 William Pulte presented a paper on "The position of Chickasaw in Western Muskogean" in which he illustrated some of the lexical and phonological differences between Choctaw and Chickasaw. Some of the same lexical differences were reported on by Gatschet (1884:96) and this means that Chickasaw is maintaining its distinctness — even though this is slight — from Choctaw. The Chickasaw Council has prepared a small dictionary of their language, using Byington's orthography, which they expect to publish soon.

### 1.1.2 *Apalachee*

Apalachee is extinct and probably died out early in the eighteenth century. About all that we have of the language is contained in a letter in the Spanish and Apalachee languages, written to be transmitted to King Charles II and dates January 21, 1688 (Swanton 1922:120). A facsimile is found in Buckingham Smith (1860a) and a part was published (Smith 1860b). Gatschet says that 'other documents written in Apalachi are preserved in the archives of Havana, the seat of the archbishoporic, to which Apalachi and all the other settlements comprised within the diocese of St. Helena belonged' (1884:76). Pilling adds, 'Mr. Gatschet informs me further that M. Pinart [a well-known collector of American Indian vocabularies] saw these documents at Havana; but their nature I am unable to learn' (1889:3).

Apalachee has long been known to be a Muskogean language, but its closest affiliations were for a time in doubt. Gatschet (1884:74) thought it might be closest to Hitchiti, probably because the Creeks held that their town known as Apalachicola had formerly been Hitchiti-speaking. Finally, in "The position of Apalachee in the Muskogean family" (1949), Haas demonstrated that it belongs in the Eastern division of Muskogean on the basis of sound correspondences worked out for all the extant languages (Haas 1941a). In addition it was possible to show that it is probably most closely related to Alabama and Koasati, particularly on the basis of its method of verb inflection.

More information on Apalachee can still be gleaned from a more thoroughgoing analysis of the available material. This can best be done after more analytic work on Alabama and Koasati has been carried out.

### 1.1.3 *Alabama and Koasati*

Haas collected considerable grammatical and lexical material on Koasati in 1938, but most of this remains unpublished. Unlike other Muskogean languages which have only one conjugational class of verbs, Koasati (and probably also Alabama) has three, as described in "A proto-Muskogean paradigm" (Haas 1946b). It has also preserved clear distinctions between men's and women's speech (Haas 1944) while only traces of this remain in Creek, for example. Other lexical material is included in several papers on comparative Muskogean (Haas 1941a, 1947a, 1950a, 1956).

A variety of Koasati, containing quite a few lexical items from Alabama, is spoken by a few people living among the Alabama in Texas and is accordingly known as Texas Koasati. Haas recorded a brief vocabulary of this in 1934. Haas and Morris Swadesh also recorded vocabularies of Louisiana Koasati and of Alabama at the same time (see item 1890 in Freeman and Smith, 1966).

Swanton acquired the services of an Alabama speaker, Harden Sylestine, to record a very full vocabulary of his language. This material remains in the BAE archives. There are a number of inconsistencies in orthography, some of which can probably not be straightened out without reelicitation, but the work contains much useful material. Quite recently Earl Rand (1968) has published a phonemic analysis of Alabama. Densmore has published on "The Alabama Indians and their music" (1937), while the folklore of the two tribes is given in translation by Swanton in *Myths and tales of the Southeastern Indians* (1929c) and more recently in H.N. Martin's *Folktales of the Alabama-Coushatta Indians* (1946).

## 1.1.4 Hitchiti and Mikasuki

On the basis of a few days' work with a speaker of Hitchiti in 1937, Haas prepared a manuscript containing Hitichiti notes and vocabulary (n.d., c. 1938–40). Some of her material on Hitchiti verb inflection appeared in "A proto-Muskogean paradigm" (1946b). Mikasuki, which is only dialectally different from Hitchiti, has been worked on quite extensively by William C. Sturtevant, who occasionally quotes some words in his articles (Sturtevant 1954, 1962). He has also published a list of Spanish loanwords in the language (1962:51). More recently David West has also worked extensively on the language and has published on the phonology (1962). More work remains to be done on the tonal accents which probably can be stated less redundantly in terms of certain key syllables, as in Creek (Haas 1940b:149–50).

Hitchiti was also one of the many languages worked on by Gatschet in the late nineteenth century. He published some lexical and grammatical material in *A migration legend of the Creek Indians* (1884:80–5) as well as text and lexical material in *Tchikilli's Kasi'hta legend in the Creek and Hitchiti languages* (1888a:163–211). An early vocabulary of Mikasuki was published by Buckingham Smith (1866). Swanton also collected materials on Hitchiti and prepared a sketch of the language which remains in manuscript in the BAE archives.

## 1.1.5 Creek and Seminole

Creek is also known as Muskogee (also spelled Muskokee, Maskogi, etc.) from the name /ma·sko·ki/ which the Creeks apply to themselves. Of all the Muskogean languages, this is the one that has received the most attention. In large part this is probably due to the fact that this was the chief language of the once powerful Creek Confederacy. Tribes of the Confederacy speaking other languages, both Muskogean (e.g., Alabama, Koasati, Hitchiti, and Mikasuki) and non-Muskogean (e.g. Yuchi), also learned to speak Creek and their languages have many Creek loanwords.

H. F. Buckner and G. Herrod published *A grammar of the Maskωke or Creek language* in 1860 and Brinton published "Contributions to a grammar of the Muskokee language" in 1870. Gatschet provided text material in *A migration legend of the Creek Indians* (1884:237–43) as well as grammatical notes (198–213), and he often referred to Creek in general linguistic articles. Additional text material is in *Tchikilli's Kasi'hta legend in the Creek and Hitchiti languages* (Gatschet 1888a).

A dictionary of Creek by Robert McGill Loughridge and David M. Hodge (English-Muskokee and Muskokee-English) appeared in 1890 and was reprinted in 1914. Under missionary influence the Creeks had adopted an alphabet for their language and many Indians were thus enabled to read and write their language. In addition to Biblical translations and religious treatises, Creek articles were printed in newspapers and the Constitution and Laws of the Creek Nation was also published in this alphabet. The alphabet was entirely satisfactory for consonants since ordinary Roman letters could be used in their usual values for everything except [ł] and [č]. For these last, the otherwise unneeded letter r was used for [ł] and c was used for [č]. The symbols for vowels, however, were troublesome (e.g. i for [ay]) and vowel length was inconsistently and inadequately indicated in spite of its great importance. Tonal accents were also not indicated. It is this alphabet that is used in the Loughridge and Hodge dictionary.

During field trips in 1936, 1937, and 1938–39 Haas collected extensive materials on the grammar, texts, and lexicon of Creek. Very little of this material has been published. However, a Creek vocabulary was prepared (n.d., c. 1938–40) and several articles on phonology and grammar have appeared. These include "Geminate consonant clusters in Muskogee" (1938), "Ablaut and its function in Muskogee [with an appendix on the phonemes]" (1940b), "A popular etymology in Muskogee "(1941b), "Noun incorporation in the Muskogean languages" (1941d), and "Classificatory verbs in Muskogee" (1948). The formerly existing distinction between men's and women's speech has now disappeared in Creek but a few traces of earlier special usage by women appears in certain tales. This is described, along with the much fuller material on Koasati, in "Men's and women's speech in Koasati" (1944). Some material on Creek verb inflection appears in "A proto-Muskogean paradigm" (1946b). Creek avoidance of certain words in their own language which bear some phonetic resemblance to English 'four-letter' words is discussed in "Interlingual word taboos" (1951b:338) along with similar examples from other parts of the world. The original dialect boundaries were seriously disturbed by the removal, but many dialect differences still remain and some of these are described in "Dialects of the Muskogee language" (1945). Although Creek contact with the Spanish was very early — in the sixteenth century, in fact — there are some Spanish loanwords in Creek which probably go back to this early period, as Sturtevant shows in "Spanish-Indian relations in southeastern North America" (1962:50–4). Some place names have been treated by William A. Read in "Indian place-names in Alabama" (1937) and "Indian stream-names in Georgia" (1949), but some of the etymologies are dubious.

There is an extensive historical and ethnographic literature, including Swanton's *Early history of the Creek Indians and their neighbors* (1922), "Social organization and social usages of the Indians of the Creek Confederacy" (1928a), "Religious beliefs and medical practices of the Creek Indians" (1928b); Speck's "The Creek Indians of Taskigi town" (1907c), "Ceremonial songs of the Creek and Yuchi Indians" (1911); and Haas's "Creek inter-town relations" (1940c).

Seminole is one of the dialects of Creek and not much has been written about it separately. Actually, the Seminole Indians are partly Creek-speaking and partly Mikasuki-speaking, but the term 'Seminole' used in referring to a language generally refers to Creek. The word is from Creek *simaló·ni ~ simanó·li* which in turn is borrowed from Spanish *cimarrón*. An early vocabulary appeared in "Comparative vocabularies of the Seminole and Mikasuki tongues" (B. Smith 1866). There is considerable ethnographic literature, including Clay MacCawley's "The Seminole Indians of Florida" (1887), Alexander Spoehr's "Camp, clan, and kin among the Cow Creek Seminole" (1941) and "The kinship system of the Seminole" (1942), and Sturtevant's "The medicine bundles and busks of the Florida Seminole" (1954). R. F. Greenlee has provided a few "Folktales of the Florida Seminole" (1945) and Read has written on "Florida place names of Indian origin and Seminole personal names" (1934). Sturtevant has collected vocabulary materials among the Florida Seminole and Haas among the Oklahoma Seminole. Some of the latter material is quoted in various comparative papers which are taken up later.

### 1.2 *Natchez*

Natchez is one of several language isolates in the Southeast. Although it is a distant relative of the Muskogean languages, it may not be any closer to them than, say, Tunica is. Its position is often misunderstood in the general literature (e.g., in dictionaries and textbooks) and it is frequently incorrectly named as a Muskogean language alongside Choctaw, Alabama, etc., especially since 1924 when Swanton published "The Muskhogean connection of the Natchez language". But Swanton himself seems always to have been clear about the distance of the relationship, for he says, 'One of the interesting points brought out in this investigation is the fact that the languages [Natchez and the Muskogean languages] may be related although on first inspection they show few resemblances' (1924:47). In another publication he points out (1946:239):

> The Natchez of western Mississippi, and the Taensa and Avoyel [languages on which we have no certain information], two smaller peoples in neighboring parts of Louisiana, constituted a widely varying branch of this [the Muskogean] stock which probably extended at one time over much more territory toward the north.

It would be more accurate to say that Natchez was one branch and the Muskogean languages were another branch of the Natchez-Muskogean stock. Moreover, in terms of a Gulf stock, (Haas 1951a), Natchez is considered one of five branches: Muskogean, Natchez, Tunica, Chitimacha, and Atakapa.

The Natchez Indians had the highest culture of any Indians north of Mexico but their numbers were unfortunately seriously depleted in the wars with the French and with other Indians in the eighteenth century. After this time remnant groups appear to have taken refuge among the Creek and the Cherokee. Swanton has brought together from several early sources much information about their culture and early history in *Indian tribes of the Lower Mississippi Valley and adjacent coast of the Gulf of Mexico* (1911:45–257). Vocabularies appear in the early literature (e.g. Gallatin 1848) and Brinton published "On the language of the Natchez" in 1873.

In 1907 Swanton found a few speakers living in the old Cherokee Nation (Oklahoma). He collected a large amount of linguistic material and prepared a grammatical sketch which remains in manuscript in the BAE Archives. He published translations of the texts he collected in his monograph *Myths and tales of the Southeastern Indians* (1929c:214–66). In 1936 only two of the speakers discovered by Swanton remained and Haas collected extensive grammatical, text, and lexical materials from them. Most of this material remains unpublished. A list of Natchez phonemes, some grammatical remarks, and a number of lexical items appear in "Natchez and the Muskogean languages" (1956) and the kinship terms are presented in "Natchez and Chitimacha clans and kinship terminology" (1939). Additional vocabulary items appear in some other papers concerned with more distant relationships (Haas 1951a, 1952, 1958a, 1959, 1960).

## 1.3 *Tunica*

Tunica, like Natchez, is a language isolate. Discussion of its possible distant relatives is taken up in a separate section. No linguistic information was available until 1886 when Gatschet collected a sizable body of material in Louisiana. Gatschet published some information in "Sex-denoting nouns in American languages" (1889) having discovered that Tunica is one of a very few American Indian languages to have sex gender distinctions in its grammar. Another unexpected feature was the presence of both /l/ and /r/ as distinct phonemes. Many years later Swanton checked Gatschet's materials and collected more on his own. The grammatical information was then presented in a paper on "The Tunica language" (1921). He also provides some information on the history and culture of the tribe in *Indian tribes of the Lower Mississippi Valley ...* (1911:306–26). He includes here some information on mythology with translations of parts of two or three myths.

Haas undertook fieldwork with the last remaining speaker in 1933 and made four return visits between then and 1939. In many respects this speaker appears to have had a very much better knowledge of the language than informants used by Gatschet and Swanton. All of the linguistic material collected by Haas has been published.

This includes a grammar, *Tunica* (1940a), "A grammatical sketch of Tunica" (1946a), *Tunica texts* (1950b), and, finally, *Tunica dictionary* (Tunica-English and English-Tunica) (1953). The latter contains words from the unpublished Gatschet-Swanton Vocabulary, especially those which could not be reelicited from the last speaker (1953:179–81). A study of "Some French loan-words in Tunica" has also been published (1947b). Implications of the solar myth are discussed in "The solar deity of the Tunica" (1942).

## 1.4 Chitimacha

Chitimacha is a language isolate of southern Louisiana. In some ways it stands out as being rather different from other languages of the area. For example, it is the only southeastern language except Yuchi to have a glottalized series of consonants. (Unlike some Siouan languages lying outside the Southeast, those in the Southeast are not known to have had a glottalized series.) In other respects, however, it bears certain similarities to its neighbors.

The chief workers on the language have been Gatschet, Swanton, and Swadesh. Gatschet reported on the tribe in "The Shetimasha Indians of St. Mary's Parish, in southern Louisiana" (1883). The most extensive treatment of the history and culture of the tribe is in Swanton's *Indian tribes of the lower Mississippi Valley* ... (1911:337–60). He also wrote about them in "Mythology of the Indians of Louisiana and the Texas coast" (1907b) and in "Some Chitimacha myths and beliefs" (1917b). Densmore has written about "A search for songs among the Chitimacha Indians in Louisiana" (1943b) and includes a few stories told to her in English.

Beginning in 1932 and on two or three followup visits, Swadesh collected extensive materials on the grammar, texts, and lexicon of this language. All of this has been written up in manuscript form and is to be found in the collections of the American Philosophical Society (732 in Freeman and Smith 1966). Swadesh's important theoretical article on "The phonemic principle" (1934a) was largely prompted by the problems he encountered in working out a phonemic analysis of Chitimacha. The specific results of the analysis as applied to Chitimacha were, however, reported separately in "The phonetics of Chitimacha" (1934b). Another early article was "Chitimacha verbs of derogatory or abusive connotation" (1933) which contains considerable material on linguistic usage not to be found in his other works. Although the full grammar remains unpublished, "Chitimacha" (1946a) is an excellent grammatical sketch of the language. Haas gives the kinship terminology, on the basis of material provided by Swadesh, in "Natchez and Chitimacha clans and kinship terminology" (1939). Various vocabulary items have appared in comparative articles by Toomey (1914), Swanton (1919), Swadesh (1946b, 1947), Haas (1951a, 1952, 1958a, 1959, 1960), and Gursky (1968, 1969).

### 1.5 *Atakapa*

Atakapa is a Choctaw word meaning 'man-eater' and was probably applied to more than one tribe of western Louisiana and eastern Texas before it became attached to a particular tribe from which a vocabulary had been obtained. Although there were at least three dialects of Atakapa, their divergence is not great and together they constitute a single language isolate. The most extensive material is on the Western dialect and was collected by Gatschet in 1885. The Eastern dialect is the most divergent and is known from a vocabulary recorded (or perhaps copied) by Martin Duralde in 1802 (422 in Freeman and Smith 1966), a part of which was printed in Gallatin (1836). Although Akokisa was the last dialect to become known, it was the earliest recorded and was reported on by M. de Villiers du Terrage and Paul Rivet in "Les Indiens du Texas et les expéditions françaises de 1720 et 1721" (1919).

Since the material on the Western dialect as recorded by Gatschet was the most extensive it formed the basis for Swanton's "A sketch of the Atakapa language" (1929a). All of the available material, including a few texts, was brought together in *A dictionary of the Atakapa language* by Gatschet and Swanton (1932). Swanton also provides a little historical and cultural information in *Indian tribes of the lower Mississippi Valley* ... (1911:360–3). Lexical material quoted from the published sources appears in various comparative studies by Swanton (1919), Swadesh (1946b, 1947), Haas (1951a, 1958a, 1959, 1960), and Gursky (1968, 1969).

Atakapa seems to have died out around the turn of the twentieth century. Unlike what was done in the case of Tunica, Swanton was not able to obtain any new Atakapa material or to check over what Gatschet had obtained. In the fall of 1934 Haas and Swadesh attempted to discover whether any speakers of the language were left. Descendants of former speakers were located but their knowledge of the language was limited to a few fragments (423 in Freeman and Smith 1966). Fortunately, there is considerable illustrative material in *A dictionary of the Atakapa language* and this could profitably be subjected to reanalysis. If properly done this would provide a better understanding of the material that is available. In general the problems encountered in using this dictionary are similar to those that have recently been described by Haas (1969b) in regard to the proper use of the Biloxi and Ofo dictionaries (Dorsey and Swanton 1912).

### 1.6 *Timucua*

The earliest texts and grammatical materials on any language of the Southeast were prepared on the Timucua language of central and northern Florida at the beginning of the seventeenth century.[2] These were the work of Francisco Pareja. His *Cathecismo*

---

[2] As far as is known these are the earliest text materials. Vocabulary notes on Powhatan appear a little earlier, for a few words of the language were written down late in the sixteenth century by John White. See the section on Powhatan and Pamlico below.

and *Confessionario* were published in 1612 and 1613, respectively, in Mexico City. His *Arte de la lengua timuquana, compuesta en 1614* was edited by Lucien Adam and Julien Vinson and published in Paris in 1886. Other early works are the writings on Christian doctrine in Timucua by Gregorio de Moville (Granberry 1956:98) and a letter composed on January 28, 1688 to be transmitted to Charles II of Spain (Smith 1860a).

A great deal has been written on the Timucua language since the seventeenth century but all of it is based on these early sources. Gatschet wrote "Volk und sprache der Timucua" (1877), "The Timucua language" (1877–80), and, with Raoul La Grasserie, "Textes timucua" (1889). La Grasserie wrote "Esquisse d'une grammaire du timucua, langue de la Floride" (n.d.), "Textes analysés et vocabulaire de la langue timucua" (1890), and "Vocabulaire timucua" (1892). Vinson published a brief paper "Sur la langue timucua" in 1885.

"Terms of relationship in Timucua" was published in 1916 by Swanton. He also wrote an important paper on Tawasa (1929b), which is one of the Timucuan dialects. In addition he had prepared an extensive file of Timucua words from all available sources and this remains in the BAE Archives. Julian Granberry made a significant start toward the preparation of a modern treatment of the language in "Timucua I: Prosodies and phonemics of the Mocama dialect" (1956), but nothing more has appeared since that time. He also provides a list of dialects (99). Vocabulary items from the printed sources appear in various comparative studies, e.g. Swanton (1929b), Haas (1951a), Swadesh (1964).

### 1.7 Representatives of the Siouan Family

Except for the Catawba, Siouan-speaking tribes in the Southeast were always small in numbers and much of what we know of the languages is by lucky accident. Biloxi, Ofo, and Tutelo comprise a subgroup of the Siouan family known as Ohio Valley Siouan (Voegelin 1941b) or Southeastern Siouan (Haas 1968:84). There has been debate about Catawba, but the best arguments for including it in the Siouan family have been presented by Siebert (1945). Moreover, all agree that it comprises a separate branch (perhaps even on the level of Catawba-Siouan) and that it is not a member of the Ohio Valley or Southeastern subgroup.

There were probably still other small Siouan tribes in the Southeast (e.g. Swanton 1923b; Sturtevant 1958), but there is true linguistic evidence for only one of these, Woccon. A vocabulary of about 140 items was first published by John Lawson (1937) in 1709 (also given by Gallatin 1836). It seems to have been closest to Catawba, but Sturtevant, who has examined manuscript comparisons made by earlier workers, states that it is 'evident that they are far from being dialects of the same language' (1958:741). In 1957 Carl F. Miller reopened debate on the problem of whether or not languages in the Southeast said to be Siouan are in fact Siouan. Sturtevant (1958) effectively answers that wherever we have actual linguistic materials, as we do for the four languages mentioned above, linguists are not in any doubt whatever about the presence of Siouan languages in the Southeast. Part of the problem arises from the fact that the presence of Siouan languages in the Southeast was so very late in being recognized, as is shown in the following discussion of the separate languages.

1.7.1 *Tutelo*

Tutelo was the first language of the Southeastern branch to be identified as Siouan. The most extensive materials that we have were obtained by Horatio Hale and presented in "The Tutelo tribe and language" (1883b). Although the language was originally spoken in Virginia, he obtained his information from a few Indians living among the Iroquois of the Six Nations Reserve in Ontario. Twenty years later only a few words and phrases were still remembered there, as reported by Edward Sapir (1913a) and Leo J. Frachtenberg (1913). The identification of Tutelo as Siouan came as a surprise, because the Tutelo tribe had been known for some time. However, because actual linguistic material was lacking, it was classified on the basis of circumstantial evidence, namely presence on the Six Nations Reserve, as being Iroquoian. It should be emphasized that from the beginning, Hale's evidence was sufficient to establish its Siouan affinity.

1.7.2 *Biloxi*

The Biloxi, when first encountered, were living along the Gulf of Mexico near the modern city that bears their name. In 1886 Gatschet discovered a few speakers living in Louisiana and for the first time secured some actual linguistic material. This, too, occasioned surprise, for this language was also clearly of Siouan affiliation. James Owen Dorsey, well versed in other Siouan languages, undertook the task of collecting more material on Biloxi and in 1893 (a) published "The Biloxi Indians of Louisiana". Much lexical and text material remained unpublished at the time of his death. Swanton assumed responsibility for this and the result was *A dictionary of the Biloxi and Ofo languages, accompanied with thirty-one Biloxi texts and numerous Biloxi phrases* (Dorsey and Swanton 1912). For a discussion of the way to make the best use of this material, see "Swanton and the Biloxi and Ofo dictionaries" (Haas 1969c).

Dorsey also published "Two Biloxi tales" (1893b) and K. W. Porter wrote "A legend of the Biloxi" (1946). In the introduction to *Tunica texts* Haas discusses the similarity between the thunder myths of the Biloxi and the Tunica (1950b: 2–3).

It is possible that even after Dorsey's work more material on the language could have been obtained from other speakers scattered in various parts of Louisiana and East Texas, but nothing was done. In 1934 Haas and Swadesh found a single speaker from whom a brief vocabulary could still be extracted. This has been analyzed and compared with the same material in Dorsey and Swanton (Haas 1968). Choctaw and other loanwords into Biloxi are discussed in the same article (81–3). Biloxi lexical materials quoted from printed sources are also to be found in various comparative studies by Charles F. Voegelin (1939), Nils Holmer (1947), Hans Wolff (1950–51),

G. Hubert Matthews (1958, 1959, 1970), Wallace L. Chafe (1964), and Haas (1968, 1969c).

### 1.7.3 *Ofo*

Ofo was the last Southeastern Siouan language to be discovered. The tribe had long been known by name but it was usually assumed that their language was of Muskogean affiliation. Swanton found a Tunica Indian who recalled a single word of their language and since the word began with /f/, this was thought to clinch the matter since this is such a common sound in Muskogean languages. Later on Swanton found a speaker of the language and, to his own surprise as well as others, Ofo turned out to be incontrovertably Siouan, as he reported in "A new Siouan dialect" (1909). All of the material that he was able to collect was published in the same volume with the Dorsey material on Biloxi (Dorsey and Swanton 1912). Swanton emphasized the presence of heavily aspirated consonants in Ofo, but this has usually been overlooked by recent Siouanists who have rewritten the forms without indicating the aspiration. This is a mistake, as is shown in "Swanton and the Biloxi and Ofo dictionaries" (Haas 1969c: 289-90). Nils Holmer had also earlier pointed out the importance of Ofo aspiration in "An Ofo phonetic law" (1947:2, footnote 3). Probable Tunica and Muskogean loanwords in Ofo are discussed in "The last words of Biloxi" (Haas 1968:82-3). Ofo lexical materials, frequently in changed orthography eliminating, among other things, aspiration, are quoted in many comparative studies, e.g., by Voegelin, Holmer, Wolff, Matthews, Chafe, and Haas, as shown above for Biloxi.

### 1.7.4 *Catawba*

Frank T. Siebert, Jr., gives a fine thumbnail history of attempts to record and place the Catawba language genetically (1945:100-1). Benjamin Smith Barton gives the earliest vocabulary in "New views of the origin of the tribes and nations of America" (1797). Gallatin (1836) published a vocabulary collected by J.L. Miller, and O.M. Lieber published another vocabulary in 1856. More serious work was finally undertaken by Gatschet in 1881 but only a part of his material, "A grammatic sketch of the Catawba language" (1900), has been published. Frank G. Speck, a devoted student of their culture and language, published many ethnographic papers. In 1928 he wrote about "Recording the Catawba language", issued a volume of texts in 1934, and discussed a single text in 1946. With Claude E. Schaeffer he also published "Catawba kinship and social organization with a resume of Tutelo kinship terms" (1942). The remainder of his linguistic materials are in the collection of the American Philosophical Society (546, 547, and 548 in Freeman and Smith 1966).

Since the late 1930s several linguists have worked on the language but very little of this material has been published. Swadesh was one of the collectors and he speaks of this in "Sociologic notes on obsolescent languages" (1948). His notes are also in the collection of the American Philosophical Society (551 in Freeman and Smith 1966). Raven I. McDavid has collected extensive materials and copies of these are in the possession of Haas and of James M. Crawford of the University of Georgia. The most detailed collection of material is that taken down by Siebert but he has published nothing since his excellent paper on "Linguistic classification of the Catawba", in two parts, appeared in 1945. He still has firm plans to write up his materials in due course (p.c.).

A.L. Pickens has made a study of Indian place names in upper South Carolina (1937, 1938) and has also collected zoological nomenclature among the Catawba (1954, 1957). Some Catawba text material by G. Hubert Matthews and Red Thunder Cloud has appeared recently (1967).

### 1.8 *Yuchi*

Yuchi is a language isolate which is usually thought to belong in a larger stock known as Siouan-Yuchi (Sapir 1929). The language is phonologically far more elaborate than other languages in the Southeast, having unaspirated, aspirated, and glottalized stops, plain and glottalized spirants, and plain and glottalized sonorants (Haas, unpublished fieldnotes of 1938). In some of these respects it is more similar (whether for genetic or earlier contact reasons, or both) to Dakota, a Siouan language of the Plains, than to any of the surrounding languages in the Southeast (Haas 1969a: 90–1). Whatever the more remote connections of the Yuchi may have been, they are known to have become affiliated with the Creeks in the Creek Confederacy by the eighteenth century. Their speech is entirely un-Muskogean and the Creeks often comment on its strangeness. Consequently, the Yuchi had to learn Creek and bilingualism was common among them. Now, of course, many are trilingual since English has been added as a third language.

Little was done on the Yuchi language before the twentieth century. Gatschet did some work but did not publish much beyond "Some mythic stories of the Yuchi Indians" (1893). In 1904, 1905, and 1908 Speck undertook fieldwork on the language and culture of these people and published a monograph on "Ethnology of the Yuchi Indians" (1909). There is a brief description of the language (15–17) without examples but Yuchi words are scattered throughout the rest of the book. There is now only one dialect though at one time there may have been two (15). Other publications by Speck include "Ceremonial songs of the Creek and Yuchi Indians" (1911) and some remarks on changes in the kinship system (1939b).

The most extensive linguistic work to date is that done by Günter Wagner who has published a collection of texts, *Yuchi tales* (1931), and a grammar (1933). A few years later Hans Wolff also collected linguistic material and published "Yuchi phonemes and morphemes, with special reference to person markers" (1948) and a text with analysis (1951). In 1950 Émile Benveniste published a careful study of "La négation en Yuchi" based on Wagner's text materials. There are still many speakers of Yuchi living in the old Creek Nation in Oklahoma. In the summer of 1970 James M. Crawford began a new intensive study of the language, and we can expect a new grammatical treatment with texts and dictionary in due course.

### 1.9 *Representatives of the Iroquoian Family*

There were at least two representatives of the Iroquoian family residing in the Southeast, the Cherokee and the Tuscarora. Cherokee constitutes 'a lone southern branch' while Tuscarora is more closely allied with the northern languages (Lounsbury 1961).

#### 1.9.1 *Cherokee*

An early grammar of Cherokee is that by John Pickering (1830)[3] who hoped also to have devised an alphabet that the Cherokee would use. This hope was dashed by Sequoya's invention of the Cherokee syllabary (around 1821) which was soon learned and widely used by the Indians (Mooney 1900:109–12 with a plate showing the syllabary opposite to 112).[4] Many Cherokee became literate in their own language almost overnight and used their writing system to write letters and manuscripts and to print books and newspapers. The *Cherokee Phoenix* (1828–34) was the earliest Indian newspaper. In a famous article by Alfred L. Kroeber (1940:2–4) Sequoya's invention has been described as an outstanding case of 'stimulus diffusion' since he had no knowledge of English or the value of the letters of the Roman alphabet; instead he simply used them in his own way and ascribed to them values unrelated to anything in English.

Mooney's *Myths of the Cherokee* (1900) is an extensive body of material in translation (3–427) and includes also a glossary (506–48). This comprises only a part of a much more extensive collection made by Mooney which included 'original Cherokee manuscripts, relating to the history, archeology, geographic nomenclature, personal names, botany, medicine, arts, home life, religion, songs, ceremonies, and language of the tribe' (11). Some of this material has since been published in transcription and translation, particularly in Mooney and Olbrechts (1932) and in several works by Jack Frederick Kilpatrick and Anna Gritts Kilpatrick (e.g. A.G. Kilpatrick and J.F. Kilpatrick 1966; J.F Kilpatrick 1966; J.F. Kilpatrick and A.G. Kilpatrick 1966). The Kilpatricks use a special transcription 'devised by Floyd G. Lounsbury and Jack Frederick Kilpatrick in March 1963' (A.G. Kilpatrick and J.F. Kilpatrick 1966: 9). Speck has also published "Some Eastern Cherokee texts" (1927). William Harlen Gilbert, Jr., has published an ethnographic monograph, "The Eastern Cherokee" (1943), and Speck and L. Bloom have published on "Cherokee dance and drama" (1951).

Recent works on the grammar of Cherokee include "The phonemes of North Carolina Cherokee" by Ernest Bender and Zellig S. Harris (1946), "Cherokee II" by Bender (1949), and a study of "Cherokee verb morphology", in three parts, by William

---

[3] This has been reprinted by John R. Kreuger, 1963.
[4] A more recent reproduction of the Cherokee syllabary is to be found in John K. White 1962:512.

D. Reyburn (1953-54). Haas gives a list of Cherokee classificatory verbs (1948:24) and some comments on loanwords between Creek and Cherokee (1961:22 and 1969a: 81).[5] Sturtevant has pointed out a couple of Spanish loans in Cherokee (1962:54). Other materials on the language have been collected by Haas, Lounsbury, Chafe, and, most recently, William H. Cook. Materials in the collection of the American Philosophical Society include those of Harris (661 in Freeman and Smith 1966), Olbrechts (681, 683 in Freeman and Smith), and Reyburn (684, 685 in Freeman and Smith).

### 1.9.2 *Tuscarora*

The amount of material available on Tuscarora is regretably very small. George Catlin published an early vocabulary (1841:262-5). Frans M. Olbrechts made an extensive collection in 1928 (3804-14 in Freeman and Smith 1966) but published only "De pronominale prefixen in het Tuscarora" (1929). Later on William D. Reyburn collected some material (3815, 3816 in Freeman and Smith) and Anthony F.C. Wallace also collected linguistic materials in connection with other kinds of investigation (3819, 3820 in Freeman and Smith). In 1951 Wallace and Reyburn collaborated on a text, "Crossing the ice: A migration legend of the Tuscarora Indians". A recent paper on "The phonology of Tuscarora" (1967) is by Joan Gleason Fickett. Floyd G. Lounsbury has also collected materials; a few words appear in Lounsbury (1961).

## 1.10 *Representatives of the Algonkian Family*

Algonkian is now known to be the most widespread linguistic family of North America. Except for the important Iroquoian enclave in the Great Lakes region, it stretched with little interruption from the Rocky Mountains to the Atlantic Ocean and from Labrador to Pamlico Sound. However, it was only weakly represented in the Southeast. Shawnee is the only extant language known to have been spoken there and its intrusion is held to be post-Columbian. All other representatives of the family in this area are extinct. There may have been several Algonkian languages in Virginia and Carolina but information on only two has come down to us.

### 1.10.1 *Powhatan and Pamlico*

John White, who visited Virginia in the period 1587-90, left us a set of beautiful watercolors of Virginia birds and fishes (Hulton and Quinn 1964) which also contained, in some cases, the Virginia Indian (Powhatan) names. The famous vocabulary

---

[5] For example, the Creek word *acína* 'cedar' may very well be a borrowing from Cherokee *atsina*. The Hitchiti have in turn borrowed their word *acin-i* (*-i*, noun suffix) from Creek. In other cases the direction of borrowing is much less certain. The word for 'buffalo' is similar in many Southeastern languages, regardless of genetic boundaries, viz., Creek *yanása* (also Choctaw *yaniš*, Alabama-Koasati *yanasa*, Hitchiti *yanas-i*), Cherokee *yahnsə*, Natchez *yanasah*, and Tunica *yániši* (Haas 1969a:81-2). What is clearly the same word occurs also in some of the Caddoan languages, e.g. Caddo *tánaha* (Allan R. Taylor, 1963, "Comparative Caddoan", *IJAL* 29:120).

of Captain John Smith was published in 1612. Another vocabulary of the same period, that of William Strachey, did not appear until 1849 when a copy (not the original) of his manuscript on "Historie of Travaile into Virginia Britannia ..." was issued by the Hakluyt Society. A little over a century later, John P. Harrington, recognizing the importance of the original vocabulary over a copy, published "The original Strachey vocabulary of the Virginia Indian language" (1955). By far the most commendable thing about this effort of Harrington's is that he provides a facsimile of the original as well as his own reading of the vocabulary. This enables the reader to make his own interpretation of the original, a very important advantage since there are, in fact, a great many misreadings.[6] James A. Geary has made a careful analysis of the Hakluyt Society's version in "Strachey's vocabulary of Indian words used in Virginia, 1612" (1953) and has concluded that more than one dialect is represented. A task that remains to be done is to compare Harrington's facsimile with the Hakluyt Society's version in order to throw new light on several doubtful points noted by Geary. Geary has also contributed "The language of the Carolina Algonkian tribes" (1955) based on a study of several early vocabularies. Speck has written "Chapters on the ethnology of the Powhatan tribes" (1928b) and a paper on "The ethnic position of the South-eastern Algonkian" (1924). Sturtevant has made a special study of "John White's contribution to ethnology" (1964).

J. Garland Pollard reprints the Pamlico (Pamticough) vocabulary collected by Lawson (1709) in "The Pamunkey Indians of Virginia" (1894).

1.10.2 *Shawnee*

The Shawnee language has been well-studied in recent times, especially by Charles F. Voegelin. He has written papers on "Shawnee phonemes" (1935), "Productive paradigms in Shawnee" (1936), and presentations of texts (1953; and with Robinett and Hickerson, 1953). By far his most important work is *Shawnee stems and the Jacob P. Dunn Miami dictionary* (1937–40) which is one of the best dictionaries available on an Algonkian language. However, a grammar and a full set of texts are still very much needed. In connection with Voegelin's work on Shawnee stems, Benjamin L. Whorf wrote a very interesting study of "Gestalt technique of stem composition in Shawnee" (1940). Working with taped material collected by Voegelin, Nancy P. Hickerson wrote "An acoustic analysis of Shawnee" as her doctoral dissertation (Indiana University) and much of this was published in a series of four papers (1958–59). Little work of this kind had previously been done on an American Indian language. Other papers will be mentioned in connection with a later section on comparative studies.

---

[6] For example, in place of Harrington's reading *Quautamu* 'to swallow', I read *Quantamū* which is from PA (proto-Algonkian) *$kwantamwa$ 'he swallows it'. In place of *vsquasenis* 'girls', I read *Vsquasenisoc*, which is derived from PA *$e\theta kwe\cdot w$- 'woman' (plus a diminutive suffix) and the animate plural suffix *-aki*. In place of *Racaioh* 'sand', I read *Racawh*, which is from PA *$le\cdot kawi$. Many other instances could be cited.

Much has been written about the history and culture of the Shawnee. A very thorough study of these people has been made by Erminie Wheeler Voegelin. Among other things, she has written papers on their agriculture and subsistence economy (1941), their musical instruments (1942), and their mortuary customs (1944), and, with C. F. Voegelin, papers on name groups (1935) and the female diety (1946). "The Shawnee musical style" (1953) is the subject of an important paper by Bruno Nettl.

## 2. UNCLASSIFIED LANGUAGES

The full extent of linguistic diversity in the Southeast may never be known. Names like Avoyel, Taensa, Koroa, Grigra, Yazoo, Tiou, Yamacraw, Yamasee, Ais, Tequesta, Calusa, and many, many others remain to haunt us. Even though some of these have been asserted to be the 'same as' or 'closely related to' other known languages, we can never be sure in any case where no vocabularies exist. In case after case, when identifications were made on the basis of circumstantial evidence or of the statements of travellers or missionaries, the information was found to be incorrect when actual linguistic material was finally obtained. After all, Ofo was thought to be Muskogean because a Tunica Indian recalled one word of the language which began with an /f/ and this was taken to be diagnostic; but when a full vocabulary was finally obtained it was seen to be incontrovertably Siouan (Swanton 1909; Dorsey and Swanton 1912). Similarly, the Tutelo were taken in by the 'Six Nations' who spoke Iroquoian languages and on this basis their language was also thought to be Iroquoian; but once more an actual vocabulary revealed that the language was indubitably Siouan (Hale 1883b). In both of these cases the result was totally surprising, since no Siouan peoples had been thought to live east of the Mississippi prior to Hale's discovery about Tutelo. But not all early mistakes were solved in favor of Siouan. Tawasa, for example, was said to be Muskogean (Swanton 1911:9), but the discovery of a vocabulary showed it to be a Timucuan dialect (Swanton 1929b). With so many misses — misses very wide of the mark —, it hardly behooves us to make any statements of affiliation or identification without linguistic documentation.

In one case, an even more exasperating problem exists. Taensa has been the subject of a grammar and vocabulary (Haumonté, Parisot, and Adam 1882) which is generally considered to be a hoax (Brinton 1890:452–67; Swanton 1911:10–13), though Gatschet attempted to defend a portion, though not all, of it (Gatschet 1888b, 1889). Perhaps the most damning evidence against the work is that the original manuscript (from which the copy that formed the basis of the publication was made) was never produced. An undisputably authentic vocabulary, if one ever turned up, is perhaps the only thing that could settle the matter completely. Swanton is convinced that the Taensa spoke a language which was the same as Natchez on the basis of statements made by early eighteenth century missionaries (1911:20–2). The dubious material on Taensa bears no resemblance to Natchez, but this does not help us in determining whether or not Taensa is or is not like Natchez as long as it remains dubious. At the same time, mere statements about sameness likewise do not help because there was also in existence a trade jargon, 'Mobilian', known to the tribes along the Mississippi and in much of the Southeast, and statements of identity could be in reference to the use of the jargon and not the tribal language. Another language said to be the same as or related to Natchez is Avoyel (or Avoyelles), but here again we do not know. The Avoyel were well known to the Tunica, who have even transmitted one of their myths in Tunica (Haas 1950b:18–21), but no words of their language have come down to us.

Koroa, Grigra, Yazoo, and Tiou are said to have been related to Tunica, but again we cannot be sure. The strongest evidence for this appears to be that Du Pratz, the early historian of Louisiana, maintained that all these languages had an /r/, a sound unpronounceable for surrounding tribes (Swanton 1911:33). But such evidence is no better than was the use of the presence of /f/ in Ofo as evidence for a Muskogean affiliation of the latter. At any rate, if Koroa, Grigra, Yazoo, and Tiou were separate languages related to Tunica (and not merely mutually intelligible dialects), their loss is perhaps even greater than if they were totally unrelated, for material on them would enable us to reconstruct a proto-Tunican instead of having to deal with Tunica as a language isolate.

The Ais, Calusa, and Tequesta were tribes in southern Florida, south of the Timucua. No specimens of their languages are known to us, but South Florida may have been linguistically even more complex than these three names suggest. Goggin and Sturtevant tell us something about the situation (1964:187):

> The short-lived sixteenth-century Spanish post was established at Calos, the "court" of the Calusa chief. ... Around this center were other villages ... whose chiefs were "subject to" Carlos. ... The extent of this territory is variously described ... [among others, as an area] including thirty chiefdoms speaking twenty-four "languages" some of which were not mutually intelligible.

Even though some languages thought to be Muskogean have turned out not to be Muskogean, there still were probably more Muskogean languages in the Southeast than the five we have records for. But which names of which tribes or towns were Muskogean-speaking and which were not is impossible to determine without linguistic records. The Yamasee and Yamacraw are among those said to have been Muskogean-speaking without evidence.

Other problematical examples could be adduced, but nothing really new would be added. Swanton's "Unclassified languages of the Southeast" (1917a) should be referred to, but it should be remembered that Swanton was always trying very hard to identify tribes known by names only with better known languages and families. In other words, he was trying to minimize the linguistic complexity. This makes the ethnographer's and the historian's task simpler but has nothing to do with the truth. When more early Spanish mission records have become known, new vocabularies may be discovered. Indeed it is not impossible that some manuscript material on the problematical Mississippi River tribes is in uncatalogued archives in Quebec.

Sturtevant has rightly stressed that 'archives are our last hope for some of the linguistic data which are badly needed for an understanding of the culture history of North America' (1962:76-7). I strongly endorse his plea (1952:77):

Any archival worker who can discover even half a dozen words, with translation, in any of the various languages spoken here [South Florida], will earn the gratitude of all anthropologists at all concerned with eastern North America — and such a discovery could even be of crucial importance for knowledge of the culture history of the Antilles and eastern South America.

The remarks are not limited in applicability to South Florida, of course. The whole of the Southeast is involved, but especially the Carolina-Virginia coast and the lower Mississippi River area.

## 3. PROBLEMS OF CLASSIFICATION

Near the turn of the nineteenth century, spurred by the publication of Pallas's *Vocabularia Comparativa* (1786–87) and Adelung and Vater's *Mithradates* (1816), a great deal of attention among scholars was directed to the problem of classifying North American languages. The determination of 'how many principal stocks, or families there are in North America' (Pickering 1831:581) was a pressing problem. In 1787 Jefferson (1964:97) had surmised that their number would be very great. Pickering, unfortunately swayed in part by theological beliefs about the recency of creation, believed they would be 'very few in number'. Following Duponceau, he surmised that there were only 'three, or at most, four principal stocks' east of the Mississippi (including the Northeast). Most of the Southeast was lumped into one stock, the 'Floridian' or 'Southern' (Pickering 1833). Although Barton (1797:lxvii-lxviii) had correctly postulated the affiliation between Cherokee and the languages of the 'Six Nations' (of the Iroquois) and also that between Muskogee or Creek and Choctaw-Chickasaw as early as 1797, his correct guesses were lost in a maze of incorrect ones and therefore the opportunity to begin a proper evaluation of the Southeastern situation was lost (Haas 1970). Duponceau's Floridian stock ignored Barton's surmises and lumped Cherokee in with Creek and Choctaw and other southern languages.

The first reasonably comprehensive vocabulary of most of the indigenous languages north of Mexico was that compiled by Gallatin (1836). At that time he believed that he had been able to ascertain the languages of all the tribes east of the Mississippi except one. This was the Alabama-Koasati which, though known to be a part of the Creek Confederacy, was not known to have had its language recorded. Gallatin believed that Creek and Choctaw-Chickasaw were related but he kept them separate until 1848. Even then he had identified only part of the Muskogean family, for, still lacking vocabularies of Alabama and Koasati, he left them unclassified.

Gallatin's 1836 classification included a classification of the languages of the Southeast that was the most accurate that had been achieved to that time. He dispensed with Duponceau's 'Floridian' and strictly separated all languages whose affinity was in the slightest doubt. This gave him the following list (arranged in alphabetical order):

Atakapa
Catawba (and Woccon)
Cherokee (possibly related to Iroquois)
Chitimacha
Choctaw (possibly related to Muskogee)
Muskogee (Muskogee proper [Creek], Hitchiti, and Seminole; possibly related to Choctaw)
Natchez
Timucua
Tunica (but not yet verified by actual linguistic material)
Yuchi

It is interesting that at this time no Siouan tribe was known to live east of the Mississippi, since Biloxi and Tutelo had not yet been identified, and Ofo was not known still to exist. Catawba, though known, was too divergent to be recognized as being related to the known Siouan languages west of the Mississippi. Lewis Henry Morgan (1870) was the first to suggest a Siouan connection for Catawba (Siebert 1945:100).

By the time Powell published his comprehensive scheme for North America north of Mexico (1891), several problems had been cleared up and his basic results for the Southeast have been little modified since. Cherokee was shown to be the southernmost branch of the Iroquoian family by Horatio Hale (1883a) and this was corroborated by Gatschet (1886) with additional evidence, particularly of a grammatical nature. Once he had obtained linguistic materials on Alabama and Koasati, it was easy for Gatschet (1884), to identify these languages as belonging in the Muskogean family. In much the same way Tutelo was clearly shown to be Siouan by Hale (1883b) after he had succeeded in obtaining some good linguistic material. Gatschet discovered speakers of Biloxi and recognized that the language was Siouan. James Owen Dorsey made a special study of the language and published positive identification (1893a). At this time Ofo still remained unclassified since no specimen of the language had ever been recorded. Its ultimate and positive identification as Siouan came when Swanton discovered a speaker of the language in 1908 (Dorsey and Swanton 1912:12).

Powell's scheme had set up 58 (later reduced to 55) linguistic stocks in North America north of Mexico. Within a couple of decades, however, a flurry of reductionism set in. It seems to have started with Roland B. Dixon and Alfred L. Kroeber (1913a-b) who, not content to allow the aboriginal languages of California to be divided up into twenty-two unrelated Powellian families, sought to establish interrelationships among them. At about the same time Swanton began trying to find interrelationships among the language isolates and language families of the Southeast. The best known language isolates of the Southeast are Tunica, Chitimacha, Atakapa, Natchez, Yuchi, and Timucua. The earliest suggested amalgamation in the area, Daniel G. Brinton's attempt to relate Natchez to Muskogean (1873), disavowing his earlier attempt to connect it with Huastec Maya (1967), was not accepted in the Powellian classification, and Natchez was placed as an independent stock. Swanton, however, reaffirmed Brinton's conclusions (1907a) and later, using some newly collected materials, presented considerable evidence for a Natchez-Muskogean connection (1924). It should be noted in passing that the Natchez-Muskogean relationship is much less close than the Algonkian-Wiyot-Yurok connection proposed by Sapir in 1913c, and yet Sapir's proposal stirred up a bitter controversy while Swanton's proposal was widely accepted (Haas 1958b:161). Another amalgamation in the area was also suggested by Swanton, namely that of Tunica, Chitimacha, and Atakapa, which he placed in a stock he named 'Tunican' (Swanton 1919). This proposal, too, was accepted without question in spite of the fact that the languages are very different in a number of fundamental respects and the relationship must therefore be quite distant. Moreover, the proposal had a strong geographical basis, but this situation seems to make more readily acceptable proposals which would otherwise be questioned. Still another proposed amalgamation was Sapir's suggestion that Yuchi was a relative of the Siouan family (1921). The basis for this suggestion is not known, but Haas presented some possible cognates in 1951a (79). By 1929, then, of language isolates for which linguistic material was available, this left only Timucua unplaced, though Swanton argued that it might be an outlying relative of Muskogean (Swanton 1929b).

The greatest reduction for North America was finally achieved by Sapir (1921, 1929) who divided up all the languages north of Mexico into six superstocks. The grandest amalgamation of all was the one called 'Hokan-Siouan' which encompassed not only many California and Texas languages and language families but also all of the various groupings that had been arrived at for the Southeast. In California, as it turned out, Sapir's scheme still allowed the appearance of several different colors on the map (since five of his superstocks were represented there), but in the Southeast all differentiation was obliterated in the one color assigned to Hokan-Siouan (Voegelin and Wheeler Voegelin 1941).

Whatever the final judgment may be about the eventual accuracy of Sapir's classification, the immediate result was unfortunate for Southeastern linguistics since it greatly oversimplified the picture and seemed to give assurance that the classificatory problems of the area had been settled.

In recent years there have been some changes in our thinking about the linguistic classification of the Southeastern languages. It was natural that this work should begin with a rechecking of some of the proposals made by Swanton, particularly in regard to Tunica (Tunica-Chitimacha-Atakapa) and to Natchez-Muskogean. Swadesh made a sophisticated study of a part of the first of these in his "Phonologic formulas for Atakapa-Chitimacha" (1946b) and in "Atakapa-Chitimacha *$k^w$" (1947). A decade later Haas presented new evidence for a relationship between "Natchez and the Muskogean languages" (1956). Two interesting points are (1) the demonstration of the presence of prothetic vowels in Natchez and (2) the morphological and phonological similarity between two of the auxiliary verbs in Natchez and two of the verb-class suffixes of proto-Muskogean.

A few years earlier Haas had also proposed putting both of Swanton's groupings into one larger one called 'Gulf' in two papers which traced the etymologies of single words, viz., "The proto-Gulf word for *water* (with notes on Siouan-Yuchi)" (1951a) and "The proto-Gulf word for *land* (with a note on proto-Siouan)" (1952). As the titles of these papers suggest, similarities to Siouan languages were also brought in. This was in line with the implications of Sapir's 'Eastern group' (Siouan-Yuchi, Natchez-Muskogean, and the queried addition of Timucua) within the larger Hokan-Siouan. Consequently all of this remained ostensibly within the framework of Sapir's Hokan-Siouan except for the rearrangement of Tunica, Chitimacha, and Atakapa. Indeed Haas carried her studies of the word for 'water' into other branches of Hokan-Siouan in "The proto-Hokan-Coahuiltecan word for 'water'" (1954). Nevertheless, in spite of such attempts to validate Sapir's farflung superstock, it became clear that the results were not as impressive as might be desired and that it might be well to look for connections between the Gulf languages and linguistic families outside of Hokan-Siouan. As a result of one such effort Haas proposed that the Gulf languages might be related to the Algonkian family and its near relatives, the Wiyot and Yurok languages of California, in "A new linguistic relationship in North America: Algonkian and the Gulf languages" (1958a).

By this time it was clear that Sapir's classification of the languages of North America into six superstocks had become more of a hindrance than a help in furthering progress in the area of linguistic relationships of the continent. Ironically enough, Sapir's classification had come to have the same effect that he had earlier (1917) lamented in regard to the Powell classification (1917:80):

While nothing is further from my mind than to minimize the great usefulness of Powell's [substitute Sapir's] classification, I may be pardoned for regretting the too definitive and dogmatic form in which it was presented. *This has had the effect until recently of discouraging further researches into the problem of linguistic groupings in America.* It is always dangerous to erect a formidable structure on a largely negative basis, *for one tends to interpret it as a postitive and finished accomplishment.* [Emphasis added.]

An important result of the proposal that Algonkian might be related to the Gulf languages was that it allowed us to break out of the restraints that Sapir's superstocks had imposed for so long. Specifically, it had the effect of raising doubts about the constituency of two of the superstocks, Hokan-Siouan (in which the Gulf languages had been included) and Algonkian-Mosan. Elmendorf (1965:100) has expressed it this way:

Haas has not only reassigned certain Hokan-Siouan components, she has entirely regrouped them. In other words, whatever the wider relations of these components may ultimately turn out to be, they are not the relations one would infer from Sapir's subgrouping.

Some of the problems posed by this turn of events are explored by Haas in "Some genetic affiliations of Algonkian" (1960). It is important to stress that suggestions about new affiliations for Algonkian do not in themselves invalidate earlier theories about other connections. The chief obstacle is that no evidence was ever given for the earlier theories. In this paper, then, it was necessary first to explore a possible relationship between Algonkian and Wakashan, Algonkian and Salishan, and Algonkian and Chimakuan (Wakashan, Salishan, and Chimakuan being the constituents of Sapir's Mosan) (see also Haas 1965). The results are interesting and worth exploring further, but at present they are not definitive. As a consequence of Haas's Algonkian-Gulf paper (1958a) and another paper on "Tonkawa and Algonkian" (1959), Gursky has explored the possibility that Algonkian may also be related to still other languages previously assigned to Hokan-Siouan in several papers, viz., "Ein lexikalischer Vergleich der Algonkin-Golf- und Hoka-Subtiaba-Sprachen" (1965), "Ein Vergleich der grammatikalischen Morpheme der Golf-Sprachen und der Hoka-Subtiaba-Sprachen" (1966), and "Algonkian and the languages of southern Texas" (1963).

In recent years still other changes involving the regrouping of constituents in the old Hokan-Siouan have been suggested. In 1931 Louis Allen proposed a special relationship between Siouan and Iroquoian. Today our knowledge of both of these families is greater than in 1931. Recently Wallace L. Chafe (1964) has followed up Allen's suggestion with new material supporting his thesis. Chafe believes this 'relationship has been established' (1965:104). This regrouping takes Iroquoian out of Sapir's Iroquois-Caddoan group and Siouan out of Sapir's 'Eastern group'. Because he also knows a great deal about Caddoan, Chafe has also commented on this (1965:105):

[I]f there is a relationship, it is an extremely remote one. I am inclined to think, though, that Caddoan and Siouan are related and if that is true, then Caddoan and Iroquoian must be related too. The hardest one to get hold of is the link between Iroquoian and Caddoan.

Other, geographically more remote affiliations for the Siouan family have also been proposed in recent years. Yukian, a small linguistic family of northern California, was something of a problem to Sapir, who placed it in Hokan-Siouan as a totally separate branch. In 1963 Elmendorf published a paper on "Yukian-Siouan lexical similarities", followed by another paper, "Item and set comparison in Yuchi, Siouan, and Yukian" (1964). In another paper he added the comment that 'it is not impossible that this grouping, if valid, will turn out to affiliate with certain Penutian groupings, rather than with Hokan' (1965:101). In this same period, at least one other suggestion about Siouan was postulated, namely, "Athapaskan, Tlingit, Yuchi, and Siouan" (Haas 1964).

Timucua, long extinct, still remains of doubtful affiliation. Gatschet (1884) argued that it showed some Carib and some Muskogean connections. Swanton (1929b) argued for a Muskogean connection and this was accepted but queried by Sapir (1929). More recently, Swadesh has argued for an Arawakan connection (1964:548) but Haas points out (1971) that an equally good case could be made for a Siouan connection.

The problem of genetic affiliations for the languages and language families of the

Southeast is thus in process of active reconsideration. A raft of new possibilities has been opened. It is important to remember that most of these new suggestions are actually supported by better evidence than was ever presented for many of the old, long-taken-for-granted assumptions enshrined in the Sapir superstocks. This does not mean that we do not need to look for more and better evidence but only that we are freed of the constraints that prevented us from looking for new possibilities for so long.

### 4. COMPARATIVE STUDIES

Linguistic prehistory is often thought of in terms of language classification, as discussed in the preceding section, but there are other more painstaking kinds of problems to be attacked by the linguistic prehistorian. The most important of these is the reconstruction of protolanguages. The optimum conditions for the reconstruction of a protolanguage require adequate synchronic descriptions of several languages the time depth of whose relation is around 2000–3000 years. The reconstructed result is parts of a language that was spoken around two or three millennia ago.

#### 4.1 *Muskogean*

The only linguistic family lying wholly within the Southeast is Muskogean and here considerable progress has been made, especially by Haas. In 1941 (a) she published "The classification of the Muskogean languages" in which most of the sound correspondences were presented though no actual reconstructions were given. Two major divisions of the family were set up, the Western Division, consisting of Choctaw-Chickasaw, and the Eastern Division, consisting of Alabama-Koasati, Hitchiti-Mikasuki, and Creek-Seminole. "A proto-Muskogean paradigm" (1946b) presents a reconstructed paradigm in which morphological as well as phonological differences between the daughter languages are accounted for. Refinements of sound correspondences and further reconstructions are presented in "Development of proto-Muskogean *$k^w$*" (1947a), "The position of Apalachee in the Muskogean family" (1949), and "The historical development of certain long vowels in Creek" (1950a). Much of this material is recapitaluted in "The prehistory of languages" (1969a: 34–42 and 52–8). Other reconstructions are also to be found in papers making comparisons outside the family, e.g. "Natchez and the Muskogean languages" (1956) and "A new linguistic relationship ..." (1958a). Many other reconstructions have been made but remain unpublished. Eventually a comparative dictionary of the Muskogean languages will be prepared. The work is being hampered by the lack of full synchronic materials on Choctaw, Alabama, and Mikasuki.

## 4.2 *Other Linguistic Families*

Several other linguistic families which have branches extending into the Southeast have also seen important progress in the reconstruction of their protolanguages. Foremost among these is Algonkian, for which we have the largest body of reconstructed material of any protolanguage north of Mexico (e.g. Bloomfield 1946; Hockett 1957; Siebert 1967; and many other papers). Special to a Southeastern language is Wick R. Miller's study, "An outline of Shawnee historical phonology" (1959) in which he starts with the reconstructions of Bloomfield and others and traces their development in Shawnee. Much more work of this sort, with other languages, needs to be done.

Much progress has also been made in the reconstruction of proto-Siouan, particularly in the work of Wolff (1950–51) and Matthews (1958 ms., 1970). Work pertinent to the Southeast in particular includes Voegelin's "Ofo-Biloxi sound correspondences" (1939) and Holmer's "An Ofo phonetic law" (1947). It also involves the attempt to reconstruct Southeastern Siouan (Biloxi-Ofo-Tutelo). A few such reconstructions are given in Haas (1968, 1969c) and others remain unpublished.

Although it seems clear enough that Catawba is related to Siouan at some level, either within the Siouan family proper or at a deeper level which might be called 'Catawba-Siouan', Siouanists to date have noted that cognates are not as easy to find as might be wished. However, Frank T. Siebert's papers on "Linguistic classification of Catawba" (1945) give impressive morphological evidence of Siouan affinity. Particularly noteworthy are his comparative tables of Siouan instrumental prefixes (102) and of Siouan modal suffixes (213). When more of his material becomes available, it seems likely that more cognate material will also be discovered.

Proto-Iroquoian could also be reconstructed in the same way as proto-Muskogean, proto-Algonkian, and proto-Siouan, and Floyd Lounsbury has actually worked out quite a lot of it. Unfortunately, he has published almost nothing of this (but see 1961).

## 4.3 *For the Future*

The work of reconstructing these protolanguages is a new phase in the progress and development of Southeastern linguistic studies. Nothing of any significance had been done in the reconstruction of any American Indian protolanguage prior to 1913 (Sapir's Uto-Aztecan) and most of the work has been done in the past twenty or thirty years. As this work progresses it will be possible to compare protolanguage with protolanguage and language isolates with protolanguages, and thus achieve new depths in genetic relationship. Some work of this sort has already been attempted, as in the comparison of proto-Algonkian and proto-Muskogean (Haas 1958a), but many new possibilities are sure to open up when it is possible to compare many protolanguages with one another. Moreover, even though little has been done in the way of comparisons of North and South American languages, the possibility of finding connections should be good in the Southeast because of its proximity to the Caribbean area. However, greater certainty in regard to any proposals of more distant connections must await a greater accumulation of actual reconstructions in the strategic protolanguages of both continents, a task which may require decades. Southeastern Indian linguistics is clearly not a thing of the past but an endeavor which is only seriously beginning and which has a very bright future indeed.

BIBLIOGRAPHY

ADAIR, JAMES. 1775. The history of the American Indians; particularly those nations adjoining to the Missisippi [sic], east and west Florida, Georgia, South and North Carolina, and Virginia. London.

ADELUNG, J.C., and J.S. VATER. 1816. Mithridates oder allgemeine Sprachenkunde. Berlin. [3.]

ALLEN, LOUIS. 1931. Siouan and Iroquoian. IJAL 6.185–93. [3.]

BARTON, BENJAMIN SMITH. 1797. New views of the origin of the tribes and nations of North America. Philadelphia, John Bioren. [1.7.4, 3.]

BARTRAM, WILLIAM. 1791. Travels through North and South Carolina, Georgia, east and west Florida, the Cherokee country, the extensive territories of the Muscogulges or Creek Confederacy, and the country of the Chactaws. Philadelphia, James and Johnson. Reissued New York (1940), New Haven (1958).

BEACH, W.W., ed. 1877. Indian miscellany. Albany.

BENDER, ERNEST. 1949. Cherokee II. IJAL 15.223–8. [1.9.1]

BENDER, ERNEST, and ZELLIG S. HARRIS. 1946. The phonemes of North Carolina Cherokee. IJAL 12.14–16. [1.9.1]

BENVENISTE, ÉMILE. 1950. La négation en Yuchi. Word 6.99–105. [1.8]

BERLANDIER, JEAN LOUIS. 1969. The Indians of Texas in 1830. Edited by John C. Ewers. Washington, D.C., Smithsonian Institution Press.

BLOOMFIELD, LEONARD. 1946. Algonquian. Linguistic structures of native America (= VFPA, no. 6), by Harry Hoijer and others, pp. 85–129. [4.2]

BRINTON, DANIEL G. 1859. Notes on the Floridian peninsula, its literary history, Indian tribes and antiquities. Philadelphia.

——. 1867. The Natchez of Louisiana, an offshoot of the civilized nations of Central America. Historical Magazine, second series, 1.16–18. Morrisania, N.Y. [3.]

——. 1870. Contributions to a grammar of the Muskogee language. PAPS 11. 301–9. [1.1.5]

——. 1873. On the language of the Natchez. PAPS 13.483–99. [1.2, 3.]

——. 1885. The Taensas grammar and dictionary. AAOJ 7.108–13.

——. 1890. The curious hoax of the Taensa language. Essays of an Americanist, pp. 452–67. Philadelphia, David McKay. [2.]

———. 1891. The American Race. Philadelphia, David McKay. Reprinted in 1901.
BUCKNER, H. F., and G. HERROD. 1860. A grammar of the Maskωke or Creek language. Marion. [1.1.5]
BUSHNELL, DAVID I., JR. 1909. The Choctaw of Bayou Lacomb, St. Tammany Parish, Louisiana. BAE-B 48. [1.1.1]
———. 1910. Myths of the Louisiana Choctaw. AmA 12.526–35.
BYINGTON, CYRUS A. 1870. A grammar of the Choctaw language. Edited by Daniel G. Brinton. PAPS 11.317–67. [1.1.1]
———. 1915. A dictionary of the Choctaw language. Edited by John R. Swanton and Henry S. Halbert. BAE-B 46. [1.1.1]
CATLIN, GEORGE. 1841. [Vocabulary of Tuscarora]. Letters and notes on the manners, customs, and condition of the North American Indians, vol. 2, pp. 262–65. London. [1.9.2]
CHAFE, WALLACE L. 1964. Another look at Siouan and Iroquoian. AmA 66.852–62. [1.7.2, 1.7.3, 3.]
———. 1965. Discussion of Elmendorf 1965. CJL/RCL 10.104–5 passim. [3.]
CROFT, KENNETH. 1948. A guide to source material on extinct North American Indian languages. IJAL 14.260–8.
DENSMORE, FRANCES. 1934a. A study of Indian music in the Gulf states. AmA 36.386–8. [1.1.1]
———. 1934b. Studying Indian music in the Gulf states. ExSI 1933.57–9. [1.1.1]
———. 1937. The Alabama Indians and their music. Straight Texas, pp. 270–93. Publication of the Texas Folk-lore Society, no. 13. [1.1.3]
———. 1943a. Choctaw music. BAE-B 136.101–88.
———. 1943b. A search for songs among the Chitimacha Indians in Louisiana. BAE-B 133.1–15. [1.4]
———. 1956. Seminole music. BAE-B 161.
DIXON, ROLAND B., and ALFRED L. KROEBER. 1913a. Relationships of the Indian languages of California. Science 37.225. [3.]
———. 1913b. New linguistic families in California. AmA 15.647–55. [3.]
DORSEY, JAMES OWEN. 1893a. The Biloxi Indians of Louisiana. AAAS-P 43.267–87. [1.7.2, 3.]
———. 1893b. Two Biloxi tales. JAF 6.48–50. [1.7.2]
DORSEY, JAMES OWEN, and JOHN R. SWANTON. 1912. A dictionary of the Biloxi and Ofo languages, accompanied with thirty-one Biloxi texts and numerous Biloxi phrases. BAE-B 47. [1.5, 1.7.2, 1.7.3, 2., 3.]
EGGAN, FRED. 1937. Historical changes in the Choctaw kinship system. AmA 39.34–53. [1.1.1]
ELMENDORF, WILLIAM W. 1963. Yukian-Siouan lexical similarities. IJAL 29.300–9. [3.]
———. 1964. Item and set comparison in Yuchi, Siouan, and Yukian. IJAL 30.328–40. [3.]

——. 1965. Some problems in the regrouping of Powell units. CJL/RCL 10.93–104. [3.]
FICKETT, JOAN GLEASON. 1967. The phonology of Tuscarora. SIL 19.33–57. [1.9.2]
FOREMAN, GRANT. 1932. Indian removal: The emigration of the five civilized tribes. Norman, University of Oklahoma Press. [0.]
——. 1934. The five civilized tribes. Norman, University of Oklahoma Press. [0.]
FRACHTENBERG, LEO J. 1913. Contributions to a Tutelo vocabulary. AmA 15. 477–9. [1.7.1]
FREEMAN, JOHN F. (compiler), and MURPHY D. SMITH (ed. consultant). 1966. A guide to the manuscripts relating to the American Indian in the Library of the American Philosophical Society (= APS-M 65). Philadelphia, The American Philosophical Society.
GALLATIN, ALBERT. 1836. A synopsis of the Indian tribes within the United States east of the Rocky Mountains, and in the British and Russian possessions in North America. TCAAS 2.1–422. Cambridge. [1.5, 1.7, 1.7.4, 3.]
——. 1848. Hale's Indians of North-West America, and vocabularies of North America. AES-T 2.xxiii-clxxx, 1–130. New York. [1.2]
GATSCHET, ALBERT S. 1877. Volk und Sprache der Timucua. VBGA 245–60. [1.6]
——. 1877–80. The Timucua language. PAPS 41.626–42, 42.490–504, 43.465–502. [1.6]
——. 1880. La langue Maskōki et ses dialectes. PICAm 3/2.742–58.
——. 1883. The Shetimasha Indians of St. Mary's Parish, southern Louisiana. TASW 2.148–58. Washington, D.C. [1.4]
——. 1884. A migration legend of the Creek Indians. Vol. 1 (= Brinton's Library of aboriginal American literature, no. 4). Philadelphia. [1.1.1, 1.1.2, 1.1.4, 3.]
——. 1886. On the affinity of the Cheroki to the Iroquois dialects. TAPA 16.xl-xlv. [3.]
——. 1888a. Tchikilli's Kasi'hta legend in the Creek and Hitchiti languages. Transactions of the Academy of Science of St. Louis 5.33–239. [1.1.4, 1.1.5]
——. 1888b. Réplique à M.D.G. Brinton, au sujet de son article "Linguistique Américaine". Revue de Linguistique 21.203–7. Paris. [2.]
——. 1889. Sex-denoting nouns in American languages. TAPA 20.159–71. [1.3, 2.]
——. 1891. Removal of the Taensa Indians. AAOJ 13.252–4.
——. 1893. Some mythic stories of the Yuchi Indians. AmA o.s. 6.279–82. [1.8]
——. 1900. A grammatic sketch of the Catawba language. AmA 2.527–49. [1.7.4]
GATSCHET, ALBERT S., and RAOUL DE LA GRASSERIE. 1889. Textes Timucua. RLPC 22.320–46. [1.6]
GATSCHET, ALBERT S., and JOHN R. SWANTON. 1932. A dictionary of the Atakapa language accompanied by text material. BAE-B 108. [1.5]
GEARY, JAMES A. 1953. Strachey's vocabulary of Indian words used in Virginia, 1612. HSS 103.208–14. [1.10.1]

——. 1955. The language of the Carolina Algonkian tribes. HSS 105.873–900. [1.10.1]
GERARD, W. R. 1904. The Tapehaneck dialect of Virginia. AmA 6.313–30.
GILBERT, WILLIAM HARLEN, JR. 1943. The Eastern Cherokees. BAE-B 133.169–413. [1.9.1]
GILLIAM, C. E. 1947. Powhatan Algonkian bird names. JWAS 37.1–2.
GODDARD, IVES. 1967. The Algonquian independent indicative. Contributions to Anthropology: Linguistics I. NMC-B 214.66–106.
GOGGIN, JOHN M., and WILLIAM C. STURTEVANT. 1964. The Calusa: A stratified, nonagricultural society (with notes on sibling marriage). Explorations in cultural anthropology: Essays in honor of George Peter Murdock, ed. by Ward H. Goodenough, pp. 179–219. New York, McGraw Hill. [2.]
GRANBERRY, JULIAN. 1956. Timucua I: Prosodies and phonemics of the Mocama dialect. IJAL 22.97–105. [1.6]
GREENLEE, R. F. 1945. Folktales of the Florida Seminole. JAF 58.138–44.
GURSKY, KARL-HEINZ. 1963. Algonkian and the languages of southern Texas. AnL 5/9.17–21. [3.]
——. 1965 [1966]. Ein lexikalischer Vergleich der Algonkin-Golf- und Hoka-Subtiaba-sprachen. Orbis 14.160–215. [3.]
——. 1966 [1967]. Ein Vergleich der grammatikalischen Morpheme der Golfsprachen und der Hoka-Subtiaba-sprachen. Orbis 15.511–37. [3.]
——. 1968. Gulf and Hokan-Subtiaban: New lexical parallels. IJAL 34.21–41. [1.4, 1.5]
——. 1969. A lexical comparison of the Atakapa, Chitimacha, and Tunica languages. IJAL 35.83–107. [1.4, 1.5]
HAAS, MARY R. [n.d.]. Hitchiti grammatical notes and vocabulary. MS c. 1938–40. [1.1.4]
——. [n.d.]. Creek vocabulary. MS c. 1938–40. [1.1.5]
——. 1938. Geminate consonant clusters in Muskogee. Lg 14.61–5. [1.1.5]
——. 1939. Natchez and Chitimacha clans and kinship terminology. AmA 41. 597–610. [1.2, 1.4]
——. 1940a. Tunica. Extract from HAIL 4.1–143. New York, J. J. Augustin. [1.3]
——. 1940b. Ablaut and its function in Muskogee. Lg 16.141–50. [1.1.4, 1.1.5]
——. 1940c. Creek inter-town relations. AmA 42.479–89. [1.1.5]
——. 1941a. The classification of the Muskogean languages. Language, culture, and personality, ed. by Leslie Spier, A. Irving Hallowell, and Stanley S. Newman, pp. 41–56. Menasha, Wisconsin. [1.1.3, 4.1]
——. 1941b. A popular etymology in Muskogee. Lg 17.340–1. [1.1.2, 1.1.5]
——. 1941c. The Choctaw word for 'rattlesnake'. AmA 43.129–32.

———. 1941d. Noun incorporation in the Muskogean languages. Lg 17.311–15. [1.1.5]
———. 1942. The solar deity of the Tunica. Papers of the Michigan Academy of Science, Arts, and Letters 28.531–35. [1.3]
———. 1944. Men's and women's speech in Koasati. Lg 20.142–9. Reprinted in Hymes 1964:228–33. [1.1.3, 1.1.5]
———. 1945. Dialects of the Muskogee language. IJAL 11.69–74. [1.1.5]
———. 1946a. A grammatical sketch of Tunica. Linguistic structures of native America (= VFPA, no. 6), by Harry Hoijer and others, pp. 337–66. [1.3]
———. 1946b. A proto-Muskogean paradigm. Lg 22.326–32. [1.1.3, 1.1.4, 1.1.5, 4.1]
———. 1947a. The development of proto-Muskogean *k$^w$. IJAL 13.135–7. [1.1.3, 4.]
———. 1947b. Some French loan-words in Tunica. RomPh 1.145–8. [1.3]
———. 1947c. Southeastern Indian folklore. Folklore research in North America. JAF 60.402–6.
———. 1948. Classificatory verbs in Muskogee. IJAL 14.244–6. [1.1.5, 1.9.1]
———. 1949. The position of Apalachee in the Muskogean family. IJAL 15.121–7. [1.1.2, 4.1]
———. 1950a. On the historical development of certain long vowels in Creek. IJAL 16.122–5. [1.1.3, 4.1]
———. 1950b. Tunica texts. UCPL 6.1–174. [1.7.2, 2.]
———. 1951a. The proto-Gulf word for *water* (with notes on Siouan-Yuchi). IJAL 17.71–9. [1.2, 1.4, 1.5, 1.6, 3.]
———. 1951b. Interlingual word taboos. AmA 53.338–44. Reprinted in Hymes 1964:489–94. [1.1.5]
———. 1952. The proto-Gulf words for *land* (with a note on proto-Siouan). IJAL 18.238–40. [1.4, 1.5, 1.6, 2., 3.]
———. 1953. Tunica dictionary. UCPL 6.175–332. [1.3]
———. 1954. The proto-Hokan-Coahuiltecan word for 'water'. Papers from the Symposium on American Indian Linguistics. UCPL 10.57–62. [3.]
———. 1956. Natchez and the Muskogean languages. Lg 32.61–72. [1.1.3, 1.2, 3., 4.1]
———. 1958a. A new linguistic relationship in North America: Algonkian and the Gulf languages. SJA 14.231–64. [1.2, 1.4, 1.5, 3., 4.1, 4.3]
———. 1958b. Algonkian-Ritwan: The end of a controversy. IJAL 24.159–73. [3.]
———. 1958c. Notes on some PCA stems in /k-/. IJAL 24.241–5.
———. 1959. Tonkawa and Algonkian. AnL 1/2.1–6. [1.2, 1.4, 1.5, 3.]
———. 1960. Some genetic affiliations of Algonkian. Culture in history: Essays in honor of Paul Radin, ed. by Stanley Diamond, pp. 977–92. New York, Columbia University Press. [1.2, 1.4, 1.5, 3.]
———. 1961. Comment on Lounsbury 1961. Symposium on Cherokee-Iroquois culture, BAE-B 180.21–3. [1.9.1]
———. 1963. The Muskogean and Algonkian words for *skunk*. IJAL 29.65–6.

———. 1964. Athapaskan, Tlingit, Yuchi, and Siouan. PICAm 35/2.495–500. Mexico. [3.]

———. 1965. Is Kutenai related to Algonkian? CJL/RCL 10.77–91. [3.]

———. 1966. Historical linguistics and the genetic relationship of languages. CTL 3.113–54. (Revised, expanded as Haas 1969a.)

———. 1968. The last words of Biloxi. IJAL 34.77–84. [1.7, 1.7.2, 1.7.3, 4.2]

———. 1969a. The prehistory of languages. JanL, series minor, no. 57. (Revision and expansion of Haas 1966.) [1.8, 1.9.1, 4.1]

———. 1969b. Grammar or lexicon? The American Indian side of the question from Duponceau to Powell. IJAL 35.239–55. [1.1.1, 1.4]

———. 1969c. Swanton and the Biloxi and Ofo dictionaries. IJAL 35.286–90. [1.7.2, 1.7.3, 4.2]

———. 1970. Review of Benjamin Smith Barton, New views of the origin of the tribes and nations of North America (Ann Arbor, Michigan, University Microfilms, 1968). IJAL 36.68–70. [3.]

———. 1971. Southeastern Indian linguistics. Red, white, and black: Symposium on Indians in the Old South, ed. by Charles M. Hudson, pp. 4454. Athens, University of Georgia. [0., 3.]

HALE, HORATIO. 1883a. Indian migrations, as evidenced by language. Part I: The Huron-Cherokee stock. AAOJ 5.18–28. [3.]

———. 1883b. The Tutelo tribe and language. PAPS 21.1–45. [1.7.1, 2., 3.]

HARRINGTON, JOHN P. 1955. The original Strachey vocabulary of the Virginia Indian language. BAE-B 157.189–202. [1.10.1]

HAUMONTÉ, J.D., M.J. PARISOT, and LUCIEN ADAM. 1882. Grammaire et vocabulaire de la langue Taensa. Bibliothèque Linguistique Américaine, vol. 9. Paris. [2.]

HICKERSON, NANCY P. 1958–59. An acoustic analysis of Shawnee. IJAL 24.20–9, 130–42; 25.22–31, 97–104. [1.10.2]

HOCKETT, CHARLES F. 1957. Central Algonquian vocabulary: Stems in /k-/. IJAL 23.247–68. [4.2]

HOIJER, HARRY, ERIC P. HAMP, and WILLIAM BRIGHT. 1965. Contributions to a bibliography of comparative Amerindian. IJAL 31.346–52. [0.]

HOIJER, HARRY, and others. 1946. Linguistic structures of native America. (= VFPA, no. 6). New York.

HOLMER, NILS M. 1947. An Ofo phonetic law. IJAL 13.1–8. [1.7.2, 1.7.3, 4.2]

HOXIE, W.J. 1903. A Seminole vocabulary. Atlantic Slope Naturalist 1.64–5.

HULTON, PAUL, and DAVID BEERS QUINN. 1964. The American drawings of John White 1577–1590. 2 vols. London, The Trustees of the British Museum, and Chapel Hill, The University of North Carolina Press. [1.10.1]

HYMES, DELL H., ed. 1964. Language in culture and society. New York/Evanston/London, Harper and Row.

JEFFERSON, THOMAS. 1964. Notes on the state of Virginia. Harper Torchbooks

TB 3052. New York/Evanston/London, Harper and Row. [3.]
KILPATRICK, ANNA GRITTS, and JACK FREDERICK KILPATRICK. 1966. Chronicles of Wolftown: Social documents of the North Carolina Cherokees, 1850–1862. BAE-B 196.1–112. [1.9.1]
KILPATRICK, JACK FREDERICK. 1966. The Wahnenauhi manuscript: Historical sketches of the Cherokee together with some of their customs, traditions, and superstitions. BAE-B 196.175–213. [1.9.1]
KILPATRICK, JACK FREDERICK, and ANNA GRITTS KILPATRICK. 1966. Eastern Cherokee folktales: Reconstructed from the field notes of Frans M. Olbrechts. BAE-B 196.379–447. [1.9.1]
KROEBER, ALFRED L. 1940. Stimulus diffusion. AmA 42.1–20. [1.9.1]
KRUEGER, JOHN R. 1963. Two early grammars of Cherokee. AnL 5/3.1–57. [1.9.1]
LA GRASSERIE, RAOUL DE. [n.d.]. Esquisse d'une grammaire du Timucua, langue de la Floride. Orléans. [1.6]
——. 1890. Textes analysés et vocabulaire de la langue Timucua. PICAm (7th session, 1888) 403–37. [1.6]
——. 1892. Vocabulaire Timucua. Orléans. [1.6]
LAWSON, JOHN. 1937. History of North Carolina. Richmond, Virginia. [First published in 1709.] [1.7, 1.10.1]
LIEBER, O. M. Vocabulary of the Catawba language. Collections of the South Carolina Historical Society 2.327–42. [1.7.4]
LORIOT, JAMES. 1964. A selected bibliography of comparative American Indian linguistics. IJAL 30.62–80. [0.]
LOUGHRIDGE, ROBERT MCGILL, and DAVID M. HODGE. 1890. English and Muskokee dictionary. St. Louis. Reprinted, Philadelphia, The Westminster Press (1914). [1.1.5]
LOUNSBURY, FLOYD G. 1946. Stray number systems among certain Indian tribes. AmA 48.672–5.
——. 1961. Iroquois-Cherokee linguistic relations. Symposium on Cherokee-Iroquois culture, BAE-B 180.1–20. [1.9, 1.9.2, 4.2]
MACCAWLEY, CLAY. 1887. The Seminole Indians of Florida. BAE-R 5.469–531. [1.1.5]
MARTIN, H. N. 1946. Folktales of the Alabama-Coushatta Indians. 75 pp. Livingston (Texas). [1.1.3]
MATTHEWS, G. HUBERT. 1958. Handbook of Siouan languages. University of Pennsylvania dissertation. [1.7.2, 1.7.3, 4.2]
——. 1959. Proto-Siouan kinship terminology. AmA 61.252–78. [1.7.2, 1.7.3]
——. 1970. Some notes on the proto-Siouan continuants. IJAL 35.98–109. [1.7.2, 1.7.3, 4.2]

MATTHEWS, G. HUBERT, and RED THUNDER CLOUD. 1967. Catawba texts. IJAL 33.7–24. [1.7.4]

MICHELSON, TRUMAN. 1933. The linguistic classification of Powhatan. AmA 35.549.

MILLER, CARL F. 1957. Revaluation of the Eastern Siouan problem with particular emphasis on the Virginia branches — the Occaneechi, the Saponi, and the Tutelo. BAE-B 164.115–211. [1.7]

MILLER, WICK R. 1959. An outline of Shawnee historical phonology. IJAL 25.16–21. [4.2]

MOONEY, JAMES. 1900. Myths of the Cherokee. BAE-R (1897–1898) 19 (pt. 1). [1.9.1]

MOONEY, JAMES, and FRANS M. OLBRECHTS. 1932. The Swimmer manuscript. BAE-B 99. [1.9.1]

MORGAN, LEWIS HENRY. 1870. Indian migrations. The North American Review, Jan., 1870. Boston. Reprinted in W.W. Beach, 1877. [3.]

———. 1871. Systems of consanguinity and affinity. SCK 17. [1.1.1]

MURDOCK, GEORGE PETER. 1960. Ethnographic bibliography of North America. 3rd edition. New Haven, Human Relations Area Files. [0.]

NETTL, BRUNO. 1953. The Shawnee musical style: Historical perspective in primitive music. SJA 9.277–85. [1.10.2]

OLBRECHTS, FRANS M. 1929. De pronominale prefixen in het Tuscarora. Donum Natalicum Schrijnen 154-61. [1.9.2]

NEUMAN, ROBERT W., and LANIER A. SIMMONS. 1969. A bibliography relative to the Indians of the State of Louisiana. Anthropological Study no. 4. Baton Rouge, Louisiana Geological Survey.

PALLAS, P.S. 1786–87. Vocabularia Comparativa. [3.]

PAREJA, FRANCISCO. 1612. Cathecismo y breve exposicion de la doctrina christiana ... en lengua castellana, y timuquana. México. [1.6]

———. 1613. Confessionario, en lengua castellana, y timuquana. México. [1.6]

———. 1886. Arte de la lengua timuquana, compuesta en 1614. Bibliothèque Linguistique Américaine, vol. 11. Edited by Lucien Adam and Julien Vinson. Paris. [1.6]

PICKENS, A.L. 1937. Dictionary of Indian place-names in upper South Carolina. South Carolina Natural History 51–53.1–10. [1.7.4]

———. 1938. Supplementary list for the dictionary of Indian place-names in upper South Carolina. Neighborhood Research 2.1. Charlottesville, N.C., Queens College. [1.7.4]

———. 1943. A comparison of Cherokee and Pioneer bird-nomenclature. Southern Folklore Quarterly 7.213–21.

———. 1954. Seeking Carolina Indian names for beasts. Neighborhood Research, Feb., 1954. Charlotteville, N.C., Queens College. [1.7.4]

———. 1957. Contributions to Catawba ethnozoology. Neighborhood Research, Spring, 1957, 1–5. Charlotteville, N.C., Queens College. [1.7.4]

PICKERING, JOHN. 1830. A grammar of the Cherokee language. 48 pp. Boston. Reprinted in Krueger, 1963. [1.9.1]

——. 1831. Indian languages of America. Encyclopaedia Americana, 4 (Appendix). 581–900. [3.]

——. 1833. Introductory memoir. A dictionary of the Abnaki language, by Father Sebastian Rasles. AAcadAS-M 1.371–2.

PILLING, JAMES C. 1887. Bibliography of the Siouan languages. B[A]E-B 5. [0., 1.1]

——. 1888. Bibliography of the Iroquoian languages. B[A]E-B 6. [0., 1.1]

——. 1889. Bibliography of the Muskhogean languages. B[A]E-B 9. [0., 1.1.2]

——. 1891. Bibliography of the Algonquian languages. B[A]E-B 13. [0., 1.1]

POLLARD, J. GARLAND. 1894. The Pamunkey Indians of Virginia. B[A]E-B 17. [1.10.1]

PORTER, K.W. 1946. A legend of the Biloxi. JAF 59.168–73. [1.7.2]

POWELL, JOHN WESLEY. 1891. Linguistic families of North America north of Mexico. B[A]E-R (1885–86) 7.1–142. [3.]

PULTE, WILLIAM. 1970. The position of Chickasaw in Western Muskogean. Presented to the Symposium on Southeastern linguistics, Southern Anthropological Society, Athens, Georgia. [1.1.1]

RAND, EARL. 1968. The structural phonology of Alabama, a Muskogean language. IJAL 34.94–103. [1.1.3]

READ, WILLIAM A. 1927. Louisiana place-names of Indian origin. University Bulletin, Louisiana State University, vol. 9, no. 2. Baton Rouge.

——. 1928. More Indian place-names in Louisiana. Louisiana Historical Quarterly 11.445–62. Baton Rouge.

——. 1934. Florida place names of Indian origin and Seminole personal names. Louisiana State University Studies, no. 11. Baton Rouge. [1.1.5]

——. 1937. Indian place-names in Alabama. Louisiana State University Studies, no. 29. Baton Rouge. [1.1.5]

——. 1940. Notes on an Opelousas manuscript of 1862. AmA 42.546–8. [1.1.1]

——. 1945. Some fish names of Indian origin. IJAL 11.234–8.

——. 1949. Indian stream-names in Georgia. IJAL 15.128–32. [1.1.5]

REYBURN, WILLIAM D. 1953–54. Cherokee verb morphology. IJAL 19.172–80, 259–73; 20.44–64. [1.9.1]

SAPIR, EDWARD. 1913a. A Tutelo vocabulary. AmA 15.295–7. [1.7.1]

——. 1913b. Southern Paiute and Nahuatl, a study in Uto-Aztekan, pt. 1. JSAm n.s. 10.379–425.

——. 1913c. Wiyot and Yurok, Algonkin languages of California. AmA 15.617–46. [3.]

——. 1917. Linguistic publications of the Bureau of American Ethnology, a general review. IJAL 1.76–81. [3.]

——. 1920. The Hokan and Coahuiltecan languages. IJAL 1.280–90.

——. 1921. A bird's-eye view of languages north of Mexico. Science 54.408. [3.]
——. 1929. Central and North American Indian languages. Encyclopaedia Britannica, 14th ed., 5.138–41. London/New York/Toronto, The Encyclopaedia Britannica Co., Ltd. Reprinted SWES, pp. 169–78. [1.8, 3.]
SIEBERT, FRANK T., JR. 1945. Linguistic classification of Catawba. IJAL 11.100–4, 211–18. [1.7, 1.7.4, 3., 4.2]
——. 1967. The original home of the proto-Algonquian people. *In* Contributions to Anthropology: Linguistics I. NMC-B 214.13–47. [4.2]
[SMITH, BUCKINGHAM], compiler. [1860a]. [Documents in the Spanish and two of the early tongues of Florida, Apalachian and Timuquan.] [Washington, D.C.] [1.1.2, 1.6]
——. 1860b. Specimen of the Appalachian language. Historical Magazine 4.40–1. Morrisania, N.Y. [1.1.2]
——. 1866. Comparative vocabularies of the Seminole and Mikasuki tongues. Historical Magazine, 10.239–43. Morrisania, N.Y. Reprinted in Indian Miscellany, ed. by W.W. Beach, pp. 120–6. Albany. [1.1.4, 1.1.5]
SMITH, JOHN. 1612. A map of Virginia. Oxford. [1.10.1]
SPECK, FRANK G. 1907a. Some comparative traits of the Maskogian languages. AmA 9.470–83.
——. 1907b. Notes on Chickasaw ethnology and folk-lore. JAF 20.50–8. [1.1.1]
——. 1907c. The Creek Indians of Taskigi town. MAAS 2, pt. 2. [1.1.5]
——. 1909. Ethnology of the Yuchi Indians. UPMAP 1.1–154. [1.8]
——. 1911. Ceremonial songs of the Creek and Yuchi Indians. UPMA-P 1.157–245. [1.1.5, 1.8]
——. 1913. Some Catawba texts and folk-lore. JAF 26.319–30.
——. 1924. The ethnic position of the South-eastern Algonkian. AmA 26.184–200. [1.10.1]
——. 1925. The Rappahannock Indians of Virginia. INM 5/3.i-xii, 25–83.
——. 1927. Some eastern Cherokee texts. IJAL 4.111–12. [1.9.1]
——. 1928a. Recording the Catawba language. EP 24.307–8. [1.7.4]
——. 1928b. Chapters on the ethnology of the Powhatan tribes of Virginia. INM 1.227–455. [1.10.1]
——. 1934. Catawba texts. CUCA 24.1–91. New York. [1.7.4]
——. 1935. Siouan tribes of the Carolinas as known from the Catawba, Tutelo, and documentary sources. AmA 37.201–25.
——. 1938. The cane blowgun in Catawba and southeastern ethnology. AmA 40.198–204.
——. 1939a. Catawba religious beliefs, mortuary customs, and dances. Primitive Man 12.21–57.
——. 1939b. Eggan's Yuchi kinship interpretation. AmA 41.171–2. [1.8]

———. 1939c. The Catawba Nation and its neighbors. The North Carolina Historical Review 16.404–17.

———. 1941. Gourds of the Southeastern Indians. The New England Gourd Society, Horticultural Hall. Boston.

———. 1946. Catawba text. IJAL 12.64–5. [1.7.4]

SPECK, FRANK G., and LEONARD BLOOM. 1951. Cherokee dance and drama. Berkeley and Los Angeles: University of California Press. [1.9.1]

SPECK, FRANK G., and CLAUDE E. SCHAEFFER. 1942. Catawba kinship and social organization with a resume of Tutelo kinship terms. AmA 44.555–75. [1.7.4]

SPENCER, JOAB. 1909. Shawnee folk-lore. JAF 22.319–26.

SPOEHR, ALEXANDER. 1941. Camp, clan, and kin among the Cow Creek Seminole. FMAS 33.1–27. [1.1.5]

———. 1942. The kinship system of the Seminole. FMAS 33.31–113. [1.1.5]

———. 1947. Changing kinship systems. FMAS 33.153–235.

STURTEVANT, WILLIAM C. 1954. The medicine bundles and busks of the Florida Seminole. Florida Anthropologist 7.31–70. [1.1.4]

———. 1958. Siouan languages in the East. AmA 60.738–43. [1.7]

———. 1962. Spanish-Indian relations in southeastern North America. Ethnohistory 9.41–94. [1.1.4, 1.1.5, 1.9.1, 2.]

———. 1964. John White's contribution to ethnology. In Hulton and Quinn, 1964: 37–46. [1.10.1]

SWADESH, MORRIS. 1933. Chitimacha verbs of derogatory or abusive connotation. Lg 9.192–201. [1.4]

———. 1934a. The phonemic principle. Lg 10.117–29. Reprinted in Readings in linguistics, ed. by Martin Joos, pp. 32–7. Washington, American Council of Learned Societies (1957). [1.4]

———. 1934b. The phonemics of Chitimacha. Lg 10.345–62. [1.4]

———. 1937. The phonemic interpretation of long consonants. Lg. 13.1–10.

———. 1939. Chitimacha grammar, texts, and vocabulary. MS. (732 in Freeman and Smith 1966).

———. 1946a. Chitimacha. Linguistic structures of native America (= VFPA, no. 6), by Harry Hoijer and others, pp. 312–36. New York. [1.4]

———. 1946b. Phonologic formulas for Atakapa-Chitimacha. IJAL 12.113–32. [1.4, 1.5, 3.]

———. 1947. Atakapa-Chitimacha *$k^w$. IJAL 13.120–1. [1.4, 1.5, 3.]

———. 1948. Sociologic notes on obsolescent languages. IJAL 14.226–35. [1.7.4]

———. 1964. Linguistic overview. Prehistoric Man in the new world, ed. by Jesse D. Jennings and Edward Norbeck, pp. 527–56. Chicago, The University of Chicago Press. [1.6, 3.]

SWANTON, JOHN R. 1907a. Ethnological position of the Natchez Indians. AmA 9.513–28. [3.]

——. 1907b. Mythology of the Indians of Louisiana and the Texas coast. JAF 20.285–9. [1.4]
——. 1908. The language of the Taënsa. AmA 10.24–32.
——. 1909. A new Siouan dialect. In Putnam Anniversary Volume, pp. 477–86. New York. [1.7.3]
——. 1911. Indian tribes of the lower Mississippi Valley and adjacent coast of the Gulf of Mexico. BAE-B 43. [1.2, 1.3, 1.4, 1.5, 2.]
——. 1913. Animal stories from the Indians of the Muskhogean stock. JAF 26. 193–218.
——. 1916. Terms of relationship in Timucua. Holmes Anniversary Volume, 451–63. Washington, D.C. [1.6]
——. 1917a. Unclassified languages of the Southeast. IJAL 1.47–9. [2.]
——. 1917b. Some Chitimacha myths and beliefs. JAF 30.474–8. [1.4]
——. 1919. A structural and lexical comparison of the Tunica, Chitimacha, and Atakapa languages. BAE-B 68. [1.4, 1.5, 3.]
——. 1921. The Tunica language. IJAL 2.1–39. [1.3]
——. 1922. Early history of the Creek Indians and their neighbors. BAE-B 73. [1.1.2, 1.1.5]
——. 1923a. Aboriginal culture of the Southeast. BAE-R 42.673–726.
——. 1923b. New light on the early history of the Siouan peoples. Journal of the Washington Academy of Sciences 13.33–43. [1.7]
——. 1924. The Muskhogean connection of the Natchez language. IJAL 3.46–75. [1.2, 3.]
——. 1928a. Social organization and social usages of the Indians of the Creek Confederacy. BAE-R 42.23–472. [1.1.5]
——. 1928b. Social and religious beliefs and usages of the Chickasaw Indians. BAE-R 44.169–273. [1.1.1, 1.1.5]
——. 1929a. A sketch of the Atakapa language. IJAL 5.121–49. [1.5]
——. 1929b. The Tawasa language. AmA 31.435–53. [1.6, 2., 3.]
——. 1929c. Myths and tales of the Southeastern Indians. BAE-B 88. [1.1.3, 1.2]
——. 1931. Source material for the social and ceremonial life of the Choctaw Indians. BAE-B 103. [1.1.1]
——. 1932. Indian language studies in Louisiana. ExSI 1930, 195–200.
——. 1934. Newly discovered Powhatan bird names. Journal of the Washington Academy of Sciences 24.96–9.
——. 1946. The Indians of the Southeastern United States. BAE-B 137. [1.2]
TOOMEY, T. NOXON. 1914. Relationships of the Chitimacha linguistic family. BHLAL 4.1–12. St. Louis. [1.4]
——. 1918. Analysis of a text in the Apalachi language. BHLAL 6.1–18.
VILLIERS DU TERRAGE, M. DE, and PAUL RIVET. 1919. Les Indiens du Texas et les expéditions françaises de 1720 et 1721. JSAm n.s. 11.403–42. [1.5]
VINSON, M. 1885. Sur la langue Timucua. PICAm (5th session, 1884) 362–5.[1.6]

VOEGELIN, CHARLES F. 1935. Shawnee phonemes. Lg 11.23–37. [1.10.2]
——. 1936. Productive paradigms in Shawnee. Essays in anthropology presented to A. L. Kroeber, pp. 391–403. Berkeley, University of California Press. [1.10.2]
——. 1937–40. Shawnee stem and the Jacob P. Dunn Miami dictionary. PRSIHS 1.63–108, 135–67, 289–341, 345–406, 409–78. [1.10.1]
——. 1939. Ofo-Biloxi sound correspondences. PIAcadS 48.23–6. [1.7.2, 1.7.3, 4.2]
——. 1941a. North American Indian languages still spoken and their genetic relationships. Language, culture, and personality, ed. by Leslie Spier, A. Irving Hallowell, and Stanley S. Newman, pp. 15–40. Menasha, Wisconsin.
——. 1941b. Internal relationships of Siouan languages. AmA 43.246–9. [1.7]
——. 1953. From FL (Shawnee) to TL (English): Autobiography of a woman. IJAL 19.1–25. [1.10.2]
VOEGELIN, CHARLES F., FLORENCE M. ROBINETT, and NANCY P. HICKERSON. 1953. From FL (Shawnee) to TL (English): some differences between two versions of the autobiography. IJAL 19.106–17. [1.10.2]
VOEGELIN, CHARLES F., and ERMINIE WHEELER VOEGELIN. 1935. Shawnee name groups. AmA 37.617–35. [1.10.2]
——. 1941. Map of North American Indian languages. PAES 20. [3.]
——. 1946. The Shawnee female deity in historical perspective. AmA 46.370–5. [1.10.2]
VOEGELIN, ERMINIE WHEELER. 1941. The place of agriculture in the subsistence economy of the Shawnee. PMA 24.513–20. [1.10.2]
——. 1942. Shawnee musical instruments. AmA 44.463–75. [1.10.2]
——. 1944. Mortuary customs of the Shawnee and other eastern tribes. PRSIHS 2.227–444. [1.10.2]
VOEGELIN, CHARLES F., and FLORENCE M. VOEGELIN. 1966. Map of North American Indian languages. American Ethnological Society: Rand, McNally, and Co.
WAGNER, GÜNTER. 1931. Yuchi tales. PAES 13. New York. [1.8]
——. 1933–38. Yuchi. In HAIL 3.293–384. Edited by Franz Boas. Glückstadt/Hamburg-New York, Augustin. [1.8]
WALLACE, ANTHONY F. C., and WILLIAM REYBURN. 1951. Crossing the ice: A migration legend of the Tuscarora Indians. IJAL 17.42–7. [1.9.2]
WEER, PAUL. 1939. Preliminary notes on the Muskhogean family. PRSIHS 1.245–86.
WEST, JOHN DAVID. 1962. The phonology of Mikasuki. SIL 16.77–91. [1.1.4]
WHITE, JOHN K. 1962. On the revival of printing in the Cherokee language. CAnthr 3/5.511–14. [1.9.1]
WHORF, BENJAMIN L. 1940. Gestalt technique of stem composition in Shawnee. PRSIHS 1.391–406. Reprinted in Language, thought, and reality: Selected writings of Benjamin Lee Whorf, ed. by John B. Carroll, pp. 160–72. 1956. New York, Wiley. [1.10.2]

WOLFF, HANS. 1948. Yuchi phonemes and morphemes, with special reference to, person markers. IJAL 14.240–3. [1.8]
——. 1950–51. Comparative Siouan I, II, III, IV. IJAL 26.61–6, 113–21, 168–78 27.197–204. [1.7.2, 1.7.3, 4.2]
——. 1951. Yuchi text with analysis. IJAL 17.48–53. [1.8]

# INDEX OF NAMES

Aberle, David F., 471, 496
Ačirgin, 194, 234, 260
Adair, James, 599
Adam, Lucien, 583, 590, 604, 606
Adams, William Y., 66, 68
Adamson, Thelma, 388, 393, 409
Adelung, Johann Christoph, 4, 18, 533, 542, 546, 551, 592, 599
Adler, Fred W., 104, 105, 363, 381, 386, 409
Afcan, Anna Rose, 246
Afcan, Paschal, 178, 202, 203, 204, 205, 233, 234, 235, 246, 257, 266, 273, 274
Aghnaghaghpik: *see* Badten, Adelinda Womkon.
Aginsky, Ethel G., 183, 234, 246, 383, 409
Ahmaogak, Rev. Roy, 209, 210, 211, 216, 235, 265, 268, 269
Aiken, Marsha, 275
Aiken, Martha, 211
Aïnana, L., 195
Aivukhak, 191
Ajnan, L., 260
Akmajian, Adrian, 260, 308, 345, 353
Albright, Robert W., 76, 88
Alcan, P., 233
Alexie, Anna, 205, 235
Alexie, Joe, 205, 235
Alford, Thomas Wildcat, 82, 88
Allen, C., 233
Allen, Louis, 25, 44, 553, 562, 596, 599
Alpher, Bary, 476
Alvarez, Albert, 470, 496
Amoss, Pamela Thorsen, 390, 393, 409
Anal'kvasak, Vera A., 192, 195, 235, 260, 261
Andersen, Karl Peter, 223, 280
Anderson, Alexander Caulfied, 298
Anderson, Stephen R., 308, 345, 353
Andrade, Manuel J., 11, 380, 381, 409, 416, 423
Andrew, Willie, 297
Andrews, H. A., 363, 409
Andrews, Margaret Hunt, 201, 235
Angaiak, John, 205, 234, 235, 266
Angalgaam, 273

Angalgaq, 273
Anko, Yuriĭ M., 192, 196, 235
Annis, Dean, 292
Antoine, R. P. Joseph, O. M. I., 219, 235
Antropova, V. V., 236
Aoki, Haruo, 31, 40, 44, 129, 168, 359, 368, 369, 370, 372, 373, 374, 377, 402, 409, 440, 451
Aoki, Paul K., 318, 347
Arima, Eugene, 214, 236, 257, 379
Arrowsmith, Gary, 384
Arroyo de la Cuesta, Father Felipe, 427, 436, 455
Ashkamakyn, 194, 263
Atcitty, Marlene, 309, 345, 355
Aupaumut, Hendrick, 82
Austerlitz, Robert, 28, 313, 314
Avey, O., 233
Avrorin, V. A., 186, 196, 197, 236
Ayakhta, 195, 236
Ayarua, Jean, 276
Ayaruaq, John, 216, 217, 236
Ayer, Edward E., 98, 106, 418

Baba, Osamu, 186, 271
Bach, Emmon, 170, 378, 410
Badten, Adelinda Womkon, 200, 272
Badten, Linda, 274
Bahr, Donald, 470
Bailey, Flora, L., 308, 357, 503
Bajdukov, G., 234, 246
Ballard, Arthur C., 389, 410
Balle, J., 222, 236
Balmès, Joseph, O. M. I., 217, 276
Barabaš, I. I., 236
Barabaš-Nikiforov, I. I., 271
Baraga, Frederic, 523
Barbeau, C. Marius, 297, 533, 534, 540, 562, 563
Barfod, H. P., 224, 236
Barfod, P., 258
Barker, M. A. R., 369, 410, 436, 438, 451
Barnes, Will C., 69
Barnett, Homer G., 360, 392, 410

Barnum, Francis P., S. J., 201, 236
Barratt, Joseph, 521
Barrett, S. A., 447, 451
Barrett, S. M., 443
Bartholet, Joel, 274
Barton, Benjamin Smith, 48, 94, 106, 536, 540, 542, 546, 550, 562, 585, 592, 599, 604
Bartram, William, 599
Bascom, Burton William, Jr., 484, 496
Basina, M. Ja., 235
Basmanova, N. G., 234
Basso, Keith H., 66, 68, 311, 322, 345, 471, 472, 473, 475, 496, 497
Bastian, 11
Bates, Henry W., 567
Bates, Reed, 378, 410
Bauer, Evelyn, 62, 68
Baumhoff, M. A., 44
Beach, W. W., 599, 606, 608
Beauchamp, William M., 536, 562
Beaumont, Ronald, 393
Bechler, Theodor, 222, 236
Becker, Alton L., 307, 354
Beeler, Madison S., 30, 31, 38, 40, 44, 64, 68, 106, 428, 431, 436, 437, 442, 446, 451
Begishe, Kenneth Y., 308, 309, 357, 472, 473, 502
Bell, Whitfield J., Jr., 94, 95, 106
Bellet, P., 498
Bender, Ernest, 539, 562, 587, 599
Benveniste, Émile, 285, 286, 318, 345, 586, 599
Berendt, 95
Bergsland, Knut, 175, 178, 183, 184, 185, 189, 211, 221, 223, 227, 228, 229, 230, 231, 232, 236, 237, 263, 265, 266, 270
Berlandier, Jean Louis, 574, 599
Berlin, Brent, 105, 106
Bernot, Lucien, 424
Berreman, J. V., 363, 410
Berthelsen, Alfred, 221, 280
Berthelsen, Christian, 237
Beukenkamp, Erik J., 388
Beyer, John Frederic, 224, 280
Bibles, Eliot, 97
Biggar, H. P., 532, 562
Billy, Matilda, 299
Binney, George, 279
Binnick, Robert I., 498, 499
Bird, Charles, 237, 249
Birket-Smith, Kaj, 202, 207, 227, 232, 237, 313, 314, 337, 339, 345
Bittany, Adolph E., 306, 308, 345, 354
Bittle, William E., 45, 48, 50, 56, 57, 311, 345, 352, 354, 357, 454, 459, 496, 497, 499, 501, 502

Black, Robert A., 470, 497
Blackman, Margaret B., 318
Blair, Robert W., 309, 345
Blaker, Margaret, 93, 100, 299
Blanchard, Ira D., 81, 82, 88
Blanchett, Marie Nick, 205, 233, 257, 266, 270, 273, 274, 275
Bloch, B., 109
Bloom, Leonard, 587, 609
Bloomfield, Leonard, 8, 11, 12, 13, 15, 16, 17, 18, 20, 27, 34, 35, 44, 54, 83, 87, 88, 89, 103, 106, 109, 115, 127, 168, 203, 449, 451, 482, 506, 508, 509, 510, 511, 512, 513, 514, 516, 517, 518, 520, 521, 522, 523, 524, 525, 598, 599
Boas, Franz, 8, 9, 10, 11, 12, 13, 16, 18, 19, 20, 21, 22, 24, 27, 28, 41, 44, 56, 63, 68, 73, 76, 83, 89, 90, 91, 94, 102, 103, 105, 106, 107, 109, 110, 114, 117, 118, 122, 123, 124, 125, 126, 127, 128, 142, 168, 170, 296, 297, 298, 299, 315, 320, 325, 326, 334, 335, 345, 362, 363, 365, 367, 372, 374, 375, 376, 378, 380, 381, 382, 383, 385, 386, 387, 394, 395, 396, 397, 398, 399, 400, 401, 405, 409, 410, 411, 414, 416, 418, 423, 436, 439, 451, 455, 535, 543, 545, 546, 562, 569
Bodine, James, 489
Bodine, John James, 62, 68, 497
Boggs, R. S., 102, 106
Bogoraz, V. G., 187, 188, 189, 190, 191, 197, 238
Boilvin, Nicholas, 545
Bojcova, A. F., 238
Bollinger, J., 499
Bolodin, L. N., 260, 261
Bolognesi, Giancarlo, 244
Borgstrøm, Carl Hj., 255
Boskbojnikov, M. G., 253
Bossu, 546
Bouchard, Randy, 318, 345, 365, 385, 386, 406, 411
Bouda, K., 267
Bourquin, Theodor, 213, 217, 238, 244, 279
Bowers, Alfred W., 84, 89
Bowman, Elizabeth, 391
Bradbury, John, 546, 563
Brandt, Elizabeth A., 80, 89, 474, 489, 497
Breckman, Kathleen, 257
Breiby, John, 205, 273, 274
Bright, Elizabeth, 66, 68, 436, 437, 452
Bright, Jane O., 36, 44, 131, 168, 301, 321, 345, 450, 451
Bright, Marcia, 63, 68
Bright, William, 29, 30, 38, 42, 44, 45, 46, 48, 49, 50, 51, 52, 55, 56, 57, 59, 63, 64, 65, 66,

Bright, William (cont'd)
  67, 68, 75, 83, 84, 89, 96, 102, 103, 104, 106, 110, 121, 128, 131, 168, 172, 357, 363, 415, 424, 429, 431, 437, 441, 442, 443, 444, 446, 450, 451, 452, 453, 454, 456, 457, 458, 479, 481, 497, 499, 574, 604
Brinton, Daniel G., 10, 18, 23, 33, 45, 82, 89, 95, 98, 107, 112, 531, 575, 578, 580, 590, 593, 594, 599, 600, 601
Broadbent, Sylvia M., 31, 40, 45, 77, 89, 436, 437, 452, 453
Bross, Michael G., 311
Brown, R. P. Bernard, O. M. I., 292
Brown, John Carter, 98, 99
Bruce, Tommy: see Opartok.
Bruyas, Jacques, 534, 563
Bucca, Salvador, 529, 563
Buckner, H. F., 578, 600
Buechel, Eugene, S. J., 543, 563
Bugge, Aage, 223, 224, 225, 238, 244
Buliard, Roger, O. M. I., 276
Bursill-Hall, G., 318
Buschmann, Johann Carl Eduard, 427, 531, 563
Bushnell, David I., Jr., 575, 600
Butler, Ruth Lapham, 106
Byčkov, A., 194, 258
Byington, Cyrus A., 7, 18, 103, 112, 575, 576, 600

Callaghan, Catherine A., 31, 40, 45, 63, 64, 68, 104, 106, 128, 129, 159, 168, 436, 437, 440, 452, 459
Campanius, Johan, 532, 563
Campbell, Rev. Edgar O., 199, 239
Campbell, Rev. John, 343, 344, 346, 353
Campbell, Lillian Nakai, 386
Canestrelli, P. Philippo, S. J., 103, 107, 398, 411
Carlos, 591
Carlson, Barry, 384
Carrière, Gaston, O. M. I., 212, 217, 276, 289, 346
Carroll, John B., 62, 68
Cartier, Jacques, 532, 562
Čarušin, E. I., 195, 239, 263
Carver, Jonathan, 542, 563
Casagrande, Joseph B., 62, 65, 68, 472, 497
Cass, General, 542
Catherine the Great, Empress of Russia, 4, 99
Catlin, George, 531, 538, 542, 548, 549, 563, 588, 600
Cearley, Alvin, 175, 178, 223, 239
Chafe, Wallace L., 25, 33, 37, 55, 104, 107, 290, 305, 317, 346, 507, 525, 527, 528, 531, 533, 535, 536, 537, 540, 553, 560, 563, 585, 588, 596, 600
Chamberlain, Alexander F., 398, 551, 563

Chamberlain, Montague, 521
Chambers, Rev. John R., 209, 239
Champlain, Samuel de, 533, 534
Chapman, John W., 7, 18
Charles II, King of Spain, 576, 583
Charput, Thérèse, 239
Chaumonot, Pierre Joseph Marie, 533
Chikoyak, Andrew, 205, 233, 234, 246, 250, 266, 274
Chomsky, Noam, 105, 107, 109, 203, 226, 369, 411
Christensen, N. O., 178
Claiborne, Judge J. F. H., 528, 563
Clark, Elaine, 310
Clark, George Rogers, 94, 530, 549
Clifton, Ernest, 379
Cline, Howard, 96
Cline, Walter, 384, 411
Codere, Helen, 417
Cohen, Marcel, 57, 99, 104, 107, 112, 114
Coleman, Phyllis, 292
Coleman, William L., 446, 454
Collins, Henry B., 56, 229, 239, 264
Collins, John, 489
Collins, June M., 381, 411
Collins, Raymond, 286, 287, 346
Collins, Sally Jo, 286, 287, 346
Collins, T., 498
Collis, Dermot Rónan F., 175, 178, 214, 217, 222, 225, 232, 239, 276, 280
Colson, Elizabeth, 379, 411
Commons, Rachel S., 411
Conklin, Harold C., 537, 563
Connors, Maureen E., 103, 107
Cook, Curtis, 495
Cook, Eung-Do, 290, 294, 295, 346
Cook, Mary Jane, 62, 69
Cook, William H., 588
Coolidge, Joseph, Jr., 205, 239, 274
Coronado, Francisco Vasquez, 529
Correll, Thomas C., 178, 211, 219, 228, 239, 275, 276
Cotton, Josiah, 6, 20, 522
Cowan, William, 35, 45
Cox, Bruce, 475, 497
Crapo, Richley H., 42, 45
Crawford, James M., 442, 446, 452, 476, 479, 497, 586, 587
Crequi-Montfort, Georges de, 115
Croft, Kenneth, 104, 107, 117, 574, 600
Cross, Marion E., 542, 564
Crowe, Keith J., 216, 276
Crowley, Cornelius J., 66, 69
Cuoq, Jean-André, 523, 534, 564

Curtain, Jeremiah, 21, 375, 427, 446, 456, 537, 564
Curtis, Edward S., 298, 300, 346, 400, 411, 529, 531, 564

da Cruz, Daniel, 528, 564
Darden, B. J., 350
Darnell, Regna, 95, 103, 105, 107, 121
Dart, Diane S., 205, 233, 234, 245, 265, 266, 267, 273, 274
Dauenhauer, Richard, 207, 316, 342
Daulby, Rev. Canon T., 239
Davidson, William, 36, 45, 291, 292, 294, 304, 322, 346
Davis, Clark A., 286, 296, 299, 346
Davis, Irvine, 33, 39, 42, 45, 52, 104, 107, 329, 495, 519
Davis, John H., 394, 406, 411
Davis, Philip, 386
Davis, Wilbur A., 52, 107
Dawson, G. M., 115
Day, Gordon M., 64, 69, 104, 107, 506, 518, 521
D'Azevedo, Warren L., 52, 70, 107, 168, 170, 171, 500
de Angulo, Jaime, 369, 411
DeBlois, A. D., 515
de Brébeuf, Jean, 533
Dejnek, A., 234
Deloria, Ella, 543, 562, 564
de Moville, Gregorio, 583
Dennison, Gene, 309, 357
Denniston, Carter, 293, 347
Denniston, Glenda, 293, 347
Densmore, Frances, 379, 381, 411, 530, 564, 575, 577, 581, 600
de Ridder, Peter, vii
Deserontyon, John, 566
DeSoto, Hernando, 528, 538
de Villiers du Terrage, M., 582
Dexterev, B., 246
Diamond, Stanley, 47, 49, 56, 349, 356, 413, 415, 454, 603
Didier, R. P., O.M.I., 219, 240
Diebold, A. Richard, Jr., 108, 396, 411
Dion, 217
Dixon, Roland B., 13, 14, 15, 18, 21, 24, 27, 29, 31, 45, 81, 88, 121, 123, 124, 125, 128, 136, 164, 168, 427, 430, 431, 432, 433, 434, 436, 438, 440, 441, 450, 452, 593, 600
Dockstader, Frederick J., 66, 69
Dorais, Louis-Jacques, 218, 276
Dorsey, James Owen, 7, 9, 10, 18, 46, 300, 302, 303, 373, 374, 543, 544, 545, 546, 549, 550, 552, 564, 569, 582, 584, 585, 590, 593, 600

Downs, James F., 161, 168
Dozier, Edward P., 61, 63, 65, 66, 67, 69, 164, 169, 471, 489, 497
Drachman, Angeliki Malikouti, 389
Drachman, Gaberell, 389, 411
Drebert, Frederick, 201, 202, 240
Driver, Harold E., 121, 128, 130, 131, 133, 137, 142, 144, 147, 149, 151, 169, 302
Drucker, Philip, 142, 143, 169, 300
Duc de Loubat: see Florimond, Joseph.
Ducharme, R. P. Lionel, O.M.I., 219, 240, 245, 276
Duff, Wilson, 392, 394, 411, 424
Dumond, Don, 230, 232, 240
Dunbar, John Brown, 530
Dunn, Caroline, 521
Dunn, Jacob Piatt, 521, 524, 589
Dunn, John, 376, 412
Duponceau, Peter Stephen, 4, 5, 6, 10, 18, 19, 48, 93, 94, 108, 592, 593, 604
Du Pratz, 591
Duralde, Martin, 582
Durbin, Marshall E., 285, 310, 322, 347
Duthilly, Arthème, 212
Dybowskiego, B., 271
Dyen, Isidore, 396, 397, 412
Dyk, Walter, 375, 412

Eames, Wilberforce, 98
Eastman, Carol M., 318, 347
Eastman, P. D., 233, 275
Eber, Dorothy Harley, 279
Edel, Abraham, 387
Edel, May Mandelbaum, 386, 387, 404, 411, 412
Edgerton, Faye E., 310, 347
Edgerton, Franklin, 5, 6, 8, 19
Edmondson, 489
Edwards, Jonathan, 6, 20
Edwards, Mary, 520
Efrat, Barbara S., 359, 391, 393, 398, 404, 412
Egede, Hans, 4, 225, 237
Egede, Paul, 4, 19, 222, 224, 240
Eggan, Dorothy, 470, 497
Eggan, Fred, 56, 229, 240, 264, 470, 494, 497, 499, 575, 600, 608
Ekholm, Gordon F., 56, 264
Elford, L. W., 36, 45, 291, 292, 304, 322, 346
Eliot, John, 3, 6, 19, 20, 78, 82, 522
El'konin, D. B., 251
Ellis, C. Douglas, 520
Elmendorf, William W., 33, 45, 46, 55, 359, 360, 370, 380, 384, 385, 389, 392, 396, 397, 405, 412, 423, 448, 450, 452, 561, 562, 595, 596, 600
Elson, Benjamin, 366
Embry, Jonathan, 355

## INDEX OF NAMES

Emel'yanova, I. M., 192, 240
Emeneau, Murray B., 12, 19, 121, 126, 132, 169
Erdmann, Friedrich, 217, 240
Ericksen, Michelle, 223, 240
Erkloo, Elijah, 216, 240, 267, 276
Erkloo, Rachel, 215, 239, 240
Ermeloff, Afenogin K., 184, 240, 263
Ernest Billy, 299
Erslew Thomas Hansen, 103, 108
Ervin, Susan M., 62, 69
Essene, F., 300
Evans, 212
Everett, Michael W., 471, 497, 499
Ewbank, Thomas, 531
Ewers, John C., 574, 599

Fabricius, Otho, 222, 224, 241
Fafard, R. P. Eugene, O.M.I., 213, 219, 241
Faineberg, L. A., 197, 271
Fairbanks, Gordon H., 395, 412
Fantin, Mario, 280
Faries, R., 520
Farrand, Livingston, 374
Fauske, David, 208, 211
Featherly, Bernadine, 274
Feldman, Lawrence H., 108
Fenton, William N., 537, 564, 565
Ferguson, Charles, A., 108, 403, 412
Fetzer, Paul, 393
Fickett, Joan Gleason, 538, 564, 588, 601
Fidelholtz, James, 522
Fishman, Joshua A., 169, 474
Fleischer, Jørgen, 225, 241
Fletcher, Alice C., 530, 547, 564
Flint, Rev. Maurice S., 212, 241, 277
Florendo, Nora, 316, 342
Florimond, Joseph, 97
Ford, Richard, 471
Ford, Samuel G., 277
Foreman, Grant, 574, 601
Forshaug, Jean, 257
Foršteĭn, Aleksandr S., 190, 191, 194, 241, 262
Foster, Michael K., 241, 536
Fowler, Don D., 52, 107
Fox, Robin, 62, 69
Frachtenberg, Leo J., 298, 360, 370, 371, 372, 373, 374, 377, 381, 387, 404, 405, 412, 436, 439, 452, 550, 564, 584, 601
Frank, Jeannette, 309, 357
Franklin, Benjamin, 94, 116
Frantz, Donald G., 519
Fraser, Alexander, 533, 564
Frederiksen, Svend, 202, 218, 222
Fredson, John, 285
Freeland, Lucy S., 369, 411, 433, 436, 452, 453

Freeman, John Finley, 86, 89, 94, 95, 108, 347, 365, 382, 413, 574, 577, 581, 582, 585, 588, 601
French, David, 375, 413
French, Kay, 375
Friederici, Georg, 64, 69
Friedrich, Paul, 105, 108
Frigout, Arlette, 470, 497
Frishberg, Nancy, 308, 347
Frobischer, Martin, 230
Fuglsang-Damgaard, Ad., 238, 241
Fulton, Sylvia, 257
Fulwiler, Minnie, 447

Gabelentz, Hans Georg Conon von der, 539, 543, 564
Gad, Finn, 221, 241
Gagné, Raymond C., 209, 214, 215, 216, 217, 226, 241, 242, 259
Gallatin, Albert, 6, 8, 19, 23, 46, 93, 94, 99, 100, 108, 112, 428, 453, 520, 528, 530, 531, 532, 533, 534, 535, 536, 537, 538, 539, 540, 542, 544, 545, 546, 547, 548, 550, 551, 565, 580, 582, 583, 585, 592, 601
Galloway, Brent, 392
Gamboa, Marilyn, 275
Gardiner, John Lyon, 522
Garfield, Viola E., 55, 376, 413
Garvin, Paul L., 37, 66, 69, 102, 108, 110, 118, 398, 399, 405, 413, 529, 565
Gates, William, 96, 102
Gatschet, Albert S., 9, 10, 19, 34, 46, 83, 98, 110, 370, 371, 427, 429, 531, 540, 549, 550, 551, 565, 575, 576, 577, 578, 580, 581, 582, 583, 584, 585, 586, 590, 593, 596, 601
Gaudefroy-Demombynes, J., 108
Geary, James A., 35, 46, 66, 69, 519, 589, 601
Geoghegan, Richard Henry, 183, 242, 243, 249
George, King, 217
Gerard, W. R., 602
Gibbs, George, 76, 89, 99, 298, 300, 303, 389, 413
Gibson, James A., 386, 388, 413
Gifford, E. W., 300, 445
Gilbert, William Harlen, Jr., 587, 602
Gillespie, Beryl, 291, 292
Gilliam, C. E., 602
Gilmore, Melvin R., 530, 531, 544, 545, 547, 565
Giorda, Joseph, 384, 413
Gipper, Helmut, 349
Gleason, H. A., Jr., 286, 347
Goddard, Ives, 35, 46, 73, 78, 81, 82, 85, 89, 96, 97, 99, 103, 108, 115, 507, 510, 513, 514, 515, 516, 517, 520, 525, 602

## INDEX OF NAMES

Goddard, Pliny Earle, 3, 4, 10, 12, 13, 18, 19, 24, 28, 46, 89, 103, 106, 111, 296, 298, 300, 302, 334, 338, 345, 347, 352, 378, 400, 411, 427, 450, 453
Goggin, John M., 591, 602
Golla, Victor K., 36, 40, 46, 141, 285, 300, 301, 302, 305, 321, 347, 437, 450, 453
Gondatti, N. L., 188, 189, 190, 242, 256
Goodenough, Edwin R., 94, 116
Goodenough, Ward H., 49, 602
Goosen, Irvy, 309, 347
Goss, James A., 365, 383, 465, 466, 471, 480, 497
Graburn, Nelson H., 218, 242
Grace, George W., 81, 84, 90, 450, 455
Granberry, Julian, 77, 89, 495, 498, 583, 602
Granger, Byrd H., 64, 68, 69
Grant, Rena V., 376, 413
Gray, Arthur, 210, 242
Gray, George, 528
Gray, Minnie, 210, 242
Greenberg, Joseph H., 30, 46, 105, 109, 122, 130, 139, 169, 170, 412
Greenfield, Philip J., 311, 347
Greenlee, R. F., 579, 602
Gregg, Josiah, 531, 565
Gregg, R. J., 359, 386
Grekoff, George V., 46, 364, 379, 390, 393, 442, 443, 446, 453
Grinnell, George Bird, 530, 565
Gross, Feliks, 66, 69
Grubb, David McC., 378, 413
Gruber, Jacob W., 8, 9, 19
Gubser, N. J., 211, 242
Gudde, Erwin G., 64, 68, 69
Guess, George, 539
Gukhuge, S. M., 192, 195, 196, 242, 260, 261
Gukhuv'e, Taĭsiya, 195
Gulick, John, 540, 565
Gulick, R. H. van, 519
Gumperz, John J., 166, 169
Gunther, Erna, 389, 390, 405, 413, 414, 419
Gursky, Karl-Heinz, 26, 28, 37, 47, 447, 448, 453, 581, 582, 596, 602
Gurvich, I. S., 186, 197, 271

Haas, Mary R., 5, 6, 8, 11, 15, 16, 17, 18, 19, 23, 26, 27, 28, 29, 30, 33, 34, 35, 36, 37, 39, 41, 43, 47, 48, 66, 69, 77, 81, 83, 89, 98, 105, 109, 121, 129, 131, 154, 169, 285, 291, 300, 322, 328, 344, 347, 359, 364, 378, 379, 380, 399, 401, 402, 403, 413, 414, 428, 433, 436, 441, 444, 445, 446, 449, 453, 479, 498, 500, 502, 505, 516, 522, 525, 539, 550, 561, 565, 573, 575, 576, 577, 578, 579, 580, 581, 582, 583, 584, 585, 586, 588, 591, 592, 594, 595, 596, 597, 598, 602, 604

Hackenberg, R., 499
Haeberlin, Herman(n) K., 41, 44, 372, 389, 394, 395, 397, 402, 411, 414
Haile, Father Berard, 7, 19, 305, 306, 309, 348, 349, 471
Halbert, Henry S., 575, 600
Hale, G., 491
Hale, Horatio, 6, 8, 9, 19, 46, 48, 99, 108, 453, 534, 538, 540, 542, 543, 545, 546, 547, 548, 550, 551, 565, 584, 590, 593, 601, 604
Hale, Kenneth L., 32, 42, 49, 58, 118, 294, 295, 298, 307, 308, 310, 348, 353, 472, 480, 481, 482, 483, 484, 485, 487, 489, 490, 497, 498, 502
Halfmoon, Mary, 407
Hall, G. K., 99
Hall, Robert A., Jr., 61, 66, 69, 378, 414
Halle, Morris, 203, 226, 369, 411
Hallowell, A. Irving, 47, 49, 57, 110, 117, 602
Halpern, A. M., 29, 38, 49, 442, 443, 444, 453, 476, 498
Hamilton, William, 530, 544, 565
Hammerich, Louis L., 66, 69, 178, 199, 202, 207, 227, 228, 230, 232, 236, 242, 266, 267, 281
Hammermeister, E., 233
Hamp, Eric P., 27, 49, 50, 84, 104, 108, 109, 110, 112, 178, 231, 243, 359, 363, 381, 387, 388, 399, 402, 414, 437, 446, 453, 547, 566, 574, 604
Hamy, 97
Hankinson, Cathy, 205, 234
Hans, Fred M., 544, 566
Hanzeli, Victor E., 79, 80, 89, 103, 109, 506, 525
Harbeck, Warren, 544
Harms, Robert T., 170, 475, 498
Harp, Rev. George, 243
Harrington, John Peabody, 24, 29, 30, 32, 38, 40, 49, 51, 84, 109, 110, 183, 184, 242, 243, 270, 283, 296, 297, 298, 299, 300, 301, 313, 314, 315, 330, 335, 348, 363, 365, 373, 374, 400, 431, 437, 440, 442, 488, 490, 498, 589, 604
Harrington, Mark R., 520, 537, 566
Harris, Herbert, 394
Harris, Jimmy G., 392, 414
Harris, S. K., 308, 357, 503
Harris, Zellig S., 12, 22, 94, 102, 103, 117, 223, 243, 264, 305, 348, 411, 437, 453, 539, 548, 562, 567, 587, 588, 599
Harry, Anna Nelson, 313, 314
Harvey, Bert, 243
Harvey, Judy, 355
Harvey, Pauline, 210, 243, 264, 270
Harwell, Henry, 476

INDEX OF NAMES

Hascall, Dudley, 204, 272, 274
Hasler, Juan, 67, 69
Hattori, Shirō, 237
Hattori, Takeshi, 184, 243
Haudricourt, André G., 63, 69, 306, 348
Haugen, Einar, 59, 65, 66, 69, 399, 414
Haumonté, J. D., 590, 604
Haury, Emil W., 56, 264
Hawthorne, Gary, 301
Hay, C. L., 111, 454, 455
Hayden, Ferdinand Vandeveer, 84, 89, 530, 531, 543, 544, 545, 546, 547, 548, 549, 566
Hays, George, 243
Hazen, W. G., 303
Heckewelder, John, 5, 19
Heinrich, Albert, 178, 211, 218, 243, 277
Heizer, Robert F., 104, 109, 436, 453
Helm, June, 90, 170, 292
Hennepin, Louis, 542, 564
Henry, David C., 287, 322, 348
Henry, Kay, 287, 322, 348
Henry, Victor, 183, 243
Henshaw, Henry W., 100, 436, 453
Herrod, G., 578, 600
Herzog, George, 65, 66, 69, 76, 89, 405, 414
Herzog, Marvin L., 166, 173
Hess, Thomas M., 359, 367, 389, 390, 391, 394, 402, 406, 414, 415
Hewitt, J. N. B., 80, 85, 535, 536, 537, 538, 540, 564, 566
Hewson, John, 27, 42, 49, 103, 109, 218
Hickerson, Harold, 540, 566, 589
Hickerson, Nancy P., 540, 589, 604
Hiel, Louis, 470
Higgins, Rober, 310, 348
Hilbert, Violet, 390
Hildebrandt, Henry, 294, 296
Hill, Archibald A., 105, 109, 112, 223, 244, 264, 540, 566
Hill, Faith, 310, 311, 348
Hill, Jane H., 45, 49, 454, 481, 497, 498
Hill, Kenneth C., 42, 49, 102, 109, 450, 454, 481, 485, 498
Hill-Tout, C., 382, 385
Hinton, Leanne, 446, 454
Hinz, Rev. John, 201, 202, 204, 244, 268
Hirsch, David I., 229, 232, 244
Hirschy, John, 118
Hoard, James E., 41, 367, 381, 383, 389, 396, 406, 414, 415
Hockett, Charles F., 16, 20, 35, 49, 103, 105, 107, 109, 110, 127, 169, 223, 244, 264, 437, 449, 454, 508, 516, 517, 518, 524, 545, 566, 598, 604
Hodge, David M., 578, 605
Hodge, Frederick Webb, 100, 110, 420

Hoenigswald, Henry M., 118
Hoff, B. J., 111
Hoffman, Bernard G., 540, 566
Hofmann, T. R., 219, 277, 278
Hofseth, Edward, 205, 234, 265
Höhn, Emil Otto, 329, 348
Hoijer, Harry, viii, 3, 9, 15, 16, 17, 20, 21, 24, 36, 44, 45, 49, 50, 66, 70, 76, 103, 104, 106, 110, 112, 126, 169, 264, 285, 291, 292, 294, 295, 298, 301, 302, 303, 304, 305, 306, 307, 310, 311, 312, 313, 319, 321, 322, 323, 324, 326, 330, 331, 332, 333, 334, 335, 345, 346, 348, 350, 351, 352, 355, 356, 363, 400, 415, 450, 451, 454, 493, 498, 500, 518, 520, 525, 574, 599, 603, 604
Holdstock, Marshall E., 294, 295
Holliday, Babette, 355
Hollow, Robert C., Jr., 549, 566
Holm, Agnes, 350, 355
Holm, Wayne, 309, 350, 355
Holmer, Nils M., 41, 50, 218, 232, 244, 537, 547, 549, 566, 584, 585, 598, 604
Holtved, Erik, 202, 217, 222, 223, 225, 232, 244, 266
Honigmann, John, 294, 350
Hopkins, Jerry, 118
Hopkins, Nicholas A., 465, 498
Hopson, Alice, 211, 275
Horden, John, 520
Horsford, E. N., 98, 536, 566
Houston, James A., 244, 277
Howard, Philip, 293, 350
Howren, Robert, 291, 292, 293, 294, 295, 319, 321, 326, 330, 350
Hoxie, W. J., 604
Hudson, Charles M., 48, 604
Hughes, Charles C., 197, 252, 271
Hulton, Paul, 588, 604
Humboldt, Wilhelm von, 5, 105, 108, 112, 123
Hunns, Derek, 228, 244
Hunt, George, 83, 378, 410, 411
Huntington, Arabella, 97
Huntington, Archer M., 97
Huntington, Collis P., 97
Huntington, Henry E., 97, 98
Huot, Martha Champion, 66, 70, 535, 566
Hyde, Villiana, 454, 475, 481, 498
Hyer, Joseph K., 543, 566
Hymes, Dell H., 9, 22, 29, 30, 31, 36, 45, 48, 50, 56, 57, 65, 69, 72, 73, 75, 76, 84, 89, 95, 102, 103, 104, 108, 110, 111, 117, 121, 122, 125, 132, 136, 166, 169, 170, 172, 331, 332, 333, 335, 336, 340, 350, 352, 354, 357, 359, 367, 369, 373, 374, 375, 377, 395, 401, 402, 405, 406, 412, 428, 436, 438, 439, 440, 454, 459, 496, 497, 499, 501, 502, 603, 604

Hymes, Virginia Dosch, 36, 50, 128, 170, 322, 350, 372, 400, 415

Idlout, Leah, 215, 216, 244
Illauq, Leah: *see* Idlout, Leah.
Ingestad, Helge, 211
Innocent, R. P., 178, 183, 184, 229, 245, 248, 249, 286, 293, 294, 319, 352
Irkrowaktok, Bernard, 217, 277
Irniq, Peter, 279
Irvin, Samuel M., 544, 565
Irving, Laurence, 211, 218, 245
Isham, James, 84, 90

Jack, Noah, 205, 245
Jackson, Halliday, 537, 566
Jacobs, Elizabeth D. Langdon, 300, 302, 335, 350, 387, 400, 416
Jacobs, Melville, 11, 50, 63, 70, 103, 107, 127, 142, 147, 170, 298, 300, 301, 315, 328, 335, 350, 359, 360, 363, 367, 368, 370, 371, 372, 374, 375, 376, 381, 387, 389, 391, 400, 401, 405, 406, 416, 418, 423, 436, 454
Jacobs, Roderick, 475
Jacobsen, William H., Jr., 29, 30, 40, 43, 50, 63, 70, 121, 126, 128, 129, 139, 140, 144, 160, 170, 359, 364, 369, 379, 402, 403, 405, 416, 442, 445, 446, 454, 479, 480, 484, 498
Jacobson, Steven, 204, 273
Jacomet, Ida, 205, 249, 265
Jakobson, A., 263
Jakobson, Roman, 48, 109, 110, 121, 170, 183, 231, 237, 245, 525
Jamassee, Nicotye, 245
James, Edwin, 530
James, Robert, 209, 245
Jaquith, James R., 110
Jefferson, Thomas, 6, 20, 94, 108, 520, 528, 530, 592, 604
Jenness, Diamond, 111, 189, 202, 209, 227, 230, 245
Jennings, Jesse D., 56, 135, 144, 160, 172, 424
Jensen, Bent, 178, 221, 246
Jensen, G. Nyborg, 246
Jensen, James, 487
Jesus Christ, 88, 257, 269, 270
Jetté, Julius, 7, 20
Jimmy, 81
Jochelson, V. I., 184, 245, 246, 249, 271
Jochelson, Waldemar, 183, 234, 235
Joe, 246
Joe, Anna Rose Afcan, 205
Joël, Janet, 295, 350
Joel, Judith Dina, 38, 50, 445, 454, 476, 498
Johannsen, Uwe, 314, 351

Johnson, Andrew P., 316, 351
Johnson, Frederick, 104, 111, 118, 433, 454
Johnson, George, 313
Johnson, J. B., 66, 70
Johnson, Lizzie, 297
Johnson, Robert, 383
Johnson, Mrs. Tom, 90
Johnston, Jane, 8
Jones, Elizabeth Orton, 231
Jones, Virginia W., 274
Jones, William M., 64, 70, 87, 90, 521, 524
Jordan, Julia A., 311
Jørgensen, H. F., 20, 247
Jorgensen, Joseph G., 397, 404, 417
Joxel'son, V. I.: *see* Jochelson, V. I.
Judd, Neil M., 100, 111

Kachru, Braj, 348
Kacyga, 255
Ḳaǧakpak: *see* Kagak, D. O.
Kagak, D. O., 210, 246
Kahane, Henry, 348
Kahane, Renee, 348
Kaklya, 194, 246, 260
Kalluak, Mark, 246, 267, 276, 277
Kalya, 192, 194, 195, 246, 260, 261
Kalyanga, 192
Kamerling, Leonard, 246
Kaschube, Dorothea V., 547, 566
Kasuga, Keoru, 184, 246
Kasyga, 194, 246, 247
Kaufman, Terrence S., 376, 552, 561
Kava, Tiiu, 392, 417
Kavauge, A. M., 192
Kayutak, Michael J., 209, 235, 247
Keane, Augustus H., 531, 567
Keim, Geri Rudolph, 205, 234, 257, 273
Keller, Kathryn C., 118
Kelly, John W., 269
Kelly, Mrs. Peter, 318
Kendall, Martha B., 446, 454
Kendall, Bonnie, 476
Kennard, Edward A., 67, 70, 470, 498, 549, 567
Kennedy, Edward, 204
Kermal, Alain, O. M. I., 213, 277
Kess, Joseph, F., 318, 351
Kew, Mike, 365, 411
Kiddle, Lawrence B., 66, 70
Kilpatrick, Anna Gritts, 82, 90, 540, 567, 571, 587, 605
Kilpatrick, Jack Frederick, 82, 90, 540, 563, 567, 571, 587, 605
King, Harry, 474
King, Quindel, 290, 296, 351
Kingsborough, Lord, 96, 97

## INDEX OF NAMES

Kinkade, M. Dale, 41, 50, 104, 111, 129, 170, 359, 364, 366, 380, 385, 387, 388, 393, 398, 402, 403, 404, 417
Kiparsky, Paul, 122, 170, 369, 402, 417
Kipp, James, 549
Kjer, O., 224, 247
Klausen, A., 247
Klein, Sheldon, 50, 450, 454
Kleinschmidt, Samuel Petrus, 6, 7, 20, 21, 55, 103, 114, 178, 183, 202, 213, 217, 222, 223, 224, 225, 226, 229, 236, 244, 247, 249, 259, 260, 264, 268
Kleivan, Inge, 221, 247
Klerekoper, F. G., 209
Klokeid, Terry J., 111, 293, 379, 380, 405, 417
Kluckhohn, Clyde, 309, 351
Kolesnikov, V. D., 251
Kolonov, A., 247
Königseer, 217, 222
Koo, Jang H., 204, 272, 273, 274
Koolerk, Paul, 242
Korolev, 263
Kotschar, Vincent F., 360, 417
Kowalczyk, Emil, 247
Kožin, B., 223
Kozlowski, Edwin, 442, 446, 454, 476
Kramer, Marvin, 399
Krasinskaja-Voblova, L. A., 247
Krauss, Michael E., 28, 29, 36, 37, 50, 121, 133, 134, 135, 137, 170, 175, 178, 183, 188, 189, 191, 200, 202, 203, 204, 207, 210, 247, 272, 273, 283, 285, 286, 287, 292, 293, 294, 297, 298, 301, 304, 305, 307, 311, 314, 316, 317, 318, 319, 320, 321, 322, 323, 324, 325, 326, 327, 330, 331, 332, 333, 335, 336, 339, 340, 341, 342, 343, 344, 351, 399, 475, 476, 478, 486, 491, 493, 498
Kristiansen, Karl, 216, 247
Kroeber, Alfred Louis, 11, 12, 13, 14, 15, 18, 24, 27, 29, 30, 31, 36, 38, 40, 45, 51, 52, 63, 70, 76, 80, 81, 84, 89, 90, 103, 111, 121, 123, 124, 125, 127, 128, 131, 134, 135, 136, 142, 143, 147, 152, 153, 159, 164, 168, 169, 170, 300, 331, 332, 333, 352, 396, 412, 417, 427, 430, 431, 432, 433, 434, 436, 437, 438, 440, 441, 445, 447, 450, 452, 455, 478, 481, 498, 518, 524, 571, 587, 593, 600, 605
Krueger, John R., 385, 417, 539, 567, 587, 605, 607
Ktug'e, 196
Kuiper, F. B. J., 418
Kuipers, Aert H., 41, 386, 393, 397, 403, 404, 406, 417, 418, 424
Kunitz, S. J., 473, 474, 498, 499
Kuroda, S. Y., 437, 455

Kutscher, G., 99, 111
Kuyapa, F., 195, 248

Labadie, Hélène, 291
Labov, William, 166, 173
Lacombe, Albert, 7, 20, 520
Lafayette, Marquis de, 99
Laflèche, F.: see LaFlesche, Francis
LaFlesche, Francis, 547, 553, 564, 567
Lafortune, Bernard, 209, 211, 240, 275
LaGrasserie, Raoul de, 583, 601, 605
Laguna, Frederica de, 285, 286, 312, 313, 314, 315, 337, 339, 345
Lamb, Sydney M., 42, 51, 64, 70, 102, 111, 369, 447, 450, 455, 465, 466, 480, 484, 499
Landar, Herbert, viii, 33, 51, 66, 70, 93, 102, 103, 104, 105, 109, 111, 178, 201, 232, 248, 286, 307, 308, 310, 322, 345, 352, 405, 418
Lane, George Sherman, 48
Langacker, Ronald W., 42, 51, 204, 450, 455, 475, 476, 481, 482, 485, 487, 498, 499
Langdon, Margaret, 38, 51, 129, 171, 442, 445, 446, 455, 476, 499
Larsen, H., 202
LaSalle, S. de, 528
Latham, Robert G., 428, 429, 430, 455, 531, 551, 553, 556, 567
Laufer, Berthod, 343
Laughlin, William S., 184, 248, 249
Laurent, Joseph, 518
Lauridsen, P., 232, 248
Law, Howard W., 38, 51
Lawson, John, 519, 538, 541, 567, 583, 589, 605
Lawson, Virginia, 291, 293, 294, 295
Lazuko, S. M., 235, 248
Leap, William L., 471, 489, 499
Lecht, 217
Lee, Dorothy D., 66, 70
Lee, May, vii
Leechman, Douglas, 61, 69
Leer, Jeffrey A., 207, 275, 316, 342, 352
Lefebvre, Gilles R., 214, 216, 248, 277
Legoff, Laurent, 7, 20, 289
Legta, Lejta: see Leïta, B.
Lehmann, Walter P., 99, 111, 173
Leighton, Dorothea, 309, 351
Leïta (Legta), B., 194, 248, 258
Lemer, R. P. Louis, O. M. I., 213, 248, 257
Lemert, Edwin M., 404, 418
Lemoine, Geo., 523, 524
Lenin, Nikolai, 195, 247
Leon, Nicolás, 98
Leslie, Adrian, 392
Lessa, William A., 406, 418

Lesser, Alexander, 37, 529, 531, 563, 567
Levin, Norman Balfour, 544, 567
Levine, Robert D., 319
Lévi-Strauss, Claude, 406, 470, 502
Levy, Jerrold E., 473, 474, 498, 499
Levy, Richard, 431, 437, 440
Lewis, Rev. Arthur, 212, 249
Lewis, Meriweather, 94, 530, 549
L'Helgouac'h, Buliard, 219
L'Helgouac'h, R. P. Jean, O.M.I., 249
Li, Fang-Kuei, 28, 34, 36, 37, 51, 103, 116, 290, 295, 300, 302, 313, 314, 319, 321, 330, 335, 352, 450, 455
Lieber, Oscar M., 550, 567, 585, 605
Lightner, 487
Liljeblad, Sven S., 410, 412, 422, 480
Lindenfeld, Jacqueline, 66, 70, 499
Lipkind, William, 545, 554, 555, 567
Lisker, Leigh, 370, 418
Ljapidevskij, A. V., 223
Loewen, Jacob A., 104, 111
Lomack, Mary Ann, 205, 249, 270, 274
Lomack, Molly, 270, 274
Long, Stephen A., 545
Longacre, Robert E., 42, 51, 483, 484, 495, 499
Lonneux, Martin J., S. J., 201, 249
Loriot, James, 51, 104, 110, 111, 116, 363, 418, 574, 605
Lot-Falck, E., 261
Lotz, J., 108
Loughridge, Robert McGill, 578, 605
Loukotka, Čestmir, 104, 111, 114, 117
Lounsbury, Floyd G., 39, 47, 51, 64, 70, 76, 90, 183, 242, 249, 535, 536, 538, 540, 558, 559, 567, 587, 588, 598, 603, 605
Lowie, Luella Cole, 98, 103, 115
Lowie, Robert H., 84, 90, 98, 103, 115, 117, 152, 171, 300, 543, 544, 547, 548, 567
Lushbaugh, B. F., 530
Lynge, Kristoffer, 238, 249

MacAllester, David, 471
McCawley, Clay, 579, 605
McCawley, James D., 487, 499
McCay, Bonnie, 392
McClellan, Catherine, 293, 294, 315, 319
Maccoby, Eleanor, 68
MacCurdy, George Grant, 103, 112
McDavid, Raven I., 585
Macgregor, Roderick, 249
McGuff, Pete, 83, 375
McIlwraith, Thomas F., 386, 418
McKay, 67
McKennan, Robert, 285
McKenney, Edward, 546, 567
Mackenzie, Kenneth, 531
McLendon, Sally V., 29, 38, 51, 65, 66, 70, 442, 443, 446, 456
McLuhan, Marshall, 67, 70
MacMillan, Donald Baxter, 249
McNair, Peter L., 365, 411
MacPherson, Andrew, 218, 249
McQuown, Norman, 96, 401, 418
McRoy, Nancy, 286
Madigan, Robert, 476
Makik, 217, 249, 266, 267
Malaurie, Jean, 248
Malécot, André, 84, 450, 455
Malkiel, Yakov, 173
Mallon, S. T., 178, 216, 249, 278
Mandelbaum, David G., 15, 20, 112, 115, 171, 172
Mandelbaum, May: see Edel, May Mandelbaum.
Mansfield, A. W., 249
Mansur, Guérios, 112
Marcoux, Joseph, 534
Marc-Uqittuq, 217
Marcy, Randolph B., 528, 529, 567
Maring, Joel M., 472, 476, 495, 499
Marino, Mary Carolyn, 545, 567
Marr, N. Ja., 250
Maršak, S. Ja., 195, 249, 263
Marsh, Gordon H.: see Innocent, R. P.
Marten, Anita Elma, 545, 568
Martin, A., 247
Martin, Frederica I., 183, 242
Martin, H. N., 577, 605
Martinet, 215
Masayesva, LaVerne, 474
Mase, Hideo, 224, 280
Mason, J. Alden, 42, 52, 433, 436, 455
Mason, Otis T., 528, 563
Massey, William C., 128, 137, 142, 147, 169
Masta, Henry Lorne, 518
Mather, Elsie, 205, 250, 270
Mathevet, Jean-Claude, 521
Mathiot, Madeleine, 470, 499
Matsuda, Tokuichiro, 105, 118
Matthews, G. Hubert, 41, 52, 118, 544, 547, 548, 551, 552, 568, 585, 586, 598, 605, 606
Matthews, Washington, 548
Mattina, Anthony, 250, 385
Maximilian, Alexander Philip, Prince of Wied, 530, 531, 542, 546, 547, 548, 549, 568
Mayers, Marvin K., 112
Méeus, 217
Meeusen, A. E., 35, 52, 517, 519, 525
Meganack, Seraphim, 275
Meillet, Antoine, 57, 104, 112, 114

## INDEX OF NAMES

Mengarini, P. Gregorio, S. J., 384, 418
Menovščikov, Georgij Alekseevič, 175, 177, 178, 179, 185, 186, 188, 189, 190, 191, 192, 193, 194, 195, 196, 197, 202, 204, 211, 213, 228, 229, 232, 237, 238, 243, 250, 251, 252, 253, 254, 255, 259, 260, 266, 271, 272
Merriam, Alan P., 384, 418
Merriam, C. Hart, 81, 224, 300, 302, 353
Meščaninov, I. I., 192, 255
Métayer, R. P. Maurice, O.M.I., 213, 219, 249, 255, 278
Metcalf, Leon V., 366, 387
Mey, Jacob, 178, 213, 223, 225, 228, 239, 255, 262, 280
Michelson, Truman, 15, 20, 24, 27, 35, 52, 74, 81, 83, 85, 87, 432, 449, 456, 506, 508, 509, 518, 521, 523, 525, 606
Mierau, Eric, 61, 70
Milanowski, Paul, 287, 353
Milanowski, Trude, 287
Milewski, Tadeusz, 140, 171
Milke, Wilhelm, 331, 332, 353
Miller, B. F., 255
Miller, Carl F., 583, 606
Miller, D. Gary, 178, 185, 189, 190, 227, 256, 281
Miller, J. L., 550, 585
Miller, Mary R., 474, 500
Miller, Patsy, 243
Miller, Paul, 243
Miller, V. F., 188
Miller, Wick R., 32, 33, 35, 39, 42, 45, 52, 66, 70, 107, 109, 161, 171, 450, 456, 463, 464, 465, 480, 481, 484, 485, 489, 490, 495, 500, 598, 606
Mitchell, Marjorie R., 391, 418
Mithridates, 334, 562
Mitiarjuk of Wakeham, 217, 256
Mixco, Mauricio, 442, 446, 456
Miyaoka, Osahito, 175, 178, 184, 186, 202, 203, 204, 206, 227, 228, 229, 232, 256, 271, 274, 275
Modrow, Ruth, 388, 418
Mohrmann, Christine, 20, 112
Moll, T. A., 257
Montgomery, William B., 546, 568
Montour, Nelles, 82
Monus, Anita, 293
Monus, Victor, 293
Mooney, James, 528, 539, 568, 587, 606
Moore, Bruce R., 112
Morack, Kathy, 205, 233
Morgan, Lawrence, 399
Morgan, Lewis Henry, 99, 530, 531, 532, 534, 535, 537, 538, 539, 543, 544, 546, 547, 548, 549, 551, 553, 568, 575, 593, 606

Morgan, William, 306, 307, 309, 357
Morice, Adrien-Gabriel, O.M.I., 7, 289, 296, 343, 346, 353
Morice, William G., 20
Morozov, V., 246
Moser, Edward, 480, 500
Moshinsky, Julius, 442, 446, 456
Moulton, William G., 17
Mueller, Richard J., 287, 290, 353
Mumixtyx, K., 263
Murdock, George Peter, 49, 102, 104, 112, 364, 382, 418, 518, 574, 602, 606
Murphy, Penny, 309, 353, 355
Murray, Dr., 546
Mylerberg, Duane, 391

Nackedhead, Calvin, 83, 91
Nacktan, Lena, 313, 314
Nagata, Shuichi, 470, 500
Nageak, James, 210
Naish, Constance, 315, 316, 333, 340, 342, 353
Napolean, Dorothy, 205, 266, 274
Nasaaluk, Marie, 217
Nashoalook, Alva, 210, 257, 265
Nbyluvak, Amkagun, 272
Neck, Helper, 202
Nelson, Galushia, 313
Nesbitt, Paul, 383
Nettl, Bruno, 590, 606
Netsvetov, Jakov, 182, 184, 271
Neuman, Robert W., 606
Nevin, Bruce E., 446, 456
Newcombe, C. F., 317
Newman, Stanley S., 14, 17, 20, 32, 40, 47, 49, 52, 57, 105, 110, 113, 117, 378, 386, 402, 404, 418, 428, 436, 437, 439, 440, 453, 456, 495, 500, 602
Nichols, Johanna, 105, 113, 401, 419
Nichols, Michael, 450
Nick, Marie: *see* Blanchett, Marie Nick.
Nick, Moses, 205, 246, 274
Nicklas, T. Dale, 575
Nicodemus, Lawrence, 383, 406
Nida, Eugene A., 118, 209
Nielsen, Frederik, 223, 225, 238, 257
Nikitin, N. N., 260, 261
Nolte, Nancy, 234, 235
Nomland, G. A., 300, 302
Norbeck, Edward, 56, 424
Norman, F., 112
Numylen, 196
Nungak, Zebedee, 214, 257, 279
Nurse Big Joe, 277
Nynijuvak, Amkaun V., 194, 235, 262, 263

O'Brien, Michael, 385, 419
Odoroff, C. L., 499
O'Grady, Geoffrey N., 105, 118, 285, 292, 294, 295, 365, 378, 379, 392, 406
Ohannessian, Sirarpi, 62, 70
Okrand, Marc, 437, 440
Olbrechts, Frans M., 538, 539, 568, 587, 588, 605, 606
O'Leary, Timothy J., 104, 113
Oliver, Symmes C., 149, 165, 171
Olmstead, David L., 29, 37, 44, 52, 55, 61, 62, 70, 71, 306, 353, 429, 431, 442, 444, 446, 456
Olsen, Carl Christian, 178, 223, 225, 257, 261
Olson, Ronald L., 387, 419
Onenko, S. N., 196, 197, 257
Oozeva, Elinor, 200, 257
Òpartok (Tommy Bruce), 217, 239, 257, 266, 278
Opler, Morris, 497
Orlova, Elizaveta Porfir'evna, 185, 194, 257, 258, 271, 272
Ornstein, Jacob, 355
Orr, Sharon Pungowiyi, 200
Ortiz, Alfonso, 470, 471, 472, 500, 501
Orton, Wolverton, 301
Osgood, Cornelius, 285, 286, 292, 323, 337, 353
Oso, Juan del, 69
Oswalt, Helen, 202, 258
Oswalt, Robert L., 38, 52, 64, 66, 70, 442, 443, 444, 446, 456

Pacifique, Révérend Père, 522
Pageau, Christiane, 216, 258, 278
Pageau, Serge, 213, 278
Pallas, P. S., 592, 606
Panegoosho, Mary, 216, 240
Papik, 239, 257
Pareja, Francisco, 77, 582, 606
Parisot, M. J., 590, 604
Parker, Arthur C., 537, 568
Parker, Ely S., 537
Parks, Douglas R., 530, 531
Parks, Sophie, 270
Parrett, W. W., 247
Parrish, James E., 308, 353
Parsons, Elsie Clews, 528, 568
Pastor, Jens Olsen, 222
Paxomov, A., 263
Peabody, Robert S., 58
Peacock, Rev. Frederick W., 218, 258, 266, 278
Pearce, Terry M., 64, 68, 71, 278
Pearson, Clara, 298
Peck, Rev. Edmund J., 212, 217, 238, 241, 249, 258
Peden, William, 20
Pedtke, Dorothy, 309, 353

P'ei, Ts'ai Yuan, 51
Peirson, Abraham, 520
Penfield, Susan, 476
Penn, William, 382, 419
Perchonock, Norma, 100, 113, 308, 354, 473, 500
Perrett, Rev. Walter Whatley, 217, 218, 266, 279
Petersen, H. C., 223, 280
Petersen, Jonathan, 224, 258
Petersen, K. Helveg, 246
Petersen, Kjeld Thor, 223, 280
Petersen, Robert O. H., 221, 223, 225, 258, 280, 286
Petitot, R. P. Emile, O.M.I., 7, 20, 213, 289, 292, 343
Petrohelos, Eileen, 178
Petter, Rudolphe, 519
Pfizmaier, A., 183, 259
Phelps, Elaine, 391
Phinney, Archie, 368, 419
Pickens, A. L., 586, 606
Pickering, John, 5, 6, 20, 23, 52, 76, 90, 518, 539, 569, 587, 592, 607
Pidgeon, Michael, 391, 419
Pierce, Joe E., 31, 53, 102, 105, 113, 300, 301, 302, 354, 364, 367, 372, 374, 401, 404, 419, 552, 569
Pierce, Larry, 406
Pike, Kenneth L., 110, 307, 310, 354, 546
Pilling, James Constantine, 7, 21, 81, 82, 90, 98, 99, 100, 103, 113, 224, 232, 259, 300, 364, 382, 419, 508, 518, 525, 533, 534, 535, 356, 537, 538, 539, 540, 543, 545, 547, 548, 549, 569, 574, 576, 607
Pinart, Alphonse, 436, 453
Pinart, M., 576
Pinnow, Heinz-Jürgen, 29, 35, 47, 53, 63, 71, 113, 286, 308, 309, 315, 322, 335, 336, 337, 338, 339, 340, 341, 342, 343, 354, 402, 419, 478, 501
Pisani, Vittore, 244
Pitkin, Harvey, 31, 39, 40, 45, 53, 104, 113, 129, 171, 435, 436, 438, 440, 452, 457
Pitseolak, 279
Plaut, W. Gunther, 542, 569
Polgar, Steven, 62, 71
Poljak, G. B., 260, 261
Pollard, J. Garland, 589, 607
Pond, Samuel W., 542
Popova, N. S., 259, 260, 263, 272
Porter, K. W., 584, 607
Post, Richard H., 411
Postal, Paul M., 535, 561, 569
Potier, Rev. Pierre, 533, 564
Potter, Beatrix, 234

# INDEX OF NAMES

Pottier, Bernard, 102, 114
Poulsen, Jens, 225
Powell, James V., 359, 368, 370, 373, 374, 381, 382, 406, 412, 419, 478, 593, 595, 601, 604
Powell, John Wesley, 6, 9, 10, 12, 14, 19, 21, 23, 45, 46, 48, 53, 76, 90, 98, 100, 110, 114, 116, 124, 125, 126, 171, 428, 429, 430, 431, 432, 457, 531, 551, 569, 607
Powers, 428
Preston, Luke, 472
Preston, W. D., 114, 183, 223, 259, 262, 370, 420, 537
Price, P. David, 105, 114
Prince, J. Dyneley, 82, 90, 521, 522
Prokofiev, S., 233
Pryde, Duncan, 219, 259
Puhvel, Jaan, 109
Pulte, William, 576, 607
Pyle, Charles, 223, 259, 292, 321, 354
Pyrlaeus, Johann Christoph, 534

Quáy-Lem u En-Chów-men, 384, 420
Quimby, George I., 56, 229, 264
Quinn, David Beers, 519, 588, 604
Quinney, John, 82

Radin, Paul, 13, 24, 47, 49, 53, 56, 83, 356, 433, 447, 448, 454, 457, 545, 562, 569, 603
Radliński, Ignacy, 271
Raffo, Yolanda Adela, 391, 420
Rafinesque, Constantine S., Jr., 99, 549, 569
Rãle, Sébastien: see Rasles, Sebastian.
Ramanujan, A. K., 118
Ramos, Elaine, 316
Rand, Earl, 577, 607
Rand, Silas T., 522
Randall, Arne, 257
Ransom, Jay Ellis, 82, 90, 183, 184, 240, 242, 259, 271, 389, 420
Rask, Rasmus, 228, 266
Rasles, Sebastian, 6, 20, 518, 607
Rasmussen, Christian, 223, 224, 247, 259
Rasmussen, Knud, 189, 202, 209, 227, 259
Ratmanova, Ostrov, 187
Ray, Dorothy Jean, 211, 275
Ray, Verne F., 360, 363, 368, 369, 370, 384, 420
Read, William A., 575, 578, 579, 607
Reagan, Albert B., 420
Red Thunder Cloud, 551, 568, 586, 606
Redden, James E., 442, 446, 457, 476, 500
Reed, E. Irene, 175, 178, 202, 203, 204, 205, 207, 234, 259, 273, 274
Regan, P., 175

Reichard, Gladys A., 27, 41, 53, 306, 348, 349, 353, 354, 356, 383, 394, 395, 420, 422, 449, 457
Reid, Russell M., 463, 500
Renville, Michel, 569
Requa, W. C., 546, 568
Rey, H. A., 234
Reyburn, William D., 538, 539, 540, 569, 571, 588, 607
Reynolds, Norman, 313
Rice, Stuart A., 54, 115
Rich, E. E., 84, 90
Richardson, Murray W., 291, 354
Riggs, Mary Ann Clark, 543, 569
Riggs, Stephen Return, 7, 21, 542, 543, 569, 572
Rigsby, Bruce J., 31, 40, 53, 129, 171, 300, 359, 368, 369, 370, 374, 376, 377, 378, 402, 406, 407, 420, 421, 440
Rioux, Louis-Philippe Marcel, 114
Rischel, Jorgen, 224, 280
Ritchie, Priscilla, 406
Ritter, John, 285
Rivet, Paul, 12, 114, 115, 582
Rjabušinskij, F. P., 271
Roberts, Helen H., 379, 421
Robinett, Florence M.: see Voegelin, Florence M.
Robins, R. H., 68, 168, 403, 421, 449, 457
Robinson, Dow F., 100, 114
Roehrig, F. L. O., 543, 569
Rogers, Jean H., 523, 524
Rohner, Ronald P., 9, 21, 83, 90, 103, 114
Rood, David S., 529, 531, 569
Rosing, Jens, 222
Rosing, Nikolaj, 221, 223, 259
Rosing, Otto, 6, 7, 21, 103, 114, 222, 259
Rousseau, Jacques, 114, 248
Rousselière, R. P. Guy Mary, O.M.I., 213, 218, 260, 262, 279
Rowe, John Howland, 10, 21, 24, 53, 104, 117
Rubcova, Ekatèrina Semenovna, 189, 190, 191, 192, 194, 195, 196, 200, 223, 234, 238, 260, 261, 272
Rudolph, Geri, 273, 274
Rumberger, J. P., Jr., 371, 421
Rutherford, Phillip R., 101, 114
Ryherd, James M., 113, 300, 302, 354, 401, 419

Sabean, B., 261, 264
Sadock, Jerrold, 178, 223, 261
Sagard-Théodat, Gabriel, 533, 569, 570
St. Clair, H. H., 372
Saladin d'Anglure, Bernard, 178, 213, 216, 217, 218, 261, 279
Salamatov, 182

Salisbury, Edward E., 112
Salomonie, Joanassie, 267, 276
Salzmann, Zdeněk, 66, 71, 104, 112, 114, 518
Sam, Pauline, 407
Sánchez García, Daniel, 115
Sapir, Edward, 9, 11, 12, 13, 14, 15, 16, 18, 20, 21, 24, 25, 26, 27, 28, 29, 30, 31, 32, 33, 34, 36, 37, 42, 53, 54, 56, 63, 70, 71, 83, 89, 90, 98, 100, 103, 106, 109, 110, 112, 114, 115, 117, 123, 124, 125, 126, 127, 131, 136, 164, 165, 166, 168, 169, 171, 172, 285, 295, 300, 301, 303, 305, 306, 307, 311, 312, 313, 317, 318, 319, 320, 321, 322, 323, 324, 326, 330, 333, 334, 335, 339, 340, 343, 351, 354, 355, 356, 360, 363, 368, 370, 374, 375, 376, 377, 379, 380, 382, 383, 394, 398, 399, 401, 402, 405, 421, 422, 423, 424, 427, 428, 431, 432, 433, 435, 436, 438, 439, 440, 441, 442, 443, 444, 447, 448, 449, 450, 456, 457, 458, 475, 478, 479, 483, 487, 493, 498, 500, 505, 511, 512, 515, 525, 550, 553, 556, 561, 570, 584, 586, 594, 595, 596, 597, 598, 607
Saporta, Sol, 105, 115
Sasaki, Tom T., 62, 71
Saunders, Ross, 386
Sauvageot, Aurelien, 229, 230, 261
Saville, Muriel, 307, 309, 355, 476
Savok, Lilli, 210
Sawyer, Jesse O., Jr., 50, 66, 71, 171, 424, 437, 447, 455, 457, 502, 522
Say, Thomas, 530, 539, 542, 544, 546, 547, 548
Schaeffer, Claude E., 419, 550, 551, 570, 585, 609
Scheppers, Emile, 105, 115
Schmeckebier, Laurence F., 99, 115
Schmitt, Alfred, 202, 261
Schmitt, Iva Osanai, 529, 570
Schmitt, Karl, 529, 570
Schneider, R. P. Lucien, O.M.I., 175, 212, 213, 214, 217, 219, 255, 260, 261
Schoenberg, Rev. Wilfred P., S. J., 365
Schoolcraft, Henry Rowe, 8, 21, 97, 99, 449, 505, 525, 528, 529, 534, 535, 536, 537, 538, 539, 544, 548, 549, 570
Schuller, Rudolf, 102, 115
Schultz, John, 383
Schultz-Lorentzen, C. W., 213, 214, 223, 224, 259, 262
Schultze, Augustus, 201, 262
Schutz, Noel W., Jr., 61, 72, 466, 502
Scott, Richard B., 62, 71
Seaburg, William, 391
Sebeok, Thomas A., vii, viii, 96, 97, 102, 108, 115, 545, 570
Secoy, Frank Raymond, 148, 172

Seiden, William, 476, 500
Seiler, Hansjakob, 42, 54, 450, 457, 481, 500
Seler, 97
Sequoya, 587
Serejnegmi, Wbje, 272
Sergeev, M. A., 196, 272
Sergeeva, Katerína Semenovna, 191, 194, 196, 246, 250, 251, 260, 262, 263, 272
Shade, Charles E., 184, 263
Shafer, Robert, 54, 55, 115, 343, 355, 434, 438, 458, 490, 500
Shannon, George, 549
Sharp, Margaret Amy, 62, 69
Shaterian, Alan, 442, 446, 458
Shaterian, Robert, 476
Shaw, George C., 63, 71
Shea, John Gilmary, 535, 570
Sherzer, Joel, 60, 63, 95, 105, 107, 115, 121, 129, 133, 137, 139, 143, 147, 149, 152, 155, 160, 162, 164, 172, 402, 422, 483
Shimkin, Dmitri B., 184, 231, 237, 263, 463, 500
Shinen, David C., 199, 200, 257, 263, 264
Shinen, Marilene, 199, 200, 263, 264
Shipley, William F., 31, 33, 39, 40, 53, 54, 66, 71, 86, 87, 88, 90, 129, 171, 172, 369, 370, 377, 422, 427, 435, 436, 437, 438, 440, 447, 450, 457, 458, 459
Shorey, Hazel, 489
Shuy, Roger W., 62, 71
Sibley, John, 528
Siebert, Frank T., Jr., 35, 41, 55, 115, 449, 458, 506, 510, 516, 518, 525, 551, 570, 583, 585, 586, 593, 598, 608
Siegel, Bernard J., 102, 115
Sikupsigak: see Harvey, Pauline
Silentman, Irene, 355
Silver, Shirley, 29, 35, 38, 55, 78, 90, 129, 172, 431, 442, 443, 446, 458
Silverstein, Michael, 40, 53, 129, 171, 178, 223, 264, 359, 368, 369, 370, 373, 376, 377, 402, 421, 422, 435, 439, 458
Simmons, Hoxie, 301
Simmons, Lanier A., 606
Simmons, Leon V., 309, 322, 345, 355
Simmons, Samuel, 209, 239, 264, 268
Siniard, Roy, 447
Sirois, Luc, 523
Skorik, P. Ja., 196, 254, 264
Sloat, Clarence, 383, 398, 417, 422
Smith, Allan H., 363, 384, 422
Smith, Buckingham, 574, 576, 577, 579, 581, 582, 583, 585, 588, 608
Smith, Erminnie A., 538, 570
Smith, John, 524, 589, 608
Smith, Lawrence, 218

## INDEX OF NAMES

Smith, M. Estellie, 475, 489, 498, 500
Smith, Marian W., 55, 389, 405, 411, 414, 418, 422, 423
Smith, Marie, 314
Smith, Murphy D., 94, 95, 106, 108, 365, 382, 413, 601
Smith, N. P., 112
Snow, Charles T., 388, 422
Snyder, Sally, 390, 422
Snyder, Warren A., 389, 422
Soboleff, Walter, 316
Sokolow, Jane, 373
Somersal, Laura Fish, 447
Sommerfelt, Alf, 20, 112
Sorsby, William, 104
Sozzo, Ciro, 280
Spade, Watt, 83, 90
Spalding, Alec E., 215, 216, 264
Sparkman, Philip S., 81, 84, 90, 455
Speck, Frank G., 463, 500, 518, 522, 523, 536, 539, 550, 551, 576, 579, 585, 586, 587, 589, 608, 609
Speirs, Randall H., 489, 501
Spencer, Joab, 609
Spencer, Robert F., 66, 71, 135, 144, 145, 146, 150, 157, 158, 160, 172
Sperry, Archdeacon John, 219, 235, 264
Spicer, Edward H., 61, 66, 69, 71
Spier, Leslie, 47, 49, 57, 70, 110, 117, 169, 172, 363, 369, 375, 411, 423, 528, 529, 570, 602
Spinden, H. J., 549, 572
Spoehr, Alexander, 499, 579, 609
Spolsky, Bernard, 102, 108, 118, 309, 350, 355, 476
Stalin, I. V., 194, 234
Stammbaum, 177, 228, 293, 304, 311, 312, 323
Stanley, Richard, 295, 305, 307, 356
Stark, Donald S., 544, 570
Stark, Louisa, 102, 104, 116
Starring, William, 543, 566
Steedman, Elsie, 405
Stefansson, 232, 241, 247
Steinmann, Rev., 264
Steinthal, 123
Stern, Theodore, 369, 370, 423
Stetson, R. H., 548, 570
Steuben, 5
Stevens, Jedediah Dwight, 542, 570
Stevens, Minnie, 313, 314
Stevens, Scar, 313, 314
Stevens, Wallace, 94, 116
Stewart, Joseph L., 405, 423
Stocking, George W., Jr., 9, 21, 101
Story, Gillian, 315, 316, 333, 340, 342, 353, 356

Stout, David, 489
Strachey, William, 46, 524, 589, 601, 604
Stresser-Péan, G., 114
Strom, R. P., 211, 275
Stross, Brian, 121
Stuart, C. I. J. M., 104, 116
Stuart, Dawn, 392
Sturtevant, William C., 66, 71, 96, 100, 104, 116, 487, 537, 551, 563, 570, 577, 578, 579, 583, 588, 589, 591, 592, 602, 609
Suárez, Jorge A., 116
Sue, Hiroko, 292, 356
Sunik, O. P., 196, 264, 265, 272
Susman, Amelia, 545, 570
Suttles, Wayne, 52, 55, 107, 142, 172, 359, 360, 381, 384, 390, 391, 392, 396, 397, 405, 412, 423
Sutton, Grace, 310
Suvorov, E. K., 271
Sverdlov, V. S., 234
Swadesh, Morris, 21, 26, 30, 31, 32, 33, 34, 37, 41, 43, 45, 46, 51, 54, 55, 62, 71, 83, 90, 94, 95, 99, 102, 103, 116, 117, 127, 128, 172, 183, 184, 208, 213, 223, 227, 228, 229, 230, 231, 237, 239, 244, 249, 264, 265, 266, 301, 319, 329, 330, 331, 332, 333, 343, 344, 356, 360, 368, 370, 373, 377, 378, 379, 380, 381, 382, 391, 394, 395, 396, 397, 402, 404, 409, 414, 421, 423, 431, 434, 435, 436, 438, 439, 442, 443, 447, 448, 457, 458, 466, 487, 500, 501, 512, 525, 550, 577, 581, 582, 583, 584, 585, 594, 596
Swanson, Earl H., Jr., 49, 52, 55, 169, 410, 412, 422, 497, 500, 501, 502
Swanton, John R., 20, 24, 26, 30, 34, 46, 48, 56, 77, 83, 104, 116, 123, 125, 172, 317, 318, 334, 337, 356, 374, 424, 543, 545, 546, 549, 550, 551, 552, 562, 564, 565, 570, 574, 575, 576, 577, 579, 580, 581, 582, 583, 584, 585, 590, 591, 593, 594, 595, 596, 600, 601, 604
Swartz, B. K., Jr., 369, 424
Swimmer, 606
Swoboda, Leo, 386
Sylestine, Harden, 577

Tabios, Derenty, 207, 275
Tac, Pablo, 81, 84
Tagarook, Peter, 210, 265
Tagliavini, Carlo, 81, 90
Talmy, Leonard, 442, 446, 458
Tambi, B., 235
Tanous, Louise, 38, 58
Tansy, Ruby, 286
Tanuta, 195, 260, 265
Taptto, Mary Helen, 308, 356

Tatak, 194, 247, 260, 265
Tate, Henry W., 376
Tax, Sol, 102, 103, 116, 237
Taylor, Allan R., 37, 57, 66, 71, 80, 90, 202, 265, 516, 519, 527, 531, 561, 571, 588
Taylor, Herbert C., 394, 424
Tayu, 194, 263, 265
Tedlock, Dennis, 471, 472, 501
Teeluk, Martha, 202, 204, 205, 234, 265, 266, 270, 273, 274
Teeter, Karl V., 27, 35, 57, 64, 71, 89, 103, 109, 431, 449, 458, 505, 508, 509, 522, 525
Teit, James A., 135, 136, 137, 172, 178, 298, 299, 382, 385, 405, 424
Tereščenko, N. M., 251, 268
Thalbitzer, William, 12, 177, 221, 222, 227, 228, 229, 230, 231, 266, 267, 280
Tharp, George W., 116, 292, 293, 294, 297, 321, 325, 326, 356
Thibert, R. P., Arthur, O.M.I., 213, 217, 219, 252, 265, 266, 276, 277, 278, 279
Thiel, R. A., 67, 68
Thomas, Alex, 83, 378, 379
Thomas, Cyrus, 116
Thomas, Jacqueline M. C., 424
Thompson, Laurence, C., 41, 103, 116, 359, 387, 391, 393, 398, 403, 404, 424
Thompson, M. C., 391
Thompson, M. Terry, 41, 359, 387, 403, 404, 424
Thompson, Stith, 154, 172
Thorning, Gába, 223, 267
Thwaites, Reuben G., 530, 531, 533, 539, 542, 544, 545, 546, 547, 548, 549, 571
Tiffany, Warren, 211, 267
Tikhon, 182
Timberlake, Alan H., 227, 281
Titiev, Mischa, 470, 501
Tobias, Gottlieb, 82
Tooker, Elisabeth J., 533, 571
Toomey, 581
Topp, Albert, 222, 267
Tovar, Antonio, 103, 105, 116
Townsend, William Cameron, 56
Toyukak, Mary, 205, 267
Trager, Edith Crowell, 32, 42, 57
Trager, Felicia Harben, 471, 489, 501
Trager, George L., 15, 22, 24, 32, 42, 57, 58, 64, 66, 71, 102, 104, 112, 116, 117, 165, 172, 306, 356, 433, 458, 471, 475, 488, 489, 490, 491, 495, 496, 501, 502
Trinel, Ernest, O.M.I., 213, 217, 279
Troike, Rudolph C., 30, 42, 57, 66, 71, 96, 117, 121, 128, 172, 309, 355, 446, 458, 478, 490, 501
Trumbull, James Hammond, 8, 22, 508, 522, 525

Ts'ai, Yüan P'ei, 352
Turner, Glen D., 540, 566
Turner, J. M., 238
Turner, Nancy, 317, 318
Turner, Paul R., 30, 57, 446, 459, 472, 478, 501
Turner, William W., 103, 112, 531, 572
Turney-High, Harry H., 384, 399, 424
Turquetil, Mgr. S. E., O.M.I., 213, 267
Tweddell, Colin Ellidge, 389, 394, 424
Tyler, Stephen, 84, 90
Tyznov, Il'ja, 275

Uhlenbeck, C. C., 12, 27, 57, 112, 227, 229, 230, 243, 266, 267, 519
Uĺgakhpak, G. I., 195, 255, 260, 261, 267
Uldall, H. J., 436, 447, 459
Ultan, Donald, 436
Ultan, Russell, 40, 57, 129, 172, 431, 436, 438, 459
Ulving, Tor, 104, 107, 117, 193, 227, 267, 272, 459
Umfreville, Edward, 542, 571
Underhill, Robert, 175, 178, 222, 223, 227, 267, 281
Uqittuq, Paulusi, 216, 258, 268, 278
Uyakoq, 268

Vaillancourt, Louis-Philippe, 117
Valentine, Victor F., 242
Vallee, Frank G., 242
Valory, Dale, 300, 301, 352
Van de Velde, R. P., F., O.M.I., 218, 268, 277
Varkovickaja, L. A., 238
Vater, Johann Severin, 4, 18, 533, 542, 546, 551, 562, 571, 592, 599
Vdovin, I. S., 183, 190, 192, 196, 220, 232, 238, 268, 272
Velten, Harry V., 127, 132, 172, 315, 356, 368
Veniaminov, I. E., 182, 183, 184, 268
Verhaar, John W. M., 111, 255, 352
Veseleckij, V. V., 268
Vibaek, Paul, 223, 268
Vihman, Eero, 442, 446, 459
Vinay, Jean-Paul, 114
Vinson, Julien, 583, 606
Virchow, 11
Voblova, L. A., 238, 268
Voegelin, Charles F., 12, 22, 24, 27, 32, 35, 41, 42, 57, 58, 61, 62, 63, 64, 65, 66, 71, 72, 80, 94, 96, 97, 102, 103, 104, 105, 106, 117, 118, 128, 172, 202, 244, 268, 322, 332, 356, 364, 369, 424, 449, 450, 451, 458, 459, 461, 481, 482, 483, 484, 485, 501, 502, 517, 520, 521, 524, 537, 545, 548, 549, 552, 567, 571, 583, 584, 585, 589, 590, 594, 598

Voegelin, Erminie Wheeler, 24, 27, 57, 58, 104, 117, 458, 501, 590, 594
Voegelin, Florence M., 32, 42, 58, 64, 72, 97, 104, 105, 114, 118, 364, 420, 424, 461, 481, 482, 483, 484, 485, 501, 502, 548, 569, 571, 589
Voevodskiĭ, 206
Vogt, Hans, 41, 58, 221, 237, 383, 384, 385, 394, 409, 425
Voorhis, Paul H., 80, 87, 90, 521
Voss, Janice, 211, 275

Wagner, Günter, 561, 571, 586
Wahrhaftig, Albert L., 83, 91
Wainman, Alex, 385
Walker, Douglas, 477, 499, 502
Walker, James R., 544, 571
Walker, Richard, 294, 296, 357
Walker, Willard, 83, 90, 471, 495, 502, 540, 571
Wall, Carolyn W., 38, 58
Wall, Leon, 306, 309, 357
Wallace, Anthony F. C., 416, 538, 571, 588
Walters, L. V. W., 411, 420
Walton, W. G., 238
Wares, Alan Campbell, 8, 22, 38, 58, 118, 445, 455, 459, 476, 502
Warkentyne, Henry J., 365
Wartes, Rev. William C., 209, 268
Washington, George, 99
Waterhouse, Viola, 58, 446, 459
Waterman, T. T., 13
Watkins, Calvert, 84, 87, 91
Watkins, Donald, 385
Watkins, E. A., 520
Watson, G., 64, 72
Watt, Daisy, 277
Wauchope, Robert, 95, 106
Waugh, Frederick W., 537, 571
Webb, Nancy M., 38, 58
Webster, Donald H., 178, 204, 209, 210, 211, 214, 216, 235, 268, 269
Webster, Thelma, 275
Weinreich, Uriel, 132, 166, 173
Weisel, George F., 384, 425
Weisgerber, Leo, 349
Wells, Rulon, 105, 118
Wells, Roger, 269
Weltfish, Gene, 37, 530, 531, 567, 571
Werner, Oswald, 100, 102, 113, 118, 308, 309, 353, 354, 357, 472, 473, 500, 502
West, David, 577
Whatmough, Joshua, 20, 112
Wheeler, Everett Pepperell, 218, 269
Whipple, Amiel Weeks, 112, 528, 529, 531, 571, 572
Whitbread, Rev. D. H., 279
White, Douglas R., 102, 104, 113
White, John K., 540, 582, 587, 588, 589, 604, 609
White, Leslie A., 83, 91
Whiting, Alfred F., 470, 502
Whitman, William, 545, 572
Whitney, William Dwight, 9, 21, 22, 76, 90, 100, 508
Whorf, Benjamin Lee, 15, 22, 24, 32, 42, 52, 58, 168, 433, 434, 438, 459, 481, 483, 485, 488, 490, 491, 495, 502, 589
Wickersham, James, 298
Wilkie, John, 533, 572
Wilkinson, David B., 290, 294, 296
Will, G. F., 549, 572
Williams, Roger, 3, 22, 48, 523, 525
Williamson, A. W., 543, 572
Williamson, John P., 543, 572
Williamson, Robert, 240
Williamson, Thomas S., 542, 543, 572
Wilmeth, R., 111
Wilson, Alan, 309, 357
Wilson, Woodrow, 121
Wingnek, Cyril, 277
Winishut, Linton, 407
Winship, George Parker, 98
Winter, Werner, 58, 442, 445, 446, 459, 477, 502
Wippel, Mary, 385
Wissler, Clark, 164, 173
Witherspoon, Gary, 309, 322, 345, 357
Witkowski, Stanley, 293
Wolfart, H. Christopher, 3, 8, 10, 22
Wolff, Hans, 41, 58, 104, 107, 118, 131, 173, 547, 552, 561, 572, 584, 585, 586, 598
Wonderly, William L., 104, 108, 116, 118
Woodrow, Frederick, 277
Woodruff, Fred, 382, 419
Woodward, Mary, 301, 357
Worcester, Samuel A., 539
Worm, Elizabeth, 205, 235, 269
Worth, Dean Stoddard, 72, 202, 269
Worth, Sol, 66, 67
Wright, Asher, 537, 539, 572
Wulfila, 86
Wurm, Stephen, 105, 118
Wyman, Leland C., 308, 357, 502, 503

Xammerix, L., 252
Xrakovskij, V. S., 247, 255
Xromčenko, G., 271

Yamachika, Raymond, 540, 572
Yampolsky, Helene Boas, 103, 118, 411
Yarmolinsky, Avrahm, 183, 190, 232, 269
Yata, 192

Yegerlehner, John, 105, 118, 489, 503
Young, Philip, 385
Young, Robert W., 306, 307, 309, 357

Zavatti, Silvio, 270
Zeisberger, David, 5, 22, 81, 536, 566, 572
Zibell, Wilfred, 178, 210, 211, 214, 242, 269, 270, 275
Zimmer, Karl E., 369, 425
Zimmerman, Herbert, 292
Zinder, L. R., 193, 252, 270
Zisa, Charles A., 101, 118
Zobarskas, Nola M., 272
Zuk, William M., 270
Zulev, P. N., 262
Zwicky, Arnold M., 129, 173, 369, 425